MAINE

HILARY NANGLE

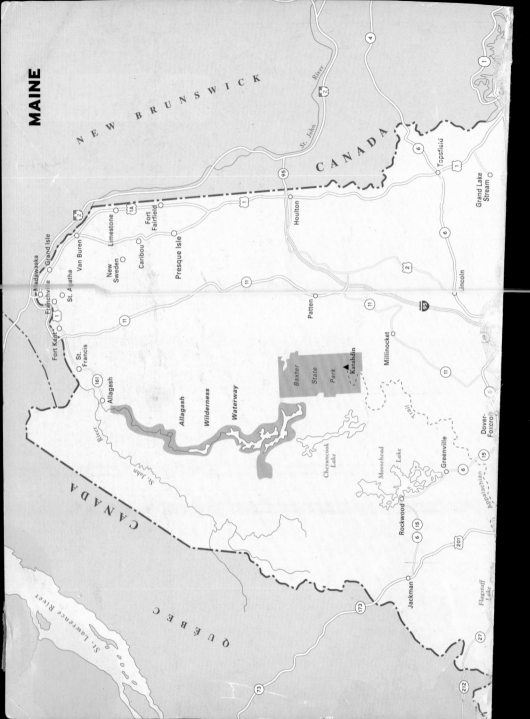

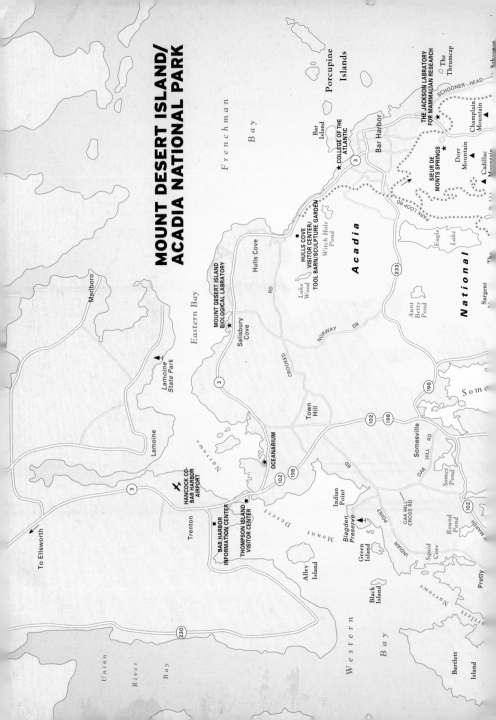

MOUNT DESERT ISLAND/ ACADIA NATIONAL PARK

Porcupine Islands

The Thrumcap

THE JACKSON LABRATORY FOR MAMMALIAN RESEARCH

SCHOONER—HEAD

Champlain Mountain

Frenchman Bay

Bar Island

COLLEGE OF THE ATLANTIC

Bar Harbor

SIEUR DE MONTS SPRINGS

Dorr Mountain

Cadillac Mountain

3

PARK LOOP RD.

HULLS COVE VISITOR CENTER/ TOOL BARN/SCULPTURE GARDEN

Witch Hole Pond

Lake Wood

Acadia

Eagle Lake

MOUNT DESERT ISLAND BIOLOGICAL LABRATORY

Hulls Cove

RD

233

NORWAY

DR

Aunt Betty Pond

National

Sargent

Eastern Bay

Salisbury Cove

3

CROOKED

Some

Marlboro

Lamoine State Park

Town Hill

102

198

198

Lamoine

Narrows

OCEANARIUM

102

198

RD

Somesville

OAK HILL RD

Somes Pond

HANCOCK CO-BAR HARBOR AIRPORT

Indian Point

OAK HILL CROSS RD

102

Trenton

BAR HARBOR INFORMATION CENTER

THOMPSON ISLAND VISITOR CENTER

Mount

Desert

Blagden Preserve

INDIAN POINT

Round Pond

MARSH

3

To Ellsworth

Green Island

Squid Cove

Pretty

Alley Island

230

Black Island

Western

Bay

Union River Bay

Bartlett Island

Great Head

Sand Beach

THUNDER HOLE
OVERLOOK

Otter
Cliffs

▲ Gorham
Mountain

Otter
Creek

BLACKWOODS △

Park

Day
Mountain

Seal
Harbor

Mountain

WILDWOOD
STABLES ★

Little Long
Pond

Penobscot
Mountain

Jordan
Pond

JORDAN POND
HOUSE ★

Hadlock
Ponds

ASTICOU AZALEA
GARDEN ★

★ THUYA
GARDEN

3

GREAT HARBOR
MARITIME MUSEUM ★

★ PETITE
PLAISANCE

Bear
Island

Greening
Island

Eastern Way

Sutton
Island

Little
Cranberry
Island

○ Islesford

Great
Cranberry
Island

Green Nubble

Crow Island

Baker
Island

Acadia
National
Park

ATLANTIC

OCEAN

Mountain

3 198

ARGENT

Norumbega
Mountain ▲

Mountain ▲

DR

Asticou

Northeast
Harbor

Western Way

Great Gott
Island

Sound

Quarry

Acadia
Mountain ▲

102

FERNALD
POINT RD

SOUTHWEST HARBOR/
TREMONT CHAMBER
OF COMMERCE

WENDELL GILLEY
MUSEUM ★

Southwest
Harbor

CLARK
POINT RD

Manset

National

Park

SEAWALL △

102A

Bass Harbor

BASS HARBOR
LIGHT ■

Echo
Lake

Beech
Mountain ▲

LONG
POND RD

Long
Pond

Mansell
Mountain ▲

Bernard
Mountain ▲

WESTERN
MOUNTAIN RD

RD

SEAL COVE

Tremont

Bernard

SWANS ISLAND
FERRY TERMINAL ■

Acadia

Seal
Cove
Pond

Hodgdon
Pond

Seal Cove

West
Tremont

102

Blue   Hill   Bay

Marsh
Harbor

Folly
Island

Moose
Island

PARK LOOP ROAD

TWO-WAY

ONE-WAY

© AVALON TRAVEL

N

2 mi

2 km

0

0

Contents

DISCOVER
Maine

Tipping the northeasternmost corner of the United States and comprising 33,215 square miles, Maine boldly promotes itself as "The Way Life Should Be." Not to say that everything's perfect, mind you, but Maine is an extraordinarily special place, where the air is clear, the water is pure, and the traditional traits of honesty, thrift, and ruggedness remain refreshingly appealing.

From the glacier-scoured beaches of the Southern Coast, around spruce-studded islands and Acadia's granite shores to the craggy cliffs Down East, Maine's coastline follows a zigzagging route that would measure about 5,500 miles if you stretched it taut. Eons ago, glaciers came crushing down from the north, squeezing Maine's coastline into a wrinkled landscape with countless bony fingers reaching toward the sea. Each peninsula has its own character, as does each island, each city, and each village.

But don't stop at the coast. Venture into Maine's inland playground: 6,000 lakes and ponds, 32,000 miles of rivers, and 17 million acres of timberlands for hiking and biking, skiing and snowmobiling, paddling and fishing. This is where intrepid Appalachian Trail hikers finish at the summit of Katahdin, Maine's tallest peak, and determined canoeists can spend a week on the Allagash, a water lifeline through the wilderness.

Pair natural highs with human pleasures: fine and quirky museums, theatrical and musical performances, artisan studios and art galleries, designer boutiques and specialty shops.

Lobster, of course, is king, but don't overlook luscious wild blueberries, sweet Maine maple syrup, delicious farmstead cheeses, and the homemade pies and preserves sold at roadside stands and farmers markets. Access to this bounty is why talented chefs are drawn here. But balance a fancy meal with a beanhole or chowder *suppah,* where you can share a table with locals, the umpteenth-generation Mainers who add character to this special place: the fishermen who make their living from the bone-chilling waters, the lumbermen who know every nook and cranny of the forested wilderness, the farmers who tame the rocky fields. If you're lucky, you might hear a genuine Maine accent (hint: *Ayuh* isn't so much a word as a sharp two-part intake of breath).

A student of Maine-born author Mary Ellen Chase once mused, "Maine is different from all other states, isn't it? I suppose that's because God never quite finished it." Maine may indeed be a work in progress, but it's a masterwork.

Planning Your Trip

Lay of the Land

SOUTHERN COAST

Sandy beaches, occasionally punctuated by rocky headlands, are the jewels of the Southern Coast, but this region also oozes history. Colonial roots are preserved in historical buildings while the arts legacy is preserved in museums and galleries. Route 1's endless shopping opportunities provide plenty of distraction.

GREATER PORTLAND

Brine-scented air, cackling gulls, lobster boats, and fishing trawlers give notice that this is a seafaring town, but it's also Maine's cultural center, rich in museums and performing-arts centers, and earns national kudos as a culinary destination.

MID-COAST REGION

No region of Maine has more lobster shacks or as rich a maritime history as this peninsula-rich stretch of coastline, dotted with traditional fishing villages and once-thriving ports and shipbuilding centers. The Maine Maritime Museum preserves that heritage; Bath Iron Works continues it; and the brick townscapes, renovated mills, and plentiful shops brimming with maritime treasure keep it alive.

PENOBSCOT BAY

Island-studded Penobscot Bay is the Maine coast in microcosm. Boat-filled harbors, sandy pocket beaches, soaring spruce trees, and lighthouses pepper the shoreline. Gentrifying fishing villages neighbor cosmopolitan towns. Antiques shops, art galleries,

Lobster shacks, ilke this one in Spruce Head, dot Maine's coastline.

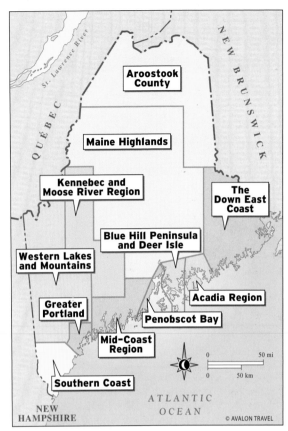

crashing upon granite ledges, serene lakes, and soaring cliffs—Acadia has it all. Watch the sun rise out of the Atlantic from Cadillac Mountain's summit, mosey along the iconic Park Loop Road, pedal the famed carriage roads, and paddle coastal nooks and crannies. Intimate yet expansive, Acadia is as accessible or as remote as you desire.

THE DOWN EAST COAST

Here the pace slows, traffic subsides, and traffic lights all but disappear. Blueberry barrens color the landscape; huge tides rule daily life. Two national wildlife reserves and numerous preserves lure hikers and bird-watchers, but the main attraction is the rugged and wild coastline.

AROOSTOOK COUNTY

Vast, rural, undeveloped, this is Maine's original melting pot, home to Acadian heritage sites, Maine's Swedish Colony, and Amish settlements. Remnants of the bloodless Aroostook War with Canada dot the border. In winter, world-class trails and training centers lure cross-country skiers, and 1,600 miles of groomed snowmobile trails connect to an international network.

artisans' studios, and museums are as plentiful as lobster boats.

BLUE HILL PENINSULA AND DEER ISLE

Water, water everywhere. Around nearly every bend is a river or stream, a cove, a boat-filled harbor, or a serene pond. This inspired and inspiring landscape hosts historic homes and forts, classic fishing villages, and a remote section of Acadia National Park. Locals, a blend of summer rusticators, genteel retirees, artists, and back-to-the-landers, have worked diligently to preserve not only the landscape but also the heritage.

ACADIA REGION

Mountains tumbling to the sea, ocean waves

MAINE HIGHLANDS

The Highlands are home to Baxter State Park, with miles of hiking trails, including those on mile-high Katahdin, the official terminus of the Appalachian Trail; the Allagash Wilderness Waterway, a paddling route through the wilderness; the Penobscot River, a favorite for white-water fans and anglers; and Moosehead Lake, where you can cruise in historical fashion aboard the *Kate*.

Fishing is popular in the wilderness waters of Maine.

KENNEBEC AND MOOSE RIVER REGION

"Benedict Arnold Slept Here" signs are posted all along the Old Canada Road National Scenic Byway, which follows his famous march on Québec. In Augusta, the Maine State Museum is an excellent introduction to the state, and Old Fort Western is the nation's oldest stockade fort. Of course, a white-water rafting trip down the Kennebec is a must.

WESTERN LAKES AND MOUNTAINS

Generations of campers have favored the lakes pocketed in the mountains of western Maine. Cruise Long Lake on the *Songo River Queen II*, cast a line in the Rangeley Lakes, hike through Grafton Notch State Park, or spend a leisurely afternoon splashing in Sebago and you'll understand why. In winter, major alpine resorts keep things hopping.

High and Low Seasons

Late May–mid-October is prime season, with July and August, the warmest months, the busiest. Of course, that means peak-season rates, congested roads, and difficulty getting reservations. Late June and late August tend to be a bit quieter, and everything is still in full swing. Prices and hours or operation throughout this book are for peak season. In the off-season, prices can drop dramatically and operating hours are much more limited. It's not uncommon for a restaurant to close early on a quiet night. In general, days and hours of operation are subject to change, so it's a good idea to call ahead or make a reservation.

September–mid-October is arguably the best season to travel in Maine. Days are warm and mostly dry, nights are cool, fog is rare, the bugs are gone, and the crowds are few. Foliage is turning by early October, usually reaching its peak by mid-month.

In winter, especially inland, skiing, snow-shoeing, and ice-skating replace hiking, biking, and boating. On the coast, choices in lodging, dining, and activities are fewer, but rates are generally far lower. In areas with solid year-round populations, life goes on full tilt.

The Best of Maine

It's a tough job to single out Maine's sightseeing icons. It offers so many. Unless you have years to spend, such a big chunk of real estate needs some whittling to be made explorable. This itinerary exposes you to a good part of Maine while taking in many of the state's icons in 20 days.

The downside: You'll be doing a fair bit of driving, primarily on two-lane roads where speeds through towns are often 25 mph or lower, and during the season when road construction is a fact of life. While this itinerary is planned as 20 days, if your schedule permits, you'll be rewarded if you spend longer in any of the locations.

Book your first two nights' lodging in Portland, then book nights 3 and 4 in Rockland or vicinity; 5 and 6 on Mount Desert Island; 7 and 8 in the Millinocket area; 9 and 10 in the Moosehead region; 11 and 12 in The Forks; 13 and 14 in Rangeley; 15 and 16 in Bethel; and 17-19 in the Sebago area.

Day 1

Stretch your legs after your journey to Maine with a refreshing walk on Ogunquit Beach, one of Maine's prettiest and proof that there's plenty of sand along Maine's fabled rockbound coast. Afterward, head to Kennebunkport and indulge your passions: shopping in the boutiques and galleries that crowd Dock Square, taking a walking tour to view the historic homes, or enjoying a leisurely drive along the waterfront.

Day 2

Begin the day with a visit to Portland Head Light, a Cape Elizabeth landmark and Maine's oldest lighthouse (1791) at the edge of 94-acre Fort Williams Park. Spend the afternoon in the Portland Museum of Art, Maine's premier art museum, smack in the heart of the state's largest city. End the day with a sunset cruise on Casco Bay.

On a calm, clear day, there's no better place to be than Monhegan Island.

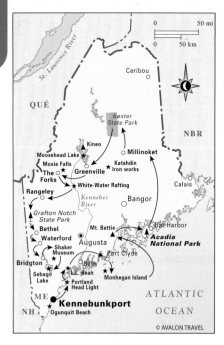

your explorations of Acadia National Park. If you've arrived on the island before noon, pick up a picnic lunch and then drive the Park Loop Road, a perfect introduction to Acadia that covers many of the highlights.

Day 6

Welcome the day by watching the sunrise from the summit of Cadillac Mountain. Afterward, if you haven't either driven or bicycled the Park Loop, do so. If you have, then explore the park: Go hiking, bicycling, or sea kayaking, take a carriage ride, or book an excursion boat to Islesford or for whale-watching.

Day 7

Depart Mount Desert Island and head inland to Millinocket, perhaps detouring to see Katahdin Iron Works but arriving in time for a late-afternoon moose safari.

Day 8

Venture into Baxter State Park for a day of hiking or rent a canoe and paddle one of the many lakes and rivers.

Day 9

Drive across the Golden Road to Greenville and Moosehead Lake. If time permits, continue to Rockwood and take the shuttle over to Kineo for a hike.

Day 10

Take a cruise on the Kate and prowl around the area, perhaps driving to Pittston Farm or hiking.

Day 11

Drive to The Forks via the Moosehead Scenic Byway and Old Canada Road National Scenic Byway and stretch your legs on a hike into Moxie Falls.

Day 12

Go white-water rafting on the Kennebec River.

Day 3

Make a pilgrimage to giant sports retailer and outfitter L. L. Bean, hub of the hubbub in Freeport's outlet bonanza. Either spend the morning shopping or taking a Walk-on Adventure class. In the afternoon, visit the Maine Maritime Museum in Bath, 10 acres of indoor and outdoor exhibits celebrating the state's nautical heritage.

Day 4

Take a day trip to Monhegan Island from Port Clyde. This car-free, carefree gem, about a dozen miles off the coast, is laced with hiking trails and has earned a place in art history books as the Artists' Island.

Day 5

Drive or hike to the top of Mount Battie, in Camden Hills State Park on the northern fringe of Camden. The vistas are magnificent, with the broad sweep of Penobscot Bay for a backdrop. Then continue up the coast to Mount Desert Island and begin

The Lobster Experience

a perfect Maine lunch

No Maine visit is complete without a "lobsta dinnah" at a lobster wharf, a rough-and-tumble operation within sight and scent of the ocean. If you spot a place with "Restaurant" in its name, keep going. You want to eat outside, at a picnic table, with a knockout view of boats, islands, and the sea. "Dinners" are served from noonish until around sunset.

Dress casually so you can manhandle the lobster without messing up your clothes. If you want beer or wine, call ahead and ask if the place serves it; you may need to bring your own. Lobster devotees cart picnic baskets with hors d'oeuvres, salads, and baguettes—even candles and champagne. Save room for dessert. Many lobster shacks are as renowned for their pies as the crustacean itself.

Here are my favorite lobster shacks:

- **Chauncey Creek Lobster Pier, Kittery Point:** For more than 40 years, the Spinney family has operated this popular spot with views toward Pepperrell Cove.

- **The Lobster Shack, Cape Elizabeth:** Ocean views, crashing surf, and a lighthouse have enticed lobster-lovers to this location since the 1920s.

- **Harraseeket Lunch and Lobster Company, South Freeport:** Take a break from L.L. Bean and head to this unfussy spot on the working harbor.

- **Five Islands Lobster Company, Georgetown:** Watch sailboats playing hide-and-seek amid the spruce-topped islands in the harbor.

- **Round Pond Lobster Co-op and Muscongus Bay Lobster, Round Pond:** These two overlook dreamy Round Pond Harbor. The co-op keeps it simple, with lobsters only. Muscongus Bay earns kid-friendly points for its touch tank filled with sea critters.

- **Waterman's Beach Lobster, South Thomaston:** The James Beard Foundation named this place overlooking island-studded Mussel Ridge Channel an "American Classic."

- **Miller's Lobster Company, Spruce Head:** Watch lobstermen unload their catches and savor the views of Wheeler's Bay at this spot.

- **McLoon's Lobster Shack, Spruce Head:** Pair mighty fine lobster with spruce-fringed island views.

- **Fish House Fish, Monhegan Island:** It doesn't get much more in the rough than this shack overlooking Monhegan's harbor.

- **Perry Lobster Shack and Pier, Surry:** It's worth the drive down Surry Neck to find this tucked-away gem with views to Mount Desert Island.

- **Thurston's Lobster Pound, Bernard:** The two-story dining area tops a wharf above Bass Harbor.

- **Lunt's Dockside Deli, Frenchboro:** It's hard to beat this spot on an island off Mount Desert Island.

- **Quoddy Bay Lobster, Eastport:** Watch the tide change and boats unload their catches on Passamaquoddy Bay.

Maine's Kennebec River is a whitewater roller coaster.

Day 13

Take the scenic drive to Rangeley via Route 16, keeping an eye out for moose along the way. Work out the driving kinks with either an afternoon paddle or a hike.

Day 14

Visit the Rangeley Outdoor Sporting Heritage Museum and then take a lazy—or not—afternoon: Hike, swim, paddle, explore, or simply sit and enjoy the environment.

Day 15

Head south on Route 17 over Height of Land, perhaps stopping in Coos Canyon to try your hand at panning for gold. Continue to Grafton Notch State Park.

Day 16

Prowl around Bethel's historic district and explore the Mahoosuc section of the White Mountains.

Day 17

Snake southward through the White Mountain foothills, perhaps exploring Paris Hill, Norway, or Waterford.

Day 18

Poke around Bridgton and Naples, and perhaps take a cruise on the Songo River Queen II.

Day 19

Visit the Shaker Museum, the world's last inhabited Shaker colony, and tour Poland Spring; there's a lot more here than bottled water.

Day 20

Head home after a dip in Sebago Lake.

Lighthouses, Lobster, and L. L. Bean

Maine's biggest draws are the three L's: lighthouses, lobster, and L. L. Bean. Maine's 64 lighthouses stretch from York's Nubble to candy-striped West Quoddy Head in Lubec. Lobster, of course, can be found practically everywhere along the coast, but the best way to enjoy it is at a no-fuss lobster shack. L. L. Bean's ever-expanding campus in Freeport is the massive outdoor retailer's mother ship, but it also has an outlet in Ellsworth.

This six-day tour concentrates on the Greater Portland, Mid-Coast, and Penobscot Bay regions. Book your first night's lodging in Portland, the second two in Damariscotta or Newcastle, and the next two in the Thomaston-Rockland area. For a real lighthouse immersion, consider splurging on an extra two nights on Isle au Haut. If you're arriving by air, use Portland International Jetport.

Day 1

Try to arrive in Portland in time to enjoy an afternoon cruise with Lucky Catch Lobster Tours; perhaps you'll catch your dinner. If not, you can still enjoy a lobster on the waterfront.

Day 2

Loop out to South Portland and Cape Elizabeth to visit Spring Point Ledge Light and Portland Head Light, a Maine icon. You won't find a better setting for lunch than The Lobster Shack, with views of crashing surf and Cape Elizabeth Light. In the afternoon, consider visiting the Portland Museum of Art to view masterworks by Maine-related artists or book a sail amid the islands of Casco Bay. Still craving lobster? Try an inspired version by one of Maine's nationally recognized chefs (reservations required).

Portland Head Light was commissioned by George Washington and first lighted in 1791.

Fall Foliage

Mountains, lakes, and few crowds are just a few reasons to visit during autumn's foliage season.

Shhh! Don't tell too many people, but Maine gets fewer leaf peepers than other New England states, so roads are less congested and lodging and dining reservations are easier. But do plan in advance. For help in planning, consult www.mainefoliage.com.

MOOSEHEAD AND THE KENNEBEC RIVER

Leaf peepers who make it as far north as Greenville are well rewarded. Plan a minimum of two nights, ideally three or longer, and spend one full day driving one of the state's most spectacular foliage routes.

The Route: Loop from Greenville over to the Kennebec River and back on Routes 5 to Jackman, 201 south to Bingham, 16 east to Abbott, then 5 north to return to Greenville. You'll parallel the shorelines of Moosehead Lake and the Moose River on the Moosehead Lake Scenic Byway before arriving in Rockwood. As you head south the views are spectacular along the Old Canada Road Scenic Byway. Dip into the Attean View rest area for views extending toward Canada. Need to stretch your legs? Consider the relatively easy hike to Moxie Falls. From here to Bingham, Route 201 can be truly spectacular, as it snakes along the Kennebec River.

Diversions: Cruise Moosehead Lake aboard the *Kate,* take a flightseeing tour or a moose safari, or drive to a remote sporting camp for lunch.

BETHEL AND RANGELEY

Combine New England's trees with lakes and mountains and you have the best of nature's palette. Divide your lodging between Bethel and Rangeley.

The Route: From Bethel, take Route 26 north to Errol, New Hampshire, then Route 16 north to Rangeley. Return via Route 17 south to Route 2 west. Heading north, you'll cut through Grafton Notch State Park on the Grafton Notch Scenic Byway; the rest of the drive is speckled with mountains, lakes, and streams. Returning south from Rangeley, the Rangeley Lakes National Scenic Byway passes over Height of Land, providing dazzling views. The entire route is through prime moose country, so keep alert.

Diversions: Hike in Grafton Notch or Rangeley, paddle the Rangeley Lakes, or pan for gold in Coos Canyon.

ACADIA AND DOWN EAST

To the magic foliage mix, add the ocean and top it off with wild blueberry barrens, which turn crimson in foliage season. Book lodging in the Schoodic region.

The Route: From Hancock, mosey inland on Route 182 along the Blackwoods Scenic Byway to Cherryfield. Then head south on Route 1A to Milbridge, continuing south on Route 1. In Steuben, dip down Pigeon Hill Road to the Petit Manan section of the Maine Coastal Islands National Wildlife Reserve before continuing south on Route 1 to Route 186, which loops around the Schoodic Peninsula via the Schoodic Scenic Byway.

Diversions: Bike the Schoodic Loop, hike Black or Schoodic Mountains, detour north from Cherryfield to Deblois to see the blueberry barrens, or browse art galleries.

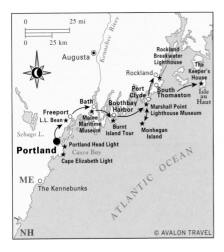

to Pemaquid Point to view Pemaquid Point Lighthouse, perhaps climbing to the top. Be sure to visit the Fisherman's Museum in the keeper's house. End the day with lobster in the rough in Round Pond.

Day 5

Begin the day with a visit to Marshall Point Lighthouse Museum in Port Clyde, and then board the mail boat to Monhegan Island. Be sure to visit the museum in the lighthouse keeper's house. Lunch? Lobster at Fish House Fish, of course.

Day 6

Greet the day with a sunrise walk out on the breakwater to Rockland Breakwater Lighthouse. Afterward, tour the Maine Lighthouse Museum and Farnsworth Art Museum. In the afternoon, take a light-house-themed cruise or sea kayak tour out of Rockport or Rockland. End the day and your lobster-infused vacation at the James Beard Award-winning lobster shack Waterman's Beach Lobster in South Thomaston. En route, take the short side jaunt out to Owls Head Light in Owls Head.

Days 7-8

Splurge with a two-night stay at The Keeper's House on Isle au Haut. The rustic accommodations are in the keeper's house, oil house, and woodshed at Robinson Point Light, and access is via a passenger ferry.

Day 3

Get an early start and begin at famed outlet store L. L. Bean in Freeport. You might even take a Walk-on Adventure with Bean's Outdoor Discovery School. In the afternoon, visit the Maine Maritime Museum in Bath, and if time permits, take a lighthouse cruise on the Kennebec River. Perhaps mosey down to Georgetown for dinner at Five Islands or stop in Wiscasset for a lobster roll.

Day 4

Spend the morning in Boothbay Harbor, stepping back in time for a visit with light keeper Joseph Muise and his family on a Burnt Island Tour. In the late afternoon, drive down

Off the Beaten Path

You've been there, done that, and seen all the icons. If you have a sense of adventure, poke around some of the state's nooks and crannies.

Aroostook Loop

Few visitors make it to Aroostook County, and that's a pity, because it is a rural gem with great outdoor resources, including Aroostook State Park and rich Acadian and Swedish heritage sites. Because of the sheer immensity of the county, you'll want to plan at least four days to a full week.

Be sure to explore the back roads for big views and surprises. Along Route 2 between Sherman Mills and Houlton are Golden Ridge with panoramic views, a railroad museum, and an Amish colony. Route 164 loops out to the Salmon Brook Historical Society and Woodland Bog Preserve. And tucked just off Route 161 is Maine's Swedish Colony.

The Adventure Decathlon

Hkers approach the summit of mile-high Katahdin, the terminus of the Appalachian Trail.

Maine is a vast outdoor playground. While you can work one or perhaps more of these adventures into a vacation, completing all 10 will require either moving here or returning again and again. Many aren't for the faint of heart or weak of muscle; almost all require planning well ahead.

- **Hiking:** Mile-high **Katahdin,** terminus of the **Appalachian Trail,** is Maine's tallest peak. Although it tops out on Baxter Peak, it also comprises several neighboring ones. The infamous **Knife Edge** provides the 1.1-mile connection between **Baxter Peak** and **Pamola Peak.**

- **Mountain Biking:** Pedal between **Carrabassett Valley** and **The Forks** via the **Maine Huts and Trails** system, a 12-foot-wide corridor through the wilderness. Connecting the points are four full-service huts, each roughly 12 miles apart.

- **Rafting:** Maine is blessed with three dam-controlled white-water roller coasters: the **Kennebec River,** the **Penobscot River,** and the **Dead River.**

- **Canoeing:** The **Allagash Wilderness Waterway** stretches 92 miles from Telos Lake to East Twin Brook through pristine lakes, rapids, and a portage around **Allagash Falls.** The biggest challenges are the distance and the weather.

- **Sea Kayaking:** Paddle along Maine's coast from Kittery to Machias Bay on the **Maine Island Trail,** a 375-mile-long waterway past more than 180 island and mainland sites available for backcountry camping.

- **Sailing:** No exercise or experience is required to sail aboard a **Maine windjammer.** All-inclusive sails on vessels both historic and new range from two days to a week.

- **Dogsledding:** Mush a team of huskies across the frozen **Lake Umbagog** wilderness north of Bethel. Sample the sport with a day trip, or immerse yourself in winter with a multiple-day trek.

- **Alpine Skiing and Snowboarding:** Crowning the summit of **Sugarloaf** are the **Snowfields,** the only lift-serviced skiing in the East above the tree line. This is backcountry, experts-only, out-of-bounds terrain, but when the gate's open these fields are worth braving the natural obstacles.

- **Cross-Country Skiing:** Ski a groomed trail through the forested wilderness between three trail-linked sporting camps in the land edging the Appalachian Trail's famed **100-Mile Wilderness.**

Maine's Swedish Colony

Way Down East

Few folks travel northeast of the Acadia region, but those who do are rewarded with a more authentic Maine experience. From Milbridge through Calais, the Maine Coast has a much different feel than points south. Fishing villages have yet to be gussied up or gentrified, and harbors are filled with working boats, not yachts. Museums, such as the Burnham Tavern in Machias, the Ruggles House in Columbia Falls, and the Tides Institute and Museum of Art in Eastport, are small in size but deep in local heritage. Bring a passport, and Campobello Island International Park is yours too.

Coastal hiking trails and wildlife preserves attract birders, and if you continue inland to Grand Lake Stream, you'll stumble upon an anglers' paradise.

Sporting Camp Adventure

There's no finer way to experience Maine's forested wilderness than to immerse yourself in it at a traditional sporting camp. Created more than a century ago to cater to the needs of hunters and anglers, today most are wonderful family destinations during the summer. You can hike, fish, paddle, swim, search for moose or other wildlife, or simply relax and enjoy the away-from-it-all experience.

Sporting camps dot Maine's North Country, with concentrations around the Rangeley Lakes and along the waterways surrounding Baxter State Park and Moosehead Lake.

SOUTHERN COAST

Drive over the I-95 bridge from New Hampshire into Maine's Southern Coast region on a bright summer day and you'll swear the air is cleaner, the sky is bluer, the trees are greener, and the roadside signs are more upbeat—"Welcome to Maine: The Way Life Should Be." (Or is it the way life *used* to be?)

Most visitors come to this region for the spectacular attractions of the justly world-famous Maine Coast—the inlets, villages, and especially the beaches—but it's also rich in history. Southernmost York County, part of the Province of Maine, was incorporated in 1636, only 16 years after the *Mayflower* pilgrims reached Plymouth, Massachusetts, and reeks of history: ancient cemeteries, musty archives, and architecturally stunning homes and public buildings. Probably the best places to dive into that history are the sites of the Old York Historical Society in York Harbor.

Geological fortune smiled on this 50-mile ribbon, endowing it with a string of sandy beaches—nirvana for sun worshippers but less enchanting to swimmers, who need to steel themselves to be able to spend much time in the ocean, especially in early summer before the water temperature has reached a tolerable level.

Complementing those beaches are amusement parks and arcades, fishing shacks-turned-chic boutiques, a surprising number of good restaurants given the region's seasonality, and some of the state's prettiest parks and preserves. Spend some time poking around the small villages that give the region so much character. Many have been gussied up and gentrified quite a bit yet retain their seafaring or farming bones.

HIGHLIGHTS

LOOK FOR **(** TO FIND RECOMMENDED
SIGHTS, ACTIVITIES, DINING, AND
LODGING.

(Old York Historical Society: York dates
from the 1640s, and on this campus of historic
buildings you can peek into early life in the area
(page 34).

(Nubble Light and Sohier Park: You'll
likely recognize this often-photographed Maine
Coast icon, which is the easiest lighthouse to
see in the region (page 34).

(Ogunquit Museum of American Art:
It's hard to say which is more jaw-dropping, the
art or the view (page 42).

(Marginal Way: Escape the hustle and bustle of Ogunquit with a stroll on this paved shorefront path (page 43).

(Wells Reserve at Laudholm Farm:
Orient yourself at the visitors center, where you
can learn about the history, flora, and fauna,
and then take a leisurely walk to the seashore,
passing through a variety of habitats (page 43).

(Seashore Trolley Museum: Ding-ding-
ding goes the bell, and zing-zing-zing go your
heartstrings, especially if you're a trolley fan
(page 53).

(Dock Square: Brave the shopping
crowds and browse the dozens of fishing shacks-turned-boutiques in the heart of
Kennebunkport (page 56).

(St. Anthony's Franciscan Monastery:
It's hard to believe this oasis of calm is just a
short stroll from busy-busy Dock Square (page
56).

(Wood Island Lighthouse: Tour Maine's
second-oldest lighthouse and perhaps even
climb the tower (page 71).

Some Mainers refer to the Southern Coast
as northern Massachusetts. Sometimes it can
seem that way, not only for the numbers of
Massachusetts plates in evidence but also because many former Massachusetts residents
have moved here for the quality of life but continue to commute to jobs in the Boston area.
The resulting downside is escalating real-estate prices that have forced folks off land that
has been in their families for generations and

pushed those in traditional seafaring occupa-
tions inland. Still, if you nose around and get
off the beaten path, you'll find that real Maine
is still here.

PLANNING YOUR TIME

Maine's Southern Coast is a rather compact region, but it's heavily congested, especially in
summer. Still, with a minimum of four days,
you should be able to take in most of the key

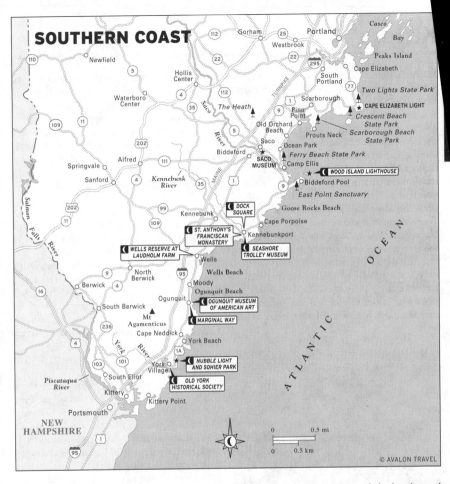

SOUTHERN COAST

© AVALON TRAVEL

sights, including beaches and museums, as long as you don't spend too many hours basking in the sun.

Route 1, the region's primary artery, often has bumper-to-bumper traffic. If you're hopscotching towns, consider using I-95, which has exits for York, Kennebunk, and Saco-Biddeford-Old Orchard Beach. Parking can also be a challenge and expensive, but a trolley system operates in summer and connects most towns, making it easy to avoid the hassles and help the environment.

July and August are the busiest months, with the best beach weather. Spring and fall are lovely, and most attractions are open. In winter, you can walk the beaches without running into another soul, it's easy to get dinner reservations, and lodging prices plummet; the trade-off is that fewer businesses are open.

...ery

...is home to a lot of well-kept secrets, ...y (pop. 9,490) being one of them. ...ers rarely get beyond the 120-plus out... ...long Route 1, but there's equal value in ex... ...ing the back roads of Maine's oldest town, ...led in 1623 and chartered in 1647. Parks, ...small nautical museum, historic architec... ...ire, and foodie finds are only a few of the at... ...ractions in Kittery and its "suburb," **Kittery Point.** It was also on Kittery's Badger Island where the sloop *Ranger* was launched in 1777. The shipbuilding continues at Portsmouth Naval Shipyard on Kittery's Dennet's Island, the first government shipyard in the United States.

SIGHTS

Avoid the outlet sprawl and see the prettiest part of the area by driving along squiggly Route 103 from the Route 1 traffic circle in Kittery through Kittery Point (administratively part of Kittery) and on to Route 1A in York. You can even make a day of it, stopping at the sights mentioned here. Be very careful to watch for cyclists and pedestrians, as there are no shoulders and lots of blind corners and hills.

Kittery Historical and Naval Museum

Maritime history buffs shouldn't miss the small but well-stocked **Kittery Historical and Naval Museum** (200 Rogers Rd. Ext., near the junction of Rte. 1 and Rte. 236, Kittery, 207/439-3080, www.kitterymuseum.com, 10am-4pm Tues.-Sat. June-Oct., $5 adults, $3 ages 7-15, $10 family). A large exhibit hall and a small back room contain ship models, fishing gear, old photos and paintings, and an astonishing collection of scrimshaw (carved whale ivory).

Lady Pepperrell House

The 1760 Georgian **Lady Pepperrell House** (Pepperrell Rd./Rte. 103, just before the Fort McClary turnoff, Kittery Point) is privately owned and not open to the public, but it's worth admiring from afar. Nearby, across from the First Congregational Church, is the area's most-visited burying ground. Old-cemetery buffs should bring rubbing gear here for some interesting grave markers. The tomb of Levi Thaxter (husband of poet Celia Thaxter) bears an epitaph written for him by Robert Browning.

Fort McClary State Historic Site

Since the early 18th century, fortifications have stood on this 27-acre headland protecting Portsmouth Harbor from seaborne foes. Contemporary remnants at **Fort McClary** (Rte. 103, Kittery Point, 207/439-2845, daily, $3 nonresident adults, $2 Maine adults, $1 ages 5-11 and nonresident seniors, free resident

© TOM NANGLE

Fort McClary has guarded Portsmouth Harbor since the early 18th century.

seniors) include several outbuildings, an 1846 blockhouse, granite walls, and earthworks—all with a view of Portsmouth Harbor. Opposite are the sprawling buildings of the Portsmouth Naval Shipyard. Bring a picnic (covered tables and a lily pond are across the street) and turn the kids loose to run and play. It's officially open May 30-October 1, but the site is accessible in the off-season. The fort is 2.5 miles east of Route 1.

Fort Foster

The only problem with **Fort Foster** (Pocahontas Rd., off Rte. 103, Gerrish Island, Kittery Point, 207/439-3800, 10am-8pm daily late May-early Sept., 10am-8pm Sat.-Sun. Sept.-May, $10 vehicle pass, $5 adults walk-in, $1 children walk-in) is that it's no secret, so parking can be scarce at this 90-acre municipal park at the entrance to Portsmouth Harbor. On a hot day, arrive early. You can swim, hike the nature trails, fish off the pier (state registration required for ages 16 and older), picnic, and investigate the tidepools. Bring a kite; there's almost always a breeze.

ENTERTAINMENT

Kittery Recreation (207/439-3800, www.kitterycommunitycenter.org) presents a **summer concert series** on the common, which varies year to year; most of the concerts are free.

SHOPPING

There is no question that you'll find bargains at Kittery's 120-plus factory outlets (www.thekitteryoutlets.com), which are actually a bunch of mini-malls clustered along Route 1. You'll find Calvin Klein, Eddie Bauer, J. Crew, Mikasa, Esprit, Lenox, Timberland, Tommy Hilfiger, Gap, Villeroy & Boch, and plenty more (all open daily). Anchoring the scene is the **Kittery Trading Post** (301 Rte. 1, Kittery, 207/439-2700 or 888/587-6246, www.kitterytradingpost.com), a humongous sporting-goods and clothing emporium. Try to avoid the outlets on weekends, when you might need to take a number for the fitting rooms.

RECREATION
Brave Boat Harbor

One of the Rachel Carson National Wildlife Refuge's 11 Maine coastal segments is **Brave Boat Harbor** (207/646-9226), a beautifully unspoiled 560-acre wetlands preserve in Kittery Point. There are hiking trails, but the habitat is particularly sensitive here, so be kind to the environment. Take Route 103 to Chauncey Creek Road and continue past the Gerrish Island bridge to Cutts Island Lane. Just beyond it and across a small bridge is a pullout on the left. You have a couple of options for hikes: a 1.8-mile loop trail, including a spur, or a half-mile loop. Bring binoculars to spot waterfowl in the marshlands.

Captain and Patty's Piscataqua River Tours

Take a spin around the Piscataqua River Basin with **Captain and Patty's Piscataqua River Tours** (Town Dock, Pepperrell Rd., Kittery Point, 207/439-3655, www.capandpatty.com, $19 adults, $10 under age 10). The 80-minute historical tour aboard an open launch departs six times daily. En route, Captain Neil Odams points out historic forts, lighthouses, and the Naval Shipyard.

ACCOMMODATIONS

Put a little *ooh* and *aah* into your touring with a visit to the **Portsmouth Harbor Inn and Spa** (6 Water St., Kittery, 207/439-4040, www.innatportsmouth.com, $165-195). The handsome brick inn, built in 1889, looks out over the Piscataqua River, Portsmouth, and the Portsmouth Naval Shipyard. Five attractive Victorian-style guest rooms, most with water views, are furnished with antiques and have air-conditioning, TVs, Wi-Fi, and phones. There's an outdoor hot tub, and beach chairs are available. Breakfasts are multicourse feasts. Request a back room if you're noise sensitive, although air-conditioning camouflages traffic noise in summer. Rooms on the third floor have the best views, but these also have handheld showers. Now for the "aah" part: The inn also has a full-service spa.

FOOD
Local Flavors

Kittery has an abundance of excellent specialty food stores that are perfect for stocking up for a picnic lunch or dinner. Most are along the section of Route 1 between the Portsmouth bridge and the traffic circle, and five are within steps of one another. At **Beach Pea Baking Co.** (53 Rte. 1, Kittery, 207/439-3555, www.beachpeabaking.com, 7:30am-6pm Mon.-Sat., 8am-4pm Sun.) you can buy fabulous breads and pastries. Sandwiches and salads are made to order 11am-3pm daily. There's pleasant seating indoors and on a patio. Next door is **Golden Harvest** (47 State Rd./Rte. 1, Kittery, 207/439-2113, 7am-6:30pm Mon.-Sat., 9am-6pm Sun.), where you can load up on luscious produce. Across the street is **Terra Cotta Pasta Co.** (52 Rte. 1, Kittery, 207/475-3025, www.terracottapastacompany.com, 10am-7pm Mon., 9am-7pm Tues.-Sat., 10am-5pm Sun.), where in addition to handmade pastas you'll find salads, soups, sandwiches, prepared foods, and lots of other goodies. You can count on **Carl's Meat Market** (25 State. Rd., Kittery, 207/439-1557), a butcher shop, for awesome burgers and sandwiches. Let your nose guide you into **Byrne & Carlson** (60 Rte. 1, Kittery, 888/559-9778, www.byrneandcarlson.com), which makes elegant and delicious chocolate for connoisseurs.

Here's a twofold find. **When Pigs Fly** (460 Rte. 1, Kittery, 207/439-4114, www.sendbread.com) earned renown for its old-world artisanal breads made from organic ingredients. Now it's also home to **When Pigs Fly Wood-Fired Pizzeria** (207/438-7036, www.whenpigsflypizzeria.com, 11:30am-9pm Sun.-Wed., 11:30am-10pm Thurs.-Sat., $12-22). Of course there's pizza—Neopolitan style in creative flavor combos—but there are other choices, including house-made charcuterie.

Want a down-home breakfast or lunch? The **Sunrise Grill** (182 State Rd./Rte. 1, Kittery traffic circle, Kittery, 207/439-5748, www.sunrisegrillinc.com, 6:30am-2pm daily, $5-13) delivers with waffles, granola, omelets, Diana's Benedict, salads, sandwiches, and burgers.

Casual Dining

The commitment to using fresh and local foods and the flair for bringing big flavors out of simple ingredients have earned **Anneke Jans** (60 Wallingford Sq., Kittery, 207/439-0001, www.annekejans.net, from 5pm daily, $20-35) kudos far beyond Kittery. Signature dishes include mussels prepared with bacon, shallots, and blue cheese, available as an appetizer or entrée. This is a local hot spot with a lively crowd; reservations are recommended. Gluten-free options are available.

Farm-to-table meets gastropub at **The Black Birch** (2 Government St., Kittery, 207/703-2294, www.theblackbirch.com, 3:30pm-10pm Tues.-Thurs., 3:30pm-11pm Fri.-Sat., $8-19). Upscale comfort foods, such as lamb meatballs, poutine and duck confit, and grilled cheddar and tomato soup, are presented in a menu designed to mix and match, accompanied by a geek-worthy beer list.

Ignore the kitschy lighthouse; **Robert's Maine Grill** (326 Rte. 1, Kittery, 207/439-0300, www.robertsmainegrill.com, from 11:30pm daily, $14-28) is a fine place to duck out of the shopping madness and enjoy well-prepared seafood that goes far beyond the usual fried choices, as well as a few landlubber options. Kids' menu available.

Ethnic Fare

Craving Cal-Mex? Some of the recipes in Luis Valdez's **Loco Coco's Tacos** (36 Walker St., Kittery, 207/438-9322, www.lococococos.com, 11am-9pm daily) have been passed down for generations, and the homemade salsas have flavor and kick. If you're feeling really decadent, go for the artery-busting California fries. There are gluten-free and kids' menus too. Most choices are less than $10. Choose from self-serve, dining room, or bar seating.

Chef Rajesh Mandekar blends techniques drawn from Indian, French, and Italian cuisines to create rave-worthy Indian fare at **Tulsi** (20 Walker St., Kittery, 207/451-9511, www.tulsiindianrestaurant.com, from 5pm Tues.-Sun. and noon-2:30pm Sun., $11-23).

Lobster and Clams

If you came to Maine to eat lobster, **Chauncey Creek Lobster Pier** (16 Chauncey Creek Rd., off Rte. 103, Kittery Point, 207/439-1030, www.chaunceycreek.com, 11am-8pm daily mid-May-early Sept., to 7pm daily early Sept.-Columbus Day) is the real deal. Step up to the window, place your order, take a number, and grab a table (you may need to share) overlooking tidal Chauncey Creek and the woods on the close-in opposite shore. It's a particularly picturesque—and extremely popular—place; parking is a nightmare. BYOB and anything else that's not on the menu.

If clams are high on your must-have list, pay a visit to **Bob's Clam Hut** (315 Rte. 1, Kittery, 207/439-4233, www.bobsclamhut. com, from 11am daily, $10-23), next to the Kittery Trading Post. An institution in these parts since 1956, Bob's is *the* place for fried seafood, especially clams; the tartar sauce is the secret weapon.

GETTING THERE AND AROUND

Kittery is 60 miles or just over an hour via I-95 from Boston, although it can take longer in summer when traffic backs up at tolls. It's about eight miles or 15 minutes via I-95. Allow about 20 minutes via Route 1, to York, although traffic can be bumper-to-bumper in the stretch by the outlets.

The Berwicks

Probably the best known of the area's present-day inland communities is the riverside town of South Berwick, thanks to a historical and literary tradition dating to the 17th century, with antique cemeteries to prove it. The 19th- and 20th-century novels of Sarah Orne Jewett and Gladys Hasty Carroll have lured many a contemporary visitor to explore their rural settings, an area aptly described by Carroll as "a small patch of earth continually occupied but never crowded for more than three hundred years."

A ramble through the Berwicks—South Berwick and its siblings—makes a nice diversion from the coast, and because it's off most visitors' radar screens, it's a good alternative for lodging and dining too.

SIGHTS

Don't blink or you might miss the tiny sign outside the 1774 **Sarah Orne Jewett House** (5 Portland St./Rte. 4, South Berwick, 207/384-2454, www.historicnewengland.org, 11am-5pm Fri.-Sun. June 1-Oct. 15, $5) smack in the center of town. Park on the street and join one of the tours to learn details of the Jewett family and its star, Sarah (1849-1909), author of

The Country of the Pointed Firs, a New England classic. Books by and about her are available in the gift shop. House tours are at 11am, 1pm, 2pm, 3pm, and 4pm. The house is one of two local Historic New England properties.

The other property is the 18th-century **Hamilton House** (40 Vaughan's Lane, South Berwick, 207/384-2454, www.historicnewengland.org, 11am-5pm Wed.-Sun. June 1-Oct. 15, $8), which crowns a bluff overlooking the Salmon Falls River and is flanked by handsome Colonial Revival gardens. Knowledgeable guides relate the house's fascinating history. It was the setting for Sarah Orne Jewett's *The Tory Lover,* among other things. Tours begin only on the hour, the last at 4pm. In July the **Sunday in the Garden** concert series takes place on the lawn ($10, includes a free pass to come back and see the house). Pray for sun; the concert is moved indoors on rainy days. From Route 236 at the southern edge of South Berwick (watch for a signpost), turn left onto Brattle Street and take the second right onto Vaughan's Lane.

Also here is the 150-acre hilltop campus of **Berwick Academy,** Maine's oldest prep school,

© TOM NANGLE

Sarah Orne Jewett House, South Berwick

chartered in 1791 with John Hancock's signature. The coed school's handsome gray-stone William H. Fogg Memorial Library ("The Fogg") is named for the same family connected with Harvard's Fogg Art Museum. The building's highlight is an incredible collection of dozens of 19th-century stained-glass windows, most designed by Victorian artist Sarah Wyman Whitman, who also designed jackets for Sarah Orne Jewett's books. Thanks to a diligent fundraising effort, the windows have been restored to their former glory.

WORTHWHILE DETOUR

About 25 minutes north of Berwick, via Route 4, is the quiet community of Alfred, home to a Shaker community begun in 1793. In 1931, the Alfred Shakers sold their assets to the Brothers of Christian Instruction and moved in with the Sabbathday Lake Shaker Community. The classic Shaker song *Simple Gifts* is attributed to Alfred Elder Joseph Brackett. Eight original Shaker buildings and a cemetery remain on Shaker Hill, part of the National Register of

Historic Places Alfred Shaker Historic District. The Friends of Alfred Shaker Museum maintain the former carriage house as the **Alfred Shaker Museum** (118 Shaker Hill Rd., Alfred, www.alfredshakermuseum.com, 1pm-4pm Wed. and Sat., May-mid-Nov., free). Afterward, treat yourself at **Shaker Pond Ice Cream** (148 Waterboro Rd., Alfred, 207/459-5070).

RECREATION

When you're ready to stretch your legs, head to **Vaughan Woods State Park** (28 Oldfields Rd., South Berwick, 207/384-5160, 9am-8pm daily late May-early Sept., park trails accessible year-round, $3 adults, $1 ages 5-11, free over age 65 or under age 5) and wander along the three miles of trails in the 250-acre riverside preserve. It adjoins Hamilton House and is connected via a path, but there's far more parking at the park itself.

ENTERTAINMENT

Another reason to venture inland is to catch a production at the **Hackmatack Playhouse**

(538 School St./Rte. 9, Berwick, 207/698-1807, www.hackmatack.org), midway between North Berwick and Berwick. The popular summer theater, operating since 1972, is based in a renovated barn reminiscent of a past era and has 8pm performances Wednesday-Saturday, a 2pm matinee Thursday, and children's shows. Tickets are $25 adults, $23 seniors, $10 younger than 20.

ACCOMMODATIONS

These two inns are sleepers (sorry, couldn't resist). Both are within easy striking distance of the coast yet provide far more value than similar properties in seaside communities.

Once the headmaster's residence for nearby Berwick Academy, the elegant turn-of-the-20th-century **Academy Street Inn Bed and Breakfast** (15 Academy St., South Berwick, 207/384-5633, year-round, $105-130) has crystal chandeliers, leaded-glass windows, working fireplaces, and high-ceilinged rooms full of antiques. Paul and Lee Fopeano's handsome home has five guest rooms with private baths. Full breakfast or afternoon lemonade on the 60-foot screened porch is a real treat.

Innkeepers Ben Gumm and Sally McLaren have turned the outstanding 25-room Queen Anne-style Hurd mansion into the **Angel of the Berwicks** (2 Elm St., North Berwick, 207/676-2133, www.angeloftheberwicks.com, $109-165), an elegant antiques-filled inn. The property, listed on the National Register of Historic Places, has 11-foot ceilings, stained-glass windows, hand-carved friezes, and ornate mantelpieces. There's even a baby grand piano in the music room. Rates include a full breakfast.

FOOD

A local institution since 1960, **Fogarty's** (471 Main St., South Berwick, 207/384-8361, www.fogartysrestaurant.net, 11am-9pm daily, $8-20) has expanded through the years from a simple take-out place to a local favorite for inexpensive, family-friendly dining. Ask for a river-view table in the back room.

Locals swear that the area's best breakfast spot is **Mayo's Family Restaurant** (43 Rte. 236, Berwick, 207/715-0320, 4am-2pm Mon.-Fri., 4am-11:30am Sat.-Sun.).

Nature's Way Market (271 Main St., South Berwick, 207/384-3210, 9am-9pm Mon.-Fri., 8am-8pm Sat.-Sun.) isn't your ordinary health-food store. In addition to carrying healthful fare, it also specializes in locally made specialty foods and a wide array of wine and beer, is a state-licensed liquor store, and also contains a butcher shop, where you can purchase made-to-order sandwiches. Stock up here for a picnic in the park.

Relish (404 Main St., South Berwick, 207/384-8249, 5:30pm-9pm Wed.-Sat., $20-33) is an intimate, low-key neighborhood bistro where Linda Robinson and Christine Prunier serve well-crafted dinners with a French accent. A gluten-free menu is available. Make reservations: It's worth it.

GETTING THERE

South Berwick is about 11 miles or 20 minutes from Kittery via Route 236. It's about 10 miles or 20 minutes from South Berwick to York via Routes 236 and 91.

The Yorks

Four villages with distinct personalities—upscale **York Harbor,** historic **York Village,** casual **York Beach,** and semirural **Cape Neddick**—make up the **Town of York** (pop. 12,529). First inhabited by Native Americans, who named it Agamenticus, the area was settled as early as 1624, so history is serious business here. High points were its founding by Sir Ferdinando Gorges and the arrival of well-to-do vacationers in the 19th century. In between were Indian massacres, economic woes, and population shuffles. The town's population explodes in summer, which is pretty obvious in July-August when you're searching for a free patch of York Beach sand or a parking place. York Beach, with its seasonal surf and souvenir shops and amusements, has long been the counterpoint to genteel York Village, but that's changing with the restoration and rebirth of York Beach's downtown buildings and the arrival of tony restaurants, shops, and condos.

History and genealogy buffs can study the headstones in the Old Burying Ground or comb the archives of the Old York Historical Society. For lighthouse fans, there are Cape Neddick Light Station ("Nubble Light") and Boon Island, six miles offshore. You can rent horses or mountain bikes on Mount Agamenticus, board a deep-sea fishing boat in York Harbor, or spend an hour hiking the Cliff Path in York Harbor. For the kids there's a zoo, a lobster-boat cruise, a taffy maker, and, of course, the beach.

SIGHTS
◖ Old York Historical Society
Based in York Village, the **Old York Historical Society** (207 York St., York Village, 207/363-4974, www.oldyork.org, museum buildings 10am-5pm Tues.-Sat., 1pm-5pm Sun., early June-mid-Oct., $12 adults or $6 one building, $10 seniors or $5 one building, $5 ages 4-16 or $3 one building, $25 family or $15 one building) is the driving force behind a collection of

eight colonial and postcolonial buildings plus a research library open throughout the summer. Start at the **Jefferds' Tavern Visitor Center** (5 Lindsay Rd., York Village), where you'll need to buy tickets. Don't miss the **Old Burying Ground,** dating from 1735, across the street (rubbings are not allowed). Nearby are the **Old Gaol** and the **School House** (both fun for kids), **Ramsdell House,** and the **Emerson-Wilcox House.** About 0.5 mile down Lindsay Road on the York River are the **John Hancock Warehouse** and the **George Marshall Store Gallery** (140 Lindsay Rd.), operated in the summer as a respected contemporary-art gallery; across the river is the **Elizabeth Perkins House.** Antiques buffs shouldn't miss the Wilcox and Perkins Houses. These two and the Ramsdell House are open by guided tour; other buildings are self-guided. Visit some or all of the buildings at your own pace; no one leads you from one to another. You can walk to some of the sites from the tavern; to reach others you'll need a car, and parking may be limited.

◖ Nubble Light and Sohier Park
The best-known photo op in York is the distinctive 1879 lighthouse known formally as **Cape Neddick Light Station,** familiarly "The Nubble." Although there's no access to the lighthouse's island, the **Sohier Park Welcome Center** (Nubble Rd., off Rte. 1A, between Long and Short Sands Beaches, York Beach, 207/363-7608, www.nubblelight.org, 9am-7pm daily mid-May-mid-Oct.) provides the perfect viewpoint (and has restrooms). Parking is limited, but the turnover is fairly good. It's not a bad idea, however, to walk from the Long Sands parking area or come by bike, even though the road has inadequate shoulders. Weekdays this is also a popular spot for scuba divers.

Sayward-Wheeler House
Owned by the Boston-based Historic New

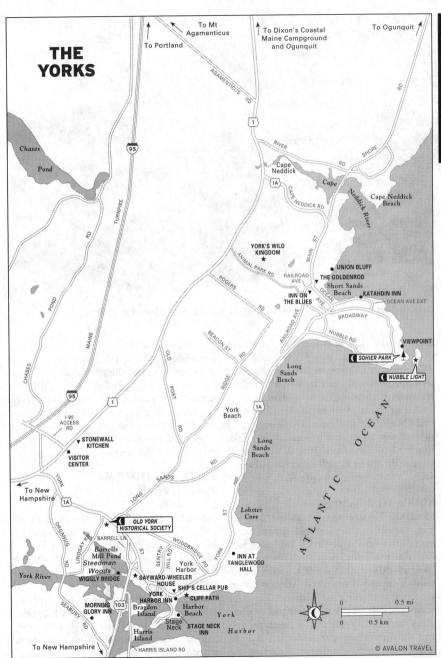

© TOM NANGLE

The Old Gaol is one of the sites maintained by the Old York Historical Society.

England, the 1718 **Sayward-Wheeler House** (9 Barrell Lane Ext., York Harbor, 207/384-2454, www.historicnewengland.org, $5) occupies a prime site at the edge of York Harbor. It's open with tours on the hour 11am-4pm the second and fourth Saturday of the month June-mid-October. In the house are original period furnishings, all in excellent condition. Take Route 1A to Lilac Lane (Rte. 103) to Barrell Lane and then to Barrell Lane Extension, or access it from the Fisherman's Walk.

York's Wild Kingdom

More than 250 creatures—including tigers, zebras, llamas, deer, lions, elephants, and monkeys—find a home at **York's Wild Kingdom** (102 Railroad Ave., off Rte. 1, York Beach, 207/363-4911 or 800/456-4911, www.yorkzoo.com). It's not what you'd call a state-of-the-art zoo, but it keeps the kids entertained. Elephant shows and other animal "events" occur three times daily in July-August. Between the zoo and the amusement-park rides, it's easy to spend a day here. Admission (covering the zoo and some of the rides) is in the neighborhood of $21 adults, $16 ages 4-12, $5 under age 4; an unlimited-rides day pass is $11. Zoo-only admission is $15 adults, $9 ages 4-12, $1 under age 4. The zoo is open 10am-6pm daily, late June to late August, closing at 5 pm from late May to late June and late August to late September. Amusement park hours are noon-9:30pm from late June until late August.

ENTERTAINMENT AND EVENTS
Live Music

Inn on the Blues (7 Ocean Ave., York Beach, 207/351-3221, www.innontheblues.com) has live music or a DJ (acoustic, blues, reggae) every night during the summer. The **Ship's Cellar Pub** (480 York St., York Harbor, 800/343-3869) in the York Harbor Inn frequently has live entertainment too. Free concerts are often held at the **Ellis Park Gazebo**, by Short Sands Beach, usually 7pm-9pm early July-early September; check local papers for schedule.

© HILARY NANGLE

Cape Neddick Light Station, known as "The Nubble," is an icon on Maine's coastline.

Festivals and Events

Each year, the Old York Historical Society invites decorators to transform a local house for the **Decorator Show House,** culminating in an open house mid-July–mid-August.

Late July–early August, the **York Days** festivities enliven the town with concerts, a road race, sand-castle contests, crafts shows, and fireworks.

York Village's **Annual Harvestfest,** in October, includes entertainment, crafts, hayrides, entertainment, and food.

The annual **Lighting of the Nubble** in late November includes cookies, hot chocolate, music, and an appearance by Santa Claus. The best part, though, is seeing the lighthouse glowing for the holidays.

RECREATION
Walks

Next to Harbor Beach, near the Stage Neck Inn, a sign marks the beginning of the **Cliff Path,** a walkway worth taking for its dramatic harbor views in the shadow of elegant summer cottages. On the one-hour round-trip, you'll pass the York Harbor Reading Room, an exclusive club. The path is on private property, traditionally open to the public courtesy of the owners, but controversy surfaces periodically about property rights, vandalism, and the condition of some sections of the walk. Note that it's called the Cliff Path for a reason; it's not a good choice for little ones. Another access point is the Hartley Mason Reservation parkland on Route 1A.

A less strenuous route is known variously as the **Shore Path, Harbor Walk,** or **Fisherman's Walk,** running west along the harbor and river from Stage Neck Road and passing the Sayward-Wheeler House before crossing the tiny green-painted Wiggly Bridge leading into the **Steedman Woods** preserve. Carry binoculars for good boat-watching and birding in the 16-acre preserve, owned by the Old York Historical Society. A one-mile double-loop trail takes less than an hour of easy strolling.

Mount Agamenticus

Drive to the summit of **Mount Agamenticus** ("The Big A") and you're at York County's highest point. It's only 692 feet, but on a clear day you'll have panoramic views of ocean, lakes, woods, and sometimes the White Mountains. The 10,000-acre preserve (www.agamenticus.org), one of the largest remaining expanses of undeveloped forest in coastal New England, is considered among the most biologically diverse wildernesses in Maine. It includes vernal pools and ponds and is home to rare and endangered species. At the summit are a billboard map of the 40-mile trail network and a curious memorial to Saint Aspinquid, a 17th-century Algonquian Indian leader. Mountain biking is also hugely popular on Agamenticus. Take a picnic, a kite, and binoculars. In the fall, if the wind is from the northwest, watch for migrating hawks; in winter, bring a sled for the best downhill run in southern Maine. From Route 1 in Cape Neddick, take Mountain Road (also called Agamenticus Road) 4.2 miles west to the access road.

Golf

The **Ledges Golf Club** (1 Ledges Dr., off Rte. 91, York, 207/351-9999, www.ledgesgolf.com) is an 18-hole course with daily public tee times.

Swimming

Sunbathing and swimming are big draws in York, with four beaches of varying sizes and accessibility. Bear in mind that traffic can be gridlocked along the beachfront (Rte. 1A) in midsummer, so it may take longer than you expect to get anywhere. **Lifeguards** are usually on duty 9:30am-4pm mid-June-Labor Day at Short Sands Beach, Long Sands Beach, and Harbor Beach. **Bathhouses** at Long Sands and Short Sands are open 9am-7pm daily in midsummer. The biggest **parking area** (metered) is at Long Sands, but that 1.5-mile beach also draws the most visitors. The scarcest parking is at Harbor Beach near the Stage Neck Inn and at Cape Neddick (Passaconaway) Beach near the Ogunquit town line.

Sea Kayaking

Kayak rentals begin at $55/day single, $75 double, from **Excursions: Coastal Maine Outfitting Company** (1740 Rte. 1, Cape Neddick, 207/363-0181, www.excursionsinmaine.com). Or sign up for a half-day tour ($60 ages 14 and older, $50 children). A four-hour basics clinic for ages 16 and older is $85. Excursions is based at Dixon's Campground on Route 1, four miles north of the I-95 York exit.

Harbor Adventures (Harris Island Rd., York Harbor, 207/363-8466, www.harboradventures.com) offers instruction and guided sea-kayaking trips from Kittery through Kennebunkport. Prices begin around $45 for a two-hour harbor tour.

Surfing

Want to catch a wave? For surfing or paddleboard information, lessons, or rentals, call **Liquid Dreams Surf Shop** (171 Long Beach Ave., York, 207/351-2545, www.liquiddreamssurf.com, 8am-8pm daily). It's right across from Long Sands Beach.

Bicycling

The **Berger's Bike Shop** (241 York St., York, 207/363-4070) rents hybrid bikes for $40 full day, $30 half day; lock and helmet are *not* included.

Fishing

A local expert on fly-fishing, spin fishing, and conventional tackle is **Eldredge Bros. Guide Service** (1480 Rte. 1, Cape Neddick, 207/373-9269, www.eldredgeflyshop.com). Four-hour guided trips for one or two anglers begin at $250 in freshwater, $350 in saltwater.

ACCOMMODATIONS
Bed-and-Breakfasts

.A boutique bed-and-breakfast catering to romantics, the **Morning Glory Inn** (120 Seabury Rd., York Harbor, 207/363-2062, www.morninggloryinnmaine.com, $175-235) has just three guest rooms, all very spacious and private and all with doors to private patios or yards, air-conditioning, TVs with DVD players, fridges, Wi-Fi, and plentiful other little amenities. The living room, in the original section of the house, was a 17th-century cottage, barged over from the Isles of Shoals; the newer post-and-beam great room doubles as a dining area, where a hot breakfast buffet is served. The property is quiet—listen to the birds singing in the gardens; it's truly a magical setting, far removed yet convenient to everything York offers.

Everything's casual and flowers are everywhere at the brightly painted **Katahdin Inn** (11 Ocean Ave., York Beach, 207/363-1824, www.thekatahdininn.com, year-round, $165-195), overlooking the breakers of Short Sands Beach. Longtime owners Rae and Paul LeBlanc appropriately refer to it as a "bed and beach." It was built in 1863 and has always been a guesthouse. Nine smallish guest rooms on three floors, eight of them with water views, have four-poster beds and mostly shared baths. Breakfast is not included, but coffee is always available, the rooms have refrigerators, and several eateries are nearby.

Built in 1889, **The Inn at Tanglewood Hall** (611 York St., York Harbor, 207/351-1075, www.tanglewoodhall.com, $175-235) was once the summer home of bandleaders Jimmy and Tommy Dorsey. More recently, it was a York Historical Society Decorator Show House. It's an elegant, gracious property within walking distance of the beach, yet a world away. All rooms TV/DVDs and Wi-Fi, some have gas fireplaces, refrigerators, or private porches. Beautiful woodland gardens are another plus.

Inns

York Harbor Inn (Rte. 1A, York Harbor, 207/363-5119 or 800/343-3869, www.yorkharborinn.com, $179-349) is an accommodating spot with a country-inn flavor and a wide variety of guest-room and package-plan options throughout the year. The oldest section of the inn is a 17th-century cabin from the Isles of Shoals. Accommodations are spread out in the inn, the adjacent Yorkshire House, and four elegantly restored houses, all with resident innkeepers: Harbor Hill and Harbor Cliffs are within steps, and the pet-friendly 1730 Harbor Crest and the Chapman Cottage are about a half mile away. All have TVs, phones, free Wi-Fi, and air-conditioning; some have four-poster beds, fireplaces, and whirlpools; many have water views. Rates include a generous continental breakfast.

You can't miss the **Stage Neck Inn** (100 Stage Neck Rd., York Harbor, 207/363-3850 or 800/340-9901, www.stageneck.com, year-round, from $325), occupying its own private peninsula overlooking York Harbor. Modern resort-style facilities include an indoor and an outdoor pool, tennis courts, golf privileges, a spa, a fitness center, and spectacular views from balconies and terraces. The formal Harbor Porches restaurant (no jeans, entrées $26-30) and the casual Sandpiper Bar and Grille are open to nonguests.

Hotels

For more than 150 years, **The Union Bluff** (8 Beach St., York Beach, 207/363-1333 or 800/833-0721, www.unionbluff.com, from $210) has stood sentry like a fortress overlooking Short Sands Beach. Guest rooms are split between three buildings, all within spitting distance of the beach. Most have ocean views. All have TVs, air-conditioning, and phones; some have fireplaces, whirlpool baths, or oceanview decks. Also on the premises are the Beach Street Grill dining room and a pub serving lighter fare. The best deals are the packages, which include breakfast and dinner. The hotel and pub are open year-round; the restaurant is seasonal. It's probably best to avoid dates when there's a wedding in-house.

Condominium Suites

Fabulously sited on the oceanfront and overlooking the Nubble Light, the high-end **ViewPoint** (229 Nubble Rd., York Beach, 207/363-2661 or 888/363-4087, www.viewpointhotel.com, from $305 night, $1,975 week) comprises luxuriously appointed 1-3-bedroom suites. All have gas fireplaces; fully equipped kitchens; washer-dryers; TVs; phones; private patios, porches, or decks; and Wi-Fi. On the premises are an outdoor heated pool, a grilling area, gardens, and a playground.

Camping

Dixon's Coastal Maine Campground (1740 Rte. 1, Cape Neddick, 207/363-3626, www. dixonscampground.com, $34-40) has more than 100 well-spaced sites on 26 wooded and open acres. It can accommodate tents and small RVs. Electric and water hookups are available. Facilities include a playground and a good-size outdoor heated pool. It's also the base for Excursions sea kayaking.

FOOD
Local Flavors

Stonewall Kitchen (Stonewall Lane, York, 207/351-2712 or 800/207-5267, www.stonewallkitchen.com) concocts imaginative condiments and other food products, many of which have received national awards. Go hungry: An espresso bar and an excellent café are on the premises. Stonewall is open daily for breakfast and lunch and light fare in the late afternoon.

Sometimes the line runs right out the door of the low-ceilinged, reddish-brown roadside shack that houses local institution **Flo's Steamed Dogs** (1359 Rte. 1, opposite the Mountain Rd. turnoff, Cape Neddick, no phone, www.floshotdogs.com, 11am-3pm, Thurs.-Tues.). Founder Flo Stacy died in 2000 at age 92, but her legend and her family live on. There is no menu—just steamed Schultz wieners, buns, chips, beverages, and an attitude. The secret? The spicy, sweet-sour hot-dog sauce, allegedly once sought by the H. J. Heinz corporation, but the Stacy family isn't telling or selling. The cognoscenti know to order their dogs only with mayonnaise and the special sauce, nothing heretical such as ketchup or mustard. It's open 11am-3pm, and not a minute later, Thursday-Tuesday year-round.

See those people with their faces pressed to the glass? They're all watching the taffy makers inside **The Goldenrod** (2 Railroad Ave., York Beach, 207/363-2621, www.thegoldenrod. com, 11am-8pm), where machines spew out 180 Goldenrod Kisses a minute, 65 tons a year, and have been at it since 1896. The Goldenrod is an old-fashioned place with a tearoom, a gift shop, an old-fashioned soda fountain with 135 ice cream flavors, and a rustic dining room as well as equally old-fashioned prices.

After viewing The Nubble, head across the road to **Brown's Ice Cream** (232 Nubble Rd., York Beach, 207/363-1277), where unusual flavors complement the standards.

Craving jerk chicken or curried goat? Stop by **Jamaican Jerk Center** (1400 Rte. 1, Cape Neddick, 207/351-3033, www.jamaicanjerkcenter.com, 11am-9pm daily), a seasonal takeout with tables under a tent and on the lawn. There's live reggae music on weekends beginning at 4pm. Yes, it's a dive, but the food's good.

Stop in at the **Gateway Farmers Market** (Greater York Region Chamber of Commerce Visitors Center, Rte. 1, York, 9am-1pm Sat. mid-June-early Oct. and Thurs. July-Aug.) and stock up for a picnic. If you still need more, head next door to Stonewall Kitchen.

Family Favorites

The York Harbor Inn's **Ship's Cellar Pub** (11:30am-11:30pm Mon.-Thurs., 11:30am-midnight Fri.-Sat., 3pm-11:30pm Sun.) attracts even the locals. The menu is the same as in the main dining room (burgers to lobster, $10-36), but the setting is far more casual. The space is designed to resemble the interior of a yacht. The pub doubles as a favorite local watering hole, with live music Wednesday-Sunday. Happy hour, with free munchies, is 4pm-6pm weekdays and sometimes draws a raucous crowd.

Wild Willy's (765 Rte. 1, York, 207/363-9924, www.wildwillysburgers.com, 11am-8pm Mon.-Sat., $7-9) has turned burgers into an art form. More than a dozen hefty mouthwatering burgers, all made from certified Angus or natural (chem-free) beef or bison, are available, from the classic Willy burger to the Rio Grande, with roasted green chilies from New Mexico and cheddar cheese. Don't miss the hand-cut fries. Order at the counter before grabbing a seat in the dining area or out on the back deck; the servers will find you when it's ready.

Locals swear by **Rick's All Seasons Café** (240 York St., York, 207/363-5584, 6am-2pm Tues.-Sun.), where the prices are low, the food is good, and the gossip is even better. Have patience: Almost everything is cooked to order.

Casual Dining

"Food that loves you back" is the slogan for **Frankie and Johnny's Natural Foods** (1594 Rte. 1 N., Cape Neddick, 207/363-1909, www.frankie-johnnys.com, from 5pm Wed.-Sun. Feb.-Dec., $23-36). Inside the shingled restaurant, wood floors and pine-colored walls provide the background for the vibrant, internationally seasoned fare of chef John Shaw, who trained at the Culinary Institute of America. Vegetarian and vegan choices are always on the menu, along with fish, seafood, and chicken options, and many dishes can be modified for the gluten-sensitive. Portions are huge, breads and pastas are made in-house, and everything is cooked to order, so plan on a leisurely meal. All entrées come with a soup or salad (opt for the house salad—it's gorgeous). Plan on leftovers. Bring your own booze, but leave the credit cards behind, since "plastic is not natural."

The Tavern at Chapman Cottage (370 York St., York Harbor, 207/363-5119, 4pm-9pm daily, $12-15), owned by the York Harbor Inn, serves a light menu, with options such as crab cakes and spicy lamb pizza.

For ocean views paired with a finer dining atmosphere, book a table at the York Harbor Inn's main dining room, **1637** (Rte. 1A, York Harbor, 207/363-5119, www.yorkharborinn. com, 5pm-10pm Thurs.-Sun., $20-35).

GiGi's (2 Beach St., York Beach, 207//351-8147, www.gigisyorkbeach.com, from 5pm daily), opened in 2013, shows a lot of promise, but suffered from first-season inconsistencies in food and service. That said, ask locally and give it a try. The balcony is ideal for people watching. Inside, the dining areas are sharp and simple. The fare is upscale Italian; think antipasto,

house-made gnocchi, and osso bucco. The bar earns raves, and happy hour (3pm-5pm daily) draws a crowd for food and drink specials.

Lobster

Friends praise the lobster roll from **The Maine Lobster Outlet** (360 Rte. 1, York, 207/363-9899, www.mainelobsteroutlet.com, 10am-5pm daily) as one of the state's best, and say the clam chowder is excellent. It's takeout only. Another good choice for a lobster roll is **Four Mile Lobster** (1902 Rte. 1, Cape Neddick, 207/251-0001, 11am-7pm Wed.-Sun.), located behind Knight's Quilt Shop. Yes, strange location, but it's a family operation, with Dad being the lobsterman and Mom owning the quilt shop.

Grab an oceanfront seat at **Lobster Cove** (756 York St., York Beach, 207/351-1100, www.lobstercoverestaurant.com, from 8am daily year-round) and watch the waves roll into Long Sands Beach while enjoying lobster or fried seafood.

INFORMATION AND SERVICES

The Maine Tourism Association operates a **Maine State Visitor Information Center** (1 Rte. 95, Kittery, 207/439-1319) in Kittery between Route 1 and I-95, with access from either road. It's chock-full of brochures and has restrooms and a picnic area.

For York-area information, head for the Shingle-style palace of the **Greater York Region Chamber of Commerce** (1 Stonewall Lane, off Rte. 1, York, 207/363-4422, www. gatewaytomaine.org), at I-95's York exit. Inside are restrooms. It's open daily in summer.

GETTING THERE AND AROUND

York is about eight miles or 15 minutes via I-95/ The Maine Turnpike; allow at least 20 minutes via Route 1, from Kittery. It's about seven miles or 15 minutes via Route 1 to Ogunquit, but allow more time in summer.

The Maine Turnpike, a toll road, is generally the fastest route if you're trying to get between two towns. Route 1 parallels the turnpike on the ocean side. It's mostly two lanes and is lined with shops, restaurants, motels, and other visitor-oriented sites, which means stop-and-go traffic that often slows to a crawl. If you're traveling locally, it's best to walk or use the local trolley systems, which have the bonus of saving you the agony of finding a parking spot.

The seasonal **Shoreline Explorer** (207/324-5762, www.shorelineexplorer.com) trolley system makes it possible to connect from York to Kennebunkport without your car. Each town's system is operated separately and has its own fees. The **York Trolley/York Beach Shuttle** (207/748-3030, www.yorktrolley.com) operates between Long and Short Sands Beaches late June-early September. The service ($1.50 one-way) runs every 30 minutes 10am-10:15pm. **The Shore Road Shuttle** (207/324-5762, www.shorelineexplorer.com) operates hourly between York's Short Sands Beach and Ogunquit's Perkins Cove late June-Labor Day; check for an exact schedule; $1 each way; $3 day pass, $10 for 12-ride pass; ages 18 and younger ride free.

Ogunquit and Wells

Ogunquit (pop. 892) has been a holiday destination since the indigenous residents named it "beautiful place by the sea." What's the appeal? An unparalleled, unspoiled beach, several top-flight albeit pricey restaurants, a dozen art galleries, and a respected art museum with a view second to none. The town has been home to an art colony attracting the glitterati of the painting world starting with Charles Woodbury in the late 1880s. The summertime crowds continue, multiplying the minuscule year-round population. These days it's an especially gay-friendly community too. Besides the beach, the most powerful magnet is Perkins Cove, a working fishing enclave that looks more like a movie set. The best way to approach the cove is via trolley-bus or on foot, along the shoreline Marginal Way from downtown Ogunquit; midsummer parking in the cove is madness.

Wells (pop. 9,589), once the parent of Ogunquit and since 1980 its immediate neighbor to the north, was settled in 1640. Nowadays it's best known as a long, skinny, family-oriented community with seven miles of splendid beachfront and lots of antiques and used-book shops strewn along Route 1. It also claims two spectacular nature preserves worth a drive from anywhere. At the southern end of Wells, abutting Ogunquit, is **Moody,** an enclave named after 18th-century settler Samuel Moody.

SIGHTS
◖ Ogunquit Museum of American Art (OMAA)

Not many museums can boast a view as stunning as the one at the **Ogunquit Museum of American Art** (543 Shore Rd., Ogunquit, 207/646-4909, www.ogunquitmuseum.org, 10am-5pm daily, early May-Oct. 31, $10 adults, $9 seniors and students, free under age 12), nor can many communities boast such renown as a summer art colony. Overlooking Narrow Cove 1.4 miles south of downtown Ogunquit, the museum prides itself on its distinguished permanent 2,000-piece American art collection. Works by Marsden Hartley, Rockwell Kent, Walt Kuhn, Henry Strater, and Thomas Hart Benton, among others, are displayed in five galleries. Special exhibits are mounted each summer, when there is an extensive series of lectures, concerts, and other programs, including the annual "Almost Labor Day Auction," a social season must. OMAA has a well-stocked gift shop, wheelchair access, and landscaped grounds with sculptures, a pond, and manicured lawns.

© HILARY NANGLE

No visit to Ogunquit is complete without walking the Marginal Way.

[Marginal Way

No visit to Ogunquit is complete without a lei-surely stroll along the **Marginal Way**, the mile-long footpath edging the ocean from Shore Road (by the Sparhawk Resort) to Perkins Cove. It has been a must-walk since Josiah Chase gave the right-of-way to the town in the 1920s. The best times to appreciate this shrub-lined shorefront walkway are early morning or when everyone's at the beach. En route are tidepools, intriguing rock formations, crash-ing surf, pocket beaches, benches (although the walk's a cinch and is even partially wheelchair-accessible), and a marker listing the day's high and low tides. When the surf's up, keep a close eye on the kids—the sea has no mercy. A mid-point access is at Israel's Head (behind a sewage plant masquerading as a tiny lighthouse), but getting a parking space is pure luck. The only wheels allowed are strollers and wheelchairs.

Perkins Cove

Turn-of-the-20th-century photos show Ogunquit's **Perkins Cove** lined with gray-shingled shacks used by a hardy colony of local fishermen, fellows who headed offshore to make a tough living in little boats. They'd hardly recognize it today. Although the cove re-mains a working lobster-fishing harbor, several old shacks have been reincarnated as boutiques and restaurants, and photographers go crazy shooting the quaint inlet spanned by a little pedestrian drawbridge. In the cove are galler-ies, gift shops, a range of eateries (fast food to lobster to high-end dining), boat excursions, and public restrooms. I enjoy it best in the early morning, before the crowds arrive. Only a cof-fee shop at the tip is open then, but you can watch the fishing boats gear up and head out. Parking in the cove is $3 for two hours, but there are some spaces in the back that open up after noon (reserved for local fishermen in the morning).

[Wells Reserve at Laudholm Farm

Known locally as Laudholm Farm (the name of the restored 19th-century visitors center),

Wells National Estuarine Research Reserve (342 Laudholm Farm Rd., Wells, 207/646-1555, www.wellsreserve.org) occupies 1,690 acres of woods, beach, and coastal salt marsh on the southern boundary of the Rachel Carson National Wildlife Refuge, just 0.5 mile east of Route 1. Seven miles of trails wind through the property. The best trail is the Salt Marsh Loop, with a boardwalk section leading to an overlook with panoramic views of the marsh and Little River inlet. Another winner is the Barrier Beach Walk, a 1.3-mile round-trip that goes through multiple habitats all the way to beautiful Laudholm Beach. Allow 1.5 hours for either; you can combine the two. Some trails are wheelchair-accessible. The informative exhibits in the **visitors center** (10am-4pm Mon.-Sat., noon-4pm Sun. late May-mid-Oct., 10am-4pm Mon.-Fri. Oct.-Mar., closed mid-Dec.-mid-Jan.) make a valuable prelude for enjoying the reserve. An extensive program schedule (Apr.-Nov.) includes lectures, nature walks, and children's programs. Reservations are required for some programs. Trails are accessible 7am-dusk. Late May-mid-October, admission is charged: $4 adults, $1 ages 6-16, maximum $10/car.

Rachel Carson National Wildlife Refuge

Eleven chunks of coastal Maine real estate between Kittery Point and Cape Elizabeth make up the **Rachel Carson National Wildlife Refuge** (321 Port Rd./Rte. 9, Wells, 207/646-9226, www.fws.gov/refuge/rachel_carson) headquartered at the northern edge of Wells near the Kennebunkport town line. Pick up a *Carson Trail Guide* at the refuge office (parking is very limited) and follow the mile-long wheelchair-accessible walkway past tidal creeks, salt pans, and salt marshes. It's a bird-watcher's paradise during migration seasons. Office hours are 8am-4:30pm Monday-Friday year-round; trail access is sunrise-sunset daily year-round. Leashed pets are allowed.

Ogunquit Arts Collaborative Gallery

Closer to downtown Ogunquit is the **Ogunquit**

Arts Collaborative Gallery (Shore Rd. and Bourne Lane, Ogunquit, 207/646-8400, www.barngallery.org, 11am-5pm Mon.-Sat., 1pm-5pm Sun. late May-early Oct., free), also known as the Barn Gallery, featuring the works of member artists, an impressive group. The OAC is the showcase for the Ogunquit Art Association, established by Charles Woodbury, who was inspired to open an art school in Perkins Cove in the late 19th century. Special programs throughout the season include concerts, workshops, gallery talks, and an art auction.

Ogunquit Heritage Museum

Ogunquit's history is preserved in the **Ogunquit Heritage Museum** (86 Obeds Lane, Dorothea Jacobs Grant Common, Ogunquit, 207/646-0296, www.ogunquitheritagemuseum.org, 1pm-5pm Tues.-Sat. June-Sept., donation), which opened in 2001 in the restored Captain James Winn House, a 1785 cape house listed on the National Register of Historic Places. Exhibits here and in a new ell focus on Ogunquit's role as an art colony, its maritime heritage, town history, and local architecture.

ENTERTAINMENT
Ogunquit Playhouse

Having showcased top-notch professional theater since the 1930s, the 750-seat **Ogunquit Playhouse** (Rte. 1, Ogunquit, 207/646-5511, www.ogunquitplayhouse.org), a summer classic, knows how to do it right: It presents comedies and musicals, late May-late Oct. with big-name stars. The air-conditioned building is wheelchair-accessible. The box office is open daily in season, beginning in early May; tickets range $39-78. The playhouse also presents a children's series. You can also take a guided **Backstage Tour** ($5 for 45 minutes or $10 for 90 minutes) taking in the dressing rooms, green room, and backstage while picking up insider info on the stars who have played here over the years; call for current schedule. Parking can be a hassle during shows; consider walking the short distance from the Bourne Lane trolley-bus stop.

© TOM NANGLE

The Ogunquit Playhouse has showcased top-notch professional entertainment since the 1930s.

Live Music

Ogunquit has several nightspots with good reputations for food and live entertainment. Best known is **Jonathan's** (2 Bourne Lane, Ogunquit, 207/646-4777 or 800/464-9934 in Maine), where national headliners often are on the schedule upstairs. Advance tickets are cheaper than at the door, and dinner guests (entrées $24-34; gluten-free menu available) get preference for seats; all show seats are reserved.

Ogunquit Performing Arts (207/646-6170, www.ogunquitperformingarts.org) presents a full slate of programs, including classical concerts, ballet, and theater, at the **Dunaway Center** (23 School Street). The **Wells Summer Concert Series** runs most Saturday evenings early July-early September at the Hope Hobbs Gazebo in Wells Harbor Park. A wide variety of music is represented, from sing-alongs to swing.

FESTIVALS AND EVENTS

During **Restaurant Week** in early June, Ogunquit-area restaurants offer specials.

Harbor Fest takes place in July in Harbor Park in Wells and includes a concert, a crafts fair, a parade, a chicken barbecue, and children's activities.

In August Ogunquit hosts the annual **Sidewalk Art Show and Sale.**

Capriccio is a performing arts festival in Ogunquit with daytime and evening events held during the first week of September. The second weekend that month, the Wells National Estuarine Research Reserve (Laudholm Farm) hosts the **Laudholm Nature Crafts Festival,** a two-day juried crafts fair with children's activities and guided nature walks.

SHOPPING

Antiques are a Wells specialty. You'll find more than 50 shops with a huge range of prices. The majority are on Route 1. **R. Jorgensen Antiques** (502 Post Rd./Rte. 1, Wells, 207/646-9444) is a phenomenon in itself, filling 11 showrooms in two buildings with European and American 18th- and 19th-century furniture and accessories. **MacDougall-Gionet Antiques and Associates** (2104 Post

Rd./Rte. 1, Wells, 207/646-3531) has been in business since 1959, and its reputation is stellar. The 65-dealer shop, in an 18th-century barn, carries American and European country and formal furniture and accessories.

If you've been scouring antiquarian bookshops for a long-wanted title, chances are you'll find it at **Douglas N. Harding Rare Books** (2152 Post Rd./Rte. 1, Wells, 207/646-8785 or 800/228-1398). Well cataloged and organized, the sprawling bookshop at any given time stocks upward of 100,000 books, prints, and maps, plus a hefty selection of Maine and New England histories.

Fans of fine craft, especially contemporary art glass, shouldn't miss **Panache** (307 Main St., Ogunquit, 207/646-4878).

RECREATION
Water Sports
BEACHES

One of Maine's most scenic and unspoiled sandy beachfronts, Ogunquit's 3.5-mile stretch of sand fringed with sea grass is a magnet for hordes of sunbathers, spectators, swimmers, surfers, and sand-castle builders. Getting there means crossing the Ogunquit River via one of three access points. For Ogunquit's **Main Beach**—with a bathhouse and big crowds—take Beach Street. To reach **Footbridge Beach,** marginally less crowded, either take Ocean Street and the footbridge or take Bourne Avenue to Ocean Avenue in adjacent Wells and walk back toward Ogunquit. **Moody Beach,** at Wells's southern end, is technically private property, a subject of considerable legal dispute. Lifeguards are on duty all summer at the public beaches, and there are restrooms in all three areas. The beach is free, but parking is not. Rates range $15-25/day and lots fill up early on warm midsummer days. After 3:30pm some parking is free. It's far more sensible to opt for the frequent trolley-buses.

Wells beaches continue where Ogunquit's leave off. **Crescent Beach** (Webhannet Dr. between Eldredge Rd. and Mile Rd.) is the tiniest, with tidepools, no facilities, and limited parking. **Wells Beach** (Mile Rd. to Atlantic Ave.) is the major (and most crowded) beach, with lifeguards, restrooms, and parking. Around the other side of Wells Harbor is **Drakes Island Beach** (take Drakes Island Rd. at the blinking light), a less crowded spot with restrooms and lifeguards. Walk northeast from Drakes Island Beach and you'll eventually reach **Laudholm Beach**, with great birding along the way. Summer beach-parking fees (pay-and-display) are $16/day or $8/afternoon for nonresidents ($5 for a motorcycle, $25 for an RV); if you're staying longer, a 10-token pass ($75) is a better bargain.

BOAT EXCURSIONS

Depending on your interests, you can go deep-sea fishing, whale-watching, or just gawking out of Perkins Cove in Ogunquit.

Between April and early November, Captain Tim Tower runs half-day (departing 4pm, $50 pp) and full-day (departing 7am, $85 pp) **deep-sea fishing trips** aboard the 40-foot **Bunny Clark** (207/646-2214, www.bunnyclark.com), moored in Perkins Cove. Reservations are necessary. Tim has a science degree, so he's a wealth of marine biology information. All gear is provided, and the crew will fillet your catch for you; dress warmly and wear sunblock.

Barnacle Billy's Dock at Perkins Cove is home port for the Hubbard family's **Finestkind Cruises** (207/646-5227, www.finestkind-cruises.com, no credit cards). Motorboat options consist of 1.5-hour, 14-mile Nubble Lighthouse cruises; one-hour cocktail cruises; a 75-minute breakfast cruise, complete with coffee, juice, and a muffin; and 50-minute lobster-boat trips. Rates run $17-26 adults, $8-13 children. Also available are 1.75-hour sails ($30 pp) aboard **The Cricket**, a locally built wooden sailboat. Reservations are advisable but usually unnecessary midweek.

EQUIPMENT RENTALS

At **Wheels and Waves** (579 Post Rd./Rte. 1, Wells, 207/646-5774, www.wheelsnwaves.com), bike or surfboard rentals are $30/day, including delivery to some hotels; a stand-up

© HILARY NANGLE

Ogunquit's 3.5-mile stretch of sand is a magnet for beach lovers.

paddleboard is $40, a single kayak is $65, and a double is $75.

Put in right at the harbor and explore t`he estuary from **Webhannet River Kayak and Canoe Rentals** (345 Harbor Rd., Wells, 207/646-9649, www.webhannetriver.com). Rates begin at $25 solo, $40 tandem for two hours.

Golf

The 18-hole Donald Ross-designed **Cape Neddick Country Club** (650 Shore Rd., Cape Neddick, 207/361-2011, www.capeneddickgolf. com) is a semiprivate 18-hole course with a restaurant and a driving range.

ACCOMMODATIONS

Most properties are open only seasonally.

Ogunquit
MOTELS

You're almost within spitting distance of Perkins Cove at the 37-room **Riverside Motel** (159 Shore Rd., 207/646-2741, www.

riversidemotel.com, $199-249), where you can perch on your balcony and watch the action or, for that matter, join it. Guest rooms have phones, air-conditioning, refrigerators, Wi-Fi, cable TV, and fabulous views. Rates include continental breakfast. The entire 3.5-acre property is smoke-free.

Juniper Hill Inn (336 Main St., 207/646-4501 or 800/646-4544, www.ogunquit.com, year-round, $149-264) is a well-run motel-style lodging on five acres close to downtown Ogunquit, with a footpath to the beach. Amenities include refrigerators, cable TV, coin-operated laundry, a fitness center, indoor and outdoor pools and hot tubs, and golf privileges.

The frills are few, but the **Towne Lyne Motel** (747 Main St./Rte. 1, 207/646-2955, www. townelynemotel.com, $139-184) is a charmer set back from the highway amid manicured lawns. Rooms are air-conditioned and have free Wi-Fi and phone, refrigerators, and microwaves; some have screened porches. Request a riverside room.

COTTAGES

It's nearly impossible to land a peak-season cottage at **The Dunes** (518 Main St., 207/646-2612, www.dunesonthewaterfront.com $150-250), but it's worth trying. The property is under its third generation of ownership, and guests practically will their weeks to their descendants. Nineteen tidy, well-equipped one- or two-bedroom housekeeping cottages with screened porches and wood-burning fireplaces as well as 17 guest rooms are generously spaced on shady, grassy lawns that roll down to the river, with the dunes just beyond. Facilities include a dock with rowboats, a pool, and lawn games. Amenities include Wi-Fi, TVs, phones, and refrigerators. It's all meticulously maintained. In peak season, the one- or two-bedroom cottages require a one- or two-week minimum stay; guest rooms require three nights.

ECLECTIC PROPERTIES

The Beachmere Inn (62 Beachmere Pl., 207/646-2021 or 800/336-3983, www.

beachmereinn.com, year-round, $170-440) occupies an enviable oceanfront location on the Marginal Way, yet is just steps from downtown. The private family-owned and operated property comprises an updated Victorian inn, a new seaside motel, and other buildings, all meticulously maintained and often updated. Pocket beaches are just outside the gate. All rooms have air-conditioning, TVs, phones, and kitchenettes; most have balconies, decks, or terraces; some have fireplaces; almost all have jaw-dropping ocean views. There's also a small spa with a hot tub, steam sauna, and fitness room; and a pub serving light fare and drinks. Morning coffee and pastries are provided.

It's not easy to describe the **Sparhawk Oceanfront Resort** (41 Shore Rd., 207/646-5562, www.thesparhawk.com, $210-330), a sprawling one-of-a-kind place popular with honeymooners, sedate families, and seniors. There's lots of tradition in this thriving six-acre complex—it has had various incarnations since the turn of the 20th century—and the "Happily Filled" sign regularly hangs out

The Beachmere Inn has a prime location overlooking Ogunquit Beach on Marginal Way.

© HILARY NANGLE

front. Out back is the Atlantic Ocean with forever views, and the Marginal Way starts right here. It offers a tennis court, gardens, and a heated pool; breakfast is included. The 87 guest rooms in four buildings vary from motel-type (best views) rooms and suites to inn-type suites. There's a seven-night minimum during July-August.

INNS AND BED-AND-BREAKFASTS

When you want to be at the center of the action, book a room at **2 Village Square Inn** (14 Village Square Ln., 207/646-5779, www.2vsquare.com, $189-269). The walk-to-everything location puts the beach, the Marginal Way, shops, restaurants, and more all within footsteps, if you can tear yourself away from the dreamy views, heated outdoor pool, hut tub, and even an on-site massage room. Owners Scott Osgood and Bruce Senecal have earned a reputation as conscientious innkeepers who aim to please. They also operate the **Nellie Littlefield Inn & Spa** (27 Shore Rd., 207/646-1692, www.nliogunquit.com, $229-319), a magnificently restored in-town Victorian, and the **Gazebo Inn** (572 Main St., 207/646-3773, www.gazeboinnogt.com, $159-499), a carefully renovated 1847 farmhouse and barn within walking distance of Footbridge Beach. All serve a full breakfast buffet. None welcome children.

Jacqui Grant's warm welcome, gracious hospitality, and stellar breakfasts combined with a quiet residential location within walking distance of both the village and Footbridge Beach have earned **Almost Home** (27 King's Ln., 207/641-1754, www.almosthomeinnogunquit.com, $155-235) a stellar reputation. She often serves afternoon cheese with wine from her son's California winery. Rooms are spacious and have nice seating areas, and the backyard makes a quiet retreat.

Built in 1899 for a prominent Maine lumbering family, **Rockmere Lodge** (40 Stearns Rd., 207/646-2985, www.rockmere.com, year-round, $175-245) underwent a meticulous six-month restoration in the early 1990s and has frequent updates since. Near the Marginal Way on a peaceful street, the handsome home has

eight comfortable Victorian guest rooms, all with CD players and cable TV (a massive library of films and CDs is available) and most with ocean views. Rates include a generous breakfast. A wraparound veranda, decks, gardens, a gazebo, and "The Lookout," a third-floor windowed nook with comfy chairs, make it easy to settle in and just watch the passersby on the Marginal Way. Beach towels, chairs, and umbrellas are provided for guests. Pets are not allowed; there are dogs in residence.

The historical **Colonial Inn** (145 Shore Rd., 207/646-5191, www.thecolonialinn.com, from $199) reopened in 2013 after a $4 million restoration that brought the Victorian-era inn in to the 21st century, with amenities including air-conditioning and Wi-Fi. Rooms in the main inn are bright and airy, and some have water views. Family-oriented rooms are located in separate buildings, and some have kitchenettes. It's an easy walk to the beach, but if the ocean's too chilly, the hotel has a heated outdoor pool and hot tub. A continental breakfast buffet is provided. The location puts the best of Ogunquit within footsteps.

RESORTS

Founded in 1872, **The Cliff House Resort and Spa** (Shore Rd., 207/361-1000, www.cliff-housemaine.com, late Mar.-early Dec., $275-370), a self-contained complex, sprawls over 70 acres topping the edge of Bald Head Cliff midway between the centers of York and Ogunquit. Fourth-generation innkeeper Kathryn Weare keeps updating and modernizing the facilities. Among the most recent additions is a spa building with oversize rooms with king beds, gas fireplaces, and balconies as well as a full-service spa, an indoor pool, an outdoor infinity pool, and a glass-walled fitness center overlooking the Atlantic. A central check-in building with an indoor amphitheater connects the main building to the spa building. The 150 guest rooms and suites vary widely in decor, from old-fashioned to contemporary; all have cable TV and phones, some have gas fireplaces, and most have a spectacular ocean view. Other facilities include a dining room, a lounge, family indoor and outdoor pools, a games room, and tennis courts. Eight pet-friendly rooms ($25) have a bowl, a bed, and treats, and there's a fenced-in exercise area. Packages offer the best bang for the buck.

Wells

Once part of a giant 19th-century dairy farm, the **Beach Farm Inn** (97 Eldredge Rd., 207/646-8493, www.beachfarminn.com, year-round, $100-150) is a 2.5-acre oasis in a rather congested area 0.2 mile off Route 1. Guests can swim in the pool, relax in the library, or walk 0.25 mile down the road to the beach. Five of the eight guest rooms have private baths (two are detached); third-floor rooms have air-conditioning. Rates include a full breakfast; a cottage rents for $725/week.

Even closer to the beach is **Haven by the Sea** (59 Church St., Wells Beach, 207/646-4194, www.havenbythesea.com, from $240), a heavenly bed-and-breakfast in a former church. Innkeepers John and Susan Jarvis have kept the original floor plan, which allows for some surprises. Inside are hardwood floors, cathedral ceilings, and stained-glass windows. The confessional is now a full bar, and the altar has been converted to a dining area that opens to a marsh-view terrace—the bird-watching is superb. Guest rooms have sitting areas, and the suite has a whirlpool tub and a fireplace. Guests have plenty of room to relax, including a living area with a fireplace. Rates include a full breakfast and afternoon hors d'oeuvres.

FOOD
Ogunquit
LOCAL FLAVORS

The Egg and I (501 Maine St./Rte. 1, 207/646-8777, www.eggandibreakfast.com, 6am-2pm daily, no credit cards) has more than 200 menu choices and earns high marks for its omelets and waffles. You can't miss it; there's always a crowd. Lunch choices are served after 11am.

Equally popular is **Amore Breakfast** (309 Shore Rd., 207/646-6661, www.amorebreakfast.com, 7am-1pm daily). Choose from 14 omelets, eight versions of eggs Benedict (including

lobster and a spirited rancheros version topped with salsa and served with guacamole), as well as French toast, waffles, and all the regulars and irregulars.

Eat in or take out from **Village Food Market** (Main St., Ogunquit Center, 207/646-2122, www.villagefoodmarket.com). A breakfast sandwich is less than $3, subs and sandwiches are available in three sizes, and there's even a children's menu. The Pick Three prepared dinner special includes an entrée and two side dishes for $9.95.

Scrumptious baked goods, tantalizing salads, and vegetarian lunch items are available to go at **Bread and Roses** (246 Main St., 207/646-4227, www.breadandrosesbakery.com, 7am-7pm daily), a small bakery right downtown with a few tables outside.

Harbor Candy Shop (26 Main St., 207/646-8078 or 800/331-5856) is packed with decadent chocolates. Fudge, truffles, and turtles are all made on-site.

ETHNIC FARE

The best and most authentic Italian dining is at **Angelina's Ristorante** (655 Main St./Rte. 1, 207/646-0445, www.angelinasogunquit.com, 4:30pm-10pm daily year-round, $16-34). Chef-owner David Giarusso uses recipes handed down from his great-grandmother, Angelina Peluso. Dine in the dining room, wine room, lounge, or out on the terrace, choosing from pastas, risottos (the house specialty), and other classics.

Another Italian outpost is **Caffe Prego** (44 Shore Rd., 207/646-7734, www.caffepregoogt.com, 11:30am-9pm daily, $10-23). Owners Donato Tramuto and Jeffrey Porter have created an authentic taste of Tuscany. They've imported Italian equipment and use traditional ingredients to create coffees, pastries, panini, brick-oven pizzas, pastas, salads, and gelati, served inside or on the terrace.

CASUAL DINING

Gypsy Sweethearts (10 Shore Rd., 207/646-7021, www.gypsysweethearts.com, dinner from 5:30pm Tues.-Sun., entrées $19-32) serves inside a restored house, on a deck, and in a garden. It's one of the region's most reliable restaurants, and the creative menu is infused with ethnic accents and includes vegetarian choices. Reservations are advised in midsummer.

Mediterranean fare is finessed with a dollop of creativity and a pinch of Maine flavors at **Five-O** (50 Shore Rd., 207/646-6365, www.five-oshoreroad.com, dinner 5pm-10pm daily, brunch 8am-11:30am Sat.-Sun.), one of the region's top restaurants for casual dining. The menu changes frequently, but the housemade pastas and entrées usually run $20-40. Lighter fare ($10-24) is available until 11pm in the lounge, where martinis are a specialty. In the off-season, multicourse regional dinners are held about once a month ($70). Valet parking is available.

Boisterous and lively, **The Front Porch** (9 Shore Rd., 207/646-4005, www.thefrontporch. net, dinner from 4pm Wed.-Sat., from noon Sun., $10-29) is not for those looking for romantic dining, but it is a good choice for families with divergent tastes. The menu ranges from flatbread pizzas to rack of lamb.

DINING WITH A VIEW

There's not much between you and Spain when you get a window seat at **MC** (Oarweed Lane, Perkins Cove, 207/646-6263, www.markandclarkrestaurants.com, 11:30am-3:30pm and from 5pm daily late May-mid-Oct., Wed.-Sun. mid-Oct.-Dec. and Feb.-late May, dinner entrées $25-37). Almost every table on both floors has a view. Service is attentive, and the food is tops and in keeping with James Beard Award-winning chefs Mark Gaier and Clark Frasier, fresh. The bar menu ($11-20), also served in the dining room by request, is available until closing. There's often live music on Wednesday night. A jazz brunch is served beginning at 11am Sunday September-June. Reservations are essential for dinner.

Equally if not more impressive are the views from the dining room at **The Cliff House** (Shore Rd., 207/361-1000, entrées $20-36). Go for the breakfast buffet 7:30am-1pm Sunday.

Service can be so-so. Before or after dining, wander the grounds.

LOBSTER

Creative marketing, a knockout view, and efficient service help explain why more than 1,000 pounds of lobster bite the dust every summer day at **Barnacle Billy's** (Perkins Cove, 207/646-5575 or 800/866-5575, www.barnbilly.com, 11am-9pm daily seasonally). Billy's has a full liquor license; try for the deck, with a front-row seat on Perkins Cove.

Less flashy and less pricey is **The Lobster Shack** (Perkins Cove, 207/646-2941, www. lobster-shack.com, 11am-9pm daily), serving lobsters, stews, chowders, and some landlubber choices too.

Wells
LOCAL FLAVORS

For scrumptious baked goods and made-to-order sandwiches, head to **Borealis Bread** (Rte. 1, 8:30am-5:30pm Mon.-Sat., 9am-4pm Sun.), in the Aubuchon Hardware plaza.

Pick up all sorts of fresh goodies at the **Wells Farmers Market** (1pm-5pm Wed.) in the Town Hall parking lot (208 Sanford Rd.).

CASUAL DINING

Pair a handcrafted microbrew with your meal, perhaps beer-battered local fish-and-chips, vegan-curried vegetables, or chargrilled house-cut steak tips at **The Boon Island Ale Restaurant** (124 Post Rd./Rte. 1, 207/641-8489, www.boonislandale.com, from 4pm daily, $15-28). While here, pick up a copy of *Boon Island,* by Kenneth Roberts, a good read about a fascinating shipwreck.

FAMILY FAVORITES

For fresh lobster, lobster rolls, fish-and-chips, chowders, and homemade desserts, you can't go wrong at the Cardinali family's **Fisherman's Catch** (Harbor Rd./Rte. 1, 207/646-8780, www.fishermanscatchwells. com, 11:30am-9pm daily early May-mid-Oct., $8-24). Big windows in the rustic dining room frame the marsh; some even have binoculars for wildlife spotting. It might seem out of the way, but trust me, the locals all know this little gem.

A good steak in the land of lobster? You betcha: **The Steakhouse** (1205 Post Rd./Rte. 1, 207/646-4200, www.the-steakhouse.com, 4pm-9:30pm Tues.-Sun., entrées $15-30) is a great big barn of a place where steaks are hand cut from USDA prime and choice corn-fed Western beef that has never been frozen. Chicken, seafood, lobster (great stew), and even a vegetarian stir-fry are also on the menu, and a children's menu is available. Service is efficient, but they don't take reservations, so be prepared for a wait.

FINE DINING
Chef Joshua W. Mather of 🝋 **Joshua's** (1637 Rte. 1, 207/646-3355, www.joshuas.biz, from 5pm daily, entrées $22-35) grew up on his family's nearby organic farm, and produce from that farm highlights the menu. In a true family operation, his parents not only still work the farm, but also work in the restaurant, a converted 1774 home with many of its original architectural elements. Everything is made on the premises, from the fabulous bread to the hand-churned ice cream. The Atlantic haddock, with caramelized onion crust, chive oil, and wild mushroom risotto, is a signature dish, and it alone is worth coming for. A vegetarian pasta entrée is offered nightly. Save room for the maple walnut pie with maple ice cream. Yes, it's gilding the lily, but you can always walk the beach afterward. Reservations are essential for the dining rooms, but the full menu is also served in the bar.

INFORMATION AND SERVICES

At the southern edge of Ogunquit, right next to the Ogunquit Playhouse, the **Ogunquit Chamber of Commerce's Welcome Center** (Rte. 1, Ogunquit, 207/646-2939, www.ogunquit.org) provides all the usual visitor information and has public restrooms. Ask for the Touring and Trolley Route Map, showing the

Marginal Way, beach locations, and public restrooms. The chamber of commerce's annual visitor booklet thoughtfully carries a high-tide calendar for the summer.

Just over the Ogunquit border in Wells (actually in Moody) is the **Wells Information Center** (Rte. 1 at Bourne Ave., 207/646-2451, www.wellschamber.org).

The handsome fieldstone **Ogunquit Memorial Library** (74 Shore Rd., Ogunquit, 207/646-9024) is downtown's only building on the National Register of Historic Places. Or visit the **Wells Public Library** (1434 Post Rd./Rte. 1, Wells, 207/646-8181, www.wells.lib.me.us).

GETTING THERE AND AROUND

Ogunquit is about seven miles or 15 minutes via Route 1, from York. Wells is about six miles or 12 minutes via Route 1 from Ogunquit. From York to Wells, it's about 15.5 miles or 20 minutes on I-95. When traveling in summer, expect heavy traffic and delays on Route 1.

Amtrak Downeaster (800/872-7245, www.amtrakdowneaster.com), which connects Boston's North Station with Portland, Maine, stops in Wells. The Shoreline Explorer trolley connects in season.

The seasonal **Shoreline Explorer** (207/324-5762, www.shorelineexplorer.com) trolley system makes it possible to connect from York to Kennebunkport without your car. Each town's system is operated separately and has its own fees. The **Shoreline Trolley Line 2/Shore Road Shuttle** ($1 one way, $3 day pass, $10 12-ride multipass, free for children under 18) operates between Short Sands Beach, in York, and Perkins Cove, Ogunquit; **Shoreline Trolley Route 3/Ogunquit Trolley** ($1.50 one way, $1 ages 10 and under) connects to **Shoreline Trolley Route 4** ($1 one way, $3 day pass, $10 12-ride multipass, free for children under 18), which serves Wells and the Wells Transportation Center, where the Amtrak Downeaster train stops.

The Kennebunks

The world may have first learned of Kennebunkport when George Herbert Walker Bush was president, but Walkers and Bushes have owned their summer estate here for three generations. Visitors continue to come to the Kennebunks (the collective name for **Kennebunk, Kennebunkport, Cape Porpoise,** and **Goose Rocks Beach**) hoping to catch a glimpse of the former first family, but they also come for the terrific ambience, bed-and-breakfasts, boutiques, boats, biking, and beaches.

The Kennebunks' earliest European settlers arrived in the mid-1600s. By the mid-1700s, shipbuilding had become big business in the area. Two ancient local cemeteries—North Street and Evergreen—provide glimpses of the area's heritage. Its Historic District reveals Kennebunk's moneyed past—the homes where wealthy ship owners and shipbuilders once lived, sending their vessels to the Caribbean and around the globe. Today, unusual shrubs and a dozen varieties of rare maples still line Summer Street—the legacy of ship captains in the global trade. Another legacy is the shiplap construction in many houses—a throwback to a time when labor was cheap and lumber plentiful. Closer to the beach in Lower Village stood the workshops of sailmakers, carpenters, and mast makers whose output drove the booming trade to success.

Although **Kennebunkport** (pop. 3,474) draws most of the sightseers and summer traffic, **Kennebunk** (pop. 10,798) feels more like a year-round community. Its old-fashioned downtown has a mix of shops, restaurants, and attractions. Yes, its beaches are also well known, but many visitors drive right through the middle of Kennebunk without stopping to enjoy its assets.

SIGHTS
◖ Seashore Trolley Museum
There's nothing quite like an antique electric trolley to dredge up nostalgia for bygone days.

With a collection of more than 250 transit vehicles (more than two dozen trolleys on display), the **Seashore Trolley Museum** (195 Log Cabin Rd., Kennebunkport, 207/967-2800, www.trolleymuseum.org, $10 adults, $8 seniors, $7.50 ages 6-16) verges on trolley mania. Whistles blowing and bells clanging, restored streetcars do frequent trips (10:05am-4:15pm) on a 3.5-mile loop through the nearby woods. Ride as often as you wish, and then check out the activity in the streetcar workshop and go wild in the trolley-oriented gift shop. Bring a picnic lunch and enjoy it here. Special events are held throughout the summer, including **Ice Cream and Sunset Trolley Rides** (7pm Wed.-Thurs., July-Aug. $5, includes ice cream). And here's an interesting wrinkle: Make a reservation, plunk down $60, and you can have a one-hour "Motorman" experience driving your own trolley (with help, of course). The museum is 1.7 miles southeast of Route 1. It's open 10am-5pm daily late May-mid-October and on weekends in May, late October, and the Christmas Prelude festival.

Walker's Point: The Bush Estate
There's no public access to Walker's Point, but you can join the sidewalk gawkers on Ocean Avenue overlooking George and Barbara Bush's summer compound. The 41st president and his wife lead a low-key laid-back life when they're here, so if you don't spot them through binoculars, you may well run into them at a shop or restaurant in town. Intown Trolley's regular narrated tours go right past the house—or it's an easy, scenic family walk from Kennebunkport's Dock Square. On the way, you'll pass **St. Ann's Church,** whose stones came from the ocean floor, and the paths to **Spouting Rock** and **Blowing Cave,** two natural phenomena that create spectacular water fountains if you manage to be there midway between high and low tides.

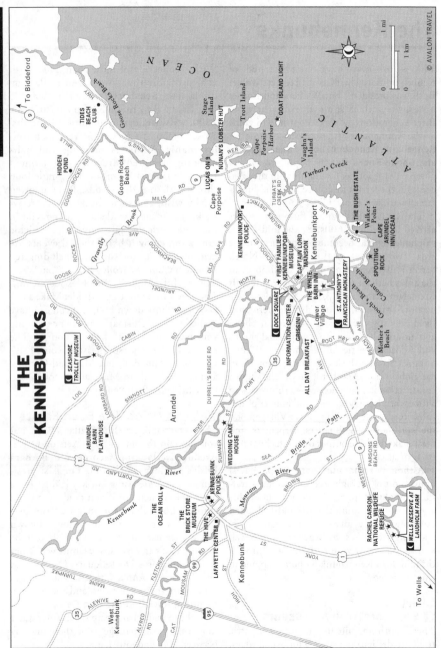

© AVALON TRAVEL

THE KENNEBUNKS

© HILARY NANGLE

Don't miss wandering the oceanfront property of St. Ann's Church in Kennebunkport.

Wedding Cake House

The **Wedding Cake House** (104 Summer St., Kennebunk) is a private residence, so you can't go inside, but it's one of Maine's most-photographed buildings. Driving down Summer Street (Rte. 35), midway between the downtowns of Kennebunk and Kennebunkport, it's hard to miss the yellow-and-white Federal mansion with gobs of gingerbread and Gothic Revival spires and arches. Built in 1826 by shipbuilder George Bourne as a wedding gift for his wife, the Kennebunk landmark remained in the family until 1983.

Cape Porpoise

When your mind's eye conjures an idyllic lobster-fishing village, it probably looks a lot like **Cape Porpoise,** only 2.5 miles from busy Dock Square. Follow Route 9 eastward from Kennebunkport; when Route 9 turns north, continue straight and take Pier Road to its end. From the small parking area, you'll see lobster boats at anchor, a slew of working wharves,

and 19th-century **Goat Island Light,** now automated, directly offshore.

Local History Museums and Tours

Occupying four restored 19th-century buildings in downtown Kennebunk, including the 1825 William Lord store, **The Brick Store Museum** (117 Main St., Kennebunk, 207/985-4802, www.brickstoremuseum.org, 10am-4:30pm Tues.-Fri., 10am-1pm Sat., $5 donation) has garnered a reputation for unusual exhibits: a century of wedding dresses, a two-century history of volunteer firefighting, and life in southern Maine during the Civil War. The museum encourages appreciation for the surrounding Kennebunk Historic District with 50-90-minute **architectural walking tours** ($5), usually May-mid-October but call for a current schedule. If the schedule doesn't suit, the museum sells a walk-it-yourself booklet ($16) and a simple map ($5). There are also Museum in the Streets signs at 25 historical locations throughout Kennebunk.

The First Families Kennebunkport Museum (8 Maine St., Kennebunkport, 207/967-2751, www.kporthistory.org, 11am-5pm Mon., Sat., mid-July-mid-Oct., $7), also known as the Nott House or White Columns, is owned and maintained by the Kennebunkport Historical Society. The mid-19th-century Greek Revival mansion is filled with Victorian furnishings and artifacts and memorabilia covering 200 years of local history. On 45-minute tours, guides relate stories of sea captains, shipbuilders, summerfolk, and presidents. Be sure to visit the restored gardens.

The Kennebunkport Historical Society also offers local walking tours. Hour-long **Kennebunkport Historic District walking tours** depart from the museum; **Cape Arundel Walking Tours** depart from St. Ann's Church on Ocean Ave. Either tour is $10; combination tickets, which include the museum, are $15. At the museum, you can buy a guidebook ($4) for a do-it-yourself tour.

Dock Square

Even if you're not a shopper, make it a point to meander through the heart of Kennebunkport's shopping district, where onetime fishing shacks have been restored and renovated into upscale shops, boutiques, galleries, and dining spots. Some shops, especially those on upper floors, offer fine harbor views. If you're willing to poke around a bit, you'll find some unusual items that make distinctive souvenirs or gifts—pottery, vintage clothing, books, specialty foods, and yes, T-shirts.

St. Anthony's Franciscan Monastery

Long ago, 35,000 Native Americans used this part of town as a summer camp. So did a group of Lithuanian Franciscan monks who in 1947 fled war-ravaged Europe and acquired the 200-acre **St. Anthony's Franciscan Monastery** (Beach St., Kennebunk, 207/967-2011). They ran a high school here 1956-1969, and the monks still occupy the handsome Tudor great house, but the well-tended grounds (sprinkled with shrines and a recently restored sculpture

created by Vytautas Jonynas for the Vatican Pavilion at the 1964 World's Fair) are open to the public sunrise-sunset daily. A short path leads from the monastery area to a peaceful gazebo overlooking the Kennebunk River. Pets and bikes are not allowed; public restrooms are available.

ENTERTAINMENT AND EVENTS
Performing Arts

MaineStage Shakespeare (www.mainestage-shakespeare.com) performs the bard's works free in Kennebunk's Lafayette Park.

Live professional summer theater is on tap at the **Arundel Barn Playhouse** (53 Old Post Rd., Arundel, 207/985-5552, www.arundelbarnplayhouse.com, $32-42), with productions staged in a renovated 1888 barn June-September.

River Tree Arts

The area's cultural spearhead is **River Tree Arts** (RTA, 35 Western Ave., Kennebunk, 207/967-9120, www.rivertreearts.org), a volunteer-driven organization that sponsors concerts, classes, workshops, exhibits, and educational programs throughout the year.

The Hive

With a gallery, performance space, studio, and food and bar service, **The Hive** (84 Main St., Kennebunk, 207/985-0006, www.thehive-kennebunk.com) is a beehive of arts-related activities.

Festivals and Events

The **Kennebunkport Festival** in early June celebrates art and food with exhibits, social events, food and wine tastings, celebrity chef dinners, and live music. The first two weekends of December mark the festive **Christmas Prelude,** during which spectacular decorations adorn historic homes, candle-toting carolers stroll through the Kennebunks, stores have special sales, and Santa Claus arrives via lobster boat.

Kennebunk Parks and Recreation sponsors

Concerts in the Park, a weekly series of free concerts 6:30pm-7:30pm Wednesday late June-mid-August in Rotary Park on Water Street. **Third Friday ArtWalks** are held June-September in downtown Kennebunk.

The Colony Hotel offers a **summer concert series** on Sunday afternoons ($5).

SHOPPING

Lots of small, attractive boutiques surround **Dock Square,** the hub of Kennebunkport, and flow over the bridge into Kennbunk's Lower Village. Gridlock often develops in midsummer. Avoid driving through here at the height of the season. Take your time and walk, bike, or ride the local trolleys. This is just a sampling of the shopping opportunities.

Antiques and Art

English, European, and American furniture and architectural elements and garden accessories are just a sampling of what you'll find at **Antiques on Nine** (Rte. 9, Lower Village, Kennebunk, 207/967-0626). Another good place for browsing high-end antiques as well as home accents is **Hurlburt Designs** (Rte. 9, Lower Village, Kennebunk, 207/967-4110). More than 30 artists are represented at **Wright Gallery** (Pier Rd., Cape Porpoise, 207/967-5053).

Jean Briggs represents nearly 100 artists at her topflight **Mast Cove Galleries** (Maine St. and Mast Cove Lane, Kennebunkport, 207/967-3453, www.mastcove.com), in a handsome Greek Revival house near the Graves Memorial Library. Prices vary widely, so don't be surprised if you spot something affordable. The gallery often sponsors 2.5-hour evening jazz concerts in July-August ($15 donation includes light refreshments). Call for a schedule.

The Gallery on Chase Hill (10 Chase Hill Rd., Kennebunkport, 207/967-0049), in the stunningly restored Captain Chase House, mounts rotating exhibits and represents a wide variety of Maine and New England artists. It's a sibling of the **Maine Art Gallery** (14 Western Ave., Kennebunkport, 207/967-0049, www.maine-art.com), which is right down the street.

Compliments (Dock Sq., Kennebunkport, 207/967-2269) has a truly unique and fun collection of contemporary fine American crafts, with an emphasis on glass and ceramic ware.

Cape Porpoise Outfitters (8 Langsford Rd., Cape Porpoise, 207/200-3737) is hip enough to get a nod from *GQ.* Jared Paul Stern has filled a huge red barn with vintage Americana, from books to clothing, nautical doodads to military artifacts. This is no junk shop; it's a curated collection that earns points for cultural cool. Call first; schedule is quirky.

Specialty Shops

Since 1968, **Port Canvas** (9 Ocean Ave., Kennebunkport, 207/985-9765 or 800/333-6788) has been turning out the best in durable cotton-canvas products. Need a new double-bottomed tote bag? It's here. Also available are golf-bag covers, belts, computer cases, day packs, and, of course, duffel bags.

Quilt fans should make time to visit **Mainely Quilts** (108 Summer St./Rte. 35, Kennebunk, 207/985-4250), behind the Waldo Emerson Inn. The shop has a nice selection of contemporary and antique quilts.

Most of the clothing shops clustered around Dock Square are rather pricey. Not so **Arbitrage** (28 Dock Sq., Kennebunkport, 207/967-9989), which combines designer consignment clothing with new fashions, vintage designer costume jewelry, shoes, and handbags.

Irresistible eye-dazzling costume jewelry, hair ornaments, handbags, lotions, cards, and other delightful finds fill every possible space at **Dannah** (123 Ocean Ave., Kennebunkport, 207/967-8640), in the Breakwater Spa building, with free customer-only parking in the rear.

For a good read, stop by **Kennebooks** (149 Port Rd., Lower Village, Kennebunk, 207/967-6136), which carries books and a whole lot more.

Scalawags is a bonanza for pet owners, with wonderful presents to bring home to furry pals. If traveling with your pooch, ask about local pet-friendly parks, inns, and restaurants, as well as favorite places for walkies.

RECREATION
Parks and Preserves

Thanks to a dedicated coterie of year-round and summer residents, the foresighted **Kennebunkport Conservation Trust** (KCT, 57 Gravelly Brook Rd., Kennebunkport, 207/967-3465, www.kporttrust.org), founded in 1974, has become a nationwide model for land-trust organizations. The KCT has managed to preserve from development several hundred acres of land, including 11 small islands off Cape Porpoise Harbor, and most of this acreage is accessible to the public, especially with a sea kayak. The trust has even assumed ownership of 7.7-acre Goat Island, with its distinctive lighthouse visible from Cape Porpoise, and other coastal vantage points. Check the website for special events and activities.

VAUGHN'S ISLAND PRESERVE

To visit **Vaughn's Island** you'll need to do a little planning, tide-wise, since the 96-acre island is about 600 feet offshore. Consult a tide calendar and aim for low tide close to the new moon or full moon, when the most water drains away. Allow yourself an hour or so before and after low tide, but no longer, or you may need a boat rescue. Wear treaded rubber boots, since the crossing is muddy and slippery with rockweed. Keep an eye on your watch and explore the ocean (east) side of the island, along the beach. It's worth the effort, and there's a great view of Goat Island Light off to the east. From downtown Kennebunkport, take Main Street to Wildes District Road. Continue to Shore Road (also called Turbat's Creek Road), go 0.6 mile, jog left 0.2 mile more, and park in the tiny lot at the end.

EMMONS PRESERVE

Also under Kennebunkport Conservation Trust's stewardship, the **Emmons Preserve** has six trails meandering through 146 acres of woods and fields on the edge of Batson's River (also called Gravelly Brook). The yellow trail gives best access to the water. Fall colors here are brilliant, birdlife is abundant, and you can do a loop in half an hour. But why

rush? This is a wonderful oasis in the heart of Kennebunkport. From Dock Square, take North Street to Beachwood Avenue (right turn) to Gravelly Brook Road (left turn). The trailhead is on the left.

PICNIC ROCK

About 1.5 miles up the Kennebunk River from the ocean, Picnic Rock is the centerpiece of the **Butler Preserve,** a 14-acre enclave managed by The Kennebunk Land Trust. Well named, the rock is a great place for a picnic and a swim, but don't count on being alone. A short trail loops through the preserve. Consider bringing a canoe or kayak (or renting one) and paddling with the tide past beautiful homes and the Cape Arundel Golf Club. From Lower Village Kennebunk, take Route 35 west and hang a right onto Old Port Road. When the road gets close to the Kennebunk River, watch for a Nature Conservancy oak-leaf sign on the right. Parking is along Old Port Road; walk down through the preserve to Picnic Rock, right on the river.

Water Sports
BEACHES

Ah, the beaches. The Kennebunks are well endowed with sand but not with parking spaces. Parking permits are required, and you need a separate pass for each town. Many lodgings provide free permits for their guests—ask when making room reservations. You can avoid the parking nightmare altogether by hopping aboard the Intown Trolley, which goes right by the major beaches.

The main beaches in **Kennebunk** (east to west, stretching about two miles) are 3,346-foot-long **Gooch's** (the most popular), Kennebunk (locally called **Middle Beach** or **Rocks Beach**), and **Mother's** (a smallish beach next to Lords Point, where there's also a playground). Lifeguards are on duty at Gooch's and Mother's Beaches July-Labor Day. Ask locally about a couple of other beach options. Mid-June-mid-September you'll need to buy a **parking permit** ($15/day, $50 per/week, $100 for the season) from the **Kennebunk Town Hall**

© TOM NANGLE

The Kennebunks have a number of prime swaths of sand.

(4 Summer St., 207/985-3675) or the Chamber of Commerce.

Kennebunkport's claim to beach fame is three-mile-long **Goose Rocks Beach,** one of the loveliest in the area. Parking spaces are scarce, and a permit is required. **Permits** ($12/day, $50/week, $100 for the season) are available from the **Kennebunkport Police Station** (101 Main St., 207/967-4243, 24 hours daily), **Kennebunkport Town Hall** (6 Elm St.), and Goose Rocks General Store (3 Dyke Rd., 207/967-4541). To reach the beach, take Route 9 from Dock Square east and north to Dyke Road (Clock Farm Corner). Turn right and continue to the end (King's Hwy.).

The prize for tiniest beach goes to **Colony Beach** (officially Arundel Beach), near The Colony resort complex. It's close to many Kennebunkport lodgings and an easy walk from Dock Square; no permit is necessary.

BOAT EXCURSIONS

Join Captain Gary aboard the 87-foot *Nick's Chance* (4 Western Ave., Lower Village,

Kennebunk, 207/967-5507 or 800/767-2628, www.firstchancewhalewatch.com, $48 adults, $28 ages 3-12, $10 under age 3, cash only) for the 4.5-hour whale-watching trip to Jeffrey's Ledge, weather permitting. The destination is the summer feeding grounds for finbacks, humpbacks, minkes, the rare blue whale, and the endangered right whale. The boat departs daily late June–early September, weekends only spring and fall, from Performance Marine, behind Bartley's Restaurant, in Kennebunk Lower Village.

Under the same ownership and departing from the same location is the 65-foot open lobster boat *Kylie's Chance,* which departs three times daily in July-August for 1.5-hour scenic lobster cruises ($20 adults, $15 ages 3-12, cash only); the schedule is reduced in spring and fall. A lobstering demonstration is given on most trips but never on the evening one.

The handsome 55-foot gaff-rigged schooner *Eleanor* (Arundel Wharf, 43 Ocean Ave., Kennebunkport, 207/967-8809, www.gwi.net/schoonersails), built by its captain, Rich

© HILARY NANGLE

Head out on a whale-watching trip from Dock Square.

Woodman, heads out for two-hour sails ($45 pp), weather and tides willing, one to three times daily during the summer.

CANOEING, KAYAKING, AND PADDLEBOARDING

Explore the Kennebunk River by canoe or kayak. **Kennebunkport Marina** (67 Ocean Ave., Kennebunkport, 207/967-3411, www. kennebunkportmarina.com) rents canoes and single kayaks ($30 for two hours, $50/half day) and double kayaks ($50 for two hours, $70/ half day). Check the tide before you depart, and plan your trip to paddle with it rather than against it.

   Coastal Maine Kayak (8 Western Ave., Lower Village, Kennebunk, 207/967-6065, www.coastalmainekayak.com) offers a daylong guided Cape Porpoise Tour ($85), including guide, instruction, equipment, and lunch; other options are available. Rental kayaks are $35 for three hours, $60 full day, and $350/week; doubles are $60, $80, and $500.

Take a half-day sea kayaking tour ($50 pp) or do it yourself with a rental kayak or paddleboard (from $35) with **Southern Maine Kayaks** (888/925-7495, www.southernmainekayaks.com).

SURFING AND PADDLEBOARDING

If you want to catch a wave, stop by **Aquaholics Surf Shop** (166 Port Rd., Kennebunk, 207/967-8650, www.aquaholicsurf.com). The shop has boards, wetsuits, and related gear both for sale and rental, and it offers lessons and surf camps.

Bicycling

Coastal Maine Kayak (8 Western Ave., Lower Village, Kennebunk, 207/967-6065, www. coastalmainekayak.com) rents bikes starting at $10/hour or $35/day.

Golf

Three 18-hole golf courses make the sport a big deal in the area. **Cape Arundel Golf Club** (19 River Rd., Kennebunkport, 207/967-3494), established in 1897, and **Webhannet Golf Club** (8 Central Ave., Kennebunk, 207/967-2061), established in 1902, are semiprivate and open to nonmembers; call for tee times at least 24 hours ahead. In nearby Arundel, **Dutch Elm Golf Course** (5 Brimstone Rd., Arundel, 207/282-9850) is a public course with rentals, pro shop, and putting greens.

ACCOMMODATIONS

Most stay open through the Christmas Prelude festival.

Inns and Hotels

Graciously dominating its 11-acre spread at the mouth of the Kennebunk River, **The Colony Hotel** (140 Ocean Ave. at King's Hwy., Kennebunkport, 207/967-3331 or 800/552-2363, www.thecolonyhotel.com/maine, from $230) springs right out of a bygone era, and its distinctive cupola is an area landmark. It has had a longtime commitment to the environment, with recycling, waste-reduction, and educational programs. There's a special feeling here, with cozy corners for reading, lawns

© TOM NANGLE

The Colony Hotel is one of the last historical grand resorts still operating on the Maine Coast.

and gardens for strolling, an oceanview heated swimming pool, room service, putting green, tennis privileges at the exclusive River Club, bike rentals, massage therapy, and lawn games. The price of rooms includes breakfast. Pets are $30/night. There are no in-room TVs in the main inn.

The White Barn Inn and its siblings specialize in the high-end boutique inn market, with four in this category. Most renowned is the exclusive **White Barn Inn GRACE** (37 Beach Ave., Kennebunk, 207/967-2321, www.whitebarninn.com, from $465). Also part of the empire are **The Beach House Inn** (211 Beach Ave., Kennebunk, 207/967-3850, www.beachhseinn.com, from $209), **The Breakwater Inn, Hotel, and Spa** (127 Ocean Ave., Kennebunkport, 207/967-3118, www.thebreakwaterinn.com, from $249), **The Yachtsman Lodge and Marina** (Ocean Ave., Kennebunkport, 207/967-2511, www.yachtsmanlodge.com, from $309), and two restaurants. Guest rooms in all properties have air-conditioning, phones, satellite TV, and video and CD players; bikes and canoes

are available for guests. Rates include bountiful continental breakfasts and afternoon tea, but check out the off-season packages, especially if you want to dine at one of the restaurants. All but the Beach House are within walking distance of Dock Square.

The White Barn Inn is the most exclusive, with Relais & Châteaux status. It's home to one of the best restaurants in the *country*. Many rooms have fireplaces and marble baths with separate steam showers and whirlpool tubs (you can even arrange for a butler-drawn bath). Service is impeccable, and nothing has been overlooked in terms of amenities. There's an outdoor heated European-style infinity pool, where lunch is available, weather permitting, as well as a full-service spa. The inn also has a Hinckley Talaria-44 yacht available for charter.

The Beach House Inn faces Middle Beach and is less formal than the White Barn (splurge on upper-floor guest rooms with views). The Breakwater, at the mouth of the Kennebunk River, comprises a beautifully renovated historical inn with wraparound porches and an

© HILARY NANGLE

Guests staying at the Cape Arundel Inn have views over the open Atlantic and the Bush estate at Walker Point.

adjacent, more modern, newly renovated building with guest rooms and a full-service spa. The complex is also home to Stripers Restaurant. Finally, there's the Yachtsman, an innovative blend of a motel and bed-and-breakfast, with all rooms opening onto patios facing the river and the marina where George H. W. Bush keeps his boat. Pets are allowed here by advance reservation for $25/night.

Families, especially, favor the sprawling riverfront **Nonantum Resort** (95 Ocean Ave., Kennebunkport, 207/967-4050 or 888/205-1555, www.nonantumresort.com, from $249) complex, which dates from 1884. It includes a bit of everything, from gently updated rooms and suites in the main building to modern family suites with kitchenettes in the newer Portside building, where some third-floor rooms have ocean views. Recreational amenities include a small outdoor heated pool, docking facilities, lobster-boat and sailing tours, fishing charters, and kayak rentals. A slew of activities are offered daily, including a children's program. All

115 guest rooms have air-conditioning, Wi-Fi, and TVs; some have refrigerators. Rates include a full breakfast. The water-view dining room is also open for dinner and, in July-August, lunch. Packages, many of which include dinner, are a good choice. Note that weddings take place here almost every weekend.

The **Kennebunkport Resort Collection** (www.kennebunkportresortcollection.com) comprises nine upscale or luxury accommodations in the area, all with the expected amenities. A seasonal dinner shuttle provides transportation between them. Fanciest is **Hidden Pond** (354 Goose Rocks Rd., Kennebunkport, 888/967-9050, from $760), which shares amenities with nearby **Tides Beach Club** (254 Kings Hwy., Kennebunkport, 855/632-3324, www.tidesbeachclubmaine.com, from $460). The family-oriented Hidden Pond resort, tucked in the woods about a mile from Goose Rocks Beach, comprises chic designer-Victorianesque cottages and bungalows, gardens, a spa, a wellness center, outdoor pools,

© HILARY NANGLE

The Nonantum Resort is an excellent family resort with a wide array of programs and facilities.

a pool grill, and the fine-dining restaurant Earth. The renovated Victorian Tides Beach Club is a hip boutique hotel with restaurant/lounge on Goose Rocks Beach. A tender oversees beach chairs and umbrellas, provides water, and even delivers lunch. All but two guest rooms at the **Cape Arundel Inn** (208 Ocean Ave., Kennebunkport, 207/967-2125, www.capearundelinn.com, Mar.-Jan. 1, from $320) overlook crashing surf and the Bush estate. The compound comprises the Shingle-style main inn building, the Rockbound motel-style building, and the Carriage House Loft, a large suite on the upper floor of the carriage house; breakfast is included. All guest rooms are air-conditioned and most have fireplaces. Bikes and beach passes, towels, and chairs are provided. Every table in the inn's restaurant (entrées $27-40) has an ocean view. Sixteen additional rooms are in the **Olde Fort Inn** (8 Old Fort Ave., Kennebunkport, 207/967-5353, from $270), the former stable house of a grand summer resort on 15 acres with an outdoor

heated pool. The meticulously renovated 1899 **☾ Kennebunkport Inn** (1 Dock Sq., Kennebunkport, 207/967-2621, from $250) comprises three buildings in the heart of Dock Square. It also has an excellent restaurant, One Dock, as well as piano bar. Rates include a continental breakfast. The **Boathouse Waterfront Hotel** (21 Ocean Ave., Kennebunkport, 207/967-8233, from $290) hangs over the river and is home to David's Restaurant.

Bed-and-Breakfasts

Three of Kennebunkport's loveliest inns are rumored to have been owned by brothers-in-law, all of whom were sea captains. Rivaling the White Barn Inn for service, decor, amenities, and overall luxury is the three-story **☾ Captain Lord Mansion** (Pleasant St., Kennebunkport, 207/967-3141 or 800/522-3141, www.captainlord.com, from $279), which is one of the finest bed-and-breakfasts anywhere. And no wonder: Innkeepers Rick and Bev Litchfield have been at it since 1978, and they're never content to rest on their laurels. Each year the inn improves upon seeming perfection. If you want to be pampered and stay in a meticulously decorated and historical bed-and-breakfast with marble bathrooms (heated floors, many with double whirlpool tubs), fireplaces, original artwork, phones, TVs, Wi-Fi, air-conditioning in all guest rooms, and even a few cedar closets, look no further. A multicourse breakfast is served to shared tables. Bicycles as well as beach towels and chairs are available. Afternoon treats are provided.

The elegant Federal-style **Captain Jefferds Inn** (5 Pearl St., Kennebunkport, 207/967-2311 or 800/839-6844, www.captainjefferdsinn. com, $199-399), in the historic district, provides the ambience of a real captain's house. Each of the 15 guest rooms and suites (11 in the main house and 4 more in the carriage house) has plush linens, fresh flowers, down comforters, TVs and DVD players, CD players, Wi-Fi, and air-conditioning; some have fireplaces, whirlpool tubs, and other luxuries. A three-course breakfast and afternoon tea are included. Five rooms are dog-friendly, at $30/day/dog; pet sitting is available.

The Captain Fairfield Inn (8 Pleasant St., Kennebunkport, www.captainfairfield.com, from $329) is perhaps the most modest architecturally of the three, but it doesn't scrimp on amenities. Guest rooms are divided between traditional and contemporary decor, but all have flat-screen TVs, air-conditioning, and Wi-Fi; some have gas fireplaces, double whirlpools, and rainfall showers. The lovely grounds are a fine place to retreat for a snooze in the hammock or a game of croquet. Rates include a four-course breakfast and afternoon cookies.

The original 1860s Greek Revival architecture of the **English Meadows Inn** (141 Port Rd., Lower Village, Kennebunk, 207/967-5766, www.englishmeadowsinn.com, from $279) was married to the Victorian Queen Anne style later in the century, but the interior decor is contemporary and clutter-free, with accents such as Asian art, Picasso lithographs, and art deco lighting. Guest rooms are split between the main house, the carriage house, and

a pet-friendly ($30) two-bedroom cottage. All have flat-screen TVs, some have fireplaces or whirlpool tubs. Rates include a full breakfast and afternoon snacks.

Slip away from the crowds at the Gott family's antiques-filled ◖ **Bufflehead Cove Inn** (B18 Bufflehead Cove Lane, Kennebunkport, 207/967-3879, www.buffleheadcove.com, from $165), a secluded riverfront home in the woods, less than one mile from K'port's action. Really, with a location like this and pampering service, you just might not want to stray from the front porch or dock. Rooms have Wi-Fi, flat-screen TVs, and air-conditioning; some have fireplaces and whirlpool tubs. Rates include a full breakfast and afternoon treats and use of beach chairs, umbrellas, and passes.

Neighboring the Wedding Cake House, **The Waldo Emerson Inn** (108 Summer St./Rte. 35, Kennebunk, 207/985-4250, www.waldoemersoninn.com, from $170) has a charming colonial feel, as it should, since the main section was built in 1784. Poet Ralph Waldo Emerson spent many a summer here; it was his great-uncle's home. Three of the six attractive guest rooms have working fireplaces. Rates include a full breakfast. Quilters, take note: In the barn is Mainely Quilts, a well-stocked quilt shop.

Traveling with a pooch? **The Hounds Tooth Inn** (82 Summer St., Kennebunk, 207/985-0117, www.houndstoothinn.biz, from $170, plus $30/pet) extends a welcome paw, allowing dogs in public rooms (but not the kitchen) and providing a fenced-in play area. Rates include a full breakfast.

Motels

Patricia Mason is the ninth-generation innkeeper at **The Seaside Motor Inn** (80 Beach Ave., Kennebunk, 207/967-4461 or 800/967-4461, www.kennebunkbeach.com, $249-349), a property that has been in her family since 1667. What a location! The 22-room motel is the only truly beachfront property in the area. Rooms are spacious, with TVs, Wi-Fi, air-conditioning, and refrigerators. Guests have use of an oceanview hot tub and bicycles. A continental breakfast is included in the rates. Kids ages 12 and younger stay free.

Second-generation innkeepers David and Paula Reid keep the **Fontenay Terrace Motel** (128 Ocean Ave., Kennebunkport, 207/967-3556, www.fontenaymotel.com, from $140) spotless. It borders a tidal inlet and has a private grassy and shaded lawn, perfect for retreating from the hubbub of busy Kennebunkport. Each of the eight guest rooms has air-conditioning, a mini-fridge, a microwave, Wi-Fi, cable TV, and a phone; some have water views. A small beach is 300 yards away, and it's a pleasant one-mile walk to Dock Square.

The clean and simple **Cape Porpoise Motel** (12 Mills Rd./Rte. 9, Cape Porpoise, 207/967-3370, www.capeporpoisemotel.com, from $129) is a short walk from the harbor. All rooms have TV and air-conditioning, and some have kitchenettes; rates include a continental breakfast, with homemade baked goods, fresh fruit, cereals, and bagels. Also available by the week or month are efficiencies with full kitchens, phones, and one or more bedrooms.

Here's a bargain: The nonprofit **Franciscan Guest House** (28 Beach Ave., Kennebunk, 207/967-4865, www.franciscanguesthouse.com), on the grounds of the monastery, has accommodations spread among two buildings and three other Tudor-style cottages. Decor is vintage 1970s, frills are few, and yes, it's in need of updating, but there are some nice amenities, including TVs, air-conditioning, a saltwater pool, Wi-Fi, and beach passes. The location is within walking distance of the beach and Dock Square. A continental breakfast is included in the rates (hot buffet available, $3), and a buffet dinner is often available (around $17). There is no daily maid service, but fresh towels are provided. Rooms are $99-195, and 1-3-bedroom suites are $109-270.

FOOD

The Kennebunkport Resort Collection operates a dining shuttle between its properties in Kennebunkport and Goose Rocks Beach. It's free for guests at its hotels, but anyone can hop aboard for $5.

Get the lowdown on K'port's food scene on a walking or trolley culinary tasting tour with **Maine Foodie Tours** (207/233-7485, www.mainefoodietours.com). Tickets, available online, cost about $50 for either.

Local Flavors

All Day Breakfast (55 Western Ave./Rte. 9, Lower Village, Kennebunk, 207/967-5132, 7am-2pm daily) is a favorite meeting spot, offering such specialties as invent-your-own omelets and crepes, Texas French toast, and the ADB sandwich.

H. B. Provisions (15 Western Ave., Lower Village, Kennebunk, 207/967-5762, www.hb-provisions.com, 6am-9pm daily) has an excellent wine selection, along with plenty of picnic supplies, newspapers, and all the typical general-store inventory. It also serves breakfast and prepares hot and cold sandwiches, salads, and wraps.

Equal parts fancy food and wine store and gourmet café, **Cape Porpoise Kitchen** (Rte. 9, Cape Porpoise, 207/967-1150, 7am-6pm daily) sells sandwiches, salads, prepared foods, desserts, and everything to go with.

Pair a fine wine with light fare at **Old Vines** (141 Port Rd., Lower Village, Kennebunk, 207/967-5766, www.oldvineswinebar.com, 5pm-11pm Wed.-Mon.), an Old World-meets-New World European-style wine bar and tapas restaurant housed in a renovated barn. The food is creative and excellent.

Prefer ales? **Federal Jack's** (8 Western Ave., Lower Village, Kennebunk, 207/967-4322, www.federaljacks.com, 11:30am-12:30am) is the brewpub that gave birth to the Shipyard label. Aim for a seat on the riverfront deck. Call in advance for a free tour, and if you're serious about brewing, ask about the Maine Brewing Vacation.

The **Kennebunk Farmers Market** sets up shop 8am-1pm Saturday mid-May-mid-October in the Grove Street municipal parking lot off Route 1 (adjacent to Village Pharmacy).

Family Favorites

A bit off the beaten track is **Lucas on 9** (62

Mills Rd./Rte. 9, Cape Porpoise, 207/967-0039, www.lucason9.com, noon-9pm Wed.-Mon., $9-30), a family-friendly restaurant operated by the Lane family. Chef Jonathan Lane makes everything from scratch and delivers on his mother Deborah's mission of "Good American food at affordable prices." Jonathan's travels have infused his preparations with more than a bow toward his work on Southern riverboats (Louisiana spicy crab soup, bread pudding with whiskey).

Burgers, pizza, sandwiches, even a turkey dinner with the trimmings—almost everything on the menu is less than $12 at **Duffy's Tavern & Grill** (4 Main St., Kennebunk, 207/985-0050, www.duffyskennebunk.com, from 11am daily). Extremely popular with locals, Duffy's is inside a renovated mill in Lafayette Center. It's an inviting space with exposed beams, gleaming woodwork, brick walls, and big windows framing the Mousam River. And if you want to catch the game while you eat, big-screen high-def TVs make it easy.

Casual Dining
The views complement the food at **Hurricane Restaurant** (29 Dock Sq., Kennebunkport, 207/967-9111, www.hurricanerestaurant.com, from 11:30am daily, entrées $20-50). Thanks to a Dock Square location and a dining room that literally hangs over the river, it reels in the crowds for both lunch and dinner.

Eat well and feel good about it at **Bandaloop** (2 Dock Sq., Kennebunkport, 207/967-4994, www.bandaloop.biz, 5pm-10pm Sun.-Thurs., 5pm-11pm Fri.-Sat. year-round, $17-29), a hip, vibrant restaurant where chef-owner W. Scott Lee likes to push boundaries. Lee named the restaurant for author Tom Robbins's fictional tribe that knew the secret to eternal life. Lee believes the secret is fresh, local, organic, and cruelty-free. Selections vary from meats and fish to vegetarian and vegan prepared with creativity.

Floor-to-ceiling windows frame the Kennebunk River breakwater, providing perfect views for those indulging at **Stripers** (Breakwater Inn, 127 Ocean Ave.,

Kennebunkport, 207/967-5333, from noon daily), another White Barn Inn sibling, where fish and seafood are the specialties. Most entrées range $23-31. Dress is casual; valet parking is available.

Dine in the heart of the action at **Dock Square** (1 Dock Sq., Kennebunkport, 207/967-2621, www.onedock.com, from 5:30pm daily), in the Kennebunkport Inn. Choose from patio dining (in season), the cozy dining room, or pub, with live entertainment nightly in season. Although there are small plates, most entrées run $24-36.

Chef Peter and his wife, Kate, operate **Pier 77** (77 Pier Rd., Cape Porpoise, 207/967-8500, www.pier77restaurant.com, 11:30am-2:30pm and 5pm-9pm daily, entrées $18-32), which overlooks Cape Porpoise Harbor with lobster boats hustling to and fro. The menu varies from paella to seafood mixed grill. There's frequent live entertainment, which can make conversation difficult. Reservations are advisable. Practically hidden downstairs is the always-packed **Ramp Bar and Grille** (11:30am-9pm daily), with lighter fare as well as the full menu and a sports-pub decor.

Local is the key word at **50 Local** (50 Main St., Kennebunk, 207/985-0850, www.localkennebunk.com, from 5:30pm daily, $10-36), a bright spot in downtown Kennebunk specializing in local and organic fare. The menu changes daily, but it's easy to cobble together a meal here that fits your appetite and budget.

Portland chef David Turin has expanded his culinary empire with **David's KPT** (207/967-8224, boathouseme.com/davids, from 11:30am daily), a fabulous addition to K'port's restaurant scene. Located at the Boathouse, David's pairs excellent food with the best views in the Dock Square area. David's menu ranges from pizza and lobster rolls to crispy skin duck breast and mixed grill ($15-34), but if you're in the mood for a special experience, book a table at **Opus Ten,** Turin's signature restaurant-within-a-restaurant concept, with a fixed, nine-course menu ($75), with optional wine pairings ($50).

The views from **Ocean** (208 Ocean Ave., 855/346-5700, www.capearundelinn.com, $25-38) at the Cape Arundel Inn compete for raves with the Chef Pierre Gignac's menu. Savor entrées such as rabbit confit, swordfish paillard, or fisherman stew while gazing out at open ocean and Walker Point. A tapas menu is served in the bar, and the Sunday afternoon Tapas on the Lawn social pairs music, wine, and hors d'oeuvres for $12/person.

Fine Dining

European country cuisine reigns at **On the Marsh** (46 Western Ave./Rte. 9, Lower Village, Kennebunk, 207/967-2299, www.onthemarsh.com, from 5:30pm daily, entrées $22-40), a restored barn overlooking marshlands leading to Kennebunk Beach. Lighter fare is served in the bar. The space is infused with arts and antiques and European touches courtesy of owner Denise Rubin, an interior designer with a passion for the continent. Dining locations include the two-level dining area, an "owner's table" with a chef's menu, and in the kitchen. Quiet piano music adds to the elegant but unstuffy ambience on weekends; service is attentive. Reservations are essential in midsummer.

Destination Dining

One of Maine's biggest splurges and worth every penny is ◖ **The White Barn Inn** (37 Beach Ave., Kennebunkport, 207/967-2321, www.whitebarninn.com, 6:30pm-9:30pm daily), with haute cuisine and haute prices in a haute-rustic barn. In summer, don't be surprised to run into members of the senior George Bush clan (probably at the back window table). Soft piano music accompanies impeccable service and chef Jonathan Cartwright's outstanding four-course (plus extras) fixed-price menu (about $106 pp, add $58 or $85 for wine pairings). For gourmands, consider the nine-course tasting menu (about $160, wine pairings around $89). Reservations are essential—well ahead during July-August—and you'll need a credit card (cancel 24 hours ahead or you'll be charged). Jackets are required, and no jeans

or sneakers are allowed. Although the price is high, the value for the dollar far exceeds that. If you can afford it, dine here.

Also splurge-worthy is **Earth** (at Hidden Pond resort, 354 Goose Rocks Rd., Kennebunkport, 207/967-6550, www.earthathiddenpond.com, from 5:30pm daily, $18-40), where consulting chef Ken Orringer hangs his toque in Maine. The farm-to-fork cuisine includes handmade pastas, house-made charcuteries, wood-oven pizzas, and entrées such as local seafood paella and grilled skirt steak. The dining room is rustic, and the garden views are sublime.

Lobster and Clams

Nunan's Lobster Hut (9 Mills Rd., Cape Porpoise, 207/967-4362, www.nunanslobster-hut.com, 5pm-close daily) is an institution. Sure, other places might have better views, but this casual dockside eatery with indoor and outdoor seating has been serving lobsters since 1953.

Adjacent to the bridge connecting Kennebunkport's Dock Square to Kennebunk's Lower Village is another time-tested classic, **The Clam Shack** (Rte. 9, Kennebunkport, 207/967-2560, www.theclamshack.net, lunch and dinner from 11am daily May-Oct.). The tiny take-out stand serves perhaps the state's best lobster rolls, jam-packed with meat and available with either butter or mayo, and deelish fried clams.

Lobster and crab rolls and chowders are the specialties at **Port Lobster** (122 Ocean Ave., Kennebunkport, 207/967-2081, www.portlobster.com, 9am-6pm daily), a fresh-fish store with takeout just northeast of Dock Square.

Pair your lobster with a view of Goat Island Light at **Cape Pier Chowder House** (79 Pier Rd., Cape Porpoise, 207/967-0123, www.capeporpoiselobster.com, from 11am daily).

The Ocean Roll (207/985-8824, www.mainelobsterrolls.com) an extremely popular food truck, selling fresh lobster rolls and fried seafood, is often parked at the corner of Ross Avenue and Route 1, Kennebunk.

© HILARY NANGLE

The best fried clams in the Kennebunks come from The Clam Shack, just across the bridge from Dock Square.

INFORMATION AND SERVICES

The **Kennebunk and Kennebunkport Chamber of Commerce** (17 Western Ave./Rte. 9, Lower Village, Kennebunk, 207/967-0857, www.visitthekennebunks.com) produces an excellent area guide to accommodations, restaurants, area maps, bike maps, tide calendars, recreation, and beach parking permits.

Check out **Louis T. Graves Memorial Public Library** (18 Maine St., Kennebunkport, 207/967-2778, www.graveslibrary.org) or **Kennebunk Free Library** (112 Main St., 207/985-2173, www.kennebunklibrary.org).

Public restrooms are at Gooch's and Mother's Beaches and at St. Anthony's Franciscan Monastery, the chamber of commerce building (17 Western Ave.), and at the chamber's Dock Square Hospitality Center.

GETTING THERE AND AROUND

Kennebunk is about five miles or 10 minutes via Route 1 from Wells. Kennebunkport is about 6.5 miles or 12 minutes via Routes 1 and 9 from Wells. Connecting Kennebunk and Kennebunkport are four miles of Route 9. From Kennebunk to Biddeford, it's about nine miles or 17 minutes via Route 1. Allow longer for summer congestion in each town.

Amtrak Downeaster (800/872-7245, www.amtrakdowneaster.com) connects Boston's North Station with Portland, Maine, with stops in Wells, Saco, and Old Orchard Beach (seasonal). It connects with the seasonal **Shoreline Explorer** (207/324-5762, www.shorelineexplorer.com) trolley system, which operates between York and Kennebunkport. Each town's system is operated separately and has its own fees. The **Shoreline Trolley Line 7/Kennebunk Shuttle** ($1 one way, $3 day pass, $10 12-ride multipass, free for children under 18) connects Line 4 (serving the Wells Transportation Facility and the Downeaster) with downtown Kennebunk, Lower Village, and Kennebunk's beaches.

Shoreline Trolley Line 6/Intown Trolley

(207/967-3686, www.intowntrolley.com, $16, $6 ages 3-17) operates as a narrated sightseeing tour throughout Kennebunk and Kennebunkport. It originates in Dock Square and makes regular stops at beaches and other attractions. The entire route takes about 45 minutes, with the driver providing a hefty dose of local history and gossip. Seats are park bench-style. You can get on or off at any stop.

Old Orchard Beach Area

Seven continuous miles of white sand beach have been drawing vacation-oriented folks for generations to the area stretching from Camp Ellis in Saco to Pine Point in Scarborough. Cottage colonies and condo complexes dominate at the extremities, but the center of activity has always been and remains Old Orchard Beach.

In its heyday, **Old Orchard Beach's pier** reached far out into the sea, huge resort hotels lined the sands, and wealthy Victorian folk (including Rose Fitzgerald and Joe Kennedy, who met on these sands in the days when men strolled around in dress suits and women toted parasols) came each summer to see and be seen.

Storms and fires have taken their toll through the years, and the grand resorts have been replaced by endless motels, many of which display "Nous parlons français" signs to welcome the masses of French Canadians who arrive each summer. They're joined by young families who come for the sand and surf along with T-shirted and body-pierced young pleasure seekers who come for the nightlife.

Although some residents are pushing for gentrification and a few projects are moving things in that direction, **Old Orchard Beach**

The Pier at Old Orchard Beach has survived since 1898.

(pop. 8,624) remains somewhat honky-tonk, and most of its visitors would have it no other way. French fries, cotton candy, and beach-accessories shops line the downtown, and as you get closer to the pier, you pass arcades and amusement parks. There's not a kid on earth who wouldn't have fun in Old Orchard—even if some parents might find it all a bit much.

Much more sedate are the villages on the fringes. The **Ocean Park** section of Old Orchard, at the southwestern end of town, was established in 1881 as a religious summer-cottage community. It still offers interdenominational services and vacation Bible school, but it also has an active cultural association that sponsors concerts, Chautauqua-type lectures, films, and other events throughout the summer. All are open to the public.

South of that is **Camp Ellis.** Begun as a small fishing village named after early settler Thomas Ellis, it is crowded with longtime summer homes that are in a constant battle with the sea. A nearly mile-long granite jetty—designed to keep silt from clogging the Saco River—has taken the blame for massive beach erosion since it was constructed. But the jetty is a favorite spot for wetting a line and for panoramic views off toward Wood Island Light (built in 1808) and Biddeford Pool. Camp Ellis Beach is open to the public, with lifeguards on duty in midsummer. Parking—scarce on hot days—is $2/hour.

As you head north from Old Orchard, you'll pass **Pine Point,** another longtime community of vacation homes. Services are few, and parking is $10/day.

Most folks get to Old Orchard by passing through **Saco** (pop. 18,482) and **Biddeford** (pop. 21,277), which have long been upstairs-downstairs sister cities, with wealthy mill owners living in Saco and their workers and workplaces in Biddeford. But even those personalities have always been split—congested commercial Route 1 is part of Saco, and the exclusive enclave of Biddeford Pool is, of course, in below-stairs Biddeford.

Saco still has an attractive downtown, with boutiques and stunning homes on Main Street and beyond. Blue-collar Biddeford is working hard to change its mill-town image. It's home to the magnificent Biddeford City Theater and the University of New England, and as a Main Street community it's getting a much-needed sprucing up. Another Biddeford hallmark is its Franco-American tradition, thanks to the French-speaking workers who sustained the textile and shoemaking industries in the 19th century. The mills on the Saco River island between the two cities are being rehabbed to house restaurants, shops, offices, and condos.

SIGHTS
Saco Museum

Founded in 1866, the **Saco Museum** (371 Main St., Saco, 207/283-3861, www.dyerlibrarysacomuseum.org, noon-4pm Tues.-Thurs. and Sun., noon-8pm Fri., 10am-4pm Sat. June-Dec., $5 adults, $3 seniors, $2 students and children ages 7 and older) rotates selections from its outstanding collection, including 18th- and 19th-century paintings, furniture,

© HILARY NANGLE

You never know who you'll see at Old Orchard Beach.

and other household treasures. Lectures, workshops, and concerts are also part of the annual schedule. Admission is free after 4pm Friday.

◖ Wood Island Lighthouse

The all-volunteer **Friends of Wood Island Light** (207/200-4552, www.woodislandlighthouse. org) is restoring Maine's second-oldest lighthouse, which was commissioned by President Thomas Jefferson, built in 1808 (reconstructed in 1858) on 35-acre Wood Island, and abandoned in 1986. In July-August the Friends offer 1.5-hour guided tours ($15 adults, $8 children, recommended donation) of the two-story keeper's house and 42-foot-tall stone tower, relating tales of former keepers and their families to bring the site to life. You can even climb the 60 stairs to the tower's lantern room for splendid views. The tour departs from Vine's Landing in Biddeford Pool. Once on the island, it's about a half-mile walk to the site. Reservations are accepted within one week of the tour date; see the website or call for a current schedule.

Harmon Museum

Dip into Old Orchard Beach's history at the Old Orchard Beach Historical Society's **Harmon Museum** (4 Portland Ave., Old Orchard Beach, 207/934-9319, www.harmonmuseum.org, 10am-4pm Tues.-Fri., 10am-2pm Sat., free). Religious groups, the famed Pier, destructive fires, Ocean Park, transportation, and celebrities are all covered with displays, artifacts, and memorabilia. Interesting anytime, but a great rainy-day activity.

TOURS

Hop aboard an **Old Orchard Beach Trolley Tour** (207/205-5327, www.shuttlebus-zoom. com, $10 adults, $7 children and seniors). Tours depart up to four times daily from near the downtown railroad crossing.

ENTERTAINMENT

At 6pm every Thursday late June-Labor Day **free concerts** are staged in Old Orchard's Memorial Park, followed by **fireworks** set off by the pier at 9:45pm.

Family concerts and other performances are staged at the outdoor **Seaside Pavilion** (8 Sixth St., Old Orchard Beach, 207/934-2024, www. seasidepavilion.org).

The BallPark (E. Emerson Cummings Blvd., Old Orchard, 207/205-6160, www. oldorchardbeachballpark.com) hosts concerts, shows, and other events and doubles as home field for the Raging Tides, which competes in the Futures Collegiate Baseball League.

The **Temple,** (Temple Avenue, Ocean Park), a 19th-century octagon that seats more than 800, is the venue for Saturday- or Sunday-night concerts (7:30pm, $12 adults) and many other programs throughout the summer.

Designed by noted architect John Calvin Stevens in 1896, the 500-seat **City Theater** (205 Main St., Biddeford, 207/282-0849, www.citytheater.org) on the National Register of Historic Places, has been superbly restored, and the acoustics are excellent even when Eva Gray, the resident ghost, mixes it up backstage.

A rainy-day godsend, **IMAX Theater** (779 Portland Rd./Rte. 1, Saco, 207/282-6234, www.cinemagicmovies.com) has digital sound, stadium seating, a restaurant, and online ticketing.

Pair burritos and other Tex-Mex faves with live music at **Bebe's Burritos** (140 Main St., Biddeford, 207/283-4222, www.bebesburritos. com, 6pm-10pm Thurs.-Sun.), with trivia on Sunday nights.

EVENTS

La Kermesse (www.lakermessefestival. com), meaning "the fair" or "the festival," is Biddeford's summer highlight, when nearly 50,000 visitors pour into town in late June to celebrate the town's Franco-American heritage. Local volunteers go all out to plan block parties, a parade, games, a carnival, live entertainment, and traditional dancing. Then there's *la cuisine franco-américaine;* you can fill up on *boudin, creton, poutine, tourtière, tarte au saumon,* and crepes (although your arteries may rebel).

The **Biddeford+Saco Art Walk** (www.biddefordartwalk.com) takes place the last Friday of each month.

AMUSEMENT PARKS AND AMUSING PLACES

Palace Playland is a kid magnet at Old Orchard Beach.

If you've got kids or just love amusement parks, you'll find Maine's best in the Old Orchard area, where sand and sun just seem to complement arcades and rides perfectly. (All of these parks are seasonal, so call or check websites for current schedule.)

In July the parishioners of St. Demetrios Greek Orthodox Church (186 Bradley St., Saco, 207/284-5651) mount the annual **Greek Heritage Festival,** a three-day extravaganza of homemade Greek food, traditional Greek music and dancing, and a crafts fair. Be sure to tour the impressive $1.5 million domed church building.

The beaches come to life in July with the annual **Parade and Sandcastle Contest** in Ocean Park.

One weekend in mid-August, Old Orchard Beach's **Beach Olympics** is a family festival of games, exhibitions, and music benefiting Maine's Special Olympics program.

RECREATION
Parks and Preserves

Saco Bay Trails (www.sacobaytrails.org), a local land trust, has produced a very helpful trail guide ($10) that includes the Saco Heath, the East Point Sanctuary, and more than a dozen other local trails. The Cascade Falls trail, for example, is a half-mile stroll ending at a waterfall. Copies are available at a number of Biddeford and Saco locations, including the Dyer Library, or from Saco Bay Trails. Trail information is also on the organization's website.

EAST POINT SANCTUARY

Owned by Maine Audubon (207/781-2330, www.maineaudubon.org), the 30-acre **East Point Sanctuary** is a splendid preserve at the eastern end of Biddeford Pool. Crashing

The biggie is **Funtown/Splashtown USA** (774 Portland Rd./Rte. 1, Saco, 207/284-5139 or 800/878-2900, www.funtownsplashtownusa.com). Ride Maine's only wooden roller coaster; fly down New England's longest and tallest log flume ride; free-fall 200 feet on Dragon's Descent; get wet and go wild riding speed slides, tunnel slides, raft slides, and river slides or splashing in the pool. Add a huge kiddie-ride section as well as games, food, and other activities for a full day of family fun. Ticketing options vary by the activities included and height, ranging $25-36 for "Big" (48 inches and taller), $20-27 for "Little" (38-48 inches tall) and "Senior" (over age 60), and free for kids under 38 inches tall.

Three miles north of Funtown/Splashtown USA, **Aquaboggan Water Park** (980 Portland Rd./Rte. 1, Saco, 207/282-3112, www.aquabogganwaterpark.com, 10am-6pm daily late June-Labor Day) is wet and wild, with such stomach turners as the Yankee Ripper, the Suislide, and the Stealth, with an almost-vertical drop of 45 feet—enough to accelerate to 30 mph on the descent. Wear a bathing suit that won't abandon you in the rough-and-tumble. Also, if you wear glasses, safety straps and plastic lenses are required. Besides all the water stuff, there are mini-golf, an arcade, go-karts, and bumper boats. A day pass for all pools, slides, and mini-golf is $20 (48 inches and taller), $16 (under 48 inches tall), and $5 (under 38 inches tall). Monday is $12 general admission. A $30 superpass also includes two go-kart rides and unlimited bumper-boat rides.

The biggest beachfront amusement park, **Palace Playland** (1 Old Orchard St., Old Orchard, 207/934-2001, www.palaceplayland.com) has more than 25 rides and attractions packed into four acres, including a giant waterslide, a fun house, bumper cars, a Ferris wheel, roller coasters, and a 24,000-square-foot arcade with more than 200 games. An unlimited pass is $32/day; a kiddie pass good for all two-ticket rides is $24; two-day, season, and single tickets are available.

The **Old Orchard Beach's pier,** jutting 475 feet into the ocean from downtown, is a mini-mall of shops, arcades, and fast-food outlets. Far longer when it was built in 1898, it has been lopped off gradually by fires and storms. The current incarnation has been here since the late 1970s.

surf, beach roses, bayberry bushes, and offshore Wood Island Light are all features of the two-part perimeter trail, which skirts the exclusive Abenakee Club's golf course. Allow at least an hour; even in fog, the setting is dramatic. During spring and fall migrations it's one of southern Maine's prime birding locales, so you'll have plenty of company at those times, and the usual street-side parking may be scarce. It's poorly signposted (perhaps deliberately), so you'll want to follow the directions: From Route 9 (Main Street) in downtown Biddeford, take Route 9/208 (Pool Road) southeast about five miles to the Route 208 turnoff to Biddeford Pool. Go 0.6 mile on Route 208 (Bridge Road) and then turn left onto Mile Stretch Road. Continue to Lester B. Orcutt Boulevard, turn left, and go to the end. Be careful: There's poison ivy on the point.

THE HEATH

Owned by The Nature Conservancy, 1,000-plus-acre **Saco Heath Preserve** is the nation's southernmost "raised coalesced bog," where peat accumulated through eons into two above-water dome shapes that eventually merged into a single natural feature. A bit of esoterica: It's the home of the rare Hessel's hairstreak butterfly. Pick up a map at the parking area and follow the mile-long self-guided trail through the woods and then into the heath via a boardwalk. The best time to visit is early-mid-October, when the heath and woodland colors are positively brilliant and insects are on the wane. You're likely to see deer and perhaps even spot a moose. The preserve entrance is on Route 112 (Buxton Road), two miles west of I-95. Pets are not allowed in the preserve.

FERRY BEACH STATE PARK

When the weather's hot, arrive early at **Ferry Beach State Park** (95 Bay View Rd., off Rte. 9, Saco, 207/283-0067, $6 nonresident adults, $4 Maine resident adults, $2 nonresident seniors, $1 ages 5-11), a pristine beach backed by dune grass on Saco Bay. In the 117-acre park are changing rooms, restrooms, a lifeguard, picnic tables, and five easy interconnected nature trails winding through woodlands, marshlands, and dunes. Later in the day, keep the insect repellent handy. It's open daily late May-late September but accessible all year; trail markers are removed in winter.

Golf

Tee off at the **Biddeford-Saco Country Club** (101 Old Orchard Rd., Saco, 207/282-5883) or the challenging 18-hole par-71 **Dunegrass Golf Club** (200 Wild Dunes Way, Old Orchard Beach, 207/934-4513 or 800/521-1029).

Water Sports

Moose County Music & Surf (67 E. Grand Ave., Old Orchard Beach, 207/729-1656, www.moosecounty.us) rents surfboards ($10 for one hour, $25 for three hours), wetsuits for $5, and kayaks ($20 for one hour, $35 for two hours).

Gone with the Wind (Yates St., Biddeford Pool, 207/283-8446, www.gwtwonline.com) offers two tours, afternoon and sunset, with prices varying with the number of people on the tour (for two people it's about $85 pp). Wetsuits are supplied. The most popular trip is to Beach Island. Also available are rentals ($40 half day, $65 full day).

ACCOMMODATIONS

The area has hundreds of beds—mostly in motel-style lodgings. The chamber of commerce is the best resource for motels, cottages, and the area's more than 3,000 campsites.

The Old Orchard Beach Inn (6 Portland Ave., Old Orchard Beach, 207/934-5834 or 877/700-6624, www.oldorchardbeachinn.com, year-round, $135-200) was rescued from ruin, restored, and reopened in 2000. Built in 1730, and most recently known as the Staples Inn, the National Historic Register building has 18 antiques-filled guest rooms with air-conditioning, phones, and TVs. Continental breakfast and afternoon tea are included in the rates; a two-bedroom suite is $425-450.

Practically next door is **The Atlantic Birches Inn** (20 Portland Ave./Rte. 98, Old Orchard Beach, 207/934-5295 or 888/934-5295, www.atlanticbirches.com, $136-220), with 10 air-conditioned guest rooms in a Victorian house and a separate cottage. Decor leans toward froufrou, breakfast is hearty continental, and there's a swimming pool. The beach is an easy walk. It's open all year, but call ahead off-season.

Two family-owned, beachfront motels, both with pools, have been recently renovated: **The Beachwood Motel** (29 W. Grand Ave., Old Orchard Beach, 207/934-2291, www.beachwood-motel.com, $210-265) and **The Edgewater Motor Inn** (57 W. Grand Ave., Old Orchard Beach, 800/203-2034, www.theedgewatermotorinn.com, $189-289). Both are in Old Orchard's hub, so don't expect quiet nights.

FOOD
Old Orchard Beach

Dining is not Old Orchard's strong point, but it is a bonanza for cheap eats. Stroll Main Street and out the pier for hot dogs, fries, pizza, and ice cream.

For casual dining, **Joseph's by the Sea** (55 W. Grand Ave., 207/934-5044, www.josephsbythesea.com, 7am-11am and 5pm-9pm daily, entrées $19-33) is a quiet shorefront restaurant amid all the hoopla. Request a table on the screened patio. The menu is heavy on seafood, but there are choices for steak lovers. Reservations are advisable in midsummer.

Camp Ellis

At **Huot's Seafood Restaurant** (Camp Ellis Beach, Saco, 207/282-1642, www.

huotsseafoodrestaurant.com, 11:30am-8:30pm Tues.-Sun., $6-27), under third-generation management, the menu is huge, portions are large, and prices are reasonable. It's a good value for fresh seafood; children's menu available.

Saco

Craving fast-ish food? The Camire family operates Maine's best homegrown option, **Rapid Ray's** (189 Main St., 207/283-4222, www. rapidrays.biz, 11am-12:30am Mon.-Thurs., 11am-1:30am Fri.-Sat., 11am-11pm Sun., $2-8), a downtown institution for more than 50 years. Burgers, steamed dogs, lobster rolls, and clam cakes are served at the standing-room-only joint.

Super soups and sandwiches come from **Vic & Whits** (206 Main St., 207/284-6710, 8am-8pm Mon.-Sat., 8am-1pm Sun.), which also has a nice selection of retail wine, beer, and Maine cheeses.

The New Moon Restaurant (17 Pepperell Sq., 207/282-2241, 7:30am-2pm Wed.-Fri., 7:30am-1pm Sat.-Sun., and 5pm-9pm Fri.-Sat.) serves rave-worthy breakfasts and lunches in a cheerful yellow house. On Friday and Saturday nights, it offers dinners with entrées such as chicken saltimbocca and filet mignon medallions ($16-22).

Located on Saco Island in renovated factory building #3, **The Run of the Mill Public House & Brewery** (100 Main St., 207/571-9648, www.therunofthemill.net, 11:30am-9pm Sun.-Thurs., to 10pm Fri.-Sat., $8-17) is a 14-barrel brewpub with seasonal outdoor deck seating overlooking the river. Expect pub-fare classics with a few surprises.

Biddeford and Biddeford Pool

For a town grounded in Franco-American culture, Biddeford has some intriguing ethnic choices, including a few that garner praise far beyond city limits: For well-prepared Indian cuisine, seek out **Jewel of India** (26 Alfred St., 207/282-5600, www.thejewelofindia. com, 11am-10pm Tues.-Sun., entrées $13-16). If you're longing for pho and Vietnamese coffee, head into **Que Huong** (49 Main St.,

207/571-8050, www.quehuongmaine.com, 11am-8pm Mon.-Thurs., to 9pm Fri.-Sat., $7-10).

Maine's oldest diner is the **Palace Diner** (18 Franklin St.), a 1926 Pollard that was towed to Maine from Lowell, Massachusetts, by horses in the same year that Lindberg flew over the Atlantic. Today, it's tucked off Main Street next to City Hall. New owners plan to reopen it in 2014. Dine in or take it to the adjacent park. It's tucked off Main Street next to City Hall. Plans called for classic diner fare for breakfast and lunch as well as fancier dinners on weekends. Ask locally for details.

Dahlia's Delights (137 Main St., 207/710-2119, www.dahliasdelights.com, 11am-7pm Tues.-Sat., 10am-2pm Sun., $6-10) serves vegetarian salads, sandwiches, soups, and specials.

Buffleheads (122 Hills Beach Rd., 207/284-6000, www.buffleheadsrestaurant.com, 11:30am-2pm and 5pm-9pm daily, closed Mon. off-season, $10-28) is an off-the-tourist-trail family dining find with spectacular ocean views. Ray and Karen Wieczoreck opened the restaurant in 1994 and have built a strong local following through the years. The kids can munch on pizza, burgers, spaghetti, and other favorites while adults savor well-prepared seafood with a home-style spin or landlubber classics. Lobster pie is a perennial favorite. Hills Beach Road branches off Route 9 at the University of New England campus.

Take your lobster or fried seafood dinner to an oceanfront picnic table on the grassy lawn behind **F. O. Goldthwaite's** (3 Lester B. Orcott Blvd., Biddeford Pool, 207/284-8872, 7am-7:30pm daily, $4-market rates), an old-fashioned general store. Salads, fried seafood, sandwiches, and kid-friendly fare round out the menu.

INFORMATION AND SERVICES

Sources of visitor information are **Biddeford-Saco Chamber of Commerce and Industry** (207/282-1567, www. biddefordsacochamber.org), **Old Orchard Beach Chamber of Commerce**

© TOM NANGLE

The Palace Diner is Maine's oldest diner.

(207/934-2500 or 800/365-9386, www.oldorchardbeachmaine.com), and **Ocean Park Association** (207/934-9068, www.oceanpark.org).

The **Dyer Library** (371 Main St., Saco, 207/282-3031, www.sacomuseum.org), next door to the Saco Museum, attracts scads of genealogists to its vast Maine history collection. Also check out **Libby Memorial Library** (Staples St., Old Orchard Beach, 207/934-4351, www.ooblibrary.org).

GETTING THERE AND AROUND

Biddeford is about five miles or 10 minutes via Route 1 from Kennebunk. From Biddeford to Portland, it's about 18 miles or 25 minutes via I-95 and I-295; allow at least a half hour via Route 1. Downtown Biddeford is about a mile via Route 9 from downtown Saco. From Saco to Old Orchard Beach is about four miles or at least 10 minutes via Route 9, the Old Orchard Beach Road, and Route 5, but it can take twice that in summer traffic.

Amtrak Downeaster (800/872-7245, www.amtrakdowneaster.com) connects Boston's North Station with Brunswick, Maine, with stops in Wells, Saco, Old Orchard Beach (seasonal), Portland, Freeport, and Brunswick. If you're thinking day trip, take the train and avoid the traffic and parking hassles.

The **Biddeford-Saco-Old Orchard Beach Transit Committee** (207/282-5408, www.shuttlebus-zoom.com) operates three systems that make getting around simple. The **Old Orchard Beach Trolley** (10am-midnight daily late June-Labor Day) operates two routes on a regular schedule that connects restaurants and campgrounds. You can flag it down anywhere en route. Fare is $1-2/ride; children under age five ride free. **ShuttleBus Local Service** provides frequent weekday and less-frequent weekend service (except on national holidays) between Biddeford, Saco, and Old Orchard Beach. One-way fare is $1.25 ages five and older, exact change required. **ShuttleBus InterCity** **Service** connects Biddeford, Saco, and Old Orchard with Portland, South Portland, and Scarborough. Fares vary by zones, topping out at $5 for anyone over age five.

GREATER PORTLAND

Whenever national magazines highlight the 10 best places to live, eat, work, or play, Greater Portland often makes the list. The very things that make the area so popular with residents make it equally attractive to visitors. Small in size but big in heart, Greater Portland entices visitors with the staples—lighthouses, lobster, and L. L. Bean—but wows them with everything else it offers. It is the state's cultural hub, with performing arts centers, numerous festivals, and varied museums; it's also a dining destination, with nationally recognized chefs as well as an amazing assortment and variety of everyday restaurants; and despite its urban environment it has a mind-boggling number of recreational opportunities. No wonder the National Heritage Trust named it a Distinctive Destination.

Portland's population hovers around 66,000, but when the suburbs are included, it climbs to nearly 250,000, making it Maine's largest city by far. Take a swing through the bedroom communities of Scarborough (pop. 18,919), Cape Elizabeth (pop. 9,015), and South Portland (pop. 25,002), and you'll better understand the area's popularity: easily accessible parks, beaches, rocky ledges, and lighthouses all minutes from downtown along with a slew of ferry-connected islands dotting Casco Bay. Head north through suburban Falmouth (pop. 11,185) and Yarmouth (pop. 8,349), and you'll arrive in Freeport (pop. 7,879), home of megaretailer L. L. Bean. En route you'll still see the vestiges of the region's heritage: sailboats and lobster boats, traps and buoys piled on lawns

COURTESY OF PORTLAND CONVENTION & VISITORS BUREAU

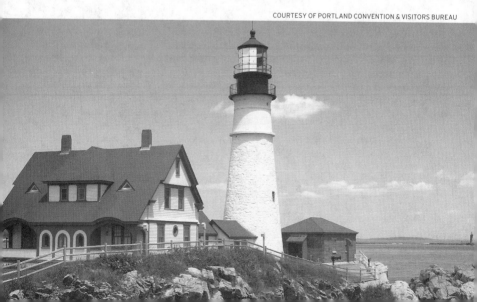

HIGHLIGHTS

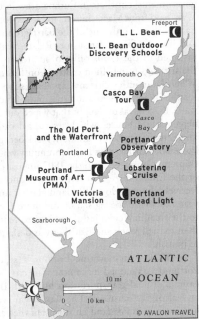

L. L. Bean
Freeport

L. L. Bean Outdoor
Discovery Schools

Yarmouth

Casco Bay
Tour

Casco
Bay

The Old Port
and the Waterfront

Portland
Observatory

Portland

Lobstering
Cruise

Portland
Museum of Art
(PMA)

Victoria
Mansion

Portland
Head Light

Scarborough

ATLANTIC

OCEAN

0   10 mi

0   10 km

© AVALON TRAVEL

LOOK FOR 【 TO FIND RECOMMENDED
SIGHTS, ACTIVITIES, DINING, AND
LODGING.

【 **The Old Port and the Waterfront:** Plan to spend at least a couple of hours browsing the shops, dining, and enjoying the energy of this restored historic district (page 82).

【 **Portland Museum of Art (PMA):** This museum houses works by masters such as Winslow Homer, John Marin, Andrew Wyeth, Edward Hopper, and Marsden Hartley as well as works by Monet, Picasso, and Renoir (page 85).

【 **Victoria Mansion:** This house is considered one of the most richly decorated dwellings of its period remaining in the country (page 85).

【 **Portland Observatory:** Climb the 103 steps to the orb deck of the only remaining maritime signal tower on the eastern seaboard, and you'll be rewarded with views from the White Mountains to Casco Bay's islands (page 85).

【 **Portland Head Light:** This lighthouse, commissioned by President George Washington, is fabulously sited on the rocky ledges of Cape Elizabeth (page 87).

【 **Casco Bay Tour:** Take a three-hour tour on the mail boat, which stops briefly at five islands en route (page 96).

【 **Lobstering Cruise:** Go out on a working lobster boat in Portland Harbor, see the sights, and perhaps return with a lobster for dinner (page 97).

【 **L. L. Bean:** The empire's flagship store is in Freeport, and no trip to this shopping mecca is complete without a visit (page 112).

【 **L. L. Bean Outdoor Discovery Schools:** Don't miss the opportunity for an inexpensive introduction to a new sport (page 115).

GREATER PORTLAND

or along driveways, and tucked here and there, farms with stands brimming with fresh produce.

Greater Portland also marks a transitional point on Maine's coastline. The long sandy beaches of the Southern Coast begin to give way to islands and a coastline edged with a jumble of rocks and ledges spliced with rivers and coves.

It's tempting to dismiss Portland in favor of seeking the "real Maine" elsewhere along the coast, but the truth is, the real Maine is here. And although Portland alone provides plenty to keep a visitor busy, it's also an excellent base for day trips to places such as the Kennebunks, Freeport, Brunswick, and Bath, where more of that real Maine flavor awaits.

PLANNING YOUR TIME

July and August are the most popular times to visit, but Greater Portland is a year-round destination. Spring truly arrives by mid-May, when most summer outfitters begin operations at least on weekends. September is perhaps the loveliest month of the year weather-wise, and by mid-October those fabled New England maples are turning crimson.

To do the region justice, you'll want to spend at least three or four days, more if your plans call for using Greater Portland as a base for day trips to more distant points. You can easily kill two days in downtown Portland alone, what with all the shops, museums, historical sites, waterfront, and neighborhoods to explore. If you're staying in town and are an avid walker, you won't need a car to get to the in-town must-see sights.

You will need a car to reach beyond the city (although the Amtrak Downeaster train connects to Wells, Old Orchard, Freeport, and Brunswick. Allow a full day for a leisurely tour through South Portland and Cape Elizabeth and on to Prouts Neck in Scarborough.

Rabid shoppers should either stay in Freeport or allow at least a day for L. L. Bean and the 100 or so outlets in its shadow. If you're traveling with a supershopper, don't despair. Freeport has parks and preserves that are light-years removed from the frenzy of its downtown, and the fishing village of South Freeport offers seaworthy pleasures.

HISTORY

Portland's downtown, a crooked-finger peninsula projecting into Casco Bay and today defined vaguely by I-295 at its "knuckle," was named Machigonne (Great Neck) by the Wabanaki, the Native Americans who held sway when English settlers first arrived in 1632. Characteristically, the Brits renamed the region Falmouth (it included present-day Falmouth, Portland, South Portland, Westbrook, and Cape Elizabeth) and the peninsula Falmouth Neck, but it was 130 years before they secured real control of the area. Anglo-French squabbles spurred by the governments' conflicts in Europe drew in the Wabanaki from Massachusetts to Nova Scotia. Falmouth was only one of the battlegrounds, and it was a fairly minor one. Relative calm resumed in the 1760s only to be broken by the stirrings of rebellion centered on Boston. When Falmouth's citizens expressed support for the incipient revolution, the punishment was a 1775 naval onslaught that wiped out 75 percent of the houses, which created a decade-long setback. In 1786, Falmouth Neck became Portland, a thriving trading community where shipping flourished until the 1807 imposition of the Embargo Act. Severing trade and effectively shutting down Portland Harbor for a year and a half, the legislation did more harm to the fledgling colonies of the United States than to the French and British it was designed to punish.

In 1820, when Maine became a state, Portland was named its capital. The city became a crucial transportation hub with the arrival of the railroad. The Civil War was barely a blip in Portland's history, but the year after it ended, the city suffered a devastating blow: Exuberant Fourth of July festivities in 1866 sparked a conflagration that virtually leveled the city. The Great Fire spared only the Portland Observatory and a chunk of the West End. Evidence of the city's Victorian rebirth remains today in many downtown neighborhoods.

After World War II, Portland slipped into decline for several years, but that is over. The city's waterfront revival began in the 1970s and continues today, despite commercial competition from South Portland's Maine Mall. Congress Street has blossomed as an arts and retail district, public green space is increasing, and an influx of immigrants is changing the city's cultural makeup. With the new century, Portland is on a roll.

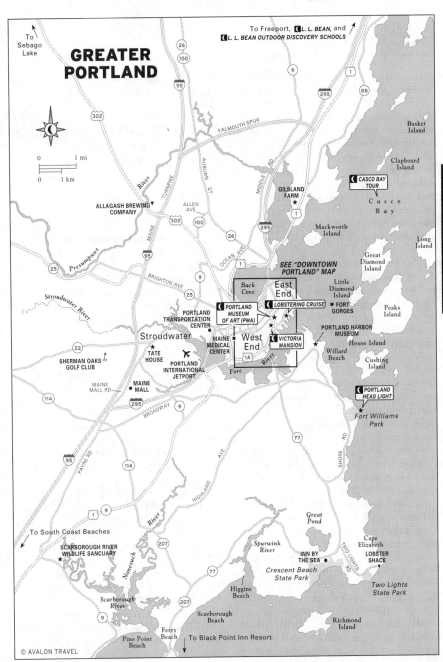

GREATER PORTLAND

To Freeport, **(** L. L. BEAN, and
(L. L. BEAN OUTDOOR DISCOVERY SCHOOLS

To
Sebago
Lake

GREATER PORTLAND

26
100
95
302

FALMOUTH SPUR

0   1 mi

0   1 km

AUBURN ST

MIDDLE RD

9

1

295

88

Basket
Island

Clapboard
Island

**ALLAGASH BREWING
COMPANY**

ALLEN
AVE

302
100
26

GILSLAND
FARM

1

**(CASCO BAY
TOUR**

C a s c o
B a y

Long
Island

River

MAINE

TURNPIKE

25

Presumpscot

95

OCEAN AVE

1

295

Mackworth
Island

Great
Diamond
Island

Stroudwater River

BRIGHTON AVE

9

25

Back
Cove

**East
End**

SEE "DOWNTOWN
PORTLAND" MAP

Little
Diamond
Island

Peaks
Island

22

**SHERMAN OAKS
GOLF CLUB**

**PORTLAND
TRANSPORTATION
CENTER**

**(PORTLAND
MUSEUM
OF ART (PMA)**

(LOBSTERING CRUISE

■ **FORT
GORGES**

**★
TATE
HOUSE**

**PORTLAND
INTERNATIONAL
JETPORT**

**MAINE
MEDICAL
CENTER**

**West
End**

**(VICTORIA
MANSION**

**PORTLAND HARBOR
MUSEUM**

House Island

Cushing
Island

1A

Fore

River

Willard
Beach

MAINE
MALL RD

**MAINE
MALL**

295

BROADWAY

9

**(PORTLAND
HEAD LIGHT**

**★
Fort Williams
Park**

114

77

SHORE RD

95

PAYNE RD

114

HIGHLAND AVE

River

Nonesuch

1

9

207

To South Coast Beaches

**SCARBOROUGH RIVER
WILDLIFE SANCTUARY**

★

77

207

Spurwink
River

Higgins
Beach

Great
Pond

**INN BY
THE SEA** ●

*Crescent Beach
State Park*

TWO LIGHTS RD

Cape
Elizabeth

**LOBSTER
SHACK**

*Two Lights
State Park*

Scarborough
River

9

Pine Point
Beach

Ferry
Beach

Scarborough
Beach

To Black Point Inn Resort

Richmond
Island

© AVALON TRAVEL

Portland

Often compared to San Francisco (an oft-cited but never verified statistic boasts that it vies with San Francisco for the title of most restaurants per capita), Portland is small, friendly, and easily explored on foot, although at times it may seem that no matter which direction you head, it's uphill. The heart of Portland is the peninsula jutting into Casco Bay. Bordering that are the Eastern and Western Promenades, Back Cove, and the working waterfront. Salty sea breezes cool summer days and make winter ones seem even chillier. Unlike that other city by the bay, snow frequently blankets Portland December–March.

Portland is Maine's most ethnically diverse city, with active refugee resettlement programs and dozens of languages spoken in the schools. Although salty sailors can still be found along the waterfront, Portland is increasingly a professional community with young, upwardly mobile residents spiffing up Victorian houses and infusing new energy and money into the city's neighborhoods.

The region's cultural hub, Portland has world-class museums and performing arts centers, active historical and preservation groups, an art school and a university, a symphony orchestra, numerous galleries and coffeehouses, and enough activities to keep culture vultures busy well into the night, especially in the thriving, handsomely restored Old Port and the up-and-coming Arts District.

Portland is also a playground for lovers of the sports and outdoors, with trails for running, biking, skating, and cross-country skiing, water sports aplenty, and a beloved minor-league baseball team, the Sea Dogs. When city folks want to escape, they often hop a ferry for one of the islands of Casco Bay or head to one of the parks, preserves, or beaches in the suburbs.

Still, Portland remains a major seaport. Lobster boats, commercial fishing vessels, long-distance passenger boats, cruise ships, and local ferries dominate the working waterfront, and the briny scent of the sea—or bait—seasons the air.

PORTLAND NEIGHBORHOODS

The best way to appreciate the character of Portland's neighborhoods is on foot. So much of Portland can (and should) be covered on foot that it would take a whole book to list all the possibilities, but several dedicated volunteer groups have produced guides to facilitate the process.

Greater Portland Landmarks (207/774-5561, www.portlandlandmarks.org) is the doyenne, founded in 1964 to preserve Portland's historic architecture and promote responsible construction. The organization has published more than a dozen books and booklets, including *Discover Historic Portland on Foot*, a packet of four well-researched walking-tour guides to architecturally historic sections of Portland's peninsula: Old Port, Western Promenade, State Street, and Congress Street. It's available online or for $6 at local bookstores, some gift shops, and the **Visitor Information Center** (14 Ocean Gateway Pier, 207/772-5800). Ask about guided walking tours highlighting neighborhoods or sights. Self-guided tours can be downloaded from the Landmarks website.

◖ The Old Port and the Waterfront

Tony shops, cobblestone sidewalks, replica streetlights, and a casual upmarket crowd (most of the time) set the scene for a district once filled with derelict buildings. Scores of boutiques, enticing restaurants, and spontaneous street-corner music make it a fun area to visit year-round. Nightlife centers on the Old Port, and a few dozen bars keep everyone hopping until after midnight. Police keep a close eye on the district, but it can get a bit dicey after 11pm on weekends.

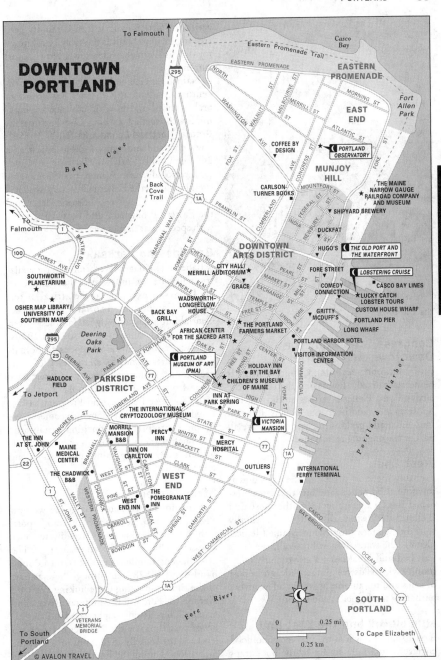

DOWNTOWN PORTLAND

To Falmouth
Casco Bay
Eastern Promenade Trail
EASTERN PROMENADE
295
EASTERN PROMENADE
NORTH ST
WASHINGTON AVE
MELBOURNE ST
MERRILL ST
MORNING ST
Fort Allen Park
EAST END
ATLANTIC ST

Back Cove

Back Cove Trail

FOX ST
COFFEE BY DESIGN
★ ◖ PORTLAND OBSERVATORY
FORE ST
MUNJOY HILL
THE MAINE NARROW GAUGE RAILROAD COMPANY AND MUSEUM
CARLSON-TURNER BOOKS
MOUNTFORT ST
FEDERAL ST
▼ SHIPYARD BREWERY
1A
FRANKLIN ST
CUMBERLAND
INDIA ST
NEWBURY
▼ DUCKFAT
To Falmouth
1
100
FOREST AVE
BAXTER BLVD
MARGINAL WAY
SOMERSET ST
CHESTNUT ST
DOWNTOWN ARTS DISTRICT
▼ HUGO'S
◖ THE OLD PORT AND THE WATERFRONT
SOUTHWORTH PLANETARIUM ★
CITY HALL/ MERRILL AUDITORIUM ★
ELM ST
PEARL ST
FORE STREET
◖ LOBSTERING CRUISE
OSHER MAP LIBRARY/ UNIVERSITY OF SOUTHERN MAINE ★
PREBLE ST
★ GRACE
MARKET ST
EXCHANGE ST
TEMPLE ST
MILK ST
COMEDY CONNECTION
■ CASCO BAY LINES
★ LUCKY CATCH LOBSTER TOURS
CUSTOM HOUSE WHARF
25
FOREST AVE
PORTLAND ST
BACK BAY GRILL
WADSWORTH-LONGFELLOW HOUSE
FREE ST
UNION ST
FORE ST
GRITTY MCDUFF'S
PORTLAND PIER
Deering Oaks Park
PARK AVE
STATE ST
★ AFRICAN CENTER FOR THE SACRED ARTS
★ THE PORTLAND FARMERS MARKET
CENTER ST
SPRING ST
PORTLAND HARBOR HOTEL
LONG WHARF
295
DEERING AVE
OAK ST
FREE ST
◖ PORTLAND MUSEUM OF ART (PMA) ★
VISITOR INFORMATION CENTER
HADLOCK FIELD
To Jetport
PARKSIDE DISTRICT
77
CONGRESS ST
HIGH ST
HOLIDAY INN BY THE BAY
YORK ST
COMMERCIAL ST
CUMBERLAND AVE
CHILDREN'S MUSEUM OF MAINE
Portland Harbor
★ INN AT PARK SPRING
PARK ST
THE INTERNATIONAL CRYPTOZOOLOGY MUSEUM
STATE ST
◖ VICTORIA MANSION
THE INN AT ST. JOHN
CONGRESS ST
MORRILL MANSION B&B
■ PERCY INN
WINTER ST
★ MERCY HOSPITAL
22
MAINE MEDICAL CENTER
BRAMHALL ST
VAUGHAN ST
INN ON CARLETON
BRACKETT ST
77
1A
THE CHADWICK B&B ■
CHADWICK ST
CLARK ST
▼ OUTLIERS
INTERNATIONAL FERRY TERMINAL
1
VALLEY ST
WEST ST
PINE ST
CARLETON ST
THE POMEGRANATE INN
WEST END
NEAL ST
WEST END INN
WESTERN PROMENADE
ST JOHN ST
CARROLL ST
SPRING ST
DANFORTH ST
CASCO BAY BRIDGE
BOWDOIN ST
WEST COMMERCIAL ST
OCEAN ST
SOUTH PORTLAND
77
1A
Fore River
To South Portland
1
VETERANS MEMORIAL BRIDGE
N
0   0.25 mi
0   0.25 km
To Cape Elizabeth

© AVALON TRAVEL

the Old Port

Congress Street and the Downtown Arts District

Bit by bit, once-declining Congress Street is being revitalized, showcasing the best of the city's culture. Galleries, artists' studios, coffeehouses, cafés, and bistros as well as libraries, museums, and performing arts centers are all part of the ongoing renaissance.

West End

Probably the most diverse of the city's downtown neighborhoods, and one that largely escaped the Great Fire of 1866, the West End includes the historically and architecturally splendid Western Promenade, Maine Medical Center (the state's largest hospital), the city's best bed-and-breakfasts, a gay-friendly community with a laissez-faire attitude, and a host of cafés and restaurants as well as a few niches harboring the homeless and forlorn.

Munjoy Hill and the East End

A once slightly down-at-the-heels neighborhood enclave with a pull-'em-up-by-the-bootstraps attitude, Portland's East End is rapidly gentrifying. Munjoy Hill is probably best known for the distinctive wooden tower crowning its summit.

Named for George Munjoy, a wealthy 17th-century resident, this district has a host of architectural and historic landmarks, making it well worth a walking tour. Fortunately, **Greater Portland Landmarks** (207/774-5561, www.portlandlandmarks.org) has produced a 24-page booklet, *Munjoy Hill Historic Guide* ($3), which documents more than 60 notable sites, including the Eastern Cemetery, which is on the National Register of Historic Places, and the Eastern Promenade and Fort Allen Park, with spectacular harbor views.

Bayside and Parkside

A Babel of languages reverberates in these districts just below and west of Portland City Hall. Bayside experienced the arrival of refugees—Cambodian, Laotian, Vietnamese, Central European, and Afghan families—from war-torn lands during the 1980s and 1990s. Nowadays you'll hear references to Somali Town, an area named for all the resettled refugees from that shattered country. Others have come from Sudan and Ethiopia. Portland's active Refugee Resettlement Program has assisted all of them, and many newcomers have become entrepreneurs, opening restaurants and small markets catering to their compatriots but increasingly gaining customers among other residents.

Stroudwater

Off the downtown peninsula at the western edge of Portland, close to the Portland Jetport, is the historic area known as Stroudwater, once an essential link in Maine water transport. The 20-mile-long **Cumberland and Oxford Canal,** hand-dug in 1828, ran through here as part of the timber-shipping route linking Portland Harbor, the Fore and Presumpscot Rivers, and Sebago Lake. Twenty-eight wooden locks allowed vessels to rise the 265 feet between sea level and the lake. By 1870 trains took over the route, condemning the canal to oblivion. The centerpiece of the Stroudwater area today is the historic 18th-century Tate House.

SIGHTS

◖ Portland Museum of Art (PMA)

Three centuries of art and architecture can be discovered at Maine's oldest (since 1882) and finest art museum, the **Portland Museum of Art** (7 Congress Sq., 207/775-6148, recorded info 207/773-2787 or 800/639-4067, www.portlandmuseum.org, 10am-5pm Sat.-Sun. and Mon.-Thurs., 10am-9pm Fri., closed Mon. mid-Oct.-late May, $12 adults, $10 seniors and students, $6 ages 6-17, free 5pm-9pm every Fri.). The museum's topflight collection of American and impressionist masters and fine and decorative arts is displayed in three architecturally stunning connected buildings: the award-winning Charles Shipman Payson building, designed by I. M. Pei and opened in 1983; the newly restored Federal-era McLellan House; and the Beaux Arts L. D. M. Sweat Memorial Galleries, designed by noted Maine architect John Calvin Stevens. The museum also has a well-stocked gift shop and an excellent café that's open for lunch daily (11am-4pm) and dinner Friday until 8pm. Check the website for current family activities, lectures, and other events, including **Movies at the Museum** ($7), showcasing foreign, classical, and art films. Plan well in advance if you want to pair a museum visit with a tour of the **Winslow Homer Studio** on nearby Prouts Neck. The 2.5-hour tours ($55) depart from the museum and are limited to 10 participants. Call for the current schedule. The studio is a don't-miss for fans of the American master.

◖ Victoria Mansion

The jaws of first-time visitors literally drop when they enter the Italianate **Victoria Mansion** (109 Danforth St., 207/772-4841, www.victoriamansion.org, 10am-4pm Mon.-Sat., 1pm-5pm Sun. May 1-Oct. 31, special hours in Dec., $15 adults, $13.50 seniors, $5 ages 6-17, $35 family, no senior discount in holiday season), also called the Morse-Libby Mansion. It's widely considered the most magnificently ornamented dwelling of its period remaining in the country. The National Historic Landmark is rife with Victoriana: carved marble fireplaces, elaborate porcelain and paneling, a freestanding mahogany staircase, gilded glass chandeliers, a restored 6-by-25-foot stained-glass ceiling window, and unbelievable trompe l'oeil touches. It's even more spectacular at Christmas, with yards of roping, festooned trees, and carolers; this is the best time to bring kids, as the house itself may not particularly intrigue them. The mansion was built in the late 1850s by Ruggles Sylvester Morse, a Maine-born entrepreneur whose New Orleans-based fortune enabled him to hire 93 craftspeople to complete the house. The interior, designed by Gustave Herter, still boasts 90 percent of the original furnishings. Guided 45-minute tours begin every half hour on the quarter hour in season; tours are self-guided during the holidays.

◖ Portland Observatory

Providing a head-swiveling view of Portland (and the White Mountains on a clear day), the octagonal red-painted **Portland Observatory** (138 Congress St., 207/774-5561, www.portlandlandmarks.org, 10am-5pm daily late May-mid-Oct., last tour at 4:30pm, sunset tours 5pm-8pm Thurs. July-Aug., $9 adults, $8 seniors, $5 ages 6-16) is the only remaining marine signal tower on the eastern seaboard. Built in 1807 at a cost of $5,000 by Captain Lemuel Moody to keep track of the port's shipping activity, the tower has 122 tons of rock ballast in its base. Admission in those days (only men were allowed to climb the 103 interior steps) was 12.5 cents. Today, admission includes the small museum at the tower's base and a guided tour to the top.

The Longfellow Connection

A few blocks down Congress Street from the PMA you can step back in time to the era of Portland-born poet Henry Wadsworth Longfellow, who lived in the accurately restored **Wadsworth-Longfellow House** (485 Congress St., 207/774-1822, www.

GREATER PORTLAND

© HILARY NANGLE

Longfellow Square honors poet Henry Wadsworth Longfellow, who spent his boyhood in Portland.

mainehistory.org, 10am-5pm Mon.-Sat., noon-5pm Sun. May 1-Oct. 31, last tour 4pm, special holiday hours Nov.-Dec., $12 adults, $10 seniors and students, $3 ages 5-17, includes the museum) as a child in the early 1800s, long before the brick mansion was dwarfed by surrounding high-rises. Wadsworth and Longfellow family furnishings fill the three-story house, owned by the Maine Historical Society. Hour-long tours by savvy guides provide insight into Portland's 19th-century life. Don't miss the urban oasis—a wonderfully peaceful garden—behind the house (same hours, free). Buy tickets at the adjacent **Maine Historical Society Museum**, where you can take in the Maine Historical Society's current exhibits chronicling five centuries of life in Maine and find an extensive collection of Maine history books in the gift shop. Admission for the museum alone is $8 adults, $7 seniors, $2 children.

Maine Narrow Gauge Railroad Company and Museum

A three-mile ride along Portland's waterfront is the highlight of a visit to the **Maine Narrow Gauge Railroad Company and Museum** (58 Fore St., 207/828-0814, www.mngrr.org, 10am-4pm daily early May-late Oct., $3 adults, $2 seniors and ages 3-12, free with train ticket) owns more than three dozen train cars and has others on long-term loan, most from Maine's five historic narrow-gauge railroads, the last of which closed in 1943. You can board a number of the cars and see others undergoing restoration. Train rides along the two-foot rails operate on the hour, 10am-3pm, $10 adults, $9 seniors, $6 ages 3-12. The track edges Casco Bay along the Eastern Promenade; it's a short but enjoyable excursion that's a real kid pleaser. The museum also operates Polar Express trains in December ($20-40).

African Center for the Sacred Arts

Here's a little treasure: Founded in 1998, as the Museum of African Culture, the **African Center for the Sacred Arts** (13 Brown St., 207/871-7188, www.museumafricanculture. org, 10:30am-4pm Tues.-Fri., noon-4pm Sat., $5 suggested donation) is the brainchild of Nigerian-born Oscar Mokeme (the director) and Arthur Aleshire. It's devoted to sub-Saharan African arts and culture. Among the museum's 1,500 or so treasures—not all on display at once—are Nigerian tribal masks and Beninese lost-wax bronzes.

Children's Museum of Maine

Here's the answer to parents' prayers: a whole museum in downtown Portland catering to kids. At the **Children's Museum of Maine** (142 Free St., 207/828-1234, www.kitetails. com, 10am-5pm Mon.-Sat., noon-5pm Sun., $9, free for children under 18 months, $2 admission 5pm-8pm first Fri. of each month, $4 for Camera Obscura only) lots of hands-on exhibits encourage interaction and guarantee involvement for a couple of hours.

The International Cryptozoology Museum

An eight-foot-tall likeness of a bigfoot greets visitors at former university professor and author Loren Coleman's **International Cryptozoology Museum** (11 Avon St., 207/518-9496, www.cryptozoologymuseum.com, noon-4pm Mon., 11am-4pm Wed.-Sat., noon-3:30pm Sun., call to confirm hours, $7 adults, $5 ages 12 and younger). Coleman is a renowned expert in cryptozoology, the story of hidden animals such as bigfoot, the Loch Ness monster, and the abominable snowman. He has amassed a collection of artifacts such as skulls and footprint castings that lend credence to the existence of these rumored beasts, as well as kitsch that includes movie props and souvenir memorabilia. This is always a big hit with kids.

Southworth Planetarium

Under a 30-foot dome with comfy theater seats and a state-of-the-art laser system, the **Southworth Planetarium** (Science Building, University of Southern Maine, 70 Falmouth St., 207/780-4249, www.usm.maine.edu/planet) presents astronomy shows, with ticket prices around $6. Take Exit 6B off I-295 and go west on Forest Avenue to Falmouth Street (a left turn). The Science Building is on the left past the parking lot.

Osher Map Library

Love maps? You'll love the University of South Maine's **Osher Map Library** (314 Forest Ave., 207/780-4850, www.oshermaps.org, call for current hours, free) with more than 300,000 maps, including works on cosmography, astronomy, navigation, geography, and history, as well as globes, atlases, books, and scientific instruments dating from the late 15th century. Exhibitions feature rare and historic works drawn from the collection. Bring a sweater; the air-conditioning is set for preservation standards. There's free parking in the USM garage on Surrender Street, off Bedford Street.

Tate House

Just down the street from the Portland International Jetport, in the Stroudwater district, is the 1755 **Tate House** (1270 Westbrook St., 207/774-6177, tatehouse.org, 10am-4pm Wed.-Sat., 1pm-4pm Sun., last tour 3pm, mid-June-mid-Oct., $10 adults, $8 seniors, $5 ages 6-12), a National Historic Landmark owned by the Colonial Dames of America. Built by Captain George Tate, who was prominent in shipbuilding, the house overlooks the Stroudwater River and has superb period furnishings and a lovely 18th-century herb garden with more than 70 species. Tours last 40 minutes. Cellar-to-attic architecture tours are offered roughly once a month, $12 adults, $10 seniors, $8 children.

Portland Head Light

Just four miles from downtown Portland in Cape Elizabeth, Fort Williams feels a world away. This oceanfront town park, a former military base, is home to **Portland Head Light** (1000 Shore Rd., Cape Elizabeth, 207/799-2661, www.portlandheadlight.com, dawn-dusk daily). Commissioned by President George Washington and first lighted in 1791, it has been immortalized in poetry, photography, and philately. The surf here is awesome—perhaps too awesome, as the *Annie C. Maguire* was shipwrecked below the lighthouse on Christmas Eve 1886. There's no access to the 58-foot automated light tower, but the restored keeper's house has become **The Museum at Portland Head Light** (10am-4pm daily late May-Oct. 31, 10am-4pm Sat.-Sun. late spring and late fall, call to confirm dates, $2 adults, $1 ages 6-18). It's filled with local history and lighthouse memorabilia. From downtown Portland, take Route 77 and then Broadway, Cottage Road, and Shore Road; the route is marked.

ENTERTAINMENT AND EVENTS

The best places to find out what's playing at area theaters, cinemas, concert halls, and nightclubs are the *Portland Phoenix* (www.portland-phoenix.com) and the *Go* supplement in the Thursday edition of the *Portland Press Herald* (www.mainetoday.com). Both have online

LIGHTHOUSES TOUR

Whether in a car or on a bike, it's easy to loop through South Portland and Cape Elizabeth on a lighthouse tour.

Begin just over the Casco Bay Bridge from downtown Portland on Route 77, take Broadway, and continue to Spring Point Marina, turning left at the stop sign and then right onto Madison Street to nine-acre Bug Light Park. A paved walkway leads to Portland Breakwater Lighthouse, also known as Bug Light, built in 1875. Also here is a memorial commemorating the Liberty ships built on this site during World War II. There's a plan to build an outdoor performing arts center adjacent to the park.

Retrace your route to Broadway and cross it, turning left on Fort Street until it ends at **Southern Maine Community College (SMCC),** overlooking the bay. The best time to come here is evenings and weekends, when there's ample parking. Unless it's foggy (when the signal is deafening) or thundering (when you'll expose yourself to lightning), walk out along the 9,000-foot granite breakwater to the **Spring Point Ledge Light** (207/699-2676, www.springpointlight.org), with fabulous views in every direction. Volunteers usually open it 11am-3pm Saturday and usually Sunday, mid-June-early September, $5 (children must be at least 51 inches tall to enter the light). Also here are picnic benches, the remains of Fort Preble,

and the **Spring Point Shoreline Walkway,** a scenic three-mile path with views to House, Peaks, and Cushings Islands. At the end of the path you'll reach crescent-shaped **Willard Beach,** a neighborhood place with restrooms, a snack bar, and those same marvelous views.

From the SMCC campus, return on Broadway to the major intersection with Cottage Road and bear left. Cottage Road becomes Shore Road at the Cape Elizabeth town line. Loop into Fort Williams Park and make a pilgrimage to **Portland Head Light,** with **Ram Island Ledge Light** in the distance, before continuing on Shore Road to its intersection with Route 77. Bear left, follow it to Two Lights Road, and follow the signs to 40-acre **Two Lights State Park.** Almost a pocket park, it has picnicking and restroom facilities, but its biggest asset is the panoramic ocean view from atop a onetime gun battery. Summer admission is $4.50 nonresident adults, $3 Maine resident adults, $1.50 nonresident seniors, $1 ages 5-11.

Before or after visiting the park, continue on Two Lights Road to the parking lot at the end, where you'll see the signal towers for which Two Lights is named. There's no access to either, and only one still works. If you haven't brought a picnic for the state park, there are few places finer to enjoy the view and a lobster than at **The Lobster Shack.**

listings; hard copies are available at bookstores and supermarkets. The *Phoenix* is free.

Nightlife
LIVE MUSIC
The Portland Conservatory of Music presents free weekly **Noonday Concerts** at First Parish Church (425 Congress St., 207/773-5747, www.portlandconservatory.net) at 12:15pm most Thursdays October-early April. The music varies widely—perhaps jazz, classical, or choral.

Portland Parks and Recreation sponsors **Summer in the Parks** (207/756-8275, www.portlandmaine.gov/rec/summer.htm,

July-Aug., free), a number of evening concert series and a midday kids' performance series in downtown parks.

In summer, take the ferry to Peaks Island for Reggae Sundays on the deck at **Jones Landing** (at the ferry landing, Peaks Island, 207/766-4400).

BREWPUBS AND BARS
Portland is a beer town, with an ever-increasing number of microbreweries and brewpubs. It's also vigilant about enforcing alcohol laws, so bring valid identification. Bars close at 1am.

Not only is **Gritty McDuff's** (396 Fore

GREATER PORTLAND

COURTESY OF PORTLAND CONVENTION & VISITORS BUREAU

Portland Head Light

St., Old Port, 207/772-2739) one of Maine's most popular breweries, but its brewpub was the state's first—opened in 1988. The menu includes pub classics such as fish-and-chips and shepherd's pie as well as burgers, salads, and sandwiches. Gritty's also books live entertainment fairly regularly. Tours are available by appointment. Gritty's also has a branch in Freeport.

A longtime favorite pub, **$3 Dewey's** (241 Commercial St., Old Port, 207/772-3310, www.threedollardeweys.com) is so authentic that visiting Brits, Kiwis, and Aussies often head here to assuage their homesickness. Inexpensive fare, 36 brews on tap, free popcorn, and frequent live music make it a very popular spot.

Far newer on the scene is **Little Tap House** (106 High St., 207/528-9283), a bright spot with 14 taps and a farm-to-table gastropub menu.

Especially popular in the late afternoon and early evening is **J's Oyster** (5 Portland Pier, 207/772-4828), a longtime fixture (some might

call it a dive) on the waterfront known for its raw bar and for pouring a good drink.

Of all Portland's neighborhood hangouts, **Ruski's** (212 Danforth St., 207/774-7604) is the most authentic—a small, usually crowded onetime speakeasy that rates just as highly for breakfast as for nighttime schmoozing. Expect basic homemade fare for well under $10, plus darts and a big-screen TV. Dress down or you'll feel out of place.

Other dress-down neighborhood bars are **Rosie's** (330 Fore St., 207/772-5656), **Mama's Crowbar** (189 Congress St., 207/357-7678), and **Blackstones** (6 Pine St., 207/775-2885, www. blackstones.com), Portland's oldest neighborhood gay bar.

For more upscale tippling, head for **Gingko Blue** (455 Fore St., 207/541-9190, www. gingkoblue.com), with some of the city's top mixologists.

Beer geeks, here's your happy place. Family-friendly **Novare Res Bier Cafe** (4 Canal Plaza, 207/761-2437, www.novareresbiercafe.com) carries nearly 500 bottled beers from around the world and has more than 25 rotating taps. Pair them with selections from the meat-and-cheese bar, sandwiches, or small plates.

West of I-295, **The Great Lost Bear** (540 Forest Ave., 207/772-0300, www.greatlost-bear.com) has 69 brews on tap, representing 15 Maine microbreweries and 50 others from the Northeast. The bear motif and the punny menus are a bit much, but the 15 or so varieties of burgers aren't bad. It's a kid pleaser.

BARS WITH ENTERTAINMENT

Scope out the scene when you arrive; the *Portland Phoenix* has the best listings. Most clubs have cover charges. The coolest venue with the hottest acts is **Port City Music Hall** (504 Congress St., 207/899-4990, www.portcitymusichall.com), a three-floor entertainment emporium. **Asylum** (121 Center St., 207/772-8274, www.portlandasylum.com) caters to a young crowd with dance jams, CD release parties, DJ nights, and live bands. **Geno's** (625 Congress St., 207/221-2382) has been at it for years—an old reliable for rock music with an emphasis on local bands. Ever popular for its Wednesday Rap Night hip-hop and weekend bands is **The Big Easy** (55 Market St., 207/871-8817, www.bigeasyportland.com). **Blue** (650A Congress St., 207/774-4111, www.portcityblue.com) presents local artists and musicians in intimate, cozy space and serves beer, wine, tea, and light fare; traditional Irish music is always featured on Wednesday evening, and jazz on Saturday.

Performing Arts

MERRILL AUDITORIUM

The magnificently restored **Merrill Auditorium** (20 Myrtle St., box office 207/874-8200, www.porttix.com) is a 1,900-seat theater inside Portland City Hall on Congress Street with two balconies and one of the country's only municipally owned pipe organs, the magnificent **Kotzschmar Organ** (207/553-4363, www.foko.org), returning to the stage in 2014 after a two-year restoration.

Special events and concerts are common at Merrill, and the auditorium is also home to a number of the city's arts organizations. The **Portland Symphony Orchestra** (207/842-0800, www.portlandsymphony.org) and presenting organization **Portland Ovations** (207/773-3150, www.portlandovations.org) have extensive, well-patronized fall and winter schedules; the PSO presents three summer Independence Pops concerts as well. The **Portland Opera Repertory Theatre** (207/879-7678, www.portopera.org) performs a major opera each summer. In addition there are films, lectures, and other related events throughout July.

Tickets for these organizations are available through **PortTix** (207/942-0800, www.porttix.com).

ONE LONGFELLOW SQUARE

Diverse programming is the hallmark of **One Longfellow Square** (207/761-1757, www.onelongfellowsquare.com), an intimate venue for performances and lectures at the corner of Congress and State Streets.

STATE THEATER

The **State** (609 Congress St., 207/956-6000, www.statetheatreportland.com), built in 1929 with art deco, Spanish, and Italian decor elements, hosts national touring artists as well as up-and-comers.

PORTLAND STAGE COMPANY

Innovative staging and controversial contemporary dramas are typical of the **Portland Stage Company** (Portland Performing Arts Center, 25A Forest Ave., 207/774-0465, www.portlandstage.org), established in 1974 and going strong ever since. Equity pros present half a dozen plays each winter season in a 290-seat performance space.

Spectator Sports

A pseudo-fierce mascot named Slugger stirs up the crowds at baseball games played by the **Portland Sea Dogs** (Hadlock Field, 271 Park Ave., 207/879-9500 or 800/936-3647, www.portlandseadogs.com, $80-10), a AA Boston

© HILARY NANGLE

The renovated Victorian buildings of the Old Port and Waterfront are filled with independent shops.

In mid-August the **Italian Street Festival** showcases music, Italian food, and games at St. Peter's Catholic Church (72 Federal St.). Artists from all over the country set up in 350 booths along Congress Street for the annual **Sidewalk Arts Festival** in late August.

The big October wingding is the **Harvest on the Harbor,** a celebration of all things food- and wine-related with tastings, dinners, exhibits, and special events.

The **Maine Brewers' Festival,** the first weekend in November at the Portland Exposition Building, is a big event that expands every year thanks to the explosion of Maine microbreweries; there are samples galore. From Thanksgiving weekend to Christmas Eve, **Victorian Holiday** in downtown Portland harks back with caroling, special sales, concerts, tree lighting, horse-drawn wagons, and Victoria Mansion tours and festivities.

SHOPPING

The Portland peninsula is thick with non-cookie-cutter shops and galleries. The Old Port/Waterfront and Arts District have the highest concentration, but more and more are opening on the East End.

Bookstores

Longfellow Books (1 Monument Way, 207/772-4045) sells new and used books and hosts readings. **Carlson-Turner Books** (241 Congress St., 207/773-4200 or 800/540-7323), on Munjoy Hill, has an extensive used-book inventory.

Art Galleries

Portland has dozens upon dozens of studios and galleries. A great way to discover them is on the **First Friday Artwalk** (www.firstfridayartwalk.com) on the first Friday evening of each month, when in-town galleries host exhibition openings, open houses, meet-the-artist gatherings, and other artsy activities.

Galleries specializing in contemporary art include **June Fitzpatrick Gallery** (112 High St., 522 Congress St., 207/699-5083, www.

Red Sox farm team. The season schedule (early Apr.-Aug.) is available after January 1.

The home court for the **Red Claws** (207/210-6655, www.maineredclaws.com, $6-30), an NBA development team for the Boston Celtics, is the **Portland Expo** (239 Park Ave.).

Events

Summer brings plentiful events, including the **Old Port Festival,** one of the city's largest festivals, usually the first weekend of June. It has entertainment, food and crafts booths, and impromptu fun in Portland's Old Port. The **Greek Heritage Festival,** usually the last weekend of June, features Greek food, dancing, and crafts at Holy Trinity Church (133 Pleasant St.).

Some of the world's top runners join upward of 500 racers in the **Beach to Beacon Race,** held in late July-early August. The 10K course goes from Crescent Beach State Park to Portland Head Light in Cape Elizabeth.

junefitzpatrickgallery.com), **Aucocisco** (89 Exchange St., 207/553-2222, www.aucocisco.com), specializing in contemporary fine art, and **Greenhut Galleries** (146 Middle St., 207/772-2693, www.greenhutgalleries.com), specializing in contemporary Maine art and sculpture. More than 15 Maine potters—with a wide variety of styles and items—market their wares at the **Maine Potters Market** (376 Fore St., 207/774-1633, www.mainepottersmarket.com).

Specialty Shops

Check out the latest home accessories from Maine-based designer **Angela Adams** (273 Congress St., 207/774-3523).

Woof: The company outlet **Planet Dog** (211 Marginal Way, 207/347-8606, www.planetdog.com) is a howling good time for dogs and their owners. You'll find all sorts of wonderful products, and Planet Dog, whose motto is to "think globally and act doggedly," has established a foundation to promote and serve causes such as dog therapy, service, search and rescue, bomb sniffing, and police dogs.

Ferdinand (243 Congress St., 207/761-2151) is chock-full of eclectic finds, including screen prints, jewelry, vintage clothing, and cards created on the owner's letterpress.

The stained-glass artwork is irresistible at **Laura Fuller Design Studio** (129 Congress St., 207/650-6989).

Follow your nose into **2 Note Botanical Perfumery** (97 Exchange St., 207/838-2815) for handcrafted, all-natural perfumes and bath and body products.

RECREATION
Parks, Preserves, and Beaches

Greater Portland is blessed with green space, thanks largely to the efforts of 19th-century mayor James Phinney Baxter, who had the foresight to hire the famed Olmsted Brothers to develop an ambitious plan to ring the city with public parks and promenades. Not all the elements fell into place, but the result is what makes Portland such a livable city.

TRAIL NETWORK

Portland Trails (305 Commercial St., 207/775-2411, www.trails.org), a dynamic membership conservation organization incorporated in 1991, is dedicated to creating and maintaining a 50-mile network of hiking and biking trails in Greater Portland. It already has 31 mapped trails to its credit, including the 2.1-mile Eastern Promenade Trail, a landscaped bay-front dual pathway circling the base of Munjoy Hill and linking East End Beach to the Old Port, and a continuing trail connecting the Eastern Prom with the 3.5-mile Back Cove Trail, on the other side of I-295. Trail maps are available on the website. Snowshoe rentals ($10/day) are available weekdays from the office. The group also holds organized walks ($5 nonmembers)—a great way to meet some locals. Better still, join Portland Trails ($35/year) and support its ambitious efforts.

DOWNTOWN PENINSULA

Probably the most visible of the city's parks, 51-acre **Deering Oaks** (Park Ave. between Forest Ave. and Deering Ave.) is best known for the quaint little duck condo in the middle of the pond. Other facilities and highlights here are tennis courts, a playground, horseshoes, rental paddleboats, a snack bar, the award-winning Rose Circle, a worth-attending farmers market (7am-noon Sat.), and, in winter, ice skating. After dark, steer clear of the park.

At one end of the Eastern Promenade, where it meets Fore Street, **Fort Allen Park** overlooks offshore Fort Gorges (coin-operated telescopes bring it closer). A central gazebo is flanked by an assortment of military souvenirs dating as far back as the War of 1812. All along the Eastern Prom are walking paths, benches, play areas, and even an ill-maintained fitness trail—all with that terrific view. Down by the water is **East End Beach,** with parking, token sand, and the area's best launching ramp for sea kayaks or powerboats. Friends of the Eastern Promenade (www.easternpromenade.org), founded in 2006, helps restore and preserve the landscape and sponsors a free summer concert series on Thursday evenings.

WINSLOW HOMER

© HILARY NANGLE

Plan in advance to tour the masterfully restored Prouts Neck studio of painter Winslow Homer.

Discovering Maine in his early 40s, Winslow Homer (1836-1910) was smitten—enough to spend the last 27 years of his life on Prouts Neck, a granite-tipped thumb of land edged with beaches reaching into the Atlantic in Scarborough, just south of Portland. Homer painted some of his greatest works—masterpieces such as *Weatherbeaten, The Fog Warning,* and *The Gulf Stream*—at this oceanfront studio, taking inspiration from the crashing surf, craggy shores, stormy seas, and dense fog. Standing in the studio puts you right at the scene, and the docent-led tours will explain the artist's importance in American art.

Originally the carriage house for Homer's *The Ark,* the adjacent house owned by Homer's brother Charles, the studio was moved 100 feet and converted to living quarters in 1883 by Portland architect John Calvin Stevens, one of the founders of the Shingle style. The piazza, pergola, and later the painting room were added.

The simplicity of the studio, with its beadboard wall and ceiling, tongue-and-groove floor, and brick fireplace, is pure Maine cottage. Some original furnishings and artifacts add context to understanding Homer. These include the *Snakes! Snakes! Mice!* sign he painted to scare off ladies who might be inclined to visit; the window in which he etched his name; the writings on the wall, such as *Oh what a friend chance can be when it chooses;* and a book of family photographs. Copies of his artwork, displays, and a slide show of images are exhibited in the painting room, or "the factory," as he called it. Especially intriguing are the Civil War sketches he made for *Harper's Weekly* while embedded with the Army of the Potomac.

The views from the second-floor piazza are the same as when Homer lived here. Gazing at the open Atlantic, listening to waves crash, gulls cry, and the wind rustling the trees, and maybe wrapped in the damp hush of fog, is perhaps the best place to begin to truly understand Homer's inspiration. After absorbing the view and walking to the oceanfront, you'll see the Homer works at the museum with a far deeper understanding of what made this genius tick.

Homer's ties with the Portland Museum of Art date back to his 1893 exhibition, which included *Signal of Distress.* On the centennial of Homer's death, the museum opened its Charles Shipman Payson wing, honoring the man who funded it and donated 17 paintings by the artist. The museum acquired Homer's studio, a National Historic Landmark, in 2006, opening it to the public after a six-year project to restore it to its 1910 appearance. The 2.5-hour tours are limited to 10 participants and cost $55 for the public, $30 for museum members. They depart the museum on a schedule that varies by season and permissions. It's wise to make reservations months in advance.

WEST OF THE DOWNTOWN PENINSULA

Looping around tidal **Back Cove** is a 3.5-mile trail for walking, jogging, or just watching the sailboards and the skyline. Along the way, you can cross Baxter Boulevard and spend time picnicking, playing tennis, or flying a kite in 48-acre **Payson Park,** where parking is available.

Talk about an urban oasis. The 85-acre **Fore River Sanctuary** (sunrise-sunset daily), managed by Portland Trails, has two miles of blue-blazed trails that wind through a salt marsh, link with the historic Cumberland and Oxford Canal towpath, and pass near **Jewell Falls,** Portland's only waterfall. From downtown Portland, take Congress Street West (Rte. 22) past I-295 to the Maine Orthopedic Center parking lot at the corner of Frost; park in the far corner.

Listed on the National Register of Historic Places, 239-acre **Evergreen Cemetery** (207/797-4597, 672 Stevens Ave., www.friendsofevergreen.org) is Portland's largest urban space. Begun in the mid-1850s and modeled after Mount Auburn Cemetery in Cambridge, Massachusetts, it's an excellent example of a rural cemetery, a garden-like place favored by 19th-century romantics. You'll find tree-lined paths, hiking trails, ponds, vistas, and plenty of history. Docents offer **historic walking tours** (5pm Thurs., 2pm Sun., $7), or download a map and explore on your old. In May, birdwatchers are here to see warblers, thrushes, and other migratory birds that gather in the ponds and meadows. During peak periods it's possible to see as many as 20 warbler species in a morning, including the Cape May, bay breasted, mourning, and Tennessee. Naturalists from Maine Audubon often are on-site helping to identify birds.

CAPE ELIZABETH

Fort Williams (www.fortwilliamspark.com, free), a 90-acre, town-owned oceanfront park on the site of a former military base, offers much more to explore beyond Portland Head Light. Walk the trails, explore ruins of the Goddard Mansion, prowl through fortifications, play tennis, or dip your toes into the surf at the rocky beach. Warning: There's a strong undertow here. The grassy headlands are great places to watch the boat traffic going in and out of Portland Harbor. Bring a picnic lunch or purchase food from one of the food trucks, and don't forget a kite.

Crescent Beach State Park (Rte. 77, www.parksandlands.com, $6.50 nonresident adults, $4.50 Maine resident adults, $1.50 senior nonresidents, $1 ages 5-11), a 243-acre park with a mile-long beach, changing rooms, a lifeguard, restrooms, picnic tables, and a snack bar, is a favorite with families.

Directly offshore is **Richmond Island** (www.ramislandfarm.com), a 226-acre private preserve that's accessible by boat and open to visitors who respect the island's ecology; do not walk on the breakwater or use the island's dock; no dogs permitted. A two-mile path skirts the perimeter, taking in four beaches, dunes, a lake, woodlands, and grasslands. Wildlife includes sheep, deer, bald eagle, blue herons, and more. Primitive camping is available on four sites with a permit; call 207/799-0011. An island map is available on the website.

SCARBOROUGH

Scarborough Beach Park (Black Point Rd./Rte. 207, 207/883-2416, www.scarborough-beachstatepark.com, $6.50 nonresident adults, $4.50 Maine resident adults, $2 children), a long stretch of sand, is the best beach for big waves. Between the parking area and the lovely stretch of beach you'll pass Massacre Pond, named for a 1703 skirmish between resident Native Americans and wannabe residents (score: Indians 19, wannabes 0). The park is open all year for swimming, surfing (permit required), beachcombing, and ice skating, but on weekends in summer the parking lot fills early. Lifeguards are on duty on sunny days from mid-June to early September. Purchase snacks or rent chairs, umbrellas, and boogie boards ($5 each) at The Shack.

At 3,100 acres, **Scarborough Marsh** (Pine Point Rd./Rte. 9, 207/883-5100, www.maineaudubon.org, 9:30am-5:30pm daily mid-June-early Sept., 9:30am-5:30pm Sat.-Sun.

late May and Sept.), Maine's largest salt marsh, is prime territory for bird-watching and canoeing. Rent a canoe (from $16 for 1 hour) at the small nature center operated by Maine Audubon and explore on your own. Or join one of the 90-minute guided tours (call for the schedule, $13). Other special programs, some geared primarily for children, include wildflower walks, art classes, and dawn bird-watching trips; all require reservations and very reasonable fees. Also here is a walking-tour trail of less than one mile. Pick up a map at the center.

Overlooking the marsh is 52-acre **Scarborough River Wildlife Sanctuary** (Pine Point Rd./Rte. 9), with 1.5 miles of walking trails that loop to the Scarborough River and past two ponds.

FALMOUTH

A 65-acre wildlife sanctuary and environmental center on the banks of the Presumpscot River, **Gilsland Farm** (20 Gilsland Farm Rd., 207/781-2330, www.maineaudubon.org, dawn-dusk daily) is state headquarters for Maine Audubon. More than two miles of easy, well-marked trails wind through the grounds, taking in salt marshes, rolling meadows, woodlands, and views of the estuary. Observation blinds allow inconspicuous spying during bird-migration season. In the **education center** (9am-5pm Mon.-Sat., noon-4pm Sun.) are hands-on exhibits, a nature store, and classrooms and offices. Fees are charged for special events, but otherwise it's all free. The center is 0.25 mile off Route 1.

Once the summer compound of the prominent Baxter family, Falmouth's 100-acre **Mackworth Island** (sunrise-sunset daily year-round), reached via a causeway, is now the site of the Governor Baxter School for the Deaf. Limited parking is just beyond the security booth on the island. On the 1.5-mile vehicle-free perimeter path, which has great Portland Harbor views, you'll meet bikers, hikers, and dog walkers. Just off the trail on the north side of the island is the late governor Percival Baxter's stone-circled pet cemetery, maintained by the state at the behest of Baxter, who donated this island as well as Baxter State Park to the people of Maine. From downtown Portland, take Route 1 across the Presumpscot River to Falmouth Foreside. Andrews Avenue (third street on the right) leads to the island.

Walking Tours
PORTLAND FREEDOM TRAIL

Pick up a copy of this free map and brochure (also available online) detailing a **self-guided walking tour** of 16 marked sights related to Portland's role in Maine's Underground Railroad (www.portlandfreedomtrail.org). Among the highlights are the Abyssinian Meeting House, the third-oldest African American meetinghouse still standing in the United States (a National Historic Landmark placed on the National Trust's 11 Most Endangered Properties list in 2013); the First Parish Unitarian Universalist Church, where abolitionist William Lloyd Garrison spoke in 1832; and Mariners' Church, location of an antislavery bookstore and print shop that printed the first Afrocentric history of the world.

PORTLAND WOMEN'S HISTORY TRAIL

Another **self-guided walking tour**, this one details four loops—Congress Street, Munjoy Hill, State Street, and the West End—with about 20 stops on each. Among the sites: a long-gone chewing-gum factory where teenage girls worked 10-hour shifts. The trail guide is available online for $8.50 in selected bookstores and at the **Maine History Museum gift shop** (489 Congress St., 207/879-0427).

GREATER PORTLAND LANDMARKS

Greater Portland Landmarks (207/774-5561, www.portlandlandmarks.org) offers seasonal walking tours of various Portland neighborhoods or themes. These change frequently, so call. It also offers downloads for self-guided tours of the Churches on the Peninsula, Congress Street, The Old Port, and Western Promenade.

Food and Beverage Tours

Maine's culinary renown has sprouted a number of tour options.

Just as the name promises, **Maine Foodie Tours** (10 Moulton St., 207/233-7485, www.mainefoodietours.com) delivers a taste of Maine. The **Culinary Walking Tour** ($45) visits vendors selling everything from cheese to lobster to chocolate in the Old Port; **Culinary Delights Trolley Tour** ($49) includes both onboard and in-shop tastings; **Sips, Smugglers, and Speakeasies** ($49) crawls through the city's pubs. Other options include **Eat Dessert First!**, **Bike and Brews,** and a progressive island dinner cruise.

Look for the keg topping the flagpole at **Shipyard Brewery** (86 Newbury St., 207/761-0807, www.shipyard.com). Full brewery tours are offered on Tuesday evenings; make reservations well in advance. Free, 30-minute tours at **Allagash Brewing Company** (50 Industrial Way, 207/878-5385, www.allagash.com) are by online reservation. **Geary's Brewing Company** (38 Evergreen Dr., 207/878-2337, www.gearybrewing.com) offers tours by appointment. You can also get a personal tour at **Rising Tide Brewing Co.** (103 Fox St., 207/370-2337).

For a more thorough immersion into the local brew scene, book a tour on **The Maine Brew Bus** (207/200-9111, www.mainebrewbus.com, $40-75) or **Maine Beer Tours** (207/553-0898, www.mainebeertours.com, $54). Minimum age is 21; ID required.

What? You'd rather have wine? Step out on a guided, two-hour, educational wine walk (from $40) or cruise (from $65) with sommelier Erica Archer of **Wine Wise** (207/619-4630, www.winewiseevents.com).

Stop by **Maine Mead Works** (51 Washington Ave., 207/773-6323, www.mainemeadworks.com) for a tour and tasting of the company's fermented honey drinks; call for a current schedule.

Land-and-Sea Tours

Various commercial operators offer area land-and-sea tours, but frankly, none is first-rate. Guides on each often present incorrect information. Still, such tours are a good way to get the city's general layout.

The best of the lot is the 1.75-hour narrated Portland City and Lighthouse Tour in a trolley-bus by **Portland Discovery Land and Sea Tours** (Long Wharf, 207/774-0808, www.portlanddiscovery.com, $22 adults, $16 children). You can combine this tour with a 90-minute Lighthouse Lovers cruise on Casco Bay. The combined price is $40 adults, $48 children.

◖ CASCO BAY TOUR

Casco Bay Lines (Commercial St. and Franklin St., Old Port, 207/774-7871, www.cascobaylines.com), the nation's oldest continuously operating ferry system (since the 1920s), is the lifeline between Portland and six inhabited Casco Bay islands. What better way to sample the islands than to take the three-hour ride along with mail, groceries, and island residents? The Casco Bay Lines Mailboat Run stops—briefly—at **Long Island, Chebeague, Cliff,** and **Little Diamond** and **Great Diamond Islands.** Departures are 10am and 2:15pm daily mid-June-early Sept., 10am and 2:45pm in other months. Fares are $15.50 adults, $13.50 seniors, and $7.75 ages 5-9. The longest cruise on the Casco Bay Lines schedule is the nearly six-hour narrated summertime trip (late June-early Sept., $25 adults, $22 seniors, $12 ages 5-9) with a two-hour stopover on **Bailey Island,** departing from Portland at 10am daily. Dogs ($3.75) on leashes and bicycles ($7) need separate tickets.

Bicycling

The **Bicycle Coalition of Maine** (207/623-4511, www.bikemaine.org) has an excellent website with info on trails, events, organized rides, bike shops, and more. Another good resource is **Casco Bay Bicycle Club** (www.cascobaybicycleclub.org), a recreational cycling club with rides several times weekly. Check the website for details.

For rentals (hybrids $25/day) and repairs, visit **Cycle Mania** (59 Federal St., 207/774-2933, www.cyclemania1.com).

© HILARY NANGLE

Hop on one of the Casco Bay ferries for an island excursion.

The best locales for island bicycling—fun for families and beginners but not especially challenging for diehards—are Peaks and Great Chebeague Islands, but do remember to follow the rules of the road.

Golf

Public courses are plentiful in Greater Portland, but you'll need an "in" to play the private ones. Free advice on helping you choose a course is offered by **Golf Maine** (www.golfme.com).

Consider just Greater Portland's 18-hole courses. **Sable Oaks Golf Club** (505 Country Club Dr., South Portland, 207/775-6257, www.sableoaks.com) is considered one of the toughest and best of Maine's public courses. Since 1998, **Nonesuch River Golf Club** (304 Gorham Rd./Rte. 114, Scarborough, 207/883-0007 or 888/256-2717, www.nonesuchgolf.com) has been drawing raves for the challenges of its par-70 championship course and praise from environmentalists for preserving wildlife habitat; there's also a full-size practice range and green. The City of Portland's **Riverside**

Municipal Golf Course (1158 Riverside St., 207/797-3524) has an 18-hole par-72 course (Riverside North) and a nine-hole par-35 course (Riverside South). Opt for the 18-hole course.

Sea Kayaking

With all the islands scattered through Casco Bay, Greater Portland is a sea-kayaking hotbed. The best place to start is out on Peaks Island, 15 minutes offshore via Casco Bay Lines ferry. **Maine Island Kayak Company** (MIKCO, 70 Luther St., Peaks Island, 207/766-2373, www.maineislandkayak.com) organizes half-day, all-day, and multiday local kayaking trips as well as national and international adventures. An introductory half-day tour in Casco Bay is $70 pp; a full day is $110 pp and includes lunch. Reservations are essential. MIKCO also does private lessons and group courses and clinics (some require previous experience).

◖ Lobstering Cruise

Learn all kinds of lobster lore and maybe even

catch your own dinner with **Lucky Catch Lobster Tours** (170 Commercial St., 207/233-2026 or 888/624-6321, www.luckycatch.com, $25 adults, $22 seniors, $20 ages 13-18, $15 ages 2-12). Captain Tom Martin offers three different 80-90-minute cruises on his 37-foot lobster boat. On each cruise (except late Saturday and all day Sunday, when state law prohibits it), usually 10 traps are hauled and the process and gear are explained. You can even help if you want. Any lobsters caught are available for purchase after the cruise for wholesale boat price (and you can have them cooked nearby for a reasonable rate). Wouldn't that make a nice story to tell the folks back home?

Boat Excursions

Down on the Old Port wharves are several excursion-boat businesses. Each has carved out a niche, so choose according to your interest and your schedule. Dress warmly and wear rubber-soled shoes. Remember that all cruises are weather-dependent.

Portland Discover–Land & Sea Tours

(Long Wharf, 207/774-0808, www.portland-discovery.com) offers a Lighthouse Lovers Cruise and a Sunset Lighthouse Cruise ($22 adults, $16 children).

Cruise up to 20 miles offshore seeking whales with **Odyssey Whale Watch** (Long Wharf, 170 Commercial St., 207/775-0727, www.odysseywhalewatch.com, $48 adults, $38 under age 12). Four- to five-hour whale watches aboard the *Odyssey* depart daily June-early September as well as on spring and fall weekends. (Go easy on breakfast that day, and take preventive measures if you're motion sensitive.) Odyssey also offers Deep Sea Fishing trips for cod ($69) and mackerel ($35); bait and tackle are provided.

Sail quietly across the waters of Casco Bay aboard a windjammer with **Portland Schooner Company** (Maine State Pier, 56 Commercial St., 207/766-2500, www.portlandschooner.com, late May-Oct., $39 adults, $15 age 12 and under). Four to six two-hour sails are offered daily on two schooners, the 72-foot *Bagheera* and the 88-foot *Wendameen*, both historical

sightseeing on a Portland boat tour

vessels designed by John G. Alden and built in East Boothbay. Overnight windjammer trips also are available for $250 pp, including dinner and breakfast.

ACCOMMODATIONS
Downtown Portland

Portland's peninsula doesn't have an overwhelming amount of sleeping space, but it does have good variety in all price ranges.

INNS AND BED-AND-BREAKFASTS

All of these are in older buildings without elevators; stairs may be steep. With the exception of the Inn at St. John, all are in the West End.

Railroad tycoon John Deering built **The Inn at St. John** (939 Congress St., 207/773-6481 or 800/636-9127, www.innatstjohn.com, $110-260) in 1897. The comfortable (if somewhat tired) moderately priced 39-room hostelry is a good choice for value-savvy travelers who aren't seeking fancy accommodations. Some rooms share baths. The inn welcomes children and pets and even has bicycle storage. Cable TV, Wi-Fi, air-conditioning, free local calls, free parking, and a meager continental breakfast are provided. Reimbursement for taxi from the airport or transportation center is available at a fixed price. Most guest rooms have private baths (some are detached); some have fridges and microwaves. The downside is the lackluster neighborhood—in the evening you'll want to drive or take a taxi when going out. It's about a 35-minute walk to the Old Port or an $8 taxi fare.

Staying at **The Pomegranate Inn** (49 Neal St. at Carroll St., 207/772-1006 or 800/356-0408, www.pomegranateinn.com, $279-359) is an adventure in itself, with faux paintings, classical statuary, contemporary art, antiques, and whimsical touches everywhere—you'll either love it or find it a bit much. The elegant 1884 Italianate mansion has seven guest rooms and a suite, all with air-conditioning, TV, and Wi-Fi, some with fireplaces.

Take a carefully renovated 1830s town house, add contemporary amenities and a service-oriented innkeeper, and the result is the

Morrill Mansion Bed and Breakfast (249 Vaughan St., 207/774-6900 or 888/566-7745, www.morrillmansion.com, $149-239), on the West End. Six guest rooms and one suite are spread out on the second and third floors. No frilly Victorian accents here—the decor is understated yet tasteful, taking advantage of hardwood floors and high ceilings. You'll find free Wi-Fi and local calls and a TV with a DVD player in each room. It's near Maine Medical Center.

In the same neighborhood is **The Chadwick Bed & Breakfast** (140 Chadwick St., 800/774-2137, www.thechadwick.com, $250). All four rooms have flat-screen TVs with DVD players, iPod docking stations, and Wi-Fi, and a DVD library is available. Guests have use of a lovely backyard garden. Here's a nice service: If you need to depart before the full breakfast is served, a bagged breakfast is provided.

Guests are treated like royalty with plush linens and memorable breakfasts at **The Inn on Carleton** (46 Carlton St., 207/775-1910 or 800/639-1779, www.innoncarleton.com, $195-210), a masterfully updated and decorated 1869 Victorian with a convenient location in the city's West End. Although all guest rooms have private baths, two are detached.

Former travel writer Dale Northrup put his experience to work in opening the **Percy Inn** (15 Pine St., 207/871-7638 or 888/417-3729, www.percyinn.com, $149-209), conveniently located just off Longfellow Square. The air-conditioned guest rooms are furnished with phones, CD players, TV/VCRs, wet bars, and refrigerators. There's even a 24-hour pantry. It's best suited for independent-minded travelers who don't desire much contact with the host or other guests, as public rooms are few and the innkeeper, although always accessible, is rarely on-site. Breakfast is a continental buffet. If you're noise sensitive, avoid accommodations that open directly into the pantry, kitchen, or breakfast room.

Built in 1835, **The Inn at Park Spring** (135 Spring St., 207/774-1059 or 800/427-8511, www.innatparkspring.com, $149-205) is one of Portland's longest-running bed-and-breakfasts.

GREATER PORTLAND

The location is excellent, just steps from most Arts District attractions. Six somewhat quirky guest rooms are spread out on three floors. All have air-conditioning and phones, and some have Internet access; one has a private patio and entrance. There's a guest fridge on each floor. Rates include a full breakfast served around a common table.

The handsome Georgian-style **West End Inn** (146 Pine St. at Neal St., 800/338-1377, www.westendbb.com, $180-215), built in 1877, has six guest rooms on three floors; one with detached bath, one with private deck. The decor blends traditional furnishings with contemporary accents. A full breakfast and afternoon refreshments are served.

FULL-SERVICE HOTELS

The 🜂 **Portland Harbor Hotel** (468 Fore St., 207/775-9090 or 888/798-9090, www.portlandharborhotel.com, from $299), an upscale boutique hotel in the Old Port, is built around a garden courtyard. Rooms are plush, with chic linens, duvets, down pillows on the beds, Wi-Fi, and digital cable TV; marble and granite bathrooms have separate soaking tubs and showers. Complimentary bike rentals are available, and the hotel offers a free local car service. Valet parking is $16. There's a cozy lounge, and the excellent restaurant has 24-hour room service. Also on the premises are a fitness room and spa services. The best splurge is the suites. Ice Bar, which features bars made of ice, is held the last weekend of January in the hotel's courtyard and draws a crowd.

You might have trouble finding the **Portland Regency** (20 Milk St., 207/774-4200 or 800/727-3436, www.theregency.com, from $290): This hotel, registered with the National Trust for Historic Preservation as a historic property, is secreted in a renovated armory in the heart of the Old Port. The nicest rooms are the renovated ones, especially those on the fourth floor with decks. Perks include Wi-Fi and free shuttles to all major Portland transportation facilities. Be forewarned: Room configurations vary widely—some provide little natural window light or are strangely shaped. All have LCD TVs, minibars, and air-conditioning. A restaurant, spa, and fitness center are on-site. Parking is $10 in July-August.

Yes, it's a chain, and yes, it's downright ugly, but the **Holiday Inn by the Bay** (88 Spring St., 207/775-2311 or 800/345-5050, www.innbythebay.com, from $175) provides a lot of bang for the buck. It's conveniently situated between the waterfront and the Arts District. Rooms on upper floors have views either over Back Cove or Portland Harbor; Wi-Fi is free, as is a local shuttle service. It also has an indoor pool, a sauna, a fitness room, on-site laundry facilities, a restaurant, and a lounge.

The Burbs

South of Portland are two upscale beachfront inns. Especially splurge-worthy and well suited for families is the oceanfront 🜂 **Inn by the Sea** (40 Bowery Beach Rd./Rte. 77, Cape Elizabeth, 207/799-3134 or 800/888-4287, www.innbythesea.com, from around $490), just seven miles south of downtown Portland. Guests stay in handsome rooms, suites, and cottages, most with kitchens or expanded wet bars, comfy living rooms, and big views. This is perhaps southern Maine's most contemporary luxury property, with a cozy lounge, a full-service spa, and a small cardio room. Big windows frame ocean views at **Sea Glass** (207/299-3134, entrées $24-34), where chef Mitchell Kaldrovich favors Maine ingredients in his creative breakfasts, lunches, and dinners. Other facilities include an outdoor pool, a *boules* court, wildlife habitats, and a private boardwalk winding through a salt marsh to the southern end of Crescent Beach State Park. By reservation, dogs are honored guests; they're welcomed with bowls and bed, receive turndown treats, and have their own room-service and spa menus.

The **Black Point Inn Resort** (510 Black Point Rd., Prouts Neck, Scarborough, 207/883-2500 or 800/258-0003, www.blackpointinn.com, from $240 pp, includes breakfast and dinner) is a classic, unpretentious

The Inn by the Sea, in Cape Elizabeth, edges Crescent Beach and the Atlantic.

seaside hotel with a genteel vibe. The historic Shingle-style hotel opened in 1878 at the tip of Prouts Neck, overlooking Casco Bay from one side and down to Old Orchard from the other. Now owned by a local partnership, the inn has returned to its roots, catering to wealthy rusticators. The **Point Restaurant** (6pm-8:30pm daily, $28-38) is open to nonguests by reservation, and the less-fussy **Chart Room** (11:30am-9pm daily, $10-18) serves lighter fare—but first, enjoy cocktails on the porch at sunset, with views over beach and water to distant Mount Washington. Guests have access to a private, oceanfront 18-hole golf course and tennis courts, the Cliff Walk around the point (passing American master Winslow Homer's studio, recently opened to the public by reserved guided tour departing from the Portland Museum of Art), and a lovely trail-laced woodland sanctuary that has ties to Homer's family. A hefty 18 percent service charge is added to daily rates.

Only a narrow byway separates **The Breakers Inn** (2 Bay View Ave., Higgins Beach, Scarborough, 207/883-4820, www.thebreakersinn.com, $195 daily, from $1,100 weekly) from the sands of Higgins Beach. This is an old-timey bed-and-breakfast in a turreted, porch-wrapped three-story Victorian. It was built in 1900, converted to an inn in the 1930s, and has been operated by the Laughton family since 1956. Every room in the main inn has an ocean view, including two in the basement. Interior stairways are steep and narrow. Fancy or frilly, this isn't; you're paying for location, not amenities or decor. Picnic lunches are available. No credit cards.

FOOD

Named "America's Foodiest Small Town" by *Bon Appétit* magazine in 2009, downtown Portland alone has more than 100 restaurants, so it's impossible to list even all the great ones—and there are many. The city's proximity to fresh foods from both farms and the sea makes it popular with chefs, and its growing immigrant population means a good choice of ethnic dining too. Here is a choice selection, by

© HILARY NANGLE

The Black Point Inn Resort is located on Prouts Neck, near the studio of painter Winslow Homer.

neighborhood, with open days and hours provided for peak season. Some restaurants don't list a closing time; that's because they shut the doors when the crowd thins. Make reservations, especially in July-August.

If you're especially into the food scene, check www.portlandfoodmap.com. You can also check the "Community News" listings in each Wednesday's *Portland Press Herald.* Under "Potluck," you'll find listings of **public meals,** usually benefiting nonprofit organizations. Prices are always quite low (under $10 for adults, $2-4 for children), mealtimes quite early (5pm or 6pm), and the flavor quite local.

When you need a java fix, **Coffee by Design** (620 Congress St.; 67 India St.; 43 Washington Ave., 207/879-2233) is the local choice, not only for its fine brews but also for its support of local artists and community causes.

The Portland Farmers Market sets up on Wednesday on Monument Square and on Saturday in Deering Oaks Park.

The Old Port and the Waterfront
LOCAL FLAVORS

All of these venues are west of the Franklin Street Arterial between Congress and Commercial Streets.

Best known for the earliest and most filling breakfast, **Becky's Diner** (390 Commercial St., 207/773-7070, www.beckysdiner.com, 4am-9pm daily) has more than a dozen omelet choices, just for a start. It also serves lunch and dinner, all at downright cheap prices.

Enjoy pizza with a view at **Flatbread Company** (72 Commercial St., 207/772-8777, www.flatbreadcompany.com, 11:30am-10pm daily), part of a small New England chain. The all-natural pizza is baked in a primitive wood-fired clay oven and served in a dining room with a wall of windows overlooking the ferry terminal and Portland Harbor. Vegan options are available.

For gourmet goodies, don't miss **Browne Trading Market** (Merrill's Wharf, 262

Commercial St., 207/775-7560). Owner Rod Mitchell became the Caviar King of Portland by wholesaling Caspian caviar, and now he's letting the rest of us in on it. Fresh fish and shellfish fill the cases next to the caviar and cheeses. The mezzanine is literally wall-to-wall wine, specializing in French.

When you're craving carbs, want pastries for breakfast, or need to boost your energy with a sweet, follow your nose to **Standard Baking Company** (75 Commercial St., 207/773-2112), deservedly famous for its handcrafted breads and pastries.

Humble sandwiches, hot dogs, and fries get treated like adults at **Blue Rooster Food Co**. (5 Dana St., 207/747-4157, www.blueroosterfoodcompany.com, 11am-6pm Sun.-Tues., 11am-2am Wed.-Sat.), a good spot for cheap eats anytime, but especially appreciated for its after-the-bars-close hours.

CASUAL DINING

Walter's (2 Portland Sq., 207/871-9258, www.waltersportland.com, 11:30am-9pm Mon.-Fri., 5pm-9pm Sat., $24-28) has been serving creative fusion fare since the 1990s (although in a chic new location as of late 2009). Despite the longevity, it's never tiresome and retains well-earned status as a favored go-to among the city's foodie set.

Chef-entrepreneur Harding Lee Smith's **The Grill Room** (84 Exchange St., 207/774-2333, www.thefrontroomrestaurant.com, 11:30am-2:30pm Mon.-Sat. and from 5pm daily, $18-39) turns out excellent wood-grilled meats and seafood.

Small plates and big flavors come from the open kitchen of **The Salt Exchange** (245 Commercial St., 207/347-5687, www.thesaltexchange.net, 11:30am-3pm Mon.-Sat. and 5:30pm-9pm Mon.-Thurs., 5:30pm-10pm Fri.-Sat.), a contemporary restaurant and lounge decorated with local artwork that changes quarterly. You'll probably want to order at least three plates ($9-26 each) to make a meal. The restaurant also has Maine's largest bourbon selection.

SEAFOOD

Ask around and everyone will tell you the best seafood in town is at **Street and Company** (33 Wharf St., 207/775-0887, www.streetandcompany.net, opens 5:30pm daily, $22-32). Fresh, beautifully prepared fish is what you get, often with a Mediterranean flair. Tables are tight, and it's often noisy in the informal brick-walled rooms.

For a broader seafood menu and more landlubber options, consider **Old Port Sea Grille and Raw Bar** (93 Commercial St., 207/879-6100, www.theoldportseagrill.com, from 11:30am daily, from $23), a sleek, modern spot near the waterfront with a fabulous raw bar and a 500-gallon aquarium inside.

For lobster in the rough, head to **Portland Lobster Company** (180 Commercial St., 207/775-2112, www.portlandlobstercompany.com, 11am-10pm daily). There's a small inside seating area, but it's much more pleasant to sit out on the wharf and watch the excursion boats come and go. Expect to pay in the low $20 range for a one-pound lobster with fries and slaw. Other choices ($8-23) and a kids' menu are available.

ETHNIC FARE

Sushi approaches an art form at **Miyake** (468 Fore St., 207/871-9170, www.miyakerestaurants.com, 11:30am-2:30pm and 5:30pm-10pm Mon.-Sat.). Trained in both French and classical Japanese techniques, chef Masa Miyake has developed a following far beyond Maine for his innovative sushi, crafted from primarily local ingredients, including vegetables, fowl, and pork raised on his farm. A four-course tasting menu is $40-50, à la carte is $12-18.

Top-notch for northern Italian is **Vignola Cinque Terre Ristorante** (36 Wharf St., 207/347-6154, www.cinqueterremaine.com, from 5pm daily, 10am-3pm Sat.-Sun., $12-34). Chef Lee Skawinski is committed to sustainable farming, and much of the seasonal and organic produce used comes from the restaurant owners' Laughing Stock Farm and other Maine farms.

The Corner Room Kitchen and Bar (110

Exchange St., 207/879-4747, www.thefrontroomrestaurant.com, from 11:30am Mon.-Sat., 10am-3pm and 4pm-9pm Sun., $15-29), another of popular local chef Harding Lee Smith's restaurants, takes its cue from rustic Italian fare, with hearty and delicious pizzas, pastas, and panini.

Pasta doesn't get much more authentic than that served at **Paciarino** (468 Fore St., 207/774-3500, www.paciarino.com, 11:30am-2:30pm and 6pm-9pm daily, $13-20). Owners Fabiana De Savino and Enrico Barbiero moved here from Milan in 2008, and they make their pastas and sauces fresh daily using recipes from De Savino's *nonna*.

Chef Damian Sansonetti arrived in Portland with a distinguished pedigree and he's living up to expectations with his rustic, authentic, southern Italian fare at **Piccolo** (111 Middle St., 207/747-5307, www.piccolomaine.com, 5pm-10:30pm Wed.-Sun., $19-25). The restaurant only seats 20, so reservations are a must.

You might think you've landed in Paris at Jean Claude Vassalle's **Merry Table Creperie** (43 Wharf St., 207/899-4494, 11:30am-2:30pm and 5pm-9pm Mon.-Sat., 11am-3pm Sun.), a charming French country bistro specializing in savory and sweet crepes ($9-13).

Irish fare with a Maine accent fills the menu at **Ri-Ra** (72 Commercial St., 207/761-4446, www.rira.com/portland, 11:30am-10pm daily). Entrées in the glass-walled second-floor dining room, overlooking the Casco Bay Lines ferry terminal, are $10-22. The ground-floor pub, elegantly woody with an enormous bar, is inevitably stuffed to the gills on weekends—a great spot for such traditional fare as corned beef and cabbage as long as you can stand the din. They don't take reservations, so be prepared to wait, especially on weekends.

For New World flavors in an Old World setting, dine at **Sonny's** (83 Exchange St., 207/772-7774, www.sonnysportland.com, lunch 11:30am-2pm and from 5pm daily, $7-22), in a former bank, serving Southwestern and South American foods such as a tri-pork Cuban sandwich or banana-leaf-baked whitefish.

DESTINATION DINING

Plan well in advance to land a reservation at ◖ **Fore Street** (288 Fore St., 207/775-2717, www.forestreet.biz, 5:30pm-10pm Sun.-Thurs., 5:30pm-10:30pm Fri.-Sat., entrées from $20). Chef Sam Hayward, renowned for his passionate and creative use of Maine-sourced ingredients, won the James Beard Award for Best Chef in the Northeast in 2004 and has been featured in most of the foodie publications. Hayward excels at elevating simple foods to rave-worthy dishes. The renovated former warehouse has copper-topped tables, an open kitchen, and industrial decor chic—quiet it's not. Make reservations well in advance, or show up early to try to land one of the handful of unreserved tables.

Arts District and Downtown

These restaurants are clustered around Danforth Street and along and around Congress Street.

LOCAL FLAVORS

Can't make up your mind? Peruse the reasonably priced fare available at **Public Market House** (28 Monument Sq., 207/228-2056, www.publicmarkethouse.com, 8am-7pm Mon.-Sat., 10am-5pm Sun.), with vendors selling meats, cheeses, breads, sandwiches, pizzas, burritos, coffees, and soups.

Be sure to have a reservation if you're going before the theater to **BiBo's Madd Apple Café** (23 Forest Ave., 207/774-9698, www.bibosportland.com, 11:30am-2pm Wed.-Fri. and 5:30pm-9pm Wed.-Sat., 10am-2pm Sun., $17-20)—it's right next to the Portland Performing Arts Center. On the other hand, it's popular anytime thanks to chef Bill Boutwell ("BiBo"). There's no way of predicting what will be on the bistro-fusion menu.

Well off most visitors' radar screens is **Artemisia Café** (61 Pleasant St., 207/761-0135, 11am-2pm Tues.-Fri., 9am-2pm Sat.-Sun., and 5pm-8:30pm Fri.-Sat., $15-25), a cheery neighborhood café with a creative menu drawing on international influences.

Nosh (551 Congress St., 207/553-2227, www.noshkitchenbar.com, 11:30am-1am

Mon.-Sat., 4pm-1am Sun.) updates the concept of New York-style deli fare with a fresh-and-local twist. The setting is sleek, with a granite bar on one side, copper-topped tables on the other, and comfy lounge-like seating at the entry. Nosh serves inspired salads, sandwiches, and burgers by day ($9-20). At night, the menu expands to include charcuterie and artisanal cheese plates and other offerings. Fries are offered in flavors including bacon-dusted and salt-and-vinegar, and accompanied by a choice from a tempting array of mayos, cheese sauces, and even Sriracha hot sauce.

ETHNIC AND VEGETARIAN FARE

Slip into sleek **Emilitsa** (547 Congress St., 207/221-0245, www.emilitsa.com, from 5pm Tues.-Sat., $18-35) for finely crafted authentic Greek food paired with Greek wines.

Duck into chef-owner Asmeret Teklu's **Asmara** (51 Oak St., 207/253-5122, 11:30am-2pm and 5pm-9pm Tues.-Fri., 5pm-9pm Sat., entrées $9-14) to be transported to eastern Africa. Traditional Eritrean and Ethiopian dishes, a mix of mild to spicy curried stews, and vegetarian plates are served on *injera,* spongy flat bread made from teff flour that doubles as an eating utensil (silverware is available, if you ask). Entrées are generous and come with a salad and choice of vegetable. Service is leisurely; this is a one-woman show.

Masa Miyake's **Pai Men Miyake** (188 State St., 207/541-9204, www.miyakerestaurants.com, 11:30am-midnight Mon.-Fri., 9am-midnight Sat.-Sun., $7-16) is a traditional Japanese noodle bar serving miso and ramen soup along with amazing pork gyoza and pork buns.

Ever-popular **Local 188** (685 Congress St., 207/761-7909, www.local188.com, from 5:30pm daily and 9am-2pm Sat.-Sun.) serves fabulous Mediterranean-inspired food with a tapas-heavy menu. It doubles as an art gallery with rotating exhibits. Most tapas selections are less than $10; heartier choices and entrées begin at $18. There is free parking behind the building.

Authentic Thai—not the Americanized version but the kind of food you might purchase from a street vendor in Bangkok—is served in a very non-Thai, cool-yet-sophisticated space at **Boda** (671 Congress St., 207/347-7557, www.bodamaine.com, 5pm-1am Tues.-Sun.). Make a meal out of small plates, or opt for an entrée ($12-19); vegetarian and gluten-free dishes are available.

Hearty, homestyle German fare is the draw at **Schulte & Herr** (349 Cumberland Ave., 207/773-1997, 11:30am-2pm Wed.-Fri., 8:30am-2pm Sun., and 5pm-9pm Wed.-Sat., $15-18).

Vegan and vegetarian cuisine comes with an Asian accent at **Green Elephant** (608 Congress St., 207/347-3111, www.greenelephantmaine.com, 11:30am-2:30pm Tues.-Sat. and from 5pm daily, $9-14). There's not one shred of meat on the creative menu, but you won't miss it.

Just outside the Arts District, **El Rayo Taqueria** (101 York St., 207/780-8226, www.elrayotaqueria.com, 11am-9pm daily), in a former gas station, delivers Cal-Mex flavors, with almost everything costing less (often far less) than $10. The prices go up a bit in the fancier and adjacent **Cantina El Rayo** (www.elrayo-cantina.com, 5pm-10pm Thurs.-Sat., $12-21).

Little Lad's (482 Congress St., 207/871-1636, www.littlelads.com, 11am-6pm Sun.-Fri.) is a no-frills vegan café, where the $4.99 lunch buffet, served 11am-3pm Mon.-Fri., might include chick-in cacciatore or bean stroganoff. Also available are sandwiches and sweets. Don't miss the herbal popcorn.

CASUAL DINING

Fun, whimsical, and artsy describes most restaurants in the Arts District, but not **Five Fifty-Five** (555 Congress St., 207/761-0555, www.fivefifty-five.com, from 5pm daily and 9:30am-2pm Sun., $10-32), where chef Steve Corry was named by *Food & Wine* magazine as one of the top 10 Best New Chefs in the country. Fresh, local, and seasonal are blended in creative ways on his ever-changing menu, which is divided into small plates, green plates, savory plates, cheese plates, and sweet plates. A five-course tasting menu is around $60. If you can't afford to splurge in the main restaurant, Corry serves lighter fare in the lounge.

A longtimer in the Portland dining scene, **David's** (22 Monument Sq., 207/773-4340, www.davidsrestaurant.com, 11:30am-4pm Mon.-Fri. and from 5pm daily, $10-30) serves pizzas, pastas, and updated familiar fare. Never one to rest on his laurels, chef-owner David Turin opened **David's Opus 10,** an 18-seat fixed-price restaurant within this one in 2012, and has an equally popular restaurant in South Portland.

Dining at **Grace** (15 Chestnut St., 207/828-4422, www.restaurantgrace.com, from 5pm Tues.-Sat., $18-36) is a heavenly experience. The restaurant is located in a masterfully renovated mid-19th-century Gothic Revival church that's listed on the National Register of Historic Places. Equally well thought out is the menu, which draws from local foods.

West End

Have breakfast or lunch or pick up prepared foods at **Aurora Provisions** (64 Pine St., 207/871-9060, www.auroraprovisions.com, 8am-6:30pm Mon.-Sat.), a combination market and café with irresistible goodies, most made on the premises.

Superb thin-crust pizzas made from all-natural ingredients in usual and unusual flavor combos emerge from the wood-fired oven at **Bonobo** (46 Pine St., 207/347-8267, www.bonobopizza.com, 11:30am-2:30pm Wed.-Fri., noon-4pm Sat., and from 4pm daily, $10-17).

Chef Abby Harmon's **Caiola's Restaurant** (58 Pine St., 207/772-1110, www.caiolas.com, from 5:30pm Mon.-Sat. and 9am-2pm Sun., entrées from $14) delivers comfort food with pizzazz in a cozy neighborhood bistro. This little gem is off most visitors' radar screens, but locals fill it nightly.

The decor is chic and sophisticated without being stuffy and the fare matches it at **Outliers** (231 York St., 207/747-4166, www.outlierseatery.com, 5pm-11pm Tues.-Sat., 10am-3pm Sun., $24-27). The menu is simple, with servers explaining that day's preparation. It's all fresh and local. Not a place for a quiet meal.

Bayside

Portlanders have long favored **Bintliff's American Café** (98 Portland St., 207/774-0005, www.bintliffscafe.com, 7am-2pm daily) for its breakfasts and brunches ($7-12); the menu is humongous. It doesn't take reservations on weekends, so expect to wait in line.

Breakfast is served all day at the **Miss Portland Diner** (140 Marginal Way, 207/210-6673, www.missportlanddiner.com, 7am-3pm Mon.-Tues., 7am-9pm Wed.-Sat.), a 1949 Worcester Diner (car no. 818) that was rescued, restored, and reopened in 2007. Snag a counter stool or a booth in the original dining car, not the addition, then treat yourself to breakfast for dinner. Sure, there are more traditional choices—soups, sandwiches, wraps, burgers, dogs, comfort foods, seafood plates and platters, or nightly dinner specials (most choices range $7-12)—but breakfast and diners go together like bacon and eggs. An added bonus: Parking is plentiful and free.

For an elegant meal in a true fine-dining setting, reserve a table at the **◖ Back Bay Grill** (65 Portland St., near the main post office, 207/772-8833, www.backbaygrill.com, from 5:30pm Tues.-Sat.). A colorful mural accents the serene dining room; arts and crafts wall sconces cast a soft glow on the white linen-draped tables. The menu, which highlights fresh, seasonal ingredients, ranks among the best in the city, and the wine list is long and well chosen. Service is professional. Entrées are $19-36 and worth every penny.

East End

These dining spots are all east of the Franklin Street Arterial. Poke around this end of the city and you'll find quite a few ethnic hole-in-the-wall places on and around Washington Avenue. It's an ever-changing array, but if you're adventurous or budget confined, give one a try.

LOCAL FLAVORS

Chocoholics take note: When a craving strikes, head to **Dean's Sweets** (82 Middle St., 207/899-3664) for adult-flavored dark-chocolate truffles made without nuts.

If you're a tea fan, don't miss **Homegrown Herb & Tea** (195 Congress St., 207/774-3484, www.homegrownherbandtea.com), an ayurvedic shop that blends black, green, and herbal teas and serves light fare, including a delightful lavender shortbread.

The most incredible fries come from ❶ **Duckfat** (43 Middle St., 207/774-8080, www.duckfat.com, 11am-10pm daily $8-14), a casual joint owned by James Beard Award-winning chef Rob Evans. Fries—fried in duck fat, of course—are served in a paper cone and accompanied by your choice of six sauces; the truffle ketchup is heavenly. Want to really harden those arteries? Order the *poutine*, Belgian fries topped with Maine cheese curd and homemade duck gravy. In addition, Duckfat serves panini, soups, salads, and really good milk shakes; wine and beer are available.

Mainers love their Italian sandwiches, and **Amato's** (71 India St., 207/773-1682, www.amatos.com, 6:30am-11pm daily, entrées $10-16) is credited with creating this drool-worthy sub, usually made with ham, cheese, tomatoes, green peppers, black olives, and onions wrapped in a doughy roll and drizzled with olive oil. Also available are calzones, salads, and other Italian-inspired foods. Amato's has outlets throughout southern Maine; this one has outdoor patio seating.

Micucci's Grocery Store (45 India St., 207/775-1854) has been serving Portland's Italian community since 1949. It's a great stop for picnic fixings, slabs of pizza, and a nice selection of inexpensive wines.

Ever had a mashed potato pizza? You can get one as well as other intriguing choices at **Otto Pizza** (225 Congress St., 207/358-7551, www.ottoportland.com, from 11:30am daily).

Huge portions at rock-bottom prices make **Silly's** (40 Washington Ave., 207/772-0360, www.sillys.com, 11am-9pm Tues.-Fri., 9am-9pm Sat.-Sun.) an ever-popular choice among the young and budget-minded. The huge menu has lots of international flair along with veggie, vegan, gluten-free, and dairy-free options. A separate menu lists milk shakes in dozens of wacky flavors. The decor: vintage kitsch,

1950s Formica and chrome, and Elvis. The same menu is served at adjacent **Silly's with a Twist,** which also serves alcohol.

Traditional Salvadorian foods (think Mexican with attitude) have turned hole-in-the-wall **Tu Casa** (70 Washington Ave., 207/828-4971, www.tucasaportland.com, 11am-9pm Sun.-Fri.) into a must-visit for in-the-know foodies. It's also a budget find, with almost everything on the menu going for less than $10.

Just try *not* to walk out with something from **Two Fat Cats Bakery** (47 India St., 207/347-5144)—oh, the cookies! The breads! The pies!

CASUAL DINING

Blue Spoon (89 Congress St., 207/773-1116, www.bluespoonme.com, 11:30am-3pm Mon.-Fri., 4:30pm-9pm daily, 9am-8pm Sun., $11-25) was one of the first upscale eateries on Portland's gentrifying East End. Chef-owner David Iovino, who studied at the French Culinary Institute, has created a warm and welcoming neighborhood gem.

Primo rustic Italian fare is the rule at **Ribollita** (41 Middle St., 207/774-2972, www.ribollitamaine.com, from 5pm Mon.-Sat., $13-20). You'll want reservations at this small, casual trattoria that's justly popular for delivering good food at fair prices; just be in the mood for a leisurely meal.

You never know what'll be on the menu (Indonesian chicken, North African stuffed peppers, maybe Caribbean shrimp cakes) at funky **Pepperclub** (78 Middle St., 207/772-0531, www.pepperclubrestaurant.com, from 5pm-9pm Sun.-Thurs., 5pm-10pm Fri.-Sat., $13-20), but take the risk. Vegetarian and vegan specials are always available, as are local and organic meats and seafood. If your kids are even vaguely adventuresome, they'll find food to like—and the prices are reasonable. In the morning, it morphs into **The Good Egg** (7am-noon Tues.-Fri., 8am-1pm Sat.-Sun.), serving breakfast, including gluten-free foods.

The weekly changing menu at **Hugo's** (88 Middle St. at Franklin St., 207/774-8538, www.hugos.net, from 5:30pm Tues.-Sat.)

showcases fresh and local fare. Expect to mix and match at least two or three of the choices ($13-17), which might include fried mussels, grilled swordfish belly, or skirt steak.

Love oysters? Don't miss **Eventide Oyster Co.** (86 Middle St., 207/774-8538, www.eventideoysterco.com, 11am-midnight daily), where the menu includes nearly two dozen oysters and other shellfish paired with sauces, as well as other seafood; mix and match from $3, with entrées around $25.

The Burbs

Gorgeous presentation, rare cheeses, a ripening room, and a knowledgeable staff all add up to making **The Cheese Iron** (200 Rte. 1, 207/883-4057, www.thecheeseiron.com) a major destination for cheeseheads. Add wine, sandwiches, and a handful of other gourmet goodies and you've got a first-class picnic or party.

Pair a visit to Portland Headlight and Fort Williams with a lobster roll from **Bite Into Maine** (Fort Williams, Cape Elizabeth, 207/420-0294, www.biteintomaine.com, noon-6pm daily), a mobile food truck also serving vegetarian sandwiches, ice cream, and desserts.

Great sunset views over Portland's skyline, a casual atmosphere, and excellent fare have earned **Saltwater Grille** (231 Front St., South Portland, 207/799-5400, www.saltwatergrille. com, from 11:30am daily, dinner entrées $13-30) an excellent reputation. Dine inside or on the waterfront deck.

If you're venturing out to Cape Elizabeth, detour into **The Good Table** (527 Ocean House Rd./Rte. 77, Cape Elizabeth, 207/799-4663, www.thegoodtablerestaurant.net, 8am-9pm Tues.-Sun., entrées $8-20). Lisa Kostopoulos's popular local restaurant serves home-style favorites as well as Greek specialties.

Dine al fresco at **The Well at Jordan's Farm** (21 Wells Rd., Cape Elizabeth, 207/831-9350, 5pm-9pm Tues.-Sat., $18-25), where Jason Williams, a Culinary Institute of America grad, creates dinners from the working farm's bounty and other ingredients sourced locally. Everything is made from scratch. Seating is on picnic tables on the lawn and in a gazebo or at the four-stool kitchen bar. In an interesting twist, all prices on the four- or five-item menu are suggested. Cash only.

Sea Glass (40 Bowery Beach Rd./Rte. 77, Cape Elizabeth, 207/299-3134, entrées $24-34), at the Inn by the Sea, is a sleeper. Chef Mitchell Kaldrovich serves Maine-inspired fare with an Argentinian accent; his gaucho steak and his paella are each worth the trip, as is the oceanview setting. Dine indoors or on the deck. Sea Glass is open for breakfast, lunch, and dinner daily and also offers a vegetarian menu and lobster tasting menu in addition to the regular one.

Every Mainer has a favorite lobster eatery (besides home), but **The Lobster Shack** (222 Two Lights Rd., Cape Elizabeth, 207/799-1677, www.lobstershacktwolights.com, 11am-8pm daily late Mar.-mid-Oct.) tops an awful lot of lists. Seniority helps—it has been here since the 1920s. There is scenery as well: a panoramic vista in the shadow of Cape Elizabeth Light. The menu has seafood galore along with burgers and hot dogs for those who'd rather not have lobster. Opt for a sunny day; the lighthouse's foghorn can kill your conversation when the fog rolls in.

INFORMATION AND SERVICES

The **Visitor Information Center of the Convention and Visitors Bureau of Greater Portland** (14 Ocean Gateway Pier, 207/772-5800, www.visitportland.com) has info and public restrooms. The **Portland Downtown District** (207/772-6828, www.portlandmaine. com) and **LiveWork Portland** (www.liveworkportland.org) have helpful sites.

Check out the **Portland Public Library** (5 Monument Sq., 207/871-1700, www.portlandlibrary.com).

In the Old Port area, you'll find **public restrooms** at the Visitor Information Center (14 Ocean Gateway Pier), Spring Street parking garage (45 Spring St.), Fore Street Parking Garage (419 Fore St.), and Casco Bay Lines ferry terminal (Commercial St. and Franklin St.). On

Congress Street, find restrooms at Portland City Hall (389 Congress St.) and the Portland Public Library (5 Monument Sq.). In Midtown, head for the Cumberland County Civic Center (1 Civic Center Sq.). In the West End, use Maine Medical Center (22 Bramhall St.).

GETTING THERE AND AROUND

Portland is about 100 miles or two hours via I-95 from Boston, although during peak travel periods it can take longer because of congestion and toll lines. It's about 26 miles or 45 minutes via Route 1 from Kennebunk. It's about 17 miles or 20 minutes via Route 295 to Freeport.

The clean and comfortable **Portland Transportation Center** (100 Thompson Point Rd., 207/828-3939) is the base for **Concord Coachlines** (800/639-3317, www.concord-coachlines.com) and the **Amtrak Downeaster** (800/872-7245, www.amtrakdowneaster. com). Parking is $4/day, and the terminal has free coffee, free newspapers (while they last), and vending machines. Route 5 of the **Metro**

(207/774-0351, www.gpmetrobus.net $1.50/ride, $5/day pass, exact change required) stops here and connects with **Portland International Jetport** (207/774-7301, www.portlandjetport. org), **Greyhound Bus** (www.greyhound.com), and **Casco Bay Lines ferry service** (www.cascobaylines.com). Taxis charge $1.90 for the first 0.1 mile plus $0.30 for each additional 0.1 mile; minimum fare is $5; airport fares add $1.50 surcharge.

Parking

Street parking (meters or pay stations) is $1/hour. Parking garages and lots are strategically situated all over downtown Portland, particularly in the Old Port and near the civic center. Some lots accept Park and Shop stickers, each valid for one free hour, from participating merchants. A day of parking generally runs $8-16. The Casco Bay Lines website (www.cascobaylines.com) has a very useful parking map listing parking lots and garages and their fees.

For winter parking-ban information, call 207/879-0300.

Casco Bay Islands

Casco Bay is dotted with so many islands that an early explorer thought there must be at least one for every day of the year and so dubbed them the Calendar Islands. Truthfully, there aren't quite that many, even if you count all the ledges that appear at low tide. No matter; the islands are as much a part of Portland life as the Old Port.

Casco Bay Lines (207/774-7871, www.cascobaylines.com) is the islands' lifeline, providing car and passenger service daily in summer. For an island taster, take the daily mail-boat run. Indeed, on hot days it may seem as if half the city's population is hopping a ferry to enjoy the cool breezes and calming views.

PEAKS ISLAND

Peaks Island is a mere 20-minute ferry ride from downtown Portland, so it's no surprise

that it has the largest year-round population. Historically a popular vacation spot—two lodges were built for Civil War veterans—it's now an increasingly popular suburb.

Although you can walk the island's perimeter in 3-4 hours, the best way to see it is via bike (extra ferry cost $6.50 adults, $3.25 children), pedaling around clockwise. It can take less than an hour to do the five-mile island circuit, but plan to relax on the beach, savor the views, and visit the museums. Rental bikes are available on the island from Brad Burkholder at **Brad and Wyatt's Bike Shop** (115 Island Ave., Peaks Island, 207/766-5631, 10am-6pm daily, $15/day, hourly rentals available).

Another way to see the island is on a 90-minute golf-cart tour with **Island Tours** (207/653-2549, www.peaksislandtours.com, $18 adults, $12 children); reservations advised.

Civil War buffs have two museums worth visiting. The **Fifth Maine Regiment Center** (45 Seashore Ave., Peaks Island, 207/766-3330, www.fifthmainemuseum.org, noon-4pm Mon.-Fri., 11am-4pm Sat.-Sun. July 1-early Sept., 11am-4pm Sat.-Sun. late May-July 1 and early Sept.-mid-Oct., $5 donation) is a Queen Anne-style cottage built by Civil War veterans in 1888 that now houses exhibits on the war and island history. Just a few steps away is the **Eighth Maine Regimental Memorial** (13 Eighth Maine Ave., Peaks Island, 207/766-5086, www.eighthmaine. com, 11am-4pm daily, $5 requested donation). Tours detail the building's fascinating history and its collection of artifacts pertaining to the Eighth Maine as well as material on the island, World War II, and more. Rustic lodging is available.

Another museum perhaps worthy of a visit just for its quirkiness is the **Umbrella Cover Museum** (207/766-4496, www.umbrellacovermuseum.org, call for hours, donation), where owner Nancy 3. Hoffman (yes, 3) displays her Guinness World Record collection.

Accommodations

The **Inn on Peaks Island** (33 Island Ave., 207/766-5100, www.innonpeaks.com, $200-300) overlooks the ferry dock and has jaw-dropping sunset views over the Portland skyline; no island roughing it here. The spacious cottage-style suites have fireplaces, sitting areas, and whirlpool baths.

On the other end of the Peaks Island luxury scale is the extremely informal and communal **Eighth Maine Living Museum and Lodge** (13 Eighth Maine Ave., 207/766-5086, mid-May-mid-Sept., 914/237-3165 off-season, www. eighthmaine.com, from $280), a rustic shore-front living-history lodge overlooking White Head Passage. Fifteen bedrooms sharing three baths and a huge shared kitchen allow you to rusticate in much the same manner as the Civil War vets who built this place in 1891 with a gift from a veteran who had won the Louisiana Lottery.

Food

Both **The Cockeyed Gull** (78 Island Ave., 207/766-2880, www.cockeyedgull.com, noon-8:30pm daily, entrées $10-27) and the **Shipyard Brewhaus** (33 Island Ave., www.innonpeaks.com, $9-24) have inside dining as well as outdoor tables with water views.

GREAT CHEBEAGUE

Everyone calls Great Chebeague just "Chebeague" (shuh-BIG). Yes, there's a Little Chebeague, but it's a state-owned park and no one lives there. Chebeague is the largest of the bay's islands—4.5 miles long by 1.5 miles wide—and the relatively level terrain makes it easy to get around. Don't plan to bring a car; it's too complicated to arrange. You can bike the leisurely 10-mile circuit of the island in a couple of hours, but unless you're in a hurry, allow time to relax and enjoy your visit.

If the tide is right, cross the sand spit from The Hook and explore **Little Chebeague.** Start out about two hours before low tide (preferably around new moon or full moon, when the most water drains away) and plan to be back on Chebeague no later than two hours after low tide.

Back on Great Chebeague, when you're ready for a swim, head for **Hamilton Beach,** a beautiful small stretch of sand lined with dune grass and not far from the Chebeague Island Inn. Also on this part of the island is **East End Point,** with a spectacular panoramic view of Halfway Rock and the bay.

Chebeague Transportation Company, from Cousins Island, Yarmouth, also serves the island. Its boats dock near Chebeague Island Inn, which is within walking distance of Calder's Clam Shack.

Accommodations

Get that old-timey island experience at the **Chebeague Island Inn** (61 South Rd., Chebeague Island, 207/846-5155, www.chebeagueislandinn.com, from $210), a nicely up-dated historical inn that charms guests with an artsy spirit, comforts them with down duvets and fancy sheets, and feeds them a full breakfast and house-made snacks. The inn's dining room serves all meals. Some rooms have shared baths.

Food

Visitors to Chebeague Island have two food choices. For simple home-cooked fare, head to **Calder's Clam Shack** (108 North Rd., Chebeague Island, 207/846-5046, www.caldersclamshack.com, 11:30am-8pm Tues.-Sun.), a takeout serving burgers, pizza, chowders, salads, sandwiches, and of course, fried seafood. On the fancier side is **Chebeague Island Inn** (61 South Rd., Chebeague Island, 207/846-5155, www.chebeagueislandinn.com, 7am-9pm). Dinner entrées, such as an organic cheeseburger and butter-poached lobster, run $23-38.

EAGLE ISLAND

Seventeen-acre Eagle Island (207/624-6080, www.pearyeagleisland.org, 10am-5pm mid-June-early Sept.) juts out of Casco Bay, rising to a rocky promontory 40 feet above the crashing surf. On the bluff's crest, Robert Edwin Peary, the first man to lead a party to the North Pole without the use of mechanical or electrical devices, built his dream home. It's now a state historic site that's accessible via excursion boats from Portland or Freeport. The half-day trip usually includes a narrated cruise to the island and time to tour the house, filled with Peary family artifacts, and wander the nature trails. Trails are usually closed until approximately mid-July to protect nesting eider ducks.

Peary envisioned the island's rocky bluff as a ship's prow and built his house to resemble a pilot house. Wherever possible, he used indigenous materials from the island in the construction, including timber drift, fallen trees, beach rocks, and cement mixed with screened beach sand and small pebbles. From the library, Peary corresponded with world leaders, adventurers, and explorers such as Teddy Roosevelt, the Wright brothers, Roald Amundsen, and Ernest Shackleton, and planned his expeditions. Peary

GREATER PORTLAND

Robert Edwin Peary's Eagle Island home is open to visitors who arrive via Atlantic Seal Cruises.

© HILARY NANGLE

reached the North Pole on April 6, 1909, and his wife, Josephine, was on Eagle Island when she received word via telegraph of her husband's accomplishment. After Peary's death in 1920, the family continued to spend summers on Eagle until Josephine's death in 1955. The family then decided to donate the island to the state of Maine.

Freeport

Freeport has a special claim to historic fame—it's the place where Maine parted company from Massachusetts in 1820. The documents were signed on March 15, making Maine its own state.

At the height of the local mackerel-packing industry, countless tons of the bony fish were shipped out of South Freeport, often in ships built on the shores of the Harraseeket River. Splendid relics of the shipbuilders' era still line the streets of South Freeport, and no architecture buff should miss a walk, cycle, or drive through the village. Even downtown Freeport still reflects the shipbuilders' craft, with contemporary shops tucked in and around handsome historic houses. Some have been converted to bed-and-breakfasts, others are boutiques, and one even disguises the local McDonald's franchise.

Today, Freeport is best known as the mecca for the shop-till-you-drop set. The hub, of course, is sporting giant L. L. Bean, which has been here since 1912 when founder Leon Leonwood Bean began making his trademark hunting boots (and also unselfishly handed out hot tips on where the fish were biting). More than 120 retail operations now fan out from that epicenter—including many shops carrying Maine-made products, and you can find almost anything in Freeport, except maybe a convenient parking spot in midsummer.

The town offers plenty for nonshoppers too. You can always find quiet refuge in the town's preserves and parks, along with plenty of local color at the Town Wharf in the still honest-to-goodness fishing village of South Freeport.

An orientation note: Don't be surprised to receive directions (particularly for South Freeport) relative to "the Big Indian"—a 40-foot-tall landmark at the junction of Route 1 and South Freeport Road. If you stop at the Maine Visitor Information Center in Yarmouth and continue on Route 1 toward Freeport, you can't miss it.

SHOPPING

In Freeport, shopping is the biggest game in town. Anyone who visits intends to darken the door of at least one shop.

◖ L. L. Bean

If you visit only one store in Freeport, it's likely to be "Bean's." The whole world beats a path to **L. L. Bean** (95 Main St./Rte. 1, 207/865-4761 or 800/341-4341, www.llbean.com)—or so it seems in July-August and December. Established as a hunting and fishing supply shop, this giant sports outfitter now sells everything from kids' clothing to cookware on its ever-expanding downtown campus, with separate Hunting & Fishing; Home; and Bike, Boat & Ski stores. Look for the outlet store—a great source for deals on equipment and clothing—in the Village Square Shops across Main Street.

Until the 1970s, Bean's remained a rustic store with a creaky staircase and a closet-size women's department. Then a few other merchants began arriving, Bean's expanded, and a feeding frenzy followed. The Bean reputation rests on a savvy staff, high quality, an admirable environmental consciousness, and a no-questions-asked return policy. Bring the kids—for the indoor trout pond and the aquarium-viewing bulb, the clean restrooms, and the "real deal" outlet store. The main store's open-round-the-clock policy has become its signature; if you show up at 2am, you'll have much of the store to yourself, and you may even spy

© HILARY NANGLE

Giant outdoor retailer and outfitter L. L. Bean put Freeport on America's shopping map.

$10.50 adults, $7.75 ages 13-16, $6.75 ages 5-12). When they receded, they scoured the landscape, pulverizing rocks and leaving behind a sandy residue that was covered by a thin layer of topsoil. Jump forward to 1797, when William Tuttle bought 300 acres and moved his family here along with his house and barn and cleared the land. Now jump forward again to the present and tour where a once-promising farmland has become a desert wasteland. The 30-minute guided safari-style tram tours combine history, geology, and environmental science and an opportunity for children to hunt for "gems" in the sand. Decide for yourself: Is the desert a natural phenomenon? A human-made disaster? Or does the truth lie somewhere in between?

Freeport Historical Society

A block south of L. L. Bean is the **Harrington House** (45 Main St./Rte. 1, 207/865-3170, www.freeporthistoricalsociety.org, 10am-5pm Mon.-Fri., free), home base of the Freeport Historical Society. You can pick up walking maps detailing Freeport's architecture for a small fee. Better yet, take a guided, 50-minute walking tour of the village (call for schedule, $10). Displays pertaining to Freeport's history and occasionally exhibits by local artists are presented in two rooms in the restored 1830 Enoch Harrington House, a property on the National Register of Historic Places.

Also listed on the register is the society's Pettengill Farm, a 140-acre 19th-century saltwater farm comprising a circa-1810 saltbox-style house, woods, orchards, a salt marsh, and lovely perennial gardens. The farmhouse is open only during the annual Pettengill Farm Days in the fall, but the grounds are open at all times. From Main Street, take Bow Street 1.5 miles and turn right onto Pettengill Road. Park at the gate, and then walk along the dirt road for about 15 minutes to the farmhouse.

Eartha

She's a worldly woman, that Eartha. The **DeLorme Mapping Co.** (Rte. 1, Yarmouth, 207/846-7000, www.delorme.com/about/

vacationing celebrities or the rock stars who often visit after Portland shows.

Outlets and Specialty Stores

After Bean's, it's up to your whims and your wallet. The stores stretch for several miles up and down Main Street and along many side streets. Pick up a copy of the *Official Map and Visitor Guide* at any of the shops or restaurants, at one of the visitor kiosks, or at the **Hose Tower Information Center** (23 Depot St., two blocks east of L. L. Bean). All the big names are here, as are plenty of little ones. Don't overlook the small shops tucked on the side streets.

SIGHTS
Desert of Maine

Okay, so maybe it's a bit hokey, but talk about sands of time: More than 10,000 years ago, glaciers covered the region surrounding the **Desert of Maine** (95 Desert Rd., 207/865-6962, www.desertofmaine.com, early May-mid-Oct.,

eartha.aspx) is home to the world's largest rotating and revolving globe, a three-story-tall spherical scale model of Earth. Eartha, as she's known, measures 41 feet in diameter with a 130-foot waist and weighs nearly three tons. She spins in DeLorme's glass-walled lobby, making her visible to passersby, but she's best appreciated up close and, well, as personal as you can get with a monstrous globe. Each continent is detailed with mountains and landforms, vegetation and civilization. She can be viewed 9:30am-5pm Monday-Friday. Take Route 1 south from downtown Freeport to the I-295 Exit 17 interchange; DeLorme is on the left.

Blueberry Pond Observatory

Prepare to be wowed by the night sky at the **Blueberry Pond Observatory** (355 Libby Rd., Pownal, 207/688-4410, www.blueberryobservatory.com), where you'll get exclusive viewings of constellations, planets, nebulas, asteroids, and galaxies. Guided two-hour tours, which include extensive viewing and digital astronomy pictures, cost $140 for the first adult and $20 for each additional adult; children 12 and younger are free. One-hour tours, which don't include photography, are half the cost.

ENTERTAINMENT

Shopping seems to be more than enough entertainment for most of Freeport's visitors, but don't miss the **L. L. Bean Summer Concert Series** (800/341-4341, ext. 37222). At 7:30pm most Saturdays early July-Labor Day weekend, Bean's hosts free big-name family-oriented events in Discovery Park, in the Bean's complex (95 Main St./Rte. 1). Arrive early—these concerts are *very* popular—and bring a blanket or a folding chair.

RECREATION
Parks, Preserves, and Other Attractions
MAST LANDING AUDUBON SANCTUARY

Just one mile from downtown Freeport, **Mast Landing Audubon Sanctuary** (Upper Mast Landing Rd., 207/781-2330, www.

maineaudubon.org, free) is a reprieve from the crowds. Situated at the head of the tide on the Harraseeket River estuary, the 140-acre preserve has 3.5 miles of signed trails weaving through an apple orchard, across fields, and through pines and hemlocks. The name? Ages ago it was the source of masts for the Royal Navy. To find it, take Bow Street (across from L. L. Bean) one mile to Upper Mast Landing Road and turn left. The sanctuary is 0.25 mile along on the left.

WOLFE'S NECK WOODS STATE PARK

Five miles of easy to moderate trails meander through 233-acre **Wolfe's Neck Woods State Park** (Wolfe's Neck Rd., 207/865-4465, www.parksandlands.com, $4.50 nonresident adults, $3 Maine resident adults, $1 ages 5-11), just a few minutes' cycle or drive from downtown Freeport. You'll need a trail map, available near the parking area. The easiest route (partly wheelchair-accessible) is the Shoreline Walk, about 0.75 mile, starting near the salt marsh and skirting Casco Bay. Sprinkled along the trails are helpful interpretive panels explaining various points of natural history—bog life, osprey nesting, glaciation, erosion, and tree decay. Guided tours are offered at 2pm daily mid-July-late August, weather permitting. Leashed pets are allowed. Adjacent **Googins Island,** an osprey sanctuary, is off-limits, but you can spy the nesting birds from the mainland; binoculars help. From downtown Freeport, follow Bow Street (across from L. L. Bean) for 2.25 miles; turn right onto Wolfe's Neck Road (also called Wolf Neck Rd.) and go another 2.25 miles.

WOLFE'S NECK FARM

Kids love **Wolfe's Neck Farm** (10 Burnett Rd., 207/865-5433, www.wolfesneckfarm.org), a 626-acre saltwater farm dedicated to sustainable agriculture and environmental education. Visit with farm animals and enjoy the farm's trails and varied habitats—fields, forests, seashore, and gardens—at no charge. **Family Farm Programs** (10am-noon, Sat., $8) introduce visitors to the animals both in the barn and the pastures, and include a tractor ride. On the **Tractor-pulled Haywagon History Tours** (10am-noon Sat., $14 ages 13 and older, $8 ages 3-12) of the farmlands and Wolfe's Neck point, guides enthusiastically share Freeport's history and the region's ecology, and weave in plenty of entertaining stories; advance reservations are requested, and a minimum of six guests is required. **Lobster & Clam Bakes** are held most Saturday evenings in the summer and include a hay-wagon ride; reservations are required by noon. Bicycle ($18-22) and kayak ($30) rentals are available. Pumpkin hayrides are offered in the fall.

WINSLOW MEMORIAL PARK

Bring a kite. Bring a beach blanket. Bring a picnic. Bring a boat. Bring binoculars. Heck, bring a tent. Freeport's 90-acre oceanfront town-owned playground, **Winslow Memorial Park** (207/865-4198, www.freeportmaine. com, $3) has a spectacular setting on a peninsula extending into island-studded Casco Bay. Facilities include a boat launch ($3-5), a campground ($23-33, no hookups), a fishing pier, a volleyball court, scenic trails, a playground, restrooms, picnic facilities, and a sandy beach—the best swimming is at high tide, and there is no lifeguard. On Thursday evenings in July-August, local bands play. The park is 5.5 miles from downtown. Head south on Route 1 to the Big Indian (you'll know it when you see it), go left on South Freeport Road for one mile to Staples Point Road, and follow it to the end.

BRADBURY MOUNTAIN STATE PARK

Six miles from the hubbub of Freeport you're in tranquil, wooded 590-acre **Bradbury Mountain State Park** (Rte. 9, Pownal, 207/688-4712, www.parksandlands.com, $4.50 nonresident adults, $3 Maine resident adults, $1 ages 5-11), with facilities for picnicking, hiking, mountain biking, and rustic camping, but no swimming. Pick up a trail map at the gate and take the easy 0.4-mile round-trip Mountain Trail to the 485-foot summit, with superb views east to the ocean and southeast to Portland. It's gorgeous in fall. Or take the Tote Road Trail, on the western side of the park, where the ghost

of Samuel Bradbury allegedly occasionally brings a chill to hikers in a hemlock grove. A playground keeps the littlest tykes happy. The camping fee is $19/site for nonresidents, $11 for residents. The park season is May 15-October 15, but there's winter access for cross-country skiing. Hawk Watch takes place mid-March-mid-May. From Route 1, cross over I-95 at Exit 20 and continue west on Pownal Road to Route 9 and head south.

◖ L. L. Bean Outdoor Discovery Schools

Since the early 1980s, the sports outfitter's **Outdoor Discovery Schools** (888/552-3261, www.llbean.com) have trained thousands of outdoors enthusiasts to improve their skills in fly-fishing, archery, hiking, canoeing, sea kayaking, winter camping, cross-country skiing, orienteering, and even outdoor photography. Here's a deal that requires no planning. **Discovery Series Courses** ($20, includes equipment) provide 1.5-2.5-hour lessons in sports such as kayak touring, fly casting, archery, clay shooting, snowshoeing, and cross-country skiing. All of the longer fee programs, plus canoeing and camping trips, require preregistration well in advance. Some of the lectures, seminars, and demonstrations held in Freeport are free, and a regular catalog lists the schedule. Bean's waterfront **Flying Point Paddling Center** hosts many of the kayaking, saltwater fly-fishing, and guiding programs and is home to the annual **PaddleSports Festival** in June, with free demonstrations, seminars, vendors, lessons, and more.

L. L. Bean Kids' Camp

No need to drag your little ones through the outlets or find a sitter when you want to enjoy an adult-oriented experience. Enroll your child, ages 6-12, for a day or a week in Bean's summer **Kids' Camp** (888/552-3261, www.llbean.com, 9am-4pm Mon.-Fri., $100/day, $350/week). They'll have a blast exploring Maine's great outdoors with skilled instructors and counselors. Activities include canoeing, kayaking, stand-up paddleboarding, archery, fishing, crafts, nature walks, and more. All equipment is provided; you'll need to provide lunch and snacks. You can even arrange for early or late pickup at an additional fee.

Boat Excursions

Atlantic Seal Cruises (Town Wharf, South Freeport, 207/865-6112, www.atlanticseal-cruises.com), owned and operated by Captain Tom Ring, makes two 2.5-hour cruises ($35 adults, $25 ages 5-12, $20 ages 1-4) daily to 17-acre **Eagle Island** (www.pearyeagleisland.org), a State Historic Site once owned by Adm. Robert Peary, the North Pole explorer. The trip includes a lobstering demonstration (except Sunday, when lobstering is banned). Once a week he offers a daylong excursion to **Seguin Island** ($55 ages 10 and older, $40 children), off the Phippsburg Peninsula, where you can climb the light tower and see Maine's only first-order Fresnel lens, the largest on the coast.

Kayak, Canoe, and Bike Rentals

Ring's Marine Service (Smelt Brook Rd., South Freeport, 207/865-6143, www.rings-marineservice.com) rents single kayaks for $35, tandems for $50, and canoes for $30/day, with longer-term rentals and delivery available. Bikes are $18 for a half day.

ACCOMMODATIONS
Downtown

One of Freeport's pioneering bed-and-breakfasts is on the main drag but away from much of the traffic in a restored house where Arctic explorer Adm. Donald MacMillan once lived. The 19th-century **White Cedar Inn** (178 Main St., 207/865-9099 or 800/853-1269, www.whitecedarinn.com, $175-370) has seven attractive guest rooms and a two-bedroom suite with antiques, air-conditioning, and Wi-Fi; some have gas fireplaces. The full breakfast will power you through a day of shopping.

Two blocks north of L. L. Bean, the **Harraseeket Inn** (162 Main St., 207/865-9377 or 800/342-6423, www.harraseeke-tinn.com, $185-315) is a splendid 84-room country inn with an indoor pool, cable TV,

air-conditioning, phones, and Wi-Fi; many rooms have fireplaces and hot tubs. One room is decorated with Thomas Moser furnishings; otherwise, decor is colonial reproduction in the two historical buildings and a modern addition; some rooms have a fireplace, woodstove, or whirlpool tub. The inn is especially accessible, so it's a prime choice for anyone with mobility issues. Rates include a hot-and-cold buffet breakfast and afternoon tea with finger sandwiches and sweets—a refreshing break. Pets are permitted in some guest rooms for $25, which includes a dog bed, a small can of food, a treat, and dishes. Ask about packages, which offer great value. Children 12 and younger stay free. The inn is home to two excellent dining venues, and it's long been a leader in the farm-to-table movement. Free transportation is provided to and from the Amtrak station.

Three blocks south of L. L. Bean on a quiet side street shared with a couple of other bed-and-breakfasts is **The James Place Inn** (11 Holbrook St., 207/865-4486 or 800/964-9086, www.jamesplaceinn.com, $165-195). Innkeepers Robin and Tori Baron welcome guests to seven comfortable guest rooms, all with air-conditioning, Wi-Fi, flat-screen TVs, and DVD players; a few have double whirlpool tubs, and one has a private deck and fireplace. If the weather is fine, enjoy breakfast on the inn's deck. After shopping, collapse on the hammock for two with a home-baked treat.

Beyond Downtown

Three miles north of downtown is the **Maine Idyll** (1411 Rte. 1, 207/865-4201, www.main-eidyll.com, $72-131), a tidy cottage colony operated by the Marstaller family for three generations. It is a retro throwback and a find for budget-bound travelers. Twenty studio to three-bedroom pine-paneled cottages are tucked under the trees. The Ritz this is not, but all have refrigerators, microwaves, Wi-Fi, and TVs; some have kitchenettes; most have fireplaces. A light breakfast is included. Well-behaved pets are welcome for $4.

The family-run **Casco Bay Inn** (107 Rte. 1, 207/865-4925 or 800/570-4970, www.

cascobayinn.com, $106-137) is a bit fancier than most motels. It has a pine-paneled lounge with a fieldstone fireplace and a guest Internet station as well as Wi-Fi throughout. The spacious guest rooms have double sinks in the bath area, and some have a refrigerator and a microwave. A continental breakfast with a newspaper is included.

Camping

For anyone seeking peace, quiet, and low-tech camping in a spectacular setting, **Recompence Shore Campsites** (134 Burnett Rd., 207/865-9307, www.freeport-camping.com, $26-46) is it. Part of Wolfe's Neck Farm Foundation, the eco-sensitive campground has 130 wooded tent sites and a few hookups, many on the farm's three-mile-long Casco Bay shorefront. Kayak and canoe rentals are available; swimming depends on the tides. Facilities include a playground and snack bar with Wi-Fi. Take Bow Street (across from L. L. Bean) to Wolfe's Neck Road, turn right, go 1.6 miles, then turn left on Burnett Road. Three pet-friendly oceanfront camping cabins are $125-165, plus $10/pet. Lobster bakes are held most Saturday evenings.

FOOD

Freeport has an ever-increasing number of places to eat, but there are nowhere near enough to satisfy hungry crowds at peak dining hours on busy days. Go early or late for lunch, and make reservations for dinner.

Local Flavors

South of downtown, **Royal River Natural Foods** (443 Rte. 1, 207/865-0046) has a small selection of prepared foods, including soups, salads, and sandwiches, and there is a seating area.

Craving a proper British tea? **Jacqueline's Tea Room** (201 Main St., 207/865-2123, www.jacquelinestearoom.com) serves a four-course Afternoon Tea, by reservation only, for about $25 pp in an elegant setting. Seatings for the two-hour indulgence are between 11am and 1pm Tuesday-Friday and every other weekend. No reservations are necessary for the Cream Tea, which includes two scones, condiments, and a pot of tea. It is served 10:30am-2:30pm.

At the Big Indian **Old World Gourmet Deli and Wine Shop** (117 Rte. 1, 207/865-4477, www.oldworldgourmet.com), the offerings are just as advertised, with sandwiches, soups, salads, and prepared foods. There are a few tables inside, but it's mostly a to-go place.

When you want to grab a quick lunch, **Li's Chinese Express Food Cart** (corner of Middle and Bow Streets, 347/323-5341, 11am-6pm daily) is just the spot for spring rolls and wok dishes.

The prices are fair, the service is efficient, the food is good, and you can eat in or take out at **The Fresh Batch** (20 Bow St., 207/865-5511, 8am-4pm daily).

Pair climbing Bradbury Mountain with breakfast or lunch at **Edna and Lucy's** (407 Hallowell Rd., Pownal, 207/688-3029, 7am-3pm Wed.-Fri., 8am-4pm Sat.-Sun.). The house-made doughnuts are a must.

Casual Dining

The Harraseeket Inn (162 Main St., 207/865-9377 or 800/342-6423) has two restaurants. The woodsy-themed **Broad Arrow Tavern** (from 11:30am daily $10-30), just two blocks north of L. L. Bean but seemingly a world away, is a perfect place to escape shopping crowds and madness. The food is terrific, with everything made from organic and naturally raised foods. Can't decide? Opt for the extensive all-you-can-eat lunch buffet ($18) that highlights a bit of everything. In early 2013, the inn teamed with the Maine Organic Farmers and Gardeners Association and the Maine Farmland Trust and completely renovated and enlarged its main restaurant, renaming it **Maine Harvest** (5:30pm-9pm daily, dinner entrées $20-38). The restaurant showcases not only farm-to-table fare but also the people who make it happen and the story behind preserving and cultivating organic farmland in the state. The menu emphasizes creative pairings and artistic presentations.

Brunch (11:45am-2pm Sun., $26) is a seemingly endless buffet, with whole poached salmon and Belgian waffles among the highlights.

Good wine and fine martinis are what reels them into **Conundrum Wine Bistro** (117 Rte. 1, 207/865-0303, from 4:30pm Tues.-Sat., $12-32), near Freeport's Big Indian, but the food is worth noting too. Dozens of wines by the glass, more than 20 martinis, and 20 champagnes will keep most oenophiles happy. The food, varying from fish tacos and cheese platters to burgers and pan-roasted salmon, helps keep patrons sober.

Ethnic Fare

Dine indoors or out on the tree-shaded patio at **Azure Italian Café** (123 Main St., 207/865-1237, www.azurecafe.com, from 11:30am daily). Go light, mixing selections from antipasto, *insalate,* and *zuppa* choices, or savor the heartier entrées ($18-33). The service is pleasant, and the indoor dining areas are accented by well-chosen contemporary Maine artwork. Live jazz is a highlight some evenings.

Down the side street across from Azure is **Mediterranean Grill** (10 School St., 207/865-1688, www.mediterraneangrill.biz, 11:30am-9pm Tues.-Sun., entrées $16-30). Because it's off Main Street, the Cigri family's excellent Turkish-Mediterranean restaurant rarely gets the crowds. House specialties such as moussaka, lamb chops, and *tiropetes* augment a full range of kebab and vegetarian choices. Or simply make a meal of the appetizers—the platters are meals in themselves. Sandwiches and wraps are available at lunch.

China Rose (23 Main St., 207/865-6886, 11am-9:30pm daily, entrées $10-16) serves Szechuan, Mandarin, and Hunan specialties in a pleasant first-floor dining area. Lunch specials run around $7.

Good food and attentive service has made **Thai Garden** (491 Rte. 1, 207/865-6005, 11am-9pm daily, $8-15) an ever-popular choice.

Lobster

In South Freeport, order lobster in the rough at **Harraseeket Lunch and Lobster Company** (36 Main St., Town Wharf, South Freeport, lunch counter 207/865-4888, lobster pound 207/865-3535, www.harraseeketlunchandlobster.com, 11am-8:45pm daily summer, 11am-7:45pm daily spring and fall, no credit cards). Grab a picnic table, place your order, and go at it. Be prepared for crowds and a wait in midsummer. Fried clams are particularly good here, and they're prepared either breaded or battered. BYOB.

Far more peaceful is **Day's Seafood Takeout** (1269 Rte. 1, Yarmouth, 207/836-3436, www.dayscrabmeatandlobster.com, from 11am daily), with a few picnic tables out back overlooking a tidal estuary.

INFORMATION AND SERVICES

Freeport Merchants Association (Hose Tower, 23 Depot St., 207/865-1212 or 800/865-1994, www.freeportusa.com) produces an invaluable foldout map-guide showing locations of all the shops, plus sites of lodgings, restaurants, visitor kiosks, restrooms, and car and bike parking.

Just south of Freeport is the **Maine Visitor Information Center** (Rte. 1 at I-95 Exit 17, Yarmouth, 207/846-0833), part of the statewide tourism-information network. Also here are restrooms, phones, picnic tables, vending machines, and a dog-walking area.

GETTING THERE AND AROUND

Freeport is about 18 miles or 20 minutes via Route 295 from Portland. It's about 10 miles or 15 minutes via Route 295 to Brunswick.

Some **Amtrak Downeaster** (800/872-7245, www.amtrakdowneaster.com) trains stop in Freeport. The station is downtown, eliminating the need for a car unless you want to explore beyond the shops and in-town activities.

MID-COAST REGION

In contrast to the Southern Coast's gorgeous sandy beaches, the Mid-Coast Region is characterized by a deeply indented shoreline with snug harbors and long gnarled fingers of land. Even though these fingers are inconvenient for driving and bicycling, this is where you'll find picture-book Maine in a panorama format. Lighthouses, fishing villages, country inns, and lobster wharves pepper the peninsulas. The Mid-Coast, as defined in this chapter, stretches from Brunswick to Waldoboro.

The Bath-Brunswick area is one of the least touristy areas of the coast. Not that visitors don't come, but this area has a strong and varied economic base other than tourism, which means that no matter when you visit, you'll find shops, restaurants, and lodgings open and activities scheduled. Bowdoin College and Bath Iron Works also contribute to a population more ethnically diverse than in most of Maine, and there's an active retiree population. Still, as you drive down the peninsulas that reach seaward from Bath and Brunswick, the vibrancy gives way to traditional fishing villages pressed by the hard realities of maintaining such lifestyles in the modern world and hanging on to waterfront properties in the face of escalating real-estate values.

Wiscasset still clings to the nickname of prettiest village in Maine, but for many travelers heading through on Route 1, Wiscasset is nothing but a headache. Traffic often backs up for miles, inching forward through the bottleneck village. Although many are just glad to get through it, those who take time to explore

HIGHLIGHTS

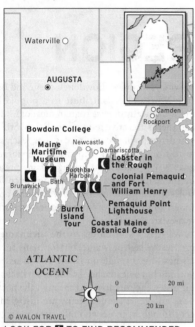

Waterville ○

AUGUSTA ◉

○ Camden
Rockport ○

Bowdoin College

Maine Maritime Museum   Newcastle ○ ○ Damariscotta

Lobster in the Rough

Boothbay Harbor

Brunswick   Bath

Colonial Pemaquid and Fort William Henry

Pemaquid Point Lighthouse

Burnt Island Tour   Coastal Maine Botanical Gardens

ATLANTIC OCEAN

0   20 mi

0   20 km

© AVALON TRAVEL

LOOK FOR ◖ TO FIND RECOMMENDED SIGHTS, ACTIVITIES, DINING, AND LODGING.

◖ **Bowdoin College:** This beautiful shady

campus is home to the Bowdoin College Museum of Art, the Peary-MacMillan Arctic Museum, and the Maine State Music Theater (page 122).

◖ **Maine Maritime Museum:** It's easy to while away a half day touring the exhibits in this museum's main and outer buildings and just enjoying the riverfront setting (page 134).

◖ **Burnt Island Tour:** Step back in history and visit with a lighthouse keeper's family circa 1950 on a living-history tour (page 153).

◖ **Coastal Maine Botanical Gardens:** This seaside garden comprises 250 acres of well-planned exhibits, trails, and art (page 156).

◖ **Pemaquid Point Lighthouse:** It's hard to say which is Maine's prettiest lighthouse, but Pemaquid's is right up there. It's also depicted on the Maine state quarter (page 166).

◖ **Colonial Pemaquid and Fort William Henry:** A beautiful setting overlooking John's Bay, a partially reconstructed fort, and remnants from archaeological digs researching one of the first English settlements in America make this site well worth a visit (page 166).

◖ **Lobster in the Rough:** Lobster wharves abound in Maine, but the Pemaquid Peninsula has a concentration of scenic spots for lobster lovers (page 178).

Wiscasset are rewarded with multitudes of antiques shops and lovely architecture.

The tempo changes northeast of Wiscasset. Traffic eases, and there's less roadside development. Detour down the Boothbay and Pemaquid Peninsulas, and you'll be rewarded with the Maine of postcards. These two peninsulas appear unchallenged as home to more lobster-in-the-rough spots than elsewhere on the coast, and Maine's creative economy is blossoming here, as evidenced by the abundant artists' and artisans' studios.

PLANNING YOUR TIME

Route 1 is the primary artery connecting all the points in the Mid-Coast Region, and Wiscasset, a major bottleneck, is smack-dab in the middle. For this reason, it's best to split your lodging and explorations into two parts: south of Wiscasset and north of Wiscasset. Even then, driving down the long fingers of land requires patience. The towns south of Wiscasset are less touristy than those on the Boothbay or Pemaquid Peninsulas, with Orr's and Bailey's Islands and the Phippsburg Peninsula being the

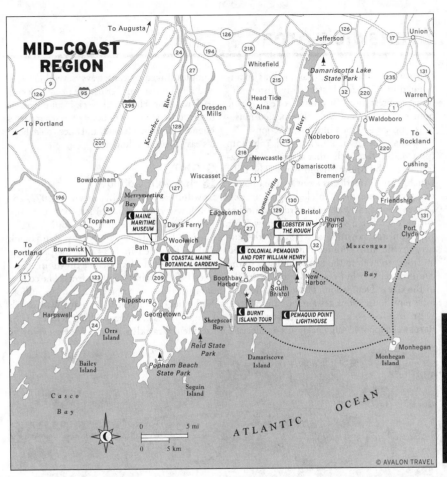

MID-COAST REGION

To Augusta
To Portland
To Portland
To Rockland

Jefferson
Union
Whitefield
Head Tide
Alna
Damariscotta Lake State Park
Warren
Waldoboro
Nobleboro
Newcastle
Damariscotta
Bremen
Cushing
Friendship
Dresden Mills
Wiscasset
Bowdoinham
Merrymeeting Bay
Topsham
Edgecomb
Bristol
Round Pond
Port Clyde
Bath
Day's Ferry
Woolwich
MAINE MARITIME MUSEUM
BOWDOIN COLLEGE
Brunswick
COASTAL MAINE BOTANICAL GARDENS
COLONIAL PEMAQUID AND FORT WILLIAM HENRY
LOBSTER IN THE ROUGH
Boothbay
Boothbay Harbor
New Harbor
Muscongus Bay
South Bristol
Phippsburg
Georgetown
Sheepscot Bay
BURNT ISLAND TOUR
PEMAQUID POINT LIGHTHOUSE
Harpswell
Orrs Island
Reid State Park
Damariscove Island
Monhegan
Monhegan Island
Bailey Island
Popham Beach State Park
Seguin Island
Casco Bay
Kennebec River
Damariscotta River

ATLANTIC OCEAN

0   5 mi
0   5 km

© AVALON TRAVEL

MID-COAST REGION

best places to sprout roots for old-time summer flavor.

To cover the region, you'll need 4-5 days. Antiques mavens should concentrate their efforts in Bath, Wiscasset, and Damariscotta. Allow at least two days to appreciate the fine museums in Brunswick and Bath, and another day to tour Wiscasset's historical house museums and nearby fort. If you're an avid or even aspiring kayaker, you'll want time to puzzle through the nooks and crannies of the coastline in a boat, and if you value parks and preserves, this region offers plenty worth your time.

Brunswick Area

Brunswick, straddling Route 1, was incorporated in 1738 and is steeped in history. It's home to prestigious Bowdoin College, classic homes and churches, several respected museums, and year-round cultural attractions.

Brunswick (pop. 20,278) and **Topsham** (pop. 8,784) face each other across roiling waterfalls on the Androscoggin River. The falls, which Native Americans knew by the tongue-twisting name of Ahmelahcogneturcook ("place abundant with fish, birds, and other animals"), were a source of hydropower for 18th-century sawmills and 19th-20th-century textile mills. Franco-Americans arrived in droves to beef up the textile industry in the late 19th century but eventually lost their jobs in the Great Depression. Those once-derelict mills now house shops, restaurants, and offices.

Brunswick is also the gateway to the **Harpswells** (pop. 4,740), a peninsula-archipelago complex linked by causeways, several bridges, and a unique granite cribstone bridge. Scenic back roads on Harpswell Neck inspire detours to the fishing hamlets of **Cundy's Harbor, Orr's Island,** and **Bailey Island,** and once you're here, it's easy to want to linger.

SIGHTS
◖ Bowdoin College
Bowdoin College (Brunswick, 207/725-3000, www.bowdoin.edu) got its start nearly 150 years before the now-defunct Naval Air Station landed on the nearby Brunswick Plains. Founded in 1794 as a men's college with a handful of students, Bowdoin, coed since 1969, now has 1,750 students. The college has turned out such noted graduates as authors Nathaniel Hawthorne and Henry Wadsworth Longfellow, sex pioneer Alfred Kinsey, U.S. president Franklin Pierce, Arctic explorers

© HILARY NANGLE

An unusual cribstone bridge connects Orr's and Bailey Islands.

Robert Peary and Donald MacMillan, U.S. senators George Mitchell and William Cohen, and a dozen Maine governors. Massachusetts Hall, the oldest building on the 110-acre campus, dates from 1802. The stately Bowdoin pines, on the northeast boundary, are even older. The striking **David Saul Smith Union**, occupying 40,000 square feet in a former athletic building on the east side of the campus, has a café, a pub, a lounge, and a bookstore open to the public. Call for information on admissions and **campus tours** (207/725-3100) and on **concerts, lectures,** and **performances** open to the public (207/725-3375).

Photos and artifacts bring Arctic expeditions to life at the small but fascinating **Peary-MacMillan Arctic Museum** (Hubbard Hall, 207/725-3416, www.bowdoin.edu/arctic-museum, 10am-5pm Tues.-Sat., 2pm-5pm Sun., free). Among the specimens are animal mounts, a skin kayak, fur clothing, snow goggles, and Inuit carvings—most collected by Arctic pioneers Robert E. Peary and Donald B. MacMillan, both Bowdoin grads. Permanent exhibits highlight the natural and cultural diversity of the Arctic. The small gift shop specializes in Inuit books and artifacts.

An astonishing array of Greek and Roman artifacts is only one of the high points at the **Bowdoin College Museum of Art** (Walker Art Building, 207/725-3275, www.bowdoin.edu/art-museum, 10am-5pm Tues.-Sat., 10am-8:30pm Thurs., 2pm-5pm Sun., free). Designed in the 1890s by Charles McKim of the famed McKim, Mead, and White firm, it's a stunning neoclassical edifice with an interior rotunda and stone lions flanking the entry. In 2007 the museum was expanded and modernized, adding a striking bronze-and-glass entry pavilion to preserve the facade while also achieving accessibility. The college's prized Assyrian reliefs, previously in the magnificent rotunda, were moved to a glass-walled addition facing Brunswick's Park Row. The renovated museum is far more user-friendly and a fitting setting for

© TOM NANGLE

The Bowdoin College Museum of Art's architecture pairs a neoclassical building with a bronze-and-glass entry pavilion.

MID-COAST REGION

JOSHUA L. CHAMBERLAIN, CIVIL WAR HERO

When the American Civil War began in 1861, Joshua Chamberlain was a 33-year-old logic instructor at Bowdoin College in Brunswick; when it ended, in 1865, Chamberlain earned the Medal of Honor for his "daring heroism and great tenacity in holding his position on the Little Round Top." He was designated by Ulysses S. Grant to formally accept the official surrender of Confederate General John Gordon (both men represented the infantry). He later became governor of Maine (1867-1871) and president of Bowdoin College, but Chamberlain's greatest renown, ironically, came more than a century later—when 1990s PBS filmmakers focused on the Civil War and highlighted his strategic military role.

Joshua Lawrence Chamberlain was born in 1828 in Brewer, Maine, the son and grandson of soldiers. After graduating from Bowdoin in 1852, he studied for the ministry at Bangor Theological Seminary and then returned to his alma mater as an instructor.

With the nation in turmoil in the early 1860s, Chamberlain signed on to help, receiving a commission as a lieutenant colonel in the Twentieth Maine Volunteers in 1862. After surviving 24 encounters and six battle wounds and having been promoted to general (brigadier, then major), Chamberlain was elected Republican governor of Maine in 1866—by the largest margin in the state's history—only to suffer through four one-year terms of partisan politics. In 1871, Chamberlain became president of Bowdoin Col-

lege, where he remained until 1883. He then dove into speechmaking and writing, his best-known work being *The Passing of the Armies*, a memoir of the Civil War's final campaigns. From 1900 to 1914, Chamberlain was surveyor of the Port of Portland, a presidential appointment that ended only when complications from a wartime abdominal wound finally did him in. He died at the grand old age of 86.

Brunswick's Joshua L. Chamberlain Museum, in his onetime home at 226 Maine Street, commemorates this illustrious Mainer, and thousands of Civil War buffs annually stream through the door in search of Chamberlain "stuff." To make it easier, the Pejepscot Historical Society has produced a helpful map titled "Joshua Chamberlain's Brunswick," highlighting town and college ties to the man—his dorm rooms, his presidential office, his portraits, even his church pew (number 64 at First Parish Church). Chamberlain's gravesite, marked by a reddish granite stone, is in Brunswick's Pine Grove Cemetery, just east of the Bowdoin campus.

Biennially, the museum celebrates **Chamberlain Days** with a symposium that concentrates on his roles in the war and in Maine. Typically, events include lectures by authors and scholars; field trips to places of interest connected with Chamberlain's life; tours of his home, concentrating on the most recent restoration work; musical or dramatic performances; and group discussions.

---

the impressive permanent collection of 19th- and 20th-century American art and other works.

Pejepscot Historical Society Museums

Side by side in an unusual cupola-topped duplex facing Brunswick's Mall (village green) are two museums operated by the **Pejepscot Historical Society** (207/729-6606, www.pejepscothistorical.org): the **Pejepscot Museum & Research Center** (159 Park Row, Brunswick,

10am-4pm Tues.-Sat., free) and the **Skolfield-Whittier House** (161 Park Row, Brunswick, tours on the hour 10am-3pm Wed.-Sat. late May-mid-Oct., $8.50 adults, $4 ages 6-16). Focusing on local history, the museum has a collection of more than 50,000 artifacts and mounts an always-interesting special exhibit each year. The 17-room Skolfield-Whittier House, on the right side of the building, looks as though the owners just stepped out for the afternoon. Unoccupied 1925-1982, the onetime sea captain's house has elegant Victorian furnishings and lots of exotic artifacts collected on global seafaring stints.

The Pejepscot Historical Society also operates the **Joshua L. Chamberlain Museum** (226 Maine St., Brunswick, 207/729-6606, tours on the hour 10am-3pm Tues.-Sat., 1pm-3pm Sun., $8.50 adults, $4 ages 6-16), across from First Parish Church, commemorates the Union Army hero of the Civil War's Battle of Gettysburg, who's now gaining long-overdue respect. The partly restored house where Chamberlain lived in the late 19th century (and where Henry Wadsworth Longfellow had lived 30 years earlier) is a peculiar architectural hodgepodge with six rooms of exhibits of Chamberlain memorabilia, much of it Civil War-related. A gift shop stocks lots of Civil War publications, especially ones covering the Twentieth Maine Volunteers. A combination ticket for both historical houses is $13 adults, $4 children.

Also under the museum's umbrella is the **Brunswick Women's History Trail.** With more than 20 points of interest, the trail covers such national notables as authors Harriet Beecher Stowe and Kate Douglas Wiggin along with lesser-known lights, including naturalist Kate Furbish, pioneering Maine pediatrician Dr. Alice Whittier, and the Franco-American women who slaved away in the textile mills at the turn of the 20th century. The museum offers guided tours lasting about one hour once a month June-August (donation requested); the tour is also mapped online.

Uncle Tom's Church

Across the street from the Chamberlain museum is the historic 1846 **First Parish Church** (9 Cleveland St. at Bath Rd., Brunswick, 207/729-7331), a Gothic Revival (or carpenter Gothic) board-and-batten structure crowning the rise at the head of Maine Street. Scores of celebrity preachers have ascended this pulpit, and Harriet Beecher Stowe was inspired to write *Uncle Tom's Cabin* while listening to her husband deliver an antislavery sermon here. Arrive here before noon any Tuesday early July-early August, when guest

organists present 40-minute lunchtime concerts (12:10pm-12:50pm) on the 1883 Hutchings-Plaisted tracker organ, followed by a building tour. A $5 donation is requested. At other times, the church is open by appointment.

Brunswick Literary Art Walk

Cast your eyes downward while walking along Maine Street. Four bronze plaques recognize Brunswick's most famous writers: Henry Wadsworth Longfellow, Nathaniel Hawthorne, Harriet Beecher Stowe, and Robert P. T. Coffin. Each plaque bears a quote from the author commemorated.

Brunswick Fish Ladder

If you're in town mid-May-late June, plan to visit **Central Maine Power's Brunswick Hydro** generating station, straddling the falls on the Androscoggin River and the Brunswick-Topsham town line (Lower Maine St., next to Fort Andross). A glass-walled viewing room lets you play voyeur during the annual ritual of anadromous fish heading upstream to spawn. Amazingly undaunted by the obstacles, such species as alewives (herring), salmon, and smallmouth bass make their way from saltwater to freshwater via a 40-foot-high, 570-foot-long artificial fish ladder. The viewing room, which maxes out at about 20 people, is open 1pm-5pm Wednesday-Friday June-September.

ENTERTAINMENT

Five Rivers Arts Alliance (108 Main St., Brunswick, 207/798-6964, http://5raa.org) maintains a calendar of area concerts, gallery openings, art shows, lectures, exhibits, and other arts-related events and also sponsors a few key events.

The **Maine State Music Theatre** (Pickard Theater, Bowdoin College, box office 1 Bath Rd., Brunswick, 207/725-8769, www.msmt. org) has been a summer tradition since 1959. The renovated state-of-the-art air-conditioned theater brings real pros to its stage for four musicals (mid-June-late Aug., $36-50). Nonsubscription tickets go on sale in early May. Performances are at 8pm Tuesday-Saturday;

matinees are staged at 2pm on an alternating schedule—each week has matinees on different days. No children under age four are admitted, but special family shows ($7-12) are performed during the season.

The **Bowdoin International Music Festival** (box office 12 Cleveland St., Brunswick, 207/725-3895, www.bowdoinfestival.org) is a showcase for an international array of classical talent of all kinds late June-early August. The six-week festival, part of an international music school, presents a variety of concert opportunities—enough that there's music almost every night of the week. Venues vary and tickets range from free to $40. Call or check the website for the current schedule.

Second Friday Art Walks (207/725-4366) take place in downtown Brunswick 5pm-8pm on the second Friday of the month May-November. Gallery openings, wine tastings, light refreshments, and other activities are usually part of the mix.

Music on the Mall presents family band concerts at 6pm-8pm Wednesday (Thursday if it rains) in July-August on the Brunswick Mall, the lovely park in the center of town.

FESTIVALS AND EVENTS

The first full week of August, the **Topsham Fair** is a weeklong agricultural festival with exhibits, demonstrations, live music, oxen pulls, contests, harness racing, and fireworks at the Topsham Fairgrounds.

The third Saturday of August, the **Maine Highland Games,** sponsored by the St. Andrew's Society of Maine, mark the annual wearing of the plaids—but you needn't be Scottish to join in the games, watch the Highland dancing, or browse the arts and crafts booths. (Only a Scot, however, can appreciate that unique concoction called haggis.)

SHOPPING

Downtown Brunswick invites leisurely browsing, with most of the shops concentrated on Maine Street. Take special care when crossing the four-lane-wide street, and do so only at marked crosswalks.

Art, Crafts, and Antiques Galleries

The **Bayview Gallery** (58 Maine St., Brunswick, 800/244-3007) specializes in contemporary New England artists.

Facing the Mall, **Day's Antiques** (153 Park Row, Brunswick, 207/725-6959) occupies five rooms and the basement of the handsome historic building known as the Pumpkin House.

More than 140 dealers show and sell their wares at **Cabot Mill Antiques** (14 Maine St., 207/725-2855), in the renovated Fort Andross mill complex next to the Androscoggin River.

Part gallery, part resource center, **Maine Fiberarts** (13 Maine St., Topsham, 207/721-0678, www.mainefiberarts.org) is a must-stop for anyone interested in fiber-related artwork: knitting, quilting, spinning, and basketry. If you're really interested in finding artists and resources statewide, buy a copy of its resource book.

Nearly two dozen local artists exhibit their works in varied media at **Sebascodegan Artists Gallery** (Rte. 24, Great Island, Harpswell, 207/833-6260).

Bookstore

With an eclectic new-book inventory that includes lots of esoterica, **Gulf of Maine Books** (134 Maine St., Brunswick, 207/729-5083) has held the competition at bay since the early 1980s. The fiction selection is particularly good, as are the religion, health, and poetry sections. Poet, publisher, and Renaissance man Gary Lawless oversees everything.

RECREATION
Parks and Preserves

In the village of Bailey Island, a well-maintained path edges the cliffs and passes the **Giant Stairs,** a waterfront stone stairway of mammoth proportions. To get there, take Route 24 from Cooks Corner toward Bailey Island and Land's End, keeping an eye out for Washington Avenue, on the left about 1.5 miles after the cribstone bridge. (Or drive to Land's End, park the car with the rest of the crowds, survey the panorama, and walk 0.8 mile back along Route

24 to Washington Avenue from there.) Turn onto Washington Avenue, go 0.1 mile, and park at the Episcopal church (corner of Ocean St.). Walk along Ocean Street to the shorefront path. Watch for a tiny sign just before Spindrift Lane. Don't let small kids get close to the slippery rocks on the surf-tossed shoreline. The same advice holds for Land's End, where the rocks can be treacherous.

Thank the **Brunswick-Topsham Land Trust** (108 Maine St., Brunswick, 207/729-7694, www.btlt.org), founded in 1985, for access to the 11-acre shorefront **Alfred Skolfield Preserve,** historically a portage site for Native Americans and later home to a shipyard. One of the two blue-blazed nature-trail loops skirts a salt marsh, where you're apt to see egrets, herons, and ospreys in summer. Take Route 123 (Harpswell Rd.) south from Brunswick about three miles; when you reach the Middle Bay Road intersection (on the right), continue on Route 123 for 1.1 miles. Watch for a small sign and a small parking area on the right.

Tucked behind the Harpswell town office, off the Mountain Road linking Route 123 with Route 24, the **Cliff Trail** is a 1.5-mile loop that follows the shoreline along Strawberry Creek, passes through forests with fairy houses, and rises to 150-foot cliffs with dreamy views over Long Reach.

Nearly four miles of trails wind through fields and forests and edge cliffs on the 118-acre **Bowdoin College Coastal Studies Center,** a spectacular chunk of oceanfront tipping an Orr's Island peninsula. It's likely you'll have the seven trails practically to yourself. To find it, take Route 24 south and then turn right on Bayview Road, just after the Orr's Island Store (just under two miles beyond the bridge). Keep right at the fork. When the road turns to gravel, continue to a parking area with an info kiosk where you can pick up a trail map.

Swimming

Thomas Point Beach (29 Meadow Rd., Brunswick, 207/725-6009 or 877/872-4321, www.thomaspointbeach.com, 9am-sunset mid-May-Sept., $3.50 adults, $2 under age 12) is actually 85 acres of privately owned parkland with facilities for swimming (lifeguard on duty, bathhouses), fishing, field sports, picnicking (500 tables), and camping (75 tent and RV sites for $26; no water or sewer hookups, but electricity and a dump station are available). No pets, skateboards, or motorcycles are allowed. The sandy beach is tidal, so the swimming "window" is about two hours before high tide until two hours afterward; otherwise, you're wallowing in mudflats. The same timing applies to kayakers and canoeists. Toddlers head for the big playground; teenagers gravitate to the arcade and the ice cream parlor. From Cooks Corner, take Route 24 south 1.5 miles, turn left, and follow signs for less than two miles to the park.

A very popular, family-oriented spot for freshwater swimming is **White's Beach** (Durham Rd., Brunswick, 207/729-0415, www.whitesbeachandcampground.com, $3.50 adults, $2.50 seniors and under age 13). The sandy-bottomed pond maxes out at nine feet. In mid-July the campground hosts a popular family bluegrass festival. Park facilities include a snack bar, a playground, hot showers, and campsites ($22-33). From Route 1 just south of the I-95 exit into Brunswick, take Durham Road 2.2 miles northwest.

Boat Excursions

Departing at noon from the Cook's Lobster House wharf (Cook's Landing) in Bailey Island (off Rte. 24), a large sturdy **Casco Bay Lines ferry** (207/774-7871, www.cascobaylines.com, $16 adults, $7.50 ages 5-9) does a 1.75-hour nature-watch circuit of nearby islands, including Eagle Island, the onetime home of Admiral Robert Peary (there are no stopovers on these circuits). Reservations aren't needed.

For a more intimate excursion in a smaller boat, Captain Les McNelly, owner of **Sea Escape Charters** (Bailey Island, 207/833-5531, www.seaescapecottages.com), operates two-hour on-demand sightseeing cruises throughout the summer (weather permitting) for $85 pp (two people) or $55 (four people). Or he'll take you out to

Island for $160/couple (cheaper if there are more passengers). He also offers fishing trips: $225 for four hours, including bait and tackle ($110 for each additional person); bring your own lunch. Trips operate out of Sea Escape Cottages, one- or two-bedroom well-equipped cottages with full kitchens and oceanside decks that rent for $160-190/night or $955-1,150/week, including linens and one change of towels.

Sea Kayaking

H2Outfitters (Orr's Island, 207/833-5257 or 800/205-2925, www.h2outfitters.com) has been a thriving operation since 1978. Based in a wooden building on the Orr's Island side of the famed cribstone bridge, this experienced company organizes guided trips, including island camping; all gear is included. A three-hour tour is $75 pp for two. If you're up for a full day of paddling, opt for the Eagle Island tour, $125 pp for two.

Seaspray Kayaking (207/443-3646 or 888/349-7772, www.seaspraykayaking.com) has

bases on the New Meadows River in Brunswick and Sebasco Harbor Resort in Phippsburg as well as rental centers in Georgetown and at Hermit Island Campground, Small Point. The New Meadows base is particularly good for those nervous about trying the sport. Rentals are $15-25 for the first hour, $5-10 for each additional hour, and $25-50/day. Equipment options include solo and tandem kayaks, recreational kayaks, surf kayaks, paddleboards, and canoes. Tours, led by Registered Maine Guides, vary from sunset paddles to three-day expeditions and include moonlight paddles, island-to-island tours, and inn-to-inn tours. Rates begin at $50 adults. A striper-fishing kayak tour, including tackle and instruction, is $85.

If you're an experienced sea kayaker, consider exploring Harpswell Sound from the boat launch on the west side of the cribstone bridge; kayaks can also be put in at Mackerel Cove, near Cook's Lobster House. A launch with plentiful parking is at Sawyer Park on the New Meadows River, on Route 1 just before you cross the river heading north.

H2Outfitters offers guided sea-kayaking trips from its Orr's Island location.

ACCOMMODATIONS
Motels and Inns

The Inn at Brunswick Station (4 Noble St., Brunswick, 207/837-6565, www.innatbrunswickstation.com, $170-310), opened in 2011, is adjacent to the train station where Amtrak's Downeaster and the Maine Eastern Railroad dock, across from the town green, and within steps of Bowdoin College. Historical photographs hung throughout offset the contemporary decor. Breakfast is available in the tavern.

Continue another mile down Route 24, cross the cribstone bridge, and you'll come to Chip Black's **Bailey Island Motel** (Rte. 24, Bailey Island, 207/833-2886, www.baileyislandmotel.com, $140), a congenial, clean, no-frills waterfront spot with 11 guest rooms and wowser views. Kids under 10 stay for free; age 10 and older are $15 extra. Continental breakfast is included, and guest rooms have Wi-Fi, cable TV, and a small fridge. A dock is available for boat launching.

Looking rather like the film set of an old-fashioned tearjerker, the family-run **Driftwood Inn** (81 Washington Ave., Bailey Island, 207/833-5461, www.thedriftwoodinnmaine.com, no credit cards) has 25 very rustic pine-paneled guest rooms in four buildings (some with a private toilet and sink; all with shared showers), six housekeeping cottages, a saltwater pool, a stunning view, a dining room, and a determinedly take-us-as-we-are ambience. There are no frills, period, but it has oceanfront porches, games, and an old-fashioned simplicity that you rarely find anymore. You'll sleep at night listening to the waves crash on the rocky shore. It's all on three oceanfront acres near the Giant Stairs. The dining room, open to nonguests by reservation, serves a set home-cooked meal nightly (usually with a fish-of-the-day alternative), late June-early September, for $18-30; breakfast is $7.25. Meals aren't offered during spring and fall. Rooms are $85-130, and cottages rent by the week ($685-1,000). Dogs are allowed in the cottages.

Bed-and-Breakfasts

Right downtown, facing the tree-shaded Mall, is ◖ **The Brunswick Inn** (165 Park Row, Brunswick, 207/729-4914 or 800/299-4914, www.brunswickbnb.com, year-round, $149-219), a stately 30-room Federal mansion built in 1848. Fine art from a local gallery hangs throughout the inn, complementing the handsome decor. Fifteen comfortable guest rooms are split between the main house and the renovated Carriage House (with two fully accessible guest rooms); all have Wi-Fi and phones, and some have TVs. There's also a pet-friendly ($20) small cottage with a kitchen ($260). Inside the main inn is a laid-back lounge with occasional entertainment.

Within walking distance of downtown Brunswick, but across the bridge spanning the Androscoggin River, is the **Black Lantern B&B** (57 Elm St., Topsham, 888/306-4165, www.blacklanternbandb.com, $110-125), Tom and Judy Connelie's lovely 1860s riverfront home. All guest rooms are decorated with an emphasis on comfort, and two have water views. Judy's quilts will warm you on a cool night.

On the outskirts of town, in a rural location smack-dab on Middle Bay, is **Middle Bay Farm Bed and Breakfast** (287 Pennellville Rd., Brunswick, 207/373-1375, www.middlebayfarm.com, year-round, $170-190), lovingly and beautifully restored by Phyllis Truesdell, who bought the property after it sat all but abandoned for a decade. Once the site of the Pennell Brothers Shipyard, the farmhouse and sail loft now house guests seeking an away-from-it-all yet convenient location. Four water-view guest rooms in the 1834 farmhouse are decorated with antiques and have TVs and video players. Also in the main house is a living room with fireplace and grand piano. Two suites in the sail loft each have a living room with a kitchenette and two tiny bedrooms, and they share an open porch. All guests receive a full breakfast in the water-view dining room. Bring a sea kayak to launch from the dock.

At the 1761 **Harpswell Inn** (108 Lookout Point Rd., South Harpswell, 207/833-5509 or 800/843-5509, www.harpswellinn.com, year-round), innkeepers Anne and Dick Moseley operate a comfortable, welcoming, antiques-filled

© TOM NANGLE

The Brunswick Inn faces the Town Mall and is within walking distance of the train station and downtown shops and restaurants.

oasis on 2.5 secluded water-view acres. It's tough to break away from the glass-walled great room, but Middle Bay sunsets from the porch can do it. And just down the hill is Allen's Seafood, a take-out fish shack, where you can watch lobstermen unload their catches in a gorgeous cove and grab a lobster roll. In fall, the foliage on two little islets in the cove turns brilliant red. The bed-and-breakfast has seven guest rooms ($155-180), three suites ($235-259), and four cottages ($975-1,500/week). Prices are slightly higher for one-night stays.

Thirteen miles south of Cooks Corner, **The Log Cabin** (Rte. 24, Bailey Island, 207/833-5546, www.logcabin-maine.com, $179-339) has nine nicely decorated guest rooms with phones, TVs and video players, private decks facing the bay, and, weather permitting, splendid sunset views to the White Mountains. Four guest rooms have kitchen facilities; some have gas fireplaces or whirlpool tubs. There's also an outdoor heated pool. Full breakfast is included; dinner ($18-34) is available.

FOOD
Local Flavors

Wild O.A.T.S. Bakery and Café (149 Maine St., Tontine Mall, Brunswick, 207/725-6287, www.wildoatsbakery.com, 7am-5pm daily) turns out terrific made-from-scratch breads and pastries, especially the breakfast kind, in its cafeteria-style place. (Just so you know, the name stands for Original and Tasty Stuff.) It has inside and outside tables, moderate prices, good-for-you salads, and great sandwiches.

For food on the run—no-frills hot dogs straight from the cart—head for Brunswick's Mall, the village green where **Danny's on the Mall** (no phone) has been cooking dirt-cheap tube steaks since the early 1980s.

Fat Boy Drive-In (Bath Rd./Old Rte. 1, Brunswick, 207/729-9431, 11am-8pm daily, no credit cards) is a genuine throwback—a landmark since 1955, boasting carhops, window trays, and a menu guaranteed to clog your arteries. Onion rings, frappés, and BLTs are specialties. Aim for the second Saturday in August, when the annual Sock Hop takes place.

Pizzas by the slice or pie in both the usual and specialty flavors and made from mostly organic and locally sourced ingredients emerge from the ovens at **Flipside** (111 Main St., Brunswick, 207/373-9448, 11:30am-9pm Mon.-Sat., noon-9pm Sun.). Possible toppings include local greens, slow-roasted tomatoes, smoked chicken, and maple-cured bacon.

Choose from about 30 flavors of gelato and *sorbetto* at **The Gelato Fiasco** (74 Maine St., Brunswick, 207/607-4002, 11am-11pm daily). You can find these to-die-for gelati statewide, but this is ground zero.

A favorite for chowder is **Salt Cod Cafe** (1894 Harpswell Islands Rd., Orr's Island, 207/833-6210, 8am-5pm daily), with a primo location overlooking the cribstone bridge. Sandwiches, wraps, rolls, and baked goods are also available.

The chocolates, truffles, and bark made by Melinda Harris Richter are divine at **Island Candy Company** (Harpswell Islands Rd., Orr's Island, 207/833-6639, 11am-8pm daily in season), and there are baked goods and ice cream too.

Family Favorites

Just over the bridge from Brunswick, in the renovated Bowdoin Mill complex overlooking the Androscoggin River, the **Sea Dog Brewery** (1 Main St., Topsham, 207/725-0162, www. seadogbrewing.com, 11:30am-1am daily, $10-20) has seating inside and on a deck overhanging the river. The menu ranges from burgers and sandwiches to full-plate entrées. It offers frequent acoustic entertainment, and there are games for kids, a video arcade, and pool tables.

The **Brunswick Farmers Market** sets up rain or shine on the Mall (village green) 8am-2pm Tuesday and Friday May-November; Friday is the bigger day. On Saturday the market moves to Crystal Spring Farm, Pleasant Hill Road (8:30am-12:30pm). You'll find produce, cheeses, crafts, condiments, live lobsters, and serendipitous surprises, depending on the season.

Ethnic and Eclectic Fare

Greek fisherman's stew, saltimbocca alla Romana, handmade organic pastas, and *arancini* are just a few of the Greek and Italian choices that might appear on the seasonally changing menu at ◖ **Trattoria Athena** (25 Mill St., Brunswick, 207/721-0700, www.trattoriaathena.com, 5pm-9pm Tues.-Sat., 4pm-8pm Sun. $18-26). The dining area is small, with a cozy rustic vibe that complements the cuisine. This gem, about a block off Maine Street, is worth finding.

Although the owners are Chinese, they do a decent job with the sushi and Japanese specialties at **Little Tokyo** (72 Maine St., Brunswick, 207/798-6888, www.littletokyomaine.com, 11:30am-9:30pm daily, entrées $12-25).

◖ **Tao Yuan** (22 Pleasant St., Brunswick, 207/725-9002, 11:30am-2pm Wed.-Fri., 5pm-9:30pm Tues.-Thurs., 5pm-10:30pm Fri.-Sat., $6-16), an Asian tapas-style restaurant, wows guests with fresh and innovative cuisine masterfully prepared by chef-owner Cara Stadler, who trained with master chefs in France and China. A dim sum brunch is held 11am-3pm on the last Sunday of the month.

Generous portions, moderate prices, efficient service, and narrow aisles are the story at **The Great Impasta** (42 Maine St., Brunswick, 207/729-5858, www.thegreatimpasta.com, 11am-9pm Mon.-Thurs., 11am-10pm Fri.-Sat., $13-22), a cheerful, informal eatery where the garlic meets you at the door. There are gluten-free choices and a "bambino menu" for the kids.

Eclectic doesn't begin to describe **Frontier Cafe** (Mill 3, Fort Andross, 14 Maine St. at Rte. 1 overpass, Brunswick, 207/725-5222, www.explorefrontier.com, 11am-9pm Sun. and Tues.-Thurs., 11am-10pm Fri.-Sat., kitchen closes one hour earlier, entrées $12-26), a combination café, gallery, and cinema inspired by founder Michael Gilroy's world travels. The menu includes wonderful market plates emphasizing the cuisine of a country or region—Spain, France, the Middle East, Italy, or global—as well as other worldly flavors, burgers, and vegetarian and vegan options.

Desserts are homemade, and there's also a kids' menu. Wine and beer are served. Films are screened, and there are frequent events and entertainment.

World-class beer is the focus at **Lion's Pride** (112 Pleasant St., Brunswick, 207/373-1840, www.lionspridepub.com, 11:30am-10pm Sun.-Thurs., 11:30am-12:30am Fri.-Sat.), where the expansive menu ($8-30) is geared around the brews. Some rather obscure pours (emphasis on Belgian) are drawn from the 35 handblown glass taps.

Hip, funky, and full of personality describe **El Camino** (15 Cushing St., Brunswick, 207/725-8228, www.elcaminomaine.com, 5pm-9pm Tues.-Sat.), which uses fresh, local, and often organic ingredients to create innovative Cal-Mex fare such as crabmeat-and-avocado quesadillas. Prices top out around $18.

Pho fans will find it as well as other Vietnamese fare at **Lemongrass** (212 Maine St., 207/725-9008, www.lemongrassme.com, 11am-9pm Tues.-Sun., $8-15).

Lobster and Seafood

In 2006 the Holbrook Community Foundation took ownership of Holbrook's Wharf, site of **Holbrook's Wharf and Grille** (984 Cundy's Harbor Rd., 207/729-0848, 11am-8pm daily), along with Holbrook's General Store and the Trufant mansion, preserving this slice of Maine fishing-village life for future generations. The wharf lobster shack is a leased operation, and quality varies year to year; ask locally. When it's on, this is the real thing for authentic lobster in the rough, and the view is superb.

You want fresh? You want simple? **Erica's Seafood** (Basin Point Rd., Harpswell, 207/833-7354, www.ericasseafood.com, 11am-7pm daily), a seasonal takeout overlooking Casco Bay, delivers on both counts. Head to the garage for lobster, to the shack for chowders, fried fish, and burgers. The only seating is on wharf-side picnic tables.

Arguments rage endlessly about who makes the best chowder in Maine, but ◖ **The Dolphin Marina and Chowder House** (Dolphin Marina, 515 Basin Point Rd., South Harpswell,

207/833-6000, www.dolphinmarinaandrestaurant.com, 11:30am-8pm daily May 1-Oct. 31, $6-30) tops lots of lists for its fish chowder, accompanied by a blueberry muffin. Equally famed is its lobster stew, plus you can't beat the scenic 13-mile drive south from Brunswick or the spectacular sea and island views through the rounded row of windows of its new, waterfront building.

Two other good bets for lobster, along with chowders and fried seafood, are **Gurnet Trading Co.** (602 Gurnet Rd./Rte. 24, Brunswick, 207/729-7300, www.gurnettrading.com), serving lunch and dinner daily overlooking Buttermilk Cove; and **Morse's Cribstone Grill** (1945 Harpswell Islands Rd., Bailey Island, 207/833-7775, 11am-8pm daily), perched on the shorefront adjacent to the bridge.

INFORMATION AND SERVICES

Area information is provided by the **Southern Midcoast Chamber of Commerce** (877/725-8797, www.midcoastmaine.com) and the **Harpswell Business Association** (www.harpswellmaine.org).

Check the website of **Curtis Memorial Library** (23 Pleasant St., Brunswick, 207/725-5242, www.curtislibrary.com) for excellent local resources and guides.

GETTING THERE AND AROUND

Brunswick is about 10 miles or 15 minutes via Route 295 from Freeport. It's about nine miles or 15 minutes via Route 1 to Bath.

The **Amtrak Downeaster** (800/872-7245, www.amtrakdowneaster.com) makes two daily trips between Boston and Brunswick, with Maine stops in Saco, Wells, Old Orchard (seasonal), and Portland en route.

Ride in restored vintage railcars on the scenic **Maine Eastern Railroad** (207/596-6725 or 800/637-2457, www.maineeasternrailroad.com), operating between Brunswick and Rockland with stops in Bath, Wiscasset, and Newcastle, and connecting with the Amtrak Downeaster. The train operates Friday-Sunday, early July through mid-October. Adult fares range $26-37 round-trip, $17-24 one way; kids 4-11 are $16-22/$10-15. A shuttlebus connects Wiscasset to Boothbay for $8/4.

Bath Area

One of the smallest in area among Maine's cities, **Bath** (pop. 8,514), packs a wallop in only nine square miles. Like Brunswick, it straddles Route 1 and edges a river, but Bath's centuries of historical and architectural tradition and well-preserved Victorian downtown have earned it a prized designation: The National Trust for Historic Preservation named it a Distinctive Destination.

Giant cranes dominate the riverfront cityscape at the huge Bath Iron Works complex, source of state-of-the-art warships—your tax dollars at work. Less evident (but not far away) is the link to the past: Just south of Bath, in Popham on the Phippsburg Peninsula, is the poorly marked site where a trouble-plagued English settlement, a sister colony to Jamestown, predated the Plymouth Colony by 13 years. (Of course, Champlain arrived before that, and Norsemen left calling cards even earlier.) In 1607-1608 settlers in the Popham Colony managed to build a 30-ton pinnace, *Virginia of Sagadahoc,* designed for transatlantic trade, but they lost heart during a bitter winter and abandoned the site.

Bath is the jumping-off point for two peninsulas to the south—**Phippsburg** (pop. 2,216, of Popham Colony fame) and **Georgetown** (pop. 1,042). Both are dramatically scenic, with glacier-carved farms and fishing villages. Drive (bicycling is best left to experienced pedalers) a dozen miles down any of these fingers and you're in different worlds.

Across the Sagadahoc Bridge from Bath is **Woolwich** (pop. 3,072), from where you can continue northeastward along the coast or detour northward on Route 128 to the hamlet of Day's Ferry. Named after 18th-century resident Joseph Day, who shuttled back and forth in a gondola-type boat across the Kennebec River, the picturesque village has a cluster of 18th- and 19th-century homes and churches—all part of the Day's Ferry Historic District. The village's Old Stage Road saw many a stagecoach in its day; passengers would ferry from Bath and pick up the stage here to travel onward.

SIGHTS
Bath Iron Works
Known locally as BIW or The Yard, **Bath Iron Works** has been building ships on this 50-acre riverfront site since 1890. Currently its roughly 5,700 employees build destroyers for the U.S. Navy. BIW is open to the public for launchings, when it's a mob scene with hordes of politicos, townsfolk, and military pooh-bahs in their scrambled eggs and brass. The best way

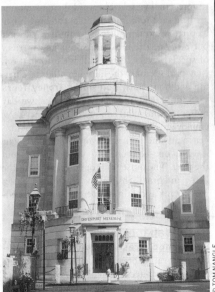

Bath City Hall

© TOM NANGLE

MID-COAST REGION

to get a peek at the workaday world behind the gates is on a Bath Iron Works Trolley Tour with the Maine Maritime Museum.

◖ Maine Maritime Museum

Spread over 25 acres on the Kennebec River is the state's premier marine museum, the **Maine Maritime Museum** (243 Washington St., Bath, 207/443-1316, www.mainemaritimemuseum. org, 9:30am-5pm daily, $15 adults, $12 seniors and students, $10 ages 6-16). On the grounds are five original 19th-century buildings from the Percy and Small Shipyard (1897-1920), a late-Victorian home, and hands-on exhibits, but the first thing you see is the architecturally dramatic Maritime History Building, locale for permanent and temporary displays of marine art and artifacts and a shop stocked with nautical books and gifts. Bring a picnic (or purchase lunch at the seasonal Even Keel Snack Bar) and let the toddlers loose in the children's pirate's play area. Then either wander the campus on your own or join one of the guided tours. Don't miss the boat shop, where volunteers build and restore small vessels. Shipyard demonstrations are held on a rotating schedule, and brown-bag lectures are often given. In summer, weather permitting, the museum sponsors a variety of special river cruises; call for information. May-mid-October the museum offers fascinating one-hour **Bath Iron Works Trolley Tours** ($35 adults, $17 under age 17, includes two-day museum admission) conducted by former BIW employees. You'll need to reserve a week or longer in advance; it's well worth the effort. Pair it with a one-hour cruise to view the yard from the river. The museum is open year-round; the Percy and Small Shipyard is year-round but in winter only as conditions permit, with reduced-price admissions.

Bath Walking Tours

Sagadahoc Preservation (www.sagadahocpreservation.org), founded in 1971 to rescue the city's architectural heritage, has produced podcasts of three different self-guided walking and driving architectural tours that can be downloaded from www.cityofbath.com.

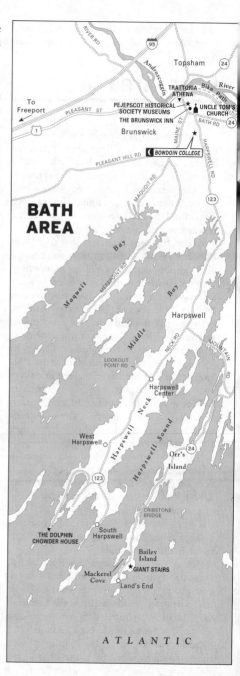

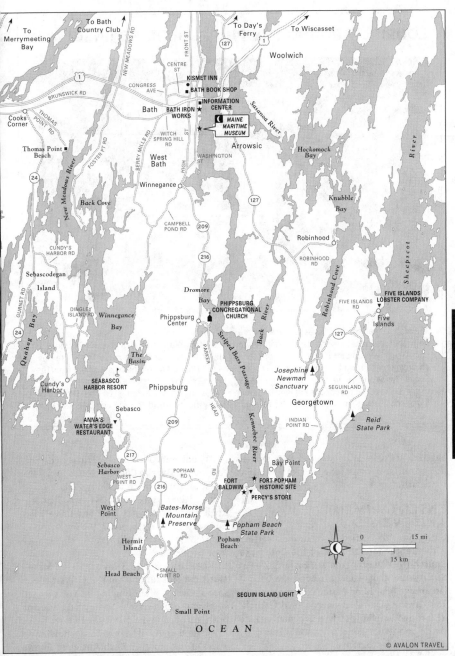

MID-COAST REGION

© AVALON TRAVEL

LOOPING AROUND THE PHIPPSBURG PENINSULA

© HILARY NANGLE

Adults as well as kids love exploring the passageways of Fort Popham.

Thanks to a map and brochures produced by the Phippsburg Business Association and Phippsburg Land Trust (www.phippsburglandtrust.org) and an online guide from the Phippsburg Historical Society (www.phippsburghistorical.com), it's easy to spend the better part of a day or longer exploring the peninsula that extends south from Bath.

About two miles south of Bath is a causeway known as **Winnegance,** a Wabanaki name usually translated as "short carry" or "little portage." Native Americans crossed here from the Kennebec River to the New Meadows River.

It's another 1.3 miles to the **Dromore Burying Ground** (on the right), with head-

Sagadahoc Preservation also offers an annual house tour, usually in June; check the website for details.

ENTERTAINMENT AND EVENTS

Bath's most diversified entertainment setting is the **Center for the Arts at the Chocolate Church** (804 Washington St., Bath, 207/442-8455, www.chocolatechurch.com), a chocolate-brown board-and-batten structure built in 1846 as the Central Congregational Church. Year-round activities at the arts center include music and dance concerts, dramas, exhibits, and children's programs.

At 7pm every Tuesday and Friday mid-June-August, the **Gazebo Concert Series** brings live entertainment to Bath's Library Park.

Five Rivers Arts Alliance (www.5raa.org) holds **Third Friday Art Walk and Drive** (various locations, Bath, 207/798-6964, 5pm-8pm) on the third Friday of the month June-September.

Throughout the summer, the **Maine Maritime Museum** (207/443-1316) schedules special events, often hinging on visits by tall ships and other vessels. Some of the visiting boats are open to the public for an extra fee.

November-April, 50 dealers show their wares at the monthly **Bath Antiques Shows**

stones dating from 1743. The next mile opens up with terrific easterly views of Dromore Bay. Right in the line of sight is state-owned, 117-acre Lee Island, which is off-limits May-mid-July to protect nesting eagles and waterfowl.

Next you're in **Phippsburg Center,** alive with shipbuilding from colonial days until the early 20th century. Hang a left onto Parker Head Road. After the Phippsburg Historical Museum (2pm-4pm Mon.-Fri. summer), in an 1859 schoolhouse, and the Alfred Totman Library, turn left onto Church Lane to see the "Constitution Tree," a huge English linden planted in 1774, in front of the 1802 **Phippsburg Congregational Church.**

Parker Head Road continues southward and meets Route 209, which leads to **Popham Beach State Park.** Continue to the end of Route 209 for **Fort Popham Historic Site,** where parking is woefully inadequate in summer. Youngsters love this place—they can fish from the rocks, explore the 1865 stone fortress, picnic on the seven-acre grounds, and create sand castles on the tiny beach next to the fort. Resist the urge to swim, though; the current is dangerous and there's no lifeguard. Across the river is Bay Point, a lobstering village at the tip of the Georgetown Peninsula. **Percy's Store** (207/389-2010), by the way, with a handful of tables, is a good bet for pizza, picnic fare, fried dough, and fishing tackle.

Across the cove from the fort is Fort Baldwin Road, a one-lane-wide winding road leading to the shorefront site of the 1607 Popham Colony. Climb the path up Sabino Hill to what's left of World War I-era **Fort Baldwin,** the best vantage point for panoramic photos.

Backtrack about four miles on Route 209, turn left onto Route 216, and head toward **Small Point.** Go about 0.9 mile to Morse Mountain Road, on the left, which leads to the parking area and trailhead for the **Bates-Morse Mountain Preserve.** Farther south are Head Beach and Hermit Island.

Returning northward on Route 216, you'll hook up with Route 209 and then see a left turn (Rte. 217) to Sebasco Harbor Resort. Take the time to go beyond the resort area. When the paved road goes left (to the Water's Edge Restaurant), turn right at a tiny cemetery and continue northward on the Old Meadowbrook Road, which meanders for about four miles along the west side of the peninsula. About midway along is **The Basin,** regarded by sailors as one of the Maine Coast's best "hurricane holes" (refuges in high winds). As you skirt The Basin and come to a fork, bear right to return to Route 209; turn left and return northward to Bath.

(www.bathantiquesshows.com, $4) at the Bath Middle School.

SHOPPING

Front and Center Streets are lined with fun, independent shops, including a number of shops selling antiques and antiquarian books clustered on lower Front Street.

Bath is home to a good independent bookstore successfully bucking the megastore trend, the **Bath Book Shop** (96 Front St., Bath, 207/443-9338). For cheap beach reads and eclectic finds, visit **The Library Bookstore** (194 Front St., Bath, 207/443-1161).

Smack downtown is **Renys** (86 Front St.,

207/443-6251), an only-in-Maine department store that's always worth a look-see.

Right in the shadow of the Route 1 overpass is an incredible resource for knitters and weavers, **Halcyon Yarn** (12 School St., Bath, 207/442-7909 or 800/341-0282), a huge warehouse of a place that carries domestic and imported yarns, looms, spinning wheels, how-to videos, kits, and pattern books.

About nine miles down Route 127, you'll come to **Georgetown Pottery** (Rte. 127, Georgetown, 207/371-2801), a top-quality ceramics studio and shop. A second shop is on Route 1 in Woolwich.

Anyone who appreciates fine woodworking

tools *must* visit the Shelter Institute's **Woodbutcher Tools** (873 Rte. 1, Woolwich, 207/442-7938), a retail shop and bookstore, five miles north of Bath.

Flea Market

One of Maine's biggest and most enduring flea markets is right on Route 1 north of Bath, often creating near-accidents as rubbernecking motorists slam to a halt. **Montsweag Flea Market** (Rte. 1 at Mountain Rd., Woolwich, 207/443-2809) is a genuine treasure trove about seven miles northeast of Bath's Sagadahoc bridge. It's open from 6:30am weekends May-mid-October, plus on Wednesday in summer (antiques and collectibles only from 5:30am).

RECREATION
Golf

The 18-hole **Bath Country Club** (Whiskeag Rd., Bath, 207/442-8411) has moderate greens fees, a pro shop, and a restaurant serving lunch and dinner.

The **Sebasco Harbor Resort** has a nine-hole course, open to nonguests on a space-available basis; call the resort's pro shop (207/389-9060) to inquire. Watch out for the infamous second hole, which gives new meaning to the term *water hole,* and say good morning to Sarah on the sixth tee: If you look nearby, you'll find a gravestone inscribed "Sarah Wallace—1862." A local rhyme goes like this:

> Show respect to Sarah
> You golfers passing by;
> She's the only person on this course
> Who can't improve her lie.

Parks and Preserves

The **Kennebec Estuary Land Trust** (KELT, 207/442-8400, www.kennebecestuary.org) maintains two preserves worth a visit; maps of each can be downloaded. Bath's **Thorn Head Preserve** at the end of High Street, is located on the point where Whiskeag Creek meets the Kennebec River. Allow a

half hour for the easy walk to the headland and its stone "picnic" table with views toward Merrymeeting Bay. Allow longer if you want to explore any of the side trails. The **Whiskeag Trail,** a five-mile nonmotorized multiuse urban path, connects the preserve to the Bath YMCA. For terrific views of this section of coast, hike the loop trail to the bedrock summit of Georgetown's **Higgins Mountain.** The Route 127 trailhead is on the right, 7.6 miles south of Route 1.

BATES-MORSE MOUNTAIN CONSERVATION AREA

Consider visiting Phippsburg's lovely 600-acre **Bates-Morse Mountain Conservation Area** only if you are willing to be conscientious about the rules for this private preserve. A relatively easy four-mile round-trip hike takes you through marshland (you'll need insect repellent) and to the top of 210-foot Morse Mountain, which has panoramic views, and down to privately owned Seawall Beach. On a clear day you can see New Hampshire's Mount Washington from the summit. No pets or vehicles are allowed, and there are no facilities; stay on the preserve road and the beach path at all times, as the side roads are private. Least terns and piping plovers—both endangered species—nest in the dunes, so avoid this area, especially mid-May-mid-August. Morse Mountain is a great locale for spotting hawks during their annual September migration southward. Pick up a map (and the rules) from the box in the parking area on Morse Mountain Road, off Route 216 just under a mile south of the intersection with Route 209.

PHIPPSBURG HIKING TRAILS

The **Phippsburg Land Trust** (207/443-5993, www.phippsburglandtrust.org) has prepared a handy free brochure with a map detailing 16 preserves, most with trails. Four—Center Pond, Ridgewell, Spirit Pond, and Sprague Pond—have trail guides available at trailhead boxes. The land trust also hosts guided walks mid-June-mid-September.

JOSEPHINE NEWMAN SANCTUARY

A must-see for any nature lover, the 119-acre **Josephine Newman Sanctuary** (Rte. 127, Georgetown), has 2.5 miles of blazed loop trails winding through 110 wooded acres and along Robinhood Cove's tidal shoreline. Josephine Oliver Newman (1878-1968), a respected naturalist, bequeathed her family's splendid property to Maine Audubon (207/781-2330, www. maineaudubon.org), which maintains it today. The 0.6-mile self-guided trail is moderately difficult, but the rewards are 20 informative markers highlighting special features: glacial erratics, reversing falls, mosses, and marshes. The easiest route is the 0.75-mile Horseshoe Trail, which you can extend for another mile or so by linking into the Rocky End Trail. No pets or bikes are allowed. To find this hidden gem, take Route 127 from Route 1 in Woolwich (the road to Reid State Park) for 9.1 miles. Turn right at the sanctuary sign and continue up the narrow, rutted dirt road (ideally no one will be coming the other way) to the small parking lot. A map of the trail system is posted at the marsh's edge and available in the box.

ROBERT P. TRISTRAM COFFIN WILDFLOWER SANCTUARY

The New England Wildflower Society (www. newfs.org) owns the 177-acre trail-laced **Robert P. Tristram Coffin Wildflower Sanctuary** bordering Merrymeeting Bay in Woolwich. It is home to more than 100 species of wildflowers. To find it, take Route 127 north for 2.2 miles, then Route 128 for 4.5 miles, and look for a small parking area on the left.

Swimming
POPHAM BEACH

On hot July and August weekends, the parking lot at **Popham Beach State Park** (Rte. 209, Phippsburg, 207/389-1335, www.parksand-lands.com, $6 nonresident adults, $4 Maine resident adults, $2 nonresident seniors, free Maine resident seniors, $1 ages 5-11), 14 miles south of Bath, fills up by 10am, so plan to arrive early at this huge crescent of sand backed by sea grass, beach roses, and dunes. Facilities include changing rooms, outside showers, restrooms, and seasonal lifeguards. It's officially open April 15-October 30, but the beach is accessible all year.

HEAD BEACH

Just off Route 216, about two miles south of the Route 209 turnoff to Popham Beach, is **Head Beach**, a sandy crescent that's open daily until 10pm. A day-use parking fee ($7) is payable at the small gatehouse; there's a restroom on the path to the beach and a store within walking distance.

REID STATE PARK

If I had to pick my favorite coastal state park, it would be **Reid** (Seguinland Rd., Georgetown, 207/371-2303, www.parksandlands.com, $6.50 nonresident adults, $4.50 Maine resident adults, $2 nonresident seniors, free Maine resident seniors, $1 ages 5-11). Surf crashes on One Mile and Half Mile beaches, eagles and osprey soar overhead, kids splash in the lagoon or hunt for seaborne treasures in pools left by the receding tide, birds nest in the sand dunes and marshlands. Trails lace the 765 acres, but for the biggest reward for the smallest effort, ascend Griffith Head and take in the sweeping seascape views. Facilities include changing rooms with showers, picnic tables, restrooms, and snack bars. The park—14 miles south of Route 1 in Woolwich and two miles off Route 127—is open daily year-round. In winter, bring cross-country skis and glide along the shoreline. Plan to arrive early on summer weekends, when parking is woefully inadequate.

Just 0.5 mile beyond the road to Reid State Park is **Charles Pond,** where the setting is unsurpassed for freshwater swimming in the long, skinny pond. You'll wish this were a secret too, but it isn't. There are no facilities.

Boat Excursions

The 50-foot *Yankee* operates out of Small Point's Hermit Island Campground Monday-Saturday throughout the summer. You can go on nature cruises, enjoy the sunset, or visit Eagle Island; the schedule is different each day,

MID-COAST REGION

© HILARY NANGLE

Rocky headlands and a gorgeous beach make it easy to spend a day at Reid State Park.

and rates vary widely by trip. Call for information and reservations (207/389-1788).

The **MV Ruth,** a 38-foot excursion boat, runs cruises out of Sebasco Harbor Resort late June-Labor Day. You don't need to be a Sebasco guest to take the trips, but reservations are essential. The schedule changes weekly, but possible options are a nature cruise, a Cundy's Harbor lunch cruise, lobstering demos, a sunset cruise, and a trip to Pirate Island, with trips ranging 1-2 hours. Call the resort (207/389-1161) for the current week's schedule and rates.

If you prefer a custom tour, call **River Run Tours** (207/504-2628, www.riverruntours. com). Whether you want to view lighthouses or wildlife or cruise upriver to Swans Island, Captain Ed Rice has a cruise for you. Boat rate is $120/hour while cruising, $50/hour for standby. His comfortable pontoon boat accommodates six; plan on at least two hours.

The easiest access to Seguin Island (www.seguinisland.org) is via the **Seguin Island Ferry** (207/841-7977, www.fishntripsmaine.com, $30), which departs from the harbor near Fort Popham; call for current schedule. Most trips allow about three hours to tour the lighthouse, hike the trails, visit the museum, and picnic.

Canoeing and Kayaking

Close to civilization yet amazingly undeveloped, 392-acre **Nequasset Lake** is a great place to canoe. You'll see a few anglers, a handful of houses, and near-wilderness along the shoreline. Personal watercraft and motors over 10 hp are banned. Take Route 1 from Bath across the bridge to Woolwich. Continue to the flashing caution light at Nequasset Road; turn right and go 0.1 mile. Turn left, and left again, into the parking area for the Nequasset Stream Waterfront Park, a popular swimming hole. Launch your canoe and head upstream, under Route 1, to the lake.

Seaspray Kayaking (888/349-7774, www. seaspraykayaking.com) operates from bases at the New Meadows Kayaking Center in West Bath and Sebasco Harbor Resort in Sebasco Estates, with rentals available at Hermit Island Campground on Small Point. Hourly rentals begin at $15-25 plus $5-10 for each additional hour, up to $25-50 daily, with longer-term rates and delivery available. A variety of guided tours are also offered, with half-day options for $50 adults, $25 children, and specialty paddles, such as sunset or moonlight, for $40 pp.

Fishing Charters

Cast a line for stripers, bluefish, pike trout, and smallmouth bass with **Kennebec Tidewater Charters** (207/737-4695, www.kennebectidewater.com). Captain Robin Thayer, a Master Maine Guide, offers freshwater and saltwater cruises beginning at $300 for four hours. Tackle is provided, and instruction is available. Catch-and-release is encouraged.

ACCOMMODATIONS
Bath

Most of Bath's in-town bed-and-breakfasts and inns are in historic residences built by shipping magnates and their families, giving you a chance to appreciate the quality of craftsmanship they demanded in their ships and their homes alike. All are open year-round.

The flamboyant pink-and-plum Italianate **Galen Moses House** (1009 Washington St., Bath, 207/442-8771 or 888/442-8771, www.galenmoses.com, $139-259) is a standout in the city's Historic District. Original architectural features—soaring ceilings, friezes, chandeliers, elaborate woodwork, stained-glass windows—and period antiques make it equally appealing inside, as do hosts Jim Haught and Larry Kieft. All guest rooms have air-conditioning and Wi-Fi. The inn has common rooms for relaxing, including one with a TV and video player. A fancy, full breakfast served at a communal table and afternoon refreshments are included. Pets are allowed in one guest room for $15/night.

Innkeeper Elizabeth Knowlton blends elegance and comfort at the **Inn at Bath** (969 Washington St., Bath, 207/443-4294 or 800/423-0964, www.innatbath.com, $170-245). Her culinary skills, honed as chef and co-owner of a Montana fly-fishing lodge, have garnered national attention. Guest rooms in the 1810 Greek Revival-style inn are decorated with antiques, and each has air-conditioning, a TV and video player, Wi-Fi, and a phone. Two have wood-burning fireplaces, and two have two-person whirlpool tubs. Kids over age four and dogs are welcome. One room is wheelchair-accessible.

When you want to be truly pampered, book a room at the ◖ **Kismet Inn** (44 Summer St., Bath, 207/443-3399, www.kismetinnmaine.com, $265-305), where innkeeper Shadi Towfighis offers five lovely guest rooms, each with either a Japanese soaking tub or a steam shower. The inn is decorated with a contemporary old world style. The beds are covered with organic-cotton linens and were designed specifically for each guest room. Guests can arrange for in-room spa services. Reserve a private dinner; it's a treat. Shadi uses natural and organic ingredients to create meals that go beyond the usual B&B fare. Not only that, but breakfast is served whenever you're ready; there are no set mealtimes. Guests must leave outdoor shoes in the entry to avoid bringing outside pollutants indoors. The inn faces Library Park and is just around the corner from Front Street's shops.

Phippsburg Peninsula

The trouble with staying at the ◖ **Sebasco Harbor Resort** (Rte. 217, Sebasco Estates, 207/389-1161 or 800/225-3819, www.sebasco.com), a self-contained resort on 575 waterfront acres, is that between the beautiful setting and the bountiful offerings, you might not set foot off the premises during your entire vacation. Situated at the mouth of the saltwater New Meadows River, 12 miles south of Bath, Sebasco has attracted families who return year after year since 1930, when it opened. Sebasco changed hands in 1997, and owner Bob Smith has brought the resort up to 21st-century standards while keeping its old-style rusticity. You'll have to look far and wide to find a better family resort. Scattered around the well-tended property are the main lodge and a variety of cottages (1-10 bedrooms; the two-bedroom units with a shared living room are a great choice for families), a main lodge, a four-story cupola-topped lighthouse building

© HILARY NANGLE

Sebasco Harbor Resort has pet-friendly accommodations.

edging the harbor, and two suites buildings, Harbor Village and the waterfront Fairwinds Spa, with more contemporary amenities. All have private baths, phones, and cable TV; many have water views; some have refrigerators or kitchenettes or full kitchens. Rates begin around $125; kids under age 12 are free; pets are $25/night. Rates that include breakfast and dinner are an additional $48 pp (no charge for children under age 11 when dining with an adult and from the kids' menu). Weekly summer events include a Sunday-evening reception and grand buffet, lobster bakes, family barbecues, bingo, live entertainment, and the Camp Merrit children's program ($18/day, includes lunch). Recreational facilities include two all-weather tennis courts, a nine-hole championship golf course and a three-hole regulation course for beginners and families, the state's largest outdoor saltwater pool, boat tours aboard the *Ruth,* sailing trips, sea-kayak excursions, mountain-bike tours, candlepin bowling, horseshoes, a playground, a well-equipped fitness center, and as much or as little organized activity as you want.

Magnificent gardens surround **Edgewater Farm Bed and Breakfast** (71 Small Point Rd./Rte. 216, Sebasco Estates, 207/389-1322 or 877/389-1322, www.ewfbb.com, $130-225), Carol and Bill Emerson's comfy, unfussy 19th-century farmhouse, just south of the turnoff to Popham Beach and close to the access for Morse Mountain. Families usually choose the carriage house, where kids can play in the huge recreation room. A brunch-size breakfast served in the solarium benefits from organic produce grown on the four-acre grounds. And then there's the four-foot-deep indoor lap pool, a hot tub outside on the deck, and the Benedictine labyrinth Bill created in a wooded grove. English, Spanish, a bit of French, and German are all spoken. Pets are welcome for $25.

Rock Gardens Inn (Rte. 218, Sebasco Estates, Phippsburg, 207/389-1339, www.rock-gardensinn.com, from $155 pp d) hosts numerous artists' workshops, and no wonder: It sits on its own peninsula, and the pretty grounds are landscaped with wild and cultivated flowers. Guests stay in one of three inn rooms or 10 cottages and have use of an outdoor heated pool and sea kayaks. Rates include breakfast and dinner—and the weekly lobster cookout. After the minimum rate is reached per cottage, kids cost $16-88, depending on their age. Sebasco Harbor Resort is just steps away, and guests have access to its facilities as well. Ask about all-inclusive art workshops.

Step back in history at **The 1774 Inn** (44 Parker Head Rd., Phippsburg Center, 207/389-1774, www.1774inn.com, $160-240), a magnificently restored four-square Georgian colonial property, listed on the National Register of Historic Places, with an 1870 ell and barn. Many colonial details have been preserved, including shutters with peepholes and strong bars to defend against attack, paneled wainscoting, ceiling moldings, fluted columns, and wide-plank pine floors. Most of the eight guest rooms (all but two with private baths) have views of the Kennebec River. All are spacious

This lighthouse is one of the buildings at Sebasco Harbor Resort.

and furnished with antiques. Outside, the inn's four acres roll down to the river. Rates include a full breakfast.

You can walk to beaches or forts from **Stonehouse Manor** (907 Popham Rd., Phippsburg, 877/389-1141, www.stonehousemanor.com, $220-320), a National Historic Register-listed bed-and-breakfast with lovely gardens and an enviable location on Silver Lake. The graceful 1896 mansion-style cottage's architectural features include leaded stained-glass windows and oak pocket doors. Rooms are spacious, and the feeling is like being on a private estate. Breakfasts are a treat.

Georgetown Peninsula

Imagine the perfect Maine seaside inn, and likely it resembles **Grey Havens Inn** (96 Seguinland Rd., Georgetown, 855/473-9428 or 207/371-2616, www.greyhavens.com, $200-350). Innkeepers Eve and Dick Roesler and Chuck Papachristos have thoroughly renovated and updated this 1904 Shingle-style classic with two turrets, front porch, and dreamy views over lobster boats, spruce-fringed islands, and rockbound coast. Public rooms flow, with a massive stone hearth dominating the living room. Guest rooms are comfy and simply decorated in coastal cottage style. Rates include a full breakfast in Blue, which also serves dinner Tuesday-Saturday.

It's hard to tear yourself away from the scenery and sanctuary at **The Mooring Bed and Breakfast** (132 Seguinland Rd., Georgetown, 207/371-2790 or 866/828-7348, www.themooringb-b.com, $165-210), the original home of Walter Reid, who donated Reid State Park to the state. His great-granddaughter Penny Barabe and her husband, Paul, have beautifully restored the house, situated on lovely oceanfront grounds with island-studded views. Each guest room has a water view and air-conditioning. There's plenty of room to spread out, including the appropriately named Spanish room. A full breakfast, afternoon wine and cheese, and sweets are included.

Even more secluded is **Coveside Bed & Breakfast** (6 Gotts Cove Lane, Georgetown,

The view from Grey Havens Inn's expansive porch takes in islands and lobster boats.

207/371-2807 or 800/232-5490, www. covesidebandb.com, $160-225), an enviable spot on five oceanfront acres near Five Islands. Tom and Carolyn Church have four guest rooms in the main house and three in the adjacent cottage. Some rooms have fireplaces; one has a whirlpool tub. Carolyn's pastry-chef skills are evident at breakfast. Wi-Fi is available, and a separate building has a TV and exercise room. Guests have use of bicycles and a canoe, gardens, and the dock on Gotts Cove.

Camping

Plan to book in January if you want a waterfront campsite in midsummer at the Phippsburg Peninsula's **Hermit Island Campground** (6 Hermit Island Rd., Phippsburg, 207/443-2101, www.hermitisland.com, no credit cards). With 275 campsites (no vehicles larger than pickup campers; no hookups) spread over a 255-acre causeway-linked island, this is oceanfront camping at its best. The well-managed operation has a store, a snack bar, a seasonal post office, boat rentals, boat excursions, trails,

and seven private beaches. The hub of activity (and registration) is the Kelp Shed, next to the campsite entrance. Open and wooded sites run $37-60 mid-June-Labor Day, $35 early and late in the season. Reservations for a week's stay or longer and for Memorial Day and Labor Day weekends can be made by mail beginning in early January and by phone in early February (call for the exact date). Reservations for stays of less than one week are accepted after March 1. It's open mid-May-Columbus Day, but full operation is really June-Labor Day. The campground is at the tip of the Phippsburg Peninsula. Pets are not allowed.

FOOD
Local Flavors

In Waterfront Park on Commercial Street, the **Bath Farmers Market** operates 8:30am-noon every Saturday May-October.

For breakfast, lunch, or sweets, drop into the **Starlight Café** (15 Lambard St., 207/443-3005, 7am-2pm Mon.-Fri., 8am-2pm Sat.), a too-cute and too-tiny daylight-basement space across a side street from the Customs House. It's bright and cheerful, and the food is hearty and creative.

A wonderful multifaceted find is Susan Verrier's **North Creek Farm** (24 Sebasco Rd., Phippsburg, 207/389-1341, www.northcreek-farm.org, 9am-6:30pm daily, lunch 11:30am-3:30pm daily), an 1850s saltwater farm with fabulous organic gardens, including ornamental display gardens and lots of rugosa roses (a specialty—Susan has written two books on them). Visitors can meander down by a waterfall, creek, and salt marsh. Inside the barn is a small store stocked with garden and gourmet goodies and a small café, where delicious soups and sandwiches are made to order. There are tables indoors, but there also are chairs and tables scattered in the gardens.

On the Georgetown Peninsula, **Five Islands Farm** (1375 Rte. 127, Five Islands, 297/371-9383, www.fiveislandsfarm.com) is a fine stop for picnic fixings, with an excellent assortment of Maine cheeses along with breads, meats, chips, salsa, and even wine.

Some argue that the state's best thin-crust pizza (and praiseworthy garlic knots) comes from the ovens at **The Cabin** (552 Washington St., Bath, 207/443-6224, www.cabinpizza.com, 10am-10pm Sun.-Thurs., 10am-11pm Fri.-Sat., no credit cards), a somewhat rough-and-tumble working-class joint that's been a local fave since 1973. It's across from Bath Iron Works. Avoid it during BIW shift changes (3pm-5pm Mon.-Fri.).

Barbecue

Finger-licking Memphis-style barbecue, along with other Southern specialties, is served in big quantities at **Beale Street Barbeque and Grill** (215 Water St., Bath, 207/442-9514, www.mainebbq.com, 11am-9pm Sun.-Thurs., 11am-10pm Fri.-Sat., $10-26). Everything's made on the premises. Find it next to the municipal parking lot.

Casual Dining

Kate and Andy Winglass operate **Mae's Café and Bakery** (160 Centre St. at High St., Bath,

207/442-8577, www.maescafeandbakery.com, 8am-3pm daily), a longtime local favorite bakery and café with seating indoors and on a front deck. It's *the* place to go for brunch (reservations are essential on weekends). Most choices are in the $9-13 range. Rotating art shows enliven the open and airy dining rooms.

The cool and contemporary Danish decor matches the food at **Solo Bistro** (128 Front St., Bath, 207/443-3373, www.solobistro.com, 11:30am-2pm Mon.-Sat. and 5pm-close daily, $15-28), a sophisticated storefront restaurant downtown where the choices might range from a bistro burger to miso-roasted halibut. A nightly three-course fixed-price menu is usually around $25. There's live jazz most Friday nights.

Dining with a View

All the places listed here are seasonal.

Even if you're not staying at **Sebasco Harbor Resort** (Rte. 217, Sebasco Estates, 207/389-1161 or 800/225-3819, www.sebasco.com), you can dine in either of its two waterfront restaurants, both with gasp-producing sunset views and both with children's menus. Binoculars hang by windows in the **Pilot House** (5:30pm-9pm Mon.-Sat., dinner entrées $18-32), the more formal of the two, so diners can get a better view of the boats or birds happening by. Below it is the casual **Ledges** (11:30am-2pm and 5pm-10pm daily, $8-24), with indoor and outdoor seating and a menu including sandwiches, pizzas, lobster, and comfort favorites.

A few notches above a seafood shack, **Anna's Water's Edge Restaurant** (75 Black's Landing Rd., Sebasco Estates, 207/389-1803, www.thewatersedgerestaurant.com, 11am-8:30pm daily $5-35) has serene views over island-salted Casco Bay. The menu ranges from hot dogs to lobster, with plentiful fried fish, sandwiches, and even pastas and steak. Keep it simple for the best experience.

Gaze at seals playing in the Kennebec River, Fort Popham, and out to open ocean from **Spinney's Restaurant** (987 Rte. 209, Popham Beach, 207/389-2052, www.spinneysrestaurant.com, 8am-8pm daily, entrées $12-30, sandwiches and hot dogs less). Food varies in quality from year to year. (Best advice: Keep it simple.) You can't beat the view, and you can keep it budget-friendly by coming for breakfast.

Big windows frame sigh-worthy views at **Blue,** the restaurant at the Grey Havens Inn (96 Seguinland Rd., Georgetown, 855/473-9428 or 207/371-2616, www.greyhavens.com, 5:30pm-9pm Tues.-Sun.). Tables are comfortably spaced in the wood-floored and bead-board walled and ceilinged dining room. The dinner menu emphasizes locally sourced fare and may include choices such as lobster, tournedos of beef, or vegetarian risotto, most running $20-30.

Lobster in the Rough

The rustic buoy-draped **Lobster House** (395 Small Point Rd./Rte. 216, Small Point, 207/389-1596 or 207/389-2178, www.thelobsterhouse.net, 4pm-10pm Tues.-Fri., 11:30am-10pm Sat.-Sun. late May-early Sept.) overlooks a scenic tidal cove; the view is best when the tide is in. No surprise that lobster and seafood

are featured, but sandwiches, soups, salads, pizza, and a few grilled items make the menu wallet-friendly for anyone. There's often live music on weekends.

Just over a mile beyond the turnoff to Reid State Park, you'll reach the end of Route 127 at Five Islands. Here you'll find **☾ Five Islands Lobster Company** (1447 Five Islands Rd., Five Islands, Georgetown, 207/371-2990, www.fiveislandslobster.com, 11:30am-7pm daily, weekends only spring and fall.), known for its slogan: "Eat on the dock with the fishermen, but best avoid the table by the bait-shack door." Here you can pig out on lobster rolls, better-than-usual onion rings, crab cakes, and, if you must, burgers and hot dogs. Dress down, BYOB, and enjoy the end-of-the-road ambience of this idyllic spot.

INFORMATION AND SERVICES
Visitor Information

A visitors center is located in Bath's renovated train station (restrooms available), adjacent to

Five Islands Lobster Company, near the tip of Georgetown Peninsula, is an especially idyllic spot to enjoy the tasty crustacean.

the Bath Iron Works main yard. It's open year-round with brochure racks, and staffed by volunteers May-October. Request copies of the *City of Bath Downtown Map and Guide* and the *Guide to Southern Midcoast Maine.*

Online information is available from **Main Street Bath** (www.visitbath.com), the city's website (www.cityofbath.com), and the **Southern Midcoast Chamber of Commerce** (877/725-8797, www.midcoastmaine.com).

Check out **Patten Free Library** (33 Summer St., Bath, 207/443-5141, www.patten.lib.me.us).

Find **public restrooms** at Bath City Hall (55 Front St.), Patten Free Library (33 Summer St.), Sagadahoc County Courthouse (752 High St.), the visitors center, and in summer only at Waterfront Park (Commercial St.).

GETTING THERE AND AROUND

Bath is about 10 miles or 15 minutes via Route 1 from Brunswick. It's about 12 miles or 20 minutes via Route 1 to Wiscasset, but allow up to double that in summer for congestion in Wiscasset.

The **Bath Trolley** (www.cityofbath.com) circulates through the area, with each one-way trip costing $1.

The scenic **Maine Eastern Railroad** (207/596-6725 or 800/637-2457, www.maineeasternrailroad.com) stops in Bath.

Wiscasset Area

Billing itself as "The Prettiest Village in Maine," **Wiscasset** (pop. 3,732) works hard to live up to its slogan, with quaint street signs, well-maintained homes, and an air of attentive elegance.

Wiscasset ("meeting place of three rivers"), incorporated as part of Pownalborough in 1760, has had its current name since 1802. In the late 18th century it became the shire town of Lincoln County and the largest seaport north of Boston. Countless tall-masted ships sailed the 12 miles up the Sheepscot River to tie up here, and shipyards flourished, turning out vessels for domestic and foreign trade. The 1807 Embargo Act and the War of 1812 delivered a one-two punch that shut down trade and temporarily squelched the town's aspirations, but Wiscasset yards soon were back at it, producing vessels for the pre-Civil War clipper-ship era—only to face a more lasting decline with the arrival of the railroads and the onset of the Industrial Revolution.

The Davey Bridge, built in 1983, is the most recent span over the Sheepscot. The earliest, finished in 1847, was a toll bridge that charged a horse and wagon $0.15 to cross, pedestrians $0.03 each, and pigs $0.01 apiece. Before that,

ferries carried passengers, animals, and vehicles between Wiscasset and Edgecomb's Davis Island (then named Folly Island).

Wiscasset is notorious for midsummer gridlock. Especially on weekends, traffic backs up on Route 1 for miles in both directions—to the frustration of drivers, passengers, and Wiscasset merchants. The state Department of Transportation has tested traffic medians, stoplights, and other devices, but nothing has solved the problem. A bypass has been under discussion for years, but not-in-my-backyard opposition to every route has halted progress. (When you stop in town, try to park pointed in the direction you're going; it's impossible to make turns across oncoming traffic.)

SIGHTS

In 1973 a large chunk of downtown Wiscasset was added to the National Register of Historic Places, and a walking tour is the best way to appreciate the Federal, Classical Revival, and even prerevolutionary homes and commercial buildings in the Historic District. Listed here are a few of the prime examples. See www.wiscasset.org for 28 properties listed on the National Historic Register and a walking map. If you

The Nickels-Sortwell House in Wiscasset is open for tours.

© TOM NANGLE

do nothing else, swing by the homes on High Street.

Historic Houses

Historic New England (207/882-7169, www. historicnewengland.org) owns two Wiscasset properties within easy walking distance of each other, and both are open for tours (every half hour 11am-4pm Wed.-Sun. June-mid-Oct., $5 each).

Once known as the Lee-Tucker House, **Castle Tucker** (Lee St. and High St.) was built in 1807 by Judge Silas Lee and bought by sea captain Richard Tucker in 1858. The imposing mansion has Victorian wallpaper and furnishings, Palladian windows, an amazing elliptical staircase, and a dramatic view over the Sheepscot River. In 1997, Jane Tucker, Richard's granddaughter, magnanimously deeded the house to Historic New England.

The three-story **Nickels-Sortwell House** (121 Main St.) looms over Route 1, yet it's so close to the road that many motorists miss it. Sea captain William Nickels commissioned the mansion in 1807 but died soon after its completion. For 70 or so years it was the Belle Haven Hotel before Alvin and Frances Sortwell's meticulous Colonial Revival restoration in the early 20th century.

Lincoln County Jail and Museum

Wiscasset's Old Jail (133 Federal St., Wiscasset, 207/882-6817, noon-4pm Sat.-Sun. June-mid-Oct., $5 adults, free under 16), completed in 1811, was the first prison in the District of Maine (then part of Massachusetts). Amazingly, it remained a jail—mostly for short-timers—until 1953. Two years after that the Lincoln County Historical Association took over, so each summer you can check out the 40-inch-thick granite walls, floors, and ceilings; the 12 tiny cells; and historic graffiti penned by the prisoners. Attached to the prison is the 1837 jailer's house, now the Lincoln County Museum, containing antique tools, the original kitchen, and various temporary exhibits. A Victorian gazebo overlooking the Sheepscot River is a great spot for a picnic. From Main Street (Rte. 1) in downtown Wiscasset, take Federal Street (Rte. 218) 1.2 miles.

Musical Wonder House

The treasures in the **Musical Wonder House** (18 High St., Wiscasset, 207/882-7163, www.musicalwonderhouse.com), an 1852 sea captain's mansion, are indeed astonishing, and eccentric Austrian-born museum founder Danilo Konvalinka delights in sharing them—for a price. The best way to appreciate the collection of 5,000-plus 19th-century European music boxes, player pianos, and musical rarities is to take a guided tour (available 10am-5pm Mon.-Sat., noon-5pm Sun. late May-Oct. or by appointment, $20-40), which includes up to two-dozen player-piano and music-box demonstrations.

Fort Edgecomb

Built in 1808 to protect the Sheepscot River port of Wiscasset, the **Fort Edgecomb State Historic Site** (Eddy Rd., Edgecomb, 207/882-7777, 9am-5pm daily late May-early Sept., $3 nonresident adults, $2 Maine resident adults, $1 ages 5-11) occupies a splendid three-acre riverfront spread ideal for picnicking and fishing (no swimming). Many summer weekends, the encampments on the grounds of the octagonal blockhouse make history come alive with Revolutionary reenactments, period dress, craft demonstrations, and garrison drills. It's off Route 1; take Eddy Road just north of Wiscasset Bridge and go 0.5 mile to Fort Road.

Wiscasset, Waterville, and Farmington Railway

Also historic, but a bit more lively and fun for kids, is the **Wiscasset, Waterville, and Farmington Railway** (97 Cross Rd., Sheepscot, 207/882-4193, www.wwfry.org, 9am-5pm Sat. year-round and Sun. late May-Oct.), a museum commemorating a two-foot-gauge common carrier railroad that operated in the early part of the 20th century, from Wiscasset in the south to Albion and Winslow in the north. On the grounds are a museum in the old station (free admission) and train rides along the mainline track running north from Cross Road, on the original roadbed ($7 adults, $4 children 4-12). Trains depart Sheepscot hourly 10am-3:30pm on weekends; the schedule is a bit complicated, check the website for spring and fall operation. From Route 1 in Wiscasset, take Route 218 north 4.7 miles to a four-way intersection and turn left on Cross Road to the museum.

Head Tide Village

Head Tide Village, an eminently picturesque hamlet at the farthest reach of Sheepscot River tides, is worth a detour, especially in autumn. From Wiscasset, follow Rte. 218 north for about eight miles and then turn right on Rte. 194 to find this idyllic pocket listed on the National Register of Historic Places. From the late 18th century to the early 20th, Head Tide (now part of the town of Alna) was a thriving mill town, a source of hydropower for the textile and lumber industries. All that's long gone, but hints of that era come from the handful of well-maintained 18th- and 19th-century homes in the village center.

Up the hill, the stunning 1838 **Head Tide Church,** another fine example of local prosperity, is usually open 2pm-4pm Saturday July-August. Volunteer tour guides point out the original pulpit, a trompe l'oeil window, a kerosene chandelier, and walls lined with historic Alna photographs.

Head Tide's most famous citizen was the poet **Edwin Arlington Robinson,** born here in 1869. His family home, at the bend in Route 194, is not open to the public. Perhaps his Maine roots inspired these lines from his poem "New England":

> Here where the wind is always north- northeast
> And children learn to walk on frozen toes.

Just upriver from the bend in the road is a favorite swimming hole, a millpond where you can join the locals on a hot summer day. Not much else goes on here, and there are no restaurants or lodgings, so Head Tide can't be termed a destination, but it's a village frozen in time—and an unbeatable opportunity for history buffs and shutterbugs.

FESTIVALS AND EVENTS

Wiscasset's daylong **Annual Strawberry Festival and Country Fair** (St. Philip's Episcopal Church, Hodge St., 207/882-7184) celebrates with tons of strawberries along with crafts and an auction on the last Saturday in June. The church is also the site of **Monday-night fish-chowder suppers,** mid-July-mid-August. Reservations are advised (207/882-7184) for these very popular 5:30pm suppers.

An **Art Walk** takes place 5pm-8pm the last Thursday of the month June-September.

A summer highlight at Watershed Center for the Ceramic Arts (207/882-6075, www.watershedceramics.org) is its annual **Salad Days,** a fundraising event held on a Saturday in July. For a $35 donation, you choose a handmade pottery plate, fill it from a piled-high buffet of fruit and veggie salads, and are part of an old-fashioned picnic social—and you even get to keep the plate. Afterward, there's plenty of time to explore the center's 32 acres.

SHOPPING

The oldest commercial building in town is **Wiscasset Old General Store** (Water St., Wiscasset, 207/882-6622), built in 1797 as a ship chandlery on the east side of Water Street. These days the store sells gifty items and hardware, and dishes out homemade ice cream downstairs.

Natural beauty products and bamboo clothing fill Kelley Belanger's fun shop, **In the Clover** (85A Main St., Wiscasset, 207/882-9435).

Antiques and Art

It's certainly fitting that a town filled end-to-end with antique homes should have more than two dozen solo and group antiques shops.

Right downtown, **Blythe House Antiques** (161 Main St., Wiscasset, 207/882-1280) has multiple dealers exhibiting in room settings.

French and English antiques are the specialty at **Daybreak Manor** (106 Rte. 1, Wiscasset, 207/882-9786), which also has formal gardens, a winery, and an apiary. Both fine art and antiques are sold at **French and Vandyke** (8 Federal St., Wiscasset, 207/882-8302).

European and American 19th- and 20th-century painters are the broad focus at **Wiscasset Bay Gallery** (67 Main St./Rte. 1, Wiscasset, 207/882-7682 or 888/622-9445, www.wiscassetbaygallery.com), which schedules high-quality rotating shows throughout the season.

In the handsome open spaces of an early-19th-century brick schoolhouse, the **Maine Art Gallery** (15 Warren St., Wiscasset, 207/882-7511, www.maineartgallery.org) was founded in 1954 as a nonprofit organization to showcase contemporary Maine artists.

Two miles south of town is **Avalon Antiques Market** (563 Rte. 1, Wiscasset, 207/882-4239, www.avalonantiquesmarket.com), a huge red barn of a place filled with more than 100 dealers showing on three floors.

ACCOMMODATIONS
Bed-and-Breakfasts

Named after a famous Maine clipper ship, Paul and Melanie Harris's **Snow Squall Inn** (5 Bradford Rd. at Rte. 1, Wiscasset, 207/882-6892 or 800/775-7245, www.snowsquallinn.com, $100-170) is a renovated mid-19th-century house on the edge of downtown. Inside are four lovely guest rooms and three family suites, all with phones, air-conditioning, and Wi-Fi, and two with fireplaces. Melanie is a licensed massage therapist and a *vinyasa* yoga instructor; Paul is a professionally trained chef. It's open all year, but only by reservation November-April.

Wiscasset's antiques shops are within easy walking distance of the pet-friendly **Newkirk Inn** (33 Washington St., Wiscasset, 207/522-3127, www.newkirkinn.com, $99-139), an 1870 Greek Revival with four air-conditioned guest rooms. Breakfast is continental.

Then there's **The Squire Tarbox Inn** (1181 Main Rd./Rte. 144, Westport Island, 207/882-7693 or 800/818-0626, www.

squiretarboxinn.com, mid-Apr.-Dec., $139-199), an elegantly casual bed-and-breakfast and inn that doubles as a working organic farm. Accomplished Swiss chef-owner Mario De Pietro and his wife, Roni, have continued the inn's reputation for dining excellence. Eleven rooms, some with fireplaces, are divided between the late-18th-century main house and the early-19th-century carriage house; those in the main house are more formal. Rates include breakfast, and the dining room is open to nonguests by reservation for dinner. Also on the property are walking paths, a rowboat, mountain bikes, a working pottery, and a working farm, with organic vegetable gardens, chickens, and goats. A few guest rooms are pet-friendly ($15/stay). From downtown Wiscasset, head southwest four miles on Route 1 to Route 144. Turn left and go about 8.5 scenic miles to the inn.

Step back in time at **Wabi Sabi Cottage** (111 Sheepscot Rd., Alna, 207/687-2200, www.wabisabicottage.com, $125-175), Joan Thompson's combination bed-and-breakfast, café, and antiques shop in a riverside cottage designed by the former resident architect of Colonial Williamsburg. The decor is pure 19th century, and one of the two guest rooms has back-to-back Victorian clawfoot tubs in the oversized bathroom. The café is open to the public by reservation for breakfast (7am-10:30am Tues.-Sun.), afternoon tea (1pm-3pm Wed.-Sun.), and occasionally for dinners.

Motels

Fairly close to Route 1, but buffered a bit by century-old hemlocks, is the well-maintained **Wiscasset Motor Lodge** (Rte. 1, Wiscasset, 207/882-7137 or 800/732-8168, www.wiscassetmotorlodge.com, $79-108), which has been updated over the years with pine and red oak harvested and milled on the eight-acre property. Guest rooms have phones, TVs, Wi-Fi, and air-conditioning; a light breakfast is included in summer. Ask for a room in the back building if you're sensitive to noise. Pet-friendly rooms are available.

FOOD

Across Federal Street from the Nickels-Sortwell House in downtown Wiscasset is the lovely **Sunken Garden,** an almost-unnoticed pocket park created around the cellar hole of a long-gone inn. It's a fine place for a picnic.

Local Flavors

Let's start with the obvious: **Red's Eats** (Main St. and Water St., Wiscasset, 207/882-6128, 11am-11pm Mon.-Sat., noon-6pm Sun., early May-mid-Oct.). This simple take-out stand has garnered national attention through the decades for its lobster rolls stuffed with the meat from a whole lobster. It's easy to spot because of the line. Expect to wait, perhaps for an hour or more. Is it worth it? I don't think so, but others rave about the cold lobster rolls, the fried fish, the hot dogs, and the wraps. If you're planning on one of Red's lobster rolls, ask someone who has just bought one the price before you get in line and make sure you have enough cash (no credit cards). Of course, you can skip the wait with a quick walk across Main Street to the Town Wharf, where **Sprague Lobster** (22 Main St., Wiscasset, 207/882-2306) has set up a competing stand. Many locals prefer Sprague's. Lines are rare, and the lobster rolls also contain the meat from an entire crustacean.

Back up the street, across a side road from the post office, is **Treat's** (80 Main St., Wiscasset, 207/882-6192, 10am-6pm Mon.-Sat., noon-5pm Sun.), a superb source of gourmet picnic fixings: sandwiches, soups, wine, cheese, condiments, and artisanal breads.

Family Favorites

Two miles southwest of downtown Wiscasset, **The Sea Basket Restaurant** (303 Rte. 1, Wiscasset, 207/882-6581, www.seabasket.com, 11am-8pm Wed.-Mon. Mar.-Dec., $4-22) has been serving hearty bowls of lobster stew and good-size baskets of eminently fresh seafood since 1981. The fried fish is almost healthful, thanks to convection-style frying using trans fat-free oil. Not a place to seek out, but decent on-the-road food.

In a high-visibility location across Route 1

© TOM NANGLE

Red's Eats is renowned for its lobster rolls.

from Red's Eats, **Sarah's Cafe** (Main St./Rte. 1 and Water St., Wiscasset, 207/882-7504, www.sarahscafe.com, 11am-8pm daily, $7-16) is the home of huge "whaleboat" and "dory" sandwiches, homemade soups, pizza, vegetarian specials, and an ice cream fountain. Lobster meat shows up in salads, burritos, quesadillas, wraps, croissants, and more. The deck has front-row seats on the Sheepscot River. Food is reliably mundane; the service can be sluggish and indifferent, but crayons keep kids busy.

Casual Dining

Well off the beaten path on an island connected to the mainland by a bridge is **The Squire Tarbox Inn** (1181 Main Rd./Rte. 144, Westport Island, 207/882-7693 or 800/818-0626, www.squiretarboxinn.com, dinner Wed.-Mon. mid-June-mid-Oct., Thurs.-Sat. mid-Apr.-mid-June and mid-Oct.-Dec., entrées $25-33), a working organic farm where Swiss chef Mario De Pietro serves memorable meals. The Continental entrées, such as rack of lamb, Swiss-style veal, and a fish of the day, are served in an elegantly rustic dining room. Off-season, Thursday nights

are Swiss night, with appropriate cuisine served. Ask about cooking classes.

INFORMATION AND SERVICES

The **Wiscasset Area Chamber of Commerce** (207/882-9600, www.wiscassetchamber.com) has info on members.

Check out **Wiscasset Public Library** (21 High St., Wiscasset, 207/882-7161, www.wiscasset.lib.me.us).

Find **public restrooms** on the Town Wharf, Water Street, and the Lincoln County Court House.

GETTING THERE AND AROUND

Wiscasset is about 12 miles or 20 minutes via Route 1 from Bath, but allow up to twice that in summer. It's about 13 miles or 20 minutes via Routes 1 and 27 to Boothbay Harbor. It's about 8 miles or 15 minutes via Route 1 to Damariscotta. The scenic **Maine Eastern Railroad** (207/596-6725 or 800/637-2457, www.maineeasternrailroad.com) stops in Wiscasset.

Boothbay Peninsula

East of Wiscasset, en route to Damariscotta, only a flurry of signs along Route 1 in Edgecomb hints at what's down the peninsula bisected by Route 27 and framed by the Sheepscot and Damariscotta Rivers. Drive southward down the Boothbay Peninsula Memorial Day-Labor Day and you'll find yourself in one of Maine's longest-running summer playgrounds.

The three peninsula towns of **Boothbay** (pop. 3,120), **Boothbay Harbor** (pop. 2,165), and, connected by a bridge, **Southport Island** (pop. 606) are a maze of islands and peninsulas. When Route 27 arrives at the water, having passed through Boothbay, you're at Boothbay Harbor ("the Harbor"), scene of most of the action. The harbor itself is a boat fan's dream, loaded with working craft and pleasure yachts. Ashore are shops and galleries, restaurants and inns, and one-way streets, traffic congestion, and pedestrians everywhere. But don't despair; it's easy to escape the peak-season crowds in one of the numerous parks and preserves, fine places for a hike or a picnic. Hop on an excursion boat to an offshore island, for a whale watch, or for an evening sail around the bay.

Try to save time for quieter spots: East Boothbay, Ocean Point, Southport Island, the Coastal Maine Botanical Gardens, or even just over the 1,000-foot-long footbridge stretching across one corner of the harbor. Cross the bridge and walk down Atlantic Avenue to the Fishermen's Memorial, a bronze fishing dory commemorating the loss of hardy souls who've earned a rugged living here by their wits and the sea. Across the street is Our Lady Queen of Peace Catholic Church, with shipwright-quality woodwork.

SIGHTS
Boothbay Railway Village
Boothbay Railway Village (Rte. 27, Boothbay, 207/633-4727, www.railwayvillage.org, 9:30am-5pm daily early June-mid-Oct., $10

adults, $5 ages 2-16) feels like a life-size train set. More than two dozen, old and new, exhibit-filled buildings have been assembled here since the museum was founded in 1964, and a restored narrow-gauge steam train makes a 1.5-mile, 20-minute circuit throughout the day. Also here is an exceptional collection numbering more than 50 antique cars and trucks. Train rides also operate on weekends from late May until daily opening in June and for a Halloween ride on the last weekend in October.

C Burnt Island Tour
Visit with a lighthouse keeper's family, climb the tower into the lantern room, and explore an island during a living- and natural-history program presented by the Maine Department of Marine Resources on **Burnt Island** (207/633-9559, www.maine.gov/dmr/education.htm, $22 adults, $12 under age 12). The tour is offered in July-August; call for current schedule. Travel via excursion boat from 21st-century Boothbay Harbor to Burnt Island, circa 1950, where actors portray the family of lighthouse keeper Joseph Muise, who lived here 1936-1951. During the three-hour program, you'll spend time with the light keeper, his wife, and each of his children, learning about their lifestyles and views on island life. Historical documents, photographs, and lenses, from 1821 to the present, are displayed in the 45-foot covered walkway between the house and tower. You may climb the spiral stairway up to the lantern room and see how the lighthouse actually functions. On an easy hike, a naturalist explains the island's flora, fauna, and geology and recounts legends. During free time, you may hike other trails, listen to a program on present-day lobstering and Maine fisheries, go beachcombing, fish for mackerel off the dock, or just relax and enjoy it all.

Marine Resources Aquarium
A 20-foot touch tank, with slimy but pettable

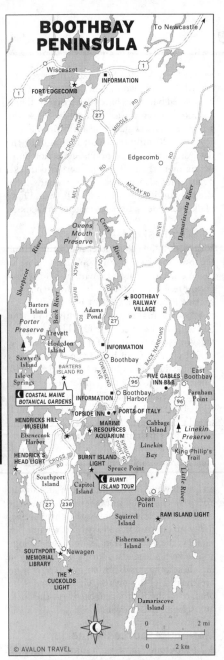

BOOTHBAY PENINSULA

To Newcastle

Wiscasset

INFORMATION

FORT EDGECOMB

Edgecomb

Damariscotta River

Ovens Mouth Preserve

Sheepscot River

Cross River

Back River

Dover River

BOOTHBAY RAILWAY VILLAGE

Adams Pond

Barters Island

Porter Preserve

Trevett

Hodgdon Island

Sawyer's Island

BARTERS ISLAND RD

INFORMATION

Boothbay

Isle of Springs

BACK NARROWS

COASTAL MAINE BOTANICAL GARDENS

INFORMATION

FIVE GABLES INN B&B

East Boothbay

Boothbay Harbor

Farnham Point

TOPSIDE INN

PORTS OF ITALY

HENDRICKS HILL MUSEUM

MARINE RESOURCES AQUARIUM

Cabbage Island

Linekin Preserve

Ebenecook Harbor

Linekin Bay

King Philip's Trail

HENDRICK'S HEAD LIGHT

BURNT ISLAND LIGHT

Spruce Point

Southport Island

Capitol Island

BURNT ISLAND TOUR

Little River

Ocean Point

Squirrel Island

RAM ISLAND LIGHT

Fisherman's Island

SOUTHPORT MEMORIAL LIBRARY

Newagen

THE CUCKOLDS LIGHT

Damariscove Island

0   2 mi

0   2 km

© AVALON TRAVEL

specimens, is a major kid magnet at the **Marine Resources Aquarium** (McKown Point Rd., West Boothbay Harbor, 207/633-9559, www. maine.gov/dmr/education.htm, 10am-5pm daily late May-early Sept., 10am-5pm Wed.-Sun. Sept., $5 adults, $3 seniors and ages 5-16), operated by the Maine Department of Marine Resources. Exhibits in the hexagonal aquarium include rare lobsters (oversize, albino, and blue) and other Gulf of Maine creatures; new residents arrive periodically. Self-guiding leaflets are available. Consider bringing a picnic—it's a great setting. At the height of summer, parking is limited, and it's a longish walk from downtown around the west side of the harbor, so plan to take the free local trolley-bus.

Southport Island

The nautical shortcut of Townsend Gut separates Boothbay Harbor from **Southport Island**. The island is ideal for a drive-about (or a pedal-about for experienced cyclists), following Route 27 south to the island's tip, returning north on Route 238. En route are plentiful glimpses of island-salted ocean waters, especially if you explore some of the side roads. Here are a few other noteworthy sights.

A historic 1810 Cape-style building, carefully restored, is the 11-room home of the **Hendricks Hill Museum** (Rte. 27, West Southport, 207/633-1102, www.hendrickshill. org, 11am-3pm Tues., Thurs., and Sat. July-Aug., donation), a community attic filled with all kinds of workaday tools and utensils and fascinating maritime memorabilia. The museum is about two miles south of the Southport Island bridge, on the right, in the center of West Southport.

From the Southport Village General Store, where you can pick up sandwiches for a picnic, decent lobster rolls, and baked goodies, among other treats, it's just a hop down Beach Road to **Hendricks Head,** with a nice sandy beach and lighthouse views.

At the island's tip is the **Southport Memorial Library** (207/633-2741, 9am-4pm and 7pm-9pm Tues. and Thurs., 9am-4pm

Sat.). Displayed inside is a huge collection of mounted butterflies.

ENTERTAINMENT

The renovated 1894 **Opera House** (86 Townsend Ave., Boothbay Harbor, 207/633-5159, www.boothbayoperahouse.com) hosts concerts, lectures, dramas, and special events.

The **Boothbay Playhouse** (275 Rte. 27, Boothbay, 207/633-3379, www.boothbayplayhouse.com, $23 adults, $19 under age 13) is a vibrant family-oriented community theater.

The **Lincoln Arts Festival** (207/633-3913, www.lincolnartsfestival.net) presents concerts—classical, pops, choral, and jazz—and other arts-related events at various locations on the Boothbay Peninsula late June-late September.

Early July-August is a great time for music in Boothbay Harbor. Free **band concerts** at 7:30pm on Thursday are performed on the Memorial Library lawn (4 Oak St.). Bring a blanket or folding chair.

Mid-June-mid-October there's live entertainment weekends at **McSeagulls** (14 Wharf St., Boothbay Harbor, 207/633-5900), which also serves decent food 11:30am-10pm daily.

Mine Oyster (16 Wharf St., 207/633-6616) does double duty: raw seafood bar and live entertainment venue, with an emphasis on dance bands.

EVENTS

The **Fishermen's Festival** is a colorful early-season celebration, held the third weekend of April, and includes the Miss Shrimp Princess pageant, a lobster-crate race, plentiful seafood and chowder, contests such as trap hauling, scallop and clam shucking, fish filleting, and net mending (plus a real steal—a lobster-eating contest you can enter for about $5), and the blessing of the fleet to ensure a successful summer season.

June is the month for **Windjammer Days,** two days of festivities centering on traditional windjammer schooners. Highlights are the Windjammer Parade, harbor-front concerts, plenty of food, and a fireworks extravaganza.

In early August the **Boat Builders Festival** features shipyard and boat tours, food, and kids' activities.

RECREATION
Parks and Preserves
BOOTHBAY REGION LAND TRUST

The **Boothbay Region Land Trust** (137 Townsend Ave., Boothbay Harbor, 207/633-4818, www.bbrlt.org) has preserved more than 1,700 acres, including six islands, with more than 30 miles of trails available. Individual preserve maps as well as a general brochure-map with driving directions are available at the information centers, the trust office, and at trailhead kiosks. The trust also offers a free series of summertime guided walks and paddles in the various preserves along with talks. A free guide, available at local businesses and info centers, provides details and access points. Here's just a sampling of the possibilities.

Most popular is the **Porter Preserve,** a 19-acre property bordering the Sheepscot River. Follow the moderately easy 0.86-mile loop trail and be rewarded with spectacular views, especially at sunset. You might even spy some seals lolling in the ledges at low tide. To get there, take Route 27 south to the monument in Boothbay Center. Bear right on Cory Lane and go 0.3 mile, bearing right again on Barters Island Road for 12.2 miles (perhaps stopping at the Trevett Country Store for lobster rolls or subs to go). Turn left on Kimballtown Road, for 0.5 mile, then left at the fork onto Porter Point Road. Park in the small lot just beyond the cemetery.

The 146-acre **Ovens Mouth Preserve** has almost five miles of trails on two peninsulas linked by a 93-foot bridge. The 1.6-mile trail on the east peninsula is much easier than the 3.7 miles of trails on the west peninsula. To get there, from the monument in Boothbay Center, travel 1.7 miles north and then go left on Adams Pond Road. Bear right at the fork and then continue 2.2 miles. To get to the east peninsula, bear right at the junction onto the Dover Road Extension. Proceed to the end of the tarred road to the parking lot on the left.

To get to the west peninsula, bear left at the junction and continue 0.15 mile to the parking area on the right.

In East Boothbay, on the way to Ocean Point, is the 94.6-acre **Linekin Preserve,** stretching from Route 96 to the Damariscotta River. The 2.3-mile white-blazed River Loop (best done clockwise) takes in an old sawmill site, a beaver dam, and great riverfront views. You'll meet a couple of moderately steep sections on the eastern side, near the river, but otherwise it's relatively easy. To get there, take Route 96 for 3.8 miles and look for the parking area and trailhead on the left.

KNICKERCANE ISLAND

This gem is ideal for a picnic, perhaps with a lobster roll from the Trevett Country Store. The island is connected via a bridge, making it a pleasant place to stroll or, if you're brave, swim. Also here is an honest-to-God lobster pound (no, not the kind that serves the tasty crustaceans, but rather the impoundment area for them). The island is off the Barters Island Road causeway. To find it, from Boothbay Center follow signs for the Coastal Maine Botanical Center, then continue until you come to open water on both sides of the road; the parking area is on the left.

BARRETT PARK

On the east side of the harbor, Barrett Park is an oceanfront park on Linekin Bay, with shade trees, picnic tables, swimming, and restrooms. To find it, take Atlantic Avenue and turn left on Lobster Cove Road (at the Catholic church).

◖ Coastal Maine Botanical Gardens

The shorefront **Coastal Maine Botanical Gardens** (Barters Island Rd., Boothbay, 207/633-4333, www.mainegardens.org, 9am-5pm daily year-round, $14 adults, $12 seniors, $6 ages 3-17) are masterful and magical, yet still in their youth. The nonprofit project, designed to preserve more than 125 acres of woodlands with a trail network and landscaped pocket "theme" gardens, has

grown to encompass 250 acres, with formal gardens, paths, herb and kitchen gardens, woods walks, a fairy village, a five-senses garden, and nearly a mile of waterfront. Artwork is placed throughout. A magical children's garden encourages imagination, play, and discovery in a setting drawing from Maine-related children's literature such as *Blueberries for Sal* and *Miss Rumphius*. The visitors center has an excellent café (9am-3pm May 1-Oct. 15), a library, and a gift shop. Pick up a map and explore your own, or join a free docent-led tour (11am and 1pm Thurs. and Sat.). Allow at least two hours, although you could easily spend a full day here. Other garden activities include lectures, the Maine Fairy House Festival, and a Kitchen Garden Dinner series. Entrance to the preserve is on Barters Island Road, about 1.3 miles west of Boothbay Center.

Boat Excursions

Two major fleet operators provide practically every type of sea adventure imaginable. Boothbay Harbor's veteran excursion fleet is **Cap'n Fish's Cruises** (Pier 1, Wharf St., Boothbay Harbor, 207/633-3244 or 800/636-3244, www.boothbayboattrips.com, $19-30 adults, $10-15 children). Cap'n Fish's 150-passenger boats do nine varied, mostly 2-3-hour cruises. There is bound to be a tour length and itinerary (seal-watching, lobster-trap hauling, lighthouses, Damariscove Harbor, puffin cruises, and more) that piques your interest. Pick up a schedule at one of the information centers and call for reservations.

The harbor's other big fleet is **Balmy Days Cruises** (Pier 8, Commercial St., Boothbay Harbor, 207/633-2284 or 800/298-2284, www.balmydayscruises.com), operating three vessels on a variety of excursions. The *Novelty* does daily one-hour harbor tours (late June-Labor Day, $16 adults, $8 ages 3-11). Reservations usually are not necessary. The 31-foot Friendship sloop *Bay Lady* offers 90-minute sailing trips ($24 adults, $18 children) daily in summer. Reservations are wise for the *Bay Lady* as well as for the fleet's most popular cruise, a

DAMARISCOVE ISLAND

Summering Wabanakis knew it as Aquahega, but Damerill's Cove was the first European name attributed to the secure, fjord-like harbor at the southern tip of 210-acre Damariscove Island in 1614, when Captain John Smith of the Jamestown Colony explored the neighborhood. By 1622, Damerill's Cove fishermen were sharing their considerable codfish catch with starving Plimoth Plantation colonists desperate for food. Fishing and farming sustained resident Damariscovers during their up-and-down history, and archaeologists have found rich deposits for tracing the story of this early island settlement about seven miles south of Boothbay Harbor.

Rumors persist that the ghost of Captain Richard Pattishall, decapitated and tossed overboard by Indians in 1689, still roams the island, accompanied by the specter of his dog. The fog that often overhangs the bleak, almost-treeless low-slung island makes it easy to fall for the many ghost stories about Pattishall and other onetime residents. In summer, the island is awash with wildflowers, bayberries, raspberries, blackberries, and rugosa roses.

Since 2005, most of 1.7-mile-long Damariscove has been owned by **The Boothbay Region Land Trust** (1 Oak St., 2nd Fl., Boothbay Harbor, 207/633-44818, www.bbrlt.org). Day-use visitors are welcome on the island anytime, but the northern section (called Wood End) protects the state's largest nesting colony of eiders—nearly 700 nests. Damariscove Island became a National Historic Landmark in 1978. Dogs are not allowed.

Access to the island is most convenient if you have your own boat. Enter the narrow cove at the southern end of the island. You can disembark at the dock on the west side of the harbor, but don't tie up here or at the adjacent stone pier. Two guest moorings and two courtesy dinghies are available. The Boothbay Region Land Trust sometimes offers special trips. Summertime caretakers live in the small cabin above the dock, where a trail map is available. Stay on the trail (watch out for poison ivy) or on the shore and away from any abandoned structures; the former Coast Guard station is privately owned.

daylong trip to Monhegan Island ($34 adults, $18 children) on the *Balmy Days II,* departing at 9:30am and returning at 4:15pm daily early June-late September, plus extended weekends in late May and early October. The three-hour round-trip allows about 3.5 hours ashore on idyllic Monhegan Island.

Sailing

A trip aboard *Schooner Eastwind,* a 65-foot traditional wooden schooner built in 2004, with **Appledore Cruises** (20 Commercial St., Boothbay Harbor, 207/633-6598, www.schoonereastwind.com, $30) is more than a day sail—it's an adventure. Herb and Doris Smith not only built this schooner, but have sailed around the world in their previous boats through the years, providing fodder for many tales. They take passengers on 2.5-hour cruises to the outer islands and Seal Rocks

up to four times daily. The boat departs from Fisherman's Wharf.

Whale-Watching and Puffin-Watching

Variations in Gulf of Maine whale-migration patterns have added whale-watching to the list of Boothbay Harbor boating options as the massive mammals travel northeastward within reasonable boating distance. **Cap'n Fish's** (Pier 1, Wharf St., Boothbay Harbor, 207/633-3244 or 800/636-3244, www.mainewhales.com) is the best choice. Three-four-hour trips depart daily mid-June-mid-October. Tours cost $48 adults, $32 ages 11-16, $25 ages 6-10, with a rain check if the whales don't show up. Reservations are advisable, especially early and late in the season and on summer weekends. No matter what the weather on shore, dress warmly and carry more clothing than

© HILARY NANGLE

Find great shopping, dining, and boating excursions at Boothbay Harbor.

you think you'll need. Motion-sensitive children and adults need to plan ahead with appropriate medication.

Cap'n Fish's also runs 2.5-hour puffin-sighting tours to Easter Egg Rock, circling the island once or twice for the best views. Cruises are offered once weekly in June, then three times weekly in July–late August, for $29 adults, $15 children.

Sea Kayaking

From Memorial Day weekend through September, **Tidal Transit** (18 Granary Way, Chowder House Building, Boothbay Harbor, 207/633-7140, www.kayakboothbay.com), near the footbridge, will get you afloat with 2-3-hour guided lighthouse, wildlife, or sunset tours for around $50; full and multiday tours are available too. No experience is necessary. Reservations are required. For do-it-yourselfers, Tidal Transit rents single kayaks ($20 one hour, $55/day) and tandems ($30 one hour, $75/day); other time options are available.

SHOPPING

Artisans' galleries pepper the peninsula. Galleries, boutiques, and novelty shops crowd Boothbay Harbor, providing plenty of browsing for all budgets and tastes. Here are a few worth seeking out.

A visit to the **Villard Gallery** (57 Campbell St., Boothbay Harbor, 207/633-3507, www. villardstudios.com) is a must for fans of fine-art crafts. Kim and Philippe Villard split their lives between Boothbay Harbor and southern France, where they live in an abandoned village in the midst of a national park. Philippe is a talented sculptor, and Kim is an equally talented painter. They collaborate on woodcuts and handmade books, and the results are in collections and museums. Call in advance if you want a demonstration of the process. They have works in all price ranges, from poster prints to the actual woodblocks themselves.

Antiques store or museum, you decide. The **Palabra Shop** (53 Commercial St., Boothbay Harbor, 207/633-4225) has 10 rooms chock-full of antiques and collectibles. It's also home to the world's largest collection of Moses bottles, viewable by appointment.

One of the state's best fine-art galleries, **Gleason Fine Art** (31 Townsend Ave., Boothbay Harbor, 207/633-6849, www.gleasonfineart.com) specializes in Maine art from the 19th-21st centuries. The gallery is light, bright, and a pleasure to browse. Even if you have no interest in buying, stop in to see works by some of Maine's top talents.

At **Eventide Epicurean Specialties** (5 Boothbay House Hill, Boothbay Harbor, 207/350-4244), you can taste your way through dozens of olive oils and balsamic vinegars, and pick up other gourmet items.

ACCOMMODATIONS

If you want to concentrate your time in downtown Boothbay Harbor, shopping or taking boat excursions, stay in town and avoid the parking hassles. Although the town practically rolls up the sidewalks in the winter, a few businesses do stay open year-round. Lodgings that do so are noted; others are seasonal, usually mid-May-mid-October.

Classic Inns

To get away from it all, book in at the **Newagen Seaside Inn** (Rte. 27, Southport, 207/633-5242 or 800/654-5242 outside Maine, www.newagenseasideinn.com, mid-May-Sept., $189-305), an unstuffy full-service inn with casual fine dining and views that go on forever. Renovated guest rooms are split among the Main Inn; the Little Inn, where rooms have private decks, TVs, and kitchenettes; and seven cottages. There's a long rocky shore, a nature trail, and a spa, plus tennis courts, a pool and hot tub, cruiser bikes, guest rowboats, a game room, candlepin bowling, and porches just for relaxing. Rates include a generous buffet breakfast. The dining room is open to nonguests by reservation for dinner 5:30pm-9pm daily; entrées run $16-28. The inn is six miles south of downtown Boothbay Harbor.

Over in East Boothbay, the **Ocean Point Inn** (Shore Rd., East Boothbay, 207/633-4200 or 800/552-5554, www.oceanpointinn.com,

$99-299) wows with spectacular sunset views and an easygoing ambience that keeps guests returning generation after generation. The sprawling complex includes eclectic lodgings: an inn, a lodge, a motel, apartments, and cottages. Most guest rooms have ocean views; all have mini-fridges, phones, cable TV, Wi-Fi, and air-conditioning; some have kitchenettes. The rates, which include a light continental breakfast, reflect that this is an older property, and some accommodations are tired; updating is in progress. Also on the premises are a restaurant and tavern with fabulous ocean views, a pier, an outdoor heated pool, a hot tub, and Adirondack-style chairs set just so on the water's edge. The best deals are the packages.

For those who require luxury touches, the **Spruce Point Inn and Spa** (Atlantic Ave., Boothbay Harbor, 207/633-4152 or 800/553-0289, www.sprucepointinn.com) is the answer. Accommodations are traditional inn rooms and cottages and condos, all with private decks, mini-fridges, and TVs; some have fireplaces, kitchenettes, and whirlpool tubs. Decor and prices vary widely. The inn holds big weddings on many weekends, so try for midweek. Rates begin around $300. Amenities at the 57-acre resort include a full-service spa and fitness center, freshwater and saltwater pools, tennis courts, rocky shorefront, and a shuttle bus to downtown (about 1.5 miles, although it seems farther). Children's programs are available. Dining choices range from poolside to pub-style to fine dining, with prices to match each setting.

Here's a real throwback. **Linekin Bay Resort** (92 Wall Point Rd., Boothbay Harbor, 207/633-2494 or 866/847-2103, www.linekinbayresort.com), which occupies 20 wooded oceanfront acres, began operating in 1919 as a summer camp for girls. Don't be fooled by the term *resort*. The accommodations, in five lodges and 35 cottages, are dated, worn, and camp-style rustic, although all have private baths (some detached), heating and fans, Wi-Fi, and private decks or porches. So why consider it? Summer season rates ($155-190/adults, $50-115/children, plus 10 percent amenity fee) include lodging, all meals, recreational programs,

MID-COAST REGION

kids' camp, sailing instruction, and use of the tennis courts, outdoor saltwater pool, sailboats, canoes, and kayaks. There's even a weekly lobster bake. Pet-friendly accommodations are available, $40/stay.

Bed-and-Breakfasts

Topping an in-town hill with sigh-producing views over the inner and outer harbors and yet just a two-minute walk to shops and restaurants is **Topside Inn** (60 McKown St., Boothbay Harbor, 207/633-5404 or 888/633-5404, www.topsideinn.com, from $185), a solid 19th-century sea captain's home with two annexes. Innkeepers Brian Lamb and Ed McDermott have completely renovated the three-building complex with an emphasis on comfort. Guest rooms in the three-story main inn are mostly spacious with nice views. Good books are everywhere, and the rockers on the wraparound porch and Adirondack chairs on the lawn are perfect places to read or relax. The annexes have motel-type guest rooms done in bed-and-breakfast style; all have decks and most

have at least glimpses of the ocean. All guest rooms have flat-screen TVs and Wi-Fi. Rates in all buildings include breakfast: a self-serve cold buffet with a hot entrée that's served to the table. Hot beverages are available all day; on most afternoons home-baked cookies magically appear in the living room or guest pantry.

Next door is **The Harbor House** (80 McKown St., Boothbay Harbor, 800/856-1164, www.harborhouse-me.com, $45-195), a mansard-roofed house with six rooms (one pet-friendly, one with detached bath) and a great wraparound porch. Breakfast is a buffet, with a hot entrée. Some rooms have great water views.

In town and on the water, the **Blue Heron Seaside Inn** (65 Townsend Ave., Boothbay Harbor, 207/633-7020 or 866/216-2300, www.blueheronseasideinn.com, year-round, $240-275) opened in 2003 after a complete restoration. The uncluttered, bright interior belies the Victorian vintage. Large guest rooms are accented with antiques and collectibles from Boothbay natives Phil and Laura Chapman's years overseas. Each room has a waterfront

The Blue Heron Seaside Inn is within steps of the harbor and downtown shops.

© HILARY NANGLE

deck, air-conditioning, a fridge, a microwave, an LCD HDTV, Wi-Fi, and a phone; some also have a fireplace and a whirlpool tub. A dock with kayaks and a paddleboat is available. A full breakfast is elegantly served on Wedgwood china.

On the east side of the harbor, up a side street but within walking distance of in-town shops and restaurants, is Mary Huntington's **Pond House** (7 Bay St., Boothbay Harbor, 207/633-5842, www.pondhousemaine.com, $90-120). The 1920s barn-red home is just one block off the harbor, surrounded by beautiful gardens and edging a pond. The five guest rooms, some with shared or detached baths, have beautiful oak woodwork and are decorated with a mix of antiques and country pieces, including quilts topping most beds. Rotating artwork covers the walls, and studio space is available to visiting artists. Wi-Fi is accessible throughout the inn. Mary's breakfasts are legendary.

Escape the hustle and bustle of Boothbay Harbor at the **❰ Five Gables Inn B&B** (107 Murray Hill Rd., East Boothbay, 207/633-4551 or 800/451-5048, www.fivegablesinn.com, $165-245), which began life as a no-frills summer hotel in the late 19th century. It's gone steadily upmarket since then. Unique touches include wonderful murals throughout and window seats in the gable rooms. All but one of the 16 light and airy guest rooms have Linekin Bay views, and some have fireplaces. The living room is congenial, the gardens are gorgeous, and the porch goes on forever. Rates include a multicourse breakfast and afternoon treats. The inn, on a side road off Route 96 in the traditional boatbuilding hamlet of East Boothbay, is 3.5 miles from downtown Boothbay Harbor. Arriving by boat? One mooring is available for guests.

Another peaceful retreat from the madding crowds is found at **The Hodgdon Island Inn** (374 Barters Island Rd., Boothbay, 800/633-7474, www.boothbaybb.com, $159-225). Richard and Pam Riley have given new life to this early-19th-century home with an Italianate addition, creating an especially comfy oasis, complete with heated outdoor pool and

Adirondack chairs on the waterfront. Niceties include robes, evening desserts, and in-room refrigerators. All rooms have water views, and some have flat-screen TVs, whirlpool tubs, or electric fireplaces. Breakfast will more than fuel you for a day of exploring the nearby preserves or botanical garden.

Quiet, private, and out of another era, **Sprucewold Lodge** (4 Nahanada Rd., Boothbay Harbor, 800/732-9778, www.sprucewoldlodge.com, $117-125) is reputed to be the largest existing log structure east of the Mississippi. The hand-hewn lodge with a covered porch was built in the 1920s. Inside are vintage, no-frills guest rooms along with a living room anchored by a huge stone fireplace. An expansive hot-and-cold buffet breakfast is served in the dining lodge at large communal tables; dinner is often also available. Also here are a massive stone fireplace, games, and the property's only TV. General manager Richard Pizer goes all out to make guests welcome. One consideration: The lodge is popular with tour groups.

Motels and Hotels

Five in-town harbor-front buildings, including one on a pier built over the ocean, are the big draws for the **Tugboat Inn** (80 Commercial St., Boothbay Harbor, 800/248-2628, www.tugboatinn.com, $165-280), part of a complex that includes a marina and restaurant. Decor is vintage motel. All rooms have TV, Wi-Fi, and air-conditioning; some have kitchens. Rates include a continental breakfast, and kids under 12 stay free.

Since 1955 the Lewis family has owned and operated the **Mid-Town Motel** (96 McKown St., Boothbay Harbor, 207/633-2751, www.midtownmaine.com, $95), a spotless, no-frills vintage motel that's within steps of everything. It's a classic: clean, convenient, and relatively cheap, and the owners couldn't be nicer folks.

Every room at the lakefront **Beach Cove Hotel & Resort** (38 Lakeview Rd., Boothbay Harbor, 207/633-0353 or 866/851-0450, www.beachcovehotel.com, $99-220) has a water view, a balcony or deck, air-conditioning, Wi-Fi, a mini-fridge, and a microwave. The renovated property, about one mile from downtown, is extremely popular with families who appreciate its beach, dock, heated saltwater pool, canoes, and rowboats. A light continental breakfast is included.

Camping

With 150 well-maintained wooded and open sites on 45 acres, **Shore Hills Campground** (Rte. 27, Boothbay, 207/633-4782, www. shorehills.com, $29-52) is a popular big-rig destination where reservations are essential in midsummer. Tenters should request a wooded site away from the biggest RVs. Leashed pets are allowed. Facilities include a laundry and free use of canoes.

Much smaller and smack on the ocean is the **Gray Homestead Oceanfront Camping** (21 Homestead Rd., Southport, 207/633-4612, www.graysoceancamping.com, $37-50), a family-run campground with 40 RV and tenting sites as well as cottages and condos. A stone beach, a pier, laundry facilities, kayak rentals, and lobsters—live or cooked—are available. There's even a small sandy beach.

FOOD
Local Flavors

Three general stores deliver local flavors with some fancy touches. It's worth the drive over to Trevett to indulge in a lobster roll from the **Trevett Country Store** (207/633-1140), just before the bridge connecting Hodgdon and Barters Islands.

"Free beer tomorrow" proclaims the sign in front of **Bet's Famous Fish Fry** (Village Common, Rte. 27, Boothbay), a take-out stand that's renowned for its very generous portions of fresh haddock fish-and-chips. Picnic tables are available. Stop into the **Southport General Store** (443 Hendricks Hill Rd., 207/633-6666), serving Southport Island since 1882, for breakfast, pizzas, sandwiches, baked goods, and a decent wine selection. On the east side, the **East Boothbay General Store** (255 Ocean Point Rd./Rte. 96, East Boothbay, 207/633-4503) has been

serving locals since 1893. These days, it sells wine and specialty foods in addition to pizzas, sandwiches, and baked goods.

The seasonal **Boothbay Area Farmers Market** sets up on the Town Commons, Boothbay, 9am-noon Thursday.

Doughnuts and pho? Must be **Baker's Way** (90 Townsend Ave., Boothbay Harbor, 207/633-1119, 6am-9pm daily). Known locally as The Doughnut Shop, this hole-in-the-wall turns out the unusual combo of excellent baked goods and Vietnamese food. The breakfast sandwiches are good, and the sticky buns are renowned not only for their size but for their taste. After 11:30am, Vietnamese dishes are available, most for less than $10. Whereas the inside dining area is purely functional, there's also seating in a pleasant backyard garden with harbor views.

Daily tours with tastings ($5) are available at the **Boothbay Craft Brewery** (301 Adams Pond Rd., Boothbay, 207/633-3411, www. boothbaycraftbrewery.com). Reliably good and reasonably priced breakfasts and lunches are turned out by **D'Ellie's** (Pier 1, Boothbay Harbor, 207/633-0277, 9am-3pm daily). Sandwiches come in full and half sizes on a choice of homemade breads.

Another locals' favorite serving breakfast, lunch, and dinner is the unassuming **Ebb Tide Restaurant** (43 Commercial St., Boothbay Harbor, 207/633-5692, 7am-9pm daily). Booths line the tiny pine-paneled dining area where decent homestyle cooking is served. Look for the red-and-white awning.

Casual Dining

Real Northern Italian fare prepared by a real Italian chef is the lure for **❰ Ports of Italy** (47 Commercial St., Boothbay Harbor, 207/633-1011, www.portsofitaly.com, 4:30pm-9:30pm daily, $20-32). Owner Sante Calandri hails from Perugia but more recently spent 23 years in New York City. This isn't a red-sauce place; expect well-prepared and innovative fare, with delicious homemade pastas and especially good seafood.

© HILARY NANGLE

The fish is fresh and the portions are huge at Bet's Famous Fish Fry in Boothbay.

The Watershed Tavern (301 Adams Pond Rd., Boothbay, 207/633-3411 11am-8:30pm Tues.-Sat., www.watershedtavern.com, $10-15), at the Boothbay Craft Brewery, serves panini, burgers, wood-oven pizzas, and small plates.

For spectacular sunset views, take a spin out to the **Ocean Point Inn** (Shore Rd., East Boothbay, 207/633-4200 or 800/552-5554, www.oceanpointinn.com, 7:30am-10am and 6pm-8:30pm daily, $10-30). The lobster stew is rave-worthy, and a children's menu is available.

The tapas menu complements the views from the third-floor deck at **Boat House Bistro** (12 The By-Way, Boothbay Harbor, 207/633-0400, www.theboathousebistro.com, 11:30am-10pm daily). There are plenty of other options, but the tapas, pizzas, soups, and salads ($3-15) are the way to go.

Lobster in the Rough

Boothbay Harbor and East Boothbay seem to have more eat-on-the-dock lobster shacks per square inch than almost anywhere else on the coast, but frankly they're all overcrowded, overpriced, and don't deliver an authentic experience.

The best of the in-town lot is **The Lobster Dock** (49 Atlantic Ave., Boothbay Harbor, 207/635-7120, www.thelobsterdock.com, 11:30am-8:30pm daily), where lobsters are delivered twice daily; now, that's fresh. Although there are a few choices for landlubbers—even PBJ for kids—lobster and fish are the prime attraction. It's right on the harbor, so the views are superb.

Far more authentic and well worth the splurge is **Cabbage Island Clambakes** (Pier 6, Fisherman's Wharf, Boothbay Harbor, 207/633-7200, www.cabbageislandclambakes. com). Touristy, sure, but it's a delicious adventure. Board the excursion boat *Bennie Alice* at Pier 6 in Boothbay Harbor, cruise for about an hour past islands, boats, and lighthouses, and disembark at 5.5-acre Cabbage Island. Watch the clambake in progress, explore the island, or play volleyball. When the feast is ready, pick up your platter, find a picnic table, and dig in.

A cash bar is available in the lodge, as are restrooms. When the weather's iffy, the lodge and covered patio have seats for 100 people. For about $60 (no credit cards), you'll get two lobsters (or half a chicken), chowder, clams, corn, an egg, onions, potatoes, blueberry cake, a beverage, and the boat ride. Clambake season is mid-June-mid-September. The 3.5-hour trips depart at 12:30pm Monday-Friday, 12:30pm and 5pm Saturday, and 11am and 1:30pm Sunday.

INFORMATION AND SERVICES

Providing info about their members are the **Boothbay Harbor Region Chamber of Commerce** (207/633-2353, www.boothbayharbor.com) and the **Boothbay Chamber of Commerce** (207/633-4743, www.boothbay.org).

Check out **Boothbay Harbor Memorial Library** (4 Oak St., Boothbay Harbor, 207/633-3112, www.bmpl.lib.me.us). Thursday evenings in July-August there are band concerts on the lawn.

Find **public restrooms** at the municipal parking lot on Commercial Street (next to Pier 1), the municipal lot at the end of Granary Way, Saint Andrews Hospital, the town offices, the library, and the Marine Resources Aquarium.

GETTING THERE AND AROUND

Boothbay Harbor is about 13 miles or 20 minutes via Routes 1 and 27 from Wiscasset. It's about 15 miles or 35 minutes to Damariscotta via Routes 27 and 1.

The Rocktide Inn operates free trolleybuses on continuous scheduled routes during the summer.

The scenic **Maine Eastern Railroad** (207/596-6725 or 800/637-2457, www.maineeasternrailroad.com) operates between Brunswick and Rockland and connects with the Amtrak Downeaster. A shuttlebus connects Wiscasset to Boothbay for $8/4.

Pemaquid Region

At the head of the Pemaquid Peninsula, the riverfront towns of **Damariscotta** (pop. 2,218) and her conjoined twin, **Newcastle** (pop. 1,752), anchor the southwestern end of the Pemaquid Peninsula; **Waldoboro** (pop. 5,075) anchors the northeastern end. Along the peninsula are **New Harbor** (probably Maine's most photographed fishing village), **Pemaquid Point** (site of one of Maine's most photographed lighthouses), and historic ports reputedly used by Captain John Smith, Captain Kidd, and assorted less-notorious types. Here too are a restored fortress, Native American historic sites, antiques and crafts shops galore, boat excursions to offshore Monhegan, and one of the best pocket-size sandy beaches in Mid-Coast Maine.

On Christmas Day 1614, famed explorer Captain John Smith anchored on Rutherford Island, at the tip of the peninsula, and promptly named the spot Christmas Cove. Today it is one of three villages that make up the town of South Bristol, the southwestern finger of the Pemaquid Peninsula. **Bristol** (pop. 2,755) and **South Bristol** (pop. 892), covering eight villages on the bottom half of the peninsula, were named after the British port city.

As early as 1625, settler John Brown received title to some of this territory from the Wabanaki sachem (chief) Samoset, an agreeable fellow who learned snippets of English from English cod fishermen. *Damariscotta* (dam-uh-riss-COT-ta), in fact, is a Wabanaki word for "plenty of alewives [herring]." The settlement here was named Walpole but was incorporated in 1847 under its current name.

Newcastle, incorporated in 1763, earned fame and fortune from shipbuilding and brickmaking—which explains the extraordinary number of brick homes and office buildings

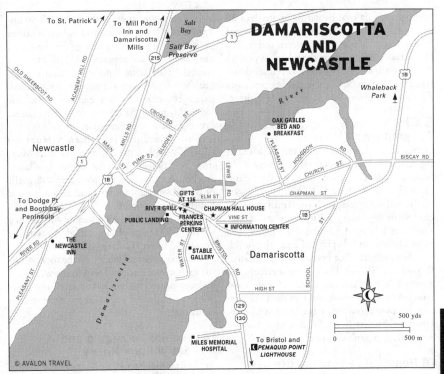

DAMARISCOTTA
AND
NEWCASTLE

© AVALON TRAVEL

throughout the town. In the 19th century, Newcastle's shipyards sent clippers, Down Easters, and full-rigged ships down the ways and around the world.

Route 1 cuts a commercial swath through Waldoboro without revealing the attractive downtown—or the lovely Friendship Peninsula, south of the highway. Duck into Waldoboro and then follow Route 220 south 10 miles to Friendship for an off-the-beaten-track drive.

Waldoboro's heritage is something of an anomaly in Maine. It's predominantly German, thanks to 18th-century Teutons who swallowed the blandishments of General Samuel Waldo, holder of a million-acre "patent" stretching as far as the Penobscot River. In the cemetery at the Old German Church, on Route 32, the inscription on a 19th-century marker sums up the town's early history:

> This town was settled in 1748, by Germans who emigrated to this place with the promise and expectation of finding a populous city, instead of which they found nothing but a wilderness; for the first few years they suffered to a great extent by Indian wars and starvation. By perseverance and self-denial, they succeeded in clearing lands and erecting mills. At this time [1855] a large proportion of the inhabitants are descendants of the first settlers.

It sure makes you wonder why Waldo's name stuck to the town.

After the mill era, the settlers went into shipbuilding in a big way, establishing six shipyards and producing more than 300 wooden vessels, including the first five-masted schooner, the 265-foot *Governor Ames,* launched in 1888. Although the *Ames's* ill-supported masts collapsed on her maiden voyage, repairs allowed her to serve as a coal hauler for more than 20 years, and many more five-masters followed in her wake. It's hard to believe today, but Waldoboro once was the sixth-busiest port in the United States. At the Town Landing, alongside the Medomak River, a marker describes the town's shipyards and shipbuilding heritage.

SIGHTS
Chapman-Hall House

Damariscotta's oldest surviving building is the Cape-style **Chapman-Hall House** (270 Main St., Damariscotta, noon-4pm Sat.-Sun. early June-mid-Oct., $5), built in 1754 by Nathaniel Chapman, whose family tree includes the legendary John Chapman, better known as Johnny Appleseed. Highlights are a 1754 kitchen and displays of local shipbuilding memorabilia. The house, on the National Register of Historic Places, was meticulously restored in the styles of three different eras. Don't miss the antique roses in the back garden. It's now cared for by the Lincoln County Historical Society (www.lincolncountyhistory. org), which organizes docent-led tours.

◖ Pemaquid Point Lighthouse

One of the icons of the Maine Coast, Pemaquid Point's lighthouse has been captured for posterity by gazillions of photographers and is depicted on a Maine state quarter. The lighthouse, adjacent keeper's house, and picnic grounds are a town park. Also on the premises is an art gallery. Admission to the grounds, payable at the gatehouse, is $2 age 12 and older. The lighthouse grounds are accessible all year, even after the museum closes for the season, when admission is free. The point is 15 miles south of Route 1 via winding two-lane Route 130.

Commissioned in 1827, **Pemaquid Point Light** (www.lighthousefoundation.org) stands sentinel over some of Maine's nastiest shoreline—rocks and surf that can reduce any wooden boat to kindling. Now automated, the light tower is licensed to the American Lighthouse Foundation and is managed by the Friends of Pemaquid Point Lighthouse.

Volunteers *aim* to open the tower 10:30am-5pm daily late May-mid-October, weather permitting. There is no charge for the tower, but donations are appreciated. Still can't get enough? Newcastle Square Vacation Rentals (207/563-6500, www.mainecoastcottages.com) manages a one-bedroom apartment available for weekly rental ($1,200) in the keeper's house. Proceeds benefit preservation.

The adjacent **Fisherman's Museum** (207/677-2494, 9am-5pm daily mid-May-mid-Oct., donation), in the former light keeper's house, points up the pleasures and perils of the lobstering industry and also has some lighthouse memorabilia.

While here, visit the **Pemaquid Art Gallery** (207/677-2752), displaying juried works by the Pemaquid Group of Artists since 1928.

Bring a picnic and lounge on the rocks below the light tower, but don't plan to snooze. You'll be busy protecting your food from the dive-bombing gulls and your kids from the treacherous surf.

◖ Colonial Pemaquid and Fort William Henry

At the **Colonial Pemaquid State Historic Site** (end of Huddle Rd., 207/677-2423, friendsof-colonialpemaquid.org, 9am-6pm daily late May-early Sept., $3 nonresident adults, $2 Maine resident adults, $1 ages 5-11), signed from Route 130 in New Harbor, visitors can gain a basic understanding of what life was like in an English frontier settlement. The 19-acre complex, listed on the National Register of Historic Places, comprises a museum-visitors center, Fort William Henry, the Fort House, the remnants of a village, an 18th-century cemetery, a picnic area, a pier and boat ramp, and restrooms, all spread out on a grassy point sloping to John's Bay and bordered by McCaffrey's Brook, the Pemaquid River, and Pemaquid Harbor. Bring a picnic, bring a kite, bring a kayak, let the kids run—but do take time to visit the historic sites (a kids' activity book is available for $1). Demonstrations, tours, lectures, and reenactments are part of the site's summer schedule.

Three national flags fly over the ramparts of **Fort William Henry,** a reconstruction of a fort dating from 1692, the second of three that stood here between 1677 and the late 18th century. The forts were built to defend the English settlement of Pemaquid, settled between 1625 and 1628, from the French. From the rebuilt western tower, you'll have fantastic views of John's Bay and John's Island, named for none other than Captain John Smith; inside are artifacts retrieved from archaeological excavations of the 17th-century trading outpost.

The square white Fort House, which dates to the late 1700s, houses a research library and archaeology lab as well as a gift shop.

Exhibits at the museum-visitors center focus on regional history, from early Native American life through the colonial period. Selections from the more than 100,000 artifacts uncovered during archaeological digs here are displayed along with a diorama of Pemaquid Village.

Take time to wander the village, 14 cellar holes of 17th- and 18th-century dwellings, a forge, a trading post, a jail, and other early buildings, all marked with interpretive signs. Also visit the burying ground. Note that rubbings are not permitted, as they could damage the fragile old stones.

Historical Houses of Worship

One of the oldest houses of worship in Maine that still holds services, **The Old Walpole Meeting House** (Rte. 129, Bristol Rd., Walpole), built in 1772, remains remarkably unchanged, with original hand-shaved shingles and handmade nails and hinges. The balcony—where African American servants were once relegated—is paneled with boards more than two feet wide. The meetinghouse is 3.5 miles south of Damariscotta and 0.25 mile south of where Routes 129 and 130 fork.

The **Harrington Meeting House** (Old Harrington Rd., off Rte. 130, 2pm-4:30pm Mon., Wed., and Fri. July-Aug., donation), begun in 1772 and completed in 1775, now serves as Bristol's local-history museum— town-owned and run by the Pemaquid

Historical Association. Behind it is an old cemetery that's fascinating to explore.

A remnant of Waldoboro's German connection is the **Old German Church** (Rte. 32, Waldoboro, 207/832-7742, 1pm-3pm daily July-Aug.) and its cemetery. The Lutheran church, built in 1772 on the opposite side of the Medomak River, was moved across the ice in the winter of 1794. Inside are box pews and a huge hanging pulpit. One of the three oldest churches in Maine, it lost its flock in the mid-19th century when new generations no longer spoke German. An annual German service is held at 3pm the first Sunday of August.

Built in 1808, **St. Patrick's Catholic Church** (Academy Hill Rd., Damariscotta Mills, Newcastle, 207/563-3240, 9am-sunset daily), a solid brick structure with 1.5-foot-thick walls, a rare crypt-form altar, and a Paul Revere bell, is New England's oldest Catholic church in continual use. Academy Hill Road starts at Newcastle Square in downtown Newcastle; the church is 2.25 miles from the square and one mile beyond Lincoln Academy.

St. Andrew's Episcopal Church (Glidden St., Newcastle, 207/563-3533), built in 1883, is nothing short of exquisite, with carved-oak beams, a stenciled ceiling, and, for the cognoscenti, a spectacular Hutchings organ.

Frances Perkins Center

For insight into the life of the first female presidential cabinet member in U.S. history, visit the **Frances Perkins Center** (170A Main St., 207/563-3374, www.francesperkinscenter.org, 10am-2pm Tues.-Sat.). In addition to the small museum honoring the U.S. Secretary of Labor, 1933-45, the center often organizes guided tours ($12-15) of the nearby Perkins Homestead, a 57-acre working farm and brickyard under consideration as a National Historic Landmark.

The Thompson Ice House

On a Sunday morning in February (weather and ice permitting), several hundred helpers and onlookers gather at Thompson Pond, next to the **Thompson Ice House** (Rte. 129, South

RETURN OF THE ALEWIVES

If you're in the Damariscotta area in May and early June, don't miss a chance to go to Damariscotta Mills to see the annual **Alewife Run.** During this time more than 250,000 alewives (*Alosa pseudoharengus,* a kind of herring) make their way from Great Salt Bay to their spawning grounds in freshwater Damariscotta Lake, 42 feet higher. Waiting eagerly at the top are ospreys, gulls, cormorants, and sometimes eagles, ready to feast on the weary fish. Connecting the bay and the lake is a man-made stone-and-masonry "fish ladder" (www.damariscottamills.org), a zigzagging channel where you can watch the foot-long fish wriggle their way onward and upward. The ladder was built in 1807; restoration is ongoing. A walkway runs alongside the route, and informative display panels explain the event. It's a fascinating historical ecology lesson. To reach the fishway, take Route 215 for 1.6 miles west of Route 1. When you reach a small bridge, cross it and take a sharp left down a slight incline to a small parking area. Walk behind the fish house to follow the path to the fish ladder. Try to go on a sunny day—the fish are more active, and their silvery sides glisten as they go.

Bristol, www.thompsonicehouse.com), for the annual ice harvest. Festivity prevails as a crew of robust fellows marks out a grid and saws out 12-inch-thick ice cakes, which are pushed up a ramp to the ice-storage house. More than 60 tons of ice is harvested each year. Sawdust-insulated 10-inch-thick walls keep the ice from melting in this building first used in 1826 and now listed on the National Register of Historic Places. In 1990 the house became part of a working museum (1pm-4pm Wed. and Fri.-Sat. July-Aug., donation), with ice tools and a window view of the stored ice cakes. The grounds, including a photographic display board depicting a 1964 harvest, are accessible for free all year. The site is 12 miles south of Damariscotta on Route 129.

Waldoborough Historical Society Museum

The **Waldoborough Historical Society Museum** (1164 Main St., Waldoboro, www.waldoborohistory.us, noon-3pm Wed.-Mon. late June-early Sept., free) is a three-building roadside complex just 0.1 mile south of Route 1 at the eastern end of town. On the grounds are the 1857 one-room **Boggs Schoolhouse,** the 1819 **Town Pound** (to detain stray livestock), and two buildings filled with antique tools, toys, and utensils along with period costumes, antique fire engines, and artifacts from the shipbuilding era.

Maine Antique Toy and Art Museum

Indulge your inner child at the **Maine Antique Toy and Art Museum** (Rte. 1, Waldoboro, 207/832-7398, noon-4pm Thurs.-Mon. late May-mid-Oct., noon-4pm Sat.-Sun. mid-Oct.-Christmas, $5). The museum houses an extensive collection of antique toys and original comic art. See how Mickey Mouse first appeared or browse a collection of Lone Ranger memorabilia. You'll find all the old favorites, including Popeye, Felix the Cat, Betty Boop, Snow White, Pogo, and Yoda. This museum is geared to nostalgic adults, not kids.

ENTERTAINMENT

Two struggling arts centers provide year-round concerts, plays, workshops, classes, and exhibits. **River Arts** (170 Business Rte. 1, Damariscotta, 207/563-1507, www.riverartsme.org) doubles as a gallery. Neoclassic on the outside, art deco within, the **Waldo Theatre** (916 Main St., Waldoboro, 207/832-6060, www.thewaldo.org) was built as a cinema in 1936. Restored in the mid-1980s, it now operates as a nonprofit organization and presents concerts, plays, films, lectures, and other year-round community events.

Lincoln County Community Theater (Theater St., Damariscotta, 207/563-3424, www.lcct.org) owns and operates the historic Lincoln Theater, dating from 1867. It also presents musicals and dramas, concerts, films, and more.

Salt Bay Chamberfest (207/522-3749, www.saltbaychamberfest.org) presents concerts in August.

FESTIVALS AND EVENTS

In mid-August, **Olde Bristol Days** features a crafts show, a parade, road and boat races, live entertainment, and fireworks. October brings **Pumpkinfest** to Damariscotta, a family pleaser with food, entertainment, and competitions.

SHOPPING

Downtown Damariscotta has a nice selection of independent shops, galleries, and boutiques. Downtown parking in summer is a major headache; the municipal lot behind the storefronts has a three-hour limit, and it's often full. You'll usually find spots on some of the side streets.

Antiques and Antiquarian Books

Antiques shops are numerous along Bristol Road (Rte. 130), where many barns have been turned into shops selling everything from fine antiques to old stuff. Serious antiques aficionados will find plenty to browse and buy along this stretch of road.

The multidealer **Nobleboro Antique Exchange** (104 Atlantic Hwy./Rte. 1, Nobleboro, 207/563-6800, www.antiquex. net) is housed in a light blue building that goes on and on, with more than 100 display areas on three levels. The selection is diverse, from period antiques to 20th-century collectibles.

Art Galleries

Worth a visit for the building alone, the **Stable Gallery** (26 Water St., Damariscotta, 207/563-1991, www.stablegallerymaine.com), just off Main Street, was built in the 19th-century clipper-ship era and still has original black-walnut

MID-COAST REGION

© TOM NANGLE

Damariscotta's annual Pumpkinfest draws crowds to the Pemaquid Peninsula in October.

stalls—providing a great foil for the work of dozens of Maine craftspeople. Lining the walls are paintings and prints from the gallery's large stable of artists.

You'll find a carefully curated selection of Maine-made fine and folk arts and crafts at **Gifts at 136** (136 Main St., Damariscotta, 207/563-1011), with works in all price ranges. They also sell artisan chocolates.

In his **River Gallery** (79 Main St., Damariscotta, 207/563-6330), dealer Geoff Robinson specializes in 19th- and early-20th-century European and American fine art—a connoisseur's inventory.

Betcha can't leave without buying something from **Pemaquid Craft Co-op** (Rte. 130, New Harbor, 207/677-2077), with 15 rooms filled with high-quality works by 50 Maine artisans.

A delightful little off-the-beaten-path find is **Tidemark Gallery** (902 Main St., Waldoboro, 207/832-5109), showing fine arts and crafts from local artists.

Head south from Waldoboro down the Friendship Peninsula to find **Old Point Comfort** (28 Pitcher Rd./Rte. 220 S., Waldoboro, 207/832-8188), the gallery and showroom where weaver Sara Hotchkiss displays her tapestry-woven carpets.

Specialty and Eclectic Shops

The Pemaquid Peninsula is fertile ground for crafts and gifts, and many of the shop locations provide opportunities for exploring off the beaten path. Artists' studios and galleries are plentiful.

The inventory at the **Maine Coast Book Shop and Café** (158 Main St., Damariscotta, 207/563-3207) always seems to anticipate customers' wishes, so you're unlikely to walk out empty-handed. You'll find a superb children's section, helpful staff, and always something tempting in the café.

Weatherbird (Main St. and 72 Courtyard St., Damariscotta, 207/563-8993) is a double find. The Main Street shop specializes in women's clothing, and off the alley behind it is the original store, stocked with housewares, wines, toys, cards, and gourmet specialties.

All sorts of finds fill the **Walpole Barn** (Rte. 129, Walpole, 207/563-7050, www.thewalpolebarn.com), Warren and Deb Storch's retirement fun. Browse home and garden products, whimsies, gourmet foods, and even wines.

The Granite Hall Store (9 Backshore Rd., off Rte. 32, Round Pond, 207/529-5864) is an old-fashioned country store with merchandise ranging from toys to Irish imports. The "penny" candy, fudge, ice cream, and the old-fashioned peanut-roasting machine captivate the kids.

Bells reminiscent of lighthouses, buoys, and even wilderness sounds are crafted by **North Country Wind Bells** (544 Rte. 32, Round Pond, 877/930-5435, www.northcountrybells.com). Factory seconds are a bargain.

Renys

Whatever you do, don't leave downtown Damariscotta without visiting **Renys** (207/563-5757 or 207/563-3011), with stores on each side of Main Street; one sells clothing, the other everything else (although that mix might change). If you can recognize the edges of cutout labels, you'll find clothes from major retailers at very discounted prices. Stock up on housewares, munchies, puzzles, toiletries, shoes, and whatever else floats your boat; the prices can't be beat.

RECREATION
Parks and Preserves

Residents of the Pemaquid Peninsula region are incredibly fortunate to have several foresighted local conservation organizations, each with its own niche and mission. The result is dozens of trail-webbed preserves. For good descriptions of trails throughout Lincoln County, purchase Paula Roberts's *On the Trail in Lincoln County* ($15.75), which describes and provides directions to more than 60 area walking trails. It's available at Salt Bay Farm, which benefits from its sale. Another excellent resource is *PWA Hike and Paddle Pocket Guide,* available for a $2 donation from the Pemaquid Watershed Association (207/563-2196, www.pemaquidwatershed.org).

SALT BAY FARM

Headquarters of the **Damariscotta River Association** (DRA, 110 Belvedere Rd., Damariscotta, 207/563-1393, www.damariscottariver.org, 9am-5pm Mon.-Fri.), founded in 1973, is the Salt Bay Farm Heritage Center, a late-18th-century farmhouse on a farm site. Here you can pick up maps, brochures, and other information on the more than 2,900 acres and 22 miles of shoreline protected and managed by the DRA. More than two miles of trails cover Salt Bay Farm's fields, salt marsh, and shore frontage and are open to the public sunrise-sunset daily year-round. DRA also has a healthy calendar of events, including bird-watching tours, natural-history trips, and concerts. To reach the farm from downtown Newcastle, take Mills Road (Rte. 215) to Route 1. Turn right (north) and go 1.4 miles to the blinking light (Belvedere Rd.). Turn left and go 0.4 mile.

SALT BAY PRESERVE HERITAGE TRAIL

Across Great Salt Bay from the DRA Salt Bay Farm is the trailhead for the **Salt Bay Preserve Heritage Trail,** a relatively easy three-mile loop around Newcastle's Glidden Point that touches on a variety of habitat and also includes remnants of oyster-shell middens (heaps) going back about 2,500 years. This part of the trail is protected by the federal government; do not disturb or remove anything. To reach the preserve from Newcastle Square, take Mills Road (Rte. 215) about two miles to the offices of the *Lincoln County News* (just after the post office). The newspaper allows parking in the northern end of its lot, but stay to the right, as far away from the buildings as possible, and be sure not to block any vehicles or access ways. Walk across Route 215 to the trailhead and pick up a brochure-map.

WHALEBACK PARK

How often do you get to see ancient shell heaps? **Whaleback Park** is an eight-acre public preserve designed to highlight what remains of the Glidden Midden, ancient oyster-shell heaps across the river from the park viewpoint.

(The midden is also visible, but not as easily, from the Salt Bay Preserve Heritage Trail.) Informational signs explain the history of the midden, allegedly the largest such human artifact north of Florida. The "mini mountain" of castoffs was even vaster until the 1880s, when a factory harvested much of it to make lime. The trailhead and parking is on Business Route 1 opposite and between the Great Salt Bay School and the Central Lincoln County YMCA.

DODGE POINT PRESERVE

In 1989 the state of Maine acquired the now 521-acre **Dodge Point Preserve**—one of the stars in its crown—as part of a $35 million bond issue. To sample what the Dodge Point Preserve has to offer, pick up a map at the entrance and follow the Old Farm Road loop trail, and then connect to the Shore Trail (Discovery Trail), heading clockwise, with several dozen highlighted sites. Consider stopping for a riverside picnic and swim at Sand Beach before continuing back to the parking lot. Hunting is permitted in the preserve, so November isn't the best time for hiking. The Dodge Point parking area is on River Road, 2.6 miles southwest of Route 1 and 3.5 miles southwest of downtown Newcastle.

TRACY SHORE PRESERVE

Walk through a woodland wonderland that extends to ledgy shorefront along Jones Cove in South Bristol. Old cellars, moss-covered trails, lichen-covered rocks, a vernal pool, old pasture grounds, and spectacular views highlight this little-known gem, owned by the DRA. It has cliffs and lots of slippery rocks, so be watchful of children. You can connect to another preserve, Library Park, on a link crossing busy Route 129. The trailhead and parking are at the intersection of Route 129 and the S Road, 8.7 miles south of the split from Route 130.

LA VERNA PRESERVE

Roughly 3.5 miles south of the Round Pond post office on Route 130 you'll find this splendid 120-acre **shorefront preserve,** with 2.5 miles of hiking trails passing through woodlands, overgrown farmland, and forested wetlands to 3,600 feet of spectacular, bold ocean frontage. Download a map from the Pemaquid Watershed Association (www.pemaquidwatershed.org).

RACHEL CARSON SALT POND

If you've never spent time studying the variety of sea life in a tidal pool, the **Rachel Carson Salt Pond** is a great place to start. Named after the famed author of *Silent Spring* and *The Edge of the Sea,* who summered in this part of Maine, the salt pond was one of her favorite haunts. The whole point of visiting a tidepool is to see what the tide leaves behind, so check the tide calendar (in local newspapers, or ask at your lodging) and head out a few hours after high tide. Wear rubber boots and beware of slippery rocks and rockweed. Among the many creatures you'll see in this 0.25-acre pond are mussels, green crabs, periwinkles, and starfish. Owned by The Nature Conservancy, the salt pond is on Route 32 in the village of Chamberlain, about a mile north of New Harbor. Parking is limited. Across the road is a trail into a 78-acre inland section of the preserve, most of it wooded. Brochures are available in the registration box.

Golf

The nine-hole **Wawenock Country Club** (Rte. 129, Walpole, 207/563-3938), established in the 1920s, is a challenging and popular public course.

Swimming

The best bet (but also the most crowded) on the peninsula for saltwater swimming is town-owned **Pemaquid Beach Park** (www.bristolparks.org), a lovely tree-lined sandy crescent. There is no lifeguard, but there are cold-water showers and bathrooms and a nature center with exhibits, and the snack bar serves decent food. Admission is $4 for anyone over age 12. The gates close at 7pm (restrooms close at 5pm). The beach is just off Snowball Hill Road, west of Route 130.

A much smaller beach is the pocket-size sandy area in **Christmas Cove** on Rutherford Island. Take Route 129 around the cove and turn to the right, and then right again down the hill.

One of the area's most popular freshwater swimming holes is **Biscay Pond,** a long, skinny body of water in the peninsula's center. From Business Route 1 at the northern edge of Damariscotta, take Biscay Road (turn at McDonald's) three miles to the pond (on the right, heading east). On hot days, this area sees plenty of cars; pull off the road as far as possible.

Farther down the peninsula, on Route 130 in **Bristol Mills,** is another roadside swimming hole, between the dam and the bridge.

Boat Excursions

At 9am each day mid-May–early October, the 60-foot powerboat *Hardy III* departs for **Monhegan,** a Brigadoon-like island a dozen miles offshore where passengers can spend the day hiking the woods, picnicking on the rocks, bird-watching, and inhaling the salt air. At 3:15pm everyone reboards, arriving in New Harbor just over an hour later. The cost is $35 adults, $18 ages 3-11, and reservations are required. Trips operate rain or shine, but heavy seas can affect the schedule. Early June–late September there's also a second Monhegan trip—used primarily for overnighters—departing New Harbor at 2pm daily. Early and late in the season, Monhegan trips operate only Wednesday, Saturday, Sunday, and holidays. The *Hardy III* also operates daily 1.5-hour **puffin-watching tours** (5:30pm mid-May–late Aug., $26 adults, $15 children), one-hour **seal-watching tours** (noon daily mid-June–early Sept. and Sept. weekends, $15 adults, $10 children), and one-hour **lighthouse cruises** (noon, mid-June–early Sept., $15 adults, $10 children). **Hardy Boat Cruises** (Rte. 32, New Harbor, 207/677-2026 or 800/278-3346, www.hardyboat.com) is 19 miles south of Route 1, based at Shaw's Fish and Lobster Wharf. Parking is $3/day at the baseball field near Shaw's.

Sea kayaking is a great way to explore the waters of the Pemaquid Peninsula.

Sea Kayaking and Canoeing

Pemaquid Paddlers, a local group, welcomes visitors to its weekly paddles, usually held beginning at 9am Saturday and lasting for about two hours. Check local papers or www.pemaquidpaddlers.blogspot.com for the schedule.

Midcoast Kayak (47 Main St., Damariscotta, 207/563-5732, www.midcoastkayak.com) has rentals and offers guided tours and lessons on Muscongus Bay and the Damariscotta River. Three-hour to full-day tours range $45-100 and include all sorts of options. If you would rather do it yourself, recreational kayaks and sea kayaks are available at rates beginning at $25 for two hours. Instruction is also available.

Operating from a base near Colonial Pemaquid is **Maine Kayak** (113 Huddle Rd., New Harbor, 866/624-6351, www.mainekayak.com). Guided options include sunset paddles, wildlife paddles, puffin paddles, paddle-and-sail, half-day and full-day trips, and a variety of overnights. Rates begin at $69 for the shorter trips. Rentals begin at $25

single, $35 tandem for two hours, with free delivery in the New Harbor area.

If you have your own boat or just want to paddle the three-mile length of **Biscay Pond,** you can park at the beach area and put in. Another good launching site is a state ramp off Route 1 in **Nobleboro,** at the head of eight-mile-long **Lake Pemaquid.**

Two preserves are accessible if you have your own boat. Owned by the Damariscotta River Association, 30-acre **Menigawum Preserve (Stratton Island)** is also known locally as Hodgdon's Island. It's at the entrance to Seal Cove on the west side of the South Bristol peninsula. The closest public boat launch is at The Gut, about four miles downriver—a trip better done *with* (in the same direction as) the tide. The best place to land is Boat House Beach, in the northeast corner—also a great spot for shelling. Pick up a map from the small box at the north end of the island and follow the perimeter trail clockwise. At the northern end, you'll see osprey nests; at the southern tip are Native American shell middens—discards from hundreds of years of marathon summer lunches. (Do not disturb or remove anything.) You can picnic in the pasture, but camping and fires are not allowed. Stay clear of the abandoned home site on the island's west side. The preserve is accessible sunrise-sunset.

Named for a 19th-century local woman dubbed "The Witch of Wall Street" for her financial wizardry, **Witch Island Preserve** is owned by Maine Audubon. The wooded 19-acre island has two beaches, a perimeter trail, and the ruins of the "witch's" house. A quarter of a mile offshore, it's accessible by canoe or kayak from the South Bristol town landing, just to the right after the bridge over The Gut. Put in, paddle under the bridge, and go north to the island.

ACCOMMODATIONS
Inns

Innkeeper Julie Bolthuis has breathed new life into (**The Newcastle Inn** (60 River Rd., Newcastle, 207/563-5685 or 800/832-8669, www.newcastleinn.com, $190-275), an 1860s sea captain's home with 14 guest rooms and suites (all with air-conditioning and Wi-Fi, some with TV, fireplace, or whirlpool tub) spread out between the main inn and carriage house. The lovely grounds descend to the edge of the Damariscotta River. Julie serves a full breakfast, on the patio when the weather cooperates, and stocks a pantry that includes a bottomless cookie jar. Two rooms are dog-friendly ($35/day).

Within easy walking distance of Pemaquid Light and 16 miles south of Route 1, **The Bradley Inn** (3063 Bristol Rd./Rte. 130, New Harbor, 207/677-2105 or 800/942-5560, www.bradleyinn.com, $180-475) is a restored late-19th-century three-story inn with restaurant, carriage house, and a cottage amid lovely gardens. Some accommodations have a water view and/or fireplace, one with a full kitchen. Room rates include full breakfast.

Almost on top of Pemaquid Light is the rambling and delightfully old-fashioned **Hotel Pemaquid** (3098 Bristol Rd./Rte. 130, New Harbor, 207/677-2312, www.hotelpemaquid.

com, mid-May-mid-Oct., $85-160, no credit cards). Seventeen miles south of Route 1 but just 450 feet from the lighthouse (you can't see it from the inn, but you sure can hear the foghorn), the hotel has been welcoming guests since 1900; it's fun to peruse the old guest registers. Hang out in the large, comfortable parlor or on the wraparound veranda. The owners have gently renovated the property, updating and improving everything without losing the Victorian charm or quirks of an old seaside hotel. Don't expect fancy or fussy. The inn building has guest rooms with private and shared baths as well as suites. Other buildings have motel-style units with private baths. Apartments in the annex are $165-205. A beautiful second-floor suite in the carriage house, with a full kitchen and a deck, is $215, or $1,400/week. For the Victorian flavor of the place, request an inn room or a suite. There is no restaurant, but The Bradley Inn and The Sea Gull Shop are nearby.

Bed-and-Breakfasts

Martha Scudder provides a warm welcome for her guests at **Oak Gables Bed and Breakfast** (Pleasant St., Damariscotta, 207/563-1476 or 800/335-7748, www.oakgablesbb.com, year-round, $120). At the end of a pretty lane, this 13-acre hilltop estate overlooks the Damariscotta River. Despite a rather imposing setting, everything's homey, informal, and hospitable. Four second-floor rooms, which can be joined in pairs, share a bath; a guest wing ($175/night, $975/week) has a full kitchen, a private bath, and a separate entrance. The heated swimming pool is a huge plus, as is the boathouse deck on the river. Guests can harvest blackberries from scads of bushes. Also on the grounds are a three-bedroom cottage ($1,400/week), a river-view one-bedroom apartment ($185/night, $1,100/week), and a studio apartment ($175/night, $975/week), which is usually booked up well ahead.

Wake up with a dip after a restful sleep at the (**Mill Pond Inn** (50 Main St./Rte. 215, Damariscotta Mills, Nobleboro, 207/563-8014, www.millpondinn.com, $140, no credit cards). The 1780 colonial was restored and converted into an inn in 1986 by delightful owners Bobby and Sherry Whear. After a full breakfast, snooze in a hammock, watch for eagles and great blue herons, pedal a bicycle into nearby Damariscotta, or canoe the pond, which connects to 14-mile-long Damariscotta Lake. Bobby, a Registered Maine Guide, offers fishing trips and scenic tours of the lake in his restored antique Lyman lapstrake (clinker-built) boat. Use of bicycles and a canoe is free for guests. The inn is just a five-minute drive from downtown Damariscotta, but a world away.

The mansard-roofed **Inn at Round Pond** (1442 Rte. 32, Round Pond, 207/809-7386, www.theinnatroundpond.com, year-round, $165-195) commands a sea captain's view of the harbor as it presides over the pretty village of Round Pond. It's an easy walk to a waterfront restaurant, two dueling lobster pounds, an old-timey country store, and a few galleries and shops. Each of four good-sized, air-conditioned rooms has harbor views and sitting areas. There are no TVs and no locks, but there's no reason for either. A full breakfast is included.

About three miles south of town is **Blue Skye Farm** (1708 Friendship Rd., Waldoboro, 207/832-0300, www.blueskyefarm.com, $120-165), Jan and Peter Davidson's bed-and-breakfast in a gorgeous 18th-century farmhouse set amid 100 acres with trails, gardens, and lawns (but close to the road, so noise can be a problem for the sensitive). Original wall stencils by Moses Eaton decorate the entry. Breakfast is provided, and guests have full use of the country kitchen to prepare other meals. Other common rooms include the dining room, screened-in sunroom, and a sitting room that's stocked with games and a fireplace. Five guest rooms, three with private baths, are meticulously decorated.

Cozy, comfy, and cluttered with good reads and beloved treasures, **La Vatout** (218 Kaler's Corner, Waldoboro, 207/832-5150, www.levatout.com, $105-145) is a find for those who want a taste of down-home Maine. Innkeeper Dominika Spetsmann and resident artist Linda Mahoney provide a warm welcome to their 1830s farmhouse with four guest rooms (two sharing a bath) surrounded by organic gardens and home to a resident cat and dog. The only indoor public area is the dining room, where hearty breakfasts are crafted from local eggs, meats, fish, and grains, along with garden produce. For a real treat, consider the art workshops or nature packages, including one that allows you to forage for wild mushrooms with Maine mushroom guru David Spahr, and then return to the inn to prepare a meal.

Motels and Cottage Colonies

You'll have to plan well in advance to snag one of the humble **Ye Olde Forte Cabins** (18 Old Fort Rd., Pemaquid Beach, 207/677-2261, www.yeoldefortecabins.com, $115-216/day, $575-1,262/week). These rustic, no-frills cabins have edged a grassy lawn dropping to John's Bay since 1922. Each has at least a toilet and a sink, but a shower house and a well-equipped cookhouse are part of the colony. Although guests are expected to clean up after themselves when using the kitchen, management keeps the place immaculate. The small private beach is a great place to launch a kayak. The cabins are less than 25 yards from Colonial Pemaquid and Fort William Henry.

Dan Thompson is the third-generation innkeeper at **The Thompson House and Cottages** (95 South Side Rd., New Harbor, 207/677-2317, www.thompsoncottages.net, $600-1,700/week), a low-key, step-back-in-time complex of mostly waterfront rooms, apartments, and cottages split between two mini peninsulas. Most have fireplaces; none has a TV. Rowboats are available, and there's a library with games, books, and puzzles.

Now, here's a bargain. Up a long winding driveway behind Moody's Diner is **Moody's Motel** (Rte. 1, Waldoboro, 207/832-5362, www.moodysdiner.com, $62-82), in business since 1927; it's likely that little has changed in the meantime. Expect nothing more than a clean and well-run property, and you'll be content. The retro motel and tourist cabins all have screened porches, TVs, and Wi-Fi; a few have kitchenettes. Pets are $5.

Camping

A favorite with kayakers is **Sherwood Forest Camping** (Pemaquid Trail, New Harbor, 800/274-1593, www.sherwoodforestcampsite. com, $28-41). Facilities include a playground, a sundeck, and a pool, but the campground is just 800 feet from Pemaquid Beach. Two-bedroom rental cabins are $750/week.

FOOD
Local Flavors
DAMARISCOTTA

The absolute best breakfasts and mighty fine lunches come from **Crissy's Breakfast and Coffee Bar** (212 Main St., 207/563-6400, www.cbandcb.com, 8am-2pm daily, $5-12). Savor killer croissants, excellent eggs, and gluten-free rice bowls, along with internationally inspired lunch items in one of three pleasant dining rooms.

For baked goods, sandwiches, soups, and gourmet goodies to go, head to **Weatherbird** (1168 Elm St., 207/563-8993, 8am-5:30pm Mon.-Sat.). Eat at one of the handful of tables out front or take it to the waterfront.

Check out the Moxie memorabilia while enjoying breakfast, lunch, sweets, and coffee at **S. Fernald's Country Store** (50 Main St., Damariscotta, 207/563-8484, 8am-6pm Mon.-Sat., 9am-5pm Sun.). The candy by the pound is a real kid pleaser.

The burgers, lobster rolls, and sweet-potato fries earn raves at **Larson's Lunch Box** (430 Main St., 207/563-5755, 11am-4pm Thurs.-Tues., to 7pm July-Aug.), a no-frills take-out stand with a few picnic tables.

In a barn-style building at the northern edge of Damariscotta, **Round Top Ice Cream** (Business Rte. 1, 207/563-5307) has been dishing out homemade ice cream since 1924.

Rising Tide Natural Foods Market (323 Main St., 207/563-5556, www.risingtide.coop, 8am-8pm daily), a thriving co-op organization since 1978, has all the natural and organic usuals, plus a self-service deli section with soups, sandwiches, salads, and entrées; indoor seating is available.

The **Damariscotta Area Farmers Market** sets up 9am-noon on Friday mid-May-October at Salt Bay Heritage Center (Belvedere Rd., just off Route 1) and 3pm-6pm Monday at Rising Tide Market (323 Main St.).

DOWN THE PENINSULA

You won't find a cozier, less expensive, or more welcoming home-based bakeshop than **Dot's Bakery** (1233 Rte. 32, Round Pond, 207/529-2514, 6am-8pm Thurs.-Mon.). Muffins, pies, doughnuts, soups, breads, and even buttermilk pancakes, sandwiches, and pizza are on the menu. Dine in on the central table or take it to go. Call ahead to order pie.

Homemade frozen custard, delicious baked goods, prepared dishes, and sandwiches to go are just a few of the reasons to stop by the seasonal **Island Grocery** (12 West Side Rd., South Bristol, 207/644-8552, www.islandgrocery. net). It also has breads, cheeses, and all kinds of gourmet goodies—stock up for a picnic. To find it, take the first right after the Gut.

Just around the corner from Colonial Pemaquid, **The Cupboard Cafe** (137 Huddle Rd., New Harbor, 207/677-3911, www.the-cupboardcafe.com, 8am-3pm Tues.-Sat., 8am-noon Sun.) is a homey cabin serving fresh-baked goods, breakfasts, and a nice choice of fresh salads, burgers, sandwiches, and specials. Almost everything is made on the premises; the cinnamon and sticky buns are so popular, they've spurred a mail-order business.

Pair exploring Fort William Henry with lunch or dinner at **The Contented Sole** (at Fort William Henry, 207/677-3000, www.thecontentedsole.com, 11:30am-9pm daily, $9-25), a quirky waterfront seafood shack with oyster bar, kids' menu, and a menu ranging from seafood to pizza.

WALDOBORO

At the corner of Routes 1 and 220, opposite Moody's Diner, is the warehouse-y building that turns out **Borealis Breads** (1860 Atlantic Hwy./Rte. 1, 207/832-0655, 8:30am-5:30pm

Mon.-Sat., 9am-4pm Sun.). Using sourdough starters (and no oils, sweeteners, eggs, or dairy products), owner Jim Amaral and his crew produce baguettes, olive bread, lemon fig bread, rosemary focaccia, and about a dozen other inventive flavors; each day has its specialties. A refrigerated case holds a small selection of picnic fixings (sandwich spreads, juices). Great soups, salads, and excellent sandwiches are available to go.

Each fall around mid-September, a tiny, cryptic display ad appears in local newspapers: "Kraut's Ready." Savvy readers recognize this as the announcement of the latest batch of Morse's sauerkraut—an annual ritual since 1918. The homemade kraut is available in stores and by mail order, but it's more fun (and cheaper) to visit the shop, the **Kraut House** (3856 Washington Rd./Rte. 220, 207/832-5569 or 800/486-1605, www.morsessauerkraut. com, 9am-6pm Thurs.-Tues.), which also has a small restaurant (10:30am-4pm Mon.-Tues., 8am-4pm Thurs.-Sun.) serving traditional German fare, including sandwiches such as a classic Reuben, liverwurst, or Black Forest ham; homemade pierogies; sausages; and stuffed cabbage rolls, all less than $12. Big serve-yourself jars of Morse's pickles are on the tables. While waiting, feast on tastings in the shop. The red-painted farm store also carries Aunt Lydia's Beet Relish, baked beans, mustard, maple syrup, and other Maine foods as well as a mind-boggling selection of hard-to-find and unusual northern European specialties, cheeses, meats, and preserved fish. It's eight miles north of Route 1.

Truck drivers, tourists, locals, and notables have been flocking to **Moody's Diner** (Rte. 1 and Rte. 220, 207/832-7785, www.moodys-diner.com, 5am-9:30pm Mon.-Sat., 6am-9pm Sun., $5-15) since the early 1930s, when the Moody family established this classic diner on a Waldoboro hilltop. The antique neon sign has long been a Route 1 beacon, especially on a foggy night, and the crowds continue, with new generations of Moodys and considerable expansion of the premises. It has gone beyond dinerdom; expect hearty, no-frills fare and such

calorific desserts as peanut butter or walnut pie. After eating, you can buy the cookbook.

The Narrows Tavern (15 Friendship St., 207/832-2210, 11:30am-1am daily, $8-18) is a convivial watering hole with a family-friendly attitude and nightly activities ranging from cribbage or table tennis to live music.

Casual Dining
DAMARISCOTTA
A reliable standby in downtown Damariscotta, next to the Damariscotta Bank and Trust, the **Salt Bay Café** (88 Main St., 207/563-3302, www.saltbaycafe.com, 7:30am-9pm daily) has a loyal following thanks to its imaginative, reasonably priced cuisine and cheerful, plant-filled setting. Vegetarians have their own menu, with more than two dozen choices. Most dinner entrées are $15-22, but hefty sandwiches are also available.

Chef Rick and Jean Kerrigan own **Damariscotta River Grill** (155 Main St., 207/563-2992, www.damariscottarivergrill. com, 11am-8:30pm daily, bar menu until 9:30pm Sat.-Sun., entrées $17-27), a reliable favorite where the open kitchen offers carefully prepared foods with an emphasis on fresh seafood. The artichoke fondue is worth fighting over. Choose a table in the back with a river view, if available.

Bridging the gap between pub and restaurant is the **Newcastle Publick House** (52 Main St., Newcastle, 207/563-3434, www.newcastlepublickhouse.com, 11am-11pm Sun.-Thurs., 11am-midnight Fri.-Sat., $8-24). Emphasis is on organic, natural, and local foods, including Pemaquid oysters, and pub favorites such as shepherd's pie or lamb shanks braised in Geary's London porter. The craft beer menu is another draw.

DOWN THE PENINSULA
The informal and rustic **Anchor Inn** (Harbor Rd., Round Pond, 207/529-5584, www.anchorinnrestaurant.com, 11:30am-2:30pm and 5pm-9pm daily mid-May-mid-Oct., entrées $18-25), tucked away on the picturesque harbor in Round Pond, always attracts a crowd with

a menu that emphasizes seafood, but has other options too. Reservations are advisable on summer weekends. After Labor Day, the schedule can be a bit erratic; call to confirm the hours.

Coveside Restaurant (105 Coveside Rd., Christmas Cove, South Bristol, 207/644-8282, www.covesiderestaurant.com, 11am-9pm daily, $10-28), based at a marina on Rutherford Island, just off the end of the South Bristol peninsula, is open for lunch and dinner as well as light meals. Grab a seat on the deck and watch a steady stream of boaters and summer vacationers during the cruising season. The food quality and service efficiency varies as it's a leased operation, but when it's on, it's hard to beat.

Location, location: Right next to Pemaquid Light is **The Sea Gull Shop** (3119 Bristol Rd., Pemaquid Point, 207/677-2374, www.seagullshop.com, 7:30am-8pm daily mid-May-mid-Oct., entrées $17-33), an oceanfront place with touristy prices but decent food—pancakes and muffins, for instance, overflowing with blueberries. BYOB; call ahead for hours in spring and fall.

◖ Lobster in the Rough

The Pemaquid Peninsula must have more eat-on-the-dock places per capita than any place in Maine. Some are basic no-frills operations; others are big-time commercial concerns. Each has a loyal following.

The biggest and best-known lobster wharf is **Shaw's Fish and Lobster Wharf** (Rte. 32, New Harbor, 207/677-2200 or 800/772-2209, 11am-8pm daily). You can also order steak, margaritas, and oysters at the wharf raw bar. Fried seafood dinners run $8-20.

Facing each other across the dock in the hamlet of Round Pond are two of my all-time favorite lobster shacks, **Round Pond Lobster Co-Op** (207/529-5725) and **Muscongus Bay Lobster** (207/529-5528). Muscongus has enlarged in recent years, so it has a bigger menu and covered seating, but tiny Round Pond

Lobster keeps it simple and oh-so-fresh. Both usually open around 10am daily for lunch and dinner and close around sunset. At either, bring the go-withs, from wine and cheese to bread and chocolates.

Other seasonal lobster wharves salting the peninsula are **Pemaquid Fishermen's Co-Op** (32 Co-Op Rd., Pemaquid Harbor, 207/677-2642), **South Bristol Fishermen's Co-op** (35 Thompson Inn Rd., South Bristol, 207/644-8224), and **Broad Cove Marine Services** (374 Medomak Rd., Bremen, 207/529-5186), a low-key sleeper.

INFORMATION AND SERVICES

The **Damariscotta Region Chamber of Commerce** (15 Courtyard St., 207/563-8340, www.damariscottaregion.com) publishes a free annual information booklet about the area.

Skidompha Library (Main St., Damariscotta, 207/563-5513, www.skidompha.org) also operates a used-book shop and a gallery and offers a film series and talks. Incidentally, if you're puzzled by the name, it comes from the names of the members of a local literary society who founded the library at the turn of the 20th century. You can also check out **Waldoboro Public Library** (958 Main St., Waldoboro, 207/832-4484, www.waldoborolibrary.org).

GETTING THERE AND AROUND

Damariscotta is about eight miles or 15 minutes via Route 1 from Wiscasset. It's about 10 miles or 15 minutes via Route 1 to Waldoboro, and about 15 miles or 30 minutes via Route 130 to Pemaquid Point. From Pemaquid Point it's about 23 miles or 40 minutes via Route 32 to Waldoboro. From Waldoboro, it's about 12 miles or 20 minutes via Route 1 to Thomaston or about 20 miles via Routes 1 and 90 to Camden.

PENOBSCOT BAY

The rugged and jagged shoreline edging island-studded Penobscot Bay is the image that has lured many a visitor to Maine. The coastline here ebbs and flows, rising to rocky headlands, dropping to protected harbors, and linking fishing villages with comparatively cosmopolitan towns. Although the state considers this to be part of the Mid-Coast, this region has a different feel and view, one framed by coastal mountains in Camden and Lincolnville and accented by an abundance of islands.

From Thomaston through Prospect, no two towns are alike except that all are changing, as traditional industries give way to arts- and tourism-related businesses. Thomaston's Museum in the Streets, Rockland's art galleries, Camden's picturesque mountainside harbor, Lincolnville's pocket beach, Belfast's inviting downtown, Searsport's sea captains' homes, and Prospect's Fort Knox all invite exploration, as do offshore, ferry-linked islands.

From salty Port Clyde, take the mail boat to Monhegan, an offshore idyll known as the Artists' Island. From Rockland and Lincolnville Beach, car and passenger ferries depart to Vinalhaven, North Haven, Matinicus, and Islesboro. All are occupied year-round by hardy souls joined in summer by less-hardy ones. Except for Matinicus, they're great day-trip destinations.

If what appeals to you about a ferry trip is traveling on the water, you can get a taste of the Great Age of Sail by booking a multiday cruise aboard one of the classic windjammer schooners berthed in Rockland, Rockport,

© HILARY NANGLE

HIGHLIGHTS

LOOK FOR ◖ TO FIND RECOMMENDED SIGHTS, ACTIVITIES, DINING, AND LODGING.

◖ **Monhegan Historical and Cultural Museum:** View an impressive collection of masters at this museum adjacent to the light-house, then visit contemporary studios and find inspiration by hiking island trails (page 192).

◖ **The Farnsworth Art Museum and the Wyeth Center:** Three generations of Wyeths are represented in this recently expanded mu-

seum, which also boasts an excellent collection of works by Maine and American masters (page 197).

◖ **Owls Head Transportation Museum:** View a fabulous collection of vintage airplanes, automobiles, and even bicycles, many of which are flown, driven, or ridden during weekend special events (page 197).

◖ **Rockland Breakwater:** Take a walk on this nearly mile-long breakwater to the light-house at the end (open on weekends). It's an especially fine place to watch the windjammers sail in or out of Rockland Harbor (page 198).

◖ **Owls Head Light State Park:** The views of Penobscot Bay are spectacular, and it's a great place for a picnic lunch (page 200).

◖ **Camden Hills State Park:** If you have time, hike the moderate trail to the summit for a gull's-eye view over Camden Harbor and Penobscot Bay. If not, take the easy route and drive (page 221).

◖ **Penobscot Marine Museum:** Learn what life was *really* like during the Great Age of Sail in a town renowned for the number and quality of its sea captains (page 238).

◖ **Fort Knox:** A good restoration, frequent events, and secret passages to explore make this late-19th-century fort one of Maine's best (page 238).

◖ **Penobscot Narrows Bridge and Observatory:** On a clear day, the views from the 420-foot-high tower, one of only three in the world, extend from Mount Katahdin to Cadillac Mountain (page 239).

and Camden. Or simply book a day sail or sea-kayak excursion.

Although it's easy to focus on the water, this region is rich in museums and art galleries, antiques and specialty shops, some of the state's nicest inns, and many of its better restaurants. Most folks arrive in July-August, but

autumn, when turning leaves color the hills and are reflected in the sea, the days remain warm, and nights are cool, is an ideal season to visit, especially for leaf peepers who want to get off the beaten track. And in winter, when snow blankets the Camden Hills, you can ski while gazing out to Camden Harbor.

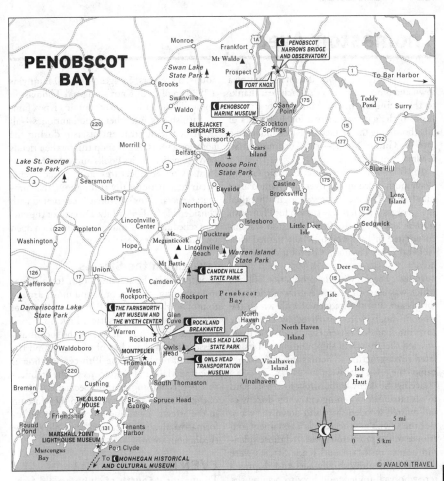

PLANNING YOUR TIME

To hit just the highlights, you'll need at least three days. If you want to relax a bit and enjoy the area, plan on 4-5 days. Make it a full week if you plan on overnighting on any of the offshore islands. In general, lodging is less expensive in Rockland, Belfast, and Searsport than it is in Camden. In any case, head for Monhegan or Vinalhaven on a fine day and save the museums for inclement ones.

Two-lane Route 1 is the region's central artery, with veins running down the peninsula limbs. Yes, traffic backs up, especially in Camden (and in Thomaston on the Fourth of July, when it's closed for a parade), but it rarely stops moving. If your destination is Rockland, take I-95 to Augusta and then Route 17 East; if it's Belfast or north, take I-95 to Augusta and then Route 3 East. Route 90 is a nifty bypass around Thomaston and Rockland, connecting Route 1 from Warren to Rockport. For a less direct route, the **Georges River Scenic Byway** is a 50-mile rural inland route, mostly along Route 131, between Port Clyde and Liberty. It parallels the coast, but it meanders through farmlands and tiny villages and by lakes and rivers, with antiques shops and farm stands along the way. It's simply gorgeous in autumn.

Thomaston Area

Thomaston (pop. 1,558) is a little gem of a town and is becoming more so each year thanks to the razing of the old Maine State Prison. It's also the gateway to two lovely fingers of land bordering the St. George River and jutting into the Gulf of Maine—the Cushing and St. George Peninsulas.

In 1605, British adventurer Captain George Waymouth sailed up the river now named after him (the St. George River was originally called the Georges River). A way station for Plymouth traders as early as 1630, Thomaston was incorporated in 1777 and officially named after General John Thomas, a Revolutionary War hero.

Industry began with the production of lime, which was used for plaster. A growing demand for plaster, and the frequency with which the wooden boats were destroyed by fire while carrying loads of extremely flammable lime, spurred the growth of shipbuilding and its related infrastructure. Thomaston's slogan became "the town that went to sea."

Seeing the sleepy harbor-front today, it's hard to visualize the booming era when dozens of tall-masted wooden ships slid down the ways. But the town's architecture is a testament and tribute to the prosperous past. All those splendid homes on Main and Knox Streets were funded by wealthy shipowners and shipmasters who well understood how to occupy the idle hands of off-duty carpenters.

SIGHTS
Montpelier

As you head north out of Thomaston on Route 1, you'll come face-to-face with an imposing colonial hilltop mansion at the junction with Route 131 South. Dedicated to the memory of General Henry Knox, President George Washington's secretary of war, **Montpelier** (Rte. 1 and Rte. 131, Thomaston, 207/354-8062, www.generalknoxmuseum.org, 10am-4pm Thurs.-Fri. late May-mid-Oct., $10 adults, $8 seniors, $4 ages 5-13, $20 family) is a 1930s replica of Knox's original Thomaston home. The mansion today contains Knox family furnishings and other period antiques—all described with great enthusiasm during the hour-long tours. A gift shop run by the Friends of Montpelier carries books and other relevant items. Concerts, lectures, and special events occur here periodically throughout the summer; General Knox's birthday is celebrated with considerable fanfare in July. Do call for the current schedule, as the museum is also often open on weekends for special events.

Museum in the Streets

Montpelier is the starting point for a three-mile walking, cycling, or, if you must, driving tour of nearly 70 sites in Thomaston's **National Historic Landmark District.** Pick up a copy of the tour brochure at one of the local businesses. Included are lots of stories behind the facades of the handsome 19th-century homes that line Main and Knox Streets; the architecture here is nothing short of spectacular. Much of this history is also recounted in the Museum in the Streets, a walking tour taking in 25 informative plaques illustrated with old photos throughout town.

EVENTS

Thomaston's **Fourth of July,** an old-fashioned hometown celebration reminiscent of a Norman Rockwell painting, draws huge crowds. A spiffy parade—with bands, veterans, kids, and pets—starts off the morning at 11am, followed by races, crafts and food booths, and lots more. If you need to get *through* Thomaston on the Fourth of July, do it well before the parade or well after noon; the marchers go right down Main Street (Rte. 1), and gridlock forces a detour.

The region's Finnish heritage is celebrated at **Finn Fling Day** at the Finnish Heritage House in mid-September.

SHOPPING

Thomaston has a block-long shopping street (on Rte. 1), with ample free parking out back behind the stores.

The **Maine State Prison Showroom Outlet** (Main St./Rte. 1 at Wadsworth St., Thomaston, 207/354-9237) markets the handiwork of inmate craftsmen. Some of the souvenirs verge on kitsch; the bargains are wooden bar stools, toys (including dollhouses), and chopping boards. You'll need to carry your purchases with you; prison-made goods cannot be shipped.

At the southern end of Thomaston, in a renovated chicken barn, is **Thomaston Place Auction Gallery** (51 Atlantic Hwy./Rte. 1, Thomaston, 207/354-8141, www.thomastonauction.com), the home of Kaja Veilleux, a longtime dealer, appraiser, and auctioneer. Auctions occur frequently with previews beforehand.

Just south of Thomaston is **Lie-Nielsen Toolworks** (Rte. 1, Warren, 800/327-2520, www.lie-nielsen.com), crafting heirloom-quality hand tools for connoisseurs; tours are available.

CAMPING

Located on the Thomaston-Cushing town line, 35-acre **Saltwater Farm Campground** (Wadsworth St./Cushing Rd., Cushing, 207/354-6735, www.saltwaterfarmcampground.com) has 37 open and wooded tent and RV sites ($35-48) overlooking the St. George River. Cabins go for $75. Facilities include a bathhouse, heated pool, hot tub, laundry, store, and play area. The river is tidal, so swimming is best near high tide; otherwise, you're dealing with mudflats.

FOOD

Often overlooked by visitors (but certainly not by locals) is casual **Thomaston Café and Bakery** (154 Main St./Rte. 1, Thomaston, 207/354-8589, www.thomastoncafe.com, 7:30am-2pm Tues.-Sat., 8:30am-2pm Sun., and 5:30pm-8pm Wed.-Sat., entrées $18-28). German-born chef Herb Peters and his wife, Eleanor, produce superb pastries, breads, and desserts (eat here or take them out). Everything's homemade, there are children's options, and the café uses only organic poultry. Try the incredible wild-mushroom hash. Reservations are essential.

Fresh seafood, including a raw bar and to-die-for fried oysters have earned **The Slipway** (24 Public Landing, Thomaston, 207/354-4155, 11:30am-9:30pm daily and 10:30am-2pm Sun., $10-24) must-go status. Aim for a fine day, when you can dine on the dock, although the views are equally fine from the porch and dining room.

INFORMATION AND SERVICES

The **Penobscot Bay Region Chamber of Commerce** (800/223-5459, www.mainedreamvacation.com) is the area's best resource.

The **Thomaston Public Library** (42 Main St., Thomaston, 207/354-2453) occupies part of the Greek Revival Thomaston Academy.

GETTING THERE AND AROUND

Thomaston is 12 miles or 18 minutes via Route 1 from Waldoboro. It's about 15 miles or 25 minutes via Route 131 to Port Clyde, and about 5 miles or 10 minutes via Route 1 to Rockland.

PENOBSCOT BAY

Cushing Peninsula

Cushing's recorded history goes back at least as far as 1605, when someone named "Abr [maybe Abraham] King"—presumably a member of explorer George Waymouth's crew—inscribed his name here on a ledge (now private property). Since 1789, settlers' saltwater farms have sustained many generations, and the active Cushing Historical Society keeps the memories and memorabilia from fading away. But the outside world knows little of this. **Cushing** (pop. 1,534) is better known as "Wyeth country," the terrain depicted by the famous artistic dynasty of N. C., Andrew, and Jamie Wyeth and assorted other talented relatives.

If you're an Andrew Wyeth fan, visiting Cushing will give you the feeling of walking through his paintings. The flavor of his Maine work is here—rolling fields, wildflower meadows, rocky tidal coves, broad vistas, character-filled farmhouses, and some well-hidden summer enclaves.

SIGHTS
Broad Cove Church

Andrew Wyeth aficionados will recognize the **Broad Cove Church** as one of his subjects—alongside Cushing Road en route to the Olson House. It's open most days, so step inside and admire the classic New England architecture. The church is also well known as the site of one of the region's best beanhole bean suppers, held on a Saturday in mid-July and attracting several hundred appreciative diners. From Route 1 in Thomaston, at the Maine State Prison Showroom Outlet, turn onto Wadsworth Street and go six miles, then bear left at the fork; the church is 0.4 mile farther, on the right.

Fans of artist Andrew Wyeth shouldn't miss The Olson House in Cushing.

© TOM NANGLE

BEANHOLE BEANS

"To be happy in New England," wrote one Joseph P. MacCarthy at the turn of the 20th century, "you must select the Puritans for your ancestors. . .[and] eat beans on Saturday night." There is no better way to confirm the latter requirement than to attend a beanhole bean supper—a real-live legacy of colonial times, with dinner baked in a hole in the ground.

Generally scheduled, appropriately, for a Saturday night (check local newspapers), a beanhole bean supper demands plenty of preparation from its hosts—and a secret ingredient or two. (Don't even think about trying to pry the recipe out of the cooks.) The supper always includes hot dogs, coleslaw, relishes, home-baked breads, and homemade desserts, but the beans are the star attraction. Typically, the suppers are also alcohol-free. They are not only feasts, but also bargains, never setting you back more than about $8.

The beans at the Broad Cove Church's annual mid-July beanhole bean supper, served family-style at long picnic tables, are legendary—attracting nearly 200 eager diners. Minus the secrets, here's what happens:

Early Friday morning: Church volunteers load 10 pounds of dry pea and soldier (yellow eye) beans into each of four large kettles and add water to cover. The beans are left to soak and soften for 6-7 hours. Two or three volunteers uncover the churchyard's four rock-lined beanholes (each about three feet deep), fill the holes with hardwood kindling, ignite the wood, and keep the fires burning until late afternoon, when the wood is reduced to red-hot coals.

Early Friday afternoon: The veteran chefs parboil the beans and stir in the seasonings. Typical additions are brown sugar, molasses, mustard, salt, pepper, and salt pork (much of the secret is in the exact proportions). When the beans are precooked to the cooks' satisfaction, the kettle lids are secured with wire and the pots are lugged outdoors.

Friday midafternoon: With the beans ready to go underground, some of the hot coals are quickly shoveled out of the pits. The kettles are lowered into the pits and the coals replaced around the sides of the kettles and atop their lids. The pits are covered with heavy sheet metal and topped with a thick layer of sand and a tarpaulin. The round-the-clock baking begins, and no one peeks before it's finished.

Saturday midafternoon: Even the veterans start getting nervous just before the pits are uncovered. Was the seasoning right? Did too much water cook away? Did the beans dry out? Not to worry, though—failures just don't happen here.

Saturday night: When a pot is excavated for the first of three seatings (about 5pm), the line is already long. The chefs check their handiwork and the supper begins. No one seems to mind waiting for the second and third seatings—while others eat, a sing-along gets under way in the church, keeping everyone entertained.

The Olson House

Many an art lover makes the pilgrimage to the **Olson House** (11am-4pm Tues.-Sun., July 1-early Oct., noon-5pm late May-July, $10, $17 with Farnsworth admission), a famous icon near the end of Hathorne Point Road. The early-19th-century farmhouse appears in Andrew Wyeth's 1948 painting *Christina's World* (which hangs in New York's Museum of Modern Art), his best-known image of the disabled Christina Olson, who died in 1968. In 1991, two philanthropists donated the Olson House to the Farnsworth Art Museum in Rockland, which has retained the house's sparse, lonely, and almost mystical ambience. The clapboards outside remain unpainted, the interior walls bear only a few Wyeth prints (hung close to the settings they depict), and it is easy to sense Wyeth's inspiration for chronicling this place. To find it, from the Broad Cove Church, continue just over one mile, then turn left onto Hathorne Point Road. Go another 1.9 miles to the house. Tours are offered on the hour.

PENOBSCOT BAY

St. George Peninsula

Even though the Cushing and St. George Peninsulas face each other across the St. George River, they differ dramatically. Cushing is far more rural, seemingly less approachable, and with little access to the surrounding waters; **St. George** (pop. 2,591) has a slew of things to do and see, places to sleep and eat, and shore access in various spots along the peninsula.

The St. George Peninsula is actually better known by some of the villages scattered along its length—**Tenants Harbor, Port Clyde, Wiley's Corner, Spruce Head**—plus the smaller neighborhoods of Martinsville, Smalleytown, Glenmere, Long Cove, Hart's Neck, and Clark Island. Each has a distinct personality, determined partly by the different ethnic groups—primarily Brits, Swedes, and Finns—who arrived to work the granite quarries in the 19th century. Wander through the Seaview Cemetery in Tenants Harbor and you'll see the story: row after row of gravestones with names from across the sea.

A more famous former visitor was 19th-century novelist Sarah Orne Jewett, who holed up in an old schoolhouse in Martinsville, paid a weekly rental of $0.50, and wrote *The Country of the Pointed Firs,* a tale about "Dunnet's Landing" (Tenants Harbor).

Today the picturesque peninsula has saltwater farms, tidy hamlets, a striking lighthouse, spruce-edged tidal coves, an active yachting harbor, and at the tip, the tiny fishing village of Port Clyde, which serves as a springboard to offshore Monhegan Island.

Port Clyde is likely the best-known community here. (Fortunately, it's no longer called by its unappealing 18th-century name: Herring Gut.) George Waymouth explored Port Clyde's nearby islands in 1605, but you'd never suspect its long tradition. It's a sleepy place, with a general store, low-key inns, a few galleries, and pricey parking.

SIGHTS
Marshall Point Lighthouse Museum

Not many settings can compare with the spectacular locale of the **Marshall Point Lighthouse Museum** (Marshall Point Rd., Port Clyde, 207/372-6450, www.marshall-point.org, 1pm-5pm Sun.-Fri., 10am-5pm Sat. late May-mid-Oct., free), a distinctive 1857 lighthouse and park overlooking Port Clyde, the harbor islands, and the passing lobster-boat fleet. Bring a picnic and let the kids run on the lawn (but keep them well back from the shoreline). The museum, in the 1895 keeper's house, displays lighthouse and local memorabilia. The grounds are accessible year-round. Take Route 131 to Port Clyde and watch for signs to the museum.

© TOM NANGLE

Marshall Point Lighthouse has a spectacular setting in Port Clyde.

but well-organized shed that has been here since the 1960s, has 50,000 or so treasures for used-book fans. For a few dollars, you can stock up on a summer's worth of reading. The shop, noon-5pm Sat.-Sat., is just under a mile east of Route 73, with eye-catching vistas in several directions (except, of course, when Spruce Head's infamous fog sets in).

General Store

Despite periodic ownership changes, **Port Clyde General Store** (Rte. 131, Port Clyde, 207/372-6543) remains a characterful destination, a two-century-old country store with ever-increasing upscale touches. Stock up on groceries, pick up a newspaper, order breakfast or a pizza, or buy a sweatshirt (you may need it on the Monhegan boat). The current owner has gussied it up even more and added a shop and a gallery featuring Wyeth works upstairs. She also operates the wharf-top restaurant out back.

RECREATION
Swimming and Beachcombing

Drift Inn Beach, on Drift Inn Beach Road (also called Candy's Cove Road), isn't a big deal as beaches go, but it's the best public one on the peninsula, so it gets busy on hot days. The name comes from the Drift Inn, an early-20th-century summer hotel. Drift Inn Beach Road parallels Route 131, and the parking lot is accessible from both roads. Heading south on the peninsula, about 3.5 miles after the junction with Route 73, turn left at Drift Inn Beach Road, then continue 0.2 mile.

Sea Kayaking

The St. George Peninsula is especially popular for sea kayaking, with plenty of islands to add interest and shelter. **Port Clyde Kayaks** (Rte. 131, Port Clyde, 207/372-8128, www.portclydekayaks.com) offers half-day, sunset, and full-moon ($60) guided tours around the tip of the peninsula, taking in Marshall Point lighthouse and the islands.

If you have kayaking experience, you can launch on the ramp just before the causeway that links the mainland with Spruce Head

© TOM NANGLE

The Port Clyde General Store not only sells merchandise, but also has an upstairs art gallery.

SHOPPING
Art

The St. George Peninsula has been attracting artists for decades, and galleries are abundant. Some have been here for years, and others started up yesterday; most are worth a stop, so keep an eye out for their signs. In early August, a number of renowned artists usually coordinate an open-studio weekend.

Overlooking the reversing falls in downtown South Thomaston, **The Old Post Office Gallery** (Rte. 73, South Thomaston, 207/594-9396, www.artofthesea.com) has 11 rooms filled with marine art and antiques: ship models, prints, paintings, sculpture, scrimshaw, and jewelry.

Used Books

Drive up to the small parking area at **Lobster Lane Book Shop** (Island Rd., Spruce Head, 207/594-7520) and you'll see license plates from everywhere. The tiny shop, in a crammed

Island, in Spruce Head (Island Rd., off Rte. 73). Parking is limited. A great paddle goes clockwise around Spruce Head Island and nearby Whitehead (there's a lighthouse on its southeastern shore) and Norton Islands. Duck in for lunch at Waterman's Beach Lobster. Around new moon and full moon, plan your schedule to avoid low tide near the Spruce Head causeway, or you may become mired in mudflats.

Boat Excursions

The best boating experience on this peninsula is a passenger-ferry trip from Port Clyde to off-shore **Monhegan Island**—for a day, overnight, or longer. The trip isn't cheap, and parking adds to the cost, but it's a "must" excursion, so try to factor it into the budget. Port Clyde is the nearest mainland harbor to Monhegan; this service operates all year. **Monhegan-Thomaston Boat Line** (Port Clyde, 207/372-8848, www.monheganboat.com) uses two boats, the *Laura B.* (70 minutes each way) and the newer *Elizabeth Ann* (50 minutes). Round-trip tickets are $35 adults, $20 ages 2-12. Leave your bicycle in Port Clyde; you won't need it on the island. Reservations are essential in summer, especially for the 10:30am boat. With advance payment, tickets are held until one-half hour before departure; there's a $5 fee for cancellations, with no refunds within 24 hours. Parking in Port Clyde is $5/day. If a summer day trip is all you can manage, aim for the first or second boat and return on the last one; don't go just for the boat ride.

During the summer, the Monhegan-Thomaston Boat Line also offers 2.5-hour sightseeing cruises, on a varied schedule, including a Puffin and Nature Cruise and a Lighthouse Cruise. Each costs $30 adults, $10 children.

The *Linderin Losh* lobster boat tours depart from the Port Clyde General Store for 2-3-hour Wyeths by Water excursions highlighting locations featured in works by N. C. and Andrew Wyeth. For reservations and details, call 207/372-6600.

ACCOMMODATIONS

No accommodations on the peninsula are contemporary or modern; for upscale lodgings, stay in Rockland or Camden.

Inns

The East Wind Inn (Mechanic St., Tenants Harbor, 207/372-6366, www.eastwindinn.com, $148-225) overlooks a dreamy island-dotted harbor. Built in 1860 and originally used as a sail loft, it has a huge veranda, a cozy parlor, harbor-view rooms, and a quiet dining room. Eighteen guest rooms, suites, and apartments are divided between the main inn and the spiffed-up 19th-century former sea captain's home; all have Wi-Fi, and TVs are available upon request. Rates include a full breakfast.

The decidedly old-fashioned **Craignair Inn** (Clark Island Rd., off Rte. 71, Spruce Head, 800/320-9997, www.craignair.com, $115-200), built in 1928 to house granite workers, is an unfussy, unpretentious spot with a quiet oceanfront location overlooking the causeway connecting Spruce Head to Clark Island and beyond to open seas. Guest rooms are split between the main inn and the vestry annex; some share baths. Rates include breakfast. Pets are allowed in some rooms for $15/night. The inn has an excellent water-view dining room (entrées $19-28).

Bed-and-Breakfasts

In the center of South Thomaston village but overlooking the reversing falls on the tidal Wessaweskeag River, the 1830 **Weskeag at the Water** (14 Elm St./Rte. 73, South Thomaston, 207/596-6676 or 800/596-5576, www.weskeag.com, year-round, $135-150) has eight guest rooms, four with in-room private baths. All are pleasantly old-fashioned, decorated with antiques, quilts, and knickknacks. Third-floor rooms are tucked under the eaves. Innkeeper Gary Smith is an antique car buff, and the inn is 1.5 miles from the Owls Head Transportation Museum.

If you stay at the circa 1820s **Ocean House** (870 Rte. 131, Port Clyde, 207/372-6691 or 800/269-6691, www.oceanhousehotel.com,

$120-158), you can plan to roll out of bed, eat breakfast, and head down the hill to the Monhegan boat. Several of the 10 unpretentious guest rooms (seven with private baths) have great harbor views. Expect steep stairs and no a/c. Also available is a two-bedroom oceanview suite ($273). The downsides: Rooms are small, stairs are steep, and screens are few.

Smack-dab in the middle of Port Clyde, the **Seaside Inn** (5 Cold Storage Rd., Port Clyde, 207/372-0700 or 800/279-5041, www.seasideportclyde.com, $120-200) is an 1850s sea captain's home with both private and shared baths. A first-floor library has books, puzzles, a TV, and a fireplace. Rates include a continental breakfast.

Camping

The third generation now operates **Lobster Buoy Campsites** (280 Waterman's Beach Rd., South Thomaston, 207/596-7546, $22-32), a no-frills oceanfront campground with 40 sites, 28 with water and electric, all with fire ring and picnic table. You can launch a canoe or kayak from the small, sandy beach. Most sites are open, and Lookout Beach is reserved for tenting. Eleanor's homemade doughnuts are a treat.

FOOD
Local Flavors

Don't be surprised to see the handful of tables occupied at the **Keag Store** (Rte. 73, Village Center, South Thomaston, 207/596-6810, 5am-9pm Mon.-Sat., 6am-8pm Sun.), one of the most popular lunch stops in the area. (Keag, by the way, is pronounced "gig"—short for "Wessaweskeag.") Roast-turkey sandwiches with stuffing are a big draw, as is the pizza, which verges on the greasy but compensates with its flavor—no designer toppings, just good pizza. Order it all to go and head across the street to the public wharf, where you can hang out and observe all the comings and goings.

Eat in or just pick up excellent pastries, sandwiches, and even fried foods to go at the **Schoolhouse Bakery** (Rte. 73, Tenants Harbor, 207/372-9608, 7am-2pm Mon.-Sat.).

Casual Dining

For a relaxing dinner with a gorgeous view, mosey on over to the **Craignair Inn Restaurant** (Clark Island Rd., off Rte. 71, Spruce Head, 800/320-9997, www.craignair.com, from 5:30pm daily in season, entrées $19-30). Big windows in the dining room frame Clark Island and the ocean beyond, and the food complements the view.

Lobster in the Rough

These open-air lobster wharves are the best places in the area to get down and dirty and manhandle a steamed or boiled lobster.

Poking right into Wheeler's Bay, **Miller's Lobster Company** (Eagle Quarry Rd., off Rte. 73, Spruce Head, 207/594-7406, www.millerslobster.com, 11am-7pm daily) is the quintessential lobster pound, a well-run operation that draws crowds all summer long. There are lobster rolls, steamed clams, crabmeat rolls, homemade pies, and even hot dogs if you need them. Several picnic tables are under cover for chilly or rainy weather; beer and wine are served.

A broad view of islands in the Mussel Ridge Channel is the bonanza at ◖ **Waterman's Beach Lobster** (343 Waterman's Beach Rd., South Thomaston, 207/596-7819, www.watermansbeachlobster.com, 11am-7pm Wed.-Sun., no credit cards). This tiny operation has a big reputation: It won a James Beard Award. It turns out lobster, clam, and mussel dinners, fat lobster and crabmeat rolls, and superb pies as well as hot dogs and grilled cheese. Step up to the window and place your order. Service can be slow, but why rush with a view like this? Choose a good day; there's no real shelter from bad weather. BYOB. The wharf is on a side road off Route 73 between Spruce Head Village and South Thomaston; watch for signs on Route 73.

The dreamy spruce-cropped island views alone are worth the trip to **McLoon's Lobster Shack** (327 Island Rd., Spruce Head, 207/593-1382, www.mcloonslobster.com, 11am-7pm daily), but this off-the-beaten-path shack dishes out mighty fine lobster, lobster rolls, lobster stew, crab cakes, and house-made desserts.

Doug's Seafood (686 Port Clyde Rd., Port Clyde, 207/372-8533, 11am-7pm Mon.-Sat.), a roadside stand, is a good bet for reasonably priced lobster rolls and fried seafood.

GETTING THERE AND AROUND
Port Clyde is about 15 miles or 25 minutes via Route 131 from Thomaston.

Monhegan Island

Eleven or so miles from the mainland lies a unique island community with gritty lobstermen, close-knit families, a longstanding summertime artists' colony, no cars, astonishingly beautiful scenery, and some of the best birdwatching on the eastern seaboard. Until the 1980s the island had only radiophones and generator power; with the arrival of electricity and real phones, the pace has quickened a bit—but not much. Welcome to **Monhegan Island.**

But first a cautionary note: Monhegan has remained idyllic largely because generations of residents, part-timers, and visitors have been sensitive to its fragility. When you buy your ferry ticket, you'll receive a copy of the regulations, all very reasonable, and the captain of your ferry will repeat them. *Heed them, or don't go.*

Many of the regulations have been developed by The Monhegan Associates, an island land trust founded in the 1960s by Theodore Edison, son of inventor Thomas Edison. Firmly committed to preservation of the island in as natural a state as possible, the group maintains and marks the trails, sponsors natural-history talks, and insists that no construction be allowed beyond the village limits.

The origin of the name *Monhegan* remains up in the air; it's either a Maliseet or Micmac name meaning "out-to-sea island" or

Artists capture iconic scenes on Monhegan Island.

© HILARY NANGLE

PENOBSCOT BAY

TEN RULES FOR MONHEGAN VISITORS

- Smoking is banned everywhere except in the village.

- Rock climbing is not allowed on the wild headlands on the back side of the island.

- Preserve the island's wild state–do not remove flowers or lichens.

- Bicycles and strollers are not allowed on island trails.

- Camping and campfires are forbidden island-wide.

- Swim only at Swim Beach, just south of the ferry landing–if your innards can stand the shock. Wait for the incoming tide, when the water is warmest (and this warmth is relative). It's wise not to swim alone.

- Dogs must be leashed; carry bags to remove their waste.

- Be respectful of private property; stay on the trails. (As the island visitors guide puts it, "Monhegan is a village, not a theme park.")

- If you're staying overnight, bring a flashlight; the village paths are very dark.

- Carry the island trail map when you go exploring; you'll need it.

- Carry a trash bag, use it, and take it off the island when you leave.

an adaptation of the name of a French explorer's daughter. In any case, Monhegan caught the attention of Europeans after English explorer John Smith stopped by in 1614, but the island had already been noticed by earlier adventurers, including John Cabot, Giovanni da Verrazzano, and George Waymouth. Legend even has it that Monhegan fishermen sent dried fish to Plimoth Plantation during the Pilgrims' first winter on Cape Cod. Captain Smith returned home and carried on about Monhegan, catching the attention of intrepid souls who established a fishing and trading outpost here in 1625. Monhegan has been settled continuously since 1674, with fishing as the economic base.

In the 1880s, lured by the spectacular setting and artist Robert Henri's enthusiastic reports, gangs of artists began arriving, lugging their easels here and there to capture the surf, the light, the tidy cottages, the magnificent headlands, fishing boats, even the islanders' craggy features. American, German, French, and British artists have long come here, and they still do; well-known painters associated with Monhegan include Rockwell Kent, George Bellows, Edward Hopper, James Fitzgerald, Andrew Winter, Alice Kent Stoddard, Reuben Tam, William Kienbusch, and Jamie Wyeth.

Officially called Monhegan Plantation, the island has about 70 year-rounders. Several hundred others summer here. A handful of students attend the tiny school through eighth grade; high-schoolers have to pack up and move "inshore" to the mainland during the school year.

At the schoolhouse, the biggest social event of the year is the Christmas party, when everyone brings casseroles, salads, and desserts to complement a big beef roast. Kids perform their Christmas play, Santa shows up with presents, and dozens of adults look on approvingly. The islanders turn out en masse for almost every special event at the school, and the adults treat the island kids almost like common property, feeling free to praise or chastise them any time it seems appropriate—a phenomenon unique to isolated island communities.

For years, Monhegan's legislated lobster-fishing season perversely began on December 1 (locally known as Trap Day), but in 2007 it was moved forward to October 1, making it possible for visitors to view the action. An air of nervous anticipation surrounds the dozen or so lobstermen after midnight the day before as they prepare to steam out to set their traps on the ocean floor. Of course, with less competition from mainland fishermen that time of year, and a supply of lobsters fattening up since the previous season, there's a ready market for their catch. But success still depends on a smooth "setting." Meetings are held daily during the month beforehand to make sure everyone will be ready to "set" together. The season lasts into June.

Almost within spitting distance of Monhegan's dock (but you'll still need a boat) is whale-shaped **Manana Island,** once the home of a former New Yorker named Ray Phillips. Known as the Hermit of Manana, Phillips lived a solitary sheepherding existence on this barren island for more than half a century until his death in 1975. His story had spread so far afield that even the *New York Times* ran a front-page obituary when he died. (Photos and clippings are displayed in the Monhegan Museum.) In summer, youngsters with skiffs often hang around the harbor, particularly Fish Beach and Swim Beach, and you can usually talk one of them into taking you over for a fee. (Don't try to talk them down too much or they may not return to pick you up.) Some curious inscriptions on Manana (marked with a yellow *X* near the boat landing) have led archaeologists to claim that Vikings even made it here, but cooler heads attribute the markings to Mother Nature.

One last note: Monhegan isn't for the mobility impaired. There's no public transportation, and roads are rough and hilly.

When to Go

If a day trip is all your schedule will allow, visit Monhegan between Memorial Day weekend and mid-October, when ferries from Port Clyde, New Harbor, and Boothbay Harbor operate daily, allowing 5-8 hours on the island—time enough to do an extensive trail loop, visit the museum and handful of shops, and picnic on the rocks. Other months, there's only one ferry per day from Port Clyde, and only three per week November-April, so you'll need to spend the night—not a hardship, but it definitely requires planning.

Almost any time of year, but especially in spring, fog can blanket the island, curtailing photography and swimming (although usually not the ferries). A spectacular sunny day can't be beat, but don't be deterred by fog, which lends an air of mystery you won't forget. Rain, of course, is another matter; some island trails can be perilous even in a misty drizzle.

Practicalities

Monhegan has no bank, but there are a couple of ATMs. Credit cards are not accepted everywhere. Personal checks, traveler's checks, or cash will do.

The only public restroom is on Horn Hill, at the southern end of the village (behind the Monhegan House). A donation of $0.50 is requested; don't complain, just drop what you can into the slot to help defray maintenance costs. It's a mere pittance to help keep the island clean.

Electricity is *very* expensive on the island (about $0.70/kilowatt hour compared with a national average of $0.09). Ask before plugging in a charger for your phone at any restaurant, shop, or other private biz, and don't be surprised if you're turned down.

SIGHTS

Monhegan is a getaway destination, a relaxing place for self-starters, so don't anticipate organized entertainment beyond the occasional lecture or narrated nature tour. Bring sturdy shoes (maybe even an extra pair in case trails are wet), a windbreaker, binoculars, a camera, and perhaps a sketchpad or a journal. If you're staying overnight, bring a flashlight for negotiating the unlighted island walkways, even in the village. For rainy days, bring a book. (If you forget, there's an amazingly good library.) In winter, bring ice skates for use on the Ice Pond.

Monhegan Historical and Cultural Museum

The **Monhegan Lighthouse**—activated in July 1824, automated in 1959, and now on the National Register of Historic Places—stands at the island's highest point, Lighthouse Hill, an exposed summit that's also home to the **Monhegan Historical and Cultural Museum** (207/596-7003, www.monheganmuseum. org, 11:30am-3:30pm daily July-Aug., hours

© HILARY NANGLE

Climb Lighthouse Hill to the Monhegan Historical and Cultural Museum for panoramic views of the village, Manana Island, and beyond.

vary June and Sept., $5) in the former keeper's house and adjacent buildings. Overseen by the Monhegan Historical and Cultural Museum Association, the museum has been updated in recent years and is well worth visiting. Exhibits displayed throughout the Keeper's House blend artwork by American icons such as Rockwell Kent and James Fitzgerald with historical photos and artifacts downstairs and an emphasis on flora, fauna, and the environment upstairs. The lighthouse tower is open one day weekly; call or check the website for current schedule. Two outbuildings have tools and gear connected with fishing and ice cutting, traditional island industries. The assistant light keeper's house, restored top to bottom as a handsome art gallery, provides a climate-controlled environment for the museum's impressive art collection. A volunteer is usually on hand to answer questions. Interesting note: Only works by deceased artists are shown as otherwise there are so many talented artists on the island. The museum also owns two buildings designed and built

by Rockwell Kent and later owned by James Fitzgerald (www.jamesfitzgerald.org). The house is maintained as a historic house museum and Fitzgerald's works are displayed in the studio. It's open twice weekly; call for current schedule.

Artists' Studios

Nearly 20 artists' studios are open to the public during the summer (usually July-August), but not all at once. At least five are open most days—most in the afternoon (Monday has the fewest choices). Sometimes it's tight timewise for day-trippers who also want to hike the trails, but most of the studios are relatively close to the ferry landing. An annually updated map-schedule details locations, days, and times. It's posted on bulletin boards in the village and is available at lodgings and shops.

Winter Works is a crafts co-op and **Lupine Gallery** (207/594-8131) showcases works by Monhegan artists. When you get off the ferry, walk up the hill, and one's on the left and the

PENOBSCOT BAY

other is dead ahead. You can't miss them—and shouldn't.

Monhegan Brewing Company

Lobsterman Matt Weber, son of a brewer, and his wife, Mary, a teacher, operate the seasonal **Monhegan Brewing Company** (1 Boody Ln., 207/975-3958, www.monheganbrewing. com, 11am-6pm daily, July-Aug.). Opened in 2013, they began with Lobster Cove APA and Shipwreck IPA as well as two nonalcoholic sodas, Trapyard Root Beer and ginger beer. The Webers are working with the Monhegan Island Farm Project, which composts the waste barley. Stop by the tasting room to see what's brewing.

RECREATION
Hiking and Walking

Just over half a mile wide and 1.7 miles long, barely a square mile in area, Monhegan has 18 numbered hiking trails, most of them easy to moderate, covering about 12 miles. All are described in the *Monhegan Associates Trail Map* (www.monheganassociates.org), available at mainland ferry offices and island shops and lodgings or on the website. (The map is not to scale, so the hikes can take longer than they may appear.)

The footing is uneven everywhere, so Monhegan can present major obstacles to those with disabilities, even on the well-worn but unpaved village roads. Maintain an especially healthy respect for the ocean here, and don't venture too close; through the years, rogue waves on the island's back side have claimed victims young and old.

A relatively easy **day-tripper loop,** with a couple of moderate sections along the back side of the island, takes in several of Monhegan's finest features starting at the southern end of the village, opposite the church. To appreciate it, allow at least two hours. From the Main Road, go up Horn Hill, following signs for the **Burnthead Trail** (no. 4). Cross the island to the **Cliff Trail** (no. 1). Turn north on the Cliff Trail, following the dramatic headlands on the island's back side. There are lots of great picnic rocks in this area. Continue to Squeaker Cove,

where the surf is the wildest, but be cautious. Then watch for signs to the **Cathedral Woods Trail** (no. 11), carpeted with pine needles and leading back to the village.

When you get back to Main Road, detour up the **Whitehead Trail** (no. 7) to the museum. If you're spending the night and feeling energetic, consider circumnavigating the island via the **Cliff Trail** (nos. 1 and 1-A). Allow at least 5-6 hours for this route; don't rush it.

Bird-Watching

One of the East Coast's best bird-watching sites during spring and fall migrations, Monhegan is a migrant trap for exhausted creatures winging their way north or south. Avid bird-watchers come here to add rare and unusual species to their life lists, and some devotees return year after year. No bird-watcher should arrive, however, without a copy of the superb *Birder's Guide to Maine*.

Predicting exact bird-migration dates can be dicey, since wind and weather aberrations can skew the schedule. Generally, the best times are mid-late May and most of September into early October. If you plan to spend a night (or more) on the island during migration seasons, don't try to wing it—reserve a room well in advance.

Around-the-Island Tour

On most days, the **Balmy Days excursion boat** makes a half-hour circuit around the island 2pm-2:30pm for a nominal fee. Ask at the ferry dock.

ACCOMMODATIONS

The island has a variety of lodgings from rustic to comfortable, but none are luxurious. Pickup trucks of dubious vintage meet all the ferries and transport luggage to the lodgings. For cottage renters, Monhegan Trucking charges a small fee for each piece of luggage.

The best lodging is the **Island Inn** (207/596-0371, www.islandinnmonhegan.com, $170-420), an imposing three-story hotel dating from 1816 that commands a prime chunk of real estate overlooking the harbor. Most guest rooms have been updated but retain the simplicity of another era, with painted floors, antique oak furnishings, and comfy beds covered with white down duvets. Just try to resist the siren song of the Adirondack chairs on the expansive veranda and lawns overlooking the ferry landing. Rates for the 32 harbor- and meadow-view guest rooms and suites (some with shared baths) include full breakfast. Add $5 pp daily gratuity and $10/room for a one-night stay.

In the heart of the village, **Monhegan House** (207/594-7983 or 800/599-7983, www.monheganhouse.com, late May-Columbus Day, $154-189), built in 1870, is a large four-story building with 28 guest rooms. All but two suites ($224) have shared baths; most are on the second floor, with a few powder rooms on the third floor. Don't miss the loose-leaf notebook in the lobby. Labeled *A Monhegan Novel,* it's the ultimate in shaggy-dog sagas, created by a long string of guests since 1992. A $3 pp service fee covers breakfast and housekeeping; there may be a $5 pp surcharge for one-night stays. Children are welcome; ages 4-12 are $19, ages 13 and older are $29.

A more modernized hostelry, **Shining Sails** (207/596-0041, www.shiningsails.com, $135-220) lacks the quaintness of the other inns, but the two guest rooms and five efficiencies are comfortable, convenient to the dock, and have private baths. Breakfast (included only in season) is meager continental. "Well-supervised" children are welcome. An additional four apartments ($165-230) are in a separate building. Shining Sails also manages more than two dozen weekly-rental cottages and apartments, with rates beginning around $800/week in season.

The funkiest lodging, and not for everyone, is **The Trailing Yew** (207/596-0440, www.trailingyew.com, $240, no credit cards). Spread among six rustic buildings are 35 guest rooms, most with shared baths (averaging five rooms per bath and not always in the same building) and lighted with kerosene (about 12 have electricity). Rates include breakfast, dinner, taxes, and gratuities; kids are $65-85, depending on age. The old-fashioned, low-key 50-seat dining

room is open to nonguests by reservation for dinner at 5:45pm, served family-style, and for breakfast at 7:45am. Bring a sleeping bag in spring or fall; rooms are unheated.

FOOD

Everything is quite casual, and food is hearty and ample, albeit pricey. None of the restaurants have liquor licenses, so buy beer or wine at one of the stores or the Barnacle Café, or bring it from the mainland. In most cases hours change frequently, so call first.

Prepared foods, varying from pastries to sandwiches and salads, are available from **Barnacle Café** (207/596-0371), under the same ownership as the nearby Island Inn; **The Novelty** (207/594-4926), behind and operated by The Monhegan House; **Black Duck Emporium** (207/596-7672); and **Monhegan Store**. The restaurant at the **Island Inn,** open to nonguests for breakfast and dinner from 6pm, has an excellent dinner menu with entrées ($19-36) emphasizing seafood; BYOB. It's also open for lunch Thursday-Sunday.

Islanders and visitors flock to the **Monhegan House Café,** overlooking the village, for breakfast and dinner (entrées $22-27).

You can't get much rougher for lobster in the rough than **Fish House Fish** (Fish Beach, 11:30am-7pm daily). Lobster and crabmeat rolls, locally smoked fish, and homemade stews and chowders are on the menu as well as fresh lobster. Take it to the picnic tables on the beach and enjoy.

INFORMATION AND SERVICES

Several free brochures and flyers, revised annually, will answer most questions about planning a day trip or overnight visit to Monhegan. Ferries supply visitors with the *Visitor's Guide to Monhegan Island* and sell the Monhegan Associates Trail Map ($1). Both are also available at island shops, galleries, and lodgings. Info is also available at www.monheganwelcome.com and www.monhegan.info.

Monhegan's pleasant little Jackie and Edward Library was named after two children who drowned in the surf in the 1920s. The fiction collection is especially extensive, and it's open to everyone.

Also check the Rope Shed, the community bulletin board next to the meadow, right in the village. Monhegan's version of a bush telegraph, it's where everyone posts flyers and notices about nature walks, lectures, excursions, and other special events. You'll also see the current Monhegan Artists Studio Locations map.

GETTING THERE AND AROUND

Ferries travel year-round to Monhegan from Port Clyde at the end of the St. George Peninsula. Seasonal service to the island is provided from New Harbor by **Hardy Boat Cruises** and from Boothbay Harbor by **Balmy Days Cruises.**

Part of the daily routine for many islanders and summer folk is a stroll to the harbor when the ferry comes in, so don't be surprised to see a good-size welcoming party when you arrive. You're the live entertainment.

Monhegan's only vehicles are a handful of pickup trucks owned by local lobstermen and li'l ol' trucks used by **Monhegan Trucking.** If you're staying a night or longer and your luggage is too heavy to carry, they'll be waiting when you arrive at the island wharf.

Rockland

A "Share the Pride" campaign—kicked off in the 1980s to boost sagging civic self-esteem and the local economy—was the first step in the transformation of **Rockland** (pop. 7,297). Once a run-down county seat best known for the aroma of its fish-packing plants, the city has undergone a sea change and in 2010 was named a Distinctive Destination by the National Trust for Historic Preservation. The expansion of the Farnsworth Museum of American Art and the addition of its Wyeth Center was a catalyst. Benches and plants line Main Street (Rte. 1), independent stores offer appealing wares, coffeehouses and more than a dozen art galleries attract a diverse clientele, and Rockland Harbor is home to more windjammer cruise schooners than neighboring Camden (which had long claimed the title "Windjammer Capital"). If you haven't been to Rockland in the last decade, prepare to be astonished.

Foresighted entrepreneurs had seen the potential of the bayside location in the late 1700s and established a tiny settlement here called "Shore Village" (or "the Shore"). Today's commercial-fishing fleet is one of the few reminders of Rockland's past, when multimasted schooners lined the wharves, some to load volatile cargoes of lime destined to become building material for cities all along the eastern seaboard, others to head northeast—toward the storm-racked Grand Banks and the lucrative cod fishery there. Such hazardous pursuits meant an early demise for many a local seafarer, but Rockland's 5,000 or so residents were enjoying their prosperity in the late 1840s. The settlement was home to more than two dozen shipyards and dozens of lime kilns, was enjoying a construction boom, and boasted a newspaper and regular steamship service. By 1854, Rockland had become a city.

Today, Rockland remains a commercial hub—with Knox County's only shopping plazas (no malls, but the big-box stores have arrived), a fishing fleet that heads far offshore, and ferries that connect nearby islands. Rockland also claims the title of "Lobster Capital of the World" thanks to Knox County's shipment nationally and internationally of 10 million pounds of lobster each year. The weathervane atop the police and fire department building is a giant copper lobster.

Rockland is more year-round community than tourist town, which adds to its appeal. But visitors pour in during two big summer festivals—the North Atlantic Blues Festival in mid-July and the Maine Lobster Festival in early August. A highlight of the Lobster Festival is King Neptune's coronation of the Maine Sea Goddess—carefully selected from a bevy of local young women—who then sails off with him to his water domain.

SIGHTS
◖ The Farnsworth Art Museum and the Wyeth Center

Anchoring downtown Rockland is the nationally respected **Farnsworth Art Museum** (16 Museum St., 207/596-6457, www.farnsworthmuseum.org), established in 1948 through a trust fund set up by Rocklander Lucy Farnsworth. With an ample checkbook, the first curator, Robert Bellows, toured the country, accumulating a splendid collection of 19th- and 20th-century Maine-related American art, the basis for the permanent *Maine in America* exhibition.

The 6,000-piece collection today includes works by Fitz Hugh Lane, Gilbert Stuart, Eastman Johnson, Childe Hassam, John Marin, Maurice Prendergast, Rockwell Kent, George Bellows, and Marsden Hartley. Best known are the paintings by three generations of the Wyeth family (local summer residents) and sculpture by Louise Nevelson, who grew up in Rockland. Sculpture, jewelry, and paintings by Nevelson form the core of the third-floor Nevelson-Berliawsky Gallery for 20th Century Art. (The only larger Nevelson collection is in New York's Whitney Museum of American Art.) The **Wyeth Center,** across Union Street in a former church, contains the work of Andrew, N. C., and Jamie Wyeth. The 6,000-square-foot Jamien Morehouse Wing hosts rotating exhibits.

In the Farnsworth's library—a grand, high-ceilinged oasis akin to an English gentleman's reading room—browsers and researchers can explore an extensive collection of art books and magazines. The museum's education department annually sponsors hundreds of lectures, concerts, art classes for all ages, poetry readings, and field trips. Most are open to non-members; some require an extra fee. A glitzy gift shop stocks posters, prints, note cards, imported gift items, and art games for children.

Next door to the museum is the mid-19th-century Greek Revival **Farnsworth Homestead** ($12 adults, $10 seniors and students age 17 and older, free under age 17), with original high-Victorian furnishings. Looking as though William Farnsworth's family just took off for the day, the house has been preserved rather than restored. The Farnsworth is open year-round, including summer holidays. Farnsworth hours are 10am-5pm Thursday-Tuesday, 10am-8pm Wednesday in summer; 10am-5pm Tuesday-Sunday in spring and fall, and 10am-5pm Wednesday-Sunday in winter. The Homestead (10am-5pm daily) and the Olson House (11am-4pm daily) are open late May-mid-October.

The Farnsworth also owns the Olson House, 14 miles away in nearby Cushing, where the whole landscape looks like a Wyeth diorama. Pick up a map at the museum to help you find the house; it's definitely worth the side trip.

◖ Owls Head Transportation Museum

Don't miss this place, even if you're not an old-vehicle buff. A generous endowment has made the **Owls Head Transportation Museum** (Rte. 73, Owls Head, 207/594-4418, www.ohtm.org, 10am-5pm daily, $10 adults, $8 seniors, free under age 18, special events are extra) a premier facility for celebrating wings and wheels; it draws more than 75,000 visitors per year. Scads of eager volunteers help restore the vehicles and keep them running. On weekends May-October, the museum sponsors air shows (often including aerobatic displays) and car and truck meets for hundreds of enthusiasts. The season highlight is the annual rally and aerobatic show (early Aug.), when more than 300 vehicles gather for two days of festivities. Want your own vintage vehicle? Attend the antique, classic, and special-interest auto auction (third Sun. in Aug.). The gift shop carries transportation-related items. If the kids get bored (unlikely), there's a play area outside with picnic tables. In winter, groomed cross-country-skiing trails wind through the museum's 60-acre site; ask for a map at the information desk.

Maine Lighthouse Museum

The headliner at the **Maine Discovery Center** (1 Park Dr.) is the **Maine Lighthouse Museum** (207/594-3301, www.mainelighthousemuseum.org, 9am-5pm Mon.-Fri., 10am-4pm Sat.-Sun. in summer, by appt. in winter, $5 adults, $4 seniors, free under age 12), home to the nation's largest collection of Fresnel lenses, along with a boatload-plus of artifacts related to lighthouses, the Coast Guard, and the sea. On view are foghorns, ships' bells, nautical books and photographs, marine instruments, ship models, scrimshaw, and so much more.

Project Puffin Visitor Center

If you can't manage a trip to see the puffins, Audubon's **Project Puffin Visitor Center** (311 Main St., 207/596-5566 or 877/478-3346, www.projectpuffin.org, 10am-5pm daily to 7pm Wed., June 1-Oct. 31, call for off-season hours) will bring them to you. Live videos of nesting puffins are just one of the features of the center, which also includes interactive exhibits, a gallery, and films, all highlighting successful efforts to restore and protect these clowns of the sea. Ask about children's programs and lecture series.

◖ Rockland Breakwater

Protecting the harbor from wind-driven waves, the 4,346-foot-long **Rockland Breakwater** took 18 years to build with 697,000 tons of locally quarried granite. In the late 19th century it was piled up, chunk by chunk, from a base 175 feet wide on the harbor floor (60 feet below the surface) to the 43-foot-wide cap. The Breakwater Light—now automated— was built in 1902 and added to the National Register of Historic Places in 1981. The city of Rockland owns the keeper's house, but the Friends of the Rockland Harbor Lights (www.rocklandharborlights.org) maintain it. Volunteers usually open the lighthouse to the public 10am-5pm Saturday-Sunday late May-mid-October and for special events. The breakwater provides unique vantage points for photographers as well as a place to picnic or catch sea breezes or fish on a hot day, but it is extremely dangerous during storms. Anyone on the breakwater risks being washed into the sea or struck by lightning (ask the local hospital staff; it has happened). Do not take chances when the weather is iffy.

To reach the breakwater, take Route 1 North to Waldo Avenue and turn right. Take the next right onto Samoset Road and drive to the end to **Marie Reed Memorial Park** (with a tiny beach, benches, and limited parking). Or go to the Samoset Resort and walk the path to the breakwater from there.

Sail, Power & Steam Museum

Opened in 2009, the **Sail, Power & Steam Museum** (Sharp's Point South, 75 Mechanic St., 207/701-7626, www.sailpowerandsteammuseum.org, 10am-3:30pm Wed.-Sat., 1pm-4pm Sun.) is Captain Jim Sharp's labor of love. Built on the grounds of the former Snow Shipyard, the museum displays highlight Rockland's maritime heritage and include half models of boats used by shipbuilders in the 19th century, vintage photos, tools of the trade, and other artifacts. Concerts are frequently held on the site. Free guided tours are offered 2pm-3pm Wednesday; musical jams take place 2pm-4pm Sunday.

Main Street Historic District

Rocklanders are justly proud of their **Main Street Historic District,** lined with 19th- and early-20th-century Greek and Colonial Revival structures as well as examples of mansard and Italianate architecture. Most now house retail shops on the ground floor; upper floors have offices, artists' studios, and apartments. The chamber of commerce has a map and details.

ENTERTAINMENT AND EVENTS

The historic **Strand Theater** (339 Main St., 207/594-7266, www.rocklandstrand.com), opened in 1923, underwent an extensive restoration in 2005. Films as well as live

© HILARY NANGLE

A nearly mile-long breakwater tethers the Samoset Resort to Rockland Breakwater Light.

entertainment are scheduled. It's also the venue for many **Bay Chamber Concerts** (207/236-2823 or 888/707-2770, www.baychamberconcerts.org) events.

The Historic Inns of Rockland coordinate the annual **January Pies on Parade,** when the inns and dozens of downtown businesses serve a variety of sweet and savory pies as a fundraiser for the local food pantry. It's always a sellout.

In mid-July the **North Atlantic Blues Festival** means a weekend of festivities featuring big names in blues. Thousands of fans jam Harbor Park for the nonstop music.

August's **Maine Lobster Festival** is a five-day lobster extravaganza with live entertainment, the Maine Sea Goddess pageant, a lobster-crate race, crafts booths, boat rides, a parade, lobster dinners, and megacrowds (the hotels are full for miles in either direction). Tons of lobsters bite the dust during the weekend despite annual protests by People for the Ethical Treatment of Animals. (The protests, however, only seem to increase the crowds.)

SHOPPING
Galleries

Piggybacking on the fame of the Farnsworth Museum, or at least working symbiotically, art galleries line Rockland's main street and many side streets. Ask around and look around. During the summer, many of them coordinate monthly openings to coincide with **First Friday Art Walks** (www.artsinrockland.org), so you can meander, munch, and sip from one gallery to another.

Across from the Farnsworth's side entrance, the **Caldbeck Gallery** (12 Elm St., 207/594-5935, www.caldbeck.com) has gained a top-notch reputation as a must-see (and must-be-seen) space. Featuring the work of contemporary Maine artists, the gallery mounts more than half a dozen solo and group shows in May-September each year.

Eric Hopkins Gallery (21 Winter St., 207/594-1996) shows the North Haven artist's colorful aerial-view paintings.

Archipelago (386 Main St., 207/596-0701), on the ground floor of the Island Institute, a

© TOM NANGLE

Owls Head Light State Park

nonprofit steward of Maine's 4,617 offshore islands, is an attractive retail outlet for talented craftspeople from 14 year-round islands.

Other eminently browsable downtown Rockland galleries are **Harbor Square Gallery** (374 Main St., 207/594-8700 or 877/594-8700, www.harborsquaregallery.com), **Dowling Walsh Gallery,** 365 Main St., 207/596-0084, www.dowlingwalsh.com), **Landing Gallery** (8 Elm St., 207/594-4544), and **Playing with Fire! Glassworks & Gallery** (497 Main St., 207/594-7805, www.playingwithfireglassworks.com).

RECREATION
Parks
◖ OWLS HEAD LIGHT STATE PARK

On Route 73, about 1.5 miles past the junction of Routes 1 and 73, you'll reach North Shore Road in the town of Owls Head. Turn left toward Owls Head Light State Park. Standing 3.6 miles from this turn, Owls Head Light occupies a dramatic promontory with panoramic views over Rockland Harbor and Penobscot

Bay. The **Keeper's House Interpretive Center & Gift Shop** (10am-4pm Wed.-Sun., Mon.-Tues. by chance) doubles as headquarters for the American Lighthouse Foundation (www.lighthousefoundation.org). The light tower is usually open 11am-4pm Wednesday and 10am-4pm Saturday-Sunday. The park surrounding the tower has easy walking paths, picnic tables, and a pebbly beach where you can sunbathe or check out Rockland Harbor's boating traffic. If it's foggy or rainy, don't climb the steps toward the light tower: The view evaporates in the fog, the access ramp can be slippery, and the foghorn is dangerously deafening. Follow signs to reach the park. From North Shore Road, turn left onto Main Street, then left onto Lighthouse Road, and continue along Owls Head Harbor to the parking area. This is also a particularly pleasant bike route—about 10 miles round-trip from downtown Rockland—although, once again, the roadside shoulders are poor along the Owls Head stretch.

HARBOR PARK

If you're looking for a park with more commotion than quiet green space, spend some time at **Harbor Park.** Boats, cars, and delivery vehicles come and go, and you can corner a picnic table, a bench, or a patch of grass and watch all the action. During the holidays, a lobster-trap Christmas tree presides over the park. Public restrooms (late May-mid-Oct.) are available. The park is just off Main Street.

Swimming

Lucia Beach is the local name for **Birch Point Beach State Park,** one of the best-kept secrets in the area. In Owls Head, just south of Rockland—and not far from Owls Head Light—the spruce-lined sand crescent (free) has rocks, shells, tidepools, and very chilly water. There are outhouses but no other facilities. There's ample room for a moderate-size crowd, although parking and turnaround space can get a bit tight on the access road. From downtown Rockland, take Route 73 one mile to North Shore Drive (on your left). Take the next right, Ash Point Drive, and continue

PENOBSCOT BAY

past Knox County Regional Airport to Dublin Road. Turn right, go 0.8 mile, then turn left onto Ballyhac Road (opposite the airport landing lights). Go another 0.8 mile, fork left, and continue 0.4 mile to the parking area.

If frigid ocean water doesn't appeal, head for freshwater **Chickawaukee Lake,** on Route 17, two miles inland from downtown Rockland. Don't expect to be alone, though; on hot days, **Johnson Memorial Park**'s pocket-size sand patch is a major attraction. A lifeguard stands watch, and there are restrooms, picnic tables, a snack bar, and a boat-launch ramp. In winter, iceboats, snowmobiles, and ice-fishing shacks take over the lake. A signposted bicycle path runs alongside the busy highway, making the park an easy pedal from town.

Golf

The semiprivate **Rockland Golf Club** (606 Old County Rd., 207/594-9322, www.rockland-golf.com, Apr.-Oct.) is an 18-hole course 0.2 mile northeast of Route 17.

For an 18-hole course in an unsurpassed waterfront setting (but with steep rental and greens fees), tee off at the **Samoset Resort** (220 Warrenton St., Rockport, 207/594-2511 or 800/341-1650).

Sea Kayaking

Veteran Maine Guide and naturalist Mark DiGirolamo is the spark plug behind **Breakwater Kayak** (Rockland Public Landing, 207/596-6895 or 877/559-8800, www.breakwaterkayak.com), which has a full range of tours, even multiday ones. A two-hour Rockland Harbor tour is $45, and the all-day Owls Head Lighthouse tour is $110, including lunch. Reservations are advisable. This outfit is particularly eco-sensitive—Mark has a degree in environmental science—and is definitely worth supporting. Maine Audubon often taps Mark to lead natural-history field trips. Dress warmly and bring a filled water bottle.

Boat Excursions

Marine biologist Captain Bob Pratt is the skipper of *A Morning in Maine* (207/594-1844

or 207/691-7245 seasonal boat phone, www.amorninginmaine.com), a classic 55-foot ketch designed by noted naval architect R. D. (Pete) Culler and built by Concordia Yachts. June-October, *Morning* departs from the middle pier at the Rockland Public Landing three times daily for two-hour sails ($35), with plenty of knowledgeable commentary from Captain Pratt. A 6pm sunset sail is available in July-August.

Watch Captain Steve Hale set and haul lobster traps during a 1.25-hour cruise ($30 adults, $18 under age 12) aboard the *Captain Jack* (Rockland Harbor, 207/594-1048, www.captainjacklobstertours.com), a 30-foot working lobster boat. Cruises depart up to six times daily Monday-Saturday May-October. Note that there are no toilets aboard. Captain Jack offers a lobster-roll lunch cruise for $45 pp. Reservations required; minimum two people for a trip.

Maine State Ferry Service

Car and passenger ferries service the islands of Vinalhaven, North Haven, and Matinicus. The Vinalhaven and North Haven routes make fantastic day trips (especially with a bike), or you can spend the night; the Matinicus ferry is much less predictable, and island services are few.

Bicycling

Rentals (from $25), sales, and repair are provided by **Sidecountry Sports** (481 Main St., 207/701-5100, www.sidecountrysports.com).

ACCOMMODATIONS

If you're planning an overnight stay in the Rockland area the first weekend in August—during the Maine Lobster Festival—make reservations well in advance. Festival attendance runs close to 100,000, so "No Vacancy" signs extend from Waldoboro to Belfast.

Samoset Resort

The 221-acre **Samoset Resort** (220 Warrenton St., Rockport, 207/594-2511 or 800/341-1650, www.samoset.com, from about

WINDJAMMING

© TOM NANGLE

Don't miss the opportunity to view windjammers under full sail.

In 1936, Camden became the home of the "cruise schooner" (sometimes called "dude schooner") trade when Captain Frank Swift restored a creaky wooden vessel and offered sailing vacations to paying passengers. He kept at it for 25 years, gradually adding other boats to the fleet. Now, more than a dozen sail Penobscot Bay's waters. Rockland wrested the Windjammer Capital title from Camden in the mid-1990s and so far has held onto it.

Named for their ability to "jam" into the wind when they carried freight up and down the New England coast, windjammers trigger images of the Great Age of Sail. Most member vessels of the Maine Windjammer Association are rigged as schooners, with two or three soaring wooden masts; their lengths range 64-132 feet. Seven are National Historic Landmarks.

These windjammers head out for 2-6 days late May-mid-October, tucking into coves and harbors around Penobscot Bay and its islands. They set their itineraries by the wind, propelled by stiff breezes to Buck's Harbor, North Haven, and Deer Isle. Everything's totally informal, geared for relaxing.

You're aboard for the experience, not for luxury, so expect basic accommodations with

$275) commands a spectacular oceanfront site straddling the boundary between Rockland and Rockport, the next town to the north. Built on the ashes of a classic 19th-century summer hotel, the Samoset is a full-service, modern family-oriented resort. Most of its 178 guest rooms and suites, all refurbished since 2007, and four cottages have knock-out ocean views and all the expected bells and whistles. Facilities include a fitness center with an indoor heated pool, an outdoor zero-entry heated pool with a bar and food service, lighted tennis courts, a children's day camp (ages 5-12, morning and evening sessions), daily planned activities, access to the adjacent famed Rockland Breakwater, a fabulous 18-hole waterfront golf course, full-service spa, and casual restaurant and lounge

with outdoor terrace seating. For a real treat, book the Flume cottage.

Bed-and-Breakfasts

These bed-and-breakfasts are in Rockland's historic district, within easy walking distance of downtown attractions and restaurants; all are members of the **Historic Inns of Rockland Maine** (www.historicinnsofrockland.com), which coordinates the January Pies on Parade event—a blast.

Most elegant is **☾ The Berry Manor Inn** (81 Talbot Ave., 207/596-7696 or 800/774-5692, www.berrymanorinn.com, $145-310), on a quiet side street a few blocks from downtown. Cheryl Michaelsen and Michael LaPosta have totally restored the manse built in 1898 by wealthy Rocklander Charles Berry as a wedding

few frills, although newer vessels were built with passenger trade in mind and tend to be a bit more comfy. Below deck, cabins typically are small and basic, with paper-thin walls—sort of a campground afloat (earplugs are often available for light sleepers). It may not sound romantic, but be aware that the captains keep track of postcruise marriages. Most boats have shared showers and toilets. If you're Type A, given to pacing, don't inflict yourself on the cruising crowd; if you're flexible, ready for whatever, go ahead and sign on. You can help with the sails, eat, curl up with a book, inhale salt air, snap photos, eat, sunbathe, bird-watch, chat up fellow passengers, sleep, eat, or just settle back and enjoy spectacular sailing you'll never forget.

When you book a cruise, you'll receive all the details and directions, but for a typical trip, you arrive at the boat by 7pm for the captain's call to meet your fellow passengers. You sleep aboard at the dock that night and then depart midmorning and spend the next nights and days cruising Penobscot Bay, following the wind, the weather, and the whims of the captain. (Many of the windjammers have no engines, only a motorized yawl boat used as a pusher and a water taxi.) You might anchor in a deserted cove and explore the shore, or you might pull into a harbor and hike, shop, and barhop. Then it's back to the boat for chow—windjammer cooks are legendary for creating three hearty all-you-can-eat meals daily, including at least one lobster feast. When the cruise ends, most passengers find it hard to leave.

On the summer cruising schedule, several weeks coincide with special windjammer events, so you'll need to book a berth far in advance for these: mid-June (Boothbay Harbor's Windjammer Days), Fourth of July week (Great Schooner Race), Labor Day weekend (Camden's Windjammer Weekend), and the second week in September (WoodenBoat Sail-In).

Most windjammers offering sails out of Camden, Rockland, and Rockport are members of the **Maine Windjammer Association** (800/807-9463, www.sailmainecoast.com), a one-stop resource for vessel and schedule information. One that isn't but is renowned for its onboard cuisine is the **Schooner J. & E. Riggin** (207/594-1875, www.mainewindjammer.com), captained by the husband-wife team of Annie Mahle, author of two cookbooks, and Jon Finger.

gift for his wife (thoughtful fellow). High ceilings and wonderful Victorian architectural touches are everywhere, especially in the enormous front hall and two parlors. Guest rooms and suites are spread between the main house and adjacent carriage house. Most have gas fireplaces and whirlpool tubs. All have air-conditioning, flat-screen TVs and video players, and Wi-Fi. A guest pantry is stocked with free soft drinks and juices and sweets—not that you'll be hungry after the extravagant breakfast.

Opened in 1996, the **Captain Lindsey House Inn** (5 Lindsey St., 207/596-7950 or 800/523-2145, www.lindseyhouse.com, $198-228) is more like a boutique hotel than a bed-and-breakfast. The Barnes family gutted the 1835 brick structure and restored it dramatically, adding such modernities as phones,

air-conditioning, Wi-Fi, and TVs. The decor is strikingly handsome, not at all fussy or frilly. Don't miss the 1926 safe in the front hall or the hidden-from-the-street garden patio—not to mention the antiques from everywhere that fill the nine comfortable guest rooms. It's smack downtown, and a few rooms have glimpses of the water. Rates include an extensive hot-and-cold breakfast buffet and afternoon refreshments.

The Limerock Inn (96 Limerock St., 207/594-2257 or 800/546-3762, www.limerockinn.com, $159-239) is a lovely painted lady. The 1890s Queen Anne mansion, with wraparound porch and turret, is listed on the National Register of Historic Places. Each of the eight guest rooms has its own distinctive flavor—such as the Turret Room, with

PENOBSCOT BAY

a wedding canopy bed, and the pet-friendly Island Cottage Room, with a private deck overlooking the back gardens. All are elegantly furnished with an emphasis on guest comfort. Three have whirlpool tubs, and one has a fireplace; there's Wi-Fi and air-conditioning throughout. The inviting decor blends family antiques with mid-century modern furnishings and original art.

Traveling with Fido and the kiddos? Check into the kid- and pet-friendly **Granite Inn** (546 Main St., Rockland, 800/386-9036, www.old-graniteinn.com, $95-215), where you can practically roll out of bed and onto an island ferry. Unlike most historical inns, the decor leans to contemporary and a bit artsy.

FOOD

Rockland is gaining a reputation as a foodie town, with new options opening regularly.

Local Flavors

The local hot spot for breakfast and lunch is **Home Kitchen Cafe** (650 Main St., 207/596-2449, www.homekitchencafe.com 7am-3pm Mon. and Wed.-Sat., 7am-9pm Wed.-Sat., and 8am-2pm Sun., $4-10), where the huevos rancheros and lobster tacos earn raves. The menu is extensive and creative. Breakfast and lunch are served all day long, and dinner specials are available in the evening.

Holding down the other end of Main Street is the **Brass Compass Café** (305 Main St., 207/596-5960, 5am-3pm Mon.-Sat., 6am-3pm Sun.), a great choice for Maine fare. The portions are big, the prices are small, and most of the ingredients are locally sourced. Sit indoors or on the dog-friendly patio. If you go for breakfast, the fish cakes are a real taste of Maine.

Taking an early ferry? Grab breakfast at **The Brown Bag** (606 Main St., 207/596-6372 or 800/287-6372), a café and bakery just up the street from the terminal. The bakery (6:30am-4pm) serves light breakfasts until 10:30am; lunch is available 10am-3pm.

Hot diggity dog! Backed up against an outside wall of The Brown Bag is a long-standing Rockland lunch landmark—**Wasses Hot Dogs** (2 N. Main St., 207/594-7472, 10:30am-6pm Mon.-Sat., 11am-4pm Sun. year-round), source of great chili dogs. This onetime lunch wagon is now a permanent modular building—only for takeout, though.

Lots of Rockland-watchers credit **Rock City Cafe** (252 Main St., 207/594-4123, www.rockcitycoffee.com), with sparking the designer-food renaissance in town. Lunch is served 11am-3pm daily

Scratch-made bread, pastries, and grab-and-go sandwiches have made **Atlantic Baking Co.** (351 Main St., 207/596-0505, www.atlanticbakingco.com, 7am-6pm Mon.-Sat., 8am-4pm Sun.) a popular spot for a quick informal lunch. There are plenty of tables to enjoy your treats, or take it to the waterfront park.

If you're craving a decent breakfast or lunch and are up for a little foray "down the peninsula," head for the **Owls Head General Store** (2 S. Shore Dr., Owls Head, 207/596-6038, 7am-3pm Sun.-Thurs., 7am-7pm Fri.-Sat.), where the atmosphere is friendly and definitely contagious. If you get lost, the helpful staff will steer you the right way, and they will even take your photograph in front of the store. Despite all the competition from lobster-in-the-rough places, the lobster roll here is among the best around, and more than one critic has proclaimed the 7-Napkin Burger as the state's best.

The **Rockland Farmers Market** sets up 9am-1pm every Thursday June-September at Harbor Park on Rockland's Public Landing.

Fiore (503 Main St., 207/596-0276, www.fioreoliveoils.com), an artisan olive oil and vinegar tasting room and retail store, is a delicious addition to downtown Rockland.

Ethnic Fare

Ask local pooh-bah chefs where they go on their night off, and the answer often is Keiko Suzuki Steinberger's **Suzuki's Sushi Bar** (419 Main St., 207/596-7447, www.suzukisushi.com, from 5pm Tues.-Sat.). The food matches the decor: simple yet sophisticated. Sashimi, *nigiri, maki,* and *temaki* choices range $6-10; hot entrées are $14-28. Both hot and cold sake are served, or try a saketume, made with gin or vodka, sake, and an *ume* plum. Reservations are essential.

An avocado-and-gold dining room is the appropriate setting for the Cal-Mex food dished out at **Sunfire Mexican Grill** (488 Main St., 207/594-6196, 11am-3pm Tues.-Sat., and 5pm-8pm Wed.-Sat.). You'll find all the usuals, from tacos to seafood specialties; most choices run $8-17. Everything is prepared fresh on-site.

Authentic Italian cuisine draws repeat customers to **Rustica** (315 Main St., 207/594-0025, www.rusticamaine.com, 5pm-9pm Mon.-Sat., $13-24). The two dining areas are comfortable yet refined, with candles on the tables; the fare is fresh and plentiful.

Hard to say which is better, the views or the fare at **La Bella Vita & The Enoteca Lounge** (220 Warrenton St., 207/594-2511, www.labellavitaristorante.com) at the Samoset Resort. Ocean Properties operates this restaurant at other properties, but this one really shines. The flavor is Italian, with pastas, pizzas from the wood-fired oven, and other specialties. Views from the restaurant and deck over the golf course to the ocean are terrific. It's open daily for breakfast, lunch, and dinner; Sunday brunch is served noon-2:30pm.

Casual Dining

Big flavors come out of the tiny kitchen at **Café Miranda** (15 Oak St., 207/594-2034, www.cafemiranda.com, 11:30am-2pm and 5pm-9:30pm Mon.-Sat., 10:30am-2pm Sun.). The menu is overwhelming in size and hard to read; it's even harder to digest the flavor contrasts, which will make your brain spin. When it works, it shines, but when it doesn't, it can be painful. Entrées are $18-27, but many of the appetizers ($6.50-12.50) are enough for a meal. Fresh-from-the-brick-oven focaccia comes with everything. If you sit at the counter, you can watch chef-owner Kerry Altiero's creations emerging from the oven. Beer and wine only. Reservations are essential throughout the summer and on weekends off-season; there is patio dining in season.

At the end of a day exploring Rockland, it's hard to beat **In Good Company** (415 Main St., 207/593-9110, www.ingoodcompanymaine.com, from 4:30pm daily), a chic and casual wine and tapas bar. Sit at the bar and watch chef-owner Melody Wolfertz, a Culinary Institute of America grad, concoct her creative tapas-style selection of small and large plates; entrées are $19-25.

There's a decidedly Southern accent to chef-owner Josh Hixson's menu **3 Crow** (449 Main St., 207/593-0812, www.3crow.com, 5pm-9pm daily), which has options such as ribs, hush puppies, and lobster 'n' grits. Most entrées are around $20. Fourteen craft brews rotate on the taps, and there's an extensive selection of whiskeys.

Destination Dining

Arriving in Rockland trailing a James Beard Award-winning reputation, chef Melissa Kelly opened **Primo** (2 S. Maine St./Rte. 73, 207/596-0770, www.primorestaurant.com) in 2000 and hasn't had time to breathe since. She has gone on to open two other restaurants, and in 2007 expanded this one, in an air-conditioned Victorian home. In 2013 she earned her second Beard Award for Best Chef in the Northeast. Fresh local ingredients, many from the restaurant's gardens, are a high priority, and unusual fish specials appear every day; pork and chicken are raised on the premises. Primo is really three experiences under one roof: the intimate and elegant dining rooms downstairs; the upstairs bar, with a handful of tables; and an upstairs counter, with seating by an open kitchen as well as at tables. There are two menus, one for the dining room (entrées from $32) and the counter menu, which highlights cheeses and charcuterie and small plates, making it possible to mix and match a meal of tapas-size portions and stay within a budget. Upstairs you can dine from either menu. Kelly's partner, Price Kushner, produces an impressive range of breads and desserts. Reservations are essential for the dining rooms, usually at least a week ahead on midsummer weekends—and you still may have to wait when you get there; no reservations are taken for the upstairs bar or counter. Primo opens at 5pm daily June-December, with fewer days off-season.

Lobster

Both Waterman's and Miller's are within easy reach. For a no-frills on-the-dock-with-the-bait experience, head to **Ship to Shore Lobster Co.** (7 Wharf St., Owls Head, 207/594-4606, www.shiptoshorelobster.com, 10am-6pm daily). They'll cook up a lobster for you, but you need to bring everything else. Ask about their Adopt-a-Lobster program.

INFORMATION AND SERVICES

For visitor information visit the **Penobscot Bay Regional Chamber of Commerce** (Gateway Center, 207/596-0376 or 800/223-5459, www.mainedreamvacation.com) or **Rockland Public Library** (80 Union St., 207/594-0310, www.rocklandlibrary.org).

Find **public restrooms** at the Gateway Center; the Knox County Courthouse (Union St. and Masonic St.); the Rockland Recreation Center (Union St. and Limerock St.), across from the courthouse, next to the playground; the Rockland Public Library; and the Maine State Ferry Service terminal.

GETTING THERE AND AROUND

Rockland is about five miles or 10 minutes via Route 1 from Thomaston. It's about eight miles or 15 minutes via Route 1 to Camden.

The scenic **Maine Eastern Railroad** (207/596-6725 or 800/637-2457, www.maineeasternrailroad.com), operates between Brunswick and Rockland with stops in Bath and Wiscasset, and Newcastle; and connects with the Amtrak Downeaster. The train operates Friday-Sunday, early July through mid-October. Adult fares range $26-37 round-trip; $17-24 one way; kids 4-11 are $16-22/$10-15. A shuttlebus connects Wiscasset to Boothbay for $8/4.

Vinalhaven and North Haven Islands

Vinalhaven (pop. 1,165) and neighboring **North Haven** (pop. 355) have been known as the Fox Islands ever since 1603, when English explorer Martin Pring sailed these waters and allegedly spotted gray foxes in his search for sustenance. Nowadays, you'll find reference to that name only on nautical charts, identifying the passage between the two islands as the Fox Islands Thorofare—and there's nary a fox in sight.

Each island has its own distinct personality. To generalize, Vinalhaven is bustling, whereas North Haven is sedate and exclusive.

VINALHAVEN

Five miles wide, 7.5 miles long, and covering 10,000 acres, Vinalhaven is 13 miles off the coast of Rockland—a 75-minute ferry trip. The shoreline has so many zigs and zags that no place on the island is more than a mile from the water.

The island is famed for its granite. The first blocks headed for Boston around 1826, and within a few decades quarrymen arrived from as far away as Britain and Finland to wrestle out and shape the incredibly resistant stone. Schooners, barges, and "stone sloops" left **Carver's Harbor** carrying mighty cargoes of granite destined for government and commercial buildings in Boston, New York, and Washington DC. In the 1880s, nearly 4,000 people lived on Vinalhaven, North Haven, and Hurricane Island. After World War I, demand declined, granite gave way to concrete and steel, and the industry petered out and died. But Vinalhaven has left its mark in ornate columns, paving blocks, and curbstones in communities as far west as Kansas City.

Vinalhaven is a serious working community, not primarily a playground. Lobster and fishing are the island's chief industry. Shopkeepers

© KATHRYN OSGOOD

Carver's Harbor

cater to locals as well as visitors, and increasing numbers of artists and artisans work away in their studios. For day-trippers, there's plenty to do—shopping, picnicking, hiking, biking, swimming—but an overnight stay provides a chance to sense the unique rhythm of life on a year-round island.

Sights

One Main Street landmark that's hard to miss is the three-story cupola-topped **Odd Fellows Hall,** a Victorian behemoth with American flag motifs on the lower windows and assorted gewgaws in the upper ones. Artist Robert Indiana, who first arrived as a visitor in 1969, owns the structure, built in 1885 for the Independent Order of Odd Fellows Star of Hope Lodge. It's not open to the public.

At the top of the hill just beyond Main Street (School St. and E. Main St.) is a greenish-blue replica **galamander,** a massive reminder of Vinalhaven's late-19th-century granite-quarrying era. Galamanders, hitched to oxen or horses, carried the stone from island quarries

to the finishing shops. (By the way, the origin of the name remains unexplained.) Next to the galamander is a colorful wooden bandstand, site of very popular evening band concerts held sporadically during the summer.

The **Vinalhaven Historical Society** (207/863-4410, www.vinalhavenhistoricalsociety.org, 11am-4pm Mon.-Sat., noon-3pm Sun. July-Aug. or by appointment, free) operates a delightful museum in the onetime town hall on High Street, just east of Carver's Cemetery. The building itself has a tale, having been floated across the bay from Rockland, where it served as a Universalist church. The museum's documents and artifacts on the granite industry are particularly intriguing, and special summer exhibits add to the interest. Donations are welcome. At the museum, request a copy of *A Self-guided Walking Tour of the Town of Vinalhaven and Its Granite-quarrying History,* a handy little brochure that details 17 in-town locations related to the late-19th-early-20th-century industry.

For another dose of history, stop by the **Old**

PENOBSCOT BAY

Engine House (Main St., 10am-2pm Mon. and Wed., 1pm-3pm Sat.) to see old firefighting equipment.

Built in 1832 and now owned by the town of Vinalhaven, **Brown's Head Light** guards the southern entrance to the Fox Islands Thorofare. There is no access to the light itself, and the keeper's house is a private residence for the town manager, but to reach the grounds, take the North Haven Road about six miles, at which point you'll see a left-side view of the Camden Hills. Continue about another mile to the second road on the left, Crockett River Road.

Turn and take the second road on the right, continuing past the Brown's Head Cemetery to the hill overlooking the lighthouse.

Entertainment

No one visits Vinalhaven for nightlife, but concerts (the Fox Island series and others), films, and lectures (most organized by the Vinalhaven Land Trust or the Vinalhaven Historical Society) are frequent. Check *The Wind* to see what's on the docket during your visit. The **Sand Bar** (Main St., 207/863-4500, 11am-9pm daily) often has entertainment.

Shopping

Vinalhaven's shops change regularly, but here are a few that have withstood the test of time. **The Paper Store** (18 Main St., 207/863-4826) carries newspapers, gifts, film, maps, and odds and ends. **Five Elements Gallery + Studio** (Main St., 207/863-2262) is filled with art-ist-owner Alison Thibault's jewelry creations and other finds. **New Era Gallery** (Main St., 207/863-9351) has a well-chosen selection of art in varied media representing primarily is-land artisans. A few doors away is **Second Hand Prose,** a used-books store run by the Friends of the Vinalhaven Public Library. **Vinalhaven Candy Co.** (35 W. Main St., 207/863-2041) is a kid magnet, but it pleases adults, too, with hard- and soft-serve ice cream and candy galore.

The Saturday-morning anything-goes **flea markets** are an island must, as much for the browsing and buying as for the gossip.

Recreation

PARKS AND PRESERVES

Vinalhaven is loaded with wonderful hikes and walks, some deliberately unpublicized. Since the mid-1980s, the **Vinalhaven Land Trust** (207/863-2543, www.vinalhavenlandtrust. org) has expanded the opportunities. When you reach the island, pick up maps at the land trust's office at **Skoog Memorial Park** (Sands Cove Rd., west of the ferry terminal) or inquire at the town office or the Paper Store. The trust also offers a seasonal series of educational walks and talks.

Some hiking options are the Perry Creek Preserve, which has a terrific loop trail; Middle Mountain Park; Tip-Toe Mountain; Polly Cove Preserve; Isle au Haut Mountain; Arey's Neck Woods; Huber Preserve; and Sunset Rock Park.

The Maine chapter of **The Nature Conservancy** (207/729-5181) owns or man-ages several islands and island clusters near Vinalhaven. **Big Garden** (formerly owned by Charles and Anne Morrow Lindbergh) and **Big White Islands** are easily accessible and great for shoreline picnics if you have your own boat. Other Nature Conservancy holdings in this area are fragile environments, mostly nesting islands off-limits mid-March–mid-August. Contact The Nature Conservancy for specifics.

No, you're not on the moors of Yorkshire, but you could be fooled in the 45-acre **Lane's Island Preserve,** one of The Nature Conservancy's most-used island preserves. Masses of low-lying ferns, rugosa roses, and berry bushes cover the granite outcrops of this sanctuary—and a foggy day makes it even more moorlike and mystical, like a set-ting for a Brontë novel. The best (albeit busi-est) time to come is early August, when you can compete with the birds for blackberries, raspberries, and blueberries. Easy trails wind past old stone walls, an aged cemetery, and along the surf-pounded shore. The preserve is a 20-minute walk (or five-minute bike ride) from Vinalhaven's ferry landing. Set off to the right on Main Street, through the vil-lage. Turn right onto Water Street and then right on Atlantic Avenue. Continue across the causeway on Lane's Island Road and left over a salt marsh to the preserve. The large white house on the harbor side of Lane's Island is privately owned.

Next to the ferry landing in Carver's Harbor is **Grimes Park,** a wooded pocket retreat with a splendid view of the harbor. Owned by the American Legion, the 2.5-acre park is perfect for picnics or for hanging out between boats, especially in good weather.

Just behind the Island Community Medical Center, close to downtown, is 30-acre **Armbrust Hill Town Park,** once the site of granite-quarrying operations. Still pockmarked with quarry pits, the park has beautifully landscaped walking paths and native flowers, shrubs, and trees—much of it thanks to late island resident Betty Roberts, who made this a lifelong endeavor. From the back of the medi-cal center, follow the trail to the summit for a southerly view of Matinicus and other offshore islands. If you're with children, be especially careful about straying onto side paths, which go perilously close to old quarry holes. Before the walk, lower the children's energy level at the large playground off to the left of the trail.

PENOBSCOT BAY

SWIMMING

Two town-owned quarries are easy to reach from the ferry landing. **Lawson's Quarry** is one mile from downtown on the North Haven Road; **Booth Quarry** is 1.6 miles from downtown via East Main Street. Both are signposted. You'll see plenty of sunbathers on the rocks and swimmers on a hot day, but there are no lifeguards, so swimming is at your own risk. There are no restrooms or changing rooms. Note that pets and soap are not allowed in the water; camping, fires, and alcohol are not allowed in the quarry areas.

Down the side road beyond Booth Quarry is **Narrows Park,** a town-owned space looking out toward Narrows Island, Isle au Haut, and, on a clear day, Mount Desert Island.

For saltwater swimming, take East Main Street 2.4 miles from downtown to a crossroads, where you'll see a whimsical bit of local folk art—the Coke lady sculpture. Turn right (east) and go 0.5 mile to **Geary's Beach** (also called **State Beach**), where you can picnic and scour the shoreline for shells and sea glass.

BICYCLING

Even though Vinalhaven's 40 or so miles of public roads are narrow, winding, and poorly shouldered, they're relatively level, so a bicycle is a fine way to tour the island. Bring your own, preferably a hybrid or mountain bike, or rent one ($15/day for a clunky one-speed) at the **Tidewater Motel** (207/863-4618) on Main Street. If you choose to bring a bike from the mainland, know that it costs extra to bring one on the ferry.

A 10-mile, 2.5-hour bicycle route begins on Main Street and goes clockwise out on the North Haven Road (rough pavement), past Lawson's Quarry, to Round the Island Road (some sections are dirt), then Poor Farm Road to Geary's Beach and back to Main Street via Pequot Road and School Street. Carry a picnic and enjoy it on Lane's Island, stop for a swim in one of the quarries, or detour down to Brown's Head Light. If you're here for the day, keep track of the time so you don't miss the ferry.

Far more rewarding view-wise, and far shorter, is the one-way-and-back pedal out along the Old Harbor Road to The Basin, which is rich in wildlife and serves as a seal nursery. There's also a nice trail at the road's end to The Basin's shorefront and across to an island; ask Phil at the Tidewater Motel for directions.

SEA KAYAKING

Sea-kayak rentals are available at the Tidewater Motel for $30/day, plus delivery. A guide can be arranged, but it's not necessary to have one to poke around the harbor or, even better, paddle through The Basin, which is especially popular with birders and wildlife-watchers.

BIRDING AND WILDLIFE-WATCHING

Join ornithologist **John Drury** (207/596-1841, $80/hour) aboard his 36-foot lobster boat on a birding and wildlife-watching cruise through the islands of Penobscot Bay. Sightings have included Arctic terns, guillemots, shearwaters, petrel, puffins, and eagles, along with seals, dolphins, minke whales, and perhaps even an albatross.

Accommodations

If you're planning on staying overnight, don't even consider arriving in summer without reservations. If you're coming for the day, pay attention to the ferry schedule and allow enough time to get back to the boat. The island has no campsites. Rates listed are for peak season.

Your feet practically touch the water when you spend the night at the ◖ **Tidewater Motel and Gathering Space** (12 Main St., Carver's Harbor, 207/863-4618, www.tidewatermotel. com, year-round, $175-299), in two buildings cantilevered over the harbor. Owned by Phil and Elaine Crossman (she operates the New Era Gallery down the street), the 19-room motel was built by Phil's parents in 1970. It's the perfect place to sit on the deck and watch the lobster boats do their thing. Be aware, though, that commercial fishermen are early risers, and lobster-boat engines can rev up as early as 4:30am on a summer morning—all part of the pace of Vinalhaven. Phil can recommend hikes and other activities, and since he maintains the island's calendar of events, he always knows what's happening and when. Continental breakfast and use of bicycles (clunky one-speeds) are included in the rates; sea-kayak rentals are available. Kids 10 and under are free; seven units are efficiencies. Also on the premises is **Island Spirits,** a small gourmet-foods store stocked with wines, beers, cheeses, breads, other goodies, and even picnic baskets to pack it all in. If you want to get a better sense of island life, pick up a copy of Phil's book *Away Happens,* a collection of humorous essays about island living. You can see a sample from it on the motel's website.

Also convenient to downtown is **The Libby House** (Water St., 207/863-4696, www.libby-house1869.com, $110-150, no breakfast), an 1869 Victorian with a two-bedroom apartment and five guest rooms, some sharing a bath.

Food

Island restaurant hours change frequently; call for current schedules.

LOCAL FLAVORS

Vinalhaven Farmer's Market sets up 8am-noon Saturday in conjunction with the Flea Market. Look for Creelman Creamery Cheese made on the island.

Baked bean suppers are regularly held at a couple of island locations. Check *The Wind* for details.

The island's best breakfast place is **Surfside** (Harbor Wharf, 207/863-2767), generally open from the wee hours through lunch daily. Eat inside or on the wharf. The fish cakes earn raves and are always available on Sunday.

Craving a cappuccino or a latte? Want brunch or lunch? Vinalhaven's student-run **ARCafé** (50B Main St., 207/867-6225) is the island's best coffee source and provides free Internet access.

Trickerville Sandwich Shop (15 Water St., 207/863-9344, 5am-4pm Mon.-Sat., 11am-3pm Sun.) has a few tables inside and out, but no views. If the weather's fine, look for **Greet's Eats**, a takeout on the wharf by the Co-op.

The Tidewater Motel hangs over Vinalhaven's Carver's Harbor.

PENOBSCOT BAY

FAMILY FAVORITES

The order-at-the-counter **Harbor Gawker** (Main St., 207/863-9365, 11am-8pm Mon.-Sat., $9-18), a local landmark since 1975, has seating indoors and out. **The Pizza Pit** (207/863-4311, 4pm-8pm Wed.-Sun.) is an easy-on-the-budget choice.

CASUAL DINING

For casual dining, book a table at **The Haven Restaurant** (Main St., 207/863-4969), with two options: Harborside (Tues.-Sat., seatings at 6pm and 8:15pm) delivers on its name and serves a creative menu that changes nightly. Streetside (6:30pm-9pm Wed.-Sat.) doesn't take reservations and serves lighter fare. The restaurant is a one-woman show, and Torry Pratt doubles as a popular local caterer, so it's wise to call.

Information and Services

Vinalhaven Chamber of Commerce (www. vinalhaven.org) produces a handy flyer-map showing locations in the Carver's Harbor area. Also helpful for trip planning is a guidebook published by Phil Crossman at the Tidewater Motel (207/863-4618, $3.50). On the island, pick up a copy of Vinalhaven's weekly newsletter, *The Wind,* named after the island's original newspaper, first published in 1884. It's loaded with island flavor: news items, public-supper announcements, editorials, and ads. A year's subscription is $50; free single copies are available at most downtown locales.

Check out the **Vinalhaven Public Library** (E. Main St. and Chestnut St., 207/863-4401). **Public restrooms** are at the ferry landing and in town at the big red fire barn.

Getting Around

I can't emphasize this enough: Don't bring a car unless it is absolutely necessary. If you're day-tripping, you can get to parks and quarries, shops, restaurants, and the historical society museum on foot. If you want to explore farther, a bicycle is an excellent option, or you can rent a car ($50) or reserve a **taxi** through

the Tidewater Motel (207/863-4618; call well ahead).

NORTH HAVEN

Eight miles long by three miles wide, **North Haven** (pop. 355) is 12 miles off the coast of Rockland—70 minutes by ferry. The island has sedate summer homes, open fields where hundreds of sheep once grazed, an organic farm, about 350 year-round residents, and a yacht club called the Casino.

Originally called North Island, North Haven had much the same settlement history as Vinalhaven, but being smaller (about 5,280 acres) and more fertile, it has developed—or not developed—differently. In 1846, North Haven was incorporated and severed politically from Vinalhaven, and by the late 1800s, the Boston summer crowd began buying traditional island homes, building tastefully unpretentious new ones, and settling in for a whole season of sailing and socializing. Several generations later, "summer folk" now come for weeks rather than months, often rotating the schedules among slews of siblings. Informality remains the key, though—now more than ever.

The island has two distinct hamlets—North Haven Village, on the Fox Islands Thorofare, where the state ferry arrives; and Pulpit Harbor, particularly popular with the yachting set. The village is easily explored on foot in a morning.

North Haven doesn't offer a lot for the day visitor, and islanders tend not to welcome them with open arms.

Entertainment

Waterman's Community Center (Main St., 207/867-2100, www.watermans.org) provides a place for island residents and visitors to gather for entertainment, events, and even coffee and gossip. It's home to North Haven Arts & Enrichment. Check the schedule on the website to see what's planned.

Shopping

Fanning out from the ferry landing is a delightful cluster of substantial year-round clapboard homes—a marked contrast to the weathered-shingle cottages typical of so many island communities. It won't take long to stroll and visit the handful of shops and galleries.

Recreation

North Haven has about 25 miles of paved roads that are conducive to **bicycling,** but, just as on most other islands, they are narrow, winding, and nearly shoulderless. Starting near the ferry landing in North Haven Village, take South Shore Road eastward, perhaps stopping en route for a picnic at town-owned Mullin's Head Park (also spelled Mullen Head) on the southeast corner of the island. Then follow the road around, counterclockwise, to North Shore Road and Pulpit Harbor.

Accommodations and Food

Within walking distance of the ferry is **Nebo Lodge** (11 Mullins Lane, 207/867-2007, www.nebolodge.com, $145-275). Nine rooms, some with shared baths, are decorated with island art, and many have rugs by Angela Adams. There's Wi-Fi throughout. Rates include a full breakfast and use of inn bikes. Dinner is available from 5pm Mon.-Sat., entrées $15-18. Nebo also runs a lobster-boat dinner shuttle from Rockland twice weekly in summer; call for schedule.

For burgers, dogs, fries, shakes, lobster rolls, ice cream, and more, duck into **Cooper's Landing** (9 Main St., 207/867-2060, 11am-8pm daily), an order-at-the-window joint within steps of the ferry. Also here is **Little Urchin Bakery** (8am-11am Tues.-Sun.), a great source for breads and breakfast.

If you have wheels, head over to **Turner Farm** (73 Turner Farm Rd., 207/867-4962, www.turner-farm.com), an organic farm dating back 200 years. The location is spectacular, with fields rolling down to the Fox Island Thorofare, and the Farm Stand (10am-1pm Tues. and Thurs.) is a great place to pick up fresh meats, produce, and goat cheese.

Information

The best source of information about North Haven is the **North Haven Town Office** (Upper

© HILARY NANGLE

Purchase organic produce and fresh goat cheese at Turner Farm on North Haven.

© TOM NANGLE

Ferries connect Rockland to offshore islands, including Vinalhaven and North Haven.

Main St., 207/867-4433, www.northhaven-maine.org).

GETTING THERE

The Maine State Ferry Service (207/596-2202, www.exploremaine.org) operates six round-trips daily between Rockland and Vinalhaven (75-minute crossing) in summer and three round-trips between Rockland and North Haven (70-minute crossing). Round-trip tickets are $17.50 adults, $8.50 children. Both ferries take cars ($49.50 round-trip, plus $14 reservation fee), but a bicycle ($16.50 round-trip/adult bike, $9.50/child bike) will do fine unless you have the time or inclination to see every corner of the island. Getting car space on the ferry during midsummer can be a frustrating—and complicated—experience, so *avoid taking a car to the island.* Give yourself time to find a parking space and perhaps to walk from it to the terminal. If you leave a car at the Rockland lot (space is limited and availability varies), it's $10/24 hours or $50/week. You can also park on some of Rockland's side streets and walk, or, for a day trip, park in the city lot between Main Street and the water or Harbor Park.

No official ferry service travels between Vinalhaven and North Haven, even though the two islands are almost within spitting distance. Fortunately, the **J. O. Brown and Sons boat shop** on North Haven provides shuttles 7am-5pm daily. Call the boat shop (207/867-4621) to arrange a pickup on the Vinalhaven side. The fee is $5 pp round-trip. Don't let anyone persuade you to return to Rockland for the ferry to North Haven.

Penobscot Island Air (207/596-7500, www.penobscotislandair.net) flies twice daily to Vinalhaven and North Haven, weather permitting, from Knox County Regional Airport in Owls Head, just south of Rockland. Seat availability is dependent on mail volume.

Greater Camden

Camden (pop. 4,850), flanked by **Rockport** (pop. 3,330) to the south and **Lincolnville** (pop. 2,164) to the north, is one of the Mid-Coast's—even Maine's—prime destinations.

Camden is the better known of the three and typifies Maine nationwide, even worldwide, on calendars, postcards, and photo books. Much of its appeal is its drop-dead-gorgeous setting—a deeply indented harbor with parks, a waterfall, and a dramatic backdrop of low mountains. That harbor is a summer-long madhouse, jammed with dinghies, kayaks, windjammers, mega-yachts, minor yachts, and a handful of fishing craft.

Driven apart by a local squabble in 1891, Camden and Rockport have been separate towns for more than a century, but they're inextricably linked. They share school and sewer systems and an often-hyphenated partnership. On Union Street, just off Route 1, a white wooden arch reads Camden on one side and Rockport on the other. Rockport has a much lower profile, and its harbor is relatively peaceful—with yachts, lobster boats, and a single windjammer schooner.

Two distinct enclaves make up Lincolnville: oceanfront Lincolnville Beach ("the Beach") and, about five miles inland, Lincolnville Center ("the Center"). Lincolnville is laid-back and mostly rural; the major activity center is a short strip of shops and restaurants at the Beach, and few visitors realize there's anything else.

SIGHTS
Self-Guided Historical Tour

Historic Downtown Camden is an illustrated map and brochure detailing historical sites and businesses in and around downtown. To cover it all, you'll want a car or bike; to cover segments and really appreciate the architecture, don your walking shoes. Pick up a copy of the brochure at the chamber of commerce.

Old Conway Homestead and Cramer Museum

Just inside the Camden town line from Rockport, the **Old Conway Homestead and Cramer Museum** (Conway Rd., Camden, 207/236-2257, www.conwayhouse.org, 11am-3pm Tues.-Fri. July-Aug., $5 adults, $2 children) is a six-building complex owned and run by the Camden-Rockport Historical Society. The 18th-century Cape-style Conway House, on the National Register of Historic Places, contains fascinating construction details and period furnishings; in the barn are carriages and farm tools. Two other buildings—a blacksmith shop and an 1820 maple sugarhouse used for making maple syrup—have been moved to the grounds and restored. In the contemporary Mary Meeker Cramer Museum (named for the prime benefactor) are displays from the historical society's collection of ship models, old documents, and period clothing. For local color, don't miss the Victorian outhouse. Also here is an education center for workshops and seminars. The museum and sap house are also open for maple-syrup demonstrations on Maine Maple Sunday (fourth Sunday in March).

Vesper Hill

Built and donated to the community by a local benefactor, the rustic open-air **Vesper Hill Children's Chapel** is dedicated to the world's children. Overlooking Penobscot Bay and surrounded by gardens and lawns, the nondenominational chapel is an almost mystical oasis in a busy tourist region. Except during weddings or memorial services, there's seldom a crowd, and if you're lucky, you might have the place to yourself. From Central Street in downtown Rockport, take Russell Avenue east to Calderwood Lane (the fourth street on the right). On Calderwood, take the second right (Chapel St.) after the private golf course. If the sign is down, look for a boulder with "Vesper Hill" carved in it. From downtown Camden,

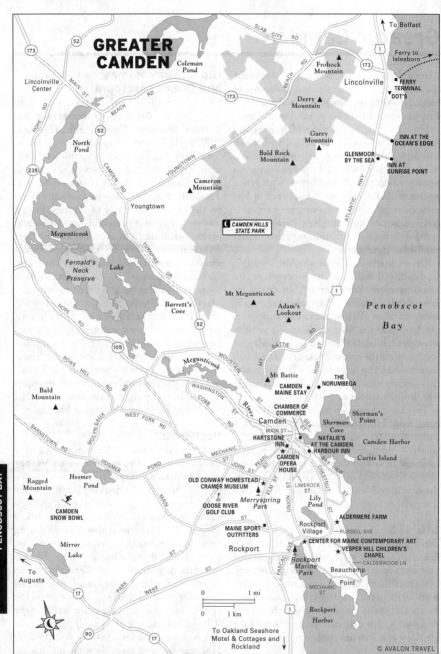

PENOBSCOT BAY

WINE TASTING

The number of wineries is increasing throughout Maine, and they're especially concentrated in this region. Tour on your own, armed with maps and a passport from **The Maine Winery Guild** (www.mainewinetrail.com), or sit back, relax, and enjoy the sipping experience at three wineries on a guided **Nap-Ah Valley Wine Tour** with All Aboard Trolley (207/691-9300, www.meetthefleet.com, $30).

Draft horses power Brian Smith's **Oyster River Winegrowers** (929 Oyster River Rd., Warren, 207/354-7177, call for hours), a small farm with vineyard and tasting room. Ask about pizza and taco nights in the barn.

More than 3,000 vines are growing on 32 acres at **Breakwater Vineyards** (35 Ash Point Dr., Owls Head, 207/594-1721, www.breakwatervineyards.com, noon-5pm Mon.-Sat.), which donates a portion of its profits to lighthouse restoration efforts. Tastings offer fruit and grape wines and mead. Tours are offered; call for details.

Head inland on Route 17 and then noodle off on the back roads to discover not one but two wineries. At **Sweetgrass Farm Winery and Distillery** (347 Carroll Rd., Union, 207/785-3024, www.sweetgrasswinery.com, 11am-5pm daily late May-late Dec.), owner Keith Bodine uses Maine-grown fruits to produce both wines and spirits, and he is eager to show interested folks how. Bring a picnic to enjoy while hiking the winery's trails. Carroll Road is between Shepard Hill Road and North Union Road, both north of Route 17, west of Route 131.

Nearby is **Savage Oakes** (174 Barrett Hill Rd., Union, 207/785-5261, www.savageoakes.com, 11am-5pm daily mid-May-late Oct.), where Elmer and Holly Savage and their sons have added winemaking to their second-generation Belted Galloway cattle farm. They grow nine varieties of grapes, both red and white, and produce more than half a dozen wines. Guided farm tours are $7 and by appointment. Barrett Hill Road is off Route 17 directly opposite Route 131 South.

Gaze out the back door of the **Cellardoor Vineyard** (367 Youngtown Rd., Lincolnville, 207/763-44778, www.mainewine.com, call for hours) and it's possible to think you're in Sonoma Valley. Tucked in the folds of the rolling hills, just inland of Lincolnville Beach, Cellardoor occupies a 200-year-old farmhouse and barn overlooking six acres of grapes. During the summer, the retail shop offers free wine tastings daily and food and wine pairings on Sunday afternoons; winery tours are offered twice daily. Cooking classes are often held in the commercial kitchen. You can pick up cheeses and other munchies for an impromptu picnic on the deck. The winery has another retail shop, The Villa, at the intersection of Routes 1 and 90 in Rockport.

take Chestnut Street to just past Aldermere Farm; turn left at Calderwood Lane and take the second right after the golf course.

Aldermere Farm (20 Russell Ave., Rockport, 207/236-2739, www.aldermere.org), by the way, is the home of the first U.S. herd of Belted Galloway cattle—Angus-like beef cattle with a wide white midriff. First imported from Scotland in 1953, the breed now shows up in pastures all over the United States. The animals' startling "Oreo-cookie" hide pattern never fails to halt passersby—especially in spring and early summer, when the calves join their mothers in the pastures. Maine Coast Heritage Trust, a state conservation organization based in Brunswick, owns the 136-acre farm. Call for information on tours or other events.

Center for Maine Contemporary Art

Once a local firehouse, this attractive building has been totally rehabbed to provide display space for the work of Maine's best contemporary artists. The nonprofit **Center for Maine Contemporary Art** (62 Russell Ave., Rockport, 207/236-2875, www.cmcanow.org, 10am-5pm Tues.-Sat., 1pm-5pm Sun., donation) mounts

ISLESBORO

Lying three miles offshore from Lincolnville Beach, 20 minutes via car ferry, is 12-mile-long Islesboro, a year-round community with a population of about 600—beefed up annually by a sedate summer colony. Car ferries are frequent enough to make Islesboro an ideal day-trip destination—and that's the choice of most visitors, partly because food options are few and overnight lodging isn't available. The only camping is on nearby Warren Island State Park—and you have to have your own boat to get there.

The best way to get an island overview is to do an end-to-end auto or bike tour. Pick up an island map at the ferry terminal and explore, heading down to Dark Harbor and Town Beach at the island's bottom, then up to Pripet and Turtle Head at its top. You won't see all the huge "cottages" tucked down long driveways, and you won't absorb island life and its rhythms, but you'll scratch the surface of what Islesboro is about.

En route, you'll pass exclusive summer estates, workaday homes, spectacular seaside vistas, a smattering of shops, and the **Historical Society Museum** (388 Main St., 207/734-6733, www.islesborohistorical.org, 12:30pm-4:30pm Sat.-Wed. July-Aug. or by appointment, donation only). On the up-island circuit, watch for a tiny marker on the west side of the road (0.8 mile north of the Islesboro Historical Society building). It commemorates the 1780 total eclipse witnessed here—the first recorded in North America. At the time, British loyalists still held Islesboro, but they temporarily suspended hostilities, allowing Harvard astronomers to lug their instruments to the island and document the eclipse.

Allow time before the return ferry to visit the **Sailors' Memorial Museum,** a town-owned museum filled with seafaring memorabilia and allegedly home to a benevolent ghost or two. It's in the keeper's house adjacent to **Grindle Point Light** (207/734-2253, www.lighthouse.cc/grindle), built in 1850, rebuilt in 1875, and now automated.

The car ferry *Margaret Chase Smith* (207/789-5611, www.exploremaine.org) departs Lincolnville Beach almost every hour on the hour, 8 or 9am-5pm, and departs Islesboro on the half hour, 7:30am-4:30pm. Round-trip fares are $25 for a car, $8.50 adults, $3.25 kids, $7 adult bicycles, and $4 kids' bikes. Reservations are $5 extra. A slightly reduced schedule prevails late October-early May. The 20-minute trip crosses a stunning three-mile stretch of Penobscot Bay, with views of islands and the Camden Hills. In summer, avoid the biggest bottlenecks: Friday afternoon (to Islesboro), Sunday afternoon and Monday holiday afternoons (from Islesboro). The *Smith* remains on Islesboro overnight, so don't miss the last run to Lincolnville Beach.

as many as a dozen shows each summer, along with special lectures and a wildly popular art auction (early August). An exceptional gift shop carries high-end crafts. In 2015, after more than 50 years in Rockport, CMA plans to move to Rockland. It's new home will be a 12,143-square-foot building located on Winter Street, adjacent to the Strand Theatre and designed by Toshiko Mori, who made *Architectural Digest*'s 2014 list of the world's preeminent architects.

Hope Elephants

In 2012, brothers Jim and Tom Laurita opened the nonprofit **Hope Elephants** (49 Hatchet Mountain Rd., Hope, 207/230-7830, www.hopeelephants.org), a purpose-built center dedicated to the care and rehabilitation of Rosie and Opal, two retired circus elephants. Visitors are welcome by advance reservation. There is no fee, but suggested donation is $15 pp, $10 under age 12.

ENTERTAINMENT

Founded in the 1960s as a classical series, **Bay Chamber Concerts** (207/236-2823 or 888/707-2770, www.baychamberconcerts.org) has expanded to include world music, jazz, and dance. The summer concerts feature a resident quartet, prominent guest artists, and outstanding programs and draw sell-out audiences to venues in Camden, Rockland, and Rockport. Seats are reserved (from $30 adults, from $8 under 19, plus $5 processing fee per order, unless purchased online).

The beautifully renovated **Camden Opera House** (29 Elm St., Camden, 207/236-7963, box office 207/236-4884, www.camdenoperahouse.com) is the site of many performances by renowned performers.

The Lincolnville Band, one of the oldest town bands in the country, occasionally plays in the park's Bicentennial Bandstand, built to commemorate the town's 200th birthday.

FESTIVALS AND EVENTS

One weekend in February is given over to the **Camden Conference,** an annual three-day foreign-affairs conference with nationally and internationally known speakers. Also in February, the **National Toboggan Championships** features two days of races and fun at the nation's only wooden toboggan chute at the Camden Snow Bowl.

The third Thursday of July is **House and Garden Day,** when you can take a self-guided tour (10am-4:30pm) of significant homes and gardens in Camden and Rockport. Proceeds benefit the Camden Garden Club. **HarborArts,** on the third weekend in July, draws dozens of artists and craftspeople displaying and selling their wares at the Camden Amphitheatre, Harbor Park.

Labor Day weekend is also known as **Windjammer Weekend,** with cruises, windjammer open houses, fireworks, and all kinds of live entertainment in and around Camden Harbor. Twenty top artisans open their studios for the annual **Country Roads Artists and Artisans Tour** in September.

Dozens of artists and craftspeople display and sell their wares at the **Fall Festival and Arts and Crafts Show,** the first weekend in October at the Camden Amphitheatre in Harbor Park.

A who's who of entrepreneurs show up for the annual **PopTech** conference in October.

Christmas by the Sea is a family-oriented early-December weekend featuring open houses, special sales, concerts, and a visit from Santa Claus.

SHOPPING
New and Old Books

The Owl and Turtle Bookshop (33 Bayview St., Camden, 207/230-7335), one of Maine's best independent new-books stores, has thousands of books and a wonderful children's selection.

Another source for books and a whole lot more is **Sherman's** (14 Main St., Camden, 207/236-2223), part of a small Maine chain.

If you want a good read at a great price, **Stone Soup Books** (33 Main St., Camden, no phone), a tiny second-floor shop across from the Lord Camden Inn, is Camden's best source for contemporary used fiction.

Dolls

Antique and handcrafted museum-quality dolls and dollhouses fill **Lucy's Doll House** (49 Bay View St., Camden, 207/236-4122).

Art, Crafts, and Gifts

You'll need to wander the streets to take in all the gift and crafts shops, particularly in Camden. Some are obvious; others are tucked away on side streets and back alleys, so explore.

A downtown Camden landmark since 1940, **The Smiling Cow** (41 Main St., Camden, 207/236-3351) is as good a place as any to pick up Maine souvenirs—a few slightly kitschy, but most reasonably tasteful. Before or after shopping here, head for the rear balcony for coffee and a knockout view of the harbor and the Megunticook River waterfall.

Also downtown is **Ducktrap Bay Trading Co.** (20 Main St., Camden, 207/236-9568), source of decoys, wildlife, and marine art and other fine crafts.

At **Danica Candleworks** (Rte. 90, West Rockport, 207/236-3060), owner Erik Laustsen learned the hand-dipping trade from his Danish relatives.

The **Messler Gallery** (25 Mill St., Rockport, 207/594-5611), just off Route 90 and on the campus of the Center for Furniture Craftsmanship, presents rotating shows that focus on woodworking.

Handsome dark wood buildings 0.2 mile north of the Beach are home to **Windsor Chairmakers** (Rte. 1, Lincolnville, 207/789-5188 or 800/789-5188). You can observe the operation, browse the display area, or order some of the well-made chairs, cabinets, and tables.

Professional boatbuilder Walt Simmons has branched out into decoys and wildlife carvings, and they're just as outstanding as his boats. Walt and his wife, Karen, run **Duck Trap Decoys** (Duck Trap Rd., Lincolnville, 207/789-5363), a gallery-shop that features the work of more than 60 other woodcarvers.

It's a lot easier to get soft, wonderful hand-woven and hand-dyed **Swans Island Blankets** (231 Rte. 1, Northport, 297/338-9691) since the company moved its sales operation off the island near Mount Desert to the mainland, just 2.7 miles north of Lincolnville Beach. Such quality comes at a sky-high price.

Discount Shopping

How could anyone resist a thrift shop with the name **Heavenly Threads** (57 Elm St./ Rte. 1, Camden, 207/236-3203)? Established by Camden's community-oriented First Congregational Church (next door to the shop), Heavenly Threads carries high-quality pre-owned clothing, books, and jewelry. It's staffed by volunteers, with proceeds going to such local ecumenical causes as Meals on Wheels.

RECREATION
Parks and Preserves
COASTAL MOUNTAINS LAND TRUST
Founded in 1986 **Coastal Mountains Land Trust** (CMLT, 101 Mt. Battie St., Camden, 207/236-7091, www.coastalmountains.org) has preserved more than 9,100 acres. Maps and information about trails open to the public as well as information about guided hikes and other events are available on the website.

CMLT preserves more than 600 acres on 1,280-foot-high **Bald Mountain**, the fifth-highest peak on the eastern seaboard. The somewhat strenuous two-mile round-trip hike accesses the open summit ledges, with grand views over Penobscot Bay. Bald Mountain is home to rare subalpine plants and is a great spot to view migrating hawks in fall. From Route 1 at the southern end of town, take John Street for 0.8 mile. Turn left and go 0.2 mile to a fork. Continue on the left fork (Hosmer Pond Rd.) for two miles. Bear left onto Barnestown Road (passing the Camden Snow Bowl) and go 1.4 miles to the trailhead on the right, signposted Georges Highland Path Barnestown Access. Maps are available in the box; the parking lot holds half a dozen cars. The blue-blazed trail is relatively easy, requiring just over an hour round-trip; the summit views are spectacular, especially in fall. Carry a picnic and enjoy it at the top. Avoid this trail in late May-early June, when the blackflies take command, and dress appropriately during hunting season.

The views are almost as fine, but the hiking is easier on the 1.5-mile round-trip Summit Road Trail up the **Beech Hill Preserve**, in Rockport. The trailhead is on the Beech Hill Road about a mile off Route 1 (turn across from Hoboken Gardens).

FERNALD'S NECK
Three miles of Megunticook Lake shoreline, groves of conifers, and a large swamp ("the Great Bog") are features of 328-acre **Fernald's Neck Preserve**, on the Camden-Lincolnville line (and the Knox-Waldo County line). Shoreline and mountain views are stupendous, even more so during fall foliage season. The easiest trail is the 1.5-mile Blue Loop at the northern end of the preserve; from it, you can access the 1-mile Orange Loop. From the Blue Loop, take the 0.2-mile Yellow Trail offshoot to Balance Rock for a great view of the lake and hills. Some sections can be wet; wear boots or rubberized shoes, and use insect repellent. From Route 1 in Camden, take

Route 52 (Mountain St.) about 4.5 miles to Fernald's Neck Road, about 0.2 mile beyond the Youngtown Inn. Turn left and then bear left at the next fork and continue to the parking lot at the road's end. Pick up a map-brochure at the trailhead register. A map is also available at the chamber of commerce office. Dogs are not allowed, and the preserve closes and the gate is locked at 7:30pm.

THE GEORGES RIVER LAND TRUST

A Rockland-based group, **The Georges River Land Trust** (207/594-5166, www.georgesriver. org), whose territory covers the Georges (St. George) River watershed, is the steward for **The Georges Highland Path,** a 40-mile low-impact footpath that reaches Rockport and Camden from the back side of the surrounding hills.

◉ CAMDEN HILLS STATE PARK

A five-minute drive and a small fee gets you to the top of Mount Battie, centerpiece of 5,650-acre **Camden Hills State Park** (Belfast Rd./ Rte. 1, 207/236-3109, www.parksandlands. com, $4.50 nonresident adults, $3 Maine resident adults, $1.50 nonresident seniors, free Maine resident seniors, $1 children 5-11) and the best place to understand why Camden is "where the mountains meet the sea." The summit panorama is breathtaking and reputedly the inspiration for Edna St. Vincent Millay's poem "Renascence" (a bronze plaque marks the spot); information boards identify the offshore islands. Climb the summit's stone tower for an even better view. The 20 miles of hiking trails (some for every ability) include two popular routes up Mount Battie—an easy hour-long hike from the base parking lot (Nature Trail) and a more strenuous 45-minute hike from the top of Mount Battie Street in Camden (Mount Battie Trail). Or drive up the paved Mount Battie Auto Road. The park has plenty of space for picnics. In winter, ice climbers use a rock wall near the Maiden's Cliff Trail, reached via Route 52 (Mountain St.). The park entrance is two miles north of downtown Camden. Request a free trail map. The park is open mid-May-mid-October, but hiking trails are accessible all year, weather permitting.

MERRYSPRING PARK

Straddling the Camden-Rockport boundary, 66-acre **Merryspring Park** (Conway Rd., Camden, 207/236-2239, www.merryspring. org) is a magnet for nature lovers. More than a dozen well-marked trails wind through woodlands, berry thickets, and wildflowers; near the preserve's parking area are lily, rose, and herb gardens. Admission is free, but donations are welcome. Also free are family programs. Special programs (fee charged) include lectures, workshops, and demonstrations. The entrance is on Conway Road, 0.3 mile off Route 1, at the southern end of Camden. Trails are open dawn-dusk daily.

IN-TOWN PARKS

Just behind the Camden Public Library is the **Camden Amphitheatre** (also called the Bok Amphitheatre, after a local benefactor), a sylvan spot resembling a set for *A Midsummer Night's Dream* (which has been performed here). Concerts, weddings, and all kinds of other events take place in the park. Across Atlantic Avenue, sloping to the harbor, is **Camden Harbor Park,** with benches, a couple of monuments, and some of the best waterfront views in town. The noted landscape firm of Frederick Law Olmsted designed the park in 1931, and it is listed on the National Register of Historic Places. Both the park and the amphitheater were restored to their original splendor in 2004.

Rockport's in-town parks include **Marine Park,** off Pascal Avenue, at the head of the harbor; **Walker Park,** on Sea Street, on the west side of the harbor; **Mary-Lea Park,** overlooking the harbor next to the Rockport Opera House; and **Cramer Park,** alongside the Goose River just west of Pascal Avenue. At Marine Park are the remnants of 19th-century lime kilns, an antique steam engine, picnic tables, a boat-launching ramp, and a polished granite sculpture of André, a harbor seal adopted by a local family in the early 1960s. André had been honorary harbormaster, ring bearer at weddings, and the subject of several books and a film—and even did the honors at the unveiling of his statue—before he was fatally wounded in a mating skirmish in 1986 at the age of 25.

CURTIS ISLAND

Marking the entrance to Camden Harbor is town-owned **Curtis Island,** with a 26-foot automated light tower and adjoining keeper's house facing into the bay. Once known as Negro Island, it's a sight made for photo ops; the views are stunning in every direction. A kayak or dinghy will get you out to the island, where you can picnic (take water; there are no facilities), wander around, gather berries, or just watch the passing fleet. Land on the Camden (west) end of the island, allowing for the tide change when you beach your boat. Respect the privacy of the keeper's house in summer; it's occupied by volunteer caretakers.

AVENA BOTANICALS MEDICINAL HERB GARDEN

Visitors are welcome to visit Deb Soule's one-acre **Avena Botanicals Medicinal Herb Garden** (519 Mill St., Rockport, 207/594-2403, www.avenabotanicals.com, noon-7:30pm Mon.-Fri., free), part of an herbal and healing-arts teaching center. Pick up a garden map and guide at the entrance, then stroll the paths. More than 125 species of common and medicinal herbs are planted, and everything is labeled. Mill Street is just shy of one mile south of the intersection of Routes 17 and 90 in West Rockport. Turn left on Mill Street and continue for almost one mile. Avena is on the right, down a long dirt driveway.

Recreation Centers

More than an alpine ski area, the **Camden Snow Bowl** (207/236-3438, www.camdensnowbowl.com) is a four-season recreation area with tennis courts, public swimming in Hosmer Pond, and biking and hiking trails, as well as alpine trails for day and night skiing and riding, a tubing park, and Maine's only toboggan chute. The hill is small, but you get

glimpses of island-studded Penobscot Bay when descending the trails.

Maine Sport Outfitters

Local entrepreneurs Stuart and Marianne Smith have made **Maine Sport Outfitters** (Rte. 1, Rockport, 207/236-7120 or 888/236-8796, www.mainesport.com) a major destination for anyone interested in outdoor recreation. The knowledgeable staff can lend a hand and steer you in almost any direction, for almost any summer or winter sport. The store sells and rents canoes, kayaks, bikes, skis, and tents, plus all the relevant clothing and accessories. Bicycle rentals begin at $20/day, and calm-water canoes and kayaks are $30-40/day. Sea kayaks are $50/day single, $65/day tandem.

Maine Sport Outdoor School (207/236-8797 or 800/722-0826), a division of Maine Sport, has a full schedule of canoeing, kayaking, and camping trips. A two-hour guided Camden Harbor tour departs at least three or four times daily in summer and costs $35 adults, $30 ages 10-15. A four-hour guided harbor-to-harbor tour (Rockport to Camden) is offered once each day for $75 adults, $60 children, including a picnic lunch. Multiday instructional programs and tours are available. The store is 0.5 mile north of the junction of Routes 1 and 90.

Sea Kayaking

Ducktrap Kayak (2175 Rte. 1, Lincolnville Beach, 207/236-8608, www.ducktrapkayak.com) runs guided coastal tours, with rates beginning at $30 pp. Rentals are also available, beginning at $25-45, depending on the type and size; delivery can be arranged.

If you have your own boat, good saltwater launch sites include Eaton Point, at the end of Sea Street in Camden, and Marine Park in Rockport. For freshwater paddling, put in at Megunticook Lake, west and east sides; Bog Bridge on Route 105, about 3.5 miles from downtown Camden; Barrett's Cove on Route 52, also about 3.5 miles from Camden; or in Lincolnville's Norton Pond and Megunticook Lake. You can even paddle all the way from the head of Norton Pond to the foot of Megunticook Lake, but use care navigating the drainage culvert between the two.

Swimming
FRESHWATER
The Camden area is blessed with several locales for freshwater swimming—a real boon, since Penobscot Bay can be mighty chilly, even at summer's peak. **Shirttail Point,** with limited parking, is a small sandy area on the Megunticook River. It's shallow enough for young kids and has picnic tables and a play area. From Route 1 in Camden, take Route 105 (Washington Street) 1.4 miles; watch for a small sign on the right. **Barrett's Cove,** on Megunticook Lake, has more parking spaces, usually more swimmers, and restrooms, picnic tables, and grills, as well as a play area. Diagonally opposite the Camden Public Library, take Route 52 (Mountain St.) about three miles; watch for the sign on the left. To cope with the parking crunch on hot summer days, bike to the beaches. You'll be ready for a swim after the uphill stretches, and it's all downhill on the way back.

Lincolnville has several ponds (some would call them lakes). On Route 52 in Lincolnville Center is Breezemere Park, a small town-owned swimming and picnic area on **Norton Pond.** Other Lincolnville options are **Coleman Pond, Pitcher Pond,** and **Knight's Pond.**

SALTWATER
The region's best ocean swimming is at **Lincolnville Beach,** where Penobscot Bay flirts with Route 1 on a sandy stretch of shorefront in the congested hamlet of Lincolnville Beach. On a hot day, the sand is wall-to-wall people; during one of the coast's legendary nor'easters, it's quite a wild place.

Another place for an ocean dip is **Laite Beach Park,** on Bay View Street about 1.5 miles from downtown Camden. It edges Camden Harbor and has a strip of sand, picnic tables, a playground, a float, and a children's amphitheater.

In Rockport, dip your toes into the ocean

at **Walker Park,** tucked away on the west side of the harbor. From Pascal Avenue, take Elm Street, which becomes Sea Street. Walker Park is on the left, with picnic tables, a play area, and a small pebbly beach.

Golf
On a back road straddling the Camden-Rockport line, the nine-hole **Goose River Golf Club** (50 Park St., Rockport, 207/236-8488) competes with the best for outstanding scenery.

Day Sails and Excursions
Most day sails and excursion boats operate late May-October, with fewer trips in the spring and fall than in July-August. You can't compare a two-hour day sail to a weeklong cruise on a Maine windjammer, but at least you get a hint of what could be—and it's a far better choice for kids, who aren't allowed on most windjammer cruises.

The classic wooden schooner *Olad* (207/236-2323, www.maineschooners.com, $37 adults, $27 under age 12) does several two-hour sails daily from Camden's Public Landing, weather permitting, late May-mid-October. Capt. Aaron Lincoln is a Rockland native, so he's got the local scoop on all the sights.

Another historic Camden day sailer is the 57-foot, 18-passenger schooner *Surprise* (207/236-4687, www.camdenmainesailing. com, $38, no credit cards) built in 1918 and skippered by congenial educator Jack Moore and his wife, Barbara. May-October they do daily two-hour sails departing from Camden's Public Landing; the minimum age is 12.

The 49-passenger *Appledore* (207/236-8353, www.appledore2.com), built in 1978 for round-the-world cruising, sails from Bay View Landing beginning around 10am three or four times daily June-October. Most cruises last two hours and cost $38 adults, $27 children. Cocktails, wine, and soft drinks are available.

Over in Rockport, the schooner *Heron* (207/236-8605 or 800/599-8605, www. woodenboatco.com) is a 65-foot John Alden-designed wooden yacht launched in 2003. Sailing options include a lobster-roll lunch sail, lighthouse sail, and sunset dinner sail ($50-65 adults, $25-35 under age 12).

If time is short, Camden Harbor Cruises (207/236-6672, www.camdenharborcruises. com, $28) offers one-hour cruises aboard the classic motor launches *Betselma* and the *Lively Lady Too,* operating from the Public Landing.

ACCOMMODATIONS

Many of Camden's most attractive accommodations (especially bed-and-breakfasts) are on Route 1 (variously disguised as Elm Street, Main Street, and High Street), which is heavily trafficked in summer. If you're sensitive to noise, request a room facing away from the street.

Camden
BED-AND-BREAKFASTS

A baker's dozen of Camden's finest bed-and-breakfasts have banded together in the **Camden Bed and Breakfast Association** (www.camdeninns.com), with an attractive brochure and website. Some of them are described here.

The 1874 **Camden Harbour Inn** (83 Bayview St., 207/236-4200 or 800/236-4200, www. camdenharbourinn.com, from $425) underwent a masterful renovation and restoration by new Dutch owners, partners Raymond Brunyanszki and Oscar Verest, reopening in 2007 as a boutique bed-and-breakfast complete with 21st-century amenities. It retains the bones of a 19th-century summer hotel, but the decor is contemporary European, with worldly accent pieces and velour furnishings in purples, reds, and silvers. Guest rooms, some with fireplaces, patios, decks, or balconies, have at least a glimpse of Camden's harbor or Penobscot Bay. All have air-conditioning, Wi-Fi, flat-screen TVs, refrigerators, and king beds. Service is five-star, right down to chocolates and slippers at turndown. At breakfast, which is included, the menu includes choices such as lobster Benedict as well as a buffet with fresh-baked items, smoked salmon, and other goodies. Snacks are always available. And the restaurant, Natalie's, is top-notch. The owners

also speak Dutch, German, some French, and rudimentary Indonesian and Thai.

The **Ⓒ Hartstone Inn** (41 Elm St., Rte. 1, 207/236-4259 or 800/788-4823, www. hartstoneinn.com, $135-309) is Michael and Mary Jo Salmon's imposing mansard-roofed Victorian close to the heart of downtown. Although some guest rooms face the street (and these are insulated with triple-pane windows), most do not, and all have air-conditioning. Once inside, you're away from it all. Even more removed are guest rooms in two other buildings under the Hartstone's umbrella. Suites in the Manor House, tucked behind the main inn, have contemporary decor. Guest rooms and suites in The Hideaway, in a residential neighborhood about a block away, have country French flair. All are elegant (Wi-Fi, air-conditioning); some have fireplaces and whirlpools. Make reservations for dinner. And then, there's the incredible breakfast. If you get hooked, the Salmons organize culinary classes during the winter, and you can even arrange for a one-on-one cooking experience with Michael.

After years of neglect, new owners Sue Walser and Phil Crispo have returned Camden's castle, **The Norumbega** (63 High St., 207/236-4646, www.norumbegainn.com, from $225) to its former opulence, but this time, they promise, there's no pretentiousness. Eleven spacious, air-conditioned guest rooms and two suites, some with balconies and terraces, many with panoramic ocean views, are on three floors of this turreted stone mansion by the sea. Phil, a former chef instructor at the Culinary Institute of America and winner on Chopped, makes the breakfasts. Five-course tasting dinners (served Thurs.-Tues.) are available to guests.

Opened to guests in 1901, the **Whitehall Inn** (52 High St./Rte. 1, 207/236-3391 or 800/789-6565, www.whitehall-inn.com, $125-274) retains its century-old genteel air. Lovely gardens, rockers on the veranda, a tennis court, and attentive service all add to the appeal of this historic country inn. Ask to see the Millay Room, commemorating famed poet Edna St. Vincent Millay, who graduated

© HILARY NANGLE

Most of the rooms at the Camden Harbour Inn offer at least a glimpse of the harbor.

from Camden High School and first recited her poem "Renascence" to Whitehall guests in 1912. It also played a role in *Peyton Place,* and enlarged movie photos are displayed throughout. Spread out between the main inn and the annex are 45 unpretentious guest rooms, all with flat-screen TVs, Internet access, and imported linens; a few share baths. Rates include a full-menu breakfast. The dining room, Vincent's, is open to nonguests for breakfast (7am-10am daily) and dinner (5pm-9pm Thurs.-Tues., entrées $10-25). Also on the premises is Gossip, a bar serving pub fare; it's open mid-May-late October.

Claudio and Roberta Latanza, both natives of Italy, became the fourth innkeepers at the ◖ **Camden Maine Stay** (22 High St./Rte. 1, 207/236-9636, www.mainestay.com, $170-290) in 2009. Like their predecessors, they do everything right, from the comfortable yet elegant decor to the delicious breakfasts and afternoon snacks to the welcoming window candles and garden retreats. The stunning residence, built in 1802, faces busy Route 1 and is just

a bit uphill from downtown, but inside and out back, behind the carriage house and barn, you'll feel worlds away.

In the heart of downtown Camden, **The Lord Camden Inn** (24 Main St./Rte. 1, 207/236-4325 or 800/336-4325, www.lord-camdeninn.com, $200-300) is a hotel alternative in a historic four-story downtown building (with an elevator). Top-floor rooms have harbor-view balconies. Rates include a breakfast buffet. Pooches are pampered in pet-friendly rooms for $25/night, including a bed, biscuits, bowls, and local dog info.

MOTEL

It's a short stroll into Merryspring Gardens from the **Cedar Crest Motel** (115 Elm St./Rte. 1, 207/236-4839, www.cedarcrestmotel.com, $134-149), a nicely maintained, older property on 3.5 wooded and landscaped acres on the southern edge of downtown. Each of the 37 guest rooms has air-conditioning, Wi-Fi, a phone, and a TV. Some have mini-fridges. On the premises are an outdoor heated pool, playground, laundry, and restaurant serving all meals, with live music on Friday evenings.

Frills are few at the easy-on-the-budget, two-story **Towne Motel** (68 Elm St., Rte. 1, 207/236-3377, www.camdenmotel.com, $124-139), but it's just steps from downtown, all rooms are air-conditioned, and there's free Wi-Fi. A continental breakfast is provided.

CAMPING
Camden Hills State Park (Belfast Rd./Rte. 1, 207/236-3109, $3 adults, $1 ages 5-11, camping $25 nonresidents, $15 Maine residents for basic site; $37.45 nonresidents, $26.75 Maine residents with water and electric) has a 112-site camping area and is wheelchair-accessible. Pets are allowed, showers are free, and the sites are large.

Rockport
MOTELS AND COTTAGE COLONIES
Step back in time at the oceanfront **◖Oakland Seashore Motel & Cottages** (112 Dearborn Ln., 207/594-8104, www.oaklandseashorecabins.com, $80-130), a low-key throwback on 70 mostly wooded acres that dates back more than a century. It was originally a recreational park operated by a trolley company, but its heyday passed with the arrival of the automobile. In the late 1940s, shorefront cabins were added, and in the 1950s, the dance pavilion was renovated into a motel. The rooms and cabins are simple, comfortable, clean, and right on the ocean's edge; some have kitchenettes, and a few have full kitchens. The bathrooms are tiny, and there are no phones or TVs. The grounds are gorgeous, with big shade trees, grassy lawns, and well-placed benches and chairs, and there's a rocky beach that's ideal for launching a kayak. This place isn't for those who need attentive service or fluffy accommodations, but it's a gem for those who appreciate quiet simplicity with a big view. Pets are a possibility ($30/stay).

Clean rooms, a convenient location, lovely ocean views from most rooms, and reasonable prices have made the Beale family's **Ledges by the Bay** (930 Rte. 1, Glen Cove, 207/594-8944, www.ledgesbythebay.com, $89-199)

a favorite among budget-conscious travelers. Guest rooms have air-conditioning, TVs, Wi-Fi, and phones; most have private balconies. Other pluses include a private shorefront, a small heated pool, and a light continental breakfast. Kids under 13 stay free in parents' room.

Family-owned and -operated, the all-suites **Country Inn** (8 Country Inn Way/Rte. 1, 207/236-2725 or 888/707-3945, www.countryinnmaine.com, $189-239) is an especially good choice for families, thanks to an indoor pool, play areas, a guest laundry, and a fitness room. Rooms are divided between a main inn and cottage suites. Some units have fireplaces, whirlpool tubs, and microwaves; all have air-conditioning, phones, fridges, Wi-Fi, and TVs. A continental breakfast buffet and afternoon tea and cookies are included. Kids ages 6-16 are $5/night; older kids are $10. On-site massage and yoga classes are available.

Lincolnville
INNS AND RESORTS
Private, secluded, and surrounded by 22 acres of woods and gardens, the oceanfront Shingle-style **Inn at the Ocean's Edge** (Rte. 1, Lincolnville Beach, 207/236-0945, www.innatoceansedge.com, from $250) is splurge-worthy. Every room has a king bed, a fireplace, and a whirlpool tub for two, as well as TV, air-conditioning, Wi-Fi, and superb ocean views. The grounds are lovely, with lounge chairs placed just so to take in the views. Facilities include an outdoor heated pool that makes it seem as if you're almost in the ocean, a hot tub, massage service, a sauna, and a fitness room. Rates include breakfast and afternoon snacks.

Even more private and secluded is **The Inn at Sunrise Point** (Rte. 1, Lincolnville, Camden, 207/236-7716 or 800/435-6278, www.sunrisepoint.com, from $395), an elegant retreat with all the bells and whistles you'd expect at these rates. The three handsome rooms in the main lodge, five separate cottages, and two lofts are all named after Maine authors or artists. Breakfast in the conservatory is divine.

On 12 hillside acres rolling down to the

oceanfront, **Glenmoor by the Sea** (2143 Atlantic Hwy./Rte. 1, 855/706-7905, www.glenmoorbythesea.com, $100-310) is a destination in itself with 19 cottages and 14 rooms, all recently renovated, two heated outdoor pools, and a nice lawn for activities. Other plusses include Wi-Fi, an oceanfront deck, tennis court, exercise room, fire pit, and a guest laundry. The motel rooms are close to Route 1 and noise may be a problem; opt for a cottage near the water if you can. A continental breakfast is included. Dogs are $10/night.

MOTEL AND COTTAGES

The family-run **Mount Battie Inn** (2158 Atlantic Hwy./Rte. 1, Lincolnville, 207/236-3870 or 800/224-3870, www.mountbattie.com, $126-219) has 22 charming motel-style guest rooms with air-conditioning, TVs, phones, Wi-Fi, fridges, and continental breakfast, including home-baked treats.

Another family-run gem, the **Ducktrap Motel** (12 Whitney Rd., Lincolnville, 207/789-5400 or 877/977-5400, www.ducktrapmotel.com, $95-115) is set back from Route 1 and screened by trees. Both the grounds and the rooms are meticulously maintained. All rooms have TVs, fridges, coffeemakers, and air-conditioning; deluxe rooms have microwaves, and the cottage has an efficiency kitchen.

Completely renovated for 2010, with individual cottages designed by college interns, the **Bay Leaf Cottages & Bistro** (2372 Rte. 1, Lincolnville, 207/706-7929 or 888/902-7929, www.bayleafcottages.com, $100-220) welcomes families and some pets ($20) in a variety of cottages and motel rooms. Note that rooms are not serviced daily by housekeeping. A continental breakfast buffet is served in the bistro; Saturday lobster dinners are available. Cooking classes and other workshops and adventures are offered.

FOOD
Local Flavors
ROCKPORT

The best source for health foods, homeopathic remedies, and fresh seasonal produce is **Fresh Off the Farm** (495 Rte. 1, 207/236-3260, 8am-7pm Mon.-Sat., 9am-5:30pm Sun.), an inconspicuous red-painted roadside place that looks like an overgrown farm stand (which it is). Watch for one of those permanent-temporary signs highlighting the latest arrivals, which might include native blueberries or native corn. The shop is 1.3 miles south of the junction of Routes 1 and 90.

At the southern Rockport town line, a sprawling red building is the home of **The Rockport Marketplace and the State of Maine Cheese Company** (461 Commercial St./Rte. 1, 207/236-8895 or 800/762-8895, 9am-6pm Mon.-Sat., noon-4pm Sun.) and **Maine Street Meats** (207/236-6328, 10am-6pm Mon.-Sat.). Inside are locally made varieties of cows' milk hard cheeses, all named after Maine locations (Aroostook Jack, Allagash Caraway, St. Croix Black Pepper, and so on) as well as hundreds of Maine-made products, from food to crafts. Maine Street Meats, a separate business within the marketplace, is a full-service butcher shop and specialty food market, selling drool-worthy local and imported meats, cheeses, charcuterie, and prepared foods, including soups, sandwiches, and flatbread pizzas.

At the junction of Routes 1 and 90, a colorfully painted barn is the home of **The Market Basket** (Rte. 1, 207/236-4371, 7am-6:30pm Mon.-Sat., 9am-4pm Sun.), the best take-out source for creative sandwiches, homemade soups, cheeses, exotic condiments, pastries, wine (large selection), beer, and entrées to go.

Locals know one of the area's best spots for lobster rolls and fried seafood is **Graffam Bros. Seafood Shack** (211 Union St., 207/236-8391, 8:30am-6pm Mon.-Sat.). There's some seating at picnic tables, but take it to Harbor Park for the oceanside setting.

Love doughnuts? The ones from **Willow Bake Shoppe** (1084 Rte. 1, 207/596-0564, 6am-noon Mon.-Sat.) earn raves.

CAMDEN

The **Camden Farmers Market** (3:30pm-6pm Wed. June-late Sept. and 9am-noon Sat. early

May-late Oct.) holds forth at the Knox Mill Complex on Washington Street.

Made-to-order sandwiches and wraps, homemade soups, veggie burgers, and baked goods are the draws at the **Camden Deli** (37 Main St., 207/236-8343, 7am-10pm daily), in the heart of downtown, but its biggest asset is the windowed seating overlooking the Megunticook River waterfall. The view doesn't get much better than this (go upstairs for the best angle).

Since the early 1970s, **Scott's Place** (85 Elm St./Rte. 1, 207/236-8751, 10:30am-4pm Mon.-Fri., to 3pm Sat.), a roadside lunch stand near Renys at the Camden Marketplace, has been dishing up inexpensive ($2-10) burgers and dogs, nowadays adding veggie burgers and salads. Call ahead and it'll be ready.

Peek behind the old-fashioned facade at **Boynton-McKay Food Company** (30 Main St., 207/236-2465, 7am-5pm daily, kitchen closes 3pm daily) and you'll see an old-fashioned soda fountain, early-20th-century tables, antique pharmacy accessories, and a thoroughly modern café menu. Restored and rehabbed in 1997, Boynton-McKay had been *the* local drugstore for more than a century. The new incarnation features bagels, creative salads, homemade soups, superb wrap sandwiches, an espresso bar, and the whole works from the soda fountain. It's open for breakfast and lunch.

Artisan pizzas, such as prosciutto, fig, and Gorgonzola, emerge from the wood-fired ovens of **Seabright** (1 Public Landing, 207/230-1414, from noon daily, $13-18, cash only), a cozy spot owned by James Beard nominee Brian Hill.

Facing downtown Camden's five-way intersection, **French and Brawn** (1 Elm St., 207/236-3361, 6am-7pm Mon.-Sat., 8am-7pm Sun.) is an independent market that earns the description *super*. Ready-made sandwiches, soups, and other goodies complement the oven-ready take-out meals, high-cal frozen desserts, esoteric meats, and staff with a can-do attitude.

LINCOLNVILLE

Need a sandwich before heading for the hills or beach? **Dot's** (2457 Rte. 1, 207/706-7922, 7am-6pm Mon.-Sat., 8am-3pm Sun.) is the place. It also bakes breakfast goods and treats, makes salads and prepared meals, and sells cheeses and wines. There's seating inside.

Local chef Annemarie Ahearn's oceanfront **Salt Water Farm** (25 Woodward Hill Rd., 207/230-0966, www.saltwaterfarm.com) is a haven for serious foodies. Hands-on cooking classes (around $85 for a half-day class) and multiday workshops are offered. The second location in Rockport serves dinner in the evenings and brunch on the weekends.

Family Favorites
CAMDEN

With a menu ranging from burgers to pastas and pizzas, the **Elm Street Grille** (Cedar Crest Motel, 115 Elm St./Rte. 1, 207/236-4839, www.elmstreetgrille.com, 7am-11am and 4pm-9pm Tues.-Sun.) is a popular spot for families seeking a good meal at a fair price. Breakfast also get high marks. Dinner choices range from pizzas to a broiled seafood platter ($10-22); kids' menu available. There's live music most Friday nights.

In the heart of Camden, **Cappy's** (1 Main St., 207/236-2254, www.cappyschowder.com, 11am-11pm daily, $10-22) has two locations, the original corner spot—small, cramped, and buzzing with locals and out-of-towners alike—and the new in 2013 **Cappy's Harborview,** just a few doors down. It's a bit pricey for food that's rather ordinary, but the chowder earns raves. It's a burger-and-sandwich menu with some heartier seafood choices. During summer, Cappy's operates a bakery with take-out pastries, sandwiches, and other goodies underneath the original store, facing on the alley that runs down to the public parking lot.

CASUAL DINING
ROCKPORT

When **Shepherd's Pie** (18 Central St., 207/236-8500, www.shepherdspierockport. com, from 5pm daily, $13-24) opened in spring 2010, it already had a cult following thanks to chef-owner Brian Hill's successful Francine Bistro in Camden. Here in a historical building with high tin ceilings and beautiful dark wood walls, Hill has created a delicious and inviting spot serving pub- and home-style favorites updated with verve; think duck hot dogs, smoked alewife Caesar, fried clam tacos, and baked beans with candied bacon. They don't take reservations; expect to wait for a table.

Overlooking Rockport Harbor, **Salt Water Farm at Union Hall** (23 Central St., www.saltwaterfarm.com, 8am-10pm Tues.-Sun.) is an extension of chef-owner Annemarie Ahearn's local foodie haven in Lincolnville. A combo café and marketplace, the menus highlight the day's deliveries from local farmers, fishermen, and foragers. Brunch is served Saturday-Sunday, there is a family-style dining in the evening ($12-18), and Full Moon Suppers ($65) are served once a month. Best seats are on the back deck overlooking Rockport Harbor.

CAMDEN

Chef-owner Brian Hill has created one of the region's hottest restaurants with **Francine Bistro** (55 Chestnut St., 207/230-0083, www.francinebistro.com, 5:30pm-10pm Tues.-Sat., entrées $24-30). The well-chosen menu is short and focused on whatever's fresh and (usually) locally available that day. In addition to the dining room, there's seating at the bar and, when the weather cooperates, on the front porch. Be forewarned, it can get quite noisy.

Down on the harbor is the informal, art-filled **Atlantica** (1 Bay View Landing, 207/236-6011 or 888/507-8514, www.atlanticarestaurant.com, 5pm-9pm daily, $14-29), two floors of culinary creativity with an emphasis on seafood. In summer, try for a table on the deck hanging over the water.

The Waterfront Restaurant (Bay View St., 207/236-3747, 11:30am-9pm daily, $18-30) has the biggest waterside dining deck in town, but you'll need to arrive early to snag one of the tables. Lunches are the most fun, overlooking lots of harbor action; at high tide, you're eye to eye with the boats. Most folks rave about the place, but I've found it inconsistent.

The word is out about **Long Grain** (31 Elm St., 207/236-9001, 11:30am-3pm and 4:30pm-9pm Tues.-Sat.), a tiny restaurant that's earned kudos far and wide for its outstanding and authentic Pan-Asian cuisine. Flavors are fresh, complex, and layered, and presentation is gorgeous. Most items are $10-18. Do make reservations or opt for takeout.

The often-changing Latin-fusion menu at Culinary Institute of America-trained chef Tom Sigler's **Comida Latin Kitchen** (31 Elm St./Rte. 1, 207/230-7367, www.comidarestaurant.com, $13-18, 5pm-9pm Mon.-Sat.) draws from Spanish, Cuban, Mexican, and Central and South American influences. Everything's made from scratch, so don't expect fast service. This place is tiny; make reservations. Lunch is served 11:30am-3pm during summer.

The fish-and-chips alone are worth the mosey inland along Route 105 from Camden to find the **Hatchet Mountain Publick House** (42 Hatchet Mountain Rd., Hope, 207/763-4565, www.hatchetmountain.com, from 5:15pm Tues.-Sat., $9-24), a combination tavern and antiques shop in a beautifully renovated barn.

Go for Happy Hour at **40 Paper** (40 Washington St., 207/230-0111, 5pm-9pm daily), located in the renovated Knox Mill, and then maybe stick around for the handmade pastas, flatbread pizzas, and other Italian fare. Food is generally quite good; service is mediocre at best.

LINCOLNVILLE

Maine fare with an unpretentious French accent paired with Penobscot Bay views have drawn diners to **Chez Michel** (2530 Rte. 1, 207/789-5600, 4pm-9pm Tues.-Sun.) for decades. Early-bird specials are served until 5:45pm; otherwise, most entrées top out around $22. This isn't a French restaurant, but there are French-inspired preparations, such as *coquille* St. Jacques and duck au poivre, as well as fried and broiled seafood, steak, and pastas. There's a children's menu too.

Fine Dining
CAMDEN

Reservations are a must for the intimate restaurant at the **Hartstone Inn** (41 Elm St., 207/236-4259 or 800/788-4823, www.

PENOBSCOT BAY

hartstoneinn.com, 5:30pm-8:30pm daily). Michael Salmon, named Caribbean chef of the year when he lived in Aruba, has cooked at the Beard House by invitation. Even Julia Child dined here. The menu changes weekly to use the freshest ingredients. The nightly chef's tasting menu is $55; entrées on the lighter, à la carte menu run $20-30.

Since opening in 2007 to rave reviews, **❰ Natalie's at the Camden Harbour Inn** (83 Bayview St., 207/236-4200, www.nataliesrestaurant.com, 5pm-9:30pm daily in season, call off-season) has become one of the state's top tables. The dining room was designed to be reminiscent of the Left Bank in Paris a century ago. The ambience is fancy here, but casual attire is fine. Instead of looking out at the Seine, you're gazing over Camden Harbor. Dining options are a three-course à la carte menu ($68) or a seven-course chef's tasting menu ($97). A more casual tapas menu is available at the bar or in the lounge.

LINCOLNVILLE

For a romantic, classic French experience, head a bit inland to **Youngtown Inn and Restaurant** (581 Youngtown Rd., 207/763-4290 or 800/291-8438, www.youngtowninn.com, 6pm-9pm Tues.-Sun., $27-34), where chef-owner Manuel Mercier draws on his Parisian heritage and European training. The best deal is the four-course $45 chef's menu. Upstairs are six guest rooms (from $170, includes breakfast).

Lobster

Lincolnville's best-known landmark is **The Lobster Pound Restaurant** (Rte. 1,

Lincolnville Beach, 207/789-5550, www.lobsterpoundmaine.com, 11:30am-10pm daily, $12-35). About 300 people—some days, it looks like more than that—can pile into the restaurant and enclosed patio, so make reservations on summer weekends. Despite the crowds, food and service are reliably good. In 2014, it merged with Andrews Brewing Co. and turned half the space into a brewpub. Lobster, of course, is still king, but the huge menu will satisfy everyone.

INFORMATION AND SERVICES

For planning, contact **Penobscot Bay Regional Chamber of Commerce** (207/236-4404 or 800/223-5459, www.mainedreamvacation.com). Also handy is a map and guide published by the **Lincolnville Business Group** (www.visitlincolnville.com).

Check out the **Camden Public Library** (Main St./Rte. 1, Camden, 207/236-3440, www.camden.lib.me.us) or **Rockport Public Library** (1 Limerock St., Rockport, 207/236-3642, www.rockport.lib.me.us).

Find **public restrooms** in Camden at the Public Landing, near the chamber of commerce, and at the Camden Public Library; in Rockport at Marine Park; and in Lincolnville, at the ferry terminal.

GETTING THERE AND AROUND

Camden is about eight miles or 15 minutes via Route 1 from Rockland. It's about six miles or 10 minutes via Route 1 from Lincolnville or about 20 miles or 30 minutes via Route 1 from Belfast.

Belfast

Belfast (pop. 6,668) is relatively small as cities go, but it's officially cool: *Budget Travel* magazine named it one of the top 10 coolest towns in the United States. Even before that, Belfast was one of those off-the-beaten-track destinations popular with tuned-in travelers. Chalk that up to its status as a magnet for left-over back-to-the-landers and enough artistic types to earn the city a nod for cultural cool. Belfast has a curling club, a food co-op, and a green store, meditation centers, an increasing number of art galleries and boutiques, dance and theater companies, the oldest shoe store in the country, and half a dozen different 12-step, self-help groups. There's a festival nearly every weekend during the summer. It even has a poet laureate.

This eclectic city is a work in progress, a study in Maine-style diversity. It's also a gold mine of Federal, Greek Revival, Italianate, and Victorian architecture. Take the time to stroll the well-planned backstreets, explore the shops, and hang out at the gussied-up waterfront.

Separating Belfast from East Belfast, the Passagassawakeag River (puh-sag-gus-uh-WAH-keg) fortunately is known more familiarly as "the Passy." The Indian name has been translated as both "place of many ghosts" and the rather different "place for spearing sturgeon by torchlight." You choose. No matter, you can cross it via a pedestrian bridge.

Many travelers make Belfast a day stop on their way between Camden and Bar Harbor. Truly, Belfast is worth more time than that. Spend a full day or two here and it's likely you'll be charmed, like many of the other urban refugees, into resettling here.

SIGHTS
Historic Walking Tour
No question, the best way to appreciate Belfast's fantastic architecture is to tour by ankle express. At the Belfast Area Chamber of Commerce, pick up the well-researched *Belfast Historic Walking Tour* map-brochure. Among more than 40 highlights on the mile-long self-guided route are the 1818 Federal-style **First Church,** handsome residences on **High Street** and **Church Street,** and the 1840 **James P. White House** (Church St. and Northport Ave.), now an elegant bed-and-breakfast and New England's finest Greek Revival residence. Amazingly for a community of this size, the city actually has three distinct listed districts on the National Register of Historic Places: Belfast Commercial Historic District (47 downtown buildings), Church Street Historic District (residential), and Primrose Hill Historic District (also residential). Another walking tour is presented by the Belfast Historical Society's **Museum in the Streets,** comprising two large panels and 30 smaller ones highlighting historic buildings and people. Signs are in English and French.

Bayside
Continuing the focus on architecture, just south of Belfast in Northport is the Victorian enclave of Bayside, a neighborhoody sort of place with small, well-kept gingerbread-trimmed cottages cheek-by-jowl on pint-size lots. Formerly known as the Northport Wesleyan Grove Campground, the village took shape in the mid-1800s as a summer retreat for Methodists. In the 1930s the retreat was disbanded and the main meeting hall was razed, creating the waterfront park at the heart of the village. Today, many of the colorfully painted homes are rented by the week, month, or summer season, and their tenants are more likely to indulge in athletic rather than religious pursuits. The camaraderie remains, though, and a stroll (or cycle or drive) through Bayside is like a visit to another era. Bayside is four miles south of Belfast, just east of Route 1. If you want to join the fun, try **Bayside Cottage Rentals** (539 Bluff Rd., Northport, 207/338-5355, www.baysidecottagerentals.com).

VISITING LIBERTY

Seventeen miles west of Belfast, off Route 3, is **Liberty** (www.historicliberty.com), a tiny town with a funky tool store, a quirky museum, a bargain T-shirt shop, and a great state park. Everything is seasonal, running about mid-May–mid-October. Call before visiting if you want to be sure everything's open.

It's a store! It's a museum! It's amazing! More than 10,000 "useful" tools—plus used books and prints and other choice items—fill the three-story **Liberty Tool Company** (Main St., Liberty, 207/589-4771). Drawn by nostalgia and a compulsion for handmade adzes and chisels, thousands of vintage-tool buffs arrive at this eclectic emporium each year; few leave empty-handed. Nor do the thousands of everyday home hobbyists looking to pick up a hammer or find a missing wrench to fill out a set. Nor do the antiques-seekers, who browse the trash and treasures on the upper floors. The collection is beyond amazing, especially in its organization. Owner Skip Brack brings back vanloads of finds almost every week, and after sorting and cleaning, many make it into this store.

The best-of-the-best make it into Brack's **Davistown Museum** (Main St., 207/589-4900, www.davistownmuseum.org), on the third floor of the building housing Liberty Graphics, across the street. The museum houses not only a history of Maine and New England hand tools but also local, regional, Native American, and environmental artifacts and information and an amazing collection of contemporary art, highlighted by works by artists such as Louise Nevelson (who used to buy tools across the street), Melitta Westerlund, and Phil Barter.

Downstairs is **Liberty Graphics Outlet Store** (1 Main St., 207/589-4035, www.lg-tees.com), selling the eco-sensitive company's overstocks, seconds, and discontinued-design T-shirts. Outstanding silk-screened designs are done with water-based inks, and many of the shirts are organic cotton; prices begin at $7.

Just down Main Street is the old **Liberty Post Office,** a unique octagonal structure that looks like an oversize box. It was built in 1867 as a harness-maker's shop and later used as the town's post office.

Two miles west of downtown, **Lake St. George State Park** (Rte. 3, 207/589-4255, $6 nonresident adults, $4 Maine resident adults, $1 ages 5-11) is a refreshing find. This 360-acre park has wooded picnic sites with grills along the lake, a beach, rental boats, a playground, volleyball and basketball courts, and five miles of hiking trails. Also available are campsites ($25 nonresidents, $15 Maine residents). Afterward, head to **John's Ice Cream** (Rte. 3, 207/589-3700) for amazing flavors handcrafted ("homemade" is too pedestrian to describe it) on the premises, or good country cooking at the **Olde Mill Diner** (143 Belfast Ave./Rte. 3, Searsmont, 207/342-2999).

If you're up for more inland exploring, weave your way along the **Georges River Scenic Byway,** a 50-mile auto route along the St. George River (a.k.a. Georges River) from its inland headwaters to the sea in Port Clyde. It's lovely anytime but is especially pretty during foliage season. The official start is at the junction of Routes 3 and 220 in Liberty, but you can follow the trail in either direction or pick it up anywhere along the way. Road signs are posted, but it's far better to obtain a map-brochure at a chamber of commerce or other information locale. Or contact the architects of the route, **The Georges River Land Trust** (207/594-5166, www.georgesriver.org).

Temple Heights

Continue south on Shore Road from Bayside to **Temple Heights Spiritualist Camp** (Shore Rd., Northport, 207/338-3029, www.templeheightscamp.org), yet another religious enclave—this one still ongoing. Founded in 1882, Temple Heights has become a shadow of its former self, reduced primarily to the funky 12-room Nikawa Lodge on Shore Road ($45, shared bath, some with ocean views), but the summer program continues thanks to prominent mediums from all over the country. Even a temporary setback in 1996—when the camp president was suspended for allegedly putting a hex on Northport's town clerk—failed to derail the operation. Camp programs mid-June–early September are open to the public; a schedule is published each spring. Spiritualist church services and group healing circles are by donation; Saturday-morning workshops are $25. Better yet, sign up for a 1.5-hour or longer **group message circle** (7:30pm Wed. and Sat., $15), when you'll sit with a medium and a dozen or so others and receive insights—often uncannily on target—from departed relatives or friends; reservations are requested, and you should plan to arrive a half hour early. Private half-hour readings can be arranged for $40.

Belfast & Moosehead Railroad

The nonprofit Brooks Preservation Society operates the **Belfast & Moosehead Railroad** (207/722-3899, www.brookspreservation.org), which rolls through the inland countryside west of Bethel. The 1.5-hour trips ($12 adults, $6 ages 3–14) aboard vintage trains depart from the **City Point Central Railroad Museum** (13 Oak Hill Rd., Belfast); call for current schedule.

ENTERTAINMENT

It's relatively easy to find nightlife in Belfast—not only are there theaters and a cinema, but there are usually a couple of bars open at least until midnight and sometimes later. Some spots also feature live music, particularly on weekends.

If you don't feel like searching out a newspaper to check the entertainment listings, just go to the **Belfast Co-op Store** (123 High St., 207/338-2532) and study the bulletin board. You'll find notices for more activities than you could ever squeeze into your schedule.

Open-mike nights, jazz jams, classes, and lectures pepper the calendar for **Waterfall Arts** (265 High St., 207/338-2222, www.waterfallarts.org).

Just south of Belfast, the funky **Blue Goose Dance Hall** (Rte. 1, Northport, 207/338-3003)

is the site for folk concerts, contra dances, auctions, and other events. Check local papers or the Belfast Co-op Store bulletin board.

Street entertainers perform and about a dozen galleries participate in Belfast Arts' **Friday Gallery Walk** (www.belfastartwalk.com), held 5:30pm-8pm the first Friday in June-December.

Check local papers for the schedule of the **Belfast Maskers** (207/338-9668, www.belfastmaskerstheater.com), a community theater group that never fails to win raves for its interpretations of contemporary and classical dramas.

The Belfast Garden Club sponsors **Open Garden Days** (www.belfastgardenclub.org) once a week mid-May–mid-September at the homes of club members and friends in and around Belfast. Gardens are usually open 10am-3pm rain or shine; a $5 pp donation is requested to benefit local beautification projects. Check local newspapers or ask at the chamber of commerce for the schedule.

EVENTS

Belfast is a hotbed of events, with a festival scheduled nearly every weekend during the summer.

The **Free Range Music Festival** in April draws fans from across the spectrum, with everything from a capella to rock.

In early July, soon after the Fourth of July, the **Arts in the Park** festival gets under way at Heritage Park, on the Belfast waterfront. It's a weekend event with two days of music, juried arts and crafts, children's activities, and lots of food booths.

In late July, the **Belfast Bound Book Festival** celebrates traditional books, with readings, storytelling, author signings, and talks.

Cheese-rolling, Highland games, and music are just a few of the activities at the midsummer **Maine Celtic Celebration.**

Dachshunds rule during September's **Wienerfest,** complete with a parade and costume contest.

In October, the **Belfast Poetry Festival**

PENOBSCOT BAY

© HILARY NANGLE

America's oldest shoe store is in downtown Belfast.

pairs poets with artists for workshops and readings.

SHOPPING

It's easy and fun to shop in downtown Belfast, a town that has so far managed to keep the big boxes away, providing fertile ground for entrepreneurs. Downtown shops reflect the city's population, with galleries and boutiques, thrift and used-goods stores, and eclectic shops, including a number specializing in books: new, used, and antiquarian.

Specialty Shops

Even if shoes aren't on your shopping list, stop in at "the oldest shoe store in America": Founded in the 1830s, **Colburn Shoe Store** (81 Main St., 207/338-1934 or 877/338-1934) may be old, but it isn't old-fashioned, and it has a bargain basement.

Brambles (69 Main St., 207/338-3448) is a gardener's delight, with fun, whimsical, and practical garden-themed merchandise.

Left Bank Books (109 Church St., 207/338-9009) is one of those wonderful bookstores that not only has a well-curated selection, but also presents readings and signings.

Seeking an out-of-print treasure or a focused tome? **Old Professor's Bookshop** (99 Main St., 207/338-2006) specializes in new, used, and rare books that answer the big questions: What is? And what matters?

Books are just one part of the eclectic mix at **Beyond the Sea** (74 Main St., 207/338-2100), but each book carried is chosen by the owner. Of special note are the Persephone Books, new editions of out-of-print classics.

Wooden toys are just one reason to visit **Out of the Woods** (48 Main St., 207/338-2692), which specializes in Maine-made wood products.

Calling itself a "general store for the 21st century," **The Green Store** (71 Main St., 207/338-4045) carries a huge selection of environmentally friendly products. Whether you're thinking of going off the grid, need a composting toilet, or just want natural-fiber clothing or other natural-living products, this is the place. A very knowledgeable staff can answer nearly any question on environmentally sustainable lifestyles.

About two miles east of Belfast's bridge, on the right, is the small roadside shop of **Mainely Pottery** (181 Searsport Ave./Rte. 1, 207/338-1108). Since 1988, Jeannette Faunce and Jamie Oates have been marketing the work of more than two dozen Maine potters, each with different techniques, glazes, and styles. It's the perfect place to select from a wide range of reasonably priced work.

RECREATION
Parks

Belfast is rich in parks and picnic spots. One of the state's best municipal parks is just on the outskirts of downtown. Established in 1904, **Belfast City Park** (87 Northport Ave., 207/338-1661, free) has lighted tennis courts, an outdoor pool, a pebbly beach, plenty of picnic tables, an unusually creative playground, lots of green space for the kids, and fantastic views of Islesboro, Blue Hill, and Penobscot Bay. For more action right in the heart of Belfast, head for **Heritage Park,** at the bottom of Main Street, with front-row seats on waterfront happenings. Bring a picnic, grab a table, and watch the yachts, tugs, and lobster boats. Every street between the two parks that ends at the ocean is a public right of way.

Hiking

Here's an easy amble, with just enough rise and fall to make you think you got a bit of a workout: The blue-blazed **Little River Community Trail** parallels the east bank of the Little River, departing from a trailhead at the Water District complex on Route 1 and ebbing and flowing just shy of a mile to the Perkins Road. You can cross the road and continue for nearly another three miles to another trailhead near the YMCA on Route 52.

Golf

Just south of Belfast is the nine-hole **Northport Golf Club** (581 Bluff Rd., Northport, 207/338-2270), established in 1916.

Boat Excursions

Sail aboard the Friendship sloop **Amity** (207/323-1443, www.belfastbaycompany.com), based at the Belfast Public Landing, for two-hour shared-charter sails ($45 pp) or for private charters, from $350. The classic sloop, built in 1901 in Friendship, was originally used for lobstering. Now beautifully restored, it carries up to six passengers.

Kayaking

If you don't have your own kayak, **Water Walker** (152 Lincolnville Ave., 207/338-6424, www.kayak-tour-maine.com) has a full range of options. Owner Ray Wirth, a Registered Maine Guide and American Canoe Association-certified open-water instructor, will arrange customized trips from a few hours to multiple days, as well as provide instruction. A 2-3-hour custom tour for two people is $120.

Curling

The Scottish national sport of curling has dozens of enthusiastic supporters at Maine's only curling rink, the **Belfast Curling Club** (Belmont Ave./Rte. 3, 207/338-9851, www.belfastcurlingclub.org), an institution here since the late 1950s. Leagues play regularly on weeknights, and the club holds bonspiels (tournaments) and open houses several times during the season, which runs early November-early April.

ACCOMMODATIONS
Bed-and-Breakfasts and Inns

On a quiet side street, **The Jeweled Turret** (40 Pearl St., 207/338-2304 or 800/696-2304, www.jeweledturret.com, $130-170) is one of Belfast's pioneer bed-and-breakfasts. Carl and Cathy Heffentrager understand the business and go out of their way to make guests comfortable. The 1898 inn is loaded with handsome woodwork and Victorian antiques—plus an astonishing stone fireplace, one of four in the house. The wraparound porches are a fine place to settle and view the gardens while enjoying afternoon tea.

Over three years, beginning in 2005, professional innkeepers Ed and Judy Hemmingsen renovated adjacent mid-19th-century row houses into an elegant boutique hotel, the **Belfast Bay Inn** (72 Main St., 207/338-5600, www.belfastbayinn.com, from $300). The two guest rooms and six suites differ in size and design, some with fireplaces, others with balconies, but all have original art, expanded wet bars, and high-quality furnishings that invite relaxation. In-room spa services are available. A full breakfast is included. The Hemmingsens delight in surprising guests with unexpected extras.

Motels

The 61 guest rooms at the oceanfront **Belfast Harbor Inn** (91 Searsport Ave., 207/338-2740 or 800/545-8576, www.belfastharborinn.com, $79-159) have TVs, air-conditioning, and free Wi-Fi and local calls; there's an outdoor heated pool—a real plus for families, as is the laundry.

Pets are allowed in some guest rooms for $10/night. Rates include a light continental breakfast buffet. If you can swing it, request an oceanview room.

In 2012, new owners completely renovated the **Yankee Clipper Motel** (50 Searsport Ave., 207/338-2353, www.yankeeclippermotelbelfast.com, $89-149), giving the vintage 1950s strip motel on Route 1 a boutique vibe. All rooms have laminated wood floors, contemporary decor, and neutral colors along with a microwave and mini-fridge.

FOOD
Local Flavors
Wraps are fast food at **Bay Wrap** (20 Beaver St., 207/338-9757, 11am-7pm Mon.-Fri., 11am-4pm Sat.). There's no limit to what the staff can stuff into various flavors of tortillas. Eat here or get them to go.

Industrial chic, casual, and laid-back best describe **Three Tides** (2 Pinchy Lane, on Marshall Wharf, 207/338-1707, www.3tides.com, 4pm-9pm Tues.-Sun.). Grab a booth inside, a seat at the bar, or a table on the deck overlooking the working harbor, and then choose from the tapas-style menu ($3.50-14). You might even play a game of boccie while waiting. Beers and ales are brewed on the premises. Also part of the operation is **LB,** a lobster pound, so lobster is often on the menu.

Love cheese? You'll love **Eat More Cheese** (33 Main St., 207/358-9701), which carries a selection from around the world. Although it has a Main Street address, the entry is around back.

The **Belfast Co-op Store** (123 High St., 207/338-2532, www.belfast.coop, 7:30am-8pm daily) is an experience in itself. You'll have a good impression of Belfast after one glance at the clientele and the bulletin board. Open to members and nonmembers alike (with lower prices for members), the co-op is a full-service organic and natural foods grocery, with a deli-café serving breakfast, lunch, and take-out fare.

Food trucks arrived in Belfast with **Good N You** (parking lot behind Main St., 11:30am-3pm Mon.-Sat. and 6:30pm-9pm Sat.), which

dishes out tacos, falafel, burritos, and other street food ($2-7).

The **Chocolate Drop Candy Shop** (64 Main St., 207/338-0566) is a kid-pleasing, retro-themed ice cream parlor and candy shop.

Siinfully delicious scratch-made croissants, bagels, and pastries emerge from the ovens at **Moonbat City Baking Co.** (137 Main St., 207/218-1039, 7am-2pm Mon.-Sat., to 1pm Sun.).

The Belfast Farmers Market (Waterfall Arts, 256 High St., 9am-1pm Fri.) provides the perfect opportunity for stocking up for a picnic. On the first Friday of the month, it relocates downtown on Main Street.

Ethnic and Vegetarian Fare
Excellent Thai food is paired with a fabulous view of Penobscot Bay at **Seng Thai** (139 Searsport Ave./Rte. 1, 207/338-0010, 11:30am-9pm daily, entrées $8-18).

Fresh food prepared in creative ways has earned **Chase's Daily** (96 Main St., 207/338-0555, 7am-5pm Tues.-Thurs. and Sat., 7am-8pm Fri., 8am-2pm Sun.) a devoted local following. The emphasis is on vegetarian fare, and most of the produce comes from the Chase family farm in nearby Freedom. Most choices are in the $7-12 range; dinner entrées range $15-22. The restaurant also serves as an art gallery, farmers market, and bakery. It's not the place for a quiet dinner, as the space is large and tends to be noisy.

Delvino's Grill and Pasta House (32 Main St., 207/338-4565, www.delvinos.com, 11am-9pm daily, entrées $13-23) satiates cravings for Italian fare with a menu that includes lasagna, lobster ravioli, seafood pomodoro, and gluten-free grilled vegetable medley.

Laan Xang Cafe (18 Main St., 207/338-6338, www.laanxangcafe.com, 9am-3pm and 5pm-7pm Mon.-Sat., $10-14), specializing in Thai, Laotian, and Vietnamese fare, is a tiny, mostly take-out spot with a handful of tables on a deck.

Casual Dining
Celebrity chef Matthew Kenney now hangs his

toque at **The Gothic** (108 Main St., 207/930-4684, from 5pm daily, $18-25), in the meticulously restored flatiron building at the head of Main Street. Kenney was a pioneer in the raw food movement, but his menus here are designed to appeal to a wider audience. The daily changing menu is divided into categories for soil, sea, and land, and the choices are limited.

A longtime standby for world cuisine, including vegetarian items, **Darby's Restaurant and Pub** (155 High St., 207/338-2339, www.darbysrestaurant.com, 11:30am-3:30pm and 5pm-9pm daily and 7:30am-9pm Fri.-Sun., entrées $12-20) served tofu before tofu was cool. This place has been providing food and drink since just after the Civil War; the tin ceilings and antique bar are reminders of that.

Lobster
Young's Lobster Pound (2 Fairview Ave., 207/338-1160), a barn of a place on the east side of the harbor, is the place to go for fresh-from-the-sea lobster. BYOB.

INFORMATION AND SERVICES
The **Belfast Area Chamber of Commerce** (16 Main St., 207/338-5900, www.belfastmaine.org) produces a regional guide.

Check out the **Belfast Free Library** (106 High St., 207/338-3884, www.belfast.lib.me.us).

Find **public restrooms** at the waterfront Public Landing, in the railroad station, at the Waldo County Courthouse, and at the Waldo County General Hospital.

GETTING THERE AND AROUND
Belfast is about 20 miles or 30 minutes via Route 1 from Camden and about 45 miles or one hour from Augusta and I-95 via Route 3. It's about 6.5 miles or 10 minutes via Route 1 to Searsport.

Searsport Area

Searsport (pop. 2,615) is synonymous with the sea, thanks to an enduring oceangoing tradition that's appropriately commemorated here in the state's oldest maritime museum. The seafaring heyday occurred in the mid-19th century, but settlers from the Massachusetts Colony had already made inroads here 200 years earlier. By the 1750s, Fort Pownall, in nearby **Stockton Springs,** was a strategic site during the French and Indian War (the North American phase of Europe's Seven Years' War).

Shipbuilding was under way by 1791, reaching a crescendo 1845-1866, with six year-round shipyards and nearly a dozen more seasonal ones. Ten percent of all full-rigged American-flag ships on the high seas were under the command of Searsport and Stockton Springs captains by 1885—a significant number of them bearing the names Pendleton, Nichols, or Carver. Many of these ships were involved in the perilous China trade, rounding notorious Cape Horn with great regularity.

All this global contact shaped Searsport's culture, adding a veneer of cosmopolitan sophistication. Imposing mansions of seafaring families were filled with fabulous Oriental treasures, many of which eventually made their way to the Penobscot Marine Museum. Brick-lined Main Street is more evidence of the mid-19th-century wealth, and local churches reaped the benefits of residents' generosity. The Second Congregational Church, known as the Safe Harbor Church and patronized by captains and shipbuilders (most ordinary seamen attended the Methodist church), is ornamented with recently restored Tiffany-style windows and a Christopher Wren steeple.

Another inkling of this area's oceangoing superiority comes from visits to local burial grounds: Check out the headstones at Gordon,

© HILARY NANGLE

Rodman cannon at Fort Knox

Bowditch, and Sandy Point cemeteries. Many have fascinating tales to tell.

Today the Searsport area's major draws are the Penobscot Marine Museum, the still-handsome brick Historic District, several bed-and-breakfasts, a couple of special state parks, and wall-to-wall antiques shops and flea markets.

The Maine Historic Preservation Commission considers the buildings in Searsport's Main Street Historic District the best examples of their type outside Portland—a frozen-in-time mid-19th-century cluster of brick-and-granite structures. The ground floors of most of the buildings are shops or restaurants; make time to stop in and admire their interiors.

SIGHTS
◖ Penobscot Marine Museum

Exquisite marine paintings, historical photographs, ship models, boats, and unusual China-trade objets d'art are just a few of the 10,000 treasures at the **Penobscot Marine Museum** (5 Church St. at Rte. 1, Searsport, 207/548-2529, www.penobscotmarinemuseum.org, 10am-5pm Mon.-Sat., noon-5pm Sun. late May-mid-Oct., $12 adults, $10 seniors, $8 ages 7-15, $30 family), Maine's oldest maritime museum—founded in 1936. Allow several hours to explore the exhibits, housed in five separate buildings on the museum's downtown campus. For a start, you'll see one of the nation's largest collections of paintings by marine artists James and Thomas Buttersworth. And the 1830s Fowler-True-Ross House is filled with exotic artifacts from foreign lands. Call or check the website for the schedule of lectures, concerts, and temporary exhibits. This isn't a very sophisticated museum, but it is a treasure.

◖ Fort Knox

Looming over Bucksport Harbor, the *other* **Fort Knox** (Rte. 174, Prospect, 207/469-7719, www.fortknox.maineguide.com, 9am-sunset May 1-Oct. 31, $4.50 nonresident adults, $3 Maine residents, $1 ages 5-11) is a 125-acre state historic site just off Route 1. Named for Major General Henry Knox, George Washington's first secretary of war, the sprawling granite fort was begun in 1844. Built to protect the upper Penobscot River from attack, it was never finished and never saw battle. Still, it was, as guide Kathy Williamson said, "very well thought out and planned, and that may have been its best defense." Begin your visit at the Visitor and Education Center, operated by the Friends of Fort Knox, a nonprofit group that has partnered with the state to preserve and interpret the fort. Guided tours are sometimes available. The fort's distinguishing features include two complete Rodman cannons. Wear rubberized shoes and bring a flashlight to explore the underground passages; you can set the kids loose. The fort hosts Civil War reenactments several times each summer as well as a Medieval Tournament, a paranormal-psychic fair, and other events (check the website). The Halloween Fright at the Fort is a ghoulish event for the brave. The grounds are accessible all year. Bring a picnic; views over the river to Bucksport are fabulous.

◀ Penobscot Narrows Bridge and Observatory

On a clear day, do not miss the **Penobscot Narrows Bridge and Observatory** (9am-5pm daily late May-June and Sept.-Nov. 1, 9am-6pm daily July-Aug., $7 nonresident adults, $5 Maine resident adults, $3 ages 5-11, includes fort admission), accessible via Fort Knox. The observatory tops the 420-foot-high west tower of the new bridge spanning the Penobscot River. It's one of only three such structures in the world and the only one in the United States. You'll zip up in an elevator, and when the doors open, you're facing a wall of glass—it's a bit of a shocker, and downright terrifying for anyone with a serious fear of heights. Ascend two more flights (an elevator is available) and you're in the glass-walled observatory; the views on a clear day extend from Mount Katahdin to Mount Desert Island. Even when it's hazy, it's still a neat experience.

Museum in the Streets

Walk through Searsport's history by visiting a dozen placards detailing historic sites with text in both French and English. Pick up a brochure at the downtown info booth, the Penobscot Maritime Museum, or other local businesses.

BlueJacket Shipcrafters

Complementing the collections at the museum are the classic and contemporary models built by **BlueJacket Shipcrafters** (160 E. Main St./Rte. 1, Searsport, 800/448-5567, www.bluejacketinc.com). Even if you're not a hobbyist, stop in to see the incredibly detailed models on display. Shipcrafters is renowned for building one-of-a-kind museum-quality custom models—it's the official model-maker for the U.S. Navy—but don't despair, there are kits here for all abilities and budgets. It's easy to find: Just look for the inland lighthouse on Route 1.

SHOPPING

Shopping in Searsport usually applies to antiques—from 25-cent flea-market collectibles to well-used tools to high-end china, furniture, and glassware. The town has more than a dozen separate businesses, some of them group shops with multiple dealers.

More than two dozen dealers supply the juried inventory for the **Pumpkin Patch** (15 W. Main St./Rte. 1, Searsport, 207/548-6047), with a heavy emphasis on Maine antiques. Specialties include quilts (at least 80 are always on hand), silver, paint-decorated furniture, Victoriana, and nautical and Native American items.

In excess of 70 dealers sell their antiques and collectibles at **Searsport Antique Mall** (149 E. Main St./Rte. 1, Searsport, 207/548-2640), making it another worthwhile stop for those seeking oldies but goodies.

The **Waldo County Craft Co-op** (307 E. Main St./Rte. 1, Searsport, 207/548-6686) features the work of about 30 Mainers: quilts, jams, bears, dolls, jewelry, baskets, pottery, floorcloths, and lots more.

RECREATION
Parks
MOOSE POINT STATE PARK

Here's a smallish park with a biggish view—183 acres wedged between Route 1 and a dramatic Penobscot Bay panorama. **Moose Point State Park** (Rte. 1, Searsport, 207/548-2882, $3 nonresident adults, $2 Maine resident adults, $1 ages 5-11) is 1.5 miles south of downtown Searsport. Bring a picnic, let the kids hang out and play (there's no swimming, but there's good tidepooling at low tide), or walk through the woods or along the meadow trail.

MOSMAN PARK

Southeast of busy Route 1, the four-acre town-owned **Mosman Park** has picnic tables, a traditional playground, lots of grassy space, a pocket-size pebbly beach, seasonal toilets, and fabulous views of the bay. Turn off Route 1 at Water Street and continue to the end.

SEARS ISLAND

After almost two decades of heavy-duty squabbling over a proposed cargo port on Searsport's 936-acre **Sears Island** (http://friendsofsearsisland.org), the state bought the island for $4 million in 1997. In 2009, a conservation ease-ment was created, forever protecting 601 acres on one of the largest uninhabited islands on the East Coast. The island is a fine place for bird-watching, picnicking, walking, fishing, and cross-country skiing; pick up a brochure at the kiosk. It's linked to the mainland by a causeway. From downtown Searsport, continue northeast on Route 1 two miles to Sears Island Road (on the right). Turn and go 1.2 miles to the beginning of the island, where you can pull off and park before a gate; cars aren't allowed on the island. An easy 1.5-mile walk will take you to the other side of the island, overlook-ing Mack Point (a cargo port) and hills off to the left. Bring a picnic and binoculars—and a swimsuit if you're hardy enough to brave the water.

FORT POINT STATE PARK

Continuing northeast on Route 1 from Sears Island will get you to the turnoff for **Fort Point State Park** (Fort Point Rd., Stockton Springs, 207/567-3356, $3 nonresident adults, $2 Maine resident adults, $1 ages 5-11) on Cape Jellison's eastern tip. Within the 154-acre park are the earthworks of 18th-century **Fort Pownall,** a British fortress built during the French and Indian War; **Fort Point Light,** a square 26-foot, 19th-century tower guarding the mouth of the Penobscot River, with an adjacent bell tower; shoreline trails; and a 200-foot pier where you can fish or watch birds or boats. Bird-watchers can spot waterfowl—especially ruddy ducks but also eagles and ospreys. Bring picnic fixings, but stay clear of the keeper's house—it's private. At the Route 1 fork for Stockton Springs, bear right onto Main Street and continue to Mill Road, in the village cen-ter. Turn right and then left onto East Cape Road, and then take another left onto Fort Point Road, which leads to the parking area.

SANDY POINT BEACH

There's a nice swath of sand on **Sandy Point Beach,** a 100-acre town-managed preserve at the mouth of the Penobscot River with walk-ing trails, osprey nests, and a beaver pond. It's at the end of Steamboat Wharf Road (off Route 1) in Stockton Springs.

Bicycling

Birgfeld's Bicycle Shop (184 E. Main St./Rte. 1, Searsport, 207/548-2916 or 800/206-2916), in business since the 1970s, is a mandatory stop for any cyclist, novice or pro. Local informa-tion on about 15 biking loops, supplies, maps, weekly group rides, sales (also skateboards and scooters), and excellent repair services are all part of the Birgfeld's mix.

An especially good ride in this area is the **Cape Jellison** loop in Stockton Springs. Park at Stockton Springs Elementary School and do the loop from there. Including a detour to Fort Point, the ride totals less than 10 miles from downtown Stockton Springs.

The **Belfast Bicycle Club** (www.belfastbi-cycleclub.org) has group rides for all abilities.

ACCOMMODATIONS
Inns and Bed-and-Breakfasts

The **Captain A. V. Nickels Inn** (127 E. Main St./Rte. 1, Searsport, 207/548-1104, www.captain-a-v-nickels-inn.com, $165-250) is an oceanside stunner. The cupola-topped man-sion, built by the good captain in 1874 as a gift to his bride, is elegantly furnished with European and American antiques. Public rooms range from cozy to expansive. Guest rooms, some with shared or detached baths, are named after ports of call; two suites have decks overlooking the ocean. Rates include an extravagant three-course breakfast and after-noon refreshments. There's also an on-site res-taurant and lounge.

New owners have completely renovated the **Homeport Inn** (121 E. Main St., Searsport, 207/548-2259, www.homeporthistoricinn.com, $120-165), a commanding former sea captain's home with endless antiques-fur-nished public rooms and guest rooms updated with flat-screen TVs and Wi-Fi. Some rooms share baths. Although the property no longer is oceanfront, shore access is only 100 yards down the road. Also on the premises is the Mermaid Restaurant.

Motels

The **Yardarm** (172 E. Main St./Rte. 1, Searsport, 207/548-2404, www.searsport-maine.com, $80-125), a small motel set back from the road, is next door to BlueJacket Shipcrafters. Each of the 18 pine-paneled units has a TV, air-conditioning, Wi-Fi, and a phone; suites (perfect for families) have a dinette, a microwave, and a small fridge. A continental breakfast is served in a cheery breakfast room in the adjacent farmhouse. Two rooms are pet-friendly.

Here's a find: **Bait's Motel** (215 E. Main St./Rte. 1, Searsport, 207/548-7299, $79-129) doesn't look like much from the exterior, but inside, the recently renovated guest rooms are outfitted with high-quality, comfortable furniture, down duvets and pillows, and nice toiletries. Add fridges, cable TV, and individually controlled heat and air-conditioning. Standard rooms are dog-friendly ($20). It's adjacent to Angler's Restaurant.

Camping

How can you beat 1,100 feet of tidal oceanfront and unobstructed views of Islesboro, Castine, and Penobscot Bay? **Searsport Shores Camping Resort** (216 W. Main St./Rte. 1, Searsport, 207/548-6059, www.campocean.com) gets high marks for its fabulous setting. About 100 good-size sites (including walk-in oceanfront tenting sites) go for $40-82. Facilities include a private beach, a small store, free showers, laundry, play areas, a recreation hall, nature trails, and a volleyball court. Request a site away from organized-activity areas. Bring a sea kayak and launch it here. Leashed pets are allowed. In early September, the campground hosts Fiber Arts College, a weekend of classes, demonstrations, and camaraderie for spinners, hookers, weavers, and the like.

FOOD
Local Flavors

Good home cooking with an emphasis on fried food has made **Just Barb's** (Main St./Rte. 1, Stockton Springs, 207/567-3886, 6am-7:30pm daily) a dandy place for an unfussy meal at a low price. Fried clams and scallop stew are both winners; finish up with a slab of pie or shortcake. The $7.99 all-you-can-eat fish fry is available daily after 11am.

Pick up sandwiches for a picnic at Fort Knox along with soups, wine, cheeses, prepared entrées, baked goods, and homemade marmalades and chutneys at **The Good Kettle** (247 Rte. 1, Stockton Springs, 207/567-2035, 8:30am-6pm Mon.-Sat.). There's also an indoor seating area.

Family Favorites

The **Anglers Restaurant** (215 E. Main St./Rte. 1, Searsport, 207/548-2405, www.anglersrestaurant.net, 11am-8pm daily, $7-20) is probably the least assuming and one of the most popular restaurants around. Expect hearty New England cooking, hefty portions, local color, no frills, and a bill that won't dent your wallet. Big favorites are the chowders, stews, and lobster rolls. The "minnow menu" for smaller appetites runs $6-13. Desserts are a specialty: The gingerbread with whipped cream is divine, and kids love the "bucket o' worms." If it's not too busy and you've ordered a lobster, ask owner Buddy Hall if he'll demonstrate hypnotizing it. It's adjacent to the Bait's Motel, 1.5 miles northeast of downtown Searsport.

The menu at the casual **Mermaid Restaurant & Pub** (121 E. Main St., 207/548-0084, 11am-9pm Tues.-Sun., $7-22), in the Homeport Inn, ranges from burgers to lobster, and there's a kids' menu too. There's entertainment on weekends.

Fine Dining

Relax and savor the views over Penobscot Bay along with a fine wine and dinner at **The Captain's Table** (127 E. Main St./Rte. 1, Searsport, 207/548-1104, www.captain-a-v-nickels-inn.com, 6pm-9pm Thurs.-Sat.), an elegant, white-tablecloth restaurant in the magnificently restored Capt. A. V. Nickels Inn. The four-course continental-inspired menu is $49; add $38 for wine pairings. For a lighter meal, dine in the less formal **Port of Call** tapas lounge (entrées $16-28).

INFORMATION AND SERVICES

The **Searsport Business and Visitors Guide** (www.searsportme.net) publishes a visitors guide and maintains a small self-serve info center in a shedlike building on Route 1 (at Norris St.), across from the Pumpkin Patch antiques shop.

The **Belfast Area Chamber of Commerce** (207/338-5900, www.belfastmaine.org) has information about the Belfast area.

Check out the **Carver Memorial Library** (Mortland Rd. and Union St., Searsport, 207/548-2303, www.carver.lib.me.us).

GETTING HERE AND AROUND

Searsport is about six miles or 10 minutes via Route 1 from Belfast. It's about 13 miles or 18 minutes to Bucksport.

Bucksport Area

The new Penobscot Narrows Bridge provides an elegant entry to the Bucksport area, a longtime river port and papermaking town. **Bucksport** (pop. 4,924) is no upstart. Native Americans first gravitated to these Penobscot River shores in summers, finding here a rich source of salmon for food and grasses for basket making. In 1764 it was officially settled by Col. Jonathan Buck, a Massachusetts Bay Colony surveyor who modestly named it Buckstown and organized a booming shipping business here. His remains are interred in a local cemetery, where his tombstone bears the distinct outline of a woman's leg; this is allegedly the result of a curse by a witch whom Buck ordered executed, but in fact it's probably a flaw in the granite. (The monument is across Route 1 from the Hannaford supermarket, on the corner of Hinks Street.)

Just south of Bucksport, at the bend in the Penobscot River, **Verona Island** (pop. 544) is best known as the mile-long link between Prospect and Bucksport. Just before you cross the bridge from Verona to Bucksport, hang a left and then a quick right to a small municipal park with a boat launch and broad views of Bucksport Harbor (and the paper mill). In the Buck Memorial Library is a scale model of Admiral Robert Peary's Arctic exploration vessel, the *Roosevelt*, built on this site.

Bucksport has a nice riverfront walkway, a historical theater, and the best views of Fort Knox. Route 1 east of Bucksport leads to **Orland** (pop. 2,225) with an idyllic setting on the banks of the Narramissic River. It's also the site of a unique service organization called H.O.M.E. (Homeworkers Organized for More Employment). East Orland (officially part of Orland) claims the Craig Brook National Fish Hatchery and Great Pond Mountain (you can't miss it, jutting from the landscape on the left as you drive east on Route 1).

SIGHTS
Alamo Theatre

Phoenixlike, the 1916 **Alamo Theatre** (85 Main St., Bucksport, 207/469-0924 or 800/639-1636, event line 207/469-6910, www.friendsofsearsisland.org, 9am-4pm Mon.-Fri. year-round) has been retrofitted for a new life—focusing on films about New England produced or revived by the unique Northeast Historic Film, which is headquartered here. Stop in, survey the restoration, visit the displays (donation requested), and browse the Alamo Theatre Store for antique postcards, T-shirts, toys, and reasonably priced videos on ice harvesting, lumberjacks, maple sugaring, and other traditional New England topics. A half mile west of Route 1, the Alamo has also become an active cinema, screening classic and current films regularly in the 120-seat theater, usually on weekends. Each summer there's also a silent film festival.

the town of Bucksport

Bucksport Waterfront Walkway

Stroll the one-mile paved walkway from the Bucksport-Verona Bridge to Webber Docks. Along the way are historical markers, picnic tables, a gazebo, restrooms, and expansive views of the harbor and Fort Knox.

H.O.M.E.

Adjacent to the flashing light on Route 1 in Orland, **H.O.M.E.** (207/469-7961, www.home-coop.net) is tough to categorize. Linked with the international Emmaus Movement founded by a French priest, H.O.M.E. (Homeworkers Organized for More Employment) was started in 1970 by Lucy Poulin, still the guiding force, and two nuns at a nearby convent. The quasi-religious organization shelters refugees and the homeless, operates a soup kitchen and a car-repair service, runs a day-care center, and teaches work skills in a variety of hands-on cooperative programs. Seventy percent of its income comes from sales of crafts, produce, and services. At the Route 1 store (Rte. 1 and Upper Falls Rd., 9am-4:30pm daily) you can

buy handmade quilts, organic produce, maple syrup, and jams—and support a worthwhile effort. You can also tour the craft workshops on the property.

SHOPPING

Locals come just as much for the coffee and conversation as the selection of new and used reads at **BookStacks** (71 Main St., Bucksport, 207/469-8992).

RECREATION
Craig Brook National Fish Hatchery

For a day of hiking, picnicking, swimming, canoeing, and a bit of natural history, pack a lunch and head for 135-acre **Craig Brook National Fish Hatchery** (306 Hatchery Rd., East Orland, 207/469-6701), on Alamoosook Lake. Turn off Route 1 six miles east of Bucksport and continue 1.4 miles north to the parking area. The **visitors center** (8:30am-3:30pm Mon.-Fri., 8am-3:30pm Sat.-Sun. summer, free) offers interactive displays on

Atlantic salmon (don't miss the downstairs viewing area), maps, and a restroom. The grounds are accessible 6am-sunset daily year-round. Established in 1889, the U.S. Fish and Wildlife Service hatchery raises sea-run Atlantic salmon for stocking six Maine rivers. The birch-lined shorefront has picnic tables, a boat-launching ramp, an Atlantic salmon display pool, additional parking, and a spectacular cross-lake view. Watch for eagles, ospreys, and loons. Also on the premises is the small **Atlantic Salmon Heritage Museum,** housed in a circa-1896 ice house and operated by the Friends of Craig Brook (call the hatchery for current hours). Inside are salmon and fly-fishing artifacts and memorabilia.

Great Pond Mountain Conservation

The **Great Pond Mountain Conservation Trust** (207/469-7190, www.greatpondtrust. org) acts as local steward for Great Pond Mountain and **Great Pond Wildlands.** It also hosts hikes and other activities.

Encompassing two parcels of land and nearly 4,300 acres, the Great Pond Wildlands is a jewel. The larger parcel totals 3,420 acres and surrounds Hothole Valley, including Hothole Brook, prized for its trout, and shoreline on Hothole Pond. The smaller 875-acre tract includes two miles of frontage on the Dead River (not to be confused with the Dead River of rafting fame in northwestern Maine) and reaches up Great Pond Mountain and down to the ominously named Hell Bottom Swamp. The land is rich with wildlife: Black bears, moose, bobcats, and deer are just a few of the species, and the pond, swamp, and river make it ideal for bird-watching. With 14 miles of woods roads lacing the land, it's prime territory for walking, mountain biking, and snowshoeing, and the waterways invite fishing and paddling. Avoid the area during hunting season. Snowmobiling is permitted; ATVs are banned. Access to the Dead River tract is from the Craig Brook National Fish Hatchery; follow Don Fish Road to the Dead River Gate and Dead River Trail. The South

Gate to Hothole Pond Tract is on Route 1, just southwest of Route 176.

The biggest rewards for the 1.8-mile easy-to-moderate hike up 1,038-foot **Great Pond Mountain** are 360-degree views and lots of space for panoramic picnics. On a clear day, Baxter State Park's Mount Katahdin is visible from the peak's north side. In fall, watch for migrating hawks. Access to the mountain is via gated private property beginning about a mile north of Craig Brook National Fish Hatchery on Hatchery Road in East Orland. Roadside parking is available near the trailhead, but during fall foliage season you may need to park at the hatchery. Pick up a brochure from the box at the trailhead, stay on the trail, and respect the surrounding private property.

Canoeing

If you've brought a canoe, **Silver Lake,** just two miles north of downtown Bucksport, is a beautiful place for a paddle. There's no development along its shores, and the bird-watching is excellent. Swimming is not allowed (there's a $500 fine); this is Bucksport's reservoir. To get to the public launch, take Route 15 north off Route 1. Go 0.5 mile and turn right on McDonald Road, which becomes Silver Lake Road, and follow it 2.1 miles to the launch site.

Golf

Bucksport Golf Club (Duck Cove Rd./Rte. 46, 1.5 miles north of Rte. 1, 207/469-7612, mid-Apr.-Sept.), running 3,397 yards, prides itself on having Maine's longest nine-hole course.

ACCOMMODATIONS
Inns and Bed-and-Breakfasts

The **Orland House** (10 Narramissic Dr., Orland, 207/469-1144, www.orlandhousebb. com, $110-125), Alvion and Cindi Kimball's elegant yet comfortable 1820 Greek Revival home, overlooks the Narramissic River. It has been beautifully restored, preserving the architectural details but adding plenty of creature comforts.

Location, location, location: If only the six simple rooms at the old-timey **Alamoosook**

Lakeside Inn (off Rte. 1, Orland, 207/469-6393 or 866/459-6393, www.alamoosook-lakesideinn.com, year-round, $139) actually overlooked the lake, it would be the perfect rustic lakeside lodge. The property is gorgeous and the location is well suited for exploring the area, but the guest rooms have tiny bathrooms. All have windows and doors opening onto a long sunporch overlooking the lake. There's also a basement recreation room with a massive stone hearth, games, and a guest kitchenette. The upside: The lodge has 0.25 mile of lakefront, and guests have access to canoes and kayaks. Paddle across the lake to the fish hatchery for a hike up Great Pond Mountain. A full breakfast is served, and there is free Wi-Fi.

Bliss! Escape everything at **Williams Pond Lodge Bed and Breakfast** (327 Williams Pond Rd., Bucksport, 207/460-6064, www.williamspondlodge.com, $120-155), a secluded, solar-powered, eco-conscious, off-the-grid retreat on 20 wooded acres with 3,000 feet of frontage on spring-fed Williams Pond. Three guest rooms are decorated in cozy lodge style. Canoes and kayaks are provided for guests. Access is via a long dirt road through the woods, something to keep in mind when arriving after dark.

Motels

In downtown Bucksport, the **Fort Knox Park Inn** (64 Main St., Bucksport, 207/469-3113, www.fortknoxparkinn.com, $125-199) is a four-story motel right at the harbor's edge. It's a bit tired, but the 40 guest rooms have phones, air-conditioning, free Wi-Fi, and satellite TV. Request a water view, or you'll be facing a parking lot.

Camping

Balsam Cove Campground (286 Back Ridge Rd., East Orland, 207/469-7771 or 800/469-7771, www.balsamcove.com, late May-late Sept., $29-48) fronts on 10-mile-long Toddy Pond. Facilities on the 50 acres include 60 wooded waterfront or water-view tent and RV sites, a one-room rental cabin ($74), on-site rental trailers ($93), a dump station, a store,

laundry, free showers and Wi-Fi, boat rentals, and freshwater swimming. Dogs are welcome on camping sites for $2/day. It's six miles east of Bucksport, off the Back Ridge Road.

FOOD

MacLeod's (Main St., Bucksport, 207/469-3963, 11:30am-8:30pm Tues.-Sat., 4pm-8:30pm Sun.-Mon., $10-34) is Bucksport's most enduring restaurant. Some tables in the pleasant dining room have glimpses of the river and Fort Knox. The wide-ranging menu has choices for all tastes and budgets. Reservations are wise for Saturday nights.

In what passes as downtown Orland (hint: don't blink), **Orland Market and Pizza** (91 Castine Rd./Rte. 175, Orland, 207/469-9999, www.orlandmarket.net, 7am-8pm daily) is a delight. Established in 1860, the old-fashioned country store has a little of this and a bit of that along with breakfast sandwiches, hot and cold sandwiches, grilled foods, salad, and all kinds of pizza. Call or drop by to find out the day's homemade specials, perhaps lasagna or spaghetti and meatballs. Smoked ribs are the specialty every other Thursday, weather permitting.

Carrier's Mainely Lobster (corner Rtes. 1 and 46, 207/469-1011, 10am-8pm daily) doesn't look like much, but it's the best local spot for lobster. A local fave that's stood the test of time, **Crosby's Drive-In and Dairy Bar** (Rte. 46, Bucksport, 207/469-3640, www.crosbysdrivein.com, 10:30am-8pm daily) has been dishing out burgers, dogs, fried seafood, and ice cream since 1938. Thursday night is Cruise Night.

INFORMATION AND SERVICES

The best source of local info is the **Bucksport Bay Area Chamber of Commerce** (52 Main St., Bucksport, 207/469-6818, www.bucksport-chamber.org).

Find **public restrooms** next to the town dock (behind the Bucksport Historical Society) and in the Bucksport Municipal Office on Main Street.

GETTING THERE AND AROUND

Bucksport is about 13 miles or 18 minutes from Searsport. It's about 18 miles or 25 minutes via Routes 1 and 15 to Blue Hill, about 20 miles or 30 minutes via Route 1 to Ellsworth, and about 20 miles or 35 minutes via Route 15 to Bangor and I-95.

BLUE HILL PENINSULA AND DEER ISLE

The Blue Hill Peninsula, once dubbed "The Fertile Crescent," is unique. Few other Maine locales harbor such a high concentration of artisans, musicians, and on-their-feet retirees juxtaposed with topflight wooden-boat builders, lobstermen, and umpteenth-generation Mainers. Perhaps surprisingly, the mix seems to work.

Anchored by the towns of Bucksport to the east and Ellsworth to the west, the peninsula comprises several enclaves with markedly distinct personalities. Blue Hill, Brooklin, Brooksville, Sedgwick, Castine, Deer Isle, and Stonington are stitched together by a network of narrow, winding country roads. Thanks to the mapmaker-challenging coastline and a handful of freshwater ponds and rivers, there's a view of water around nearly every bend.

You can watch the sun set from atop Blue Hill Mountain; tour the home of the fascinating Jonathan Fisher; stroll through the village of Castine (charming verging on precious), whose streets are lined with dowager-like homes; visit *WoodenBoat* magazine's world headquarters in tiny Brooklin; and browse top-notch studios and galleries throughout the peninsula. Venture a bit inland of Route 1, and you find lovely lakes for paddling and swimming and another hill to hike.

After weaving your way down the Blue Hill Peninsula and crossing the soaring pray-as-you-go bridge to Little Deer Isle, you've entered the realm of island living. Sure, bridges and causeways connect the points, but the farther down you drive, the more removed from civilization you'll feel. The pace slows; the

HIGHLIGHTS

LOOK FOR ◖ TO FIND RECOMMENDED SIGHTS, ACTIVITIES, DINING, AND LODGING.

◖ **Parson Fisher House:** More than just another historic house, the Parson Fisher House is a remarkable testimony to one man's ingenuity (page 250).

◖ **Blue Hill Mountain:** It's a relatively easy hike for fabulous 360-degree views from the summit of Blue Hill Mountain (page 253).

◖ **Flash! In the Pans Community Steelband:** Close your eyes and you might think you're on a Caribbean island rather than in Maine when you hear this phenomenal steelpan band (page 259).

◖ **Holbrook Island Sanctuary State Park:** Varied hiking trails and great birding are the rewards for finding this off-the-beaten-path preserve (page 262).

◖ **Castine Historic Tour:** A turbulent history detailed on signs throughout town makes Castine an irresistible place to tour on foot or by bike (page 265).

◖ **Sea Kayaking:** Hook up with "Kayak Karen" in Castine for a tour (page 269).

◖ **Haystack Mountain School of Crafts:** Don't miss an opportunity to visit this internationally renowned crafts school with an award-winning architectural design in a stunning setting (page 272).

◖ **Nervous Nellie's:** Sculptor Peter Beerits's ever-expanding whimsical world captivates all ages, and it's free (page 274).

◖ **Arts and Crafts Galleries:** Given Haystack's presence and the inspiring scenery, it's no surprise to find dozens of fabulously talented artisans on Deer Isle (page 276).

◖ **Guided Island Tours:** Captain Walter Reed knows these waters and is an expert on the flora and fauna (page 281).

◖ **Acadia National Park:** Isle au Haut's limited access makes this remote section of the park truly special. It's unlikely you'll have to share the trails—or the views—with more than a few other people (page 285).

population dwindles. Fishing and lobstering are the mainstays; lobster boats rest near many homes, and trap fences edge properties. If your ultimate destination is the section of Acadia National Park on Isle au Haut, the drive down Deer Isle to Stonington serves to help disconnect you from the mainland. To reach the park's acreage on Isle au Haut, you'll board the Isle au Haut ferryboat for the trip down Merchant Row to the island.

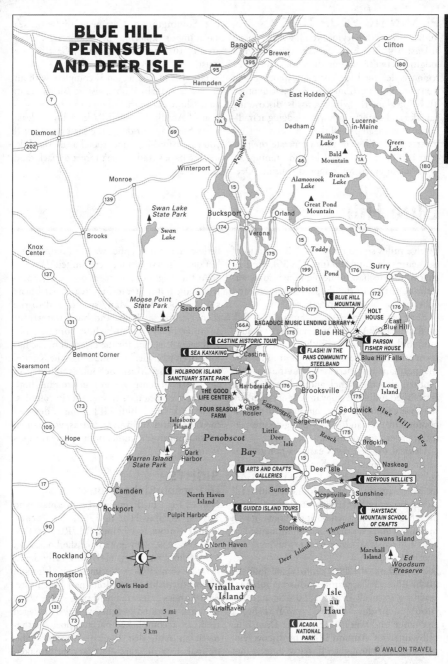

© AVALON TRAVEL

PLANNING YOUR TIME

To truly enjoy this region, you'll want to spend at least 3-4 days here, perhaps splitting your lodging between two or three locations. The region is designed for leisurely exploring; you won't be able to zip from one location to another. Traveling along the winding roads, discovering galleries and country stores, and lodging at traditional inns are all part of the experience.

Arts fans will want to concentrate their efforts in Blue Hill, Deer Isle, and Stonington. Outdoor-oriented folks should consider Deer Isle, Stonington, or Castine as a base for sea kayaking or exploring the area preserves. For architecture and history buffs, Castine is a must.

No visit to this region is complete without at least a cruise by if not a visit to Isle au Haut, an offshore island that's home to a remote section of Acadia National Park. Allow at least a few hours for a ride on the mail boat, but if you can afford the time, spend a full day hiking the park's trails. Don't forget to pack food and water.

Blue Hill

Twelve miles south of Route 1 is the hub of the peninsula, **Blue Hill** (pop. 2,686), exuding charm from its handsome old homes to its waterfront setting to the shops, restaurants, and galleries that boost its appeal.

Eons back, Native American summer folk gave the name Awanadjo (small, hazy mountain) to the mini-mountain that looms over the town and draws the eye for miles around. The first permanent settlers arrived in the late 18th century, after the French and Indian War, and established mills and shipyards. More than 100 ships were built here between Blue Hill's incorporation in 1789 and 1882—bringing prosperity to the entire peninsula.

Critical to the town's early expansion was its first clergyman, Jonathan Fisher, a remarkable fellow who has been likened to Leonardo da Vinci. In 1803, Fisher founded Blue Hill Academy (predecessor of today's George Stevens Academy), then built his home (now a museum), and eventually left an immense legacy of inventions, paintings, engravings, and poetry.

Throughout the 19th century and into the 20th, Blue Hill's granite industry boomed, reaching its peak in the 1880s. Scratch the Brooklyn Bridge and the New York Stock Exchange and you'll find granite from Blue Hill's quarries. Around 1879, the discovery of gold and silver brought a flurry of interest, but little came of it. Copper was also found here, but quantities of it, too, were limited.

At the height of industrial prosperity, tourism took hold, attracting steamboat-borne summer boarders. Many succumbed to the scenery, bought land, and built waterfront summer homes. Thank these summer folk and their offspring for the fact that music has long been a big deal in Blue Hill. The Kneisel Hall Chamber Music School, established in the late 19th century, continues to rank high among the nation's summer music colonies. New York City's Blue Hill Troupe, devoted to Gilbert and Sullivan operettas, was named for the longtime summer home of the troupe's founders.

SIGHTS

◖ Parson Fisher House

Named for a brilliant Renaissance man who arrived in Blue Hill in 1794, the **Parson Fisher House** (44 Mines Rd./Rte. 15/176, 207/374-2459, www.jonathanfisherhouse.org, 1pm-4pm Thurs.-Sat. early July-early Sept., Fri.-Sat. to mid-Oct., $5) immerses visitors in period furnishings and Jonathan Fisher lore. And Fisher's feats are breathtaking: He was a Harvard-educated preacher who also managed to be an accomplished painter, poet, mathematician, naturalist, linguist, inventor, cabinetmaker, farmer, architect, and printmaker.

Blue Hill village is sited by Blue Hill Falls.

In his spare time, he fathered nine children. Fisher also pitched in to help build the yellow house on Tenney Hill, which served as the Congregational church parsonage. Now it contains intriguing items created by Fisher, memorabilia that volunteer tour guides delight in explaining, including a camera obscura. Don't miss it.

Historic Houses

A few of Blue Hill's elegant houses have been converted to museums, inns, restaurants, and even some offices and shops, so you can see them from the inside out. To appreciate the private residences, you'll want to walk, bike, or drive around town. Also ask at the Holt House about village walking tours.

In downtown Blue Hill, a few steps off Main Street, stands the **Holt House** (3 Water St., www.bluehillhistory.org, 1pm-4pm Tues. and Fri., 11am-2pm Sat. July-mid-Sept., $3 adults, free under age 13), home of the Blue Hill Historical Society. Built in 1815 by Jeremiah Holt, the Federal-style building contains restored stenciling, period decor, and masses of memorabilia contributed by local residents. In the carriage house are even more goodies, including old tools, a sleigh, carriages, and more.

Walk or drive up Union Street (Rte. 177), past George Stevens Academy, and wander **The Old Cemetery,** established in 1794. If gnarled trees and ancient headstones intrigue you, there aren't many good-size Maine cemeteries older than this one.

Bagaduce Music Lending Library

At the foot of Greene's Hill in Blue Hill is one of Maine's more unusual institutions, the **Bagaduce Music Lending Library** (3 Music Library Lane/Rte. 172, 207/374-5454, www.bagaducemusic.org, 10am-4pm Mon.-Fri. or by appointment), where you can borrow from a collection of more than 250,000 titles. Somehow this seems appropriate for a community that's a magnet for music lovers. Annual membership is $20 ($10 for students); fees range $1-4/piece.

Scenic Routes

Parker Point Road (turn off Rte. 15 at the Blue Hill Library) takes you from Blue Hill to Blue Hill Falls the back way, with vistas en route toward Acadia National Park. For other serene views, drive the length of **Newbury Neck** in nearby Surry, or head west on Route 15/176 toward Sedgwick, Brooksville, and beyond.

ENTERTAINMENT AND EVENTS

Variety and serendipity are the keys here. Check local calendar listings and tune in to **radio station WERU** (89.9 and 102.9 FM, www.weru.org), the peninsula's own community radio; there might be announcements of concerts by local resident pianist Paul Sullivan or the Bagaduce Chorale, or maybe a contra dance. **George Stevens Academy** has a free Tuesday evening lecture series in July-August.

The October **Foliage Food & Wine Festival** has workshops, lectures, music, and plentiful dining opportunities.

Live Music

Since 1922, chamber-music students have been spending summers perfecting their skills and demonstrating their prowess at the **Kneisel Hall Chamber Music School** (Pleasant St./Rte. 15, 207/374-2811, www.kneisel.org). Faculty concerts run Friday evening and Sunday afternoon late June-late August. The concert schedule is published in the spring, and reserved-seating tickets ($30 inside, $20 on the porch outside, nonrefundable) can be ordered online or by phone. Other opportunities to hear the students and faculty exist, including young-artist concerts, children's concerts, open rehearsals, and more. Kneisel Hall is about 0.5 mile from the center of town.

The Blue Hill Congregational Church is the site for the **Vanderkay Summer Music Series** (207/374-2891), whose offerings range from choral music from the Middle Ages to bluegrass. Tickets are $15.

Chamber music continues in winter thanks to the volunteer **Blue Hill Concert Association** (207/326-4666, www. bluehillconcertassociation.org), which presents five concerts January-March at the Congregational church. Recommended donation is $30.

Lectures

The **Marine Environmental Research Institute Center for Marine Studies** (55 Main St., 207/374-2135, www.meriresearch.org) sponsors the monthly Ocean Environment evening lecture series, which tackles subjects such as Changing Oceans: Exploring the Depths.

Events

WERU's annual **Full Circle Fair** is usually held in mid-August at the Blue Hill Fairgrounds (Rte. 172, north of downtown Blue Hill). Expect world music, good food, crafts, and socially and environmentally progressive talks.

On Labor Day weekend, the **Blue Hill Fair** (Blue Hill Fairgrounds, Rte. 172, 207/374-9976) is one of the state's best agricultural fairs.

The **Foliage, Food & Wine Festival** takes place in October.

SHOPPING

Perhaps it's Blue Hill's location near the renowned Haystack Mountain School of Crafts. Perhaps it's the way the light plays off the rolling countryside and onto the twisting coastline. Perhaps it's the inspirational landscape. Whatever the reason, numerous artists and artisans call Blue Hill home, and top-notch galleries are abundant.

The **Liros Gallery** (14 Parker Point Rd., Blue Hill, 207/374-5370 or 800/287-5370, www.lirosgallery.com) has been dealing in Russian icons since the mid-1960s. Prices are high, but the icons are fascinating. The gallery also carries Currier & Ives prints, antique maps, and 19th-century British and American paintings. Just up the street is the **Cynthia Winings Gallery** (24 Parker Point Rd., 917/204-4001, www.cynthiawiningsgallery.com), which shows contemporary works by local artists. From here it's a short walk to **Blue Hill Bay Gallery** (Main St., Blue Hill, 207/374-5773, www.bluehillbaygallery.com), which represents contemporary artists in various media.

Don't miss **Jud Hartmann** (79 Main St., at Rte. 15, Blue Hill, 207/374-9917, www.judhartmanngallery.com). The spacious, well-lighted, in-town gallery carries Hartmann's limited-edition bronze sculptures of the woodland Native Americans of the Northeast. Hartmann often can be seen working on his next model in the gallery—a real treat. He's a wealth of information about his subjects, and he loves sharing the mesmerizing stories he's uncovered during his meticulous research.

Also on Main Street are two other fun, artsy gallery-shops. **Handworks Gallery** (48 Main St., Blue Hill, 207/374-5613, www.handworksgallery.org) sells a range of fun, funky, utilitarian, and fine-art crafts, including jewelry, furniture, rugs, wall hangings, and clothing, by more than 50 Maine artists and craftspeople. Browse **North Country Textiles** (Main St., Blue Hill, 207/374-2715, www.northcountrytextiles.com) for fine handwoven throws, rugs, clothing, and table linens as well as other fine crafts.

Pottery is abundant in Blue Hill. **Rackliffe Pottery** (Rte. 172, Blue Hill, 207/374-2297 or 888/631-3321, www.rackliffepottery.com), noted for its vivid blue wares, also makes its own glazes and has been producing lead-free pottery since 1969.

About two miles from downtown is another don't-miss: **Mark Bell Pottery** (Rte. 15, Blue Hill, 207/374-5881), in a tiny building signaled only by a small roadside sign, is the home of exquisite, award-winning porcelain by the eponymous potter. It's easy to understand why his wares have been displayed at the Smithsonian Institution's Craft Show as well as at other juried shows across the country. The delicacy of each vase, bowl, or piece is astonishing, and the glazes are gorgeous. Twice each summer he has kiln openings—must-go events for collectors and fans.

Blue Hill Books (26 Pleasant St./Rte. 15, 207/374-5632, www.bluehillbooks.com) is a wonderful independent bookstore that organizes an "authors series" during the summer.

RECREATION
Parks and Preserves

Blue Hill Heritage Trust (101 Union St., 207/374-5118, www.bluehillheritagetrust.org, 8am-5pm Mon.-Fri.) works hard at preserving the region's landscape. It also presents a Walks and Talks series, with offerings such as kayaking by preservation land along Eggemoggin Reach, a full-moon hike up Blue Hill Mountain, and walks through other trust properties, such as 700-acre Kingdom Woods Conservation Preserve and Cooper Farm at Caterpillar Hill. Many include talks by knowledgeable folks on complementary topics. Trail maps for all sites can be downloaded from the website.

◖ BLUE HILL MOUNTAIN

Mountain seems a fancy label for a 943-footer, yet **Blue Hill Mountain** stands alone, visible from Camden and even beyond. On a clear day, head for the summit and take in the wraparound view encompassing Penobscot Bay, the hills of Mount Desert, and the Camden Hills. Climb the fire tower and you'll see even more. In mid-June the lupines along the way are breathtaking; in fall the colors are spectacular—with reddened blueberry barrens added to the variegated foliage. Go early in the day; it's a popular easy-to-moderate hike. A short loop on the lower slopes takes only half an hour. Take Route 15 (Pleasant St.) to Mountain Road. Turn right and go 0.8 mile to the trailhead (on the left) and the small parking area (on the right). You can also walk (uphill) the mile from the village.

BLUE HILL TOWN PARK

At the end of Water Street is a small park with a terrific view, along with a small pebble beach, picnic tables, a portable toilet, and a playground.

Outfitters

The Activity Shop (61 Ellsworth Rd., 207/374-3600, www.theactivityshop.com) rents bicycles for $65/week and Old Town canoes and kayaks for $45 single, $55 double per day, including delivery within a reasonable area.

ACCOMMODATIONS

If you're trying to imagine a classic country inn, **The Blue Hill Inn** (Union St./Rte. 177, 207/374-2844 or 800/826-7415, www.blue-hillinn.com, mid-May-late Oct., $185-235) would be it. Sarah Pebworth graciously welcomes guests to her antiques-filled inn, open since 1840 and located steps from Main Street's shops and restaurants. Ten air-conditioned guest rooms and a suite have real chandeliers, four-poster beds, down comforters, fancy linens, and braided and Oriental rugs; three have wood-burning fireplaces. Rear rooms overlook the extensive cutting garden, with chairs and a hammock. A three-course breakfast is served in the elegant dining room (also available to nonguests, $16). Afternoon refreshments with sweets appear in the living room daily, and superb hors d'oeuvres are served 6pm-7pm in two elegant parlors or the garden. Also available are two year-round, pet-friendly suites with cooking facilities in the elegant Cape House ($285-315).

What's old is new at **Barncastle** (125 South St., Blue Hill, 207/374-2330, www.barn-castle.com, $135-185), a late-19th-century Shingle-style cottage that's listed on the National Register of Historic Places. It opens to a two-story foyer with a split stairway and balcony. Rooms and suites open off the balcony, and all are spacious and minimally decorated and have contemporary accents, including flat-screen TVs, Wi-Fi, a fridge, and a microwave. Rates include a continental breakfast. The downstairs tavern serves pizza, salads, and sandwiches; noise can be a factor.

The **Wavewalker Bed and Breakfast** (28 Wavewalker Lane, Surry, 207/667-5767, www.wavewalkerbedandbreakfast.com, $160-225) has a jaw-dropping location near the tip of Newbury Neck. It sits on 20 private acres with 1,000 feet of shorefront as well as woods and blueberry fields. The newly built inn is smack on the oceanfront, with views across the water to Mount Desert Island. Four spacious guest rooms have wowser views as well as Wi-Fi, DIRECTV, and a DVD player; some have fireplaces and/or oversized whirlpool tubs. The first-floor room is a good choice for those with mobility problems. Guests also have use of a living room, sunroom, and oceanfront deck. A full, hot breakfast is served. Kayaks are available. A separate two-bedroom-plus-loft rental cottage rents for $850-1,200/week.

FOOD
Local Flavors

Picnic fare and pizza are available at **Merrill & Hinckley** (11 Union St., 207/374-2821, 6am-9pm Mon.-Fri., 7am-9pm Sat., 8am-8pm Sun.), a quirky 150-year-old family-owned grocery and general store.

Craving chocolate? **Black Dinah Chocolatiers** (5 Main St., 207/374-5621) has a mainland home, sharing space with Fairwinds Florist. Here you'll find the Isle au Haut confectioner's freshly made to-die-for chocolates, ice cream, and sorbet, as well as a coffee/tea/hot chocolate bar. While here, don't miss the Art Box, a vending machine with $10 works by 10 local artists—perfect gift for someone back home, perhaps?

The **Blue Hill Wine Shop** (138 Main St., 207/374-2161), tucked into a converted horse barn, carries more than 1,000 wines, plus teas, coffees, breads, and cheeses. Monthly wine tastings (usually 2:30pm-6pm last Sat. of the month) are always an adventure.

The **Blue Hill Co-op and Cafe** (4 Ellsworth Rd./Rte. 172, 207/374-2165, café 207/374-8999, 7am-7pm daily) sells organic and natural foods. Breakfast items, sandwiches, salads, and soups—many with ethnic flavors—are available in the café.

Local gardeners, farmers, and craftspeople peddle their wares at the **Blue Hill Farmers Market** (9am-11:30am Sat. and 3pm-5pm Wed. late May-mid-Oct.). It's a particularly enduring market, well worth a visit. Demonstrations by area chefs and artists are often on the agenda. Late May-late August the Saturday market is at the Blue Hill Fairgrounds; the Wednesday market is at the First Congregational Church.

Eat in or pick up sandwiches, salads, soups,

FOREVER FARMS

Despite popular perception, family farms are experiencing a resurgence in Maine. According to the **Maine Farmland Trust** (207/338-6575, www.mainefarmlandtrust.org), since 2002 Maine has gained more than 1,000 farms and attracted many young farmers. It leads the New England states in agricultural production, contributing $2 billion to the state's economy each year.

Maine is the world's largest producer of brown eggs and wild blueberries; it ranks eighth in the country in production of potatoes and second in production of maple syrup, and it ranks second in New England for both milk and livestock production. Farm stands and farmers markets, community-supported agriculture programs, demand for fresh local fare in local restaurants, and growing public awareness of the importance of knowing where food originates all contribute to the strength of Maine's farms. Impressive statistics, yes, but there's a cloud on the horizon. The rising cost of land combined with the aging of the farmers who own much of the state's agricultural land threatens Maine's farming future.

Maine Farmland Trust is working to bridge that gap. The nonprofit organization's mission is to protect Maine's farmland and to support farmers and the future of farming in Maine. It does this through four programs: Forever Farms helps interested landowners place conservation easements on their land, often in partnership with the local or regional land trust; Buy/Protect/Sell purchases vulnerable farms, protects them with an easement, then resells the land to a farmer at its farmland value; Farm-

Link helps place incoming farmers on land; and Farm Viability projects are designed to help farmers prosper.

The seedbed of farmland preservation in Maine was on the Blue Hill Peninsula, where the **Blue Hill Heritage Trust** (207/374-5118, www.bluehillheritagetrust.org) has preserved more than 2,000 acres of farmland since 1989. One of the driving forces behind the BHHT's efforts is local farmer Paul Birdsall, who helped found the organization in 1985 and then went on to help found Maine Farmland Trust in 1999. Birdsall's 360-acre Horsepower Farm is one of 13 permanently preserved agricultural properties on the peninsula. Birdsall is the elder of four generations on the family farm in Penobscot. Back in the 1980s, when he recognized that development was pushing the cost of land higher than farmers could afford, he began to purchase available farmland, preserve it with easements, and then resell it to farmers, such as Philip and Heather Retberg of Quills End Farm, a 105-acre property in Penobscot.

The battle to preserve Maine's farmland is at a crucial stage. Over the next 10 years, ownership of as much as 400,000 acres of farmland is expected to change as aging farmers die or sell. Since its founding, the Maine Farmland Trust has helped protect more than 34,000 acres of farmland. It is working to protect 100,000 acres by 2014. Doing so is expected to cost $50 million, but it will help ensure Maine's food security, and the economic impact of that investment is projected to be more than $50 million each year.

---

and baked goods to go at **The Mill Stream Deli, Bakery & BBQ** (58 Main St., Blue Hill, 207/374-1049, 8am-5pm Mon.-Sat.) or **The De-Li** (25 Water St., 207/374-9354, 6am-3pm Mon.-Fri., 8am-3pm Sat.).

Deep Water Brew Pub (33 Tenney Hill Rd., 207/374-2441, www.deepwaterbrewing.com, 5:30pm-9pm Wed.-Sun.), Blue Hill's first microbrewery, serves pub-style fare such as ribs, burgers, and tacos ($9-14).

Family Favorites

Marlintini's Grill (83 Mines St./Rte. 15, 207/374-2500, www.marlintinisgrill.com, from 11:30am daily, $8-22) is half sports bar and half restaurant. You can sit in either, but the bar side can get raucous. Best bet: the screened-in porch. The menu includes soups, salads, burgers, fried seafood, rib eye, and nightly home-style specials; there's a kids' menu too. The portions are big; the service is good; the food is okay.

Just south of town is **Barncastle** (125 South St., 207/374-2300, www.barn-castle. com, 3pm-8pm daily, entrées $8-20), serving a creative selection of wood-fired pizzas in three sizes as well as sandwiches, subs, panini, calzones, and salads in a lovely Shingle-style cottage. There are vegetarian options. Expect to wait for a table; this is one popular spot.

The menu at **66 Steak & Seafood** (66 Main St., 207/374-1055, www.66steakandseafood. com, 11am-midnight Mon.-Fri. 9am-midnight Sat.-Sun., $7-45) also includes sandwiches, salads, pastas, and even a roasted veggie platter, but stick to the basics.

Elevated pub fare is served at the **Black Anchor Village Pub** (50 Main St., 207/374-7012, $8-19, 11am-9pm daily), with dining in airy front rooms or the cozy bar area. The menu includes salads such as cold duck and pecan, blackened salmon, and artichoke; a range of burgers and hearty sandwiches, and entrées such as pot pies, fried fish, and a meatloaf dinner. It's also the local hot spot for live entertainment.

Fine Dining

For a lovely dinner by candlelight, make reservations at **(Arborvine** (33 Upper Tenney Hill/Main St., 207/374-2119, www.arborvine. com, 5:30pm-9pm Wed.-Sun., entrées $28-35), a conscientiously renovated two-century-old Cape-style house with four dining areas, each with a different feel and understated decor. Chef-owner John Hikade and his wife, Beth, prepare classic entrées such as crispy roasted duckling and roasted rack of lamb. Their mantra has been fresh and local for more than 30 years.

Seafood

For lobster, fried fish, and the area's best lobster roll, head to **The Fish Net** (163 Main St.,

207/374-5240, 11am-9pm daily), an inexpensive, mostly take-out joint on the eastern end of town.

It's not easy to find **(Perry's Lobster Shack and Pier** (1076 Newbury Neck Rd., Surry, 207/667-1955, 10am-7pm daily), but for a classic lobster-shack experience, make the effort. The traditional Maine lobster shack is about five miles down Newbury Neck, just after the Causeway Place beach. Expect lobster, lobster and crab rolls, corn, chips, mussels, and clams. From the pier-top picnic tables, you're overlooking the water with Mount Desert Island as a backdrop. Save room for the ice cream sandwiches, made from local farm ice cream and homemade chocolate cookies.

INFORMATION AND SERVICES

The **Blue Hill Peninsula Chamber of Commerce** (207/374-3242, www.bluehillpeninsula.org) is the best source for information on Blue Hill and the surrounding area.

At the **Blue Hill Public Library** (5 Parker Point Rd., 207/374-5515, www.bluehill.lib. me.us), ask to see the suit of armor, which *may* have belonged to Magellan. The library sponsors a summer lecture series.

Public restrooms are in the Blue Hill Town Hall (Main St.), Blue Hill Public Library (Main St.), and Blue Hill Memorial Hospital (Water St.).

GETTING THERE AND AROUND

Blue Hill is about 17 miles or 25 minutes via Routes 1 and 15 from Bucksport. It's about 14 miles or 20 minutes via Route 172 to Ellsworth, about 8 miles or 15 minutes via Route 15 to Brooksville, and about 20 miles or 35 minutes via Routes 15, 175, 199, and 166 to Castine.

Brooklin, Brooksville, and Sedgwick

I'm going to let you in on a secret, a part of Maine that seems right out of a time warp, a place with general stores and family farms, a place where family roots go back generations and summer rusticators have returned for decades. Nestled near the bottom of the Blue Hill Peninsula and surrounded by Castine, Blue Hill, and Deer Isle, this often-missed area offers superb hiking, kayaking, and sailing, plus historic homes and unique shops, studios, lodgings, and personalities.

The best-known town is **Brooklin** (pop. 824), thanks to two magazines: *The New Yorker* and *WoodenBoat.* Wordsmiths extraordinaire E. B. and Katharine White "dropped out" to Brooklin in the 1930s and forever afterward dispatched their splendid material for *The New Yorker* from here. (The Whites' former home, a handsome colonial not open to the public, is on Route 175 in North Brooklin, 6.5 miles from the Blue Hill Falls bridge.) In 1977, *WoodenBoat* magazine moved its headquarters to Brooklin, where its 60-acre shoreside estate attracts builders and dreamers from all over the globe.

Nearby **Brooksville** (pop. 934) drew the late Helen and Scott Nearing, whose book *Living the Good Life* made them role models for back-to-the-landers. Their compound now verges on must-see status. **Buck's Harbor,** a section of Brooksville, is the setting for *One Morning in Maine,* one of Robert McCloskey's beloved children's books.

Incorporated in 1789, the oldest of the three towns is **Sedgwick** (pop. 1,196), which once included all of Brooklin and part of Brooksville. Now wedged between Brooklin and Brooksville, it includes the hamlet of Sargentville, the Caterpillar Hill scenic overlook, and a well-preserved complex of historic buildings. The influx of pilgrims—many of them artists bent on capturing the spirit that has proved so enticing to creative types—continues in this area.

SIGHTS

WoodenBoat Publications

On Naskeag Point Road, 1.2 miles from Route 175 in downtown Brooklin, a small sign marks the turn to the world headquarters of **WoodenBoat** (Naskeag Point Rd., Brooklin, 207/359-4651, www.woodenboat.com). Buy magazines, books, clothing, and all manner of nautical merchandise at the handsome store, stroll the grounds, or sign up for one of the dozens of one- and two-week spring, summer, and fall courses in seamanship, navigation, boatbuilding, sail making, marine carving, and more; tuition varies by course and duration. Special courses are geared to kids, women, pros, and all-thumbs neophytes; the camaraderie is legendary, and so is the cuisine. School visiting hours are 8am-5pm Monday-Saturday June-October.

Historical Sights

Now used as the museum and headquarters of the Sedgwick-Brooklin Historical Society, the 1795 **Reverend Daniel Merrill House** (Rte. 172, Sedgwick, 207/359-8900, 2pm-4pm Sun. July-Aug. or by appointment, donation) was the parsonage for Sedgwick's first permanent minister. Inside the house are period furnishings, old photos, toys, and tools; a few steps away are a restored 1874 schoolhouse, an 1821 cattle pound (for corralling wandering bovines), and a hearse barn. Pick up a brochure during open hours and guide yourself around the buildings and grounds. The **Sedgwick Historic District,** crowning Town House Hill, comprises the Merrill House and its outbuildings, plus the imposing 1794 Town House and the 23-acre Rural Cemetery (the oldest headstone dates from 1798) across Route 172.

The **Brooksville Historical Society Museum** (150 Coastal Rd./Rte. 176, Brooksville, 207/326-8987, 1pm-4pm Wed. and Sun.) houses a collection of nautical doodads, farming implements, blacksmith tools,

© TOM NANGLE

Shop for all things wooden-boat-related at the *WoodenBoat*'s shop.

and quilts in a converted boathouse. The museum is restoring a local farmhouse for more exhibits.

The Good Life Center

Forest Farm, home of the late Helen and Scott Nearing, is now the site of **The Good Life Center** (372 Harborside Rd., Harborside, 207/326-8211, www.goodlife.org). Advocates of simple living and authors of 10 books on the subject, the Nearings created a trust to perpetuate their farm and philosophy. Resident stewards lead tours (usually 1pm-5pm Thurs.-Mon. late June-early Sept., $5 donation suggested). Ask about the schedule for the traditional Monday-night meetings (7pm), featuring free programs by gardeners, philosophers, musicians, and other guest speakers. Occasional work parties, workshops, and conferences are also on the docket. The farm is on Harborside Road, just before it turns to dirt. From Route 176 in Brooksville, take Cape Rosier Road, go eight miles, passing Holbrook Islands Sanctuary. At the Grange Hall, turn right and

follow the road 1.9 miles to the end. Turn left onto Harborside Road and continue 1.8 miles to Forest Farm, across from Orrs Cove.

Four Season Farm

About a mile beyond the Nearings' place is **Four Season Farm** (609 Weir Cove Rd., Harborside, 207/326-4455, www.fourseasonfarm.com, 1pm-5pm Mon.-Sat. June-Sept.), the lush organic farm owned and operated by internationally renowned gardeners Eliot Coleman and Barbara Damrosch. Both have written numerous books and articles and starred in TV gardening shows. Coleman is a driving force behind the use of the word *authentic* to mean "beyond organic," demonstrating a commitment to food that is local, fresh, ripe, clean, safe, and nourishing. He's successfully pioneered a "winter harvest," developing environmentally sound and economically viable systems for extending fresh vegetable production October-May in cold-weather climates. The farm is a treat for the eyes as well as the taste buds—you've never seen such gorgeous produce. Ask about dinners on the farm and other events. Also here is the **Cape Rosier Artist Collective,** a gallery showing works by local artisans.

Scenic Routes

No one seems to know how **Caterpillar Hill** got its name, but its reputation comes from a panoramic vista of water, hills, and blueberry barrens—with a couple of convenient picnic tables where you can stop for lunch, photos, or a ringside view of sunset and fall foliage. From the 350-foot elevation, the views take in Walker Pond, Eggemoggin Reach, Deer Isle, Swans Island, and even the Camden Hills. The signposted rest area is on Route 175/15, between Brooksville and Sargentville; watch out for the blind curve when you pull off the road. If you want to explore on foot, the one-mile Cooper Farm Trail loops through the blueberry barrens and woods. From the scenic overlook, walk down to and out Cooper Farm Road to the trailhead.

Between Sargentville and Sedgwick, Route 175 offers nonstop views of Eggemoggin Reach, with shore access to the Benjamin River just before you reach Sedgwick village.

Two other scenic routes are **Naskeag Point** in Brooklin and **Cape Rosier,** the westernmost arm of the town of Brooksville. Naskeag Point Road begins off Route 175 in "downtown" Brooklin, heads down the peninsula for 3.7 miles past the entrance to WoodenBoat Publications, and ends at a small shingle beach (limited parking) on Eggemoggin Reach. Here you'll find picnic tables, a boat launch, a seasonal toilet, and a marker commemorating the 1778 Battle of Naskeag, when British sailors came ashore from the sloop *Gage,* burned several buildings, and were run off by a ragtag band of local settlers. Cape Rosier's roads are poorly marked, perhaps deliberately, so keep your DeLorme atlas handy. The Cape Rosier loop takes in Holbrook Island Sanctuary, Goose Falls, the hamlet of Harborside, and plenty of water and island views. Note that some roads are unpaved, but they usually are well maintained.

ENTERTAINMENT AND EVENTS
◖ Flash! In the Pans Community Steelband

If you're a fan of steel-band music, the **Flash! In the Pans Community Steelband** (207/374-2172, www.flashinthepans.org) usually performs somewhere on the peninsula 7:30pm-9pm Monday mid-June-early September. Local papers carry the summer schedule for the nearly three-dozen-member band, which deserves its devoted following. Admission is usually a small donation to benefit a local cause.

Eggemoggin Reach Regatta

Wooden boats are big attractions hereabouts, so when a huge fleet sails in for the **Eggemoggin Reach Regatta** (usually the first Saturday in August, but the schedule can change), crowds gather. Don't miss the parade of wooden boats. The best locale for watching the regatta itself is on or near the bridge to Deer Isle or near the Eggemoggin Landing grounds on Little Deer Isle. For details, see www.erregatta.com.

SHOPPING

Most of these businesses are small, owner-operated shops, which means they're often catch-as-catch-can.

Antiques

When you need a slate sink, a claw-foot tub, brass fixtures, or a Palladian window, **Architectural Antiquities** (52 Indian Point Lane, Harborside, 207/326-4938, www.arch-antiquities.com), on Cape Rosier, is just the ticket—a restorer's delight. Prices are reasonable for what you get, and they'll ship your purchases. It's open all year by appointment; ask for directions when you call. Antiques dating from the Federal period through the turn of the 20th century are the specialties at **Sedgwick Antiques** (775 N. Sedgwick Rd./Rte. 172, Sedgwick, 207/359-8834). Early furniture, handmade furniture, and a full range of country accessories and antiques can be found at **Thomas Hinchcliffe Antiques** (26 Cradle Knolls Lane, off Rte. 176, West Sedgwick,

E. B. WHITE: SOME WRITER

Every child since the mid-1940s has heard of E.B. White–author of the memorable *Stuart Little*, *Charlotte's Web*, and *Trumpet of the Swan*– and every college kid for decades has been reminded to consult his copy of *The Elements of Style*. But how many realize that White and his wife, Katharine, were living not in the big city but in the hamlet of North Brooklin, Maine? It was Brooklin that inspired Charlotte and Wilbur and Stuart, and it was Brooklin where the Whites lived very full, creative lives.

Abandoning their desks at *The New Yorker* in 1938, Elwyn Brooks White and Katharine S. White bought an idyllic saltwater farm on the Blue Hill Peninsula and moved here with their young son, Joel, who became a noted naval architect and yacht builder in Brooklin before his untimely death in 1997. Andy (as E.B. had been dubbed since his college days at Cornell) produced 20 books, countless essays and letters to editors, and hundreds (maybe thousands?) of "newsbreaks"–those wry clipping-and-commentary items sprinkled through each issue of *The New Yorker*. Katharine continued wielding her pencil as the magazine's standout children's-book editor, donating many of her review copies to Brooklin's Friend Memorial Library, one of her favorite causes. (The library also has two original Garth Williams drawings from *Stuart Little*, courtesy of E. B., and a lovely garden dedicated to the Whites.) Katharine's book, *Onward and Upward in the Garden*, a collection of her *New Yorker* gardening pieces, was published in 1979, two years after her death.

Later in life, E.B. sagely addressed the young readers of his three award-winning children's books:

Are my stories true, you ask? No, they are imaginary tales, containing fantastic characters and events. In real life, a family doesn't have a child who looks like a mouse; in real life, a spider doesn't spin words in her web. In real life, a swan doesn't blow a trumpet. But real life is only one kind of life–there is also the life of the imagination. And although my stories are imaginary, I like to think that there is some truth in them, too–truth about the way people and animals feel and think and act.

E.B. White died on October 1, 1985, at the age of 86. He and Katharine and Joel left large footprints on this earth, but perhaps nowhere more so than in Brooklin.

207/326-9411). Painted country furniture, decoys, and unusual nautical items are specialties at Peg and Olney Grindall's **Old Cove Antiques** (106 Caterpillar Rd./Rte. 15, Sargentville, 207/359-2031 or 207/359-8585), a weathered-gray shop across from the Eggemoggin Country Store.

Artists' and Artisans' Galleries

Small studio-galleries pepper Route 175 (Reach Rd.) in Sedgwick and Brooklin; most are marked only by small signs, so watch carefully. First up is **Eggemoggin Textile Studio** (off Rte. 175/Reach Rd., Sedgwick, 207/359-5083, www.chrisleithstudio.com), where the incredibly gifted Christine Leith weaves scarves, wraps, hangings, and pillows with hand-dyed silk and wool; the colors are magnificent. You might catch her at work on the big loom in her studio shop, a real treat.

Continue along the road to find **Reach Road Gallery** (Reach Rd., Sedgwick, 207/359-8803, www.reachroadgallery.com), where Holly Meade sells her detailed woodblock prints as well as prints from the children's books she has illustrated.

Continue over to Brooklin, where Virginia G. Sarsfield handcrafts paper products, including custom lampshades, calligraphy papers, books, and lamps, at **Handmade Papers** (113 Reach Rd., Brooklin, 207/359-8345, www.handmadepapersonline.com).

In what passes as downtown Brooklin, glass artist Sihaya Hopkins sells her handmade glass beads and jewelry at **Blossom Studio** (Naskeag Building, Brooklin, 207/359-8560).

In Brooksville, more finds await on Route 176. You'll need to watch carefully for the sign marking the long drive to **Paul Heroux and Scott Goldberg Pottery** (2032 Coastal Rd./ Rte. 176, Brooksville, 207/326-9062). The small gallery is a treat for pottery fans.

Continue southwest on Route 176 and watch closely for signs for **Bagaduce Forge** (140 Ferry Rd., Brooksville, 207/326-9676); it isn't easy to find. Joseph Meltreder is both blacksmith and farrier, and his small forge, with big views, is the real thing. He turns out whimsical pieces. Especially fun are the nail people—you'll know them when you see them.

Wine, Books, and Gifts

Three varieties of English-style hard cider are specialties at **The Sow's Ear Winery** (Rte. 176 at Herrick Rd., Brooksville, 207/326-4649, no credit cards), a minuscule operation in a funky two-story shingled shack. Winemaker Tom Hoey also produces sulfite-free blueberry, chokecherry, and rhubarb wines; he'll let you sample it all. Ask to see his cellar, where everything happens. Lining the walls in the tiny tasting room/shop are books, also for sale, that concentrate on architecture and history, with specialty areas highlighting Gothic arches and Russian history, but including plenty of other esoteric topics.

Betsy's Sunflower (12 Reach Rd., 207/359-5030), in Brooklin village, is a browser's delight filled with garden and kitchen must-haves and books. Her motto: "It has to be affordable, useful, and fun."

Don't miss the "world's smallest bookstore," Bill Henderson's **Pushcart Press Bookstore** (Rte. 172, Sedgwick, 207/359-2427), behind Sedgwick Antiques. It's a trove of literary fiction both used (paperbacks $2, hardbacks $5) and new, including editions of the *Pushcart Prize: Best of the Small Presses* annual series. Sales help support Pushcart fellowships.

Nautical books, T-shirts, gifts, food

© HILARY NANGLE

Pushcart Press Bookstore is the world's tiniest bookstore.

(including fresh lobsters and key lime pie), and boat gear line the walls and shelves of the shop at **Buck's Harbor Marine** (on the dock, South Brooksville, 207/326-8839, www.bucksharbor. com).

RECREATION
◖ Holbrook Island Sanctuary State Park

In the early 1970s, foresighted benefactor Anita Harris donated to the state 1,230 acres in Brooksville that would become the **Holbrook Island Sanctuary** (207/326-4012, www.parksandlands.com, free). From Route 176, between West Brooksville and South Brooksville, head west on Cape Rosier Road, following brown-and-white signs for the sanctuary. Trail maps and bird checklists are available in boxes at trailheads or at park headquarters. The easy Backshore Trail (about 30 minutes) starts here, or go back a mile and climb the steepish trail to **Backwoods Mountain** for the best vistas. Other attractions include shorefront picnic tables and grills, four old cemeteries, super bird-watching during spring and fall migrations, a pebble beach, and a stone beach. Leashed pets are allowed, but no bikes are allowed on the trails, and camping is not permitted. The park is officially open May 15-October 15, but the access road and parking areas are plowed in winter for cross-country skiers.

Swimming

A small, relatively little-known beach is Brooklin's **Pooduck Beach.** From the Brooklin General Store (Rte. 175), take Naskeag Point Road about 0.5 mile, watching for the Pooduck Road sign on the right. Turn right and drive to the end; parking is very limited. You can also launch a sea kayak here into Eggemoggin Reach.

Bicycling

Bicycling in this area is for confident, experienced cyclists. The roads are particularly narrow and winding, with poor shoulders. Best bets for casual pedal pushers are the **Naskeag**

scenic route or around **Cape Rosier,** where traffic is light.

Boating

Buck's Harbor Marine (on the dock, South Brooksville, 207/326-8839, www.bucksharbor. com) offers morning, afternoon, and evening excursions aboard sailboats and powerboats. Each lasts up to two hours and costs $65/person. Minimum party size is four (max is six), but the marina will try to match you with another party if your group is smaller. Buck's Harbor rents Ensign-class Antares day sailboats for $200/day ($1,200/week) and charters bareboat sail and power yachts to qualified skippers.

Picnicking

You can take a picnic to the **Bagaduce Ferry Landing,** in West Brooksville off Route 176, where there are picnic tables and cross-river vistas toward Castine. Another good spot is **Holbrook Island Sanctuary State Park on Cape Rosier.**

ACCOMMODATIONS
Bed-and-Breakfast

Best known for its restaurant and pub, **The Brooklin Inn** (Rte. 175, Brooklin, 207/359-2777, www.brooklininn.com, $105-125 with breakfast; add $10 for a one-night stay) also has five comfortable bedrooms; two share a bath. It's open year-round and often offers packages including meals; ask.

Cottage Colonies

The two operations in this category feel much like informal family compounds—where you quickly become an adoptee. These are extremely popular spots, where successive generations of hosts have catered to successive generations of visitors, and reservations are usually essential for July-August. Many guests book for the following year before they leave. We're not talking fancy; the cottages are old-shoe rustic, of varying sizes and decor. Most have cooking facilities; one colony includes breakfast and dinner in July-August. Both have hiking trails, playgrounds, rowboats, and East Penobscot Bay on the doorstep.

The fourth generation manages the **Hiram Blake Camp** (220 Weir Cove Rd., Harborside, 207/326-4951, www.hiramblake.com, Memorial Day-late Sept., no credit cards), but other generations pitch in and help with gardening, lobstering, maintenance, and kibitzing. Thirteen cottages and a duplex line the shore of this 100-acre property, which has been in family hands since before the Revolutionary War. The camp itself dates from 1916. Don't bother bringing reading material: The dining room has ingenious ceiling niches lined with countless books. Guests also have the use of rowboats, and kayak rentals are available. Home-cooked breakfasts and dinners are served family-style; lobster is always available at an additional charge. Much of the fare is grown in the expansive gardens. Other facilities include a dock, a recreation room, a pebble beach, and an outdoor chapel. There's a one-week minimum (beginning Saturday or Sunday) in July-August, when cottages go for $1,050-3,400/week (including breakfast, dinner, and linens). Off-season rates (no meals or linens, but cottages have cooking facilities) are $650-1,075/week. The best chances for getting a reservation are in June and September. Dogs are welcome.

Sally Littlefield is the hostess at ◖ **Oakland House Seaside Resort** (435 Herrick Rd., Brooksville, 207/359-8521 or 800/359-7352, www.oaklandhouse.com). Much of this rolling, wooded land, fronting on Eggemoggin Reach, was part of the original king's grant to her late husband Jim's ancestors, way back in 1765. Jim was the eighth generation on the property. Ten one- and two-bedroom nicely furnished and well-equipped cottages are tucked along the shoreline or in the trees. All but one have ocean views; five have kitchenettes, and four have full kitchens. One is pet-friendly ($10/night). Weekly rates begin around $900, varying with month and by cottage; nightly rates begin around $185. Other pluses are trails threading through the woods and providing access to viewpoints and a pocket beach.

FOOD
Local Flavors

The **Brooklin General Store** (1 Reach Rd., junction of Rte. 175 and Naskeag Point Rd., Brooklin, 207/359-8817), vintage 1872, carries groceries, beer and wine, newspapers, take-out sandwiches, and local chatter. Also here is the **Village Café,** serving breakfast and lunch Tuesday-Sunday, and dinner Thursday-Saturday.

Wine, cheese, espresso, and chocolate—what's not to like about **Sandy's Provisions** (123 Reach Rd., Brooklin, 207/359-8008, www.thecavebrooklin.com), which also serves breakfast and lunch.

Millbrook Company bakery and restaurant (160 Snow's Cove. Rd./Rte. 15, 207/359-8344, www.millbrookcompany.com, Sedgwick, 7am-2pm Tues.-Sun.) is a good bet for reasonably priced breakfasts and lunches, as well as occasional dinners.

Lunch is the specialty at **Buck's Harbor Market** (Rte. 176, South Brooksville, 207/326-8683), a low-key, marginally gentrified general store popular with yachties in summer. Pick up sandwiches, cheeses, breads, and treats for a Holbrook Island adventure.

You often can find **Tinder Hearth's** (1452 Coastal Rd., Brooksville, 207/326-8381) organic, wood-fired, European-style breads in local shops and at farmers markets, but you can buy it right at the bakery on Tuesday and Friday, when you also can purchase thin-crust pizzas in the evenings. It's on the western side of Route 176 north of the Cape Rosier road. It's not well marked, so keep an eye out for the Open sign.

In North Brooksville, where Route 175/176 crosses the Bagaduce River, stands the **Bagaduce Lunch** (11am-7pm daily, to 3pm Wed., early May-mid-Sept.), a take-out shack named an "American Classic" by the James Beard Foundation in 2008. Owners Judy and Mike Astbury buy local fish and clams. Check the tide calendar and go when the tide is changing; order a clam roll or a hamburger, settle in at a picnic table, and watch the reversing falls. If you're lucky, you might sight an eagle, osprey, or seal. The food is so-so, but the setting is tops.

Ethnic Fare

⟨ El El Frijoles (41 Caterpillar Rd./Rte. 15, Sargentville, 207/359-2486, www.elelfrijoles. com, 11am-8pm Wed.-Sun., $5-16)—that's *L. L. Beans* to you gringos—gets raves for its made-from-scratch California-style empanadas, burritos, and tacos, many of which have a Maine accent. Try the spicy lobster burritos or a daily special, such as ranchero shrimp tacos. Dine in the screen house or on picnic tables on the lawn; there's a play area for children.

Casual Dining

Behind the Buck's Harbor Market is **⟨ Buck's Restaurant** (6 Cornfield Hill Rd., Brooksville, 207/326-8688, 5:30pm-8:30pm daily, $22-25), where guests dine at white-clothed tables inside or on a screened porch. Chef Jonathan Chase's menu reflects what's locally available and changes frequently. Possibilities include grilled marinated swordfish or pan-seared duck breast. Service is excellent.

What's not organic is local, and what's not local is organic at **The Brooklin Inn** (Rte. 175, Brooklin, 207/359-2777, www.brooklininn. com, 5:30pm-9pm daily, $12-28). The upstairs restaurant is old-school genteel. A children's menu is available. In addition to à la carte selections, a three-course fixed-price menu usually is offered daily for about $25. Downstairs, the less formal **Irish pub** (5:30pm-10pm daily) serves burgers, Guinness stew, and pizza in addition to the upstairs menu. On Friday night,

it's all the fresh baked hake you can eat for $11 in the pub, or $14 in the dining room.

INFORMATION AND SERVICES

The best source of information about the region is the **Blue Hill Peninsula Chamber of Commerce** (207/374-2281, www.bluehillpeninsula.org).

Local **Penobscot Bay Press** (www.penobscotbaypress.com), which publishes a collection of local newspapers, also maintains an excellent site, with listings for area businesses as well as articles highlighting area happenings.

The **public libraries** in this area are small and welcoming, but hours are limited. Most have Wi-Fi and restrooms. **Friends Memorial Library** (Rte. 175, Brooklin, 207/359-2276) has a lovely Circle of Friends Garden, with benches and a brick patio. It's dedicated to the memory of longtime Brooklin residents E. B. and Katharine White. Also check out **Free Public Library** (1 Town House Rd./Rte. 176, Brooksville, 207/326-4560) and **Sedgwick Village Library** (Main St., Sedgwick, 207/359-2177).

GETTING THERE AND AROUND

Brooksville is about eight miles or 15 minutes via Route 15 from Castine. It's about 11 miles or 25 minutes to Deer Isle Village.

Castine

Castine (pop. 1,366) is a gem—a serene New England village with a tumultuous past. It tips a cape, surrounded by water on three sides, including the entrance to the Penobscot River, which made it a strategic defense point. Once beset by geopolitical squabbles, saluting the flags of three different nations (France, Britain, and Holland), its only crises now are local political skirmishes. This is an unusual community, a National Register of Historic Places enclave that many people never find. The town celebrated its bicentennial in 1996. Today a major presence is Maine Maritime Academy, yet Castine remains the quietest college town imaginable. Students in search of a party school won't find it here; naval engineering is serious business.

What visitors discover is a year-round community with a busy waterfront, an easy-to-conquer layout, a handful of traditional inns, wooded trails on the outskirts of town, an astonishing collection of splendid Georgian and Federalist architecture, and water views nearly every which way you turn. If you're staying in Blue Hill or even Bar Harbor, spend a day here. Or book a room in one of the town's lovely inns, and use Castine as a base for exploring here and beyond. Either way, you won't regret it.

HISTORY

Originally known as Fort Pentagouet, Castine received its current name courtesy of Jean-Vincent d'Abbadie, Baron de St-Castin. A young French nobleman manqué who married a Wabanaki princess named Pidiwamiska, d'Abbadie ran the town in the second half of the 17th century and eventually returned to France.

A century later, in 1779, occupying British troops and their reinforcements scared off potential American seaborne attackers (including Col. Paul Revere), who turned tail up the Penobscot River and ended up scuttling their more than 40-vessel fleet—a humiliation known as the Penobscot Expedition and still regarded as one of the worst naval defeats for the United States.

When the boundaries for Maine were finally set in 1820, with the St. Croix River marking the east rather than the Penobscot River, the last British Loyalists departed, some floating their homes north to St. Andrews in New Brunswick, Canada, where they can still be seen today. For a while, peace and prosperity became the bywords for Castine—with lively commerce in fish and salt—but it all collapsed during the California gold rush and the Civil War trade embargo, leaving the town down on its luck.

Of the many historical landmarks scattered around town, one of the most intriguing must be the sign on "Wind Mill Hill," at the junction of Route 166 and State Street:

> On Hatch's Hill there stands a mill. Old Higgins he doth tend it. And every time he grinds a grist, he has to stop and mend it.

In smaller print, just below the rhyme, comes the drama:

> Here two British soldiers were shot for desertion.

Castine has quite a history indeed.

SIGHTS
◖ Castine Historic Tour

To appreciate Castine fully, you need to arm yourself with the Castine Merchants Association's visitors brochure-map (all businesses and lodgings in town have copies) and follow the numbers on bike or on foot. With no stops, walking the route takes less than an hour, but you'll want to read dozens of historical plaques, peek into public buildings, shoot some photos, and perhaps even do some shopping.

MAINE MARITIME ACADEMY

© HILARY NANGLE

Maine Maritime Academy's training vessel is docked in Castine. When the ship is at dock, tours are available on weekdays during the summer.

The state's only merchant-marine college and one of only seven in the nation occupies 35 acres in the middle of Castine. Founded in 1941, the academy awards undergraduate and graduate degrees in such areas as marine engineering, ocean studies, and marina management, preparing a student body of about 850 men and women for careers as ship captains, naval architects, and marine engineers.

The academy owns a fleet of 60 vessels, including the historic gaff-rigged research schooner *Bowdoin*, flagship of Arctic explorer Admiral Donald MacMillan, and the 499-foot training vessel *State of Maine*, berthed down the hill at the waterfront. In 1996-1997, the *State of Maine*, formerly the U.S. Navy hydrographic survey ship *Tanner*, underwent a $12 million conversion for use by the academy. It is still subject to deployment, and in 2005 the

school quickly had to find alternative beds for students using the ship as a dormitory when it was called into service in support of rescue and rebuilding efforts after Hurricane Katrina in New Orleans. Midshipmen conduct free 30-minute tours of the vessel on weekdays in summer (mid-July-late Aug.). The schedule is posted at the dock, or call 207/326-4311 to check; photo ID is required.

Weekday tours of the campus can be arranged through the admissions office (207/326-2206 or 800/227-8465 outside Maine, www.mainemaritime.edu). Campus highlights include the three-story Nutting Memorial Library, in Platz Hall; the Henry A. Scheel Room, a cozy oasis in Leavitt Hall containing memorabilia from late naval architect Henry Scheel and his wife, Jeanne; and the well-stocked bookstore (Curtis Hall, 207/326-9333).

Highlights of the tour include the late-18th-century **John Perkins House,** moved to Perkins Street from Court Street in 1969 and restored with period furnishings. It's open in July-August for guided tours (2pm-5pm Sun. and Wed., $5).

Next door, **The Wilson Museum** (107 Perkins St., 207/326-8545, www.wilsonmuseum.org, 10am-5pm Mon.-Fri. and 2pm-5pm Sat.-Sun. late May-late Sept., free), founded in 1921, contains an intriguingly eclectic two-story collection of prehistoric artifacts, ship models, dioramas, baskets, tools, and minerals assembled over a lifetime by John Howard Wilson, a geologist-anthropologist who first visited Castine in 1891 (and died in 1936). Among the exhibits are Balinese masks, ancient oil lamps, cuneiform tablets, Zulu artifacts, pre-Inca pottery, and assorted local findings.

Open the same days and hours as the Perkins House are the **Blacksmith Shop,** where a smith does demonstrations, and the **Hearse House,** containing Castine's 19th-century winter and summer funeral vehicles. Both have free admission.

At the end of Battle Avenue stands the 19th-century **Dyce's Head Lighthouse,** no longer operating; the keeper's house is owned by the town. Alongside it is a public path (signposted; pass at your own risk) leading via a wooden staircase to a tiny patch of rocky shoreline and the beacon that has replaced the lighthouse.

The highest point in town is **Fort George,** site of a 1779 British fortification. Nowadays, little remains except grassy earthworks, but there are interpretive displays and picnic tables.

Main Street, descending toward the water, is a feast for historic architecture fans. Artist Fitz Hugh Lane and author Mary McCarthy once lived in elegant houses along the elm-lined street (neither building is open to the public). On Court Street between Main and Green Streets stands turn-of-the-20th-century **Emerson Hall,** site of Castine's municipal offices. Since Castine has no official information booth, you may need to duck in here (it's open weekdays) for answers to questions.

Across Court Street, **Witherle Memorial Library,** a handsome early-19th-century building on the site of the 18th-century town jail, looks out on the Town Common. Also facing the Common are the Adams and Abbott Schools, the former still an elementary school. The **Abbott School** (10am-4pm Tues.-Sat., 1pm-4pm Sun. July-early Sept., reduced schedule spring and fall, donation), built in 1859, has been carefully restored for use as a museum and headquarters for the **Castine Historical Society** (207/326-4118, www.castinehistoricalsociety.org). A big draw at the volunteer-run museum is the 24-foot-long Bicentennial Quilt, assembled for Castine's 200th anniversary in 1996. The historical society, founded in 1966, organizes lectures, exhibits, and special events (some free) in various places around town.

On the outskirts of town, across the narrow neck between Wadsworth Cove and Hatch's Cove, stretches a rather overgrown canal (signposted British Canal) scooped out by the occupying British during the War of 1812. Effectively severing land access to the town of

© TOM NANGLE

The Abbott School is now home to the very active Castine Historical Society.

© TOM NANGLE

Fort Madison dates from the early 1800s.

Castine, the Brits thus raised havoc, collected local revenues for eight months, then departed for Halifax with enough funds to establish Dalhousie College, now Dalhousie University. Wear waterproof boots to walk the canal route; the best time to go is at low tide.

If a waterfront picnic sounds appealing, settle in on the grassy earthworks along the harbor-front at **Fort Madison,** site of an 1808 garrison (then Fort Porter) near the corner of Perkins and Madockawando Streets. The views from here are fabulous, and it's accessible all year. A set of stairs leads down to the rocky waterfront.

ENTERTAINMENT AND EVENTS

Possibilities for live music include **Dennett's Wharf** (15 Sea St., 207/326-9045), where some performances require a ticket, and **Danny Murphy's Pub** (on the wharf, tucked underneath the bank and facing the parking area and harbor).

The **Castine Town Band** often performs free concerts on the Common; check www.castine. org for its schedule.

A different band performs on the Town Dock every Wednesday evening for free **Waterfront Wednesdays.**

The **Wilson Museum** (107 Perkins St., 207/326-8545, www.wilsonmuseum.org) frequently schedules concerts, lectures, and demonstrations.

The **Trinitarian Church** often brings in high-caliber musical entertainment.

Castine sponsors the intellectual side of the early August Wooden Boat Regatta, The **Castine Yacht Club** brings in a who's who of big-name sail-related designer and racers for this annual lecture series. Other events include on-the-dock boat tours and limited sailing opportunities.

Another source of intellectual stimulation is the **Castine Library,** which presents lectures and other programs.

Gardening fans should ask about **Kitchen and Garden Tours,** which take place every few years.

SHOPPING

Tucked into the back of the 1796 Parson Mason House, one of Castine's oldest residences, **Leila Day Antiques** (53 Main St., 207/326-8786, www.leiladayantiques.com) is a must for anyone in the market for folk art, period furniture, and quilts.

Clustered downtown along Main Street are **Tarratine Gallery,** a cooperative of Castine-area artists; **Lucky Hill,** a combination gallery and home-goods boutique; and **Castine Handwovens,** a weaving studio using historical looms. Down on the town wharf, **SaraSara's** carries a fun selection geared toward women.

Oil paintings by local artists Joshua and Susan Adam are on view at **Adam Gallery** (140 Battle Ave., 207/326-8272).

RECREATION
Witherle Woods

The 185-acre **Witherle Woods,** owned by Maine Coast Heritage Trust (www.mcht.org), is a popular walking area with a 4.2-mile maze

© HILARY NANGLE

Kayaking provides a different perspective on Castine's harbor.

of trails and old woods roads leading to the water. Many Revolutionary War-era relics have been found here; if you see any, do not remove them. Access to the preserve is via a dirt road off of Battle Avenue, between the water district property (at the end of the wire fence) and the Manor's exit driveway and diagonally across from La Tour Street. You can download a map from the website.

Sea Kayaking

Right near Dennett's Wharf is **Castine Kayak Adventures** (17 Sea St., 207/866-3506, www. castinekayak.com), spearheaded by Maine Guide Karen Francoeur. All skill levels are accommodated; "Kayak Karen," as she's known locally, is particularly adept with beginners, delivering wise advice from beginning to end. Three-hour half-day trips are $55; six-hour full-day tours are around $105 and include lunch. Two-hour sunset tours are $45; the sunrise tour includes a light breakfast for $55. Friday and Saturday nights, there are special two-hour phosphorescence tours under the stars (weather permitting) for $55 pp. Longer trips are available for $150/day. If you have your own boat, call Karen; she knows these waters. She offers instruction for all levels as well as a Maine Sea Kayak Guide course. Karen also rents bikes for $20/day.

Swimming

Backshore Beach, a crescent of sand and gravel on Wadsworth Cove Road (turn off Battle Ave. at the Castine Golf Club), is a favorite saltwater swimming spot, with views across the bay to Stockton Springs. Be forewarned, though, that ocean swimming in this part of Maine is not for the timid. The best time to try it is on the incoming tide, after the sun has had time to heat up the mud. At mid- to high tide, it's also the best place to put in a sea kayak.

Golf

The nine-hole **Castine Golf Club** (200 Battle Ave., 207/326-8844, www.castinegolfclub. com) dates to 1897, when the first tee required a drive from a 30-step-high mound. Willie Park Jr. redesigned it in 1921.

Boat Excursions

Glide over Penobscot Bay aboard the handsome and quite comfortable wooden motor sailer *Guildive* (207/701-1421, www.guildivecruises. com), captained by Kate Kana and Zander Parker. The two-hour to full-day sails cost $40-60; options include sunset sails and day sails to Searsport. Note: The Guildive took the summer of 2013 off, but planned to return for 2014.

ACCOMMODATIONS
Inns

Castine is not the place to come if you require in-room phones, air-conditioning, or fancy bathrooms. The pace is relaxed and the accommodations reflect the easy elegance of a bygone era.

The three-story Queen Anne-style ◖ **Pentagöet Inn** (26 Main St., 207/326-8616 or 800/845-1701, www.pentagoet. com, May-late Oct., $140-285) is the perfect Maine summer inn, right down to the lace curtains billowing in the breeze, the soft floral wallpapers, and the intriguing curiosities that accent but don't clutter the guest rooms. Congenial innkeepers Jack Burke, previously with the U.S. Foreign Service, and Julie Van de Graaf, a pastry chef, took over the century-old inn in 2000 and have given it new life, upgrading rooms and furnishing them with Victorian antiques, adding handsome gardens, and carving out a niche as a dining destination. Their enthusiasm for the area is contagious. The inn's 16 guest rooms are spread between the main house (with Wi-Fi service) and the adjoining 1791 Federal-style Perkins House (newly renovated, with marble baths, Wi-Fi, and in-room TVs). A hot buffet breakfast, afternoon refreshments, and evening hors d'oeuvres are provided. Jack holds court in Passports Pub (chock-full of vintage photos and prints as well as exotic antiques), advising guests on activities and opportunities. Borrow one of the inn's bikes and explore around town or simply walk—the Main Street location is convenient to everything Castine offers. Better yet, just sit on the wraparound porch and take it all in.

In 2010 a group of local residents purchased the venerable **Castine Inn** (41 Main St., Castine, 207/326-4365, www.castineinn. com, $135-235), with 19 second- and third-floor guest rooms and suites; all have Wi-Fi and TV, and some have water views. Public space includes a formal living room as well as a wraparound porch overlooking the gardens. Breakfast is served in the dining room, which features a wraparound mural of Castine.

Rental Properties

Several Castine real estate agents have listings for summer cottage rentals; start with **Saltmeadow Properties** (7 Main St., Castine, 207/326-9116, www.saltmeadowproperties. com).

FOOD
Local Flavors

The **Castine Farmers Market** takes place on the Town Common 9am-11:30am Thursday.

The **Breeze** (Town Dock, 207/326-9200, 10am-8pm daily), a waterfront take-out stand, serves good basics such as homemade doughnuts, burgers, fried clams, and ice cream, but it also dishes out some intriguing specials, such as Korean teriyaki chicken, Hawaiian beef tenderloin, and Thai curry chicken, for less than $10. You can't beat the location or the view.

Castine Variety (5 Main St., 207/326-9920, 7:30am-8pm daily), The Breeze's sister operation, serves pizza, seafood, and burgers in a restored general store.

When everything else in town is closed, your best bet for late-night eats is **Danny Murphy's Pub** (2 Sea St., on the wharf, tucked underneath the bank facing the parking area and harbor, 207/326-1004, 11am-1am daily), a sports bar with the usual pub grub.

On a warm summer day, it's hard to find a better place to while away a few hours than **Dennett's Wharf** (15 Sea St., 207/326-9045, www.dennettswharf.net, 11am-11pm daily May-mid-Oct., $10-25), and that's likely what

Craving fried clams or a lobster roll? The Breeze is the place.

you'll do here, as service can be slow. Next to the Town Dock, it's a colorful barn of a place with an outside deck and front-row windjammer-watching seats in summer. The best advice is to keep your order simple.

New ownership promises few changes at **MarKels** (26 Water St., 207/326-9510, 7am-3pm daily), a higgledy-piggledy eatery of three rooms and a deck at the end of an alleyway tucked between Main and Water Streets. Stop here for coffee, cold juices, pastries, interesting snacks and salads, homemade soups, specials, and delicious sandwiches.

Casual Dining

Jazz music plays softly and dinner is by candlelight at the **C Pentagöet** (26 Main St., 207/326-8616 or 800/845-1701, www.pentagoet.com, from 6pm Tues.-Sat., entrées $18-29). In fine weather you can dine on the porch. Choices vary from roasted *loup de mer* to slow-cooked lamb shank, or simply make a meal of bistro plates, such as lamb lollipops

and crab cakes and a salad. Don't miss the lobster bouillabaisse or the chocolate *budino,* a scrumptious warm Italian pudding that melts in your mouth (a must for chocoholics). On Tuesday night, there's live jazz on the porch during dinner.

INFORMATION AND SERVICES

Castine has no local information office, but all businesses and lodgings in town have copies of the Castine Merchants Association's visitors brochure-map. For additional information, go to the **Castine Town Office** (Emerson Hall, 67 Court St., 207/326-4502, www.castine.me.us, 8am-3:30pm Mon.-Fri.).

Check out **Witherle Memorial Library** (41 School St., 207/326-4375, www.witherle.lib.me.us). Also accessible to the public is the Nutting Memorial Library, in Platz Hall on the Maine Maritime Academy campus.

Find **public restrooms** by the dock, at the foot of Main Street.

GETTING THERE AND AROUND

Castine is about 16 miles or 25 minutes via Routes 1, 175, and 166 from Bucksport. It's about 20 miles or 35 minutes via Routes 166, 199, and 175 from Blue Hill.

Deer Isle

"Deer Isle is like Avalon," wrote John Steinbeck in *Travels with Charley*—"it must disappear when you are not there." **Deer Isle,** the name of both the island and its midpoint town, has been romancing authors and artisans for decades, but it is unmistakably real to the quarrymen and fishermen who've been here for centuries. These longtimers are a sturdy lot, as even Steinbeck recognized: "I would hate to try to force them to do anything they didn't want to do."

Early-18th-century maps show no name for the island, but by the late 1800s nearly 100 families lived here, supporting themselves first by farming, then by fishing. In 1789, when Deer Isle was incorporated, 80 local sailing vessels were scouring the Gulf of Maine in pursuit of mackerel and cod, and Deer Isle men were circling the globe as yachting skippers and merchant seamen. At the same time, in the once-quiet village of Green's Landing (now called Stonington), the shipbuilding and granite industries boomed, spurring development, prosperity, and the kinds of rough high jinks typical of commercial ports the world over.

Green's Landing became the "big city" for an international crowd of quarrymen carving out the terrain on Deer Isle and nearby Crotch Island, source of high-quality granite for Boston's Museum of Fine Arts, the Smithsonian Institution, a humongous fountain for John D. Rockefeller's New York estate, and less showy projects all along the eastern seaboard. The heyday is long past, but the industry did extend into the 20th century (including a contract for the pink granite at President John F. Kennedy's Arlington National Cemetery gravesite). Today, Crotch Island is the site of Maine's only operating island granite quarry.

Measuring about nine miles north to south (plus another three miles for Little Deer Isle), the island of Deer Isle today has a handful of hamlets (including **Sunshine, Sunset, Mountainville,** and **Oceanville**) and two towns—**Stonington** (pop. 1,043) and **Deer Isle** (pop. 1,975). Road access is via Route 15 on the Blue Hill Peninsula. A huge suspension bridge, built in 1939 over Eggemoggin Reach, links the Sargentville section of Sedgwick with Little Deer Isle; from there, a sinuous 0.4-mile causeway connects to the northern tip of Deer Isle.

Deer Isle remains an artisans' enclave, anchored by the Haystack Mountain School of Crafts. Studios and galleries are plentiful, although many require tooling along back roads to find them. Stonington, a rough-and-tumble fishing port with an idyllic setting, is slowly being gentrified, as each season more and more galleries and upscale shops open for the summer. Locals are holding their collective breaths, hoping that any improvements don't change the town too much (although most visitors could do without the car racing on Main Street at night). Already, real-estate prices and accompanying taxes have escalated way past the point where many a local fisherman can hope to buy, and in some cases maintain, a home.

SIGHTS

Sightseeing on Deer Isle means exploring back roads, browsing the galleries, walking the trails, hanging out on the docks, and soaking in the ambience.

Haystack Mountain School of Crafts

The renowned **Haystack Mountain School**

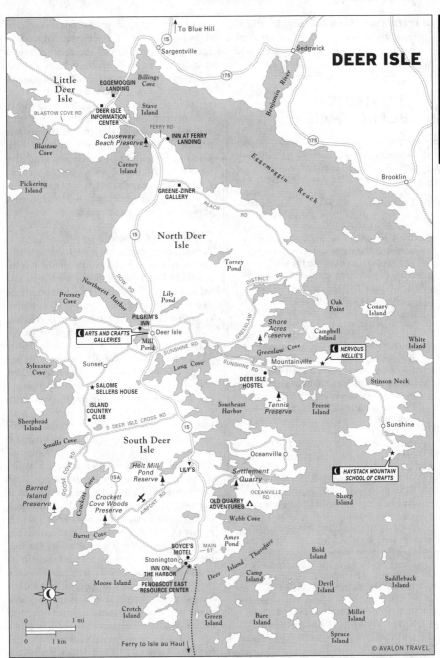

DEER ISLE

To Blue Hill

Sargentville

Sedgwick

Little Deer Isle

BLASTOW COVE RD

EGGEMOGGIN LANDING

Billings Cove

DEER ISLE INFORMATION CENTER

Stave Island

Blastow Cove

FERRY RD

Causeway Beach Preserve

INN AT FERRY LANDING

Carney Island

Pickering Island

Benjamin River

Eggemoggin Reach

Brooklin

GREENE-ZINER GALLERY

REACH RD

North Deer Isle

DOW RD

Torrey Pond

DISTRICT RD

Pressey Cove

Northwest Harbor

Lily Pond

PILGRIM'S INN

ARTS AND CRAFTS GALLERIES

Deer Isle

Mill Pond

GREENLAW RD

Shore Acres Preserve

Oak Point

Conary Island

SUNSHINE RD

Greenlaw Cove

Mountainville

NERVOUS NELLIE'S

Campbell Island

White Island

Sylvester Cove

Sunset

SALOME SELLERS HOUSE

ISLAND COUNTRY CLUB

Long Cove

SUNSHINE RD

DEER ISLE HOSTEL

Southeast Harbor

Tennis Preserve

Stinson Neck

Freese Island

Sunshine

Sheephead Island

S DEER ISLE CROSS RD

15

South Deer Isle

Smalls Cove

GOOSE COVE RD

Holt Mill Pond Reserve

LILY'S

Oceanville

Settlement Quarry

HAYSTACK MOUNTAIN SCHOOL OF CRAFTS

Barred Island Preserve

15A

Crockett Cove Woods Preserve

AIRPORT RD

OCEANVILLE RD

OLD QUARRY ADVENTURES

Sheep Island

Burnt Cove

Crockett Cove

Webb Cove

BOYCE'S MOTEL

Ames Pond

MAIN ST

Stonington

Moose Island

INN ON THE HARBOR

PENOBSCOT EAST RESOURCE CENTER

Deer Island Thorofare

Camp Island

Bold Island

Devil Island

Saddleback Island

Crotch Island

Green Island

Bare Island

Millet Island

Spruce Island

Ferry to Isle au Haut

0   1 mi

0   1 km

© AVALON TRAVEL

of Crafts (Sunshine Rd., Deer Isle, 207/348-2306, www.haystack-mtn.org) in Sunshine is open to the public on a limited basis, but if it

---

THE MAINE ISLAND TRAIL

In the early 1980s, a "trail" of coastal Maine islands was only the germ of an idea. By the end of the millennium, the **Maine Island Trail Association** (MITA) counted some 4,000 members dedicated to conscientious (i.e., low- or no-impact) recreational use of more than 180 public and private islands along 375 miles of Maine coastline from the New Hampshire border to Machias Bay. Access to the trail is only by private boat, and the best choice is a sea kayak, to navigate shallow or rock-strewn coves.

The trail's publicly owned islands—supervised by the state Bureau of Public Lands—are open to anyone; the private islands are restricted to MITA members, who pay $45/individual or $65/family/year for the privilege (and, it's important to add, the responsibility). With the fee comes the **Maine Island Trail Guidebook,** providing directions and information for each of the islands. With membership comes the expectation of care and concern. "Low impact" means different things to different people, so MITA experienced acute growing pains when enthusiasm began leading to "tent sprawl."

To cope with and reverse the overuse, MITA has created an "adopt-an-island" program, in which volunteers become stewards for specific islands and keep track of their use and condition. MITA members are urged to pick up trash, use tent platforms where they exist, and continue elsewhere if an island has reached its assigned capacity (stipulated on a shoreline sign and/or in the guidebook).

Membership information is available from the **Maine Island Trail Association** (207/761-8225, www.mita.org).

---

fits into your schedule, go. Anyone can visit the school store or walk down the central stairs to the water; to see more of the campus, take a tour (1pm Wed., $5), which includes a video, viewing works on display, and the opportunity to visit some studios. Beyond that, there are slide programs, lectures, demonstrations, and concerts presented by faculty and visiting artists on varying weeknights early June-late August. Perhaps the best opportunities are the End-of-Session auctions, held on Thursday night every 2-3 weeks, when you can tour the studios for free at 7pm before the auction at 8pm. It's a great opportunity to buy craftwork at often very reasonable prices.

◖ Nervous Nellie's

Part museum, part gallery, part jelly kitchen, and part tearoom: **Nervous Nellie's** (600 Sunshine Rd., 800/777-6845, www.nervous-nellies.com) is all that and more. Sculptor Peter Beerits is the mastermind behind this creative enterprise that invites exploration. Beerits has built a fantasy world that complements his book series called The Nervous Nellie Story. The comic-book-format illustrated stories are aimed at 13-year-old boys, he says, adding, "but then, doesn't everyone have a 13-year-old boy inside them?" Judging by the popularity of this place, it's true. The meadows teem with whimsical wood and metal sculptures, including dragons, Huns on horseback, a lobster and crab playing checkers, pigs waving from windows, and more. King Arthur and the Knights of the Round Table inhabit the woods. And between the tearoom and Beerits's workshop is a growing interactive village, with a Mississippi blues joint, a Western saloon with hotel above, Hardy's General Store, a Chinese laundry, a jail, and a sheriff's office, with more planned. Beerits builds each from his junkyard finds and populates them with characters. He's not only the creator and curator, but often doubles as guide for those who want to know more. You can easily spend an hour here, and there's no admission; wander freely. The property is also home to Beerits's other enterprise, **Nervous Nellie's Jams and Jellies,** known for outstanding, creative condiments; sampling is encouraged. The best time to come is 9am-5pm daily May-early October, when the shop operates the casual **Mountainville Cafe,** serving tea, coffee, and delicious scones—with, of course, delicious Nervous Nellie's products. Stock up, because they're sold in only a few shops. Also sold is a small, well-chosen selection of Maine products. Really, trust me, you must visit this place.

Historic Houses and Museums

There's more to the 1830 **Salome Sellers House** (416 Sunset Rd./Rte. 15A, Sunset Village, 207/348-6400, www.dis-historicalsociety.org, 1pm-4pm Wed., Fri., Sat., July-Sept., donation) than first meets the eye. A repository of local memorabilia, archives, and intriguing artifacts, it's also the headquarters of the **Deer Isle-Stonington Historical Society.** Sellers, matriarch of an island family, was a direct descendant of *Mayflower* settlers. She lived to be 108, a lifetime spanning 1800-1908, earning

Museum, theme park, or snack stop? Nervous Nellie's is all of the above.

© TOM NANGLE

the record for oldest recorded Maine resident. The house contains Sellers's furnishings, and in a small exhibit space in the rear is a fine exhibit of baskets made by Maine Native Americans. Behind the house are the archives, heritage gardens, and an exhibit hall filled with nautical artifacts. Bringing all this to life are enthusiastic volunteer guides, many of them island natives. They love to provide tidbits about various items; seafarers' logs and ship models are particularly intriguing, and don't miss the 1920s peapod, the original lobster boat on the island. The house is just north of the Island Country Club and across from Eaton's Plumbing.

Close to the Stonington waterfront, the **Deer Isle Granite Museum** (51 Main St., Stonington, 207/367-6331, www.deerisle-granitemuseum.org, 9am-5pm Sat.-Tues., and Thurs., July-Aug.) was established to commemorate the centennial of the quarrying business hereabouts. The best feature of the small museum is a 15-foot-long working model of Crotch Island, center of the industry, as it appeared at the turn of the 20th century. Flatcars roll, boats glide, and derricks move—it all looks very real. Donations are welcome.

Another downtown Stonington attraction is a Lilliputian complex known as the **Miniature Village.** Some years ago, the late Everett Knowlton created a dozen and a half replicas of local buildings and displayed them on granite blocks in his yard. Since his death, they've been restored and put on display each summer in town—along with a donation box to support the upkeep. The village is set up on East Main Street (Rte. 15), below Hoy Gallery.

Pumpkin Island Light

A fine view of Pumpkin Island Light can be had from the cul-de-sac at the end of the Eggemoggin Road on Little Deer Isle. If heading south on Route 15, bear right at the information booth after crossing the bridge and continue to the end.

Penobscot East Resource Center

The purpose of the **Penobscot East Resource Center,** in Stonington (13 Atlantic Ave.,

207/367-2708, www.penobscoteast.org, 10am-5pm Mon.-Fri.), is "to energize and facilitate responsible community-based fishery management, collaborative marine science, and sustainable economic development to benefit the fishermen and the communities of Penobscot Bay and the Eastern Gulf of Maine." Bravo to that! At the center are educational displays and interactive exhibits, including a touch tank, highlighting Maine fisheries and the Gulf of Maine ecosystem.

One of the driving forces behind the venture is Ted Ames, who won a $500,000 MacArthur Fellowship "genius grant" in 2005.

ENTERTAINMENT AND EVENTS

Stonington's National Historic Landmark, the 1912 **Opera House** (207/367-2788, www.operahousearts.org), is home to Opera House Arts, which hosts films, plays, lectures, concerts, family programs, and workshops year-round.

Mid-June, when lupines in various shades of

© HILARY NANGLE

Stonington's Opera House can be spotted from the harbor.

pink and purple seem to be blooming everywhere, brings the **Lupine Festival** (207/348-2676 or 207/367-2420), a weekend event that includes art openings and shows, boat rides, a private garden tour, and entertainment ranging from a contra dance to movies.

Early July-September is the season for **First Friday,** an open-house night held on the first Friday evening of each month, with demonstrations, music, and refreshments sponsored by the Stonington Galleries (www.stonington-galleries.com).

Seamark Community Arts (207/348-5208, www.seamarkcommunityarts.com) hosts arts workshops for children and adults in areas such as book arts, nature crafts, pottery, drawing and painting, film and video, printmaking, basketry, textile arts, and more.

Mid-July brings the **Stonington Lobsterboat Races** (207/348-2804), very popular competitions held in the harbor, with lots of possible vantage points. Stonington is one of the major locales in the lobster-boat race circuit.

In mid-September is **Deer Isle Lighthouse Weekend,** when eight local beacons are open for tours and local businesses and galleries offer lighthouse-themed activities.

The **Peninsula Potters Studio Tour and Sale** (207/348-5681, www.peninsulapotters.com) is held in October, when more than a dozen potters from Blue Hill to Stonington welcome visitors.

Want to meet locals and learn more about the area? **Island Heritage Trust** sponsors a series of walks, talks, and tours late May-mid-September. For information and reservations, call 207/348-2455.

SHOPPING

The greatest concentration of shops is in Stonington, where galleries, clothing boutiques, and eclectic shops line Main Street.

◖ Arts and Crafts Galleries

Thanks to the presence and influence of Haystack Mountain School of Crafts, super-talented artists and artisans lurk in every corner of the island. Most galleries are tucked away on back roads, so watch for roadside signs. Many have studios open to the public where you can watch the artists at work. Here's just a sampling.

NORTH END OF DEER ISLE
Greene-Ziner Gallery (73 Reach Rd., 207/348-2601, www.melissagreene.com) is a triple treat. Melissa Greene turns out incredible painted and incised pottery (she's represented in the Smithsonian's Renwick Gallery), and Eric Ziner works magic in metal sculpture and furnishings. Your budget may not allow for one of Melissa's pots (in the four-digit range), but I guarantee you'll covet them. In addition to the works of this talented couple, there's also a working organic farm with a farm stand.

DEER ISLE VILLAGE AREA
One of the island's premier galleries is Elena Kubler's **The Turtle Gallery** (61 N. Deer Isle Rd./Rte. 15, 207/348-9977, www.turtlegallery. com), in a handsome space formerly known as the Old Centennial House Barn (owned by the late Haystack director Francis Merritt) and the adjacent farmhouse. Group and solo shows of contemporary paintings, prints, and crafts are hung upstairs and down in the barn; works by gallery artists are in the farmhouse, and there's usually sculpture in the gardens both in front and in back. It's just north of Deer Isle Village, across from the Shakespeare School.

The **Hutton Gallery** (89 N. Deer Isle Rd./Rte. 15, 207/348-6171, www.huttongallery. com) offers a nice range of fine art and craft work, including prints, jewelry, paintings, basketry, glass, and fiber art.

The **DOW Gallery** (19 Dow Rd., 207/348-6498, www.dowstudiodeerisle.com) shows pottery, metalwork, jewelry, prints, and drawings by Ellen Wieske, Carole Ann Fer, and other artists and artisans.

In the village, **Deer Isle Artists Association** (5 Main St., 207/348-2330, www.deerisleartists.com) features two-week exhibits of paintings, prints, drawings, and photos by member artists.

Just a bit south is **John Wilkinson Sculpture** (41 Church St., 207/348-2363, www.sculptor1.com), open by chance or appointment. Wilkinson works in concrete, wood, and plaster.

Detour down Sunshine Road to view sculptor **Peter Beerits Sculpture at Nervous Nellie's** (600 Sunshine Rd., 800/777-6845, www.nervousnellies.com), a world of whimsy that will entertain all ages, and if the timing works, catch the Wednesday tour at Haystack.

STONINGTON
Cabinetmaker Geoffrey Warner features his work as well as that of other local woodworkers in rotating shows at **Geoffrey Warner Studio** (431 N. Main St., 207/367-6555, www.geoffreywarnerstudio.com). Warner mixes classic techniques with contemporary styles and Eastern, nature-based, and arts and crafts accents to create some unusual and rather striking pieces. He also crafts the budget-friendly ergonomic Owl stool as well as offers kits and workshops.

Bright and airy **Isalos Fine Art** (Main St., Stonington, 207/367-2700, www.isalosfineart.com) shows the work of local artists in rotating shows.

Debi Mortenson shows her paintings, photography, and sculptures at **D Mortenson Gallery** (10 W. Main St., 207/367-5875, www.debimortenson.com) year-round, by chance or appointment.

The **Watson Gallery** (68 Main St., 207/367-2900, www.gwatsongallery.com) is a fine-art gallery representing a number of top-notch painters and printmakers. Occasionally it hosts live performances.

More paintings, many in bold, bright colors, can be found at Jill Hoy's **Hoy Gallery** (80 Main St., 207/367-2368, www.jillhoy.com).

On the other end of Main Street, **Marlinespike Chandlery** (58 W. Main St., 207/348-2521, www.marlinespike.com) specializes in rope work, both practical and fancy.

A bit off the beaten path but worth seeking out is the **Siri Beckman Studio** (115 Airport Rd., 207/367-5037), Beckman's home studio-gallery featuring her woodcuts, prints, and watercolors.

Antiques, Books, and Gifts

In downtown Stonington, below the Opera House, **Dockside Books & Gifts** (62 W. Main St., Stonington, 207/367-2652) carries just what its name promises, with a specialty in marine and Maine books. The rustic two-room shop has spectacular harbor views.

Janice Glenn's emporium, **Old Schoolhouse Antiques at Burnt Cove** (194 Burnt Cove Rd., Stonington, 207/367-2849, no credit cards), is across from the grocery store. It's a funky shop jam-packed with vintage clothing, kitchenware (organized by color), textiles, cookbooks, and other collectibles, with an especially nice collection of quilts, rugs, and samplers.

Eclectic Shops

At the bottom of the island, **The Seasons of Stonington** (6 Thurlow's Hill Rd., Stonington, 207/367-6348) sells wine, fine foods, art, and other finds.

Shoppers need to be cautious going into **The Dry Dock** (24 Main St., Stonington, 207/367-5528), where the merchandise instantly sells itself. Imported women's clothing from Nigerian, Tibetan, and Indian cottage industries; unique jewelry; and unusual note cards are just some of the options in one large room and a smaller back room.

RECREATION
Parks and Preserves

Foresighted benefactors have managed to set aside precious acreage for respectful public use on Deer Isle. The Nature Conservancy (207/729-5181, www.nature.org) owns two properties, **Crockett Cove Woods Preserve** and **Barred Island Preserve**. The conscientious steward of other local properties is the **Island Heritage Trust** (420 Sunset Rd., Sunset, 207/348-2455, www.islandheritagetrust.org). At the office, 8am-4pm Monday-Friday, you can pick up note cards, photos, T-shirts, and helpful maps and information on hiking trails and nature preserves. Proceeds benefit the Island Heritage Trust's efforts; donations are appreciated.

SETTLEMENT QUARRY

Here's one of the easiest, shortest walks in the area, leading to an impressive vista. From the parking lot on Oceanville Road (just under one mile off Rte. 15), marked by a carved granite sign, it's about five minutes to the top of the old **Settlement Quarry**, where the viewing platform (a.k.a. the "throne room") takes in the panorama—all the way to the Camden Hills on a good day. In early August, wild raspberries are an additional enticement. Three short loop trails lead into the surrounding woods from here. A map is available in the trailhead box.

EDGAR TENNIS PRESERVE

The 145-acre **Edgar Tennis Preserve,** off Sunshine Road, has very limited parking, so don't try to squeeze in if there isn't room; schedule your visit for another hour or day. But do go, and bring at least a snack if not a full picnic to enjoy on one of the convenient rocky outcroppings (carry out what you carry in). Allow at least 90 minutes to enjoy the walking trails, one of which skirts Pickering Cove, providing sigh-producing views. Another trail leads to an old cemetery. Parts of the trails can be wet, so wear appropriate footwear. Bring binoculars for bird-watching. The preserve is open sunrise-sunset. To find it, take Sunshine Road 2.5 miles to Tennis Road, and follow it to the preserve.

SHORE ACRES PRESERVE

The 38-acre **Shore Acres Preserve,** a gift in 2000 from Judy Hill to the Island Heritage Trust, comprises old farmland, woodlands, clam flats, a salt marsh, and granite shorefront. Three walking trails connect in a 1.5-mile loop, with the Shore Trail section edging Greenlaw Cove. As you walk along the waterfront, look for the islands of Mount Desert rising in the distance and seals basking on offshore ledges. Do not walk across the salt marsh, and try to avoid stepping on beach plants. To find the preserve, take Sunshine Road 1.2 miles and then bear left at the fork onto Greenlaw District Road. The preserve's parking area is just shy of one mile down the road. Park only in the parking area, not on the paved road.

CROCKETT COVE WOODS PRESERVE

Donated to The Nature Conservancy by benevolent eco-conscious local artist Emily Muir, 98-acre **Crockett Cove Woods Preserve** is Deer Isle's natural gem—a coastal fog forest laden with lichens and mosses. Four interlinked walking trails cover the whole preserve, starting with a short nature trail. Pick up the helpful map-brochure at the registration box. Wear rubberized shoes or boots, and respect adjacent private property. The preserve is open sunrise-sunset daily year-round. From Deer Isle Village, take Route 15A to Sunset Village. Go 2.5 miles to Whitman Road and then to Fire Lane 88.

BARRED ISLAND PRESERVE

Owned by The Nature Conservancy but managed by the Island Heritage Trust, **Barred Island Preserve** was donated by Carolyn Olmsted, grandniece of noted landscape architect Frederick Law Olmsted, who summered nearby. A former owner of adjacent Goose Cove Lodge donated an additional 48 acres of maritime boreal fog forest. A single walking trail, one mile long, leads from the parking lot to the point. At low tide, and when eagles aren't nesting, you can continue out to Barred Island. Another trail skirts the shoreline of Goose Cove, before retreating inland and rejoining the main trail. From a high point on the main trail, you can see more than a dozen islands, many of which are protected from development, as well as Saddleback Ledge Light, 14 miles distant. To get to the preserve, follow Route 15A to Goose Cove Road and then continue to the parking area on the right. If it's full, return another day.

HOLT MILL POND PRESERVE

The Stonington Conservation Commission administers the town-owned **Holt Mill Pond Preserve,** where more than 47 bird species

have been identified (bring binoculars). It comprises four habitats: upland spruce forest, lowland spruce-mixed forest, freshwater marsh, and saltwater marsh. A self-guiding nature trail is accessible off the Airport Road (off Route 15 at the intersection with Lily's Café). Look for the Nature Trail sign just beyond the medical center. The detailed self-guiding trail brochure, available at the trailhead registration kiosk, is accented with drawings by noted artist Siri Beckman.

AMES POND

Ames Pond is neither park nor preserve, but it might as well be. On a back road close to Stonington, it's a mandatory stop in July-August, when the pond wears a blanket of pink and white water lilies. From downtown Stonington, take Indian Point Road just under a mile east to the pond.

CAUSEWAY BEACH AND SCOTT'S LANDING

If you're itching to dip your toes into the water, stop by **Causeway Beach** along the causeway linking Little Deer Isle to Deer Isle. It's popular for swimming and is also a significant habitat for birds and other wildlife. On the other side of Route 15 is **Scott's Landing,** with more than 20 acres of fields, trails, and shorefront.

ED WOODSUM PRESERVE AT MARSHALL ISLAND

The Maine Coast Heritage Trust (www.mcht. org) owns 985-acre **Marshall Island,** the largest undeveloped island on the eastern seaboard. Since acquiring it in 2003, the trust has added 10 miles of hiking trails. After exploring, picnic on Sand Cove beach on the southeastern shore. **Old Quarry Ocean Adventures** (Stonington, 207/367-8977, mobile 207/266-7778, www. oldquarry.com) offers full-day trips on select dates for $50/person. Or, charter a trip aboard Captain Steve Johnson's **Bert & I** (207/460-8679). Johnson will transport you to Marshall on weekends for about $140 pp round-trip plus $35 pp for each additional person or hour. Primitive camping is available by **reservation**

207/729-7366) at designated sites; fires require a **permit** (207/827-1800).

Sporting Outfitters and Guided Trips

The biggest operation is **Old Quarry Ocean Adventures** (Stonington, 207/367-8977 www.oldquarry.com), with a broad range of outdoor adventure choices. Bill Baker's ever-expanding enterprise rents canoes, kayaks, sailboats, bikes, moorings, platform tent sites, and cabins. Bicycle rentals are $22/day or $110/week. Sea-kayak rentals are $58/day for a single, $67 for a tandem. Half-day rates (based on a four-hour rental) are $42 and $52, respectively. Overnight 24-hour rental is available for a 10 percent surcharge. Other options include canoes, rowboats, and sailboats; check the website for details. For all boat rentals, you must demonstrate competency in the vessel. They'll deliver and pick up anywhere on the island for a fee of $40. All-day guided tours in single kayaks are $110; tandems are $195. Half-day tours are $60 and $120, respectively. Plenty of other options are available, including sunset tours, family trips, and gourmet picnic paddles.

Overnight kayaking camping trips on nearby islands are led by a Registered Maine Guide. Rates, including meals, begin around $300/adult for one night, with a three-person minimum. If you're bringing your own kayak, you can park your car ($7/night up to two nights, $6/night for three or more nights) and launch from here ($5/boat for launching); they'll take your trash and any trash you find. Old Quarry is off the Oceanville Road, less than a mile from Route 15, just before you reach the Settlement Quarry preserve. It's well signposted.

Guided Walks

The Island Heritage Trust (402 Sunset Rd., Sunset, 207/348-2455, www.islandheritage-trust.org), along with the Stonington and Deer Isle Conservation Commissions, sponsors a Walks and Talks series. Guided walks cover topics such as "Bird Calls for Beginners," "Salt Marsh Ecology," and "Geocache Introduction." Call for information and reservations.

Sea Kayaking

The waters around Deer Isle, with lots of islets and protected coves, are extremely popular for sea kayaking, especially off Stonington.

If you sign up with the **Maine Island Trail Association** (207/761-8225, www.mita.org, $45/year), you'll receive a handy manual that steers you to more than a dozen islands in the Deer Isle archipelago where you can camp, hike, and picnic—eco-sensitively, please. Boat traffic can be a bit heavy at the height of summer, so to best appreciate the tranquility of this area, try this in September after the Labor Day holiday. Nights can be cool, but days are likely to be brilliant. Remember that this is a working harbor.

The six-mile paddle from Stonington to Isle au Haut is best left to experienced paddlers, especially since fishing folks refer to kayakers as "speed bumps."

Swimming

The island's only major freshwater swimming hole is the **Lily Pond,** northeast of Deer Isle Village. Just north of the Shakespeare School, turn into the Deer Run Apartments complex. Park and take the path to the pond, which has a shallow area for small children.

Golf and Tennis

About two miles south of Deer Isle Village, watch for the large sign (on the left) for the **Island Country Club** (Rte. 15A, Sunset, 207/348-2379, early June-late Sept.), a nine-hole public course that has been here since 1928. Also at the club are three Har-Tru tennis courts. The club's cheeseburgers and salads are among the island's best bargain lunches.

Boat Excursions
ISLE AU HAUT BOAT COMPANY

The *Miss Lizzie* departs at 2pm Monday-Saturday mid-June-late August from the **Isle au Haut Boat Company** (Seabreeze Ave., Stonington, 207/367-5193 or 207/367-6516,

One of the best ways to tour Deer Isle is by boat, perhaps aboard the Isle au Haut passenger ferry.

www.isleauhaut.com) dock in Stonington for a narrated 1.25-hour Lobster Fishing Scenic Cruise, during which the crew hauls a string of lobster traps. Cost is $20 adults, $8.50 under age 12. Special puffin and lighthouse cruises are offered on a limited basis. Another option is to cruise over and back to Isle au Haut without stepping foot off the boat ($20 adults). Reservations are advisable, especially in July-August. Dockside parking is around $10, or find a spot in town and save the surcharge.

🅒 GUIDED ISLAND TOURS

Captain Walter Reed's **Guided Island Tours** (207/348-6789, www.guidedislandtours. com) aboard the *Gael* are custom designed for a maximum of four passengers. Walt is a Registered Maine Guide and professional biologist who also is a steward for Mark Island Lighthouse and several uninhabited islands in the area. He provides in-depth perspective and the local scoop. The cost is $35 pp for the first hour plus $25 pp for each additional hour

(no credit cards); kids under 12 are half price. Reservations are required; box lunches are available for an additional fee.

OLD QUARRY OCEAN ADVENTURES

Yet another aspect of the **Old Quarry Ocean Adventures** (Stonington, 207/367-8977, www. oldquarry.com) empire are sightseeing tours on the *Nigh Duck.* The three-hour trips, one in the morning (9am-noon) and one in the afternoon (1pm-4pm), are $40 adults and $30 under age 12. Both highlight the natural history of the area as Captain Bill navigates the boat through the archipelago. Lobster traps are hauled on both trips (but not on Sunday); the morning trip visits Isle au Haut. The afternoon excursion features an island swimming break in a freshwater quarry. Also available is a 1.5-hour sunset cruise, departing half an hour before sunset, for $36 adults and $26 under age 12. And if that's not enough, Old Quarry also offers puffin-watching, lighthouse, whale-watching, and island cruises, with rates beginning at

$65 adults, $45 children. Of course, if none of this floats your boat, you can also arrange for a custom charter for $200/hour.

Old Quarry also offers a number of special trips in conjunction with Island Heritage Trust. Most are noted on Old Quarry's website, but for reservations or more info, call 207/348-2455.

SUNSET BAY CO.

Cruise through East Penobscot Bay aboard the mail boat *Katherine* (207/701-9316, $24 adults, $12 under age 12), which departs the Deer Isle Yacht Club at 9am, Mon.-Sat., for a two-hour excursion taking in Eagle, Butter, Barred, and Great Spruce Head islands.

ACCOMMODATIONS

Inns and Bed-and-Breakfasts

Pilgrim's Inn (20 Main St., Deer Isle, 207/348-6615, www.pilgrimsinn.com, early May–mid-Oct., $149-259) comprises a beautifully restored colonial building with 12 rooms and three newer cottages overlooking the peaceful Mill Pond. The inn, on the National Register of Historic Places, began life in 1793 as a boardinghouse named The Ark. Rates include a full breakfast. The Whale's Rib Tavern serves dinner.

◖ The Inn on the Harbor (45 Main St., Stonington, 207/367-2420 or 800/942-2420, www.innontheharbor.com, $150-240) is exactly as its name proclaims—its expansive deck hangs right over the harbor. Although recently updated, the 1880s complex still has an air of unpretentiousness. Most of the 14 guest rooms and suites, each named after a windjammer, have fantastic harbor views and private or shared decks where you can keep an eye on lobster boats, small ferries, windjammers, and pleasure craft; binoculars are provided. Streetside rooms can be noisy at night. Rates include a continental buffet breakfast. An espresso bar is open 11am-4:30pm daily. Nearby are antiques, gift, and crafts shops; guest moorings are available. The inn is open all year, but call ahead in the off-season, when rates are lower.

Eggemoggin Reach is almost on the doorstep at **The Inn at Ferry Landing** (77 Old Ferry Rd., Deer Isle, 207/348-7760, www.ferrylanding.com, $130-185), overlooking the abandoned Sargentville-Deer Isle ferry wharf. The view is wide open from the inn's great room, where guests gather to read, play games, talk, and watch passing windjammers. Professional musician Gerald Wheeler has installed two grand pianos in the room; it's a treat when he plays. His wife, Jean, is the hospitable innkeeper, managing three water-view guest rooms and a suite. A harpsichord and a great view are big pluses in the suite. The Mooring, an annex that sleeps five, is rented by the week ($1,700 without breakfast). The inn is open year-round except Thanksgiving and Christmas; Wi-Fi is available throughout.

Motel

Right in downtown Stonington, just across the street from the harbor, is **Boyce's Motel** (44 Main St., Stonington, 207/367-2421 or 800/224-2421, www.boycesmotel.com, year-round, $70-145). Eleven units all have TVs, phones, and refrigerators; some have kitchens and living rooms, and one has two bedrooms. Across the street, Boyce's has a private harborfront deck for its guests. Ask for rooms well back from Main Street to lessen the noise of locals cruising the street at night.

Hostel and Bunkhouse

In 2009 the rustic, bordering on primitive **Deer Isle Hostel** (65 Tennis Rd., Deer Isle, 207/348-2308, www.deerislehostel.com, $25 adults, $15 under age 12, $30 pp private room, no credit cards) opened near the Tennis Preserve. Owner Dennis Carter, a Surry, Maine, native and local stoneworker and carpenter, modeled it on The Hostel in the Forest in Brunswick, Georgia. It's completely off the grid, with a pump in the kitchen for water, an outhouse, watering-can shower, and woodfired hot tub. Carter expects guests to work in the extensive organic gardens, using produce for shared meals prepared on a woodstove, the sole source of heat. The three-story timberframe design is taken from a late-17th-century home in Massachusetts. Carter hand-cut the granite for the basement, and the timbers in the nail-free frame are hand-hewn from local blown-down spruce. The goal is sustainability, not profit. Communal dinners are available nightly.

Old Quarry Ocean Adventures Bunkhouse (130 Settlement Rd., Stonington, 207/367-8977, www.oldquarry.com) sleeps up to eight in three private rooms, $50-60 double; weekly rates as well as whole-building rates are available. Guests use the campground bathhouse facilities. Bring your own sleeping bag or linens, or rent them for $4.

Camping

Plan ahead if you want to camp at **Old Quarry Ocean Adventures Campground** (130 Settlement Rd., Stonington, 207/367-8977, www.oldquarry.com), with both oceanfront and secluded platform sites for tents and just three RV sites. Rates range $40-54 for two people, plus $17 for each additional adult, varying with location and hookups. Children ages 5-11 are $6. Leashed pets are permitted ($2/stay); Wi-Fi is $3/stay. Parking is designed so that vehicles are kept away from most campsites, but you can use a garden cart to transport your equipment between your car and your site. The campground is adjacent to Settlement Quarry Park.

FOOD

Options for dining are few, and restaurants suffer from a lack of consistency. Patience is more than a virtue here; it's a necessity.

Local Flavors

Craving sweets? Head to **Susie Q's Sweets and Curiosities** (40 School St., Stonington, 207/367-2415, 8am-3pm Wed.-Sun.). Susan Scott bakes a fine selection of cookies and pies, offers a limited selection of breakfast and lunch choices (including homemade doughnuts), and also carries antiques, books, quilts, toys, and other fun items. It's a Wi-Fi hotspot.

Hot coffee and light goodies are usually available at **44 North Coffee** (11 Church St./

Rte. 15, Deer Isle, 207/348-5208), which roasts all-organic Fair Trade beans.

Burnt Cove Market (Rte. 15, Stonington, 207/367-2681, 6am-8pm Mon.-Thurs., to 9pm Fri.-Sat., 7am-8pm Sun.) sells pizza, fried chicken, and sandwiches, plus beer and wine.

Although chef-owner Kyra Alex no longer operates **Lily's House** (450 Airport Rd. at Rte. 15, Stonington, 207/367-5936) as a traditional restaurant, she still offers food-themed and other special events and serves farmhouse lunches usually once a week during the summer.

The Island Community Center (6 Memorial Lane, just off School St., Stonington) is the locale for the lively **Island Farmers Market** (10am-noon Fri. late May-late Sept.), with more than 50 vendors selling smoked and organic meats, fresh herbs and flowers, produce, gelato and yogurt, maple syrup, jams and jellies, fabulous breads and baked goods, chocolates, ethnic foods, crafts, and so much more. Go early; items sell out quickly.

Family Favorites

Harbor Cafe (36 Main St., Stonington, 207/367-5099, 6am-8pm Mon.-Sat., 6am-2pm Sun., $5-20) is *the* place to go for breakfast (you can eavesdrop on the local fisherfolk if you're early enough), but it's also reliable for lunch and dinner (especially on Friday night for the seafood fry, with free seconds).

The views are top-notch from the harborfront **Fisherman's Friend Restaurant** (5 Atlantic Ave., Stonington, 207/367-2442 www.fishermansfriendrestaurant.com, from 11am daily). The restaurant turns out decent fried food, generous portions, fresh seafood, and outstanding desserts, but it seems to have lost its soul since it moved from its old digs to this larger and more modern space. Still, where else can you get lobster prepared 18 different ways? Prices are reasonable—the Friday-night fish fry, with free seconds, is around $11.

Dine downstairs in the tavern, upstairs in the dining rooms, outside at **The Factory Tavern** (25 Seabreeze Ave., Stonington, 207/367-2600, www.thefactorytavern.com, 11:30am-10pm

Wed.-Sun., $8-28), located just steps from the Isle au Haut ferry terminal. The menu ranges from burgers and pizzas to prime rib. Don't miss the sticky toffee pudding.

Casual Dining

The **Whale's Rib Tavern** (20 Main St./Sunset Rd., Deer Isle Village, 207/348-5222, 5pm-8:30pm daily, $15-30) is a comfy white-tablecloth tavern with a rustic feel in the lower level of the Pilgrim's Inn. Well-prepared entrées may include seared halibut with lobster risotto, rack of lamb, and vegetarian fare.

Views! Views! Views! Gaze over lobster boats toing-and-froing around spruce-and-granite-fringed islands and out to Isle au Haut from **C Aragosta** (27 Main St., Stonington, 207/367-5500, www.aragostamaine.com, 11am-2pm and 5pm-9pm Mon.-Sat., $21-30), a culinary bright spot fronting on the harbor in downtown Stonington. The emphasis is on seafood—the lobster ravioli earns raves—but Chef Devin Finigan's oft-changing menu draws from what's currently available from local farms. Lunch is served on the harbor-hugging deck; dinner in the unpretentiously elegant dining room. Reservations are wise.

INFORMATION AND SERVICES

The **Deer Isle-Stonington Chamber of Commerce** (207/348-6124, www.deerisle-maine.com) has a summer information booth on a grassy triangle on Route 15 in Little Deer Isle, 0.25 mile after crossing the bridge from Sargentville (Sedgwick).

Across from the Pilgrim's Inn is the **Chase Emerson Memorial Library** (Main St., Deer Isle Village, 207/348-2899). At the tip of the island is the **Stonington Public Library** (Main St., Stonington, 207/367-5926).

Find **public restrooms** at the Atlantic Avenue Hardware pier and the Stonington Town Hall on Main Street; Chase Emerson Library in Deer Isle Village; and behind the information booth on Little Deer Isle.

GETTING THERE AND AROUND

Deer Isle Village is about 12 miles or 25 minutes via Route 15 from Brooksville. Stonington is about six miles or 15 minutes via Route 15 from Deer Isle Village.

Isle au Haut

Eight miles off Stonington lies 4,700-acre **Isle au Haut,** roughly half of which belongs to Acadia National Park. Pronounced variously as "I'll-a-HO" or "I'LL-a-ho," the island has nearly 20 miles of hiking trails, excellent birding, and a tiny village.

Fewer than 50 souls call Isle au Haut home year-round, and most of them eke out a living from the sea. Each summer, the population temporarily swells with day-trippers, campers, and cottagers—then settles back in fall to the measured pace of life on an offshore island.

Samuel de Champlain, threading his way through this archipelago in 1605 and noting the island's prominent central ridge, named it Isle au Haut (High Island). Appropriately, the tallest peak (543 feet) is now named Mount Champlain.

First settled in 1792, then incorporated in 1874, Isle au Haut earned a world record during World War I, when all residents were members of the Red Cross. Electricity came in 1970, and phone service in 1988.

More recent fame has come to the island thanks to island-based authors Linda Greenlaw, of *Perfect Storm* fame, who wrote *The Lobster Chronicles,* and more recently Kate Shaffer, of Black Dinah Chocolatiers, who shared her recipes along with island tales, in *Desserted.* Although both books piqued interest in the island, Isle au Haut remains uncrowded and well off the beaten tourist track.

© TOM NANGLE

Boats of all types ply the waters of the Isle au Haut Thorofare.

Most of the southern half of the six-mile-long island belongs to Acadia National Park, thanks to the wealthy summer visitors who began arriving in the 1880s. It was their heirs who, in the 1940s, donated valuable acreage to the federal government. Today, this offshore division of the national park has a well-managed 18-mile network of trails, a few lean-tos, several miles of unpaved road, a lighthouse inn, and summertime passenger-ferry service to the park entrance.

In the island's northern half are the private residences of fishing families and summer folk, a minuscule village (including a market, chocolate shop café, and post office), and a five-mile stretch of paved road. The only vehicles on the island are owned by residents.

If spending the night on Isle au Haut sounds appealing (it is), you'll need to plan well ahead; it's no place for spur-of-the-moment sleepovers. (Even spontaneous day trips aren't always possible.) The best part about staying on Isle au Haut is that you'll have much more than seven hours to enjoy this idyllic island.

Folk singer Gordon Bok penned the lyrics to *The Hills of Isle au Haut:*

> The winters drive you crazy
> And the fishin's hard and slow
> You're a damn fool if you stay
> But there's no better place to go

◖ ACADIA NATIONAL PARK

Mention **Acadia National Park** and most people think of Bar Harbor and Mount Desert Island, where more than three million visitors arrive each year. The Isle au Haut section of the park sees maybe 5,000 visitors a year. The limited boat service, the remoteness of the island, and the scarcity of campsites contribute to the low count, leaving the trails and views for only a few hardy souls.

About a third of a mile from the town landing, where the year-round mail boat and another boat dock, is the **Park Ranger Station** (207/335-5551), where you can pick up trail maps and park information—and use the island's only public facilities. (Do yourself a favor, though: Plan ahead by downloading Isle au Haut maps and information from the Acadia National Park website, www.nps.gov/acad).

ENTERTAINMENT AND EVENTS

Although Isle au Haut is pretty much a make-your-own-fun place, summer events usually include a Fourth of July parade, which all islanders participate in, so there are few spectators, and an island talent show in August. Look also for signs at the town landing dock about themed cook-offs, which might include such gourmet items as Spam.

RECREATION

Hiking

Hiking on Acadia National Park trails is the major recreation on Isle au Haut, and even in the densest fog you'll see valiant hikers going for it. A loop road circles the whole island; an unpaved section goes through the park, connecting with the mostly paved nonpark section. Walking on that is easy. Beyond the road, none of the park's 18 miles of trails could be labeled "easy"; the footing is rocky, rooty, and often squishy. But the park trails are well marked, and the views—of islets, distant hills, and the ocean—make the effort worthwhile. Go prepared with proper footwear.

The most-used park trail is the four-mile one-way **Duck Harbor Trail,** connecting the town landing with Duck Harbor. You can either use this trail or follow the island road—mostly unpaved in this stretch—to get to the campground when the summer ferry ends its Duck Harbor runs.

Even though the summit is only 314 feet, **Duck Harbor Mountain** is the island's toughest trail. Still, it's worth the 1.2-mile one-way effort for the stunning 360-degree views from the summit. Option: Rather than return via the trail's steep, bouldery sections, cut off at the Goat Trail and return to the trailhead that way.

For terrific shoreline scenery, take **Western Head Trail** and **Cliff Trail** at the island's southwestern corner. They form a nice loop around Western Head. The route follows the coastline,

ascending to ridges and cliffs and descending to rocky beaches, with some forested sections. Options: Close the loop by returning via the Western Head Road. If the tide is out (and only if it's out), you can walk across the tidal flats to the quaintly named Western Ear for views back toward the island. Western Ear is privately owned, so don't linger. The **Goat Trail** adds another four miles (round-trip) of moderate coastline hiking east of the Cliff Trail; views are fabulous and bird-watching is good, but if you're here only for a day, you'll need to decide whether there's time to do this and still catch the return mail boat. If you do have the time and the energy, you can connect from the Goat Trail to the **Duck Harbor Mountain Trail.**

Guided Nature Tour

Isle au Haut-based naturalist Kathie Fiveash offers **custom guided tours** (207/235-2171) of the island. With a master's degree in environmental science and years of experience teaching island ecology at the local school, she's a great choice for anyone looking to learn more about the island's habitats, birds, flora, or fauna. Rate is $50 pp for four hours, with a $100 minimum.

Bicycling

Pedaling is limited to the 12 or so miles of mostly unpaved, hilly roads, and although it is a way to get around, frankly, the terrain is neither exciting, fun, nor view-worthy. Mountain bikes are not allowed on the park's hiking trails, and rangers try to discourage park visitors from bringing them to the island. You can rent a bike (about $25/day) on the island from the Isle au Haut Ferry Service or Old Quarry Ocean Adventures. It costs $20 round-trip to bring your own bike aboard the Isle au Haut ferry. Both boats carry bikes *only* to the town landing, not to Duck Harbor.

Swimming

For freshwater swimming, head for **Long Pond,** a skinny, 1.5-mile-long swimming hole running north-south on the east side of the island, abutting national park land. You can bike over there, clockwise along the road, almost five miles, from the town landing. Or bum a ride from an island resident. There's a minuscule beach-like area on the southern end with a picnic table and a float. If you're here only for the day, though, there's not enough time to do this *and* get in a long hike. Opt for the hiking—or do a short hike and then go for a swim (the shallowest part is at the southern tip).

ACCOMMODATIONS AND FOOD

Options for food are extremely limited on Isle au Haut, so if you're coming for a day trip, bring sufficient food and water. If you want to stay overnight, plan well in advance.

Inn

Escape to **The Keeper's House** (P.O. Box 26, Lighthouse Point, Isle au Haut 04645, 207/335-2990, www.keepershouse.com, from $350), a light-station inn. Attached to the automated Point Light and within night sight of three other lighthouses, the inn and outlying rustic cottages reopened under new ownership in 2013. This is a truly special, all-inclusive, rustic retreat. The top-floor Garret Room has the only private bath. The three other rooms in the main building share two baths. The best view is from The Keeper's Room, overlooking the light tower and Isle au Haut Thorofare. Detached from the main house are the rustic Oil House, with a private outhouse, and The Woodshed, with two bedrooms, kitchenette, and bath. Guests relax outdoors or gather in the small living room. Rates include breakfast, lunch, and candlelight dinners as well as use of bicycles and a rowboat. Adding to the yesteryear ambiance is the owner's collection of antique autos. BYOB and pack light. No electricity, no phones, no smoking, no credit cards, no pets, no stress. Nirvana.

Camping

You'll need to get your bid in early to reserve one of the five six-person lean-tos at **Duck Harbor Campground,** open May 15-October

15. Before April 1, contact the park for a reservation request form (207/288-3338, www.nps.gov/acad). From April 1 on *(not before, or the park people will send it back to you),* return the completed form, along with a check for $25, covering camping for up to six people for a maximum of five nights May 15-June 14, three nights June 15-September 15, and five nights again September 16-October 15. Competition is stiff in the height of summer, so list alternative dates. The park refunds the check if there's no space; otherwise, it's nonrefundable and you'll receive a "special-use permit" (*do not* forget to bring it along). There's no additional camping fee.

Unless you don't mind backpacking nearly five miles to reach the campground, try to plan your visit between mid-June and late September, when the mail boat makes a stop in Duck Harbor. It's wise to call the **Isle au Haut Company** (207/367-5193) for the current ferry schedule before choosing dates for a lean-to reservation.

Trash policy is carry-in/carry-out, so pack a trash bag or two with your gear. Also bring a container for carting water from the campground pump, since it's 0.3 mile from the lean-tos. It's a longish walk to the general store for food—when you could be off hiking the island's trails—so bring enough to cover your stay.

The three-sided lean-tos are big enough (8-by-12 feet, 8 feet high) to hold a small (two-person) tent, so bring one along if you prefer being fully enclosed. A tarp will also do the trick. (Also bring mosquito repellent—some years, the critters show up here en masse.) No camping is permitted outside of the lean-tos, and nothing can be attached to trees.

Food

Isle au Haut is pretty much a BYO place—and for the most part, that means BYO food.

Thanks to the seasonal **Isle au Haut General Store** (207/335-5211, www.theislandstore.net), less than a five-minute walk from the town landing, you won't starve. The inventory isn't extensive, but it can be intriguing, because of

© TOM NANGLE

Satiate any chocolate cravings at Black Dinah Chocolatiers, a tiny shop and café.

the store manager, who travels worldwide and stocks the shop with her finds.

Even more intriguing is **Black Dinah Chocolatiers and Seasonal Cafe** (207/335-5010, www.blackdinahchocolatiers.com), just shy of a mile from the town landing. Steve and Kate Shaffer's little shop doubles as a café, serving pastries, organic coffees and teas, a few lunch-type offerings, exquisite ice cream, and, of course, decadent handmade chocolates. Eat inside or on the deck. The café has free Wi-Fi.

And then there's **The Maine Lobster Lady** (207/669-2751), a seasonal takeout serving lobster, fried seafood, blueberry pie, and ice cream, of course.

GETTING THERE

Two companies offer transportation to Isle au Haut's town landing. Use Isle au Haut Boat Company if your destination is the park, as it lands right at Duck Harbor twice daily during peak season. If money's no object, you can always arrange a private charter.

Isle au Haut Boat Company

The **Isle au Haut Boat Company** (Seabreeze Ave., Stonington, 207/367-5193, www.isleauhaut.com) generally operates five daily trips Monday-Saturday, plus two on Sunday from mid-June to early September. Other months, there are two or three trips Monday-Saturday. The best advice is to request a copy of the current schedule, covering dates, variables, fares, and extras.

Round-trips April-mid-October are $38 adults, $19.50 kids under 12 (two bags per adult, one bag per child). Round-trip surcharges include bikes ($21), kayaks/canoes ($46 minimum), and pets ($10.50). If you're considering using a bike, inquire about on-island bike rentals ($25/day). Weather seldom affects the schedule, but be aware that heavy seas could cancel a trip.

There is twice-daily ferry service, from mid-June to Labor Day, from Stonington to Duck Harbor, at the edge of Isle au Haut's Acadia National Park campground. For a day trip, the schedule allows you 6.5 hours on the island Monday-Saturday and 4.5 hours on Sunday. No boats or bikes are allowed on this route, and no dogs are allowed in the campground. A ranger boards the boat at the town landing and goes along to Duck Harbor to answer questions and distribute maps. Before mid-June and after Labor Day, you'll be off-loaded at the Isle au Haut town landing, about five miles from Duck Harbor. The six-mile passage from Stonington to the Isle au Haut town landing takes 45 minutes; the trip to Duck Harbor is 1.25 hours.

Ferries depart from the Isle au Haut Boat Company dock (Seabreeze Ave., off E. Main St. in downtown Stonington). Parking around $10 is available next to the ferry landing. Arrive at least an hour early to get all this settled so you don't miss the boat. Better yet, spend the night on Deer Isle before heading to Isle au Haut.

Old Quarry Ocean Adventures

Also offering seasonal service to Isle au Haut is **Old Quarry Ocean Adventures** (Stonington, 207/367-8977, www.oldquarry.

com) which transports passengers on the *Nigh Duck*. The boat usually leaves Old Quarry at 9am and arrives at the island's town landing at 10am, returning from the same point at 5pm. The fee is $38 round-trip for adults, $20 for children under 12. You can add an island bike rental for an additional $22 or a kayak for $20. Old Quarry also offers a taxi service to Isle au Haut for $175/hour for up to six people.

INFORMATION AND SERVICES

Information about the section of Acadia National Park on Isle au Haut is available both online (www.nps.gov/acad) and at the Ranger Station (207/335-5551), about one-third of a mile from the town landing boat dock. General information on the island is available online from **Isle au Haut Boat Company** (www.isleauhaut.com).

ACADIA REGION

Summer folk have been visiting Mount Desert Island (MDI) for millennia. The earliest Native Americans discovered fabulous fishing and clamming, good hunting and camping, and invigorating salt air. Today's arrivals find variations on the same theme: thousands of lodgings and campsites, hundreds of restaurant seats, dozens of shops, plus 40,000 acres of Acadia National Park.

It's no coincidence that artists were a large part of the 19th-century vanguard here: The dramatic landscape, with both bare and wooded mountains descending to the sea, still inspires all who see it. Once the word got out, painterly images began confirming the reports, and the surge began. Even today, no saltwater locale on the entire eastern seaboard can compete with the variety of scenery on Mount Desert Island.

Those pioneering artists brilliantly portrayed this area, adding romantic touches to landscapes that really need no enhancement. From the 1,530-foot summit of Cadillac Mountain, preferably at an off hour, you'll sense the grandeur of it all—the slopes careening toward the bay and the handful of islands below looking like the last footholds between Bar Harbor and Bordeaux.

For nearly four centuries, controversy has raged about the pronunciation of the island's name, and we won't resolve it here. French explorer Samuel de Champlain apparently gets credit for naming it l'Ile des Monts Deserts (island of bare mountains) when he sailed by in 1604. The accent in French would be on the second syllable, but today "De-SERT" and "DES-ert" both have their advocates, although

HIGHLIGHTS

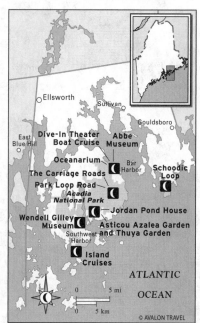

© AVALON TRAVEL

century, afternoon tea and popovers on the lawn of the Jordan Pond House have been a tradition. Make reservations for an afternoon pick-me-up, perhaps after walking or biking the many carriage roads that lead here (page 306).

◖ **Abbe Museum:** The downtown Abbe Museum and its seasonal museum at Sieur de Monts Spring are fascinating places to while away a few hours and learn about Maine's Native American heritage (page 308).

◖ **Oceanarium:** A fabulous introduction to the coastal ecology is provided at this low-tech, kid-friendly site (page 310).

◖ **Dive-In Theater Boat Cruise:** Got kids? Don't miss this tour, where Diver Ed brings the undersea world aboard (page 316).

◖ **Asticou Azalea Garden and Thuya Garden:** "Magical and enchanting" best describes these two peaceful gardens. Whereas Zen-like Asticou is best seen in spring, Thuya delivers color through summer and also has hiking paths (page 326).

◖ **Wendell Gilley Museum:** Gilley's intricately carved birds, from miniature shorebirds to life-size birds of prey, are a marvel to behold (page 332).

◖ **Island Cruises:** Kim Strauss shares his deep knowledge of island ways and waters on the lunchtime cruise that allows time to explore Frenchboro (page 335).

◖ **Schoodic Loop:** A scenic six-mile road edges the pink-granite shores of Acadia National Park's only mainland section and accesses hiking trails and picnic spots (page 347).

LOOK FOR ◖ TO FIND RECOMMENDED SIGHTS, ACTIVITIES, DINING, AND LODGING.

◖ **Park Loop Road:** If you do nothing else on Mount Desert, drive this magnificent road that takes in many of Acadia National Park's highlights (page 301).

◖ **The Carriage Roads:** Whether you walk, bike, or ride in a horse-drawn carriage, do make a point of seeing Mr. Rockefeller's roads and bridges (page 302).

◖ **Jordan Pond House:** For more than a

the former gets the accuracy nod. In any case, the island is anything but deserted today. Even as you approach it, via the shire town of **Ellsworth** and especially in **Trenton,** you'll run the gauntlet of big-box stores, amusements, and

enough high-cholesterol eateries to stun the surgeon general. Don't panic: Acadia National Park lies ahead, and amid the thick of consumer congestion there are glimpses of the prize. Even on the most crowded days, if you

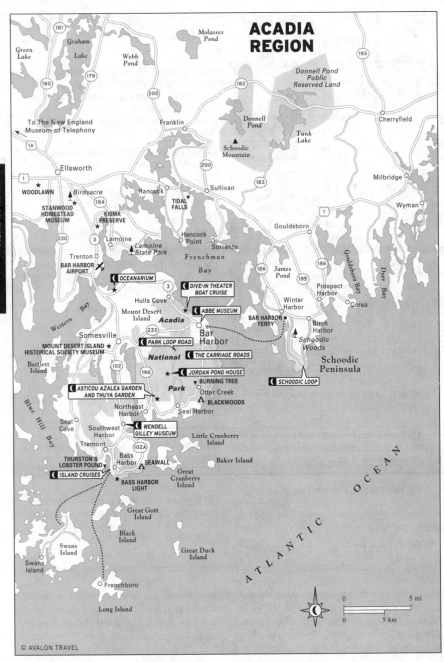

ACADIA REGION

181

Green
Lake

Graham
Lake

179

Webb
Pond

Molasses
Pond

193

180

200

182

Donnell Pond
Public
Reserved Land

Cherryfield

To The New England
Museum of Telephony

1A

Franklin

200

Donnell
Pond

Tunk
Lake

Schoodic
Mountain

Milbridge

Ellsworth

1

WOODLAWN ★

★ Birdsacre

STANWOOD
HOMESTEAD
MUSEUM ★

184

Hancock

Sullivan

183

Wyman

Gouldsboro

1

230   3   KISMA
PRESERVE ★

Lamoine

TIDAL
FALLS

Hancock
Point

Sorrento

186   James
Pond

186

Gouldsboro Bay

Dyer
Bay

Trenton
BAR HARBOR
AIRPORT ✈

Lamoine
State Park

Frenchman

195

Prospect
Harbor

Corea

Western
Bay

OCEANARIUM

3

Bay

DIVE-IN THEATER
BOAT CRUISE

Winter
Harbor

Hulls Cove

ABBE MUSEUM ★

BAR HARBOR
FERRY ■

Birch
Harbor

Mount Desert
Island   *Acadia*

BAR
Harbor

Schoodic
Woods

Somesville

233

Schoodic
Peninsula

MOUNT DESERT ISLAND
HISTORICAL SOCIETY MUSEUM

PARK LOOP ROAD

National   THE CARRIAGE ROADS

Bartlett
Island

102

198   JORDAN POND HOUSE

SCHOODIC LOOP

Blue Hill Bay

ASTICOU AZALEA GARDEN
AND THUYA GARDEN ★

Park   BURNING TREE ▼
Otter Creek
BLACKWOODS ⬠

Northeast
Harbor

Seal Harbor

Seal
Cove

Southwest
Harbor

WENDELL
GILLEY MUSEUM

Little Cranberry
Island

Tremont

102A

Baker Island

THURSTON'S
LOBSTER POUND ▼

Bass
Harbor   SEAWALL

ISLAND CRUISES

BASS HARBOR
LIGHT ★

Great
Cranberry
Island

Great Gott
Island

Black
Island

Great Duck
Island

Swans
Island

Frenchboro

Long Island

A T L A N T I C   O C E A N

0   5 mi
0   5 km

© AVALON TRAVEL

venture more than a few steps into the park, you'll find you have it nearly to yourself.

As you drive or bike around Mount Desert—vaguely shaped like a lobster claw and indented by Somes Sound (the only fjord on the U.S. East Coast)—you'll cross and recross the national-park boundaries, reminders that Acadia National Park, covering a third of the island, is indeed the major presence here. It affects traffic, indoor and outdoor pursuits, and, in a way, even the climate.

The other major presence is **Bar Harbor,** largest and best known of the island's communities. It's the source of just about anything you could want, from T-shirts to tacos, books to bike rentals. The contrast with Acadia is astonishing as the park struggles to maintain its image and character. And yet, even in Bar Harbor, the park's presence is felt. Bar Harbor shares the island with **Southwest Harbor, Tremont,** and a number of small villages: **Bass Harbor, Bernard, Northeast Harbor, Seal Harbor, Otter Creek, Somesville,** and **Hall Quarry.** From Bass, Northeast, and Southwest Harbors, private and state ferries shuttle bike and foot traffic to offshore **Swans Island, Frenchboro** (Long Island), and the **Cranberry Isles** (and cars to Swans Island).

Stay on Route 1 instead of taking Route 3 to the island and the congestion disappears. The towns lining the eastern shore of Frenchman Bay—**Hancock, Sullivan, Winter Harbor,** and **Gouldsboro**—have some of the best views of all: front-row seats facing the peaks of Mount Desert Island. It's no wonder many artists and artisans make their homes here. And at the tip of the **Schoodic Peninsula,** a stunning pocket of Acadia National Park sees only a fraction of the visitors who descend on the main part of the park.

PLANNING YOUR TIME

So much to do, so little time—that's the lament of most visitors. You can circumnavigate Mount Desert Island in a day, hitting the highlights along the Park Loop with just enough time to *ooh* and *aah* at each, but to appreciate Acadia, you need time to hike the trails, ride the carriage roads, get afloat on a whale-watching cruise or a sea kayak, visit museums, and explore an offshore island or two. A week or longer is best, but you can get a taste of Acadia in 3-4 days.

The region is very seasonal, with most restaurants, accommodations, and shops open mid-May-mid-October. May and June bring the new greens of spring and blooming rhododendrons and azaleas in Northeast Harbor's Asticou Garden, but mosquitoes and black-flies are at their worst and weather is temperamental—perhaps sunny and hot one day, damp and cold the next, a packing nightmare. July and August bring summer at its best, along with the biggest crowds. September is a gem of a time to visit: few bugs, fewer people, less fog, and autumn's golden light. Foliage usually begins turning in early October, making it an especially beautiful time to visit (the Columbus Day holiday weekend brings a spike in visitors). Winter is Acadia's silent season, best left for independent travelers who don't mind making do or perhaps making a meal of peanut-butter crackers if an open restaurant can't be found.

The only way onto Mount Desert Island is Route 3. Unless you're traveling in the wee hours of the morning or late at night, expect traffic. Avoid it during shift changes on-island, 8am-9am and 3pm-4pm weekdays, when traffic slows to a crawl. On the island, use the Island Explorer bus system to avoid parking hassles.

Ellsworth

The punch line to an old Maine joke is "Ya cahn't get they-ah from he-ah." The truth is, you can't get to Acadia without going through **Ellsworth** (pop. 7,741) and **Trenton** (pop. 1,481). Indeed, when you're crawling along in bumper-to-bumper traffic, it might seem as if all roads lead to downtown Ellsworth. And the truth is that many do.

Although there are ways to skirt around a few of the worst bottlenecks, the region does have its calling cards. Ellsworth, Hancock County's shire town, has mushroomed with the popularity of Acadia National Park, but you can still find handsome architectural remnants of the city's 19th-century lumbering heyday (which began shortly after its incorporation in 1800). Brigs, barks, and full-rigged ships—built in Ellsworth and captained by local fellows—loaded lumber here and carried it around the globe. Despite a ruinous 1855 fire that swept through downtown, the lumber trade thrived until late in the 19th century, along with factories and mills turning out shoes, bricks, boxes, and butter.

These days, Ellsworth is the region's shopping mecca. Antiques shops and small stores line Main Street, which doubles as Route 1 in the downtown section; supermarkets, strip malls, and big-box stores line Routes 1 and 3 between Ellsworth and Trenton.

Other pluses for the area include inexpensive lodging and the Bar Harbor Chamber of Commerce Information Center location on Route 3 in Trenton. If you're day-tripping to Mount Desert Island, you can leave your car here and hop aboard the free Island Explorer bus, eliminating driving and parking hassles.

SIGHTS
Woodlawn
Very little has changed at **Woodlawn** (Surry Rd./Rte. 172, 207/667-8671, www.woodlawnmuseum.com, 10am-5pm Tues.-Sun., 1pm-4pm Sun. June-Sept., 1pm-4pm Tues.-Sun.

May and Oct., $10 adults, $3 ages 5-12, grounds free) since George Nixon Black donated his home, also known as the Black Mansion, to the town in 1928. Completed in 1828, the Georgian house is a marvel of preservation—one of Maine's best—filled with Black family antiques and artifacts. House highlights include a circular staircase, rare books and artifacts, canopied beds, a barrel organ, and lots more. After taking an audio tour, plan to picnic on the manicured grounds, and then explore two sleigh-filled barns, the Memorial Garden, and the two miles of mostly level trails in the woods up beyond the house. Consider timing a visit with one of the frequent events: There's a farmers market on Sunday and on several Wednesday afternoons in July-August there are elegant teas ($25 pp) in the garden (or in the carriage house if it's raining), with china, silver, linens, special-blend tea, sandwiches, pastries, and live music; reservations are required. On Route 172, watch for the small sign 0.25 mile southwest of U.S. 1, and turn into the winding uphill driveway.

Birdsacre
En route to Bar Harbor, watch carefully on the right for the sign that marks **Birdsacre** (Rte. 3/Bar Harbor Rd., 207/667-8460, www.birdsacre.com, sunrise-sunset daily, donation), a 200-acre urban sanctuary. Wander the trails in this peaceful preserve, spotting wildflowers, birds, and well-labeled shrubs and trees, and you'll have trouble believing you're surrounded by prime tourist territory. One trail, a boardwalk loop through woods behind the nature center, is accessible for wheelchairs and strollers.

At the sanctuary entrance is the 1850 **Stanwood Homestead Museum** (tours by chance or by appointment 10am-4pm daily June-late Sept., donation appreciated), with period furnishings and wildlife exhibits. Once owned by noted ornithologist Cordelia

© HILARY NANGLE

Shops and restaurants line Ellsworth's Main Street.

the biology of the animals, how they came to be here, and whether they'll be returned to the wild. For serious animal lovers, the preserve offers behind-the-scenes tours and close-ups; there are even options for staying in the preserve overnight. It truly is a special place, home to more than 100 exotic and not-so-exotic creatures, with an emphasis on wolves and big cats, including one of the rarest tigers in the world. Donations are essential to Kisma's survival, and yes, it's pricey, but so is feeding and caring for these animals.

Downeast Scenic Railroad

All aboard! The all-volunteer **Downeast Rail Heritage Preservation Trust** (245 Main St., 866/449-7245, www.downeastscenicrail.org) has restored a 1948 diesel engine and rehabilitated the Calais Branch Line from Ellsworth to Ellsworth Falls and then back and on to Washington Junction. Saturday-Sunday (late May-mid-Oct.) you can board the two vintage coaches, an open flatcar, or caboose for a roughly 13-mile, 90-minute scenic excursion ($15 adults, $8 ages 3-12). Work continues on the track to Green Lake, which will allow a 24-mile round-trip. Boarding takes place behind The Maine Community Foundation (245 Main St.). If you're a train buff, ask about volunteer opportunities.

Telephone Museum

What was life like before cell phones? Find out at the **Telephone Museum** (166 Winkumpaugh Rd., 207/667-9491, www.thetelephonemuseum.org, $10 adults, $5 children), a hands-on museum with the largest collection of old-fashioned switching systems in the East. To find the museum, head 10 miles north on U.S. 1A toward Bangor, then go left on Winkumpaugh Road for one mile. Call for schedule.

Flightseeing

Two businesses provide options for getting an eagle's-eye view of the area. Both are based on the Route 3 side of Hancock County/Bar Harbor Airport, just north of Mount Desert Island.

Stanwood, the volunteer-operated museum and preserve doesn't charge an admission fee, but donations are needed and greatly appreciated. Birdsacre is also a wildlife rehabilitation center, so expect to see all kinds of winged creatures, especially hawks and owls, in various stages of recuperation. Some will be returned to the wild, and others remain here for educational purposes. Stop by the Nature Center for even more exhibits.

Kisma Preserve

I can't stress this enough: **Kisma Preserve** (446 Bar Harbor Rd./Rte. 3, 207/667-3244, www.kismapreserve.org, 10am-6pm daily mid-May-late fall, basic tour $14) is not a zoo; it's a nonprofit educational facility, and everything revolves around preserving and protecting the animals, most of which are either rescues or retirees. Rules are strictly enforced—no running, loud voices, or disruptive behavior is permitted. The easiest way to view the animals is on a one-hour guided tour. Guides educate visitors about

© TOM NANGLE

Ellsworth's handsome city hall is easy to spot.

Scenic Flights of Acadia (Bar Harbor Rd./ Rte. 3, 207/667-6527, www.scenicflightsofacadia.com) offers low-level flightseeing services in the Mount Desert Island region. Flights range 15-75 minutes and cost from $46 pp with a two-passenger minimum.

Scenic Biplane and Glider Rides (968 Bar Harbor Rd./Rte. 3, 207/667-7627, www.acadiaairtours.com) lets you soar in silence with daily glider flights. The one- or two-passenger gliders are towed to an altitude of at least 2,500 feet and then released. An FAA-certified pilot guides the glider. Rates begin at $220 for a 15-minute flight for two. Or ride in a biplane: A 20-minute ride in an open-cockpit plane is $25 for two. Or for a different twist, consider experiencing a World War II-era T-6 fighter plane, with flights beginning at $275 for 15 minutes. All flights are subject to an airport fee.

ENTERTAINMENT

Ellsworth has three free summer series (www. downtownellsworth.com). The **Ellsworth Concert Band** performs Wednesday evening in the plaza outside Ellsworth City Hall (City Hall Ave.). If it rains, it's held inside City Hall. Practice begins at 6:30pm, concerts start at 8pm, and the 30-member community band even welcomes visitors with talent and instruments—just show up at practice time. **Outdoor family movies** are shown at sunset Thursday at the Knowlton Playground on State Street (donations appreciated). **Concerts** are staged at Waterfront Park at 6pm on Friday.

Ace lumberjack "Timber" Tina Scheer has been competing around the world since she was seven, and she shows her prowess at **The Great Maine Lumberjack Show** (Rte. 3, 207/667-0067, www.mainelumberjack.com, 7pm daily mid-June-early Sept., 4pm Sat. and 2pm Sun. early Sept.-mid-Oct., $11 adults, $10 over age 62, $7.50 ages 4-11). During the 75-minute "Olympics of the Forest," you'll watch two teams compete in 12 events, including ax throwing, crosscut sawing, log rolling, speed climbing, and more. Some events are open to participation. (Kids can learn some skills by appointment.) Performances are held rain or shine. Seating is under a roof, but dress for the weather if it's inclement. The ticket office opens at 6pm.

The carefully restored art deco **Grand Auditorium of Hancock County** (100 Main St., 207/667-9500, www.grandonline.org) is the year-round site of films, concerts, plays, and art exhibits.

SHOPPING
Specialty Shops

You're unlikely to meet a single person who has left **Big Chicken Barn Books and Antiques** (1768 Bucksport Rd./U.S. 1, 207/667-7308, www.bigchickenbarn.com) without buying something. You'll find every kind of collectible on the vast first floor, courtesy of more than four dozen dealers. Climb the stairs for books, magazines, old music, and more. With free coffee, restrooms, and 21,000 square feet of floor space, this place is addictive. The Big Chicken is 11 miles east of Bucksport, 8.5 miles west of Ellsworth.

Just south of downtown, in a property listed on the National Register of Historic Places, the 1838 courthouse at the corner of Court Street and Route 1 is **Courthouse Gallery Fine Art** (6 Court St., 207/667-6611, www.courthousegallery.com), showcasing works by some of Maine's top contemporary artists.

The 40-plus-dealer **Old Creamery Antique Mall** (13 Hancock St., 207/667-0522) fills 6,000 square feet on two jam-packed floors.

Around the corner is **Atlantic Art Glass** (25 Pine St., 207/664-0222, www.atlanticartglass.com), where you can watch Linda and Ken Perrin demonstrate glassblowing and buy their contemporary creations.

Don't miss **Rooster Brother** (29 Main St./Rte. 1, 800/866-0054, www.roosterbrother.com) for gourmet cookware, cards, and books on the main floor; coffee, tea, candy, cheeses, a huge array of exotic condiments, fresh breads, and other gourmet items on the lower level; and discounted merchandise on the second floor, open seasonally. You can easily pick up all the fixings for a fancy picnic here.

It's hard to categorize **J&B Atlantic Company** (142 Main St./Rte. 1, 207/667-2082). It takes up a good part of the block, with room after room filled with furniture, home accessories, gifts, books, and antiques.

John Edwards Market (158 Main St., 207/667-9377) is a twofold find: Upstairs is a natural-foods store; downstairs is the Wine Cellar Gallery, a terrific space showcasing Maine artists throughout the year.

Stock up on Maine-made jams, syrups, honeys, and other specialty foods at **Maine's Own Treats** (68 Rte. 3/Bar Harbor Rd., 207/667-8888).

Discount Shopping

You can certainly find bargains at the **L. L. Bean Factory Store** (150 High St./Rte. 1, 207/667-7753), but this is an outlet, so scrutinize the goods for flaws and blemishes before buying.

Across the road is **Renys Department Store** (Ellsworth Shopping Center, 175 High St./Rte. 1, 207/667-5166, www.renys.com), a Maine-based discount operation with a "you never know what you'll find" philosophy. Trust me, you'll find something here.

Marden's (461 High St./Rte. 3, 207/669-6035, www.mardenssurplus.com) is another Maine "bit of this, bit of that" enterprise with the catchy slogan "I shoulda bought it when I saw it." Good advice.

ACCOMMODATIONS

These updated motels and cottage colonies along Routes 1 and 3 provide cheap sleeps, with a few frills, but fussbudgets should look elsewhere.

If all you want is a good bed in a clean room, the family-owned and operated **Sunset Motor Court** (210 Twin Hill Rd., Ellsworth, 207/667-8390, www.sunsetmotorcourtmotel.com, $80-125), a pet-friendly tourist court facing U.S. 1 south of town, fits the bill. It's also well situated for exploring the Blue Hill Peninsula region. Each of the comfortably renovated rainbow-colored one- and two-bedroom cabins has heat, air-conditioning, a TV, a microwave, a refrigerator, and in-room coffee with pre-packaged pastries. French and Polish are also spoken.

The Kelley family's **Isleview Motel** (1169 Bar Harbor Rd./Rte. 3, Trenton, 207/667-5661 or 866/475-3843, www.isleviewmotelandcottages.com, $65-135) comprises a motel, one- and two-bedroom cottages, and a few "sleep-and-go" rooms above the office, all decorated in country style. At these prices and with this location—eight miles from the park entrance, on the Island Explorer shuttle route, across from a lobster restaurant, and just 0.5 mile from the Thompson Island picnic area—don't go looking for fancy, but wallet-conscious travelers will be tickled with it. Although small, most guest rooms are equipped with mini-refrigerator, a microwave, Wi-Fi, a coffeemaker, air-conditioning, and a TV. Outside are picnic tables and grills. Rates include breakfast pastries, juice, and coffee.

New owners, since 2009, have been upgrading and updating the pet-friendly **Acadia Sunrise Motel** (952 Bar Harbor Rd./Rte. 3, Trenton, 207/667-8452, www.acadiasunrisemotel.com, $69-105), originally built in 1985 as a strip mall. All guest rooms have air-conditioning, cable TV, phones, refrigerators, microwaves, and coffeemakers; efficiency units have kitchenettes with stoves. Perks include an outdoor heated pool and a guest laundry. Ask for a room at the back, away from the street noise and overlooking the airport with the ocean and Acadia's mountains in the distance.

Camping

Equally convenient to the Schoodic Region and Mount Desert Island is the 55-acre **Lamoine State Park** (23 State Park Rd./ Rte. 184, Lamoine, 207/667-4778, www.parksandlands.com, day-use $4.50 nonresident adults, $3 Maine resident adults, $1 ages 5-11). Park facilities include a pebble beach and a picnic area with a spectacular view, a boat-launch ramp, and a children's play area. Camping (mid-May-mid-Sept., $25 nonresidents, $15 Maine residents, reservations $2/night) is available at 62 sites. No hookups are

available, and the minimum stay is 2 nights, with a 14-night maximum. Reserve online with a credit card, or call 207/624-9950 or 800/332-1501 weekdays within Maine. Leashed pets are allowed, but not on the beach, and cleanup is required.

FOOD
Local Flavors

Order breakfast anytime at **The Riverside Café** (151 Main St., 207/667-7220, www.maineriversidecafe.com, 6am-3pm Mon.-Wed., 6am-9pm Thurs.-Fri., 7am-9pm Sat., 7am-3pm Sun.). Lunch service begins at 11am. On weekend nights there's often entertainment. And the café's name? It used to be down the street, overlooking the Union River.

Less creative but no less delicious are the home-style breakfasts at **Martha's Diner** (Renys Plaza, 151 High St., 207/664-2495, www.marthasdiner.com, 6am-2pm Tues.-Fri., 6am-1pm Sat., 7am-1pm Sun., under $10), where lunch is also served 11am-2pm Tuesday-Friday. Booths are red leatherette and Formica, and the waitresses may call you "doll."

Big flavors come out of tiny **86 This** (2 State St., 207/610-1777, 11am-8pm Tues.-Sat.), a wrap and burrito joint with a handful of tables. The flavors are rich, the portions are generous, and wraps are named after the owners' favorite indie bands.

Jordan's Snack Bar (200 Down East Hwy./ U.S. 1, 207/667-2174, www.jordanssnackbar.com, 10:30am-9pm daily) has an almost cult following for its crabmeat rolls and fried clams. Wednesday Cruise-Ins, beginning at 6pm, usually feature live entertainment and draw up to 50 vintage cars.

Ice cream doesn't get much finer than that sold at **Morton's Moo** (9 School St., 207/266-9671), a family-run spot with a deservedly giant reputation for homemade Italian gelato, *sorbetto,* and ice cream in creative flavors. It's half a block off Main Street behind The Maine Grind.

Mighty fine pizza is served at **Finelli Pizzeria** (12 U.S. 1, 207/664-0230, www.finellipizzeria.com, from 11am daily) where the pizza dough and focaccia bread are made fresh daily. The specialty is New York-style thin-crust pizza, but other options include calzones, pastas, subs, and salads.

The **Ellsworth Farmers Market** sets up in the parking lot behind the Maine Community Foundation (245 E. Main St., 2pm-5:30pm Mon. and Thurs. mid-June-late Oct.). The **Woodlawn Farmers Market** (11am-2pm Sun. year-round) takes place at the Woodlawn museum (Surry Rd./Rte. 172).

Casual Dining

Cleonice at The Maine Grind (192 Main St., 207/664-7554, www.cleonice.com, 7:30am-8:30pm Mon.-Sat., 10am-5pm Sun.) is a double find. While the counter-service at this congenial spot, dubbed Ellsworth's Living Room, operates in half of the space during the day, Cleonice operates in the other half for lunch and takes over the full restaurant, with its open kitchen, in the evening. Chef-owner Richard Hanson sources ingredients locally, including much from his own farm and seafood from local fishing coops, and he creates almost everything from scratch. At night, the Mediterranean-influenced menu includes both small and large plates, and blackboard specials are always intriguing; entrées run $18-28, but you can make a meal from the incredible tapas selections ($5-15), covering the Mediterranean circuit (spanakopita, hummus, manchego cheese with pear sauce, and even *brandade de morue*). The restaurant is named after Hanson's mother, Cleonice Renzetti. (It helps if you learn how to pronounce it: klee-oh-NEESE.)

Down East meets Far East at **Shinbashi** (139 High St., 207/667-6561, www.myshinbashi.com, 11:30am-9:30pm daily, $8-24), serving an extensive menu of Japanese, Chinese, Vietnamese, and Thai specialties, including sushi and Peking duck; there's also a children's menu.

Lobster

It's hard to say which is better—the serene views or the tasty lobster—at Brian and Jane Langley's **Union River Lobster Pot** (8 South St., 207/667-5077, www.lobsterpot.com, 4pm-9pm daily June-mid-Oct., $15-24). It's tucked behind Rooster Brother, right on the banks of the Union River. The menu includes far more than lobster, with chicken, fish, meat, and pasta dishes, and a kids' menu is available. Remember to save room for the pie, especially the blueberry.

Far more touristy is **Trenton Bridge Lobster Pound** (Bar Harbor Rd./Rte. 3, 207/667-2977, www.trentonbridgelobster.com, 11am-7:30pm Mon.-Sat. late May-mid-Oct.), on the right next to the bridge leading to Mount Desert Island. Watch for the "smoke signals"—steam billowing from the huge vats.

INFORMATION AND SERVICES

The **Thompson Island Visitors Center** (Rte. 3, Thompson Island, 207/288-3411) represents the Mount Desert Island Regional Chambers of Commerce, which includes the Trenton Chamber of Commerce. An Acadia National Park ranger is usually stationed here, and park passes are available.

The **Ellsworth Area Chamber of Commerce** (207/667-5584, www.ellsworthchamber.org) also covers Trenton.

En route from Ellsworth on Route 3, on the right shortly before you reach Mount Desert Island, you'll see the **Bar Harbor Chamber of Commerce** (Rte. 3, 207/288-5103 or 888/540-9990, www.barharbor-maine.com). You'll find all sorts of info on the island and other locations, plus restrooms, phones, and helpful staff.

George Nixon Black, grandson of the builder of the Woodlawn Museum, donated the National Register of Historic Places-listed Federalist **Ellsworth Public Library** (46 State St., 207/667-6363, www.ellsworth.lib.me.us) to the city in 1897.

Find **public restrooms** in City Hall (City Hall Ave.) in downtown Ellsworth, open 24 hours daily, seven days a week; the library (46 State St.); the Chamber of Commerce; and the picnic area and boat launch (Water St.).

GETTING THERE AND AROUND

Ellsworth is about 14 miles via Route 172 from Blue Hill. It's about 20 miles or 30-45 minutes, depending upon traffic, to Bar Harbor.

Route 1 of the **Island Explorer** (www.exploreacadia.com) bus system, which primarily serves Mount Desert Island with its fleet of propane-fueled fare-free vehicles, connects the Hancock County/Bar Harbor Airport in Trenton with downtown Bar Harbor. Operated by Downeast Transportation, the Island Explorer runs late June-mid-October.

Before or after visiting Mount Desert Island, if you're headed farther Down East—to Lamoine, the eastern side of Hancock County, and beyond—there's a good shortcut from Trenton. About five miles south of Ellsworth on Route 3, just north of the Kisma Preserve, turn east onto Route 204.

Acadia National Park on Mount Desert Island

Rather like an octopus, or perhaps an amoeba, **Acadia National Park** extends its reach here and there on Mount Desert Island. The first national park east of the Mississippi River and the only national park in the northeastern United States, it was created from donated parcels—a big chunk here, a tiny chunk there—and slowly but surely fused into its present-day size of more than 46,000 acres. Within the boundaries of this splendid space are mountains, lakes, ponds, trails, fabulous vistas, and several campgrounds. Each year more than two million visitors bike, hike, and drive into and through the park. Yet even at the height of summer, when the whole world seems to have arrived, it's possible to find peaceful niches and less-trodden paths.

Acadia's history is unique among national parks and is indeed fascinating. Several books have been written about some of the high-minded (in the positive sense) and high-profile personalities who provided the impetus and wherewithal for the park's inception and never flagged in their interest and support. Just to spotlight a few, we can thank George B. Dorr, Charles W. Eliot, and John D. Rockefeller Jr. for the park we have today.

The most comprehensive guide to the park and surrounding area is *Moon Acadia National Park*.

NATIONAL PARK INFORMATION

Anyone entering the park by any means should buy a pass. Entrance fees, covering pedestrians, bicyclists, and motorized vehicles, are $20 late June-early October, and $10 May 1-late June and most of October. That covers one vehicle for seven days. If you're traveling alone, an individual seven-day pass is $5. An annual pass to Acadia is $40, the America the Beautiful pass covering all federal recreation sites is $80, a lifetime senior pass (age 62 and older) is $10, and an access pass for citizens with disabilities is free. Passes are available at the visitors centers.

Hulls Cove Visitor Center

The modern **Hulls Cove Visitor Center** (Rte. 3, Hulls Cove, 207/288-3338, 8am-4:30pm daily Apr. 15-June 30 and Oct., 8am-6pm daily July-Aug., 8am-5pm daily Sept.) is eight miles southeast of the head of Mount Desert Island and well signposted. Here you can buy your park pass, make reservations for ranger-guided natural- and cultural-history programs, watch a 15-minute film about Acadia, study a relief map of the park, and buy books, park souvenirs, and guides. Pick up a copy of the *Beaver Log,* the tabloid-format park newspaper, with a schedule of park activities plus tide calendars and the entire schedule for the excellent **Island**

© TOM NANGLE

Any road trip in the Acadia region must include the Park Loop Road.

Explorer shuttle-bus system, which operates late June-early October. The Island Explorer is supported by entrance fees (park pass required), as well as by Friends of Acadia and L. L. Bean. If you have children, enroll them in the park's **Junior Ranger Program** (a nominal fee may be charged). They'll receive a booklet. To earn a Junior Ranger Patch, they must complete the activities and join one or two ranger-led programs or walks.

Thompson Island Visitor Center

As you cross the bridge from Trenton toward Mount Desert Island, you might not even notice that you arrive first on tiny **Thompson Island,** site of a visitors center (8am-6pm daily mid-May-mid-Oct.) established jointly by the chambers of commerce of Mount Desert Island's towns and Acadia National Park. In season, a park ranger is usually posted here to answer questions and provide basic advice on hiking trails and other park activities, but consider this a stopgap—be sure to continue to the park's main visitors center.

Acadia National Park Headquarters

November-April, information is available at **Acadia National Park Headquarters** (Eagle Lake Rd./Rte. 233, 8am-4:30pm Mon.-Fri.), about 3.5 miles west of downtown Bar Harbor.

SIGHTS
◖ Park Loop Road

The 27-mile **Park Loop Road** takes in most of the park's big-ticket sites. It begins at the visitors center, winds past several of the park's scenic highlights (with parking areas), ascends to the summit of **Cadillac Mountain,** and provides overlooks to magnificent vistas. Along the route are trailheads and overlooks as well as **Sieur de Monts Spring** (Acadia Nature Center, Wild Gardens of Acadia, Abbe Museum summer site, and the convergence of several spectacular trails), **Sand Beach, Thunder Hole, Otter Cliffs, Fabbri picnic area** (there's one wheelchair-accessible picnic table), **Jordan Pond House, Bubble Pond, Eagle Lake,** and the summit of **Cadillac Mountain.** Just before

WITH A LITTLE HELP FROM OUR FRIENDS

As we watch federal funding for national parks lose headway year after year, every park in the United States needs a safety net like **Friends of Acadia** (FOA, 207/288-3340 or 800/625-0321, www.friendsofacadia.org), a dynamic organization headquartered in Bar Harbor. Propane-powered shuttle-bus service needs expanding? FOA finds a million-dollar donor. Well-used trails need maintenance? FOA organizes volunteer work parties. New connector trails needed? FOA gets them done. No need seems to go unfilled.

FOA—one of Acadia National Park's greatest assets—is both reactive and proactive. It's an amazingly symbiotic relationship. When informed of a need, the Friends stand ready to help; when they themselves perceive a need, they propose solutions to park management and jointly figure out ways to make them happen. It's hard to avoid sounding like a media flack when describing this organization.

Friends of Acadia was founded in 1986 to preserve and protect the park for resource-sensitive tourism and myriad recreational uses. Since then, FOA has contributed almost $20 million to the park and surrounding com-munities for trail upkeep, carriage-road maintenance, seasonal park staff funding, and conservation projects. FOA also cofounded the Island Explorer bus system and instigated the Acadia Trails Forever program, a joint park-FOA partnership for trail rehabilitation. In 2003, for instance, FOA and the park announced the reopening (after considerable planning and rebuilding) of the Homans Path, on the east side of Dorr Mountain. The trail, built around 1916 and named after Eliza Homans, a generous benefactor, fell into disuse in the 1940s. It ascends via a granite stairway to a ledge with a commanding view of the Great Meadow and Frenchman Bay. More recently, the Schooner Head Path, the wheelchair-accessible Jesup Path, and the Canada Cliffs Connector Trail have been reconstructed through Acadia Trails Forever; altogether, more than 40 trails have been rehabilitated or built through the program.

As part of its efforts to reduce traffic congestion on Mount Desert Island, FOA purchased land in Trenton for an off-island transit and welcome center and has sold approximately 150 acres to the Maine Department of Trans-

you get to Sand Beach, you'll see the Park Entrance Station, where you'll need to buy a pass if you haven't already done so. If you're here during nesting and fledging season—April-mid-August—be sure to stop in the Precipice Trailhead parking area.

Start at the parking lot below the Hulls Cove Visitor Center and follow the signs; part of the loop is one-way, so you'll be doing the loop clockwise. Traffic gets heavy at midday in midsummer, so aim for an early-morning start if you can. Maximum speed is 35 mph, but be alert for gawkers and photographers stopping without warning, and pedestrians dashing across the road from stopped cars or tour buses. If you're out here at midday in midsummer, don't be surprised to see cars and RVs parked in the right lane in the one-way sections; it's permitted.

Allow a couple of hours so you can stop along the way. You can rent an audio tour on cassette or CD for $13 (including directions, an instruction sheet, and a map) at the Hulls Cove Visitor Center. Another option is to pick up the drive-it-yourself tour booklet **Motorist Guide: Park Loop Road** ($1.50), available at the Thompson Island and Hulls Cove Visitor Centers.

⬛ The Carriage Roads

In 1913, John D. Rockefeller Jr. began laying out what eventually became a 57-mile carriage-road system, and he oversaw the project through the 1940s. Motorized vehicles have never been allowed on these lovely graded byways, making them real escapes from the auto world. Devoted now to multiple uses, the "Rockefeller roads" see hikers, bikers, baby

portation for the facility. The organization constructed a community trail on the remaining land. The Acadia Land Legacy Partnership between FOA, Acadia National Park, Maine Coast Heritage Trust, and conservation donors, purchases or protects privately held lands in or adjacent to Acadia's borders; recent achievements include the purchase of 37 acres on Lower Hadlock Pond and a conservation easement that will protect 1,400 acres of intact woods and wetland bordering Acadia's Schoodic District. FOA also funds more than 130 seasonal staff serving the park.

You can join FOA and its 3,500 members and support this worthy cause; memberships start at $35/year. You can also lend a hand while you're here: FOA and the park organize volunteer work parties for Acadia trail, carriage-road, and other outdoor maintenance three times weekly (8:20am-12:30pm Tues., Thurs., and Sat.) between June and Columbus Day. Call the recorded information line (207/288-3934) for the work locations, or call the FOA office for answers to questions. The meeting point is Park Headquarters (Eagle Lake Rd./Rte. 233, Bar Harbor), about three miles west of town.

This is a terrific way to give something back to the park, and the camaraderie is contagious. Take your own water, lunch, and bug repellent. Dress in layers and wear closed-toe shoes. More than 10,000 volunteer hours go toward this effort each year.

Each summer, Friends of Acadia also sponsors a handful of **Ridge Runners,** who work under park supervision and spend their days out and about on the trails repairing cairns, watching for lost hikers, and handing out Leave No Trace information. FOA also hires more than a dozen area teens each summer for the Acadia Youth Conservation Corps, which does trail and carriage-road work, and the Acadia Youth Technology Team, a youth-powered think tank coming up with new ways to get young people excited about the park.

If you happen to be in the region on the first Saturday in November, call the FOA office to register for the annual carriage-road cleanup, which usually draws up to 500 or so volunteers. Bring water and gloves; there's a free hot lunch at midday for everyone who participates. It's dubbed Take Pride in Acadia Day—indeed an apt label.

strollers, wheelchairs, and even horse-drawn carriages. Fortunately, a $6 million restoration campaign, undertaken during the 1990s, has done a remarkable job of upgrading surfaces, opening overgrown panoramas, and returning the roads to their original 16-foot width.

Pick up a free copy of the carriage-road map at any of the centers selling park passes. The busiest times are 10am-2pm.

The most crowded carriage roads are those closest to the visitors center—the Witch Hole Pond Loop, Duck Brook, and Eagle Lake. Avoid these, opting instead for roads west of Jordan Pond, or go early in the morning or late in the day. Better still, go off-season, when you can enjoy the fall foliage (late Sept.-mid-Oct.) or winter's cross-country skiing.

If you need a bicycle to explore the carriage roads, you can rent one in Bar Harbor,

Northeast Harbor, or Southwest Harbor. Be forewarned that hikers are allowed on the carriage roads that spill over onto private property south of the Jordan Pond House, but these are off-limits to bicyclists. The no-biking areas are signaled with Green Rock Company markers. The carriage-road map clearly indicates the biking and no-biking areas. Bicyclists must be especially speed-sensitive on the carriage roads, keeping an eye out for hikers, horseback riders, small children, and the hearing impaired.

HORSE-DRAWN CARRIAGE RIDES

To recapture the early carriage-roads era, take one of the horse-drawn open-carriage tours run by **Carriages of Acadia** (Park Loop Rd., Seal Harbor, 877/276-3622, www.carriagesofacadia.com), based at Wildwood Stables, a mile south of the Jordan Pond House. Four one- and two-hour tours start at 9am daily mid-June-mid-October. Reservations are not required, but they're encouraged, especially in midsummer. The best outing is the two-hour **Day Mountain Summit** ($26 adults, $10 ages 6-12, $7 ages 2-5) sunset ride. Other routes are around $20-26 adults, $9-10 children, $7 little kids. If you take the two-hour carriage ride to Jordan Pond House departing at 1:15pm on weekends ($20 adults, not including food and beverages), you're guaranteed a reserved lawn chair for tea and popovers.

Bass Harbor Head Light

At the southern end of Mount Desert's western "claw," follow Route 102A to the turnoff toward Bass Harbor Head. Drive or bike to the end of Lighthouse Road, walk down a steep wooden stairway, and look up and to the right. Voilà! **Bass Harbor Head Light**—its red glow automated since 1974—stands sentinel at the eastern entrance to Blue Hill Bay. Built in 1858, the 26-foot tower and light keeper's house are privately owned, but the dramatic setting captivates photographers.

Baker Island

The best way to get to—and to appreciate—history-rich Baker Island is on the ranger-narrated Acadia National Park Baker Island Tour aboard the *Miss Samantha,* booked through **Bar Harbor Whale Watch Co.** (1 West St., Bar Harbor, 207/288-2386 or 888/942-5374, www.barharborwhales.com, $46 adults, $27 ages 6-14, $9 under age 6). The half-day tours are offered mid-June-mid-September and include access via skiff to the 130-acre island with a farmstead, a lighthouse, and intriguing rock formations. The return trip provides a view from the water of Otter Cliffs (bring binoculars and look for climbers), Thunder Hole, Sand Beach, and Great Head. Call for the current schedule.

RECREATION
Hikes

If you're spending more than a day on Mount Desert Island, plan to buy a copy of *A Walk in the Park: Acadia's Hiking Guide,* by Tom St. Germain, which details more than 60 hikes, including some outside the park. Remember that pets are allowed on park trails, but only on leashes no longer than six feet. Four of the Island Explorer bus routes are particularly useful for hikers, alleviating the problems of backtracking and car-jammed parking lots. Here's a handful of favorite Acadia hikes, from easy to rugged.

These three easy trails are ideal for young families. **Jordan Pond Nature Trail** starts at the Jordan Pond parking area. This is an easy, wheelchair-accessible, one-mile wooded loop trail; pick up a brochure. Include Jordan Pond House (for tea and popovers) in your schedule. **Ship Harbor Nature Trail** starts at the Ship Harbor parking area, on Route 102A between Bass Harbor and Seawall Campground, in the southwestern corner of the island. The easy 1.3-mile loop trail leads to the shore; pick up a brochure at the trailhead. Ship Harbor is particularly popular among bird-watchers seeking warblers, and you just might spot an eagle while you picnic on the rocks. An even easier trail, with its parking area just east of the Ship Harbor parking area, **Wonderland** is 1.4 miles round-trip.

A moderate 1.4-mile loop, the **Great Head Trail** starts at the eastern end of Sand Beach, off the Park Loop Road. Park in the Sand Beach parking area, and cross the beach to the trailhead. Or take Schooner Head Road from downtown Bar Harbor and park in the small area where the road dead-ends. There are actually two trail loops here, both of which have enough elevation to provide terrific views.

Another moderate hike with great views is the 1.8-mile round-trip **Gorham Mountain Trail.** It's a great family hike, as kids especially love the Cadillac Cliffs section. Access is off the Park Loop Road, just beyond Thunder Hole.

The moderate hike to **Beech Mountain**'s summit has an abandoned fire tower, from which you can look out toward Long Pond and the Blue Hill Peninsula. A knob near the top is a prime viewing site for the migration of hawks and other raptors in September. Round-trip on the wooded route is about 1.2 miles, although a couple of side trails can extend it. You'll have less competition here in a quieter part of the park. Take Route 102 south from Somesville, heading toward Pretty Marsh. Turn left onto Beech Hill Road and follow it to the parking area at the end.

Beehive Trail and **Precipice Trail** are the park's toughest routes, with sheer faces and iron ladders; Precipice is often closed (usually mid-Apr.-late July) to protect nesting peregrine falcons. If challenges are your thing and these trails are open (check beforehand at the visitors center), go ahead. But a fine alternative in the difficult category is the **Beachcroft Trail** on Huguenot Head. Also called the Beachcroft Path, the trail is best known for its 1,500 beautifully engineered granite steps. Round-trip is 2.4 miles, or you can continue a loop at the top, taking in the **Bear Brook Trail** on Champlain Mountain, for about 4.4 miles. The parking area is just north of Route 3, near Sieur de Monts Spring.

Rock Climbing

Acadia has a number of splendid sites prized by climbers: the sea cliffs at Otter Cliffs and Great Head; South Bubble Mountain; Canada Cliff (on the island's western side); and the South Wall and the Central Slabs on Champlain Mountain. If you haven't tried climbing, never do it yourself without instruction. **Acadia Mountain Guides Climbing School** (228 Main St., Bar Harbor, 207/288-8186 or 888/232-9559, www.acadiamountainguides.com) and **Atlantic Climbing School** (ACS, 24 Cottage St., 2nd fl., Bar Harbor, 207/288-2521, www.acadiaclimbing.com) both provide instruction and guided climbs. Costs vary on the site, experience, session length, and number of climbers.

Swimming

Slightly below the Park Loop Road (take Island Explorer Route No. 3—Sand Beach), **Sand Beach** is the park's and the island's biggest sandy beach. Lifeguards are on duty during the summer, and even then, the biggest threat can be hypothermia. The

ACADIA REGION

© HILARY NANGLE

Otter Cliffs

saltwater is terminally glacial—in mid-July it still might not reach 60°F. The best solution is to walk to the far end of the beach, where a warmer shallow stream meets the ocean. Avoid the parking lot scramble by taking the Explorer bus.

The park's most popular freshwater swimming site, staffed with a lifeguard and inevitably crowded on hot days, is **Echo Lake,** south of Somesville on Route 102 and well signposted (take Island Explorer Route No. 7—Southwest Harbor).

If you have a canoe, kayak, or rowboat, you can reach swimming holes in **Seal Cove Pond** and **Round Pond,** both on the western side of Mount Desert. The eastern shore of **Hodgdon Pond** (also on the western side of the island) is accessible by car via Hodgdon Road and Long Pond Fire Road. **Lake Wood,** at the northern end of Mount Desert, has a tiny beach, restrooms, and auto access. To get to Lake Wood from Route 3, head west on Crooked Road to unpaved Park Road. Turn left and continue to the parking area, which will be crowded on a hot day, so arrive early.

Park Ranger Programs

Pick up a copy of *Acadia Weekly,* which details the ranger programs available. Don't miss these possibilities for learning more about the park's natural and cultural history.

The park ranger programs, lasting 1-3 hours, are great—and most are free. During July-August there are dozens of weekly programs, all listed in the *Beaver Log.* Included are early-morning (7am) bird-watching walks; moderate-level mountain hikes; tours of the historic Carroll Homestead, a 19th-century farm; Cadillac summit natural-history tours; children's expeditions to learn about tidepools and geology (an adult must accompany kids); trips for those in wheelchairs; and even a couple of tours a week in French. Some tours require reservations, but most do not; a few, including boat tours, have fees.

Park rangers also give the evening lectures during the summer in the amphitheaters at Blackwoods and Seawall Campgrounds.

CAMPING

Mount Desert Island has at least a dozen commercial campgrounds, but there are only two—Blackwoods and Seawall—within park boundaries on the island; neither has hookups. Both have seasonal restrooms with no showers, dumping stations, and seasonal amphitheaters, where rangers present evening programs.

Blackwoods Campground

Year-round **Blackwoods,** just off Route 3, five miles south of Bar Harbor, has 306 sites. Because of its location on the east side of the island, it's also the more popular of the two campgrounds. **Reservations** (877/444-6777, www.recreation.gov, credit card required) are suggested May 1-October 31, when the fee is $20/site/night. Reservations can be made up to six months ahead. In April and November, camping is $10; December-March it's free. A new trail, under construction in 2013, will connect the campground to the Ocean Drive trail system.

Seawall Campground

Reservations (877/444-6777, www.recreation.gov, credit card required) are accepted for half of the 214 sites at **Seawall Campground,** on Route 102A in the Seawall district, four miles south of Southwest Harbor, but the rest are first-come, first-served. In midsummer you'll need to arrive as early as 8:30am (when the ranger station opens) to secure one of the 200 or so sites. Seawall is open late May-September. The cost is $20/night for drive-up sites and $14/night for walk-in tent sites.

RV length at Seawall is limited to 35 feet, with the width limited to an awning extended no more than 12 feet. Generators are not allowed in the campground.

FOOD
◖ Jordan Pond House

The only restaurant within the park is the **Jordan Pond House** (Park Loop Rd., 207-276-3316, www.thejordanpondhouse.com, 11:30am-8pm daily mid-May-late Oct.,

JORDAN POND HOUSE

In the late 19th century, when Bar Harbor was in the throes of becoming "the great new place" to escape the heat of Washington DC, New York, Philadelphia, and the Midwest, gentle ladies and men patronized an unassuming farmhouse-teahouse on the shores of Jordan Pond. By 1895 or 1896, under the stewardship of Thomas McIntire, it became Jordan Pond House—a determinedly rustic establishment, with massive fieldstone fireplaces, serving afternoon tea and leisurely luncheons during the summer and fall.

And rustic it remained, well into the late 20th century—until leveled by a disastrous fire in the summer of 1979. At that point, it was owned by Acadia National Park. John D. Rockefeller Jr. had bought it in the 1930s and donated it to the park in the early 1940s. Since then it has been managed on behalf of the park by concessionaires.

Today, Jordan Pond House, the only restaurant within Acadia National Park, must rely on its framed antique photos to conjure up a bit of nostalgia for the bygone era. The building is modern and open, the pace in summer is frenetic, and the food is average. But the view from the lawn over Jordan Pond and the astounding Bubbles is incredible. Surely that hasn't changed.

So, at least once, brave the crowds and have afternoon tea on the lawn at Jordan Pond House (make reservations so you won't have to wait). Order tea or Oregon Chai or even cappuccino and fresh popovers (two) with extraordinary strawberry jam. You might even splurge and add a scoop of Jordan Pond ice cream.

Lunch (salads, sandwiches, and entrées include a popover) and afternoon tea are served 11:30am-5:30pm daily, inside or on the lawn. Dinner begins at 6pm, inside or on the porch.

You can buy a package of popover mix along with the jam in the gift shop, but if you don't and need a popover fix when you return home, here's the Jordan Pond House recipe:

JORDAN POND HOUSE POPOVERS

- 2 large eggs
- 1 cup whole milk
- 1 cup all-purpose flour (sifted)
- 1/2 teaspoon salt
- 1/8 teaspoon baking soda
- Preheat oven to 425°F. Beat eggs with electric mixer at high speed for three minutes. Reduce mixer speed to lowest setting and very gradually pour in half the milk. In separate bowl, combine sifted flour, salt, and baking soda and sift again.
- With mixer still running at slowest speed, add dry ingredients to egg-and-milk mixture. Turn off mixer and use rubber spatula to blend mixture thoroughly.
- Set mixer to medium speed and very gradually pour in remaining milk, blending for one minute. Raise mixer speed to highest setting and beat 10 minutes.
- Strain batter through fine-mesh strainer to remove lumps, then pour into well-buttered popover or custard cups. Bake 15 minutes. Without opening oven, reduce heat to 350°F and bake 15 more minutes (20 minutes if oven door has a window).
- Serve immediately, with fresh jam and room-temperature butter. Recipe makes two popovers. Increase as desired, but measure carefully. Popovers turn out significantly better if baked in ovenproof cups rather than in metal or glass.

11:30am-9pm late June-early Sept.), a modern facility in a spectacular waterside setting. Jordan Pond House began life as a rustic 19th-century teahouse; wonderful old photos still line the walls of the current incarnation, which went up after a disastrous fire in 1979. Afternoon tea is still a tradition, with tea, popovers, and extraordinary strawberry jam served on the lawn until 5:30pm daily in summer, weather permitting. It is not exactly a bargain at nearly $11, but it's worth it. However, Jordan Pond is far from a secret, so expect to wait for seats at the height of summer. Better yet, plan ahead and make reservations. Jordan Pond House is on the Island Explorer's Route No. 5. Note: The locally based Acadia Corporation managed Jordan Pond House for 80 years, but in a controversial 2013 decision, the park service awarded the contract to an out-of-state concessionaire beginning in 2014. Prices and recommendation reflect the previous operator.

Bar Harbor and Vicinity

In 1996, **Bar Harbor** (pop. 5,235) celebrated the bicentennial of its founding (as the town of Eden). In the late 19th century and well into the 20th, the town grew to become one of the East Coast's fanciest summer watering holes.

In those days, ferries and steam yachts arrived from points south, large and small resort hotels sprang up, and exclusive mansions (quaintly dubbed "cottages") were the venues of parties thrown by summer-resident Drexels, DuPonts, Vanderbilts, and prominent academics, journalists, and lawyers. The "rusticators" came for the season with huge entourages of servants, children, pets, and horses. The area's renown was such that by the 1890s, even the staffs of the British, Austrian, and Ottoman embassies retreated here for the summer from Washington DC.

The establishment of the national park in 1919 and the arrival of the automobile changed the character of Bar Harbor and Mount Desert Island; two World Wars and the Great Depression took an additional toll in myriad ways; but the coup de grâce for Bar Harbor's era of elegance came with the Great Fire of 1947, a wind-whipped conflagration that devastated more than 17,000 acres on the eastern half of the island and leveled gorgeous mansions, humble homes, and more trees than anyone could ever count. Only three people died, but property damage was estimated at $2 million. Whole books have been written about the October inferno; fascinating scrapbooks in Bar Harbor's Jesup Memorial Library dramatically relate the gripping details of the story. Even though some of the elegant cottages have survived, the fire altered life here forever.

SIGHTS
◖ Abbe Museum
The **Abbe Museum** is a superb introduction to prehistoric, historic, and contemporary Native American tools, crafts, and other cultural artifacts, with an emphasis on Maine's Micmac, Maliseet, Passamaquoddy, and Penobscot people. Everything about this privately funded museum, established in 1927, is tasteful. It has two campuses: The main campus (26 Mt. Desert St., Bar Harbor, 207/288-3519, www.abbemuseum.org, 10am-5pm daily late May-early Nov., call for off-season hours, $6 adults, $2 ages 6-15) is home to a collection spanning nearly 12,000 years. Museum-sponsored events include crafts workshops, hands-on children's programs, archaeological field schools, and the **Native American Festival** (held at the College of the Atlantic, usually the first Saturday after the Fourth of July).

Admission to the in-town Abbe also includes admission to the museum's original site in the park, about 2.5 miles south of Bar Harbor, at Sieur de Monts Spring, where Route 3 meets the Park Loop Road (10am-5pm daily late May-mid-Oct.). Inside a small but handsome National Historic Register building are displays from a 50,000-item collection. Admission to only the Sieur de Monts Spring Abbe is $3 adults, $1 ages 6-15; admission here can be credited to main museum fees.

While you're at the original Abbe Museum site, take the time to wander the paths in the adjacent **Wild Gardens of Acadia,** a 0.75-acre microcosm of more than 400 plant species native to Mount Desert Island. Twelve separate display areas, carefully maintained and labeled by the Bar Harbor Garden Club, represent

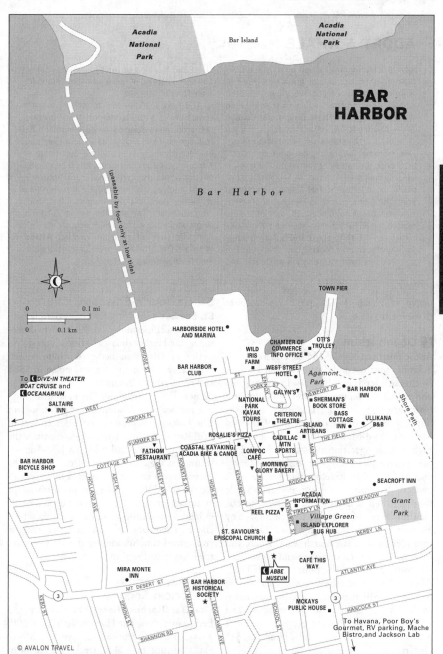

Acadia National Park

Bar Island

Acadia National Park

BAR HARBOR

Bar Harbor

(passable by foot only at low tide)

0   0.1 mi
0   0.1 km

TOWN PIER

HARBORSIDE HOTEL AND MARINA

WILD IRIS FARM

CHAMBER OF COMMERCE INFO OFFICE

OTT'S TROLLEY

BAR HARBOR CLUB

WEST STREET HOTEL

Agamont Park

To ◖DIVE-IN THEATER BOAT CRUISE and ◖OCEANARIUM

SALTAIRE INN

GALYN'S

NEWPORT DR

BAR HARBOR INN

NATIONAL PARK KAYAK TOURS

SHERMAN'S BOOK STORE

CRITERION THEATRE

BASS COTTAGE INN

ULLIKANA B&B

ISLAND ARTISANS

JORDAN PL

ROSALIE'S PIZZA

CADILLAC MTN SPORTS

THE FIELD

BAR HARBOR BICYCLE SHOP

SUMMER ST

FATHOM RESTAURANT

COASTAL KAYAKING/ ACADIA BIKE & CANOE

LOMPOC CAFE

STEPHENS LN

MORNING GLORY BAKERY

SEACROFT INN

COTTAGE ST

ACADIA INFORMATION

ALBERT MEADOW

Grant Park

REEL PIZZA

Village Green

ISLAND EXPLORER BUS HUB

DERBY LN

ST. SAVIOUR'S EPISCOPAL CHURCH

MIRA MONTE INN

★ ◖ABBE MUSEUM

CAFÉ THIS WAY

ATLANTIC AVE

MT DESERT ST

BAR HARBOR HISTORICAL SOCIETY

3

MCKAYS PUBLIC HOUSE

3

HANCOCK ST

SHANNON RD

To Havana, Poor Boy's Gourmet, RV parking, Mache Bistro, and Jackson Lab

WEST ST

BRIDGE ST

KEBO ST

HOLLAND AVE

ASH PL

GREELEY AVE

ROBERTS AVE

HIGH ST

KENNEBEC ST

RODICK ST

RODICK PL

FIREFLY LN

KENNEBEC PL

MAIN ST

YORK ST

LENOX ST

SPRING ST

GLEN MARY RD

LEDGELAWN AVE

SCHOOL ST

Shore Path

© AVALON TRAVEL

ADOPT A WHALE

Here's a trump card: When everyone else is flashing photos of kids or grandkids, you can whip out images of your very own adopted whale. And for that, you can thank Allied Whale's **Adopt-a-Whale** program at College of the Atlantic (COA) in Bar Harbor.

In 1972, COA established Allied Whale, a marine-mammal laboratory designed to collect, interpret, and apply research on the world's largest mammal. Although Allied Whale's primary focus is the Gulf of Maine, its projects span the globe, involving international scientific collaboration. Since 1981, part of the research has involved assembling an enormous photo collection (more than 25,000 images) for identification of specific humpback and finback whales (with names such as Quartz and

Elvis) and tracking of their migration routes. The photo catalog of finbacks already numbers more than 1,000.

And here's where the adoption program comes in—it's a way to support the important research being done by Allied Whale and its colleagues. If you sign up as an adoptive "parent" for a year, you'll receive a Certificate of Adoption, a large color photo and a biography of your whale, its sighting history, an informational booklet, and an Adopt a Whale-Allied Whale bumper sticker. It's a superb gift for budding scientists. The adoption fee is $30 for a single whale or $40 for a mother and calf.

For further information, contact **Allied Whale** (207/288-5644, www.barharborwhalemuseum.org/adopt2.php).

---

native plant habitats; pick up the map-brochure that explains each.

🄲 Oceanarium

At the northern edge of Mount Desert Island, 8.5 miles northwest of downtown Bar Harbor, is this understated but fascinating spot, also called the **Maine Lobster Museum and Hatchery** (1351 Rte. 3, Bar Harbor, 207/288-5005, www.theoceanarium.com, 9am-5pm Mon.-Sat. mid-May-late Oct.). This low-tech, high-interest operation awes the kids, and it's pretty darn interesting for adults too. David and Audrey Mills have been at it since 1972 and are determined to educate visitors while showing them a good time. Visitors on tour view thousands of tiny lobster hatchlings, enjoy a museum, finger sea life in a touch tank, and meander along a salt marsh walk, where you can check out tidal creatures and vegetation. All tours begin on the hour and half hour. Allow 1-2 hours to see everything. Tickets are $15 adults, $10 ages 4-12, covering admission to the lobster hatchery, lobster museum, and touch tank; an expanded program includes a 45-minute Marsh Walk for $17 adults, $11 children.

St. Saviour's Episcopal Church

St. Saviour's (41 Mt. Desert St., Bar Harbor, 207/288-4215, 7am-dusk daily), close to downtown Bar Harbor, boasts Maine's largest collection of Tiffany stained-glass windows. Ten originals are here; an 11th was stolen in 1988 and replaced by a locally made window. Of the 32 non-Tiffany windows, the most intriguing is a memorial to Clarence Little, founder of The Jackson Laboratory and a descendant of Paul Revere. Images in the window include the laboratory, DNA, and mice. In July-August, volunteers regularly conduct free tours of the Victorian-era church, completed in 1878; call for the schedule or make an appointment for an off-season tour. The church is open for self-guided tours 8am-8pm daily—pick up a brochure in the back. If old cemeteries intrigue you, spend time wandering the 18th-century town graveyard next to the church.

The Bar Harbor Historical Society

The Bar Harbor Historical Society (33 Ledgelawn Ave., Bar Harbor, 207/288-0000, www.barharborhistorical.org, 1pm-4pm Mon.-Sat. mid-June-mid-Oct., free), in a Jacobean

Revival-style building listed on the National Register of Historic Places, has fascinating displays, stereopticon images, and a scrapbook about the 1947 fire that devastated the island. The photographs alone are worth the visit. Also here are antique maps, Victorian-era hotel registers, and other local memorabilia. In winter it's open by appointment.

For a sample of Bar Harbor before the great fire, wander over to upper West Street, which is on the National Register of Historic Places thanks to the remaining grand cottages that line it.

College of the Atlantic

A museum, a gallery, and a pleasant campus for walking are reasons to visit the **College of the Atlantic** (COA, 105 Eden St./Rte. 3, Bar Harbor, 207/288-5015, www.coa.edu), which specializes in human ecology, or humans' interrelationship with the environment. In a handsome renovated building that originally served as the first Acadia National Park headquarters, the **George B. Dorr Natural History Museum** (10am-5pm Tues.-Sat., donation) showcases regional birds and mammals in realistic dioramas made by COA students. The biggest attraction for children is the please-touch philosophy, allowing them to reach into a touch tank and to feel fur, skulls, and even whale baleen. The museum gift shop has a particularly good collection of books and gifts for budding naturalists.

Ask locally about the **Bar Harbor Whale Museum,** operated by research associates affiliated with the college's Allied Whale program. It closed for construction, but was expected to reopen in a new downtown location in 2014 or 2015. In the meantime, some exhibits have been relocated to the Dorr Museum.

Across the way is the **Ethel H. Blum Gallery** (207/288-5015, ext. 254, 11am-4pm Mon.-Sat. summer, 9am-5pm Mon.-Fri. during the academic year), a small space that hosts some intriguing exhibits.

Also on campus is the **Beatrix Farrand Garden,** behind Kaelber Hall. The garden, designed in 1928, contained more than 50 varieties of roses and was the prototype for the rose garden at Dumbarton Oaks in Washington DC. Both are known for Farrand's use of garden rooms, such as the walled terraces in this garden.

The first floor of **The Turrets,** a magnificent 1895 seaside cottage that's now an administration building, can be explored. Don't miss **Turrets Sea Side Garden,** fronting on the ocean, which was restored by a student in 2005. The central fountain, created by alumnus Dan Farrenkopf of Lunaform Pottery, was installed in 2009.

The college also offers excellent and very popular weeklong sessions of **Family Nature Camp** (800/597-9500, www.coa.edu/summer, July-early Aug., $900 adults, $460 ages 5-15 covers almost everything). It's essential to register well in advance; ask about early-season discounts. Families are housed and fed on the campus, and explore Acadia National Park with expert naturalist guides.

Check the college's calendar of events for lectures, conversations, and other events.

The college and its museum are 0.5 mile northwest of downtown Bar Harbor; take Island Explorer Route No. 2 (Eden Street).

Garland Farm

Fans of landscape architect Beatrix Farrand will want to visit **Garland Farm** (475 Bayview Dr., 207/288-0237, www.beatrixfarrandsociety.org), the ancestral home of Lewis Garland, who managed her Reef Point property. When Farrand dismantled that property in 1955, she moved here with the Garlands, engaging an architect to build an addition to the original farmhouse and barn using architectural elements from Reef Point. The property was sold a few times, and greatly reduced in size, until the Beatrix Farrand Society was formed in 2002 and purchased it in 2004. The society's goal is to restore Garland Farm to its Farrand-era design and condition and create a center for the study of design and horticulture. The property, now listed on the National Register of Historic Places, hosts special events and programs. Garland Farm is open for visits one or two days per week and tours by appointment.

Research Laboratories

Some of the world's top scientists live year-round or come to Bar Harbor in summer to work at two prominent scientific laboratories.

World renowned in genetic research, scientists at **The Jackson Laboratory for Mammalian Research** (600 Main St./Rte. 3, Bar Harbor, 207/288-6000, www.jax.org) study cancer, diabetes, muscular dystrophy, heart disease, and Alzheimer's disease, among others—with considerable success. The nonprofit research institution, locally called JAX or just "the lab," is also renowned for its genetics databases and for producing genetically defined laboratory mice, which are shipped to research labs worldwide. Free summer public tours (limited to 15 people; preregistration required) begin in the lab's visitors lobby and visit the lab's three main research wings. These show the evolution of facilities over the decades, beginning with the 1980s, and the guide discusses the genetic research occurring in each. The lab is 1.5 miles south of downtown Bar Harbor.

No less impressive is the **Mount Desert Island Biological Laboratory** (MDIBL, 159 Old Bar Harbor Rd., Salisbury Cove, 207/288-3605, www.mdibl.org), one of the few scientific research institutions in the world dedicated to studying marine animals to learn more about human health and environmental health. It is the only comprehensive effort in the country to sequence genomes. Tours are offered by advance reservation, with at least one week's notice. **Science Café** is a comfortable community science forum offered every other week at an off-site location. **Family Science Night,** held once or twice each summer, is an interactive program of performances, demonstrations, and hands-on science; reservations are recommended. In 2012, the lab won a $250,000 grant to work with the National Park Service and the Schoodic Education and Research Center to create a **Pathway to BioTrails,** a hands-on program to involve park visitors in scientific research. The program will monitor park flora and fauna using a genetic technique called DNA barcoding. Ultimately, the program will offer a range of citizen science projects organized around hiking, cycling, and sea-kayaking trails, allowing visitors, research scientists, and park staff to work together to assess the effect of environmental changes. The lab is six miles north of Bar Harbor off Route 3.

Bar Harbor and Park Tours

The veteran of the Bar Harbor-based bus tours is **Acadia National Park Tours** (tickets at Testa's Restaurant, Bayside Landing, 53 Main St., Bar Harbor, 207/288-0300, www.acadiatours.com, $30 adults, $15 under age 13), operating May-October. A 2.5-3-hour naturalist-led tour of Bar Harbor and Acadia departs at 10am and 2pm daily from downtown Bar Harbor (Testa's is across from Agamont Park, near the Bar Harbor Inn). Reservations are advised in midsummer and during fall-foliage season (late Sept.-early Oct.); pick up reserved tickets 30 minutes before departure.

If you have a time crunch, take the one-hour trolley-bus tour operated by **Oli's Trolley** (ticket office at 1 West St., Bar Harbor, 207/288-9899 or 866/987-6553, www.acadiaislandtours.com), which departs from the West Street boardwalk five times daily in July-August, and includes Bar Harbor mansion drive-bys and the Cadillac summit. Purchase tickets at Harbor Place (1 West St.), next to the town pier on the waterfront. Dress warmly if the air is at all cool; it's an open-air trolley. Cost is $15 adults, $10 under age 12. Reservations are advisable. The trolley also does 2.5-hour park tours two or three times daily May-October. Tickets are $29 adults, $15 under age 12. The bus and trolley routes both include potty stops.

Clip clop through downtown Bar Harbor in the same manner of those during the gilded age on a half-hour horse-drawn carriage ride with **Wild Iris Farm** ($25 adults, $12.50 children, departing from the Harborside Hotel on West St.).

Although the Island Explorer buses do reach a number of key park sights, they are not tour buses. There is no narration, the bus cuts off the Park Loop at Otter Cliffs, and it excludes the summit of Cadillac Mountain.

Bird-Watching and Nature Tours

For private tours of the park and other parts of the island, contact Michael Good at **Down East Nature Tours** (150 Knox Rd., Bar Harbor, 207/288-8128, www.downeastnaturetours.com). A biologist and Maine Guide, Good is simply batty about birds. He has spent more than 25 years studying the birds of North America, and he has even turned his home property on Mount Desert Island into a bird sanctuary. Good specializes in avian ecology in the Gulf of Maine, giving special attention to native and migrating birds. Whether you're a first-timer wanting to spot eagles, peregrine falcons, shorebirds, and warblers or a serious bird-watcher seeking to add to your life list, perhaps with a Nelson's sharp-tailed sparrow, Good's your man. Prices begin at $75 pp for four hours and include transportation from your lodging; kids are half price. Bring your own binoculars, but Good supplies a spotting scope. A two-hour wetland ecology tour is $40 adults, $20 kids.

ENTERTAINMENT

The **Bar Harbor Town Band** performs for free at 8pm Monday and Thursday evenings July-mid-August in the bandstand on the Village Green (Main St. and Mt. Desert St., Bar Harbor).

You never know quite what's going to happen at **Improv Acadia** (15 Cottage St., Bar Harbor, 207/288-2503, www.improvacadia.com, $17 adults, $12 under age 11). Every show is different, as actors use audience suggestions to create comedy sketches. Shows are staged once or twice a night late May-mid-October. Dessert, snacks, and drinks are available.

The **Bar Harbor Music Festival** (207/288-5744 in July-Aug., 212/222-1026 off-season, www.barharbormusicfestival.org), a summer tradition since 1967, emphasizes up-and-coming musical talent in a series of classical, jazz, and pop concerts and even an opera, usually Friday and Sunday early July-early August, at various island locations that include local inns and an annual outdoor concert in Acadia National Park. Tickets are $25-40 adults, $15 students, and can be purchased at the festival office building (59 Cottage St., Bar Harbor). Reservations are advised.

The nonprofit, community-based **Harborside Shakespeare Company** (207/939-6929, www.harborsideshakespeare.org) performs one of the bard's works each summer.

Theaters

Built in 1932 and listed on the National Register of Historic Places, the beautifully refurbished **Criterion Theatre and Arts Center** (35 Cottage St., Bar Harbor) is an 877-seat art deco classic, with an elegant floating balcony. In 2007 it gained nonprofit status, with a mission to make arts and theater more accessible through diverse programs, but financial pressures caused it to close. It's occasionally open for films or special events.

Combine pizza with your picture show at **Reel Pizza Cinerama** (33 Kennebec Pl., Bar Harbor, 207/288-3811 for films, 207/288-3828 for food, www.reelpizza.net). Two films are screened nightly on each of two screens. All tickets are $6; pizzas start at $9. Doors open at 4:30pm; get there early for the best seats.

EVENTS

Bar Harbor is home to numerous special events; here's just a sampling. For more, call 800/345-4617 or visit www.barharbormaine.com.

In early June, the annual **Acadia Birding Festival** (www.acadiabirdingfestival.com) attracts bird-watchers with guided walks, boating excursions, tours, talks, and meals.

In late June, **Legacy of the Arts** is a week-long celebration of music, art, theater, dance, and history, with tours, exhibits, workshops, concerts, lectures, demonstrations, and more.

The **Fourth of July** is always a big deal in Bar Harbor, celebrated with a 6am blueberry-pancake breakfast, a 10am parade, an 11am seafood festival, a band concert, and fireworks. A highlight is the Lobster Race, a crustacean competition drawing contestants such as Lobzilla and Larry the Lobster in a four-lane saltwater tank on the Village Green.

ACADIA REGION

Independence Day celebrations in the island's smaller villages always evoke a bygone era.

The Abbe Museum, the College of the Atlantic, and the Maine Indian Basketmakers Alliance sponsor the annual **Native American Festival** (10am-4pm first Sat. after July 4, free), featuring baskets, beadwork, and other handicrafts for sale as well as Indian drumming and dancing, held at College of the Atlantic.

In even-numbered years, the **Mount Desert Garden Club Tour** (www.gcmdgardenday.com) presents a rare chance to visit some of Maine's most spectacular private gardens on a Saturday in late July.

The **Directions Craft Show** fills a weekend in late July or early August with extraordinary displays and sales of crafts by members of the Maine Crafts Guild. You'll find it at Mount Desert Island High School (Rte. 233/Eagle Lake Rd., Bar Harbor).

The mid-September **Acadia Night Sky Festival** (www.acadianightskyfestival.com) celebrates Acadia's stellar stargazing with arts and science events, presentations, and activities.

SHOPPING

Bar Harbor's boutiques—running the gamut from attractive to kitschy—are indisputably visitor oriented; many shut down for the winter.

Downtown Bar Harbor's best fine crafts gallery is **Island Artisans** (99 Main St., Bar Harbor, 207/288-4214, www.islandartisans.com). More than 100 Maine artists are represented here, and the quality is outstanding. You'll find basketwork, handmade paper, wood carvings, blown glass, jewelry, weaving, metalwork, ceramics, and more.

For more than three decades, **Alone Moose Fine Crafts** (78 West St., Bar Harbor, 207/288-4229, www.finemainecrafts.com) has lured collectors and browsers with its selection of sculpture, pottery, jewelry, and other works.

Toys, cards, and newspapers blend in with the new-book inventory at **Sherman's Book Store** (56 Main St., Bar Harbor, 207/288-3161). It's just the place to pick up maps and trail guides for fine days and puzzles for foggy days.

RECREATION
Walks

A real treat is a stroll along downtown Bar Harbor's **Shore Path**, a well-trodden granite-edged byway built around 1880. Along the craggy shoreline are granite-and-wood benches, town-owned **Grant Park** (great for picnics), birch trees, and several handsome mansions that escaped the 1947 fire. Offshore are the four Porcupine Islands. The path is open 6:30am-dusk, and leashed pets are allowed. Allow about 30 minutes for the mile loop, beginning next to the town pier and the Bar Harbor Inn and returning via Wayman Lane.

Check local newspapers or the Bar Harbor Chamber of Commerce visitor booklet for the times of low tide, then walk across the gravel bar to wooded **Bar Island** (formerly Rodick's Island) from the foot of Bridge Street in downtown Bar Harbor. Shell heaps recorded on the eastern end of the island indicate that Native Americans enjoyed this turf in the distant past. You'll have the most time to explore the island during new-moon or full-moon low tides, but no more than four hours—about 1.5 hours before and after low tide. Be sure to wear a watch so you don't get trapped (for up to 10 hours). The foot of Bridge Street is also an excellent kayak-launching site.

About a mile from downtown along Main Street (Rte. 3) is **Compass Harbor,** a section of the park where you can stroll through woods to the water's edge and explore the overgrown ruins of Acadia National Park cofounder George Dorr's home.

Five trails wind through The Nature Conservancy's forested 110-acre **Indian Point-Blagden Preserve**, a rectangular parcel with island, hill, and bay vistas. Seal-watching and bird-watching are popular, and there are harbor seals on offshore rocks as well as woodpeckers and 130 other species in blowdown areas. To spot the seals, plan your hike around low tide, when they'll be sprawled on the rocks close to shore. Wear rubberized shoes. Bring binoculars or use the telescope installed here for the purpose. To keep from disturbing the seals, watch quietly and avoid jerky movements. Park near

© TOM NANGLE

Walkers on Bar Harbor's Shore Path have views of the Porcupine Islands.

the preserve entrance and follow the Big Woods Trail, which runs the length of the preserve. A second parking area is farther in, but then you'll miss much of the preserve. When you reach the second parking area, just past an old field, bear left along the Shore Trail to see the seals. Register at the caretaker's house (just beyond the first parking lot, where you can pick up bird and flora checklists), and respect private property on either side of the preserve. It's open dawn-6pm daily year-round. From the junction of Routes 3 and 102/198, continue 1.8 miles to Indian Point Road and turn right. Go 1.7 miles to a fork and turn right. Watch for the preserve entrance on the right, marked by a Nature Conservancy oak leaf.

Bicycling

With all the great biking options, including 33 miles of carriage roads open to bicycles and some of the best roadside bike routes in Maine, you'll want to bring a bike or rent one here.

The Minutolo family's **Bar Harbor Bicycle Shop** (141 Cottage St., Bar Harbor, 207/288-3886, www.barharborbike.com), on the corner of Route 3, has been in business since 1977. If you have your own bike, stop here for advice on routes—the Minutolos have cycled everywhere on the island and can suggest the perfect mountain-bike or road-bike loop based on your ability and schedule. The shop has rentals varying from standard mountain bikes to full-suspension models and even tandems as well as all the accessories and gear you might need; rates begin at about $25/day. Hours in summer are 8am-6pm daily, 9am-5pm spring and fall. The shop also can give you the schedule for local rides organized by the **Downeast Bicycle Club** (www.downeast-bicycleclub.ning.com).

Sea Kayaking

National Park Kayak Tours (39 Cottage St., Bar Harbor, 207/288-0342 or 800/347-0940, www.acadiakayak.com) limits its Registered Maine Guide-led tours to a maximum of six tandem kayaks per trip. Four-hour morning, midday, afternoon, or sunset paddles are

© TOM NANGLE

ACADIA REGION

Excursion boats and sea-kayaking trips depart from the piers in Bar Harbor.

offered, including shuttle service, a paddle and safety lesson, and a brief stop, for $48 pp in July-August, $44 off-season. Most trips cover about six miles. Multiday camping trips also are offered. Try to make reservations at least one day in advance.

Golf

Duffers first teed off in 1888 at **Kebo Valley Golf Club** (100 Eagle Lake Rd./Rte. 233, Bar Harbor, 207/288-5000, www.kebovalleyclub. com, May-Oct.), Maine's oldest club and the eighth-oldest in the nation. The 17th hole became legendary when it took President William Howard Taft 27 strokes to sink a ball in 1911.

Boat Excursions
◖ DIVE-IN THEATER BOAT CRUISE

You don't have to go diving in these frigid waters; others will do it for you. When the kids are clamoring to touch slimy sea cucumbers and starfish at various touch tanks in the area, they're likely to be primed for Diver Ed's

Dive-In Theater Boat Cruise (207/288-3483 or 800/979-3370, www.divered.com), departing from the College of the Atlantic pier (105 Eden St., Bar Harbor). Ed Monat, former Bar Harbor harbormaster and College of the Atlantic grad, heads the crew aboard the 46-passenger *Starfish Enterprise,* which goes a mile or two offshore where Ed, a professional diver, goes overboard with a video camera and a mini-Ed, who helps put things in proportion. You and the kids stay on deck, all warm and dry, along with Captain Evil, who explains the action on a TV screen. There's communication back and forth, so the kids can ask questions as the divers pick up urchins, starfish, crabs, lobsters, and other sea life. When Ed resurfaces, he brings a bag of touchable specimens—another chance to pet some slimy creatures (which go back into the water after show-and-tell). It's a great concept. Watch the kids' expressions— this is a big hit. The two-hour trips depart three times daily Monday-Friday, twice daily Saturday, and once on Sunday early July-early September; fewer trips are made in spring and fall. The cost is $40 adults, $35 seniors, $30 ages 5-12, $15 under age 5. Usually twice weekly there's a park ranger or naturalist on board and the tour lasts for three hours— check the park's *Beaver Log* newspaper or Diver Ed's website for the schedule and reservation information—these trips cost an additional $5. Advance reservations are strongly recommended.

WHALE-WATCHING AND PUFFIN-WATCHING

Whale-watching boats go as far as 20 miles offshore, so no matter what the weather in Bar Harbor, dress warmly and bring more clothing than you think you'll need—even gloves, if you're especially sensitive to cold. I've been out on days when it's close to 90°F on the island but feels more like 30°F in a moving boat on the open ocean. Motion-sensitive children and adults should plan in advance for appropriate medication, such as seasickness pills or patches. Adults are required to show a photo ID when boarding the boat.

Whale-watching, puffin-watching, and combo excursions are offered by **Bar Harbor Whale Watch Company** (1 West St., Bar Harbor, 207/288-2386 or 800/942-5374, www.barharborwhales.com), sailing from the town pier (1 West St.) in downtown Bar Harbor. The company operates under various names, including Acadian Whale Watcher, and has a number of boats. Most trips are accompanied by a naturalist (often from Allied Whale at the College of the Atlantic), who regales passengers with all sorts of interesting trivia about the whales, porpoises, seabirds, and other marine life spotted along the way. In season, some trips go out as far as the puffin colony on Petit Manan Light. Trips depart daily late May-late October, but with so many options it's impossible to list the schedule—call for the latest details. Tickets are around $60 adults, $33 ages 6-14, $9 under age 6. A portion of the ticket price benefits Allied Whale, which researches and protects marine animals in the Gulf of Maine.

Trips may extend longer than the time advertised, so don't plan anything else too tightly around the trip.

Scenic Nature Cruises (1.5-2 hours) and kid-friendly **Lobster** and **Seal Watch Cruises** (1.5 hours) are also offered. Rates for these are around $30 adults, $25 children, $18 ages 6-14, and $5 or less for little kids.

SAILING

Captain Steve Pagels, under the umbrella of **Downeast Windjammer Cruises** (207/288-4585 or 207/288-2373, www.downeastwindjammer.com), offers 1.5-2-hour day sails on the 151-foot steel-hulled *Margaret Todd,* a gorgeous four-masted schooner with tanbark sails that he designed and launched in 1998. Trips depart at 10am, 2pm, and around sunset daily mid-May-mid-October (weather permitting) from the Bar Harbor Inn pier, just east of the town pier in downtown Bar Harbor. You'll get the best wildlife sightings on the morning trip, but better sailing on the afternoon trip; there's live music on the sunset one. A park ranger narrates some morning sails. Buy tickets either at

the pier, at 27 Main St., or online with a credit card; plan to arrive at least half an hour early. The cost is $38 adults, $35 seniors, $28 ages 6-11, $5 ages 2-5. Dogs are welcome on all sails.

SEA VENTURE

Captain Winston Shaw's custom boat tour by **Sea Venture** (207/288-3355, www.svboat-tours.com) lets you design the perfect trip aboard *Reflection,* a 20-foot motor launch. Captain Shaw, a Registered Maine Guide and committed environmentalist, specializes in nature-oriented tours. He's the founder and director of the Coastal Maine Bald Eagle Project, and he was involved in the inaugural Earth Day celebration in 1970. He's been studying coastal birds for more than 25 years. You can pick from 10 recommended cruises lasting 1-8 hours, or design your own. In any case, the boat is yours. The boat charter rate is $100/hour for up to two people, $120 for three or four, and $150 for five or six. Captain Shaw can also arrange for picnic lunches. On longer trips, restroom stops are available. The boat departs from the Atlantic Oakes Motel pier, off Route 3 in Bar Harbor.

LOBSTER CRUISE

When you're ready to learn *the truth* about lobsters, sign up for a two-hour cruise aboard **Captain John Nicolai's** *Lulu* (56 West St., Bar Harbor, 207/963-2341 or 866/235-2341, www.lululobsterboat.com), a traditional Maine lobster boat that departs up to four times daily from the Harborside Hotel and Marina. Captain Nicolai provides an entertaining commentary on anything and everything, but especially about lobsters and lobstering. He hauls a lobster trap and explains intimate details of the hapless critters. Reservations are required. Cost is $30 adults, $27 seniors and active U.S. military, $17 ages 2-12. Free parking is available in the hotel's lot.

ACCOMMODATIONS

Unless otherwise noted, these properties operate seasonally; most are open May-October. Rates listed are for peak season.

© TOM NANGLE

A sail on the four-masted schooner *Margaret Todd* is a fine way to see Bar Harbor by sea.

Hotels and Motels

One of the town's best-known, most visible, and best-situated hotels is the **Bar Harbor Inn** (Newport Dr., Bar Harbor, 207/288-3351 or 800/248-3351, www.barharborinn.com, $209-385), a sprawling complex on eight acres overlooking the harbor and islands. The 153 rooms and suites vary considerably in style, from traditional inn to motel, and are in three different buildings. Continental breakfast is included (Wi-Fi is extra), and special packages, with meals and activities, are available—an advantage if you have children. The kids will appreciate the heated outdoor pool; adults might enjoy the full-service spa. Also under the same management and ownership (www.bar-harbor-hotels.com) is the family-oriented **Acadia Inn** (98 Eden St., Bar Harbor, 207/288-3500, www.acadiainn.com, $190), located between the park entrance and downtown Bar Harbor. Facilities include an outdoor heated pool, whirlpool tub, and laundry. Rates include continental breakfast, Wi-Fi, and in-room fridge.

The appropriately named **Harborside Hotel & Marina** (55 West St., Bar Harbor, 207/288-5033 or 800/238-5033, www.theharborside-hotel.com, from $290) fronts the water in downtown Bar Harbor. Most of the 187 guest rooms and suites have a water view and semi-private balcony. Some have large outdoor hot tubs. A full-service spa is located in the beautifully restored Bar Harbor Club. An Italian restaurant is in the hotel. Facilities also include an oceanfront outdoor heated pool, a hot tub, and a pier. Sharing use of those facilities is its sister property, the **West Street Hotel** (50 West St., 877/905-4498, www.theweststreethotel.com, from $289), a new and tony spot with a rooftop pool (ages 18 and older, only) overlooking downtown, harbor, islands, and ocean. Rooms have a nautical vibe, and those on the West Street-side have nice views. All have Wi-Fi, flat-screen TVs, and in-room fridge.

On the edge of downtown, across from College of the Atlantic, are two adjacent sister properties tiered up a hillside: **Wonder View Inn & Suites** (55 Eden St., Bar Harbor, 888/439-8439, www.wonderviewinn.com,

$110-260) and the **Bluenose Hotel** (90 Eden St., Bar Harbor, 207/288-3348 or 800/445-4077, www.barharborhotel.com, $220-540). The pet-friendly ($20/pet/night) Wonder View comprises four older motels on estate-like grounds with grassy lawns and mature shade, an outdoor pool, and a restaurant. Guest rooms vary widely, and rates reflect both style of accommodation and views; all have refrigerator, TV, Wi-Fi, and air-conditioning. The Bluenose, one of the island's top properties, comprises two buildings. Mizzentop is newest, and its guest rooms and suites are quite elegant, many with fireplaces, all with fabulous views and balconies. Also here are a spa, fitness center, indoor and outdoor pools, and a lounge with live music every evening. Stenna Nordica guest rooms, accessed from outdoor corridors, are more modest, but still have views.

On the edge of town, the **Cromwell Harbor Motel** (359 Main St., Bar Harbor, 207/288-3201 or 800/544-3201, www.cromwellharbor.com, $130-170) is set back from the road on nicely landscaped grounds with an outdoor pool. All guest rooms have air-conditioning, phones, TVs, microwaves, and refrigerators. The location puts all of downtown's sights within walking distance.

On the lower end of the budgetary scale are two neighboring motels: **Edenbrook Motel** (96 Eden St./Rte. 3, Bar Harbor, 207/288-4975 or 800/323-7819, www.edenbrookmotelbh.com, $80-120), with panoramic views of Frenchman Bay from some rooms, and the wee bit fancier **Highbrook Motel** (94 Eden St./Rte. 3, Bar Harbor, 207/288-3591 or 800/338-9688, www.highbrookmotel.com, $109-169), with Wi-Fi, in-room mini-fridge, and continental breakfast. Both are about 1.5 miles from Acadia's main entrance, one mile from downtown.

Clean and affordable, the **Belle Isle Motel** (910 Rte. 3, Bar Harbor, 207/288-5726, www.belleislemotel.net, $79-89), a vintage mom-and-pop roadside motel, delivers on both counts. Darren and Camille Taylor purchased the Belle in 2011 and have spruced it up. The rooms are small, but all have air-conditioning, TV, free local calls, Wi-Fi, and refrigerators;

deluxe rooms are more spacious, but closer to the road. Also on the premises are a heated pool, playground, picnic area, and guest laundry. A microwave is available for guest use.

If all you want is a room with a bed, **Robbins Motel** (396 Rte. 3, Bar Harbor, 207/288-4659 or 800/858-0769, www.robbinsmotel.com, $65), an older motel, has 30 small, unadorned (some might call them dismal) but clean, pine-paneled, queen-bed guest rooms. All have air-conditioning and TV; some have Wi-Fi. There is no charm and it's not quiet, but it's cheap. Off-season rates are as low as $36.

Inns and Bed-and-Breakfasts

Few innkeepers have mastered the art of hospitality as well as Roy Kasindorf and Hélène Harton, owners of **The Ullikana** (16 The Field, Bar Harbor, 207/288-9552, www.ullikana.com, $185-355), located in a quiet downtown location close to Bar Harbor's Shore Path. Roy and Hélène genuinely enjoy their guests. Hélène is a whiz in the kitchen; after one of her multicourse breakfasts, usually served on the water-view patio, you won't be needing lunch. She's also a decorating genius, blending antiques and modern art, vibrant color with soothing hues, and folk art with fine art. Roy excels at helping guests select just the right hike, bike route, or other activity. Afternoon refreshments provide a time for guests to gather and share experiences. Alpheus Hardy, Bar Harbor's first cottager, built the 10-room Victorian Tudor inn in 1885. The comfortable rooms all have private baths (although two are detached); many have working fireplaces, and some have private terraces with water views. The innkeepers also speak French.

Right next door is the gorgeously renovated and rejuvenated **Bass Cottage** (14 The Field, Bar Harbor, 207/288-1234 or 866/782-9224, www.basscottage.com, $230-380). Corporate refugees Teri and Jeff Anderholm purchased the 26-room 1885 cottage in 2003 and spent a year gutting it, salvaging the best of the old, and blending in the new to turn it into a luxurious and stylish 10-room inn. It retains its Victorian bones, yet is most un-Victorian

© TOM NANGLE

Even on a foggy morning, most guests dine on the harbor-view patio of The Ullikana.

balconies. All have TVs and Wi-Fi. A full breakfast is served either in the dining room or on the water-view deck. It's steps from downtown, but really, with a location like this, why leave?

Outside of town, in a serene location with fabulous views of Frenchman Bay, is Jack and Jeani Ochtera's **(Inn at Bay Ledge** (150 Sand Point Rd., Bar Harbor, summer 207/288-4204, www.innatbayledge.com, $175-400), an elegant, casual retreat tucked under towering pines atop an 80-foot cliff. Built in 1800 as a minister's home, it's been expanded and updated in the intervening years. Terraced decks descend to a pool and onto the lawn, which stretches to the cliff's edge. Stairs descend to a private stone beach below. Almost all guest rooms have water views; some have whirlpool tubs and/or private decks. A sauna and a steam shower are available. In the woods across the street are cottages, which lack the view but have use of the inn's facilities. Also on the premises is the Summer House ($475), a shingled cottage with a deck 25 feet from the edge of Frenchman Bay.

Much less pricey and a find for families is the **Seacroft Inn** (18 Albert Meadow, Bar Harbor, 207/288-4669 or 800/824-9694, www.seacroftinn.com, $109-149), well situated just off Main Street and near the Shore Path. All rooms in Bunny and Dave Brown's white multigabled cottage have air-conditioning, phones, TVs, refrigerators, and microwaves; a continental breakfast is available for $5 pp. Housekeeping is $10/day. Some rooms can be joined as family suites.

Marian Burns, a former math and science teacher, is the reason everything runs smoothly at **Mira Monte Inn** (69 Mount Desert St., Bar Harbor, 207/288-4263 or 800/553-5109, www.miramonte.com, $190-260), close (but not too close) to downtown. Born and raised here, and an avid gardener, Marian's a terrific resource for island exploring. Try to capture her during wine and cheese (5pm-7pm), and ask about her experience during the 1947 Bar Harbor fire. And don't miss her collection of antique Bar Harbor hotel photos. The 13 Victorian-style

in style. Guest rooms are soothingly decorated with cream- and pastel-colored walls and have phones, Wi-Fi, and flat-screen TVs with DVD players (a DVD library is available—valuable on a stormy day); many rooms have fireplaces and whirlpool tubs. The spacious and elegant public rooms—expansive living rooms, a cozy library, porches—flow from one to another. Teri puts her culinary degree to use preparing baked goods, fruits, and savory and sweet entrées for breakfast and evening refreshments. A guest pantry is stocked with tea, coffee, and snacks.

Situated on one oceanfront acre in the West Street Historical District, **The Saltair Inn** (121 West St., Bar Harbor, 207/288-2882, www.saltairinn.com, $195-370) was originally built in 1887 as a guesthouse. Innkeepers Kristi and Matt Losquadro and their young family now welcome guests in eight guest rooms, most of which are quite spacious, and five of which face Frenchman Bay. Frills vary by room but might include whirlpool tubs, fireplaces, and

rooms have air-conditioning, cable TV, and either a balcony or a fireplace, and some have whirlpool tubs. Also available are four suites, some with kitchen or kitchenette. Rates include an extensive hot-and-cold breakfast buffet.

Hostel

Not officially a hostel, but with a hostel-style atmosphere, and only for women, the **MDI YWCA** (36 Mount Desert St., Bar Harbor, 207/288-5008, $25-40/night; $75-100/week) has second- and third-floor single and double rooms, as well as a seven-bed solarium (dorm). Located in a historic downtown building next to the library and across from the Island Explorer bus hub, "the Y" has bathrooms on each floor, as well as a laundry room (coin-operated machines), a TV room, and shared kitchen facilities. There's zero tolerance for smoking, alcohol, and drugs (you'll need to sign an agreement). For summer and fall reservations, call way ahead, as the Y is popular with the island's young summer workers.

FOOD

You won't go hungry in Bar Harbor. The island's best collection of good, inexpensive restaurants are along Rodick Street, from Reel Pizza down to Rosalie's, which actually fronts on Cottage Street. You'll find a good ethnic mix. For sit-down restaurants, make reservations as far in advance as possible. Expect reduced operations during spring and fall; few places are open in winter.

Local Flavors

Free tastings are offered daily at **Bar Harbor Cellars** (854 Rte. 3, Bar Harbor, 207/288-3907, www.barharborcellars.com). The winery is in the early stages of using organic techniques to grow hybrid grapes. In the meantime, it's making wines from European and California grapes. Also here is a Maine chocolate room and a small selection of complementary foods, such as olives, cheese, and crackers.

Only a masochist could bypass **Ben and Bill's Chocolate Emporium** (66 Main St., Bar Harbor, 207/288-3281 or 800/806-3281),

which makes homemade candies and more than 50 ice cream flavors (including a dubious lobster flavor); the whole place smells like the inside of a chocolate truffle. It opens daily at 10am, with closing dependent on the season and crowds, but usually late in the evening.

That said, the most creative flavors come from **MDI Ice Cream** (7 Firefly Ln., Bar Harbor, 207/288-0999, and 325 Main St., Bar Harbor, 207/288-5664, www.mdiic.com). It's made in small batches, just five gallons at a time, using the finest ingredients. We're talking creamy, rich, delicious, and wild flavors.

Probably the least-expensive lunch or ice cream option in town is **West End Drug Co.** (105 Main St., Bar Harbor, 207/288-3318), where you can get grilled-cheese sandwiches, PBJ, and other white-bread basics as well as shakes, egg creams, and sundaes at the fountain.

Equally inexpensive, but with a healthful menu, is the **Take-A-Break Cafe** (105 Eden St., Bar Harbor, 207/288-5015, www.coa.edu) in Blair Dining Hall, at College of the Atlantic. If you find yourself on the college campus, perhaps for a boat tour or museum visit, consider eating here. The cafeteria-style café serves breakfast, lunch, and dinner on most weekdays, and although there are individual choices, the best deals are the all-you-can eat meals ($5-10). There are always vegetarian, vegan, gluten-free, and meat choices, and the selection is organic and local whenever possible. Even better, the food is excellent.

When it comes to pub-grub favorites, such as burgers and fish sandwiches, **The Thirsty Whale Tavern** (40 Cottage St., Bar Harbor, 207/288-9335, www.thirstywhaletavern.com, 11am-9pm daily, $6-12) does it right.

Combine a pizza with a first-run or art flick at **Reel Pizza Cinerama** (33 Kennebec Pl., Bar Harbor, 207/288-3811 for films, 207/288-3828 for food, www.reelpizza.net), where you order your pizza, grab an easy chair, and watch for your number to come up on the bingo board. Most films are screened twice nightly. Pizzas ($12-20 or by the slice) have cinematic names—Zorba the Greek, The Godfather,

Manchurian Candidate. Then there's Mussel Beach Party—broccoli, tomatoes, goat cheese, and smoked mussels. You get the idea. Reel Pizza opens daily at 4:30pm and has occasional Saturday matinees; closed Monday in winter. Arrive early; the best seats go quickly.

For breakfast or brunch, you can't beat **2 Cats** (130 Cottage St., Bar Harbor, 207/288-2808 or 800/355-2828, www.2catsbarharbor. com, 7am-1pm daily). Fun, funky, and fresh best describe both the restaurant and the food ($8-12). Dine inside or on the patio. Dinner is also served at 2 Cats—call for nights and hours. Three upstairs guest rooms are available for $165-195, less in winter—with breakfast, of course.

Escape the downtown madness at **Tea House 278** (278 Main St., Bar Harbor, 207/288-2781, www.teahouse278.com, 11am-7pm Wed.-Sun.), a traditional Chinese teahouse offering Gaiwan service, along with light fare, and even Mahjong.

Between Mother's Day and late October, the **Eden Farmers Market** operates out of the YMCA parking lot off Lower Main Street in Bar Harbor, 9am-noon each Sunday. You'll find fresh meats and produce, local cheeses and maple syrup, yogurt and ice cream, bread, honey, preserves, and even prepared Asian foods.

Picnic Fare
Although a few of these places have some seating, most are for the grab-and-go crowd.

For a light, inexpensive meal, you can't go wrong at **Morning Glory Bakery** (39 Rodick St., Bar Harbor, 207/288-3041, www.morning-glorybakery.com, 7am-5pm Mon.-Fri., 8am-5pm Sat.-Sun.). Fresh-baked goodies, breakfast and regular sandwiches, soups, and salads are all made from scratch.

Another good choice for take-out fare is **Downeast Deli** (65 Main St., Bar Harbor, 207/288-1001, 7am-4pm daily). You can get both hot and cold fresh lobster rolls as well as other sandwiches, soups, and salads.

At **Adelmann's Deli** (224 Main St., Bar Harbor, 207/288-0455, 11am-8pm)

build-your-own lunch sandwiches are $9. Choose from a variety of breads, Boar's Head-brand meats and cheeses, veggies, condiments, and more.

If you happen to be on Route 102 in the Town Hill area around lunchtime, plan to pick up picnic fare at **Mother's Kitchen** (Rte. 102, Town Hill, Bar Harbor, 207/288-4403, www.motherskitchenfoods.com, 9am-2pm Mon.-Fri.). The plain, minuscule building next to Salsbury's (look for the Real Good Food sign) is deceiving—it has been operating since 1995 and turns out 20 different sandwiches as well as deli salads, scones, breakfast sandwiches, great cookies, and pies.

Brewpubs and Microbreweries
Bar Harbor's longest-lived brewpub is the **Lompoc Cafe** (36 Rodick St., Bar Harbor, 207/288-9392, www.lompoccafe.com, 4:30pm-9:30pm daily late Apr.-mid-Dec.), with brews on tap. Go for pizzas, salads, and entrées ($8-21), along with boccie in the beer garden and live entertainment on weekends. After 9pm there's just beer and thin-crust pizza until about 1am.

Lompoc's signature Bar Harbor Real Ale and five or six others are brewed by the **Atlantic Brewing Company** (15 Knox Rd., Town Hill, in the upper section of the island, 207/288-2337, www.atlanticbrewing.com). Free brewery tours, including tastings, are given daily at 2pm, 3pm, and 4pm late May-mid-October. Also operating here in summer is **Mainely-Meat Bar-B-Q** (207/288-9200, 11:30am-7pm daily, $8-16), offering pulled pork, chicken, ribs, and similar fare for lunch and dinner.

Sip beers and sodas produced by **Bar Harbor Brewing Company** (8 Mt. Desert St., Bar Harbor, 207/288-4592, www.barharborbrewing.com) as well as wines from Bar Harbor Cellars.

Family Favorites
An unscientific but reliable local survey gives the best-pizza ribbon to **Rosalie's Pizza & Italian Restaurant** (46 Cottage St., Bar Harbor, 207/288-5666, www.rosaliespizza.

com, 4pm-10pm daily), where the Wurlitzer jukebox churns out tunes from the 1950s. Rosalie's earns high marks for consistency with its homemade pizza, in four sizes or by the slice, along with calzones and subs; there are lots of vegetarian options. If you need something a bit heartier, try the Italian dinners—spaghetti, eggplant parmigiana, and others—all less than $10, including a garlic roll. Beer and wine are available. Avoid the downstairs lines by heading upstairs and ordering at that counter, or call in your order.

Efficient, friendly cafeteria-style service makes **EPI's Pizza** (8 Cottage St., Bar Harbor, 207/288-5853, 11am-7pm daily Sept.-June, to 9pm daily July-Aug.) an excellent choice for subs, salads, pizzas, and even spaghetti. If the weather closes in, there are always the pinball machines in the back room.

Route 66 Restaurant (21 Cottage St., Bar Harbor, 207/288-3708, www.barharborroute66.com, 7am-about 8pm daily, $9-25), filled with 1950s memorabilia and old toys, is a fun restaurant that's a real hit with kids (check out the Lionel train running around just below the ceiling). The wide-ranging menu includes sandwiches, burgers, pizza, steak, chicken, seafood, and kids' choices. No raves here, just okay food in a fun atmosphere.

Good food at a fair price reels them into **Poor Boy's Gourmet** (300 Main St., Bar Harbor, 207/288-4148, www.poorboysgourmet.com, from 4:30pm daily). Until 6pm it serves an early-bird menu with about nine entrées and again as many seconds-on-us pasta choices for about $11. The price jumps just a bit after that, with most entrées running $12-20. There's even a relatively cheap lobster feast.

Savor the panoramic views over Bar Harbor, Frenchman Bay, and the Porcupine Islands along with breakfast or dinner at the **Looking Glass Restaurant** (Wonder View Inn, 50 Eden St., Bar Harbor, 207/288-5663, www.wonderviewinn.com, 7am-10:30am and 5:30pm-9pm daily, $11-38). It's quite casual, with choices ranging from sandwiches to rack of lamb. There's a children's menu, and the deck is pet-friendly.

Casual Dining

You can't go wrong at **Galyn's Galley** (17 Main St., Bar Harbor, 207/288-9706, www.galynsbarharbor.com, 11am-9pm daily Mar.-Nov., dinner entrées $12-31). Once a Victorian boardinghouse and later a 1920s speakeasy, Galyn's has been a popular restaurant since 1986. Lots of plants, modern decor, reliable service, a great downtown location, and several indoor and outdoor dining areas contribute to the loyalty of the clientele. Reservations are advisable in midsummer.

When you're craving fresh and delicious fare but not a heavy meal, the **Side Street Café** (49 Rodick St., Bar Harbor, 207/801-2591, www.sidestreetbarharbor.com, 11am-midnight daily, $8-26) delivers. It's a cheerful place with a relaxed demeanor combined with good service and a friendly attitude. The lobster roll and the crab melt earn high fives, as do the burgers.

Set back from the road behind a garden is the very popular **McKays Public House** (231 Main St., Bar Harbor, 207/288-2002, www.mckayspublichouse.com, 5pm-10pm daily, $11-26), a comfortable pub with seating indoors in small dining rooms or at the bar, or outdoors in the garden. The best bet is the classic pub fare, which includes shepherd's pie, burgers, and fish-and-chips. Fancier entrées, such as seafood risotto, are also available.

Casual, friendly, creative, and reliable defines **Cafe This Way** (14 Mt. Desert St., Bar Harbor, 207/288-4483, www.cafethisway.com, 7am-11:30am Mon.-Sat., 8am-1pm Sun., and 5:30pm-9:30pm daily, $16-25), where it's easy to make a meal out of the appetizers alone. Vegetarians will be happy here, and there's a gluten-free menu too. The breakfast menu is a genuine wake-up call ($5-9). It's not a choice for quiet dining.

Chef-owner Karl Yarborough is putting **Mache Bistro** (321 Main St., Bar Harbor, 207/288-0447, www.machebistro.com, from 5:30pm Tues.-Sat., $17-28) on the must-dine list. His interpretations of "French flavors with local flair" are creative without being over the top. This place is justifiably popular, so do make reservations.

Ethnic Fare

For Thai food, **Siam Orchid** (30 Rodick St., Bar Harbor, 207/288-9669, www.siamorchidrestaurant.net, 11am-11pm daily) gets the locals' nod, although it's a bit pricey. House specials run $14-20; curries and noodle dishes, such as pad thai, are $12-17. There are plenty of choices for vegetarians. Siam Orchid serves beer and wine only.

Sharing the same building is **Gringo's** (30 Rodick St., Bar Harbor, 207/288-2326, 11am-10pm daily), a Mexican hole-in-the-wall specializing in take-out burritos, wraps, homemade salsas, and smoothies, with almost everything—margaritas and beer included—less than $8. For a real kick, don't miss the jalapeño brownies.

For "American fine dining with Latin flair," head to ◖Havana (318 Main St., Bar Harbor, 207/288-2822, www.havanamaine.com, 5pm-10pm daily May-Nov., call for off-season hours, entrées $19-35), where the innovative Cuban-esque menu changes frequently to take advantage of what's locally available. Inside, bright orange walls and white tablecloths set a tone that's equally festive and accomplished. Outside, a wood-fired grill and open-air bar offer a tapas menu.

Fine Dining

Five miles south of Bar Harbor, in the village of Otter Creek, which itself is in the town of Mount Desert, is the inauspicious-looking **Burning Tree** (Rte. 3, Otter Creek, 207/288-9331, 5pm-10pm Wed.-Mon. late June-early Oct., closed Mon. after Labor Day, $19-30), which is anything but nondescript inside. Chef-owners Allison Martin and Elmer Beal Jr. have created one of Mount Desert Island's better restaurants, but it can get quite noisy when busy, which it usually is. Reservations are essential in summer. Specialties are imaginative seafood entrées and vegetarian dishes. The homemade breads and desserts are delicious. At the height of summer, service can be a bit rushed and the kitchen runs out of popular entrées. Solution: Plan to eat early; it's worth it.

Local fare gives a decidedly Maine twist to chef-co-owner Josh Heikkinen's creative entrées at **Fathom** (6 Summer St., 207/288-9664, www.fathombarharbor.com, 5:30pm-9pm daily). Depending on the season, you might find local halibut with fiddleheads, seared duck breast with rhubarb, drunken shrimp in tequila cream, grilled salmon with a Maine chimichurri, or his intriguing red snappah rolls, made with lobster and red hot dogs. Most entrées run $24-32.

Lobster

Nearly every restaurant in town serves some form of lobster (my top choice for a lobster roll is the Side Street Café).

Dine inside or on the dock at **Stewman's Lobster Pound** (35 West St., 207/288-0346, www.stewmanslobsterpound.com, 11am-10pm, daily), where the menu ranges from burgers to lobster.

Although it lacks the oceanfront location, **West Street Café** (76 West St., Bar Harbor, 207/288-5242, www.weststreetcafe.com, 11am-8pm daily) is a fine spot for a lobster dinner at a fair price. Dine before 6pm for the best price. There are other items on the menu, but the reason to go here is for the lobster (market price). A kids' menu is available.

INFORMATION AND SERVICES

The **Bar Harbor Chamber of Commerce** (1201 Bar Harbor Rd./Rte. 3, Trenton, 207/288-5103, www.barharbormaine.com) operates a seasonal info center at the corner of Main and Cottage Streets.

Once you're on Mount Desert, if you manage to bestir yourself early enough to catch sunrise on the Cadillac summit (you won't be alone—it's a popular activity), stop in at the chamber of commerce office later and request an official membership card for the **Cadillac Mountain Sunrise Club** (they'll take your word for it).

Jesup Memorial Library (34 Mount Desert St., Bar Harbor, 207/288-4245, www.jesup.lib.me.us) is open all year. The library holds its annual book sale on the third Saturday in August.

Find **public restrooms** at the park visitors centers, and in downtown Bar Harbor in Agamont Park, Harbor Place at the town pier, the municipal building (the fire and police station) across from the Village Green, and on the School Street side of the athletic field.

GETTING THERE AND AROUND

Bar Harbor is about 20 miles or about 30-45 minutes, depending upon traffic, via Route 3 from Ellsworth; about 45 miles or 75 minutes via Routes 1A and 3 from Bangor; and about 275 miles or five hours via Routes 195 and 3 from Boston. It's about 12 miles or 20 minutes via Routes 233 and 198 or 20 miles/35 minutes via Route 3 to Northeast Harbor.

Make it easy on yourself, help improve the air quality, and reduce stress levels by leaving your car at your lodging (or if day-tripping, at the Bar Harbor Chamber of Commerce on Route 3 in Trenton) and taking the Island Explorer bus.

RVs are not allowed to park near the town pier; designated RV parking is alongside the athletic field, on Lower Main and Park Streets, about eight blocks from the center of town.

Northeast Harbor

Ever since the late 19th century, the upper crust from Philadelphia has been summering in and around Northeast Harbor. Sure, they also show up in other parts of Maine, but it's hard not to notice the preponderance of Pennsylvania license plates surrounding Northeast Harbor's elegant "cottages" mid-July-mid-August.

Actually, even though Northeast Harbor is a well-known name with special cachet, it isn't even an official township; it's a zip-coded village within the town of **Mount Desert** (pop. 2,053), which collects the breathtaking property taxes and doles out the municipal services.

The attractive boutiques and eateries in Northeast Harbor's small downtown area cater to a casually posh clientele, and the well-protected harbor attracts a tony crowd of yachties. For their convenience, a palm-size annual directory, *The Redbook,* discreetly lists owners' summer residences and winter addresses—but no phone numbers.

Except for two spectacular public gardens and two specialized museums, not much here is geared to budget-sensitive visitors—but there's no charge for admiring the spectacular scenery.

Although all of Mount Desert Island is seasonal, Northeast Harbor is especially so, and it has a tiny and decreasing year-round population. Many businesses don't open until early July and close in early September.

SIGHTS
Somes Sound

As you head toward Northeast Harbor on Route 198 from the northern end of Mount Desert Island, you'll begin seeing cliff-lined **Somes Sound** on your right. Experts disagree as to whether Somes is a true fjord, but in any case it's a lovely chunk of real estate. The glacier-sculpted sound juts five miles into the interior of Mount Desert Island from its mouth, between Northeast and Southwest Harbors. Watch for the right-hand turn for Sargent Drive (no RVs allowed), and follow the lovely granite-lined route along the east side of the sound. Halfway along, a marker explains the geology of this spectacular natural inlet. There aren't many pullouts en route, and traffic can be fairly thick in midsummer, but don't miss it. Suminsby Park, off Sargent Drive, 0.8 mile from Route 3, is a fine place for a picnic. The park has rocky shore access, a hand-carry boat launch, picnic tables, grills, and an outhouse. An ideal way to appreciate Somes Sound is from the water—sign up for an excursion out of Northeast or Southwest Harbor.

© HILARY NANGLE

Asticou Azalea Garden

Gardens
◖ ASTICOU AZALEA GARDEN AND THUYA GARDEN

If you have the slightest interest in gardens, allow time for Northeast Harbor's two marvelous public gardens, both operated by the nonprofit **Mount Desert Land and Garden Preserve** (207/276-3727, www.gardenpreserve.org).

One of Maine's best spring showcases is the **Asticou Azalea Garden,** a 2.3-acre pocket where about 70 varieties of azaleas, rhododendrons, and laurels—many from the classic Reef Point garden of famed landscape designer Beatrix Farrand—burst into bloom. When Charles K. Savage, beloved former innkeeper of the Asticou Inn, learned the Reef Point garden was being undone in 1956, he went into high gear to find funding and managed to rescue the azaleas and provide them with the gorgeous setting they have today, across the road and around the corner from the inn. Serenity is the key—with a Japanese sand garden that's mesmerizing in any season, stone lanterns,

granite outcrops, pink gravel paths, and a tranquil pond. Try to visit early in the season and early in the morning to savor the effect. Blossoming occurs May-August, but the prime time for azaleas is roughly mid-May-mid-June. The garden is on Route 198, at the northern edge of Northeast Harbor, immediately north of the junction with Peabody Drive (Rte. 3). Watch for a tiny sign on the left (if you're coming from the north), marking access to the parking area. A small box suggests a $5 donation, and another box contains a garden guide ($2). Pets are not allowed in the garden. Take Island Explorer Route No. 5 (Jordan Pond) or Route No. 6 (Brown Mountain) and request a stop. Note: The Asticou Stream Trail, a lovely meander through fields and woods and down to the shoreline, connects the garden to the town. Look for a small signpost just north of the Asticou Inn and across from the Route 3 entrance to the garden.

Behind a carved wooden gate on a forested hillside not far from Asticou lies an enchanted garden also designed by Charles K. Savage and

THE MAINE SEA COAST MISSION

Remote islands and other isolated communities along Maine's rugged coastline may still have a church, but few have a full-time minister; fewer yet have a health-care provider. Yet these communities aren't entirely shut off from either preaching or medical assistance.

Since 1905, the **Maine Sea Coast Mission** (127 West St., Bar Harbor, 207/288-5097, www.seacoastmission.org), a nondenominational, nonprofit organization rooted in a Christian ministry, has offered a lifeline to these communities. The mission, based in Bar Harbor, serves nearly 2,800 people on eight different islands, including Frenchboro, the Cranberries, Swans, and Isle au Haut, as well as others living in remote coastal locations on the mainland. Its numerous, much-needed services include a Christmas program; in-school, after-school, and summer school programs; emergency financial assistance; food assistance; a thrift shop; ministers for island and coastal communities; scholarships; and health services.

Many of these services are delivered via the mission's Sunbeam V, a 75-foot diesel boat that has no limitations on when it can travel and few on where it can travel. In winter, it even serves as an icebreaker, clearing harbors and protecting boats from ice damage. During your travels in the Acadia region, you might see the Sunbeam V homeported in Northeast Harbor or on its rounds.

A nurse and a minister usually travel on the ship. The minister may conduct services on the island or on the boat, which also functions as a gathering place for fellowship, meals, and meetings. The minister also reaches out to those in need, marginalized, or ill, and often helps with island funerals. Onboard telemedicine equipment enables the nurse to provide much-needed health care, including screening clinics for diabetes, cholesterol, and prostate and skin cancer; flu and pneumonia vaccines; and tetanus shots.

The mission welcomes donations and volunteers. You can make a difference.

inspired by Beatrix Farrand. Special features of **Thuya Garden** are perennial borders and sculpted shrubbery. On a misty summer day, when few visitors appear, the colors are brilliant. Adjacent to the garden is **Thuya Lodge** (207/276-5130), former summer cottage of Joseph Curtis, donor of this awesome municipal park. The lodge, with an extensive botanical library and quiet rooms for reading, is open 10am-4:30pm daily late June-Labor Day. The garden is open 7am-7pm daily. A collection box next to the front gate requests a $5 donation per adult. To reach Thuya, continue on Route 3 beyond Asticou Azalea Garden and watch for the Asticou Terraces parking area (no RVs; two-hour limit) on the right. Cross the road and climb the Asticou Terraces Trail (0.4 mile) to the garden. Allow time to hang out at the three lookouts en route. Alternatively, drive 0.2 mile beyond the Route 3 parking area, watching for a minuscule Thuya Garden sign on the left.

Go 0.5 mile up the steep, narrow, and curving driveway to the parking area (but walking up reaps higher rewards). Or take Island Explorer Route No. 5 (Jordan Pond) and request a stop.

Note: It's possible to connect Asticou and Thuya Gardens by walking the Asticou Hill Trail, which follows an old road, or hiking the moderately difficult (lots of exposed roots) Eliot Mountain Trail. From the Asticou, the Asticou Hill Trail road across from the Asticou Inn provides access to both; it's a private road, but foot traffic has a right of way.

ABBY ALDRICH ROCKEFELLER GARDEN

The private **Abby Aldrich Rockefeller Garden** (207/276-3330 in season, www.rockgarden-maine.wordpress.com, free) was created in 1921, when the Rockefellers turned to renowned garden designer Beatrix Farrand to create a garden using treasures they'd brought back from Asia. The enclosed garden is a knockout, accented with secret passages, a sunken garden, English floral beds, Korean tombstone figures, a moon gate, and even yellow roof tiles from Beijing. It's open only one day a week from late July to early September, and numbers are limited, so reservations are vital; check the website for current details. A garden guide with map is provided, but you're free to explore at your own pace.

Petite Plaisance

On Northeast Harbor's quiet South Shore Road, **Petite Plaisance** is a special-interest museum commemorating noted Belgian-born author and college professor Marguerite Yourcenar (pen name of Marguerite de Crayencour), the first woman elected to the prestigious Académie Française. From the early 1950s to 1987, Petite Plaisance was her home, and it's hard to believe she's no longer here; her intriguing possessions and presence fill the two-story house, of particular interest to Yourcenar devotees. Free hour-long tours of the first floor are given in French or English, depending on visitors' preferences; French-speaking visitors often make pilgrimages here. The house is open for tours daily June 15-August 31. No children under 12 are allowed. Call 207/276-3940 at least a day ahead, between 9am and 4pm, for an appointment and directions, or write to Petite Plaisance Trust, P.O. Box 403, Northeast Harbor, ME 04662. Yourcenar admirers should request directions to Brookside Cemetery in Somesville, seven miles away, where she is buried.

Great Harbor Maritime Museum

Annual exhibits focusing on the maritime heritage of the Mount Desert Island area are held in the small, eclectic **Great Harbor Maritime Museum** (124 Main St., Northeast Harbor, 207/276-5262, www.greatharbormaritimemuseum.org, 10am-5pm Tues.-Sat. late June-Labor Day, $3), housed in the old village fire station and municipal building. ("Great Harbor" refers to the Somes Sound area—Northeast, Southwest, and Seal Harbors, as well as the Cranberry Isles.) Yachting, coastal trade, and fishing receive special emphasis. Look for the

canvas rowing canoe, built in Veazie, Maine, between 1917 and 1920; it's the only one of its kind known to exist today.

ENTERTAINMENT

Since 1964 the **Mount Desert Festival of Chamber Music** (207/276-3988, www.mtdesertfestival.org) has presented concerts in the century-old Neighborhood House on Main Street at 8:15pm Tuesday mid-July-mid-August. Tickets ($25 general admission, $10 students) are available at the Neighborhood House box office Monday-Tuesday during the concert season or by phone reservation.

SHOPPING

Upscale shops, galleries, and boutiques with clothing, artworks, housewares, antiques, and antiquarian books line both sides of Main Street, making for intriguing browsing and expensive buying (check the sale rooms of the clothing shops for bona fide bargains). The season is short, though, with some shops open only in July-August.

One must-visit is **Shaw Contemporary Jewelry** (100 Main St., 207/276-5000 or 877/276-5001, www.shawjewelry.com, year-round). Besides the spectacular silver and gold beachstone jewelry created by Rhode Island School of Design alumnus Sam Shaw, the work of more than 100 other jewelers is displayed exquisitely. Plus there are sculptures, Asian art, and rotating art exhibits. It all leads back toward a lovely light-filled garden. Prices are in the stratosphere, but appropriately so. As one well-dressed customer was overheard sighing to her companion: "If I had only one jewelry store to go to in my entire life, this would be it."

If you're traveling with children or if you have any interest in art, science, or nature, don't miss **The Naturalist's Notebook** (16 Main St., Seal Harbor, 207/801-2777, www.thenaturalistsnotebook.com) a shop and exploratorium. Owned by artist-photographer Pamelia Markwood and her *Sports Illustrated* writer/editor husband, Craig Neff, the shop has three stories full of engaging exhibits, books, and treasures. A branch operates at 15 Main St. in Northeast Harbor.

RECREATION
Boat Excursions
Northeast Harbor is the starting point for a couple of boat services headed for the **Cranberry Isles.** The vessels leave from the commercial floats at the end of the concrete municipal pier on Sea Street.

The 75-foot *Sea Princess* (207/276-5352, www.barharborcruises.com) carries visitors as well as an Acadia National Park naturalist on a 2.5-hour morning trip around the mouth of Somes Sound and out to Little Cranberry Island (Islesford) for a 50-minute stopover. The boat leaves Northeast Harbor at 10am daily mid-May-mid-October. A narrated afternoon trip departs at 1pm on the same route. Other trips operate, but not daily. These include a scenic 1.5-hour Somes Sound cruise, a three-hour sunset dinner cruise to the Islesford Dock Restaurant on Little Cranberry (Islesford), and a 1.5-hour sunset cruise of Somes Sound. Fees range $23-28 adults, $18 ages 5-12, $7 under age 5. Reservations are advisable for all trips, although even that provides no guarantee, since the cruises require a 15-passenger minimum.

The *Helen Brooks,* built in 1970, is one of two traditional Friendship sloops operated by **Downeast Friendship Sloop Charters** (Northeast Harbor Municipal Marina, 41 Harbor Dr., 207/266-5210, www.downeast-friendshipsloop.com); the other one sails out of Southwest Harbor. Private charters start at $250 for a two-hour sail, covering up to six passengers and including an appetizer and soft drinks; shared trips are $50/person for two hours, $75/person for three hours. A sunset sail is a lovely way to end a day.

ACCOMMODATIONS
Inns
For more than 100 years, the genteel **Asticou Inn** (Rte. 3, Northeast Harbor, 207/276-3344 or 800/258-3373, www.asticou.com, $195-380) has catered to the whims and weddings of Northeast Harbor's well-heeled summer rusticators. She's an elegant old gal that seems right out of a Hollywood romance movie set in the 1950s: Hardwood floors are topped with Asian and braided rugs, rooms are papered with floral or plaid wallpapers, and gauzy ruffled curtains blow in the breeze. It's all delightfully old-fashioned, and most guests would have it no other way. But it's not for everybody. The one nod to modern times is free Wi-Fi. There's no air-conditioning, no in-room phone or TV, and no soundproofing. The inn tops a lawn that slopes down to the yacht-filled harbor, and cocktails and lunch are served daily on the porch overlooking the heated pool, tennis court, and water. Accommodations are spread out between the main inn, three cottages, and four funky Topsiders, which seem inspired by the old *Jetsons* TV show. The nicest accommodations, a mix of rooms and suites, face the harbor. The inn's restaurant, Peabody's, serves breakfast, lunch, and dinner daily. Try to plan a late-May or early-June visit; you're practically on top of the Asticou Azalea Garden, Thuya Garden is a short walk away (or hike via the Eliot Mountain Trail), and the rates are lowest. Asticou is a popular wedding venue, so if you're looking for a quiet weekend, check the inn's event schedule before booking a room.

Bed-and-Breakfasts
In 1888, architect Fred Savage designed the two Shingle-style buildings that make up the three-story **Harbourside Inn** (Main St., Northeast Harbor, 207/276-3272, www.harboursideinn.com, mid-June-mid-Sept., $150-250). The Sweet family has preserved the old-fashioned feel by decorating the 11 spacious guest rooms and three suites with antiques, yet modern amenities include some kitchenettes and phones. Most rooms have working fireplaces. A continental breakfast is served. Trails to Norumbega Mountain and Upper Hadlock Pond leave from the back of the property.

The new in 2009 **Colonel's Suites** (143 Main St., Northeast Harbor, 207/288-4775, www.colonelssuites.com, $149-219), above the bakery/restaurant of the same name, provide comfortable accommodations with modern

ACADIA REGION

© HILARY NANGLE

The classic Asticou Inn overlooks the yacht-filled Northeast Harbor.

amenities. Every suite has a separate seating area, refrigerator, and flat-screen TV. Rates include a full breakfast in the restaurant.

Three miles from Northeast Harbor, in equally tony Seal Harbor, is a true bargain, the **Lighthouse Inn and Restaurant** (12 Main St./Rte. 3, Seal Harbor, 207/276-3958, www.lighthouseinnandrestaurant.com, $75-125). Sure, the three guest rooms (one small, one very large with a kitchenette, one two-room suite with a kitchenette) are a bit dated and dowdy, but at these prices, who cares? Downstairs is a restaurant (11am-8pm daily) with equally reasonable prices. It's a short walk to Seal Harbor Beach and the Seal Harbor entrance to the Park Loop Road.

Motels

Although it's long overdue for an overhaul—every guest room has two double beds, towels are tiny, and the decor is uninspired—you can't beat the location of the **Kimball Terrace Inn** (10 Huntington Rd., Northeast Harbor, 207/276-3383 or 800/454-6225, www.

kimballterraceinn.com, $190-230). The three-story motel faces the harbor, and every guest room has a patio or private balcony (ask for a harbor-facing room). Bring binoculars for yacht-spotting. The motel has a small pool, a restaurant, and a lounge, and is a short walk from Northeast Harbor's downtown. It is a popular wedding venue, so if that's a concern, ask if there are any groups in-house before you book.

FOOD

Hours listed are for peak season, early July-early September. At other times, call, most restaurants are open fewer days and hours.

Local Flavors

In the **Pine Tree Market** (121 Main St., Northeast Harbor, 207/276-3335), you'll find gourmet goodies, a huge wine selection, a resident butcher, fresh fish, a deli, homemade breads, pastries, sandwiches, and salads. The market offers free delivery to homes and boats.

Pop into **Full Belli Deli** (5 Sea St., Northeast

Harbor, 207/276-4299, 8am-8pm daily) for soups, fat sandwiches, pizzas, and breakfast fare.

A seasonal branch of **Little Notch Bakery** (Main St., Northeast Harbor, 207/276-5556) sells their famous breads and premade sandwiches.

From June well into October, the **Northeast Harbor Farmers Market** is set up each Thursday, 9am-noon, across from the Kimball Terrace Inn on Huntington Road.

Family Favorites

The homemade doughnuts are reason enough to visit **The Colonel's Restaurant and Bakery** (143 Main St., Northeast Harbor, 207/288-4775, www.colonelsrestaurant.com, 7am-9pm daily), but tucked behind the bakery is a full-service restaurant, serving everything from burgers to prime rib, as well as the usual seafood musts ($10-20). It draws families, thanks to a kids' menu and a casual atmosphere. It can be quite boisterous inside. There's also a deck out back and a separate bar area, which often is the quietest spot with the fastest service.

Casual Dining

Peabody's at the Asticou Inn (Rte. 3, 207/276-3344 or 800/258-3373, 7:30am-10am, 11:30am-9pm daily) is open to nonguests for breakfast, lunch, afternoon tea, and dinner ($28-40). When the weather cooperates, lunch and dinner are served on the deck, with serene views over Northeast Harbor. A lighter menu is served in the lounge.

INFORMATION AND SERVICES

The harbor-front information bureau of the **Mount Desert Chamber of Commerce** (18 Harbor Rd., Northeast Harbor, 207/276-5040, www.mountdesertchamber.org) covers the villages of Somesville, Northeast Harbor, Seal Harbor, Otter Creek, Pretty Marsh, Hall Quarry, and Beech Hill.

Find **public restrooms** at the end of the building housing the Great Harbor Maritime Museum, in the town office on Sea Street, and at the harbor.

GETTING THERE AND AROUND

Northeast Harbor is about 12 miles or 20 minutes via Routes 233 and 198 or 20 miles/35 minutes via Route 3 from Bar Harbor. It's about 13 miles or 25 minutes to Southwest Harbor.

Northeast Harbor is served by Route No. 5 (Jordan Pond) and Route No. 6 (Brown Mountain) of the Island Explorer bus system.

Southwest Harbor and Vicinity

Southwest Harbor (pop. 1,764) is the hub of Mount Desert Island's "quiet side." In summer, its tiny downtown district is probably the busiest spot on the whole western side of the island (west of Somes Sound), but that's not saying a great deal. "Southwest" has the feel of a settled community, a year-round flavor that Bar Harbor sometimes lacks. And it competes with the best in the scenery department. The Southwest Harbor area serves as a very convenient base for exploring Acadia National Park, as well as the island's less-crowded villages and offshore Swans Island, Frenchboro, and the Cranberry Isles.

The quirky nature of the island's four town boundaries creates complications in trying to categorize various island segments. Officially, the town of Southwest Harbor includes only the villages of **Manset** and **Seawall,** but nearby is the precious hamlet of **Somesville.** The Somesville National Historic District, with its distinctive arched white footbridge, is especially appealing, but traffic gets congested here along Route 102, so rather than just rubbernecking, plan to stop and walk around.

The "quiet side" of the island becomes even

ACADIA REGION

quieter as you round the southwestern edge into **Tremont** (pop. 1,563), which includes the villages of **Bernard; Bass Harbor,** home of Bass Harbor Head Light and ferry services to offshore islands; and **Seal Cove.** Tremont occupies the southwesternmost corner of Mount Desert Island. It's about as far as you can get from Bar Harbor, but the free Island Explorer bus service's Route No. 7 (Southwest Harbor) comes through here regularly.

Be sure to visit these small villages. Views are fabulous, the pace is slow, and you'll feel as if you've stumbled upon "the real Maine."

SIGHTS
◖ Wendell Gilley Museum
In the center of Southwest Harbor, the **Wendell Gilley Museum** (Herrick Rd. and Rte. 102, Southwest Harbor, 207/244-7555, www.wendellgilleymuseum.org, 10am-5pm Tues.-Sat. July-Aug., to 4pm June and Sept.-Oct., 10am-4pm Fri.-Sun. May and Nov.-Dec., $5 adults, $2 ages 5-12) was established in 1981 to display the life work of local woodcarver Wendell

Gilley (1904-1983), a onetime plumber who had gained a national reputation for his carvings by the time of his death. The modern, energy-efficient museum houses more than 200 of his astonishingly realistic bird specimens carved over more than 50 years. Summer exhibits also feature other wildlife artists. Many days, a local artist gives woodcarving demonstrations, and members of the local carving club often can be seen whittling away. The gift shop carries an ornithological potpourri, including books, binoculars, and carving tools. Kids over eight appreciate this more than younger ones. If you're bitten by the carving bug, workshops are available, ranging from 90-minute introductory lessons for adults and children ($30, includes kit and admission), offered most weekdays during the summer, to multiday classes on specific birds.

Somesville Historical Museum and Gardens
The tiny **Somesville Historical Museum and Gardens** (Rte. 102, Somesville, 207/276-9323,

Southwest Harbor

© HILARY NANGLE

www.mdihistory.org, 1pm-4pm Tues.-Sat., June 1-Oct. 15, donation) is adjacent to the gently curving white bridge in Somesville, so there's a good chance you're going to stop nearby, if just for a photo. In season, the heirloom garden, filled with flowering plants and herbs of the 19th and early 20th centuries, is worth a photo or two. The one-room museum has local artifacts and memorabilia displayed in a themed exhibit that changes annually. You can purchase a walking-tour guide to Somesville in the museum. If you're especially interested in history, ask about the museum's programs, which include speakers, demonstrations, and workshops.

Charlotte Rhoades Park and Butterfly Garden

It's easy to miss the **Charlotte Rhoades Park and Butterfly Garden** (Rte. 102, Southwest Harbor, 207/244-5405, www.rhoadesbutterflygarden.org), but that would be a mistake. This tiny seaside park was donated to the town in 1973, and the butterfly garden was established in 1998 to promote conservation education. The park is seldom busy, and it's a delightful place for a picnic. A kiosk is stocked with butterfly observation sheets, and there's usually a volunteer on duty on Thursday morning. Try to time a visit with the annual butterfly release in July. The park is on the water side of Route 102 between the Causeway Golf Club and the Seal Cove Road.

Country Store Museum

Stepping inside the former general store that's now headquarters for the **Tremont Historical Society** (Shore Rd., Bass Harbor, 207/244-9753, www.tremontmainehistory.us, 1pm-4pm Mon., Wed., Fri. July-mid-Oct.) is like stepping into the 1800s. Displays highlight the local heritage. If you're lucky, seventh-generation islander Muriel Davidson might be on duty and regale you with stories about her aunt, author Ruth Moore. You can buy copies of Moore's books here—good reads all. The museum is across from the Seafood Ketch.

Seal Cove Auto Museum

The late Richard C. Paine Jr.'s Brass Era (late 19th to early 20th centuries) car collection, one of the largest in the country, is nicely displayed and identified in the **Seal Cove Auto Museum** (Pretty Marsh Rd./Rte. 102, Seal Cove, 207/244-9242, www.sealcoveautomuseum.org, 10am-5pm daily May 1-Oct. 31, $6 adults, $5 seniors and teens, $2 ages 5-12). All vehicles are in as-found condition; this ranges from fresh-from-the-barn to meticulously restored. It's easy for kids of any age to spend an hour here, reminiscing or fantasizing. Among the highlights are a 1913 Peugeot with mahogany skiff body; 1915 F.R.P., the only one still in existence; an original 1903 Ford Model A, the first car commercially produced by the Ford Motor Co.; and a 1909 Ford Model T "Tin Lizzie," from the first year of production. The oldest car in the collection is an 1899 DeDion-Bouton, one of the earliest cars produced in the world. The museum is about six miles southwest of Somesville. Or, if you're coming from Southwest Harbor, take Route 102 north to Seal Cove Road (partly unpaved) west to the other side of Route 102 (it makes a giant loop) and go north about 1.5 miles. This is not on the Island Explorer route.

ENTERTAINMENT
Acadia Repertory Theatre

Somesville is home to the **Acadia Repertory Theatre** (Rte. 102, Somesville, 207/244-7260 or 888/362-7480, www.acadiarep.com, $24 adults; $19 seniors, students, and military; $10 under age 16), which has been providing first-rate professional summer stock on the stage of Somesville's antique Masonic Hall since the 1970s. Classic plays by Oscar Wilde, Neil Simon, and even Molière have been staples, as has the annual Agatha Christie mystery. Performances in the 144-seat hall run at 8:15pm Tuesday-Sunday late June-late August, with 2pm matinees on the last Sunday of each play's run. Special children's plays are performed at 10:30am Wednesday and Saturday in July-August. Tickets for children's theater programs are $9 adults, $6 children.

Lecture and Concert Series

During July-August, the Claremont Hotel (22 Claremont Rd., Southwest Harbor, 207/244-5036 or 800/244-5036, www.theclaremonthotel.com) sponsors a **free weekly lecture series** at 8pm on Thursday evening. Past topics have ranged from John Marin and Maine Modernism to Understanding Climate Change and the Climate Change Debate. It also offers a Saturday Evening Concert series ($10), with music ranging from bluegrass to classical.

EVENTS

During July-August, the Wednesday **Pie Sale** at the Somesville Union Meeting House is always a sellout. Go early; the doors open at 10am.

In early August, the annual **Claremont Croquet Classic,** held on the grounds of the classic Claremont Hotel, is open to all ages.

In September, Smuggler's Den Campground, on Route 102 in Southwest Harbor, is home to the annual **MDI Garlic Festival,** with entertainment and opportunities to savor the stinking rose, and in October the campground hosts the annual **Oktoberfest and Food Festival** (207/244-9264 or 800/423-9264, www.acadiachamber.com), a one-day celebration with crafts, food, games, music, and about two dozen Maine microbrewers presenting about 80 different brews.

The Astronomy Institute of Maine (www.astroinstitute.org) coordinates the **Maine Starlight Festival** in late September/early October. The nine-day event includes lectures, movies, sky-viewing opportunities, and other activities.

SHOPPING
Southwest Harbor

Fine art of the 19th and early 20th centuries is the specialty at **Clark Point Gallery** (46 Clark Point Rd., Southwest Harbor, 207/244-0920). Most works depict Maine and Mount Desert Island.

Jewelry approaches fine art at **Aylen & Son Jewelers** (332 Main St./Rte. 102, Southwest Harbor, 207/244-7369). For more than 25 years Peter and Judy Aylen have been crafting and selling jewelry in 18-karat gold and sterling silver and augmenting it with fine gemstones or intriguing beads.

More than 50 coastal Maine artisans sell their crafts at **Flying Mountain Artisans** (28 Main St./Rte. 102, Southwest Harbor, 207/244-0404), a cooperatively owned shop with a good range of creative goods, from quilts to blown glass. Also here is a gallery showing the works of more than 20 artists. Consider stopping in after a hike on Flying Mountain.

Bernard and Seal Cove

It's fun to poke around **Ravenswood** (McMullen Ave., Bass Harbor, 207/669-4287), a musty shop filled with old books, nautical gifts, model ship kits, and marvelous birds carved on-site.

Linda Fernandez Handknits (Bernard Rd., Bernard, 207/244-7224) sells beautiful handknit sweaters, mittens, hats, socks, Christmas stockings, and embroidered pillowcases all handcrafted by the talented and extended Fernandez family. The kids' lobster sweaters are especially cute.

When a psychic told A. Jones more than 30 years ago that she would move to an island, she thought, *Wrong.* But the psychic was right: Continue down Bernard Road, then hang a left on Columbia Avenue to find **A. Jones Gallery** (Columbia Ave., Bernard, 207/244-5634). Inside is a double find: artworks in a variety of media and styles as well as a working studio in the barn; country antiques and folk-art finds in the garage.

Potters Lisbeth Faulkner and Edwin Davis can often be seen working in their studio at **Seal Cove Pottery & Gallery** (Kelleytown Rd., Seal Cove, 207/244-3602). In addition to their functional hand-thrown or hand-built pottery, they exhibit Davis's paintings as well as crafts by other island artisans.

RECREATION
Hiking

At the Southwest Harbor/Tremont Chamber of Commerce office, or at any of the area's stores,

ACADIA REGION

© TOM NANGLE

Have fun shopping at Ravenswood.

lodgings, and restaurants, pick up a free copy of the *Trail Map/Hiking Guide,* a very handy foldout map showing more than 20 hikes on the west side of Mount Desert Island. Trail descriptions include distances, time required, and skill levels (easy to strenuous).

Bicycle Rentals
A veteran business with a first-rate reputation, **Southwest Cycle** (370 Main St., Southwest Harbor, 207/244-5856 or 800/649-5856, www.southwestcycle.com) is open all year (8:30am-5:30pm Mon.-Sat. and 9:30am-4pm Sun. July-Aug.; 9am-5pm Mon.-Sat. and 9:30am-4pm Sun.). The staff will fix you up with maps and lots of good advice for three loops (10-30 miles) on the western side of Mount Desert. Rentals begin around $18 for an afternoon and $24 for a full day, with multiday discounts available. The shop also rents every imaginable accessory, from baby seats to jogging strollers.

Golf
The nine-hole **Causeway Club** (Fernald Point Rd., 207/244-3780), which edges the ocean, is more challenging than it looks.

Boat Excursions
◖ ISLAND CRUISES
High praise goes to Captain Kim Strauss's **Island Cruises** (Little Island Marine, Shore Rd., Bass Harbor, 207/244-5785, www.bassharborcruises.com) for its narrated 3.5-hour lunch cruise to Frenchboro. The 49-passenger *R. L. Gott,* which Strauss built, departs at 11am daily during the summer. Kim has been navigating these waters for more than 55 years, and his experience shows not only in his boat handling but also in his narration. Expect to pick up lots of local heritage and lore about once-thriving and now abandoned granite-quarrying and fishing communities, the sardine industry, and lobstering; and to see seals, cormorants, guillemots, and often eagles. The trip allows enough time on Frenchboro for a picnic (or lunch at the summertime deli on the dock) and a short village stroll, then a return through the sprinkling of islands along

© HILARY NANGLE

Play a quick nine at the waterfront Causeway Club.

the 8.3-mile route. Kim also hauls a few traps and explains lobstering. He earns major points for maneuvering the boat so that passengers on both sides get an up-close view of key sights. It's an excellent, enthralling tour for all ages. Round-trip cost is $30 adults, $15 children 11 and younger. Make reservations; if the weather looks iffy, call ahead to confirm. Most of the trip is in sheltered water, but rough seas can put the kibosh on it. Island Cruises also does a two-hour **afternoon nature cruise** among the islands that covers the same topics but spends a bit more time at seal ledges and other spots ($25 adults, $15 children). On either trip, don't forget to bring binoculars. You'll find the Island Cruises dock by following signs to the Swans Island Ferry and turning right at the sign shortly before the state ferry dock.

FRIENDSHIP SLOOP CHARTERS
The *Alice E.,* built in 1899, is the oldest Friendship Sloop sailing today. It's one of two traditional Friendship sloops operated by **Downeast Friendship Sloop Charters**

(Dysert's Great Harbor Marina, Apple Lane, Southwest Harbor, 207/266-5210, www. downeastfriendshipsloop.com); the other one sails out of Northeast Harbor. Private charters start at $250 for a two-hour sail, covering up to six passengers and including an appetizer and soft drinks; shared trips are $50/person for two hours, $75/person for three hours.

DEEP SEA FISHING
Go fishing with the **Masako Queen Fishing Company** (Beal's Wharf, Clark Point Rd., Southwest Harbor, 207/244-5385, www.masakoqueen.com, $65 adults, $40 ages 5-12) aboard the 43-foot *Vagabond* and you might return with a lobster. The boat goes 8-20 miles offshore for mackerel, bluefish, codfish, and more. All equipment is included; dress warmly.

BOAT RENTALS AND LESSONS
Mansell Boat Rental Co. (135 Shore Rd., Manset, next to Hinckley, 207/244-5625, www.mansellboatrentals.com) rents sailboats and powerboats by the day or week, including

a keel day-sailer for $195/day and a 13.6-foot Boston Whaler for $175/day. Also available are sailing lessons: $195 for a two-plus-hour sail lesson cruise for two, which includes rigging and unrigging the boat; $100/hour for private lessons, minimum two hours.

Paddling
SEA KAYAKING
On the outskirts of Southwest Harbor's downtown is **Maine State Kayak** (254 Main St., Southwest Harbor, 207/244-9500 or 877/481-9500, www.mainestatekayak.com). Staffed with experienced, environmentally sensitive kayakers (all are Registered Maine Guides), the company offers four-hour guided trips departing at 8:30am, 10am, and 2pm along with a sunset tour, with a choice of half a dozen routes that depend on tides, visibility, and wind conditions. The rate is $48 pp, $44 in June and September. Most trips include island or beach breaks. Maximum group size is six tandems; minimum age is 12. Neophytes are welcome.

CALM-WATER PADDLING
Just west of Somesville (take Pretty Marsh Rd.) and across the road from Long Pond, the largest lake on Mount Desert Island, **National Park Canoe & Kayak Rental** (145 Pretty Marsh Rd./Rte. 102, Mount Desert, 207/244-5854 or 877/378-6907, www.nationalparkcanoerental.com, mid-May-mid-Oct.) makes canoeing and kayaking a snap. Just rent the boat, carry it across the road to Pond's End, and launch it. Be sure to pack a picnic. Rates begin at $32 for a three-hour canoe or solo kayak rental, $35 for a tandem kayak. A do-it-yourself sunset canoe or kayak tour (5pm-sunset) is $20 pp. The late fee is $10/half hour. Reservations are essential in July-August.

If you've brought your own canoe or kayak, launch it here at Pond's End and head off. It's four miles to the southern end of the lake. If the wind kicks up, skirt the shore; if it really kicks up from the north, don't paddle too far down the lake, because you'll have a difficult time getting back.

Another option is to launch your canoe on the quieter, cliff-lined southern end of the lake, much of which is in the park. To find the put-in, take the Seal Cove Road (on the east end of downtown Southwest Harbor). Go right on Long Cove Road to the small parking area at the end near the pumping station. You can also put in from the Long Pond Fire Road, off Route 102, in Pretty Marsh.

Almost the entire west side of **Long Pond** is Acadia National Park property, so plan to picnic and swim along here; tuck into the sheltered area west of Southern Neck, a crooked finger of land that points northward from the western shore. Stay clear of private property on the east side of the lake.

ACCOMMODATIONS
Inn
If you're pining for the *Old Maine,* stay at **The Claremont** (22 Claremont Rd., Southwest Harbor, 207/244-5036 or 800/244-5036, www.theclaremonthotel.com), an elegant, oceanfront grande dame dressed in mustard-yellow clapboard with a spectacular six-acre hilltop setting overlooking Somes Sound. Dating from 1884, the main building has 24 guest rooms, most of them refurbished yet pleasantly old-fashioned and neither fussy nor fancy; if you want techie frills, go elsewhere. Additional guest rooms are in the Phillips House and Cole Cottage. Guest rooms in these buildings begin at $185 in summer, including buffet breakfast. Also on the premises are 14 cottages ($235-370). Guests have access to croquet courts, a clay tennis court, one-speed cruiser bikes, rowboats, and a library. The boathouse bar is especially popular. The most popular time here is the first week in August, during the annual Claremont Croquet Classic. Children are welcome. The hotel and dining room are open mid-June-mid-October; cottages are open late May-mid-October.

Bed-and-Breakfasts
Many of Southwest Harbor's bed-and-breakfasts are clustered downtown, along Main Street and the Clark Point Road.

Set on a corner, well back from Clark Point Road, is **Harbour Cottage Inn** (9 Dirigo

Rd., Southwest Harbor, 207/244-5738 or 888/843-3022, www.harbourcottageinn.com, $229-290), appealingly revamped in 2002 when Javier Montesinos and Don Jalbert took over the reins. Built in 1870, it was the annex for the island's first hotel and housed the increasing numbers of rusticators who patronized this part of the island. It has evolved into a lovely bed-and-breakfast with eight guest rooms and three suites decorated in a colorful and fun cottage style. Some guest rooms have whirlpool baths and/or fireplaces, and all have TVs and Wi-Fi. Rates include a multicourse breakfast. Also part of Harbour Cottage is **Pier One,** which offers five truly waterfront suites ($1,540-1,825 weekly), including a studio cottage. All were renovated in 2009 in a comfortable cottage style; all have kitchens, TVs, and phones. Guests have private use of a 150-foot pier, and they can dock or launch canoes, kayaks, or other small boats from right outside their doors; dockage is available for larger boats. It's all within walking distance of downtown.

The linden-blossom fragrance can be intoxicating in summer at the **Lindenwood Inn** (118 Clark Point Rd., Southwest Harbor, 207/244-5335 or 800/307-5335, www.lindenwoodinn.com, $155-295). Jim King, the Australian owner, has imaginatively decorated the inn's nine guest rooms and poolside bungalow with artifacts from everywhere in a style that's sophisticated yet comfortable. After you hike Acadia's trails, the heated pool and hot tub are especially welcome, and after that, perhaps enjoy a drink while shooting pool or playing darts. Some guest rooms have harbor views.

The **Island House** (36 Freeman Ridge, Southwest Harbor, 207/244-5180, www.islandhousebb.com, year-round), in a quiet neighborhood about a mile from downtown, has two comfy guest rooms ($130) plus a guest living-dining room area where a full breakfast is served. Also here is a separate two-bedroom apartment above the garage ($185).

Even glimpsed through the trees from the road, **The Birches** (46 Fernald Point Rd., Southwest Harbor, 207/244-5182, www.thebirchesbnb.com, $135-170) is appealing. A wooded drive winds down to the large home fronting the ocean, near the mouth of Somes Sound. It's just 350 yards to the Causeway Golf Club and a short walk to the Flying Mountain trailhead. Built as a summer cottage in 1916, The Birches retains that casual summer ease, right down to the stone fireplace in the living room and the croquet court on the lawn. Guest rooms are large and minimally decorated. This is the Homer family home, and it's more of a home-stay B&B than a fancy inn.

In Manset, adjacent to the Hinckley Yacht complex and with jaw-dropping views down Somes Sound, is **The Moorings** (133 Shore Rd., Manset, 207/244-5523 or 800/596-5523, www.mooringsinn.com, $110-195), where fourth-generation innkeeper Leslie Watson is now owner. The oceanfront complex is part motel, part cottage rental, and part old-fashioned bed-and-breakfast. Rooms are named after locally built sailing vessels. The motel-style rooms in the Lighthouse View Wing have refrigerators, microwaves, Wi-Fi, waterfront decks, and incredible views (spend the afternoon counting the Hinckley yachts). A continental breakfast is available each morning. Also on the property or nearby are cottage units ($150-245). Bikes, canoes, and kayaks are available for guests, so you can paddle around the harbor; Mansell Boat Rental Co. is also on the premises. Dogs are permitted with prior approval.

Built in 1884 as the Freeman Cottage, the elegant Victorian **Inn at Southwest** (371 Main St., Rte. 102, Southwest Harbor, 207/244-3835, www.innatsouthwest.com, $150-200) has 13 dormers and a wraparound veranda furnished with wicker. Seven second- and third-floor guest rooms—named for Maine lighthouses and full of character—are decorated with a mix of contemporary and antique furnishings. Some have gas stoves or limited water views; all have Wi-Fi. Breakfast is a feast, with such treats as cheesecake crepes and eggs Florentine served indoors or on the patio. In the afternoon, cookies are available.

Across the lane is the elegant and artsy Queen Anne **Kingsleigh Inn 1904** (373 Main St., Southwest Harbor, 207/244-5302, www.

kingsleighinn.com, $165-315), with eight air-conditioned rooms, some with private harbor-facing decks, on three floors; all have Wi-Fi. The best splurge is the turret suite, with a fireplace, TV, private deck, and a telescope trained on the harbor. Breakfast is an elegant, three-course affair, served on the water-view porch, weather permitting. Afternoon refreshments are served, and chocolate truffles or chocolate-raspberry rum balls and port wine are replenished daily in guest rooms.

Motels and Cottages

Smack on the harbor and just a two-minute walk from downtown is the appropriately named **Harbor View Motel & Cottages** (11 Ocean Way, Southwest Harbor, 207/244-5031 or 800/538-6463, www.harborviewmoteland-cottages.com). The family-owned complex comprises motel rooms ($86-128/night, $540-815/week) spread out in two older, somewhat dowdy, one-story buildings and a newer three-story structure fronting on the harbor. A continental breakfast is served to motel guests July 1-early September. Also on the premises are seven housekeeping cottages with kitchenettes (weekly rentals only, $740-1,225), ranging from studios to two-bedrooms. Pets are welcome in some units.

Directly across from the famed seawall and adjacent to the park is the **Seawall Motel** (566 Seawall Rd./Rte. 102A, Southwest Harbor, 207/244-9250 or 800/248-9250, www.seawall-motel.com, $120), a budget-friendly find. The no-surprises two-story motel (upstairs guest rooms have the best views) has free Wi-Fi, in-room phones, cable TV, and service-oriented owners. Kids 12 and younger stay free. The location is excellent for bird-watchers.

Cottage Rentals

L. S. Robinson Co. (337 Main St., Southwest Harbor, 207/244-5563, www.lsrobinson. com) has an extensive list of cottage rentals in the area. The Southwest Harbor/Tremont Chamber of Commerce also keeps a helpful listing of privately owned homes and cottages available for rent.

Camping

Acadia National Park's Seawall Campground is on this side of the island.

On the eastern edge of Somesville, just off Route 198, at the head of Somes Sound, the Craighead family's **Mount Desert Campground** (516 Somes Sound Dr., Rte. 198, Somesville, 207/244-3710, www.mount-desertcampground.com) is especially centrally located for visiting Bar Harbor, Acadia, and the whole western side of Mount Desert Island. The campground has 152 wooded tent sites, about 45 on the water, spread out on 58 acres. Reservations are essential in mid-summer—one-week minimum for waterfront sites, three days for off-water sites in July-August. (Campers book a year ahead for waterfront sites here.) This deservedly popular and low-key campground gets high marks for maintenance, noise control, and convenient tent platforms. Another plus is The Gathering Place, where campers can relax, play games, and purchase coffee and fresh-baked treats or ice cream. Summer rates are $37-52 a night for two adults and two children younger than 18. Electrical hookups are $2/night. No pets are allowed July-early September, and no trailers over 20 feet are permitted. Kayak and canoe rentals are available.

Built on the site of an old quarry, on a hillside descending to rocky frontage on Somes Sound, **Somes Sound View Campground** (86 Hall Quarry Rd., Mount Desert, 207/244-3890, off-season 207/244-7452, www.ssvc. info, late May to mid-Oct., $25-60, no credit cards) is among the smallest campgrounds on the island, with fewer than 60 sites, all geared to tents and vans. Rustic camping cabins are $70/night. Facilities include hot showers (if you're camping on the lowest levels, it's a good hike up to the bathhouse), a heated pool, a boat launch, kayak and paddleboat rentals, and a fishing dock. You can swim in the sound from a rocky beach. Leashed pets are allowed. It's two miles south and east of Somesville and a mile east of Route 102.

The Worcester family's **Smuggler's Den Campground** (Rte. 102, Southwest Harbor,

207/244-3944, www.smugglersdencamp-ground.com, $34-59) is a midsized, pet-friendly campground between Echo Lake and downtown Southwest Harbor. It's also the site of the annual Oktoberfest. Trails access back roads to both Echo Lake (1.25 miles) and Long Pond (1 mile) as well as 25 miles of Acadia National Park trails. Big-rig sites are grouped in the top third; pop-ups and small campers are in the middle third; tenting sites are in the lower third and in the woods rimming the large recreation field. Also available are cabins ($550 camping, $900 with kitchen and bath, per week). Facilities include Wi-Fi; heated pool and kiddie pool; four-acre recreation field with horseshoe pit, half-court basketball, and lawn games; laundry; free hot showers; lobster and ice cream sales; and entertainment.

FOOD
Local Flavors
Lots of goodies for picnics can be found at **Sawyer's Market** (344 Main St., Southwest Harbor, 207/244-7061, 7:30am-8:30pm Sun.-Wed., to 9pm Thurs.-Sat.); for wine, cheese, and gourmet goodies, head across the street to **Sawyer's Specialties** (353 Main St., Southwest Harbor, 207/244-3317, open daily).

Good chowders, sandwiches, fried clams, lobster rolls, and even pizza are served at the cozy **Quietside Cafe** (360 Main St., Southwest Harbor, 207/244-9444, 11am-9pm Mon.-Sat., to 4pm Sun., $6-12). Do save room for the homemade pies.

Some of the island's most creative sandwiches and pizza toppings emerge from **Little Notch Cafe** (340 Main St., Southwest Harbor, 207/244-3357, 7:30am-8:30pm daily), next to the library in Southwest Harbor's downtown. Also available are Little Notch Bakery's famed breads, a couple of pasta choices, and homemade soups, stews, and chowders. Most choices run $8-16.

Good food, good coffee, and good wine mix with a Mediterranean-influenced menu at **Sips** (4 Clark Point Rd., Southwest Harbor, 207/244-4550, www.sipsmdi.com, 7am-9pm daily), a congenial place. Small- and large-plate

and tapas-style choices range $8-28; the risottos are especially good. A children's menu is available. On Thursday night during the summer season, there usually is live music.

Treat yourself to lunch overlooking Somes Sound at the **Boat House** at the Claremont Hotel (22 Claremont Rd., 207/244-5036 or 800/244-5036, noon-2pm daily July-Aug., $7-15). It's also a popular spot for cocktails, served 5:30pm-9pm, when you can watch the sun set behind Cadillac Mountain.

College of the Atlantic students run **Beech Hill Farm** (Beech Hill Rd., Mount Desert, 207/244-5204, 8am-5pm Tues.-Sat.), a five-acre farm certified organic by the Maine Organic Farmers and Gardeners Association. Also here are acres of heirloom apple trees and 65 acres of forestland. Visit the farm stand for fresh produce as well as other organic or natural foods such as cheeses and baked goods.

Ethnic Fare
Craving a taste of Mexico? **XYZ Restaurant** (80 Seawall Rd./Rte. 102A, Manset, 207/244-5221, www.xyzmaine.com, entrées $25) specializes in the flavors of interior Mexico: Xalapa, Yucatán, and Zacatecas (hence "XYZ"). The most popular dish is *cochinita*—citrus-marinated pork rubbed with achiote paste, worthy of its reputation. For dessert, try the XYZ pie. Dine inside or on the porch. The food is great, but it's pricey and served with a dose of attitude. Hours vary, often by week, so call for the current schedule.

From the outside, it doesn't look like much, but locals know you can count on **DeMuro's Top of the Hill** (Rte. 102, Southwest Harbor, 207/244-0033, www.topofthehilldining.com, 5pm-close daily, $10-28) for a good meal at a fair price. The Italian-influenced menu has something in all price ranges, and includes vegetarian fare as well as lobster. Twilight specials ($10-13) are served 5pm-6pm.

Casual Dining
By day, **Eat-a-Pita** (326 Main St., Southwest Harbor, 207/244-4344, 8am-4pm daily, dinner

5pm-9pm Tues.-Sun.) is a casual, order-at-the-counter restaurant serving breakfast and lunch. At night it morphs into **Cafe 2,** a full-service restaurant. The dining room, furnished with old oak tables and chairs, has a funky, artsy attitude; there's also patio seating outside and an outdoor bar (think pink flamingos). Start the day with a Greek or Acapulco omelet. Lunch emphasizes pita sandwiches, burgers, panini, and salads (delicious—call in advance for takeout); dinner choices ($10-26) include salads, light meals, a half-dozen pastas, and entrées.

Earning high praise for its internationally accented fare, good service, fabulous views over the harbor, and incredible martinis is **Fiddlers' Green** (411 Main St., Southwest Harbor, 207/244-9416, www.fiddlersgreenrestaurant. com, 5:30pm-10pm Tues.-Sun.). House specialties, such as Asian vegetable hot pot, trout livorese, and steaks, range $16-44, but you can also make a meal of small plates, soups, sandwiches, and salads.

Fine Dining

The dreamy views from **Xanthus** (22 Claremont Rd., 207/244-5036 or 800/244-5036, 6pm-9pm daily), at the Claremont Hotel, descend over the lawns and croquet courts, boathouse, and dock to the water backed by mountains. It's truly a special place for an elegant meal complemented by an old-fashioned grace. Jackets are not required, but men won't feel out of place wearing one. Entrées range $24-30; a three-course fixed-price dinner is $30. Dining-room reservations are advised in midsummer.

Red sky at night, diners delight: Gold walls, artwork, wood floors, and a giant hearth set a chic tone for **Red Sky** (14 Clark Point Rd., 207/244-0476, www.redskyrestaurant.com, 5:30pm-9pm daily, entrées $19-30), one of the island's tonier restaurants. Owners James and Elizabeth Geffen Lindquist's creative fare emphasizes fresh seafood, hand-cut meats, and local organic produce; there's always a vegetarian choice. The restaurant is open Valentine's Day-New Year's Eve.

Seafood and Lobster in the Rough

If you have a penchant for puns—or can tune them out—head for the family-run **Seafood Ketch Restaurant** (McMullin Ave., Bass Harbor, 207/244-7463, www.seafoodketch.com, 11am-9pm daily). The corny humor begins with "Please, no fishing from dining room windows or the deck" and "What foods these morsels be," and goes up (or down, depending on your perspective) from there. But there's nothing corny about the seafood roll, an interesting change from the usual lobster or crab roll. There are a few "landlubber delights," but mostly the menu has fresh seafood dishes—including the baked lobster-seafood casserole, a recipe requested by *Gourmet* magazine. Most entrées run $19-24, a bit pricey given the informality and service, but sandwiches and lighter fare are available. Sunday omelets are the specialty, served 11am-2pm along with the full menu. This is a prime family spot, with a kids' menu, where the best tables are on the flagstone patio overlooking Bass Harbor (bring bug repellent). Follow signs for the Swans Island ferry terminal.

Pick your lobster, then grab a picnic table overlooking the harbor at **The Captain's Galley at Beal's Lobster Pier** (182 Clark Point Rd., Southwest Harbor, 207/244-3202, 11am-sunset daily).

Few restaurants have as idyllic a setting as **(Thurston's Lobster Pound** (Steamboat Wharf Rd., Bernard, 207/244-7600, 11am-8:30pm daily, market rates), which overlooks lobster boat-filled Bass Harbor. The screened dining room practically sits in the water. Family-oriented Thurston's also has chowders, sandwiches, and terrific desserts. Beer and wine are available. Read the directions at the entrance and order before you find a table on one of two levels.

INFORMATION AND SERVICES

The **Southwest Harbor/Tremont Chamber of Commerce** (329 Main St., Southwest Harbor, 207/244-9264 or 800/423-9264, www.acadia-chamber.com) stocks brochures, maps, menus, and other local info.

ACADIA REGION

Check out **Southwest Harbor Public Library** (338 Main St., Southwest Harbor, 207/244-7065, www.swhplibrary.org).

Find **public restrooms** at the southern end of the parking lot behind the Main Street park and near the fire station. There are portable toilets at the town docks.

GETTING THERE AND AROUND

Southwest Harbor is about 13 miles or 25 minutes via Routes 198 and 102 from Northeast Harbor. It's about 14 miles or 25 minutes to Bar Harbor.

Southwest Harbor, Tremont, and Bass Harbor are serviced by Route No. 7 (Southwest Harbor) of the Island Explorer bus system.

Islands Near Mount Desert

Sure, Mount Desert is an island, but for a sampling of real island life, you'll want to make a day trip to one of the offshore islands. Most popular are the **Cranberry Isles** and **Swans Island,** but don't overlook **Frenchboro,** an off-the-radar gem.

CRANBERRY ISLES

The **Cranberry Isles** (pop. 141), south of Northeast and Seal Harbors, comprise Great Cranberry, Little Cranberry (called Islesford), Sutton, Baker, and Bear Islands. Islesford and Baker include property belonging to Acadia National Park. Bring a bike and explore the narrow, mostly level roads on the two largest islands, Great Cranberry and Islesford, but remember to respect private property. Unless you've asked permission, do not cut across private land to reach the shore.

The Cranberry name has been attributed to 18th-century loyalist governor Francis Bernard, who received these islands along with all of Mount Desert as a king's grant in 1762. Cranberry bogs (now long gone) on the two largest islands evidently caught his attention. Permanent European settlers arrived in the 1760s, and there was even steamboat service by the 1820s.

Lobstering and other fishing industries are the commercial mainstays, boosted in summer by the various visitor-related pursuits. Artists and writers come for a week, a month, or longer; day-trippers spend time on Great Cranberry and Islesford.

Largest of the islands is **Great Cranberry,** with a general store, a small historical museum with a café, and a gift shop, but not much else except pretty views.

The second-largest island is **Little Cranberry,** locally known as Islesford. It's easy to spend the better part of a day here exploring. Begin at **The Islesford Historical Museum** (207/288-3338, 9am-noon and 12:30pm-3:30pm Mon.-Sat., 10:45am-noon and 12:30pm-3:30pm Sun. late June-late Sept., free), operated by the National Park Service. The exhibits focus on local history, much of it maritime, so displays include ship models, household goods, fishing gear, and other memorabilia. Also on Islesford are public restrooms (across from the museum), a handful of galleries, and a general store. For lunch, bring a picnic or head to the **Islesford Dock** (207/244-7494, www.islesford.com, 11am-3pm Wed.-Sat., 10am-2pm Sun., dinner 5pm-9pm Tues.-Sun. late June-Labor Day), where prices are moderate, the food is home-cooked, and the views across to Acadia's mountains are incredible, especially at sunset.

Getting There

Decades-old family-run **Beal and Bunker** (207/244-3575, www.cranberryisles.com) provides year-round mail and passenger boat service to the Cranberries from Northeast Harbor. The schedule makes it possible to do both islands in one day. The summer season, with more frequent trips, runs late June-Labor Day.

© TOM NANGLE

the Islesford Dock

The first boat departs Northeast Harbor's municipal pier at 7:30am Monday-Saturday; the first Sunday boat is 10am. The last boat for Northeast Harbor leaves Islesford at 6:30pm and leaves Great Cranberry at 6:45pm. The boats make a variety of stops on the three-island route (including Sutton in summer), so be patient as they make the circuit. It's a people-watching treat. If you just did a round-trip and stayed aboard, the loop would take about 1.5 hours. Round-trip tickets (covering the whole loop, including intraisland trips if you want to visit both Great Cranberry and Islesford) are $28 adults, $14 ages 3-11, free under age 3. Bicycles are $7 round-trip. The off-season schedule operates early May-mid-June and early September-mid-October; the winter schedule runs mid-October-April. In winter, the boat company advises phoning ahead on what Mainers quaintly call "weather days."

The **Cranberry Cove Ferry** (upper town dock, Clark Point Rd., Southwest Harbor, 207/244-5882, cell 207/460-1981, www.downeastwindjammer.com) operates a summertime service to the Cranberries mid-May-mid-October. The ferry route begins at the upper town dock (Clark Point Rd.) in Southwest Harbor, with stops in Manset and Great Cranberry before reaching Islesford an hour later. (Stops at Sutton can be arranged.) In summer (mid-June-mid-Sept.) there are six daily round-trips, with two additional evening trips Wednesday-Saturday. The first departure from Southwest Harbor is 7am; the last departure from Islesford is 6pm. Round-trip fares are $28 adults, $20 children, $6 bicycles.

The **Cadillac Water Taxi** (207/801-1898), a converted lobster boat, makes frequent on-demand trips to the Cranberries.

Captain John Dwelley (207/244-5724) also operates a water-taxi service to the Cranberries. His six-passenger *Delight* makes the run from Northeast, Southwest, or Seal Harbor. Reservations are required for trips 6am-8am and 6pm-11pm. Custom cruises are available, including excursions to Baker's Island. Consider the sunset cruise to the Islesford Dock for dinner.

FRENCHBORO, LONG ISLAND

Since Maine has more Long Islands than anyone cares to count, most of them have other labels for easy identification. Here's a case in point—a Long Island known universally as Frenchboro, the name of the village that wraps around Lunts Harbor. With a year-round population hovering around 65, Frenchboro has had ferry service only since 1960. Since then, the island has acquired phone service, electricity, and satellite TV, but don't expect to notice much of that when you get here. It's a very quiet place where islanders live as islanders always have—making a living from the sea and being proud of it. In 1999, when more than half the island (914 acres, including 5.5 miles of shorefront) went up for sale by a private owner, an incredible fundraising effort collected nearly $3 million, allowing purchase of the land in 2000 by the Maine Coast Heritage Trust. Some of the funding has been put toward restoration of the village's church and one-room schoolhouse; islanders and visitors will still have full access to all the acreage, and interested developers will have to look elsewhere. Frenchboro is the subject of *Hauling by Hand,* a fascinating, well-researched "biography" published in 1999 by eighth-generation islander Dean Lunt.

Frenchboro is a delightful day trip. A good way to get a sense of the place is to take the 3.5-hour lunch cruise run by Captain Kim Strauss of **Island Cruises** (Little Island Marine, Shore Rd., Bass Harbor, 207/244-5785, www.bassharborcruises.com). For an even longer day trip to Frenchboro, plan to take the passenger ferry *R. L. Gott* during her weekly run for the Maine State Ferry Service. Each Friday early April-late October, the *R. L. Gott* departs Bass Harbor at 8am, arriving in Frenchboro at 9am. The return trip to Bass Harbor is at 6pm, allowing nine hours on the island. The **Maine State Ferry Service** (207/244-3254, daily recorded info 800/491-4883, www.exploremaine.org) uses the ferry *Captain Henry Lee,* the same vessel used on the Swans Island route, for service to Frenchboro on Wednesday, Thursday, and Sunday. On some days, the schedule allows five hours on the island, but the days and times are limited, so it's best to check the current schedule online.

When you go, take a picnic with you, or stop at **Lunt's Dockside Deli** (207/334-2902, www.luntlobsters.com), open only in July-August. It's a very casual establishment—order at the window, grab a picnic table, and wait for your name to be called. Lobster rolls and fish chowder are the specialties, but there are plenty of other choices, including sandwiches, hot dogs, and even vegetable wraps. Of course, you can get lobster too. Prices are low, the view is wonderful, and you might even get to watch lobsters being unloaded from a boat. You can also purchase humongous lobster and crab rolls on homemade bread, cheeseburgers, salads, and more at the **Offshore Store** (207/334-2943, www.offshorestoreandmore.com).

The **Frenchboro Historical Society Museum** (207/334-2924, free), just up from the dock, has interesting old tools, other local artifacts, and a small gift shop. It's usually open afternoons Memorial Day-Labor Day. The island has a network of easy and not-so-easy maintained trails through the woods and along the shore; some can be squishy, and some are along boulder-strewn beachfront. The trails are rustic, and most are unmarked, so proceed carefully. In the center of the island is a beaver pond. (You'll get a sketchy map on the boat, but you can also get one at the historical society.)

In August, Frenchboro hosts its annual **Lobster Festival** (Lunt & Lunt Lobster Company, 207/334-2922), a midday meal comprising lobster, chicken salad, hot dogs, coleslaw, homemade pies, and more, served rain or shine, with proceeds benefiting a local cause. Islanders and hundreds of visitors gather in the village for the occasion. The Maine State Ferry makes a special run that day.

SWANS ISLAND

Six miles off Mount Desert Island lies scenic, roughly 7,000-acre **Swans Island** (pop. 332), named after Col. James Swan, who bought it and two dozen other islands as an investment in 1786. As with the Cranberries, fishing is the year-round way of life here, with lobstering being the primary occupation. In summer the population practically triples with the arrival of artists, writers, and other seasonal visitors. The island has no campsites, few public restrooms, and only a handful of guest rooms. Visitors who want to spend more than a day tend to rent cottages by the week.

You'll need either a bicycle or a car to get around on the island, as the ferry comes in on one side and the village center is on the other. Should you choose to bring a car, it's wise to make reservations for the ferry, especially for the return trip. Bicycling is a good way to get around, but be forewarned that the roads are narrow, lack shoulders, and are hilly in spots.

A Swans Island summer highlight is the **Sweet Chariot Music Festival,** a three-night midweek extravaganza in early August geared to boaters.

Overnight accommodations are available at **The Harbor Watch Inn** (111 Minturn Rd., 207/526-4563 or 800/532-7928, www.swansisland.com, $95-150). The **Swans Island Tea Room** (253 Harbor Rd., 207/526-4900, www.

swansislandtearoom.com) is a double find. Baked goods, sandwiches, and ice cream are served 8am-2pm Wednesday-Sunday. Upstairs are two pet-friendly guest rooms ($110-130, including breakfast; pets $20).

Getting There and Around

Swans Island is a six-mile, 40-minute trip on the state-operated car ferry *Captain Henry Lee,* operated by the **Maine State Ferry Service** (207/244-3254, daily recorded info 800/491-4883, www.exploremaine.org). The ferry makes up to six round-trips a day, the first from Bass Harbor at 7:30am Monday-Saturday, 9am Sunday, and the last from Swans Island at 4:30pm. Round-trip fares are around $17.50 adults, $8.50 ages 5-11; bikes are $16.50 adults, $9.50 children; vehicles are $49.50. Reservations are accepted only for vehicles; be in line at least 15 minutes before departure or you risk forfeiting your space.

To reach the Bass Harbor ferry terminal on Mount Desert Island, follow the distinctive blue signs, marked Swans Island Ferry, along Routes 102 and 102A.

Southwest Cycle (Main St., Southwest Harbor, 207/244-5856 or 800/649-5856) rents bikes by the day and week and is open year-round. It also has ferry schedules and Swans Island maps. For the early-morning ferry, you'll need to pick up bikes the day before; be sure to reserve them if you're doing this in July-August.

Schoodic Peninsula

Slightly more than 2,366 of Acadia National Park's acres are on the mainland Schoodic Peninsula; the rest are all on islands, including Mount Desert. World-class scenery and the relative lack of congestion, even at the height of summer, are just two reasons to sneak around to the eastern side of Frenchman Bay. Other reasons are abundant opportunities for outdoor recreation, two scenic byways, and dozens of artists' and artisans' studios tucked throughout this region.

Still, the biggest attractions in this area are the spectacular vignettes and vistas—of offshore lighthouses, distant mountains, and close-in islands—and the unchanged villages. **Winter Harbor** (pop. 516) known best as the gateway to Schoodic, shares the area with an old-money, low-profile Philadelphia-linked summer colony on exclusive Grindstone Neck.

Gouldsboro (pop. 1,737) including the not-to-be-missed villages of **Birch Harbor, Corea,** and **Prospect Harbor,** earned its own minor

© HILARY NANGLE

Working lobster wharfs dot the Schoodic Peninsula.

fame from Louise Dickinson Rich's 1958 book *The Peninsula*, a tribute to her summers on Corea's Cranberry Point, "a place that has stood still in time." Since 1958, change has crept into Corea, but not so as you'd notice. It's still the same quintessential lobster-fishing community, perfect for photo ops. A new section of the Maine Coastal Islands National Wildlife Reserve, the 431-acre **Corea Heath Unit,** has taken over former navy lands along Route 195 in Corea. In another initiative, the Frenchman Bay Conservancy acquired the 600-acre Northern Corea Heath, across the highway, home to Grand Marsh and Grand Marsh Bay.

Between Ellsworth and Gouldsboro are **Hancock** (pop. 2,394), **Sullivan** (pop. 1,236), and **Sorrento** (pop. 274). Venture down the oceanside back roads and you'll discover an old-timey summer colony at Hancock Point, complete with a library, a post office, a yacht club, and tennis courts.

Meander inland to find the **Donnell Pond Public Reserved Lands,** a spectacular chunk of mostly undeveloped lakes for boating and fishing, peaks for hiking, and even a beach for camping.

SCHOODIC SECTION OF ACADIA NATIONAL PARK

The Schoodic section of Acadia is much smaller, less busy, and provides fewer recreational opportunities than that on Mount Desert Island, but it's still magnificent and well worth visiting.

As with so much of Acadia's acreage on Mount Desert Island, the Schoodic section became part of the park largely because of the deft diplomacy and perseverance of George B. Dorr. No obstacle ever seemed too daunting to Dorr. In 1928, when the owners objected to donating their land to a national park tagged with the Lafayette name (geopolitics being involved at the time), Dorr even managed to obtain congressional approval for the 1929 name change to Acadia National Park—and Schoodic was part of the deal.

To reach the park boundary from Route 1 in

SCENIC BYWAYS

The Schoodic region boasts not one but two designated scenic byways: the **Schoodic National Scenic Byway,** which wraps around the peninsula, and the **Blackwoods Scenic Byway,** an inland blue highway cutting through the Donnell Pond Public Reserved Lands. If time permits, drive at least one of these routes. Ideally you'd do both, because the scenery differs greatly. Best idea yet: Connect the two via U.S. 1, creating a loop that includes lakes and forests, mountains and fields, ocean and rocky coast. If you have only one day to explore this region, this route takes in the best of it. In early-mid-October, when the fall foliage is at its peak colors, the vistas are especially stunning.

The 29-mile Schoodic National Scenic Byway stretches from Sullivan on U.S. 1 to Gouldsboro,

and then south on Route 186 and around the Schoodic Peninsula, ending in Prospect Harbor. A detailed guide is available at www.schoodicbyway.org. Other information is available at www.byways.org. There is interpretive signage, explaining sights and history, along the route.

The 12.5-mile Blackwoods Scenic Byway meanders along Route 182 inland of U.S. 1, from Franklin to Cherryfield, edging lakes and passing through small villages. You'll find access to trailheads and boat launches at Donnell Pond and Tunk Lake. Although Cherryfield is beyond the Schoodic region, it's a beautiful town to visit, filled with stately Victorian homes. It's also the self-proclaimed wild blueberry capital of the world. Maps and information are available at www.blackwoodsbyway.org.

Gouldsboro, take Route 186 south to Winter Harbor. Continue through town, heading east, and then turn right and continue to the park entrance sign, just before the bridge over Mosquito Harbor.

You can also tour the park using the free Island Explorer bus, which circulates through Winter Harbor, around the Schoodic Loop, and on to Prospect Harbor, with stops along the way. It's an efficient and environmentally friendly way to go.

(Schoodic Loop

The major sights of Acadia's Schoodic section lie along the six-mile one-way road that meanders counterclockwise around the tip of the Schoodic Peninsula. You'll discover official and unofficial picnic areas, hiking trailheads, offshore lighthouses, and turnouts with scenic vistas. Also named the Park Loop Road, it's best referred to as the Schoodic Loop to distinguish it from the one on Mount Desert.

The first landmark is **Frazer Point Picnic Area,** with lovely vistas, picnic tables, and wheelchair-accessible restrooms. Other spots are fine for picnics, but this is the only official one. If you've brought bikes, leave your car

here and do a counterclockwise 12.2-mile loop through the park and back to your car via Birch Harbor and Route 186. It's a fine day trip.

From the picnic area, the road becomes one-way. Unlike on the Park Loop Road on Mount Desert, no parking is allowed in the right lane. There are periodic pullouts, but not many cars can squeeze in. Despite the fact that this is far from the busiest section of Acadia, it can still be frustrating to be unable to find a space in the summer months. The best advice is to stay in the area and do this loop early in the morning or later in the afternoon, perhaps in May or June. (The late September-early October foliage is gorgeous, but traffic does increase then.) While you're driving, if you see a viewpoint you like (with room to pull off), stop; it's a long way around to return.

From this side of Frenchman Bay, the vistas of Mount Desert's summits are gorgeous behind islands sprinkled here and there.

Drive 1.5 miles from the picnic area to Raven's Head, a Thunder Hole-type cliff with sheer drops to the churning surf below and fabulous views (there are no fences, so it's not a good place for little ones). The trail is unmarked, but there's a small pullout on the left side of the road opposite it. Be extremely careful here—stay on the path (the environment is very fragile and erosion is a major problem), and stay well back from the cliff's edge.

At 2.2 miles past the picnic area, watch for a narrow, unpaved road on the left, across from an open beach vista. It winds for a mile (keep left at the fork) up to a tiny parking circle, from which you can follow the trail (signposted "Schoodic Trails") to the open ledges on 440-foot Schoodic Head. From the circle, there's already a glimpse of the view, but it gets much better. If you bear right at the fork, you'll come to a grassy parking area with access to the Alder Trail and the Schoodic Head Trail.

Continue on the Schoodic Loop Road, and hang a right onto a short, two-way spur to **Schoodic Point.** On your right will be the **Schoodic Education and Research Center** (locally called by its acronym, SERC, 207/288-1310, www.sercinstitute.org), on the site of a former top-secret U.S. Navy base that became part of the park in 2002. At the entrance is a small info center (with ADA-accessible restroom), staffed by volunteers and park rangers. Continue up the road to the restored Rockefeller Hall, which opened in 2013 as a welcome center. Inside are exhibits highlighting Schoodic's ecology and history, the former Navy base's radio and cryptologic operations, and current research programs. SERC also offers ranger-led activities, lectures by researchers or nationally known experts addressing environmental topics related to the park and its surroundings, and other programs and events. Check the online calendar for current opportunities.

After touring SERC, continue out to Schoodic Point, the highlight of the drive, with surf crashing onto big slabs of pink granite. Be extremely cautious here: Chances of rescue are slim if a rogue wave sweeps someone offshore.

Schoodic Woods

In 2011, **Schoodic Woods LLC** (schoodicwoods.com) purchased about 3,000 prime acres, straddling Gouldsboro and Winter Harbor, at the base of the Schoodic Point peninsula. The company is working with Acadia National Park officials to develop 1,500 acres on the south side of Route 186 as a recreational area, with nonmotorized trails, a campground, amphitheater, welcome center, and day-use parking area. Maine Coast Heritage Trust has an option for a conservation easement on the portion adjacent to the park.

From Schoodic Point, return to the Loop Road. Look to your right and you'll see Little Moose Island, which can be accessed at low tide. Be careful not to get stranded here. Continue to the **Blueberry Hill** parking area (about one mile from the Schoodic Point-Loop Road intersection), a moor-like setting where the low growth allows almost 180-degree views of the bay and islands. There are a few trails in this area—all eventually converging on **Schoodic Head,** the highest point on the peninsula. (Don't confuse this with Schoodic Mountain, which is well north of here.) Across the road and up the road a bit is the trailhead for the 180-foot-high **Anvil** headland.

© TOM NANGLE

Schoodic Point is renowned for the surf crashing upon its pink granite shores.

EDUCATING FOR THE FUTURE

Maine native and Wall Street tycoon John G. Moore once owned most of the Schoodic Peninsula. After his death, his heirs donated the land to the Hancock County Trustees of Public Reservations in the 1920s, with the stipulation that the land be used as a public park and for the "promotion of biological and other scientific research." Seven years later, more than 2,000 acres of the peninsula were donated to Acadia National Park.

At that time, John D. Rockefeller Jr. was working with the National Park Service to construct the Park Loop Road on Mount Desert Island. The U.S. Naval Radio Station on Otter Point was in the way, so Rockefeller helped the National Park Service work with the U.S. Navy to relocate the station to Schoodic Point. Five buildings, including Rockefeller Hall, a French Norman Revival-style mansion now listed on the National Register of Historic Places, were constructed. In 1935, the U.S. Naval Radio Station at Schoodic Point was commissioned.

The station expanded during World War II and the Cold War, and by the late 20th century the 100-acre campus comprised more than 35 buildings and was home to 350 navy employees. When the station closed in 2002, the land was returned to the park for use as a research and education center.

After a $10 million renovation to the campus, the **Schoodic Education and Research Center Institute** (207/288-1310, www.sercinstitute.org), also known as SERC, officially opened in 2011.

SERC is one of 20 research learning centers in the country. Its mission is to "guide present and future generations to greater understanding and respect for nature by providing research and learning opportunities through its outstanding Acadia National Park setting, unique coastal Maine facilities, and innovative partnership programs." The goal is for SERC to become a "world-class research and learning institution, providing knowledge and transformational experiences necessary for harmony between humankind and the natural world."

It's well on the way. "We're building a science community of researchers and postdoctoral students that will interact with educators, teachers, students, citizen scientists, and volunteers," says president and CEO Mike Soukup, who was chief scientist for the National Park Service until 2007.

A core part of SERC's mission is education, and it works with the park to present programs, lectures, special events, and ranger-led activities; check the online calendar for current offerings. Among these are "bio blitzes," which research the park's flora and fauna in minute detail. In 2007, more than 100 specialists and volunteers participated in a blitz to catalog spiders. The findings included 60 species that had not been previously identified as being in the park, including eight that hadn't been identified as being in the state. Other blitzes have identified true bugs, flies, beetles, moths and butterflies, and ants.

SERC also sponsors an artist-in-residence program as well as a biennial sculpture symposium, in odd-numbered years, that draws sculptors from around the globe.

SERC offers education and research programs in science and math aimed not only at scientists and researchers but also at students and teachers. These include professional development and summer scholarship programs for math and science teachers, advanced-placement summer institutes for teachers, research fellowships, fellowships for scientists and educators, and school programs.

In 2009 local benefactor Edith Robb Dixon donated $1 million in the name of her late husband, Fritz Eugene Dixon Jr., to renovate the Rockefeller Hall. The hall was designed by New York architect Grosvenor Atterbury, who used a similar design for the park's carriage road gatehouses on Mount Desert Island. In 2013, it opened as a welcome center, with exhibits highlighting Schoodic's ecology and history, the former navy base's radio and cryptologic operations, and current research programs.

As you continue along this stretch of road, keep your eyes peeled for eagles, which frequently soar here. There's a nest on the northern end of Rolling Island; you can see it with binoculars from some of the roadside pullouts.

From Blueberry Hill, continue 1.2 miles to a pullout for the East Trail, the shortest and most direct route to Schoodic Head. It's about another mile to the park exit, in Wonsqueak Harbor. It's another two miles to the intersection with Route 186 in Birch Harbor. (If you didn't bring a picnic lunch or dinner, Bunker's Wharf Restaurant is a good, if slightly pricey, stop, with views of a working wharf.)

ENTERTAINMENT AND EVENTS

Winter Harbor's biggest wingding is the annual **Lobster Festival** (www.acadia-schoodic.org), the second Saturday in August. The daylong gala includes a parade, live entertainment, lobster-boat races (a serious competition in these parts), crafts fair, games, and more crustaceans than you could ever consume.

Concerts, art classes, coffeehouses, workshops, and related activities are presented year-round by **Schoodic Arts for All** (207/963-2569, www.schoodicarts.org). Many are held at historic Hammond Hall in downtown Winter Harbor. A summer series presents monthly concerts on Friday evenings May-October. In early August the two-week **Schoodic Arts Festival** is jam-packed with daily workshops and nightly performances for all ages.

The **Pierre Monteux School for Conductors and Orchestra Musicians** (Rte. 1, Hancock, 207/422-3280, www.monteuxschool.org), a prestigious summer program founded in 1943, has achieved international renown for training dozens of national and international classical musicians. It presents two well-attended concert series late June-July. The Wednesday series (7:30pm, $15 adults, free under 18) features chamber music; the Sunday concerts (5pm, $20 adults, $5 students) feature symphonies. An annual free children's concert usually is held on a Monday (1pm) in early to mid-July. All concerts are held in the school's Forest Studio.

Seeking to add more vibrancy and diversity to the peninsula's entertainment offerings and to indulge their own interests in music and the sciences, the owners of Oceanside Meadows Inn created the **Innstitute for the Arts and Sciences** (207/963-5557), which presents a series of Thursday-night events late June-late September, with a break during the Schoodic Arts Festival. The wide-ranging calendar includes lectures and concerts as well as art shows. Some are free; others are $12 in advance or $15 at the door.

On Monday evening, weather permitting, in July-August, the **Frenchman Bay Conservancy** (www.frenchmanbay.org) presents a concert series at its Tidal Falls preserve. Bring chairs or a blanket, and pack a picnic supper or purchase lobster rolls or hot dogs from the Fisherman's Inn cart. Music might range from jazz to steel pan drums, ukeleles to an orchestra.

In September, dozens of peninsula businesses open their doors for the **Schoodic Creates** Tour.

SHOPPING

You can find just about anything at the **Winter Harbor 5 and 10** (Main St., Winter Harbor, 207/963-7927). It's the genuine article, an old-fashioned five-and-dime that's somehow still surviving in the age of Walmart.

Need a good read? Duck into **Scottie's Bookhouse** (209 Rte. 1, Hancock, 207/667-6834) and choose from a wide-ranging selection of about 35,000 used books.

Galleries

From Route 1, loop down to Winter Harbor and back up on Route 186 through Prospect Harbor to find these galleries.

Architectural stoneware, with a specialty in sinks, is the drawing card at **Maine Kiln Works** (115 S. Gouldsboro Rd./Rte. 186, Gouldsboro, 207/963-5819, www.waterstonesink.com), but you'll also find functional pottery in the shop. You might also see Dan Weaver at work on the wheel in the back room.

An old post office houses **Lee Art Glass**

GALLERY HOPPING IN HANCOCK AND SULLIVAN

Artist and artisan studios and galleries are numerous, and it's easy to while away a foggy day browsing and buying. Begin by picking up copies of the *Artist Studio Tour Map*, which details and provides directions to about a dozen galleries in Franklin, Sullivan, and Hancock, as well as the *Schoodic Peninsula* brochure, which notes galleries and shops on the peninsula. Both are widely available and free. Hours and days of operation vary; it's best to call first if you really want to visit a gallery. Here's a sampling to get you started.

Take the Point Road 2.5 miles to find Russell and Akemi Wray's **Raven Tree Gallery** (536 Point Rd., Hancock, 207/422-8273). Russell specializes in wood sculpture, bronzes, prints, and jewelry; Akemi crafts pottery. Out front is a small sculpture gallery.

Return to Route 1 and take Eastside Road, just before the Hancock-Sullivan Bridge, and drive 1.5 miles south to **Gull Rock Pottery** (103 Gull Rock Rd., off Eastside Rd., Hancock, 207/422-3990, www.gullrockpottery.com), where Torj and Kurt Wray (Russell's parents) have a magical waterfront setting and sculpture gallery. Inside is wheel-thrown, hand-painted, dishwasher-safe pottery decorated with blue-and-white motifs representing local landscapes.

Cross the Hancock-Sullivan Bridge and then take the first left off Route 1 onto Taunton Drive to find **Lunaform** (Cedar Lane, West Sullivan, 207/422-0923, www.lunaform.com), which is in a class by itself. First there's the setting–the beautifully landscaped grounds surrounding an abandoned granite quarry. Then there's the realization that many of the wonderfully aesthetic garden ornaments created here look like hand-turned *pottery*, when in fact they're hand turned but made of steel-reinforced concrete. It takes a bit of zigging and zagging to get here. Go right onto Track Road; after 0.5 mile, go left onto Cedar Lane.

Bet you can't keep from smiling at the whimsical animal sculptures and fun furniture of talented sculptor-painter Philip Barter. His work is the cornerstone of the eclectic **Barter Family Gallery** (Shore Rd., Sullivan, 207/422-3190, www.bartergallery.com). But there's more: Barter's wife and seven children have put their considerable skills to work producing hooked and braided rugs, jewelry, and other craft items. Follow Taunton Road 2.5 miles from Route 1.

Continue north on Taunton Road as it loops around Hog Bay and onto Route 200 for the next three stops. Charles and Susanne Grosjean's **Hog Bay Pottery** (245 Hog Bay Rd./ Rte. 200, Franklin, 207/565-2282, www.hogbay.com) is a double treat. Inside the casual, laid-back showroom are Charles's functional nature-themed pottery and Susanne's stunning handwoven rugs.

Handwoven textiles are the specialty at **Moosetrack Studio** (388 Bert Gray Rd./Rte. 200, Sullivan, 207/422-9017, www.moosetrackhandweaving.com), where the selections vary from handwoven area rugs to shawls woven from merino wool and silk. Camilla Stege has been weaving since 1969, and her work reflects her experience and expertise.

Paul Breeden, best known for the remarkable illustrations, calligraphy, and maps he's done for *National Geographic*, Time-Life Books, and other national and international publications, displays and sells his paintings at the **Spring Woods Gallery and Willowbrook Garden** (40A Willowbrook Lane, Sullivan, 207/422-3007, www.springwoodsgallery.com, www.willowbrookgarden.com). Also filling the handsome modern gallery space are paintings by Ann Breeden and metal sculptures and silk scarves by the talented Breeden offspring. Allow time to meander through the sculpture garden, where there's even a playhouse for kids.

(679 S. Gouldsboro Rd./Rte. 186, Gouldsboro, 207/963-7280). The fused-glass tableware is created by taking two pieces of window glass and firing them on terra-cotta or bisque molds at 1,500°F. What makes the result so appealing are the colors and the patterns—crocheted doilies or stencils—impressed into the glass. The almost magical results are beautiful and delicate looking yet functional.

Winter Harbor Antiques and Works of Hand (424-426 Main St., Winter Harbor, 207/963-2547) is another double treat: Antiques fill one building, and works by local craftspeople and artists fill the other. It's across from Hammond Hall and set behind colorful, well-tended gardens.

Barbara Noel makes most of the sea-glass jewelry, mobiles, and other creations at **Harbor Treasures** (358 and 368 Main St., Winter Harbor, 207/963-7086).

Works by contemporary Maine artists, including noted painters and sculptors associated with the Schoodic International Sculpture Symposium, are shown in rotating shows at **Littlefield Gallery** (145 Main St., Winter Harbor, 207/963-6005, www.littlefieldgallery.com).

The folk-art funk begins on the exterior of the **Salty Dog Gallery/Hurdy Gurdy Man Antiques** (173 Main St., Prospect Harbor, 207/963-7575), a twofold find. The lower level is filled with fun folk-arts vintage goods. Upstairs, owner Dean Kotula displays his fine art, documentary-style photographic prints.

Visiting the **U.S. Bells Foundry and Watering Cove Pottery** (56 W. Bay Rd./Rte. 186, Prospect Harbor, 207/963-7184, www.us-bells.com) is a treat for the ears, as browsers try out the many varieties of cast-bronze bells made in the adjacent foundry by Richard Fisher. If you're lucky, he may have time to explain the process—particularly intriguing for children and a distraction from their instinctive urge to test every bell in the shop. The store also carries quilts by Dick's wife, Cindy, and wood-fired stoneware and porcelain by their daughter-in-law Liza Fisher. U.S. Bells is 0.25 mile up the hill from Prospect Harbor's post office.

Here's a nifty place: **Chapter Two** (611 Corea Rd., Corea, 207/963-7269, www.chaptertwocorea.com) is home to Spurling House Gallery, Corea Rug Hooking Company, and Accumulated Books Gallery. Spread out in three buildings is a nice selection of used and antiquarian books, fine crafts, and Rosemary's hand-hooked rugs. Yarn, rug-hooking supplies, and lessons are available. Ask Garry for info on hiking local preserve trails, and don't miss the short trail behind the shop.

Down the first dirt lane after the Corea Post Office is **The Corea Wharf Gallery** (13 Gibbs Ln., 207/963-2633, www.coreawharfgallery.com). Inside a humble wharf-top fishing shack are displayed historic photographs of Corea, taken in the 1940s-1960s by Louise Z. Young, born in Corea in 1919. She was a friend of painter Marsden Hartley, and took many candid photographs of him around the area. Young also worked with noted photographer Berenice Abbott. Also here are artifacts from Corea's history, especially ones connected to fishing. The gallery doubles as a food stand selling lobster, lobster rolls, hot dogs, and ice cream.

RECREATION
Preserves
The very active **Frenchman Bay Conservancy** (FBC, 207/422-2328, www.frenchmanbay.org) manages a number of small preserves dotting the region, and most have at least one trail providing access. The conservancy publishes a free *Short Hikes* map, available locally, that provides directions to seven of these.

TIDAL FALLS PRESERVE
FBC's four-acre **Tidal Falls Preserve** (off Eastside Rd., Hancock) overlooks Frenchman Bay's only reversing falls (roiling water when the tide turns). There are picnic tables on the lawn overlooking the falls, and ledges where seals often slumber. It's an idyllic spot. A summer concert series takes place here on Monday during the summer, when Fisherman's Inn Restaurant, in Winter Harbor, operates a food cart selling hot dogs and lobster rolls.

The Corea Wharf Gallery doubles as a lobster shack.

COREA HEATH

In 2008 FBC purchased 600 acres of land known as the **Corea Heath,** and that summer volunteers began cutting trails. *Heath* is a local word for peat land or bog, and this one is a rare coastal plateau bog, distinguished because it rises above the surrounding landscape. It's a spectacular property, with divergent ecosystems including bogs, ledges, and mixedwood forest. Natural features include pitcher plants, sphagnum mosses, rare vascular plants, and jack pines. It's an excellent place for birdwatching, and the preserve borders a section of the Maine Coastal Islands National Wildlife Refuge. Check with the conservancy or ask Garry at Chapter Two (611 Corea Rd., Corea, 207/963-7269, www.chaptertwocorea.com) for more info. The trailhead is signed on the Corea Road.

DONNELL POND PUBLIC RESERVED LAND

More than 15,000 acres of remote forests, ponds, lakes, and mountains have been preserved for public access in **Donnell Pond Public Reserved Land** (Maine Bureau of Parks and Lands, 207/827-1818, www.parksandlands.com), north and east of Sullivan. Hikers can climb Schoodic, Black, Caribou, Tunk, and Fiery Mountains; paddlers and anglers have Donnell Pond, Tunk Lake, Spring River Lake, Long Pond, Round Pond, and Little Pond, among others. Route 182, an official Scenic Highway, snakes through the Donnell Pond preserve. Hunting is permitted, so take special care during hunting season.

The hiking isn't easy here, but it isn't technical, and the options are many. The interconnecting trail system takes in Schoodic Mountain, Black Mountain, and Caribou Mountain. Follow the Schoodic Mountain Loop clockwise, heading westward first. To make a day of it, pack a picnic and take a swimsuit (and don't forget a camera and binoculars for the summit views). On a brilliantly clear day, you'll see Baxter State Park's Mount Katahdin, the peaks of Acadia National Park, and the ocean beyond. And in late July–early

© HILARY NANGLE

One of the rewards for exploring Corea Heath is seeing a beaver lodge.

August, blueberries are abundant on the summit. For such rewards, this is a popular hike, so don't expect to be alone, especially on fall weekends, when the foliage colors are spectacular.

The Black Mountain ascent begins easily enough and then climbs steadily through the woods, easing off a bit before reaching bald ledges. Continue to the true summit by taking the trail past Wizard Pond. Views take in the forested lands, nearby lakes and peaks, and out to Acadia's peaks. You can piggyback it with Schoodic Mountain, using that trailhead base for both climbs. Another possibility is to add Caribou Mountain. That loop exceeds seven miles, making a full day of hiking.

Trailheads are accessible by either boat or vehicle. To reach the vehicle-access trailhead for Schoodic Mountain from Route 1 in East Sullivan, drive just over four miles northeast on Route 183 (Tunk Lake Rd.). Cross the Maine Central Railroad tracks and turn left at the Donnell Pond sign onto an unpaved road (marked as a jeep track on the USGS map). Go about 0.25 mile and then turn left for the parking area and trailhead for Schoodic Mountain, Black Mountain, Caribou Mountain, and a trail to Schoodic Beach. If you continue straight, you'll come to another trailhead for Black and Caribou Mountains. Water-access trailheads are at Schoodic Beach and Redman's Beach.

Bicycling

The Maine Department of Transportation has mapped and provides info on area bicycle routes. These include the Schoodic Peninsula, with 10-, 12-, and 24-mile loops, and the Downeast Route/East Coast Greenway Trail, a 140-mile trail stretching from Ellsworth to Calais. PDF maps with tour details are available at www.exploremaine.org, or you can pick up a copy of *Explore Maine by Bike: 33 Loop Bicycle Tours* at any of the Maine Visitor Centers. Do be extremely careful pedaling in this region, because, as in much of Maine, shoulders are few and traffic moves swiftly.

The best choices for cycling are the **Schoodic Loop** and the quiet roads of **Grindstone Neck** and **Corea.**

SeaScape Kayaking (18 E. Schoodic Dr., Birch Harbor, 207/963-5806, www.seascape-kayaking.com) rents bicycles for $15/day.

Paddling

Experienced sea kayakers can explore the coastline throughout this region. Canoeists can paddle the placid waters of Jones Pond on the Schoodic Peninsula. In Donnell Pond Public Reserved Land, the major water bodies are **Donnell Pond** (big enough by most gauges to be called a lake) and **Tunk** and **Spring River Lakes;** all are accessible for boats (even, alas, powerboats).

To reach the boat-launching area for Donnell Pond from Route 1 in Sullivan, take Route 200 north to Route 182. Turn right and go about 1.5 miles to a right turn just before Swan Brook. Turn and go not quite two miles to the put-in; the road is poor in spots but adequate for a regular vehicle. The Narrows, where you'll put in, is lined with summer cottages ("camps" in the Maine vernacular); keep paddling eastward to the more open part of the lake. Continue on Route 182 to find the boat launches for Tunk Lake and Spring River Lake (hand-carry only). Canoeists and kayakers can access Tunk Stream from Spring River Lake.

Still within the preserve boundaries, but farther east, you can put in a canoe at the northern end of Long Pond and paddle southward into adjoining Round Pond. In early August, Round Mountain, rising a few hundred feet from Long Pond's eastern shore, is a great spot for gathering blueberries and huckleberries. The put-in for Long Pond is on the south side of Route 182 (park well off the road), about two miles east of Tunk Lake.

OUTFITTERS AND TRIPS

Paddle around the waters of Schoodic or Flanders Bay with **SeaScape Kayaking** (18 E. Schoodic Dr., Birch Harbor, 207/963-5806, www.seascapekayaking.com). Guided three-hour tours are $50 pp, including homemade blueberry snacks. Canoe rental for lake usage is $45 per 24 hours; kayaks are $45 double, $35 single.

Antonio Blasi, a Registered Maine Sea Kayak and Recreational Guide, leads guided tours of Frenchman or Taunton Bay and hiking and camping expeditions through **Hancock Point Kayak Tours** (58 Point Rd., Hancock, 207/422-6854, www.hancockpointkayak.com). A three-hour paddle, including all equipment, safety and paddling demonstrations, and usually an island break, is $45. Overnight kayak camping trips are $150 pp. Antonio also leads overnight backpacking trips for $125 pp, and cross-country skiing and snowshoe tours are available in winter.

Swimming

The best freshwater swimming in the area is at **Jones Beach,** a community-owned recreation area on Jones Pond in West Gouldsboro. Here you'll find restrooms, a nice playground, picnic facilities, a boat launch, a swim area with a float, and a small beach. Open sunrise to

sunset, the beach is at the end of Recreation Road, off Route 195, which is 0.3 mile south of Route 1. No unleashed pets are permitted.

Two beach areas on Donnell Pond are also popular for swimming—**Schoodic Beach** and **Redman's Beach**—and both have picnic tables, fire rings, and pit toilets. It's a half-mile hike to Schoodic Beach from the parking lot. Redman's Beach is accessible only by boat. Other pocket beaches are also accessible by boat, and there's a rope swing (use at your own risk) by a roadside pullout for Fox Pond.

A sandy beach on a remote freshwater pond is the reward for a quarter-mile hike into the Frenchman Bay Conservancy's **Little Tunk Pond Preserve.** From Route 1 in Sullivan, take Route 183 about five miles, then look for the parking area on your left.

Golf

Play the nine-hole **Grindstone Neck Golf Course** (Grindstone Ave., Winter Harbor, 207/963-7760, www.grindstonegolf.com) just for the dynamite scenery and for a glimpse of this exclusive late-19th-century summer enclave.

ACCOMMODATIONS

There are no lodgings in the Schoodic section of the park, but within 15 minutes are pleasant inns, bed-and-breakfasts, and an RV campground.

Country Inns

Follow Hancock Point Road 4.8 miles south of Route 1 to the three-story gray-blue **Crocker House Country Inn** (967 Point Rd., Hancock, 207/422-6806, www.crockerhouse.com, $115-180), Rich and Liz Malaby's antidote to Bar Harbor's summer traffic. Built as a summer hotel in 1884, the inn underwent rehabbing a century later, but it retains a delightfully old-fashioned air despite now offering Wi-Fi and having air-conditioning. Breakfast is included. Guests can relax in the common room or reserve spa time in the carriage house. One kayak and a few bicycles are available; clay tennis courts are nearby. If you're arriving by boat, request a mooring. The inn's dining room is a draw in itself. Some rooms are pet-friendly.

Bed-and-Breakfasts

Overlooking the Gouldsboro Peninsula's only sandy saltwater beach, **Oceanside Meadows Inn** (Rte. 195, Corea Rd., Prospect Harbor, 207/963-5557, May-mid-Oct., $149-209) is an eco-conscious retreat on 200 acres with organic gardens, wildlife habitat, and walking trails. Fourteen guest rooms are split between the 1860s captain's house and the 1820 Shaw farmhouse next door. Rooms have a comfy, old-fashioned shabby-chic decor. Note that there are no TVs or air-conditioning, and many of the bathrooms are tiny. Breakfast is a multicourse vegetarian event, usually featuring herbs and flowers from the inn's gardens. The husband-and-wife team Ben Walter and Sonja Sundaram, assisted by a loyal staff, seem to have thought of everything—hot drinks available all day, a guest fridge, beach toys, even detailed guides to the property's trails and habitats (great for entertaining kids). As if all that weren't enough, Sonja and Ben have totally restored the 1820 timber-frame barn out back—creating the **Oceanside Meadows Innstitute for the Arts and Sciences.** Local art hangs on the walls, and the 125-seat barn has a full schedule of concerts and lectures June-September on natural history, Native American traditions, and more, usually on Thursday night. Some are free, some require tickets; all require reservations. Oceanside Meadows is six miles off Route 1. There are no nearby restaurants, so expect to head out for lunch or dinner.

Watch lobster boats unload their catch at the dock opposite **Elsa's Inn on the Harbor** (179 Main St., Prospect Harbor, 207/963-7571, www.elsasinn.com, $120-165). Jeffrey and Cynthia Alley, along with their daughter Megan and her husband, Glenn Moshier, have turned the home of Jeff's mother, Elsa, into a warm and welcoming inn. The family roots in the area go back more than 10 generations, so you're guaranteed to receive solid information on where to go and what to do. Every

room has an ocean view, and Megan pampers guests with sumptuous linens, down duvets, terry robes, Wi-Fi, and a hearty hot breakfast. After a day exploring, settle into a rocker on the veranda and gaze over the boat-filled harbor out to Prospect Harbor Light. And afterward? Well, perhaps a lobster bake. With advance notice, Jeff will bring over some fresh lobster, and Megan will prepare a complete lobster dinner—corn on the cob, coleslaw, homemade rolls, and a seasonal dessert, all for about $25 pp, depending on market rates. Minimums apply, but if you're interested, ask Megan to see if other guests are too. It's open year-round.

Off the beaten path is Bob Travers and Barry Canner's **Black Duck Inn on Corea Harbor** (Crowley Island Rd., Corea, 207/963-2689, www.blackduck.com, May-mid-Oct., $140-200), literally the end of the line on the Gouldsboro Peninsula. Set on 12 acres in this timeless fishing village, the bed-and-breakfast has four handsomely decorated guest rooms and plenty of common space. Also available are a harborfront studio and cottage.

Something of a categorical anomaly, **The Bluff House Inn** (57 Bluff House Rd., Gouldsboro, 207/963-7805, www.bluffinn.com, year-round, $95-175) is part motel, part hotel, part bed-and-breakfast. The 1980s building overlooks Frenchman Bay. Verandas wrap around the first and second floors, so bring binoculars for sighting ospreys and bald eagles. Pine walls and flooring give a lodge feeling to the open first floor. Settle by the stone fireplace or grab a seat by the window. Breakfast is continental buffet, usually with one hot entrée. The eight second-floor rooms are decorated "country" fashion, with quilts on the very comfortable beds. (In hot weather, request a corner room.) Pet-friendly rooms are available for $15/stay.

Just off the peninsula, and set well back from Route 1, **Acadia View Bed and Breakfast** (175 Rte. 1, Gouldsboro, 866/963-7457, www.acadiaview.com, $145-175) tops a bluff with views across Frenchman Bay to the peaks of Mount Desert and a path down to the shorefront. Pat and Jim Close built the oceanfront house as

© HILARY NANGLE

Elsa's Inn on the Harbor overlooks working wharfs and a distant lighthouse.

a bed-and-breakfast that opened in 2005. It's filled with antique treasures from the Closes' former life in Connecticut. Each of the four guest rooms has a private deck. The Route 1 location is convenient to everything. It's open year-round.

Machias native Dottie Mace operated a bed-and-breakfast in Virginia before returning to Maine to open **Taunton River Bed & Breakfast** (19 Taunton Dr., Sullivan, 207/422-2070, www.tauntonriverbandb.com, $115-125) in a 19th-century farmhouse with river views. Rooms are carefully decorated; they're warm and inviting, formal without being stuffy. Two of the three guest rooms share a bath. It would be easy to spend the day just sitting on the porch swing, but it's an easy pedal or drive to local art galleries. The inn is just a stone's throw off Route 1, so traffic noise might bother the noise sensitive.

Sustainable living is the focus of Karen and Ed Curtis's peaceful **Three Pines Bed and Breakfast** (274 East Side Rd., Hancock, 207/460-7595, www.threepinesbandb.com,

year-round, $100-125), fronting on Sullivan Harbor, just below the Reversing Falls. Their quiet off-the-grid 40-acre oceanfront organic farm faces Sullivan Harbor and is home to a llama, rare-breed chickens and sheep, ducks, and bees as well as a large organic garden, berry bushes, an orchard, and greenhouses. Photovoltaic cells provide electricity, and appliances are primarily propane powered; satellite technology operates the phone, TV, and Wi-Fi systems. Two inviting guest rooms have private entrances and water views. A full vegetarian breakfast (with fresh eggs from the farm) is served. Bicycles and a canoe are available. You can walk or pedal along an abandoned railway line down to the point, and you can launch a canoe or kayak from the back—or is it the front?—yard. Children are welcome; pets are a possibility.

Cottages

Roger and Pearl Barto, whose family roots in this region go back five generations, have four rental accommodations on their Henry's Cove oceanfront property, **Main Stay Cottages** (66 Sargent St., Winter Harbor, 207/963-2601, www.awa-web.com/stayinn, $90-125). Most unusual is the small one-bedroom Boat House, which has stood since the 1880s. It hangs over the harbor, with views to Mark Island Light, and you can hear the water gurgling below you at high tide (but it is cramped, be forewarned). Other options include a very comfortable efficiency cottage, a one-bedroom cottage, a second-floor suite with a private entrance, and a four-bedroom house ($250/night). All have big decks and fabulous views over the lobster boat-filled harbor; watch for the eagles that frequently soar overhead. Main Stay is on the Island Explorer bus route and just a short walk from where the Bar Harbor Ferry docks.

Simple and rustic, but charming in a sweet, old-fashioned way, are **Albee's Shorehouse Cottages** (Rte. 186, Prospect Harbor, 207/963-2336 or 800/963-2336, www.theshorehouse.com, May-mid-Oct., $85-135), a cluster of 10 vintage cottages decorated with braided rugs, fresh flowers, and other homey touches. Two things make this place special: the waterfront location—and it's truly waterfront; many of the cottages are just a couple of feet from the high-tide mark—and the management. Owner Richard Rieth goes out of his way to make guests feel welcome. Pick up lobsters and say what time you want dinner, and they'll be cooked and delivered to your cottage. He's slowly fixing up the cottages, but these will never be fancy; if you're fussy, go elsewhere. In peak season, preference is given to Saturday-Saturday rentals, but shorter stays are often available. Wi-Fi is available throughout, and dogs are welcome.

The views to Mount Desert are dreamy from **Edgewater Cabins** (25 Benvenuto Ave., Sullivan, 207/422-6414 May 15-Oct. 15, 603/472-8644 rest of year, www.edgewatercabins.com, $525-850/week), a colony of seven housekeeping cottages on a spit of land jutting into Frenchman Bay. The well-tended four-acre property has both sunrise and sunset water views, big trees for shade, and lawns rolling to the shorefront. Stays of at least three nights ($85-175/night) are possible, when there's availability.

Camping

A handful of authorized primitive campsites can be found in the **Donnell Pond Public Reserved Land.** Prime sites are on Tunk Lake (southwestern corner) and Donnell Pond (at Schoodic Beach and Redman's Beach), all accessible on foot or by boat. Each has a table, a fire ring, and a nearby pit toilet. Many of the sites are on the lakefront. All are first-come, first-served with no fees or permits required; they are snapped up quickly on midsummer weekends. You can camp elsewhere within this public land, except in day-use areas, but fires are not permitted at unofficial sites.

Sites at **Mountainview Campground** (22 Harbor View Dr./Rte. 1, Sullivan, 207/422-6408, www.flandersbay.com, May-Oct., $26-40) are spread throughout an oceanfront field, so there's not a lot of privacy. The best sites edge the Frenchman Bay shorefront and are reserved for tents and small campers using 20-amp service. Other sites can accommodate full hookups with 30-50-amp service. Hot showers are free, and if you stay six days, your seventh day is free.

The Bartos, owners of **Main Stay Cottages** (66 Sargent St., Winter Harbor, 207/963-2601, www.awa-web.com/stayinn, $50), have added a 10-site campground overlooking Henry Cove. It's designed for self-contained RVs, as there are no restrooms or showers on site; sewer, water, electric, and Wi-Fi are available.

FOOD
Local Flavors

Make a point to attend one of the many **public suppers** held throughout the summer in this area and so many other rural corners of Maine. Typically benefiting a worthy cause, these usually feature beans, chowder, or spaghetti and the serendipity of plain potluck. Everyone saves room for the homemade pies. Notices of such suppers are usually posted on public bulletin boards in country stores and in libraries, on signs in front of churches, and at other places where people gather.

The **Winter Harbor Farmers Market** takes place in the parking lot at the corner of Newman Street and Route 186, Winter Harbor, on Tuesday morning, late June-early September.

This area has two excellent smokehouses. Stock up on gourmet goodies at **Grindstone Neck of Maine** (311 Newman St./Rte. 186, just north of downtown Winter Harbor, 207/963-7347 or 866/831-8734, www.grindstoneneck.com), which earns high marks for its smoked salmon, shellfish, spreads and pâtés, and smoked cheeses, all made without preservatives or artificial ingredients. Also available are fresh fish, wine, and frozen foods for campers. Defying its name, **Sullivan Harbor Smokehouse** (Rte. 1, Hancock, 207/422-3735 or 800/422-4014, www.sullivanharborfarm.com) is in spacious modern digs in Hancock. Big interior windows allow visitors to see into the production facility.

You'd be hard pressed to find a better place to enjoy a lobster or lobster roll than the **Corea Wharf Gallery** (13 Gibbs Ln., Corea, 207/963-2633), an eat-on-the-wharf food stand overlooking dreamy Corea Harbor. The menu includes lobster rolls, lobster grilled cheese, hot dogs, sausages, and ice cream.

Tracey's Seafood (Rte. 182, Sullivan, 207/422-9072) doesn't look like much from the road, but locals insist it's their favorite cheap-eats spot for meaty lobster rolls, chowders, and fried seafood. Indoor seating is available.

Craving curry? Call in your order 24 hours in advance and **Tandoor Downeast** (119 Eastbrook Rd., Franklin, 207/565-3598, www.tandoordowneast.com) will prepare authentic Indian cuisine for you to take out. Chef Gunjan Gilbert's menu is extensive, and prices are reasonable, with most choices $6-8. Or take your chances and simply stop by and choose from whatever's available.

Step into Italy at Buzzy Gioia's **Maple Knoll Pizza** (138 Blackswoods Rd./Rte. 182, Franklin, 207/565-2068, 2pm-8pm Wed.-Sun.), on the eastern edge of in-town Franklin.

Buzzy draws on his Italian heritage—his parents came from the old country—to craft authentic pizzas, submarine sandwiches, and calzones. And don't miss his special sauce.

Take Route 182 to Route 200/Eastbrook Road, and go 1.6 miles to family-operated **Shalom Orchard Organic Winery** (158 Eastbrook Rd., Franklin, 207/565-2312, www.shalomorchard.com). The certified-organic farm is well off the beaten path, but worth a visit for its organic fruit and wines, as well as for its yarns, pelts, fleece, and especially the views of Frenchman Bay from the hilltop.

German and Italian presses, Portuguese corks, and Maine fruit all contribute to the creation of Bob and Kathe Bartlett's award-winning dinner and dessert wines, just north of the Schoodic Peninsula. Founded in 1982, **Bartlett Maine Estate Winery** (175 Chicken Mill Pond Rd., Gouldsboro, 207/546-2408, www.bartlettwinery.com, 10am-5pm Mon.-Sat. June-Oct. or by appt.) produces more than 20,000 gallons annually in a handsome wood-and-stone building designed by the Bartletts. Not ones to rest on their many laurels, in 2010 the Bartletts introduced the **Spirits of Maine Distillery.** There are no tours, but you're welcome to sample the wines. Reserve wines and others of limited vintage are sold only on-site. A sculpture garden patio makes a nice spot to relax. Bartlett's is 0.5 mile south of Route 1 in Gouldsboro.

Family Favorites

Once a true old-fashioned country store, beloved **Gerrish's Store** (352 Main St., Winter Harbor) has been reborn as a café and ice cream shop, but it remains family-owned and -operated.

The best place for grub and gossip in Winter Harbor is **Chase's Restaurant** (193 Main St., Winter Harbor, 207/963-7171, 7am-8pm daily, to 2pm Sun.), a seasoned no-frills booth-and-counter operation.

Shoot pool, play darts or horseshoes, watch the game on TV, sip a cold drink, and savor a burger at **Nautica Pub** (East Schoodic Dr., at the intersection with Rte. 186, Birch Harbor,

207/963-7916, from 11am daily). There's usually live jazz on Thursday nights.

When you're craving pizza, **Sunrise Deli & Café** (27 Main St., Prospect Harbor, 207/963-9017, 7am-9pm daily) is the spot. Expect good pie, sandwiches, specials, and luscious baked goods.

Don't be put off by "Wilbur," the lobster *sculpture* outside **Ruth & Wimpy's Kitchen** (792 Rte. 1, Hancock, 207/422-3723, www.ruthandwimpys.com, 11am-9pm Mon.-Sat.); you'll probably see a crowd as well. This family-fare standby serves hefty sandwiches, lobster prepared 30 ways, pizza, pasta, and steak. Prices begin around $3.25 for a cheeseburger and climb to about $35 for a twin lobster shore dinner. Antique license plates and collections of miniature cars and trucks accent the interior. It's five miles east of Ellsworth, close to the Hancock Point turnoff.

Good food served by friendly folks is what pulls the locals into ◖ **Chester Pike's Galley** (2336 Rte. 1, Sullivan, 207/422-8200,

Ruth & Wimpy's Kitchen is a road-food classic for lobster served about two dozen ways.

6am-2pm Tues.-Thurs. and Sat., 6am-2pm and 4:30pm-8:30pm Fri., 7am-2pm Sun., $6-12). The prices are low, the portions big. If you're on a diet, don't even *look* at the glass case filled with fresh-baked pies, cakes, and cookies. Go early if you want to snag one of the homemade doughnuts on Sunday morning. It's also open Friday night for a fish fry with free seconds.

Casual Dining

The Fisherman's Inn (7 Newman St./Rte. 186, Winter Harbor, 207/963-5585, 4:30pm-9pm daily late May-mid-Oct.) has been an institution in these parts since 1947. Kathy Johnson runs the front of the house; her husband, Carl, is the chef. He's also the brains behind Grindstone Neck of Maine, the smoked-seafood operation just up the road, and diners are welcomed with a sample of smoked-salmon spread and a cheese spread. That's followed up with Carl's focaccia bread and the house dipping sauce, a tasty blend of Romano cheese, fresh garlic, roasted red pepper, and parsley with olive oil. And that all comes before any appetizers. Seafood is the specialty here, and there's a good chance that the guy at the neighboring booth caught your lobster or fish. Asian influences are evident too. Entrées range $18-30, and some dishes can top that given seasonal market rates, but it's easy to make a meal from starters. If you're on a tight budget, aim for an early dinner. Early-bird specials, served 4:30pm-5:30pm, are around $14. Carl also operates a food cart out front, serving meat-packed lobster rolls and gourmet hot dogs for lunch (11am-3pm).

Bunker's Wharf (260 East Schoodic Dr., Birch Harbor, 207/963-7488, 5pm-9pm Tues.-Sun., late May-mid-Oct.) overlooks a working wharf and lobster-boat-filled harbor. It's one mile from the end of Acadia National Park's Schoodic Loop, on a two-way section of road, so it can be approached from Birch Harbor too. Entrées such as scallops over linguine, filet mignon, and stuffed haddock run $15-34, and steamed lobster is always available.

In 2013, chef Mike Poirier and baker Alice Letcher opened **The Salt Box** (1161 Rte. 1,

© TOM NANGLE

A lobster boat turned ferry makes it easy to travel between Bar Harbor and Winter Harbor.

Hancock, 207/422-9900, www.saltboxmaine. com, 8am-10:30am Fri.-Sat., to 11:30am Sun., 11am-2:30pm Tues.-Sat., from 5pm by reservation Thurs.-Sat.), in a log building set back from the road, and they quickly earned a following. The decor is gently rustic, the food is sophisticated yet approachable and focused on fresh seasonal ingredients, and the service is excellent. A tasting dinner (about $45) is served on Thursday nights. Brunch is served 8am-noon on Sundays.

Fine Dining

The unpretentious dining rooms at the **Crocker House Country Inn** (967 Point Rd., Hancock Point, 207/422-6806, www.crockerhouse.com, 5:30pm-9pm daily May 1-Oct. 31, 5:30pm-8:30pm Fri.-Sun. Apr. and Nov.-Dec., entrées $22-32) provide the setting for well-prepared continental fare.

The wide-ranging menu at **Chipper's** (Rte. 1, Hancock, 207/422-8238, www.chippersrestaurant.com, 5pm-9pm Wed.-Sun.), a combination restaurant and pub, includes rack of

lamb and even chateaubriand, but the emphasis is on seafood; the crab cakes earn rave reviews. Meals include a sampling of tasty haddock chowder and a salad, but save room for the homemade ice cream for dessert. Entrées are in the $20-33 range, but some appetizer-salad combos provide budget options, and burgers and subs are available in the pub.

INFORMATION AND SERVICES

For advance information about eastern Hancock County, contact the **Schoodic Peninsula Chamber of Commerce** (www.acadia-schoodic.org).

To plan ahead, see the Acadia website (www. nps.gov/acad), where you can download a Schoodic map.

Check out **Dorcas Library** (Rte. 186, Prospect Harbor, 207/963-4027, www.dorcas. lib.me.us) or **Winter Harbor Public Library** (18 Chapel Ln., Winter Harbor, 207/963-7556, www.winterharbor.lib.me.us), in the 1888 beach stone and fieldstone Channing Chapel.

The inviting octagonal **Hancock Point Library** (Hancock Point Rd., Hancock Point, 207/422-6400, summer only) was formed in 1899. More than a library, it's a center for village activities. Check the bulletin boards by the entrance to find out what's happening when.

GETTING THERE AND AROUND

Winter Harbor is about 25 miles via Routes 1 and 186 from Ellsworth. It's about 20 miles or 30 minutes to Milbridge, on the Down East Coast.

By Ferry and Bus

The seasonal passenger-only **Bar Harbor Ferry** (207/288-2984, www.barharborferry. com, round-trip $32 adults, $22 children, $7 bicycle) operates four times daily late June-late August between Bar Harbor and Winter Harbor and coordinates with the free **Island Explorer** (www.exploreacadia.com) bus's summertime Schoodic route, Route 8, making a super car-free excursion in either direction. The bus covers the lower part of the peninsula, from Winter Harbor through Prospect Harbor, late June-August, circulating roughly once an hour.

A ferry alternative is **Winter Harbor Water Taxi & Tours** (207/963-7007, www.winterharborwatertaxiandtours.com). Captain Wes Shaw will squire you around Schoodic's waters or over to Bar Harbor for $75/hour, covering up to six passengers.

THE DOWN EAST COAST

The term *Down East* is rooted in the direction the wind blows—the prevailing southwest wind that powered 19th-century sailing vessels along this rugged coastline. But to be truly Down East, in the minds of most Mainers, you have to be physically here in Washington County—a stunning landscape of waterways, forests, blueberry barrens, rocky shoreline dotted with islands and lighthouses, and independent pocket-size communities, many still dependent upon fishing or lobstering for their economies.

At one time, most of the Maine Coast used to be as underdeveloped as this part of it. You can set your clock back a generation or two while you're here; you'll find no giant malls, only a couple of fast-food joints, and two—count 'em—traffic lights. Although there are a handful of restaurants offering fine dining, for the most part your choices are limited to family-style restaurants specializing in home cooking with an emphasis on fresh (usually fried) seafood and lobster rolls. Nor will you find grand resorts or even not-so-grand hotels. Motels, tourist cabins, and small inns and bed-and-breakfasts dot the region. The upside is that prices too are a generation removed. If you're searching for the Maine of your memories or your imagination, this is it.

When eastern Hancock County flows into western Washington County, you're on the Down East Coast (sometimes called the Sunrise Coast). From Steuben eastward to Jonesport, Machias, and Lubec—then "around the corner" to Eastport, Calais, Princeton, and Grand Lake Stream—Washington County is

© HILARY NANGLE

THE DOWN EAST COAST

HIGHLIGHTS

0   10 mi

0   10 km

NEW BRUNSWICK

MAINE

Roosevelt Campobello International Park

Calais

Whale-Watching   Eastport

Shackford Head State Park

West Quoddy Head State Park

Beddington

Machias

Machias Seal Island Puffin Tour

Milbridge   Beals

Bar Harbor

Great Wass Island Preserve

Maine Coastal Islands National Wildlife Refuge

© AVALON TRAVEL

LOOK FOR ◖ TO FIND RECOMMENDED SIGHTS, ACTIVITIES, DINING, AND LODGING.

◖ **Maine Coastal Islands National Wildlife Refuge:** More than 300 birds have been sighted at Petit Manan Point, but even if you're not a bird-watcher, come for the hiking and, in August, the blueberries (page 368).

◖ **Great Wass Island Preserve:** The finest natural treasure in this part of Maine is the Great Wass Archipelago, partly owned by The Nature Conservancy, with opportunities for hiking and bird-watching (page 374).

◖ **Machias Seal Island Puffin Tour:** An excursion boat departs from Cutler for Machias Seal Island, home to Atlantic puffins (the clowns of the sea), as well as razorbill auks, Arctic terns, and common murres (page 380).

◖ **West Quoddy Head State Park:** This park features the iconic candy-striped West Quoddy Head Light, with recreational opportunities like cliff-side hiking trails, beachcombing, and bird-watching (page 383).

◖ **Roosevelt Campobello International Park:** Make it an international vacation by venturing over to this New Brunswick park, home to the Roosevelt Cottage and miles of hiking trails, jointly managed by the United States and Canada (page 393).

◖ **Whale-Watching:** Cruise into Passamaquoddy Bay, pass the Old Sow whirlpool, and ogle seabirds and whales (page 396).

◖ **Shackford Head State Park:** The rewards for this easy hike are panoramic views over Cobscook Bay from Eastport to Campobello (page 401).

twice the size of Rhode Island, covers 2,528 square miles, has about 30,000 residents, and stakes a claim as the first U.S. real estate to see the morning sun. The region also includes handfuls of offshore islands—some accessible by ferry, charter boat, or private vessels. (Some, with sensitive bird-nesting sites, are off-limits during the summer.) At the uppermost point of the coast, and conveniently linked to Lubec by a bridge, New Brunswick's Campobello Island is a popular day-trip destination—the locale of Franklin D. Roosevelt's summer retreat. Other attractions in this area include festivals, concert series, art and antiques galleries, lighthouses, two Native American reservations, and the great outdoors for hiking, biking, birding, sea kayaking, whale-watching, camping, swimming, and fishing. Hook inland to Grand Lake Stream to find a remote, wild land of lakes famed for fishing and old-fashioned family-style summer vacations.

One of the Down East Coast's millennial

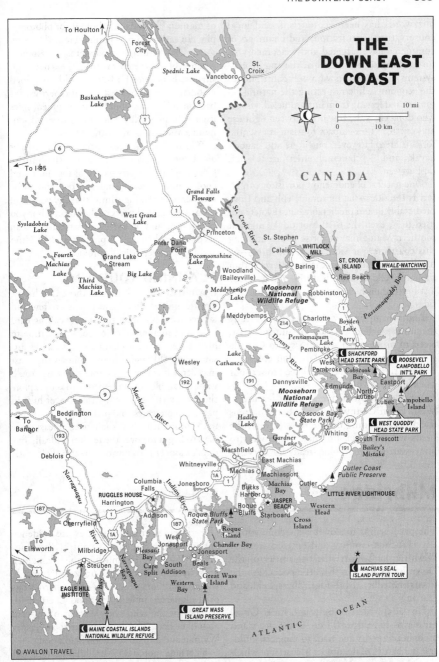

THE DOWN EAST COAST

buzzwords has been ecotourism, and local conservation organizations and chambers of commerce have targeted and welcomed visitors willing to be careful of the fragile ecosystems here—visitors who will contribute to the economy while respecting the natural resources and leaving them untrammeled, visitors who don't cross the fine line between light use and overuse. Low-impact tourism is essential for this area. However, outfitters and canoe-, kayak-, and bicycle-rental outlets are few and far between.

One natural phenomenon no visitor can affect is the tide—the inexorable ebb and flow, predictably in and predictably out. If you're not used to it, even the 6-10-foot tidal ranges of southern Maine may surprise you. But along this coastline, the tides are astonishing—as much as 28 feet difference in water level within six hours. Old-timers tell stories of big money lost betting on horses racing the fast-moving tides.

Another surprise to visitors may be how early the sun rises—and sets—on the Sunrise Coast. Keep in mind that if you cross into Canada from either Lubec or Calais, you enter the Atlantic time zone, and you'll need to set your clock ahead one hour.

Yet another distinctive natural feature of Washington County is its blueberry barrens (fields). Depending on the time of year, the fields will be black (torched by growers to jump-start the crop), blue (ready for harvest), or maroon (fall foliage, fabulous for photography). In early summer, a million rented bees set to work pollinating the blossoms. By August, when a blue haze forms over the knee-high shrubs, bent-over bodies use old-fashioned wooden rakes to harvest the ripe berries. It's backbreaking work, but the employment lines usually form quickly when newspaper ads announce the start of the annual harvest.

Warm clothing is essential in this corner of Maine. It may be nicknamed the Sunrise Coast, but it also gets plenty of fog, rain, and cool temperatures. Temperatures tend to be warmer, and the fog diminishes, as you head toward the inland parts of the county, but you can never count on that. Mother Nature is an accomplished curveball pitcher, and El Niño and La Niña periodically provide an assist.

PLANNING YOUR TIME

Down East Maine is not for those in a hurry. Traffic ambles along, and towns are few and far between. Nature is the biggest calling card here, and to appreciate it you'll need time to hike, bike, canoe, sea kayak, or take an excursion boat. Although Route 1 follows the coast in general, it's often miles from the water. You'll want to ramble down the peninsulas to explore the seaside villages, see lighthouses, or hike in parks and preserves, and perhaps wander inland to the unspoiled lakes. You'll need at least three days to begin to cover the territory, ideally five days or longer if you want to really explore it.

Milbridge

The pace begins to slow by the time you've left Hancock County and entered western Washington County, the beginning of the Down East Coast. In this little pocket are the towns of Steuben, Milbridge, Cherryfield, and Harrington.

Nowadays life can be tough here. Once, great wooden ships slid down the ways and brought prosperity and trade to shippers, builders, and barons of the timber industry, of which Cherryfield's stunning houses are evidence enough. Now the barons control the blueberry fields, covering much of the inland area of western Washington County and annually shipping millions of pounds of blueberries out of headquarters in Milbridge and Cherryfield, named for the wild cherries that once were abundant here. The big names here are Jasper Wyman and Sons and Cherryfield Foods.

Milbridge (pop. 1,353) straddles Route 1 and

the Narraguagus River (Nar-ra-GWAY-gus, a Native American name meaning "above the boggy place"), once the state's premier source of Atlantic salmon. **Cherryfield** (pop. 1,232) is at the tidal limit of the Narraguagus. Even though Route 1A trims maybe three miles off the trip from Milbridge to Harrington, resist the urge to take it. Take Route 1 from Milbridge to Cherryfield—the Narraguagus Highway—and then continue to Harrington. You shouldn't miss Cherryfield.

Steuben's (pop. 1,131) claim to fame is the Petit Manan section of the Maine Coastal Islands National Wildlife Refuge.

SIGHTS
Milbridge Historical Society Museum

A group of energetic residents worked tirelessly to establish the **Milbridge Historical Society Museum** (S. Main St., Milbridge, 207/546-4471, www.milbridgehistoricalsociety.org, 1pm-4pm Sat.-Sun. June-Sept. and also Tues. July-Aug., donation). Displays in the large exhibit room focus on Milbridge's essential role in the shipbuilding trade, but kids will enjoy such oddities as an amputation knife used by a local doctor and a re-created country kitchen. The museum also sponsors a monthly lecture series June-October.

Scenic Fall Foliage Routes

In fall—roughly early September-early October in this part of Maine—the postharvest blueberry fields take on brilliant scarlet hues. They're gorgeous. The best barren-viewing road is Route 193 between Cherryfield and Beddington, via Deblois, the link between Routes 1 and 9—a 21-mile stretch of granite outcrops, pine windscreens, and fiery-red fields.

Cherryfield Historic District

Imagine a little town this far Down East having a 75-acre National Register Historic District with 52 architecturally significant buildings. If architecture appeals, don't miss Cherryfield. The **Cherryfield-Narraguagus Historical Society** (88 River Rd., Cherryfield,

207/546-2076, www.cherryfieldhistorical.com, 1pm-4pm Sat. summer) has produced a free brochure-map, *Walking Tour of the Cherryfield Historic District,* which you can download. Architectural styles included on the route are Greek Revival, Italianate, Queen Anne, Colonial Revival, Second Empire, Federal, and Gothic Revival—dating 1803-1940, with most from the late 19th century. Especially impressive for such a small town are the Second Empire-style homes.

ENTERTAINMENT AND EVENTS

The biggest event in this end of Washington County is **Milbridge Days,** the last weekend in July, drawing hundreds of visitors. The Saturday-afternoon highlight is the codfish relay race—hilarious enough to have been featured in *Sports Illustrated* magazine and on national television. The four-member teams, clad in slickers and hip boots, really do hand off a greased cod instead of the usual baton. Race rules specify that runners must be "reasonably sober" and not carry the codfish between their teeth or legs. Also on the schedule are blueberry pancake breakfasts, a fun parade, kids' games, an auction, a dance, beano and cribbage tournaments, crafts booths, and a lobster bake. You have to be there. The relay race has been going since the mid-1980s; the festival has been going for a century and a half.

Eagle Hill Institute (59 Eagle Hill Rd., Steuben, 207/546-2821, www.eaglehill.us) offers series of community programs including lectures, sometimes preceded by optional dinners ($15-20, advance reservation required), by guest speakers, authors, and scholars on wide-ranging natural history and cultural history topics with a scientific focus. See the website or call for the current schedule. The institute is four miles off Route 1. Take Dyer Bay Road off Route 1, bearing left at the fork onto Mogador Road for a total of 3.6 miles, then left on Schooner Point Road, and then right on Eagle Hill Road. Programs take place in the dining hall lecture room.

MAINE FISHERIES TRAIL

According to the National Marine Fisheries Service, the proportion of Maine workers employed in commercial fishing is more than 10 times the percentage nationwide. Maine's **Downeast Fisheries Trail** (www.downeastfisheriestrail.org) stretches along Route 1 from Penobscot Bay to Cobscook Bay, but here in Washington County, where the percentage of fishing folks is even higher, you're in the thick of it.

Of the hundreds of sardine canneries that peppered coastal Maine's waterfront, none remain. Once, groundfish such as cod were a major fishery for boats heading to sea from ports such as Jonesport, Lubec, and Eastport, but now they're all but gone. These days, commercial fishermen harvest clams, elvers, crabs, alewives, scallops, urchins, shrimp, marine worms, and even seaweed, in addition to fish and lobster; hatcheries seek to replenish species such as sea-run salmon; and farms raise Atlantic salmon, oysters, and mussels.

The mapped trail comprises 45 sites celebrating Maine's maritime heritage and marine resources, from the Penobscot Marine Museum in Searsport to the Cobscook Bay Resource Center in Eastport. Marked sites allow you to delve into Maine's fishing and maritime heritage by visiting fish hatcheries, aquaculture facilities, active fishing harbors, processing plants, working wharves and piers, and related historical sites. You can request a printed copy of the map by calling 207/581-1435.

SHOPPING

Arthur Smith (Rogers Point Rd., Steuben, 207/546-3462) is the real thing when it comes to chain-saw carvings. He's an extremely talented folk artist who looks at a piece of wood and sees an animal in it. His carvings of great blue herons, eagles, wolves, porcupines, flamingoes, and other creatures are incredibly detailed, and his wife, Marie, paints them in lifelike colors. Don't expect a fancy studio; much of the work can be viewed roadside.

Also in Steuben, but on the other end of the spectrum, is **Ray Carbone** (460 Pigeon Hill Rd., Steuben, 207/546-2170, www.raycarbonesculptor.com), whose masterful wood, stone, and bronze sculptures and fine furniture are definitely worth stopping to see or buy. Don't miss the granite sculptures and birdbaths in the garden.

Contemporary Maine art by local artists and artisans is shown in rotating shows at **Schooner Gallery** (59 Main St., Milbridge, 207/546-3179, www.schoonergallery.com).

Just across the bridge from downtown Cherryfield, **Riverlily** (2 Wilson Hill Rd., Cherryfield, 207/546-7666) carries a little bit of everything, from lotions and potions to jewelry and scarves.

Stop by **4 Main Street Antiques** (4 Main St., Cherryfield, 207/546-2664) for European and American furniture and decorative works. **The River Bank Gallery** (8 Main St., Cherryfield, 207/546-3718) carries an eclectic selection of art and antiques.

Tunk Mountain Arts & Crafts (639 Blackswoods Rd./Rt. 182, Cherryfield, 207/546-8948) shows works in varied media by local and regional artists.

The farm store at **Black Woods Farm Alpacas** (278 Blackswoods Rd., Cherryfield, 207/546-2193) is a find for fiber fans. Purchase everything from raw fiber to finished products, including clothing and teddy bears.

RECREATION
◖ Maine Coastal Islands National Wildlife Refuge

Occupying a 2,195-acre peninsula in Steuben with 10 miles of rocky shoreline and three offshore islands is the refuge's outstandingly scenic **Petit Manan Point Division** (Pigeon Hill Rd., Steuben, 207/546-2124, www.fws.gov/refuge/maine_coastal_islands). The remote location means it sees only about 15,000 visitors a

© TOM NANGLE

The Cherryfield Historic District is a must-visit.

year, most of those likely bird-watchers, as more than 300 different birds have been sighted here. The refuge's primary focus is restoring colonies of nesting seabirds. Among the other natural highlights here are stands of jack pine, coastal raised peat lands, blueberry barrens, freshwater and salt marshes, granite shores, and cobble beaches. When asking directions locally, you might hear it called 'tit Manan.

The moderately easy 4-mile round-trip Birch Point Trail and easy 1.5-mile round-trip Hollingsworth or Shore Trail provide splendid views and opportunities to spot wildlife along the shore and in the fields, forests, and marshland. The Hollingsworth Trail, leading you to the shoreline, is the best. On clear days, you can see the 123-foot lighthouse on Petit Manan Island, 2.5 miles offshore. The Birch Point Trail heads through blueberry fields to Dyer Bay and loops by the waterfront saltmarshes, with much of the trail passing through woods.

From Route 1, on the east side of Steuben, take Pigeon Hill Road. Six miles down is the

first parking lot, for the Birch Point Trail; another half mile takes you to the parking area for the Hollingsworth Trail. Space is limited at both parking areas. If you arrive in August, help yourself to blueberries. The refuge is open sunrise-sunset daily all year; cross-country skiing is permitted in winter.

McClellan Park

You can picnic, hike, and camp at this 10-acre oceanfront park in Milbridge. Go tidepooling, clamber over rocks, or just admire the views over the rugged islands offshore. From Route 1, take Wyman Road, which is approximately four miles.

Boat Excursions

Captain Jamie Robertson's **Robertson Sea Tours and Adventures** (Milbridge Marina, Fickett's Point Rd., 207/483-6110 or 207/461-7439, www.robertsonseatours.com, May 15-Oct. 1) offers cruises from the Milbridge Marina aboard the *Kandi Leigh*, a classic Maine lobster boat. Options include puffins and seabirds, island lighthouses, and a lobstering cruise. Prices range $60-85 adults, $25-65 children for the 1.5-4-hour cruises. Boat minimums may apply. Captain Robertson also offers a **whale-watching cruise** aboard the six-passenger 33-foot *Elisabeth Rose* ($95 adults, $75 kids under 12, $360 minimum).

Captain Harry "Buzzy" Shinn's **Downeast Coastal Cruises** (207/546-7720, cell 207/598-7740, www.downeastcoastalcruises.com) depart from the Milbridge Marina aboard the comfortable *Alyce K.* for island cruises, lighthouse cruises, puffin cruises, lobster cruises (complete with a meal), sunset cruises, and charters. Cruises last 2-3.5 hours and cost $45-75 adults, $35-65 children; boat minimums apply.

ACCOMMODATIONS

One of Cherryfield's 52 buildings on the National Register of Historic Places, the 1793 Archibald-Adams House is now the **Englishman's Bed and Breakfast** (122 Main

Increasingly, many of the historical buildings in Cherryfield are being turned into shops.

© TOM NANGLE

St., Cherryfield, 207/546-2337, www.eng-lishmansbandb.com, $100-165). The magnif-icently restored, Federal-style home borders the Narraguagus River and makes a superb base for exploring inland and Down East Maine. The lovely grounds have gardens and a screened-in gazebo. Owners Peter (the Englishman) and Kathy Winham are archaeologists and seri-ous tea drinkers—they also sell fine teas on-line (www.teasofcherryfield.com) and in area specialty stores. Two guest rooms in the main house have river views. One has a private half bath but shares a full bath. A riverside guest-house, built in the 1990s, melds beautifully with the inn's architecture and is self-catering; pets are allowed here for $7/night.

Camping

Since 1958 the Ayr family has welcomed campers at its quiet, well-off-the-beaten-path property on Joy Cove. With a convenient lo-cation 15 minutes from Petit Manan National Wildlife Refuge and 20 minutes from Schoodic Point, **Mainayr Campground** (321 Village Rd.,

Steuben, 207/546-2690, www.mainayr.com, late May-mid-Oct., $29-32) has 35 mostly wooded tenting and RV sites (five with full hookups). Also on the premises are a play-ground, a laundry, a beach for tidal swimming, clamming flats, a grassy launch area for kayaks and canoes, a camp store, berries for picking, and fresh lobsters.

FOOD
Local Flavors

The **Milbridge Farmers Market** (9am-noon Sat. early June-mid-Oct.) sets up on Main Street.

Although it's cultivating a small vineyard out front, **Catherine Hill Winery** (661 Blackswoods Rd., Cherryfield, 207/546-3426, www.cathill-winery.com) is currently making small-batch wines from grapes sourced elsewhere. Stop by the tasting room to learn more.

Thank the migrant community who arrive here in summer to pick blueberries for **Vasquez Mexican Food** (High St., Milbridge, 10am-8pm Mon.-Sat., $3-7), a food truck serving

© HILARY NANGLE

The Fisherman's Wife Café is a pleasant spot in Milbridge.

authentic Mexican fare. There are just a few picnic tables for seating. Note, from late July through most of August, the truck moves to the migrant camps in Deblois.

Family Favorites

Cheery waitresses serve big portions of home-cooked fare at **44 Degrees North** (17 Main St., Milbridge, 207/546-4440, www.44-degrees-north.com, 11am-8pm Mon.-Thurs., 11am-9pm Fri.-Sat.). The front room is family oriented, with booths, tables, and cheerful decor. The back room doubles as a bar and has a big-screen TV. As is usually the case in this part of Maine, there's a case full of mouthwatering desserts. Most heartier choices are less than $17.

Tucked behind Water's Edge Realty is a find for good home cooking, **Fisherman's Wife Café** (4 School St., 207/546-7004, 6:30am-6pm Mon.-Wed., 6:30am-8pm Thurs.-Sat., 6:30am-3pm Sun.). The country-cute dining rooms are small, but you can always get it to go and take it to the waterfront. Lunch fare includes subs, sandwiches, lobster rolls, fish-and-chips, and burgers, with most choices less than $10. The small kitchen can get overwhelmed, so if it's packed, expect a lag time between ordering and eating. Friday night there's an all-you-can-eat fish fry.

More good home cooking, from shepherd's pie to fried fish, comes out of the kitchen at **Scovils Millside Dining** (1276 Main St./Rte. 1, Harrington, 207/483-6544, 7am-7pm Mon.-Sat., 7am-2pm Sun.), a cheerful family-run restaurant near the intersections of Routes 1 and 1A. The Friday all-you-can-eat fish fry is $10. Dinner choices run $8-22.

Casual Dining

Long before farm to table became mainstream, Jessie King and Alva Lowe had earned a reputation for garden-fresh fare at ⟨ **Kitchen Garden Restaurant** (35 Village Rd., 207/546-4269, www.thekitchengardenrestaurant.com, $17-30, no credit cards), based in their 1860s Cape-style home. When they closed in 2003, locals mourned, but in 2011 the talented duo reopened it, again drawing from their gardens as well as local, mostly organic sources to create authentic Jamaican fare, such as jerk chicken and curried goat, as well as seafood and vegetarian entrées. Reservations are required, and guests are requested to order their meals in advance. Bring your own wine or beer ($5 bottle fee); call for current days of operation. Lunch may be available in summer.

INFORMATION

Info on the area is available from the **Milbridge Area Merchants Association** (www.milbridge. org), **Destination Cherryfield** (www.destinationcherryfield.org), and the **Machias Bay Area Chamber of Commerce** (85 E. Main St., Machias, 207/255-4402, www.machiaschamber.org).

GETTING THERE AND AROUND

Milbridge is about 20 miles or 25 minutes via Routes 186 and 1 from Winter Harbor. It's about 25 miles or 30 minutes via Routes 1 and 187 to Jonesport.

Jonesport and Beals Area

Between western Washington County and the Machias Bay area is the molar-shaped Jonesport Peninsula, reached from the west via the attractive little town of **Columbia Falls,** bordering Route 1. Rounding the peninsula are the picturesque towns of Addison, Jonesport, and Beals Island. First settled around 1762, Columbia Falls still has a handful of houses dating from the late 18th century, but its best-known structure is the early-19th-century Ruggles House.

On the banks of the Pleasant River, just south of Columbia Falls, **Addison** (pop. 1,266) once had four huge shipyards cranking out wooden cargo vessels that circled the world. Since that 19th-century heyday, little seems to have changed, and the town today may be best known as the haunt of painter John Marin, who first came to Maine in 1914.

Jonesport (pop. 1,370) and **Beals Island** (pop. 508) are traditional hardworking fishing communities—old-fashioned, friendly, and photogenic. Beals, connected to Jonesport via an arched bridge over Moosabec Reach, is named for Manwarren Beal Jr. and his wife, Lydia, who arrived around 1773 and quickly threw themselves into the Revolutionary War effort. But that's not all they did—the current phone book covering Jonesport and Beals Island lists dozens of Beal descendants (as well as dozens of Alleys and Carvers, other early names).

Even more memorable than Manwarren Beal was his six-foot, seven-inch descendant Barnabas, dubbed "Tall Barney" for obvious reasons. The larger-than-life fellow became the stuff of legend all along the Maine Coast.

Also legendary here is the lobster-boat design known as the Jonesport hull. People "from away" won't recognize its distinctive shape, but count on the fishing pros to know it. The harbor here is jam-packed with Jonesport lobster boats, and souped-up versions are consistent winners in the summertime lobster-boat race series.

SIGHTS
Ruggles House

Behind a picket fence on a quiet street in Columbia Falls stands the remarkable **Ruggles House** (Main St., Columbia Falls, 207/483-4637, www.ruggleshouse.org, 9:30am-4:30pm Mon.-Sat., noon-4:30pm Sun. June 1-Oct. 15, $5 adults, $3 ages 6-12). Built in 1818 for Judge Thomas Ruggles—lumber baron, militia captain, even postmaster—the tiny house on a grand scale boasts a famous flying (unsupported) staircase, intricately carved moldings, a Palladian window, and unusual period furnishings. Rescued in the mid-20th century and maintained by the Ruggles House Society, this gem has become a magnet for savvy preservationists. A quarter mile east of Route 1, it's open for hour-long guided tours.

At the house, pick up a copy of the Columbia Falls walking-tour brochure, which details the intriguing history of other houses in this hamlet.

Jonesport Historical Society
In 2012, the **Jonesport Historical Society** (Sawyer Sq., Jonesport, www.peabody.lib. me.us, 11am-3pm Tues., Thurs., Sat.) began moving into a permanent home inside an 1896 building that had remained in the Sawyer family and retained original ledgers, daybooks, letters, and receipts dating back to the building's construction. Society members have delighted in finding artifacts in the basement and the original safe in a shipping clerk's office, which appears as it did circa 1900. A monthly series of lectures is held here too. Admission is free, but for $5 you can join the society, a real bargain.

Downeast Institute for Applied Marine Research and Education
University of Maine at Machias professor Brian Beal founded the Beals Island Regional Shellfish Hatchery, now the **Downeast Institute** (Black Duck Cove, Great Wass Island, 207/497-5769, www.downeastinstitute. org), a marine field station for the University of Maine at Machias. Learn everything there is to know about shellfish, especially soft-shell clams, on this eight-acre property with two natural coves. Tours are by appointment.

Wreaths Across America Museum
Wreaths Across America has earned international fame for its annual wreath-laying at Arlington National Cemetery. The **museum** (4 Point St., Columbia Falls, 877/385-9504, www. wreathsacrossamerica.org, 9am-4pm daily, free) located at its headquarters shows films and showcases items donated to the company over the years by veterans and their families. You can tour this heart-tugging memorial to American soldiers on your own or with a guide.

Wild Salmon Resource Center
Established in 1922, the **Wild Salmon Resource Center** (Columbia Falls, 207/483-4336, www.mainesalmonrivers.org, 9am-4pm Mon.-Fri., free) has a few educational displays and a library. In the basement is a volunteer-run fish hatchery that raises 50,000 Atlantic salmon fry annually. Staff welcome visitors and explain the efforts to save Maine's endangered salmon.

Moosabec Mussels
Family-owned **Moosabec Mussels** (Jonesport, 207/497-2500) processes wild harvested mussels, clams, and periwinkles. At the plant, mussels are purged, decluped, graded, washed, and inspected before being packaged for sale. Free tours are available by appointment, usually between 11am and 2pm on Tuesday, Thursday, and Saturday; call plant manager Roger Dam at 207/399-4783.

ENTERTAINMENT AND EVENTS
For a taste of real Maine, don't miss the Downeast Salmon Federation's April **Smelt Fry** (207/483-4336) held under a riverside tent in Columbia Falls.

The biggest annual wingding hereabouts is Jonesport's **Fourth of July** celebration, with several days of special activities, including barbecues, a beauty pageant, kids' games, fireworks, and the famed **Jonesport Lobster Boat Races** in Moosabec Reach.

Peabody Memorial Library (207/497-3003, www.peabody.lib.me.us) in Jonesport presents bimonthly art shows and sponsors a summer music series.

SHOPPING
You can't miss the humongous blueberry housing **Wild Blueberry Land** (1067 Rte. 1, 207/483-2583, www.wildblueberryland-maine. com). Step inside to find blueberry everything, from baked goods—including pies—to blueberry-themed merchandise ranging from scented candles to condiments. The shop, created by Dell, a research farmer, and Marie, a

chef, Emerson is to promote sustainable blueberry farming in the region.

Flower-design majolica pottery and whimsical terra-cotta items are April Adams's specialties at **Columbia Falls Pottery** (150 Main St., Columbia Falls, 207/483-4075 or 800/235-2512, www.columbiafallspottery.com), an appealing shop in a rehabbed country store next to the Ruggles House.

In downtown Jonesport, **Church's True Value** (Main St./Rte. 187, Jonesport, 207/497-2778) carries all the usual hardware items, plus gifts, souvenirs, and sportswear. Helpful owners John and Sharon Church can also answer any question about the area and solve most any problem.

Nelson Decoys Downeast Gallery (13 Cranberry Lane, Jonesport, 207/497-3488) is equal parts shop, gallery, and museum. Inside are not only hand-carved decoys but also creations by other area artists and artisans. It's in an old schoolhouse, just off Main Street downtown.

RECREATION
◖ Great Wass Island Preserve

Allow a whole day to explore 1,576-acre Great Wass Island, an extraordinary preserve, even when it's drenched in fog—a not-infrequent event. Owned by **The Nature Conservancy** (207/729-5181, www.nature.org), the preserve is at the tip of Jonesport's peninsula. Easiest hiking routes are the wooded 2.2-mile Little Cape Point and 2.3-mile Mud Hole Trails, retracing your path for each. (Making a loop by connecting the two along the rocky shoreline adds considerably to the time and difficulty, but do it if you have time; allow about six hours and wear waterproof footwear.) Expect to see beach-head irises (like a blue flag) and orchids, jack pines, a rare coastal peat bog, seals, pink granite, pitcher plants, lots of warblers, and maybe some grouse. Carry water and a picnic; wear bug repellent. No camping, fires, or pets are allowed, and there are no toilet facilities; access is during daytime only. To reach the preserve from Route 1, take Route 187 to Jonesport (12 miles) and then cross the arched bridge to Beals Island. Continue across Beals to the Great Wass causeway (locally called "the Flying Place") and then go three miles on Black Duck Cove Road to the parking area (on the left). Watch for The Nature Conservancy oak-leaf symbol. At the parking area, pick up a trail map and a bird checklist.

Also owned by The Nature Conservancy is 21-acre **Mistake Island**, accessible only by boat. Low and shrubby, Mistake has a Coast Guard-built boardwalk from the landing at the northwest corner to **Moose Peak Light**, standing 72 feet above the water at the eastern end of the island. The only negative on this lovely island is rubble left behind when the government leveled the keeper's house.

Scenic Cruises

Operating as **Coastal Cruises** (Kelley Point Rd., Jonesport, 207/497-3064 or 207/497-2699, www.cruisedowneast.com), Captain Laura Fish and her brother Harry Fish, a certified dive master, offer three-hour Moosabec Reach cruises in the 23-foot powerboat *Aaron Thomas*. Among the sights are Great Wass Island and Mistake Island. Rates begin at $200 covering up to six passengers. Custom dive trips and instruction are available with Harry, a PADI-certified diver. Reservations are required. Trips depart from Jonesport and operate May-mid-October.

Captain Paul Ferriero's **Pleasant River Boat Tours** (280 Water St., Addison, 207/483-6567 or 207/598-6993, www.pleasantriverboattours.com) offers lobster, puffin, and river cruises aboard his 34-foot lobster boat, *Honey B*, for $50-60/person; boat minimums apply.

ACCOMMODATIONS
Bed-and-Breakfasts

How about staying in a beautiful modern farmhouse overlooking the water—with llamas lolling outside? At **Pleasant Bay Bed and Breakfast and Llama Keep** (338 West Side Rd., Addison, 207/483-4490, www.pleasantbay.com, year-round, $50-150), Joan and Lee Yeaton manage to pamper more than 40 llamas and a herd of red deer as well as their two-legged guests. Three miles of trails wind through the 110 acres, and a canoe is available for guests. Three lovely guest rooms (private and shared baths) and one suite, with a microwave and a refrigerator, all have water views. Rates include a delicious breakfast. Arrange in advance for a llama walk ($15/llama). The farm borders Pleasant Bay, 3.9 miles southwest of Route 1.

Cottages and Apartments

Proprietor Dorothy Higgins's **Cranberry Cove Cottages** (56 Kelley Point Rd., Jonesport, 207/497-2139, cranberry-cove@hotmail.com, $125) comprise two, coveside efficiency lofts, each distinctively furnished in cottage style and with TVs, phones, fireplaces, and harbor views. Kayaks are provided. Pets are welcome. Rates decrease with the length of stay.

Camping

The town of Jonesport operates the low-key, no-frills **Jonesport Campground** (Henry Point, Kelley Point Rd., Jonesport, early May-Labor Day) on two acres with fabulous views over Sawyer Cove and Moosabec Reach. Basic facilities include outhouses, picnic tables, and fire rings; three power poles provide hookups. Showers and washing machines are available across the cove at Jonesport Shipyard (207/497-2701). The campground is exposed to wind off the water, so expect nights to be cool. Sites are allocated on a first-come, first-served basis for a small fee. Avoid the campground during Fourth of July festivities; it's jam-packed. From Route 187 at the northeastern edge of Jonesport, turn right onto Kelley Point Road and then right again to Henry Point.

FOOD

The choices are slim in the Jonesport/Beals area. **Bayview Takeout** (Beals, 207/497-3301, 11am-8pm daily) delivers on its slogan "Wicked Good Food." Burgers, subs, salads, and fried seafood run $3.50-16.

INFORMATION AND SERVICES

The **Machias Bay Area Chamber of Commerce** (85 E. Main St., Machias, 207/255-4402, www.machiaschamber.org) handles inquires for the Machias area as well as Jonesport.

In downtown Jonesport, **Church's True Value** (Main St./Rte. 187, Jonesport, 207/497-2778), open Monday-Saturday, is a good source for local info.

GETTING THERE AND AROUND

Jonesport is about 25 miles or 30 minutes via Routes 1 and 187 from Milbridge. It's about 22 miles or 30 minutes via Routes 187 and 1 to Machias.

Machias Bay Area

The only negative thing about **Machias** (muh-CHAI-us, pop. 1,221) is its Micmac Indian name, meaning "bad little falls" (even though it's accurate—the midtown waterfall here is treacherous). A contagious local esprit pervades this shire town of Washington County thanks to antique homes, a splendid river-valley setting, Revolutionary War monuments, and a small university campus.

If you regard crowds as fun, an ideal time to land here is during the renowned annual Machias Wild Blueberry Festival, the third weekend in August, when harvesting is under way in Washington County's blueberry fields and you can stuff your face with blueberry everything—muffins, jam, pancakes, ice cream, and pies. You can also collect blueberry-logo napkins, T-shirts, magnets, pottery, and jewelry. Biggest highlight: the annual summer musical parody.

Among the other summer draws are a chamber-music series, art shows, and semiprofessional theater performances. Within a few miles are day trips galore—options for hiking, biking, golfing, swimming, and sea kayaking.

Also included within the Machias sphere are the towns of **Roque Bluffs, Jonesboro, Whitneyville, Marshfield, East Machias,** and **Machiasport.** Just to the east, between Machias and Lubec, are the towns of **Whiting** and **Cutler.**

HISTORICAL SIGHTS

History is a big deal in this area, and since Machias was the first settled Maine town east of the Penobscot River, lots of enthusiastic amateur historians have helped rescue homes and sites dating from as far back as the Revolutionary War.

English settlers, uprooted from communities farther west on the Maine Coast, put down permanent roots here in 1763, harvesting timber to ensure their survival. Stirrings of revolutionary discontent surfaced even at this remote outpost, and when British loyalists in Boston began usurping some of the valuable harvest, Machias patriots plotted revenge. By 1775, when the armed British schooner *Margaretta* arrived as a cargo escort, local residents aboard the sloop *Unity,* in a real David-and-Goliath episode, chased and captured the *Margaretta.* On June 12, 1775, two months after the famed Battles of Lexington and Concord (and five days before the Battle of Bunker Hill), Machias Bay was the site of what author James Fenimore Cooper called "The Lexington of the Sea"—the first naval battle of the American Revolution. The name of patriot leader Jeremiah O'Brien today appears throughout the Machias area—on a school, a street, a cemetery, and a state park. In 1784, Machias was incorporated; it became the shire town in 1790.

Museums

One-hour guided tours vividly convey the atmosphere of the 1770 **Burnham Tavern** (Main St./Rte. 192, Machias, 207/255-6930, www.burnhamtavern.com, 9:30am-3:30pm Mon.-Fri. mid-June-late Sept. or by appointment, $5

adults, $1-2 kids), one of 21 homes in the entire country designated as most significant to the American Revolution. Upstart local patriots met here in 1775 to plot revolution against the British. Job and Mary Burnham's tavern-home next served as an infirmary for casualties from the Revolution's first naval battle, just offshore. Lots of fascinating history lies in this National Historic Site, maintained by the Daughters of the American Revolution. Hanging outside is a sign reading "Drink for the thirsty, food for the hungry, lodging for the weary, and good keeping for horses, by Job Burnham."

Headquarters for the Machiasport Historical Society and one of the area's three oldest residences, the 1810 **Gates House** (344 Port Rd., Machiasport, 207/255-8461, 12:30pm-4:30pm Tues.-Fri. July-Aug., or by appointment, free) was snatched from ruin and restored in 1966. The building, on the National Register of Historic Places, overlooks Machias Bay and contains fascinating period furnishings and artifacts, many related to the lumbering and shipbuilding era. The museum, four miles southeast of Route 1, has limited parking on a hazardous curve.

O'Brien Cemetery

Old-cemetery buffs will want to stop at **O'Brien Cemetery,** resting place of the town's earliest settlers. It's next to Bad Little Falls Park, close to downtown, off Route 92 toward Machiasport. A big plus here is the view, especially in autumn, of blueberry barrens, the waterfall, and the bay.

Fort O'Brien State Historic Site

The American Revolution's first naval battle was fought just offshore from **Fort O'Brien** (207/942-4014, www.parksandlands.com, free) in June 1775. Now a State Historic Site, the fort was built and rebuilt several times—originally to guard Machias during the Revolutionary War. Only Civil War-era earthworks now remain, plus well-maintained lawns overlooking the Machias River. Steep banks lead down to the water; keep small children well back from the edge. There are no restrooms or other

TWO SCENIC ROUTES

The drives described below can also be bike routes (easy to moderately difficult), but be forewarned that the roads are narrow and shoulderless, so caution is essential. Heed biking etiquette.

ROUTE 191, THE CUTLER ROAD

Never mind that Route 191, between East Machias and West Lubec, is one of Maine's most stunning coastal drives—you can still follow the entire 27-mile stretch and meet only a handful of cars. **East Machias** even has its own historic district, with architectural gems dating from the late 18th century along High and Water Streets. Farther along Route 191, you'll find fishing wharves, low moorlands, a hamlet or two, and islands popping over the horizon. The only peculiarly jarring note is the 26-tower forest of North Cutler's Naval Computer and Telecommunications Station, nearly 1,000 feet high—monitoring global communications—but you'll see this only briefly. (At night, the skyscraping red lights are really eerie, especially if you're offshore aboard a boat.) Off Route 191 are minor roads and hiking trails worth exploring, especially the coastal trails of the Cutler Coast Public Preserve. About three miles south of the Route 191 terminus, you can also check out **Bailey's Mistake,** a hamlet with a black-sand (volcanic) beach. The name? Allegedly it stems from one Captain Bailey who, misplotting his course and thinking he was in Lubec, drove his vessel ashore here one night in the late 19th century. Unwilling to face the consequences of his lapse, he and his crew off-loaded their cargo of lumber and built themselves dwellings. Whether true or not, it makes a great saga. Even though it's in the town of **Trescott,** and the hamlet is really South Trescott, everyone knows this section as Bailey's Mistake.

ROUTE 92, STARBOARD PENINSULA

Pack a picnic and set out on Route 92 (beginning at Elm Street in downtown Machias) down the 10-mile length of the Starboard Peninsula to a stunning spot known as the Point of Maine. Along the way are the villages of Larrabee, Bucks Harbor, and Starboard, all part of the town of Machiasport. In Bucks Harbor is the turnoff (a short detour to the right) to **Yoho Head,** a controversial upscale development overlooking Little Kennebec Bay.

South of the Yoho Head turnoff is the sign for **Jasper Beach.** From the Jasper Beach sign, continue 1.4 miles to two red buildings (the old Starboard School House and the volunteer fire department). Turn left onto a dirt road and continue to a sign reading Driveway. Go around the right side of a shed and park on the beach. (Keep track of the tide level, though.) You're at **Point of Maine,** a quintessential Down East panorama of sea and islands. On a clear day, you can see offshore **Libby Island Light,** the focus of Philmore Wass's entertaining narrative *Lighthouse in My Life: The Story of a Maine Lightkeeper's Family.*

facilities, but there's a playground at the Fort O'Brien School next door. Officially the park is open Memorial Day weekend-Labor Day, but it's accessible all year. Take Route 92 from Machias about five miles toward Machiasport; the parking area is on the left.

OTHER SIGHTS
Maine Sea Salt Company

Season your visit with a tour of the **Maine Sea Salt Company** (11 Church Ln., Marshfield, 207/255-3310, www.maineseasalt.com), which produces sea salt in its solar greenhouses and shallow pools using evaporation and reduction of seawater. Free tours (available most days 9am-5pm, call first) explain the process and include tastings of natural, seasoned, and smoked salts.

University of Maine at Machias

Founded in 1909 as Washington State Normal School, the **University of Maine at Machias** (UMM, 116 O'Brien Ave., Machias, 207/255-1200, www.machias.edu) is now part of the state university system. **The Art Gallery** (Powers Hall, afternoon Mon.-Fri. during school terms or by appointment) features works from the university's expanding permanent collection of Maine painters—including John Marin, William Zorach, Lyonel Feininger, and Reuben Tam. Rotating exhibits occur throughout the school year.

UMM's **Center for Lifelong Learning** has a fitness center, and a six-lane heated pool. The pool and fitness room are open to the public ($7); call for schedule.

Also open to the public is **Merrill Library** (207/255-1284).

Little River Lighthouse

Friends of the **Little River Lighthouse** (207/259-3833, www.littleriverlight.org) usually open the restored lighthouse and tower for tours a couple of times each summer. Transportation is provided to the island from Cutler Harbor. Donations benefit care and maintenance of the 1876 beacon.

ENTERTAINMENT AND EVENTS

The **University of Maine at Machias** (207/255-1384, www.machias.edu) is the cultural focus in this area, particularly during the school year.

If the UMM Ukulele Club is performing anywhere, don't miss them.

Machias Bay Chamber Concerts (207/255-3849, www.machiasbaychamberconcerts.com, $15 adults, $8 students, free under age 13) are held at 7:30pm on Tuesday evening early July-mid-August at the Centre Street Congregational Church. Art exhibits accompany concerts.

The **Machias Wild Blueberry Festival** (www.machiasblueberry.com) is the summer highlight, running Friday-Sunday the third weekend in August and featuring a pancake breakfast, road races, concerts, crafts booths, a baked-bean supper, a homegrown musical, and more. The blueberry motif is everywhere. It's organized by Centre Street Congregational Church, United Church of Christ, in downtown Machias.

A few times each summer, the **Little River Lighthouse** (Cutler, 207/259-3833, www.littleriverlight.org) is open for tours.

SHOPPING

Influenced by traditional Japanese designs, Connie Harter-Bagley markets her dramatic raku ceramics at **Connie's Clay of Fundy** (Rte. 1, East Machias, 207/255-4574, www.clayoffundy.com), on the East Machias River, four miles east of Machias. If she's at the wheel, you can also watch her work.

Need a read? **Jim's Books, Etc.** (8 Elm St., Machias, 207/255-9058), at the third house on the left on Route 92, just beyond the university campus, is open by chance or by appointment.

Fine wines, craft beers, and a nice selection of cheeses are sold at **The French Cellar** (7 Water St., Machias, 207/255-4977).

RECREATION
Parks, Preserves, and Beaches
BAD LITTLE FALLS PARK

At Bad Little Falls Park, alongside the Machias River, stop to catch the view from the footbridge overlooking the roiling falls (especially in spring). Bring a picnic and enjoy this midtown oasis tucked between Routes 1 and 92.

JASPER BEACH

Thanks to a handful of foresighted year-round and summer residents, spectacular crescent-shaped **Jasper Beach**—piled high with ocean-polished jasper and other rocks—has been preserved by the town of Machiasport. There is no sand here, just stones, in intriguing shapes and colors. Resist the urge to fill your pockets with souvenirs. Parking is limited, and there are no facilities. From Route 1 in downtown Machias, take Route 92 (Elm Street) 9.5 miles southeast, past the village of Bucks Harbor. Watch for a large sign on your left. The beach is on Howard's Cove, 0.2 mile off the road and accessible year-round.

ROQUE BLUFFS STATE PARK

Southwest of Machias, six miles south of Route 1, is **Roque Bluffs State Park** (Roque Bluffs

Rd., Roque Bluffs, 207/255-3475, www.park-sandlands.com). Saltwater swimming this far north is for the young and brave, but this park also has a 60-acre freshwater pond warm and shallow enough for toddlers and the old and timid. Facilities include primitive changing rooms, outhouses, hiking trails, a play area, and picnic tables; there is no food and there are no lifeguards. Views go on forever from the wide-open mile-long sweep of sand-and-pebble beach. Admission is $4.50 nonresident adults, $3 Maine resident adults, $1 ages 5-11. The fee box relies on the honor system. The park is open daily May 15-September 15, but the beach is accessible year-round.

CUTLER COAST PUBLIC RESERVE

On Route 191, about 4.5 miles northeast of the center of Cutler, watch for the parking area (on the right) for the **Cutler Coast Public Reserve,** a spectacular 12,234-acre preserve with nearly a dozen miles of beautifully engineered hiking trails on the seaward side of Route 191. It's popular with wildlife-watchers: Birding is great, and you might spot whales (humpback, finback, northern right, and minke), seals, and porpoises. Easiest is the 2.8-mile round-trip Coastal Trail through a cedar swamp and spruce-fir forest to an ocean promontory and back. Allow 5-6 hours to continue with the 5.5-mile Black Point Brook Loop, which progresses along a stretch of moderately rugged hiking southward along dramatic tree-fringed shoreline cliffs. Then head back via the Black Point Brook cutoff and connect with the Inland Trail to return to the parking area. Bring binoculars and a camera; the views from this wild coastline are fabulous. Also bring insect repellent—inland boggy stretches are buggy. Carry a picnic and commandeer a granite ledge overlooking the surf. Precipitous cliffs and narrow stretches can make the shoreline section of this trail perilous for small children or insecure adults, so use extreme caution and common sense. There are no facilities in the preserve. If you're here in August, you can stock up on blueberries and even some wild raspberries. Another

option, the 9.1-mile Fairy Head Loop, starts the same way as the Black Point Brook Loop but continues southward along the coast, leading to three primitive campsites (stoves only, no fires), available on a first-come, first-served basis. There's no way to reserve these, so you take your chances. Unless you have gazelle genes, the longer loop almost demands an overnight trip. Information on the preserve, including a helpful map, is available from the **Maine Bureau of Parks and Lands** (207/287-3821, www.parksandlands.com). Originally about 2,100 acres, this preserve expanded fivefold in 1997 when several donors, primarily the Richard King Mellon Foundation, deeded to the state 10,055 acres of fields and forests across Route 191 from the trail area, creating a phenomenal tract that now runs from the ocean all the way back to Route 1. Mostly in Cutler but also in Whiting, it is Maine's second-largest public-land gift after Baxter State Park.

BOG BROOK COVE PRESERVE

Adjacent to the Cutler Coast Public Reserve is Maine Coast Heritage Trust's (www.mcht.org) 1,770-acre **Bog Brook Cove Preserve.** Between the two preserves, this is the largest contiguous area of conservation land in the state outside of Acadia National Park. Bog Brook Cove's lands flow from Cutler into neighboring Trescott and include nearly three miles of ocean frontage, headlands, gravel beaches, coastal peat lands, and 10-acre Norse Pond. Trails are under construction. Already in place is a 1,100-foot wheelchair-accessible trail to an overlook in Moose Cove with smashing views of Grand Manan Island.

Multiuse Trails

The 85-mile **Down East Sunrise Trail** (www.sunrisetrail.org), a rails-to-trails conversion, stretches from Washington Junction near Ellsworth to Ayers Junction in Charlotte, southwest of Calais. It's open to pedestrians, snowmobiles, ATVs, cyclists, skiers, and equestrians. Check the website for a downloadable map.

Golf

With lovely water views and tidal inlets serving as obstacles, the nine-hole **Great Cove Golf Course** (387 Great Cove Rd., off Roque Bluffs Rd., Jonesboro, 207/434-7200) is a good challenge. You can also play a quick nine at **Barren View Golf Course** (Rte. 1, Jonesboro, 207/434-6531, www.barrenview.com).

Water Sports

If you've brought your own sea kayak, there are public launching ramps in Bucks Harbor (east of Rte. 92, the main Machiasport road) and at Roque Bluffs State Park. You can also put in at Sanborn Cove, beyond the O'Brien School on Route 92, about five miles south of Machias, where there's a small parking area. Before setting out, check the tide calendar and plan your strategy so you don't have to slog through acres of muck when you return.

Sunrise Canoe and Kayak (68 Hoytown Rd., Machias, 207/255-3375 or 877/980-2300, www.sunrisecanoeandkayak.com) rents canoes and kayaks for $25-35/day and offers half-day sea-kayak excursions on Machias Bay, including one to a petroglyph site (from $50 pp). It also offers guided day trips and fully outfitted multiday canoeing and kayaking excursions on the Machias and St. Croix Rivers and along the Bold Coast.

The **Machias River,** one of Maine's most technically demanding canoeing rivers, is a dynamite trip mid-May-mid-June, but no beginner should attempt it. The best advice is to sign on with an outfitter or guide. The run lasts from four days up to six days if you start from Fifth Machias Lake. Expect to see wildlife such as ospreys, eagles, ducks, loons, moose, deer, beavers, and snapping turtles. Be aware, though, that the Machias is probably the buggiest river in the state, and black-flies will form a welcoming party. In addition to Sunrise Canoe and Kayak, Bangor-based **Sunrise Expeditions** (207/942-9300 or 800/748-3730, www.sunrise-exp.com) also offers fully outfitted trips.

Boat Excursions
◖ MACHIAS SEAL ISLAND PUFFIN TOUR

Andy Patterson, skipper of the 40-foot *Barbara Frost,* operates the **Bold Coast Charter Company** (207/259-4484, www.boldcoast.com), homeported in Cutler Harbor. Andy provides knowledgeable narration, answers questions in depth, and shares his considerable enthusiasm for this pristine corner of Maine. He is best known for his five-hour puffin-sighting trips to Machias Seal Island (departing between 7am and 8am daily mid-May-Aug., $120, no credit cards); the trip is unsuitable for small children or adults who are susceptible to seasickness. Daily access to the island is restricted, and swells can roll in, so passengers occasionally cannot disembark, but the curious puffins often surround the boat, providing plenty of photo opportunities. No matter what the air temperature on the mainland, dress warmly and wear sturdy shoes. The *Barbara Frost's* wharf is on Cutler Harbor, just off Route 191. Look for the Little River Lobster Company sign; you'll depart from the boat-launching ramp. All trips are dependent on weather and tide conditions, and reservations are required. Note: Reserve early, because trips can sell out a month or more in advance.

ACCOMMODATIONS
Bed-and-Breakfasts and Inns

The beautifully restored 1797 **Chandler River Lodge** (654 Rte. 1, Jonesboro, 207/434-2540, www.chandlerriverlodge.com, $100-150) sits well off the highway and overlooks treed lawns that roll down to the Chandler River. It's an idyllic spot, with Adirondack-style chairs positioned just where you want to sit to take in the views. Rates include a continental breakfast. Some rooms share baths.

Victoriana rules at the **Riverside Inn** (Rte. 1, East Machias, 888/255-4344 or 207/255-4134, www.riversideinn-maine.com, $110-145), a meticulously restored early-19th-century sea captain's home with four guest rooms (one with a kitchenette). Relax on the deck overlooking the East Machias River or sit in the lovely terraced

PUFFINS

The chickadee is the Maine state bird, and the bald eagle is our national emblem, but probably the best-loved bird along the Maine Coast is the Atlantic puffin *(Fratercula arctica)*, a member of the auk (Alcidae) family. Photographs show an imposing-looking creature with a quizzical mien; amazingly, this larger-than-life seabird is only about 12 inches long. Black-backed and white-chested, the puffin has bright orange legs, "clown-makeup" eyes, and a distinctive, rather outlandish red-and-yellow beak. Its diet is fish and shellfish.

Almost nonexistent in this part of the world as recently as the 1970s, the puffin (or "sea parrot") has recovered dramatically thanks to the unstinting efforts of Cornell University ornithologist Stephen Kress and his Project Puffin (www.projectpuffin.org). Starting with an orphan colony of two on remote Matinicus Rock, Kress painstakingly transferred nearly a thousand puffin chicks (also known fondly as "pufflings") from Newfoundland and used artificial nests and decoys to entice the birds to adapt to and reproduce on Eastern Egg Rock in Muscongus Bay.

In 1981, thanks to the assistance and persistence of hundreds of interns and volunteers, and despite the predations of great black-backed gulls, puffins finally were fledged on Eastern Egg, and the rest, as they say, is history. Within 20 years, more than three dozen puffin couples were nesting on Eastern Egg Rock, and still more had established nests on other islands in the area. Kress's methods have received international attention, and his proven techniques have been used to reintroduce bird populations in remote parts of the globe. In 2001, *Down East* magazine singled out Kress to receive its prestigious annual Environmental Award.

HOW AND WHERE TO SEE PUFFINS

Puffin-watching, like whale-watching, involves heading offshore, so be prepared with warm clothing, rubber-soled shoes, a hat, sunscreen, binoculars, and, if you're motion sensitive, appropriate medication.

Maine Audubon naturalists accompany tours aboard Hardy Boat Cruises, out of New Harbor, and Cap'n Fish's, out of Boothbay Harbor, and excursion boats depart from Bar Harbor and Milridge. The best daily up-close-and-personal opportunities for puffin-watching along the Down East Coast—specifically, on Machias Seal Island—is with **Bold Coast Charters** (207/259-4484, www.boldcoast.com), which departs from Cutler May-August and costs about $120 pp. Weather permitting, you'll be allowed to disembark on the 20-acre island.

If you can't get afloat to see puffins, the next best thing is a visit to the **Project Puffin Visitor Center** (311 Main St., Rockland, 877/478-3346), where you can view exhibits, a film, and live video feeds of nesting puffins.

ADOPT-A-PUFFIN PROGRAM

Stephen Kress's Project Puffin has devised a clever way to enlist supporters via the Adopt-a-Puffin program (www.projectpuffin.org). For a $100 donation, you'll receive a certificate of adoption, vital statistics on your adoptee, annual updates, and a color photo.

perennial gardens and you'll forget you're a few steps from a busy highway. The dining room is open to nonguests. Rates include a hot, multi-course breakfast.

The barn-red **Inn at Schoppee Farm** (Rte. 1, Machias, 207/255-4648, www.schoppeefarm. com, $100) fronts on the tidal Machias River. The 19th-century farm operated as a dairy for three generations before Machias natives David and Julie Barker returned home to operate it

as a bed-and-breakfast. They welcome guests with three guest rooms, each furnished with antiques and such niceties as air-conditioning, Wi-Fi, whirlpool baths, satellite TV, and soft down comforters in addition to river views and a full breakfast. Just east of the causeway, it's a healthy walk to downtown diversions.

After a meticulous restoration, Michael and Liz Henry opened **The Talbot House Inn** (509 Main St., E. Machias, 207/259-1103, www.thetalbothouseinn.com, $65-125) in a Mansard-roofed mansion that served as a stop on the Underground Railroad. The house is rife with architectural riches, but the bathrooms (some shared) are modern.

The second generation now operates **Micmac Farm Guesthouses** (47 Micmac Ln., Machiasport, 207/255-3008, www.micmacfarm.com, $95/night, $595/week). Stay in one of Anthony and Bonnie Dunn's three rustic but comfortable and well-equipped cottages and you'll find yourself relaxing on the deck overlooking the tidal Machias River and watching for seabirds, seals, and eagles. (Note: Mosquitoes can be pesky.) No breakfast is provided, but each wood-paneled cottage has a kitchenette and dining area. Pets and children are welcome. There's also a river-view room in the restored 18th-century Gardner House, with a private bath with whirlpool tub. Guests have use of the farmhouse, including a library. A light breakfast is provided for Gardner House guests.

Motels

The best feature of the two-story **Machias Motor Inn** (109 Main St./Rte. 1, Machias, 207/255-4861, www.machiasmotorinn.com, year-round, $124) is its location overlooking the tidal Machias River; sliding doors open onto decks with a view. Twenty-eight guest rooms and six efficiencies have extralong beds as well as cable TV, air-conditioning, Wi-Fi, and phones. Next door is Helen's Restaurant—famed for seasonal fruit pies and an all-you-can-eat weekend breakfast buffet. Well-behaved dogs ($10/dog/night) are welcome. The motel is within easy walking distance of downtown, which makes it perfect if you're here for the Blueberry Festival.

For inexpensive digs, you can't beat the **Blueberry Patch** (550 Rte. 1, Jonesboro, 207/434-5411, $64-75), a clean and bright motel and tourist cabins, with three efficiency units. Robert and Tammie Alley provide homespun hospitality with a few extras. All rooms have satellite TV, air-conditioning, Wi-Fi, and phones, and there's even a pool and a small playground. If you're taller than six feet, choose a motel room rather than a cabin; the cabin bathrooms are tiny. A light continental breakfast is available.

Lighthouse

Yes, you can spend a night or more at **Little River Lighthouse** (Cutler, 207/259-3833, www.littleriverlight.org, $150-225), thanks to the Friends of Little River Lighthouse. Three guest rooms sharing two baths are available, but you have to bring food, bottled water, towels, bed linens or sleeping bags, and all personal items (soap, shampoo) and clean up after yourself. Guests have use of a kitchen. Transportation to the lighthouse is provided, but you have to coordinate your arrival with the tide.

FOOD

Watch the local papers for listings of **public suppers, spaghetti suppers,** or **baked bean suppers,** a terrific way to sample the culinary talents of local cooks. Most begin at 5pm, and it's wise to arrive early to get near the head of the line. The suppers often benefit needy individuals or struggling nonprofits, and where else can you eat nonstop for less than $10?

Local Flavors

Craving something healthful? The **Whole Life Natural Market** (4 Colonial Way, Machias, 207/255-8855, www.wholelifemarket.com, 9am-6pm Mon.-Fri., 9am-2pm Sat., 10am-noon Sun.) is home to the **Saltwater Café** (9am-2pm Mon.-Sat.) serving salads, soups, sandwiches, and baked goods made from organic fruits, vegetables, and grains as well as hormone-free dairy products. When the café isn't open, grab-and-go foods are usually available in the store.

Another source for fresh, healthful foods is the **Machias Valley Farmers Market** (3pm-6pm Wed., 10am-4pm Fri., and 9am-1pm Sat. May-Oct.). It's held on "the dike," a low causeway next to the Machias River. It's usually a good source for blueberries in late July-August.

It doesn't look like much from the outside, but

locals praise **Smoky Toast Café** (1183 Rte. 1, Jonesboro, 207/434-5910, 5am-2pm Mon.-Fri.) as a great spot to relax over breakfast or lunch. Service is friendly, the place is spotless, and the only drawback is that it isn't open on weekends.

Pop into **Aunt Millie's General Store** (Route 1, Jonesboro, 207/434-2013) for a good meal at a reasonable cost.

Family Favorites

Family-owned and very popular all day long is **The Blue Bird Ranch Family Restaurant** (78 Main St./Rte. 1, Machias, 207/255-3351, www.bluebirdranchrestaurant.com, 6am-8pm daily, $8-23), named for the Prout family's other enterprise, the Blue Bird Ranch Trucking Company. Service is efficient, the food is hearty, the desserts are homemade, and the portions are ample in the three dining rooms.

Helen's (111 Main St./Rte. 1, Machias, 207/255-8423, 6am-8pm Mon.-Sat., 7am-7:30pm Sun., $5-23) is renowned for its blueberry pie. A new generation has spruced up the restaurant, an institution in these parts since 1950. The owners are committed to supporting local farmers whenever possible.

Fine Dining

Oak furnishings and lacy white tablecloths set the tone at the ❰ **Riverside Inn** (622 Main St./Rte. 1, East Machias, 207/255-4134, www.riversideinn-maine.com, 5pm-8pm Tues.-Sun., $27-34), one of the region's most consistent and long-lasting fine-dining spots. The fare ranges from trout meunière to beef Wellington. Reservations are required. The riverside deck is open for cocktails and appetizers.

INFORMATION AND SERVICES

The **Machias Bay Area Chamber of Commerce** (85 E. Main St., Machias, 207/255-4402, www.machiaschamber.org) stocks brochures, maps, and information on area hiking trails.

GETTING THERE AND AROUND

Machias is about 22 miles or 30 minutes via Routes 1 and 187 from Jonesport. It's about 28 miles or 40 minutes via Routes 1 and 189 to Lubec.

Lubec

As the nation's easternmost point, **Lubec** (pop. 1,359) is literally the beginning of the United States. Lubec residents love to point out that the closest traffic light is 50 miles away.

Settled in 1780 as part of Eastport, it split off in 1811 and was named for the German port of Lübeck (for convoluted reasons still not totally clear). The town's most famous resident was Hopley Yeaton, first captain in the U.S. Revenue-Marine (now the U.S. Coast Guard), who retired here in 1809.

With appealing homes and more than 90 miles of meandering waterfront, Lubec conveys the aura of realness: a hardscrabble fishing community that extends a wary welcome to visitors. Along the main drag, Water Street, a number of shuttered buildings, many undergoing

restoration, reflect the town's roller-coaster history. Once the world's sardine capital, Lubec no longer has a packing plant, but new businesses are slowly arriving, and each year the town looks a bit spiffier. No longer primarily a fishing town, these days the summer residents far outnumber year-rounders. In 2010 the community reluctantly closed its high school, which will likely accelerate the transition.

Arrive here on a fine summer day and it's easy to understand why so many visitors are smitten and, seduced by the views and the real estate prices, purchase a piece of a dream.

SIGHTS

❰ West Quoddy Head State Park

Beachcombing, bird-watching, hiking,

© TOM NANGLE

West Quoddy Head's candy-striped lighthouse is a coastal Maine icon.

picnicking, and an up-close look at Maine's only red-and-white-striped lighthouse are the big draws at 541-acre **West Quoddy Head State Park** (West Quoddy Head Rd., Lubec, 207/733-0911, www.parksandlands.com, 9am-sunset May 15-Oct. 15, $3 nonresident adults, $2 Maine resident adults, $1 children), the easternmost point of U.S. land. Begin with a visit to the **Visitor Center** (207/733-2180, www.westquoddy.com, 10am-4pm daily late May-early July and early Sept.-mid-Oct., 10am-5pm daily July-Aug., free), located in the 1858 keeper's house and operated by the enthusiastic all-volunteer West Quoddy Head Light Keepers Association. Inside are exhibits on lighthouse memorabilia, local flora and fauna, and area heritage; a gallery displaying local works; and a staffed information desk.

The current **West Quoddy Head Light,** towering 83 feet above mean high water, was built in 1857. (Its counterpart, Harbour Head Lightstation, a.k.a. East Quoddy Head Light, is on New Brunswick's Campobello Island.) Views from the lighthouse grounds are fabulous, and whale sightings are common in summer. The lighthouse tower is open the Saturday after July 4 and during Maine Open Lighthouse Day, usually held in September.

The cliffs of Canada's Grand Manan Island are visible from the park's grounds. The four-mile round-trip, moderately difficult Coastal Trail follows the 90-foot cliffs to Carrying Place Cove. An easy mile-long boardwalk winds through a unique moss and heath bog; a second bog is designated as a National Natural Landmark. The one-mile Coast Guard Trail loops out to an observation point. Be forewarned that the park gate is locked at sunset. In winter the park is accessible for snowshoeing. From Route 189 on the outskirts of Lubec, take South Lubec Road (well signposted) to West Quoddy Head Road. Turn left and continue to the parking area.

Mulholland Market and McCurdy's Herring Smokehouse

Lubec Landmarks (207/733-2197, www.mccurdyssmokehouse.org) is working to preserve these two local landmarks. The **smokehouse complex** (11am-4pm daily, $3 donation), one of the last herring-smoking operations in the country (closed in 1991 and now a National Historic Landmark), can be seen on the water side of Water Street. In 2007, after years of effort, it reopened to the public. You can tour it on your own, or volunteer guides will explain the exhibits, which include hands-on ones for kids. Next door, **Mulholland Market Gallery** (50 Water St., 10am-4pm Thurs.-Tues.), which now doubles as a community center, is the organization's headquarters. Inside are displays about the smokehouses, exhibits of local art, and a small gift shop. It is volunteer operated, so hours aren't set in stone.

Robert S. Peacock Fire Museum

Worth a look-see for fans of old fire equipment, the small **museum at the fire station** (40 School St., Lubec, 207/733-2341) is open by request at the adjacent town office.

© TOM NANGLE

McCurdy's Herring Smokehouse, in Lubec

Lubec Breakwater

Even the humongous tides and dramatic sunsets over Johnson Bay can get your attention if you hang out at the breakwater. A **Lost Fishermen's Memorial Park,** honoring regional fishermen lost at sea, is planned here. Across the channel on Campobello Island is red-capped **Mulholland Point Lighthouse,** an abandoned beacon built in 1885. As the tide goes out—18 or so feet—you'll also see hungry harbor seals dunking for dinner. And if you're lucky, you might spot the eagle pair that nests on an island in the channel (bring binoculars).

ENTERTAINMENT AND EVENTS

Classical music is the focus (for the most part) at **SummerKeys** (207/733-2316 or 973/316-6220 off-season, www.summerkeys.com), a music camp for adults, no prior experience required, with weeklong programs in piano, voice, oboe, flute, clarinet, guitar, violin, and cello. Free concerts by visiting artists, faculty, and students are held at 7:30pm Wednesday evening late June-early September in the Congregational Christian Church on Church Street.

ArtworksOfMaine Visual & Performing Arts Center (10 N. Lubec Rd., 207/733-2468, www.artworksofmaine.com) opened in 2013 in the former library and grange hall. Works by regional artists are exhibited in the gallery, and performing arts classics and performances are planned.

Live music is usually on tap on weekends at Cohill's Inn and Annabell's Pub, both on Water Street.

The **Masonic Summer Music Series**, held most Thursday evenings at the town bandstand on Main Street, include an all-you-can-eat cookout ($8 adults, $4 children) and a free concert.

Timber-frame buildings built by the **Cobscook Community Learning Center** (CCLC, Timber Cove Rd., Trescott, 207/733-2233, www.theccclc.org) house an open pottery studio, a fiber-arts studio, and multipurpose classrooms. The year-round programs offered

© TOM NANGLE

Eagles are often sighted in the channel between Lubec and Campobello Island.

include open-jam music nights, workshops, talks, adult education, indigenous education, sustainable and value-added eco-ventures, youth programs, and more.

Birders flock to the Cobscook Bay area for **The Down East Spring Birding Festival** (207/733-2233, www.downeastbirdfest.org), held annually in late May. Guided and self-guided explorations, presentations, and tours fill the schedule, and participation is limited, so register early.

Downeast Coastal Conservancy (www.downeastcoastalconservancy.org) offers workshops, guided walks, boat trips, and other events throughout the summer.

SHOPPING

Most of Lubec's shops are along Water Street.

The old RJ Peacock factory is now home to **Dianne's Glass Gallery** (72 Water St., Lubec, 207/733-2458), where Dianne Larkin sells her handcrafted hot-fused glass jewelry, plates, and other creations. Also available here are the locally made, all-natural sea salts produced by

Quoddy Mist (207/733-4847, www.quoddymist.com).

Northern Tides (24 Water St., Lubec, 207/733-2500) carries intriguing works by local artisans such as sea-glass creations, pottery crafted with finds from the sea, felt work, and weaving.

Wags and Wool (83 Water St., Lubec, 207/733-4714) caters to knitters and dog lovers, with natural fibers, local yarns, handknit sweaters, socks, and gloves, and dog accessories.

Lighthouse buffs must stop at **West Quoddy Gifts** (Quoddy Head Rd., one mile before the lighthouse, 207/733-2457). It's stocked with souvenirs and gift items, most with a lighthouse theme.

Fred and Patty Hartman's **DownEast Drawings and Wildlife Art Gallery** (Rte. 189, Whiting, 207/733-0988) is filled with award-winning artwork featuring the flora and fauna of the region.

Shanna Wheelock's **Cobscook Pottery and Fiber Arts** (162 N. Lubec Rd., 207/733-2010) is worth the short detour off Route 1.

TIDES

Nowhere in Maine is the adage "Time and tide wait for no man" truer than along the Washington County coastline. The nation's most extreme tidal ranges occur in this area, so the hundreds of miles of tidal shore frontage between Steuben and Calais provide countless opportunities for observing tidal phenomena. Every six hours or so, the tide begins either ebbing or flowing. The farther Down East you go, the higher (and lower) the tides. Although tides in Canada's Bay of Fundy are far higher, the highest tides in New England occur along the St. Croix River at Calais.

Tides govern coastal life—particularly Down East, where average tidal ranges may be 10-20 feet and extremes approach 28 feet. Everyone is a slave to the tide calendar, which coastal-community newspapers diligently publish. Boats tie up with extralong lines, clammers and worm diggers schedule their days by the tides, hikers have to plan for shoreline exploring, and kayakers need to plan their routes to avoid getting stuck in the muck.

Tides, as we learned in school, are lunar phenomena, created by the gravitational pull of the moon; the tidal range depends on the lunar phase. Tides are most extreme at new and full moons—when the sun, moon, and Earth are aligned. These are spring tides, supposedly because the water springs upward (the term has nothing to do with the season). And tides are smallest during the moon's first and third quarters—when the sun, Earth, and moon have a right-angle configuration. These are neap tides (*neap* comes from an Old English word meaning "scanty"). Other lunar and solar phenomena, such as the equinoxes and solstices, can also affect tidal ranges.

The best time for shoreline exploration is on a new-moon or full-moon day, when low tide exposes mussels, sea urchins, sea cucumbers, starfish, periwinkles, hermit crabs, rockweed, and assorted nonbiodegradable trash. Rubber boots or waterproof, treaded shoes are essential on the wet, slippery terrain.

Caution is also essential in tidal areas. Unless you've carefully plotted tide times and heights, don't park a car, bike, or boat trailer on a beach. Make sure your sea kayak is lashed securely to a tree or bollard, don't take a long nap on shoreline granite, and don't cross a low-tide land spit without an eye on your watch.

A perhaps apocryphal but almost believable story goes that one flatlander stormed up to a ranger at Cobscook Bay State Park one bright summer morning and demanded indignantly to know why they had had the nerve to drain the water from her shorefront campsite during the night. When it comes to tides. . . you have to go with the flow.

THE DOWN EAST COAST

Wheelock's been featured in *American Craft* magazine.

RECREATION
Boat Excursions

Explore Cobscook, Fundy, and Passamaquoddy Bays on a tour with **Downeast Charter Boat Tours** (31 Johnson St., Lubec, 207/733-2009, www.downeastcharterboattours.com) aboard the 25-foot lobster boat *Lorna Doone*. You'll pass lighthouses and likely also spy whales.

Jet-boat whale-watching tours are offered aboard the *Tarquin* from **The Inn on the Wharf** (60 Johnson St., Lubec, 207/733-4400, www. theinnonthewharf.com). The 2.5-3-hour tours are $49 adults, $25 kids under 12.

Hiking and Walking

Tag along with Lubec's **Pathfinders Walking Group,** enthusiastic area residents who go exploring every Sunday year-round, usually meeting at 2pm for a two-hour ramble; check local papers for the schedule. Nonmembers are welcome, there's no fee, and you'll see a side of Lubec and more that most visitors never encounter.

Two preserves run by the Maine Coast Heritage Trust (www.mcht.org) are fine places for a walk. The 1,225-acre **Hamilton**

THE DOWN EAST COAST

© HILARY NANGLE

Mowry Beach is especially popular with bird-watchers.

Cove Preserve's 1.5 miles of ocean frontage are highlighted by cobble beaches, rocky cliffs, and jaw-dropping views (on a clear day) of Grand Manan. To find it, take Route 189 to South Lubec Road toward Quoddy Head, but bear right at the fork on Boot Cove Road and continue 2.4 miles to a small parking lot on the left. There's a kiosk with maps about 100 feet down the trail. It's 0.8 mile to an observation platform and another 0.5 mile to the bench at the trail's end. For more expansive views, hike 1.2 miles to the summit of Benny's Mountain.

Continue on Boot Cove Road another 1.5 miles to find 700-acre **Boot Head Preserve,** with dramatic cliffs and ravines that epitomize Maine's Bold Coast reputation. The trail passes through a rare coastal raised peat land before continuing to a viewing platform on the coast. From the parking lot to Boot Cove via the Coastal Trail, it's 1.25 miles; return via the Interior Trail for another 0.75 mile.

For information on other hikes in the area, pick up a copy of *Cobscook Trail Guide,* with maps and trail details. It's available for about $7 at local stores or from the Quoddy Regional Land Trust Office on Route 1 in Whiting. Another resource available locally is *Self-Guided Birding Explorations, Washington County, Maine,* published in conjunction with the Down East Spring Birding Festival. It lists and maps walks and hikes, and notes habitats and bird species.

In 2010, *Travel + Leisure* magazine named Lubec one of the best beach towns in the country. Where's the beach, you ask? **Mowry Beach,** managed by the Downeast Coastal Conservancy (www.downeastcoastalconservancy.org), is at the end of Pleasant Street; continue past the wastewater treatment plant to a parking lot. Follow the path over the dunes to the beach. When the tide rolls out, remnants of a drowned Ice Age forest are revealed. Also here is a wheelchair-accessible boardwalk designed for sighting nesting, migrating, and wintering birds, including warblers, finches, waxwings, hawks, and northern shrikes.

© HILARY NANGLE

Cohill's Inn overlooks the water.

Biking and Kayaking

The Wharf (60 Johnson St., Lubec, 207/733-4400) rents bikes for $18/day as well as kayaks for $25-35. **Cohill's** (7 Water St., 207/733-4300) rents bikes for $45/day.

ACCOMMODATIONS

Many visitors use Lubec as a base for day trips to Campobello Island (passport or passport card necessary), so it's essential to make reservations at the height of summer. Several lodgings are also available on Campobello.

Bed-and-Breakfasts and Inns

Built in 1860 by a British sea captain, **Peacock House Bed and Breakfast** (27 Summer St., Lubec, 207/733-2403 or 888/305-0036, www.peacockhouse.com, $98-140) has long been one of Lubec's most prestigious residences. Among the notables who have stayed here are Donald MacMillan, the famous Arctic explorer, as well as U.S. senators Margaret Chase Smith and Edmund Muskie. It has three guest rooms and four suites, which have TVs and sitting areas;

one has a gas fireplace and a refrigerator. One guest room is wheelchair-accessible.

Unusual antiques fill the guest rooms and sitting room of the 19th-century **Home Port Inn** (45 Main St., Lubec, 207/733-2077 or 800/457-2077 outside Maine, www.homeportinn.com, $95-130), ensconced on a Lubec hilltop. Each of the seven guest rooms has a private bath, although some are detached; some have water views. Rates include a buffet breakfast.

Ellen and Jack Gearrin extend a warm Irish welcome to guests at **Cohill's Inn** (7 Water St., 207/733-4300, www.cohillsinn.com, $95-140), which overlooks the Bay of Fundy on one side and the Narrows on the other. There are no frills or fuss in the simply but nicely furnished guest rooms; each has a fan and a TV, beds are covered with comforters and quilts, and a continental breakfast is included in the rates. Wi-Fi is available. Downstairs is a popular and reliable pub, but service ends at 8pm, so it's quiet at night.

Purpose-built **Whiting Bay Bed & Breakfast** (1 Cobscook Way, Whiting, 207/733-2402, www.whitingbaybb.com, $100-125) sits on 7.5 acres with water on three sides. It's a heavenly retreat, decorated with a light touch. Rates include a full breakfast.

The waterfront **Water Street Tavern & Inn** (12 Water St., Lubec, 207/733-2477, www.watersttavernandinn.com, $95-150) has three nicely appointed rooms and two suites, all with Wi-Fi, TV, and phone. All guests have access to a gathering room with comfy seating, big views, and a kitchenette.

Motel

The **Eastland Motel** (385 County Rd./Rte. 189, Lubec, 207/733-5501, www.eastlandmotel.com, $70-85) has 20 guest rooms with cable TV, Wi-Fi, and air-conditioning; some have refrigerator and microwave. Request one of the 12 rooms in the newer section. A homemade continental breakfast is included in the rates. One room is dog friendly ($10).

Apartments, Suites, and Houses

Bill Clark has rescued the former Coast Guard

Water Street Tavern & Inn is on the waterfront in downtown Lubec.

© HILARY NANGLE

station at West Quoddy Head and restored, renovated, and reopened it as (**West Quoddy Station** (S. Lubec Rd., Lubec, 207/733-4452 or 877/535-4714, www.quoddyvacation.com), with five one-bedroom units (four in the lodge and one separate cabin), plus the five-bedroom, 2.5-bath Station House. All have kitchens, Wi-Fi, and satellite TV. Views are stupendous and extend to East Quoddy Head on Campobello; you can walk to West Quoddy Head, about 0.5 mile away. Rates begin at $95/night, when available, but weekly rentals ($900-$1,900) get first preference.

Another restoration project is the former Lubec Sardine Company's Factory B, where Judy and Victor Trafford have renovated the truly waterfront complex into (**The Inn on the Wharf** (60 Johnson St., Lubec, 207/733-4400, www.theinnonthewharf.com), comprising lodging and a restaurant, while preserving the working waterfront. Guest rooms ($100) have use of a common kitchen and dining area. Two-bedroom, two-bathroom apartments ($150) have full kitchens and laundry

facilities. All have incredible views and Wi-Fi. Also on the premises are a yoga studio and bike and kayak rentals. A whale-watching boat and water taxi to Eastport departs from the wharf. That's all great, but what really distinguishes this property is that hidden on the basement level are huge tanks holding lobsters, crabs, and eels; an area for processing the periwinkle harvest; and other intriguing spots where you might catch local fishing folks bringing in their catches. Of course, a side effect of that is that there's a briny scent permeating the entire property.

Camping

A 3.5-mile network of nature trails, picnic spots, great bird-watching and berry picking, hot showers, a boat launch, and wooded shorefront campsites make **Cobscook Bay State Park** (Rte. 1, Edmunds Township, 207/726-4412, www.parksandlands.com), on the 888-acre Moosehorn Reserve, one of Maine's most spectacular state parks. It's even entertaining just to watch the 24-foot tides surging

© HILARY NANGLE

The Inn on the Wharf is located in a renovated sardine plant.

in and out of this area at five or so feet per hour; there's no swimming because of the undertow. Reserve well ahead to get a place on the shore. There are no hookups, but there's a dump station for RVs. To guarantee a site in July-August, using MasterCard or Visa, call 207/624-9950 (800/332-1501 in Maine) or visit www.campwithme.com; the reservation fee is $2/site/night with a two-night minimum. The park is open daily mid-May-mid-October; trails are groomed in winter for cross-country skiing, and one section goes right along the shore. Summer day-use fees are $4.50 nonresident adults, $3 Maine resident adults, $1.50 nonresident seniors, free Maine resident seniors, $1 ages 5-11. The nonresident camping fee is $24/site/night; the fee for Maine residents is $14.

FOOD
Local Flavors
Monica's Chocolates (100 County Rd./Rte. 189, Lubec, 866/952-4500, www.monicaschocolates.com, 8am-8pm daily) gives meaning to the term *sinfully delicious.* Monica Elliott creates sumptuous handmade gourmet chocolates using family recipes from her native Peru. Her hot chocolate, not always available, is swoon worthy.

Stave off a midday hunger attack with homebaked goodies with an organic twist from **Sun Porch Industries** (99 Johnson St., Lubec, 207/733-7587, 11am-5pm Wed.-Sun.), a tiny natural and organic foods store.

Baked goods, pizzas, freshly made sandwiches, and other light fare is served at **Atlantic House Coffee & Deli** (52 Water St., Lubec, 207/733-0906, 8am-7pm daily). Take it to one of two back decks overlooking the water.

It's a treat to visit the Bell family's 200-year-old, 1,600-acre organic saltwater farm, **Tide Mill Organic Farm** (91 Tide Mill Rd., Edmunds, 207/733-4756 or 207/733-2551, www.tidemillorganicfarm.com), now operated by the eighth generation on this land. The farm stand is open 10am-3pm Saturday. Tours of the farm are available; call for times. The fee is $5 for anyone over age 8 or $20/family.

Family Favorites

Good burgers, chowders, and other choices from the daily chalkboard menu as well as Guinness, Smithwick's, and microbrews have earned **Cohill's Inn** (7 Water St., Lubec, 207/733-4300, www.cohillsinn.com, 11am-8pm daily, $9-29) an enthusiastic two thumbs up from locals and visitors alike. The dining room has nice water views, and there's often entertainment on Saturday afternoon.

Depending on your source, **Uncle Kippy's** (County Rd./Rte. 189, Lubec, 207/733-2400, www.unclekippys.com, 11am-8pm Wed.-Mon., $5-19) gets high marks in Lubec for wholesome cooking. Steak and seafood are specialties—at unfancy prices—but there's pizza too.

Casual Dining

If the weather's nice, aim for a seat on the back deck at the **Water Street Tavern & Inn** (12 Water St., Lubec, 207/733-2477, from 7am daily, $12-28). The menu ranges from pizza to duck, but seafood is the specialty.

Craving Italian? Dine inside or on the waterside deck at **Frank's Dockside Deli** (20 Water St., Lubec, 11am-7pm Thurs.-Tues., 3pm-7pm Wed., $12-25).

Lobster

Fisherman's Wharf (69 Johnson St., Lubec, 207/733-4400, www.theinnonthewharf.com, 7am-8pm Fri.-Wed., $12-24 7am-8pm daily), at the Inn on the Wharf, is in a renovated, oceanfront sardine factory. There's seating inside and on a small deck, with panoramic views over Cobscook Bay to Eastport's Shackford Head. Seafood is the specialty, but there are landlubber choices and a full bar too.

Fresh seafood takeout is available at **Becky's Seafood** (145 Main St., 207/479-4874, 11am-8pm daily); nothing fancy, nothing fussy, but cheap.

INFORMATION AND SERVICES

The **Association to Promote and Protect the Lubec Environment** (888/347-9302, www.

Frank's Dockside Deli is a local favorite for Italian fare.

© HILARY NANGLE

visitlubecmaine.com) is the best source for local information. The **Cobscook Bay Area Chamber of Commerce** (www.cobscookbay. com) also covers the Cobscook Bay region, including Lubec.

Lubec Memorial Library (Water St. and School St., Lubec, 207/733-2491) has a public restroom.

GETTING THERE AND AROUND

Eastport Ferry (207/853-2635, www.eastportferry.com) offers passenger service between Lubec and Eastport. It departs up to six times daily, Tuesday-Sunday. Tickets are $19.50 adults, $10 children under 12. Bring a bicycle for $6; dogs are free.

The **Franklin D. Roosevelt Memorial Bridge** connects Lubec to Campobello Island (passport, passport card, or enhanced driver's license required for return).

Lubec is approximately 28 miles or 40 minutes via Routes 1 and 189 from Machias. It's about 40 miles or one hour via Routes 189, 1, and 190 to Eastport.

Campobello Island

Just over the Franklin D. Roosevelt Memorial Bridge from Lubec lies nine-mile-long, unspoiled **Campobello Island** (pop. 1,000), in Canada's New Brunswick province. Most visitors come to see the place where President Franklin D. Roosevelt, along with other wealthy Americans, summered, but few take the time to explore the charms of Roosevelt's "beloved island." Those who do find a striking lighthouse that's open for tours, hiking trails, carriage roads for biking, whale-watching excursions, and spectacular vistas.

It's interesting to note that before becoming a summer retreat for wealthy Americans, Campobello was the feudal fiefdom of a Welsh family. King George III awarded the grant to Captain William Owen in 1767, and he arrived in 1770.

SIGHTS
◀ Roosevelt Campobello International Park

Since 1964, **Roosevelt Campobello International Park**'s 2,800 acres of the island have been under joint U.S. and Canadian jurisdiction, commemorating U.S. president Franklin D. Roosevelt. FDR summered here as a youth, and it was here that he came down with infantile paralysis (polio) in 1921. The park, covering most of the island's southern end, has well-maintained trails and carriage roads, picnic sites, and dramatic vistas, but its centerpiece is the imposing Roosevelt Cottage, one mile northeast of the bridge.

Stop first at the park's **Visitor Centre** (459 Rte. 774, Welshpool, 506/752-2922 in season, www.fdr.net), where you can pick up brochures (including a trail map, bird-watching guide, and bog guide), sign up for Tea with Eleanor, and see a short video setting the stage for the cottage visit.

ROOSEVELT COTTAGE

It's a short walk from the Visitor Centre to the **Roosevelt Cottage** (10am-6pm Atlantic time, 9am-5pm eastern time, mid-May-mid-Oct., free). Little seems to have changed in the 34-room red-shingled Roosevelt "Cottage" overlooking Passamaquoddy Bay since President Roosevelt last visited in 1939. The Roosevelt Cottage grounds are beautifully landscaped, and the many family mementos—especially those in the late president's den—bring history alive. It all feels very personal and far less stuffy than most presidential memorials. You tour on your own, but guides are stationed in various rooms to explain and answer questions.

THE DOWN EAST COAST

© HILARY NANGLE

Explore the carriage roads of Roosevelt Campobello International Park to find lookouts, picnic areas, and trails.

TEA WITH ELEANOR

Twice daily, the park offers an engaging **Tea with Eleanor** in the Hubbard Cottage, which neighbors the Roosevelt cottage. During the one-hour program, park interpreters tell stories about the remarkable Eleanor, highlighting her history and her many feats, while guests enjoy tea and cookies. The program is free, but seating is limited, and reservations are required. These are made in person at the Visitor Centre, first-come/first served, so it's wise to get there early to snag seats.

THE PARK BY BICYCLE OR CAR

Carriage roads lace the park, and although you can drive them, a bike, if you have one, is far more fun. Options include **Cranberry Point Drive,** 5.4 miles round-trip from the Visitor Centre; **Liberty Point Drive,** 12.4 miles round-trip, via Glensevern Road, from the Visitor Centre; and **Fox Hill Drive,** a 2.2-mile link between the other two main routes. En route, you'll have access to beaches, picnic

sites, spruce and fir forests, and great views of lighthouses, islands, and the Bay of Fundy.

Just west of the main access road from the bridge is the **Mulholland Point picnic area,** where you can spread out your lunch next to the distinctive red-capped lighthouse overlooking Lubec Narrows. A marine biology exhibit in the red shed adjacent to it highlights seals, whale rescue, tides, and other related topics.

HIKING AND PICNICKING

Within the international park are 8.5 miles of walking-hiking trails, varying from dead easy to moderately difficult. Easiest is the 1.2-mile (round-trip) walk from the Visitor Centre to **Friar's Head picnic area,** named for its distinctive promontory jutting into the bay. For the best angle, climb up to the observation deck on the "head." Grills and tables are here for picnickers. Pick up a brochure at the Visitor Centre detailing natural sights along the route.

The most difficult—and most dramatic—trail is a 2.4-mile stretch from **Liberty Point to**

Raccoon Beach, along the southeastern shore of the island. Precipitous cliffs can make parts of this trail risky for small children or insecure adults, so use caution. Liberty Point is incredibly rugged, but observation platforms make it easy to see the tortured rocks and wide-open Bay of Fundy. Along the way is the SunSweep Sculpture, an international art project by David Barr. At broad Raccoon Beach, you can walk the sands, have a picnic, or watch for whales, porpoises, and ospreys. To avoid returning via the same route, park at Liberty Point and walk back along Liberty Point Drive from Raccoon Beach. If you're traveling with nonhikers, arrange for them to meet you with a vehicle at Con Robinson's Point.

A fascinating boardwalk, perfect for those in wheelchairs, is **Eagle Hill Bog,** 1.8 miles down the Glensevern Road. Interpretive signs explain the lichens, scrub pines, pitcher plants, and other flora and fauna within the bogs. A spur trail leads to a trail that climbs quickly to an observation deck.

You can also walk the park's perimeter, including just more than six miles of shoreline, but only if you're in good shape, have waterproof hiking boots, and can spend an entire day on the trails. Before attempting this, however, inquire at the Visitor Centre about trail conditions and tide levels.

Herring Cove Provincial Park

What a sleeper! Far too few people visit 1,049-acre **Herring Cove Provincial Park** (506/752-7010 or 800/561-0123), with picnic areas, 88 campsites, a four-mile trail system, a mile-long sandy beach, freshwater Glensevern Lake, a restaurant with fabulous views, and the nine-hole championship-level **Herring Cove Golf Course** (506/752-2467). The park is open early June-September. Admission is free.

Head Harbour Lightstation/ East Quoddy Head

Consult the tide calendar before planning your assault on **Head Harbour Lightstation** (also called East Quoddy Head Light), at Campobello's northernmost tip. The

© TOM NANGLE

THE DOWN EAST COAST

The Herring Cove Golf Course is rarely crowded.

© HILARY NANGLE

Head Harbour Lightstation has been restored and is open for tours, but the only access is by foot at low tide.

51-foot-tall light, built in 1829, is on an islet accessible only at low tide. The distinctive white light tower bears a huge red cross. (You're likely to pass near it on whale-watching trips out of Eastport or Lubec.) From the Roosevelt Cottage, follow Route 774 through the village of Wilson's Beach and continue to the parking area. A stern Canadian Coast Guard warning sign tells the story:

> Extreme Hazard. Beach exposed only at low tide. Incoming tide rises 5 feet per hour and may leave you stranded for 8 hours. Wading or swimming are extremely dangerous due to swift currents and cold water. Proceed at your own risk.

It's definitely worth the effort for the bay and island views from the lighthouse grounds, often including whales and eagles. You can walk out to the lighthouse during a four-hour window around dead low tide (be sure your watch coincides with the Atlantic-time tide calendar).

In 2005 the **Friends of the Head Harbour Lightstation** (916 Rte. 774, Welshpool, www.campobello.com/lighthouse), a local nonprofit, took over maintenance of the station to restore it. It now charges access fees to support the efforts. You can see the light from the nearby grounds at no charge, but if you want to hike out to the island or visit the light, the suggested donation is $5. Add a tour of the lighthouse, including climbing the tower, for $10; the family maximum for the walk or the tour is $25 (cash only). The Friends are restoring the interior with period furnishings and plan to rent the keeper's house for overnight guests to experience the island. You can support the efforts with a membership, available for US$15 individual or US$25 family.

Campobello Island Public Library and Museum

Campobello's **library** (306 Welshpool St., 506/752-7082) houses a small collection of artifacts and memorabilia related to island life as well as birch bark items crafted by Tomah Joseph.

TOURS

Island Discovery Tours (877/346-2225, www.islanddiscoverytours.com) offers guided tours of the island with round-trip transportation from Lubec for $55, including lunch. Transportation to and from the Roosevelt Cottage only is $10. And yes, you'll need either a passport or passport card. If you're already on island, you can join one of the tours departing from the Roosevelt Cottage.

RECREATION
◖ Whale-Watching

Island Cruises (506/752-1107 or 888/249-4400, www.bayoffundywhales.com, $50 adults, $40 children, $160 two adults and two children, $45 seniors) depart three or four times daily from Head Harbour Wharf for scenic whale-watching cruises aboard the *Mister Matthew,* a 37-foot traditional Bay of Fundy fishing boat that carries 20 passengers. Captain Mac Greene is a member of the Fundy Whale Rescue Team, so he has great insights and stories to share. Sightings might include minke, finback, humpback, and perhaps even northern right whales.

Outfitter

Campobello Island Outdoor Adventures (727 Friar's Bay Beach, Welshpool, 877/346-2225, www.campobelloislandadventures.com) is the go-to for bicycle ($8/hour, $20 half day, $30 full day) and kayak rentals. It also offers guided tours.

ACCOMMODATIONS AND FOOD

In midsummer, if you'd like to overnight on the island, reserve lodgings well in advance; Campobello is a popular destination. The nearest backup beds are in Lubec, and those fill up too.

The Owen House (11 Welshpool St., Welshpool, 506/752-2977, www.owenhouse. ca, late May-mid-Oct., $104-210 Canadian) is the island's best address, an old-shore, comfortable, early-19th-century inn on 10 acres on Deer Point overlooking Passamaquoddy Bay and Eastport in the distance. Nine guest rooms (two with shared baths) on three floors are decorated with antiques and family treasures along with owner Joyce Morrel's paintings (Joyce grew up in this house) and assorted handmade quilts. There's a first-floor guest room that's ideal for those with mobility problems. Don't expect fancy or techy amenities; there are no phones, and there are no TVs, other than one for playing movies. Joyce and innkeeper Jan Meiners are very active in the lighthouse preservation efforts. Just north of the inn is the Deer Island ferry landing.

Check into the oceanfront **Pollock Cove Cottages** (2455 Rte. 774, Wilson's Beach, 506/752-2300, www.campobello.com, $75-175), and you might never leave. The views are that spectacular. The property, spread out on a grassy bluff, offers rooms with refrigerators,

© TOM NANGLE

The Owen House commands a bluff with views over Passamaquoddy Bay.

rooms with kitchenettes, and two-bedroom cottages with full kitchens.

The campground at **Herring Cove Provincial Park** (506/752-7010, $25-40 Canadian) is a gem. It's underused, so crowds are rare. Sites are tucked in the woods near Herring Cove Beach. On the premises are a restaurant, nine-hole golf course, picnic grounds, and hiking trails that lead into adjacent Campobello International Park. Sites are available for tents to RVs.

Don't expect culinary creativity on Campobello, but you won't starve—at least during the summer season. The best choice is **Family Fisheries** (1977 Rte. 774, Wilson's Beach, 506/752-2470, 11am-9:30pm daily, $6-30 Canadian), a seafood restaurant and fish market toward the northern end of the island. Portions are huge, service is friendly, the fish is superfresh, and the homemade desserts are decadent. BYOB—wine only.

Herring Cove (136 Herring Cove Rd., Welshpool, 506/752-1092, 8am-8pm daily, $8-25), at the golf course, has a full bar and serves a full menu.

Roosevelt Campobello International Park plans to open the restored and renovated **Adams Cottage** as a restaurant, serving lunch Monday-Friday, dinner Friday and Saturday, and brunch on Sunday. Constructed in 1917 with logs cut on the island, the cottage once belonged to a cousin of FDR. If the weather's fine, aim for a seat on the deck and enjoy views of Friar's Bay. Check with the park for details (506/752-2922).

Owner Robert Calder roasts beans daily at **Jocie's Porch** (724 Rte. 774, Welshpool, 506/752-9816, 7am-7pm daily), which serves the island's best coffee as well as light fare, all overlooking Friar's Bay.

INFORMATION AND SERVICES

Be aware that there's a one-hour time difference between Lubec and Campobello. Lubec, like the rest of Maine, is on eastern time; Campobello, like the rest of New Brunswick, is on Atlantic time, an hour later. As soon as

you reach the island, set your clock ahead an hour.

There is no need to convert U.S. currency to Canadian money for use on Campobello; U.S. dollars are accepted everywhere on the island, but prices tend to be quoted in Canadian dollars.

Off the bridge, stop at the **Tourist Information Centre** (44 Rte. 774, Welshpool, 506/752-7043, May-Oct.) on your right for an island map, trail maps of the international park, tide info for lighthouse visits, and New Brunswick visitor information.

The best source of information on Campobello Island is **www.visitcampobello. com.**

Public restrooms are at the Tourist Information Centre near the bridge and the park's Visitor Centre.

GETTING THERE AND AROUND

Campobello is connected by bridge to Lubec. From Campobello you can also continue by ferry to New Brunswick's Deer Island and on to Eastport or make the Quoddy Loop and continue to Letete, N.B., and visit St. Andrews, before crossing the border at Calais and returning south to Eastport.

To visit the island, you'll have to pass immigration checkpoints on the U.S. and Canadian ends of the **Franklin D. Roosevelt Memorial Bridge** (U.S. Customs, Lubec, 207/733-4331; Canada Border Services, Campobello, 506/752-1130). Be sure to have the required identification: a passport or a passport card.

The funky two-stage boat-and-barge **East Coast Ferries** (877/747-2159, www. eastcoastferries.nb.ca, no credit cards, passport or passport card required) departs Campobello for Deer Island on the hour 9am-7pm Atlantic time late June-early September; the fare is $16/car plus $3/passenger over age 11, $23 maximum per car. It connects with the ferry from Deer Island to Eastport, which departs on the hour 9am-6pm Atlantic time, $13/car and driver plus $3/passenger over age 11, $28 maximum per car. Motorcycles on each ferry are $8. All fares are subject to a fuel surcharge. A separate free ferry connects Deer Isle to Letete, near St. Andrews. It departs Deer Isle on the hour 6am-10pm Atlantic time, and on the half hour 7:30am-6:30pm.

Eastport and Vicinity

When you leave Whiting, the gateway to Lubec and Campobello, and continue north on Route 1 around Cobscook Bay, it's hard to believe that life could slow down any more than it already has, but it does. The landscape's raw beauty is occasionally punctuated by farmhouses or a convenience store, but little else.

Edmunds Township's claims to fame are its splendid public lands—Cobscook Bay State Park and a unit of Moosehorn National Wildlife Refuge. Just past the state park, loop along the scenic shoreline before returning to Route 1.

Pembroke (pop. 840), once part of adjoining **Dennysville** (pop. 342), is home to Reversing Falls Park, where you can watch and hear ebbing and flowing tides draining and filling Cobscook Bay.

If time allows a short scenic detour, especially in fall, turn left (northwest) on Route 214 and drive 10 miles to quaintly named **Meddybemps** (pop. 157), allegedly a Passamaquoddy word meaning "plenty of alewives [herring]." Views over Meddybemps Lake, on the north side of the road, are spectacular, and you can launch a canoe or kayak into the lake here, less than a mile beyond the junction with Route 191 (take the dead-end unpaved road toward the water).

Backtracking to Route 1, heading east from Pembroke, you'll come to **Perry** (pop. 889), best known for the Sipayik Indian Reservation at Pleasant Point, a Passamaquoddy settlement, two miles east of Route 1, that has been here since 1822. Route 191 cuts through the heart of the reservation.

The city (yes, it's officially a city) of **Eastport** (pop. 1,331) is on Moose Island, connected by a causeway to the mainland at Sipayik (Pleasant Point). Views are terrific on both sides, especially at sunset, as you hopscotch from one blob of land to another and finally reach this mini-city, where the sardine industry was introduced as long ago as 1875. Five sardine canneries once operated here, employing hundreds of local residents who snipped the heads off herring and stuffed them into cans.

Settled in 1772, Eastport has had its ups and downs, mostly mirroring the fishing industry. It's now on an upswing as people "from away" have arrived to soak up the vibe of a small town with a heavy Down East accent. Artists, artisans, and antiques shops are leading the town's rejuvenation as a tourist destination, with the Tides Institute at the forefront. A big push came in 2001 when the Fox Network reality-TV series *Murder in Small Town X* was filmed here; the city morphed into the village of Sunrise, Maine, and local residents eagerly filled in as extras. The huge waterfront statue of a fisherman is a remnant of the filming.

Until 1811 the town also included Lubec, which is about 2.5 miles across the water via boat but more than 40 miles in a car. A passenger ferry connects the two.

SIGHTS
Historic Walking Tour

The best way to appreciate Eastport's history is to pick up and follow the route in *A Walking Guide to Eastport,* available locally for $2.75. The handy map-brochure spotlights the city's 18th-, 19th-, and early-20th-century homes, businesses, and monuments, many now on the National Register of Historic Places. Among the highlights are historic homes converted to bed-and-breakfasts, two museums, and a large chunk of downtown Water Street, with many handsome brick buildings erected after a disastrous fire swept through in 1886.

© HILARY NANGLE

Eastport's fishing fleet is protected from the elements by a massive breakwater.

Raye's Mustard Mill Museum

How often do you have a chance to watch mustard being made in a turn-of-the-20th-century mustard mill? Drive by **J. W. Raye and Co.** (83 Washington St./Rte. 190, Eastport, 207/853-4451 or 800/853-1903, www.rayesmustard.com, 8am-5pm Mon.-Fri., 10am-5pm Sat.-Sun.) at the edge of Eastport and stop in for a free 15-minute tour (offered as schedules permit, call first) of North America's last traditional stone-ground mustard mill. You'll get to see the granite millstones, the mustard seeds being winnowed, and enormous vats of future mustard. Raye's sells mustard under its own label and produces it for major customers under their labels. The shop stocks all of Raye's mustard varieties (samples available), other Maine-made food, and gift items, and it also has a small café where you can buy coffee, tea, and light fare. Both Martha Stewart and Rachael Ray have discovered Raye's, which took home both gold and bronze medals from the 2009 World-Wide Mustard Competition.

The Tides Institute and Museum of Art

One of the most promising additions to Eastport's downtown is the **Tides Institute** (43 Water St., 207/853-4047, www.tidesinstitute.org, 10am-4pm Tues.-Sun., donation appreciated), housed in a former bank that's being restored. The institute's ambitious goals are to build significant cultural collections and to produce new culturally important works employing printmaking, letterpress, photography, bookmaking, oral history, and other media. For its collection, the institute is focusing on works by artists associated with the U.S.-Canada northeast coast but with an eye to the broader world. It already has significant works by artists such as Martin Johnson Heade and photographers such as Paul Caponigro, a fine selection of baskets by Native Americans, and two organs made by the local Pembroke organ company in the 1880s. A series of rotating shows during the summer highlights both the permanent collections and loaned works. The research and

Raye's Mustard Mill Museum dates back to the turn of the 20th century.

reference library has more than 4,000 volumes. The institute also offers programs on a range of topics and workshops by visiting artists. These are open to the public by reservation; definitely stop in for a visit. In 2013, the institute opened **Studio Works,** a studio space with demonstrations and a visiting artist program, across the street.

Pleasant Point Reservation

To get to Eastport, you pass through the Passamaquoddy's Sipayik or **Pleasant Point Reservation** (www.wabanaki.com). Ask locally or check the website to find basket makers and other traditional artists who might sell from their homes. The decorative and work baskets are treasures that constantly escalate in price. It's a real treat to be able to buy one from the maker. For a more in-depth understanding of the culture, visit the **Waponahki Museum** (59 Passamaquoddy Rd., Perry, 207/853-4400, www.waponahkimuseum.org, 9am-4pm Mon.-Thurs.).

Downeast Observatory

The **Downeast Amateur Astronomers' Downeast Observatory** (356 Old County Rd., Pembroke, 207/214-5706, www.downeastaa. com), with an eight-inch DE8 reflector and 3-5-inch refractors, is open to the public for free by appointment, but donations are greatly appreciated. Contact Charlie Sawyer at the observatory for details.

PARKS AND PRESERVES
◖ Shackford Head State Park

Ninety-acre **Shackford Head** (off Deep Cove Rd., Eastport, www.parksandlands.com, free) is on a peninsula that juts into Cobscook Bay. The trailhead and parking area are just east of the Washington County Community College Marine Technology Center at the southern end of Eastport. The park has five miles of wooded trails. Easiest is the 1.2-mile round-trip to Shackford Head Overlook and its continuation onto the steeper Ship Point Trail, which adds another 0.4 mile. The trail rises gently to a 175-foot-high headland with wide-open

© TOM NANGLE

The Tides Institute's collection focuses on regional art.

views of Eastport and, depending on weather, Campobello Island, Lubec, Pembroke, and even Grand Manan. This state preserve is a particularly good family hike. There's a toilet near the parking area but no other facilities. Also here is a memorial with plaques detailing the history of five Civil War ships that were decommissioned and burned on Cony Beach by the U.S. government between 1901 and 1920. Eastport's huge tides allowed the ships to be brought in and beached and then taken apart as the tide receded. Fourteen Eastport men served on four of the ships.

Reversing Falls Park

There's plenty of room for adults to relax and kids to play at the 140-acre Reversing Falls Park in West Pembroke—plus shorefront ledges and a front-row seat overlooking a fascinating tidal phenomenon. It's connected via hiking trails to the Downeast Coastal Conservancy's **Reversing Falls Conservation Area** (www.downeastcoastalconservancy.org), a nearly

200-acre property with 1.5 miles of shorefront and 70 acres of coastal wetlands. Pack a picnic and then check newspapers or information offices for the tide times so that you can watch the saltwater surging through a 300-yard-wide passage at about 25 knots, creating a whirlpool and churning "falls." The park is at Mahar Point in West Pembroke, 7.2 miles south of Route 1. Coming from the south (Dennysville), bear right off Route 1 onto Old County in West Pembroke and continue to Leighton Point Road. Turn right on Young's Cove Road and continue to the park.

Gleason Cove

This quiet park and boat launch is a delightful place to walk along the shorefront or to grab a table and spread out a picnic while drinking in the dreamy views over fishing weirs and islands in Passamaquoddy Bay. To get here, take Shore Road (opposite the New Friendly Restaurant) and then take a right on Gleason Cove Road.

ENTERTAINMENT

The **Eastport Arts Center** (36 Washington St., Eastport, 207/853-4650, www.eastportartscenter.com) is an umbrella organization for local arts groups, with headquarters and performance space in a former church. You can pick up a brochure with a complete schedule, which usually includes concerts, workshops, films, puppet shows, productions by local theater group **Stage East,** and other cultural events. Also based here is the **Passamaquoddy Bay Symphony Orchestra,** formed in 2007 by conductor Trond Saeverud, who doubles as concertmaster of the Bangor Symphony Orchestra.

Concerts and other programs are sometimes held in the waterfront amphitheater between Water Street and the waterfront walkway. It's marked by *Nature's Grace,* a granite sculpture carved by New Brunswick artist Jim Boyd.

FESTIVALS AND EVENTS

For a small community, Eastport manages to pull together and put on plenty of successful events during the year.

Eastport's annual four-day **Fourth of July–Old Home Week** extravaganza includes a parade, pancake breakfasts, barbecues, a flea market, an auction, races, live entertainment, and fireworks. This is one of Maine's best Fourth of July celebrations and attracts a crowd of more than 10,000. Lodgings are booked months in advance, so plan ahead.

Indian Ceremonial Days, a three-day Native American celebration, includes children's games, canoe races, craft demos, talking circles, fireworks, and traditional food and dancing at Sipayik, the Pleasant Point Reservation in Perry, the second weekend in August.

The three-day **Eastport Pirate Festival** (www.eastportpiratefestival.com) in September features live music, parades, children's activities, reenactments, and races.

A great resource for area happenings is **CulturePass** (www.culturepass.net), which covers the entire Passamaquoddy Bay region. Pair it with the **Artsipelago Two Countries One Bay Passport** (www.artsipelago.net), a cultural guide to the international Passamaquoddy Bay region.

SHOPPING
Art, Crafts, and Antiques
Eastport has long been a magnet for artists and craftspeople yearning to work in a supportive environment, but the influx has increased in recent years. Nearly two dozen galleries line Water Street and overflow on side streets and throughout the area.

The Eastport Gallery (74 Water St., Eastport, 207/853-4166) is a cooperative with works in varied media. The gallery also sponsors the annual **Paint Eastport Day,** usually held the second Saturday in September, when anyone is invited to paint a local scene; a reception and "wet paint" auction follow.

A group of energetic women with local ties renovated a waterfront building, turning it into **The Commons** (51 Water St., Eastport, 207/853-4123), a fabulous gallery displaying works by artisans from the region and farther afield.

More than 20 artists from the region are represented at **Eastport Breakwater Gallery** (93 Water St., Eastport, 207/853-4773).

Woodworker Roland LaVallee's gallery **Crow Tracks** (11 Water St., Eastport, 207/853-2336) is filled with his intricate carvings of birds and local fauna. The tiny garden entryway doubles the pleasure of a visit.

Indulge your sweet tooth at **Sweeties Downeast** (80 Water St., 207/853-3120), where candy, nuts, and homemade fudge are sold by the pound.

Mary Creighton's **Native American Arts** (55 Bayview Drive, Pleasant Point, Perry, 207/853-4779) sells a nice selection of baskets, dream catchers, moccasins, jewelry, and other goods crafted by Maine Native Americans.

A number of very talented artists and artisans are tucked along the back roads of the area. You might get lucky and find them open, but it's wise to call before making a special trip. These include **Wrenovations** (6 Steam Mill Rd., Robbinston, 207/454-2382), with stained art creations by Mark Wren; **The Red Sleigh** (Rte. 1, Perry, 207/854-6688), filled with locally made treasures, from jewelry to pies; and **Susan Designs** (behind Loring's Body Shop, 416 Gin Cove Rd., Perry, 207/853-4315), where gifted quilt artist Susan Plachy sells her creations.

Gifts and Home
Describing **45th Parallel: The Store** (Rte. 1, Perry, 207/853-9500) is a tough assignment. You really have to go and see for yourself; the aesthetic displays are worth the trip to this eclectic emporium. Housed in a one-story log building two miles (northeast, in the Calais direction) from the junction of Routes 190 and 1, the 45th Parallel is part antiques shop, part gift shop, part global marketplace—and entirely seductive.

Stop in, if only for a few minutes, at **S. L. Wadsworth and Son** (42 Water St., Eastport, 207/853-4343), the oldest ship chandlery in the country and the oldest retail business in Maine. In addition to hardware and marine gear, you'll find nautical gifts, souvenirs, and copies of Eastport-set mysteries penned by local author Sarah Graves.

45th Parallel is part antiques shop, part gift shop, part global marketplace—and filled with intriguing merchandise.

RECREATION
Boat Excursions

Eastport Windjammers (207/853-2500 or 207/853-4303, www.eastportwindjammers. com) offers two sailing cruises aboard the *Ada C. Lore,* a historic 118-foot Chesapeake Bay oyster schooner built in 1923 and one of only three remaining in the country. The three-hour whale-watching cruise ($45 adults, $30 ages 5-12, $15 under age 5) departs at 1:30pm daily and heads out into the prime whale-feeding grounds of Passamaquoddy Bay—passing the Old Sow whirlpool (the largest tidal whirlpool in the Northern Hemisphere), salmon aquaculture pens, and Campobello Island. En route you'll see bald eagles, porpoises, possibly puffins and ospreys, and more. The best months are July and August, but Butch is a skilled spotter, so if they're there, he'll find them. A two-hour sunset cruise ($35 adults, $25 children) departs the Eastport Pier (call for times). Also available are 2.5-hour lobstering cruises and 3-hour fishing trips aboard the *Lady H* ($45 adults, $30 ages 5-12, $15 under age 5).

Sea Kayaking and Canoeing

Explore the region by sea kayak with **Cobscook Hikes and Paddles** (13 Woodcock Way, Robbinston, 207/726-4776 summer, 207/454-2130 winter, www.cobscookhikesandpaddles. com), which serves the area between Whiting and Calais. Registered Maine Guides Stephen and Tessa Ftorek lead three-hour ocean or lake paddles ($50 pp) designed to meet your interests and ability. Two-hour sunrise or sunset paddles are $40. On the Biolum trip, you can watch luminescent organisms sparkle in the water on a two-hour evening paddle ($45). The Ftoreks also offer guided full-day and half-day hikes, beachcombing experiences, and in winter, snowshoeing adventures.

ACCOMMODATIONS
Bed-and-Breakfasts

Although musician and retired teacher Greg

Noyes, innkeeper at the (**Kilby House Inn B&B** (122 Water St., Eastport, 800/853-4557, www. kilbyhouseinn.com, $85-110), grew up closer to Ellsworth, his great-great-grandfather was born in Eastport. Greg bought the Kilby House in 1992 and has masterfully updated and renovated the 1887 Victorian into a lovely four-bedroom inn filled with antiques, some original to the house, clocks, a grand piano, and an organ. Some bathrooms are small, but the hospitality and location, just one block off the ocean and two blocks from downtown, make up for that. Breakfast is served at 8am in the formal dining room.

Apartments

On the second floor of **The Commons** (51 Water St., Eastport, 207/853-4123, www. thecommonseastport.com), a newly renovated downtown building on the waterfront, are two nicely appointed two-bedroom apartments with decks and spectacular harbor views. Weeklong rentals begin around $1,050; Tide Watcher has two baths and rents for $1,150/ week; Water's Edge has one bath and rents for $1,050/week; shorter stays may be possible.

FOOD
Local Flavors

Drool-worthy pastries, breads, and sweets fill the cases at **Moose Island Bakery** (75 Water St., Eastport, 207/853-3111, from 6:30am daily). Also worth a visit for scrumptious homemade goodies is the **Irish Cow Bakery** (11 Shore Rd., Perry, 207/853-4411, 7am-noon Wed.-Sun.). The **Sunrise County Farmers Market** is held at Eastport's downtown waterfront park 11am-2pm Saturday. It's worth the slight detour off Route 1 to purchase hot- and cold-smoked salmon as well as smoked salmon sticks, and smoked haddock at **Maine-ly Smoked Salmon** (555 South Meadow Rd., Perry, 207/853-4794, 9am-5pm daily).

Ethnic Flavors

Oompah! The **Liberty Cafe** (33 Water St., Eastport, 207/853-2080, from 11am Tues.-Fri., from 7am Sat.-Sun., $6-24) specializes in Greek fare, from gyros to spanakopita, but also

offers grilled fare, such as steaks and seafood, to keep everyone happy. The combo plate is a great intro. Although there's a small deck out front, the best views are from the dining room and deck in the rear. Note: The food is very good, but the service can be painfully slow.

Family Favorites

The aptly named **New Friendly Restaurant** (1014 Rte. 1, Perry, 207/853-6610, 11am-8pm daily, $6-20) lays on home-cooked offerings for "dinnah" (a Maine-ism meaning "lunch"), specializing in steak and seafood.

Time your meal right and you can watch the Deer Isle ferry arrive and depart or view a windjammer sail by from the bi-level **Eastport Chowder House** (167 Water St., Eastport, 207/853-4700, 11am-9pm daily). Seafood, natch, is the specialty, with entrées in the $7-21 range. There's a bar downstairs and a harborfront deck too.

A downtown Eastport institution since 1924, the **WaCo Diner** (Bank Square, 207/853-9226, from 6am daily), pronounced WHACK-o, is short for Washington County *or*, the story goes, for Nelson Watts and Ralph Colwell, who started it as a lunch cart. Expect diner fare with an emphasis on seafood, and prices in the $8-20 range. If the weather's fine, aim for a seat on the waterside deck.

Lobster

When the weather's clear, there's nothing finer than lobster at (**Quoddy Bay Lobster** (7 Sea St., Eastport, 207/853-6640, 10am-6pm daily). Lobster is the headliner—watch boats unload their catch, it's that fresh—and I think the lobster rolls are the state's best, each is topped with the meat from one claw. Other options include wraps, salads, and chowders. There's even a kids' menu. Eat indoor or head to the covered outside tables on the harbor's edge.

INFORMATION AND SERVICES

One of the best resources is the free *Artsipelago: Two Countries One Bay* (www.artsipelago.net) guidebook and map, available locally and online, which details the arts and culture of the Passamaquoddy Bay region on both sides of the border, sorted by town. Listings include artists, cultural institutions, galleries, farmers markets, farms, local foods, ferries, festivals, film, historic sites, lighthouses, music, parks/natural sites, and theater.

Brochures are available at the **Quoddy Maritime Museum and Visitor Center** (70 Water St., Eastport, 10am-6pm daily June-Sept.). In the museum section of the center is a huge model of the failed 1936 Passamaquoddy Tidal Power Project, an idea whose time hadn't come when it was proposed. A new, but far, far smaller, experimental hydro tidal project was installed in 2012.

Information is also available from the **Eastport Chamber of Commerce** (64 Water St., 207/853-4644, www.eastportchamber.net) as well as online at www.cobscookbay.com.

The handsome stone **Peavey Memorial Library** (26 Water St., Eastport, 207/853-4021), built in 1893, is named after the inventor of the Peavey grain elevator.

A **public restroom** is available at the library, and in summer there are portable toilets on Eastport's breakwater.

GETTING THERE AND AROUND

Eastport is about 40 miles or one hour via Routes 189, 1, and 190 from Lubec. It's about 28 miles or 40 minutes to Calais via Routes 190 and 1.

Eastport-Lubec Ferry (207/853-2635, www.eastportferry.com) offers passenger service between Lubec and Eastport. It departs up to six times daily, Tuesday-Sunday, including on Wednesday evenings in conjunction with the SummerKeys concert series in Lubec. Tickets are $19.50 adults, $10 children under 12. Bring a bicycle for $6; dogs are free.

If your next stop is New Brunswick, Canada, consider taking the funky two-stage boat-and-barge **East Coast Ferries** (877/747-2159, www.eastcoastferries.nb.ca, no credit cards, passport or passport card required) that connect through Deer Island to Campobello Island. It departs Eastport for Deer Island on the half hour 9:30am-6:30pm Atlantic time late June-early September; fares are $13/car plus $3/passenger over age 11, $18 maximum per car. It connects with the ferry from Deer Island to Campobello, which departs on the half hour 8:30am-6:30pm Atlantic time, $16/car and driver plus $3/passenger over age 11, $23 maximum per car. Motorcycles on each ferry are $8. All fares are subject to additional fuel surcharges. A separate free ferry connects Deer Isle to Letete, near St. Andrews. It departs Deer Isle on the hour 6am-10pm Atlantic time, and on the half hour 7:30am-6:30pm.

Calais and Vicinity

Calais (CAL-us, pop. 3,123) is as far as you'll get on the coast of Maine; from here on, you're headed inland. Europeans showed up in this area as early as 1604, when French adventurers established an ill-fated colony—the root of Acadian/Cajun civilization in New World—on St. Croix Island in the St. Croix River, 16 whole years before the Pilgrims even thought about Massachusetts. After a winter-long debacle, all became relatively quiet until 1779, when the first permanent settler arrived.

Southeast of Calais is tiny **Robbinston** (pop. 574), a booming shipbuilding community in the 19th century but today little more than a blip on the map.

Calais is a major border crossing into New Brunswick, Canada.

SIGHTS
Walking Tour
Pick up a copy of the *Walking Tour Guide to Calais Residential Historic District* at the Maine Tourism Information Center (39 Union St., Calais). The guide, produced by the St. Croix Historical Society, briefly covers the town's history and maps and describes the architecture and early owners of 23 historic houses, four of which are listed on the National Register of Historic Places.

St. Croix Island International Historic Site
Acadian/Cajun civilization in North America has its roots on 6.5-acre **St. Croix Island,** an International Historic Site under joint U.S. and Canadian jurisdiction (Rte. 1, Red Beach Cove, eight miles south of Calais, 207/454-3871, www.nps.gov/sacr, free). The island is the site of the pioneering colony, the earliest European settlement in North America north of Florida, established by French explorers Samuel de Champlain and Pierre du Gua de Monts in 1604. Doomed by disease, mosquitoes, lack of food, and a grueling winter, 35

settlers died; in spring the emaciated survivors abandoned their effort and moved on to Nova Scotia. In 1969, archaeologists found the graves of 23 victims, but the only monument on the island is a commemorative plaque dating from 1904.

Unless you have your own boat, you can't get over to the island, but you can stop at the mainland visitors center, partake in interpretation programs, and enjoy the heritage trail, with bronze statues depicting various key personae or cultures in the development of the colony. The trail ends on the point with views of the island. Also here are picnic tables, restrooms, a gravel beach, and a boat launch.

Whitlock Mill Lighthouse
From the lovely Pikewoods Rest Area, beside Route 1 about four miles southeast of Calais, there's a prime view of 32-foot-high **Whitlock Mill Lighthouse** on the southern shore of the St. Croix River. Built in 1892, the green flashing light is accessible only over private land, so check it out from this vantage point. You can also have a picnic break here.

Calais-Robbinston Milestones
A quirky little local feature, the **Calais-Robbinston milestones** are a dozen red-granite chunks marking each of the 12 miles between Robbinston and Calais. Presaging today's highway mile markers, late-19th-century entrepreneur and journalist James S. Pike had the stones installed on the north side of Route 1 to keep track of the distance while training his pacing horses.

ENTERTAINMENT AND EVENTS
Music on the Green is a series of free concerts presented at 6:30pm in Triangle Park in downtown Calais.

Calais, Maine, and St. Stephen, New Brunswick, collaborate the first or second week of August for the nine-day **International Festival** of dinners, concerts, dances, a crafts fair, ball games, and a cross-border parade and road race. Newspapers carry schedules (note which events are on eastern time and which are on Atlantic time).

SHOPPING

The **Urban Moose** (80 Main St., Calais, 207/454-8277) has an eclectic inventory that invites browsing. Books new, old, and rare are sold at the **Calais Book Shop** (405 Main St., Calais, 207/454-1110).

If you stop in at **Katie's on the Cove** (Rte. 1, Mill Cove, Robbinston, 207/454-3297 or 800/494-5283), do so at your own risk—chocoholics may need a restraining order. Joseph and Lea Sullivan's family operation, begun in 1982, has become a great success story. They now produce about four dozen varieties of homemade fudge, truffles, caramels, peanut brittle, and even marzipan. The shop, 12 miles southeast of Calais and about 15 miles west of Eastport, is no place for unruly or demanding kids—space is limited and the candy is pricey. Call for hours.

RECREATION
Parks and Preserves
MOOSEHORN NATIONAL WILDLIFE REFUGE

More than 50 miles of trails and gravel roads wind through the 17,257-acre Baring Unit of the **Moosehorn National Wildlife Refuge** (Charlotte Rd., Baring, 207/454-7161, http://moosehorn.fws.gov, sunrise-sunset daily, free), on the outskirts of Calais. Start with the 1.2-mile nature trail near the refuge headquarters and get ready for major-league wildlife-watching: 35 mammal and 220 bird species have been spotted in the refuge's fields, forests, ponds, and marshes. Wear waterproof shoes and insect repellent. In August, help yourself to wild blueberries. During November deer-hunting season, either avoid the refuge Monday-Saturday or wear a hunter-orange hat and vest. Trails are accessible by snowshoe, snowmobile, or cross-country skis in winter. To reach

© HILARY NANGLE

You can't miss Katie's on the Cove, a chocolate shop in Robbinston.

refuge headquarters, take Route 1 north from downtown Calais about three miles. Turn left onto Charlotte Road, and go 2.4 miles to the headquarters sign. The office is open 8am-4pm Monday-Friday all year, except major national holidays; you can pick up free trail maps, bird checklists, and other informative brochures. Call ahead to learn about joining wildlife biologists on woodcock waterfowl banding trips. If you want to help support the conservation of wildlife in eastern Maine and educational programs, you can join Friends of Moosehorn National Wildlife Refuge (www.friendsofmoosehorn.org). A check for a mere $15 will do the trick.

By the way, if you don't have time to walk the trails, watch for the elevated artificial nesting platforms—avian high-rises for bald eagles—outside of Calais alongside Route 1 North, near the junction with Charlotte Road. Depending on the season, you may spot a nesting pair or even a fledgling. The chicks, usually twins but occasionally triplets, hatch around mid-May and try their wings by early August. A 400-square-foot observation deck across Route 1 is the best place for eagle-watching.

Continuing on Charlotte Road past the Moosehorn Refuge headquarters, you'll come to **Round Lake** (locally called Round Pond), a lovely spot where you can picnic, swim, or put in a kayak or canoe. Across the road, with a great lake view, is the interesting old Round Pond Cemetery, dating from the early 19th century. (Why do graveyards often have the best views?) Just after the cemetery, a left turn puts you on Pennamaquam Lake Road (or Charlotte Road) toward Perry; a right turn takes you to Route 214, near Pembroke.

DEVIL'S HEAD

About six miles south of Calais, watch for signs pointing to Devil's Head, and take the dirt road on the river side. The 318-acre site has a mile of frontage on the St. Croix River estuary and views to St. Croix Island. A road with two parking areas descends to the shoreline, and there are pit toilets and a marked hiking trail, approximately 1.5 miles looping from the road, leading to the highest point of coastal land north of Cadillac Mountain. The headland was originally called d'Orville Head but it morphed into Devil's Head.

PIKE'S PARK

Calais has a lovely riverfront park at the foot of North Street. Pike's is the perfect place for a picnic. From here you have access to the **Calais Waterfront Walk,** which edges the river, running for 0.9 mile upriver and 0.6 mile downriver.

Golf

At the nine-hole **St. Croix Country Club** (River Rd./Rte. 1, Calais, 207/454-8875, late Apr.-late Oct.), the toughest and most scenic hole is the seventh, one of five holes on the river side of Route 1.

ACCOMMODATIONS
Bed-and-Breakfasts

Within easy walking distance of downtown is **(** **Greystone Bed and Breakfast** (13 Calais Ave., Calais, 207/454-2848, www.greystonecalaisme.com, $95), Alan and Candace Dwelley's masterfully restored 1840 Greek Revival home. The property, listed on the National Register of Historic Places, is an architectural gem within, with Corinthian columns and black marble fireplace mantels. One of the two guest rooms can be paired with a third, smaller room. The Dwelleys serve a more-than-full breakfast and are eager to share their recommendations for local sights and shopping.

Motels

The same family has owned and operated the **International Motel** (626 Main St., Calais, 207/454-7515 or 800/336-7515, www.theinternationalmotel.com, $65-85) since 1955. The nicest guest rooms are in the newer Riverview building. Some rooms have refrigerators; all have air-conditioning, TVs, and Wi-Fi. Pet-friendly rooms are available.

The Gothic-styled, gingerbread-trimmed **Redclyffe Shore Motel and Dining Room** (Rte.

1, Robbinston, 207/454-3270, www.redclyffe-shoremotorinn.com, $85-95) sits on a bluff jutting into the St. Croix River as it widens into Passamaquoddy Bay. The 16 motel units have cable TV, phones, and sunset-facing river views. Redclyffe is locally popular for its greenhouse-style dining room with ocean views; dinner is served nightly from 5pm ($11-26). It's 12 miles south of Calais.

FOOD

Calais has few options for dining, and what's available leans toward family fare or fast food. Days and hours of operation reflect peak season and are subject to change.

If you're near downtown Calais, order picnic sandwiches to go at **Border Town Subz** (311 Main St., Calais, 207/454-8562, 10am-6pm Tues.-Fri., 10am-2pm Sat.), a reliable local favorite. Equally popular is **The Sandwich Man** (206 North St., 207/454-2460), just north of downtown on Route 1.

Fried foods, burgers, pizza, and reasonably priced dinner plates have earned **Yancy's** (332 North St., Calais, 207/454-8200, 11am-8pm daily, entrées $5-15) a solid reputation with families.

The **Nook and Cranny** (575 Airline Rd./Rte. 9, Baileyville, 207/454-3335, www.nookncran-nyrestaurant.com, 11am-9pm Tues.-Sun.) has a top-notch reputation among locals. It doesn't look like much from the outside, but the interior is cozy, and the wide-ranging menu has a bit of this and some of that, with most choices in the $12-26 range.

The **Sunrise County Farmers Market** (10am-2pm Tues. late June-early Oct.) takes place in the downtown park.

INFORMATION AND SERVICES

The **Maine Visitor Information Center** (39 Union St., Calais, 207/454-2211) has free Wi-Fi, clean restrooms, and scads of brochures, including those produced by the **St. Croix Valley Chamber of Commerce** (207/454-2308 or 888/422-3112, www.visitcalais.com). The information center is open 8am-6pm daily mid-May-mid-October, 9am-5:30pm daily the rest of the year.

Check out **Calais Free Library** (Union St., Calais, 207/454-2758, www.calais.lib.me.us).

Public restrooms are available at the Maine Visitor Information Center and at the St. Croix International Heritage Site in Red Beach.

GETTING THERE AND AROUND

Calais is about 28 miles or 40 minutes from Eastport via Routes 190 and 1. It's about 95 miles or two hours and 15 minutes to Bangor via Routes 1 and 9.

If you plan to cross into Canada, you'll have to pass immigration checkpoints on both the U.S. (Calais, 207/454-3621) and Canadian (St. Stephen, 506/466-2363) ends of the bridges. Be sure to have the required identification (passport or passport card) and paperwork.

Pay attention to your watch too—Calais is on eastern time, whereas St. Stephen and the rest of New Brunswick is on Atlantic time, one hour later.

Grand Lake Stream

For a tiny community of 109 year-rounders, Grand Lake Stream has a well-deserved, larger-than-life reputation. It's the center of a vast area of rivers and lakes, ponds and streams—a recreational paradise, and more than 35,000 acres, including 62 miles of shore frontage, has been preserved by the **Downeast Lakes Land Trust** (www.downeastlakes.org). It's the town at the end of the world, remote in every sense of the word, yet just a half hour or so inland from Calais.

The famous stream is a narrow three-mile neck of prime scenic and sportfishing water connecting West Grand Lake and Big Lake. A dam spans the bottom of West Grand, and just downstream is a state-run salmon hatchery. Since the mid-19th century, the stream and its lakes have been drawing fishing fans to trout and landlocked-salmon spawning grounds, and fourth and fifth generations now return here each year.

Fly-fishing enthusiasts arrive May-June for landlocked salmon and smallmouth bass (the stream itself is fly-fishing only); families show up July-August for canoeing, bird-watching, swimming, fishing, and hiking; hunters arrive in late October for game birds and deer; and snowmobilers, snowshoers, and cross-country skiers descend as the snow piles up.

Canoe building has contributed to the area's mystique. The distinctive Grand Lake canoe (or "Grand Laker"), a lightweight, square-sterned, motorized 20-footer, was developed in the 1920s specifically for sportfishing in these waters. In the off-season, several villagers still hunker down in their workshops and turn out these stable cedar beauties. (Interested? Call Bill Shamel, 207/796-8199.)

RECREATION

The region has the greatest concentration of Registered Maine Guides in the state, which gives you an indication of the fishing, hunting, and canoeing opportunities here. Truly the best way to experience Grand Lake Stream is with a member of the **Grand Lake Stream Guides Association** (www.grandlakestreamguides. com). The website lists members and specialties. You can arrange for one of these skilled guides to lead you on a fishing expedition, wildlife or photographic safari, or canoeing trip for a half day or longer.

Hiking

If you're in Grand Lake Stream only for the day, head for the **public landing** (bear right after the intersection with the Pine Tree Store), where you'll find a parking area, a dock, a portable toilet, and a boat launch. You can also walk the path on the eastern shore of the stream. Or, armed with a map from the Pine Tree Store, hike the 2.6-mile **Little Mayberry Cove Trail** edging the western shoreline of West Grand Lake.

Better yet, plan a day with a guide. The region has the greatest concentration of Registered Maine Guides in the state, which gives you an indication of the fishing, hunting, and canoeing opportunities here. Truly the best way to experience Grand Lake Stream is on a fishing expedition, canoeing trip, or photographic safari with a member of the **Grand Lake Stream Guides Association** (www. grandlakestreamguides.com).

Folk Art Festival

A great time to visit the village is the last full weekend in July for the annual **Grand Lake Stream Folk Art Festival** (207/796-8199, www.grandlakestreamfolkartfestival.com, 10am-5pm Sat.-Sun., $8), held on the town's grassy ball field. Tents shelter approximately 50 top-notch juried artisans. Nonstop bluegrass and folk music is another attraction. An exhibit highlights the region's canoe-building tradition, and another displays antique and contemporary quilts. Complementing the festival are lakeside lobster and chicken barbecues by the guides. A music jam, open to anyone, occurs Sunday morning. Leashed pets are welcome on festival grounds.

ACCOMMODATIONS

Cabin accommodations, with or without meals, are the lodgings of choice in Grand Lake Stream, and there's enough variety for every taste and budget. Few guests stay one night; most stay several days or a week. Rates quoted below are for two; many cabins can sleep more than that, and rates may be lower for extra people. Some housekeeping cabins require your own sheets and towels. Most camps have boat rentals for about $25-50/day (a motor brings the total to about $50-75).

Weatherby's (3 Water St., Grand Lake Stream, 877/796-5558. www.weatherbys.com), an Orvis-endorsed fly-fishing lodge with roots in the late 1800s, is an institution in these parts. Guests stay in 15 rustic cottages and cabins, all with fireplace or woodstove, screened porch, and bathroom. Meals are served in the main lodge, a comfy spot with a library of sporting books and magazines, fly-tying bench, and piano. American Plan rates (from $159 pp adults, $75 ages 10-15, $55 ages 4-9) include breakfast, lunch, and dinner; housekeeping rates, no meals, are $60 pp, $25 ages 5-15. Dogs are $15/day.

Mike and Jean Lombardo's **Shore Line Camps** (207/796-5539, www.shorelinecamps. com, no credit cards) has eight 1-3-bedroom housekeeping cabins, most fronting right on Big Lake. All have spotless pine interiors and full kitchens. The base rate is $50 pp, $25 ages 2-12, but all cabins have a minimum rate per night. Canoes, rowboats, and motorboats are available for rental.

Leen's Lodge (207/796-2929 or 800/995-3367, www.leenslodge.com, May-Oct.), on a spacious wooded shore and peninsula of West Grand Lake, has 10 small and large rustic cabins with baths. Rates, including breakfast, pack lunch, and dinner, begin around $145 pp. Children 6-12 and under pay $10 multiplied by their age; children 5 and younger are free. Housekeeping rates are

also sometimes available. Leashed pets are welcome, and kennels are provided. BYOB. Canoe and motorboat rentals should be arranged in advance.

Grand Lake Lodge (207/796-5584, www. grandlakelodgemaine.com, from $45 pp or from $500/week, no credit cards), on the shore of West Grand Lake and two blocks from the village center and with a safe swimming area, is a particularly good choice for families.

The Lakeside (14 Rolfe St., Princeton, 888/677-2874, www.thelakeside.org) is set well back from Route 1 on Lewy Lake, which flows through Long Lake into Big Lake. Gary and Jennifer Dubovick have five housekeeping cabins ($65-85) along the lakeshore plus eight housekeeping rooms (one with private bath) in the main house ($50 without breakfast). Rooms are comfy, have TVs, and there's also Wi-Fi, a living room with a TV, and a billiards room. If you want breakfast, a box lunch, dinner, and maid service, add $75 pp/day. Guide services and boat rentals are available.

FOOD

The heart of Grand Lake Stream is the **Pine Tree Store** (3 Water St., Grand Lake Stream, 207/796-5027). People have been getting their gas and groceries here for more than 60 years. It's also a good source of local information (and gossip), and it sells pizza, sandwiches, and general-store merchandise.

The **Old School Family Restaurant** (46 Main St., Princeton, 207/796-5254, 5am-2pm Mon.-Wed., 5am-7pm Thurs.-Fri., 6am-2pm Sat.-Sun.) is a find for fans for good home cookin' at reasonable prices. Go for breakfast; the homemade toast is reason enough. Dinner options range from sandwiches to a fried seafood platter ($7-19).

Both Leen's Lodge and Weatherby's open their dining rooms to guests by reservation. Expect to pay $25-35 for a full meal.

INFORMATION AND SERVICES

The volunteer-run **Grand Lake Stream Chamber of Commerce** (www.grandlake

stream.org) produces a brochure listing accommodations, shops, and services.

GETTING THERE

Grand Lake Stream is about 32 miles or 45 minutes from Calais via Route 1 and the Grand Lake Stream Road. It's about 80 miles or 1.75 hours to Houlton via Route 1 or about 115 miles or 2.25 hours to Bangor via Routes 1 and 9.

AROOSTOOK COUNTY

Welcome to the Crown of Maine. When Mainers refer to "The County," they're referring to Aroostook, a Micmac Indian word meaning "bright" or "shining." At 6,453 square miles, Maine's largest county—the largest east of the Mississippi—is bigger than Connecticut and Rhode Island combined, but its population numbers fewer than 72,000 residents (that's 11.1 per square mile), and fully a quarter of them live in only two smallish cities, Presque Isle and Caribou. People may be scarce, but Aroostook has the largest density of moose and black bear in the Lower 48.

This is Maine's big sky country, an awesome place to view the Northern Lights. In places, it seems to go on forever. Neat farmhouses and huge, half-buried potato-storage barns anchor vast undulating patches of potatoes, broccoli, and barley. Potato fields define The County— bright green in spring, pink and white in summer, dirt-brown and gold just before the autumn harvest.

Aroostook County, like the rest of Maine, has its share of hills, forests, and waterways, but the most significant hills here—Quaggy Jo, Mars, Debouillie, Haystack, Number Nine—are startling. Almost accidental, they appear out of nowhere—chunks the glaciers seem to have overlooked. Thanks to them, you'll find authentic vertical hiking, although Aroostook's trails are more often horizontal, through marshlands and woodlands and along abandoned rail beds.

Winters are long, snowy, and cold. Snowmobiling is a big deal here. Legions of snowmobilers (often called "sledders") crisscross

© HILARY NANGLE

HIGHLIGHTS

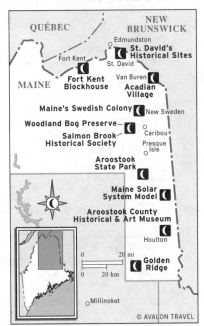

LOOK FOR **◖** TO FIND RECOMMENDED SIGHTS, ACTIVITIES, DINING, AND LODGING.

◖ Maine Solar System Model: Stretching 40 miles between Houlton to Presque Isle is a three-dimensional scale model of the solar system (page 419).

◖ Aroostook County Historical and Art Museum: There are plenty of treasures for history buffs, including military artifacts dating from the Civil War (page 420).

◖ Golden Ridge: Route 2, between Sherman Mills and Houlton, passes along the ridge top, with panoramic views from Katahdin to distant lakes (page 421).

◖ Salmon Brook Historical Society: Learn about the traditional potato-farm lifestyle at this National Historic Register property and museum (page 425).

◖ Maine's Swedish Colony: It's an authentic touch of Sweden, and the best time to visit is during the annual June Midsommar Festival (page 425).

◖ Aroostook State Park: Maine's first state park has opportunities for hiking, swimming, and boating (page 428).

◖ Woodland Bog Preserve: In early summer, schedule a walk with Nature Conservancy steward Richard Clark to learn about the flora and fauna and see rare orchids (page 429).

◖ Acadian Village: Delve into Maine's Acadian history and heritage on a guided tour of 16 antique and replica buildings (page 435).

◖ St. David's Historical Sites: Learn about Acadian heroine Tante Blanche, visit a typical homestead and school, and see where the Acadians first landed (page 436).

◖ Fort Kent Blockhouse: A relic of the bloodless Aroostook War, the 1839 blockhouse is being restored to its original design (page 436).

The County every winter, exploring hundreds of miles of the incredible Interconnecting Trail System (ITS). More recently, Aroostook has embraced a return to its cross-country skiing heritage, thanks to the Maine Winter Sports Center's mission and properties. It's home to an Olympic biathlon training center and hosts World Cup Nordic skiing events.

The County's agricultural preeminence sets it apart from the rest of Maine, but so do its immigrant cultures. Acadian culture permeates the northernmost St. John Valley, where the French dialect is unlike anything you'll ever hear in language classes (or in France). It leads to some wonderfully whimsical street and road names—for instance, Brise Culotte

Road, roughly translated as "Torn Trousers Road." Islands of Acadian or French culture exist in other parts of Maine, but it's in "the Valley" that you'll be tempted to pile on the pounds with such regional specialties as *poutine* (French fries smothered with cheese and gravy), *tourtière* (pork pie), and *tarte au saumon* (salmon tart).

Swedish surnames are prevalent too, especially around New Sweden and environs, and more recently Amish families have moved here, drawn by The County's rural farming traditions.

As often occurs with remote rural areas, The County sometimes gets a bum rap (never from the snowmobiling crowd) among downstaters and others who've never been here. But it deserves notice—for the scenery if nothing else. Admittedly, it's a long haul—it's about as far as you can get from the rockbound coast—but you're guaranteed a totally different Maine experience. For many visitors, there's a sensation of traveling back 20 or 30 years to an era when life was simpler, communities were small, and everyone greeted each other by name.

To truly appreciate The County, detour off Route 1 and explore the crossroads and often-gravel byways. Trust me, it's worth it.

PLANNING YOUR TIME

Covering such a large expanse of geography takes time. While you can loop around Aroostook's periphery in 2-3 days, you'll need 4-5 days to explore the region and tease out its many charms.

Snowmobilers and cross-country skiers come January-March, when The County measures its snow in feet, not inches.

In June, newly planted potato fields resemble Ireland in their vibrant greens, although the blackflies and mosquitoes can be annoying. Most museums and historical sites are open during the summer, so that's the best time for history buffs to visit. Days are long and temperatures moderate, also making it ideal for hikers, cyclists, and paddlers. In mid-July, the potato fields blossom, a gorgeous sight.

Autumn comes early, with leaves beginning

© AVALON TRAVEL

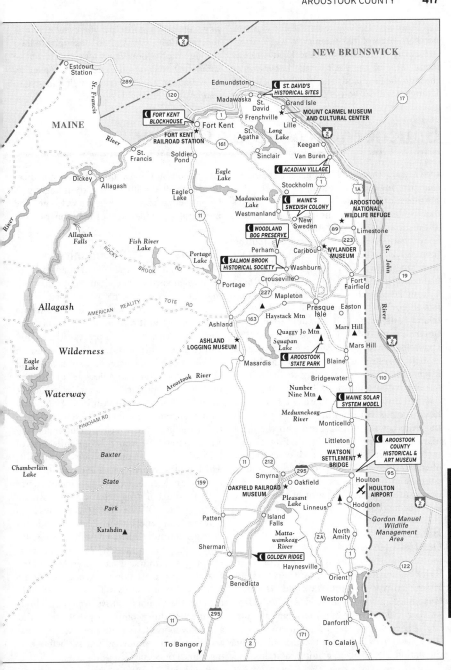

to turn color as early as late August in the northern parts of The County.

Get off Route 1 and Route 11 and mosey along some of the back roads that meander through the farmlands and by lakes and rivers. Doing so will let you experience Maine's Big Sky Country, a landscape where endless fields meet expansive sky. And do make time to loop through the St. John Valley for a taste of Maine unlike any other. From Caribou or Presque Isle, you can drive up to the crown, visit Valley sites, and return in a long day.

Southern Aroostook County

Driving north on I-95, you find the interstate petering out at Houlton, about 120 miles northeast of Bangor. That sometimes makes this feel like the end of the earth, but it's actually just the beginning of Aroostook County.

Southern Aroostook, centered on **Houlton** (pop. 6,123) is a narrow north-south corridor stretching from Sherman Mills on I-95 to the Canadian border, roughly straddling Route 1 from just north of **Danforth** to **Presque Isle** (pop. 9,692) Among its communities are **Island Falls** (pop. 837), **Oakfield** (pop. 737), **Smyrna** (pop. 442), **Monticello** (pop. 790) and **Bridgewater** (pop. 610) It's in this region that the forests and mountains of the Maine Highlands begin to give way to the rolling farmlands characteristic of The County.

Hard by the New Brunswick border, Houlton has carved out its own niche as the shire town, and, according to the local historical society, "history's hiding place." Incorporated in 1834, Houlton is quiet and not often considered a destination, but the county courts and other government offices are all here, so there's a fair amount of activity—at least during the week.

SIGHTS
Oakfield Railroad Museum
Housed in a 1910 Bangor and Aroostook Railroad station and run by the Oakfield Historical Society, the **Oakfield Railroad Museum** (Station St., Oakfield, 207/757-8575, www.oakfieldmuseum.org, 1pm-4pm Sat.-Sun. late May-early Sept., free) contains an impressive collection of iron-horse memorabilia. Tour the station, the adjacent reading room library, and the outbuildings, including a restored caboose. If you're really lucky, a train might pass by on the tracks. Donations are welcome. The museum is 17 miles west of Houlton, off I-95 Exit 286.

Smyrna Amish Community
Many folks think they've stepped back in time when visiting The County, but that feeling intensifies in Smyrna, where horse-drawn carriages signal the presence of the **Smyrna Amish community.** Seeking a quiet place to work, raise their families, practice their faith, and interact with outsiders, five Midwestern families established a community in this rural farming town about 15 miles west of Houlton in 1996. Since then, the community has grown steadily. In addition to farming, the Smyrna Amish operate a number of businesses, open to the public, all of which are clustered along a short stretch of Route 2, one mile west of I-95 Exit 295. These include Sturdi-Bilt, which builds wooden sheds and outbuildings; Kauffman Metals, which fabricates metal roofing and building; Northeastern Rustic Furniture; the Bicycle Shop; Cedar Meadows Harness Shop; and Pioneer Place, a wonderful little general store where you can purchase locally made goods and foods and just about everything else, from socks to knives. Most of the businesses are closed on weekends. While the Amish welcome visitors to their businesses, remember they're not a tourist attraction. This is a living, breathing community that has opened a window to its lifestyle. Respect their personal and community property, and ask before taking photos of people.

© HILARY NANGLE

An impressive collection of iron-horse memorabilia fills the Oakfield Railroad Museum.

€ Maine Solar System Model

Space travel is possible in Aroostook County, where the three-dimensional **Maine Solar System Model** (pages.umpi.edu/~nmms/solar/) stretches 40 miles along Route 1. The model comprises the sun, the planets, dwarf planets, and the moons for Earth, Saturn, Jupiter, and Pluto. All of the major planets are large enough to be seen while driving along Route 1, where one mile is equal to the distance between Earth and the sun, and the speed of light is 7 mph.

The 93-million-to-one scale model was masterminded by Dr. Kevin McCartney, a geology professor at the University of Maine at Presque Isle and director of the Northern Maine Museum of Science; implemented by hundreds of local volunteers, including service and school groups, businesses, and individuals; and accomplished without any formal sponsors or grants. Local students built the planets. It's really quite a marvel of can-do grassroots community spirit.

Pluto, only 1 inch in diameter, is embedded in a wall in the lobby of the Visitor Information Center in Houlton, just off Route 1, north of the I-95 interchange. Other models are mounted on 10-foot-tall posts and dot parking lots and fields along the route. The project is detailed and mapped both in a brochure, available at the center, and on the Internet. If heading north, begin in Houlton and set your odometer to zero at the info center.

Plans call for expanding the model into New Brunswick and Quebec with the addition of other dwarf planets.

Market Square Historic District

An arced pedestrian bridge across the Meduxnekeag River links Gateway Crossing, on Route 1, with Market Square's 28 turn-of-the-20th-century buildings listed on the National Register of Historic Places (the architecture is lovely, but unfortunately more than a few storefronts are empty). Along the bridge and walkway (both wheelchair-accessible) are markers detailing Houlton's downtown history. A walking guide is available at the **Greater Houlton Area Chamber of Commerce**

AROOSTOOK COUNTY

Saturn, part of the Maine Solar System Model along Rte. 1 in Aroostook County

(109 Main St., Houlton), two blocks up Main Street. On the Route 1 side, illustrated plaques detailing more history along with flora and fauna pepper an easy 0.2-mile round-trip riverside trail.

◖ Aroostook County Historical & Art Museum

The 1903 White Memorial Building, the Colonial Revival residence that houses the chamber, is also home to the **Aroostook County Historical & Art Museum** containing a fine collection of photos, books, vintage clothing, antique tools, and housewares. You can wander through on your own, but a guide will bring the collection to life. Of particular interest are military artifacts from the Hancock Barracks, the Civil War, and the Camp Houlton POW internment camp. Also on view are the ventilator cowl from the battleship *Maine,* which sank in Havana Harbor, and a Confederate battle flag captured by a Houlton member of the First Calvary Maine. Call the

chamber (207/532-4216) in advance for an appointment or stop by the chamber office and take a chance that a volunteer is available to come in and show you around. Donations are appreciated.

Museum staff can also provide information about and direct you to a number of local historical sites. Unfortunately most haven't been maintained. I've watched them deteriorate and all but disappear over the years. There is not much to see at either of these, but they are worth mentioning for their places in history.

Garrison Park, site of the **Hancock Barracks,** was established in 1828 to protect American border settlements and garrisoned troops during the 1838-1839 Aroostook War. It provided frontier training for West Point graduates, and Gen. Robert E. Lee visited here. To find the overgrown, gated site, take Route 2 toward the airport and turn left onto Garrison Road, near the top of the hill.

The still functioning **Houlton International Airport** dates from the early 1940s. Neutrality laws prevented U.S.-built planes from flying directly from the United States to Britain, so during the months before Pearl Harbor, planes were known to land in Houlton and then be towed across the border to Canada for takeoff. That all changed when the U.S. Army took over the airport during World War II and turned it into an airbase and Maine's largest **German POW camp.** About 4,000 prisoners lived here in barracks while laboring in lumber camps, canneries, potato farms, and paper mills. The original World War II airport control tower (one of the few surviving in the country), one POW camp building, a few foundations, and a small memorial are all that remain of the era. To find the site, take Route 2 east from downtown. At the T intersection, bear right and then right again on Aviation Road.

Watson Settlement Bridge

About six miles north of Houlton, amid typical Aroostook farmland in Littleton, stands Maine's northernmost (yes, and easternmost) covered bridge, built in 1911 and last used in 1985. The wood-truss bridge, straddling a

Plan in advance to tour the Aroostook County Historical & Art Museum.

branch of the Meduxnekeag River, feels quite forlorn, a remnant of the past just sitting here unused (except, unfortunately, by graffiti artists). Maine once had 120 or so covered bridges; only nine remain, and this is the only one using the Howe truss system. For the prettiest route to the bridge from Houlton, take Foxcroft Road from Route 2 and continue 6.1 miles; turn left onto Carson Road. From Route 1 in Littleton, go right on Carson Road, which winds its way down to the river (bear left at the fork). The quicker route is to head north on Route 1 four miles from the I-95 interchange and then go right on Carson Road for 2.9 miles.

Southern Aroostook Agricultural Museum

Farming memorabilia fills the **Southern Aroostook Agricultural Museum** (1664 Rte. 1, Littleton, 207/538-9300, www.oldplow. org, 1pm-4pm Thurs.-Sat. June-late Sept., $5 adults, $3 under age 10), started as a retirement project for Cedric and Emily Shaw. The collection grew, and in 2001 the museum moved

from the Shaws' farm to the former Littleton Elementary School. Local support has allowed it to continue growing, adding a tool collection and a former one-room schoolhouse as well as building a model potato barn and a new barn.

Scenic Routes
◖ GOLDEN RIDGE

The interstate is the fastest route to Houlton, but Route 2, from Sherman Mills through Oakfield and Smyrna, is the best choice for moseyers, and it really isn't that much longer. The far-less-traveled route passes through gorgeous countryside dotted with farms, lakes, and small villages. The views from Golden Ridge, a section between Island Falls and Oakfield, reach to Katahdin and beyond. Watch for potato barns, a unique barn built into the ground for cold potato storage. Most have a gambrel roof topping the landscape.

MILLION-DOLLAR VIEW SCENIC BYWAY

South of Houlton and stretching eight miles along Route 1 between Danforth and Orient is an especially scenic drive that passes over Peekaboo Mountain and offers panoramic views over the Chiputneticook chain of lakes and to Katahdin. It's also prime moose-watching country. There are two scenic pull-outs.

ENTERTAINMENT AND EVENTS

For canoeists and kayakers, the year's biggest event is the eight-mile spring-runoff **Meduxnekeag River Race,** held on a Saturday in late April-early May. Beginning in New Limerick, west of town, the route includes a short stretch of Class III rapids. For more information, contact the Greater Houlton Chamber of Commerce (207/532-4216).

Check local listings and posters for the frequent outdoor **concerts** staged in local parks.

The annual **Soapbox Derby,** held in mid-June in Community Park, always attracts a big crowd.

The early July **Houlton Fair** includes a carnival, a pig scramble, truck pulling, pageants, entertainment, baking contests, and crafts and agricultural exhibits.

RECREATION
Parks and Preserves
PIERCE PARK

Near downtown Houlton, mystery surrounds the origins of Pierce Park's quaint fountain with a centerpiece statue usually called *The Boy with the Leaking Boot.* Donated to the town in 1916, it's one of two dozen or so similar statues in the United States and Europe. Legends have it coming from Germany or Belgium or Italy, but no record exists. Benches surround the fountain, and lower- and upper-level troughs provide fresh water for pets and their owners. The Houlton Garden Club maintains the flowers in the park—a popular local spot for photographs, picnics, and coffee breaks.

GORDON MANUEL WILDLIFE MANAGEMENT AREA

Just south of Houlton in Hodgdon, the Gordon Manuel Wildlife Management Area (no phone) covers 6,482 acres of fields, woods, and marshland along the Meduxnekeag River. From Route 1, turn right (west) onto Hodgdon Road and watch for a dairy bar (there's a water access point adjacent to it). Take the first left after it onto the unpaved Horseback Road. Continue 1.7 miles and turn left at a narrow dirt road. Wind through the trees about 0.2 mile to a small parking area on the Meduxnekeag River. Watch for ospreys, green herons, even bald eagles. You can launch a canoe or kayak (no motors allowed) and explore the area. The setting is particularly gorgeous during the fall foliage season, but be forewarned that hunting is allowed here, so wear a hunter-orange vest and hat mid-October-November.

If you don't have a canoe or kayak and just want to do some birding, this is a particularly relaxing bike ride, even from Houlton.

Golf

On a clear day, Baxter State Park's Katahdin is visible from **Va-Jo-Wa Golf Club** (142-A Walker Settlement Rd., Island Falls, 207/463-2128, www.vajowa.com), a particularly scenic 18-hole, par-72 course named after Vaughn, John, and Warren Walker. Call for a starting time; this course is popular.

Southwest of Houlton is the nine-hole **Houlton Community Golf Club** (Drew's Lake Rd., New Limerick, 207/532-2662, www.houltongolf.com), built on onetime potato fields in 1921. The setting is lovely, on the shores of Nickerson Lake; the lakefront clubhouse has a snack bar. Bring a swimsuit; a dip in the lake feels great after a round of golf.

Winter Recreation

Houlton is at the fringe of prime **snowmobiling** country. The crowds tend to head up the road to Presque Isle, Caribou, and the St. John Valley, but there are plenty of trails here. For information on snowmobiling in the Houlton area, contact the chamber of commerce or the **Maine Snowmobile Association** (207/622-6983, www.mesnow.com), which can put you in touch with local snowmobile clubs. When snowmobiling in the Houlton area, you'll notice on trail maps that some routes cross into

Canada. Carry a passport or passport card when you are near the border. The Houlton border crossing is open 24 hours.

Also lacing the region are **cross-country ski trails.**

ACCOMMODATIONS

Clean, well maintained, and regularly updated, **◖ Ivey's Motor Lodge** (Rte. 1, Houlton, 207/532-4206 or 800/244-4206 in Maine, www.iveysmotorlodge.com, $86-125) wins folks over with good-size guest rooms, friendly service, and amenities unexpected in an older motel. All rooms have air-conditioning, TVs, DVD players, Wi-Fi, fridges, and microwaves; some have whirlpool tubs or efficiency kitchens. Rates include a hot-and-cold continental buffet. On the premises is a pub with big-screen TV. It's on Route 1, on the north side of I-95 Exit 302.

The **Shiretown Motor Inn** (282 North Rd./Rte. 1, Houlton, 207/532-9421 or 800/441-9421, www.shiretownmotorinn.com, $109-139) has an indoor pool, a fitness room, and Wi-Fi, but it needs updating and TLC. Ask for a room in the new building and avoid staying in the pool building. Rates include continental breakfast.

About 28 miles south of Houlton **First Settler's Lodge** (341 Rte. 1, Weston, 207/448-3000, www.firstsettlerslodge.com, $125-150) is an East Grand Lakes area spoiler with spectacular views. Four guest rooms, a loft with bunks, an efficiency apartment, and a luxury suite have Wi-Fi and satellite TV, and there's a guest kitchen. Breakfast is included. The lodge is also open for dinner by reservation on Friday and Saturday nights.

FOOD
Local Flavors

Homemade doughnuts, cinnamon buns, and other treats emerge from the kitchen at **Sadie's Bakery** (5 Water St., Houlton, 207/532-6650), a hole-in-the-wall that's been in biz since 1948. Most of Maine's farmers markets operate one or maybe two days a week; the **Houlton Farmers Market** sets up shop daily

early May-mid-October next to McDonald's on Route 1, just south of I-95 Exit 62.

Maple syrup and honey are produced at **Spring Break** (3315 Rte. 2, Smyrna Mills, 207/757-7373, www.mainemapleandhoney.com), a sugarhouse and Maine-made gift shop near the Amish colony.

Family Favorites

For humongous portions (even by County standards), home cooking, good service, and local color, **◖ Grammy's Country Inn** (1687 Bangor Rd., Linneus, 207/532-7808, 6am-9pm Mon.-Sat., 7am-9pm Sun.) is the choice. It's nothing fancy, mind you, but where else might you find deep-fried lobster on the menu? Order conservatively, and even then, plan on having leftovers. Do save room for dessert, which includes two-fisted whoopie pies. The best part though is that nearly everything on the menu is less than $12.

Another option for old-fashioned meals such as country-fried steak and liver and onions, a Friday night fish fry, and rave-worthy desserts is **Elm Tree Diner** (146 Bangor Rd., Houlton, 207/532-3777, www.elmtreediner.com, 5:30am-8pm Mon.-Thurs., 5:30am-9pm Fri.-Sat., 7am-8pm Sun., $4-18). Breakfast is served all day.

It's easy to spot **The Blue Moose** (180 Rte. 1, Monticello, 207/538-0991, 11am-8pm, Tues.-Thurs., 11am-9pm Fri., 7am-9pm Sat., 7am-7pm Sun.): Just look for the, um, blue moose. Rather nondescript on the exterior, inside it's warm, inviting, and lodge-like. The family-operated restaurant serves mighty fine home-style fare at better-than-reasonable prices, and there's a children's menu. As with most such restaurants in the region, the desserts are homemade and scrumptious.

Casual Dining

Hidden in the back of the small downtown Fishman Mall and displaying the work of local artists, Joyce Transue's **The Courtyard Café** (61 Main St., Houlton, 207/532-0787, www.thecourtyardcafe.biz, 11am-2pm Tues.-Fri. and 5pm-8pm Tues.-Thurs., 5pm-9pm

Fri.-Sat.) is well worth finding. Dine either in the main restaurant or the more casual bar. The menu changes frequently, but dinner possibilities ($14-30) might include chicken Marsala or bourbon-glazed Alaskan sockeye salmon. Reservations are recommended. There's often live music on Saturday nights.

Across the street, occupying a former bank, is **The Vault** (64 Main St., Houlton, 207/532-2222, 5pm-10pm Wed.-Sat., entrées $12-18). Entrées, such as fish tacos or veal with mushrooms, run $10-15. Be forewarned the space is small and tends to be noisy. Service is leisurely at best; don't attempt to dine here if in a hurry. Reservations highly recommended.

The Horn (382 North St., Houlton, 207/532-2260, 11am-2:30pm and 4:30pm-8pm Wed.-Sat., $12-20) is the latest incarnation of former The Horn of Plenty, which closed in 2012. Ask locally about its current reputation.

INFORMATION AND SERVICES

The **Greater Houlton Chamber of Commerce** (109 Main St., Houlton, 207/532-4216, www.

greaterhoulton.com) is in the same 1903 Colonial Revival building as the Aroostook Historical and Art Museum. Request the *Walking Guide to Market Square Historic District*.

Check out **Cary Memorial Library** (107 Main St., Houlton, 207/532-1302, www.cary.lib.me.us).

The **Maine Visitor Information Center** (28 Ludlow Rd., Houlton, 207/532-6346), with brochures and maps covering the entire state, is open 9am-5pm weekdays year-round, with weekend and extended weekday hours in summer. Restrooms are also available.

Aroostook County Tourism (888/216-2463, www.visitaroostook.com) has information on and links for the entire county.

GETTING THERE

Houlton is about 80 miles or 1.75 hours from Grand Lake Stream via Route 1 or about 120 miles or 1.75 hours from Bangor via I-95. It's about 42 miles or 50 minutes to Presque Isle.

Central Aroostook County

Ahh. Sighs of contentment are common in a region where folks know their neighbors, crime is rare, and the only traffic jams are caused by slow-moving farm equipment. In addition to road signs urging drivers to be wary of moose, there are others encouraging sharing the road with roller-skiers and Amish horse-and-buggies.

Most of the 60,000 acres planted with spuds in Maine are found in the "Potato Triangle," the region framed by **Presque Isle** (pop. 9,692) to the south, **Caribou** (pop. 8,189) to the north, and **Fort Fairfield** (pop. 3,496) on the Canadian border, tied together by the zigzagging course of the Aroostook River. Farmhouses, potato barns, and rolling fields dominate the landscape—and when those fields bloom in mid-July, it's one of the prettiest sights around. Northeast of Caribou is

Limestone (pop 2,314); south of Presque Isle is **Mars Hill** (pop. 1,493). Each is a day's stage ride from the others, about 13 miles, making it easy to explore the region from one base. South of Fort Fairfield is **Easton**, home to another Amish community.

The economic impact caused by the closing of Limestone's Loring Air Force Base in the late 1990s devastated the region, and although the population erosion continues, the base is becoming a success story with the establishment of the Loring Commerce Centre and the creation of Aroostook National Wildlife Refuge.

Outdoor enthusiasts, especially, will find plenty: 904-acre Aroostook State Park, miles of multiuse trails, two small alpine areas, and impressive cross-country facilities that have hosted World Cup events. Cross-country skiing was introduced to Maine by settlers of the Swedish Colony, the region northwest of Caribou anchored by **New Sweden** (pop. 602) and **Stockholm** (pop. 253).

A handful of intriguing low-tech museums and heritage sites entertain history buffs. What you won't find here is much in the way of interesting shopping.

SIGHTS

Most historical sights in the area are run by volunteers, so hours change frequently. It's wise to call before making a special trip.

University of Maine at Presque Isle

Established in 1903 as the Aroostook State Normal School for training teachers, the **University of Maine at Presque Isle** (UMPI, 181 Main St./Rte. 1, Presque Isle, 207/768-9400, www.umpi.edu) has more than 1,500 two-year and four-year students on its 150-acre campus at the southern end of the city. The school is noted for its training in physical education and recreation.

In the Campus Center is the **Reed Art Gallery,** a one-room gallery that overflows into the hallway, where rotating exhibits spotlight Maine and Canadian artists. During the school year, the gallery is open 9am-4pm Monday-Saturday; the summer schedule tends to be less predictable.

Science wunderkind Kevin McCartney, a geology professor and the powerhouse behind the Maine Solar System scale model, also gets credit for the **Northern Maine Museum of Science,** in Folsom Hall. Hallways in the three-story science building have been turned into a free teaching museum, where you can take a test to see if you're color blind, touch a real dinosaur bone, and take in all manner of scientific and mathematical exhibits explaining such hard-to-grasp concepts as DNA and the Fibonacci sequence and displays varying from bottle-nosed dolphins to fluorescent minerals. Also here is the sun, the epicenter of the Route 1 solar system model, as well as another scale model that extends the length of the second

floor. Nothing is high-tech, but it's enjoyable and well presented. Pick up a brochure that explains the exhibits—look for it on case tops. Also look for a guide to the **West Campus Woods Nature Trail,** protected by the museum. There are 10 interpretive stations that illustrate features of the northern forest.

🄲 Salmon Brook Historical Society

Here's a worthwhile two-for-one deal, with lots of charm and character: In tiny downtown Washburn, across from the First Baptist Church, the **Salmon Brook Historical Society** (1267 Main St./Rte. 164, Washburn, 207/455-4339) operates the **Benjamin C. Wilder Homestead,** an 1852 farmhouse on the National Register of Historic Places, and the **Aroostook Agricultural Museum** in the adjacent red barn. The well-restored 10-room house has period furnishings and displays; the barn contains old tools and antique cookware and pottery. The museums, on 2.5 acres, are open July 4-early September, call for current hours, and other times by appointment. Admission is free, but donations are welcome. Washburn is 11 miles northwest of Presque Isle and 10 miles southwest of Caribou.

Nylander Museum

If you were an eccentric self-educated geologist and needed a place to display and store everything you'd accumulated, you'd create a place like the **Nylander Museum** (393 Main St., Caribou, 207/493-4209, cariboumaine.org, 9am-5pm Fri.-Sat., donation). Swedish-born Olof Olssen Nylander traveled the world collecting specimens, settled in Caribou, and bequeathed his work, including 6,000 fossils and 40,000 shells, to the city. Since his 1943 death, the museum has acquired other collections: butterflies, mounted birds, and additional geological specimens. It's all displayed in two small galleries.

🄲 Maine's Swedish Colony

Maine's Swedish Colony (www.maineswedishcolony.info) comprises New Sweden,

ONE POTATO, TWO POTATO

Native to South America, the potato is king in Aroostook County, where 90 percent of Maine's spuds grow on more than 60,000 acres—Maine is the country's fifth- to eighth-largest producer (depending on the harvest).

Aroostook County's potato heritage dates back more than 150 years, says fourth-generation potato farmer Keith LaBrie of Labrie's Farms in St. Agatha. "It became a staple on family farms generations ago. Back 50, 60 years ago, there were thousands of small growers, with 15-20-acre farms. Those have consolidated into 300-500-acre farms, and the harvesting is mechanized now for efficiency."

In the past, he says, Maine predominantly grew the round, white table stock variety. Recently there's been more of a move toward russet types. While most of what Maine grows is used for processed French fries and potato chips, Maine potatoes are now being used to produce Cold River Vodka (www.coldrivervodka.com), made and sold in Freeport.

Potato fields are in full blossom in mid-July. Different varieties produce differently colored flowers, so there will be white in one field, red in another.

Annual festivals in Fort Fairfield and Houlton celebrate the blossoms and the harvest; potatoes appear on every restaurant menu and family table; and countless roadside stands peddle them by the bag. Although high schools still close for 2-3 weeks in September so students (and teachers!) can assist with the harvest, most of the work is done mechanically these days.

Now, if you don't get enough of this potato business while you're here in The County, there's always a membership in the **Organic Potato of the Month Sampler Club.** Eight months a year, **Wood Prairie Farm** (49 Kinney Rd., Bridgewater, 800/829-9765, www.woodprairie.com), an organic farm in Bridgewater, sends its members an eight-pound gift box of three different kinds of organic potatoes. The package comes with postcards and recipes, so you're all set. The base price for the eight-month club is $299; one month is $39.95.

Information on the potato industry is available from the **Maine Potato Board** (207/764-4148, www.mainepotatoes.com).

Stockholm, and Woodland, and spills over into neighboring towns, including Perham, Westmanland, Madawaska Lake, and Caribou.

New Sweden is eight miles northwest of downtown Caribou via Route 161. At the **New Sweden Historical Museum** (Capitol Hill Rd. and Station Rd., New Sweden, 207/896-5240), three floors of memorabilia reflect the rugged life in this frontier community. An exact replica of the colony's "Kapitoleum" (capitol), the museum was built in 1971 after fire leveled the original structure. Check out the museum's guestbook: Visitors have come from all over Scandinavia to see this cultural enclave. The museum, 0.5 mile north and east of Route 161, is open noon-4pm daily Memorial Day weekend-mid-September. Admission is free, but donations are welcome. Next door, in the **Capitol Hill School,** a gift shop carries Swedish items.

Out back is a monument with the list of the original settlers.

Continuing east on Station Road, you'll pass **W. W. Thomas Memorial Park** on the left, a great spot for a picnic, with a play area for kids and a dramatic vista over the rolling countryside. Concerts occur periodically in the band shell. About 0.2 mile farther are the circa-1870 **Larsson/Ostlund Log Home,** one of the colony's oldest buildings, and the shingled **Lars Noak Blacksmith and Woodworking Shop,** another remnant of the early settlers. Volunteers aim to open these two properties Tuesday-Sunday during the summer.

More exhibits await at the **Stockholm Historical Society Museum** (280 Main St., Stockholm), which is usually open 1:30pm-4:30pm Saturday-Sunday, July-August, but hours for it aren't formal. Ask at the post office across the street, nearby Anderson Store,

The New Sweden Historical Museum chronicles the history and heritage of Maine's Swedish Colony.

or simply call one of the names listed on the front door for access. The **Woodland Historical Society** (http://woodlandhistorical.wix.com/museum) sometimes opens the **Lagerstrom House Museum** and the **Snowman School Museum**.

A fun time to visit New Sweden is during the **Midsommar Festival,** on the closest weekend to Midsummer Day (June 21), when most sites are open for tours and residents don traditional Swedish costumes and celebrate the year's longest day. Activities include decorating a maypole, Swedish dancing, a smorgasbord, concerts, and a prayer service. Non-Scandinavians are welcome to join in.

Goughan's Farm
Goughan's Farm (872 Fort Fairfield Rd./Rte. 161, Caribou, 207/498-6565, 8am-5pm Mon.-Sat., noon-5pm Sun., Mar.-mid-Dec.) has a bit of everything, depending on when you show up. Don't miss the farm-fresh ice cream or the strawberry shortcake or fruit pies in season. Goughan's (pronounced GAWNS) has maple syrup in spring; pick-your-own strawberries, raspberries, string beans, and peas in summer; apples and choose-your-own pumpkins in fall; and Christmas wreaths and trees in winter. There's also a late summer corn maze.

Frontier Heritage Historical Society
Fort Fairfield's historical society maintains a number of local properties, but few are open except during the annual Potato Festival in July. The **Fort Fairfield Blockhouse Museum** (Main St.) is a 1976 replica of the original, and it's filled with local memorabilia. The **Friends Church Museum** (Rte. 1A), built in 1858 as a Quaker meetinghouse, is believed to have served as a station on the Underground Railroad during the Civil War. The **Railroad Museum** (Depot St., off Brown St.) comprises locomotives and cars and an 1875 Canadian-Pacific Railroad station. Also on the railroad site is the restored **Black/McIntosh One-Room School House,** built in 1848.

Double Eagle Park
Just beyond the state park access road is a **tiny park** (140 Spragueville Rd., Presque Isle) commemorating the launch of the *Double Eagle II,* the first manned helium balloon to cross the Atlantic. A replica honors the August 1978 flight, when a crew of three made the Presque Isle-Miseray, France, passage in approximately 137 hours. (The first solo transatlantic balloon flight, six years later, took off from Caribou.)

Loring Military Heritage Center
A Gam 77 hound dog air-to-ground missile stands outside the **Loring Military Heritage Center** (131 Cupp Rd., 11am-3pm Sat., noon-3pm Sun.), located on the grounds of the Loring Commerce Centre. The small, volunteer-run museum is dedicated to the history of the former air force base (1953-1994) named after Charles J. Loring, USAF, Medal of Honor winner from Maine. If you previously were stationed here or want more info, try Bill

AROOSTOOK COUNTY

Ossenfort (207/227-5265) or Cuppy Johndro (207/551-3439) to set up an appointment.

Scenic Routes

With so much open space in The County, particularly in the Potato Triangle, drivers and bicyclists can enjoy great long vistas. One route, a favorite of Senator Susan Collins, who ought to know, is **Route 164** between Caribou and Presque Isle, half of it along the Aroostook River. (Locals call it the Back Presque Isle Road; it's also the Washburn Road and the Caribou Road—just to make things totally confusing.) On the way, you can check out the museums in Washburn, detour on the multiuse trail, or loop out on Route 228 and visit the Woods Edge Gallery in Perham.

Another scenic drive is **Route 167,** between Presque Isle and Fort Fairfield; the 12-mile stretch is especially dramatic in mid-July when the rolling fields are draped with pink and white potato blossoms and Fort Fairfield puts on its annual Potato Blossom Festival.

If you're even a bit adventurous and have a trustworthy vehicle, explore the back roads in this region. Although many are quite hilly, they're worth the effort for cyclists too. Be forewarned that many have gravel sections, but they're usually well maintained. Don't be surprised to come across roller-skiers or Amish buggies. Expect to find big views from hilltop ridges and honor stands for potatoes and other fresh produce. Good choices are the roads east of Route 1 in the Easton area and the Tangle Ridge Road, in Woodland.

TOURS

The **Presque Isle Historical Society** (207/762-1151, www.pihistory.org) offers a wide range of ways to experience the city, including two-hour guided walking tours, one-hour tours of the Vera Estey House Museum, guided walking tours of the historic Fairmount Cemetery, and three-hour narrated city tours and foliage tours aboard Molly the Trolley. Fees range from free to $10.

RECREATION
Parks and Preserves
◖ AROOSTOOK STATE PARK

Aroostook State Park (State Park Rd., Presque Isle, 207/768-8341, www.parksandlands.com, $3 nonresident adults, $2 Maine resident adults, $1 ages 5-11 and nonresident seniors) has the distinction of being Maine's first state park, created in 1939, when inspired citizens of Presque Isle donated 100 acres of land to the state. The park has grown significantly since then; it now comprises nearly 800 acres, encompassing Quaggy Jo Mountain and Echo Lake and providing plentiful opportunities for hiking, water sports, snow sports, camping, and more. Quaggy Jo comes from the Micmac word *quaquajo,* which translates as "twin-peaked." Allow 2-3 hours for the moderate (with steep sections) three-mile hike (clockwise) via the North Peak, North-South Peak Ridge, and South Peak Trails to take in both summits; the views, especially from North Peak, are superb. After hiking, have a lakeside picnic and then cool off with a swim or fish for brook trout. Public boat access is available. Call it a night at one of 30 campsites ($12 Maine residents, $20 non-residents). The park is equally inviting in winter, when a selection of trails are open for cross-country skiing. These range from the one-mile Novice Trail to the four-mile Quaggy Jo Mountain Trail, which is best for advanced skiers. Groomed snowmobile trails also pass through the park. The park is open daily mid-May-mid-October. The gate is 1.5 miles west of Route 1, five miles south of downtown Presque Isle.

AROOSTOOK NATIONAL WILDLIFE REFUGE

More than 5,250 acres encompassing grasslands, forests, 10 ponds, three brooks, and one stream of the Cold War-era Loring Air Force Base have found new life as **Aroostook National Wildlife Refuge** (97 Refuge Rd., Limestone, 207/454-7161, www.fws.gov/northeast/aroostook). Established in 1998, the refuge is still actively restoring habitat by removing buildings, railroad tracks, and fencing as well as restoring wetlands. Seven trails, ranging 0.12-1.9 miles, provide excellent wildlife viewing, especially early in the morning or late in the evening. Trails are divided on two parcels, half near the visitor center and the rest near Chapman Pond. According to the Friends of Aroostook National Wildlife Refuge (www.friendsofaroostooknwr.org), Aroostook County supports the largest density of moose and black bears in the Lower 48, and sightings of each are a daily occurrence on the refuge. Migratory songbirds nest here in spring and summer, and various ducks, Canada geese, woodcocks, and ruffled grouse are also frequently sighted. Stop at the FOANWR's volunteer-staffed **Nature Store** (207/328-4634, usually open 1pm-4pm Tues.-Thurs. and 11am-3pm Sat.) for information and maps as well as nature-related gifts. The refuge is off Route 89, eight miles east of Caribou, five miles west of Limestone. Trails are open sunrise-sunset daily.

◖ WOODLAND BOG PRESERVE

About six miles west of Caribou, **Woodland Bog Preserve,** a 265-acre Nature Conservancy property, is home to several rare orchid species and 80 bird species (nearly 90 have been banded here). On weekday mornings and Sunday afternoons, mid-May-mid-July, Perham resident Richard Clark—the Nature Conservancy's on-site steward—leads fascinating free walks through this bog (technically, a calcareous fen surrounded by a cedar swamp) as well as the conservancy's 200-acre **Perham Bog Preserve.** Clark also leads walks in **Salmon Brook Lake Bog,** a 1,857-acre northern white cedar bog bought by the state under the Land for Maine's Future program. To set up a time, call Richard Clark directly (207/455-8359 days or 207/455-8060 evenings and Mon.). Wear waterproof shoes and insect repellent. Dedicated environmentalists, Richard and his wife, Susan, have donated an easement on a 135-acre parcel that connects two sections of the state's land.

TRAFTON LAKE RECREATION AREA

Swim, fish, hike, bike, boat, picnic, camp, and play at 85-acre **Trafton Lake Recreation Area** (Ward Rd., Limestone, 207/325-4707), maintained by the town of Limestone.

Multiuse Trails
COLLINS POND LOOP

In downtown Caribou, a 1.5-mile loop circles around Collins Pond, an old millpond and waterfall downtown. Walk or bike the path through a town park, with a picnic area, beside ball fields, and along city sidewalks. It passes through wetlands populated by muskrat, moose, red-winged blackbirds, and other species; bring binoculars and head out in the early morning or before sunset for the best wildlife spotting.

AROOSTOOK VALLEY AND BANGOR-AROOSTOOK TRAILS

Led by the Caribou Recreation Department, several volunteer groups have worked to open up nearly 90 miles of abandoned railroad beds for year-round use by bikers, hikers, snowmobilers, all-terrain vehicles, and cross-country skiers. The two trail systems intersect in Washburn. The trails are mostly packed gravel, so you'll want a mountain bike. The prettiest and most rural section of this impressive network is the section of the trail between Washburn and Stockholm (40 miles one-way), including a short stretch through the Woodland Bog. Park in downtown Washburn, and carry plenty of water. From Caribou, you can go to Stockholm and on to Van Buren (29 miles one-way). Or begin in Carson (just west of Caribou) and go to New Sweden (9 miles one-way).

Golf

Check out the 18-hole **Presque Isle Country Club** (Rte. 205/Parkhurst Siding Rd., Presque Isle, 207/764-0430 or 207/769-7431, www.pi-countryclub.com). Another easy-on-the budget choice is the 18-hole **Mars Hill Country Club** (75 Country Club Rd., Mars Hill, 207/425-4802, www.golfmhcc.com).

Winter Sports

Twenty miles of professionally designed world-class mountain-biking and cross-country skiing trails are available free at the **Maine Nordic Heritage Center** (Nordic Heritage Access Rd., off Rte. 167, Presque Isle, 207/492-1444, www.nordicheritagecenter.org), part of the Maine Winter Sports Center. The center is considered one of the world's best internationally licensed cross-country facilities, and it has hosted international biathlon and cross-country races. The facilities include 20.5 miles of Nordic trails, a 30-point biathlon range, 0.6-mile paved and lighted roller-ski loop, 1.5-mile lighted trail, and visitors center with equipment rentals. Afterward, finish up with a sauna in the lodge. Best of all, the trails are free. The facility has 20 miles of marked mountain bike trails.

If alpine skiing is your preference, the Maine Winter Sports Center also operates the family-oriented **Quaggy Joe Ski Area** (Rte. 167, Presque Isle, 207/764-3016), adjacent to the Nordic Heritage Center, and the **Big Rock Ski Area** (37 Graves Rd., Mars Hill, 207/425-6711, www.bigrockmaine.com). Quaggy Joe is tiny, with only a T-bar serving its 218-foot vertical range, but it's very inexpensive. Big Rock is a good-size community ski area with three lifts (a triple chair, a double chair, and a Magic Carpet) and 35 trails and glades on a 980-foot vertical range. Although the area averages 160 inches of snow, 80 percent of the terrain is covered by snowmaking. About 55 percent is open for night skiing. Unfortunately the area's future is in jeopardy as the foundation that's been supporting it is no longer doing so.

Snowmobile rentals are available at **The Sled Shop** (108 Main St., Presque Isle, 207/764-2900, www.thesledshopinc.com). Rates begin at $200/day. Links to local snowmobile clubs are on its website.

Indoor Recreation

Inside **Caroline D. Gentile Hall** (University of Maine at Presque Isle campus, 207/768-9772, www.umpi.edu) are a walking and running track, a gym, a 37-foot rock wall and bouldering wall, strength machines and free weights, cardio trainers, and a pool. A day pass is $7 adults, $4 under age 14.

Sports Outfitters

Mojo (730 North St., Presque Isle, 207/760-9500, www.mojooutdoorsports.com) rents bikes ($25/day), kayaks ($25/day), skis/boots/poles ($25/day), and river tubes ($15/day). It also organizes weekly ride groups.

Perception of Aroostook (9 Caribou Rd./Rte. 1, Presque Isle, 207/764-5506, www.perceptionofaroostook.com) rents canoes and kayaks and will provide shuttles for the easy-going, 10-mile calm-water paddle on the Aroostook River from Washburn to Presque Isle.

ENTERTAINMENT AND EVENTS

In early June, the **Aroostook State Park Birding Festival** features guided bird walks, bird-banding demonstrations, and educational programs.

One of The County's biggest wingdings is the **Maine Potato Blossom Festival** held in Fort Fairfield in mid-July. Pageantry, potatoes, crafts, potatoes, entertainment, potatoes, fireworks, and potatoes.

Agriculture exhibits, harness racing, live entertainment, and fireworks are all part of Presque Isle's **Northern Maine Fair** (www.northernmainefairgrounds.com), the biggest country fair in this part of Maine, the first full week of August.

SHOPPING

About 11 miles west of Caribou, the **Woods Edge Gallery** (High Meadow Rd., Perham, 207/455-8359, 1pm-5pm Tues.-Sat. year-round) devotes almost 1,000 feet of exhibit space to watercolor and acrylic landscapes, plus photography—mostly by Aroostook County artists. The gallery doubles as owner Richard Clark's working studio. The gallery is 1.25 miles west of Route 228. Clark, steward for the Nature Conservancy's nearby Woodland Bog, also leads seasonal nature tours there.

Monica's Scandinavian Imports (176 Sweden St., Caribou, 207/493-4600) is chock-full of imported goods, from linens to clothing, cheese, and jewelry.

ACCOMMODATIONS

Lodging choices are few, so it's smart to have advance reservations.

Bed-and-Breakfasts

Within walking distance of downtown Caribou sights and restaurants, the **C Old Iron Inn B&B** (155 High St., Caribou, 207/492-4766, www.oldironinn.com, $79-99) comes by its name honestly. Hundreds of antique irons are displayed through the in-town 1913 arts and crafts-style house, and geology professor Kevin McCartney can recount the background of each one. Three guest rooms are comfortably furnished with quilts and oak antiques. A small entertainment room has a fridge, a TV, and microwave; Wi-Fi is available. Settle into the living room with a choice from the extensive magazine selections or choose a good read—plenty of mysteries, along with Lincoln and aviation libraries—from the well-stocked bookcases. Known for her culinary talent, Kate McCartney serves a delicious breakfast in the Victorian dining room. Ask Kevin about the Maine Solar System or the Science Museum at UMPI, both of which he developed—a clever and industrious fellow he.

Motels

Patronized primarily for its convenient downtown site, the clean but dated **Northeastland Hotel** (436 Main St., Presque Isle, 207/768-5321 or 800/244-5321 in Maine, www.northeastlandhotel.com, $110-125), dating from 1934, has 50 very spacious guest rooms with air-conditioning, TVs, Wi-Fi, and phones. Pets are not allowed; children 12 and under stay free.

The 148-room **Presque Isle Inn and Convention Center** (Rte. 1, Presque Isle, 207/764-3321 or 800/533-3971, www.presqueisleinn.com, $89-150) is a bit tired, but it's the area's best full-service lodging. Amenities include a restaurant, a health club, an indoor pool, an on-site coin laundry, Wi-Fi, and cable TV. The bar is a popular local rendezvous spot, and there's live entertainment on weekends in the lounge. Some rooms have kitchenettes. In winter, when the parking lot has more snowmobiles than cars, don't even think about arriving sans reservation. Pets are welcome.

Just south of town, the two-story **Caribou Inn and Convention Center** (Rte. 1, Caribou, 207/498-3733, www.caribouinn.com, $110-155), a sister property of the Presque Isle Inn, has 72 large, comfortable guest rooms and suites with air-conditioning, cable TV, Wi-Fi, and refrigerators (suites have kitchenettes). Facilities include an indoor pool, a health club, a restaurant, and a coin-op laundry. (Request a room away from the pool area.) Kids under age 13 stay free. Pet-friendly rooms are available for a small fee.

Russell's Motel (357 Main St., Caribou, 207/498-2567, www.russellsmotel.com, $65) is a vintage motel that provides a lot of bang for the buck. The paneled rooms have TVs, air-conditioning, fridges, microwaves, and Wi-Fi. Long distance calls are free, and kids under age 12 stay free.

A bit out of the way, but ideal for snowmobilers, is the **Aroostook Hospitality Inn** (23 Langille St., Washburn, 207/455-8567, www.aroostookhospitalityinn.com, $65-90), where rates include a continental breakfast and Wi-Fi.

Camping

Campsites at **Aroostook State Park** (State Park Rd., Presque Isle, 207/768-8341, parksandlands.com) are $20 for nonresidents, $12 for Maine residents. Sites are wooded and close to Echo Lake. Campers have a shower house with free hot showers and a cookhouse with a cookstove, a sink for washing dishes, picnic tables, and a cabinet of games. To be sure of a campsite on summer weekends, make reservations online (www.campwithme.com) or by phone (207/624-9950 out of state or 800/332-1501 in Maine; MasterCard or Visa required) at least two weeks ahead; there is a two-night minimum for reservations.

The 34 lakefront RV campsites at **Trafton Lake Campground** (Ward Rd., Limestone,

207/325-4704, late May-early Sept.) have full hookups and are $20/day, $110/week. The 10 tent sites are $10/day, $60/week. The campground is 2.5 miles off Route 89.

FOOD

As with other parts of Maine, Aroostook County has frequent **public suppers** throughout the summer. Visitors are welcome, even encouraged (most suppers benefit a good cause), so check the papers, line up early, and enjoy the local food and color.

Mars Hill

For a guaranteed dose of local color—and decent food besides—pull up at **Al's Diner** (87 Main St./Rte. 1, Mars Hill, 207/429-8186, 5am-8pm Mon.-Thurs., 5am-9pm Fri.-Sat., 6am-9pm Sun., $6-18), a friendly village restaurant that started as an ice cream shop in 1937. The third generation is now running the place. For breakfast, try the Aroostook omelet, made with potatoes, of course.

Just south of Mars Hill, **The Country Bakery** (Rte. 1, 207/425-4140, 5:30am-5pm Tues.-Fri., 5:30am-4pm Sat.) is an Amish-run spot with a smattering of tables. Stop in for inexpensive breakfasts and freshly made sandwiches, pizzas, and occasionally barbecue, along with delicious doughnuts and other treats.

Presque Isle
LOCAL FLAVORS

Despite its name, the **Riverside Inn Restaurant** (399 Main St., Presque Isle, 207/764-1447, 5am-3pm Mon.-Wed., 5am-7pm Thurs. and Sat., 5am-8pm Fri., 6am-3pm Sun., $5-12) doesn't have a river view. It's a cozy neighborhood place with perhaps a dozen booths, a four-stool counter, and a glass case filled with home-baked goodies, including doughnuts and cookies. Breakfast is served all day along with the usual home-style fare. It's in downtown Presque Isle close to Riverside Park and set back from the street.

Pop into **Star City Coffee** (483 Main St., 207/554-4222, 6:30am-2pm Mon.-Tues., to

8pm Wed.-Sat.) for The County's best coffees, along with soups and sandwiches.

Stock up on picnic goodies at the **Presque Isle Farmers Market** (9am-1pm Sat. mid-May-mid-Oct.), held in the Sears parking lot at the Aroostook Center Mall.

FAMILY FAVORITES

The Whole Potato Café & Commons (428 Main St., 207/554-4258, 11am-3pm Tues., 11am-8pm Wed.-Sat., 10am-2pm Sun.) is a community-oriented spot, with a gallery, performance space, and a kitchen serving sandwiches, wraps, potato skillets, and similar fare, with as much as possible drawn from local farmers. Maine brews and wines are also available. There's an inside children's play area too.

Corned beef and cabbage, shepherd's pie, bangers and mash, and fish-and-chips are nightly dinner specials at the **Irish Setter Pub** (710 Main St., 207/764-5400, 11am-9pm Mon.-Wed., 11am-11pm Thurs.-Sat. $10-20), a congenial and popular spot just north of downtown.

CASUAL DINING

Here's a welcome change to the usual deep-fried and family fare: **Café Sorpreso** (415 Main St., Presque Isle, 207/764-1854, 11am-2pm and 5pm-8pm Tues.-Sat., $17-28) is an inviting, contemporary downtown restaurant with a menu that changes biweekly and emphasizes fresh and, when possible, local Maine foods.

Caribou
LOCAL FLAVORS

Farms Bakery & Coffee Shop (118 Bennett Dr., 207/493-4508, 6am-2pm Tues.-Sat.) is the place to go for scratch-made croissants, delicious pastries, and light lunches. On Friday and Saturday go early for the to-die-for pecan rolls.

Here's a classic and a deal: **Burger Boy** (344 Sweden St., 207/498-2329, 10:30am-9pm Mon.-Sat., 11am-9pm Sun.) has been serving fresh ground burgers, house-made fries, and decent shakes since the 1940s. There's a drive-through, but for the real flavor of the joint, eat in the dining area amid table jukeboxes (sorry, none work), 45 records, and other vintage decor. Burgers start at $2.22.

FAMILY FAVORITES

Napoli's Italian Restaurant and Pizzeria (6 Center St., 207/493-1446, 11am-8pm, Mon.-Wed., to 9pm Thurs.-Sat., $6-20) has a solid reputation for excellent salads, large portions, good pizzas, and traditional Italian fare. There's a kids' menu available. Dine in the lounge, where you can catch the game on the big-screen TV or in the dining room.

Inexpensive home cooking is the draw for **Frederick's Restaurant** (507 Main St., 207/498-3464, 11am-8pm Tues.-Sat., noon-7pm Sun.).

Check out the golf simulator or the 10 TVs while waiting for your dinner at the **Par & Grill** (118 Bennett Dr., Caribou, 207/492-0988, from 11:30am daily) sports bar. Entrées range from burritos to porterhouse steak, with most ranging $5-14; children's menu available.

Fort Fairfield

Wander well off the beaten path for an enchanted evening at 🄲 **Canterbury Royale** (182 Sam Everett Rd., 207/472-4910), a destination-dining experience. Guests are immersed in an Old World European setting for elegant seven-course diners Tuesday-Sunday featuring haute French cuisine served in a private dining room. You're provided a menu in advance, from which you choose the entrée from among nearly 20 choices, and then half-sisters and classically trained chefs Barbara Boucher and Renee O'Neill choose the other courses. The setting, presentation, and food are sublime. Tables are set with crystal, silver, elaborate candelabras, and marble accents. Some furnishings and the elaborate, decorative woodwork were hand-carved by Renee. Cost varies with menu choices, ranging $37-100 pp, plus tax, tip, and wine. Plan far in advance, as only two parties are seated each evening. Reservations are required, and jeans, T-shirts, shorts, or sneakers are not allowed. The restaurant also offers European-style five-course brunches for $25 pp.

Good food at a fair price keeps locals returning to **Boondock's Grille** (294 Main St., 207/472-6074, 11am-7pm Wed.-Thurs., to 9pm Fri.-Sat., to 3pm Sun.), with prices in the $6-18 range.

Stockholm

Time a visit to the Swedish Colony to enjoy a meal at **Eureka Hall Restaurant and Tavern** (5 School St., Stockholm, 207/896-3196, noon-11pm Thurs.-Sat., noon-9pm Sun., $6-18), serving American fare in a sit-down setting upstairs and pizza and subs downstairs. There's often live music. Do call, as hours change frequently.

INFORMATION AND SERVICES

Local info is available from the **Central Aroostook Chamber of Commerce** (207/764-6561, www.pichamber.com) and the **Caribou Chamber of Commerce** (207/498-6156 or 800/722-7648, www.cariboumaine.net). Also check out **Caribou Public Library** (30 High St., Caribou, 207/493-4214, www.caribou-public.lib.me.us) and the **Mark & Emily Turner Memorial Library** (39 Second St., Presque Isle, 207/764-1572, www.presqueisle.lib.me.us).

Aroostook County Tourism (888/216-2463, www.visitaroostook.com) and **Aroostook Outdoors** (www.goaroostookoutdoors.com) have information and Web links for the entire county.

GETTING THERE

Presque Isle is about 42 miles or 50 minutes via Route 1 from Houlton. It's about 56 miles or 1.25 hours to Fort Kent via Route 1.

PenAir operates daily nonstop flights between Boston's Logan Airport and Northern Maine Regional Airport in Presque Isle (PQI, 650 Airport Dr., 207/764-2550, www.flypresqueisle.com). While at the airport, check out the **Presque Isle Air Museum** (207/764-2542), which displays historical photos and memorabilia from Presque Isle's impressive aviation history in two corridors.

The St. John Valley

Settled by Acadians in 1785, the St. John Valley isn't quite sure whether it should be the 51st state or Canada's 11th province. Valley hallmarks are huge Roman Catholic churches, small riverside communities, tidy homes, an eclectic French patois, and a handful of unique culinary specialties—all thanks to a twist of fate.

Henry Wadsworth Longfellow's immortal epic poem *Evangeline* relates a saga of *le grand dérangement,* when more than 10,000 French-speaking Acadians tragically lost their lease on Nova Scotia after the British expelled them for disloyalty in 1755—a date engraved ever since in the minds of their thousands of descendants now living on the American and Canadian sides of the St. John River. (Thousands more of their kin ended up in Louisiana, where Acadian-Cajun traditions also remain strong.)

In this part of Maine, Smiths and Joneses are few—countless residents bear such names as Cyr, Daigle, Gagnon, Michaud, Ouellette, Pelletier, Sirois, and Thibodeau. In **Van Buren** (pop. 2,171), **Grand Isle** (pop. 467), **Madawaska** (pop. 4,035), **St. Agatha** (pop. 747), and **Frenchville** (pop. 1,087), French is the mother tongue for 97 percent of the residents, who refer to the Upper St. John Valley as *chez nous* ("our place"), their homeland. Many roadside and shop signs are bilingual—even the name board for the University of Maine branch in Fort Kent.

Religion is as pervasive an influence as language. When a Madawaska beauty represented Maine in the Miss America contest in 1995, the local *St. John Valley Times* admonished its readers: "Keep your fingers crossed and your rosaries hot."

Since the 1970s, renewed local interest in and appreciation for Acadian culture has spurred cultural projects, celebrations, and genealogical research throughout the valley, with the eventual goal of a National Park Service Acadian culture center. "Valley French," a unique archaic patois long stigmatized in Maine schools, has undergone a revival. Since the 1970s, several valley schools have established bilingual programs, and a 1991 survey estimated that 40 percent of valley schoolchildren speak both English and French. The 2014 Acadian World Congress celebrated the valley's roots.

Controversy erupts periodically over whose lineage is "true" Acadian (as opposed to Québécois—although many Acadians also fled to Québec), but valley residents all turn out en masse for the summer highlight: Madawaska's multiday Acadian Festival in mid-August. It's a local festival unlike any other in Maine. If you plan to visit then, make lodging plans far in advance. Thousands of far-flung descendants of whichever founding family is being honored each year book every room on both sides of the border.

Between Madawaska and Fort Kent, detour off Route 1, via Route 162, into the lovely lake district, locally known as the "back settlements," through the town of St. Agatha (usually pronounced the French way: "Saint a-GAHT") and the village of Sinclair. T-shaped **Long Lake** is the northernmost of the Fish River Chain of Lakes, extending southwest to Eagle Lake.

West of Fort Kent are the tiny and tinier riverside communities of **St. John** (pop. 267), **St. Francis** (pop. 485), **Allagash** (pop. 239), and Dickey, the latter two serving as endpoints for two of Maine's most popular long-distance canoe routes: the St. John River and the Allagash Wilderness Waterway.

An excellent companion when touring the St. John Valley is *Voici the Valley Cultureway,* a guidebook and CD, that highlights the heritage and sights. It can be purchased locally ($15) or ordered in advance from the **Maine Acadian Heritage Council** (207/728-6826, www.voici-thevalley.org).

The St. John River serves as the border between the United States and Canada at the tip of Aroostook County.

SIGHTS
◖ Acadian Village

In the hamlet of Keegan, about two miles northwest of downtown Van Buren, is a prominent reminder of the heritage in this valley. Begun as a small-scale bicentennial project in 1976, the **Acadian Village** (Rte. 1, Van Buren, 207/868-5042, www.connectmaine. com/acadianvillage, $6 adults, $3 children, noon-5pm daily June 15-Sept. 15) is a 2.5-acre open-air museum comprising 17 antique and replica buildings in an A-shaped layout. Included are a country store, a forge, a schoolhouse, a chapel, and several residences. This isn't a sophisticated museum, but it does convey the region's heritage. Tours by attentive guides vividly convey the daily struggles of 18th-19th-century Acadians in the valley. Kids particularly enjoy the schoolhouse and the barbershop; outside, there's plenty of letting-off-steam room.

Mount Carmel Museum and Cultural Center

As with the other religion-dominated communities in the valley, the most prominent landmark in the Lille village of **Grand Isle** (pop. 467) is the former Catholic church, a Baroque, twin golden-domed building undergoing long-term restoration as a nonprofit bilingual museum and cultural center. Built in 1910, Our Lady of Mount Carmel Church had its first mass on New Year's Day 1910 and its last in 1978. Since historian, preservationist, and renaissance man Don Cyr took over the wooden church in 1984, he has organized concerts and other events under the aegis of the nonprofit **Mount Carmel Cultural and Historic Association** (207/895-3339, www. museeculturel.org). He also shares his collection of Acadian antiques and artifacts. The church is usually open noon-4pm Sunday and Tuesday-Thursday mid-June-early September for docent-led tours. It also hosts concerts

AROOSTOOK COUNTY

THE BLOODLESS AROOSTOOK WAR

Aroostook County's major brush with historic notoriety occurred in 1839, with the skirmish known as the Aroostook War. Always described as "bloodless"–since there were no casualties (other than a farmer accidentally downed by friendly fire)–the war was essentially a boundary dispute between Maine and New Brunswick that had simmered since 1784, when New Brunswick was established.

The 1783 Treaty of Paris had set the St. Croix River as the Washington County line, but loopholes left the northernmost border ill-defined. Maine feared losing timber-rich real estate to Canada, and matters heated up when 200 burly militiamen descended on the region in early 1839 to defend the young state's territory. About 3,000 troops ended up supporting the Maine cause, and legendary war hero Gen. Winfield ("Old Fuss and Feathers") Scott was sent to Augusta for three weeks in March 1839 to negotiate the successful truce.

After the "war," Aroostook was incorporated as a county, and by 1842 the Webster-Ashburton Treaty (sometimes also called the Treaty of Washington), negotiated by Daniel Webster and Lord Ashburton, brought a long-awaited peace that opened the area for stepped-up settlement.

Among the remnants of the Aroostook War are two wooden blockhouses, one an original and a National Historic Site, on the banks of the St. John River in Fort Kent, the other a replica on the Aroostook River in Fort Fairfield.

and lectures. While here, walk 100 yards or so down Route 1 to the gallery, showing contemporary and traditional art, in the former Lawrence Parent General Store.

St. David's Historical Sites

As you reach the eastern edge of Madawaska, you can't help but notice the bell tower of the imposing brick neo-Gothic **St. David Catholic Church,** established in 1871. The building, on the National Register of Historic Places, is usually open and has a high arched ceiling, a domed altar, and stained-glass windows.

Just to the right (east) of St. David's is the one-room **Tante Blanche Museum** (Rte. 1, St. David Parish, Madawaska, 207/728-4518, free), containing Acadian artifacts. Run by the Madawaska Historical Society (www.madawaskahistorical.org), the log museum commemorates Marguerite Blanche Thibodeau Cyr ("Tante Blanche"), an Acadian heroine during a 1797 famine. The museum is usually open 11am-4pm Wednesday-Sunday mid-June-early September; on-site volunteers answer questions and provide guidance. The museum's campus also includes the 1870 **School House No. 1** and the circa 1840 **Albert House.**

Continue down the 0.5-mile gravel road to the riverfront, where a 14-foot-high marble **Acadian Cross** marks the reputed 1785 landing spot of Acadians expelled by the British from Nova Scotia and New Brunswick. During the annual Acadian Festival, the landing is reenacted.

Fort Kent Blockhouse

Built in 1839 during the decades-long U.S.-Canada border dispute known as the Aroostook War, the **Fort Kent Blockhouse** (Blockhouse Rd., Fort Kent, 9am-5pm daily late May-early Sept., free), a National Historic Landmark, is the only remnant of a complex that once included barracks, a hospital, and an ammunition hoard. On the second floor are historic artifacts plus information about the curious "bloodless" border skirmish over timber rights. Bring a picnic and commandeer a table in the pretty little riverside park just below the fort (tent camping is allowed, $4 pp or $10/carload). Early in the summer, before the river dwindles, you can also launch a canoe or kayak here. The Fort Kent Eagle Scouts maintain and staff the blockhouse and the nearby log-cabin gift shop.

© HILARY NANGLE

the Acadian Village in the St. John Valley

Fort Kent Railroad Station

The station, on the National Register of Historic Places, was in service 1902-1979 and was part of the Bangor and Aroostook Railroad's Fish River division. It's now the home of the **Fort Kent Historical Society and Gardens** (207/834-5354, noon-4pm Tues.-Fri. late June-mid-Aug.)

The First Mile

The bridge to Canada marks the northern end of Historic U.S. Route 1, with Key West, Florida, anchoring the southern end. You are 318 miles north of Portland, 368 miles north of the New Hampshire border at Kittery, and 2,209 miles north of Key West.

St. Agatha Historical House and Preservation Center

Wow! This tiny town (pop. 747), has one heck of a museum: the **St. Agatha Historical House and Preservation Center** (433 Main St., St. Agatha, 207/543-6911, 1pm-4pm Tues.-Sun. mid-June-early Sept., donation). Volunteers

assist guests touring both the oldest house in town and the museum, which is chock-full of interesting artifacts and exhibits (carvings, textiles, farm equipment, religious and school goods, and much more). It's easy to while away an hour or so here.

University of Maine at Fort Kent

Founded in 1878 as a teacher-training school, the **University of Maine at Fort Kent** (UMFK, 25 Pleasant St., Fort Kent, 207/834-7500, www.umfk.maine.edu) still prides itself on the quality of its teacher-education program. Because of its location in the Upper St. John Valley, UMFK also offers a BS degree in bilingual and bicultural studies, and the school's **Acadian Archives** (207/834-7535, www.umfk. maine.edu/archives) are the state's best resource on Maine's Acadian heritage.

Detour to Allagash

Few people visit Allagash, sited where the famed Allagash Wilderness Waterway flows into the St. John River. Contemporary author

AROOSTOOK COUNTY

Cathie Pelletier, who grew up here, called the town "Mattagash" in her entertaining novels of life in northern Maine. One doesn't visit here for the sights—there really aren't any. Or the shopping: Less than a handful of businesses cater to paddlers, hunters, anglers, and snowmobilers. One comes to Allagash for a taste of frontier life, to experience a way of life that's disappeared from most of America. Visit Allagash, and you'll feel as if you've arrived not only at the end of the road, but also at the end of the world, and in some ways you have.

Unlike the rest of the St. John Valley, Maine's largest town in terms of total land mass was settled by Irish and English immigrants, so it's not unusual to find lots of Irish surnames, such as McBrearity and Kelly. These days moose and bear far outnumber people.

As long as you're not squeamish about hunting, step into **Two Rivers Lunch** (75 Dickey Rd., Allagash, 207/398-3393, 7am-3pm daily), a down-home place decorated with animal trophies and hunting pics. Tylor and Leitha Kelly opened it as a hot dog stand in 1976, and Leitha is still at the stove. The menu tops out at around $8. Order a grilled cheese, some coleslaw, and the house-made mixed fries, and then strike up a conversation with the locals.

RECREATION
Parks and Preserves
FISH RIVER FALLS

An idyllic setting for a picnic, Fish River Falls, a Class IV rapid, is a bit of a local secret, since finding it isn't easy. Take Route 162 south, and when you see Bouchard Family Farms (which grows acres of buckwheat for *ployes,* a traditional Acadian pancake), bear right on Strip Road; watch for Airport Road on the right. There's a small sign noting falls access. Once you get to the parking area, the falls are a 10-minute stroll slightly downhill. Carry a picnic and sit on the rocks, which have potholes formed by grinding boulders and likely dating back to the glacier age.

DEBOULLIE PUBLIC RESERVE LANDS

Wildlife-watchers, hikers, anglers, campers, snowmobilers, and pretty much anyone who enjoys the great outdoors will appreciate the 21,871-acre **Deboullie Public Reserve Lands** (207/435-7963, www.parksandlands. com). Wildlife-watching is excellent throughout the reserve thanks to varied habitats that include ponds, streams, marshes, and woodlands. Watch for deer and moose, beavers and snowshoe hares, loons and bald eagles. While the northern three-quarters of the preserve is gently rolling forested ridges, the southern quarter has mountains to climb and ponds for boating and fishing. Brook trout are abundant in most of the ponds; landlocked salmon can be hooked in Togue Pond. Hike Deboullie Mountain to the inactive fire station at the top for panoramic views of the region. Along the route, keep an eye out for ice caves, deep crevices in the rocks where ice can remain year-round. Allow at least four hours for the six-mile hike. Primitive waterfront campsites dot the preserve, but for those who prefer a roof over their heads, **Red River Camps** (www. redrivercamps.com) is a traditional sporting camp on Island Pond. Deboullie gives meaning to the word *remote.* It's about 30 rugged miles southwest of Fort Kent. Access is via the **North Maine Woods** (www.northmaine-woods.org) checkpoint in St. Francis. The name Deboullie, by the way, is derived from a French term meaning "tumble down," referring to rock slides.

Multiuse Trail

The 17-mile crushed-stone **Saint John Valley Heritage Trail** edges the south bank of the St. John River between Fort Kent and St. Francis and connects to area ATV and snowmobile trails. It's also part of the National Park Service's Acadian interpretation efforts.

Canoeing the St. John River

The St. John, the longest free-flowing river east of the Mississippi, doubles as the international border. Public boat access points are plentiful, but land only on the U.S. shoreline. A good resource is **Northern Forest Canoe Trail** (www.northernforestcanoetrail.org).

Golf

The Bangor and Aroostook Railroad line runs right through the first and ninth holes at the **Fort Kent Golf Club** (St. John Rd./Rte. 161, Fort Kent, 207/834-3149). The nine-hole hilly course has dynamite views of the St. John River. The attractive clubhouse has a bar and light meals.

The ninth hole at the nine-hole **Birch Point Country Club** (Birch Point Rd., St. David, 207/895-6957) has the distinction of being New England's northernmost golfing hole. The clubhouse has a bar and a basic food menu; cart rentals are available.

Swimming and Canoeing

Birch Point Beach (Chapel Rd., St. David, on the east side of Long Lake; turnoff to the beach at St. Michael's Chapel) has a small grassy area with picnic tables; the lake views are fantastic.

A lovely **picnic and recreation area** (Rte. 162, St. Agatha) on the western shore of Long Lake has a boat launch, a beach, grills, and restrooms.

Winter Sports

CROSS-COUNTRY SKIING

One of the top cross-country skiing facilities in the world, **The 10th Mountain Center** (Paradise Circle Rd., Fort Kent, 207/834-6203, www.10thmtskiclub.org, free) has hosted World Cup Biathlon events. Another of the successful Maine Winter Sports Center facilities, this one has a biathlon and cross-country facility, with 7.5 miles of biathlon trails, plus an additional 18 miles of cross-country trails, a lighted roller-ski loop, a wax building, a stadium, and a full biathlon range with 30 shooting stations. Snowshoes and pets are permitted on 1.4-mile Volunteer's Way, also known as the Pet Loop. The lodge, with a sauna and a fireplace, is a comfy place to relax after a day on the trails. The center's access road is 1.6 miles south of downtown Fort Kent off Route 1.

ALPINE SKIING

Just a couple of blocks off Main Street is **Lonesome Pine Trails** (Forest Ave., Fort Kent, 207/834-5202, www.lonesomepines.org), a volunteer-run community hill with a 500-foot vertical drop served by two tows; there is also night skiing. Adult tickets are $20 full day, $15 half day.

SNOWMOBILING

This is prime sledding country. The best resource for trail info is **Fort Kent SnoRiders** (www.fortkentsnoriders.com). At **Top of Maine Rentals** (379 Aroostook Rd./Rte. 11, Fort Kent, 207/834-3095) expect to pay around $200 for a one-day rental.

EVENTS

Spectators crowd the snowy streets to watch Fort Kent's five-day March **Can Am Crown International Sled Dog Races** (www.can-am-crown.net). Special locations offer vantage points for watching teams competing in races for 30, 60, and 250 miles. A mushers' award ceremony is the finale.

Madawaska hosts the Franco-American **Acadian Festival** (www.acadianfestival.com) with a historical reenactment, tournaments, a fishing derby, Acadian food, music and dancing, a parade, and a featured-family reunion in mid-August.

ACCOMMODATIONS

Lodging options are slim on this side of the border.

Van Buren

The circa 1969 **Aroostook Hospitality Inn** (95 Main St., Van Buren, 207/455-8567, www.aroostookhospitalityinn.com, from $70) was renovated in 2009 and now welcomes guests with new furnishings and fixtures. Rates include a nice continental breakfast. Guests have access to a huge gathering room with a fireplace—nice for a winter's eve. Guest rooms have refrigerators, air-conditioning, and Wi-Fi. It's walking distance to downtown shops and restaurants.

Madawaska

Just across the road from the lake, the **Long Lake Motor Inn** (596 Main St./Rte. 162, St. Agatha, 207/543-5006, www.stagatha.com/longlake, $67-72) has 18 spacious guest rooms with phones, flat-screen TVs, refrigerators, and microwaves; 11 with lake views (and great sunrises) and two two-bedroom lakefront units with kitchenettes. Continental breakfast is included, and there's a lounge on the premises.

The Lakeview Camping Resort (9 Lakeview Dr., St. Agatha, 207/543-6331, www.lakeviewrestaurant.biz) has 80 mostly wooded sites, with areas for RVs ($26-42) and tents ($21 d). Also on-site are a convenience store, a shower house, and a restaurant.

New in 2013, the (**Inn of Acadia** (384 St. Thomas St., 207/728-3402, www.innofacadia.com, $89-149), a boutique inn, was created out of a former convent. This is The County's finest lodging, with 15 air-conditioned rooms and four suites decorated in a sleek, contemporary style and furnished with Wi-Fi, flat-screen TVs, and mini-fridges. Also here are a café, lounge, fitness studio, and guest laundry. Rates include a continental breakfast. Light fare may be offered in the lounge, where there's acoustical music on Friday and Saturday evenings. Airport shuttles are available.

Fort Kent

Clean, comfortable, and inexpensive, the downtown **Northern Door Inn** (356 W. Main St., Fort Kent, 207/834-3133 or 866/834-3133, www.northerndoorinn.com, $84) has a nice gathering area in the lobby, where a meager continental breakfast is served. Rooms have air-conditioning, phones, refrigerators, TVs, and Wi-Fi. There's a guest laundry. Don't look for fancy; this place is old and due for a major updating. Kids 12 and under are free; pets are $5 each per night.

The fanciest lodging in the region is the (**Four Seasons Inn of Soldier Pond** (13 Church St., Wallagrass, 207/834-4722, www.fourseasonsinnofsoldierpond.com, $99-149), a renovated merchant's house overlooking the Fishkill River about 15 minutes south of Fort

Kent. A lot of thought went into the renovations; every room has air conditioning, Wi-Fi, plush bedding, robes, and flat-screen TVs; some have jetted tubs and river views. Public spaces include a formal parlor, a comfy library, a guest pantry, and a gazebo by the river. Rates include a continental breakfast. The innkeeper doesn't live on the premises.

FOOD

Check local papers and bulletin boards for notices about **public suppers,** an inexpensive way to break bread with the locals.

Van Buren

Here's a nice surprise: **Robin's Restaurant** (44 Main St., Van Buren, 207/868-3044, 10am-8pm Mon.-Sat., 8am-7pm Sun., $3-14), an unfussy, welcoming family-owned and operated downtown spot, has a menu that ranges from burgers and pizzas to pork chops and lobster Alfredo.

Frenchville

Roughly 11 miles west of Madawaska, on Route 1 North, you'll find Frenchville. If you arrive in time for lunch or dinner, stop in at **Rosette's Restaurant** (240 Main St./Rte. 1, Frenchville, 207/543-7759, 10:30am-8pm Tues.-Thurs., 7am-9pm Fri.-Sat., 7am-8pm Sun., $3-20), a valley favorite. Almost everything's homemade, prices are very reasonable, and the color is local; expect to hear a mix of French and English.

Ask anyone in the valley: When it comes to *ployes* (buckwheat pancakes), *creton* (a meat spread), and chicken stew, no one does it better than (**Dolly's** (Rte. 1, Frenchville, 207/728-7050, 7am-8pm Wed.-Mon., 7am-8:30pm Fri.-Sat., $4-18), a Valley institution since 1988. Go early for the chicken stew as it always sells out.

St. Agatha

When it's time for a meal, head up the hill for the best panorama in town at **The Lakeview Restaurant** (9 Lakeview Dr., St. Agatha, 207/543-6331, www.lakeviewrestaurant.biz, 7am-9pm, $8-26). An awning-covered deck

© HILARY NANGLE

Purchase potatoes, *ployes* mix, farm fresh produce, and local crafts at Bouchard's Country Store.

has sweeping views over Long Lake; indoor booths and tables have plenty of visibility. The wide-ranging menu has a choice and price for every taste and budget. Lakeview doesn't take reservations.

The best view in the village of Sinclair, about six miles down the road from St. Agatha, is at the **◖ Long Lake Sporting Club Resort** (Rte. 162, Sinclair, 207/543-7584 or 800/431-7584, www.longlakesportingclub.com 5pm-9pm Mon.-Sat., noon-8pm Sun.). Seemingly in the middle of nowhere, this informal place is almost always crowded. In summer, guests come by boat or car, occasionally by floatplane; in winter, they arrive by snowmobile. The deck and dining room have fabulous views over Long Lake. Huge steaks and giant lobsters are specialties, and all meals come with *ployes,* Acadian buckwheat pancakes typically served with an artery-clogging pâté called *creton*. Most entrées are in the $20s.

Fort Kent

Purchase *ployes* mix, farm-fresh produce, and local crafts at **Bouchard's Country Store** (Rte. 161, 207/843-3237).

Prime rib is the specialty at **The Swamp Buck** (250 W. Main St./Rte. 1, Fort Kent, 207/834-3055, 11am-9pm Mon.-Sat., 9am-9pm Sun., $10-24), but the menu ranges from decent burgers to blackened haddock, and there's a kids' menu too.

Dining options expand beyond the usual burgers, fried food, and family fare at **The Custom Cake Cafe** (142 W. Main St./Rte. 1, Fort Kent, 207/834-1140, www.customcakecafe.com, 7am-3pm Mon.-Sat. and 5pm-9pm Wed.-Sat., $14-26). Sample entrées such as duck breast and filet mignon. Nightly dinners often have themes, such as Mexican, pub, or gourmet.

Walk into **Doris's Cafe** (345 Market St./Rte. 161, Fort Kent Mills, 207/834-6262, 5am-2pm Mon.-Fri., to noon Sat.), and conversation ceases as every head in the place turns to see the stranger. Not to worry; chatter quickly resumes—and you can catch all the local gossip. Expect specials such as American chop suey. If you've never had *poutine* (French fries smothered with gravy and cheese), you can order it here.

Try to snag a window table overlooking the Fish River at the **Mill Bridge Restaurant** (271 Market St., 207/834-9117, 10:30am-9pm Mon.-Sat., 8:30am-9pm Sun., $4-18), a bright spot with a menu ranging from pizza and pastas to fried seafood and steak, along with beer and wine. Kid-friendly options are $5.

INFORMATION AND SERVICES

For local information, check with the **Greater Madawaska Chamber of Commerce** (356 Main St./Rte. 1, Madawaska, 207/728-7000, www.greatermadawaskachamber.com) and the **Greater Fort Kent Area Chamber of Commerce** (76 W. Main St./Rte. 1, Fort Kent, 207/834-5354 or 800/733-3563, www.fortkentchamber.com), which serves as a clearinghouse for much of the Upper St. John Valley.

AROOSTOOK COUNTY

Aroostook County Tourism (888/216-2463, www.visitaroostook.com) has information and Web links for the entire county.

The 1994 National Park Service publication *Acadian Culture in Maine* is available online at http://acim.umfk.maine.edu.

GETTING AROUND

Fort Kent is about 56 miles or 1.25 hours from Presque Isle via Route 1. It's about 96 miles or 2.25 hours to Patten via Route 11.

If you're planning to pass through one of the three U.S.-Canada border stations, have the proper identification and paperwork. For crossings into the United States, see www.cbp.gov. For crossings into Canada, see www.cbsa-asfc.gc.ca. Remember that New Brunswick is on Atlantic time, an hour later than eastern time.

The **U.S. Customs office** maintains offices in Van Buren (207/868-3391), Madawaska (207/728-4376), and Fort Kent (207/834-5255). All are open 24 hours daily.

South from the Peak of the Crown

The rolling farmlands of northern Aroostook give way to forests and mountains as you drive south on Route 11 from Fort Kent. If you took a poll among those who know, especially photographers, the stretch from Fort Kent through Eagle Lake to Portage would probably rank near the top as a favorite fall foliage drive. What's so appealing along this 37-mile Scenic Highway? Brilliant colors roll down hills, dapple open vistas, and reflect in the smattering of lakes and ponds.

Through the years, **Eagle Lake** (pop. 864) has benefited heavily from being the home-town of John Martin, one of Maine's most influential politicians, who served an un-precedented 10 terms as speaker of Maine's House of Representatives. The town really looks as though someone has been paying at-tention. The official rest area, overlooking the lake, has picnic tables and plenty of park-ing. Many a photo has been snapped here. Eighteen-mile-long L-shaped Eagle Lake is a key link in the Fish River Chain of Lakes, starting at Long Lake in St. Agatha. In win-ter, the lake supports wall-to-wall ice-fishing shacks.

Portage (pop. 391) is particularly popular as a summer playground, and many county resi-dents have built or rented camps on the shores of Portage Lake.

Considered the "Gateway to the North Maine Woods," **Ashland** (pop. 1,302) is the home of **North Maine Woods** (207/435-6213, www.northmainewoods.org), a private organi-zation charged with managing recreational use of more than three million acres of northern Maine's working timberlands. Visit the web-site to download maps and a detailed brochure or for information on where to go, how to get there, what to do, and where to sleep.

Route 11 continues southward and out of Aroostook County to Patten, Medway, and Millinocket. One note: Don't expect to be alone with the moose and other wildlife out here; logging trucks legally own the road, and they know it, so give them a wide berth.

SIGHTS

There's not much to see at the open-air **Ashland Logging Museum** (Garfield Rd., Ashland), which has six buildings containing a blacksmith shop, old woods rigs, and other gear, as well as a fire tower, but it's worth a quick look-see. For a more in-depth look, make an appointment (AshlandLoggingMuseum@gmail.com). Just before Ashland, when Route 11 takes a sharp left, turn right onto Garfield Road and go a little less than a mile.

RECREATION
Hiking

About eight miles south of Eagle Lake is the wooded **Hedgehog Mountain Rest Area,** trail-head for the 1.5-mile round-trip Hedgehog

Mountain. It's not the most exciting climb, and the summit view is so-so, but it's fairly steep, so it's a good little workout.

About 10 miles east of Ashland on Route 163 (Presque Isle Rd.) is the trailhead (on the left) for **Haystack Mountain,** a quarter-mile climb. It begins with an easy hike through the woods then steepens near the fairly bald summit; keep left at the trail split to avoid the steepest section. Pack a picnic so you can enjoy the almost 360-degree view.

Water Sports

Eagle Lake's **town park,** down at lake level, has shorefront picnic tables and grills. The wind kicks up wildly at times, but on a calm day, this is a fine place to launch a canoe. From Route 11, turn at Old Main Street and go 0.6 mile; there's plenty of parking.

From Route 11, turn west at West Cottage Road and go 0.5 mile to reach the Portage **town beach.** The view is fabulous, and parking is ample; there are picnic tables, a grill, and a grassy "beach."

Roughly midway between Ashland and Masardis, in the town of Masardis, is an access road to the boat landing for **Squa Pan Lake,** probably the oddest-shaped lake in the state.

SHOPPING

Detour out to **Made in Aroostook** (685 Oxbow Rd., Oxbow, 207/435-6171) for a selection of fine and folk crafts, from jewelry to quilts, all locally made.

GETTING AROUND

Patten is about 96 miles or 2.25 hours from Fort Kent via Route 11. It's 40 miles or 50 minutes to Millinocket via I-95 and Route 157 or 90 miles or 1.5 hours to Bangor.

AROOSTOOK COUNTY

MAINE HIGHLANDS

Home to Maine's highest mountain and largest lake, the Maine Highlands, covering all of Piscataquis County and the northern two-thirds of Penobscot County, typify Maine's rugged North Woods. Within Piscataquis County are 40-mile-long Moosehead Lake, the appealing frontier town of Greenville, the headwaters of the Allagash Wilderness Waterway, the mile-high Katahdin, and the controlled wilds of Baxter State Park.

Sport hunters and anglers have always frequented the North Woods, and they still do. But hunters, sportfishers, and back-to-the-landers increasingly have to share their untamed turf with a new generation of visitors. Sporting camps originally built for rugged anglers and hunters now welcome photographers, birders, and families; white-water rafting, canoeing, kayaking, and snowmobiling are all big business; and hikers have found nirvana in a vast network of trails—particularly the huge, carefully monitored trail system in Baxter State Park.

In the 1970s, paper companies were forced by environmental concerns to halt the perilous river-run log drives that took their products to market. This cessation not only cleaned up the rivers but also spared the lives of the hardy breed of men who once made a living unjamming the logs in roiling waters. The alternative now is roads, lots of them, mostly unpaved—a huge network that has opened up the area to more and more outdoors enthusiasts. For generations, paper companies allowed public recreation on their lands and access via their roads, but as they sell off large chunks of wilderness,

PHOTO BY STACEY CRAMP, COURTESY OF THE MAINE OFFICE OF TOURISM.

HIGHLIGHTS

© AVALON TRAVEL

LOOK FOR ◖ TO FIND RECOMMENDED SIGHTS, ACTIVITIES, DINING, AND LODGING.

◖ **Patten Lumbermen's Museum:** A visit to this replica of a lumber camp will cure any romantic notions about being a lumberjack (page 449).

◖ **Ambajejus Boom House:** Paddle or cruise to this artifact from the log-driving era (page 449).

◖ **Hiking in Baxter State Park:** Explore Maine's gem, choosing from more than 200 miles of trails crowned by Katahdin, Maine's tallest peak (page 461).

◖ **Cruise on the *Kate*:** See Moosehead Lake from the water on a historic vessel (page 469).

◖ **Kineo:** It's worth the effort to get a close-up view of Kineo's icon cliffs and to hike to its summit (page 471).

◖ **Moose Safaris:** You can't go home without spotting at least one moose, so go with a guide who knows where they hang out (page 474).

◖ **Gulf Hagas Reserve:** Nicknamed the Grand Canyon of the East, the 3.5-mile-long gorge makes a spectacular hike (page 486).

◖ **Stephen King-dom:** Learn all about the master of horror on a guided tour to Bangor area sites (page 490).

◖ **University of Maine Museum of Art:** Bangor lured the university's collection away from the Orono campus (page 492).

◖ **Penobscot Nation Museum:** Cross the bridge to Indian Island to see this engaging collection of artifacts, videos, and artwork from Maine's Penobscot Native Americans (page 500).

the patterns are changing. Some new owners are discontinuing the open-road and open-land policies, and that's a cause for concern among many outdoor-oriented folks.

The area is rich in aquatic possibilities too. Maine's best-known classic canoe trips follow the Allagash and St. John Rivers northward, but no one can even begin to count the other lakes, rivers, and streams that have wonderful canoeing.

Stay at one of this region's primitive forest campsites and you'll really sense the wilderness—owls hoot, loons cry, frogs croak—and yes, insects annoy. No matter how much civilization intrudes, it's still remote and wild. As one writer put it, "Trees grow, die, fall, and rot, never having been seen by anyone. They litter the shores of lakes, form temporary islands, block streams, and quickly eradicate paths."

The air gateway to the region is Bangor,

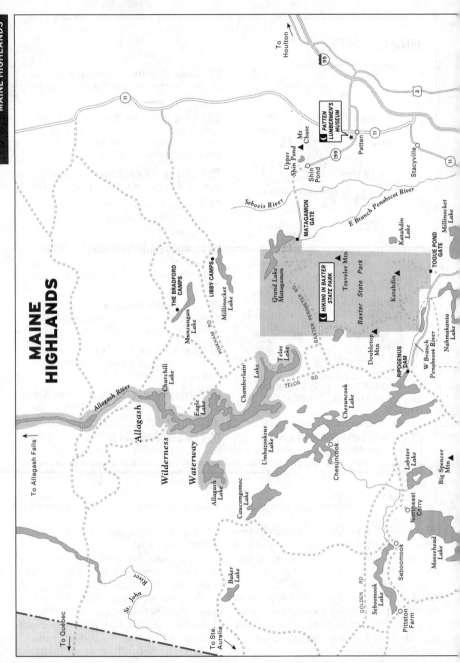

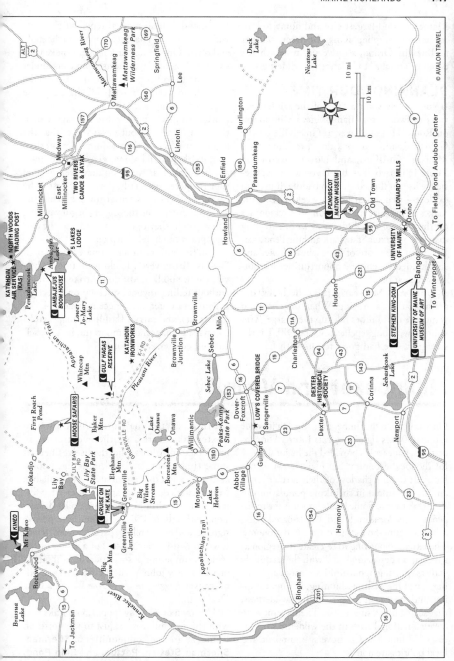

© AVALON TRAVEL

Maine's second-largest city and home to horror maven Stephen King. Between Bangor and nearby Orono, a university town, there's enough "cultcha" to balance the wilderness.

PLANNING YOUR TIME

If you merely want a taste of the wilderness, you can swoop from Bangor up to Millinocket on Route 11, segue over to Greenville on the Golden Road, and back down to Bangor via Monson, Guilford, and Dover-Foxcroft on Route 15 in two days, but if you want to experience it, you'll need time to paddle, hike, and explore—plan on at least a week. Greenville makes a fine base for exploring the region; it's on the edge of the wilderness, within striking distance of Baxter State Park and the Penobscot River, on the shore of Moosehead Lake, and surrounded by endless opportunities for outdoor recreation.

From mid-May-early July, the blackflies are more than annoying. When they begin to wane, the mosquitoes take up the charge. Arm yourself with bug repellent. While DEET is the strongest, I've had good results with Lewey's Eco-Blends, an all-natural repellent available widely in Maine. The key is applying it liberally and often. One Baxter Park ranger I spoke with swore by Bounce dryer sheets—place one under a cap and the other under your shirt around the waistline to create a "force field" that keeps the bugs from biting.

Most timber-company throughways remain there for all to use, but never forget that the logging trucks *own* them—in more ways than one. As they barrel along, give them room—and some slack as well; you may even be glad they're there, especially if you get lost. The *DeLorme Atlas* is essential for exploring the area, but every time the loggers begin working a new patch, they open new roads, so the cartographers can barely keep up.

Finally, never underestimate the North Woods: Bring versatile clothing (more than you think you'll need), don't strike out alone without telling anyone, stock up on insect repellent and water, use a decent vehicle (4WD if possible), and carry a flashlight, maps, and a compass. Perhaps most important, be a conscientious, eco-sensitive visitor.

Millinocket and Vicinity

Once crucial to the timber industry, **Millinocket** (pop. 4,506) is fighting for its future. For generations, paper mills provided the major support for the local economy, but major downsizings have left them a shadow of their former selves and have resulted in shrinking populations in the area's towns. Some locals hope for the resurgence of the local mills and woods-based work; others are gung-ho for a tourism-based economy. The latter are pushing to re-create the region as a recreation destination, and with the seemingly endless sporting opportunities—canoeing, rafting, kayaking, fishing, hunting, hiking, camping, and more—in the surrounding wilderness, that seems like a smart idea. There's a move to create a national park in the wilderness northeast of Millinocket. Controversy is rampant, and local politics are hot.

Millinocket is the closest civilization to Baxter State Park's southern entrance, so most Baxter visitors find themselves here at some time or other. Food, lodging, books, auto fuel, and other essentials are all available. Millinocket's downtown appears somewhat forlorn, but revitalization plans are under discussion, with talk of a visitor center, interpretive signage, and even a biking pathway from downtown to Millinocket Lake. For a vision of the region's timbering past, wander into the post office to view John W. Beauchamp's 1942 oil-on-canvas *Logging in the Maine Woods,* a New Deal mural.

The town of **Medway** (pop. 1,349) links I-95 with the two mill towns; just to the north on Route 11 are the communities of **Sherman, Sherman Station, Patten,** and **Shin Pond,**

© HILARY NANGLE

The Ambajejus Boom House was used as a rest stop by rivermen during the great log drives.

providing access to the less-used northeast entrance (Matagamon Gate) of Baxter State Park.

SIGHTS
◖ Patten Lumbermen's Museum

About 40 miles northeast of Millinocket, 0.5 mile west of downtown Patten and about 25 miles southeast of Baxter State Park's Matagamon Gate, is a family-oriented museum commemorating the lumberman's grueling life. The nine buildings at the open-air **Patten Lumbermen's Museum** (61 Shin Pond Rd./Rt. 159, Patten, 207/528-2650, www.lumbermensmuseum.org, 10am-4pm Tues.-Sun. July-mid-Oct., 10am-4pm Fri.-Sun. in spring, $8 adults, $7 seniors, $3 ages 4-12) tell the tale of timber in the 19th and early 20th centuries: cramped quarters, hazardous equipment, rugged terrain, and nasty weather. Lots of working gear and colorful dioramas appeal to children, and there are picnic tables, a snack bar, and room to roam. A summer highlight is the annual **beanhole bean dinner** (beans baked underground

overnight), held the second Saturday in August.

◖ Ambajejus Boom House

The only access to the **Ambajejus Boom House,** a property on Ambajejus Lake that is listed on the National Register of Historic Places, is via boat or snowmobile. You can arrange a cruise with Katahdin Cruises or a canoe rental or guided trip with New England Outdoor Center or do it yourself. It's always open and filled with incredible lumbering-era artifacts. The boom house, erected here in 1906, was used as a rest stop for 65 years by rugged river drivers, lumbermen who "boomed out" (collected with immense chains) and actually rode logs downstream to the sawmills. The meticulous restoration of the once-derelict house has been done as a personal project by Chuck Harris, a onetime river driver who is often on-site. If you go on your own, launch your boat in Spencer Cove, near Katahdin Air Service, on the west side of the Golden Road, and paddle or motor out and around to the

MAINE'S BIG DIG: THE GOLDEN ROAD

The era of nimble lumberjacks driving logs downriver ended in the early 1970s when Maine's paper companies began building roads into the wilderness for access to their timberlands. The most famous of these, The Golden Road, runs from Millinocket around the top of Moosehead Lake to the Québec border. It took nearly 1,000 workers almost five years to build the private, 96-mile, mostly unpaved road. Completed in 1975 and originally called the West Branch Haul Road, Maine's version of the Big Dig reputedly earned its current name from the megacost ($3.2 million) of construction.

The Golden Road is the most scenic link between Millinocket and Greenville, a 71-mile trip, two-thirds unpaved, through the wilderness. Red-and-white mile markers tacked to trees tick off the distance—if you can spot them. Driving this route is a true adventure, but it's not for everybody. If you're not used to driving backwoods dirt roads, this might not be the place to start. If you choose to do so, it's vital to ask about the road's condition—if there has been a lot of cutting going on along the route or if it has been a while between gradings, it could be in uncomfortably rough shape. Remember, it's a private road built for trucks and logs, not cars and people.

When driving from Millinocket, you'll exit the Golden Road after about 48 miles. Watch for a fork in the road, with a crude sign denoting Greenville Road; if you make it to the North Woods checkpoint, you've overshot it. The Greenville Road then parallels Moosehead Lake's east shore to Greenville. Keep an eye peeled for moose, deer, and even black bears.

Remember that you are entering true wilderness. There are no gas stations, restaurants, lodgings, or anything but water, trees, and wildlife, and cell phone service is spotty at best. Go prepared with a full tank of gas, bottles of water, energy bars, bug repellent, and a good spare tire. Bicycles, motorcycles, ATVs, and horses are not allowed on the road.

Should you meet a logging truck along the way, pull way, way over and let it pass. If it's loaded, it might be carrying as much as 100,000 pounds of logs (and unlike Harry Chapin's song about bananas, it's you, not the logs, that will be mashed).

---

right, to the head of the lake. Stay close to shore, as the wind can pick up unexpectedly. (If you need a canoe, you can rent one across the road at the Big Moose Inn.)

Flightseeing

Based at Ambajejus Lake, about eight miles northwest of Millinocket on the road to Baxter State Park, **Katahdin Air Service** (KAS, Millinocket, 866/359-6246, www.katahdinair.com) provides access to wilderness locations in every direction, but even if you have no particular destination, the scenic floatplane flights are fabulous. Fall-foliage trips are beyond fabulous. Rates begin at $85 pp (two-person minimum). You'll fly over Katahdin and the Penobscot River's West Branch, perhaps spotting moose en route. The best flight, though, is an hour-long trip over Baxter State Park to the Allagash Wilderness Waterway and back along the West Branch. Flights operate daily late May-October, weather permitting.

Katahdin Air Service is also a major link in the sporting-camp network, flying guests into and out of the remote camps via floatplane. When you contact a sporting camp for rate information, request the rates for floatplane access. It won't be cheap, but it's safe and fun. For a token sporting-camp experience without an overnight, sign up for one of KAS's "fly 'n' dine" trips. For $130 pp (two-person minimum, covering meals and transport), it'll fly you into a sporting camp for dinner and take you back afterward. It's a delicious adventure.

If you prefer your plane to have wheels, book a sightseeing flight with **West Branch Aviation** (Millinocket Municipal Airport, 164 Medway Rd., Millinocket, 207/723-4375, www.westbranchaviation.com). The rate is $52 pp for a half hour, $85 pp for a full hour, with a two-person minimum on all flights.

Katahdin Woods & Waters Scenic Byway

The 89-mile Katahdin Woods & Waters Scenic Byway winds between Millinocket and Patten, following the Baxter State Park Road and Routes 11 and 159, offering views of Maine's highest peak and taking in museums and sights en route. A map-brochure, detailing the byway and sights and services along it, can be picked up locally or downloaded from www.explore-maine.org.

Here's my recommended detour from the byway: On a clear day, detour west off Route 11 on the Happy Corner Road, about two miles south of downtown Patten, follow it about two miles to the Frenchville Road, on your right, and take that (gravel in sections) north to a T intersection and bear right on the Waters Road, which will connect with Route 159, turn right to return to Route 11 and Patten. The biggest rewards for this loop are the panoramic views of Katahdin from the Happy Corner Road; the rest is a delightful country byway, with some nice ridge views east from the Frenchville Road. It's simply gorgeous in autumn.

ENTERTAINMENT AND EVENTS

Family fun is the specialty at **Magic City Mini Golf** (237 Penobscot Ave., Millinocket, 207/723-4404), an indoor fun center with an 18-hole miniature golf course, golf simulator, video games, and a pool table.

Millinocket is widely known for its **Fourth of July** celebration (the fireworks display is outstanding).

Patten's **Annual Beanhole Bean Dinner** is a great celebration featuring good food (and a fascinating culinary tradition) at the Patten Lumbermen's Museum the second Saturday in August.

SHOPPING

Unless you're looking for camping or sporting supplies, shopping choices are slim in the area, but **North Light Gallery** (256 Penobscot Ave., Millinocket, 207/723-4414 or 800/970-4278, www.artnorthlight.com) is well worth a stop. Owner Marsha Donahue specializes in art from the Katahdin-and-Lakes School, and she shows the works of numerous talented artists and artisans. You can't miss the building; Donahue has painted murals on the exterior.

If you can't leave without a photograph of a moose, Mark Picard's **Moose Prints Gallery** (58 Central St., Millinocket, 207/447-6906) is a must-stop.

Stock up on last-minute head-into-the-woods needs at **North Woods Trading Post** (Baxter State Park Rd., Millinocket, 207/723-4326, 7am-9pm daily). Tom and Sandy Bell purchased the old store in 2011 and have completely renovated it into the best supply store for anyone heading into Baxter State Park. Pick up bottled water (there's no place to buy it in the park), fill the gas tank, purchase technical gear and clothing, take advantage of the free Wi-Fi (just ask for the password), find the perfect map or book, have a bit to eat (food's good), and pick Tom's brain for suggestions (he's from these parts and was a ranger at Chimney Pond for years). And stop again on the way out for the perfect souvenir. Sandy stocks the store with Maine-made gifts.

SUMMER RECREATION
Mattawamkeag Wilderness Park

Talk about a well-kept secret that shouldn't be: Check out the 1,000-acre town-owned **Mattawamkeag Wilderness Park** (Rte. 2, Mattawamkeag, 207/736-4881 or 888/724-2465, www.mwpark.com), about an hour's drive southeast of Baxter State Park's southern gate. The park's well-managed facilities include 15 miles of trails, picnic tables, restrooms, free hot showers, a recreation hall, a playground, a sandy beach (on the Mattawamkeag River), and fishing for bass, salmon, and trout. There's also access to fine canoeing, including flat water and Class V white water, on one of northern Maine's most underused rivers. And you can stay the night at one of the 56 wooded campsites and 11 lean-tos. The entrance is about

THE UNGAINLY, BELOVED MOOSE

Everyone loves Maine's state animal, *Alces alces americana*. The ungainly moose, bulbous-nosed and top-heavy, stops traffic and brings out the cameras. It also stops cars literally, usually a lose-lose situation. The moose's long legs put its head and shoulders about windshield level, and a crash can propel the animal headfirst through the glass. Human and animal fatalities are common.

State biologists estimate that Maine has nearly 30,000 moose, most in the North Woods, so it's pretty hard not to encounter one if you're driving the roads or hiking the trails in the Maine Highlands region.

Moose pay no heed to those yellow-and-black diamond-shaped moose-crossing signs, but officials post them near typical moose hangouts, so slow down when you see them. During daylight hours, especially early and late in the day, keep your binoculars and camera handy. In late spring and early summer, pesky flies and midges drive the moose from the deepest woods, so you're more likely to see them close to the roadside. At night, be even more careful, as moose don't tend to focus in on headlights (as deer do), and their eyes don't reflect at an angle that drivers can see.

Moose are vegetarians, preferring new shoots and twigs in aquatic settings, so the best places to see them are wetlands and ponds fringed with grass and shrubs. These spots are likely to be buggy too, so slather yourself with insect repellent.

Moose hunting, officially sanctioned, is somewhat controversial, partly because the creatures seem to present little sporting challenge. But they are a challenge, not because of wile or speed but because of heft. Imagine dragging one of these fellows out of the woods to a waiting truck; it's no mean feat. In Maine's annual Moose Lottery—a herd-thinning scheme concocted by the Department of Inland Fisheries and Wildlife—hunters receive permits to shoot moose in specific zones in late September-mid-October. At official state weighing stations, the hapless moose are strung up, weighed, tested for parasites, and often butchered on the spot by freelance meat packagers. Moose meat is actually tasty.

---

eight miles east of Route 2 on an unpaved logging road locally called "the park road"; it's signposted on Route 2. Day use is $3 pp, maximum $7/car. Camping fees are $22-35/site/night; seven sites have hookups. The park is open daily late May-October.

Moose-Spotting

Want some assistance finding an elusive moose? **Maine Quest Adventures** (2062 Medway Rd./Rte. 157, Medway, 207/447-5011, www.mainequestadventures.com) provides guided moose and wildlife photography tours with guaranteed moose sightings. Tours by van are $49 pp for three hours, $75 pp for a full day; three-hour sunrise/sunset canoe/kayak tours are $65 pp. All tours require a two-person minimum.

New England Outdoor Center (800/766-7238, www.neoc.com) offers three-hour, guided moose-spotting tours via canoe, touring kayaks, pontoon boats, or vans for $49-60 adults, $39 under age 12; a full-day tour is $109 adults, $89 kids. If you don't see a moose or if your tour doesn't meet your every expectation, you can return for free.

Excursion Boat

Katahdin Scenic Cruises (207/723-8391, www.bigmoosecabins.com), based at the Big Moose Inn, makes it easy to get out on the lakes to see the wildlife and Katahdin if you don't want to brave a canoe, kayak, or raft. Options include 1-3-hour trips; from $25, boat minimums may apply.

Water Sports
CANOEING AND KAYAKING

This part of Maine is a canoeist's paradise, well known as the springboard for Allagash Wilderness Waterway and St. John River trips.

Close to Millinocket, experienced canoeists and kayakers may want to attempt sections of the **East and West Branches of the Penobscot River,** but no neophyte should try them. We're talking Big Water. Refer to the *AMC River Guide* for details, or contact one of the local outfitters such as New England Outdoor Center or Maine Quest Adventures.

A relatively gentle, early-summer canoe trip ideal for less-experienced paddlers is on the **Seboeis River,** between the Shin Pond-Grand Lake Road and Whetstone Falls, about 24 miles. Even easier, and a good family trip, is the flat-water run putting in below Whetstone Falls (west of Stacyville) and taking out before Grindstone Falls. .

If you launch your canoe early in the day on **Sawtelle Deadwater,** near Shin Pond, west of Patten, you're bound to see moose. From Shin Pond, head northwest, crossing the Seboeis River at about six miles, and then turn right onto the next unpaved road and continue less than two miles to the water. You can also reach the Deadwater off the parallel paved Huber Road. Canoe rentals are also available at Shin Pond Village.

If you're itching to master a roll or better your white-water paddling techniques, **Maine Kayak** (866/624-6352, www.mainekayak. com) operates a white-water kayaking school with courses costing about $240 for a two-day course.

Most accommodations have canoes available for their guests, but if you need to rent, stop at **Maine Quest Adventures** (Rte. 157, Medway, 207/447-5011, www.mainequestadventures. com). Daily canoe and kayak rentals are $25.

WHITE-WATER RAFTING

Maine's biggest white-water rafting area is around The Forks, where the Kennebec and Dead Rivers meet, in the Kennebec Valley Region, but the second-largest area is along the West Branch of the Penobscot River near Millinocket. One-day Penobscot River rafting trips pass through Ripogenous Gorge, a rip-roaring chasm of roiling Class IV and V white water, over nine-foot Nesoudnehunk

Falls, through a few other Class IV rapids and a few ponds, all in the shadow of Katahdin. It's a fabulous adventure, and a riverside lunch is included.

The primary rafting outfitter here is the **New England Outdoor Center** (NEOC, Black Cat Rd., off Baxter State Park Rd., Millinocket, 207/723-5438 or 800/766-7238, www.neoc. com), based in updated and renovated historical sporting camp on Millinocket Lake overlooking Katahdin. NEOC organizes West Branch rafting trips ($80-120 pp, depending on day and month). Packages including meals and lodging are available. NEOC is a full-service outdoor adventure resort, with lodging, dining, and guided recreational services.

FISHING

Water, water everywhere. That means primo fishing, including streams, rivers, and walk-in and fly-in ponds for brook trout; ponds and lakes for splake and lake trout; rivers and lakes for landlocked salmon; brooks and streams for wild and native brook trout; lakes for brown trout; and streams and rivers for bass. The Maine Department of Inland Fisheries and Wildlife (www.mefishwildlife.com) produces *Fishing Opportunities in the Katahdin Region,* a brochure detailing where to fish for what. Fishing licenses and other info also are available on the website.

For local info and supplies visit **Two Rivers Canoe and Kayak** (Rte. 157, Medway, 207/746-8181, www.tworiverscanoe.com).

Guided and outfitted fishing trips for one or two anglers with **Maine Quest Adventures** (Rte. 157, Medway, 207/746-9615 or 207/290-1733, www.mainequestadventures.com) are $300 full day with lunch, $200 half day with a snack; multiday trips are also available.

Serious anglers should consider one of the sporting camps listed in *Accommodations.*

WINTER RECREATION

Winter can be magical in the North Country. Snow is usually measured in feet, not inches, so snowmobiling and cross-country skiing are big business; snowshoeing and ice fishing also draw winter sports fans. Motels in Millinocket fill up fast in snow season, so plan well ahead for winter adventures.

Snowmobiling

More than 350 miles of the Interconnecting Trail System (ITS) crisscross the Millinocket area, including some that run right through town. Local snowmobile clubs produce excellent trail maps available from the Katahdin Area Chamber of Commerce. Snowmobile enthusiasts might also want to visit the Northern Timber Cruisers Snowmobile Club's **Antique Snowmobile Museum** (Millinocket Lake Rd., Millinocket, 207/723-6203, www.northerntimbercruisers. com, weekends and by appointment), which contains about three dozen machines. The clubhouse also serves food.

Snowmobile rentals ($185-215), clothing rentals ($10-25), and guided trips are available from **The New England Outdoor Center's Twin Pine Snowmobile Rentals** (800/634-7238, www.neoc.com), based at Twin Pine Camps, near ITS 86 in Millinocket.

Cross-Country Skiing

The Northern Timber Cruisers also groom and track more than 20 miles of free wilderness cross-country trails. Begin at the clubhouse on Baxter State Park Road 1.6 miles northeast of Millinocket. For trail conditions, call 207/723-4329.

ACCOMMODATIONS

Besides in-town and area lodgings, Millinocket is also the springboard for a number of wilderness sporting camps, some of which are inaccessible, or nearly so, by road. Small planes equipped with skis or pontoons ferry clients to the remote sites—not an inexpensive undertaking, but a great adventure that's well worth the splurge.

Bed-and-Breakfasts

Whoo-ee! Millinocket's getting some fancy with the addition of **C 5 Lakes Lodge** (46 Marina Dr., South Twin Lake, Millinocket, 207/723-5045, www.5lakeslodge.com, $200-275). Area natives Rick and Debbie LeVasseur built this eye-catching two-story log lodge on a spit of land extending into South Twin Lake. Soaring windows and a stone fireplace dominate the two-story living room, with stunning views of Katahdin over the chain of lakes out front. Every guest room has a handcrafted, quilt-covered king bed, a bath with a double whirlpool tub, satellite TV, a gas stove, air-conditioning, a fridge, a data port, and that view. The LeVasseurs provide canoes and kayaks for their guests on the pebble beach out front; small fishing boats are available for rental at the dock out back, and flightseeing tours will pick up right here. Rates include a full breakfast. It's cushy, comfy, and a fine place for wildlife-watching: five pairs of eagles and 24 pairs of loons nest on the interconnecting lakes, and Rick has a few "guaranteed" moose-spotting sites. Rick and Debbie throw in a lot of extras for their guests. For example, when the weather cooperates and their schedule permits, they take guests for lake tours aboard their pontoon boat. Also available is a two-bedroom loft apartment ($300).

In downtown Millinocket is **The Young House Bed and Breakfast** (193 Central St., Millinocket, 207/723-5452, www.theyounghousebandb.com, $100). Each of the five smallish guest rooms has air-conditioning, a TV and DVD player, and Wi-Fi. Public rooms include a parlor with a baby grand. A full choice-of-menu breakfast is included.

If you're entering Baxter from the north or following the Kathadin Woods & Waters Byway, the **Bradford House** (46 Main St., Patten, 772/285-3868, www.thebradfordhousemaine.net, $125-150, no credit cards) is a fine place to call it a night. Stephen and Filena Singer's rambling 1842 farmhouse has guest rooms on the second and third floors. All are furnished with comfy antiques, down comforters, quilts, flat-screen TVs, and Wi-Fi. Only the huge third-floor room has an en suite private bath; the others are detached. Rates include a full country breakfast.

Thanks to its location on a peninsula, 5 Lakes Lodge is surrounded by water on three sides.

Motels

The two-story, 48-room **Baxter Park Inn** (935 Central St./Rte. 157, Millinocket, 207/723-9777, www.baxterparkinn.com, $100-115) is an older motel that's slowly being updated; ask for a renovated room. On-site owners keep the rooms spotless. Perks include air-conditioning, free Wi-Fi, an indoor pool and whirlpools, and continental breakfast. It's also right on ITS 83. Pets are allowed with a signed waiver for $10. Despite its name, it is in town and not near the park.

Close to I-95's Exit 56 is the **Gateway Inn** (Rte. 157, Medway, 207/746-3193, www.medwaygateway.com, $65-75), a motel with 38 rooms and suites. Accommodations on the west side have decks, great views of Katahdin (weather permitting), and higher rates. Pets are welcome. Continental breakfast is included; air-conditioning, phones, satellite TV, and an indoor pool are all available. There's even a guest kitchen with a fridge and a microwave.

Eclectic Properties

Hardest to characterize is the **Big Moose Inn** (Baxter State Park Rd., Millinocket, 207/723-8391, www.bigmoosecabins.com) on Millinocket Lake, midway between Millinocket and Baxter State Park's southern boundary. It's part inn, part sporting camp, part campground. Two white-water rafting companies are based here. This is not the place to stay if you're seeking peace and quiet, but it is a great property steeped in Maine woods traditions. The main lodge is everything you'd expect: comfy antiques and country furniture, a big stone fireplace, a moose head and other woodsy accents, and a big screened-in porch. Traditional guest rooms ($56 pp) with shared baths are inviting but very small (if you're over six feet tall, don't even think about it, as some have short beds); rates include continental breakfast. Suites with private baths are $140-199 with breakfast. On the grounds are 35 tent sites ($11 pp) and six screened lean-tos ($14 pp), plus 14 cabins that sleep 2-16, all with screened porches ($49 pp; minimum varies by cabin;

bring your own towels). Canoe or kayak rental is $5/hour or $15/day. The inn has a restaurant and pub, and next door is North Woods Trading Post, with pizza, sandwiches, and supplies. Smoking and pets are not allowed. The lodge, cabins, and campground are open May-Columbus Day.

Hikers take note: The **Appalachian Trail Lodge** (33 Penobscot Ave., Millinocket, 207/723-4321, www.appalachiantraillodge.com) provides cheap sleeps ($25 bunk, $35-55 private room with shared bath, $95 family suite with kitchen) and caters to you with hiking and Bangor airport shuttles, coin-op laundry, and a community kitchenette.

If you're approaching Baxter State Park from the north gate, **Morning Glory Farm** (199 Happy Corner Rd., Patten, 800/219-7950, www.mountaingloryfarm.com, $110) has two apartments in a beautifully renovated 1864 farmhouse on a working Amish farm. Advance reservations are required; rates decrease with length of stay.

Outdoor Adventure Resort

Ground zero for year-round sporting outfitter **New England Outdoor Center** (off Baxter State Park Rd., 800/766-7238, www.neoc.com), is its lakefront, Katahdin-view Twin Pine campus, an oasis of civilization in the wilderness just southeast of Baxter State Park. Facilities include a lodge with full-service restaurant and lounge, a recreation hall with a sauna and games, and use of canoes, kayaks, and docking facilities. The lakeside accommodations range from small cabins to green-built guesthouses, all with full kitchens. Rates begin about $250 d for a small cabin during peak season, but packages that include everything from activities to meals are available. Pets are accommodated ($20/night). During peak seasons (summer rafting and winter snowmobiling), it can get rowdy with enthusiasm.

Sporting Camps

Eight miles off the access road to Baxter's northern gate is **Bowlin Camps** (Patten, 207/528-2022, www.bowlincamps.com), a traditional fishing and hunting camp on the shore of the Penobscot River's East Branch. It now also welcomes family groups, especially in July-August. Kids love the suspension bridge across the river, and there are trails to ponds and two waterfalls. An easy 16-mile canoe run starts here (rentals are available), and someone will meet you at the other end. Cabins are rustic, heated with woodstoves; all have private baths and gas and electric lights, three have kitchenettes, one is accessible. Summer rates in cabins begin around $95 pp/night, including family-style meals served in the main lodge. Children under 16 are half price; dogs are $15. Add a four-hour moose safari for $54 pp. Snowmobiling is huge here, and there are 12 miles of cross-country trails; Bowlin is open all year.

Two excellent sporting camps with long-standing reputations off to the north are Libby Camps and Bradford Camps. Both require 60-90-minute drives on unpaved roads; it's worth the splurge to arrive by floatplane. July-August are the best times for families, as fishing is slow and hunting hasn't started.

About 150 miles north of Bangor, **❰ Libby Camps** (Millinocket Lake, 207/435-8274, www.libbycamps.com), on the east shore of a different Millinocket Lake than the one near Millinocket, is flanked by Baxter State Park and the Allagash Wilderness Waterway. Matt and Ellen Libby are the third generation to run this fishing and hunting camp, built in 1890; their son Matt and his wife, Jess, are next in line, and daughter Alison and her husband help out too—it's a serious business. If you catch a trophy salmon or brook trout at this Orvis-endorsed fly-fishing lodge, they'll even ready it for the taxidermist. Eight comfortable cabins have flush toilets, propane lights, and quilt-topped beds. The basic daily rate, including three meals, a boat, and a cabin, is $210 pp d. Pets are allowed. Hearty meals are served close to an enormous stone fireplace in the handsome log-beam lodge. (Pray that Ellen will make her peanut-butter squares for dessert and buy a copy of her cookbook.) Canoes, kayaks, and motorboats are available for guests, and there's

BE A SPORT

Although dozens of traditional sporting camps exist all over Maine, most of the veterans are in the Katahdin-Moosehead Region, with the Kennebec Valley and Western Mountains running a close second. Almost all are north of Bangor.

Sporting camps deliver an authentic wilderness experience without camping. Noise and light pollution are nonexistent; on a clear night, the stars are magnificent. They're so much more than a place to stay; they're an experience, often a throwback to the 19th century, or at least to the early 20th century.

They're so varied that it's impossible to paint them with one broad brush. All but a few are accessible by road, but the "road" might be a rutted, muddy tank trap, making passengers yearn for a floatplane. All are rustic no-frills operations, some much more so than others. (If you're a frill-seeker, forget it; seek elsewhere.) Some have electricity and flush toilets; others have kerosene lanterns and private or shared outhouses. All are on or close to freshwater, meant to be convenient for fishing. Some offer American Plan (AP) rates, serving three meals a day, usually family-style; others have housekeeping facilities, where you're on your own; some let you choose.

Most camps have on-site guides available for hire—take advantage. Guides know the woods and water, and whether you want to find the fish or simply take a long walk in the woods, they know the best places and will point out hidden sights and wildlife.

With all the logging roads crisscrossing the region, there are only a few sporting camps now inaccessible by road, but most guests opt to fly in and out. As one guide put it, "People prefer flying over dying; those logging trucks run up and over a couple of cars every year."

If all this sounds intriguing, the **Maine Sporting Camp Association** (www.mainesportingcamps.com), founded in 1987, has more info.

---

a sandy beach. The Libbys also own 10 "outpost cabins" on wildly remote ponds. (Even more remote is their Riverkeep Lodge on the Atikonak River in Labrador.) Libby Camps is open May-November. Both Matts are licensed pilots, and they'll fly you in on a seaplane from the Presque Isle Airport or Matagamon Lake near Patten, or you can arrange transport with other flying services.

The only sporting camp on a pristine 1,500-acre lake, **◖ The Bradford Camps** (Munsungan Lake, 207/746-7777, winter 207/439-6364, www.bradfordcamps.com) is owned by Igor and Karen Sikorsky. (If the name rings a bell, think helicopters). The scenery and sunsets are magnificent, the loons are mystical, and moose sightings are frequent. This is a special place. Eight good-size log cabins (with bathrooms and propane lamps), lined up along the lakefront, are $167 pp per day or $1,059/week; family rate for two adults and two kids under 18 is about $2,800/week. Rates include excellent meals served family-style in the lake-view lodge. Most fascinating is the antique ice house, containing brilliantly clear ice cut arduously from the lake the previous winter. Canoes and kayaks are free for guests, a boat with a motor and gas is $60/day, and hiking trails await. A guide (from $220/day) is essential for fishing these waters—noted for rare blue-back trout—and helpful for canoeing a nearby stretch of the Allagash. Bradford is open May-November; in October-November most guests are hunters seeking deer, moose, and grouse. If you're an aviation fan, ask about the Sikorsky Seminar weekend, usually in July. Karen and Igor can arrange flights from Millinocket Lake or you can drive 60 miles over rough logging roads and pay $30 pp gate fees (trust me: fly). No credit cards.

Camping

New England Outdoor Center's **Penobscot Outdoor Center Campground** (off Baxter State

Park Rd.), the closest private campground to the southern entrance of Baxter, has bunkhouses ($50-120), cabin tents ($40-80), and tenting sites ($11-13 pp). Frills include a hot tub, bar, and some food service in the base lodge. No hookups, no water.

Probably the closest you can get to Baxter's south gate with an RV is **Chewonki's Big Eddy Campground** (8027 Golden Rd., Greenville, 207/350-1599 Apr. 1-Oct. 15, 207/882-7323 Oct. 16-Mar. 31, www.bigeddy.org). Many of the 75-acre campground's primitive sites ($14 pp, $8 ages 13-17) edge the Penobscot River at the famed Big Eddy landlocked salmon pools. Chewonki also offers camping gear rental, canoe rentals, and shuttles. Also available are camping cabins, about $60 pp per night.

The closest campground to the north gate is the Christianson family's **Matagamon Wilderness** (Patten, 207/446-4635, www. matagamonwilderness.com), which is just a few miles from the Matagamon gate. On the premises and bordering the East Branch of the Penobscot River are 36 wilderness campsites that can accommodate up to a 42-foot RV ($20), housekeeping cabins ($30-40 pp per day), a general store with food service, and boat rentals. Pets are allowed in the campground for $10/stay.

FOOD

While the local options are improving, this isn't a destination for foodies, not by a long shot. With few exceptions, most of what's available is good home cookin', and you're welcome anywhere in jeans.

Local Flavors

For pizza, subs, pastas, and calzones, locals recommend **Angelo's** (118 Penobscot Ave., 207/723-6767, 10:30am-9pm Mon.-Sat.) downtown.

The **Appalachian Trail Café** (210 Main St., Millinocket, 207/723-6720, 5am-8pm daily) knows how to feed hungry hikers, rafters, anglers, and other outdoor adventurers. Breakfast is served all day, but burgers, fried foods, and

other budget-friendly comfort foods join the menu for lunch and dinner.

Order pizzas as well as sandwiches made on house-made bread at **The Hangar** (at the airport, Rte.11, Patten, 207/528-2555, 10am-8pm Tues.-Sat.), and then settle at a table inside or out.

Casual Dining

When locals want to celebrate, they head to one of these restaurants.

The nicest downtown restaurant is the **Scootic Inn** (70 Penobscot Ave., Millinocket, 207/723-4566, www.scooticin.com 11am-10pm Mon.-Sat., 4pm-10pm Sun., bar until 1am, $8-25). The dining areas are pleasant, there's a full bar, and kids are welcome. The menu varies from pizzas, calzones, sandwiches, burgers, and fried foods to entrées such as Cajun chicken and rib eye steak.

Dine inside on one of the antique oak tables in the airy, light-filled dining room or outdoors on the screened-in porch at **Fredericka's** in the Big Moose Inn (Baxter State Park Rd., Millinocket, 207/723-8391, www.bigmoosecabins.com, 5pm-9pm Wed.-Sat. Sept.-June, 5pm-9pm Wed.-Sun. July-Aug., $18-30). The creative menu emphasizes fresh and local ingredients. Entrée choices may include seafood casserole or Angus rib eye. Lighter fare is served at the inn's **Loose Moose Bar and Grill** (from 5pm daily, $7-11).

A tad more relaxed is **River Drivers Restaurant** (off the Baxter State Park Rd, 207/723-8475 or 800/766-7238, www.neoc. com, 6pm-9pm daily, $10-35) at the New England Outdoor Center's Twin Pine campus. The dining room and patio have eye-candy views over Millinocket Lake to Katahdin, and the fare, which emphasizes fresh and local, is well prepared. Breakfast and lunch are served in peak seasons.

INFORMATION AND SERVICES

The **Katahdin Area Chamber of Commerce** (1029 Central St./Rte. 157, Millinocket, 207/723-4443, www.katahdinmaine.com) is based in a small prefab building at the eastern edge of Millinocket.

Check out **Millinocket Memorial Library** (5 Maine Ave., Millinocket, 207/723-7020, www. millinocket.lib.me.us).

Just east of Northern Plaza in Millinocket, Baxter State Park Headquarters, open weekdays, has **public restrooms,** as does Millinocket's municipal building (197 Penobscot Ave.) and the chamber of commerce.

Pets are not allowed in Baxter State Park. For doggie day care, call Connie P. McManus of **CPM Grooming** (100 Pamola Park/Cedar St., Millinocket, 207/723-6795 or 207/731-3111).

GETTING THERE AND AROUND

Millinocket is about 72 miles or 1.25 hours from Bangor via I-95. It's about 85 miles or 2 hours to Greenville via Routes 11 and 6 or 70 miles and 2 hours via the (mostly unpaved) Baxter State Park, Golden, Greenville, and Lily Bay Roads.

Katahdin Air Service (KAS, Millinocket, 866/359-6246, www.katahdinair.com) has an excellent half-century reputation offering charter floatplane flights to remote campsites and sporting camps May-November.

A full-service shuttle provider, **Maine Quest Adventures** (Rte. 157, Medway, 207/746-9615, www.mainequestadventures.com) shuttles adventurers throughout the region. It also offers airport pickup.

Baxter State Park

Consider the foresight of Maine Governor Percival Proctor Baxter. After years of battling the state legislature to protect the area around Katahdin, Maine's highest mountain, he bade good-bye to state government in 1925 and proceeded to make his dream happen on his own. Determined to preserve this chunk of real estate for Maine residents and posterity, he pleaded the cause with landowners and managed to accumulate an initial 5,960-acre parcel—the nucleus of today's 209,501-acre Baxter State Park—and donated it to the state in 1931. From then on, he acquired and donated more and more bits and pieces, adding his last 7,764-acre parcel in 1962, just seven years before his death at the age of 90. The governor's prescience went far beyond mere purchases of land; his gift carried stiff restrictions that have been little altered since then. And thanks to interest accrued on his final bequest, as well as small and large donations from park users and supporters, park authorities have been able to add even more acreage—including a splendid 4,119-acre parcel donated in 2006.

Today this fantastic recreational wilderness has 46 mountain peaks and more than 200 miles of trails. One rough unpaved road (limited to 20 mph) circles the park; no pets or radios are allowed; cell phones may be carried but used only for emergencies. No gasoline, drinking water, or food is available; camping is carry-in, carry-out.

Camping, in fact, is the only way to sleep in Baxter—at tent sites, lean-tos, bunkhouses, or rustic log cabins. Competition for sleeping space can be fierce on midsummer weekends; it's pure luck to find an opening, so you need to plan well ahead. Guaranteeing a spot, particularly one of the coveted 22 cabins, means reserving well in advance (no refunds). The rewards are rare alpine flowers, unique rock formations, pristine ponds, waterfalls, wildlife sightings (especially moose), dramatic vistas, and in late September, spectacular fall foliage.

The hiking here is incomparable. Peakbaggers accustomed to 8,000-footers (or more) may be unimpressed by the altitudes, but no one should underestimate the ruggedness of Baxter's terrain or the vagaries of the weather in this unique microclimate.

MAINE HIGHLANDS

© HILARY NANGLE

If you want to spy a moose, the Baxter State Park region is a good bet.

Percival Baxter was by no means the first to discover this wilderness. His best-known predecessor was author Henry David Thoreau, who climbed Katahdin in 1846 from what's now Abol Campground but who never reached the summit. He didn't even reach Thoreau Spring (4,636 feet), named in his honor, but he did wax eloquent about the experience:

> This was that Earth of which we have heard, made out of Chaos and Old Night? . . . . It was the fresh and natural surface of the planet Earth, as it was made forever and ever. . . so Nature made it, and man may use it if he can.

Locked in what he called "a cloud factory," Thoreau declined to approach the summit: "Pomola [the Penobscot Indians' malevolent spirit of Katahdin] is always angry with those who climb to the summit of Ktaadn." And Native Americans traditionally stayed below the tree line, fearing the resident evil spirits. They all had a point. The current trail system didn't exist in the Native Americans' or Thoreau's days, of course (the first recorded summiteer was Charles Turner Jr. in 1804), so fatalities were probably more frequent, but even in the 21st century, climbers have died on Katahdin, and difficult rescues occur every year.

Regulations

The list of rules (www.baxterstateparkauthority.com/rules) is long at Baxter, and park rangers make the rounds to ensure enforcement. In the end, the rules are what make Baxter so splendid. Here are a few choice ones, but read through for any that might pertain to your plans.

No motorcycles, motorbikes, or ATVs are allowed in the park; **bicycles** are allowed only on maintained roads, not on trails, but the narrow, rough Perimeter Road is not particularly bike-friendly. When weather has been especially dry, bicyclists end up with mouthfuls of dust. **Snowmobiles** are restricted to certain areas; check with park rangers.

The park bans the use of **cell phones, TVs, radios,** and **CD or cassette players.** Noise levels in the park are strictly monitored by the rangers. There are no pay phones in the park, but all park rangers have radiophones.

No domestic animals are allowed in the park.

Baxter in Winter
The roads aren't plowed, campgrounds are closed, and the lakes and ponds are frozen solid, but Baxter authorities allow winter use of the park—with a multipage list of rigid restrictions. If this sounds appealing, contact the Baxter State Park Authority (www.baxterstateparkauthority.com/index.htm) for winter information.

DAY USE
Most day-use visitors are here to hike; on summer and fall weekends, you'll need to arrive early—even if you're not climbing Katahdin—because the day-use **parking areas** fill up. (There are only 284 day-use parking spots in the park; reserve in advance for $5.) On weekends, a long line forms before dawn at the Togue Pond Gate. A notice board at each gatehouse specifies which day-use parking areas are closed and which are open; there's almost always some place to park (although never alongside the Perimeter Road or campground access roads), and zillions of trails to hike, even if it may not be what you had in mind. So plan to arrive early (no later than 7am to hike Katahdin) or be prepared to be totally flexible about your hiking choice.

The northern end of the park is much less used than the southern end, so consider entering via the northern **Matagamon Gate** and hiking the wonderful trails in that part of Baxter. Take I-95 Exit 264 (Sherman) and then drive another 33 miles west, via Patten and Shin Pond, to Matagamon Gate.

Picnic areas, some with only a single table, are spotted throughout the park; most of the vehicle-accessible campgrounds also have picnic areas where noncampers are welcome. At the campgrounds, park in the day-use parking area, not the campers' lots.

◖ HIKING
Baxter's 200 or so miles of trails could occupy hikers for their entire lives. There's no such thing as "best" hikes, but some are indeed better (for various reasons) than others. Below is a range of options; consult the most recent edition of Stephen Clark's *Katahdin: A Guide to Baxter State Park and Katahdin* for details and more suggestions.

Trails originating at campgrounds all have registration clipboards; sign-in is required for Katahdin hikes and encouraged for all other hikes. All trails are blue-blazed, except for white-blazed ones that are part of the Appalachian Trail. Carved brown signs appear at all major trail junctions. All hikers are required to carry a flashlight.

Wear Polartec, polypropylene, Gore-Tex, or wool clothing, not cotton. Jeans can be a real drag (literally) if you get soaked in a stream, waterfall, or rainstorm. If you're planning to hike Katahdin, bring more layers than you think you'll need. Bring plenty of insect repellent, especially in June, when the blackflies are on the rampage. Wear light-colored long pants and a long-sleeved shirt and sweater with tight-fitting wrists and a snug collar.

Nature Trails and Family Hikes
Baxter has three easy nature trails that make ideal hikes for families with a range of age and skill levels. Nature-trail maps are available at park headquarters, the park entrance gates, and the nearest ranger stations to the trailheads. The 1.8-mile **Daicey Pond Nature Trail,** beginning at Daicey Pond Campground, circumnavigates the pond counterclockwise, taking about an hour. In August, help yourself to the raspberries near the end of the circuit. Best of all, you can extend the hike at the end by renting a canoe ($1/hour or $8/day) at the campground's ranger station, in the shadow of Katahdin's west flank. After that, take the easy 1.2-mile round-trip hike from the campground access road to Big Niagara Falls.

The other nature trails are **South Branch Nature Trail,** a 0.7-mile walk starting at South Branch Campground in the northern part of the park, and **Roaring Brook Nature Trail,** a 0.75-mile walk starting near Roaring Brook Campground, in the southeastern corner of the park, with dramatic views of Katahdin's east flank.

Other easy-to-moderate good family hikes are Trout Brook Mountain, Burnt Mountain, and Howe Brook Trail—all in the northern section of the park. Burnt Mountain has a fire tower at the top, and you'll need to climb the tower to see the view; the summit itself is quite overgrown. In the southern end of the park, a short easy trail leads from Upper Togue Pond to **Cranberry Pond.** An easy 5.2-mile round-trip from Daicey Pond Campground goes to **Lily Pad Pond** and then via canoe to **Windy Pitch Ponds.** Plan to picnic en route alongside Big Niagara Falls. (Before departing, stop at the Daicey Pond office and pick up the keys for the canoe locks at Lily Pad Pond.)

Howe Brook Trail, departing from South Branch Campground, requires fording the brook several times in summer, so wear waterproof footgear. The reward, higher up, is a series of waterfalls and little pools where the kids can swim (the water is frigid)—and flat boulders where you can picnic and sunbathe. In the fall, the foliage on this hike is especially gorgeous. For this six-mile hike, allow about four hours round-trip for lunch, a swim, and dawdling. Afterward, rent a canoe at the campground ($1/hour or $8/day) and paddle around scenic Lower South Branch Pond, in the shadow of North Traveler Mountain.

In 2006, after a multimillion-dollar fund-raising campaign, the Trust for Public Land donated 4,119 acres on the park's eastern flank to the Baxter State Park Authority. Centerpiece of the parcel is spectacular **Katahdin Lake**—long coveted by Percival Baxter for inclusion in the park. The 6.6-mile (round-trip) hike is relatively easy—via the trailhead at Avalanche Field in the southeastern corner of the park. If you're inclined to linger longer at the lake, year-round accommodations in the form of

housekeeping and American Plan (with all meals) options are available in the eight lakeside log cabins managed by Holly and Bryce Hamilton at **Katahdin Lake Wilderness Camps** (www.katahdinlakewildernesscamps.com, $125 pp adults, $55 pp ages 6-12; note, the only access is by foot or floatplane).

Moderate Hikes

Good hikes generally classified as moderate are Doubletop Mountain, Sentinel Mountain, and the Owl. If you decide to hike **Doubletop Mountain,** start at the Nesowadnehunk (Ne-SOWD-na-hunk) Field trailhead and go south to Kidney Pond Campground, an eight-mile one-way trek, up and over and down. It's much less strenuous this way. Allow about six hours.

Allow about six hours also for the **Sentinel Mountain Trail** from Daicey Pond Campground (6.6 miles round-trip) or Kidney Pond Campground (4 miles round-trip). It's not difficult; the only moderate part involves a boulder field about midway up. Take a picnic and hang out at the top; the view across to Katahdin, the Owl, and Mount O-J-I is splendid. With binoculars, you'll probably spot moose in the ponds below. Keep one eye on your lunch, however; a resident Canada jay at the summit has an acquisitive streak.

If the weather has been rainy, do not hike the Owl. It verges on being strenuous even under normal conditions.

Katahdin

Mile-high Katahdin, northern terminus of the Appalachian Trail, is the Holy Grail for most Baxter State Park hikers—and certainly for Appalachian Trail through-hikers, who have walked 2,158 miles from Springer Mountain, Georgia, to get here. Thousands of hikers scale Katahdin annually via several different routes. The climb is strenuous, requires a full day, and is not suitable for small children; kids under age six are banned above the tree line. You'll be a lot happier and a lot less exhausted if you plan to camp in the park before and after the Katahdin hike.

© HILARY NANGLE

Katahdin dominates the view from Daicey Pond Campground in Baxter State Park.

Katahdin, by the way, is a Native American word meaning "greatest mountain"—hence there's no need to refer to it as "Mount" Katahdin. The Katahdin massif actually comprises a single high point (Baxter Peak, 5,267 feet) and several neighboring peaks (Pamola Peak, 4,902 feet; Hamlin Peak, 4,756 feet; and the three Howe Peaks, 4,612-4,734 feet).

Even though Thoreau never made it to Katahdin's summit (Baxter Peak), countless others have, and the mountain sees a virtual traffic jam in summer and fall, particularly late in the season, when most of the through-hikers are nearing the end of their odyssey. Some hikers make the summit an annual ritual; others consider it a onetime rite of passage and then opt for less-trodden paths and less-strenuous climbs.

Rangers post weather reports at 7am daily at all the campgrounds. Heed them. Katahdin has its own biome, and weather on the summit can be dramatically different from that down below. At times, especially in high-wind and blowing-snow conditions, park officials close trails to the summit. They don't do it frivolously; Katahdin is literally a killer.

Besides the requisite photo next to the Baxter Peak summit sign, Katahdin's other "been there, done that" experience is a traverse of the aptly named **Knife Edge,** a treacherous 1.1-mile-long granite spine (minimum width three feet) between Baxter and Pamola Peaks. If you can stand the experience, hanging on for all you're worth next to a 1,500-foot drop, go for it; the views are incredible. But don't push beyond your personal limits; you're hours from the nearest hospital.

The most-used route to Baxter Peak is the **Hunt Trail,** a 10-mile round-trip that coincides with the Appalachian Trail from Katahdin Stream Campground; allow at least eight hours round-trip. Other routes start from Russell Pond, Chimney Pond, Roaring Brook, and Abol Campgrounds. See Stephen Clark's *Katahdin* guide for specific route information.

CAMPING

Facilities at 10 campgrounds vary from cabins to tent sites, lean-tos, and bunkhouses; there also are several backcountry campsites supervised by the nearest campground rangers.

All the campgrounds close October 15; they open on various dates beginning May 15. One hike-in campground (Chimney Pond) opens June 1. Fees are $30/night for a lean-to or tent site, $20/night for outlying tent sites, $11 pp per night in a bunkhouse, and $55/night for a two-person cabin. Fees must be prepaid and are not refundable.

The park's only cabins are in the southwest corner—at **Daicey Pond Campground** (10 cabins) and **Kidney Pond Campground** (12 cabins). Daicey Pond has the best views—Katahdin from every cabin, and the sunrises are unmatched. With two exceptions, Kidney Pond cabins overlook the pond and surrounding woods, but not the mountains; Doubletop Mountain is in back of the campground. All cabins have woodstoves (for heating only), gas lanterns, outhouses, outside fireplaces, and beds; bring your own linens, water, food, and whatever else you think you might need.

Chimney Pond and **Russell Pond Campgrounds** are hike-in; the distance from the Roaring Brook parking area to Chimney Pond is 3.3 miles, and to Russell Pond is seven miles. Chimney Pond has a bunkhouse and nine four-person lean-tos. Russell Pond has a bunkhouse, five lean-tos, and three tent sites—all arranged around the pond, where you can also rent canoes ($1/hour or $8/day).

South Branch Pond Campground, close to Matagamon Gate, has an eight-person bunkhouse, 12 lean-tos, and 21 tent sites in an especially idyllic setting; seven of the lean-tos are right next to the pond.

June-August, bring fabric screening if you're staying in a lean-to; a tarp may foil the blackflies, mosquitoes, and no-see-ums, but you don't want to suffocate.

Getting Reservations

Reservations for any campsite within the park for the dates May 15-Oct.15 operate on a rolling basis and must be made beginning four months in advance by mail, in person at park headquarters, via phone, or online. For instance, to request a site or sites for July 14, you'll need to mail your reservation to arrive no earlier than March 14 (see www.baxterstateparkauthority.com/camping/ for the reservation schedule). July gets booked up first, then August; weekends are more crowded than weekdays. Maximum length of stay is seven nights per campground, 14 nights total in the park. If you make a reservation and can't keep it, be considerate and call or email the park headquarters to cancel, even though you won't receive a refund. It will give someone else a chance to enjoy the beauty of Baxter.

PARK ACCESS, INFORMATION, AND SERVICES

Unless you're hiking the Appalachian Trail (AT), the only way to enter the park is via one of two gates. **Togue Pond Gate** at the southern end of the park is the choice for visitors from Greenville or Millinocket and is the most-used gate. At the northeast corner of the park is **Matagamon Gate,** accessible via I-95, Patten, and Shin Pond Road. Both gates are open 6am-10pm early May-mid-Oct. After Columbus Day, the gates are open 6am-7pm, weather permitting.

Before you enter the park, check your fuel gauge and fill up your tank; there are no fuel facilities in the park.

If you have camping reservations, don't arrive at the park with more people than your receipt indicates; the rangers at the gate check this, and the campground rangers even do body counts to be sure you haven't stuffed extra people into cabins or lean-tos.

Appalachian Trail through-hikers are required to register at the Abol Stream kiosk at the edge of the park as well as at Katahdin Stream Campground, before ascending Katahdin.

Maine residents have free daytime use of the park—one of Governor Baxter's stipulations. At the gates, **nonresidents** pay $14/

vehicle for a day pass; a nonresident season pass is $39. (A rental car with Maine plates no longer qualifies in the resident category.) Everyone must pay for camping. A day-use parking reservation is $5.

There is no public transportation to or within Baxter State Park, so you'll need a car, truck, or bicycle. The park's website lists a couple of enterprises that offer shuttle services. RVs are also allowed, but maximum size is nine feet high, seven feet wide, and 22 feet long (or 44 feet for a car and trailer). Baxter is not a drive-through park. The park's 43-mile unpaved **Perimeter Road,** connecting Togue Pond and Matagamon Gates, is narrow and corrugated, evidently deliberately so; it's designed for access, not joyriding.

A few trail loops include the Perimeter Road, but avoid walking on it if possible. In wet weather, you'll be splashed by cars navigating the potholes; in hot weather, the gritty dust gets in your teeth. Hitchhiking is discouraged, but you can usually get a ride if you need it.

Information

Books, maps, and information are available at **Baxter State Park Headquarters** (64 Balsam Dr., Millinocket, 207/723-4636 or 207/723-5140, www.baxterstateparkauthority.com, 8am-5pm Mon.-Fri. year-round), at campground ranger stations, and at the Togue Pond Visitor Center.

Pick up a *Day Use Hiking Guide* at the visitors center or at park headquarters. The fold-out map, quite sketchy, also has basic info on major park trails.

The Allagash and St. John Rivers

ALLAGASH WILDERNESS WATERWAY

In 1966, the state established a 92-mile stretch of the Allagash River as the Allagash Wilderness Waterway (AWW), a collection of lakes, ponds, and streams starting at Telos Lake and ending at East Twin Brook, about six miles before the Allagash meets the St. John River. Also recognized as a National Wild and Scenic River, the waterway's habitats shelter rare plants, 30 or so mammal species, and more than 120 bird species. You'll spot plenty of wildlife along the way.

Arranging a flexible schedule to do the Allagash gives you enough slack to wait out strong winds on the three largest lakes. Such a schedule also allows time for a leisurely pace, side trips, and fishing along the way.

Highlights

Allagash Lake, one of the state's most pristine lakes, feeds into Chamberlain Lake from the west via Allagash Stream. No motors are allowed on Allagash Lake, making it especially tranquil. The side trip is six miles one-way, and

water levels (too high or too low) can make it a rough go. At **Lock Dam,** built in 1841, ask about conditions. Between Chamberlain and Eagle Lakes, on a narrow spit of land seemingly in the middle of nowhere, stand two of the waterway's oddities—two old **steam engines,** relics rusted out and long abandoned. Once linked to the Eagle Lake and Umbazooksus Railroad, the short-run Lombard Hauler locomotives operated around the clock six days a week 1927-1933, hauling 125,000 cords of pulpwood annually for the timber industry.

An exhilarating white-water run is the reward for tackling **Chase Rapids,** a nine-mile stretch starting just below Churchill Dam. You can usually expect Class II white water—sometimes Class III—if you launch with the dam's water release schedule. Two hours after the dam has been closed, the route can get pretty "bony," so you're likely to be hung up temporarily several times along the way. In the afternoon, wear well-secured sunglasses to protect yourself from glare. For a fee, the Churchill rangers will portage your gear to the end of the rapids, so you have to get only yourselves and your canoes to the end of the run. If you're at all hesitant about making the run, or the water is too low, the rangers will also carry passengers to the end of the run.

Allagash Falls, eight miles before the end of the waterway and 13 miles before the river meets the St. John, is a dramatic 40-foot drop. Needless to say, you'll need to portage here (on the right)—but only 0.3 mile.

When to Go

Canoeing season on the AWW usually runs from late May (after "ice-out") to early October. Water and insect levels are high and water temperature is low in May-June; July-August are most crowded but have better weather; September can be chilly, but the foliage is fabulous. The average annual temperature in this area is 40°F; winter temperatures average 20°F. The AWW is accessible in winter for snowmobiling and ice fishing. Winter camping is permitted at the Chamberlain Thoroughfare Bridge parking lot on a first-come, first-served basis.

Camping

There are 80 signposted campsites along the waterway; all are first-come, first served. July-August, when canoe traffic is fairly heavy, don't wait too late in the day to set up camp. Sites are $12 pp per night for nonresidents, $10 pp per night for Maine residents. Children under age 15 are free. Fees are payable in advance at the ranger station where you enter the waterway. Theoretically, you're expected to stay only one night at any site, but an extension usually isn't a big problem.

Sporting Camps

Close to one of the major waterway access points, and roughly 50 miles north of Millinocket, **Nugent's Camps** (Chamberlain Lake, 207/944-5991, www.nugentscamps.com) is reachable only by boat, floatplane, or snowmobile or skis. Built in 1936, the clean cabins are determinedly rustic, all have privies, and there's a common shower. Although housekeeping rates are available (bring your own sleeping bags and towels; no meals; $50 pp per night), opt for the American Plan ($135 pp per day includes linens and all meals) to save lugging victuals and to take advantage of the hearty family-style meals in the character-full main lodge. Cabin and dinner only are $80 pp.

Also on the paddling route are **McNally's Ross Stream Camps** (207/944-9995 or 254/241-1704, www.mcnallysrossstreamcamps.com), on Chemquasabamticook Stream, better known as Ross Stream. The six circa 1940 camps have woodstoves, running water, showers, and flush toilets. Linens are provided in summer. Rates, including all meals, are $110 pp per day, kids under age 12 are $60. Canoe and kayak rentals begin at $10.

Information

The **Maine Bureau of Parks and Lands,** in the Department of Conservation (Northern Region, 106 Hogan Rd., Bangor, 207/941-4014, www.parksandlands.com), manages operations on the Allagash Wilderness Waterway. During the season, rangers are stationed at key sites all along the route. Call or write the office for a useful free map and a list of outfitters. For seasonal water-level information, call the **Forest Service** (207/435-7963, 8am-5pm daily late Apr.-mid-Dec.).

Information also is available from **North Maine Woods** (207/435-6213, www.north-mainewoods.org) and the **Northern Forest Canoe Trail** (802/496-2285, www.northern-forestcanoetrail.org).

A particularly lovely pictorial overview of the waterway is naturalist Dean Bennett's excellent book *Allagash: Maine's Wild and Scenic River.*

Getting There

The Allagash Wilderness Waterway is accessible by private logging roads at specified points. You'll need to pay the North Maine Woods gate fees when you cross onto timber-company land ($7/day Maine residents, $12 nonresidents; ages 14 and under or 70 and older have free day use; special fees apply to sporting camp visitors; cash or check only). You can get here from Greenville or Millinocket, or from the Aroostook County community of Ashland. Official access points with parking areas are Chamberlain Thoroughfare Bridge, Churchill Dam, Umsaskis Thoroughfare, and Michaud Farm. Winter access sites are different.

THE ST. JOHN RIVER

Like the Allagash, the St. John has long been associated with the timber industry—and the spring log drives when huge loads of giant logs were driven *upstream* and eventually to the mills. The history of the late-19th and early-20th-century lumbering era is especially colorful, loaded with tales of unbelievably rugged conditions and equally rugged characters. It's only a memory since the log drives ended, but you'll see remnants of the industry along the way.

When to Go

The prime season for canoeing the St. John River is May-early June, although many years there's enough water until late June. North Maine Woods (NMW) monitors daily water levels on the river, so you'll need to call a day in advance (207/435-6213) to confirm that water flow is adequate, especially after mid-June. NMW suggests that 3,000 cfs (cubic feet per second) is the minimum for enjoyable canoeing—to avoid grounding out or extensive portaging—but experienced canoeists recommend a minimum of 2,000 cfs.

June brings out the blackflies at campsites, so be prepared to combat them with high-powered bug repellent and tight-fitting, light-colored clothing.

Camping

Between Baker Lake and Allagash village, there are 28 riverside camping areas with a total of more than 60 sites. All are signposted. Most are on the left (west) side of the St. John; some require climbing the bank to reach level ground. Campsites are first-come, first-served. If a site is filled, you'll have to move on, anywhere from 2-5 more miles. Camping is allowed only at designated sites. About half of the sites have at least one sheltered picnic table, a real plus that

saves rigging tarps for meals in rainy weather. Other facilities are outhouses and fire rings. Sites are $12 pp per night for nonresidents, $10 pp per night for Maine residents. Children under age 15 are free.

Even though the St. John has no dams, a heavy rainstorm can swell the water level, causing the river to rise as much as three feet overnight. Keep this in mind when lashing your canoe for the night; secure it well and as high as possible.

Information

Download a St. John River brochure from **North Maine Woods** (207/435-6213, www.northmainewoods.org), the nonprofit recreational manager for this area. The Northwoods Maine Gate fee is $7/day Maine residents, $12 nonresidents; ages 14 and under or 70 and older have free day use; cash or check only.

Getting There

There are five main access points for the St. John River, plus the final takeout point downriver at the top of Maine. From the southernmost point, **5th St. John Pond,** it's 143 miles to the town of Allagash. The easiest way to get here is via one of Greenville's two flying services. Downstream are **Baker Lake, St. Juste Road Bridge,** and **Moody Bridge,** the latter being best for low-water conditions; drive in via Ashland (about 3.5 hours on American Realty Rd.). By the time you get to **Priestly Bridge,** you're more than halfway downriver—almost not worth the trip. Opt instead for starting at Baker Lake or Moody Bridge—or, if you're going with a guiding service, wherever your guides prefer to start. Shuttle arrangements can be complicated for St. John trips. Work out all details in advance, and include access and camping fees in your budget.

GUIDES

Neophyte canoeists should think twice before setting out without a guide on multiday canoe trips. You should have experience with Class II white water before attempting either of these rivers. Even experienced paddlers who are unfamiliar with Maine's rivers ought to assess the pluses and minuses of a do-it-yourself expedition versus a guided trip. It's rare to find a deserted campsite. The costs of provisioning, arranging shuttles, camping fees, and gear rental can add up—and guides spare you from cooking and cleanup. It's not a bad trade-off.

Most guide services have their specialties, but few specialize in only one river. Some arrange trips all over the state; others go to Canada, Alaska, and beyond. Veteran guide services that offer trips on both the St. John and the Allagash Rivers include Mike Patterson's **Wilds of Maine Guide Service** (207/338-3932, www.wildsofmaine.com), the Cochrane family's **Allagash Canoe Trips** (207/237-3077, www.allagashcanoetrips.com), and Blaine Miller's **Allagash Guide Inc.** (207/634-3748, www.allagashguide.com).

If you're planning to visit a sporting camp within reasonable distance of the Allagash River, check to see whether it arranges Allagash trips; a number of them do.

Costs vary for guided trips, usually including everything except transportation to Maine; figure around $175-200 pp per day.

Greenville and Vicinity

Greenville (pop. 1,646) is the jumping-off point for the North Woods—ground zero for floatplanes and ski-planes maintaining contact with remote hamlets and sporting camps. Although barely larger than a small town, it's the big city for tinier communities in every direction. The truth is, it's a bit like a frontier town itself. Greenville looks out over **Moosehead Lake**—Maine's largest—from its southern end. Moosehead is 40 miles long and covers 117 square miles, but counting all the niches and notches, its shoreline runs to more than 400 miles.

The origin of the lake's name has to be from the large number of antlered critters hereabouts, especially along the shore toward the outposts of **Rockwood** or **Kokadjo**. In addition to moose-watching, you can wear yourself out with all the recreational choices: swimming, boating, fishing, camping, hiking, white-water rafting, golfing, picnicking, birding, skiing, snowshoeing, and snowmobiling. In spring, summer, and fall, you can also cruise the lake aboard an antique steamer.

Moosehead has been attracting outdoors enthusiasts, primarily hunters and anglers, since the 1880s. The long haul from lower New England, ending with the passenger train from Bangor, apparently was worth it for the clean air, prime angling, and chance to rough it. That era has long passed, and the clientele has changed noticeably, but Greenville's downtown still has a rustic air, the outlying hamlets even more so.

Greenville was incorporated in 1836, just before the timber industry began to take off. Steamboats hauled huge corrals ("booms") of logs down the lake to the East Outlet of the Kennebec River (East and West Outlets are both on the west side of Moosehead Lake), where river drivers took over. All that ended fairly recently, in the 1970s. The steamer *Katahdin* is a relic of that colorful era.

Greenville's lakeshore twin, **Greenville Junction,** once a busy rail crossroads, has now become one of those blink-and-you'll-miss-it places, but you can still eat and sleep here. Twenty miles northwest of Greenville on Route 6/15 is the small and somewhat crowded hamlet of Rockwood**,** the closest spot to Kineo, a lake icon marked by cliffs that plunge to the water. One of the best Kineo views is from the public boat landing, on a loop road just off Route 6/15. Route 6/15 then continues west, along Brassua Lake and the aptly named Moose River, to **Jackman**—a lovely 30-mile drive popular with moose-watchers.

When you make inquiries about the Moosehead area, you'll hear lots of references to "ice-out." It's almost a season—the time when winter's ice releases its grip on the lake and spring and summer activities can begin. Depending on the severity of the winter, ice-out occurs anywhere in early-late May. Fisherfolk arrive, plumbing begins to work, and a few weeks later the blackfly larvae start to hatch. Spring is under way.

SIGHTS
◖ Cruise on the *Kate*

A turn-of-the-20th-century wooden vessel once used in the lumber industry, the steamboat *Katahdin,* locally called the *Kate,* has been converted to diesel and now runs cruises on 40-mile-long Moosehead Lake from its base at the bottom of the lake next to the **Moosehead Marine Museum** (12 Lily Bay Rd., Greenville, 207/695-2716, www.katahdincruises.com). The best trip for children is the regular three-hour midday run (the schedule changes annually). Tickets are $33 adults, $29 seniors, $18 ages 11-16; $3 kids under age 11. A 4.5-hour **Mount Kineo cruise** ($38 adults, $34 seniors, $21 ages 11-16; $5 kids under age 11), three

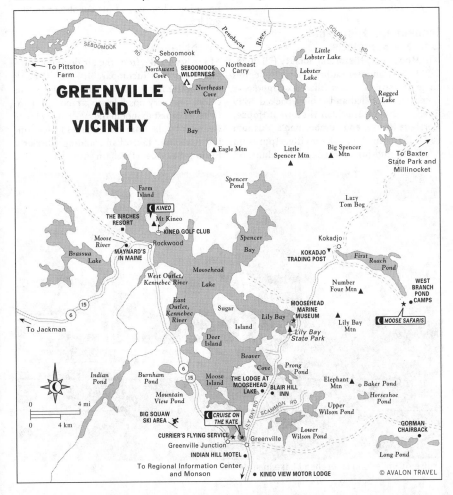

© AVALON TRAVEL

hours if passenger minimum isn't met, is offered occasionally July-early October. An all-day head-of-lake trip (call for rates) operates the last Saturday of September, when it's chilly, but the fall foliage is fantastic. There is indoor and outdoor seating, and dinner is available on board. Smoking and high-heeled shoes are not allowed; the boat is wheelchair-accessible. Cruises operate on a regular schedule July-early September, but only on weekends late May-June and on a limited schedule through September. Reservations are advisable for the longer cruises.

Moosehead Historical Society Museums

The **Moosehead Historical Society** (207/695-2909, www.mooseheadhistory.org) operates three properties in Greenville. Most impressive is the artifact-filled and exhibit-packed 1899 **Eveleth-Crafts-Sheridan Historical House, Carriage House, and Lumberman's Museum** (444 Pritham Ave., Greenville, 1pm-4pm Wed.-Fri. mid-June-early Sept., $5 adults, $2

children). Guided tours of the main house and adjacent carriage house provide a personalized glimpse into town life, leisure activities, and the roll of the logging industry; the last tour is at 3:30pm. The **Center for Moosehead History** (6 Lakeview St., Greenville, 10am-4pm Thurs.-Sat.) has a nice display of Native American artifacts. It shares a location with the **Moosehead Lake Aviation Museum**, which highlights the aviators and bush pilots who operated in the region. On the grounds are two granite sculptures, part of the Thoreau Wabanki Trail honoring Thoreau and his Penobscot Indian guides.

Flightseeing

Moosehead Lake from the air during fall-foliage season is incomparable—you'll bank over Mount Kineo, survey a palette of autumn colors, and very possibly see a moose or two. (They're easiest to spot in the sad-looking tracts clear-cut by the timber companies.) Most fun is the lakefront takeoff and landing. **Currier's Flying Service** (Pritham Ave./Rte. 6/15,

Cruise 40-mile-long Moosehead Lake in style aboard the *Kate*.

© HILARY NANGLE

Greenville Junction, 207/695-2778, www.curriersflyingservice.com) flies a whole slew of on-demand trips in vintage seaplanes over Mount Kineo, Squaw Mountain, and Katahdin. Costs range $40-165 pp with a two-passenger minimum. Call to arrange a flight schedule; planes depart from Greenville Junction, where the Currier family also operates a small gift shop, selling Sue Currier's hand-sewn wall hangings.

◖ Kineo

Moosehead Lake's most distinctive landmark, at the lake's "waistline," is Mount Kineo, a 763-foot-high chunk of green-tinged rhyolite or felsite that erupted from the bowels of the earth about 425 million years ago. Smoothed by glacial activity on the west side, Kineo has sharp cliffs on its east side. The chert-like volcanic stone (not flint; Maine has no native flint) was a major reason Native Americans glommed on to the Moosehead area thousands of years ago; its hardness served them well for weapons and fishing and hunting tools. The surrounding woodlands yielded prime birch bark, supplying raw material for canoes, carryalls, and even shelters. Stone tools and arrowheads still turn up occasionally, especially along the shore when the water level is low, but most have been carted off by amateur collectors. Resist the urge to take home samples. Once the site of a monumental summer resort hotel, Kineo is rather sleepy these days, with only a nine-hole golf course, dating from the 1860s, as a reminder of that heyday. But if your schedule permits, go; a hike up Mount Kineo is a must.

Kineo is accessible via rough roads on the east side of the lake, but just barely. It's far easier and better to rent a boat on the west side of the lake in Rockwood (but beware of fluky lake winds), or take the Rockwood Village-Kineo shuttle service, which departs regularly from the village dock ($10 adults, $5 ages 6-11). Most Wednesdays during the season, the steamboat *Katahdin* makes a 1.5-hour stop at the base of Mount Kineo—not enough time for a major hike but ample to get a sense of the site.

From the dock, the Indian and Bridle Trails lead to the top, but signposting is a bit lax; keep an eye out for blue blazes. The Bridle Trail is easier. Allow about three hours round-trip for the hike; carry a picnic. In winter, when Moosehead Lake freezes solid, you can get to the Kineo peninsula by snowmobile (weather and common sense determine the schedule), but the trails are too full of snow for hiking.

ENTERTAINMENT AND EVENTS

Moosemainea, an annual monthlong moose-oriented festival sponsored by the Moosehead Lake Region Chamber of Commerce, combines canoe, rowboat, and mountain-bike races; a family fun day; moose safaris; and even a "best moose photo" contest. Register your own moose sightings on a huge map at the chamber of commerce. Events take place in Greenville and Rockwood mid-May-mid-June.

The first full weekend in September, the **International Seaplane Fly-In Weekend** is a four-day event at Greenville and Greenville Junction drawing seaplanes from all over New England for public breakfasts, a two-day crafts fair, flightseeing, and more. Beds are very scarce during the Fly-In, so either book well ahead to be part of it or wait for another time to visit.

In February, the **100-Mile Wilderness Sled Dog Race** attracts dog teams from throughout the Northeast.

SHOPPING

The Greenville area, and especially downtown Greenville, is filled with shops selling moose-related merchandise and other goods with a woodsy theme.

If you're entering Greenville from the south, cresting the last hill you'll see on your right the **Indian Hill Trading Post** (Rte. 15, Greenville, 207/695-2104 or 800/675-4487, www.indianhill.com), one-stop shopping with camping gear, clothing, footwear, an ATM, fishing and hunting licenses, souvenirs, and a supermarket that sells ice, liquor, groceries, and even live lobsters. In short, if it doesn't have it, you don't need it.

On the main drag downtown, the

LITTLE FARM IN THE BIG WILDERNESS

© HILARY NANGLE

Head to Pittston Farm for a meal or an overnight adventure.

Trust me: If you continue up Route 6/15 from Greenville 20 miles to Rockwood, and then another 20 miles on an unpaved road, you're guaranteed to have an adventure at **Pittston Farm** (207/280-0000, www.pittstonfarm. com).

The South and North Branches of the Penobscot River wrap around Pittston Farm, which is truly an oasis in the wilderness. Once a working logging camp where teamsters were based, its two impressive barns and a three-story farmhouse remain relatively intact. Current owners Bob and Jenny Mills, along with their family, are investing in updating this National Historic Register-listed property, without losing its come-as-you-are hospitality. Although the frills are few, the welcome is warm, the price is right, and the experience is priceless. You'll likely spot a moose or two on the way; drive defensively.

This unincorporated territory, officially called the Pittston Academy Grant, once was a major center for timber operations along the Penobscot River. Now the 100-acre river-side farm is known as *the* place to go by car, flying service, or snowmobile for meals fit for lumberjacks. Dress down (suspenders will fit right in). All-you-can-eat breakfasts are served beginning at 7am, lunch from a menu is available 11am-3pm, and the huge dinner buffet is served 5pm-7pm; BYOB. It's hearty home cooking, definitely meat-oriented, and you won't eat alone. The homemade pies and cookies alone are worth the trip. Reservations are advisable. No credit cards are accepted.

After eating, spend some time in the museum, blacksmith shop, and chapel (a former potato barn), stroll the grounds, and visit the horses, goats, and cattle. Canoe and kayak rentals are available, and there are plenty of hiking trails in the area.

Accommodations include 15 shared-bath rooms in the comfy main lodge, air-conditioned rooms with private baths in the carriage house, and four no-frills cabins with private baths; rates for all begin around $60 pp with three all-you-can-eat meals, $105 pp without meals.

© HILARY NANGLE

A shuttle runs from the dock in Rockwood to Kineo, allowing visitors access to its golf course and hiking trails.

Moosehead Lake Indian Store at Kamp Kamp (Pritham Ave., Greenville, 207/695-0789), is jam-packed with woods-related merchandise, from moose and bear doodads to antiques.

Just beyond the town offices, **Joe Bolf** (Minden St., Greenville, 207/695-3002, www.joebolf.com) works magic with a chain saw; don't miss the "band."

Peter Templeton is keeping a family tradition of boatbuilding alive at **Ship Shape** (296 Pritham Ave., Greenville, 207/695-2402). Templeton specializes in building replica models of the steamships that used to ply Moosehead Lake, but he builds other models, too, and takes commissions.

For reading material, **Gabriel's Studio** (Rte. 6/15, Greenville, 207/695-3968) has a good selection of inexpensive used books.

RECREATION
Multisport Outfitters
The biggest and best outfitter in this neck of the woods is **Northwoods Outfitters** (Main St., Greenville, 866/223-1380 or 207/695-3288, www.maineoutfitter.com), in downtown Greenville right across from the *Katahdin*. Northwoods should be your first stop no matter what your choice of activity. These folks are the region's outdoor pros. Even if you have your own equipment and have no need of a guide, stop in for advice and information, maps, and perhaps a cup of java and final posting from the civilized world from its **Internet Café.** Northwoods does it all, offering rental equipment, shuttles, and guided trips: Moose safaris, lake cruises, mountain biking, hiking, sailing, canoeing, white-water rafting, fishing, dogsledding, snowmobiling, snowshoeing, and so on. Even better, it uses guides who are passionate about their individual sports. It's open 9am–5pm daily with extended hours during peak seasons.

Lily Bay State Park
Lining the eastern shore of Moosehead Lake, 925-acre **Lily Bay State Park** (Lily Bay Rd.,

Greenville, 207/695-2700, www.parksand-lands.com, $3 Maine resident adults, $4.50 nonresident adults, $1.50 nonresident seniors, $1 ages 5-11, free over age 65 and under age 5) is the place to go for moose-watching, fishing, picnicking, hiking, canoeing, swimming, birding, and camping at some of Maine's most desirable waterfront sites. The park is open 7am-11pm daily May 1-October 15, but it's accessible in winter for cross-country skiing and snowmobiling. From Greenville, head north on Lily Bay Road for eight miles; the park is on the left.

◖ Moose Safaris

Ed Mathieu is the chief honcho of **Moose Country Safaris** (191 N. Dexter Rd., Sangerville, 207/876-4907, www.moosecountrysafaris.com), usually operating in the Greenville area. Reservations are essential. Moose safaris, lasting about four hours, go out at 5:45am and 2pm mid-May-mid-October by 4WD and canoe or kayak; there's a two-person minimum, and the cost is $150 for two.

Northwoods Outfitters also offers three-hour moose safaris by land or water ($50 pp); Currier's does its moose-watching from the air.

If you go on your own, swampy **Lazy Tom Bog** is one of the region's best moose-watching haunts. Plan to go soon after sunrise or just before sunset. From Greenville, take Lily Bay Road north to Kokadjo, 18 miles. A mile later, when the road forks, take the left fork (signposted Spencer Pond Camps). Continue 0.5 mile to a small bridge. Park on either side of the bridge and have your camera ready, preferably with a long lens. If you want to emerge from your car, or even stick your lens through the open window, you may need to douse yourself with insect repellent. And try to keep the kids quiet.

Hiking

Except for early June, when blackflies torment woodland hikers as well as moose, the Greenville area is sublime for hiking. The chamber of commerce has a list that includes hiking directions for **Number Four Mountain,**

Big and Little Squaw Mountains, Big and Little Spencer Mountains, and **Elephant Mountain** (a B-52 crash site). Also ask at the chamber for directions to **Moose Mountain,** off Route 6/16, topped with the first fire tower in the United States. It's a bit rickety but still there. The hike is moderate to difficult and takes about four hours round-trip.

Northwoods Outfitters offers **guided hikes** with Registered Maine Guides for $150 for a long half day.

Mountain Biking

Given all the backwoods trails, mountain biking is very popular. You can bring a bike and strike out on your own, rent a bike, or go with a guide or group. Remember, however, that bicycles are *not* allowed on logging roads; the huge lumber trucks are intimidating enough for passenger vehicles, never mind bicycles.

Mountain bike rentals are available from **Northwoods Outfitters** for $25/day. Also available are kids' bikes, child seats, and Trail-a-Bikes.

Twenty miles north of Greenville, **The Birches Resort** (Rockwood, 207/534-7305, www.birches.com) rents mountain bikes ($50/day) and sends you off on its network of mountain-bike trails. It also offers a four-hour group trail ride ($60 pp includes lunch).

Water Sports

In addition to Lily Bay State Park, there's fine swimming at **Red Cross Beach** in downtown Greenville. The parking area is near the Masonic Temple on Pritham Avenue, and a short path through the woods leads to the beach. You'll find lifeguards, picnic tables, and even floats. Another swimming spot is at the boat launch in Greenville Junction.

CANOEING AND KAYAKING

If you're not an experienced paddler, be cautious about canoeing or kayaking on Moosehead Lake. The sheltered bays and coves are usually safe, but you can have serious trouble in the open areas—especially the stretch between Rockwood and Kineo. Do not attempt it; even

MOOSE TRIVIA

- Typical height for an adult bull moose is seven feet at the shoulders; typical weight is about 1,000 pounds, with 1,400-pounders also recorded. Cow moose run about 800 pounds.

- Moose usually lumber along, seemingly in no hurry, but they've been known to run as fast as 35 mph.

- The bull moose's rack of antlers can measure six feet across; the largest recorded was a hair under seven feet.

- Moose give birth in late May-early June, after a 35-week pregnancy; singles are normal, twins are less common, triplets are very rare. A newborn calf weighs 20-30 pounds, occasionally 35 pounds.

- Moose have extremely acute senses of hearing and smell, but their eyesight is pitiable. If you're utterly quiet and stay downwind of them, they probably won't spot you.

- Moose have no history of harming humans, but stay out of their way during "the rut," when they're charging around and out of the woods looking for females in heat. This usually occurs mid-September-mid-October, when the foliage is at its peak, hikers are out and about, and Moose Lottery winners are in hot pursuit.

MOOSE-WATCHING HOT SPOTS

- Sandy Stream Pond, Baxter State Park
- Grassy Pond, Baxter State Park
- Russell Pond, Baxter State Park
- Sawtelle Deadwater, off Shin Pond Road, about seven miles northwest of Shin Pond
- Lazy Tom Bog, off Lily Bay Road, about 19 miles north of Greenville
- Route 6/15, between Greenville Junction and Rockwood, on the west side of Moosehead Lake
- The Golden Road, between Ripogenus Dam and Pittston Farm

---

pros have been swamped by rogue winds on that route. At Lily Bay State Park, you can launch a canoe from the waterfront campsites and easily make it to Sugar Island.

At **Northwoods Outfitters,** canoe or kayak rentals begin at $25/day; weekly rentals and deliveries are available, as is shuttle service.

BOAT RENTALS

If you want to explore Moosehead Lake's numerous nooks and crannies, the best way is with a powerboat. **Beaver Cove Marina** (16 Coveside Rd., Beaver Cove, 207/695-3526, www.beavercovemarina.com) rents 14-16-foot fishing skiffs for $125/day and 18-23-foot powerboats $275-310/day. Careful: The lake is shallow.

WHITE-WATER RAFTING

From Greenville, you're well positioned to raft either the Kennebec or the Penobscot Rivers.

Check with Northwoods Outfitters, which also provides transportation.

FLY-FISHING

The best local resource for fly-fishing, hands down, is the **Maine Guide Fly Shop and Guide Service** (34 Greenville Rd., Greenville, 207/695-2266, www.maineguideflyshop.com). This veteran operation, owned by Dan Legere, will set you up with a guide and all the equipment you need to do it right. Rates for a guided drift-boat experience, including lunch and gear, are $350 for one person, $400 for two.

Golf

The most popular, scenic, and windswept course in the area is the nine-hole **Kineo Golf Club** (207/534-9012, www.mooseheadlakegolf.com), built for the 500 or so guests at the turn-of-the-20th-century Mount Kineo House. At every turn you'll see Mount Kineo, or

Moosehead Lake, or both. There are dynamite views. The course is open June-mid-October, and you'll need to get there by boat.

Built in the 1920s, nine-hole **Squaw Mountain Village Golf Course** (Rte. 6/15, Greenville Junction, 207/695-3609) is now part of a modern condo complex. Greens fees are low, and the pace is unhurried.

Winter Sports
DOGSLEDDING AND SNOWSHOEING

Former Outward Bound instructor, Certified Wilderness Responder, and Registered Maine Guide Stephen Madera is the ideal guy to head into the Maine woods with via dogsled. His company, **Song in the Woods** (207/876-4736, www.songinthewoods.com), offers trips of all lengths into the wilderness around Gulf Hagas and the Roach Ponds. You can even mush your own team. Rates for dogsledding begin at $350 for two people for a short day trip, $400 for two for a full day with lunch. Snowshoeing adventures begin at $70. Multiday trips are available. In summer, Madera also offers customized hiking and paddling trips into the region, beginning at $85 pp for a half day.

SNOWMOBILING

The biggest winter pursuit hereabouts is snowmobiling, thanks to an average 102-inch annual snowfall and 300 miles of Greenville-area trails connecting to the entire state network. It's pretty competitive trying to get a bed in winter if you don't plan well ahead; be forewarned. Incidentally, if you're curious about how people get around northern Maine in winter, check out the parking lot at the Greenville school complex (Pritham Ave.); the vehicle of choice is the snowmobile.

A particularly popular loop is the 160-mile **Moosehead Trail,** which circumnavigates Moosehead Lake: Greenville to Rockwood to Pittston Farm, Seboomook, Northeast Carry, Kokadjo, and back to Greenville. You can start at any access point along the route and go in either direction.

The chamber of commerce has snowmobile trail maps and can put you in touch with local snowmobile clubs. Thanks to these energetic clubs, trails are well maintained and signposted.

For snowmobile rentals or guided tours, contact Northwoods Outfitters. Rates begin around $180 for a rental sled. An introductory guided tour is $99.

CROSS-COUNTRY SKIING

The Birches Resort (Rockwood, 207/534-7305, www.birches.com) has 40 miles of groomed cross-country ski trails winding through an 11,000-acre nature preserve. A trail pass is $14 full day, $11 half day for adults; kids are $10 or $8. Full-day rates include use of the hot tub and sauna. Equipment rentals are available at the Birches Ski Touring Center. For lodging at the Birches, escape to one of its remote woodstove-heated trailside yurts on a guided tour for $159 pp including equipment, meals, and guide.

For a real adventure, ski between the **Appalachian Mountain Club**'s (www.outdoors.org) three wilderness lodges—Medawisla (undergoing renovation), Little Lyford, and Gorman Chairback—and privately owned West Branch Pond Camps. Groomed wilderness trails connect the properties, which all welcome adventurers with woodstove-heated cabins and hot family-style meals. Both guided and self-guided adventures are available, as is gear shuttle.

ACCOMMODATIONS

Lodging in the area varies from just a few grades above camping to exquisite country inns and lodges.

Country Inns

Wow! Combine a magnificent Victorian hillside manse with eye-popping views of Moosehead Lake with an English manor house decor and ambience, and the result is the (€ **Blair Hill Inn** (Lily Bay Rd., Greenville, 207/695-0224, www.blairhill.com, from $325), where Dan and Ruth McLaughlin (escapees from the software industry) have created a relaxing, elegant retreat. Eight spacious second- and third-floor guest rooms in the magnificent 1891 home are furnished with comfy antiques and accented with ornate woodwork, fabulous lighting, and fine paintings. Some have working fireplaces, most have expansive lake views, all have flat-screen TVs and Wi-Fi, and many of the bathrooms have separate soaking tubs and large showers. A truly gourmet breakfast is included, and a five-course dinner ($59 pp) is available Thursday-Saturday. If you want a different angle on the expansive views, relax in the dining room, living room, or comfy lounge; even better, score a seat on the front porch. The grounds include lovely gardens, greenhouses, a huge barn, and rolling lawns edged with stone walls. During summer, the inn hosts a concert series on the lawn. Service is top-notch, yet unobtrusive; the innkeepers will arrange activities and make recommendations on request.

Elegance and comfort are also bywords at Linda and Dennis Bortis's **The Lodge at Moosehead Lake** (Lily Bay Rd., Greenville, 207/695-4400, www.lodgeatmooseheadlake. com, from $275), which immerses guests in a chic version of a cabin in the woods. Perhaps the most astonishing feature is the furniture. Each of the five guest rooms in the main building has a theme—Trout, Loon, Moose, Totem, and Bear—and each has beds and mirrors hand-carved by local woodworking master Joe Bolf, plus lots of accessories, to carry it out. All but the Trout have dramatic views of Moosehead Lake. Whirlpool tubs, fireplaces, and camouflaged video players are in each room as well as in the three bi-level waterview carriage-house suites—named Allagash, Baxter, and Katahdin. In Allagash and Baxter, lumber-era boom chains hold swaying queen-size beds with incredible lake views; Katahdin has a fireplace in the *bathroom*. In the guest pantry is a small gift shop with clever moose-themed items, snacks, and dozens of videos for guests to borrow. There is Wi-Fi throughout. Upstairs is the two-bedroom Kineo suite, with a kitchen, a living-dining room, a big deck, and jaw-dropping views. Breakfast is included all year. North-country dinners are available to guests; these vary seasonally.

Just steps to downtown shops and restaurants, the 1849 **Captain Sawyer House** (18 Lakeview St., Greenville, 207/695-2369, www. captainsawyerhouse.com, $145-165) feels far removed, thanks to its side street location with lake views from the front porch. The inn also has a locally popular first-floor tavern, where dinner ($23-27) is served on weekends.

Motels

The **Kineo View Motor Lodge** (Rte. 15, Greenville, 207/695-4470 or 800/659-8439, www.kineoview.com), three miles south of Greenville, sits on a prime hilltop with a dead-on view of Mount Kineo and gorgeous sunsets. Opened in 1993, the chalet-style three-story motel has 12 good-size guest rooms with phones, TVs, fridges, microwaves, and balconies) for $89-99. Two suites, one with a full kitchen, are $179-199 each. Rates include continental breakfast late May-mid-October. This is a great place to bring kids—there's lots of acreage to run around, including nature trails. Outside are picnic tables and a grill. Some rooms accommodate pets, $10 by reservation.

Two miles closer to Greenville than Kineo View and with a hilltop view delivering elevated views down Moosehead Lake, the **Indian Hill Motel** (127 Moosehead Lake Rd./Rte. 15, Greenville Junction, 207/695-2623 or 800/771-4620, www.indianhillmotel.com, $79-119) is a vintage motel with 15 good-size guest rooms that have air-conditioning, phones, cable TV, Wi-Fi, and tiny baths. New owners in 2012 have been adding little niceties. Ask for a room far off the highway to lessen the traffic noise. In the commercial complex across Route 15 are a supermarket and the chamber of commerce.

You're practically *in* the lake at **Chalet Moosehead** (Birch St., Greenville Junction, 207/695-2950 or 800/290-3645, www. mooseheadlodging.com, $119-165). The newer two-story building is where you want to stay; first- and second-floor guest rooms have whirlpool tubs, fridges, TVs, phones, air-conditioning, and private balconies with dynamite views. The older two-story section has seven basic, somewhat tired, guest rooms, some with kitchenettes. Kids age five and under stay free; pets ($20/dog) are allowed in the older units. Dock space is free if you bring your own boat, and guests have free use of canoes, paddleboats, gas grills, and a private swimming area.

For a room with vroom, consider the **Moose Mountain Inn** (314 Rockwood Rd., Greenville, 800/792-1858, www.moosemountaininn. com, $90-110), a vintage few-frills motel at the base of Little Moose Mountain. It's owned by Northwoods Outfitters, which operates a snowmobile and ATV rental outpost here. All guest rooms have TVs, air-conditioning, microwaves, refrigerators, and Wi-Fi. There's also a pool on the premises. Rates include a continental breakfast.

Sporting Camps and Rental Cabins

Ease into sporting camp life at **Maynard's in Maine** (Rockwood, 207/534-7703 or 888/518-2055, www.maynardsinmaine.com), operated by Gail and William Maynard. Cross the Rockwood bridge, take a left, and you're on tarred road right to the property. Although it's not remote by most sporting camp standards, it's a rural gem. Meals are served in the central lodge; guests stay in the cabins, all with full baths and most with views over the Moose River to the Blue Ridge (a blaze of color during foliage season). The food is great—freshly made and home-baked. Guests choose from two entrées each night. At first glance it may seem more run-down than rustic, but the cabins are comfy, the mattresses firm, and the plumbing is inside. Rates, including breakfast, dinner, and a packed lunch, are $70 adults, $40 ages 3-12; without meals, it's $45 adults, $20 kids. Cabins have 1-3 bedrooms. Pets are allowed for $20/stay. Motorboat rental is $55/day, canoes and kayaks are $20.

Eric Stirling is the fourth-generation host at **West Branch Pond Camps** (Kokadjo, 207/695-2561, www.westbranchpondcamps.com). Lining the shore of First West Branch Pond, overlooking White Cap Mountain, are eight classically rustic cabins with indoor plumbing and evening electricity. Eric is fixing them up, adding new roofs, replacing mattresses and furnishings, and repairing screens and broken boards. For wilderness lovers who prefer a tad of comfort, this is the real thing. The camps are set upon 30 private acres surrounded by conservation lands, and the authenticity and peacefulness are all-encompassing. Fly-fishing, hiking, and canoeing are the major pursuits here. Cross-country skiers and snowshoers come in winter. If you're hoping to spot a moose, well, the gangly mammals often stroll right through the property, even peeking in the kitchen window. Speaking of the kitchen: When the bell rings for meals, guests head to the 1890 lakeside lodge and vacuum up the hearty cuisine described in one upscale national magazine as "simple, soulful Yankee cooking." Dinner ($20-30 pp, including dessert) is open to nonguests by reservation. BYOB. Most guests stay for a week, and the many repeats make it tough to book space, but the daily rate is $115 pp adults, $50 ages 5-11, which includes meals, lodging, a boat, firewood, and linens. Well-behaved pets are $20/stay. Take Lily Bay Road from Greenville 17 miles; turn right onto an unpaved road (signposted West Branch Ponds) and go 10 more miles. It's open May-September and late January-late March. In winter, heat is by woodstove and there are privies as well as two heated bathhouses with shower and toilet in each.

The **Appalachian Mountain Club** (603/466-2727, www.outdoors.org/mainelodges) operates two trail-connected traditional sporting camps in the 100-Mile-Wilderness region. Both are historical and rustic, with woodstoves providing the only cabin heat in winter. **Little Lyford,** dating from 1874, near Gulf Hagas and the Appalachian Trail, Little Lyford Pond, and the Pleasant River, is the most primitive. Guests share a central bathhouse with hot showers, a winter sauna, and composting toilets. It's a full-service lodge with three daily meals provided. **⟨ Gorman Chairback** on the shores of Long Pond is the newest and provides the most amenities. It has eight renovated log cabins, a central bathhouse with showers and a sauna, and a new environmentally friendly lodge. A third lodge, **Medawisla,** sited where the Roach

River flows into Second Roach Pond, is currently closed for renovation, but plans call for it to reopen; ask for info. Packages that include gear shuttle for lodge-to-lodge skiing are available. Rates vary by season, and you'll get the best price if you join the AMC. Nonmember rates, including meals, begin at $131 pp.

Forty-three miles northeast of Greenville is **Nahmakanta Lake Camps** (207/731-8888, www.nahmakanta.com), Don and Angel Hibbs's oasis in the wilderness on Nahmakanta Lake. Nine restored cabins right on the lake have screened porches, full kitchens, and woodstoves. There is no electricity. Each cabin has a private but separate bathroom. Choose from the full American Plan, including all meals ($150 pp per day adults, plus $8 multiplied by age for ages 1-17); the Modified American Plan, including supper ($118 pp per day adults, $6 multiplied by age for children), or housekeeping ($85 pp per day adults, $4 multiplied by age for kids). Canoes and kayaks are provided; boats and motors are $60/day; guides are available. Summer access is via 25 miles of gravel roads or floatplane. Dogs ($20/stay) are welcome with advance notice.

Fifty acres of woods etched with trails surround the new, nicely appointed **Moosehead Hills Cabins** (418 Lily Bay Rd., Greenville, 207/695-2514, www.mooseheadhills.com). Three hillside cabins have nice Moosehead views. A path and a road lead to the shoreline, where guests have use of a dock and kayaks. Also available are two cabins on seven-mile-long Loon Pond, also known as Wilson Pond, each with a private dock and water frontage. Peak rates are $210-375/night, $1,410-2,600/week with a one-week minimum in July-August and a two- or three-night minimum the rest of the year. Dogs are allowed in some cabins for $15/pooch/day.

Camping

The **Maine Forest Service** supervises and maintains free campsites with fireplaces and outhouses, many on the shores of Moosehead Lake. Most are accessible only by boat on a first-come, first-served basis. For information, contact the Maine Forest Service **office** (downtown Greenville, 207/695-3721).

At the northern end of Moosehead Lake, about 5.5 miles south of the Golden Road, **Seboomook Wilderness Campground** (Seboomook Village, 207/280-0555, www.seboomookwildernesscampground.us), has 84 wooded and open tent and RV sites, Adirondack shelters, and housekeeping cabins (no linens), many right on the water. Everything is very rustic, although there is a central bathhouse with flush toilets and free hot showers. Request a site on the eastern side, away from the long-term RV area. Facilities include a small, shallow beach and a grocery store with a lunch counter. History buffs take note: This is the site of a World War II German POW camp. Camping sites are $18-30/day; shelters are $30 d; cabins are $50-100/day. Weekly rates are also available. Seboomook's store is open all winter for snowmobilers and cross-country skiers; campsites are open mid-May-November. Canoes, kayaks, and motorboat rentals are available. The campground is about 28 unpaved miles north of Rockwood.

You can't get much closer to the water than some of the primitive sites at **South Inlet Wilderness Campground** (Frenchville Rd., Kokadjo, 207/695-2474 evenings, 207/695-3954 winter, $16-20). Although near a dirt road, many of the sites front on First Roach Pond. There's also a field for bigger RVs but no hookups. Facilities include a beach, a boat launch, privies, fire rings, and picnic tables.

Plan well in advance to snag one of the primo waterfront sites at **Lily Bay State Park** (Lily Bay Rd., Greenville, 207/695-2700); on weekends July-August, campsite reservations are essential, with a two-night minimum (call 207/287-3824 and have a MasterCard, Visa, or Discover card ready, or visit www.campwithme.com). Only the lucky will find a last-minute space, even though there are 93 sites in two clusters; none have hookups. Camping fees are $24 nonresidents, $14 Maine residents, plus the reservation fee of $2/site/night.

FOOD

The range of dining experiences in and near Greenville is surprisingly broad. While choices are plentiful in summer, they're scanty in the off-season.

Local Flavors

The gossip is as good as the grub at the **Kokadjo Restaurant & Trading Post** (3424 Lily Bay Rd., Greenville, 207/695-3993, www.kokadjo. com, 7am-9pm daily), right across the road from First Roach Pond. There might not be a sign out front; it's kind of quirky that way. Inside find a small shop, a take-out counter, and a restaurant with a menu running from burgers to prime rib. Fred and Marie Candeloro also rent seven cabins, all with whirlpool tub, a few with fireplaces (from $150).

Extremely popular among local residents for breakfast and lunch is **Flatlanders** (38 Pritham Ave., Greenville, 207/695-3373). The best choice is the broasted chicken, which one waitress described as "kinda like fried chicken but cooked in a pressure cooker so it's more healthy." Whatever; everyone agrees it's tasty.

Buy pizza and subs, beer and wine coolers, and worms and crawlers at **Jamo's** (Pritham Ave., Greenville, 207/695-2201). OK, skip the latter pairing, but the pizza's decent, and the Dagwood sandwiches, made on fresh-baked pita bread, earn raves.

Northwoods Gourmet Girl (Pritham Ave., 207/570-8112, www.northwoodsgourmet-girl.com), a.k.a. Abby Freethy, has gained a national following for her line of condiments and specialty foods, and she's now also offering comfy and stylish chef's clothing. She also offers dinners, usually once weekly in summer, in her small shop. Go! The menu is small but the choices are broad and the food is excellent. Freethy also makes take-out chicken potpies in the off-season.

Look for the **Café Crepe** food truck (207/970-8677, 11am-6pm Mon.-Thurs., to 7pm Fri.-Sat., to 4pm Sun.) parked on the lakefront in downtown Greenville. The seasonal operation serves both savory and sweet crepes, with most priced $5-8.

For cheap eats and breakfast served all day, pop into **Auntie M's Family Restaurant** (13 Lily Bay Rd., Greenville, 207/695-2238, 5am-3pm daily).

Casual Dining

A dining bright spot in downtown Greenville, **Rod-N-Reel Cafe** (44 Pritham Ave., Greenville, 207/695-0388, 4pm-9pm Wed.-Sun.) reels them in for reliable home-style food with flair. Fish is the dominant theme, from the name to the decor to the menu, but you can get steaks, chicken, and pasta as well. Dinner entrées are $12-24, but lighter fare is available. Friday and Saturday are prime rib nights. In peak summer it usually opens for lunch too.

For upscale pub food, such as wraps and salads, as well as burgers and chili, detour into the **Stress-free Moose** (65 Pritham Ave., Greenville, 207/695-3100, 11am-10pm Mon.-Thurs., 11am-midnight Fri.-Sat., 11am-9pm Sun.). While you can sit inside, the big wraparound porch is the place to while away an afternoon or evening.

In Greenville Junction, with fantastic lake views, is **Kelly's Landing** (Rte. 6/15, Greenville Junction, 207/695-4438, www.kellysatmoosehead.com, 7am-9pm daily year-round, $8-21). The food is hit or miss, but you can't beat the location. If the weather's fine, dine on the deck; if not, the dining rooms have big windows on the lake. A kids' menu is available. An all-you-can-eat buffet breakfast is served Sunday 8am-11am. There's always a crowd, and boaters can tie up at the dock.

Experience sporting-camp life and meals without getting too far into the woods at **Maynard's in Maine** (207/534-7703 or 888/518-2055, www.maynardsinmaine.com), an authentic main lodge and cabins overlooking the Moose River in Rockwood. Go for the experience, but don't expect gourmet fare, just good home cookin'. Maynard's is open to nonguests (breakfast 7am-9am daily, dinner 5:30pm-7:30pm daily, reservations required). There's a full menu for breakfast and a choice of two entrées at dinner ($13-17), which includes soup or salad, potato, vegetable, and rolls. Everything is homemade or baked and served family-style in the pleasant dining room.

Another good choice for a fine meal in a great setting is **Northern Pride Lodge** (3405 Lily Bay Rd., Frenchtown Township, 207/695-2890, www.northernpridelodge. com, 5pm-8pm daily), 18 miles north of Greenville overlooking First Roach Pond in Kokadjo. Entrées, such as pork tenderloin medallions, baked salmon, and roast duckling, are $20-28. Reservations are required by noon. If you don't want to drive the moose slalom back to Greenville, rooms ($110) are available with shared baths and include breakfast.

If you're willing to drive a good 10 miles into the woods to dine, book a table at **West Branch Pond Camps** (Kokadjo 207/695-2561, www. westbranchpondcamps.com). This is the real deal, with a set menu offered at 6pm Monday-Saturday and at noon Sunday; prices range $20-30, depending on the meal. Dining here is an adventure, and the food never disappoints; everything is made from scratch in a historical kitchen. If you're worried about making the drive at night, make reservations for the Sunday noon turkey dinner. Advance reservations are required.

Fine Dining

The elegant **◖ Blair Hill Inn** (Lily Bay Rd., 207/695-0224) serves a fixed-price five-course menu ($59) 5:30pm-8:30pm Thursday-Saturday evenings in the elegant dining room and adjacent glassed-in porch high on a hill with sweeping sunset views over Moosehead Lake. The inn has an indoor wood-burning grill, so meats and fish are grilled, and much of the produce comes from the inn's greenhouses and gardens. And almost everything is made from scratch—from sorbet and ice cream to breads and soups; special diets can be accommodated, including vegan with notice. It's open mid-June-mid-October. Arrive early to enjoy a sunset cocktail in the lounge or on the porch.

INFORMATION AND SERVICES

The **Moosehead Lake Region Chamber of Commerce** (888/876-2778, www.moosehead-lake.org) has information about member businesses and area activities.

DeLorme Mapping produces a widely available foldout *Map and Guide of Moosehead Lake,* with excellent detail and information on sightseeing and recreational pursuits.

The **Shaw Public Library** (N. Main St., Greenville, 207/695-3579) has archives loaded with North Woods lore.

State agencies with offices in Greenville are the **Maine Warden Service** (MWS, 207/695-3756) and the **Maine Forest Service** (MFS, Lakeview St., Greenville, 207/695-3721), where you can view a Smokey Bear display. The Greenville MWS office, with jurisdiction for all search-and-rescue missions of Maine's acreage, undertakes at least one search-and-rescue mission per week. The MFS, besides fire-spotting duty, is also responsible for a number of public campsites in the region.

In Greenville, the Indian Hill Trading Post has **public restrooms,** as do the chamber of commerce office and the Moosehead Marine Museum, next to the *Katahdin* wharf. In Greenville Junction and Rockwood, there are restrooms at the public boat landings.

GETTING THERE

Greenville is about 2 hours from Millinocket via Routes 11 and 6/15 or 70 miles and 2 hours via the (mostly unpaved) Baxter State Park, Golden, Greenville, and Lily Bay Roads. It's about 34 miles or 45 minutes to Dover-Foxcroft via Route 6/15 and about 50 miles or 1 hour to Jackman via Route 6/15. It's about 72 miles or 1.5 hours from Bangor via Route 15.

GETTING AROUND

Greenville flying services operating small pontoon- or ski-equipped planes act as the lifelines to remote North Woods sporting camps, campsites, rivers, lakes, and ponds inaccessible overland. In some cases, road access exists, but you'll jeopardize your vehicle, your innards, and maybe your life along the way. **Currier's Flying Service** (Pritham Ave./Rte. 6/15, Greenville Junction, 207/695-2778, www.curriersflyingservice.com) and **Jack's Air Service** (Pritham Ave., Greenville, 207/695-3020), based in downtown Greenville, provide on-demand charter service to remote locales. Both firms have flat hourly rates if you want to create your own itinerary.

You don't need a plane to get to Kineo, but you will need a boat. First, drive the 20 miles along Route 6/15 to Rockwood, where the lake is narrowest—about 4,000 feet across. The **Kineo Shuttle**, a pontoon boat, runs on a set schedule, departing hourly in July-August, less frequently spring and fall, from the Rockwood public landing (on the village loop just off the highway). Just show up and climb aboard. The fare is $10 pp round-trip.

Many of the **roads** in the Greenville area are unpaved; paper-company roads tend to be the best maintained, because access is essential for their huge log trucks and machinery. But others, especially roads leading to sporting camps, can become tank traps in spring—April-May—and after a heavy downpour. Before setting out during those times—especially if you don't have a 4WD vehicle—check on road conditions. Ask the chamber of commerce, the Maine Forest Service, the county sheriff, or the sporting camp owners.

Dover-Foxcroft Area

At the bottom of Piscataquis (piss-CAT-uh-kwiss) County, **Dover-Foxcroft** (pop. 4,213) is the county seat, hub for the surrounding towns of **Milo** (pop. 1,847), **Brownville Junction** (pop. 1,250), **Sangerville** (pop. 1,343), **Guilford** (pop. 1,521), **Abbot** (pop. 714), and **Monson** (pop. 686). Here's an area that's often overlooked, probably because Greenville, Moosehead Lake, and Baxter State Park are just up the road. But it's easy to spend a couple of days exploring here—notably for dramatic Gulf Hagas Reserve and Borestone Mountain Sanctuary, but also for a handful of out-of-the-way towns few visitors get to appreciate.

One town growing steadily in renown is Monson, 20 miles northwest of Dover-Foxcroft and 15 miles south of Greenville. Incorporated in 1822, Monson has an old reputation and a new one. The old one comes from its slate quarries, first mined in the 1870s, which shipped slate around the nation for sinks, roof tiles, blackboards, and even urinals. A considerable Finnish community grew up here to work the quarries; their descendants still celebrate traditional holidays. Although the industry has declined, and only one company still operates, Monson slate monuments adorn the gravesites of John F. Kennedy and Jacqueline Kennedy Onassis. You can still see an abandoned quarry pit on Pleasant Street, near Lake Hebron, on the western side of town.

Monson's current fame comes from Appalachian Trail (AT) through-hikers, whose energetic grapevine carries the word about the town's hospitality to the rugged outdoors folk nearing the end of their arduous trek from Springer Mountain, Georgia. The Monson stopover comes just before the AT leg known as the 100-Mile Wilderness, so it's a place to regroup, clean up, and rev up for the grueling, isolated week or 10 days ahead.

Sangerville, incorporated in 1813, is the birthplace of the infamous Sir Harry Oakes, a colorful adventurer who acquired a fortune in Canadian gold mining. Murdered in bed in his Nassau (Bahamas) mansion in 1943, gazillionaire Oakes was interred in Dover-Foxcroft. His killer was never found. Also born in Sangerville was Sir Hiram Maxim, inventor of the Maxim gun. These days, it's the East Sangerville Grange that gets the attention, especially in winter, when there's entertainment accompanied by fantastic desserts.

Dexter and Corinna are actually in the Sebasticook Valley area, but since many visitors pass through them on Route 7, they're included here.

SIGHTS
Monson

Most folks zip through this pretty little lakeside village, but lakeside **Monson** is worth a linger. It's a major stop on the Appalachian Trail, the last vestige of civilization before northbound hikers enter the infamous 100-Mile Wilderness on the way to Katahdin.

Low's Covered Bridge

In 1987, the raging Piscataquis River, swollen by spring rains, wiped out 130-foot-long **Low's Covered Bridge,** near Sangerville. Named after settler Robert Low, the original bridge was built in 1830 and replaced in 1843 and 1857. The current incarnation, a well-made replica, reopened in 1990 at a cost of $650,000. It's one of only nine covered bridges now in Maine. Close to Route 16/6/15, the bridge is 3.7 miles east of Guilford and 4.5 miles west of Dover-Foxcroft.

Katahdin Iron Works

Only a lonely stone blast furnace and a charcoal kiln remain at Katahdin Iron Works, the site of a once-thriving 19th-century community where iron mining produced 2,000 tons of ore a year and steam trains brought tourists to the three-story Silver Lake House to "take the waters" at Katahdin Mineral Springs. Today most visitors drive down the unpaved 6.5 miles from Route 11 and stop just across the road, at the North Maine Woods **KI Checkpoint,** for hiking in Gulf Hagas Reserve. Entrance to the KI site (as it's known locally) is free, but you'll have to pay a fee to proceed on the road.

Lake Onawa

Four-mile-long **Lake Onawa** is the mountain-ringed setting for the charming hamlet of Onawa, once linked to civilization only by train. Then came the road, and passenger service ceased, leaving Onawa as a summer colony with a year-round population of three. A prime attraction is an incredible 126-foot-high wooden railroad trestle (featured in one of Stephen King's films) that challenges even brave-hearted souls. Acrophobes, forget it. There's a walkway alongside, but it's still scary; don't attempt it on a windy day, and keep in mind that the tracks are still active. During World War II, the trestle was protected by African American security guards, among them Edward Brooke, the late U.S. senator from Massachusetts. The 1,400-foot-long trestle, officially the Ship Pond Stream Viaduct, soars over Ship Pond Stream at the southern end of the lake, about 0.5 mile beyond the cluster of cottages. To reach Onawa, from Route 6/16/15 at the northern edge of Monson, take the partly unpaved Elliotsville Road northeast; turn right at the Big Wilson Stream bridge, and then take the next left onto Onawa Road. Continue about three miles to the settlement.

Historical Society Museums

Locals are proud of their history, and a handful of small museums are worthy of visits if you're a history buff.

The **Dexter Historical Society** (207/924-5721) operates three museums on its downtown Grist Mill campus (off Rte. 23, 10am-4pm Mon.-Fri., 1pm-4pm Sat. mid-June-early Sept., 1pm-4pm Mon.-Sat. Sept.): the one-room Carr Schoolhouse, the 1825 Miller's house, and the water-powered Grist Mill. The society's Abbott Museum headquarters (Rte. 7/23, 10am-4pm Mon.-Sat. late May-mid-Oct., noon-4pm Wed.-Fri., 10am-4pm Sat. winter) now doubles as a shop with works by local artisans. Most of the historical exhibits are downstairs. Admission is free, but donations are encouraged.

In downtown Monson, the old town hall has been reborn as the home of the **Monson Historical Society** (Main St., 207/876-3073, 10am-2pm Sat.), with a Scandinavian gift shop downstairs and exhibits upstairs (check out the birch shoes).

ENTERTAINMENT AND EVENTS

October-May, the East Sangerville Grange Hall hosts its monthly Saturday night **Winter Coffee House Series** where the entertainment is fab and the desserts are beyond amazing as local cooks vie to outdo each other.

Live music, community theater, movies, and other entertainment are regularly scheduled at the **Center Theatre for the Performing Arts** (20 E. Main St., Dover-Foxcroft, 207/564-8943, www.centertheatre.org), which opened in 2006 in a nicely renovated 300-seat movie theater. Ask about the local doctor who was married on stage during a presentation by the Maine Hysterical Society, complete with reception line during intermission.

The last Saturday in April, the early-season **Piscataquis River Canoe Race** covers eight miles of mostly flat water between Guilford and Dover-Foxcroft. An hour-long family-oriented race goes under Low's Covered Bridge. Starting time is 11am, next to the Guilford Industries factory.

The one-day **Maine Whoopie Pie Festival** (www.mainewhoopiepiefestival.com) is held in June, with tastings, tours, crafts, and entertainment.

The **Piscataquis Valley Fair** (www.piscataquisvalleyfair.com) takes place the fourth weekend in August. A family-oriented traditional county fair, it features agricultural exhibits, a pig scramble, a homemade ice cream parlor, fireworks, and a carnival. It's at the Piscataquis Valley Fairgrounds (Fairview Ave., just south of Rte. 6/15, east side of Dover-Foxcroft).

Throughout the summer, Finn dances take place on Saturday nights at the **Finnish Farmers Club.** Look for the small sign hanging in front of the white frame building two miles south of Monson village on the west side of Route 6/15. Expect dancing, perhaps traditional costumes, coffee, and pulla bread along with Finnish folk music performed by Woodsong.

Leaping Lipizzaners! **Isaac Royal Farm** (849 Range Rd., Dover-Foxcroft, 207/564-3499) operates a renowned equestrian school with world-class instructors, holds dressage shows, and stages don't-miss themed equestrian theatrical presentations complete with music, choreography, and costumes.

SHOPPING

You'll find a handful of arts and crafts shops in Monson and Abbott.

Buy wonderful maple syrup, great dressings, and bison meat at **Breakneck Ridge Farm** (160 Mountain Rd., Blanchard Township, 207/997-3922, www.breakneckridgefarm.com). The farm has a few open houses each year; private tours are available year-round by reservation.

Bob Moore is the king of maple in these parts. At **Bob's Sugar House** (252 E. Main St./Rte. 15, Dover-Foxcroft, 207/564-2145, www.mainemaplesyrup.com), you'll find pure Maine maple syrup, maple butter, maple cream, maple popcorn, maple barbecue seasoning, and the list goes on.

Works by more than 100 artisans and crafters, from fine to schlocky, along with specialty foods and gifty items fill **Mainely Crafts** (445 Corinna Rd./Rte. 7, 207/924-5900).

RECREATION

Peaks-Kenny State Park

Get organized to arrive at **Peaks-Kenny State Park** (Sebec Lake Rd., Dover-Foxcroft, 207/564-2003, www.parksandlands.com, $6 nonresident adults, $4 Maine resident adults, $2 nonresident seniors, $1 ages 5-11, free under age 5) well before 11am on weekends in June-August—after that, you may be turned away or have to wait. This particularly scenic park on 14-mile-long Sebec Lake has 50 picnic sites, a playground, a lifeguard-staffed sandy beach, nine miles of hiking trails, and 56 campsites. Canoe rentals are $3/hour.

Hiking

For details on these or other hikes, consult *North Woods Walks* by Christopher Keene (a guide for Northwoods Outfitters) or AMC's *Maine Mountain Guide,* available in local bookstores.

CONSERVING FOR THE FUTURE

Anyone who has visited Maine's North Woods knows that this landscape of woods, water, and mountains is a treasure. While the state and federal government had protected bits and pieces, most notably Baxter State Park, Nahmakanta, and Gulf Hagas, it was a hopscotch pattern that left the connecting areas, including those sheltering the famed 100-Mile Wilderness section of the Appalachian Trail, vulnerable.

Enter the **Appalachian Mountain Club (AMC),** which in 2003 launched the Maine Woods Initiative, a strategy for land conservation that combines outdoor recreation, resource protection, sustainable forestry, and community partnerships in the 100-Mile Wilderness region. Through its work on the initiative, AMC is protecting land from development and maintaining public access for recreation in perpetuity.

In 2003, the AMC acquired the Katahdin Iron Works tract, a spectacular 37,000-acre parcel of wilderness that includes the headwaters of the West Branch of the Pleasant River and abuts federally protected Gulf Hagas. That wasn't enough. In 2009, the AMC acquired the Roach Ponds Tract, which abuts not only the Katahdin Iron Works Tract but also the state's Nahmakanta Public Reserved Land. The purchase of the 29,500-acre Roach Ponds tract was a historic transaction that marked the creation of a 63-mile-long corridor of conservation land stretching from the AMC's Katahdin Iron Works property near Greenville north to Baxter State Park. The holdings comprise nearly 650,000 acres of conservation land that's a playground for outdoor enthusiasts.

Within the AMC's 66,500-acre Maine Woods Property alone are more than two dozen ponds, more than 80 miles of managed recreational trails and ski routes, and more than 150 miles of dirt roads, and a 21,000-acre ecological reserve to protect the West Branch watershed as well as a few other special zones to protect other vital ecological resources. The remaining acreage is a working forest, maintained with sustainable techniques, and open to hunters, anglers, paddlers, mountain bikers, wildlife-watchers, skiers, snowshoers, and campers.

Even better, it's possible to immerse oneself in this chunk of heaven without sacrificing all creature comforts. Within the Maine Woods Property are three AMC-managed sporting camps: Medawisla Wilderness Lodge and Cabins, Little Lyford Lodge and Cabins, and Gorman Chairback Lodge and Cabins; the privately owned West Branch Pond Camps; and a mix of drive-in, hike-in, and paddle-in campsites.

BORESTONE MOUNTAIN SANCTUARY

Owned and maintained by the Maine Audubon Society (www.maineaudubon.org), **Borestone Mountain Sanctuary** (Elliotsville Rd., Elliotsville Plantation, 207/631-4050, Oct.-May 207/781-2330, 8am-sunset May-Oct., $5 adults, $3 ages 6-18 and over age 60) is a 1,600-acre preserve that provides a wonderful hiking experience for all ages. The two-mile (each way) moderately difficult trail to the rocky open summit delivers ample rewards at the top: full-circle views that include Lake Onawa below and the mountains of the 100-Mile Wilderness. Foliage season is especially dramatic here. Allow 4-5 hours for the four-mile round-trip, including a halfway-up stop at the Sunrise Pond visitors center, with displays on local flora and fauna; don't miss it. Pets are not allowed. From Route 6/16/15 at the northern edge of Monson, take the partly unpaved Elliotsville Road northeast 8.5 miles to the trailhead.

APPALACHIAN TRAIL

Sample the country's eastern footpath from the trailhead north of Monson on Route 6/15, just south of Spectacle Ponds. Unless you're a serious hiker, you won't want to venture too far, as this is one of the most difficult sections of the trail.

© HILARY NANGLE

Peaks-Kenny State Park borders 14-mile-long Sebec Lake.

◖ GULF HAGAS RESERVE

Hiking in and around Gulf Hagas Reserve, a spectacular 400-foot-high, 3.5-mile-long wooded and rocky gorge along the West Branch of the Pleasant River, requires registering first at the **KI Checkpoint** (207/965-8135) operated by North Maine Woods, the forest recreation-management association. (KI is short for Katahdin Ironworks.) The checkpoint is one of the entrances into the **KI Jo-Mary Multiple Use Forest,** a 175,000-acre working forest. (Jo-Mary is the name of a legendary Indian chief.) The checkpoint is open 6am-9pm (sometimes later on midsummer weekends) early May-Columbus Day. The staffers have maps of the reserve ($2) and KI Jo-Mary ($3); do not hike Gulf Hagas without the map. Access is $12 for nonresidents, $7 for Maine residents. No bicycles, motorcycles, or ATVs can go beyond this point. Camping at one of the 60 scenic primitive sites in this area costs an extra $10 pp per night, $5 for seniors. It's wise to call the checkpoint ahead of time to reserve one of the sites, which have outhouses, picnic tables, and fire rings. The policy is carry-in, carry-out. There's also a commercial campground here.

You'll need to drive about seven miles from the checkpoint to one of the two parking areas; remember that logging trucks have the right-of-way on this road. As you walk from your vehicle toward the gulf, you'll go through **The Hermitage,** a 35-acre preserve of old-growth pines. Gulf Hagas Reserve, a National Natural Landmark that's part of the Appalachian Trail corridor, is no cakewalk. Almost weekly, rangers have to rescue injured or lost hikers who underestimate the terrain. Ledges are narrow, with 100-foot drop-offs, and rain can make them perilous. Leave rambunctious children at home; the section beyond **Screw Auger Falls** is particularly dangerous for kids under 12. Wear waterproof hiking boots—you have to cross a stream to gain access to the reserve.

Caveats aside, the hike is fantastic—especially mid-September-early October, when the leaves are gorgeous and the bugs have retreated. Carry a compass and a flashlight and allow 6-8 hours for the 8.3-mile canyon circuit (although there are shortcuts if you tucker out before the end). Most hikers do the loop clockwise. North Maine Woods trails are blue-blazed; a spur of the Appalachian Trail is white-blazed. The trails are open mid-May-late October, but atypical weather can affect the schedule. The checkpoint is 11.5 miles northwest of Brownville Junction (6.5 miles northwest of Rte. 11).

The Appalachian Mountain Club's Little Lyford Camps is a convenient base for hiking Gulf Hagas.

Multiuse Trails

Stretching 27 miles, the **Newport/Dover-Foxcroft Rail Trail** is extremely popular, especially among horseback riders. From its Newport base on the north side of Route 7 to its end near Fairview Street in Dover-Foxcroft, the trail passes through towns and rural countryside, including farms, woods, and wetlands, and edges Sebasticook and Corundel Lakes, the east branch of the Sebasticook River, and the Piscataquis River.

The 10-mile Guilford Memorial River Walk edges the Piscataquis River from Guilford to Abbot. The trailheads are off Route 15 in Guilford, east of the athletic fields, and at the Sangerville Station bridge on Route 23.

Water Sports

Lakes and rivers color much of the map blue in this region. If you have your own boat, quiet-water paddling options include the Sebec River above Milo, the Piscataquis River above the dam in Guilford, Lake Hebron in Monson, and Branns Mill Pond in Dover-Foxcroft.

Kayak rentals for three-mile-long Lake Hebron are available from **Lakeshore House** (9 Tenney Hill Rd./Rte. 5/15, Monson, 207/997-7069, www.thelakeshorehouse.com) for a donation to the local charity.

ACCOMMODATIONS
Bed-and-Breakfasts

On a prominent hilltop and surrounded by gardens, the dark-red-painted **Guilford Bed and Breakfast** (Elm St./Rte. 6/15/16, Guilford, 207/876-3477, www.guilfordbandb.com,

$129-149), built by a woolen mill owner as a wedding gift for his daughter, exudes history, wealth, and prominence of a bygone era. Innkeepers Isobel and Harland Young, from Ohio, were longtime guests before buying the inn in 2006 and then undertaking a historical restoration, completed in 2009. A big, screened porch wraps around the Queen Anne-style Victorian's front, leading into the formal hall and spacious public rooms, all filled with comfortable furnishings.

Just beyond the Dover-Foxcroft area, but close enough, the **Brewster Inn** (37 Zion's Hill Rd., Dexter, 207/924-3130, www.brewsterinn.com, $69-149) is an attractive 19-room mansion, on the National Register of Historic Places, remodeled in 1934 by John Calvin Stevens, and once owned by Maine governor Ralph Brewster. The nine guest rooms all have phones, air-conditioning, TVs, Wi-Fi, and stories to tell. The knotty-pine Game Room was the governor's private hideout, and guess who once slept in the Truman Room? Breakfast is a generous buffet with one hot dish. English innkeeper Mark Stephens, who arrived in 2007, has been remodeling the rooms and bringing back the lovely gardens to their mid-20th-century splendor.

Set well back from the road but downtown, **Freedom House Bed & Breakfast** (140 E. Main St., Dover-Foxcroft, 207/564-8851, www.freedomhousebandb.com) welcomes guests in two separate buildings. In the main house is a suite, complete with kitchenette and sitting, that can be customized for one, two, or three bedrooms ($129-229, with breakfast). The adjacent cottages has a one-bedroom apartment with full kitchen ($125), and three guest rooms (from $79). All have Wi-Fi and TV; only rooms in the main house include breakfast.

Neither hostel nor B&B, Rebekah Santagata's **Lakeshore House** (9 Tenney Hill Rd./Rte. 5/15, Monson, 207/997-7069, www.thelakeshorehouse.com) is a continually evolving lakeside business housing hiker-oriented guest rooms, a pub, and canoe and kayak rentals on Lake Hebron. All guests share two baths, a living room with a TV, and a kitchenette. There is Wi-Fi on the premises with one laptop available to guests. Rates begin around $25 pp.

Hostel

Headquarters for Appalachian Trail through-hikers, a home-away-from-home since 1977 is the legendary **Shaw's Boarding Home** (Pleasant St., Monson, 207/997-3597, www.shawslodging.com). To weary hikers, this welcoming no-frills operation feels like the Hyatt Regency. Short-haul hikers are also welcome, as are snowmobilers in winter; couch potatoes will feel totally out of place. The home can accommodate nearly three dozen guests in varied arrangements—private rooms in the main house ($35 s, $56 d), bunkhouse beds ($23 pp), and tent sites ($12). A lumberjack-quality breakfast is $7, and dinner is $12. For small fees, shuttle and mail-drop service and laundry facilities are available; parking for short-haulers is $1/day.

Camping

Within the boundaries of the KI Jo-Mary Multiple Use Forest is a single commercial campground, the **Jo-Mary Lake Campground** (Upper Jo-Mary Lake, Millinocket, 207/723-8117, www.northmainewoods.org, mid-May-late Sept.), on the southern shore of five-mile-long Upper Jo-Mary Lake. Despite being remote, the campground has 70 sites, flush toilets, hot showers, laundry facilities, a snack bar, plenty of play space for kids, and a sandy beach. Sites are about $16-20 pp, two-person minimum (includes access fee). The campground is 15 miles southwest of Millinocket and 20 miles north of Brownville. From Brownville Junction, take Route 11 northwest about 15 miles, turn left onto an unpaved road, and stop at the Jo-Mary Checkpoint, and then continue six miles northwest to the campground.

Peaks-Kenny State Park (Sebec Lake Rd., Dover-Foxcroft, 207/564-2003) has 56 campsites. On weekends July-August, reservations are essential (two-night minimum; call 207/287-3824 using MasterCard or Visa). Nonresident camping fees are $25/site/night,

Maine residents $15/site/night, plus the reservation fee of $2/site/night; no hookups. Leashed pets are allowed.

FOOD
Abbott Village

The claim to fame at the **Abbott Village Bakery** (106 Rte. 6/15, 207/876-4243, 6am-6pm Wed.-Thurs. and Sun.-Mon., 6am-2pm Tues., 6am-7pm Fri.-Sat.) is the nine-inch Skidder Tire Doughnut (available by request, call). It's a homely li'l spot, but it's a good choice for homemade doughnuts, breads, sweets, and sandwiches on homemade bread.

Dover-Foxcroft

Good home cooking with a few surprises packs **The Nor'easter Restaurant** (44 North St., 207/564-2122, 11am-8pm daily, $6-18), a congenial place with country-style decor and seating both at the counter and tables. The service is warm and attentive.

Ⓒ **Stutzman's** (891 Doughty Hill Rd., 207/564-8596, 9am-6pm Mon.-Sat., 10am-1pm Sun.), on the back road between Sangerville and Dover-Foxcroft, began life as a farm market but has grown to include a justly popular restaurant. Go for the wood-fired oven pizzas, fresh salads and sandwiches, soups and specials, and the Sunday all-you-can-eat brunch ($10), as well as house-baked breads and sweets.

Some of the most popular flavors at **Butterfield's Ice Cream** (946 W. Main St., 207/564-2513) are vanilla peanut butter and chocolate peanut butter, but there are plenty of other options available.

Monson

This barbecue oasis is no secret: Even celebrity chef Anthony Bourdain has discovered Mike and Kim Witham's **Spring Creek Bar-B-Q** (26 Greenville Rd./Rte. 15, 207/997-7025, www.springcreekbar-b-qmaine.com, 10am-8pm Thurs.-Sat., 9am-5pm Sun.), although he visited the winter snowmobile-trail location. Prices and portions are geared to Appalachian Trail hikers, so you won't go hungry or poor.

There are tables inside and outside; they have no liquor license and don't take credit cards. About the hours: They stay open until the food's gone.

Reasonably priced pub fare is served at the **Lakeshore House** (9 Tenney Hill Rd./Rte. 5/15, 207/997-7069, www.thelakeshorehouse. com, noon-8pm Sun. and Tues.-Thurs., noon-9pm Fri.-Sat., noon-8pm Sun., $6-12) a casual spot overlooking Lake Hebron with seating indoors and out. Salads, sandwiches, pizza, tacos, and daily specials provide plenty of choices.

Thyme & Seasons (35 Greenville Rd./Rte. 15, 207/997-3495, 10:30am-5pm Wed.-Thurs. and Sat., 10:30am-8pm Fri., $8-12), located in the Monson Community and Commerce Center across from Spring Creek Bar-B-Q, doubles as a floral shop. Inside it's a riot of color, with brightly painted tables and wall and ceiling murals. It's truly a fun spot, serving breakfast and lunch as well as dinner on Friday nights to coincide with the Monson Jammers music jams. It also has an excellent tea selection.

Dexter

Fossa's General Store (4 Main St., Dexter, 207/924-3390, 10am-7pm Tues.-Sat., 11am-4pm Sun.), a project of the Dexter Regional Development Corp., serves brick-oven pizza, hand pies, specialty breads, and daily specials, such as soup, burgers, and salads, and doubles as a market for local grown or produced goods.

Milo

Awesome doughnuts, bismarks, cinnamon buns, cream horns, and other drool-worthy pastries are reason enough to stop at **Elaine's Cafe & Bakery** (38 Main St./Rte. 11, 207/943-2705, www.elainesbasketcafe. com, 6am-5pm daily), a cheerful, riverside spot on the north side of the bridge. In addition, inexpensive breakfasts are served until 11:30am daily.

GETTING THERE

Dover-Foxcroft is about 34 miles or 45 minutes from Greenville via Route 6/15. It's about 53 miles or just over an hour from Millinocket via Route 11. It's about 38 miles or 50 minutes to Bangor via Route 15.

INFORMATION AND SERVICES

Local information is available from the **Southern Piscataquis County Chamber of Commerce** (100 South St./Rte. 7, Dover-Foxcroft, 207/564-7533, www.spccc.org).

For information about Gulf Hagas Reserve and the KI Jo-Mary Multiple Use Forest, contact **North Maine Woods** (207/435-6213, www.northmainewoods.org).

The Town of Monson has local information posted at www.monsonmaine.org. Find Dexter info at www.downtowndexter.com.

Bangor Area

Maine's Queen City is best identified by a trio of kings, but its appeal extends to those on a pauper's budget. Home to king of horror Stephen King, Bangor was folksinger Roger Miller's destination in "King of the Road" and is home to a gigantic statue of king of the woods Paul Bunyan. One would think with so many kingly claims, Bangor (BANG-gore) would be nicknamed the King City, but for reasons now unknown, it's been promoted as the Queen City since the late 19th century.

Lumber capital of the world in the 19th century, Bangor is still northern Maine's magnet for commerce and culture—the big city for the northern three-quarters of the state. The county seat for Penobscot County, downtown Bangor is awakening from a slump dating to the 1960s, typical of many urban areas. The 2002-2004 waterfront National Folk Festivals brought excitement and major crowds to the city and dusted off its sense of possibility, and Bangor has continued the three-day late-August event as the American Folk Festival. Now you can stroll alongside Kenduskeag Stream, duck into shops and an increasing number of restaurants, and end the evening with music, a show, or perhaps trying your luck at the state's first slots.

Bangor incorporated in 1791, but when explorer Samuel de Champlain landed here in 1604 (an event commemorated by a plaque downtown, next to Kenduskeag Stream), the Queen City bore the Native American name of Kenduskeag, meaning "eel-catching place." A downtown park shadows the river.

In the late 19th century, when the lumber trade moved westward, smaller industries moved into greater Bangor to take up the slack, but a disastrous fire on April 30, 1911, leveled 55 acres of Bangor's commercial and residential neighborhoods, retarding progress for several decades.

The bloodiest shootout in Maine history occurred in 1937, when FBI agents, tipped off about the presence of the Al Brady Gang, then on the Most Wanted list, engaged in a street battle that didn't end until all the gangsters were either dead or in custody.

Bangor highlights fine specimens of Victorian, Italianate, Queen Anne, and Greek Revival architecture—and who knows, you might see legendary author Stephen King in your travels. Part of what King enjoys about Bangor is that locals are used to him and accord him "normal person" treatment.

SIGHTS
The Standpipe

A distinctive west-side landmark is the **Thomas Hill Standpipe.** The 1.75-million-gallon riveted-steel water tower and observatory, built in 1897, is a National Historic and American Water Landmark. Some say it's the queen city's crown, and a case can be made that it resembles one when viewed from afar. The Standpipe is open four days each year for tours, usually once per season, which allows visitors to climb the interior staircase circling to the top and access the great view from the observation platform. For tour information, call the **Bangor Water District** (207/947-4516, www.bangorwater. org).

Paul Bunyan Statue

Bangor's Victorian-era fortunes were built on the millions of trees felled in the North Woods and driven down the Penobscot River, then milled and shipped from its busy port. One local tall tale paints super-logger Paul Bunyan as a native son, allegedly born in Bangor on February 12, 1834. That might explain the 31-foot-tall statue of him in front of the Cross Center downtown. Weighing 3,200 pounds, the colorful statue was erected in 1959 during the city's 125th anniversary. Inside the base is a time capsule due to be opened in 2084. While Bunyan's status as a local might be questionable, the tool he holds is genuine Maine-made: After observing the difficulties river drivers were having shepherding logs down the Penobscot River with the traditional cant dog, local blacksmith Joseph Peavey invented the tool that bears his name.

◖ Stephen King-dom

Maine native and naturalized hometown boy, horror honcho Stephen King is anything but a myth. Born in Portland, he has lived in Bangor since 1980, and you may spot him around town (especially at baseball and basketball games). His turreted mansion on West Broadway looks like a set from one of the movies based on his novels and stories—complete with a wrought-iron front gate and fence festooned with iron bats and cobwebs. Heed the No Trespassing sign; the best-selling author has had his share of odd encounters with off-the-wall devotees, not to mention his 1999 encounter with an out-of-control minivan. These days, even though he's back at work, it's best to keep up with him via his website (www.stephenking.com).

The Greater Bangor Convention and Visitors Bureau offers **Tommyknockers and More bus tours** (800/916-6673, www.bangorcvb.

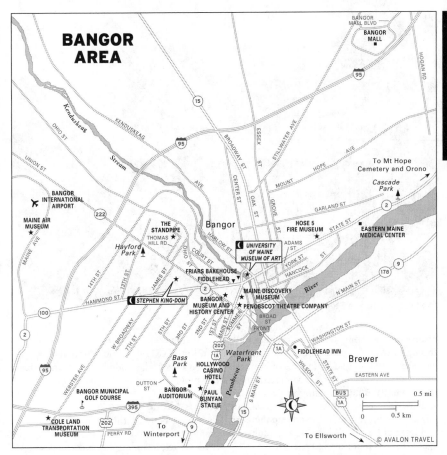

org, $20) about once a month, June-October. Advance registration and payment is required, and space is limited.

For a more personalized view of sites related to the horror master, book a private tour with Stuart Tinker's **SK Tours** (25 Thomas Hill Rd., 207/947-7193, www.sk-tours.com). Tinker, a King expert whose been featured on TV and quoted in magazines, has been offering tours for roughly two decades. A three-hour tour ($80 for two) visits about 30 sites related to the author, from places where he's lived to locations featured in his books as well as filming locations.

Bangor Museum and History Center

Built by a wealthy attorney in 1836 and listed on the National Register of Historic Places, the handsome brick Thomas A. Hill House, home of the **Bangor Museum and History Center** (159 Union St., Bangor, 207/942-1900, www.bangormuseum.com, 10am-5pm Tues.-Sat., $5 adults, $3 ages 6-18 and 55 and older), on the corner of High Street, has been restored to Victorian elegance, with period furnishings, Maine paintings, and special exhibits.

The center offers a good variety of guided walking and bus tours focused on Bangor's

© HILARY NANGLE

The best way to see Stephen King's Bangor is on a specialty tour.

history. **Devil's Half Acre** is an evening walk through the city's late 19th-century vice and violence neighborhood, with tales of brothels, tenements, and more; not recommended for kids. **Ghostly Bangor** highlights paranormal activities and is available as a guided walk or bus tour. Other bus tours include **Monuments** and **Best of Bangor**. Walks are $10 adults, $5 ages 5-12; bus tours are $20 pp.

University of Maine Museum of Art (UMMA)

Bangor scored a coup when it lured **UMMA** (Norumbega Hall, 40 Harlow St., Bangor, 207/561-3350, www.umma.umaine.edu, 10am-5pm Mon.-Sat.) downtown. The museum's primary strengths are photography and contemporary works on paper, and its focus is on modern and contemporary art. Among the significant items in the museum's collection of more than 6,500 original works are pieces by John Marin, Roy Lichenstein, Willem de Kooning, and Alex Katz. Exhibits are displayed in one permanent and three changing galleries.

Admission is usually free, thanks to an annual gift. Entrance is via a bridge from the riverside park between Hammond and Central Streets downtown.

Kenduskeag Stream Trail

Pick up a copy of the Kenduskeag Stream map at the visitors bureau and follow it to 13 marked sites, including where Portuguese navigator Esteban Gómez landed in 1525, followed by French geographer Samuel de Champlain in 1604. Also on the trail is Lovers Leap, a 150-foot-tall cliff where a Native American couple plunged to their deaths after being denied permission to marry.

Maine Discovery Museum

Here's a major kid magnet with a wide range of interactive exhibits that encourage creative play. The **Maine Discovery Museum** (74 Main St., Bangor, 207/262-7200, www.mainediscoverymuseum.org, 9:30am-5pm Tues.-Sat., noon-5pm Sun., $7.50) occupies more than 22,000 square feet on three floors of the former Freese's

Department Store. Seven permanent exhibit areas feature nature, geography, art, science, anatomy, Maine children's literature, and music. Special programs are scheduled for children and families throughout the year.

Air and Fire Museums

On the grounds of Bangor International Airport, the **Maine Air Museum** (98 Maine Ave., Bangor, 877/280-6247 in Maine or 207/941-6757, www.maineairmuseum.org, 10am-4pm Sat., noon-4pm Sun. late May-early Sept., $2) is a fledgling museum operated by the Maine Aviation Historical Society and dedicated to the history of Maine aviation.

Kids get a kick out of the firefighting artifacts and fire trucks at the **Hose 5 Fire Museum** (247 State St., Bangor, 207/945-3229, early May-late Oct., 9am-noon Sat.), in an 1897 fire station.

Cole Land Transportation Museum

Children love the **Cole Land Transportation Museum** (405 Perry Rd., Bangor, 207/990-3600, www.colemuseum.org, 9am-5pm daily May-mid-Nov., $7 adults, $5 seniors, free under age 19), a sprawling facility founded by Bangor trucking magnate Galen Cole. More than 200 19th- and 20th-century vehicles—just about anything that has ever rolled across Maine's landscape—fill the museum. Besides vintage cars, there are fire engines, tractors, logging vehicles, baby carriages, even a replica railroad station. And this being Maine, the museum believes it owns the largest collection of snow-removal equipment in the country. A gift shop stocks transportation-related items. Outside are picnic tables and a covered bridge to walk over and under. The museum is near the junction of I-95 and I-395.

Winterport

In Waldo County, 12 miles downriver from Bangor, is Winterport, a pretty little sleeper of a town tucked along the Penobscot River. It earned its name as the limit of winter navigation for Bangor's lumber trade; ice blocked shipping traffic from proceeding farther upriver. The National Register **Winterport Historic District** includes splendid 19th-century Greek Revival homes and commercial buildings on Route 1A and the short side streets descending to the river. The **Winterport Winery and Penobscot Bay Brewery** (279 S. Main St., Winterport, 207/223-4500, www.winterportwinery.com) has a tasting room for its fruit wines and a gallery for exhibiting local artists.

Mount Hope Cemetery

In a state where burial grounds usually command views to die for, the standout is **Mount Hope** (207/945-6589, www.mthopebgr.com, 7:30am-7:30pm daily Apr. 1-Nov. 1, 7:30am-4pm daily Nov. 1-Apr. 1), established in 1834, consecrated in 1836, and easily the state's loveliest. Here you can hobnob with some of Maine's dearly departed. Among the sights are unusual grave markers, including one elevated sarcophagus, and the graves of Hannibal Hamlin, Abe Lincoln's vice president during the Civil War, and gangster Al Brady, listed as Public Enemy Number 1 and killed in a firestorm of bullets in downtown Bangor in 1937. Also of note is 20-foot-tall Soldier's Monument, erected in 1864 and among the oldest Civil War monuments in the country. Inspired by the design of Mount Auburn Cemetery in Cambridge, Massachusetts, 264-acre Mount Hope is more park than cemetery—with gardens, ponds, bridges, paved paths, lots of greenery, a few picnic tables, and wandering deer. The entrance to the green-fenced cemetery is at 1048 State Street (Rte. 2), about 0.25 mile east of Hogan Road. Cemetery tours are offered by the **Bangor Museum and History Society** (207/942-1900, www.bangormuseum.com, $10 adults, $5 ages 5-12). Call or check the website for the schedule.

ENTERTAINMENT

More than a century ago, when cabin-feverish lumberjacks roared into Bangor for R&R, they were apt to patronize Fan Jones's "establishment" on Harlow Street. Adult entertainment is still available in the city, but so is higher-brow stuff. That said, nights in Bangor are pretty quiet for a city.

Bangor Symphony Orchestra (BSO)

Founded in 1896, Maine's **BSO** (207/942-5555 or 800/639-3221, www.bangorsymphony.com) has an enviable reputation as one of the country's oldest and best community orchestras. During the regular season, September-May, monthly concerts are presented weekends at the Maine Center for the Arts in Orono. The orchestra occasionally performs in summer too.

Penobscot Theatre Company

Bangor's professional theater company, **Penobscot Theatre** (131 Main St., Bangor, 207/942-3333, www.penobscottheatre.org) performs classic and contemporary comedies and dramas September-early June in the 1920 Bangor Opera House.

Concerts

On Tuesday evenings late spring-summer, the **Bangor Band** (www.bangorband.org) performs free outdoor concerts; check the website for schedule and location.

Every Thursday evening in June-July, the **Cool Sounds of Summer** free outdoor concerts are held in Pickering Square. Bangor Library also sponsors a summer concert series on its lawn.

During the summer, **Waterfront Concerts** (www.waterfrontconcerts.com) brings big-name entertainment to the open-air Waterfront Pavilion on the riverfront; most require tickets, but some are free. In the winter, the venue shifts to the downtown Cross Center.

FESTIVALS AND EVENTS

In April (usually the third Saturday), the **Kenduskeag Stream Canoe Race** is an annual 16.5-mile spring-runoff race sponsored by Bangor Parks and Recreation (207/992-4490). It draws upward of 700 canoes and thousands of spectators and finishes in downtown Bangor. The best location for spotting action is Six Mile

Falls—take Broadway (Rte. 15) about six miles northwest of downtown.

Late July-early August, the **Bangor State Fair,** held in Bass Park, is a huge 10-day affair with agricultural and crafts exhibits, a carnival, fireworks, sinful food, and big-name live music. This is a big deal and attracts thousands from all over northern Maine.

The annual **KahBang festival** (www.kahbang.com), in August, celebrates music, art, and film with a variety of events.

Multiple stages of continuous music and dance by more than two dozen performing groups representing various cultures along with dozens of artisans, many demonstrating their crafts, bring in tens of thousands for the annual and free (so far) **American Folk Festival** (207/992-2630, www.americanfolkfestival.com), held on the Bangor waterfront. It's a fabulous event and one worth making an effort to attend.

SHOPPING
Antiques and More

Browse, eat, sip, and buy at the **Antique Marketplace and Cafe** (65 Maine St., Bangor, 207/941-2111 or 877/941-2111, www.antiquemarketplacecafe.com). Filling two floors are a wide range of antiques, along with used books and a café serving breakfast and lunch daily. **The Rock & Art Shop** (36 Central St., Bangor, 207/947-2205) blends nature, art, and yes, rocks into an unusual shopping experience.

Books

If you can't decide between new or used, head to **BookMarc's Bookstore** (78 Harlow St., Bangor, 207/942-3206). Also in downtown Bangor is **Pro Libris** (10 3rd St., Bangor, 207/942-3019), billing itself as a "readers' paradise." With 35,000 used paperbacks and hardcovers, that's just about right.

Fresh Air Market

Nearly 40 vendors, including artisans, farmers, and bakers, sell their products along the Kenduskeag Stream, behind Pickering Square Garage, on Thursday evenings mid-June-early

August. It complements the Cool Sounds concert series in Pickering Square (www.downtownbangor.com).

RECREATION
Fields Pond Audubon Center
South of Bangor-Brewer (although it feels as if you're heading east) is the Maine Audubon Society's **Fields Pond Audubon Center** (216 Fields Pond Rd., Holden, 207/989-2591). About four miles of footpaths wind through 192 acres of woods, fields, marshes, and lakeshore, all open sunrise-sunset daily year-round. (Wear waterproof shoes or boots; parts of the trail can be wet.) Canoe rentals are available to explore the pond. The headquarters is the L. Robert Rolde Nature Center (10am-4pm Thurs.-Sat.), where you can pick up brochures and maps. A full schedule of programs occurs here throughout the year, including lectures, nature walks, slide talks, even a nature-book discussion group. Cost averages $5-10 pp. A nature store carries books, cards, and gifts.

Bangor City Forest and Orono Bog
Here's a double treat that's rich in flora and fauna. About nine miles of trails and more than four miles of roads meander through the 680-acre working Bangor City Forest (http://cityforest.bangorinfo.com). It's a great place for a walk or bike ride and for wildlife-spotting.

Accessible through the Bangor City Forest, the mile-long **Orono Bog Boardwalk** (Tripp Dr., Bangor, 207/581-2850, www.oronobogwalk.org), a National Natural Landmark, is wheelchair-accessible, has a restroom, benches every 200 feet, and interpretative signage. A series of **guided nature walks** (207/866-2578) are offered 9am-10:30am Saturday early June-late October. Most are free; reservations are recommended.

The forest and bog parking area are on Tripp Road, off Stillwater Avenue, about midway between the Bangor Mall and Kelly Road. Leashed pets are allowed in the forest, but not the bog.

Golf
Considered a standout among public courses, the **Bangor Municipal Golf Course** (280 Webster Ave., Bangor, 207/941-0232) has 18 holes dating from 1964 and a newer (and tougher) nine holes. Stretching over both sides of Webster Avenue, the course is also on the Bangor Airport flight path; don't flinch when a jet screams overhead.

Twelve miles southeast of Bangor, across from the Lucerne Inn, the nine-hole **Lucerne-in-Maine Golf Course** (Rte. 1A, Dedham, 207/843-6282), is worth a visit just for the spectacular view.

ACCOMMODATIONS
Bangor has all the major budget and mid-priced chains but lacks independent B&Bs or inns.

If you're flying in or out of Bangor Airport, you can't beat the convenience of the **Four Points Sheraton Hotel** (307 Godfrey Blvd., Bangor, 207/947-6721 or 800/228-4609, www.fourpointsbangorairport.com, from $155), which is linked to the terminal by a skyway. Renovated in 2009, it has a restaurant, fitness room, indoor pool, and free Internet access. Pets are permitted for $20/stay.

Hollywood Casino Hotel & Raceway (500 Main St., Bangor, 877/779-7771, www.hollywoodcasinobangor.com, $99-349) is the best downtown hotel, but it is a casino and you have to deal with the noise and hoopla that goes with it. That said, the 152 rooms have flat-screen TVs and free Wi-Fi. Facilities include two restaurants, lounge, fitness center, and the casino. The location puts all of downtown within footsteps. Airport shuttles are available.

Just over the bridge but within walking distance of downtown Bangor, **The Fiddlehead Inn** (5 E. Summer St., Brewer, 888/983-4466, www.fiddleheadinn.com, $145-155) is a meticulously renovated and decorated early-20th-century home with two guest rooms sharing one bathroom. Innkeeper Saundra Haley serves a hearty vegetarian breakfast.

Route 1A runs between Winterport and Bangor, then turns southeast and returns to the coast at Ellsworth. Twelve miles southeast of Bangor (and 25 miles northwest of Ellsworth) is **The Lucerne Inn** (Bar Harbor Rd./Rte. 1A, Dedham, 207/843-5123 or 800/325-5123, www.lucerneinn.com, $119-219), a retrofitted early-19th-century stagecoach hostelry on a 10-acre hilltop overlooking Phillips Lake and the hills beyond. Despite the highway out front, noise is no problem in the rear-facing guest rooms, which have air-conditioning, phones, TVs, and fireplaces. Rates include continental breakfast, and an on-site dining room serves dinner and a popular Sunday brunch. Outside there's a pool; pets are not allowed.

FOOD
Local Flavors
A downtown landmark since 1978, **Bagel Central** (33 Central St., Bangor, 207/947-1654, 6am-6pm Mon.-Thurs., 6am-5:30pm Fri., 6am-2pm Sun.) is a cheerful spot to meet, greet, and grab some handmade bagels (try the blueberry), great deli sandwiches, soups, and more. It's operated under Orthodox rabbinical supervision.

A few doors down at **❰ Friars Bakehouse** (21 Central St., Bangor, 207/947-3770), Brother Kent and Brother Donald, of the Franciscan Brothers of St. Elizabeth of Hungary, bake divine breads and buns along with sinful whoopie pies and other treats and offer a very limited selection of soups and sandwiches. Tables are communal; prayers are free. Days and hours of operation change frequently, and it often sells out early; call or follow the advice on the door: If the light's on, it's open. Cash only. In 2013, the friars began brewing beers, too, which are available at **Bangor Wine and Cheese** (86 Hammond St., 207/942-3338).

Just east of Bangor is the **Stonehouse Café** (1492 State St., Veazie, 207/942-9552, 7am-7pm Tues.-Thurs., 7am-8pm Fri., 7am-3pm Sat.-Sun., $4-18), a cozy hole-in-the-wall where breakfast is served all day and the fried fish is a big draw.

I scream, you scream, everyone screams for **Pete's Pretty Good Ice Cream and Café** (Rte. 1A, Holden, 207/943-0444, 11am-9pm daily), which in addition to some amazingly creative flavors of supercreamy ice cream also serves a noteworthy hand-picked lobster roll as well as fried seafood and grilled fare.

Massimo's Breads (130 Hammond St., Bangor, 207/659-7575, 10:30am-2pm Tues.-Sat.) serves panini made on authentic artisan Italian breads and specialty pizzas by the slice.

It's the 14 rotating taps of craft brews that bring most folks to **Nocturnem Draft Haus** (56 Main St., Bangor, 207/907-4380, www.nocturnemdrafthaus.com, from 3pm Mon.-Sat.). Pairing well with the world-class brews are cheeses and charcuterie, burgers, and salads pairs served by a knowledgeable staff. There's live music every weekend, and outside seating during the summer.

Look for **Pompeii Pizza** (207/745-2275, 11am-4pm Mon.-Fri., $8-10), a food truck with a wood-fired brick oven on the Bangor waterfront. Cash only.

Giacomo's (1 Central St., Bangor, 207/947-3702, www.giacomosbangor.com, 7am-6pm Mon.-Fri., 8am-4pm Sat., 11am-3pm Sun.) is a reliable choice for panini, pizza, and espresso.

Family Favorites
Convenient to I-95 Exit 180, **Dysart's** (Coldbrook Rd., Hermon, 207/947-8732, www.dysarts.com) is a truckers' destination resort—you can grab some grub, shower, shop, phone home, play video games, fuel up, and even sneak a bit of shut-eye. For real flavor, opt for the truckers' dining room, where the music is country and dozens of bleary-eyed drivers have reached the end of their transcontinental treks. If you're here with a carload, order an 18-Wheeler—18 scoops of ice cream with a collection of toppings. No question, Dysart's is unique, and it's open 24 hours daily year-round.

Mighty fine, slow-cooked barbecue comes from the pits at **4Points BBQ & Blues House** (145 Main St., Winterport, 207/223-9929, www.4pointsbbq.com, 10:30am-10:30pm Wed.-Sun., $15-25). Owner John Ramirez learned the craft of being pit boss in his home state of Oklahoma. Go early. The melt-in-your-mouth brisket, smoked turkey, and Kansas City burnt ends often sell out before 4pm. There's live music on the deck every weekend, and there's a kids' menu.

Ethnic Fare

Everything is prepared to order at **Bahaar Pakistani Restaurant** (23 Hammond St., Bangor, 207/945-5979, 5pm-9pm Thurs.-Sat.). Vegetarians find lots of options among the 70-plus appetizers, *biryanis,* and curries, which you can order hot, hotter, and hottest. Most choices are around $10. Takeout is available, and they have a full liquor license. Reservations are advisable on weekend nights. Be advised that the restaurant doesn't stick to its promised hours.

Insiders give the nod to **Yoshi Japanese Restaurant** (373 Wilson St., Brewer, 207/989-9688, www.yoshi09brewerme.com, 11am-2:30pm and 4:30pm-9pm Mon.-Wed., 11am-2:30pm and 4:30pm-10pm Thurs.-Sat., noon-9pm Sun., entrées from $10), which opened in 2009, for the region's best sushi. The dining room is minimalist in decor. Choose from regular tables, cushions on the floor around sunken tables, or the sushi bar, where you can watch the maestros at work. With a 12-page menu, the choices seem endless.

Rome-born Massimo Ranni creates authentic Italian fare (his grandmother ran a bakery in the old country) at **Massimo's Cucina Italiana** (96 Hammond St., Bangor, 207/945-5600, www.massimoscucinaitaliana.com, 5pm-9pm Mon.-Sat., $14-26). Skip the pasta in favor of the small plates or meat dishes. Be forewarned, the chef doesn't take kindly to requests to alter ingredients.

Craving pho? You'll find that as well as *banh mi,* hot pot, and other well-crafted Vietnamese fare at **Little Vietnam** (687 Hogan Rd., Bangor, 207/945-0074, www.lvrestaurantbar.com, 10:30am-10:30pm daily). Most choices run $10-15.

Casual Dining

Seasonally appropriate comfort foods with pizzazz are served at **⟨ Fiddlehead** (84 Hammond St., Bangor, 207/942-3336, www.thefiddleheadrestaurant.com, 4pm-9pm Tues.-Fri.,

5pm-10pm Sat., 5pm-9pm Sun.), a downtown restaurant with a cozy, neighborhood feel. Don't expect romantic. It can be loud, given the wood floors and brick walls, and the cross-table chatter among friends. Owners Laura Albin, who runs the front of the house, and Melissa Chaiken, the chef, are especially accommodating of vegetarians and the glucose intolerant, but the menu, which changes quarterly, ranges from burgers to seafood.

Thistle's (175 Exchange St., Bangor, 207/945-5480, www.thistlesrestaurant.com, 11am-2pm Tues.-Fri. and 5pm-9pm Tues.-Sat., entrées $16-28) is a longtime reliable place that draws an older crowd for moderately priced continental entrées with a Latin flair, plus excellent homemade breads and desserts. Paella is a specialty.

For good food and good times, the place to see and be seen is **11 Central** (11 Central St., Bangor, 207/922-5115, www.11centralbangor.com, 4pm-10pm daily, $15-30), an American bistro serving steaks, pastas, seafood, and pizzas in a casual yet stylish downtown spot with a hip vibe.

The Luna Bar & Grill (49 Park St., Bangor, 207/990-2233, 5pm-9pm Tues.-Thurs. and 5pm-10pm Fri.-Sat.), located behind City Hall, earns kudos for creative cocktails, including house-made infused vodkas, as well as entrées such as pistachio-encrusted pork loin and pan-seared scallops, most in the $18-22 range.

INFORMATION AND SERVICES

The best sources for local information are **The Bangor Region Chamber of Commerce** (519 Main St., Bangor, 207/947-0307, www.bangorregion.com) and **The Greater Bangor Convention and Visitors Bureau** (40 Harlow St., Bangor, 207/947-5205 or 800/916-6673, www.bangorcvb.org).

Two **Maine Visitor Information Centers** (8am-6pm daily) are just south of Bangor on I-95, one on each side of the highway. The modern gray-clapboard buildings have racks of statewide information, agreeable staffers, clean restrooms, vending machines, and covered picnic tables. Northbound, the center is at mile 175 (207/862-6628); southbound, it's at mile 179 (207/862-6638).

Check out **Bangor Public Library** (145 Harlow St., Bangor, 207/947-8336, www.bpl. lib.me.us).

GETTING THERE AND AROUND

Bangor International Airport (BIA, 287 Godfrey Blvd., Bangor, 207/992-4600, www. flybangor.com) is served by major U.S. carriers.

Concord Coachlines (1039 Union St./Rte. 222, Bangor, 207/945-4000 or 800/639-3317, www.concordcoachlines.com) connects Bangor with Augusta, Portland, and points south via direct and coastal routes.

Cyr Bus Line (207/827-2335 or 800/244-2335, www.johntcyrandsons.com) operates one round-trip daily between Aroostook County and Bangor, stopping in Bangor at the Greyhound and Concord bus terminals.

Operating once daily between Bangor and Calais is **West's Coastal Connection** (207/546-2823 or 800/596-2823, www.west-busservice.com), stopping in Bangor at the Concord terminal as well as at the airport.

Serving Bangor, Brewer, Old Town, Veazie, Orono, and Hampden is **BAT Community Connector** (207/992-4670). The service operates 6:15am-6:15pm Monday-Saturday, with no Hamden service on Saturday. The fare is $1.25, exact change required.

By car, Bangor is about 72 miles or 1.15 hours from Millinocket via I-95 and about 72 miles or 1.5 hours from Greenville via Route 15. It's about 10 miles or 15 minutes to Orono via I-95, about 130 miles or 2 hours to Portland via I-95, and about 48 miles or 1.25 hours to Bar Harbor via Routes 1A and 3.

Orono and Vicinity

Home of the University of Maine's flagship campus, **Orono** (pop. 10,362) is part college town, part generic Maine village, and a fine example of the tail wagging the dog. More than 11,000 university students converge on this Bangor suburb every year, fairly overwhelming the year-round population.

Called Stillwater when settled by Europeans in the 1770s, the town adopted the name of Penobscot Indian chief Joseph Orono and incorporated in 1806. By 1840, along with Bangor, eight miles to the southwest, prosperity descended, thanks to the huge Penobscot River log drives spurring the lumber industry's heyday. A stroll along Orono's Main Street Historic District, especially between Maplewood Avenue and Pine Street, attests to the timber magnates' success; the gorgeous homes are a veritable catalog of au courant architectural styles: Italianate, Greek Revival, Queen Anne, Federal, and Colonial Revival. Contact Orono's municipal office for a free copy of *Orono Tree Walk*, describing the trees of the town.

Old Town (pop. 7,840) gained its own identity in 1840 after separating from Orono. ("Old Town" is the English translation of the settlement's Wabanaki name.) In those days, sawmills lined the shores of the town's Marsh Island between the Stillwater and Penobscot Rivers—the end of the line for the log drives and the backbone of Old Town's economy. That all crumbled in 1856, though, when a devastating fire swept through the area. Occurring as residents exited from memorial services for Abraham Lincoln, it was called the "Lincoln Fire." Several decades later, Old Town finally regained its economic footing, thanks to factories making shoes, canoes, and paper products.

Under separate tribal administration and linked to Old Town by a bridge built in 1951, Indian Island Reservation is home to about 400 Penobscot Indians.

SIGHTS
University of Maine

Orono's major sights are on the 660-acre campus of the **University of Maine** (UMO, www.umaine.edu), a venerable institution founded in 1868 as the State College of Agriculture and Mechanical Arts. It received its current designation in 1897 and now awards bachelor's, master's, and doctoral degrees. The oldest building on campus is North Hall, an updated version of the original Frost family farmhouse.

Information about the campus, including guided tours, is available from the **visitors center** (Buchanan Alumni House, 160 College Ave., University of Maine, Orono, 207/581-3740, 10am-3pm Mon.-Fri. and also noon-3pm Sat. during the academic year). Guided campus tours are offered daily.

One of the newest buildings, built in 1986 and renovated in 2009, is the **Collins Center for the Arts,** scene of year-round activity. Located on the second floor is the expanded **Hudson Museum** (207/581-1901, 9am-4pm Mon.-Fri., 11am-4pm Sat. and before selected performances, free), spotlighting traditional and contemporary world cultures in three contiguous galleries. The World Cultures Gallery comprises eight display areas, organized by theme, including one devoted to the museums' superlative Palmer collection of pre-Columbian artifacts. The Maine Indian Gallery highlights the museum's impressive Maliseet, Micmac, Passamaquoddy, and Penobscot holdings. Temporary exhibitions fill the Merritt Gallery.

The Maine sky takes center stage at the **Maynard F. Jordan Planetarium** (5781 Wingate Hall, Munson Rd., University of Maine, Orono, 207/581-1341, www.galaxymaine.com), on the second floor of Wingate Hall. Multimedia presentations help explain the workings of our universe and bring astronomy to life. Comet collisions and rocketing asteroids keep the kids transfixed. Program scheduling varies; call ahead to reserve space in the 45-seat auditorium. Admission to scheduled events is $3 across the board. The public is invited to view the sky though a telescope at the **Jordan Observatory** on many clear Friday-Saturday evenings.

At the eastern edge of the campus, the seven-acre **Lyle E. Littlefield Ornamental Trial Garden** (Rangeley Rd., 207/594-2948) contains more than 2,500 plant species, many being tested for winter durability. The best time to come is early June, when crabapples and lilacs put on their perennial show. The garden is open daily; bring a picnic. Horticulture fans will also enjoy the 10-acre riverside **Fay Hyland Arboretum,** on the western edge of campus.

In the last agricultural building on campus (the barn predates UMO), the **Page Farm and Home Museum** (207/581-4100, www.pfhm.org, 9am-4pm Tues.-Sat.) houses a collection of farm implements and home items; on-site are a one-room schoolhouse, a blacksmith's shop, heritage gardens, and a general store stocked with goods made by local artisans. The museum presents an annual community picnic lunch at the end of July. Blacksmithing, old-fashioned games, and ice cream-making are part of the festivities.

Parking is a major sticking point at UMO, so you'll need a parking permit for most areas except the Maine Center for the Arts and the sports complex when events are taking place. For other times and lots, you can obtain a free one-day permit either from campus security or the parking office. For more information call 207/581-4053.

Old Town Museum

In the former St. Mary's Catholic Church, the **Old Town Museum** (353 S. Main St., Old Town, 207/827-7256, www.theoldtownmuseum.org, 1pm-4pm Fri.-Sun. early June-mid-Oct., free) has well-organized exhibit areas focusing primarily on Old Town's pivotal role in the 19th-century lumbering industry. Other displays feature woodcarvings by sculptor Bernard Langlais, an Old Town native, and an excellent collection of Native American sweetgrass baskets. Each year, temporary exhibits add to the mix. Ask about the 2pm Sunday programs—they can include anything from carving, weaving, beadwork, and quilting demonstrations to hand-bell concerts and historical lectures.

⟨ Penobscot Nation Museum

Don't be put off by the humble exterior of Indian Island's **Penobscot Nation Museum** (12 Downstreet St., Indian Island, 207/827-4153, www.penobscotculture.com, 10am-4:30pm Mon.-Thurs., other days by appointment, free, donation appreciated); inside it's jam-packed with Native American historical artifacts and artwork, including exhibits of baskets, bead-work, dress, antique tools, and birch-bark canoes. Curator James Nepture brings the collection to life and will show videos of Penobscot life, including *Penobscot: The People and Their River.* Jewelry, dream catchers, and other hand-crafted items are for sale in the small store. Posted hours aren't always maintained.

In the island's Protestant cemetery is the grave of **Louis Sockalexis,** the best Native American baseball player at the turn of the 20th century. Allegedly, his acceptance onto Cleveland's baseball team spurred management to dub the team the Indians—a name that has stuck.

After visiting the museum, if you continue to the stop sign and bear right, you'll come to a riverside park with interpretive signage and trails accented with sculptures. It's a fine place for a picnic lunch.

Leonard's Mills

Officially known as the **Maine Forest and Logging Museum** (off Rte. 9, Bradley, 207/581-2871, www.leonardsmills.com), 400-acre Leonard's Mills re-creates a 1790s logging village, with a sawmill, a blacksmith shop, a covered bridge, a log cabin, and other buildings. The site is accessible roughly sunrise-sunset year-round, but the best times to visit are during the museum's special-events days (the schedule varies) when dozens of museum volunteers don period dress and bring the village to life. Demonstrations, beanhole bean suppers, hayrides, antique games, and kids dipping candles or making cider are all part of the mix. The season's biggest events

© HILARY NANGLE

After visiting the Penobscot Nation Museum on Indian Island, walk the interpretative trails.

are **Living History Days,** a two-day festival held in mid-July and the first weekend in October. Admission varies by event but is usually about $10 adults, $5 children. An ongoing museum project is the restoration to working condition of one of the old Lombard Haulers, an important part of the North Woods story. The museum is on Penobscot Experimental Forest Road in Bradley, 1.3 miles southeast of Route 178. It's directly across the river from Orono, but the only bridges are north (Old Town-Milford) and south (Bangor-Brewer).

ENTERTAINMENT AND EVENTS

In early December, at the Hudson Museum on the Orono campus of the University of Maine, the **Maine Indian Basketmakers Sale and Demonstration** includes Maine Indian baskets, carvings, jewelry, and traditional arts. Demonstrations, drumming, and singing are all on the agenda. For more information, contact the Hudson Museum (207/581-1904).

On the UMO campus, the **Collins Center for the Arts** (207/581-1755, www.collinscenterforthearts.com) is the year-round site of concerts, dramas, and other events with big-name performers. The box office (800/622-8499 for ticket orders) is open 9am-4pm weekdays and 90 minutes prior to each event.

Orono Parks and Recreation presents a **Summer Concerts in the Park** series on Wednesday evenings.

SHOPPING

The world's oldest continuously operating canoe manufacturer, **Old Town Canoe Company** (125 Gilman Falls Rd./Rte. 43, Old Town, 207/827-1530, www.oldtowncanoefactoryoutlet.com), incorporated in 1904, was turning out as many as 400 boats a month two years later. In 1915 the list of dealers included Harrod's in London and the Hudson's Bay Company in far northern Canada, and Old Town had supplied canoes to expeditions in Egypt and the Arctic. Quality is high at Old Town, so its boats are pricey, but you can visit the **Old Town Canoe Factory Outlet Store** and look over the supply of "factory-blemished" canoe and kayak models. You may end up with a real bargain. There's also a full line of paddles, jackets, compasses, and other accessories. While here, inquire about factory tours. To find it, follow Main Street (Rte. 43) north.

RECREATION
Sunkhaze Meadows National Wildlife Refuge

The best time to visit **Sunkhaze Meadows National Wildlife Refuge** (off Rte. 2, Milford, 207/827-6138, ww.sunkhaze.org) is during the fall waterfowl migration, but hunting is allowed then, so wear a hunter-orange hat or vest. More than 200 bird species have been spotted here; moose and beavers are common. The best way to see them is to paddle the five-mile stretch of Sunkhaze Stream that bisects the refuge. Allow about six hours for this expedition, putting in on Stud Mill Road (park in the lot at the Ash Landing trailhead; do not park on Stud Mill Road) and taking out on Route 2 (you'll need two vehicles for this). Don't forget insect repellent. Another option is a 1.6-mile loop with an observation platform roughly halfway along the trail. Access is via the unpaved Stud Mill Road or County Road, north of Milford. No staff or facilities are available at the 11,672-acre refuge, but you can download maps from the website. In winter, the refuge trails are open for cross-country skiing.

University of Maine

Recreation resources are abundant at UMO. **Campus Recreation** (207/581-1082, www.umaine.edu/campusrecreation) oversees facilities including **Wallace Pool, Alfond Arena, Latti Fitness Center, Memorial Gym,** and the **Student Recreation and Fitness Center.** Hours vary at each, and a small access fee may be required.

Ask at the campus recreation center or visitors center for a map of **University Forest,** with trails for biking, walking, snowshoeing, and cross-country skiing.

ACCOMMODATIONS

Less than a mile from the university campus is **University Inn Academic Suites** (5 College Ave., Orono, 207/866-4921 or 800/321-4921, www.universityinnorono.com, $107-182), a somewhat dated but renovated and well-maintained motel overlooking the Stillwater River. All guest rooms have balconies and Wi-Fi; suites have refrigerators and microwaves. Rates include a hot breakfast buffet. Also on-site are an outdoor heated pool with bar service and a family recreation center with foosball, a pool table, and a big-screen TV. There's a dock for boat launching; canoe and kayak rentals are available.

Even closer to the university and just off I-95 is the three-story **Black Bear Inn** (4 Godfrey Dr., Orono, 207/866-7120 or 800/528-1234, www.blackbearinnorono.com, $100-275), decorated with a black bear theme, right down to the welcoming teddy bear on the bed. Opened in 1990, it has 68 motel-style rooms, a coin-op laundry, Wi-Fi, an exercise room, and a sauna. The priciest guest rooms are the hot-tub suites. Rates include continental breakfast with a waffle station. At night, the breakfast room morphs into a small but casual café serving everything from burgers and pizzas to ribs and salmon. Pets are accepted for $10.

In Milford is a real bargain for families. The **Milford Motel on the River** (154 Rte. 2, Milford, 800/282-3330, www.milfordmotelontheriver.com, $99-125) is an older but well-maintained property with accommodations ranging from guest rooms with kitchenettes to two-bedroom suites with living areas and full kitchens. There's a coin-op laundry on the premises.

FOOD

Orono's restaurants are clustered downtown on Main and Mill Streets, making it easy to window-shop the options to find one that satisfies your hunger.

Local Flavors

Burritos, quesadillas, smoothies, and bagels constitute the menu at **Verve** (2 Mill St., Orono, 207/866-4004, www.verveburritos.com, 8am-4pm daily), an order-at-the-counter joint, with both table and lounge-style seating. For burgers and hot dogs, check out **The Family Dog** (6 Mill St., Orono, 207/866-2808, www.thefamilydogorono.com, 7am-10pm Mon.-Sat., 9am-10pm Sun.), where a Sunday Jazz Brunch is served until 2pm. Fat sandwiches are the rule at **Harvest Moon Deli** (18 Mill St., Orono, 207/866-3354, 10am-4pm daily).

After visiting Leonard's Mills, head over to **Spencer's Ice Cream** (77 Main St., Bradley, 207/827-8670), which has been dishing out homemade ice cream since 1930.

Family Favorites

Orono's veteran restaurant is **Pat's Pizza** (11 Mill St., Orono, 207/866-2111, 7am-midnight Sun.-Thurs., 7am-1am Fri.-Sat.), a statewide family-owned chain founded in Orono in July 1931 by C. D. "Pat" Farnsworth. Then known as Farnsworth's Cafe, it became Pat's Pizza in 1953. Pizza toppings are endless and even include pineapple, sauerkraut, and capers. Subs, calzones, burgers, and "tomato Italian" entrées are also on the menu.

Casual Dining

Every college town needs a **Woodman's** (31 Main St., Orono, 207/866-4040, www.woodmansbarandgrill.com, 4pm-10pm daily, $9-23), a casual restaurant with a menu ranging from burgers and sandwiches to chicken marsala and New York strip. Don't go looking for culinary wonders here, just good food and service.

INFORMATION AND SERVICES

The best source of information on Orono and Old Town is the **Bangor Region Chamber of Commerce** (519 Main St., Bangor, 207/947-0307, www.bangorregion.com). Also helpful is the **Orono Town Office** (59 Main St., Orono, 207/866-2556, www.orono.org).

GETTING THERE AND AROUND

By car, Bangor is about 10 miles or 15 minutes to Orono via I-95.

Serving Bangor, Brewer, Old Town, Veazie, Orono, and Hampden is **BAT Community Connector** (207/992-4670). The service operates 6:15am-6:15pm Monday-Saturday, with no Hamden service on Saturday. The fare is $1.25, exact change required.

KENNEBEC AND MOOSE RIVER REGION

For more than 3,000 years, the Kennebec and Québec's Chaudière Rivers have been the primary routes for trade and migration between Canada's St. Lawrence River and the Gulf of Maine, between Québec City and the sea. People and goods have moved through history along this corridor: farmers migrating north, hoping to profit from the Québec market; French, Irish, and British families moving south in search of opportunity; escaping slaves following the Underground Railroad north; economic opportunists smuggling alcohol south during prohibition. The most famous traveler was Benedict Arnold, who followed the route on foot and in bateaux with a band of Colonial militia in 1775 in his ill-fated attempt to capture Québec City from the British.

The river wends its way through Somerset and Kennebec Counties from Indian Pond through The Forks, Bingham, Skowhegan, Waterville, Augusta, and Richmond, and then on toward the sea at Bath. Augusta, the state's capital, is rich in historical sights and balanced by the shops and restaurants in Hallowell. Waterville is home to Colby College, alone worth a visit for its Museum of Art. The region's lovely lakes districts—Belgrade Lakes, China Lakes, and Winthrop Lakes—have been favorite summer destinations for generations upon generations. On the outskirts are rural farming communities such as Unity, home to an Amish colony and an annual organic-foods fair that's a draw for urbanites and back-to-the-landers alike.

Many towns along the Kennebec had wood or textile mills. Locals called the rotten-egg

HIGHLIGHTS

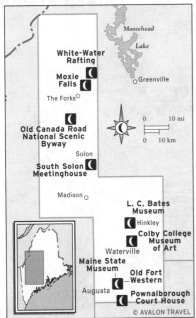

© AVALON TRAVEL

LOOK FOR ◖ TO FIND RECOMMENDED SIGHTS, ACTIVITIES, DINING, AND LODGING.

◖ **Maine State Museum:** Spend a few hours immersed in Maine's history and pick up all kinds of "Well, what do you know?" trivia (page 509).

◖ **Old Fort Western:** The nation's oldest stockaded fort hosted Benedict Arnold on his march to Québec (page 509).

◖ **Pownalborough Court House:** President John Adams once handled a trial in this pre-Revolutionary riverside courthouse (page 510).

◖ **Colby College Museum of Art:** American art is on display in this recently expanded campus museum (page 525).

◖ **L. C. Bates Museum:** View all sorts of eccentric natural-history relics and then walk the trails in the forest (page 531).

◖ **South Solon Meetinghouse:** From the exterior it looks like just another New England meetinghouse—inside, however, wow! (page 535)

◖ **Moxie Falls:** It's a short hike into one of New England's tallest waterfalls (page 536).

◖ **Old Canada Road National Scenic Byway:** Benedict Arnold marched his troops along a good stretch of this National Scenic Byway along the Kennebec River (page 536).

◖ **White-Water Rafting:** For thrills, take a wild guided ride down the Kennebec River (page 537).

stench emitted from the papermaking smokestacks "the smell of money." The region's mill-driven economy is dying, and dependent communities take a big hit with each closure or cutback. Many are finding new hope for the future in renovating old mills into new housing and business complexes or in ecotourism, especially from Skowhegan north, where the wilderness lakes, forests, and mountains provide endless opportunities for outdoors-oriented folks. And on the culinary front, Skowhegan is now Maine's bread center and Somerset

County has the distinction of being the country's top producer of maple syrup.

Traditional outdoor sports such as hunting, fishing, hiking, camping, and boating were joined by white-water rafting in 1976. That's the year timber companies stopped floating logs down the Kennebec to their lumber mills and gutsy outdoorsman Wayne Hockmeyer decided to take a rubber raft through the Kennebec Gorge. He survived, and since then, white-water rafting has mushroomed, focusing long-overdue attention on the beautiful

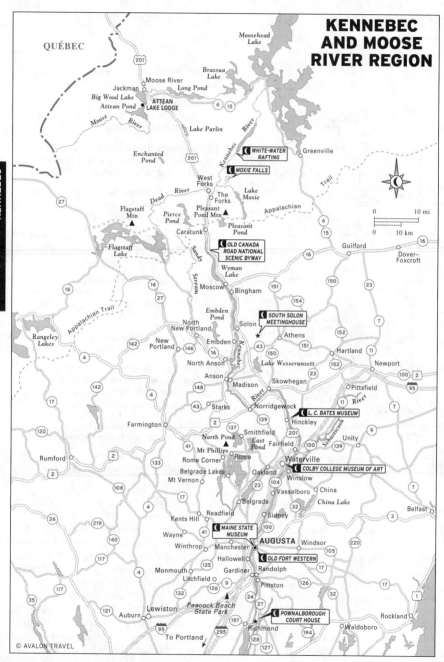

KENNEBEC

KENNEBEC AND MOOSE RIVER REGION

QUÉBEC

Moosehead Lake

Moose River
Jackman
Big Wood Lake
Attean Pond
ATTEAN LAKE LODGE

Brassua Lake
Long Pond
Lake Parlin

Enchanted Pond

WHITE-WATER RAFTING
Greenville

MOXIE FALLS

West Forks
The Forks
Lake Moxie

Flagstaff Mtn
Pierce Pond
Pleasant Pond Mtn
Appalachian

Caratunk
Pleasant Pond
Flagstaff Lake

OLD CANADA ROAD NATIONAL SCENIC BYWAY
Guilford
Dover-Foxcroft

Wyman Lake
Moscow
Bingham

Rangeley Lakes
Appalachian Trail

Embden Pond
North New Portland
Solon
SOUTH SOLON MEETINGHOUSE
Athens
Hartland
Newport

New Portland
Embden
North Anson
Lake Wesserunsett

Anson
Madison
Skowhegan
Pittsfield

Starks
Norridgewock
L. C. BATES MUSEUM
Hinckley

Farmington
North Pond
Smithfield
East Pond
Fairfield
Unity

Mt Phillips
Rome Corner
Rome
Waterville
COLBY COLLEGE MUSEUM OF ART

Rumford
Belgrade Lakes
Mt Vernon
Oakland
Winslow
Vassalboro
China

Belgrade
China Lake
Belfast

Readfield
Sidney

Kents Hill
MAINE STATE MUSEUM

Wayne
Winthrop
Manchester
AUGUSTA
Windsor

Hallowell
OLD FORT WESTERN

Monmouth
Gardiner
Randolph
Pittston

Litchfield

Peacock Beach State Park
POWNALBOROUGH COURT HOUSE

Auburn
Lewiston
Richmond
Rockland
Waldoboro

To Portland

© AVALON TRAVEL

Upper Kennebec Valley and creating a whole new crowd of enthusiasts for this region. Augmenting that is the Maine Huts Trail, which connects The Forks to Carrabassett Valley.

PLANNING YOUR TIME

Depending on your interests, you can swim, canoe, raft, hike, mountain bike, snowmobile, or cross-country ski; tour museums and historic sites; take walking tours; shop; or blend it all into one rich excursion of history, heritage, culture, and adventure.

Getting around the region is easy: Route 201 parallels the Kennebec River from one end to the other. The downside is that Route 201 is also the major highway from Québec to the U.S. coast, and it may seem as if everyone else but you is simply trying to get from point A to point B in record time. Traffic generally isn't heavy, but it can be disconcerting to have a big rig on your bumper on the narrow and winding stretches of the road. Once you're above Skowhegan, moose also become a danger. Be wary, especially around dawn and dusk or in early spring, when moose often lick salt residue on roadsides.

Think of Route 201 as the region's spine, and Routes 2, 3, 16, 17, and 27 as crucial vertebrae linking it to Maine's Western Lakes and Mountains, Highlands, and Mid-Coast regions. There's a good chance you're going to pass through the region if you're gallivanting around the state. From Norridgewock, Route 201A parallels the river on its western banks, passing through Madison and the Ansons and pretty farm country before rejoining Route 201 in Bingham.

Unless you're a snowmobiler, May-October is the best time to appreciate this part of Maine. In May-June, blackflies are notorious and can make outdoor pleasures—with the exception of fishing—true misery. July-September, when both the air and water are warm, is the best time for white-water rafting, for recreation on the lakes, and for hiking. In late September-early October, when the foliage is at its peak, driving the northern stretch of Route 201, a National Scenic Byway, is glorious.

Outdoor enthusiasts will want to spend at least 2-3 days in and around The Forks or Jackman region, where rafting, canoeing, and hiking opportunities are plentiful. Plan on another 1-2 days to visit the cultural diversions clustered in Augusta and Waterville. If you want to loop out to Unity and Thorndike, add another half day or so (but don't even consider doing so during the third weekend in September, unless you're heading to the Maine Organic Farmers and Gardeners Association's annual Common Ground Fair). Of course, generations of folk spend a week or longer every summer in the lakes regions surrounding Augusta, but you can dip your toes in for a sample in a day or two.

If you're history-minded—or just interested in "heritage touring"—consider following the **Kennebec-Chaudière International Corridor,** a historic route that stretches from Bath, Maine, to Québec City. Native Americans used it on foot and by canoe; Benedict Arnold used it; and enterprising 19th-century traders found it invaluable for moving their wares between the United States and Canada. Along the route are museums, churches, dramatic scenery, and French and American cultural centers. The heritage, people, and landscape are brought to life on a CD, *Deep Woods and River Roads,* narrated by Nick Spitzer, folklorist and host of Public Radio International's *American Routes.* It can be purchased at museums and visitors centers along the route.

KENNEBEC

Augusta and Vicinity

As the state capital, **Augusta** (pop. 19,136) is where everything is supposed to happen. A lot does happen here, but don't be surprised to find the imposing State House and lovely governor's mansion the centerpieces of a relatively sleepy city. Augusta is the seventh-largest city in Maine and no megalopolis, but it *is* the heart of state government and central Maine.

Pilgrims first settled here on the banks of the Kennebec River in the 17th century, and Boston merchants established Fort Western in the mid-18th century. Augusta was named state capital in 1827.

The three best-known communities south of Augusta—Hallowell, Gardiner, and Richmond—all scale down hillsides to the river, making their settings especially attractive. In **Hallowell** (pop. 2,381), settled in 1762, the main thoroughfare still retains the air of its former days as a prosperous port and source of granite and ice. The entire downtown, with brick sidewalks and attractive shops and restaurants, is a National Historic District.

Six miles south of Augusta, **Gardiner** (pop. 5,800), the "Tilbury Town" of noted author Edwin Arlington Robinson, claims more buildings on the National Register of Historic Places than any of its neighbors. The Gardiner Historic District includes more than 45 downtown buildings. Main Street is a gem, and although still too many storefronts are empty, there's a bit of a buzz here. Besides Robinson, another prominent Gardiner resident was Laura Howe Richards, author of *Captain January* and daughter of Julia Ward Howe, who wrote "The Battle Hymn of the Republic." (The yellow Federal-style home where Richards and her husband raised seven children, at 3 Dennis Street, is not open to the public.) Most outstanding of Gardiner's mansions (also not open to the public) is Oaklands, a Gothic Revival home built in 1836 by the grandson of founding father Dr. Sylvester Gardiner, a wealthy land speculator.

Just over the border in Sagadahoc County, **Richmond** (pop. 3,411), also flush with handsome buildings, was the site of a Russian émigré community in the 1950s. Here's a town that awaits rediscovery. Just over the bridge is a pre-Revolutionary courthouse, and north of that, also on the river, is the starting point of Benedict Arnold's march to Québec.

West of Augusta, amid the Winthrop Lakes region, the town of **Monmouth** (pop. 4,104) is the site of Cumston Hall, a dramatic turn-of-the-20th-century structure that now houses the Theater at Monmouth as well as the municipal offices and public library.

SIGHTS
Maine State House
From almost every vantage point in Augusta, your eye catches the prominent dome of the Maine State House, centerpiece of the

© TOM NANGLE

Maine's capitol is in Augusta.

KENNEBEC

government complex on the west side of the Kennebec River. Occupying the corner of State and Capitol Streets, the State House dates originally from 1832, when it was completed to the design of famed Boston architect Charles Bulfinch, who modeled it on his Massachusetts State House design. Only a dozen years had passed since Maine had separated from Massachusetts; Augusta had become the state capital in 1827. Granite for the building came from quarries in nearby Hallowell; the total construction cost was $145,000. Atop the oxidized copper dome stands a gold-gilded sculpture, *Lady Wisdom.* In the early 20th century, space needs forced a major expansion of the building, leaving only the eight-columned front portico as the Bulfinch legacy.

Visitors are welcome to wander around the State House (after clearing entry screening), but check first to see whether the legislature is in session. If so, parking becomes scarce, the hallways become congested, and access may be restricted. The best place to enter the building is on the west side, facing the more modern state office building; the entrance is marked "Maine State House." Pick up the useful brochure for a self-guided tour, or better still, take a free 45-60-minute guided tour, usually available 9am and 11am and noon weekdays. Call ahead (207/287-2301; tours are organized by the Maine State Museum) to arrange it, or ask at the kiosk.

On the Blaine House side of the State House is a replica of the **Liberty Bell,** with the same dimensions, weight, aged-oak yoke, iron straps, hand-forged bolts, and inscription. Only the crack is indicated, so this one can ring true. The bell was crafted in 1950, when the U.S. Department of the Treasury donated one to each state to promote the Savings Bond Independence Drive.

Maine State Museum

If the Smithsonian is the nation's attic, welcome to Maine's attic—and a well-organized one at that. At the **Maine State Museum** (State House Complex, Augusta, 207/287-2301, www.mainestatemuseum.org, 9am-5pm Tues.-Fri., 10am-4pm Sat., $2 adults, $1 ages 6-18 and seniors, $6 family), gears and tools spin and whir in the intriguing *Made in Maine* industrial exhibits, focusing on quarrying, ice harvesting, fishing, agriculture, lumbering, and shipbuilding. A spiraled archaeological exhibit covers the past 12 millennia of Maine's history. Some displays are interactive, and all exhibits are wheelchair-accessible. Gallery guides are available in French, German, Spanish, Japanese, and Russian. During the winter, the museum sponsors a free lecture series, and special programs occur throughout the year. A small gift shop stocks historical publications and Maine-related gifts and toys. The museum is part of the state government complex that includes the State House and the Maine State Library. The museum and library share a building, separated by a parking lot from the State House.

The Blaine House

In 1833, a year after the State House was ready for business, retired sea captain James Hall finished his elegant new home across the street. But it was not until 29 years later, when prominent politico James G. Blaine assumed ownership, that the house became the hotbed of state and national political ferment. No underachiever, Blaine was a Maine congressman and senator, Speaker of the U.S. House, U.S. secretary of state under two presidents, and Republican candidate for the presidency. Two decades after his death, Blaine's widow donated the family home to the state of Maine; it has been the governor's mansion ever since.

Free 25-minute guided tours of the ground-floor public areas of the **Blaine House** (State St. and Capitol St., Augusta, 207/287-2121, www.blainehouse.org) are given 2pm-4pm Tuesday-Thursday year-round. Reservations are required and a completed security form is required and must be submitted prior to tour date.

Old Fort Western

Built in 1754 for the French and Indian Wars and restored as recently as 1988, **Old Fort Western** (16 Cony St., Augusta, 207/626-2385,

KENNEBEC

THE RUSSIANS WERE COMING

In the 1950s, the sleepy Kennebec River town of Richmond, 12 miles south of Maine's state capital, became the center of a unique and unlikely colony as several hundred Russian-speaking refugee families settled among the area's villages and rolling farmland. The Kennebec Valley, economically depressed and remote from other Russian immigrant centers in the United States, seems an improbable choice for a Slavic enclave. Yet Richmond soon boasted a Russian restaurant, a Russian boot-maker's shop, a balalaika orchestra, and even onion domes—on St. Alexander Nevsky, Maine's first Russian Orthodox church, which celebrated its 50th anniversary in 2003. For the first time, Russian was heard on Richmond's streets, and Russian-speaking children enrolled in local schools. At the time, Richmond had the distinction of being home to the largest rural Russian-speaking population in the country.

The settlement was the brainchild of Baron Vladimir von Poushental, a swashbuckling veteran of the czar's World War I air force. Fleeing the Bolshevik Revolution, he landed in New York, where his personality and family connections gained him entry to a series of managerial jobs, if not to the wealth he had enjoyed as a Russian noble. An expert marksman and dedicated hunter, von Poushental in 1947 decided to retire to a modest cabin in the Kennebec Valley, where he had hunted and fished for many years. There he began buying up abandoned farms and promoting the valley's attractions to fellow Russian émigrés. The climate and coun-

tryside resembled Russia's, he said, and land was cheap. For a few thousand dollars, a refugee could buy a house and 30 acres. To create a nucleus for the settlers, the baron donated a 400-acre farm to the aging veterans of Russia's White armies, and he helped them establish a retirement home and an Orthodox chapel.

And so they came: Ukrainians, Russians, Belorussians, and Cossacks; professors, farmers, artists, and carpenters. Some came directly from Europe's displaced-persons camps, others from homes and jobs in U.S. cities where they had lived for years. The settlers shared a common language, their Orthodox faith, a zest for life, and a hatred of the Soviet regime. The younger émigrés worked, raised families, and became part of the larger American community around them. Their elderly parents felt more comfortable associating with other Russian-speakers.

Today the boot-maker and restaurant are gone. Most of the elderly—the old émigrés from pre-Communist Russia—are dead, their Cyrillic gravestones dotting the Richmond cemetery. Their grandchildren, Russian Americans, have merged successfully into the mainstream United States. Most have married outside their ethnic group, and many have taken jobs outside the Kennebec Valley, not necessarily by choice. Yet a fair number still live and work in the area. In a way that might have surprised even von Poushental, who died in 1978, the colony he sponsored took root and flourished in a part of the country he loved.

www.oldfortwestern.org, 1pm-4pm daily late May-early Sept., 1pm-4pm Sat.-Sun. early Sept.-mid-Oct., $6 adults, $4 ages 6-16), reputedly the nation's oldest remaining stockaded fort, has witnessed British, French, and Native Americans squabbling over this Kennebec riverfront site. Benedict Arnold and his troops camped here during their 1775 march to Québec. Today, costumed interpreters help visitors travel through time to the 18th century; hands-on demonstrations—butter churning,

musket drill, barrel building, weaving, even vinegar making—occur daily Fourth of July-Labor Day. The fort is also open 1pm-3pm on the first Sunday of the month November-January, and 1pm-3pm on Maple Syrup Day, the fourth Sunday in March. The museum is on the east bank of the Kennebec River in downtown Augusta, next to Augusta City Hall.

◖ Pownalborough Court House

If you're an architecture fan or a history buff,

don't miss the 1761 **Pownalborough Court House** (River Rd./Rte. 128, Dresden, 207/882-9628, www.lincolncountyhistory.org, 10am-4pm Tues.-Sat. and noon-4pm Sun. July-Aug., Sat.-Sun. only June and Sept.-mid-Oct., $5 ages 15 and older), a pre-Revolutionary riverfront courthouse listed in the National Register of Historic Places. President John Adams once handled a trial here—in this mid-18th-century frontier community (named Pownalborough) established by French and German settlers. During the 30-minute tour of the three-story courthouse, docents delight in pointing out the restored beams, paneling, and fireplaces, as well as the on-site tavern that catered to judges, lawyers, and travelers. Walk a few hundred feet south and you'll find a cemetery with graves of Revolutionary, War of 1812, and Civil War veterans. Also here are maintained trails along the riverfront and in the woods. From Richmond, take Route 195, crossing the river, and then Route 128 north. From here, if you continue north on 128 and then north on Route 27, you'll come to the Colburn House.

Major Reuben Colburn House

Another must-stop for history buffs, the newly restored **Major Reuben Colburn House** (13 Arnold Rd., off Rte. 27, Pittston, www.maine.gov/colburnhouse, tours 1pm-5pm Sat.-Sun., July-Aug.) was the launching point for Benedict Arnold's 1775 assault on Québec City. When Arnold and his expedition numbering more than 1,000 soldiers arrived here, they found 200 bateaux, built by Colburn upon orders of Gen. George Washington, to take them through Maine's wilderness by following the Kennebec and Dead Rivers. It was Colburn who conceived the idea for the attack and sold it to Gen. Washington, and it was Colburn, with local workmen, who built the boats in a two-week time frame, without seasoned lumber and with a nail shortage. Among those who accompanied Arnold on his march were Aaron Burr and Henry Dearborn. Colburn financed much of the expedition, but was never reimbursed by the government, which later led to his financial ruin. The Colburn House

also serves as the headquarters for the **Arnold Expedition Historical Society** (www.arnoldsmarch.com). Like the nearby Pownalborough Court House, the Colburn House is on the east side of the Kennebec.

Walking and Driving Tours

Many of Hallowell's distinctive homes have stories to tell. Stop by **Hallowell City Hall** (1 Winthrop St., 207/623-4021) to pick up a copy of the *Museums in the Streets* map or visit www.historichallowell.org to download a walking brochure.

Fans of poet Edgar Arlington Robinson will find a map of Gardiner-area ("Tilbury Town") sites at www.earobinson.com.

ENTERTAINMENT

The **Gaslight Theater,** a talented community-theater group, performs periodically throughout the year at the **Hallowell City Hall Auditorium** (Winthrop St., Hallowell, 207/626-3698, www.gaslighttheater.org).

Six miles south of Augusta, the 1864 **Johnson Hall Performing Arts Center** (280 Water St., Gardiner, 207/582-7144, www.johnsonhall.org) is the year-round site of just about anything anyone wants to present—plays, lectures, art camps, after-school programs, classes, concerts, and more.

Maine's enduring Shakespearean theater is the **Theater at Monmouth** (796 Main St./Rte. 132, Monmouth, box office 207/933-9999 or 800/769-9698 in Maine, www.theateratmonmouth.org, $28), based in Monmouth's architecturally astonishing **Cumston Hall.** Completed in 1900, the Romanesque Victorian structure has columns, cutout shingles, stained glass, and a huge square tower. The interior is equally stunning, with frescoes and a vaulted ceiling. The theater's summer season, performed by professionals in rotating repertory, runs early July-August. Shakespeare usually gets the nod for one or two of the four plays. Tickets for the family show are $15 adults, $10 children.

During the school year, the **University of Maine at Augusta** campus schedules lectures,

KENNEBEC

© HILARY NANGLE

Benedict Arnold's march to Quebec began at the Major Reuben Colburn House.

concerts, and other performances. Check with the school (student activities 207/621-3000, ext. 3442, or information center 877/862-1234, www.uma.edu) for current information.

FESTIVALS AND EVENTS

The Augusta area seems to claim more country fairs than any other part of the state; don't miss an opportunity to attend at least one. Each has a different flavor, but there are always lots of animals, games, and junk food, often a carnival, and sometimes harness racing.

In June, the Maine Alpaca Association sponsors the **Maine Fiber Frolic** (www.fiberfrolic.com), a celebration of fiber, fiber animals, and fiber arts at the Windsor Fairgrounds. Expect llamas, alpacas, angora rabbits, sheep, goats, and other livestock as well as demonstrations, workshops, and exhibits.

In mid-June, the annual **Blistered Fingers Family Bluegrass Music Festival** (www.blisteredfingers.com) takes place at the Litchfield Fairgrounds in Litchfield.

The small four-day **Pittston Fair** (www.pittstonfair.com) features agricultural exhibits, a carnival, and even a woodsman contest at the Pittston Fairgrounds, East Pittston, in mid-July. The third Saturday in July, **Old Hallowell Day** (www.oldhallowellday.org) includes a craft fair, a parade, food booths, and a road race in downtown Hallowell. The **Monmouth Fair** fills four days with agricultural exhibits, a carnival, and crafts in early August.

The last week of August, the Windsor Fairgrounds come alive with the weeklong **Windsor Fair,** with agricultural exhibits, harness racing, a demolition derby, a beauty pageant, and a carnival.

The three-day **Litchfield Fair** has farm exhibits, animal pulling, a carnival, and more the second weekend in September.

SHOPPING

Two towns south of Augusta draw shoppers. Both **Hallowell** and **Gardiner** have boutiques, restaurants, specialty shops, and antiques stores.

Art, Crafts, and Antiques

Kennebec River Artisans (130 Water St., Hallowell, 207/623-2345) shows and sells the wares of more than three dozen craftspeople. The **Harlow Gallery** (160 Water St., Hallowell, 207/622-3813), headquarters for the Kennebec Valley Art Association, serves as a magnet not only for its member artists but also for friends of art. One of Maine's best sources for vintage lighting is **Brass and Friends Antiques** (154 Water St., Hallowell, 207/626-3287).

Books

The apt slogan at **Merrill's Bookshop** (134 Water St., 2nd Fl., Hallowell, 207/623-2055) is "Good literature from Edward Abbey to Leane Zugsmith." John Merrill has an eye for unusual rare and used books, so you may walk out with a personal treasure.

General Store

"Guns. Wedding Gowns. Cold Beer." The sign outside **Hussey's General Store** (510 Ridge Rd./Rte. 32 at Rte. 105, Windsor, 207/445-2511, www.husseysgeneralstore.com) says it all. With merchandise spread out on three floors, there isn't much that Hussey's doesn't have, and that bridal department does a steady business. Its slogan: "If we don't have it, you don't need it." From Augusta, take Route 105 about 11 miles east to Route 32; Hussey's is on the corner. If you're at the Windsor Fairgrounds, the store is only about two miles farther north on Route 32.

RECREATION
Parks and Preserves

On the east side of State Street, between the State House and the river, is 10-acre **Capitol Park,** a great place for a picnic after visiting the Maine State Museum, the State House, and the Blaine House. In the park is the **Maine Vietnam Veterans Memorial,** a dramatic "you are there" walk-through monument erected in 1985.

VILES ARBORETUM

On the east side of the Kennebec River, the **Viles Arboretum** (153 Hospital St./Rte. 9, Augusta, 207/621-0031, www.vilesarboretum. org, dawn-dusk daily) devotes 224 acres to more than 300 varieties of trees and shrubs. Bring a picnic (carry-in, carry-out) and wander the nearly six-mile trail network. If you're a birder, bring binoculars; more than 150 species have been spotted here. Well-designed planting clusters include hosta and rhododendron collections, a rock garden, an antique apple orchard, and the Governors Grove, with a white pine dedicated to each Maine governor. Stop first at the **Viles Visitor Center** (8am-4pm Mon.-Fri.) to pick up a trail map. Leashed pets are allowed; smoking is not allowed on the grounds. During the winter, the trails are groomed for cross-country skiing. Admission is free; donations are appreciated.

Next to the arboretum parking lot is **Cony Cemetery** (also known as Knight Cemetery), one of Augusta's oldest, with gravestones dating from the late 18th century. Old-cemetery buffs will want to check it out, but rubbings are not permitted.

KENNEBEC VALLEY GARDEN CLUB PARK

Escape the shopping hubbub in this pocket of tranquility at the Augusta Civic Center. Designed in 1974 by Lyle Littlefield, a professor of horticulture at the University of Maine, it's now maintained by club members. Within the two-acre park's borders are a water-lily pond rimmed with cattails, two formal gardens, and trails edged by perennials. Nearby are children's butterfly and hummingbird gardens and woodlands with wildflowers.

JAMIES POND WILDLIFE MANAGEMENT AREA

Maine's Department of Inland Fisheries and Wildlife manages this 840-acre preserve with a 107-acre pond. The pond, stocked with brook trout and splake, appeals equally to anglers, birders, wildlife-watchers, and paddlers. Mapped trails weave through the surrounding woodlands. Access is from Outlet Road, just west of the Maple Hill Farm Inn in Hallowell.

VAUGHN WOODS

Just steps from downtown Hallowell is this Hobbit-like landscape, with a babbling brook, pond, stone bridges, and a dam. Paths weave through the 166 acres, which are a joy to explore. The parking area is on the corner of Middle Street and Litchfield Road.

Swan Island

The Maine Department of Inland Fisheries and Wildlife (IF&W) has established a byzantine reservation system to limit visitors to its **Steve Powell Wildlife Management Area** (207/547-5322, www.state.me.us/ifw/education/swan-island) on 1,755-acre, four-mile-long Swan Island in the middle of the Kennebec River. Don't be daunted; it's worth the effort. The entire island is on the National Register of Historic Places. Well-marked trails are everywhere; one trail takes 30 minutes, another takes three hours and goes the length of the lovely wooded island. No license is needed for fishing, but even private boats need permission to land here (near the campground); small boats are not recommended because of 10-foot tidal variations. Bikes are permitted on the center main road only, and cars and pets are not allowed.

Getting here requires taking a small ferry the very short distance from a dock in Richmond, next to the town-owned Waterfront Park on Route 24. The boat operates May 1-Labor Day. Call for reservations. Day-use admission is $8 over age 3. Pack a picnic lunch; fireplaces at the campground are available for day use if no campers are using them, but bring tinfoil for cooking. Alcohol is not allowed on the island.

The island, settled in the early 1700s, once had as many as 95 resident farmers, fishermen, ice cutters, and shipbuilders. Now there are derelict antique houses, a herd of white-tailed deer, wild turkeys, nesting bald eagles, plenty of waterfowl and other birds, and the primitive campground.

Swan Island's campground has 10 well-spaced lean-tos, each sleeping six, with picnic tables, fireplaces, and outhouses; firewood and potable water are provided. Cost is $14 over age 3, plus the state's 7 percent lodging tax. There's a two-night maximum. The policy is carry-in, carry-out, so bring trash bags. A rickety flat-bed truck with benches meets campers at the island dock and transports them the 1.5 miles to the campground. The same truck does the island tour.

Bicycling

You can walk, bike, ski, or run the **Kennebec River Rail Trail** (KRRT), keeping an eye peeled for bald eagles, salmon, and just the general flow of the Kennebec. The Friends of KRRT (www.krrt.org) maintains the 6.5-mile riverside trail connecting Augusta's Waterfront Park to Gardiner.

Golf

Ten miles north of Augusta and 12 miles south of Waterville, the **Natanis Golf Club** (Webber Pond Rd., Vassalboro, 207/622-3561, www.natanisgc.com) has been the site of many a Maine golf tournament. Named after a trusted Indian guide, the Natanis club has two separate 18-hole courses.

Water Sports

Take a look at a map of the region and you'll find plenty of blue indicating lakes, ponds, rivers, and streams. **Collins Boat Rentals** (290 Rte. 135, Monmouth, 207/933-4782) rents canoes and kayaks for $20/eight-hour day or $100/week; reservations are required. Fishing boat rentals begin at $45/day for an open 14-foot aluminum boat with 6 hp motor.

For swimming, head 12 miles south of Augusta to **Peacock Beach** (Rte. 201, Richmond, 207/737-4305), a quiet 100-acre park on long, narrow Pleasant Pond.

Fish for stripers and blue fish on the Kennebec River with Gardiner-based **Maine Experience Guide Service** (207/215-3828, www.maineexperienceguideservice.com) with Master Maine Guide Jay Farris. Rates begin at $250 for four hours and cover up to three people. In autumn, Farris also offers a five-hour foliage tour down the Kennebec, including a shore lunch, for $175, covering up to two people.

Richmond Corner Sauna

Meriting a recreational category of its own—or maybe it should qualify as entertainment—the clothing-optional **Richmond Corner Sauna** (81 Dingley Rd., Richmond, 207/737-4752 or 800/400-5751, www.richmondsauna.com, $25 pp) is one of those funky places you either like or you don't. But it has been here since 1976, and maybe you'll like it. Finnish-American owner Richard Jarvi has built a loyal clientele for his authentic wood-heated sauna house with six private rooms and a group one. In between and afterward, there's a pool and a hot tub. If nudity bothers you, don't come. If you're too relaxed to drive after the sauna, the casual, clothing-optional main house, built in 1831, has five B&B guest rooms ($85 d) with shared baths; room rates include sauna, pool, and hot tub access as well as a continental breakfast. The sauna is open 5pm-9pm Tuesday-Sunday in winter, 6pm-10pm Tuesday-Sunday in summer. From downtown Richmond, take Route 197 west about five miles and turn left (south) onto Route 138. Take an immediate left onto Dingley Road, where you'll see the sign.

ACCOMMODATIONS

On the western side of the city, close to I-95 but convenient to downtown and the Capitol complex, is the **Senator Inn and Spa** (284 Western Ave., Augusta, 207/622-5804 or 877/772-2224, www.senatorinn.com, $110-280), with a decent restaurant, a full-service spa, and indoor and outdoor heated pools. Some rooms have fireplaces or whirlpool tubs. Pets are allowed in certain rooms for $12/night. Rates include a deluxe continental breakfast.

Bed-and-Breakfasts

On a back road only 10 minutes from the State House, 130-acre **Maple Hill Farm Bed and Breakfast Inn and Conference Center** (11 Inn Rd., off Outlet Rd., Hallowell, 207/622-2708 or 800/622-2708, www.maplebb.com,

$115-209) provides a green, rural respite. Eight guest rooms (all with Wi-Fi, phones, cable TV, video players, air-conditioning, and individual heat control) in the informal renovated 1890s farmhouse overlook woods, fields, gardens, and even the Camden Hills. Some guest rooms have double whirlpool tubs, gas fireplaces, and private decks. Public areas include a living room, a hot tub, and a sauna. Breakfast is a custom-cooked affair from a menu and features the inn's own fresh eggs as an option. Coffee, tea, and baked goodies are available anytime in the inn's common guest kitchen. No pets are permitted because of the delightful farm animals, including llamas, cows, and goats. The eco-aware inn is a leader in the green movement. It has a wind-generating turbine, extensive solar panels, and other green initiatives. Maple Hill Farm is three miles west of downtown Hallowell, next to an 800-acre wildlife preserve with an extensive trail network and a wonderful pond.

About 10 miles southwest of Augusta but a world removed is **A Rise and Shine B&B** (19 Moose Run Dr./Rte. 135, Monmouth, 207/933-9876, www.riseandshinebb.com, $100-150), the former Woolworth family estate overlooking Lake Cobbosseeconte in Monmouth. Restoring the main house after it had been empty for five years has been ongoing for partners Lorette Comeau and Tom Crocker, but they're turning it into a real prize, with Lorette's hand-painted murals in a few of the eight guest rooms. The overall atmosphere is very inviting, with plenty of shared public rooms—a great room, a living room, a dining room, a huge patio, and a TV room—to spread out and relax. They welcome families and have even created a children's garden as well as a giant checkerboard court (OK, adults love it too). Rates include a full breakfast; Wi-Fi and computer access are provided. Two first-floor rooms connect through a bath for a family suite. In the evenings, Tom, a professional singer, often entertains guests—a real treat. Also on the premises is a small rental cottage with two bedrooms and a full kitchen ($300). Here's a twist on pets: The property previously was a racehorse farm, so horses can be accommodated by arrangement.

It's a short walk to downtown shops and restaurants from the colonial-style **Second Street Bed & Breakfast** (68 Second St., Hallowell, 207/622-2213, www.secondstbandb.com, $150-175). Each of the five guest rooms has individually controlled heat. There's Wi-Fi, and a full breakfast is included.

FOOD
Local Flavors

Almost everything on the menu is made in-house at the **Downtown Diner** (204 Water St., Augusta, 207/623-9695, 5am-2pm Mon.-Fri., 6am-2pm Sat., 7am-1pm Sun.), a reliable spot for inexpensive good home cookin' in the spot once occupied by Hersey's Shoe Store, which the marquee still advertises.

Expanding from its original Belfast store to a location near the State House, **Bay Wrap** (1 Hichborn St., Augusta, 207/620-9727, www.thebaywrap.com, 11am-7pm Mon.-Fri., 11am-4pm Sat.) fills tortillas with all kinds of concoctions. The Samurai Salmon is divine.

Great sandwiches, soups, salads, breads, delish cookies, and other treats come from **Slates Deli** (165 Water St., Hallowell, 207/622-4104, 7:30am-3pm Mon.-Fri., 7:30am-2pm Sat.).

Peruse used books while waiting for your order at **Lisa's Legit Burritos** (242 Water St., Gardiner, 207/203-2013, 11am-7pm Mon.-Thurs., 11am-8pm Fri.-Sat.). It's an order-at-the-counter place, decorated with artsy touches.

If you're wandering around the back roads and make it as far as Readfield Center, duck into the **Readfield Emporium** (1146 Main St., Readfield, 207/685-7348, 5pm-10pm Wed.-Sun.) for a casual dinner. Pizza is the big draw, but with options such as pizza spanakopita or pizza piccata, it's no ordinary pie shop. Other choices include Thai-grilled chicken breast and homemade grilled wine sausage; most run $8-18. The space doubles as an art gallery and wine bar, and there's often live entertainment. And here's a cool piece of trivia: Noted contemporary designer Alexis Bittar's parents own the place.

For homemade soups, sandwiches, and baked goods, tuck into **The Flaky Tart** (130 Main St., Winthrop, 207/377-8278, 8:30am-4pm Tues.-Fri., 9am-2pm Sat.). Fixed-price dinners (around $35) are offered once a month.

Put your lights on for service at **Fast Eddies** (1308 Rte. 202, Winthrop, 207/377-5550, www.fasteddiesdrivein.com, 11am-9pm daily mid-Apr.-mid-Sept.), but even if you opt for carhop service, make it a point to visit the dining room, where James Dean, Elvis, Marilyn Monroe, and Betty Boop preside over a cool collection of 1950s memorabilia. Burgers, shakes, fried foods, and homemade ice cream are the draws. Wednesday night draws antique car buffs.

Pastries, hearty breakfasts, and fat sandwiches are the lures to **Annabella's Bakery & Café** (2 Front St./Rte. 24, Richmond, 207/737-7165, www.annabellas.me, 6:30am-2:30pm Tues.-Sat., 6:30am-1pm Sun.). Take it to go and enjoy your meal in the riverside park across the street.

The yummy aromas of Old World-style baking are reason enough to venture off the beaten path to find **Black Crow Bakery** (232 Plains Rd., Litchfield, 207/268-9927, www.blackcrowbread.com, 7am-7pm Tues.-Sat.), where the specialty, a Tuscan loaf, is as pretty as it is tasty. Almost all the breads baked in the brick oven are sourdough-based, and every day features a different loaf, perhaps Sicilian, olive herb, focaccia, the fantastic apricot almond, or Greek cheese. A modern mixer is Mark and Tinker Mickalide's only high-tech tool; they operate a very traditional bakery in their 1810 farmhouse's former summer kitchen, even grinding their own grains on Maine granite. The shop, which operates on the honor system, is across from the Legion Hall, between I-495 and the Litchfield Fairgrounds.

This region is blessed with excellent homemade ice cream. Worth the trip are: **Webber's** (Rte. 201, Farmingdale); **Hamilton's** (Water St./Rte. 201, downtown Hallowell); **Tubby's** (Main St., Wayne, 207/685-8181, and 41 Main St., Winthrop, 207/377-3340), which makes outrageous flavors from scratch; and **Old**

Colony Ice Cream (28 Bowdoin St., Winthrop, 207/377-7788), just a couple of blocks from a lakeside park.

The **Augusta Farmers Market** operates 10am-1pm Wednesday and Saturday at the Turnpike Mall on Western Avenue. There's also **Farmers Market at Mill Park** at the old Edwards Mill site on the north end of Water Street, operating 2pm-6pm Tuesday. West of Augusta, the **Winthrop Farmers Market** is set up in the municipal building parking lot (Main St. in Winthrop) 9am-1pm Tuesday and Saturday.

Family Favorites

When you have a hankering for finger-lickin' Memphis-style barbecue, **Riverfront Barbeque and Grill** (300 Water St., Augusta, 207/622-8899, www.riverfrontbbq.com, 11am-9pm Mon.-Wed., 11am-10pm Thurs.-Sat., noon-9pm Sun., $9-24) delivers, serving big portions of slow-smoked goodness—and a few surprises, such as veggie risotto—at affordable prices. Everything's prepared from scratch using local ingredients, whenever possible. There's a kids' menu too.

Don't let the location inside a hotel deter you from **Cloud 9** (Senator Inn and Spa, 284 Western Ave., Augusta, 207/622-5804, 6:30am-9pm daily, $12-30). The chefs are committed to using local ingredients and take great care in preparing the fare. Choices vary from wood-oven pizzas to handmade pastas, burgers and fries to filet mignon. The brunch buffet, served 11am-2pm Sunday, brings them in from points far and wide.

Chowders, lobster stew, and fried seafood are the specialties at **Hattie's Chowder House** (103 Water St., Hallowell, 207/621-4114, 11am-9pm Mon.-Sat., 11am-8pm Sun., $7-24), but the menu has a bit of everything.

Downriver from Augusta, the **Railway Café** (64 Main St., Richmond, 207/737-2277, 6:30am-8pm Mon.-Thurs., 6:30am-9pm Fri.-Sat., 7am-4pm Sun., dinner entrées $6-20) has been the favorite local gathering spot since 1984. Looking at the original 19th-century woodwork and tin ceiling, who'd guess it had

once been a funeral parlor? Dinner entrées include steak, seafood, grilled chicken, and pizza. The café is open year-round for breakfast, lunch, and dinner.

Casual Dining

Ask anyone where to eat in the Augusta area and chances are high that the answer will be **❰ Slates** (167 Water St., Hallowell, 207/622-9575, 11am-9pm Tues.-Fri., 10am-9:30pm Sat., 10am-2pm Sun., 4:30pm-9pm Mon.), the Energizer Bunny of local restaurants. Founded in 1979, it just keeps improving. Destroyed by fire in early 2007, it rose from the ashes revitalized. Dinner options range from pizza and crepes to osso bucco and blackened haddock; most are in the $10-28 range. The weekend brunches are fabulous: grilled fish and meats, unique omelets and Benedicts, huevos rancheros, stuffed croissants, homemade granola, and salads. Vegetarian fare is available.

It's the 20-ounce pint glass, not politics, that helped christen **The Liberal Cup** (115 Water St., Hallowell, 207/623-2739, 11:30am-9pm daily, $7-14), a brewpub and restaurant where owner Geoffrey Houghton, who studied in Britain, brews great ales. Homemade is true of the food too; the place is packed with diners sampling the salads, salmon, steak, fish-and-chips, and shepherd's pie. Even the salad dressings are made on the premises.

The first-rate **❰ A-1 Diner** (3 Bridge St., Gardiner, 207/582-4804, 7am-8pm Mon.-Sat., 8am-1pm Sun., $8-16) is the real thing, a genuine classic diner with moderate prices and some added attractions, such as air-conditioning. The menu, however, goes well beyond diner fare. How about tilapia with pesto, Transylvania eggplant casserole, or Turkish lamb tagine? The soups are great too. There's also a regular diner menu, and Sunday brunch draws a big crowd.

Ethnic Fare

Café de Bangkok (272 Water St., Hallowell, 207/622-2638, www.cafedebangkokme.com, 11am-9:30pm Mon.-Thurs., 11am-10pm Fri.-Sat., 4pm-9:30pm Sun., $11-23) deserves its rep as one of Maine's best Thai restaurants. Not only is the food excellent—with great sushi—but also the setting on the Kennebec River is lovely.

If you're feeding bottomless-stomach teens, **Lucky Garden** (222 Water St., Hallowell, 207/622-3465, 11am-9pm daily, $8-26) is a great choice. The restaurant, with a nice dining room overlooking the river, is locally known for its sesame chicken. The all-you-can-eat buffets ($7.95 lunch 11am-2:30pm daily, $11.95 dinner 5pm-8:30pm Fri.-Sat.) are ideal for those with big appetites.

INFORMATION AND SERVICES

Local information is available from the **Kennebec Valley Chamber of Commerce** (207/623-4559, www.augustamaine.com), the **Hallowell Board of Trade** (207/620-7477, www.hallowell.org), and the **Kennebec Valley Tourism Council** (207/623-4884, www.kennebecvalley.org).

The Romanesque Revival **Lithgow Public Library** (Winthrop St. and State St., Augusta, 207/626-2415, www.lithgow.lib.me.us), one of Maine's handsomest libraries, was built in 1896 of Maine granite. Do not miss the gorgeous reading room, with a Tiffany clock, stained-glass windows, and French-inspired decor.

The **Maine State Library** (Maine State Cultural Building, Augusta, 207/287-5600, www.maine.gov/msl), in the State House complex, includes the Maine State Museum and the State Archives (207/287-5790) within its walls.

GETTING THERE AND AROUND

Cape Air Airlines (866/227-3247, www.capeair.com) operates flights year-round between Boston's Logan Airport and the **Augusta State Airport** (AUG, 75 Airport Rd., Augusta, 207/626-2306).

Concord Coachlines (Augusta Transportation Center, 9 Industrial Dr., Augusta, 800/639-3317, www.concordcoachlines.com) operates bus service among Portland, Augusta, and Bangor, connecting with the Maine Coast, Boston, and points south.

By car, Augusta is roughly 60 miles or 55 minutes from Portland via I-295 and I-95. It's roughly 34 miles or 1 hour from Belfast via Route 3, and roughly 75 miles or just over an hour from Bangor via I-95. It's roughly 17 miles or 30 minutes to Belgrade Lakes via Route 27.

Belgrade Lakes Area

The Belgrade Lakes area is one of those Proustian memories-of-childhood places where multigenerational family groups return year after year for idyllic summer visits full of nothing but playing, going for hikes or swims, fishing, listening for the loons, watching sunsets, and dreading the return to civilization. It was the inspiration for *On Golden Pond*—playwright Ernest Thompson spent his childhood summers here. Today's parents, recalling carefree days at one of the many Belgrade-area summer camps, now send their own kids to camp here, or they rent lakefront cottages and devote their energies to re-creating those youthful days.

Water, water everywhere: Mosey along the back roads and it seems as if there's yet another body of water around every other bend. Belgrade's chain of lakes is seven major lakes and ponds: Long Pond, North Pond, Great Pond, East Pond, Salmon Pond, McGrath Pond, and Messalonskee Lake (also known as Snow Pond), as well as numerous smaller ones; as you continue south, so do the lakes and ponds. Camps and cottages are sprinkled around their shores—you might even spot Elizabeth Arden's once-famed Maine Chance Farm. Roadside put-ins and boat-launch ramps, from which you can put in a canoe, kayak, or powerboat, can be found on every lake. This is a great area just to strap a canoe or kayak on the car and wander, stopping wherever seems interesting for a paddle. Incidentally, the village of Belgrade Lakes, heart of the region, has its own post office but is part of the towns of **Belgrade** (pop. 3,189) and **Rome** (pop. 1,010).

Since the Belgrade Lakes area is tucked in between Waterville and Augusta, those cities serve as the easily accessible commercial and cultural hubs for Belgrade visitors.

Directly west of Belgrade Lakes village is the charming, out-of-the-way hamlet of **Mount Vernon** (pop. 1,640), founded in 1792 and worth a visit by car or bike. North of that is **Vienna** (VI-enna, pop. 570); south is lovely **Kents Hill,** home to a prep school and part of the town of **Readfield** (pop. 2,598).

SIGHTS

D. E. W. Animal Kingdom

Lions and tigers and bears, oh, my! And monkeys, camels, wallabies, ostriches, a binturong, a hyena, and, well, the list goes on. Allow at least an hour to visit the 42-acre **D. E. W.** (domestic, exotic, wild) **Animal Kingdom** (9918 Pond Rd./Rte. 41, Mount Vernon, 207/293-2837, www.dewanimalkingdom.com, 10am-5pm Tues.-Sun. Apr.-mid-Sept., $15 ages 13-64, $10 ages 4-12 and 65-99), west of Belgrade Lakes village. Kids love the hands-on stuff at Julie and Bob Miner's innovative nonprofit zoo, where they raise and rehabilitate exotic and other animals, enhancing rare and endangered breeds, and educate visitors about them. Bob, a disabled Vietnam vet, has rescued animals from zoos and shows and even New York City apartments. Julie and Bob have hand-raised and bottle-fed many of these animals from infancy, and they enter every cage. Bob kisses the bears and the lions, and Julie nuzzles the panther, but visitors watch from behind a double fence; trust me, it's plenty close enough, especially when you learn such facts as that the hyena has the strongest jaw pressure of any land mammal. Tours are offered at 11am and 2pm. The zoo is midway between Mount Vernon village

© TOM NANGLE

The Belgrade Lakes region was the inspiration for the film *On Golden Pond.*

KENNEBEC

and Kents Hill. Note: Whining children are strongly discouraged.

Flightseeing

Take off from the water and cruise by air over the lakes with **Airlink** (Great Pond Marina, 207/859-0109, www.airlinkconnection.com), with flights starting at $75 pp for 20 minutes.

ENTERTAINMENT AND EVENTS

The big entertainment here is shared family time on the lakes, but there are a few nearby venues worth exploring.

Late June-mid-August, free concerts by students and faculty are offered at the **New England Music Camp** (Lake Messalonskee, Sidney, 207/465-3025, www.nemusiccamp. com). Call or check the website for current schedule. Weekend concerts are at the outdoor "Bowl-in-the-Pines" (bring a blanket or folding chair); midweek performances take place in Alumni Hall.

SHOPPING

Mosey and poke around the back roads and you'll be rewarded with a handful of galleries and whatnot shops.

Multipurpose Store

Cars and canoes are about the only things you can't buy at **Day's Store** (Main St./Rte. 27, Belgrade Lakes, 207/495-2205 or 800/993-9500, www.go2days.com), a legendary institution since 1960. From firewater to fishing tackle, sandwiches (including the Long Pond Grinder) to souvenirs, and more than a dozen kinds of homemade fudge, it's a general store par excellence. Don't expect fancy; the local flavor provides its character. Long Pond is at its back door, providing access by boat or car. Day's is in the center of the village; you can't miss it.

Gifts and Crafts

A few doors south of the Village Inn in Belgrade Lakes is the seasonal branch of Waterville's **Maine Made and More Shop**

(Main St./Rte. 27, Belgrade Lakes, 207/495-2274), a summer landmark since 1980. Here's the place to stock up on tasteful gifts and crafts: jams and maple syrup, cards and guidebooks, T-shirts and sweatshirts, stuffed moose, and even shoes.

Delivering what its name promises, **Maine Bone Carving** (Rte. 41, Mount Vernon, 877/562-6637, www.mainebonecarving.com) sells hand-carved moose bone and also sells the works of Maine and New Zealand artisans. Open by chance or by appointment.

The talented duo of potter Mark Hutton and weaver Hillary Hutton sell their gorgeous handcrafted works from their home-based **Hutton Studios** (277 Tower Rd., Vienna, 207/293-3686, www.huttonstudios.com), open by chance or by appointment.

RECREATION

Parks and Views

Just north of Day's Store in Belgrade Lakes village is a cute little picnic area on Long Pond, **Belgrade Peninsula Park** (5:30am-10:30pm), next to an old dam. Late in the day it's a great spot for sunset-watching and fishing; no camping or fires are permitted. The Belgrade Lakes Conservation Corps restored it in 1996, and there is space for five carefully parked cars.

Another scenic standout, with a super photo op of Long Pond and Belgrade Lakes village, is the state-maintained overlook at **Blueberry Hill** on the west side of Long Pond. From Route 27, just south of Belgrade Lakes village, take Castle Island Road west about three miles to Watson Pond Road. Turn right (north) and continue about 1.5 miles. (Another 2.8 miles north of Blueberry Hill is the trailhead for French's Mountain.)

Golf

Golf has taken center stage here ever since the opening of the splendid **Belgrade Lakes Golf Club** (West Rd., Belgrade Lakes, 207/495-4653, www.belgradelakesgolf.com) in 1998. Designed by noted British expert Clive Clark, the course is an 18-hole standout, and the view from the elegant clubhouse is dazzling.

Hiking

Proactive in protecting much of the region's beautiful land for hiking and responsible enjoyment, the **Belgrade Regional Conservation Alliance** (BRCA, 207/495-6039, www.belgradelakes.org) has a terrific trail map and hiking guide to the Kennebec Highlands—although it doesn't show every protected acre, since the alliance is managing to protect land faster than it can print maps.

The two good hikes listed here are included on the map, which can also be obtained at local general stores such as Day's. Both hikes are just north of Belgrade Lakes village in the town of Rome. Neither is particularly high, but their summits are isolated enough to provide panoramic vistas.

For lots of gain, little pain, and a good family hike, head for **French Mountain,** on the west side of Long Pond. To reach the trailhead from Route 27, go about 4.2 miles north of Belgrade Lakes village and turn left onto Watson Pond Road, continue for less than a mile; the trail (signposted) begins on the left. Allow about 20 minutes to reach the summit, with fantastic views of Long Pond, the village, and Great Pond. Take a picnic (and a litter bag) and stretch out on the ledges. It's less than a mile round-trip.

A marginally tougher yet still-easy hike is **Mount Phillips,** a 755-footer with summit views of Great Pond. Allow about 20 minutes to reach the top via the 1.4-mile blue-blazed loop trail from the Route 225 trailhead. Take Route 225 from Rome Corner (Logan's Country Antiques is at the fork). Continue 1.5 miles to the trailhead (on the left), across from a Hemlock Trail sign. Park as far off the road as possible.

Water Sports

Good places for swimming are **Long Pond Public Beach** on Lakeshore Drive in Belgrade Lakes village (near Sunset Grille) and at the Belgrade Community Center, on Route 27 just south of the village. In addition to the lakefront, the center also has a pool open to nonresidents for $2 during community swim hours.

FISHING

Fishing is a big deal here, particularly in May-June and September (the season runs Apr. 1-Oct. 1). Among the 20 species in the seven major lakes and ponds are landlocked salmon, brown trout, black bass, pickerel, white perch, and eastern brook trout. You'll have to stick to bag, weight, and length limits. Pick up tackle and nonresident fishing licenses at **Day's Store** (Main St., Belgrade Lakes, 207/495-2205 or 800/993-9500).

Cast a line for northern pike with **Maine Wilderness Tours** (207/465-4333, www.mainewildernesstours.com). Trips include rod, reel, tackle, and bait, with rates beginning at $175 for four hours for up to two anglers.

BOATING

Great Pond Marina (25 Marina Dr., Belgrade Lakes, 207/495-2213, www.greatpondmarina.com) rents fishing boats ($67/day), runabouts (from $164/day), pontoon boats (from $246/day), kayaks ($30/day s, $50 d), and paddleboards ($50/day). A security deposit is required.

Roller Skating

Here's a throwback: When the windows are open, it feels as if you could dive out into the water at **Sunbeam Roller Rink** (Rte. 8, Smithfield, 207/362-4951), an old-fashioned roller-skating rink edging North Pond. It's open 7pm-10pm Wednesday, Friday, and Saturday evenings in summer.

Belgrade Community Center

Belgrade's spiffy recreation center (Rte. 27, Belgrade, 207/495-3481, www.belgrademaine.com) fronts on Great Pond and has a beach as well as an outdoor pool. Inside are the town library and a full-size basketball court. Everything's open to visitors, although if you want to borrow a book or two, you'll have to join the library as a nonresident for $10 (well worth it if the weather isn't cooperating and you're in a camp or cottage for the week). The center offers a full range of programs, from pickup basketball and volleyball to a summer kids' camp to a knitting and crafts club.

ACCOMMODATIONS
Inns, Guesthouses, and Bed-and-Breakfasts

Practically hidden on a hillside just steps from downtown Belgrade Lakes is the ◖ **Wings Hill Inn and Restaurant** (Rte. 27, Belgrade Lakes, 866/495-2400, www.wingshillinn.com, $155-195). Built around the turn of the 18th century, the rambling farmhouse-turned-inn houses six guest rooms and the area's best fine-dining restaurant, thanks to hands-on chef-owners Christopher and Tracey Anderson. The downstairs Sage Suite sleeps three and has a private entrance, a TV with a DVD player, and a small fridge. All of the second-floor rooms have balconies, some shared. The best guest room is Moonlight, a spacious room with a large private deck and lake views. Relax on the screened wraparound porch or snag an Adirondack-style chair on the lawn or a patio seat or, in winter, a place inside by the fire. A TV and a guest phone are in the living room; Wi-Fi is available throughout. Rates include a full breakfast and fresh-baked treats with afternoon tea.

On the eastern side of Great Pond is the aptly named **Among the Lakes Bed and Breakfast** (58 Smithfield Rd., Belgrade, 207/465-5900, www.amongthelakes.com, $125-145). Although it doesn't have a lake view, Great Pond is about a one-mile stroll down a private lane. Each of the five guest rooms has air-conditioning; some share baths. Rates include a full breakfast.

Just west of Waterville on the eastern edge of the Belgrade Lakes region is **The Pressey House Lakeside Bed and Breakfast** (32 Belgrade Rd., Oakland, 207/465-3500, www.presseyhouse.com, $140-235), a mid-19th-century octagonal house with an ell and a barn at the head of nine-mile-long Messalonskee Lake (also known as Snow Pond). There are five good-size suites, most with kitchens; one has a balcony overlooking the lake, another has a fireplace; all have Wi-Fi. Rates include a full breakfast. The inn is family-friendly, and suites sleep as many as five. Relax in the Gallery great room, which has a huge brick fireplace dividing it in two, or on the patio. You can borrow the canoe, kayaks, or a paddleboat to explore the lake. The Pressey House, a five-minute drive from I-95 Exit 127, is open year-round.

You can almost dive into Lake Minnehonk from the back porch of the **Lakeside Loft** (386 Pond Rd./Rte. 41, Mount Vernon, 207/293-4855, www.thelakesideloft.com, $101-196). Three self-catering units with cooking facilities face the lake, and guests have access to the living room as well as a kayak, canoes, backpacks, and in winter, snowshoes. There's also Wi-Fi and a video library.

Sporting Camps

Distant from most of Maine's sporting camps, these classic Belgrade-area operations nonetheless retain the flavor of those much farther north. And it's a heck of a lot easier to reach when driving from the south.

Established in 1910 and still operated by the same family, **Bear Spring Camps** (60 Jamaica Point Rd., Rome, www.bearspringcamps.com, mid-May-early Oct.) is one of the state's largest sporting camps, with 32 rustic cottages on 400 wooded acres. All have baths and Franklin stoves and overlook the North Bay of nine-mile-long Great Pond. Each cottage has its own dock; rental motorboats, kayaks, canoes, and even a pontoon boat are available. Other facilities include a sandy beach, a tennis court, and hiking trails. Cottages have 1-4 bedrooms with rates from $1,045 d per week, including all meals, served in the main lodge. In traditional style, lunch (called "dinner") is the main meal of the day, while supper is lighter fare. The staff will cook the fish you catch. Cabins are available only by the week mid-June-Labor Day, and reservations are tough to come by; off-season, when they're available, daily rates are available. Some guests stay for a month, and they book a year ahead. Pets are not allowed. Bear Spring Camps is 0.25 mile off Route 225, four miles east of Route 27.

Founded in 1909, **Alden Camps** (3 Alden Camps Cove, Oakland, 207/465-7703, www.aldencamps.com, mid-May-late Sept.) has an incredibly loyal following that includes fourth-generation guests, which makes getting reservations tough but not impossible. The 18 rustic cottages face great sunrises across three-mile-long East Pond (a.k.a. East Lake). Most guests spend a week. Each no-frills cottage has a screened porch, electricity, a bath, a fridge, and daily maid service. The crew of college kids aims to please, and former staffers now show up as guests. Meals are hearty and surprisingly creative with about a dozen or so entrée choices nightly (limited reservations for nonguests, entrées $20, including a salad course). The Friday night lobster bake or clam bake—open to nonguests, call for reservations—is a longstanding tradition. BYOB. The 40-acre spread on Route 137 has a clay tennis court, a sandy beach, a waterskiing boat, boat rentals, and a kids' play area. Rates, which include all meals, vary with cottage size and occupancy, beginning around $130 pp per night or $780 pp per week for a one-room cottage. Children under age 13 are $21-81/day or $126-486/week, depending on age. Spring and late summer rates are lower. After the Labor Day-late September season, cottages are available without meals for $93-183/day or $558-1,098/week. Rates do not include gratuities. Low-season midweek specials are a real steal. Pets are grudgingly allowed for $30/day. Boat rentals are $20/day or $120/week; canoes and kayaks are free. Alden Camps is seven miles off I-95 Exit 127.

Occupying all of tiny Castle Island, a blip on the causeway-bridge dividing Long Lake, is **Castle Island Camps** (Castle Island Rd., Belgrade Lakes, 207/495-3312 or winter 207/293-2266, www.castleislandcamps. com, May 1-Sept. 30, no credit cards). What a location! The 12 rustic cabins are geared to anglers, but they're popular with families in summer who want a simple old-fashioned lake-based holiday. Each cabin fronts on the lake, and home-style meals, served in the lodge, are included in the rates ($92 s, $164 d per night; $615 s; kids' rates begin at $40 under age 3 and increase with age). Rental boats ($60/day with gas) and kayaks ($30/day, $20 half day) are available. Other

amenities are Wi-Fi, a swimming dock, and a games room.

Seasonal Rentals

Seasonal rentals are the preferred lodging in the Belgrade Lakes area. For possibilities, call **Belgrade Reservation Center** (207/495-2104, www.belgraderental.com).

FOOD
Local Flavors

If you're looking for picnic fare or a quick bite, stop in at **Day's Store** (Main St./Rte. 27, Belgrade Lakes, 207/495-2205 or 800/993-9500, www.go2days.com) and pick up pizza, sandwiches, and baked goodies.

Detour down by the old millstream to **The Olde Post Office Café** (366 Pond Rd., Village Center, Mount Vernon, 207/293-4978, www. oldepostofficecafe.com, 7am-2:30pm Wed.-Sun.). Sandwiches, salads, panini, and wraps fill the menu along with baked goodies. Grab a seat inside or on the screened porch overlooking the stream or lake. Don't miss the old wheel-driven mill across the street. The café also is open occasionally for Saturday night dinners with music.

Reliability is the biggest selling point for the **Sunset Grille** (4 West Rd., Belgrade Lakes, 207/495-2439, 7am-10pm Sun.-Thurs., 7am-midnight Fri.-Sat.). The local grub and gossip spot is open daily for breakfast, lunch, and dinner, and it has a full bar. Stick to the basics and the chili, and don't be in a rush.

Pete's Pig (81 Main St./Rte. 27, Belgrade Lakes, 207/495-4095, www.petespig.com, 11am-7pm daily) is just the ticket if you've got a hankering for slow-roasted and smoked Southern barbeque.

Casual Dining

Who'd a thunk a sporting camp would serve fare such as rack of lamb or wild mushroom ravioli? You'll have to call in advance to book one of the few seats on the porch available to nonguests at **Alden Camps** (3 Alden Camps Cove, Oakland, 207/465-7703, www.alden-camps.com, dinner daily late May-early Sept.).

Even though you'll hear the passing whiz of traffic, the experience is worth it. Entrées are in the $20s, and that includes a loaf of fresh-baked bread and a salad with homemade dressing choice. BYOB. On Friday nights, it's an outdoor lobster and seafood bake—a very popular choice.

Fine Dining

Fortunately for diners at the inn, innkeepers Tracey and Christopher Anderson of the **C** **Wings Hill Inn and Restaurant** (Rte. 27, Belgrade Lakes, 866/495-2400, www.wingshill-linn.com) met while attending culinary school. The five-course fixed-price menu (seatings at 6pm and 8pm Thurs.-Sun. Sept.-June, 6pm and 8pm Wed.-Sun. July-Aug., $65), changes weekly and includes appetizer, choices of soup, a salad, and main course such as grilled pork or slow-roasted Cornish hen. In the off-season, a three-course menu may be available for $43. BYOB. Reservations are strongly recommended.

INFORMATION

Local information is available from **The Belgrade Lakes Region Business Group** (www.belgradelakesmaine.com) and **Kennebec Valley Tourism Council** (207/623-4884, www.kennebecvalley.org).

Summertime in the Lakes, a free tabloid with ads, features, and calendar listings, is an especially helpful local publication that appears weekly during the summer. Copies are available at the information center and at most of the restaurants and shops in the region.

Check out the **Belgrade Public Library** (Belgrade Community Center, Rte. 27, Belgrade, 207/495-3481, www.belgrademaine.com).

GETTING THERE

By car, Belgrade Lakes is roughly 17 miles or 30 minutes from Augusta via Route 27. It's roughly 18 miles or 30 minutes to Waterville via Routes 27 and 11. It's roughly 20 miles or 30 minutes to Farmington.

Waterville and Vicinity

Most visitors come to **Waterville** (pop. 15,722) drawn by Colby College, an elite liberal arts institution whose students and faculty give a college-town flavor to this former mill town, incorporated in 1802. The school's Museum of Art is reason enough to visit this small city. Other draws include a fabulous film festival and the oldest blockhouse in the nation, in nearby **Winslow** (pop. 7,794).

As early as 1653, Europeans set up a trading entrepôt here, calling it Teconnet—the earlier version of today's Ticonic Falls, on the Kennebec River—and commerce with Native Americans thrived until the onset of the Indian Wars two decades later. In the late 19th century a contingent of Lebanese immigrants arrived, finding employment in the town's mills, and many of their descendants have become prominent community members. Best known of these is favorite son and former U.S. Senate

Majority Leader George J. Mitchell, who still returns to spend time with his many relatives here.

Venture east to the rolling farmlands of **Unity** (pop. 2,099) to find Maine's organic farming center as well as Unity College and an Amish community.

SIGHTS
Colby College

Crowning Mayflower Hill, two miles from downtown Waterville, is **Colby College** (Mayflower Hill, Waterville, 207/872-3000, www.colby.edu). Colby's 1,800 students attend a huge variety of liberal arts programs on a 713-acre campus noted for its handsome Georgian buildings. Founded by Baptists in 1813 as the all-male Maine Literary and Theological Institution, Colby received its current name in 1867 and went coed in 1871. Campus tours are available through the **Admissions Office** (207/859-4828 or 800/723-3032, 8am-5pm Mon.-Fri., 8am-noon Sat.).

COLBY COLLEGE MUSEUM OF ART

With the 2013 opening of the 26,000-foot Alfond-Lunder Family Pavillion, Colby's **Museum of Art** (207/859-5600, 10am-4:30pm Tues.-Sat., noon-4:30pm Sun., free), in the Bixler Art and Music Center, became the state's largest art museum in terms of gallery space. Over the years, it's earned an especially distinguished reputation for its remarkable permanent collection of 18th-20th-century American art, which was cemented with the donation of the Lunder Collection, valued at $100 million and comprising more than 500 objects, including works by Winslow Homer, Sol LeWitt, John Singer Sargent, and Georgia O'Keeffe, to name just a few, as well as 300 works by James McNeill Whistler.

The new galleries are just the latest in the museum's growth. In 1996, it opened its $1.5 million Paul J. Schupf Wing to house 415 paintings and sculptures created by artist Alex Katz during a 50-year period. In July 1999, the architecturally stunning $1.3 million Lunder Wing opened, expanding the museum's exhibit space to 28,000 square feet. Other significant holdings include works by Gilbert Stuart, Winslow Homer, and John Marin; special solo and group shows are mounted throughout the year. And don't miss the tasteful gift shop. The museum is on the east side of the campus's main quadrangle, just north of Mayflower Hill Drive.

Also on the campus is the 128-acre **Perkins Arboretum and Bird Sanctuary,** with three nature trails. Bring a picnic and blanket and stretch out next to Johnson Pond. In winter there's ice skating on the pond.

Fort Halifax

The two-story **Fort Halifax** (Bay St., Winslow) stands sentinel where the Sebasticook River meets the Kennebec River. The oldest blockhouse in the nation, it was built in 1754 of doweled logs during the French and Indian Wars.

In 1987, after rampaging Kennebec floodwaters swept the building away, more than three dozen of the giant timbers were retrieved downstream. Energetic fundraising allowed the blockhouse to be meticulously restored. The surrounding park is a great place for a picnic, with tables dotting shaded grassy lawns rolling to the river's edge.

Two-Cent Bridge

Spanning the Kennebec from Benton Avenue in Winslow to Front Street in Waterville (walk down Temple St. in Waterville), the 700-foot-long **Two-Cent Bridge** (officially the Ticonic Footbridge) was built in 1903 for pedestrian commuters to the Scott Paper mill in Winslow, who paid $0.02 to cross. Closed in 1973, the bridge was recently reopened and is the forerunner of a Head of Falls waterfront redevelopment effort. Possibly the only toll pedestrian bridge left in the United States, its replica tollbooth now simply an object of curiosity. A stroll over the bridge gives good views of Ticonic Falls, the waterfall that likely inspired author Richard Russo's Pulitzer prize-winning novel *Empire Falls*.

Redington Museum

Home of the Waterville Historical Society, the **Redington Museum and Apothecary** (62 Silver St., Waterville, 207/872-9439, www. redingtonmuseum.org, 10am-3pm Tues.-Sat. Memorial Day weekend-Labor Day, closed holidays, tours 10am, 11am, 1pm, 2pm, $3 adults, $2 under age 12) has a particularly intriguing replica 19th-century pharmacy filled with authentic pharmaceutical antiquities. The Federal-style Redington House was built in 1814 by early settler Asa Redington for his son, William.

OFF THE BEATEN PATH

Sometimes you really do have to see it to believe it. That's the case with the **Bryant Stove and Music/Doll Circus** (27 Stovepipe Alley, Thorndike, 207/568-3665, www.bryantstove.com, $4), a labor of love collected, created, repaired, and assembled by Joe and

© TOM NANGLE

The Two-Cent Bridge spans the Kennebec River in Waterville.

Bea Bryant. Begin with the Doll Circus. Flip a switch and the room comes alive with dolls dancing, marching, swinging, turning, and twisting to music. Airplanes fly, a Ferris wheel turns, stuffed animals swing. There's a Barbie doll fashion show, a hula show, and a line of Barbies and Kens marching to the altar. No matter which way you look, dolls and stuffed animals are actively positioned in creative scenes. It's a jaw-dropping marriage of lights and music and movement. And that's just the first room. Beyond it are a small engine room with miniature working steam engines; a music section with player pianos, nickelodeons, jukeboxes, organs, barrel pianos, hurdy-gurdies, and more. The museum is very hands-on, and visitors are encouraged to push buttons, play the instruments, and learn about the mechanisms. If that's not enough, there are also antique stoves and automobiles that Joe lovingly repaired. A separate part of the business specializes in antique stoves; quite a few celebrities have bought the

restored beauties here. To find this gem, about 22 miles east of Waterville, follow Route 201 to Route 139.

ENTERTAINMENT

Above City Hall is the refurbished turn-of-the-20th-century **Waterville Opera House** (93 Main St., 207/873-5381, tickets 207/873-7000, www.operahouse.com). Once the haunt of vaudevillians, the renovated Opera House is now the site of plays, dance performances, and concerts throughout the year.

About 20 minutes northeast in rural Unity is **Unity Centre for the Performing Arts** (42 Depot St., Unity, 207/948-7469, http://uccpa. unity.edu), a 200-seat theater built by Bert and Coral Clifford and donated to Unity College in 2007.

EVENTS

One of Maine's premier art-film houses, the two-screen **Railroad Square Cinema** (17 Railroad Sq., Waterville, 207/873-6526, www.railroadsquarecinema.com) is the home of the **Maine International Film Festival** (MIFF, 207/873-7000, www.miff.org), which has brought such luminaries as Sissy Spacek and Peter Fonda to town to receive Mid-Life Achievement Awards. The 10-day summer festival screens about 100 films representing about 50 filmmakers.

A gathering of New England's best fiddlers, the **East Benton Fiddlers' Convention** (207/453-2017, www.eastbentonfiddlers.com) draws close to 2,000 enthusiasts to open-air performances at the Littlefield farm in East Benton. The convention happens noon-dusk the last Sunday in July.

Downtown Waterville is the site of midsummer **Taste of Greater Waterville.** The food-focused one-day festival is usually held on a Wednesday. There's alfresco dining along with music for kids and adults.

During the third weekend in September, sleepy Unity comes alive with the **Common Ground Fair,** a celebration of organic foods and country life sponsored by the Maine Organic Farmers and Gardeners Association.

During the academic year, and less often in summer, **Colby College** (207/859-4353, www.colby.edu/news) is the venue for exhibits, lectures, concerts, performances, and other events.

SHOPPING

Unlike so many former mill towns, Waterville's downtown has life, with shops and restaurants and plenty of free parking in The Concourse, the triangle framed by Elm, Main, and Spring Streets.

New, Used, and Children's Books

Conveniently situated downtown and facing the square, **Re-Books** (Main St., Waterville, 207/877-2484) is a basement-level shop with a fairly extensive selection of hardcovers and paperbacks. Directly above it, despite the name, and facing Main Street is the **Children's Book Cellar** (207/872-4543), a very kid-friendly space with a great selection of books and toys.

Johnny's Selected Seeds

If you're a gardener, farmer, horticulturalist, or just plain curious, take a 15-minute drive east of Waterville to visit the research farm of **Johnny's Selected Seeds** (Foss Hill Rd., Albion). Pick up a map and then take a self-guided tour of the 40 acres of trial gardens 9am-4pm Monday-Friday July-August. Or visit the store (207/861-3999) and headquarters (955 Benton Ave., Winslow, 207/861-3900, www.johnnyseeds.com). The eponymous seed source has a national reputation. More than 2,000 varieties of herbs, veggies, and flowers are grown in the trial gardens, which were started in 1973. Known for high-quality seeds and service, the company makes good on anything that doesn't sprout.

RECREATION

Kennebec Messalonskee Trails (207/873-6443, www.kmtrails.org) has constructed a number of trails in the region, which are mapped and detailed on its website.

ACCOMMODATIONS

Chains dominate the lodging in this region, but The Pressey House, in the Belgrade Lakes area, is convenient to Waterville.

Guests at **84 The Pleasant Street Inn** (84 Pleasant St., Waterville, 207/680-2515, www.84pleasantstreet.com, $65-99) have access to a full kitchen, a dining area, and a living room, making it easy to feel at home. Five guest rooms have full baths, one has a half bath, and one has a shared bath; all have Wi-Fi and air-conditioning. It's clean and cozy, and rates include a self-serve continental breakfast. One caveat: You'll be on your own and it's unlikely you'll meet the innkeeper.

About 20 minutes northeast of Waterville is **The Copper Heron** (130 Main St., Unity, 207/948-9003, www.copperheron.com, $95), with four guest rooms in an in-town Greek Revival house built in 1842. Common areas include a library with a TV and video player as well as a dining room where full breakfasts (and dinners by arrangement) are served. You can walk to the Unity Centre for the Performing Arts, Unity College, and lovely Unity Pond (there's a boat put-in, but you'll want to drive to that). Unity is also home to the Maine Organic Farmers and Gardeners Association and its annual Common Ground Fair in September. Children are welcome.

FOOD
Local Flavors

In a local twist on the traditional Maine public suppers—thanks to Waterville's substantial Lebanese community—**St. Joseph Maronite Church** (3 Appleton St., Waterville, 207/872-8515) puts on a Lebanese supper at least once a year (the second Sunday after Easter). If you enjoy Eastern Mediterranean home cooking, be there. Call the church for details.

Jorgensen's Café (103 Main St., Waterville, 207/872-8711, 7am-6pm Mon.-Sat., 7am-4pm Sun.) is a downtown institution where you might hear French spoken. Bagels, muffins, breakfast sandwiches, and more than 25 varieties of coffee brewed daily attract morning crowds; lunch comprises specialty sandwiches,

KENNEBEC

with every kind of deli meat available, plus quiche, salads, and soups. It's also the local outlet for Kennebec Chocolates.

Nothing's finer on a hot summer day than a banana or peanut butter-chocolate chip ice cream from **North Street Dairy Cone** (127 North St., Waterville, 207/873-0977).

Prepared foods, fresh foods, and daily vegan, vegetarian, and/or gluten-free lunch specials make it easy to assemble a picnic lunch at **Barrels Community Market** (74 Main St., Waterville, 207/660-4844, www.barrelsmarket.com, 10am-6pm Mon.-Fri., 9am-4pm Sat.).

An extremely popular hangout, **Big G's Deli** (Benton Ave., Winslow, 207/873-7808, www.big-g-s-deli.com, 6am-7pm daily, no credit cards) began as a sandwich shop in 1986 and now seats 200. It's renowned for enormous "name" sandwiches such as the Miles Standwich (nearly a whole turkey dinner), all on thick slices of homemade bread (half sandwiches are available). In fact, all breads and pastries are house-made. You can enjoy breakfast until 1pm. Order at the counter and try for a seat; or get it to go for the mother of all picnics. On the east side of the Kennebec River, Big G's is about a mile north of the Route 201 bridge to Waterville.

The **Grand Central Café** (10 Railroad Sq., 207/872-9135, 5pm-8pm Mon.-Wed., 11am-8pm Thurs., 11am-9pm Fri.-Sat., 11am-2pm Sun.) is a local favorite for fancy brick-oven pizza.

Tea lovers take refuge in **Selah Tea Café** (177 Main St., Waterville 207/660-9181, www.selahteacafe.com, 8am-6:30pm daily), a cozy spot serving breakfast, sandwiches, soups, and salads in addition to fine teas.

Breakfast fans shouldn't miss **Bonnie's Diner** (972 Benton Ave., Winslow, 207/872-7712, 5:30am-2pm Mon.-Sat., 7am-2pm Sun.), a cheap-eats palace hugging the roadside.

The **Downtown Waterville Farmers Market** (2pm-6pm Thurs.) sets up in the concourse along Appleton Street downtown.

Casual Dining

Fresh, flavorful cuisine with varied ethnic inspirations makes dining at **The Last Unicorn** (98 Silver St./Rte. 201, Waterville, 207/873-6378, 11am-9pm daily, dinner entrées $18-25) a delicious adventure. Creative appetizers, an extensive wine and cocktail list, and weekend brunch are other pluses of this friendly place, which has patio dining in summer. Soups, salads, spreads, and desserts are made on the premises.

The **Riverside Farm Market** (291 Fairfield St., Oakland, 207/465-4439, www.riversidefarmmarket.com, 11am-6pm Tues.-Fri., 10am-4pm Sat.) doubles as a casual café (11am-3pm Tues.-Sat., 5:30pm-8:30pm Thurs.-Sat., 11am-2pm Sun.) serves fabulous sandwiches, soups, and salads with a Mediterranean bent, scrumptious baked goods, and designer coffees. You also can pick up baked goods or lunch—soups, salads, quiche, and sandwiches—at the deli and baked goods counter. The dinner menu ($20-26) changes might include saltimbocca or lobster.

The emphasis is on seafood at **18 Below Raw Bar** (18 Silver St., Waterville, 855/242-1665, www.18belowrawbar.com, 4pm-9pm Tues.-Sun., $12-28), but landlubbers and vegetarians will find a few options. The lounge is open to 1am.

Ethnic Fare

Linked like a conjoined twin to the Railroad Square Cinema, **Buen Apetito** (4 Chaplin St., Railroad Sq., Waterville, 207/861-4649, www.buenapetitorestaurant.com, 5pm-8pm Sun.-Mon., 4pm-8pm Tues.-Thurs., 11am-9pm Fri.-Sat., $8-15) serves Southwestern fare accented by fresh salsas and homemade tortillas.

It doesn't look like much from the outside—or on the inside, for that matter—but the little **Lebanese Cuisine** (34 Temple St., Waterville, 207/873-7813, 9am-4pm Mon.-Fri., 9am-1pm Sat.) delivers on its name, with authentic dishes including stuffed grape leaves, spinach and feta pastries, and a divine baklava.

For terrific Thai, seek out **Pad Thai too** (400 Memorial Dr., Waterville, 207/859-8900, www.padthaitoo.me, 4pm-8pm daily and 11am-2pm Tues.-Fri., $9-15), a family-owned and -operated restaurant that caters to vegetarians and vegans (although meat and seafood dishes are available) by using a gluten-free soy sauce instead of fish sauce. Every dish is prepared to order in a small kitchen, so expect a leisurely meal.

The area has numerous Asian restaurants, and one that has stood the test of time is **Asian Café** (53 Bay St., Winslow, 207/877-6688, 11am-9pm daily, $9-15), serving Japanese, Korean, Thai, and Vietnamese cuisine. Portions are generous, and service is friendly and efficient. A gluten-free menu is available.

INFORMATION AND SERVICES

The best sources of local information are the **Mid-Maine Chamber of Commerce** (207/873-3315, www.midmainechamber. com), **Waterville Main Street** (207/680-2055, www.watervillemainstreet.org), and **Kennebec Valley Tourism Council** (207/623-4884, www. kennebecvalley.org).

Check out **Waterville Public Library** (73 Elm St., Waterville, 207/872-5433, www. waterville.lib.me.us). **Miller Library** (Colby College, Waterville, 207/859-5100) has a huge Irish literature collection and a room dedicated to poet Edwin Arlington Robinson.

GETTING THERE

By car, Waterville is roughly 23 miles or 28 minutes from Augusta via I-95 and roughly 18 miles or 30 minutes from Belgrade Lakes via Routes 27 and 11. It's roughly 20 miles or 25 minutes to Skowhegan via I-95 and Route 201.

Skowhegan Area

The Wabanaki named **Skowhegan** (skow-HE-gun, pop. 8,589), meaning "the place to watch for fish," because that's just what the early Native Americans did at the Kennebec River's twin waterfalls. Their spears were ready when lunch came leaping up the river. The island between the falls later formed the core for European settlement of Skowhegan, the largest town and county seat of Somerset County. Named for England's Somerset, the county was incorporated in 1823 and covers 3,633 square miles.

Favorite daughter Margaret Chase Smith, one of Maine's preeminent politicians, put Skowhegan on the map, and even since her 1995 death, admirers and historians have made pilgrimages to her former home. During her years in the U.S. House and Senate, "The Lady from Maine" would return to her constituents—and she was never too busy to autograph place mats at her favorite local restaurant or to wave from her chair in her house's streetside solarium. Older local residents still recall the day President Dwight D. Eisenhower and his entourage visited Mrs. Smith in 1955,

when "Ike" spoke to an enthusiastic crowd at the Skowhegan Fairgrounds.

Another local institution is the nationally and internationally renowned Skowhegan School of Painting and Sculpture, founded in 1946 as a summer residency program. One of the few art schools in the United States offering workshops in fresco painting, Skowhegan provides 65 artists with a bucolic 300-acre lakeside setting for honing their skills and interacting with peers and prominent visiting artists. Gaining admission is highly competitive for the nine-week program. Skowhegan's annual summer lecture series, featuring big names in the art world, is open to the public.

These days, Skowhegan is earning fame as the state's bread-making center, thanks to the presence of Maine Grains at the Somerset Grist Mill, which is turning out flours from stone-milled local grains, and the annual Kneading Conference and companion Artisan Bread Fair in late July.

In the early 18th century, the town of **Norridgewock** (NORE-ridge-wok, pop. 3,367) was a French and Indian stronghold against the

KENNEBEC

British. A century earlier, French Jesuit missionaries had moved in among the Norridgewock Indians at their settlement here and converted them to Catholicism. Best known of these was Father Sébastien Râle, beloved of his Indian parishioners. In 1724, taking revenge for Indian forays against them, a British militia detachment marched in and massacred the priest and his followers, a major milestone during what was known as Dummer's War. Today, a granite monument to Father Râle stands at the scene, Old Point, along the Kennebec River about two miles south of downtown Madison, close to the Madison-Norridgewock town boundary.

Meaning "smooth water between rapids," Norridgewock was the last bit of civilization for Benedict Arnold and his men before they headed into the Upper Kennebec wilderness on their march to Québec in 1775. Stopping for almost a week, they spent most of their time caulking their leaky bateaux. Today the town has a slew of handsome 18th- and 19th-century homes.

More recently, some of the scenes in the 2005 movie *Empire Falls* were shot in Skowhegan. That was one of the bright spots in a town that's fighting for its economic survival. It recently received grants to spruce up its architecturally rich main street, which unfortunately doubles as Route 201, the major thoroughfare between Québec and the U.S. coast. Take care crossing the street.

SIGHTS
Margaret Chase Smith Library

Beautifully sited on Neil Hill, high above the Kennebec River, the **Margaret Chase Smith Library** (56 Norridgewock Ave., Skowhegan, 207/474-7133, www.mcslibrary.org, 10am-4pm Mon.-Fri., donation) bulges with fascinating memorabilia from the life and times of one of Maine's best-known politicians, who spent 32 years in the U.S. House and Senate and died in 1995. Over the entrance door is her signature red rose; inside is a 20-minute video describing her career. In 2000, the library held a special commemoration of the 50th anniversary of Senator Smith's "declaration of

conscience" speech, in which she courageously castigated Senator Joseph McCarthy for his "Red Scare" witch-hunting tactics. Ask if a staff member is available to show you Senator Smith's house, connected to the library on the 15-acre estate. (She was born at 81 North Ave. in Skowhegan.) The library is closed the week between Christmas and New Year's Day. The complex is 0.5 mile west of Route 201 (Madison Ave.).

Skowhegan History House

When you enter the handsome red-brick **Skowhegan History House** (66 Elm St., Skowhegan, 207/474-6632, www.skowhegan-historyhouse.org, $2 adults, $1 children and seniors), with only half a dozen rooms, you'll find it hard to believe that blacksmith Aaron Spear built it in 1839 for his family of 10 children. It must have been mighty cozy sleeping. Skowhegan treasures—antique clocks, china, and other furnishings—now fill the two-story structure, which has a commanding view over the Kennebec River and lovely gardens. The house, located just west of Route 201 at the junction of Elm and Pleasant Streets, is staffed by volunteers and open late May to mid-October; call for hours.

The Skowhegan Indian Monument

Rising 62 feet above its pedestal and weighing 24,000 pounds, the giant wooden **Skowhegan Indian statue** was carved in 1969 by Maine sculptor Bernard Langlais, a Skowhegan School of Painting alum who died in 1977. Known nationally for his work, Langlais dedicated the monument to the Native Americans who first settled this area. One hand holds a spear, the other holds a stylized fishing weir. The sculpture is in need of some repair work, but it's still a standout and fundraising is under way for restoration. It's just off Route 201, tucked in the back corner of a parking lot behind a Cumberland Farms at the intersection with High Street.

Skowhegan Historic District

Bounded roughly by Water and Russell Streets

and Madison Avenue, the **Skowhegan Historic District,** close to the Kennebec River, contains 38 turn-of-the-20th-century buildings from the town's heyday as a commercial center. After trains arrived in 1856, the wireless telegraph in 1862, and telephones in 1883, Skowhegan saw incredible prosperity. It's worth a walkabout to admire the architectural details of a bygone era, although sad to say, many of the buildings need maintenance.

◖ L. C. Bates Museum

Offbeat doesn't begin to describe this treasure chest. In a Romanesque building, listed on the National Register of Historic Places, on the Good Will-Hinckley School campus, which was established in 1889 as a school for disadvantaged children, the **L. C. Bates Museum** (Rte. 201, Hinckley, 207/238-4250, www.gwh.org, 10am-4:30pm Wed.-Sat., 1pm-4:30pm Sun. Apr. 1-mid-Nov., 10am-4:30pm Wed.-Sat. mid-Nov.-Mar. or by appointment, $3 adults, $1 under age 17) is a way-cool, way-retro museum, with a broadly eclectic collection focusing on natural history. Among the treasures in the dozen or so rooms are hundreds of mounted rare birds, priceless Native American artifacts, and a trophy marlin caught by Ernest Hemingway. Dress warmly if you visit in winter; it's not heated.

Behind the museum, visit the arboretum and nature trails, open dawn-dusk. *Forest Walking Trails* maps are available in the museum. Alongside the trails are monuments to prominent conservationists. The turreted brick-and-granite building is five miles north of I-95 Exit 133, between Fairfield and Skowhegan, and is visible from Route 201 at the southern end of the campus.

Pedestrian Bridges

Spanning the South Channel of the Kennebec River, the **Swinging Bridge** connects Skowhegan Island (from behind the ice cream stand) to Alder Street, off West Front Street. First built in 1883, floods in 1888, 1901, 1936, and 1987 damaged or destroyed the wire footbridge. Its latest incarnation was unveiled in 2006, when the town completely renovated it. The views are terrific, and the island park is a jewel.

The **Skowhegan Walking Bridge** spans the river about a block below the dam, opposite where Route 201 North and Route 2 split downtown. This one traces its history back to 1856, when it was constructed for the Somerset and Kennebec Railroad. The following year it was carried away by floodwaters. A wooden bridge followed, and then a steel one, also destroyed by floodwaters. The current bridge was built in 1988. Like the Swinging Bridge, it's worth a stroll just for the views.

ENTERTAINMENT
Theaters

For a dose of nostalgia, plan to catch a flick at the 350-car **Skowhegan Drive-In** (Waterville Rd./Rte. 201, Skowhegan, 207/474-9277, www.skowhegandrivein.com), a landmark since 1954. Nightly double features start at dusk or whenever the sun disappears. Gates open at 7:30pm.

Built in 1901, the **Lakewood Theater** (Rte. 201, Madison, 207/474-7176, www.lakewoodtheater.org), on the shores of Lake Wesserunsett six miles north of Skowhegan, has had a roller-coaster history, but it's now in a decidedly "up" phase. Maine's oldest summer theater presents nine musicals, comedies, and light dramas each season. Performances are at 8pm Thursday-Saturday and at 4pm every other Sunday, plus matinees at 2pm every other Wednesday late May-mid-September. On matinee Wednesday, there is also a 7pm evening performance. Tickets are $19-37 adults and about $18 ages 4-17.

Lectures and Concerts

Performing arts events are sometimes scheduled in Skowhegan's **Opera House** inside the circa-1909 City Hall, where Booker T. Washington spoke in 1912.

Mid-June-early August, the evening **Barbara Fish Lee Lecture Series** draws nationally and internationally noted artists to participate in

KENNEBEC

© HILARY NANGLE

Lakewood Theater is Maine's oldest summer theater.

its lecture and presentation series at the Old Dominion Fresco Barn at the Skowhegan School of Painting and Sculpture (207/474-9345, www.skowheganart.org).

A **concert series** is held at **Skowhegan's Coburn Park** at 5pm Sunday during July-August.

EVENTS

Mega-size omelets made in the world's largest omelet pan, a parade, a crafts fair, live entertainment, a carnival, and fireworks are among the features of the **Central Maine Egg Festival.** The biggest day is Saturday. It's held at Manson Park in Pittsfield mid-late July.

Artisan bread bakers and those interested in learning about growing and milling grains converge in Skowhegan for the annual late August **Kneading Conference** and its companion **Artisan Bread Fair.**

Billed as the oldest country fair in the United States, dating back more than 175 years, and also Maine's largest outdoor event, the **Skowhegan State Fair** is a 10-day

extravaganza with agricultural exhibits galore, live entertainment, harness racing, food booths, a carnival, and a demolition derby at the Skowhegan Fairgrounds (Rte. 201, Skowhegan) early-mid-August.

SHOPPING
Factory Outlet

Discounts of up to 50 percent are typical for athletic-shoe seconds at the **New Balance Factory Store** (12 Walnut St., Skowhegan, 207/474-6231). The store also carries sportswear, socks, sports bags, and such. The outlet is just off Route 201 (W. Front St.) south of the Kennebec. The turn is next to Skowhegan Savings Bank.

Antiques

The **Fairfield Antiques Mall** (382 Rte. 201, Fairfield, 207/453-4100) boasts that it's the state's largest antiques group shop. Judge for yourself; it's 2.5 miles north of the I-95 interchange.

In downtown Skowhegan, **Hilltop Antiques**

(48 Water St., 207/474-0055) has 27 rooms brimming with finds spread out on three floors.

Crafts

About 20 talented area artists show their works at the cooperatively owned **River Roads Artisans Gallery** (75 Water St., Skowhegan).

RECREATION
Parks

Donated to the town by Abner Coburn, 13-acre **Coburn Park**, a wonderful riverside oasis, has a lily pond, memorial gardens (including a hospice garden and a Margaret Chase Smith rose garden), a summer concert series at the gazebo, pagodas, and more than 100 species of trees and shrubs. Bring a picnic, grab a table, and enjoy. The park is on Water Street (Rte. 2) at the eastern edge of town.

Lake George Regional Park (off Rte. 2, Skowhegan and Canaan, 207/474-1292, $5 adults, $1 ages 5-11) has boating, swimming, two sandy beaches, hiking and walking trails, playing fields, and picnicking in two sections framing Lake George.

About three miles north of Solon, close to the Solon-Bingham town line and just north of the area known as Arnold's Landing, is **Arnold's Way Rest Area,** with covered picnic tables, grills, and an outhouse. Interpretive panels here mark the first of two dozen panels along the Old Canada Road Scenic Byway at Moscow, The Forks, Parlin Pond, and Attean, helping motorists get a feel for area history and activities such as logging.

Golf

The 18-hole **Lakewood Golf Course** (Rte. 201, Madison, 207/474-5955, www.lakewoodgolf-maine.com), five miles north of Skowhegan, dates from 1925.

ACCOMMODATIONS
Bed-and-Breakfasts

Helen Lamphere and her daughter Charlene run **Helen's Bed and Breakfast** (165 Madison Ave./Rte. 201, Skowhegan, 207/474-0066, www.helensbandb.com, Apr.-Dec., $75-105), a handsome 19th-century brick Victorian with four air-conditioned rooms. Antiques, country pieces, and Helen's hand-braided rugs create a comfy retreat. Helen also sells her rugs. Guests share the large deck and yard.

Sleep where the stars slept at **The Colony House Inn Bed and Breakfast** (79 Beach Rd., Madison, 888/268-2853, www.colonyhouse-inn.com, $45 pp), a lovely—if tired—lakefront historical B&B adjacent to the Lakeside Theater. The 1929 John Calvin Stevens-designed Shingle-style inn is wrapped in old-style elegance, with comfy public rooms, a nice screened porch, and a many-windowed dining room where a full breakfast is served. The prices reflect the old-fashioned baths and the overall need for some TLC. One guest room has a private bath, two lake-facing guest rooms are connected by a bath, and two other guest rooms share a bath. Also on the premises are two cottages ($550-650/week or $100 d per night), one lakefront, the other facing the lake. Within walking distance are the theater, golf course, and a spiritualist camp that has been running for more than 125 years. Rent a boat, or simply settle into one of the Adirondack chairs on the lawn and gaze out at Lake Wesserunsett; it's heaven.

Motels

Convenient to downtown, the **Towne Motel** (172 Madison Ave./Rte. 201 N., Skowhegan, 207/474-5151 or 800/843-4405, www.townemotel.com, $98-128 July-mid-Oct.) has 33 guest rooms, all with phones, air-conditioning, cable TV, and high-speed Internet access; some have kitchenettes. Continental breakfast is included. The large outdoor pool is great for kids. Pets are welcome in some guest rooms ($10).

For a cheap sleep, check in to the quaint but vintage **Breezy Acres Motel** (315 Waterville Rd./Rte. 201, Skowhegan, 207/474-2703, www.breezyacresmotel.com, $58-78), owned by Dennis and Nancy Willete since 1979. On the grounds are a picnic area, a trout pond with paddleboating, an outdoor pool, and even a nine-hole golf course.

FOOD
Local Flavors

Just south of downtown, the **Snack Shack** (100 Waterville Rd./Rte. 201, Skowhegan, 207/474-0550, 11am-8pm Mon.-Sat.) never disappoints for fried foods or sandwiches. It has a few tables, but most folks get takeout.

It doesn't get much more local than **The Pickup Café** (42 Court St., Skowhegan, 207/474-0708, www.thepickupcsa.com), located at the Somerset Grist Mill. The café is an offshoot of a community-supported agriculture (CSA) pickup point, and the food for the farm dinners (4pm-9pm Fri.-Sat.), coffeehouse brunches (7am-2pm, Sat.-Sun.), and wood-fired pizza day (3pm-6pm Wed.) comes from local farms.

An 1864 bank now houses **The Bankery** (87 Water St., Skowhegan, 207/474-2253, www.thebankery.com, 7:30am-6pm Mon.-Sat.), a fine source for made-from-scratch baked goods that include soups, chowders, flatbreads, quiches, breads, cookies, cakes, pies, and other treats. You can even watch the bakers at work.

More than two dozen fat sandwiches, as well as flatbread pizzas, salads, and a soup of the day, draw locals into **Kel-Matt Café** (112 Madison Ave./Rte. 201, Skowhegan, 207/474-0200, www.kelmatcafe.com, 11am-3pm Mon.-Fri., 11am- 2pm Sat.), in a Victorian house just north of downtown across from Bangor Savings Bank. Service is friendly and efficient. Be careful to park only in the restaurant's designated lot and not in that of the insurance agency next door.

I scream, you scream, and in Maine everyone screams for **Gifford's Ice Cream** (307 Madison Ave./Rte. 1, Skowhegan, no phone). At this roadside institution, you can lick whoopie pie, Maine tracks, Denali peanut butter Iditarod, or Maine wild blueberry flavors while playing a game of miniature golf.

The **Skowhegan Farmers Market** sets up at the Somerset Grist Mill, at the corner of Court and High Streets, 9am-1pm Saturday May-October.

Family Favorite

The parking lot's always busy at **Ken's Family Restaurant** (414 Madison Ave./Rte. 201, Skowhegan, 207/474-3120, www.kensfamilyrestaurant.com, 10:30am-8pm Mon.-Thurs., 7am-9pm Fri.-Sat., 7am-8pm Sun., $7-18), in its second generation of Dionne family ownership. Seafood is the specialty, and seconds are on the house when you order the jumbo fish fry. The Italian menu is equally popular; select a pasta and pair it with a sauce for $8.50. Families know they can count on good home cooking, and there's always the all-you-care-to-eat breakfast, served weekends. The children's menu lists about 10 choices for $3.99, and of course there's the kid-pleasing dirt pudding.

Casual Dining

Two doors from the Towne Motel, in a renovated 19th-century home, the **⊄ Heritage House Restaurant** (182 Madison Ave., Skowhegan, 207/474-5100, www.hhrestaurant.com, lunch buffet 11:30am-2pm Tues.-Fri., dinner 5pm-9pm daily year-round, entrées $16-25) is Skowhegan's favorite special occasion restaurant. Apricot mustard chicken breast is a specialty. Reservations are advisable on weekends.

Pair a show at the Lakewood Theatre with a meal at the **Lakewood Inn Restaurant** (76 Theatre Rd., Madison, 207/858-4403, www.lakewoodtheater.org, 5pm-9pm Thurs.-Sat., 11am-2pm and 4:30pm-8pm Wed. and Sun., $13-24). The menu changes regularly, but may include beef tenderloin or Maine haddock.

INFORMATION AND SERVICES

The **Skowhegan Area Chamber of Commerce** (23 Commercial St., Skowhegan, 207/474-3621 or 888/772-4392, www.skoweganchamber.com) has info, as does the town's website (www.skowhegan.org). More information is available from **Kennebec Valley Tourism Council** (207/623-4884, www.kennebecvalley.org).

Check out **Skowhegan Free Public Library** (9 Elm St., Skowhegan, 207/474-9072, www.skowhegan.lib.me.us).

GETTING THERE

By car, Skowhegan is roughly 20 miles or 25 minutes from Waterville via I-95 and Route 201. It's roughly 45 miles or one hour to Bingham via Route 201.

Solon to Jackman

Route 201, from **Solon** (pop. 1,053) north to **Jackman** (pop. 862), is a National Scenic Byway threading through the rural towns of **Bingham** (pop. 922), **Moscow** (pop. 512), and **The Forks** (pop. 37). Until the arrival of white-water rafting in the late 1970s, the Upper Kennebec Valley was best known to anglers, hunters, timber truckers, and families who'd been summering here for generations. And long before that, before dams changed the river's flow patterns, Native Americans used the Kennebec as a convenient chute from the interior's dense forests to summer encampments on the coast. In 1775, Col. Benedict Arnold led more than 1,000 men up this river in a futile campaign to storm the ramparts of Québec City.

Midway between Skowhegan and The Forks, 23 miles in each direction, Bingham is also right on the 45th parallel and thus equidistant between the North Pole and the equator (3,107 miles in each direction). This quiet valley town with attractive, manicured homes is a stopping point for many white-water rafters en route to Caratunk and The Forks. The town was named for William Bingham, an influential Colonial-era banker and land speculator who made a fortune in privateering. Roscoe Vernon ("Gadabout") Gaddis, TV's pioneering Flying Fisherman, built Bingham's funky grass airfield, the Gadabout Gaddis Airport, site of an annual September fly-in with plane rides and aerobatics.

Just north of Bingham is Moscow, home of the 155-foot-high Wyman Dam, harnessing the Kennebec River for hydroelectric power. Backed up behind the dam is gorgeous Wyman Lake, lined with birches, evergreens, frequent pullouts (great for shutterbugs), and a small lakeside picnic area on the west side of Route 201.

Appropriately named, The Forks stands at the confluence of the Kennebec and Dead Rivers. Although neither looks particularly menacing from the Route 201 bridge, both draw legions of white-water rafters and kayakers for the class III-IV rapids on the dam-controlled waters.

Surrounded by mountains, Jackman is the valley's frontier town, the last outpost before the Québec border, 16 miles northward. Founded as a railway stop for lumber trains, it's now a linchpin in the international snowmobile trail system. Wander into local businesses and you'll likely hear a French lilt to conversation.

From Bingham to Jackman, Route 201 is better known as "Moose Alley." Even though state transportation officials have built rumble strips into the road and littered the roadsides with flashing yellow lights and cautionary Moose Crossing signs, drivers still barrel along, and every year fatalities occur. Those who drive carefully, though, have a treat in store: Moose sightings are relatively frequent, especially early and late in the day. If you notice a car or two pulled off the road, it's likely someone has spotted a moose. (Another Moose Alley in this area—a pretty sure bet for spotting one of the behemoths—is Route 6/15 from Jackman east to Rockwood.)

SIGHTS

South Solon Meetinghouse

The **South Solon Meeting House** (www.southsolonmeetinghouse.org), a serene white clapboard, traditional circa-1842 New England meetinghouse now listed on the National Register of Historic Places, sits at a crossroads in the hamlet of South Solon. The exterior hints at the eye candy inside. One of the

KENNEBEC

KENNEBEC

founders of the Skowhegan School of Painting and Sculpture rescued the church from ruin in the 1930s; in the 1950s fresco artists selected in a stiff competition were given a free hand to paint the place. The riot of color followed until every square inch of wall and ceiling was frescoed with interdenominational religious scenes. (A fresco program still continues at the Skowhegan School.) The local caretaker is Andy Davis (207/643-2555). The meetinghouse is on the corner of South Solon Road and Meetinghouse Road, north of Route 43 and east of Route 201.

◖ Moxie Falls

Here's a big reward for little effort: One of New England's highest waterfalls, **Moxie Falls,** with drops of as much as 100 feet, is one of the easiest to reach. From Route 201, just south of the Kennebec River bridge in The Forks, drive 1.8 miles east on Lake Moxie Road to the signposted parking area. From

© HILARY NANGLE

The simple exterior of the South Solon Meetinghouse gives no clue as to the riot of color within.

here, via an easy wide trail, plus steps and a boardwalk, it's 0.6 mile to the falls in Moxie Stream. Allow a relaxed hour for the round-trip; if it's hot, cool off in the stepped pools. Avoid the falls in June, when blackflies will have you for lunch.

◖ Old Canada Road National Scenic Byway

High on everyone's list of the best roads to drive in fall is Route 201, the 78-mile officially designated **Old Canada Road Scenic Byway** (www.fhwa.dot.gov/byways) between Lakewood and the Canadian border. Every curve in the winding two-lane road reveals a red, gold, and green palette any artist would die for. But truly, it's gorgeous in any season.

It's also a historic route. Benedict Arnold marched his troops along the Kennebec River to the north of Moscow before crossing the river and turning inland. Rest stops along the route have interpretative signage and picnic tables. Two of the prettiest are **Wyman Lake Rest Area,** about midway between Bingham and The Forks, and **Attean View Rest Area,** just south of Jackman (climb the Owl's Head Trail for an even more spectacular view). The rest area in The Forks, just before the bridge, is a great place to watch rafts float by at the end of their thrilling trip down the Kennebec River. Detour into the neat little hamlet of **Caratunk,** a smidgen east of Route 201 on the way to Pleasant Pond.

For a glimpse into the region's glorious past, visit the **Old Canada Road Historical Society** (16 Sidney St., Bingham, www.oldcanadaroad.org, 1pm-4pm Fri., 11am-4pm Sat.).

RECREATION

Recreation is the big focus in this part of Maine. Among the opportunities in the Upper Kennebec Valley are hiking, canoeing, kayaking, bicycling, fishing, and snowmobiling—just for a start—but the big business is white-water rafting, based in and around The Forks.

THE BENEDICT ARNOLD TRAIL

"A tragic masterpiece of bad timing, bad maps, and bad luck" is author Ogden Tanner's summation of Col. Benedict Arnold's march to Québec. Even though Arnold's expedition has been little more than a footnote to history, it's an incredible story, and one best appreciated during a visit to this region.

Arnold marched his troops up the Kennebec River Valley before crossing it and veering inland and up along the Carrabassett River. From Pittston to the Carrying Place (10 miles north of Bingham) and along Route 27, between Kingfield and the border, Arnold Trail historical markers note the expedition's rest stops, obstacles, and other details.

When you see the terrain, you'll begin to understand some of the awful rigors endured by Arnold (before his change of heart and alliance) and his men when they chose a route through the Kennebec Valley to attack the British in Québec City in 1775. Although he later betrayed the Revolutionary cause, Arnold was in good graces when he set out that fall with 1,100 adventurers to remove the English from their Québec stronghold.

In Pittston, six miles south of Augusta, the expedition assembled 220 locally made bateaux and then continued up the Kennebec River to Augusta, camping at Old Fort Western, Skowhegan, and Norridgewock—cutting a swath through the Kennebec River Valley before portaging westward at Carrying Place Township to the Western Lakes and Mountains region and on into Canada. Afflicted by disease, hunger, cold, insects, and unforgiving terrain, the group was devastated before dragging into Québec City in December 1775.

If you're interested in Arnold, pick up a copy of *Following Their Footsteps: A Travel Guide and History of the 1775 Secret Expedition to Capture Québec* by Stephen Clark. The book includes history, maps, canoe routes, and an appendix of places to visit along the way.

Water Sports
◖ WHITE-WATER RAFTING

Carefully regulated by the state, the rafting companies have come a long way since the sport really took off in the early 1980s. Most have sprawling base complexes and have diversified year-round into other adventure sports such as mountain biking, canoeing, kayaking, camping, rock climbing, horseback riding, snowmobiling, and cross-country skiing. The state strictly monitors the number of rafts allowed on the rivers; on midsummer weekends there's a near-capacity crowd.

The focus of white-water rafting in this region is the **East Branch of the Kennebec River,** a 12-mile run from the Hydro Harris Station hydroelectric dam, below Indian Pond, to The Forks. The dam's controlled water releases produce waves of up to eight feet, and the trip begins with a bang in the Alleyway. The highlight is Magic Falls, a Class IV drop that appears as nothing more than a horizon line when approaching it but that has the punch to flip rafts. The excitement is concentrated in the first half of the trip; by the end of it you're just floating along, but that provides opportunities for swimming, water fights between rafts, and perhaps kayaking. Some companies also break for a riverside lunch. Kennebec trips operate early May-mid-October.

Most of the rafting companies also organize trips on the more challenging and oddly named **Dead River,** but serious water releases occur only half a dozen times during the season, mostly on spring weekends. Competition is stiff for space on the infrequent Dead River trips, an exhilarating 16-mile run through Class III-V white water from below Grand Falls to The Forks. The biggest thrill is Poplar Hill Falls. In July-August, the Dead River lives up to its placid name, and outfitters organize moderately priced Sport-Yak and family rafting trips.

The cost of a one-day Kennebec River trip ranges $80-130 pp, depending on whether it's a weekday, weekend, or midsummer. Prices include a hearty cookout or lunch either along the river or back at base camp. The cost of the one-day Dead River trip ranges $90-140 pp. Scads of economical package rates are available—covering lodging, meals, and other activities—especially early and late in the season. Be forewarned that all outfitters have age minimums, usually 10 on the upper Kennebec and 15 on the Dead. Some also impose a weight minimum.

If you want to make more than a day of it—definitely a good plan, since trips start early in the morning and you'll be exhilarated but dog-tired at the end of the day—bookend the trip with nearby lodging. Most of the outfitters have accommodations and dining for every budget. The camaraderie is contagious when everyone around you is about to go rafting or has just done it.

About a dozen outfitters operate on the Kennebec and Dead Rivers. The oldest and biggest is **Northern Outdoors** (1771 Route 201, The Forks, 800/765-7238, www.northernoutdoors.com), with extensive base facilities including lodging, dining, rentals, and more. Five other companies operate under the umbrella of **Raft Maine** (www.raftmaine.com), which provides info and sends out brochures.

CANOEING AND KAYAKING

If you're a neophyte canoeist, if you have never done a multiday trip, or if you want to go en famille, your baptismal expedition probably ought to be the three-day **Moose River Bow Trip,** an easy 45-mile loop (ergo "bow") with mostly flat water. Of course, you can do this yourself, and you don't even need to arrange a shuttle, but a guided trip has its advantages—not the least of which is that the guides provide the know-how for the beginners, they do the cooking and cleanup, and they're a big help for portaging.

Experienced guides Andy and Leslie McKendry operate **Cry of the Loon Kayak Adventures** (207/668-7808, www.cryoftheloon.net), which does a three-day Moose River Bow ($425 pp, with only one portage). Maximum group size is eight and minimum

four. Leslie's gourmet meals are included in the cost. Andy and Leslie will also do one-day guided trips ($60 pp with lunch). If you want to be on your own, they rent kayaks and canoes for $25/day. Avoid June, when the blackflies descend; the water level can be a problem in August for the bow trip. Cry of the Loon's base is 6.5 miles east of Jackman on Route 15.

Maine Huts and Trails

The nonmotorized multiuse **Maine Huts and Trails** (www.mainehuts.org) network, which extends about 50 miles from Carrabassett Valley to The Forks, has a full-service hut sited about two miles below Grand Falls on the Dead River, making it easy to hike or bike the trail or even hike in, then paddle out. It's also open to skiers and snowshoers.

Hiking

The **Appalachian Trail** (AT), extending 2,158 miles from Springer Mountain, Georgia, to the summit of Maine's Katahdin, crosses the Upper Kennebec Valley near Caratunk, just south of The Forks. The *Appalachian Trail Guide to Maine* provides details for reaching several sections of the white-blazed trail accessible to short-haul hikers. Crossing the 70-yard-wide Kennebec at this point would be a major obstacle were it not for the seasonal free ferry service operated for AT hikers by the Maine Appalachian Trail Club (www.matc.org). Check the website for the current schedule.

Other hikes abound, but access is often through a maze of logging roads or through territory where active logging may change landmarks. Ask locally for directions to the trailheads to **Sally Mountain, Number 5** (topped with a fire tower), **Coburn Falls,** and **Kibby Mountain** (with an observation deck).

If you're spending any time in the woods mid-October-November, do not go out without at least a hunter-orange cap to signal your presence to hunters; a hunter-orange vest is even better. Even though some properties are posted No Hunting, don't take a chance; one scofflaw can make a life-and-death difference. If you're skittish or don't have the proper clothing, you can hike on Sunday, when hunting is banned.

Mountain Biking

Mountain biking is growing in popularity here, but be forewarned that this is logging country, and on the woods roads, logging trucks and equipment have the right of way; don't mess with them. Best bet is the **Maine Huts Trail.**

The **Kennebec Valley Trail** is an easy 14.6-mile multiuse gravel trail that follows an old railroad bed (with no tracks) from between the Williams Dam public landing, alongside the Kennebec River in Solon, and Gaddis Airport, on the southern outskirts of Bingham. The route roughly shadows the river, and is especially gorgeous in autumn.

In the Jackman area, an easy-to-moderate 10-mile trip is the **Sandy Bay Loop,** beginning seven miles north of downtown Jackman. Jackman's chamber office has a recreational map detailing this route and others in the area.

Snowmobiling and ATVing

The region is a snowmobiling hotbed, with hundreds of miles of groomed snowmobile trails that connect east to the Moosehead Lake area, west to the Sugarloaf area, and north into Canada. Most double as ATV trails.

Escape into the winter wilderness with **Northern Outdoors** (1771 Rte. 201, The Forks, 800/765-7238, www.northernoutdoors.com). If you're comfortable exploring the backwoods on your own, rental sleds begin at $235/single sled. Better yet, go with a guide; full-day tours begin at $300.

ACCOMMODATIONS

Most of the white-water rafting companies have lodging, and it's convenient to stay where you play. But if you aren't rafting, staying at these places can be a bit overwhelming, especially with the après-raft party atmosphere. If you're planning to be in this area during snowmobiling season, especially in Jackman, book well in advance; the lodgings get chockablock with sledders.

The custom-designed post-and-beam **Hawk's Nest Lodge, Restaurant & Pub** (2989 Rte. 201, West Forks, 207/663-2020, www.hawksnestlodge.com, $60 pp), built in 2004, is especially popular with rafters and sledders. The pine-paneled guest rooms are spacious and comfortably furnished with custom furnishings. All have Wi-Fi, TV, and mini-fridges; most have river views. One especially family-friendly, two-story suite was constructed on the site of a climbing wall, and the hand holds remain. Chain saw carvings by Maine Guide Jeff Samudosky accent the property.

(**Attean Lake Lodge** (Birch Island, Jackman, 207/668-3792, www.atteanlodge.com, Memorial Day-Sept.) has certain trappings of a traditional sporting camp, but it's more like an upscale rustic cottage colony geared to families. Owned by the Holden family since 1900, it's on Birch Island in the center of island- and rock-sprinkled Attean Lake (also called Attean Pond). Brad and Andrea Holden now make it all work—flawlessly. Fourteen well-maintained log cabins (some old, some new, 2-6 beds) have baths, fireplaces, gas or kerosene lamps, and porches with fantastic views of the lake and surrounding mountains. Guests tend to collect in the new main lodge, with its cathedral ceiling, stone fireplaces, and window-walled dining room. Kids love the sandy beach. Meals have plenty of creativity (swordfish with ginger sauce, for instance). Motorboats are $30/day; canoes, kayaks, paddleboats, and a sailboat are free. July-Labor Day, rates for two adults are $345/day, including three meals (wine and beer are available), but nobody stays just one night. Early and late in the season, rates are $280 d per day; children's rates are much lower. Book well ahead; this is a popular getaway, and many families have been coming for years. Some guests barely leave the island the whole time they're here, but be sure to paddle across the pond and climb **Sally Mountain** (about 1.5 miles round-trip) for views that stretch as far as Katahdin; in fall, the foliage vistas are fabulous. Access to the island is via the lodge launch, a five-minute run.

The nicest motel in town is **Bishop's**

Country Inn Motel (461 Main St., Jackman, 207/668-3231 or 888/991-7669, www.bishopsmotel.com, $105 d), a newish two-story building with free Wi-Fi and HBO, air-conditioning, and continental breakfast. All rooms also have a fridge, a microwave, and a coffeemaker, and there's a coin-op laundry on the premises. It's directly across Route 201 from Bishop's Store, where you can get everything else you might possibly want or need.

Just south of downtown is **Mountainview Resort** (263 Main St., 207/668-7700), a somewhat dated timeshare resort with guest rooms and 1-3-bedroom cabins, all with woodsy decor and full kitchens. It's sited on 40 acres with seemingly endless wilderness mountain views. The resort has indoor and outdoor pools, an exercise room, a sauna, and laundry facilities. The best lodging is the cabins. Rates vary by season and accommodation.

Camping

How often do you find a campground on the National Register of Historic Places? That's the case at **The Evergreens Campground and Restaurant** (Rte. 201A, Solon, 207/643-2324, www.evergreenscampground.com), on a prehistoric site used by Native Americans about 4,000 years ago. Many stone tools and weapons excavated here are now in the Maine State Museum in Augusta; a small collection is displayed at the campground. The campground has mostly wooded sites (tent sites $15, RV sites $28, free under age 8), some right on the Kennebec River. Cabins are $45. Pets are allowed; rental canoes, kayaks, and tubes are available by the day; and shuttle service is available. There is a small launch fee for people bringing their own boats, and a guest fee. The restaurant, open 5pm-8:30pm Friday-Saturday for dinner and 8am-11am Saturday-Sunday for breakfast, has a bar and a riverfront deck. Directly across the river (technically in Embden) is a huge outcrop covered with ancient Indian petroglyphs; eagles can often be seen on this shore. The campground, a mile south of the center of Solon, is open all year, except mud season, and caters to snowmobilers in winter.

Indian Pond Campground (The Forks, 800/371-7774, mid-Apr.-mid-Oct., $14 for two adults, kids under age 14 stay free), next to Harris Station on the East Branch of the Kennebec, where Upper Kennebec rafting trips begin, has 27 tent and RV sites that have picnic tables and fire rings but no hookups. There also are 21 water-access primitive sites. Other facilities include showers, restrooms, RV dump station, laundry machines, and a boat launch. Leashed pets are allowed. You can hike from here to Magic Rock and watch Kennebec River rafters surging through Magic Falls. If hydroelectric plants pique your interest, ask at the gatehouse about a tour of Harris Station. To reach the campground from Route 201 in The Forks, take Lake Moxie Road (also called Moxie Pond Rd.) about five miles east; turn left (north) onto Harris Station Road and continue eight miles to the campground gatehouse.

On Heald Stream in Moose River, a mile east of downtown Jackman, the 24-acre **Moose River Campground and Cabins** (207/668-4400, www.mooserivercampground.org, mid-May-mid-Oct.) has 48 tent and RV sites close to a picturesque old dam site. Now crumbling from disuse, the dam was once part of a thriving turn-of-the-20th-century lumber mill that employed more than 700 workers to turn out 35 million board feet annually. Open and wooded campsites are $25-35. Housekeeping cabins are $30 pp. Canoe rentals are available. Facilities include a snack bar, a swimming pool, a trout pond, a laundry room, and a children's play area. Also on-site are three year-round cabins.

FOOD

Fine dining simply doesn't exist in this region, but you'll find good home cooking. It's always wise to ask locally about current reputations, as they do seem to change with the wind as cooks blow in and out of town or head downriver. Most of the rafting companies also operate restaurants.

Thompson's Restaurant (348 Main St./Rte. 201, Bingham, 207/672-3330, 7am-3pm Sun.-Wed., 7am-8pm Sat.-Sun.) has been

© HILARY NANGLE

Mama Bear's in Jackman dishes out hearty portions.

around forever serving inexpensive, no-nonsense fare. It's had its ups and downs, and is currently on an upswing.

Gas, food, clothing: You can get it at **Berry's Store** (Rte. 201, The Forks, 207/663-4461), an institution in these parts. Gordon Berry provides everything the sports-minded person might want or need. Or you might just want to sit down a spell in one of the rockers by the register and catch up on the local gossip.

Pizzas are the drawing card to the **Hawk's Nest Lodge, Restaurant & Pub** (2989 Rte. 201, West Forks, 207/663-2020, www.hawksnestlodge.com, $9-29), which also serves typical pub grub as well as some heftier entrées, such as mussels linguine and chicken parmesan.

Home cookin' is also the specialty at

❰ **Mama Bear's** (420 Main St., Jackman, 207/668-4222, 4am-8pm Mon.-Thurs., 4am-9pm Fri.-Sat., 6am-8pm Sun.). Slide into a booth, check out the engraved table and the historical pics lining the walls. Most menu items run $6-12. There's a full bar too. Interesting note: This tiny spot was Jackman's original A&P store.

The **Kennebec River Brew Pub** (Rte. 201, The Forks, 800/765-7238, www.northernoutdoors.com), at Northern Waters, caters to the rafting and recreating crowd, but it's one of the best bets around. The dinner menu ranges from burgers to filet tips ($10-20). It's open daily for breakfast, lunch, and dinner.

Craving Q? **Lake Parlin BBQ & Smokehouse** (Rte. 201, Parlin Pond Township, 207/668-9060, www.lakeparlinlodge.com, from 11:30am Thurs.-Mon., $8-24) does the trick and serves it in a pine-walled, lakeview dining area accented with a stone fireplace and animal trophies.

INFORMATION AND SERVICES

Local information is available from the **Upper Kennebec Valley Chamber of Commerce** (207/672-4100), **The Forks Area Chamber of Commerce** (The Forks, 207/663-4430, www.forksarea.com), the **Jackman/Moose River Region Chamber of Commerce** (207/668-4171 or 888/633-5225, www.jackmanmaine.org), and **Kennebec Valley Tourism Council** (207/623-4884, www.kennebecvalley.org).

GETTING THERE

By car, Bingham is roughly 45 miles or one hour from Skowhegan via Route 201. It's roughly 50 miles or one hour from Bingham to Jackman via Route 201. From Jackman, it's roughly 50 miles or one hour to Greenville via Route 6/15, and it's 110 miles or 2.25 hours to Québec City via Routes 201, 173, and 73.

KENNEBEC

WESTERN LAKES AND MOUNTAINS

When I tire of the summertime coastal crowds or I'm ready to hit the slopes, I head for Maine's Western Lakes and Mountains—about 4,500 outstandingly scenic square miles of Franklin, Oxford, Androscoggin, and Cumberland Counties. The recreational variety is astonishing. In winter, the state's two alpine powerhouses—Sunday River and Sugarloaf—entice skiers and riders from throughout the Northeast and even abroad. Six smaller, family-oriented ski areas—Saddleback, Shawnee Peak, Mount Abram, Black Mountain, Titcomb, and Lost Valley—deliver fewer on-mountain amenities but offer more wallet-friendly prices. Cross-country and snowshoeing trails also lace the region, dogsledding is increasingly popular, and snowmobiling is big business. There are trails for winter hiking and ponds for skating.

Still, winter is the off-season in much of this region. The multitude of lakes, ponds, rivers, and streams satisfy recreational boaters and anglers, while the mountains attract hikers and mountain bikers. One of the most rugged stretches of the 2,158-mile Appalachian Trail, which runs from Georgia to Maine, passes through this area.

Of Maine's nine covered bridges (seven originals and two carefully built replicas), five are in the Western Lakes and Mountains—including the picturesque "Artist's Covered Bridge," near Sunday River, my favorite because you can ski through the forest and suddenly come upon it.

Sprawling, mountainous Oxford County, backed against New Hampshire, has fabulous trails for hiking and rivers for canoeing. There's gold—and all kinds of other

© HILARY NANGLE

HIGHLIGHTS

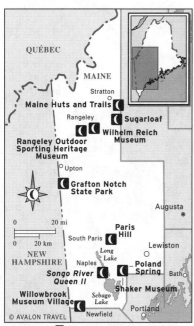

LOOK FOR ◖ TO FIND RECOMMENDED SIGHTS, ACTIVITIES, DINING, AND LODGING.

◖ **Sugarloaf:** The summit snowfields are the only lift-accessible skiing and riding above the tree line in the East (page 553).

◖ **Maine Huts and Trails:** Hike, bike, paddle, ski, or snowshoe from hut to hut on this spectacular wilderness trail (page 555).

◖ **Rangeley Outdoor Sporting Heritage Museum:** Learn about the sporting legends who made Rangeley famous (page 560).

◖ **Wilhelm Reich Museum:** You don't have to agree with the controversial scientist to enjoy the views from the estate (page 561).

◖ **Grafton Notch State Park:** This is a spectacular chunk of real estate, with hiking trails, waterfalls, and picnic areas (page 576).

◖ **Willowbrook Museum Village:** This village is preserved in time with 25 buildings on the National Register of Historic Places (page 592).

◖ *Songo River Queen II:* Take in views to Mount Washington on a cruise across Long Lake (page 596).

◖ **Poland Spring:** Tour through the history of famed Poland Spring Water and Hiram Ricker's family empire (page 605).

◖ **Shaker Museum:** Visit the world's last inhabited Shaker community (page 606).

◖ **Paris Hill:** Take a walk around this hidden hilltop National Historic District (page 610).

minerals—in the Oxford Hills; the official state gemstone, tourmaline, an intriguing stone that turns up in green, blue, or pink, is most prevalent in western Maine. Grab a digging tool or gold pan and try your hand at amateur prospecting. You're unlikely to find more than a few flakes or some pretty specimens of sparkly pyrite (fool's gold), but the fun is in the adventure.

East of Oxford County, Franklin County comprises Sugarloaf and the lovely Rangeley Lakes recreational area. Farmington is the

county seat and a university town. Mostly rural Androscoggin, fourth smallest of the state's 16 counties, takes its commercial and political cues from Lewiston and Auburn, the state's second-largest population center.

Directly west of Portland, and partly in Cumberland County, are Sebago and Long Lakes, surrounded by towns and villages that swell with visitors throughout the summer. Also here are most of the state's youth summer camps—some many generations old. During the annual summer-camp parents' weekend in

WESTERN LAKES

WESTERN LAKES

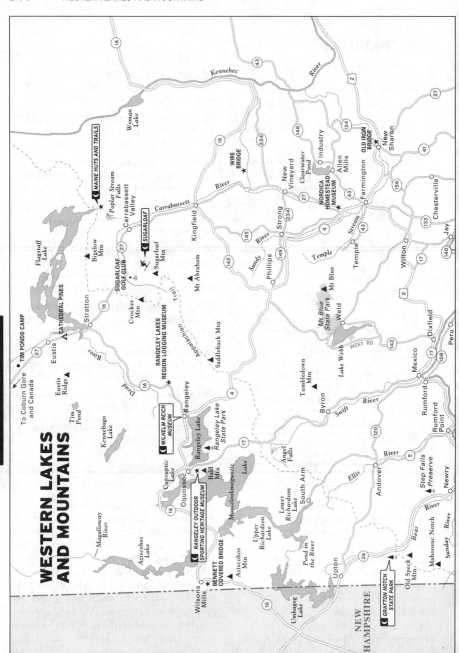

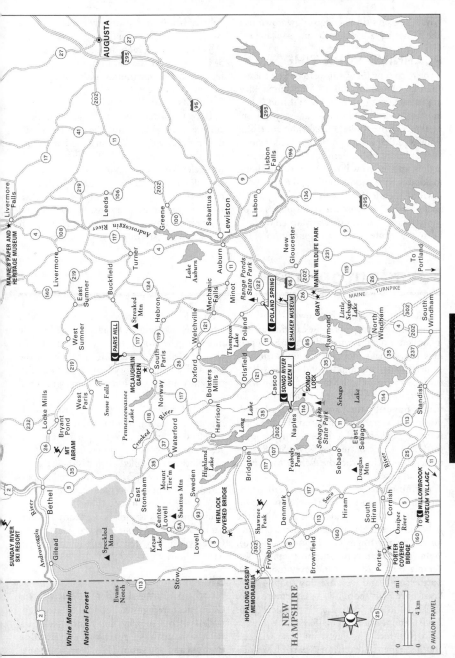

© AVALON TRAVEL

July, Bridgton's tiny besieged downtown feels like Times Square at rush hour.

PLANNING YOUR TIME

If you're coming for warm-weather recreation—boating, swimming, hiking, and simply playing in the great outdoors—you'll find it here in abundance. And in July-August, you won't be alone on the Route 302 corridor stretching from Windham through Bridgton. Skip north to the Oxford Hills, Bethel, and the Kingfield region, and the crowds diminish. Bethel, home to Sunday River, and Kingfield, the nearest big town to Sugarloaf, come to life during the ski season, but otherwise are quiet places to escape, recreate, and especially to enjoy fall's foliage. If winter sports are your priority, late February-mid-March usually brings the best combination of snow and temperatures.

While you can loop through this region in 3-4 days, to get the most out of the summer recreational opportunities, pick one spot and explore from there. Good hubs are Rangeley, Bethel, Bridgton, and Naples.

If you're interested in Franco American culture, plan on spending the better part of a day in the Lewiston-Auburn area. For antiquing, slip over to Cornish. For fishing, make Rangeley your base. No matter where you stay, don't overplan. The region's riches demand that you get off the highways and byways and onto the back roads. Wander around and you'll stumble on spectacular views, great hikes, country stores, and swimming holes.

Farmington Area

Farmington is a sleeper of a town—home to a respected University of Maine campus, an easily walkable downtown, and an unusual opera museum. What's more, mountain towns and scenery stretch out and beyond in every direction. Less than an hour's drive north of town is the Carrabassett Valley, a recreation stronghold made famous by the year-round Sugarloaf alpine resort. Off to the northwest are the fabled Rangeley Lakes, and a drive southwest leads to Bethel, home of Sunday River Ski Resort, mineral quarries, and the White Mountain National Forest.

Farmington (pop. 7,760) was incorporated in 1794 and became the county seat for Franklin County 44 years later. It remains the judicial hub but also is the commercial center for the nearby towns of **Wilton** (pop. 4,116), **Weld** (pop. 419), **New Sharon** (pop. 1,407), **Temple** (pop. 528), and **Industry** (pop. 929). To the south and west are **Jay** (pop. 4,851), **Livermore Falls** (pop. 1,843), **Livermore** (pop. 1,795), **Dixfield** (pop. 2,250), **Mexico** (pop. 2,681), and **Rumford** (pop. 5,841).

In Rumford and Jay, your nose will tell you it's paper-mill territory, part of Maine's economic lifeline; locals call the sulfuric odor "the smell of money." Residents have become inured to the aroma, but visitors may need a chance to adjust. Livermore is the site of the Norlands Living History Center, a unique participatory museum that rewards you with a real "feel" for the past.

And, lest we forget, Farmington's leading candidate for favorite son is Chester Greenwood, who, in 1873, rigged beaver fur, velvet, and a bit of wire to create "Champion ear protectors"—called earmuffs these days—when he was only 15. The clever fellow patented his invention and then went on to earn 100 more patents for such things as doughnut hooks and shock absorbers. His early-December birthday inspires the quirky annual Chester Greenwood Day celebration in downtown Farmington.

SIGHTS
Nordica Homestead Museum

Gem-encrusted gowns, opera librettos, lavish gifts from royalty, and family treasures fill the handful of rooms in the **Nordica Homestead Museum** (116 Nordica Lane,

GLOBAL MAINE

Posted almost casually on an undistinguished corner in western Maine is a roadside landmark that inevitably appears in any travel book or slide show with a sense of the whimsical. Nine markers direct bikers, hikers, or drivers to Maine communities bearing the names of international locales: **Norway, Paris, Denmark, Naples, Sweden, Poland, Mexico, Peru,** and **China.** All are within 94 miles of the sign, which stands at the junction of Routes 5 and 35 in the burg of Lynchville (part of Albany Township), about 14 miles west of Norway. If you approach the sign from the south on Route 35, you're likely to miss it; it's most noticeable when coming from the north on Route 35 or the west on Route 5.

A similar one stands next to The Lake Store in Norway. This one provides distances to **Lisbon, Belgrade, Rome, Madrid, Athens, Moscow, Belfast, Stockholm,** and **Vienna.** And speaking of Vienna, yet another distance marker stands at the crossroads of Route 41 and the Kimball Falls Road in Vienna, in the Belgrade Lakes Region. This one provides mileage details to Vienna, Austria, as well as 16 stateside towns bearing the name.

Farmington, 207/778-2042, www.lilliannordica.com, 1pm-5pm Tues.-Sun., June 1-Sept. 15, by appointment Sept. 16-Oct. 15, $2 adults, $1 children over age 5), birthplace of Lillian Norton (1857-1914), better known as Madame Lillian Nordica, the legendary turn-of-the-20th-century Wagnerian opera diva. Her influence still pervades the house, where scratchy recordings play in the background and newspaper clippings line the walls. No opera buff should miss this. A guide is on hand to answer questions. Even the kids get a kick out of the costumed mannequins, and there's lots of space on the grounds for letting off steam. Take Route 4/27 north from Farmington and turn right (east) onto Holley Road; the farm is 0.5 mile down the road.

Maine's Paper and Heritage Museum

The fledgling **Maine's Paper and Heritage Museum** (22 Church St., Livermore Falls, 207/592-1807, www.papermuseumofmaine. org, 10:30am-2:30pm, late May-early Sept.) aims to grow into an interactive experience where visitors can experience life in a papermaking community.

RECREATION
Mount Blue State Park

Mount Blue State Park (299 Center Hill Rd., Weld, 207/585-2261, www.parksandlands. com, campground 207/585-2261, www.campwithme.com), covering nearly 8,000 acres in two sections, is one of Maine's best-kept secrets. Yes, it's crowded in summer, but mostly with Mainers. It offers multilevel hiking, superb swimming, wooded campsites, mountain scenery, and daily interpretive natural-history programs in summer. There are movies on weekends, guided hikes, weekly guest speakers, even gold-panning expeditions—you'll never be bored. Swimming and camping are on Lake Webb's west side; the Center Hill section, including the trail to Mount Blue itself, is on the lake's east side. The main entrance, with a two-mile access road, is eight miles from Weld, on the lake's west side. Day-use admission is $6 nonresident adults, $4 Maine resident adults, $1 ages 5-11, nonresident seniors $1.50, resident seniors free. Canoe rentals are $3/hour. Winter activities include snowshoeing, snowmobiling, and more than a dozen miles of groomed cross-country ski trails.

Swimming and Paddling

Five miles northeast of downtown Farmington is the hamlet of Allens Mills (officially the town of Industry), where you can swim or paddle in aptly named **Clearwater Lake.** To get there from Farmington, follow Broadway (Rte. 43) until you reach the T junction and boat landing at the lake.

Another local swimming hole is at the Route 4 bridge in Fairbanks, just north of Farmington.

Hiking

You're getting into western Maine's serious mountains here, so there are plenty of great hiking opportunities, running the gamut from a cakewalk to a workout.

In Weld, a deservedly popular hiking route goes up 3,187-foot **Mount Blue,** in the eastern section of Mount Blue State Park. From Route 142 in Weld village, follow signs and take Maxwell Road and then Center Hill Road about 2.5 miles to the parking area for Center Hill itself. You can stop for a picnic (sweeping views even at this level, plus picnic tables and outhouses), follow the 0.5-mile-long self-guided nature-trail loop (pick up a brochure here), and then go on. It's also a great spot for sunset-watching. Continue up the unpaved road 3.5 miles to the parking lot for the Mount Blue trailhead. Allow about three hours for the steepish 2.8-mile round-trip (easy, then moderately difficult). In midsummer, carry plenty of water. Hope for clear air on the summit; vistas of the Longfellows and beyond are awesome.

Other good hikes around Weld, on the west side of Lake Webb, are **Tumbledown Mountain** (3,068 feet via several route options; nesting peregrines can restrict access in early summer) and **Little Jackson Mountain** (3,434 feet). Tumbledown, moderately strenuous, attracts the "been there, done that" set. A much easier hike, but likely to be more crowded, is 2,386-foot **Bald Mountain,** with a scoured summit fine for picnics if it's not too blustery. Allow about two hours for the three-mile round-trip, including a lunch break. To reach the trailhead from Weld, take Route 156 southeast about 5.5 miles. There's limited parking on the right; watch for the sign.

Multiuse Trail

The 14-mile **Whistlestop Trail,** connecting Jay, Wilton, and Farmington, passes through rural scenery, crosses rivers, and bypasses quarries. The trail can be accessed from many points.

One convenient downtown Farmington location is on Oak Street (off Rte. 2/4), adjacent to a CN Brown station.

Fitness Center

A rainy-day godsend is the $4.5 million University of Maine at Farmington **Health and Fitness Center** (152 Québec St. at Lincoln St., Farmington, 207/778-7495, www.umf.maine. edu). It's open to the public for weight training, indoor jogging, tennis, and swimming in a six-lane heated pool. Call for current hours and fees.

ENTERTAINMENT

Throughout the year, something is always happening at the **University of Maine at Farmington** (207/778-7000, www.umf.maine. edu): lectures, concerts, plays, you name it. Contact the college for schedule and details.

The free, 1.5-hour **Music on Main** summer concerts begin at 11:30am Tuesday, in the green and white octagonal bandstand.

FESTIVALS AND EVENTS

The two-day **Wilton Blueberry Festival** (www. wiltonbbf.com), in early August, is an always-crowded blueberry-oriented celebration that includes a parade, road races, games, crafts booths, a book sale, a museum open house, live entertainment, a lobster-roll lunch, a chicken barbecue, and a pig roast in downtown Wilton.

The third week of September is given over to the **Farmington Fair,** a weeklong country fair with agricultural exhibits, a parade, harness racing, and live entertainment at the Farmington Fairgrounds.

The first Saturday in December, Farmington honors a native son on **Chester Greenwood Day.** Festivities commemorating the inventor of earmuffs include a road race, an oddball earmuff parade, a polar-bear swim, and other activities.

SHOPPING

Downtown Farmington has just enough options to entertain shoppers of all budgets. Fans of fine craft simply must visit

WESTERN LAKES

SugarWood Gallery (248 Broadway, Farmington, 207/778-9105), which features the work of more than 100 western Maine artisans. Furniture, pottery, weaving, art quilts, handmade teddy bears, and more fill this cooperative gallery.

It's hard to resist the cheerful, welcoming ambience at **Devaney Doak and Garrett Booksellers** (193 Broadway, Farmington, 207/778-3454, www.ddgbooks.com), not to mention the children's corner piled high with books, toys, and games. Owner Kenny Brechner does the ordering and the website's book reviews; his eclectic taste is evident. And how many independent bookshops have a website with hilarious parodic reviews?

Around the corner, **Twice-Sold Tales** (155 Main St., Farmington, 207/778-4411) has a well-chosen and well-organized selection; Maine titles are a specialty, and prices are reasonable (paperback mysteries are only $1). Ask owner Jim Logan, an avid outdoorsman, about hiking options in Farmington and beyond.

I always introduce visiting friends to **Renys** (24 Broadway, Farmington, 207/778-4641), and they always leave with at least a bag or two. From clothing to cleaning supplies to electronics to food, Renys has it all. Part of a small statewide chain, this one is spread out on three floors—even the back corners have finds.

ACCOMMODATIONS

Surprisingly for a county seat that doubles as a college town, there are few lodgings in Farmington itself.

Just west of Farmington on Wilson Lake, **Wilson Lake Inn** (183 Lake Rd., Wilton, 207/645-3721 or 800/626-7463, www.wilson-lakeinn.com, $89-179) is a well-maintained family-owned property that's been expanded over the years to include studios and extended-stay two-bedroom suites with kitchens, in addition to basic guest rooms; all were renovated in 2012 with upgraded bedding, 32-inch flat-screens, and new decor. The grounds are lovely, with gardens and a lawn leading to the lakefront. All rooms have free HBO, air-conditioning, mini-fridges, free Wi-Fi, data ports, and phones, and there's a laundry on the premises. Rates include continental breakfast, and guests have free use of a canoe, paddleboat, and kayaks as well as outdoor grills. Sightseeing flights leave from the inn's dock.

Step back in time at **Kawanhee Inn** (12 Ann's Way/Rte. 142, Weld, 207/585-2000, www.maineinn.net, late May-mid-Oct.), a lakefront lodge-style inn and cabins tucked under the shelter of towering pines. Owners Chris and Jodi Huntington have renovated the cabins and updated the rooms, all while preserving the classic 1920s style. Don't expect TVs, cell phone reception, or frills. Sunsets in this mountain-and-lake setting on six-mile-long Lake Webb are spectacular; loons' cries add to the magic. Eleven second-floor guest rooms with shared and private baths in the large main lodge are $110-165/day with a two-night minimum stay on weekends. Cabins (rates begin at $1,350/week) vary in age, size, and facilities; all have lake views, fieldstone fireplaces, and screened-in porches. Pets are welcome for $35/dog/night plus a $200 security deposit (some restrictions, call). There's free Wi-Fi. The sandy beach is great for kids, and superb hiking is close by. Guests have use of canoes and kayaks. The lodge's lakeview dining room is open to nonguests for dinner (Wed.-Sun., $18-28) mid-June-early September. Devotees keep returning here, so book well ahead for midsummer. In mid-September, nights are coolish and it's pretty quiet, but the foliage is incredible.

Camping

Mount Blue State Park (299 Center Hill Rd., Weld, 207/585-2261, www.parksandlands. com; campground 207/585-2261, www.campwithme.com) has 136 wooded sites but no hookups. Camping fees are $25/site for nonresidents, $15 for Maine residents. Reservations are handled through the state-park reservation system; from out of state call 207/287-3824 at least two weeks ahead or book reservations online from February 1 at www.campwithme. com. The reservation fee is $2/site/night, two-night minimum.

FOOD
Local Flavors
If you'll be camping or staying in a condo or cottage with cooking facilities, swing by **Whitewater Farm** (28 Mercer Rd./Rte. 2, Mercer, 207/778-4748) for local naturally raised beef, lamb, chicken, turkey, rabbit, pork, cheeses, eggs, and produce.

There's always a line at **Gifford's Ice Cream** (Rte. 4/27, Farmington, 207/778-3617, 11am-10pm daily summer, 11am-9pm daily spring and fall), a longtime take-out spot. Besides about four dozen terrific ice cream flavors, it also has foot-long hot dogs. It's open mid-March-early November.

My favorite stop in Farmington is the order-at-the-counter **Soup for You! Cafe** (222 Broadway, Farmington, 207/779-0799, 10:30am-7pm Mon.-Sat.), which oozes college-town funk and concocts some of the best soups you'll ever taste; usually about six are made daily, with vegan, vegetarian, and gluten-free options. Also available are sandwiches, both named and create-your-own varieties. Smoothies and coffee drinks are very popular here too. Vegetarians will find plenty of choices, and kids can get PB&J. Nothing on the menu is more than $6.

The **Sandy River Farmers Market** sets up its tables in the parking lot of the Narrow Gauge Cinema (Front St., Farmington, 9am-2pm Fri., 2pm-6pm Tues. May-Oct.). You'll find herbs, homemade bread, cheeses, and organic meats and produce.

Family Favorites
Home-style fare, house-made desserts, generous portions, and all-day breakfast are the draws to **Boivins Harvest House Restaurant** (147 Pleasant St., Farmington, 207/778-6880, www.harvesthouserestaurant.com, 7am-9pm Mon.-Thurs., 6am-10pm Fri.-Sat., 6am-9pm Mon.-Sun., $6-18), an especially family-friendly spot. Don't look for culinary creativity here, just solid American food ranging from liver and onions to baked stuffed haddock.

Just east of Rumford, the **Front Porch Cafe** (6 Hall Hill Rd., Dixfield, 207/562-4646, www.thefrontporchcafe.com, 8am-3pm Wed.-Mon. and 5pm-8pm Thurs.-Sat.) has earned a solid reputation for good food, generous portions, and friendly service. It's also worth a stop to sign the covered bridge entry, see the dual handmade stone fireplaces, and visit the indoor uptown outhouse. Owners Clint Bailey and Sammie Angel make this place special, and Sammie, a professional musician, sometimes entertains in the evenings.

Casual Dining
Breakfast, lunch, dinner, even tapas— **The Homestead Bakery Restaurant** (186 Broadway, Farmington, 207/778-6162, www.homesteadbakery.com, 8am-9pm Mon.-Sat., 8am-2pm Sun., $10-24) serves it all. There's plenty of ethnic variety—Mediterranean, Mexican, Thai—as well as pub-style classics and even vegetarian. A martini and wine bar, with couches by a fireplace, provides cozier seating.

Step back in time and savor the views from the **Kawanhee Inn** (12 Ann's Way/Rte. 142, Weld, 207/585-2000, www.maineinn.net, 5pm-9pm Wed.-Sun., hours vary spring and fall, $10-28). The lakefront setting is spectacular, especially at sunset. Reservations are recommended.

The former Bass Shoe factory now houses **Calzolaio Pasta Co.** (248 Main St., Wilton, 207/645-9500, www.calzolaiopasta.com, 11am-9pm daily, $9-24), which prepares decent Italian fare from pizzas and pastas to specialty entrées such a veal saltimbocca and Sicilian chicken. There are kids', vegetarian, and gluten-free menus too. Opt for an outdoor riverside table if the weather's fine.

INFORMATION AND SERVICES
Downtown Farmington (www.downtownfarmington.com) has local information and listings.

Check out **Cutler Memorial Library** (117 Academy St., Farmington, 207/778-4312, www.farmington.lib.me.us).

GETTING THERE AND AROUND

Farmington is roughly 40 miles or 50 minutes from Augusta via Route 27. It's about 22 miles or 30 minutes to Kingfield via Route 27. It's about 40 miles or one hour to Rangeley via Route 4.

Sugarloaf Area

The thread tying together the Sugarloaf area is the lovely Carrabassett River, which winds its way through the smashingly scenic **Carrabassett Valley** from the area more or less around **Sugarloaf** through **Kingfield** (pop. 997), to **North Anson,** where it tumbles over treacherous falls and flows into the mighty Kennebec River. On both sides of the valley, the Longfellow and Bigelow Ranges boast six of Maine's ten 4,000-footers—a hiker's paradise.

Flanking the west side of the valley is the huge Sugarloaf resort. In 1951, Kingfield businessman Amos Winter and some of his pals, known locally as the "Bigelow Boys," cut the first ski trail from the snowfields above the tree line atop Sugarloaf Mountain, dubbing it "Winter's Way." A downhill run required skiing three miles to the base of the trail and then strapping on animal skins for the uphill trek. Three runs on wooden skis would be about the daily max in those days. By 1954 the prophetically named Winter and some foresighted investors had established the Sugarloaf Mountain Ski Club; and the rest, as they say, is history.

Sugarloaf is the megataxpayer in the relatively new town of **Carrabassett Valley** (pop. 781). It bills itself as a year-round resort, which is true, but winter is definitely the peak season, when the head count is highest and so are the prices. Everything's open and humming November-late April; spring skiing has been known to extend even into June.

Before Amos Winter brought fame and fortune to his hometown and the valley, Kingfield was best known as a timber center and the birthplace of the Stanley twins (designers of the Stanley Steamer). Today it's an appealing slice-of-life rural town, with handsome old homes and off-mountain beds and restaurants.

In **Stratton,** a village in **Eustis** (pop. 618), old-timers reminisce over the towns of Flagstaff and Dead River—already historic two centuries before they were consigned to the history books in the 1950s. That's when the Long Falls Dam, built on the Dead River, backed up the water behind it, inundated the towns, and created 20,000-acre Flagstaff Lake. The hydroelectric dam now controls the water flow for spring white-water rafting on the Dead River.

Flagstaff owes its name to Col. Benedict Arnold, whose troops en route to Québec in 1775 flew their flag at the site of today's Cathedral Pines Campground. After struggling up the Kennebec River to the spot known as the Carrying Place, the disheartened soldiers turned northwest along the Dead River's North Branch at Flagstaff and then on through the Chain of Ponds to Canada.

Route 27, from Kingfield to the Canadian border at Coburn Gore, is an officially designated Scenic Highway, a 54-mile stretch that's most spectacular in mid-late September. But there's no pot of gold at the end; there's not much to Coburn Gore except a Customs outpost, a convenience store (with fuel), and a few unimpressive dwellings.

SIGHTS
Stanley Museum

Here's a reason to go back to school: The small but captivating **Stanley Museum** (40 School St., Kingfield, 207/265-2729, www.stanley-museum.org, 1pm-4pm Tues.-Sun. June-Oct., 1pm-4pm Tues.-Fri. Nov.-May or by appointment, $4 adults, $3 seniors, $2 under age 12), located in the town's old schoolhouse, is dedicated to educating visitors about Kingfield's most famous native sons, twin brothers Francis

Edgar (F. E.) and Freelan Oscar (F. O.) Stanley. Although best known for the Stanley Steamer, the identical twins' legacy of invention and innovation extends far beyond either the automobile or Kingfield. These versatile overachievers also invented the photographic dry plate, eventually selling out to George Eastman. Freelan Stanley, the first to climb Mount Washington by car, later became a noted violinmaker. He was also a talented portrait artist—one of his subjects was poet Henry Wadsworth Longfellow—and he's credited with inventing the first airbrush. Also in the museum are hundreds of superb photographs (and glass-plate negatives) by the twins' clever sister, Chansonetta Stanley Emmons, and work by Chansonetta's artist-daughter, Dorothy. The museum gift shop contains auto-related books, pamphlets, and other specialty items.

Ski Museum of Maine

Established in 1995, the **Ski Museum of Maine** (256 Main St., Kingfield, 207/265-2023, www. skimuseumofmaine.org, 9am-5pm daily in winter, free) exhibits Maine-related ski artifacts and memorabilia documenting Maine's role in the growth and development of the sport, from immigrant Swedes to manufacturing to resorts. Call ahead for off-season and summer hours.

Nowetah's American Indian Museum

A bold, in-your-face sign announces the driveway to **Nowetah's American Indian Museum** (Rte. 27, New Portland, 207/628-4981, www. nowetahs.webs.com, 10am-5pm daily, free), an astonishing repository of hundreds of Maine Indian baskets and bark objects—plus porcupine-quill embroidery, trade beads, musical instruments, soapstone carvings, and other Native American esoterica. Übercollector Nowetah Cyr, a descendent of St. Francis Abenaki and Paugussett Indians, loves explaining unique details about the artifacts she's displayed here since 1969; but be forewarned: She's a talker. In the museum's gift shop are many Native American craft pieces as well as books. It's 16 miles north of Farmington.

Wire Bridge

Now here's a most unusual landmark, about seven miles south of Kingfield and not far from Nowetah's museum: Twenty-five-foot-tall shingled towers announce the entrance to the **Wire Bridge** suspended over the Carrabassett River in New Portland. Built in 1864-1866 at a cost of $2,000, with steel supports imported from England, the bridge is on the National Register of Historic Places. Locals often refer to it as "rustproof" for its stainless-steel construction, or "flood-proof" for its longtime survival despite nasty spring floods. To find the bridge from Route 146 in New Portland, turn north onto Wire Bridge Road and follow signs for less than a mile.

Dead River Historical Society Museum

Unless you're a rabid history fan or have an area connection, many local historical society museums can be a bit of a snore. Not so the **Dead River Historical Society** (11am-3pm Sat.-Sun. July-early Sept., donation), which contains fascinating memorabilia from the two villages submerged when the Dead River was dammed and Flagstaff Lake created.

Benedict Arnold Trail

In the fall of 1775, Benedict Arnold marched north from Augusta with the goal of capturing Québec. He followed the Kennebec River, then portaged to the Dead River, following it to Chain of Ponds near the Québec border. While there are dirt woods roads that ramble through this region, Route 27 roughly follows the route north from Kingfield, and there are roadside historical markers from Stratton north. It's a gorgeous drive, especially in autumn, when leaves are turning and snow might fringe the peaks.

PICNIC AND REST AREAS

Several riverside and viewpoint rest areas on or near Route 27 make picnicking almost mandatory, especially in autumn, when the leaf colors are splendid. On Route 27, roughly halfway between Kingfield and the Sugarloaf access road,

© HILARY NANGLE

Sugarloaf is the largest alpine ski area in the East.

a picnic area is sandwiched between the highway and the Carrabassett River, just north of Hammond Field Brook.

About 12 miles north of the Sugarloaf access road, turn left (west) onto Eustis Ridge Road and go two miles to the Eustis Ridge picnic area, a tiny park with an expansive view of the Bigelow Range.

Finally, on Route 27, about 23 miles north of Sugarloaf, there's another scenic picnic area, this one alongside the Dead River on the east side of the highway.

C Sugarloaf

Best known as the king of alpine resorts in Maine, **Sugarloaf** (Carrabassett, 207/237-2000 or 800/843-5623, www.sugarloaf.com) is a four-season destination resort with alpine skiing and snowboarding, snowshoeing, cross-country skiing, and ice skating December-late April; golf, hiking, and mountain biking during warmer months; and zip-lining during both seasons. A compact base village has a hotel, an inn, and gazillions of condos as well as

restaurants, a chapel, a handful of shops, and a base lodge housing a snow school and rental operations. The separate Outdoor Center, linked via shuttle and trails, houses cross-country skiing operations and has an ice-skating rink and an excellent, but very casual, café.

ALPINE SKIING AND RIDING

At 4,237 feet, Sugarloaf is not only Maine's highest skiing mountain, it also has the only lift-serviced terrain above the tree line in the East. Well over 100 named trails and glades on more than 1,000 acres, served by 15 lifts that range from a T-bar to detachable high-speed quads, ribbon its 2,820 vertical feet. Even beginners can ski from the summit, a 3.5-mile descent via the longest run. Although the resort has produced national and international ski and snowboard champions (2006 and 2010 Olympic gold snowboard-cross medalist Seth Wescott calls it home), Sugarloaf has always been especially family-friendly, with day care and all kinds of children's ski and entertainment programs. Full-day lift tickets are about

$80 adults, $68 teens, and $56 ages 6-12 and 65-80; ages 5 and younger as well as ages 80 and older ski free. Most lodging packages include lift tickets; multiday tickets are less expensive, as are those purchased online.

SUGARLOAF OUTDOOR CENTER

On Route 27 about a mile south of the Sugarloaf access road is the entrance to the **Sugarloaf Outdoor Center** (207/237-6830), geared in winter toward cross-country skiing, snowshoeing, and ice skating. Some sections of the 63-mile cross-country skiing trail network are on Maine Public Reserve Land, and some are on Penobscot Indian Nation land. Also at the Outdoor Center is an Olympic-size outdoor ice-skating rink, lighted on weekend nights and holiday weeks. The glass-walled lodge looking out on Sugarloaf Mountain has ski, snowshoe, and skate rentals, plus a casual café. Cross-country lessons are available. Call for current hours and fees for all programs, and ask about special events such as guided moonlight tours and snowshoe tours.

GOLF

Designed by Robert Trent Jones Jr., and regularly ranked in national golf magazines as Maine's top course, the 18-hole, par-72 **Sugarloaf Golf Club and Golf School** meanders through woods and alongside the Carrabassett River in the shadow of the Longfellow Range. It's actually a town-owned course but is managed by Sugarloaf. You get what you pay for; greens fees are steep. Tee times are essential; book a week or two in advance for weekends. Sugarloaf's golf school offers multiday programs all summer, with special weeks designed for Women's Golf School and Junior Golf Camp. Club rentals and private lessons are available; carts are mandatory. A driving range, a pro shop, and a café round out the facilities.

OTHER ACTIVITIES

Summer activities at Sugarloaf include guided hikes, boat trips, moose-spotting tours, mountain biking, fly-fishing, scenic chair rides, and wilderness cookouts. Zip-line tours ($39 pp) on

seven lines varying 160-260 feet in length are offered year-round.

ANTIGRAVITY CENTER

A partnership between Sugarloaf, the town, and CVA (Carrabassett Valley Academy, a ski preparatory school at the mountain's base that has produced many Olympians), the **Antigravity Center** (207/237-5566, www.carrabassettvalley.org), locally called the AGC, is the answer to a parent's frustration when the weather doesn't cooperate. It houses a gym, a climbing wall, a skate park, trampolines, a weight room, and more, and fitness classes are offered. Call for current hours and programs.

ENTERTAINMENT AND EVENTS

Sugarloaf is entertainment central in these parts. Every night in winter there's live music somewhere here, so you can hopscotch from The Bag to Gepetto's to The Rack (owned by double Olympic snowboard-cross gold medalist Seth Wescott) and back again.

The last full week in January is **White White World Week,** Sugarloaf's winter carnival, with discount lift tickets, reduced lodging rates, ski races, fireworks, a torchlight parade, and other special events.

Sugarloaf meets the Caribbean during **Reggae Fest** with spring skiing, reggae bands day and night, and lots of boisterous fun over a mid-late-April weekend.

In early July, the annual **Kingfield POPS concert** features the Bangor Symphony Orchestra, an arts and crafts festival, a garden tour, and more.

Kingfield's galleries and museums open their doors on the first Friday evening of each month for **Friday Artwalk.**

RECREATION
Multisport Trails

The town-owned **Narrow Gauge Trail** begins at Campbell Field on the east side of Route 27 near the foot of the Sugarloaf access road and continues seven miles, gradually downhill, to the Carrabassett Valley Town Park. The trail follows the abandoned narrow-gauge railway bed along the river. Pack a picnic and wear a bathing suit under your biking duds; you'll be passing swimming holes along the way. In winter, it's groomed weekly for cross-country skiing. From the trail, you can connect to the Maine Huts and Trails network.

(Maine Huts and Trails

Inch by inch, mile by mile: Imagine a 180-mile-long highway through the wilderness. When finished, the easygoing 12-foot-wide corridor through the wilderness will stretch from Newry in the Mahoosuc Mountains to Rockwood on Moosehead Lake, with offshoot dedicated hiking trails. It's not a trail for motorized vehicles, but rather for hikers, mountain bikers, snowshoers, cross-country skiers (it's groomed in winter), even paddlers.

Larry Warren, a former Sugarloaf manager, town founder, and preservation advocate, had the vision, and in 2008, after years of arm-twisting, persuasion, and major fundraising, the first section of the **Maine Huts and Trails system** (office 496 Main St., Kingfield, 207/265-2400, www.mainehuts.org) opened in Carrabassett Valley. By 2013, it had expanded to more than 50 trail miles with four full-service huts spaced roughly 10-12 miles—or a day's hike—apart.

Comfy (practically luxe) off-the-grid backwoods lodges provide beds (including a pillow and fleece blanket, but not sheets) in dorms heated to 60°F in winter (private and family rooms available) and hot meals. The main lodges have composting toilets, hot showers, and gathering rooms furnished with leather sofas and chairs, braided rugs, and other nice touches. Rates begin at $84 pp in a shared room with breakfast and dinner.

Huts are located at Stratton Brook, with views of the Bigelow Mountains, Sugarloaf, and the Carrabassett Valley, accessed from a trailhead from a spur trail just north of the Sugarloaf Mountain access road; Poplar Falls, in the shadow of Little Bigelow Mountain, accessed from the Carrabassett Valley trailhead near the town recreation center off Route 27;

on the shores of Flagstaff Lake, also accessed via a trailhead on the Long Falls Dam Road north of North New Portland or by boat across the lake; and at Grand Falls on the Dead River near The Forks, from which you can arrange a white-water paddle or raft trip. This is absolutely gorgeous territory, and the trail's design makes it welcoming to beginning hikers and mountain bikers and especially families. Pricing varies by season and choice of accommodations. Trust me: Even if you only hoof in for lunch, this is an experience that should be incorporated into every vacation in this region.

Hiking

The Sugarloaf summer website (www.sugarloaf.com/summer) has an excellent listing of area hikes under "Events & Activities."

Cathedral Pines is a fine spot for a family hike, ski, or snowshoe. Maintained paths slice and loop through a majestic red pine stand and out a boardwalk over a bog. Find the trailhead and parking across from Cathedral Pines Campground, at the corner of Route 27 and Eustis Ridge Road, about 3.5 miles north of the intersection with Route 16 in Stratton.

An easy family hike, combining a picnic and swim, goes to the twin cascades of Poplar Stream Falls. Off Route 27 in Carrabassett Valley, leave your car at the Maine Huts parking lot and walk northeast 1.5 miles to the falls, veering off the Maine Huts trail. Pack a picnic and let the kids have a swim.

Just east of Stratton (eight miles northwest of Sugarloaf) is the dedicated hiker's dream: 35,000-acre Bigelow Preserve is all public land thanks to conservationists who organized a statewide referendum and yanked it from developers' hands in 1976. Within the preserve are the multiple peaks of the Bigelow Range—the Horns Peaks (3,810 and 3,831 feet), West Peak (4,150 feet), Avery Peak (4,088 feet), and Little Bigelow (3,040 feet), as well as 3,213-foot Cranberry Peak. In the fall when the hardwoods all change colors, the vistas are incomparable. In winter, snowmobilers crisscross the preserve, and cross-country skiers often take advantage of their trails, especially along the

East Flagstaff Road, where you might be able to stop for hot chocolate at volunteer-staffed Bigelow Lodge. The trailhead for Cranberry Peak (6.6 miles round-trip, moderate to strenuous) is next to Route 27 at the southern end of Stratton village.

About five miles southeast of Stratton, the Appalachian Trail (AT) crosses Route 27 and continues north and then east across the Bigelow Peaks, the spine of the Bigelow Range. You can get to the AT here, or drive back northwest 0.5 mile on Route 27 and go 0.9 mile on rugged unpaved Stratton Brook Road to another AT trailhead. In any case, if you do the whole AT traverse, 16.5 miles from Route 27 to East Flagstaff Road, you'll probably want to arrange a shuttle at East Flagstaff Road (via Long Falls Dam Rd. from North New Portland). The white-blazed AT route is strenuous; four free campsites with lean-tos are sited along the way. (The most-used campsite is Horns Pond, where space can be tight.) You can detour to the Maine Huts' Flagstaff hut too.

Depending on your enthusiasm, your stamina level, and your time frame (and maybe the weather), there are lots of options for short hikes along the AT or on a number of side trails. Preserve maps are usually available at the Sugarloaf Area Chamber of Commerce, but for planning your hikes, request or download a copy of the Bigelow Preserve map-brochure from the **Maine Bureau of Parks and Lands** (22 State House Station, Augusta, 207/287-3821, www.parksandlands.com). Also helpful is the *Appalachian Trail Guide to Maine*.

Water Sports

Along the Carrabassett River between Kingfield and the Sugarloaf access road are half a dozen swimming holes used by generations of local residents. Several spots have natural waterslides and room for shallow dives. Not all are easy to find, and parking is limited, but a refreshing river dip on a hot day is worth the bother. Look for roadside pullouts with parked cars.

On mountain-rimmed Flagstaff Lake in Eustis, about 11 miles north of Sugarloaf, the town-owned beach next to the Cathedral Pines Campground has a playground and changing rooms. There are no lifeguards, but there's also no admission fee. (Do not use the campground's beach unless you're staying there.)

BOATING

Pines Market (927 Arnold Trail/Rte. 27, Eustis, 207/246-4221) rents single kayaks for $10/day and canoes or tandem kayaks for $20/day. You can put it right at the shop, which edges Flagstaff Lake.

Master Maine Guide Jeff Hinman's **Flagstaff Scenic Boat Tours** (Eustis, 207/246-2277, www.flagstaffboattours.com) provides pontoon boat tours on the lake, detailing the story of the flooded villages below the surface and pointing out wildlife en route. Options include a 2.5-hour historic tour ($40 pp) and a 4.5-hour luncheon cruise to the Maine Huts and Trails Flagstaff Hut ($55 pp) that includes lunch. Boat minimum is four people.

Moose-Spotting

Head up Route 27 to Route 16 and go west. Early or late in the day, perhaps en route to dinner in Rangeley, you're almost guaranteed to see a moose in the boggy areas or near the sand and salt piles stored for winter use. Just remember to drive slowly and watchfully. No one wins when you hit a moose. Sugarloaf resort offers guided moose-spotting tours.

ACCOMMODATIONS

When you've had a long day on the slopes, a bed close by can be mighty tempting—plus you can be upward bound quickly in the morning. But such convenience doesn't come cheaply, so your budget may dictate where you decide to stay. The choices are on the mountain at Sugarloaf, in Carrabassett Valley near the Sugarloaf access road, or farther afield in Kingfield, Stratton, Eustis, and beyond. On weekends and holiday periods, on-mountain beds are scarce to nonexistent, so reservations well in advance are necessary.

Many of the lodgings in the region around Sugarloaf provide discount passes for cross-country skiing out of the Sugarloaf Outdoor Center. It's a nice little perk, so if you're planning any cross-country skiing, ask when you're inquiring about a room.

Sugarloaf

Accommodations are available all year at the resort (800/843-5623), and prices vary widely depending on the property and the dates. Possibilities include condominiums and two hotels. The winter-only **Sugarloaf Inn** (207/237-6837), conveniently situated adjacent to the Sawduster double chairlift, has 42 guest rooms (some in need of a face-lift) with rates in the same ranges as the condos. The imposing **Sugarloaf Mountain Hotel** (207/237-2222 or 800/527-9879), with 119 varied guest rooms and suites and two penthouses, is in the village center. Amenities include microwaves, refrigerators, and video players. Guests have use of a small health club. Pets and smoking are not allowed. All reservations booked by Sugarloaf include use of the **Sugarloaf Sports and Fitness Club** (207/237-6946), in the Sugartree condo complex on Mountainside Road, and both properties have free Wi-Fi. In winter, packages with lift tickets are best bet.

Just south of the mountain access road but on the shuttle route is **Nestlewood Inn** (3004 Town Line, Carrabassett Valley, 207/237-2077, www.nestlewoodinn.com, $150-245), a purpose-built log structure with seven guest rooms and spacious living rooms, including one with a stone fireplace. Rates include a full breakfast, afternoon snacks, and Wi-Fi. On-site massage is available. You can walk to Hug's Restaurant and to the Narrow Gauge Trail.

Kingfield

Slumber in history at the 1918 **Herbert Grand Hotel** (246 Main St., Kingfield, 207/265-2000 or 800/843-4372, www.herbertgrand-hotel.com, from $80), an antiques-filled, three-story, 26-room Victorian hotel in downtown Kingfield. Some will find it charming; the dated rooms and facilities will put others off. Rooms vary widely; some are a bit quirky.

Rates include Wi-Fi access. Dogs are welcome for $10 each/night.

Next door to One Stanley Avenue restaurant and under the same ownership, **Three Stanley Avenue** (3 Stanley Ave., Kingfield, 207/265-5541, www.stanleyavenue.com, $70-80) has been a B&B since the early 1980s. The antiques-filled yellow Victorian (built by Bayard Stanley, younger brother of the famed Stanley Steamer twins) has three first-floor guest rooms with private baths and three second-floor guest rooms sharing two baths. It's all very welcoming, with comfortable wicker chairs on the front porch and a traditional gazebo, formerly a bandstand, in the backyard. Rates include a full breakfast served at the adjacent restaurant.

Stratton and Eustis

You can launch a canoe or kayak into Flagstaff Lake from the backyard of **Tranquility Lodge** (Rte. 27, Stratton, 207/246-2122, www.tranquillitylodgebandb.com, $76-99), an especially peaceful bed-and-breakfast in a converted 19th-century post-and-beam barn just north of Stratton village. Old farming tools decorate the walls, and there's a carriage, which keeps the feeling rural and rustic. Most rates include a continental breakfast. Free Wi-Fi is available.

A wonderful traditional sporting camp, **Tim Pond Camps** (Eustis, 207/243-2947, www.timpondcamps.com) has been operating since 1877, when guests took so long to get here that they stayed the whole summer. Harvey and Betty Calden have owned this idyllic lakeside retreat since 1981. Eleven rustic log cabins dot the woods on either side of a modern-rustic lodge (the original lodge burned down), where everyone gathers three times a day for great comfort food; the dinner bell rings promptly at 5:30pm. BYOB. Daily rates are $195 pp, including all meals and use of a classic Rangeley boat with a motor and gas, and a canoe; half price for ages 5-11. The pet fee is $10/visit. Be forewarned, though, that it's worth your life to get a reservation here—about 90 percent of the guests are repeats, and most stay at least a week. Fly-fishing for brook trout is the prime pursuit (every spring a fly-fishing school is offered), but it's a fine place just to relax and listen to the loons. Here's how one avid fisherman describes the schedule: "Fish, eat breakfast, fish, eat lunch, fish, eat supper, fish, sleep." A family discount is available in July-August. Cabins have full baths, electricity until 10pm, daily maid service, and fascinating guest journals. Tim Pond Camps is at the northern end of mile-long Tim Pond, on a dirt road about 10 miles west of Route 27. It's open mid-May-mid-October, then again in November.

Camping

With 115 wooded sites (most with hookups) on 300 acres, nonprofit **Cathedral Pines Campground** (Rte. 27, Eustis, 207/246-3491, www.gopinescamping.com, $27-35) has one of Maine's most scenic locations. It's set amid gigantic red pines and surrounded by mountains on the shore of Flagstaff Lake. Look for the marker that designates this site as one of Benedict Arnold's stops during his march to Québec City in 1775. Facilities include a recreation hall, a bathhouse, laundry, a swimming beach, basketball, a playground, canoe rentals, and paddleboat rentals. Pets are allowed. The campground is 26 miles south of the Québec border.

Just five miles south of the border, in the midst of pond-speckled, mountain-cradled wilderness, is **Natanis Point Campground** (19 Nantanis Point Rd., Chain of Ponds Township, 207/297-2694, www.natanispointcampground.com, $24), with 61 grassy sites, some waterfront on Nantanis or Round Ponds. Amenities include a sandy beach, a boat launch providing access to five miles of interconnecting lakes, and direct access to a 150-mile ATV trail.

FOOD

You can bounce around to different Sugarloaf-area restaurants in the winter season and even catch a twofer night here and there. During holidays and winter weekends, make reservations.

Sugarloaf Resort

Sugarloaf's base lodge has a number of quick eating options. Standing out from the usual concession fare is **Bob's Clam Hut** (207/237-3520), a seasonal outpost of the famed Kittery fried clam hot spot. Boyne, Sugarloaf's corporate parent, owns and operates several of the restaurants on the mountain. These include: **45 North** (Sugarloaf Mountain Hotel, 2092 Access Rd., 207/237-4220, 5pm-10pm daily, $16-28), a family-friendly restaurant with a rustic barn style and a menu that ranges from duck poutine to Scottish salmon; **Bullwinkle's Grill** (207/237-2000, sometimes open for dinner), the only on-mountain venue, located off Tote Road on the mountain's western side, with access via snowcat; and the ski-in/ski-out **Shipyard Brew Haus** (Sugarloaf Inn, Access Rd., 207/237-6834, 7am-10pm daily, $9-24).

In the base village, the independently owned **Bag and Kettle** (207/237-2451, www.thebagandkettle.com, 11am-close daily late Nov.-mid-Apr., $9-30), known locally as The Bag, is famous for its burgers, soups, and wood-fired pizzas, although the menu is much broader than that; Blues Monday features live music.

For ample sandwiches, homemade soups, salads, and hearty breakfasts, **D'Ellies** (207/237-2490, www.dellies.net), another independent, is one of Sugarloaf Village's most popular eateries. It's open for breakfast and lunch daily during ski season. Seating is extremely limited—this is more of a to-go kind of place. To avoid the swarming noontime rush, call in your sandwich order in the morning before heading for the lift line. Name a time, and it'll be ready for pickup at the express register, where you can also grab drinks, soups, and baked goods.

Two-time Olympic gold medalist is one of the partners in **The Rack** (Access Rd., 207/237-2211, from 3:45pm daily, $14-24), and you can view his memorabilia and, when he's around, chat with him while enjoying hearty ribs. This is an especially popular après-ski spot, with frequent live music.

Carrabassett Valley

Reservations are a good idea at **Hug's** (3001

Rte. 27, Carrabassett Valley, 207/237-2392, 4:30pm-9:30pm Wed.-Sun., entrées $15-24), a northern Italian restaurant, open in winter only, that's always jam-packed. Be forewarned: Tables are tight and there's little place to wait for a table. But who cares—the food is good, the atmosphere festive, the pesto breadsticks are addictive, and the family-style salad is delicious. Kids' portions are available. Hug's is a mile south of the Sugarloaf access road.

Six miles south of the Sugarloaf access road is **Tufulio's** (Rte. 27, Valley Crossing, Carrabassett Valley, 207/235-2010, 5pm-9pm daily, $10-26), another Italian-accented family favorite and producers of the valley's best pizza. The shrimp-and-artichoke pesto pie is tops. Also on the menu are seafood, chicken, and plenty of pasta dishes. Go on Sunday for the two-for-one specials. In summer you can eat on the deck. It opens at 4pm for a popular happy hour.

Kingfield

The **Orange Cat Cafe** (329 Main St., Kingfield, 207/265-2860, www.orangecatcafe.com, 7am-3pm Mon. and Wed.-Sat., 8am-3pm Sun.), in the "brick castle," is a favorite for breakfast sandwiches and pastries, homemade soups, creative sandwiches, salads, and other goodies.

An old reliable, **Longfellow's** (Rte. 27, Kingfield, 207/265-2561, www.longfellowsme.com, 11am-9pm daily, $10-18), serves a menu ranging from burgers to baked scallops, chicken enchiladas to steak. Service is friendly, prices are reasonable, and the best tables have views over the river out back. Owners Chris and Mel Doucette live on a dairy farm and grow many of the vegetables and produce their own maple syrup. Two-fer night is on Tuesday.

The area's top fine-dining restaurant is **One Stanley Avenue** (1 Stanley Ave., Kingfield, 207/265-5541, www.stanleyavenue.com, 5pm-9:30pm Tues.-Sun. mid-Dec.-mid-Apr., entrées $21-35), a Kingfield magnet since 1972 with a menu that never changes (entrées are noted with the year they are added to the menu). Cocktails in the Victorian lounge precede a dining experience: unobtrusive service, understated decor, and entrées such as roast duck with rhubarb glaze, chicken with fiddleheads, and sage rabbit. Reservations are essential on winter weekends.

Stratton

Much-better-than good home cooking at reasonable prices with some intriguing specials and an emphasis on using fresh and local products reels them into the humble **Stratton Diner** (161 Main St., 207/246-3000, 8am-2:30pm Sun.-Tues. and 8am-8pm Fri.-Sat.), which has been gussied up inside and also serves beer and wine.

The **Coplin Dinner House** (8252 Rte. 27, 207/246-0016, 5-9:30pm Wed.-Sun., 10am-2pm Sun., $19-28) occupies a restored farmhouse on the outskirts of Stratton Village. Expect entrées like roast half ducking, char-grilled rack of lamb, or sesame-encrusted tuna. Lighter fare is served at the bar.

INFORMATION AND SERVICES

Although woefully outdated, the **Sugarloaf Area Chamber of Commerce** (Rte. 27, Carrabassett Valley, www.sugarloafchamber.org) has information for the whole valley, including Sugarloaf.

Sugarloaf (5092 Access Rd., Carrabassett Valley, 207/237-2000, www.sugarloaf.com) provides information on anything and everything on the mountain. During the ski season, the free tabloid *Sugarloaf This Week,* published biweekly, carries comprehensive information about on-mountain activities. It's available everywhere on the mountain and throughout the valley and beyond.

If you're staying on the mountain or in the valley and have cable TV, tune to channel 17 (WSKI) for weather, snow, trail, and lift updates, plus an entertainment rundown.

For information about **Kingfield** visit www.kingfieldusa.com.

The **Flagstaff Area Business Association** (207/246-4221, www.eustismaine.com) has information about the Stratton-Eustis region.

GETTING THERE AND AROUND

Kingfield is roughly 22 miles or 30 minutes from Farmington via Route 27. It's about 15 miles or 25 minutes to Sugarloaf via Route 27. It's about 42 miles or one hour to Rangeley via Routes 27 and 16.

The free **Sugarloaf Explorer** shuttle service (207/237-6853, www.sugarloafexplorer.com) operates 8am-approximately midnight daily during the winter season; it's on an on-call basis midweek and on a set schedule on weekends and during holiday periods. Various routes serve the condos, outdoor center, and valley.

Rangeley Lakes Area

Rangeley (pop. 1,168), incorporated in 1855, is the centerpiece of a vast system of lakes and streams surrounded by forested mountains. Rangeley is a catchall name. First applied to the town (formerly known as the Lake Settlement), it now also refers to the lake and the entire region. "I'm going to Rangeley" could indicate a destination anywhere in the extensive network of interconnecting lakes, rivers, and streams backing up to New Hampshire. The Rangeley Lakes make up the headwaters of the Androscoggin River, which technically begins at Umbagog Lake and flows seaward for 167 miles to meet the Kennebec River in Merrymeeting Bay, near Brunswick and Topsham.

Excavations have revealed evidence of human habitation in this area as long ago as 9000 BC. More than 8,000 stone tools and other artifacts were uncovered at the Vail site, on the edge of Aziscohos Lake. Native Americans certainly left their linguistic mark here, too, with tongue-twisting names applied to the lakes and other natural features. Mooselookmeguntic means "where hunters watch moose at night"; Umbagog means "shallow water"; Mollychunkamunk (a.k.a. Upper Richardson Lake) means "crooked water"; Oquossoc means "landing place"; and Kennebago means "land of sweet water." The town's more prosaic name comes from 19th-century landowner Squire James Rangeley.

The region has been a vacation magnet since the late 1800s, drawing sports who came first by stagecoach and later by rail and steamer to breathe in the unspoiled air, paddle and fish the clear waters, hike mountain trails, and hunt in vast wild lands. Folks still come today for many of the same reasons, but to these add golf, tennis, and winter sports that include skiing, snowshoeing, ice fishing, and especially snowmobiling. Recreation is the primary attraction, but there are also cultural events, old-fashioned annual festivals and fairs, the unique Wilhelm Reich Museum, and shops that carry antiques, books, sportswear, and crafts.

Southeast of Rangeley, the town of **Phillips** (pop. 1,028), was the birthplace of fly-fishing legend Cornelia T. "Fly Rod" Crosby (1854-1946), recipient of the first Registered Maine Guide license issued by the state—the imprimatur for outdoors professionals. Crosby, who wrote columns for the local paper, was a fanatic angler and hunter who always kept a china tea set neatly stowed in her gear.

Along Route 17 about 23 miles south of Oquossoc is Coos Canyon, in the town of **Byron** (pop. 145), where gold was found in the early 1800s on the East Branch of the Swift River. Amateur prospectors still flock to the area, but don't get your hopes up—it's more play than profits.

SIGHTS

◖ Rangeley Outdoor Sporting Heritage Museum

Don and Stephanie Palmer began collecting artifacts relating to the region's rich sporting heritage back in the mid-1990s, and as the collection grew they realized they needed a museum to house it. Opened in 2010 after a major fundraising effort, the **Rangeley**

Outdoor Sporting Heritage Museum (Rte. 17, Oquossoc Village, 207/864-5647, www. rangeleyoutdoormuseum.org, 10am-2pm Fri.-Sat. June and early Sept.-mid-Oct., 10am-2pm Wed.-Sun. July-early Sept., $5 over age 11) has engaging exhibits that tell the stories of Rangeley's many sporting luminaries, including Fly-Rod Crosby; fly-tier Carrie Stevens; taxidermist, painter, and angler Herb Welch; and boatbuilder Herbie Ellis. You enter through a reconstructed 1890 log cabin, which sets the tone. An expansion in 2012 added more exhibits. This museum is a community treasure, and locals and summer residents are helping it grow its collections with finds from their attics. Don't miss it. As a five-year-old remarked when I visited, "This museum is so cool."

◖ Wilhelm Reich Museum

Controversial Austrian-born psychoanalyst and natural scientist Wilhelm Reich (1897-1957), noted expert on sexual energy, chose Rangeley for his residence and research. Hour-long guided tours of the **Wilhelm Reich Museum** (Dodge Pond Rd., Rangeley, 207/864-3443, www.wilhelmreichtrust.org, 1pm-5pm Wed.-Sun. July-Aug., 1pm-5pm Sat. Sept., $6 adults, free under age 13), his handsome fieldstone mansion, include a slide presentation covering Reich's life, eccentric philosophy, experiments, and inventions such as the orgone accumulator and the cloudbuster. Reich is buried on the estate grounds. Views are spectacular from the roof of the museum, also known as Orgonon, so bring binoculars and a camera. A nature-trail system, including a bird blind, winds through the wooded acreage. The museum hosts free outdoor-oriented natural-science programs 2pm-4pm Sunday.

Rangeley Lakes Scenic Byway

While most visitors reach Rangeley via Route 4 from the Farmington area, another popular route is Route 17 from the Rumford-Mexico area. When you reach Byron on the Swift River, you enter the 35-mile **Rangeley Lakes Scenic Byway**, stretching from Byron north to Oquossoc and then southward down Route 4 through Rangeley to Madrid. The label is unquestionably deserved, especially in autumn when the vibrant colors are unforgettable. The two-lane road winds through the rural woods of western Maine, opening up periodically to reveal stunning views of lakes, streams, forested hillsides, and the Swift River. You might even see a moose. Highlights are two signposted viewpoints—Height of Land and the Rangeley Scenic Overlook—surveying Mooselookmeguntic and Rangeley Lakes, respectively. Height of Land, 11 miles south of Oquossoc, adjoins the Appalachian Trail. An easy Conservation Walk, highlighting the natural beauty, is expected to be completed by 2014.

Rangeley Lakes Region Logging Museum

On the grounds of the three-story **Rangeley Lakes Region Logging Museum** (Rte. 16, Rangeley, 207/864-5595, www.rlrlm.org, 11am-5pm Wed.-Sun. July-early Sept. or by appointment) is an eclectic assortment of lumberjack paraphernalia, artifacts, and samples of traditional artwork created in the camps. Call first; I've found it closed even during posted open hours.

Every year on the last Friday-Saturday in July, the museum sponsors Logging Festival Days, complete with beanhole beans, music, and a woodsmen's competition.

Bennett Covered Bridge

Spanning the Magalloway River beneath Aziscohos Mountain, the 93-foot-long, Paddleford truss-type **Bennett Covered Bridge,** built in 1901 and closed to traffic in 1985, sees far fewer visitors than most of Maine's eight other covered bridges. The setting, in the hamlet of Wilsons Mills, makes for great photos, so it's worth detouring on the unpaved road next to the Aziscohos Valley Camping Area, 0.3 mile west of Route 16 and 28 miles west of Rangeley.

Narrow Gauge Railroad

The **Sandy River and Rangeley Lakes**

WESTERN LAKES

© HILARY NANGLE

The highlight of the Rangeley Lakes Scenic Byway is the Height of Land viewpoint.

Railroad (Mill Hill Rd., Phillips, 207/788-3621, www.srrl-rr.org) dates to 1879, when the first section was constructed to connect northern Franklin County with Farmington, the terminus of the Maine Central Railroad. Since 1969, volunteers have been working to restore and reopen a section of the original two-foot narrow gauge track. Visit the small shop and station, then board a restored 1884 passenger car for the quick ride to the museum and roundhouse. The round-trip excursion takes about 50 minutes. The train operates June-mid-October on an erratic schedule. Fares are $6 adults, $1 ages 6-12. Call or check the website for current season info and schedule; even then, it's dependent on the availability of equipment and operators. Rail fans might also want to check out the Railroad Room of the nearby **Phillips Historical Society** (Main St., Phillips). It's open 1pm-3pm on the first and third Sunday June-early October.

Moose-Spotting

Do-it-yourself moose-spotting is a favorite pastime in this area. The likelihood of spotting one of these gangly critters can be quite high, if conditions are ripe. Route 16 between Rangeley and Stratton is well known as "moose alley," especially in the boggy areas close to the road. Sunrise and sunset are the best times for sighting moose. Keep your camera handy, and drive slowly; no one wins in a moose-car collision, and fatal accidents are not uncommon on this unlighted stretch.

Flightseeing

The best way to put the region in perspective is from the air. **Acadian Seaplanes** (2640 Main St., 207/252-6630, www.acadianseaplanes.com) offers tours of the Rangeley region via floatplane (beginning at $65 pp for 15 minutes). Also available are moose-spotting tours ($184 pp) and Fly & Dine trips ($300/couple plus meal costs) to a remote sporting camp for dinner.

ENTERTAINMENT

The great outdoors is the Rangeley region's biggest source of entertainment, but there are some options for rainy days and evening fun. **Rangeley Friends of the Arts** (RFA, 207/864-2958, www.rangeleyarts.com) is a local cultural organization that promotes the arts in the region through concerts, events, scholarships, and school programs.

Once a week, avid readers gather for a book discussion hosted by **Books, Lines & Thinkers** (Main St., Rangeley, 207/864-4355). Call the shop for details.

Lakeside Theater (2493 Main St., Rangeley, 207/864-5000) screens major films year-round (weekends only off-season). On Sunday nights during summer, independent films are shown.

Hungry for a good time? Check out **Moose Alley** (2809 Main St., Rangeley, 207/864-9955), with a 10-lane bowling alley, an arcade, a billiards room, live music on Friday and Saturday nights, sporting events on 22 HD screens, and a menu heavy on sandwiches, salads, burgers, and pizza ($6-8). On winter weekends, there's frequently après-ski entertainment at **Saddleback.**

FESTIVALS AND EVENTS

Hardly a day goes by in July-August without something scheduled. At other times, events are less frequent.

Avid snowmobilers shouldn't miss the annual January **Snodeo.** Events at the family-oriented festival include competitions, food, games, an auction, raffles, live entertainment, radar runs, children's events, a snowmobile parade, antique snowmobile displays, fireworks, and more.

The last weekend in July, **Logging Museum Festival Days** includes a parade, a bean-hole bean supper, lumberjack events, and the Little Miss Woodchip contest. It's held on the Rangeley Logging Museum grounds on Route 16.

The juried **Arts in August** festival takes place in Lakeside Park. Downtown Rangeley comes alive the third Thursday in August for the **Annual Blueberry Festival,** a daylong celebration of the blueberry harvest, with sales of everything blueberry.

Held the first Saturday in October, the **Logging Museum Apple Festival** is a daylong apple-themed celebration that includes cider pressing. It's held on the Rangeley Logging Museum grounds on Route 16.

SHOPPING

The new-book selection is distinguished at **Books, Lines & Thinkers** (Main St., Rangeley, 207/864-4355, bltbooks@rangeley.org) thanks to owner Wess Connally, a former high school English teacher in Rangeley. The small user-friendly shop has lots of great reading; trust me, you won't leave empty-handed. Wess organizes and leads a book-discussion group year-round, and visitors are welcome.

Ecopelagicon: A Nature Store (3 Pond St., Rangeley, 207/864-2771) emphasizes eco-oriented gifts, books, toys, games, and cosmetics.

The flavors of the lakes and woods are captured at **The Gallery at Stony Batter** (Rte. 4, Oquossoc, 207/864-3373), which sells regionally themed artwork, furnishings, and antiques, from moose merchandise to fine art.

RECREATION

Parks
RANGELEY LAKE STATE PARK

With 1.2 miles of lake frontage and panoramic views toward the mountains, 869-acre **Rangeley Lake State Park** (S. Shore Dr., Rangeley, 207/864-3858, www.parksandlands.com, $4.50 nonresident adults, $3 Maine resident adults, $1.50 ages 5-11 and nonresident seniors, free for Maine seniors) gets high marks for picnicking, swimming, fishing, birding, boating, and camping. The swimming "beach" is a large patch of grass. None of the 50 campsites is at water's edge, but a dozen have easy shore access. (For camping reservations, visit www.campwithme.com; from out of state call 207/287-3824 at least two business days in advance—MasterCard and Visa only. Maine residents call 800/332-1501.) If you're doing any boating, stay close to shore until you're comfortable with the wind conditions; the wind picks up very quickly on Rangeley Lake, especially in the south and southeast coves near the park. Camping is $25/site nonresidents, $15 for Maine residents, plus $2/site/night for a reservation; there are no hookups, but there are hot showers. The park, four miles off Route 17, is open mid-May-September, but it's accessible in the winter for cross-country skiing and snowmobiling.

LAKESIDE PARK

In downtown Rangeley, overlooking both lake and mountains, lovely, grassy **Lakeside Park** has a tiny beach and a safe swim area, grills and covered picnic tables, tennis courts, a playground with plenty of swings, lots of lawn for running, and a busy boat-launching ramp. Restrooms are open when a lifeguard is on duty. Access is from Main Street (Rte. 4) near the Parkside and Main Restaurant and the chamber of commerce office.

SMALLS' FALLS

One of Maine's most accessible cascades, **Smalls' Falls** is right next to Route 4 at a state rest area 12 miles south of Rangeley. Pull into the parking area and walk a few steps to the overlook. Bring a picnic. Locals love to swim in the pools between the falls. For more of a challenge, ascend a bit farther to Chandler's Mill Stream Falls. The rest area is officially open mid-May-October, but it's easy to park alongside the highway early and late in the season.

Preserves

Since its founding in 1991, **Rangeley Lakes Heritage Trust** (RLHT, Rte. 4, Oquossoc, 207/864-7311, www.rlht.org) has preserved more than 12,800 acres, including 45 miles of water frontage, 15 islands, and Bald Mountain. Trail maps can be printed from the website.

HUNTER COVE WILDLIFE SANCTUARY

Loons, ducks, and other waterfowl are the principal residents of RLHT's **Hunter Cove Wildlife Sanctuary.** While walking the three miles of easy blazed trails, best covered in a clockwise direction, keep an eye out for the

blue flag iris, which blossoms throughout the summer. You may even spot a moose. If you launch a canoe into Hunter Cove and paddle under the Mingo Loop Road bridge early in the season, you'll come face-to-face with nesting cliff swallows! To reach the sanctuary, take Route 4 west of downtown Rangeley for about 2.5 miles, turning left into the preserve across the road from Dodge Pond. It's signposted. The preserve is open sunrise-sunset daily, and admission is free.

Hiking

Hiking opportunities in this region are plentiful, and indeed there are numerous hiking guidebooks that provide details on more serious endeavors. Here's a sampling of a few hikes that reap big rewards for basic efforts. Wear appropriate footwear and carry water, snacks or lunch, and bug repellent.

BALD MOUNTAIN

Centerpiece of a 1,953-acre parcel of Maine Public Reserve Land, **Bald Mountain** is a relatively easy two-hour round-trip hike that ascends less than 1,000 feet, yet the minimal effort leads to stunning views of Rangeley, Cupsuptic, and Mooselookmeguntic Lakes—not to mention the surrounding mountains. Even three-year-olds can tackle this without terrifying their parents. Pack a picnic. The trailhead is on Bald Mountain Road in Oquossoc, about a mile south of Route 4 and roughly across from the entrance to Bald Mountain Camps. Park well off the road.

ANGEL FALLS

Dropping 90 feet straight down, dramatic **Angel Falls** is one of New England's highest cascades, reached after a fairly short easy-to-moderate hike. Even in midsummer, you'll be fording running water, so wear rubberized or waterproof shoes or boots. The best time to come is autumn, when most of the rivulets have dried up and the woods are brilliantly colorful. Allow 1-1.5 hours for the 1.4-mile round-trip hike. The trail is mostly red-blazed, with the addition of orange strips tied at crucial points.

From Oquossoc, take Route 17 south 17.9 miles to the unpaved Houghton Road, on the right. Follow the road to a T intersection, then turn right on Bemis Road for another 3.4 miles. Park on the left before the trailhead marker. This is a popular hike, so you should see other cars. The trail leads off to the left.

PIAZZA ROCK AND SADDLEBACK MOUNTAIN

A distinctive landmark on the western slope of Saddleback Mountain, **Piazza Rock** is a giant cantilevered boulder 600 feet off the Appalachian Trail (AT). The hike up is easy to moderate, not a cakewalk but fine for families, along the white-blazed AT from Route 4. From downtown Rangeley, go seven miles southeast on Route 4 and park in the lot on the south side of the highway. Piazza Rock is 1.2 miles northeast of the highway.

If you continue on the AT from Piazza Rock, it's another four miles to the summit of 4,116-foot **Saddleback Mountain,** but most hikers take the shorter route up the mountain from the ski area's Base Lodge. To get there from Rangeley, go south on Route 4 to Dallas Hill Road and then go 2.5 miles to Saddleback Mountain Road. From the lodge, follow the orange trail markers. Expect a stiff breeze and 360-degree vistas. A trail map is available at the lodge.

CASCADE STREAM GORGE

A 16-foot cascade, a 2,000-foot gorge, and well-placed picnic tables are the rewards for this short but sometimes steep trail. Allow about 30 minutes for the one-mile round white-blazed trail without stops. From downtown Rangeley, head south 3.5 miles on Route 4, turning left on Cascade Road, left on Town Hall Road, then right up a steep drive, bearing right again into the parking area.

Other excellent hikes west and north of Rangeley are **Aziscohos Mountain** and **West Kennebago Mountain.** Both are easy to moderate, have terrific views from their summits, and require 3-4 hours round-trip from their trailheads. West Kennebago has a fire tower.

FLY ROD CROSBY TRAIL

In August 2012, the first 20 miles of the **Fly Rod Crosby Trail** opened. Eventually, the trail, named for Maine's first registered guide, Cornelia "Fly Rod" Crosby, will stretch 45 miles from Strong to Oquossoc. The first section begins at Phillips and continues northwest through Madrid and Sandy River Plantation, first following an abandoned railroad bed and then veering into the backcountry before ending at Saddleback Mountain. The sections from Strong to Phillips and continuing from Saddleback to Oquossoc are under development. The trail is being developed by the nonprofit High Peaks Alliance (www.highpeaksalliance.org); find a trail map on the website with directions to current trailheads.

Excursion Boat

Cruise the waters of Rangeley Lake aboard the 1947 antique launch *Oquossoc Lady* with **Rangeley Region Lake Cruises** (207/864-2038, www.rangeleylakecruises.com). Most cruises last one hour and cost $25 adults, $10 under age 11.

Water Sports
FISHING

The Rangeley Lakes area earned its vaunted reputation for world-class fishing. Diehard anglers will always show up in May-early June, lured by landlocked salmon and brook trout. The region boasts of being the birthplace of contemporary fly-fishing, and indeed many famous flies originated here. The best fly-fishing correlates with the waves of fly hatches late May-early July. Both the **Kennebago River** and **Upper Dam** on Mooselookmeguntic Lake are hot spots for fly-fishing. If you're very serious about fishing, arrange to be flown into a wilderness pond.

The best local source of information on fly-fishing is **Rangeley Region Sport Shop** (2529 Main St., Rangeley, 207/864-5615, www.rangeleysportshop.com), where the enthusiastic owners will get you outfitted, point you in the right direction, or help you find a guide.

PADDLE ACROSS MAINE

You can paddle an ancient Native American route through the mountains and wilderness of northern New England and Québec. The 740-mile **Northern Forest Canoe Trail** (802/496-2285, www.northernforestcanoetrail.org) begins in Old Forge, New York, and passes through 35 communities in Vermont, Québec, New Hampshire, and Maine, following lakes, rivers, and streams, both flat water and white water, before finishing in Fort Kent. While some dedicated paddlers have completed the trek from start to finish, most folks dabble in various areas.

More than 350 miles of the waterway are in Maine. The trail enters the state via Lake Umbagog in section 8 and then progresses through the Rangeley Lakes and across Flagstaff Lake to Spencer Stream before crossing into the Kennebec River Valley region, following the Moose River, and finishing section 10 in Moosehead Lake. Sections 11 through 13 pass from the lake to the West Branch of the Penobscot and on to Chesuncook Lake. From here, it follows the Allagash Wilderness Waterway to its confluence with the St. John River at the tip of Maine.

If you get serious about paddling it, the trail is mapped in 13 sections (sections 8-13 are in Maine, maps are $10 each, available online or in local shops; the full set is $60). The maps detail the waterways, portages, dams, communities en route, and natural sights. Also beneficial is the *Northern Forest Canoe Trail Guidebook* ($25). Much information is available online, with even more available to those who join Northern Forest Canoe Trail; membership is $35.

CANOEING AND KAYAKING

Canoeing and kayaking are splendid throughout this region. Be forewarned, though, that Rangeley and Mooselookmeguntic Lakes are much larger than they look, and they have wide-open expanses where fluky winds can kick up suddenly and mightily and swamp boats. Fatalities have occurred in just such circumstances. Check on wind conditions before you head out. Do not take chances.

If you're looking for pristine waters where motorboats are banned, opt for **Saddleback Lake, Loon Lake, Little Kennebago Lake,** or **Quimby Pond,** all fairly close to Rangeley.

Choices for canoeing near Rangeley are Rangeley Lake (especially around Hunter Cove), the Cupsuptic River, the lower Kennebago River, and Mooselookmeguntic Lake. Slightly farther afield are Upper and Lower Richardson Lakes, both wonderfully scenic, as is Umbagog Lake (um-BAY-gog), straddling the Maine-New Hampshire border. The Cupsuptic, Kennebago, and Magalloway Rivers are all easy Class I waters. The Rangeley Lakes Area Chamber of Commerce has produced a suggested canoeing itinerary for the Rangeley Lakes chain, including information about wilderness campsites en route. Some of the campsites require reservations and fire permits.

Besides being a fishing-gear supplier and a place that has camping and hunting gear as well as water toys, outdoor clothing, and unique gifts, **River's Edge Sports** (Rte. 4, Oquossoc, 207/864-5582, www.riversedgesports.com) also rents canoes and kayaks. Rates start at $25/day or $125/week. For $45, including canoe rental, River's Edge will shuttle you and the canoe up the Kennebago River to the start of an idyllic 2-3-hour downstream paddle to Route 16 and your car; go at sunrise for the best chance of spotting a moose.

Ecopelagicon (7 Pond St., Rangeley, 207/864-2771, www.ecopelagicon.com) rents kayaks for use on Haley Pond for a short paddle or to take to your camp. Single kayaks rent for $32/day, $25/half day, or $12/hour; doubles are $36, $28, and $15. Long-term rates are available. Delivery and pickup are available for a fee. **Mookwa** at Ecopelagicon offers guided kayak tours beginning at 8am on most Thursdays. Each week's trip visits a different waterway.

WESTERN LAKES

The four-hour, half-day tours are $65-75 pp with a snack; full-day tours are $85 pp with lunch. Minimum age is 12. By the way, *mookwa* is a Cree word for loon.

MOTORBOATING

Of course, the easiest way to explore these massive lakes is by motorboat. Most lakes have public access points, but these may be busy. Put-ins for Rangeley Lake include the state park, Lakeside Park, and off Route 4 in Oquossoc. The best one for Mooselookmeguntic is Haines Landing, at the end of Route 4. There's another ramp off Route 16 west, approximately four miles from the intersection with Route 4. Also off Route 16 is the Mill Brook access for Lake Richardson and the Black Cove Campground access for Aziscohos (be careful, as it's extremely shallow in places). Maine has strict rules about boating. For information, contact the **Maine Department of Inland Fisheries and Wildlife** (www.maine.gov/ifw) or a local outfitter.

The best place to rent a sturdy motorboat is **Saddleback Marina** (Rte. 4, Oquossoc, 207/864-3463, www.saddlebacksummer.com). Prices begin at $160/day; half-day rates begin at $100; hourly rental is $35; gas and oil are extra. Restroom and picnic facilities are available.

Biking

In downtown Rangeley, the multiuse **Railroad Trail Loop** begins on Depot Street. The 12.5-mile circuit travels over mixed terrain, including paved and unpaved roads and an abandoned railroad bed, and has some steep sections.

The **Rangeley Lakes Trails Center** (524 Saddleback Mountain Rd., 207/864-4309) has seven miles of trails on lower Saddleback Mountain; two are easy, and the rest cater to advanced cyclists.

Rent mountain bikes from **River's Edge Sports** (Rte. 4, Oquossoc, 207/864-5582, www.riversedgesports.com) for $25/day or $125/week.

Golf

Noted golfers have been teeing off at **Mingo Springs Golf Course** (Country Club Rd., Rangeley, 207/864-5021) since 1925, when the course started with nine holes. Today's 18-hole, par-70 course boasts panoramic vistas of lakes and mountains—and sometimes an annoying breeze. Golf-and-lodging packages are available at the adjacent Country Club Inn.

Gold Panning

"Gold bought, sold, and lied about here" proclaims the sign outside **Coos Canyon Rock and Gift Shop** (472 Swift River Rd., Byron, 207/364-4900, www.cooscanyonrockandgift.com), a family operation since 1956. Check out the exhibits of some of the nuggets found in the Swift River and then rent equipment and try it yourself. A pan and trowel for use on-site are free, with a $5 deposit. Off-site use is $2/day for a pan and screen, $1 for a trowel, or $15 for a fancier sluice box ($85 deposit). It's a relatively inexpensive lesson in patience.

Winter Sports

ALPINE SKIING AND SNOWBOARDING

Saddleback (207/864-5671 or 866/918-2225, www.saddlebackmaine.com) is the yin to nearby Sugarloaf's yang. Although it deserves its reputation as a low-key, wallet-friendly, family-oriented area, it's beginning to be discovered. This is big-mountain skiing, with a 2,000-foot vertical drop off a 4,116-foot summit laced with classic New England narrow and winding trails and some of the East's best gladed terrain. The base area has a full-service lodge with food service, condominiums, equipment rentals, day care, and snowsports school.

CROSS-COUNTRY SKIING AND SNOWSHOEING

The volunteer-operated nonprofit Rangeley Lakes Cross Country Ski Club (524 Saddleback Mountain Rd., 207/864-4309, www.xcski-rangeley.com) operates the **Rangeley Lakes Trails Center,** with 55 km of mapped trails lacing through the Saddleback preserve on lower Saddleback Mountain. Maps are available at the center, where a yurt serves as the lodge.

WESTERN LAKES

Trails are open 9am-4pm daily. Full-day trail passes are $18 adults, $10 ages 7-18.

The summer nature trails at **Orgonon, the Wilhelm Reich Museum** (207/864-3443), west of downtown Rangeley, are accessible for free cross-country skiing or snowshoeing 9am-4pm weekdays.

For cross-country ski or snowshoe rentals, visit **The Alpine Shop** (2504 Main St., Rangeley, 207/864-3741).

ICE SKATING

A local skating club maintains an ice rink on **Haley Pond.** Free skate rentals are available from **Ecopelagicon** (3 Pond St., Rangeley, 207/864-2771). Haley Pond is also home to a winter pond hockey tournament in February.

SNOWMOBILING

Snowmobiling is big business in Rangeley, and in winter most accommodations and lodgings cater to it. The Rangeley area, linked to the state's **Interconnected Trail System** (ITS) via ITS 84, 89, and 117, has its own well-marked 150-mile groomed network thanks to the diligent efforts of the local Rangeley Lakes Snowmobile Club (www.rangeleysnowmobile.com). A family club membership is $45; individual membership is $30. Club gatherings and events are a good way to get the local scoop. The club also operates a **conditions hotline** (207/864-7336). Popular rides include a 65-mile lake loop; all or part of the 300-mile Black Fly Loop, which circles through Franklin and Somerset Counties; Kennebago Mountain; and even into Canada on the 12,500-mile international circuit. There are no local trail fees, but support at local fundraisers is appreciated.

Rental sleds are available from **Camp Do What You Wanna** (2419 Main St., Rangeley, 207-864-3000, www.campdowhatyouwanna.com, from $200 half-day).

ACCOMMODATIONS
Inns and Motels

Next to the stunning Mingo Springs Golf Course, the **Country Club Inn** (56 Country Club Rd., Rangeley, 207/864-3831, www. countryclubinnrangeley.com, mid-May-mid-Oct. and late Dec.-Mar.) claims the same fabulous lake-and-mountain panorama as the golf course. Nineteen 1960s-style lake-view guest rooms are $143 with breakfast, $218 with breakfast and dinner, or $125 room only; ask about golf packages. Decor is classic lodge: two huge fireplaces in the living room accented by wildlife trophies, lots of pine paneling everywhere. There are no in-room TVs or phones. The inn is superbly maintained and run, and there's an outdoor pool. Pets are $10/night. The inn is 2.2 miles west of downtown Rangeley.

Owner Travis Ferland acquired the venerable **Rangeley Inn** (2443 Main St., Rangeley, 207/864-3341, www.therangeleyinn.com, $109-165) in 2013 and began updating the rambling, downtown Victorian-era hotel to restore its former glory. Rooms in the main inn retain Victorian charm, those in pet-friendly ($15/night) Haley Pond Lodge have mini-fridges and pond views. All rooms are being updated with flat-screen TVs and Wi-Fi; some rooms have whirlpools and/or fireplaces or woodstoves. The main building also houses a restaurant serving contemporary pub-style fare. Guests have free use of kayaks on Haley Pond. The main building houses a **tavern** (5-9pm Thurs.-Mon., $10-18) serving contemporary pub fare such as a cubano sandwich, seared duck breast, and gnocchi.

Completely renovated in 2007, the **Rangeley Saddleback Inn** (2303 Main St., Rangeley, 207/864-3434, www.rangeleysaddlebackinn.com, from $135) is a family pleaser thanks to an indoor pool and jetted tub, on-site restaurant and pub, in-room TVs, microwaves, and mini-fridges, and four pet-friendly guest rooms.

The sunset views over Rangeley Lake are sigh-worthy from **Loon Lodge** (16 Pickford Rd., Rangeley, 207/864-5666, www.loonlodgeme.com, $85-150), which also houses a popular restaurant and pub. Beyond the back deck, the lawn rolls down to the lake, so you can wake with a morning swim. Some guest rooms are small with shared baths; the nicest are huge, have private baths, and have access to the back lawns. Although the inn has a restaurant and lounge open most nights for dinner, you'll have to go into town for breakfast.

Bed-and-Breakfasts

On a quiet hillside less than half a mile from downtown, Rob Welch, a retired principal, and his wife, Jan, a schoolteacher, are the enthusiastic hosts at **℄ Pleasant Street Inn B&B** (104 Pleasant St., Rangeley, 207/864-5916, www.pleasantstreetinnbb.com, $145-175). The Welches have completely renovated and expanded a traditional Maine farmhouse to include five good-size guest rooms, all with Wi-Fi and satellite TV, two with whirlpool tubs. It's bright, airy, and comfy. Guests have plenty of room to spread out in the guest parlor with a TV, spacious living room, and dining area, where a full breakfast is served. Guests also have access to a pantry stocked with afternoon refreshments as well as a guest computer. The inn is on the in-town snowmobile route, and there's plenty of parking for snowmobile trailers. Children younger than 12 and pets are not allowed. In the winter, you can watch Rob feed the deer in the backyard.

Right downtown, with views over Rangeley Lake, is the **North Country Inn B&B** (2541 Main St., Rangeley, 800/295-4968, www.northcountrybb.com, $99-149). The two front guest rooms have the best views, but the two in back are quieter. All have queen beds and cable TV. The front porch is an inviting place to relax and watch the parade and fireworks during special events. Rates include Wi-Fi and a full breakfast.

Rangeley still too bustling for you? Buddy and Jeanne Conroy offer three cozy rooms at **The Conroy House Bed and Breakfast** (82 Dodge Rd., Phillips, 207/639-3000, www.conroyhouse.com, $75), in the very quiet town of Phillips. Breakfast is a treat.

Cabin Colonies

On a quiet cove about four miles west of town, **Hunter Cove on Rangeley Lake** (office 334 Mingo Loop Rd., cabins Hunter Cove Rd., Rangeley, 207/864-3383, www.huntercove.com) has eight rustically modern well-equipped waterfront cabins on six acres. Each has one or two bedrooms, a screened porch, a woodstove, a phone, and a TV. Rates are $160-220 nightly or $1,000-1,250/week. Rates cover up to four people; pets are $10/day. It's open year-round, with lower rates off-season and midweek. From here, it's an easy paddle to the western edge of the Hunter Cove Wildlife Sanctuary, and Mingo Springs Golf Course is nearby.

Far more remote is **Nioban Camps** (South Shore Dr., Rangeley, 207/864-2549, www.nioban.com). Although the sporting camp is historical, the original cottages were replaced in 2001 with nice two-bedroom lakefront cabins, each with a screened porch and a well-equipped kitchen. Table tennis, a phone, a TV, and games are available in the main lodge. Moose and deer sightings are frequent; beavers and ducks swim along the shore; and eagles fly overhead. The camps are open year-round for snowmobiling, snowshoeing, and skiing. Rates are $950/week June-August. In May and September-March, cabins are available with a two-night minimum stay for $190-210/night. Pets are $10/day. A one-bedroom honeymoon cabin is $160/night or $700/week.

Sporting Camps

Stephen Philbrick is the third-generation owner of **℄ Bald Mountain Camps** (Bald Mountain Rd., Oquossoc, 207/864-3671, www.baldmountaincamps.com), a family-oriented traditional sporting camp on the shore of Mooselookmeguntic Lake. Established in 1897, the superb operation has more than 90 percent repeat guests, some of whom have been returning since the 1930s. It's tough to get a reservation, especially in peak summer. Fourteen recently winterized, rustic waterfront log cabins can accommodate 2-8 people. Cabins are furnished, each offering a private porch, a fireplace, a living room, individual bedrooms, full housekeeping services, a mini-fridge, a microwave, and porter service. Three meals a day are served daily during peak season in the lake-view lodge. A highlight is the Friday night cookout, with lobster, ribs, corn, steamed clams, and blueberry pancakes for dessert. The informal dining room is open to nonguests for dinner year-round (book well ahead) by reservation only. Among the activities are swimming at the sandy beach, fishing, tennis, boating, and waterskiing. There's a playground for kids. May-October, meal-inclusive rates are $160-185/adult/day, $100-130/child ages 5-13; cottage rentals range $125 efficiency to $375 housekeeping per night or $650/$2,200/week. Winter rates, effective December-April, do not include meals and begin at $165/night. Pets are $15/day. Motorboat, canoe, kayak, pontoon boat, tube, and waterski rentals are available.

Grant's Kennebago Camps (Kennebago Rd., Rangeley, 207/864-3608 or 800/633-4815, www.grantscamps.com, mid-May-mid-Oct.) is a classic sporting camp built in 1905 on remote five-mile-long Kennebago Lake. Expect to hear lots of loons and see plenty of moose—if you can get a reservation. Seriously dedicated fly-fishers fill up the beds in May and September; families take their places July-August (check the family packages). Daily rates for the 18 rustic cabins, with private baths and hot showers, are $135-170/adult, including three meals daily in the water-view dining room and use of boats and bikes mid-July-mid-Sept. Children ages 7-12 are $60/night; children under 6 are free. Pets are $15/night/pet. The main lodge's lake-view dining room is open to nonguests for all meals by reservation, but the hearty cuisine makes it a popular place, so call well ahead; BYOB. Canoe, kayak, and motorboat rentals range $30-60/day. Grant's arranges a daily moose run ($40 pp) on the Kennebago River July-August. (Nonguests can also go on the moose run for a higher fee.) Access to Grant's is via a gated nine-mile road from Route 16, west of Rangeley. The gate is open 7am-6pm only; if you're coming just for dinner, Grant's will arrange for access.

Avid fly-fishers have been heading to **Lakewood Camps** (207/243-2959, www.lakewoodcamps.com, no credit cards) for more than 150 years. The lakefront cabins are by Middle Dam, which separates Lower Richardson Lake from the famed Rapid River, and are accessible only by boat. The cold and wild Rapid River, which falls nearly 1,100 feet in less than eight miles, is restricted to fly-fishing. Landlocked salmon and brook trout are found in both the lake and river, but the lake is also home to togue (lake trout). Much of this area is protected Maine Public Reserve Land. Walk the Carry Road, which parallels the river, and you'll pass the home where Louise Dickinson Rich lived when she wrote *We Took to the Woods*. The daily rate ($165 pp, $120 ages 12-16, $70 ages 6-11) includes all meals and boat transportation as well as use of canoes and kayaks; row boats are $25; a motorboat with gas is $95. Guests stay in simple lakeside cabins that have Franklin fireplaces, generator-powered electricity, and full baths. Dogs are $22/night.

Camping

In addition to the nonprofit and commercial campgrounds described here, the Rangeley Lakes Region Chamber of Commerce maintains a list of no-fee and low-fee **remote wilderness campsites** throughout the Rangeley Lakes.

The **Maine Forest Service** (Rte. 16, Oquossoc, 207/864-5545), responsible for more than a dozen no-fee primitive campsites, will provide a copy of its list on request. The office also issues fire permits.

Here's a find: The **Stephen Phillips Memorial Preserve Trust** (Oquossoc, 207/864-2003) oversees 60 primitive tent sites on both the east and west shores of Mooselookmeguntic Lake and on Students, Toothaker, and other islands, all part of a 400-acre charitable preserve that includes more than four miles of lakefront. Mainland sites are large and private; each has a fire ring, picnic table, and water access. Island sites and those on the west shore are accessible only by boat. Canoe rentals are available for $20/day. Nightly cost is $16/site for two people, teens or extra adults are $8, ages 6-12 are $5, dogs are $5 each. Two nature trails cross and circle Students Island.

At the southeast corner of Aziscohos Lake, **Black Brook Cove Campground** (Lincoln Pond Rd., Lincoln Plantation, 207/486-3828, www.blackbrookcove.com, from $25) provides three different kinds of camping experiences. The main campground has 30 tent and RV sites with hookups; the secluded east shore area has 26 wooded waterfront sites for small, self-contained units and tents. These wooded waterfront sites are 3.5 miles from the main campground and 100 feet from the water. Twenty-acre boat-accessible Beaver Island, out in the lake, has nine wilderness sites, and there are another seven wilderness sites around the lake. The remote sites include outhouses. The main campground facilities include coin-operated hot showers, a private beach, a convenience store, and rental boats and canoes.

The Rangeley Lakes Heritage Trust owns and operates **Cupsuptic Lake Park & Campground** (Rte. 16, Oquossoc, 207/864-5249, www.cupsupticcampground.com). The lakefront campground has 42 RV sites with varied hookups, 23 tent sites, 4 fully equipped cabin tents, and 6 day-use sites. Options include wilderness, island, and wooded sites, with rates beginning at $24. Rental boats are available, and dogs are permitted ($3/day). Also on-site are a recreation hall, a sandy beach, rental boat slips, and Wi-Fi hotspots. Plan to stay on a Friday night for the baked beans.

Seasonal Rentals

The **Morton and Furbish Agency** (207/864-5777 or 888/218-4882, www.rangeleyrentals.com) has a wide selection of daily, weekly, and monthly rental cottages, camps, houses, and condos for winter and summer use. The chamber of commerce can also assist with seasonal rentals.

FOOD

Check the local newspaper for announcements of **public suppers,** featuring chicken, beans, spaghetti, or just potluck. Most suppers benefit charitable causes, cost under $10 pp, and provide an ample supply of local color.

Local Flavors

While bagels are the specialty at **Moosely**

Bagels (2588 Main St., Rangeley, 207/864-5955), there's plenty more on the menu. For breakfast, choose from a full range of baked goods and simple to fanciful egg concoctions; lunch options include sandwiches, wraps, soups, and hot specials. There's seating inside or on the back, lake-view deck.

"Meet me at the Frosty" is Rangeley's summertime one-liner, a ritual for locals and visitors alike. **Pine Tree Frosty** (Main St., Rangeley, 207/864-5894), a tiny takeout near Haley Pond and the Rangeley Inn, serves ever-popular Gifford's ice cream in dozens of flavors along with good-size lobster rolls and superb onion rings.

Far more than the usual produce is available at **The Farmer's Wife** (Rte. 17 and Rangeley Ave., Oquossoc, 207/863-2492), a farm stand that also sells gourmet foods, fresh-baked breads and pies, salads, and wine. Nearby **Oquossoc Grocery** (Rte. 4, Oquossoc, 207/864-3662) has fresh-baked doughnuts, hot and cold sandwiches, and pizza.

Watch the game while chowing good burgers, nachos, hand-cut fries, and similar fare at ever-popular **Sarge's Sports Pub and Grub** (Main St., Rangeley, 207/864-5616, from 11am daily). More substantial entrées ($10-17) are served after 5pm, and there's even a kids' menu, although this place has more of a bar atmosphere. Weekends there's often live entertainment.

Family Favorites

Several sporting camps in the Rangeley area open their dining rooms to nonguests, primarily for dinner, during the summer. Grab the opportunity to sample the sporting-camp ambience and the retro comfort food that brings guests back from one generation to the next.

A notable exception to the retro comfort-food theme is the lakefront restaurant at **Bald Mountain Camps** (Bald Mountain Rd., Oquossoc, 207/864-3671, www.baldmountaincamps.com). Choose from sandwiches and burgers ($12-16) or entrées such as white fish or rib eye ($12-30). Especially popular is the Friday night cookout, with lobster, spare ribs, chicken, burgers, dogs, and all the go-withs. Make reservations well in advance, and aim for sunset.

The Red Onion (Main St./Rte. 4, Rangeley, 207/864-5022, $10-20) is a barn of a place where you can also get award-winning chili and pizza made on homemade dough. Portions are large. The Onion is open 11am-9:30pm daily year-round, unless, as the staff say, "High winds, low humidity, and plain laziness" inspire them to close the doors.

Try to snag a table on the deck overlooking the park and lake at **Parkside and Main** (2520 Main St./Rte. 4, Rangeley, 207/864-3774, 11:30am-11pm daily, $8-22). The menu varies from burgers to steak; stick with the homemade soups and salads or simpler preparations, and don't miss the homemade blue cheese dressing. In summer there's often entertainment on the deck.

Tall Tales Tavern (207/864-9737, from 11am daily, $8-20), a local favorite, is an offshoot of a meat, fish, and lobster market and a farm market, so everything's very fresh.

Casual Dining

Huge windows frame dramatic views of Rangeley Lake from the dining room of the hilltop **⟨ Country Club Inn** (56 Country Club Rd., Rangeley, www.countryclubinnrangeley.com, dinner 6pm-8pm Wed.-Sun., $10-32). White tablecloths drape the well-spaced tables, and the food complements the view. Entrées range from a portobello burger to roast duck. If the weather's fine, begin with cocktails on the deck overlooking the lake. The restaurant is open to nonguests by reservation for dinner, but tables for nonguests can be scarce when the inn is fully booked.

Call well ahead, especially for summer weekends. In winter, the dining room is open Friday-Saturday.

Cozy and inviting, **Forks in the Air Mountain Bistro** (2485 Main St., Rangeley, 207/864-2883, www.forksintheair.com, 4pm-9pm Sun.-Thurs., 4pm-10pm Fri.-Sat.) serves small and large plates ($7-28) that may include flatbreads, baked Atlantic haddock, or grilled pork tenderloin.

The sunset view over Rangeley Lake with the White Mountains as a backdrop is reason alone to reserve a table at **Loon Lodge** (16 Pickford Rd., Rangeley, 207/864-5666, www.loonlodgeme.com, 5pm-9pm Tues.-Sat., $22-31), where the restaurant menu might include lobster ravioli Florentine or country cassoulet. Or settle into the pub, and dine off either the restaurant or pub menu ($10-12).

INFORMATION AND SERVICES

The **Rangeley Lakes Region Chamber of Commerce** (Lakeside Park, Rangeley, 207/864-5364 or 800/685-2537, www.rangeleymaine.com) produces annual guides to lodgings and services; the useful *Maine's Rangeley Lakes Map* costs $4. **Public restrooms** are located in a building adjacent to the chamber.

The **Rangeley Public Library** (7 Lake St., Rangeley, 207/864-5529, www.rangeleylibrary.com) is housed in a wonderful old stone building just off Main Street.

GETTING THERE

Rangeley is roughly 42 miles or one hour from Kingfield via Routes 27 and 16. It's about 65 miles or 1.5 hours to Bethel via Routes 17 and 2.

Bethel and Vicinity

Bethel (pop. 2,607) is a sleeper. It's a classic New England village tucked in the folds of the White Mountains. White-steepled churches, an ivy-covered brick prep school (Gould Academy), lovely antique homes, a main street dotted with shops and restaurants, and a sprawling inn on the common are all easily explored on foot. Six miles away, Sunday River, one of New England's hottest alpine resorts, draws skiers and snowboarders to its modern slopes and lodges. The Ellis, Bear, and Androscoggin Rivers wind through the region, and in the river valleys are two covered bridges, a handful of ponds, and many working farms. Framing the region on two sides are two spectacular notches, Evans Notch, part of the White Mountain National Forest, and Grafton Notch, a state park, as well as the city of **Rumford** (pop. 5,841), a paper-manufacturing center whose favorite son was former Secretary of State Edmund Muskie. **Rumford Point, Center Rumford,** and **Hanover** (pop. 238) are don't-blink villages and towns between Rumford and Bethel, and each has its calling cards.

Thanks to Sunday River, winter is peak season here. In addition to skiing and riding, there's snowshoeing, snowmobiling, dogsledding, skijoring, ice skating, ice fishing, even ice climbing. Spring brings canoeists and anglers. Summer is lovely, with hiking for all abilities, biking, boating, fishing, rockhounding in local quarries, golfing, even llama trekking.

Autumn is still surprisingly undiscovered. It's perhaps the region's prettiest season, when visitors can take advantage of all the summer activities and do so under a canopy of blazing crimson, gold, and orange backed by deep evergreen.

But let's back up a bit. Bethel's "modern" history dates from 1774, when settlers from Sudbury, Massachusetts, called it Sudbury Canada, a name reflected in the annual August Sudbury Canada Days festival. Another present-day festival, Mollyockett Day, commemorates one of the area's most intriguing historical figures, a Pequawket Indian woman named Mollyockett. She practiced herbal medicine among turn-of-the-19th-century settlers, including a baby named Hannibal Hamlin. Her remedies proved effective in snatching Abraham Lincoln's future vice president from death in 1809. (The incident actually occurred in the Hamlin home on Paris Hill, southeast of Bethel.) Mollyockett died August 2, 1816, and is buried in the Woodlawn Cemetery on Route 5 in Andover.

Meanwhile, the name Bethel surfaced in 1796, when the town was incorporated. Agriculture sustained the community for another half century, until the Atlantic and St. Lawrence Railroad in 1851 connected Bethel to Portland (and later to Montreal) and access to major markets shifted the economic focus toward timber and wood products, which remain significant even today.

North of Bethel, **Andover** (pop. 821) has become a word-of-mouth favorite among through-hikers and section hikers on the Appalachian Trail (AT), which snakes by about eight miles to the west. It's Maine's southernmost town near the AT, and the hikers pile into Andover for a break in August-September after negotiating the Mahoosuc Range, one of the AT's toughest sections.

East of Bethel are the tiny communities of **Locke Mills** (officially in the town of Greenwood, pop. 830) and **Bryant Pond** (in the town of Woodstock, pop. 1,277), both with summer and winter recreational attractions.

SIGHTS
Maine Mineral and Gem Museum
When the **Maine Mineral and Gem Museum** (57 Main St. Bethel, 207/824-3036, www.mainemineralgemmuseum.org) opens in late 2014, organizers promise it will showcase one of the world's most extensive collections,

exhibits, and archival documents relating to Maine mining, minerals, and gems. In addition, meteorite, fossils, and other minerals will be displayed and explained. Tours of area mines will be available. Call or check the website for its current status.

Covered Bridges

Often called the **Artist's Covered Bridge** because so many artists have committed it to canvas, an 1872 wooden structure stands alongside a quiet country road north of the Sunday River Ski Resort. Kids love running back and forth across the disused bridge, and in summer they can swim below it in the Sunday River. The bridge is 5.7 miles northwest of Bethel; take Route 2 toward Newry, turn left at the Sunday River Road, and then bear right at the fork. The bridge is well signposted, just beyond a small cemetery.

About 20 miles north of Bethel in South Andover, the **Lovejoy Bridge,** built in 1867, is one of the lesser-visited of Maine's nine covered bridges. It's also the shortest. Spanning the Ellis River, a tributary of the Androscoggin, the 70-foot-long bridge is 0.25 mile east of Route 5 but not visible from the highway; it's about 7.5 miles north of Rumford Point. In summer, local kids use the swimming hole just below the bridge.

Historical Houses and Tours

The **Bethel Historical Society** (Bethel Common, 14 Broad St., Bethel, 207/824-2908, www.bethelhistorical.org) maintains two downtown properties. Listed on the National Register of Historic Places, the 1813 Federal-style **Dr. Moses Mason House** (1pm-4pm Tues.-Sat. July-Aug. or by appointment, $3 adults, $1.50 ages 6-12, $7/family) is a beautifully restored eight-room museum. Particularly significant in the museum are the hall murals painted by noted itinerant muralist Rufus Porter or his nephew Jonathan Poor. Dr. Moses Mason, a local physician, was elected to Congress a dozen years after Maine achieved statehood and served two terms as a Maine congressman. The Mason House is adjacent to

The Artist's Covered Bridge crosses the usually sleepy Sunday River in Newry.

the 1821 **O'Neil Robinson House** (10am-4pm Tues.-Fri. year-round and 1pm-4pm Sat. July-Aug., donation), which has exhibit galleries and a small museum shop.

Bethel Historical Society interns and volunteers lead free **Guided One-Hour Walking Tours of Bethel Hill** at 10am Saturday early July-late August. The tour departs from the bell tower on the north end of the common. Or do it yourself, armed with the society's free *Walking Tour of Bethel Hill Village* brochure, available from the society or chamber of commerce. It provides detailed information on 29 buildings and monuments in the downtown area's Historic District. Officially, more than 60 structures are included in the district. Allow an hour to appreciate the 19th- and 20th-century architecture that gives real cachet to Bethel's heart.

ENTERTAINMENT

The **Mahoosuc Arts Council** (MAC, 207/824-3575, www.mahoosucarts.org) sponsors more than a dozen performances throughout the year, plus about a dozen art residencies and other cultural events in local schools.

Free concerts take place every Sunday in August at 4pm on the **Bethel Common;** rain location is Bingham Auditorium, 45 Church St.

At **Sunday River Ski Resort** there's live entertainment in several locations weekends and during school vacations. The resort also runs the Black Diamond Family Entertainment series, with performances such as vaudeville, marionettes, storytelling, and circus acts.

The hot spots for après-ski into the night are the **Foggy Goggle** at Sunday River; **The Matterhorn** (Sunday River Access Rd., 207/824-6836, www.matterhornskibar.com), a classic ski bar accented with cool alpine memorabilia and featuring live weekend entertainment; **Suds Pub** (207/824-6558, www.thesudburyinn.com) at the Sudbury Inn, where Hoot Night has been an open-mic tradition on Thursday since 1987; and **The Jolly Drayman** (Rte. 2, 207/824-4717, www.briarleainn.com), which attracts an older clientele who appreciate its English pub style.

EVENTS

In mid-June the annual three-day **Trek Across Maine: Sunday River to the Sea** draws nearly 2,000 cyclists for the 180-mile bike expedition from Bethel to Rockland, proceeds from which benefit the Maine Lung Association. Registrations are accepted on a first-come, first-served basis, and the trek is usually fully booked by April. Pledges are required, and there's a registration fee. Call 800/458-6472 for details.

Don't like cycling? Perhaps the **Androscoggin River Source to the Sea Canoe Trek** is more your style. The annual 20-day paddle (spread over four-day weekends in midsummer) from the New Hampshire headwaters to Fort Popham near Bath—about 170 miles—is open to all canoeists, who can participate on any leg of the journey. A contribution is requested to benefit the Androscoggin Land Trust (207/583-2723, www.androscogginlandtrust.org).

Bethel's **Annual Gem, Mineral, and Jewelry Show** is a long-running mid-July event with exhibits, demonstrations, and sales of almost everything imaginable in the rock and gem line—even guided field trips to nearby quarries.

The third Saturday in July, on Bethel Common in downtown Bethel, **Mollyockett Day** commemorates a legendary turn-of-the-19th-century Native American healer with a parade, children's activities, a crafts fair, food booths, and fireworks. There's also usually an oddball race—a couple of years it was wheeled beds; another year it was spouse-carrying.

Andover presents a parade, live entertainment, children's games, art and flower shows, antique cars, a barbecue, and a beanhole bean supper the first weekend in August as part of **Andover Old Home Days.** The second weekend that month at the Moses Mason House in Bethel, **Sudbury Canada Days** commemorates Bethel's earliest settlers with traditional crafts, an art show, a parade, croquet, a bean supper, and a contra dance.

Maine artisans take center stage in the annual display and sale at the **Blue Mountains**

Arts and Crafts Festival, held the second weekend in October at the Sunday River Ski Resort in Newry.

During winter, Sunday River's calendar is chock-full of events.

SHOPPING

While Bethel doesn't have tons of shops, the ones it does have are not the run-of-the-mill variety.

Check out the strikingly unusual designs and glazes at **Bonnema Potters** (146 Main St., Bethel, 207/824-2821), in a handsomely restored studio across the street from the Sudbury Inn. Best of all are the earth colors used on tiles, dishes, vases, and lamps.

Maine Line Products (297 Main St., Greenwood, 207/875-2522) is a source of whimsical, Maine-made souvenirs for your whimsical friends, as well as serious gifts such as jams, syrup, fudge, and wind chimes.

Shoppers entering **Linda Clifford–Scottish and Irish Merchant** (91 Main St., Bethel, 207/824-6560, www.lindaclifford.com) are almost always overwhelmed by the quality and selection. Pottery, crystal, clothing, jewelry, tartans, and more are all elegantly displayed. Be prepared to drool or part with some serious bucks.

Shaker-reproduction furniture and a home store filled with decorative items and accessories and wood ware can be found at **Timberlake Home Store** (158 Rte. 2, Bethel, 207/824-6545 or 800/780-6681, www.stimberlake.com). Ask about lectures, demonstrations, and workshops.

Handcrafted wood products fill **Maine Artisans Wood Gallery** (1180 Rte. 2, Rumford, 207/364-7500), which sells hardwood goods, including furniture and accent pieces.

RECREATION
Parks and Preserves
STEP FALLS PRESERVE

The Nature Conservancy's first Maine acquisition, in 1962, the 24-acre **Step Falls Preserve** is ideal for family hiking—an easy one-hour round-trip through the woods alongside an impressive series of cascades and pools. Pick up a trail map at the box in the parking area. Bring a picnic and have lunch on the rocks along the way. The waterfalls are most dramatic in late spring; the foliage is most spectacular in fall; the footing can be dicey in winter. The trailhead for the preserve is on Route 26, eight miles northwest of Route 2 and 10 miles southeast of the New Hampshire border. Watch for The Nature Conservancy oak-leaf sign on the right, next to Wight Brook.

◖ GRAFTON NOTCH STATE PARK

Nestled in the mountains of western Maine, 3,192-acre **Grafton Notch State Park** (Rte. 26, Grafton Township, 207/824-2912 or 207/624-6080 off-season, www.parksandlands.com, $3 nonresident adults, $2 Maine resident adults, $1 ages 5-11 and nonresidents over age 64; payment is on the honor system) boasts splendid hiking trails, spectacular geological formations, and plenty of space for peace and quiet. It's hard to say enough about this lovely park, a must-visit. Bring a picnic. Highlights include **Screw Auger Falls, Mother Walker Falls,** and **Moose Gorge Cave.**

The best (but not easiest) hike is the **Table Rock Loop,** a 2.4-mile moderate-to-strenuous two-hour circuit from the main trailhead (signposted Hiking Trails) at the edge of Route 26. The trailhead parking area is four miles inside the park's southern boundary and 0.8 mile beyond the Moose Cave parking area. Part of the route follows the white-blazed Appalachian Trail; otherwise, the trail is orange- and blueblazed. Some really steep sections are indeed a challenge, but it's well worth the climb for the dramatic mountain views from aptly named Table Rock.

Another favorite moderate-to-strenuous hike goes up **Old Speck Mountain** (4,180 feet), third highest of Maine's ten 4,000-footers and part of the Mahoosuc Range. The 28-foot-high viewing platform on the recently restored fire tower gets you above the wooded summit for incredible 360-degree views of the White Mountains, the Mahoosuc Range, and other mountains and lakes. Allow a solid seven hours for the 7.8-mile round-trip from the trailhead on the west side of Route 26 in Grafton Notch. The route follows the white-blazed Appalachian Trail (AT) most of the way; the tower is about 0.25 mile off the AT. Although there's a route map at the trailhead (at the same location as for the Table Rock hike), the best trail guide for this hike is in John Gibson's *50 Hikes in Southern and Coastal Maine*.

If you're driving along Route 26 early or late in the day, keep a lookout for moose; have your camera ready and exercise extreme caution. You'll usually spot them in boggy areas munching on aquatic plants, but when they decide to cross a highway, watch out—unlike us, they don't look both ways. And their eyes don't reflect headlights, so be vigilant after dark. Moose-car collisions are too often fatal for both moose and motorists.

THE MAHOOSUC RANGE

South and east of Grafton Notch State Park is a 27,253-acre chunk of **Maine Public Reserve Land** (Bureau of Parks and Lands, 207/287-3821, www.parksandlands.com) known as The Mahoosucs, or the Mahoosuc Range, where the hiking is rugged and strenuous but the scenic rewards are inestimable. The Appalachian Trail traverses much of the reserve, and its hikers insist that the mile-long Mahoosuc Notch section, between Old Speck and Goose Eye Mountains, is one of their biggest challenges on the 2,158-mile Georgia-to-Maine route, requiring steep ascents and descents with insecure footing, gigantic boulders, and narrow passages. If you're an experienced hiker, go for it, and use reliable guidebooks and maps, preferably USGS maps. The best overview of the reserve is *Spectacular Scenic Touring Loop in the Mahoosucs* (www.mahoosuctouringmap.org). The helpful map and brochure provides info on trails, culture, campgrounds, outfitters, guides, and information sources.

WHITE MOUNTAIN NATIONAL FOREST

About 49,800 acres of the 770,000-acre **White Mountain National Forest** (www.fs.usda.gov/whitemountain) lie on the Maine side of the border with New Hampshire. Route 113,

roughly paralleling the border, bisects the **Caribou-Speckled Mountain Wilderness,** the designated name for this part of the national forest. It's all dramatically scenic, with terrific opportunities for hiking, camping, picnicking, swimming, and fishing.

A drive along Route 113, north to south between Gilead and Stow, is worth a detour. It takes about 30 minutes without stops, but bring a picnic and enjoy the mountain views from the tables at the Cold River Overlook, about a mile south of the Evans Notch highpoint. Route 113 is too narrow for bikes in midsummer, when logging trucks and visitor traffic can be fairly dense. Save this bike tour for a fall weekday, and take it south to north for a good downhill run from Evans Notch. The road is closed in winter. If you plan on stopping or hiking, Evans Notch requires a parking permit ($5 for 7 days). Some locations have an "iron ranger" allowing payment of $3/parking place/day.

An easy family hike is the **Albany Brook Trail,** one mile each way between the Crocker Pond Campground (at the end of Crocker Pond Rd.) and the northern shore of Round Pond.

Outfitters and Guide Services

These companies provide rentals, guide services, and support for many of the sports detailed below. They're also great resources if you've brought your own equipment.

The Maine Guides at **Bethel Outdoor Adventure** (BOA, 121 Mayville Rd./Rte. 2, Bethel, 207/824-4224 or 800/533-3607, www.betheloutdooradventure.com) are pros at canoeing, kayaking, and bicycling. They also offer snowmobiling tours and rent machines.

Sun Valley Sports and Guide Service (129 Sunday River Rd., Bethel, 207/824-7533 or 877/851-7533, www.sunvalleysports.com) provides Orvis-endorsed wading and drift-boat trips, fly-fishing instruction, wildlife safaris, canoe and kayak rentals, and guided ATV tours in addition to equipment. It also provides shuttle services for those with their own boats and operates a full-service fly shop.

Veteran professional guides Polly Mahoney

WESTERN LAKES

and Kevin Slater of **Mahoosuc Guide Service** (1513 Bear River Rd., Newry, 207/824-2073, www.mahoosuc.com) lead wilderness canoe trips not in the Bethel area but on the Allagash, Penobscot, and St. John Rivers as well as in Québec. With extensive wilderness backgrounds in such locales as Labrador and the Yukon Territory, management experience with Outward Bound, a flair for camp cooking, and a commitment to Native American traditions, Polly and Kevin are ideal trip leaders.

Hiking and Walking

Much of the hiking in this area is within the various parks and preserves, but a fun family hike not in that category is the easy-to-moderate ascent of **Mount Will** in Newry, on the outskirts of Bethel. The Bethel Conservation Commission has developed a 3.2-mile loop trail that provides mountain and river views; allow about 2.5 hours to do the loop. At the chamber of commerce information center, pick up a Mount Will trail-map brochure, which explains three different hiking options. There also may be maps at the trailhead, which is on the west side of Route 2/26, 1.9 miles north of the Riverside Rest Area—a terrific spot, incidentally, for a posthike picnic next to the Androscoggin River.

The wheelchair-accessible **Bethel Recreational Path** is about 1.5 miles long and parallels the Androscoggin River. It begins at Davis Park (Rte. 26 and Intervale Rd.), where there's also a skateboard park, picnic tables, a boat launch, and a playground, and ends near Bethel Outdoor Adventure on Route 2. Expect to share it with joggers, in-line skaters, and cyclists. The **Androscoggin River Recreational Walking Trail** covers 1.5 miles, beginning at the lovely Riverside Rest Area on Route 2, just east of the Sunday River access road, and continuing to the River View Resort.

Water Sports
ANDROSCOGGIN RIVER

The rivers in the Bethel area are a paddler's dream, varying from beginner and family stretches to white-water sections for intermediate and advanced canoeists. Fortunately, the major artery, the Androscoggin River, seldom has low-water problems, and you'll see lots of islands as well as eagles, moose, and a beaver dam. West of Bethel there's an old cable from a onetime ferry crossing.

The 42-mile **Androscoggin River Canoe Trail,** created in 2001 by the **Mahoosuc Land Trust** (207/824-3806, www.mahoosuc.org), provides access points to the river spaced about five miles apart, from the Shelburne Dam in New Hampshire to Rumford. The *Map and Guide to the Androscoggin Canoe Trail* is available from the trust for $4.95 plus $1 postage.

The annual, nine-day, 170-mile, **Androscoggin River Source to the Sea Canoe Trek** (http://arwc.camp7.org) celebrates the river's revival from years of unbridled pollution caused primarily by paper-mill runoff.

The best source of information on the Androscoggin is **Bethel Outdoor Adventure** (BOA, 121 Mayville Rd./Rte. 2, Bethel, 207/824-4224 or 800/533-3607, www.betheloutdooradventure.com). It offers canoe rentals, maps, shuttle service, and trip-planning advice. In addition, the BOA staff can advise on canoeing the Ellis, Little Androscoggin, and Sunday Rivers.

POND PADDLING

Just east of Locke Mills, before the **Littlefield Beaches Campground** (207/875-3290, www.littlefieldbeaches.com), you can put in at **Round Pond,** on the south side of Route 26, and continue into North and South Ponds. Bring a picnic, and before you head out, enjoy it across the road at the lovely state rest area, which has grills and covered picnic tables in a wooded setting.

FISHING

The 26-mile stretch of the Upper Androscoggin River between the New Hampshire border and Rumford Point, its tributaries, the Wild, Pleasant, Sunday, and Bear Rivers, and local brooks are popular with anglers seeking rainbows, brookies, browns, and landlocked salmon. Even during the peak of summer, it's possible to catch smallmouth bass on the Andro.

Pick up a copy of *A Guide to Local Fishing* at the Bethel Area Chamber of Commerce and also check the resources of the **Upper Andro Anglers Alliance** (www.upperandro.com).

Biking

The Bethel Area Chamber of Commerce has sheets detailing about a dozen rides in the region, with lengths varying from a five-mile Village Restaurant Ride (don't be deceived; it takes in Paradise Hill, a killer for Sunday cyclists) to the 53-mile covered bridge cruise. For an easy pedal, follow the Sunday River Road as it continues out past Artist's Covered Bridge. It's mostly level and winding, paralleling the river and providing beautiful mountain views. No matter where you ride, do follow the rules of the road, keeping right and riding single file.

Hybrid-bike rentals are available from **Bethel Bicycle** (53 Mayville Rd., Bethel, 207/824-0100, www.bethelbicycle.com) and **Bethel Outdoor Adventure** (BOA, 121 Mayville Rd./Rte. 2, Bethel, 207/824-4224 or 800/533-3607, www.betheloutdooradventure.com), a full-service shop. Expect to pay $25-30/day.

SUNDAY RIVER MOUNTAIN BIKE PARK

Looking for a real mountain biking adventure? **Sunday River's bike park** (800/543-2754, www.sundayriver.com, 10am-5pm Fri.-Sun., $29 adults, $18 under age 13; trail only $20) has 20 miles of lift-serviced mountain biking on 25 trails, accessed from its South Ridge Lodge. Terrain ranges from dirt roads to single tracks with jumps, features, and even a log ride. You'll need a bike with front and rear brakes and ideally with full suspension. Rental bikes with full suspension are $80.

Golf

Thanks to its spectacular setting, the 18-hole championship course at the **Bethel Inn and Country Club** (Bethel Common, Bethel, 207/824-2175, www.bethelinn.com) wows every golfer who plays here. Starting times

are definitely required, and caddies are available. Also based here is the **Guaranteed Performance School of Golf** (800/654-0125, www.gpgolfschool.com). It includes five hours of on-course instruction and video analysis with PGA professionals, with a maximum of three students per instructor.

The newest course in the area is the spectacular Robert Trent Jones Jr.-designed 18-hole course at **Sunday River Ski Resort** (207/824-3000, www.sundayriver.com), which opened in 2005.

BIG Adventure Center

When the weather doesn't cooperate—and even if it does—and the kids need to let off steam, **BIG Adventure Center** (12 North Rd., Bethel, 207/824-0929, www.thebigadventurecenter.com) is just the ticket. Outdoor activities include two giant waterslides and an 18-hole miniature golf course; indoor possibilities include rock climbing and laser tag.

Winter Sports
SUNDAY RIVER SKI RESORT

Sprawling octopus-like over eight connected mountains, **Sunday River** (Sunday River Rd., Newry, 207/824-3000 or 800/543-2754, snow phone 207/824-6400, www.sundayriver.com) defines the winter sports scene in this area, with downhill skiing and snowboarding, ice skating, cross-country skiing, phenomenal snowmaking capability, slope-side lodging, and plentiful amenities that include a spa, night skiing, entertainment, restaurants, and lodging. Its 743 acres are laced with 132 designated trails and glades, terrain parks and pipes, a snow-tubing area, and three base lodges (South Ridge is the main one). Serving it all are 16 lifts, including a chondula (combination gondola and chairlift) and four high-speed quads. Don't even consider leaving the base without a trail map, and make sure everyone in your party knows exactly where to meet for lunch or at day's end.

Sunday River is also home to **Maine Handicapped Skiing** (800/639-7770, www.maineadaptive.org), which provides free lessons and tickets for alpine and cross-country skiing and snowboarding for people with physical disabilities. Reservations are required.

Sunday River has day-care facilities in three locations (reservations are advised), a ski school, rental equipment, a free on-mountain trolley-bus service, and plenty of places to grab a snack or a meal at a wide range of prices. Call or check the website for current ticket prices; one-day tickets purchased at the window are priciest, so be smart and buy online in advance for the best price.

The ski season usually runs early November-early May, weather permitting; the average annual snowfall is 167 inches. There's only one road on and off the mountain, so expect delays early and late in the day during weekends and holidays.

Sunday River also has a **zip-line park** open both summer and winter.

CROSS-COUNTRY SKIING

Right in downtown Bethel, the **Bethel Inn Touring Center** (Bethel Common, 207/824-6276, www.caribourecreation.com, $19 adult day pass, $15 students and seniors) has about 25 trails groomed for classic and skate skiing and five miles of snowshoe trails on the inn's scenic golf course. The ski shop has a wax room and a snack bar with seating areas. Ski and snowshoe rentals and half-day tickets are available.

About 30 miles of trails wind through 1,000 acres along the Androscoggin River at **Carter's Cross-Country Ski Center** (Middle Intervale Rd., Bethel, 207/539-4848, www.cartersxcski.com, $14 adults, $10 children), owned and managed by Carter's Cross-Country Ski Center in Oxford (207/539-4848). In winter, the Bethel location operates a lodge and ski shop with a snack bar and rents skis and snowshoes.

ICE SKATING

Picture an old-fashioned Currier and Ives winter landscape with skaters skimming a snow-circled pond and you'll come close to the scene on Bethel Common in winter. Bring a camera. The groomed ice-skating area, in the downtown Historic District, is usually ready for skaters by Christmas vacation. Sunday River Ski Resort also has rink; skating is free, and rental skates are available.

DOGSLEDDING

When they're not off leading multiday dogsledding trips in the Mahoosucs or on Umbagog Lake (rates begin around $600 pp), or even with the Inuit in Canada's Nunavut Territory ($6,150 pp) or the Cree in Québec (from $4,260 pp), Kevin Slater and Polly Mahoney of **Mahoosuc Guide Service** (1513 Bear River Rd., Newry, 207/824-2073, www.mahoosuc.com) will bundle you in a deerskin blanket and take you on a one-day dogsled trip on Umbagog Lake, beyond Grafton Notch State Park. Wear goggles or sunglasses; the dogs kick up the snow. Insulted parkas and footwear, a campfire lunch, and warm drinks are included in the $275 pp fee. Trips are limited, and they're very popular; book well in advance. Also on the premises are Mahoosuc's **Mahoosuc Mountain Lodge** and **Farmhouse Bed & Breakfast** (207/824-2073, www.mahoosucmountainlodge.com). Bunk rates range $40-60 pp. For more privacy, opt for one of the three shared-bath guest rooms ($50 pp with breakfast), in the nicely renovated 1903 farmhouse.

In winter, there is a three-day Learn-to-Mush package at **Telemark Inn Wilderness Lodge** (591 King's Hwy., Mason Township, 207/836-2703, www.newenglanddogsledding.com, $1,025 pp d, $1,250 s, plus 10 percent gratuity) that includes three half-day guided mushing experiences, three nights' lodging, and all meals.

SNOWMOBILING

Snowmobile rentals are available from **Northeast Snowmobile** (800/458-1838, www.northeastsnowmobile.com). Expect to pay about $150 for a half day.

ACCOMMODATIONS

Conveniently, the **Bethel Area Chamber of Commerce Reservations Service** (800/442-5826, www.bethelmaine.com) provides toll-free lodging assistance for more than 1,000 beds in member B&Bs, motels, condos, and

© HILARY NANGLE

Join Mahoosuc Guide Service on a dog-sledding trip.

inns in Bethel, at Sunday River Ski Resort, and farther afield. If you're planning a winter visit, however, particularly during Thanksgiving and Christmas holidays, February school vacation, or the month of March, don't wait until the last minute. Procrastination will put you in a bed 40 miles from the slopes.

Keep in mind that peak season (ergo the highest room rates) in this part of Maine is in winter, not summer. Some lodgings also have higher rates for fall foliage in September-October.

Sunday River Lodging

On-mountain lodging options at **Sunday River** (207/824-3000, reservations 800/543-2754, www.sundayriver.com) include 425 guest rooms and suites in two full-service hotels—the **Grand Summit** and the **Jordan Grand Hotel**—as well as hundreds of slope-side condos and town houses in seven different clusters. Both hotels have restaurants and cafés, indoor and outdoor heated pools, tennis courts, video game rooms, and lots of extra amenities; the

Jordan Grand is in an isolated location. Most guest rooms have full kitchen facilities. Except for the dorm rooms, lodging packages include lift tickets. Prices for accommodations and activity packages vary widely.

Country Inns

Bethel's grande dame, **The Bethel Inn and Country Club** (21 Broad St., Bethel, 207/824-2175 or 800/654-0125, www.bethelinn.com), is the centerpiece of a classic New England village scene. It faces the Bethel Common in the historical district; out the back door is the golf course backed by the White Mountains. Rooms are spread out between the traditional main inn and outbuildings. Also on the premises are 1-3-bedroom condominiums. Guest rooms vary widely in decor and quality; be forewarned that some are tired, to put it kindly. The best choices are in the new wing of the main inn and the newly updated ones in the main inn. This is a full-service resort, and amenities include golf, tennis, a health club with a saltwater pool and a sauna, a game room, a

The Bethel Inn celebrated its 100th anniversary in 2013.

© HILARY NANGLE

lakeside outpost for swimming and boating, and a summer children's program. Inn rates, including breakfast, begin at around $100/person. Children under age 12 stay free in the same room. Rates with dinner are available, but do check packages, which provide the best bang for the buck. Some accommodations permit dogs for $20/night. It's open year-round, but the restaurant may be closed some nights during the off-season, although the tavern remains open.

Bethel's other longtime country inn, **The Sudbury Inn** (Main St., Bethel, 207/824-2174 or 800/395-7837, www.thesudburyinn.com), is best known for its dining room and pub, but it's a classic B&B too. Guest rooms and suites (and even a three-bedroom apartment with a full kitchen and a fireplace) are spread between the main house and the dog-friendly carriage house ($15/dog/day). The two-bedroom suites are especially good for families. All are comfortably furnished and have cable TV, air-conditioning, and phones. A full breakfast is included in the rates, which begin at $89-129 for a standard.

Bed-and-Breakfasts

Architect Stuart Crocker designed the lovely Shingle-style **Crocker Pond House** (917 North Rd., Bethel, 207/836-2027, www.crockerpond.com, $125-150) so that it fits naturally into its setting on 50 mostly wooded acres. It's a lovely environmentally designed inn that blends contemporary amenities, such as Wi-Fi, with traditional cottage design, Norwegian antiques, and Native American art in a restorative atmosphere (there is no TV). Crocker and his wife, Ellen, welcome guests in seven guest rooms, all south-facing with mountain views; one is wheelchair-accessible with a roll-in shower. Begin the morning with Stuart's blueberry pancakes, and after hiking or snowshoeing the trail behind the inn, relaxing by the pond, or exploring, return for afternoon tea and cookies. Pets are not allowed; two cats are in residence. Norwegian, French, and German are spoken at the inn. Children are welcome, and the loft rooms are especially good for families. Children under age 14 sharing a room are $15 each; older children are $25 each.

For a quiet stay within walking distance of downtown shops, restaurants, and attractions, opt for the Bethel Hill Bed and Breakfast (66 Broad St., Bethel, 207/824-2161, www.bethel-hill.com $139-179), a handsome inn with three, air-conditioned spacious guest rooms tastefully decorated with antiques. A separate lakefront house has two additional suites ($250-295, including continental breakfast).

Traveling with your pooch? **Paws Inn** (372 Walkers Mill Rd./Rte. 26, Bethel, 207/824-6678, www.pawsinn.net, $75-85) takes dog-friendly to the extreme. Carolyn Bailey and her sidekick, Sampson, provide two guest rooms, dog beds or crates, fenced-yard and barn play areas, doggie snacks, and plenty of love. You only need bring food for your dog and proof of vaccinations; Carolyn prepares a generous continental breakfast. It's two miles south of Bethel.

Motels

The **Inn at the Rostay** (186 Mayville Rd./Rte. 2, Bethel, 207/824-3111 or 888/754-0072, www.rostay.com) is a motel that acts like an inn. Rooms are spread between three buildings. Most have a refrigerator and microwave; all have air-conditioning or ceiling fan, phone, Wi-Fi, and TV and VCR, with a video library available. On the five-acre premises are a pool, hot tub, picnic pavilion, and quilt shop. Guests can have a full breakfast ($8), served in a dining room adjacent to a guest parlor. Rates begin at $68 d midweek and vary greatly. Winter holiday weeks are priciest at $112-135. Some rooms are pet-friendly ($20).

For clean, cheap, and convenient digs, check into Ruthie's **Bethel Village Motel** (88 Main St., Bethel, 800/882-0293, www.bethelvillagemotel.com, from $75), smack downtown in a walk-to-everything location behind Ruthie's boutique. Guest rooms are pleasantly decorated, and all have air-conditioning, TVs, fridges, and Wi-Fi.

Camping

To really escape, **South Arm Campground** (62 Kennett Dr., Andover, 207/364-5155, www.

southarm.com) has 38 lakeside wilderness sites ($15/family), including island sites accessible only by boat, with transportation available. A bit less remote on a peninsula is the full-service main campground with 65 wooded sites ($24-32), all with water and 30-amp electricity; it has a marina, modern bathhouses, and a bakery and general store. From here, you can fly-fish the Rapid River, canoe the lake, fish, paddle (rentals available), take a sunset moose cruise, walk a section of the Appalachian Trail, bike logging roads, or just relax in this little slice of heaven.

Just south of its namesake, **Grafton Notch Campground** (1471 Bear River Rd./Rte. 26, Newry, 207/824-2292, www.campgrafton.com, $25) is a small, no-frills campground with 14 wooded sites with fire rings and picnic tables, a modern bathhouse, and a dump station ($10), but no hookups. Leashed dogs are permitted. Don't expect real quiet, though; you can hear the trucks on Route 26, but you can't beat the location if you want to hike in the state park.

Thirteen miles west of Bethel is the seven-acre **Hastings Campground** (877/444-6777 for credit-card reservations, $16), one of four campgrounds along Route 113 in the White Mountain National Forest. The 24-site campground is primitive, with no hookups or showers, but it does have vault toilets, a hand pump for water, fishing and hiking, and it is wheelchair-accessible. Route 113 is especially scenic, so this is a prime location for extensive hiking in the national forest. Trail information and maps are available from the Evans Notch Ranger District office. The campground is in Gilead, three miles south of Route 2.

When you really yearn to escape, try to snag one of the first-come, first-served seven sites at **Crocker Pond Campground** ($14), located in the White Mountain National Forest. No reservations are accepted, so be prepared with a contingency plan. The campground, set amid white pines on the edge of Crocker Pond, has a hand pump for water and a vault toilet. Nonmotorized boats are permitted in the pond. To find the campground, from Route 2 in West

Bethel, take the Flat Road (across from the post office) and travel 5.8 miles, then turn right at the sign and continue another 0.5 mile down a dirt road.

FOOD
Local Flavors

You can feel good when eating at the **Good Food Store** (Rte. 2, Bethel, 207/824-3754 or 800/879-8926, www.goodfoodbethel.com, 9am-8pm daily, $5-8). The combination store and takeout sells both good food and food that's good for you, and it stocks a huge array of natural foods. Create an instant picnic with sandwiches, salads, and soups, even beer and wine. If you're renting a condo and don't feel like cooking or eating out, you can pick up homemade soups, stews, and casseroles to go.

Also on the premises is **Smokin' Good BBQ** (Rte. 2, Bethel, 207/824-4744, www. smokingoodbarbecue.com, 11:30am-7pm Thurs.-Tues., $7-27), operating from Graceland, an orange trailer. A transplanted Texan turned me onto this gem. Choices include pulled pork, beef brisket, ribs, chicken, and sides such as barbecue beans, slaw, and corn bread. Dress for the elements: There are only picnic tables for seating.

Baked goods made daily from scratch from all-natural ingredients have earned **DiCocoa's Bakery and Marketplace** (119 Main St., Bethel, 207/824-5282, www.cafedicocoa.com) a solid following. Go for the fabulous baked goods, but don't miss the lunch specials, including panini and soup. The bakery doubles as a market selling fancy foods and take-home meals. It also makes scrumptious gelato, and I think the chocolate chip cookies are among the best I've ever had.

For cheap eats at any meal, snag a table at the **Crossroads Diner & Deli** (24 Mayville Rd./Rte. 2, Bethel, 207/824-3673, 5:30am-8pm daily).

No matter what your dietary preference—vegan, vegetarian, gluten-free, carnivore—**Erin's Café on Main** (63 Main St., Bethel, 207/824-3746) has you covered. Breakfast is the specialty, although soups and salads also are served.

The **Bethel Farmers Market** sells good-for-you produce and other items 9am-1pm Saturday mid-June-mid-October, on Route 26 (at Parkway) next to Norway Savings Bank at the southern edge of town.

On-Mountain Dining

The independently owned **Phoenix House and Well** (Skiway Rd., across from the South Ridge base complex, Newry, 207/824-2222, www. phoenixhouseandwell.com, 11am-midnight daily during ski season, summer hours vary, $9-20) has a split personality: Downstairs is a pub; upstairs is a fancier dining room (weekends only). The same menu is served in both locations. Choices range from burgers to seafood fettuccine. There's live entertainment almost every weekend. Go elsewhere if you're hungry and it's busy; service can be painfully slow.

Pubs and Pizzas

Also open only in winter but farther down the access road is **Great Grizzly American Steak House/Matterhorn** (292 Sunday River Rd., Newry, 207/824-6271, www.matterhornski-bar.com, 3-11pm Mon-Fri., noon-12:30am Sat.-Sun., $10-26), an immensely popular barn-style restaurant that's *the* aprés-ski spot in Bethel, with entertainment on weekends. It's filled with co-owner Roger Beaudoin's finds, many from his travels and climbing expeditions in Switzerland (to the Matterhorn, of course). Antique mountain-climbing gear is in one room; a village motif complete with a real-estate office and old Sunoco pumps is in another; classic skis are everywhere. Check out the bar, made from 120 skis. The wide-ranging menu includes the best pizzas in the region, cooked in a wood-burning oven, as well as steaks, seafood, pastas, salads, and even sushi. There's even a kids' menu. On weekend nights, there's usually entertainment in the early evening. Reservations are not accepted, so it's wise to dine early on weekends or expect to wait. Live entertainment, usually rock bands, begins at 9:30pm on Friday-Saturday; a cover is charged unless you're already seated and have had dinner.

On the lower level of the Sudbury Inn is **Suds Pub** (151 Main St., Bethel, 207/824-2174 or 800/395-7837, www.thesudburyinn.com, from 11:30am daily), a very relaxing hangout. The moderately priced menu includes appetizers, burgers, soups, salads, pizza, and a few entrées, most in the $7-15 range. The full bar has 29 beers on tap. Thursday night is Hoot Night, an open-mic tradition since 1987 and a great chance to mingle with locals. There's also live music on Friday and Saturday nights.

For an English pub experience, head to **The Jolly Drayman English Pub and Restaurant** (Briar Lea Inn, 150 Mayville Rd./Rte. 2, Bethel, 207/824-4717 or 877/311-1299, www.briarleainn.com, 4pm-9pm Mon.-Thurs., 5pm-9pm Fri.-Sun., $13-20). Former owners remodeled the space based on a 15th-century English pub and named it for the drayman, the driver of the beer wagon. Come for the fine ales and stouts and the pub-style favorites such as Thatcher's shepherd's pie and bangers-and-mash. On Monday, it serves a half-pound burger for $5; Wednesday is trivia night, with great prizes; and Thursday features all-you-can-eat fish-and-chips.

Ethnic Fare

Cafe DiCocoa (125 Main St., Bethel, 207/824-5282, www.cafedicocoa.com, $50) is open from 6:45pm Saturday evenings during winter for **Gentle Dining,** a candlelight-dinner experience during ski season. The five-course fixed-price dinner (BYOB) is by reservation only and features an internationally inspired menu. The 2.5-hour evening workshops include an overview of the history and culture of the featured region, explanations of ingredients, cooking demonstrations, and plentiful samples. Friday nights in winter feature **Cocina Mexicana**, made-from-scratch Mexican fare ($4-10), BYOB. About once a month during winter, the restaurant also hosts tasting workshops or cooking classes ($29).

It's hard to believe, but you can even get authentic—and truly delicious—Japanese and Korean food in Bethel. **Cho Sun** (141 Main St., Bethel, 207/824-7370, www.chosunrestaurant.com, 5pm-9pm Wed.-Sun., entrées $18-26) is in a lovely New England Victorian house decorated with Asian art and antiques. Sushi is a specialty, but owner Pok Sun Lane's South Korean fare draws on her heritage.

Classic Italian fare is served at **22 Broad Street** (22 Broad St., Bethel, 207/824-3496, www.22broadstreet.com, 5pm-close daily, $17-25), located in the Greek Revival-style 1848 Gideon Hastings House across from the Bethel Inn. Choices include house-made ravioli, pork saltimbocca, and veal piccata. Martinis are a specialty, and there's a kids' menu.

Casual and Fine Dining

The Sudbury Inn (151 Main St., Bethel, 207/824-2174 or 800/395-7837, www.sudbury-inn.com,), a warmly retrofitted 1873 Victorian inn, has two dining venues. Reserve a table in the **Dining Room** (5:30pm-9pm Thurs.-Sat., $18-28) for white tablecloth dining on the glassed-in porch or fireside and a menu ranging from mushroom lasagna and baked haddock to rack of lamb and roasted duck. **Bistro 151** (from 3pm Thurs.-Sun., $7-22) aims for a casual French bistro tone, where there's Wi-Fi and HDTV. In this family-friendly space, you can order from the Dining Room, Sud's Pub, or bistro menu, the latter featuring small and large plates with a French accent.

Another longtimer, **S.S. Milton** (43 Main St., Bethel, 207/824-2589, $12-25) is an unpretentious, homey, family-friendly restaurant with a menu that ranges from veggie scampi to New Zealand lamb.

The dining room at **The Bethel Inn** (Bethel Common, Bethel, 207/824-2175, www.bethelinn.com) is open to nonguests for breakfast (7:30am-9:30am Mon.-Fri. and 7am-10am Sat.-Sun. holidays) and dinner (5:30pm-8:45pm daily through Dec. 31, weekends in winter). The dining rooms overlook the golf course to the mountains beyond, but the fare doesn't match the views. The continental menu includes duck, tenderloin, and lobster, with entrées ranging $24-44.

INFORMATION AND SERVICES

The **Bethel Area Chamber of Commerce** (Cross St., Bethel, 207/824-2282 or 800/442-5826, www.bethelmaine.com) has public restrooms. An excellent online planning tool for the region is www.westernmaine.org.

GETTING THERE AND AROUND

Bethel is roughly 65 miles or 1.5 hours from Rangeley via Routes 17 and 2. It's about 36 miles or 50 minutes to Fryeburg via Route 5, about 24 miles or 30 minutes to South Paris via Route 26, and about 70 miles or 1.5 hours from Portland via Route 26.

The free **Bethel Explorer** (www.mountainexplorer.org) bus service operates between Bethel and Sunday River. It runs 6:30am-1am daily mid-December-early April (but check the schedule).

At Sunday River, the free **Sunday River Trolley** (207/824-3000) circulates throughout the resort, operating weekends Thanksgiving-Christmas and then daily from mid-December-early April. It runs on a 30-minute cycle, 8am-1am weekdays and 7am-1am weekends and holidays.

Fryeburg Area

Fryeburg (pop. 3,449), a crossroads community on busy Route 302, is best known as the funnel to and from the factory outlets, hiking trails, and ski slopes of New Hampshire's North Conway and the White Mountains. Except during early October's annual extravaganza, the giant Fryeburg Fair, Fryeburg seldom ends up on anyone's itinerary. That's a shame: The mountain-ringed community has lots of charm, historic homes, the flavor of rural life, and access to miles of Saco River canoeing waters.

Incorporated in 1763, Fryeburg is Oxford County's oldest town; even earlier it was known as Pequawket, an Indian settlement and trading post—until skirmishes with white settlers routed the Native Americans in 1725 during Dummer's War (also known as Lovewell's War). Casualties were heavy on both sides; Lovewell and the Pequawket chief were among the fatalities.

In 1792, Fryeburg Academy, a private school on Main Street, was chartered; the school's Webster Hall is named after famed statesman Daniel Webster, whose undistinguished teaching career at the school began and ended in 1802. Among the students at the time was Rufus Porter, who later gained renown as a muralist, inventor, and founder of *Scientific American* magazine. Today the school is one of a handful of private academies in Maine that provide public secondary education, a uniquely successful private-public partnership.

Just north of Fryeburg is the town of **Lovell** (pop. 1,140), with three hamlets—known collectively as the Lovells—strung along Route 5, on the east side of gorgeous Kezar Lake. Anyone who has discovered Kezar Lake yearns to keep it a secret, but the word is out. The mountain-rimmed lake is too beautiful.

SIGHTS
Hemlock Covered Bridge

The 116-foot-long **Hemlock Bridge,** built in 1857 over the "Old Saco," or "Old Course," a former channel of the Saco River, is in the hamlet of East Fryeburg, just west of Kezar Pond. It's accessible by car, but if you have a mountain bike, this is a peaceful pedal on a nice dirt road. The best time to visit is July-October; mud or snow can prevent car access in other months, and June is buggy. From the Route 5/302 junction in Fryeburg, take Route 302 east 5.5 miles to Hemlock Bridge Road. Turn left (north) and go about three miles on a paved and then unpaved road to the bridge. Or paddle under the bridge on a detour from canoeing on the Saco River.

It's a peaceful pedal or drive out to the Hemlock Covered Bridge.

Hopalong Cassidy Memorabilia

When he died in 1956, longtime Fryeburg resident Clarence Mulford, author of the Hopalong Cassidy books, left his extensive collection of Western Americana, including models, copies of his books, research materials, and more, along with enough money to display them, to the **Fryeburg Public Library** (515 Main St., Fryeburg, 207/935-2731, www.fryeburgmaine.org/town-departments/library).

ENTERTAINMENT

Anything happening in Bethel and vicinity, Oxford Hills, or Sebago and Long Lakes is also within easy reach of the Fryeburg area, especially in the daytime.

The **Leura Hill Eastman Performing Arts Center** (Fryeburg Academy, Fryeburg, 207/935-9232, www.fryeburgacademy.org) is a year-round venue that attracts regional and national entertainers.

Singer-songwriter Carol Noonan has created a phenomenal 200-seat performing arts center on her hilltop farm. **Stone Mountain Arts Center** (695 Dug Way Rd., Brownfield, 866/227-6523, www.stonemountainartscenter.com) brings in nationally renowned performers such as Roseanne Cash, Shemekia Copeland, Sweet Honey in the Rock, Leo Kottke, and Paula Poundstone, to name a few. The calendar is jam-packed. All events take place in the barn, and preshow dinners, pizzas, and salads ($15-25) are available by reservation. Credit cards are taken for reservations, but cash or checks are preferred for actual payment. Print out a copy of the directions—this place is in the boonies.

The **Lovell Brick Church for the Performing Arts** (www.lovellbrickchurch.org) is the site of a summer entertainment series, with performances May-September.

In summer, **outdoor concerts** are held Tuesday nights at the gazebo (or in the fire barn, if it's raining). During July, The **International Musical Arts Institute** (www.imaifestival.org) presents concerts in Fryeburg Academy's Bion Cram Library.

EVENTS

The big event in these parts is the **Fryeburg Fair** (www.fryeburgfair.com) the last country fair of the season held the first week of October, sometimes including a few days in September. It's Maine's largest agricultural fair and an annual event since 1851. A parade, a carnival, craft demonstrations and exhibits, harness racing, pig scrambles, children's activities, ox pulling, and live entertainment are all here, as are plenty of food booths (it's sometimes called the "Fried-burg" Fair). More than 300,000 turn out for eight days of festivities, so expect traffic congestion. The fair runs Sunday-Sunday, and the busiest day is Saturday. No dogs are allowed on the 180-acre site. Spectacular fall foliage and mountain scenery just add to the appeal. Find it at the Fryeburg Fairgrounds (officially the West Oxford Agricultural Society Fairgrounds) on Route 5 in Fryeburg.

SHOPPING

It's hard to believe that the jewelry and crafts inside the **Harvest Gold Gallery** (Rte. 5, Center Lovell, 207/925-6502, www.harvestgoldgallery.com) are more stunning than the setting overlooking Kezar Lake. Magnificent gold jewelry, much of it accented with Maine gemstones, is made on the premises. Also here is a very well-chosen selection of high-end crafts, with an emphasis on fine glasswork. It's definitely not a place to bring young kids.

Less high-end but no lower in quality are the crafts at **Weston's** (48 River St./Rte. 113 N., Fryeburg, 207/935-2567, www.westonsfarm.com). The mostly locally made selection includes baskets, bears, pillows, candles, and more.

Log House Designs (Rte. 5, Fryeburg, 207/935-2848, www.loghousedesignsusa.com, 7am-3pm Mon.-Fri.) is a bargain-seeker's dream. You enter via the stitching room, and then progress to the bona fide outlet, where the company's Gore-Tex outdoor wear, fleece products, travel accessories, and even dog beds are sold at great prices.

RECREATION

Hiking

The easiest and therefore busiest trail in the area is the 20-minute stroll up **Jockey Cap,** named for a cantilevered ledge that has long since disappeared. At the summit, with a 360-degree view of lakes and mountains, is a monument to Admiral Robert Peary, the Arctic explorer who once lived in Fryeburg. The metal edge of the monument is a handy cheat sheet with profiles and names of all the mountains you're looking at—more than four dozen of them. The trail is fine for kids, but keep a close eye on the littlest ones; the drop-off is perilous on the south side. Jockey Cap is also popular with rock climbers and boulder mavens. The trailhead is on Route 302, about a mile east of downtown Fryeburg, on the left between the Jockey Cap Country Store and the Jockey Cap Motel. And here's a bit of trivia: Jockey Cap was the site of Maine's first ski tow.

Allow about half an hour to reach the summit of **Sabattus Mountain** in Lovell, north of Fryeburg. This is an especially good family hike, easy and short enough for small children. Carry a picnic and enjoy the views at the top—on the ledges of the more open second summit. You'll see the White Mountains, Pleasant Mountain, and skinny Kezar Lake; in fall it's fabulous. To reach the trailhead from Fryeburg, take Route 5 North to Center Lovell. About 0.8 mile after the junction of Routes 5 and 5A, turn right onto Sabattus Road. Go about 1.6 miles, bearing right at the fork onto an unpaved road. Continue another 0.5 mile to a parking area on the left; the trailhead is across the road. The round-trip loop trail is 1.4 miles.

Other good hikes in this area are **Mount Tom** (easy, about 2.5 hours round-trip), just east of Fryeburg; **Burnt Meadow Mountain** (moderately difficult, about four hours round-trip to the north peak, with good views of the Presidential Range), near Brownfield; and **Mount Cutler** (moderately difficult, about two hours round-trip), near Hiram.

Water Sports

Fryeburg has two public beaches that double

as canoe put-ins. **Weston's Beach** (River St./ Rte. 5 N., just off Rte. 302) is a swath of sand extending into the Saco River that gets wider as the summer progresses and the river level drops. Another sandy beach is adjacent to **Canal Bridge Campground,** just off Route 5 heading toward Lovell.

CANOEING

The **Saco River,** whose headwaters are in Crawford Notch, New Hampshire, meanders 84 miles from the Maine border at Fryeburg to the ocean at Saco and Biddeford. Its many miles of flat water, with intermittent sandbars and a few portages, make it wonderful for canoeing, camping, and swimming, but there's the rub: The summer weekend scene on the 35-mile western Maine stretch sometimes looks like bumper boats at Disneyland, especially weekends and holidays, and it can be quite raucous—with large parties towing canoes filled with beer. Aim for midweek or late September-early October, when the foliage is spectacular, the current is slower, noise levels are lower, and the crowds are busy elsewhere. For a relaxing trip, figure about 2 mph and you can do the Fryeburg-to-Hiram segment with two overnight stops, including a couple of interesting side-trip paddles to Hemlock Bridge, Pleasant Pond, and Lovewell's Pond. If you put in at Swan's Falls in Fryeburg (www. sacorivercouncil.org, parking $10/day), you won't have to deal with portages between there and Hiram. For multiday trips, you'll need to get a **fire permit** (free; available at some local stores), or stay at one of the commercial campgrounds.

Saco River Canoe and Kayak (Rte. 5, Fryeburg, 207/935-2369, www.sacorivercanoe. com), close to the convenient put-in at Swan's Falls, rents canoes and tandem kayaks ($45/ day Fri.-Sun. July-Aug., $30 midweek and off-season) and provides delivery and pickup service along a 50-mile stretch of the Saco River. Shuttle costs range $6-16 for two canoes (depending on location). Safety-conscious owners Fred and Prudy Westerberg know their turf— they've been in the biz since the 1970s—and

provide helpful advice for planning short and extended canoe trips.

If crowds on the Saco become a bit much, head east or north with your canoe or kayak to the area's lakes and ponds, even to **Brownfield Bog**, a favorite with birders. Prime canoeing spots are **Lovewell Pond** and **Kezar Pond** in Fryeburg; **Kezar Lake** in Lovell; and **Virginia Lake** in Stoneham. A north wind kicks up on Kezar Lake, so stay close to shore. The most spectacular is mile-long Virginia Lake, nudged up against the White Mountain National Forest. To see a house on the wooded shoreline is a rarity. The rough access road (off Rte. 5 between North Lovell and East Stoneham) is a mechanic's delight, but persevere; tranquility lies ahead.

The best way to see beautiful Kezar Lake is by renting a boat from **Kezar Lake Marina** (219 W. Lovell Rd., Lovell, 207/925-3000, www. kezarlake.com). Canoes and kayaks rent for $10/hour or $25/day. A 13-foot Boston Whaler begins at $50/half day, $90/full day.

Winter Sports
SNOWMOBILING

More than 600 miles of groomed trails are accessible from Fryeburg. For information and sled rental, try **Northeast Snowmobile Rentals** (532 Main St./Rte. 302, Fryeburg, 800/458-1838, www.northeastsnowmobile. com). Rates begin around $150 for a half day. Full clothing, including boots, pants, jacket, and gloves, is $25. A two-hour guided tour up Black Cap Mountain is $95 s, $115 d.

ACCOMMODATIONS

If you're planning to be in the area during the Fryeburg Fair, you'll need to reserve beds or campsites months ahead, in some cases a year in advance.

Inns and Bed-and-Breakfasts

◖ **The Oxford House Inn** (548 Main St./Rte. 302, Fryeburg, 207/935-3442 or 800/261-7206, www.oxfordhouseinn.com, $119-199 d) is better known for its dining, but upstairs are four spacious and inviting guest rooms, each with a TV, air-conditioning, and Wi-Fi. Rear rooms have bucolic views over the Saco River Valley farmlands to the White Mountains. Breakfasts, served in the mountain-view porch-dining room, are every bit as creative as the inn's dinner menus.

Here's a treat. **The Old Saco Inn** (125 Old Saco Ln., Fryeburg, 207/925-3737, www.the-oldesacoinn.com, $105-180) sits on 65 quiet acres bordering the old course of the Saco River. A huge lawn rolls down to the river's edge; rising beyond are the distant White Mountains. Trails meander through the woods and fields, and canoes and kayaks are provided for paddlers. Centerpiece of the main inn is a two-story living/dining room centered on a huge hearth. Just off of it is a cozy pub with wood-stove, where a light menu is served on weekends. There's a guest library with cozy nooks in the upstairs mezzanine. Guest rooms are spread out between the inn and the adjacent carriage house. All have Wi-Fi and TV, most have refrigerators and private entrances, some have decks, one has a detached but private bath. A full breakfast is included, served either indoors or on the porch.

If you love dogs or are traveling with your pooch, you'll adore the **Admiral Peary Inn Bed and Breakfast** (27 Elm St., Fryeburg, 207/935-1269, www.admiralpearyinn.com, $149-189), named for the famed Arctic explorer who briefly resided here. What distinguishes this inn are the spacious and plentiful public rooms: the front library, a parlor, a dining room, huge kitchen with dining area, great room with fireplace and 50-inch TV, pool table nook, and large three-season porch, not to mention the back deck and yard. Innkeeper Donna Pearce has updated the decor, opting for handsome and comfy over froufrou and frilly. The inn, dating from the 1860s, is located in a quiet residential area that's an easy walk to downtown restaurants. Dogs stay free as long as they can vouch for the behavior of their people. Rates include a full breakfast.

Cottage Colony

The *New York Times* once headlined a story on

Quisisana (42 Quisisana Dr., Center Lovell, 207/925-3500, www.quisisanaresort.com, no credit cards) as "Where Mozart Goes on Vacation." Amen. By day, the staff at this elegantly rustic 47-acre retreat masquerade as waiters and waitresses, chambermaids, boat crew, and kitchen help; each night, presto, they're the stars of musical performances worthy of Broadway and concert-hall ticket prices. Since 1947 it has been like this at "Quisi"—with staff recruited from the nation's best conservatories. Veteran managers literally attuned to guests' needs keep it all working smoothly.

The frosting on all this culture is the setting—a beautifully landscaped pine grove on the shores of sandy-bottomed Kezar Lake, looking off to the White Mountains and dramatic sunsets. No wonder that reservations for the lodge rooms and 38 neat white cottages are hard to come by. The New York-heavy clientele knows to book well ahead, often for the same week, and new generations have followed their parents here. In July-August, a one-week minimum Saturday-Saturday reservation is required. Rates begin at $180 pp, including meals, musical entertainment, tennis, and nonmotorized boats. Beer and wine only are available. Quisisana's season begins in mid-June and ends in late August.

Camping

Canoeing is the major focus at **Woodland Acres Campground** (Rte. 160, Brownfield, 207/935-2529, www.woodlandacres.com), with a 100-canoe fleet available for rent ($58/day includes shuttle service to one location; reduced rates for additional days). The staff makes it all very convenient, even suggesting more than half a dozen daylong and multiday canoe trips for skill levels from beginner to expert. This well-maintained campground on the Saco River has 109 wooded tent and RV sites ($34-44). Facilities include a rec hall, a beach, a camp store, and free hot showers. Leashed pets are allowed ($2.50/day). From Fryeburg, take Route 5/13 southeast to Route 160; turn left (north) and go a mile to the campground.

Also in Brownfield, and also geared toward canoeists, is **River Run** (Rte. 160, Brownfield,

207/452-2500, www.riverruncanoe.com), with 22 large primitive tent sites ($10 pp, no hookups) on 100-plus acres next to the Saco River's Brownfield Bridge. Canoe rentals and shuttle service are available—canoes run about $21/day Monday-Thursday, $40 on weekends and holidays, with the shuttle price about $9-20.

The Saco River Recreational Council maintains rustic **Swans Falls Campground** (198 Swans Falls Rd., Fryeburg, 207/935-3395, www.sacorivercouncil.org, $15 pp, $25 min./night) on the Saco River just north of Fryeburg. The wooded grounds have 18 campsites with picnic tables and fire rings. Also here are a small educational facility and a store. This is a very busy canoe and kayak access point on the Saco River.

FOOD
Local Flavors

Rosie's Restaurant at the Lovell Village Store (Rte. 5, Lovell, 207/925-1255, 5am-8pm Mon.-Sat., 6am-7pm Sun.) is always packed. Expect good food, friendly service, and a never-too-late-for-breakfast/never-too-early-for-lunch menu.

Weston's Farm, established by the Weston family in 1799 and now operated by the sixth generation, edges the Saco River and is across from Weston's Beach. Stop at **Weston's Farm Stand** (48 River St./Rte. 113 N., Fryeburg, 207/935-2567, www.westonsfarm.com, 9am-6pm daily mid-May-Dec. 24) for all kinds of picnic and cottage fixings, from fresh produce and local meats to cheese and maple syrup.

Casual Dining

Here's a sleeper: Chef-co-owner and Culinary Institute of America grad Jonathan Spak crafts contemporary American fare with international (especially Asian) accents at **◖ The Oxford House Inn** (548 Main St., Fryeburg, 207/935-3442, www.oxfordhouseinn.com, 5:30pm-9pm daily, $12-32). He offers half- and full-plate pastas, bistro plates, and full entrées, making it easy to assemble a meal that fits both your budget and cravings. The four dining rooms appear formal, but this is a casual place; request a table on the glassed-in back porch to watch the sun set behind the White Mountains. Dinner reservations are wise, especially July-August and during the Fryeburg Fair.

Beer geeks, here's your happy place. Fronting on the golf course yet hidden on a back road is a local secret with a big reputation—**Ebenezer's Restaurant and Pub** (44 Allen Rd., off W. Lovell Rd., Lovell, 207/925-3200, www.ebenezerspub.net, from noon daily summer, shorter hours off-season). Most folks come for the Belgian beer selection—easily the best in New England, some say in the entire country. And if you're not a fan of Belgian brews, there are dozens of other beer choices. Complementing that is good pub fare, burgers, sandwiches, salads, pizzas ($6-12) as well as heartier entrées ($15-22), although service can be glacial. Dine on the screened-in porch or inside the tavern and bar. Every August, Ebenezer's puts on an extravagant multicourse Belgian dinner with beer pairings as part of its weeklong Belgian Beer Festival.

Innkeeper Janice Sage won the **Center Lovell Inn and Restaurant** (1107 Main St., Center Lovell, 207/925-1575 or 800/777-2698, www.centerlovellinn.com, 6pm-9pm daily, entrées $25-30) in an essay contest and became a cover story in the *New York Times Magazine*. She has been here since 1993, serving an enthusiastic clientele drawn to the wide-ranging continental menu, which changes weekly. The best tables are on the glassed-in porch, where you can watch the sun slip behind the mountains. Reservations are advised, especially in midsummer. Prefer to tumble into bed after dining? The inn has five second-floor guest rooms with private and shared baths in the 1805 main building, plus five more with private and shared baths in the adjacent Harmon House. Room rates are $119-159. The inn and the restaurant are open May-October and December-March.

If you have a hankering for barbecue and good times, the **302 West Smokehouse & Tavern** (636 Main St., Fryeburg, 207/935-3021, www.302west.com, from 11am daily) delivers on both counts. Big portions of ribs and barbecued entrées run $10-20; burgers, quesadillas, and the like begin around $9. If there's entertainment, plan on a crowd; this place is crazy popular with locals. If the weather's nice, grab a seat on the back deck.

INFORMATION

The **Greater Bridgton Lakes Region Chamber of Commerce** (207/647-3472, www.mainelakeschamber.com) covers Fryeburg.

GETTING THERE AND AROUND

Fryeburg is roughly 36 miles or 50 minutes from Bethel via Route 5. It's about 20 miles or 25 minutes to Cornish via Route 5 and about 15 miles or 20 minutes to Bridgton via Route 302.

Cornish

Folded in the foothills of the White Mountains and well off the radar screen of most tourists, Cornish, neighboring Limerick, and Newfield are charming rural towns filled with architectural gems and dotted with antiques and eclectic shops. Lovely to visit spring through fall, they're especially treasured during foliage season, not only for the leaves but also for the apple harvest. Local historians boast that in the 1850s many of Cornish's splendid homes were moved by oxen from other parts of town to the main drag to be close to the stagecoach route. **Limerick,** which edges Lake Sokokis, provides easy access to **Newfield,** home to an amazing country museum. The Cornish area is convenient to Sebago, Portland, and the Southern Coast.

SIGHTS
Porter Covered Bridge

Just west of Cornish, this lovely bridge linking Oxford and York Counties and the towns of Porter and Parsonsfield spans the Ossipee River. Officially known as the **Parsonsfield-Porter Historical Bridge,** the current 152-foot double-pan, Paddleford construction dates from 1859. The best view is from Route 160, just south of what passes as downtown.

◖ Willowbrook Museum Village

Plan a day trip to tiny Newfield, home to the fascinating 19th-century **Willowbrook Museum Village** (Main St., just north of Rte. 11, Newfield, 207/793-2784, www.willowbrookmuseum.org, 10am-5pm Thurs.-Mon.

late May-mid-Oct., $12 adults, $7 ages 13-18, $5 ages 6-12, $9 over age 64, free under age 6). The museum, created by Don King (not the boxing promoter) and his wife, Pan, comprises 25 buildings listed on the National Register of Historic Places in a country village setting. While you can breeze through in an hour or so, you'll want to linger for half a day. What's to see? Two historical homes, a carriage house, a country store, a schoolhouse, a magnificently restored carousel, and incredible collections of carriages and sleighs, farm tools, toys, and other curious antiquities. Occasionally there are demonstrations, but for the most part Willowbrook is yours to discover, a snapshot in time. Bring a picnic (or visit the café and ice cream shop) and a camera and soak up the rural history on this incredibly peaceful site.

ENTERTAINMENT AND EVENTS

The **Ossipee Valley Fair** is an old-fashioned four-day agricultural fair with tractor pulling, animal exhibits, live entertainment, food booths, games, and a carnival. It's in South Hiram the second weekend in July.

Every summer, the **Saco River Festival Association** (Parsonfield, 207/625-7116, www.sacoriverfestival.org) sponsors a concert series at the Old Cornish Fairgrounds.

The **Ossipee Valley Music Festival** (www.ossipeevalley.com), a long weekend of bluegrass, fiddling, and acoustical music, takes place in mid-July.

Apple Acres Farm (www.appleacresfarm. com) hosts an autumn **bluegrass festival**.

A great time to visit Cornish is the last Saturday in September, when the annual **Apple Festival** (207/625-7447, www.cornish-maine. org), held in downtown Cornish, celebrates the area's major crop with music, a crafts fair, and even an apple-pie contest. You can overdose all day on apples and stock up for winter, and do it just as fall foliage is starting to appear. For a spectacular panorama of fall colors along the Ossipee and Saco River Valleys, drive up Towles Hill Road (left turn, just west of town).

SHOPPING

Antiques and artisans' shops dominate Cornish's genuinely quaint and walkable downtown. Here's a sampling. **Cornish Trading Company** (19 Main St./Rte. 25, 207/625-8387) is a terrific group antiques shop in the handsome three-story Masonic building. Across the street is **Full Circle Artisan's Gallery** (12 Main St., 207/625-7725), carrying fine craft by regional artists. For vintage commercial signage

and memorabilia, visit **The Smith Co.** (Main St., 207/625-6030). **Village Jewelers** (Main St., 207/625-8958) has a drool-worthy selection of Maine gems. **Evie's Eclectic Collections** (Main St., 207/625-8916) delivers on its name, with merchandise displayed in a beautifully restored mansion. After exhausting the Main Street shops, head up High Street. **Cottage Treasures** (47 High Rd., 207/625-2301) specializes in porcelain, glass, and vintage linens. Antiques jumble with junktiques at **Red House Antiques** (53 High Rd., 207/625-8322).

The shopping isn't limited to Cornish. **At Once All Agog** (24A Main St., Limerick, 207/793-2464) sells puzzles, toys, games, and books.

RECREATION

Back Country Excursions (43 Woodward Rd., Parsonfield, 207/625-8189, www.bikebackcountry.com) has 30 miles of dedicated mountain-biking trails for all abilities as well as a technical terrain park for thrill-seekers on an 8,800-acre private recreational and logging

Antiques shops and independent boutiques draw shoppers to downtown Cornish.

preserve. Instruction and guided rides are available. Rates are $60 for a full day with lunch, $50 without lunch, or $30 half day, which includes access to shower facilities and maps. Bikes rent for $30-45, and a helmet is $5. You also can rent a canoe for paddling local waterways for $20. Camping and lodging are available.

ACCOMMODATIONS

Smack-dab downtown is the delightfully old-fashioned **Cornish Inn** (2 High St., Cornish, 207/625-8501, www.cornishinn.com, $85-165), a three-story gently updated classic with a wraparound porch and an on-site dining room serving dinner. The 16 air-conditioned guest rooms are simple yet comfortable. Rates include a self-serve light continental breakfast, but there are options for full breakfasts within walking distance.

The barn-red **Midway Country Lodging** (712 S. Hiram Rd., Cornish, 207/625-8835, www.mainemidwaylodging.com, $84-109) is a motel-like inn, or maybe an inn-like motel. Country is the theme, and all rooms have air-conditioning, TVs, Wi-Fi, fridges, microwaves, and phones; some have a whirlpool bath, a video player, or a balcony. The outdoor pool has a nice mountain view, and the landscaped grounds even have a fountain.

Here's a budget find: The handsome brick Greek Revival-style **Jeremiah Mason Bed & Breakfast** (40 Main St., Limerick, 207/793-4858, www.jeremiahmasonhouse.com, $55-75), built by a wealthy banker in 1859, retains the elegance of a bygone era. Spacious antiques-accented guest rooms have chandeliers, marble fireplaces, and floor-to-ceiling windows. Rates include a full breakfast; less expensive rooms have half-baths.

FOOD

In addition to pick-your-own apples in autumn, **Apple Acres Farm** (363 Durgintown Rd., Hiram, 207/625-4777) is justifiably popular for apple-cider doughnuts, ice cream, doughnut ice-cream sandwiches, pies, and even lobster rolls.

Fresh and seasonal are the hallmarks at the **Cornish Inn** (2 High St., Cornish, 207/625-8501, www.cornishinn.com, 11:30am-2:30pm Sat. and 4:30pm-9pm Wed.-Sun., $13-22). The menu changes weekly to reflect what's locally available, and often is drawn from the inn's gardens.

Krista's Restaurant (2 Main St., Cornish, 207/625-3600, www.kristasrestaurant.com, 11:30am-8pm Mon., Wed., Thurs., 11:30am-9pm Fri., 7am-9pm Sat., 7am-8pm Sun., $8-26) serves fabulous fresh fare in huge portions in its cheery air-conditioned dining rooms and on a screened deck overhanging a gurgling stream. Dinner options range from burgers and salads to entrées such as Tuscan baked haddock and herb-crusted prime rib.

Fresh seafood is served at **Bay Haven Lobster Pound Two** (Maple St., Cornish, 207/625-7303, 11am-8pm daily, $10-22), operated by a fishing family. Portions are very generous; prices are reasonable. Dress down, order the humongous fisherman's platter—and plan on sharing.

Good food at a good price served in a pleasant country-style dining room across from Lake Sokokis have made **The Peppermill Restaurant** (171 Washington St., Limerick, 207/793-2500, 7am-8pm Sun.-Thurs., 7am-9pm Fri.-Sat., dinner $8-16) a local favorite for breakfast, lunch, and dinner. Dinner choices range from comfort foods to surf and turf, with prime rib a specialty on Friday and Saturday nights.

Heather and Gary Labbe have turned four antiques- and treasure-filled rooms in their lovely Carpenter-Gothic home into the **Clipper Merchant Tea House** (58 Main St., Limerick, 207/793-3500, www.clippermerchant.com, 11am-4pm Wed.-Sat. mid-May-early Dec.). Begin with the lavender lemonade, then opt either for lunch ($10-14) or, even better, the indulgent high tea ($40 for two).

INFORMATION

Area info is available from **The Cornish Association of Businesses** (207/625-8856, www.cornish-maine.org) and www.limerick-maine.com.

GETTING THERE AND AROUND

Cornish is roughly 20 miles or 25 minutes from Fryeburg via Route 5. It's about 23 miles or 35 minutes to Bridgton via Routes 5 and 117. It's about 35 miles or 50 minutes to Portland via Route 25.

Sebago and Long Lakes

Maine's Lakes region, the area along the shores of Sebago and Long Lakes, includes the two major hubs of **Bridgton** (pop. 5,210) and **Naples** (pop. 3,872), as well as the smaller communities of **Sebago** (pop. 1,719) and **Harrison** (pop. 2,730) and the larger communities of **Raymond** (pop. 4,436), **Casco** (pop. 3,742), and **Windham** (pop. 17,001). All are in Cumberland County.

Settled in 1768, Bridgton was incorporated in 1794; Naples was not incorporated until 1834. When the summer-vacation boom began in the mid-19th century and then erupted after the Civil War, visitors flowed into this area via stagecoach, the Cumberland and Oxford Canal, and later the Bridgton and Saco Railroad.

The 28-lock canal, opened in 1830 and shut down in 1870, connected the Fore River in Portland with Sebago and Long Lakes. Its only working remnant is the Songo Lock in Naples, on the Songo River between Brandy Pond and Sebago Lake.

Sebago is an apt Native American word meaning "large, open water"; it's the state's second-largest lake (after Moosehead), and fluky winds can kick up suddenly and toss around little boats, so be prudent. Now a major water source for Greater Portland, the lake reportedly served as the crossroads for major Native American trading routes, and artifacts still occasionally surface in the Sebago Basin area.

Engage in a heart-to-heart with an adult vacationing in this area and you're likely to find someone trying to recapture the past—the carefree days at summer camp in the Sebago and Long Lakes region. The shores of Sebago, Long, and Highland Lakes shelter dozens of children's camps that have created several generations of Maine enthusiasts—"people from away" who still can't resist an annual visit. Unless your own kids are in camp, however, or you're terminally masochistic, do not appear in Bridgton, Naples, or surrounding communities on the last weekend in July. Parents, grandparents, and surrogate parents all show up then for the midseason summer-camp break, and there isn't a bed or restaurant seat to be had in the entire county and maybe beyond. Gridlock is the rule.

Aside from that, this mountain-lake setting has incredible locales for canoeing, swimming, hiking, fishing, golfing, camping, biking, ice skating, snowshoeing, and skiing. Maine's first ski lift opened in 1938 on Pleasant Mountain, now the Shawnee Peak ski area.

These lakes are quite convenient to Portland—Sebago is the large body of water you'll see to the west as you descend into the Portland Jetport.

SIGHTS
Narramissic, the Peabody-Fitch Farm

Built in 1797 and converted to Federal style in 1828, the Peabody-Fitch Farm is the crown jewel of the **Bridgton Historical Society** (207/647-3699, www.bridgtonhistory.org). Still undergoing restoration—now to the pre-Civil War era—the homestead includes a carriage house, an ell, a barn, a blacksmith shop, and historic gardens. The barn has its own

WESTERN LAKES

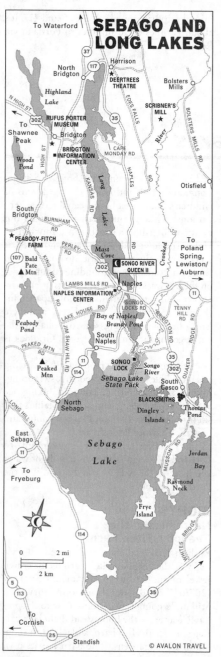

story: It's known as the Temperance Barn because the landowners were avowed teetotalers, so the volunteer barn-raisers earned only water for their efforts. Narramissic is a relatively recent name, given to it by the 20th-century owner who donated it to the historical society in 1986. The name is a Native American word meaning "hard to find," reflecting her lengthy search for a family summer home. But it also suits the circuitous route, fortunately signposted, to the South Bridgton farm from downtown Bridgton: Take Main Street to Route 117 south and turn left on Route 107, then right on Ingalls Road. A season highlight is the Woodworkers' Show in July. The grounds are open during daylight hours for hiking and picnicking; call for open house hours.

◖ Songo River Queen II

Berthed in downtown Naples is the **Songo River Queen II** (Bay of Naples Causeway/Rte. 302, Naples, 207/693-6861, www.songoriver-queen.net, $15-25 adults, $8-13 children), a 93-foot Mississippi stern-wheeler replica that operates one- and two-hour narrated cruises on Long Lake mid-May-mid-October. Onboard are restrooms and a snack bar. Cruises operate daily, rain or shine; weekends spring and fall.

Presidential Maine

Inspired by a famous western Maine signpost giving directions to nine Maine towns named for foreign cities and countries, Boy Scouts in Casco decided to create some competition—a directional sign for 10 Maine towns named for U.S. presidents. The marker stands next to the village green in **Casco,** at the corner of Route 121 and Leach Hill Road, pointing to towns such as Washington (76 miles), Lincoln (175 miles), Madison (96 miles), and Monroe (114 miles). There's even a Clinton (84 miles).

If you're here in the fall, take time to detour briefly to Casco's "million-dollar view." Continue south from the signpost less than two miles on Route 121 to Route 11 (Pike Corner), turn right (west) and go about 0.5 mile to Quaker Ridge Road and turn left (south).

Views are spectacular along here, especially from the Quaker Hill area.

Rufus Porter Museum

The early 19th-century itinerant artist's murals and paintings are the focus at the **Rufus Porter Museum and Cultural Heritage Center** (Main St., Bridgton, 207/647-2828, www.rufusportermuseum.org, 10am-4pm Tues.-Sat. late June-late Aug., noon-4pm Wed.-Sat. early Sept.-mid-Oct., $8 adults, $7 seniors, free under age 16), now located in the John and Maria Webb House. Porter, the founder of *Scientific American* magazine, painted landscapes on the walls of homes throughout New England. Most were unsigned, and some of Porter's murals are displayed in the front hall of the house. During one week in July, the museum hosts a **Cultural Heritage Series** with classes, workshops, and lectures concentrating on the arts and sciences of the 19th and 20th centuries. Other programs and classes are also offered. The museum is in a barn-red house on the northern edge of downtown Bridgton. Note that the museum is staffed by volunteers, so it's wise to verify hours.

Scribner's Mill

In use by three generations of the Scribner family between 1847 and 1962, **Scribner's Saw Mill and Homestead** (207/585-6455, Scribner's Mill Rd., Harrison, www.scribnersmill.org, 1pm-4pm Sat. July-Aug.) is an accurately reconstructed, working, sash sawmill museum. The best time to visit is during the annual Back to the Past weekend in August, with tours, demonstrations, and children's activities.

ENTERTAINMENT

Tucked away on a back road in Harrison, east of Long Lake, dramatic-looking 278-seat **Deertrees Theatre and Cultural Center** (156 Deertrees Rd., Harrison, 207/583-6747, www.deertreestheatre.org) is a must-see even if you don't attend a performance. The acoustically superior building, constructed of rose hemlock in 1936, is on the National Register of Historic Places and has seen the likes of Rudy Vallée, Ethel Barrymore, Tallulah Bankhead, and Henry Winkler; restoration of the rustic building in the 1990s has given it an exciting new life. During the summer season, there's something going on nearly every night—musicals, plays, comedy, folk, jazz, blues, and weekly children's performances. The theater is signposted off Route 117 in the Harrison woods. Also here is the **BackStage Gallery** (10am-5pm Tues.-Sat. and one hour before performances).

Mid-July-mid-August, the **Sebago-Long Lake Chamber Music Festival** (207/583-6747, www.sebagomusicfestival.org, $25 adults, free under 22) brings Tuesday evening chamber-music concerts to Harrison's Deertrees Theatre. Advance booking is essential for this popular series, founded in 1975.

Sunday evening **band concerts** around the gazebo behind the Naples Information Center are free mid-July-mid-August. Bring a chair or blanket to the Village Green (Rte. 302, Naples).

Live entertainment is scheduled most weekends at **Bray's Brewpub and Eatery** (Rte. 302 and Rte. 35, Naples, 207/693-6806, www.braysbrewpub.com).

One of a dying species, **Bridgton Drive-In** (Rte. 302, Bridgton, 207/647-8666, www.bridgtondrivein.com) screens a double feature beginning at dusk each night July-August.

FESTIVALS AND EVENTS

The **Shawnee Peak** ski area (207/647-8444, www.shawneepeak.com) has a full schedule of family-oriented special events, including races, throughout the winter; call or check the website for information.

The **Maine Blues Festival** (www.mainebluesfestival.com), in June, celebrates Maine's blues artists.

The third Saturday in July, Bridgton is the scene of the **Annual Art in the Park** exhibition and sale, a mad success since its inception. Also in July is Bridgton's annual **Chickadee Quilters Show** (www.quiltguilds.com/maine.htm), with exhibits and sales of magnificent quilts and wall hangings at the Bridgton Town Hall.

FAMILY-SIZE ALPINE AREAS

Maine's big resorts get most of the attention, but for young families or anyone on a budget, the smaller resorts provide not only a fun experience but also a good value. Perhaps the vertical range isn't as grand, but really, how often do you ski 2,000 feet without stopping? All of these little guys have night skiing, most have tubing parks, and some have cross-country trails too. If you're searching for areas with soul, for friendly faces, and places where kids matter, head to these slopes.

Lost Valley (200 Lost Valley Rd., off Young's Corner Rd., Auburn, 207/784-1561, www.lostvalleyski.com) is a vest-pocket ski area secreted in the barely rolling countryside outside Auburn. Don't be deceived by the hill's diminutive size. Although the vertical drop is only 240 feet, it was enough to produce four Olympians: Karl Anderson and Anna, Julie, and Rob Parisien. This is an especially family-friendly area; the base lodge doubles as the local babysitting service—parents just naturally watch out for one another's kids. According to Julie Parisien, who has coached local youth, you may be able to make only 10 turns from top to bottom, but that's 10 good turns. And that's what matters.

Maine's oldest ski area is **Shawnee Peak** (Rte. 302, Bridgton, 207/647-8444, www.shawneepeak.com), an increasingly popular destination given its proximity to Portland (45 miles). I have a soft spot for the area where I spent my youth—bring your family, and you'll likely understand why. The setting is rural and undeveloped, and Pleasant Mountain appears to rise out of Moose Pond. The views, which take in Mount Washington and the Presidential Range of the White Mountains, are calming, almost inspirational. It's one of the largest night-skiing facilities, acreage-wise, in New England. Arrive at night, and you'll notice that the trails spell out the word LOV in 1960s-block-style lettering. The mountain skis bigger than its 1,300-foot vertical range indicates, as it has two faces, with open slopes on one and squiggly trails ribboning the other.

For anyone weak in the wallet or overawed by megaresorts, **Mount Abram** (Howe Hill Rd., off Rte. 26, Locke Mills, 207/875-5002, www.skimtabram.com) is the solution. This longtime family favorite is something of a sleeper. Most folks drive right by on their way to glitzy Sunday River, just up the road. A savvy few turn off Route 26 in Locke Mills, drawn by this resort's commitment to family skiing and a decent 1,150-foot vertical range. The segregated learning area, tubing park, night lights, cross-country loop, low-key atmosphere, and lack of crowds make it a real gem.

A real success story is **Black Mountain of Maine** (39 Glover Rd., Rumford, 207/364-8977, www.skiblackmountain.org), where prices are low and spirit is high. Recent investments in the 1,150-vertical-foot hill include new lifts, new trails, adding snowmaking, and making it smoke-free. Another plus is the cross-country trail system, designed by two-time Olympian Chummy Broomhall.

The Farmington Ski Club operates **Titcomb Mountain Ski Area** (Morrison Hill Rd., West Farmington, 207/778-9031, www.titcombmountain.com), an all-volunteer operation with a modest 340-foot vertical range. It's the hill where two-time Olympic gold medalist Seth Wescott played as a youth. In addition to the alpine terrain, there are nine miles of groomed trails for cross-country skiing and snowboarding (a potential solution for mixed marriages or partnerships). The operating schedule coincides with school hours, so it's open late afternoon and evenings, weekends, and daily during vacation weeks. Yes, it's a club, but nonmembers are welcome.

SHOPPING

Anchored by **Renys** (Main St., 207/647-3711), where you can buy just about anything portable at great prices, Bridgton offers the best collection of interesting shops, with most housed in historic buildings along the town's main drag. But there are other stores worth seeking in the area.

Art, Crafts, Gifts, and Antiques

More than 60 member artists exhibit their work at **Gallery 302** (112 Main St., Bridgton, 207/647-2787), home of the nonprofit Bridgton Art Guild. The co-op sponsors the town's annual Art in the Park, and the gallery hosts exhibits, receptions, classes, and workshops.

About a dozen vendors sell antiques and other finds at **Harry Barker's Emporium** (142 Main St., 207/647-4500). And the name? The shop is a fundraising effort by the Harvest Hills animal shelter.

A onetime Unitarian church is the setting for the carefully chosen and superbly eclectic inventory at **Craftworks** (53 Main St., Bridgton, 207/647-5436), a Bridgton landmark since the early 1970s.

Cry of the Loon (Rte. 302, South Casco, 207/655-5060) has gifts and a tasteful, eclectic mix of gourmet condiments, Maine crafts, antiques, furniture, and much more spread out in three buildings on both sides of the road.

Since the 1970s, **Hole in the Wall Studioworks** (1544 Roosevelt Trail/Rte. 302, Raymond, 207/655-4592, www.holeinthewallstudioworks.com) has been selling an especially fine selection of American-made art and crafts. Don't miss the sculpture garden.

Maine-made crafts and a luscious selection of yarns are at **Rosemary's Gift Shop** (39 Roosevelt Trail/Rte. 302, Windham, 207/894-5770).

Books

Bridgton Books (140 Main St., Bridgton, 207/647-2122), an independent bookstore, carries an excellent selection of books (20,000 titles include new, selected used, and a large bargain-book section), cards, puzzles, and more.

Winery

Yes, there's even a winery in the region. **Blacksmiths** (Rte. 302, South Casco, 207/655-3292, www.blacksmithswinery.com) produces more than a dozen wines on the premises and offers tastings.

RECREATION
Sebago Lake State Park

Fourth largest of Maine's state parks, 1,400-acre **Sebago Lake State Park** (11 Park Access Rd., Naples, 207/693-6613 late June-Labor Day, 207/693-6231 off-season, www.parksandlands.com, $6.50 nonresident adults, $4.50 Maine resident adults, $1.50 nonresident seniors, $1 ages 5-11) is one of the most popular—so don't anticipate peace and quiet here in July-August. Swimming and picnicking are superb, fishing is so-so, and personal watercraft are an increasing hazard. During the summer, park officials organize lectures, hikes, and other activities; the schedule is posted at the gate. The park is open mid-May-October, but there's winter access to 4.5 miles of groomed cross-country skiing trails—mostly beginner terrain. It's also ideal for snowshoeing.

You can reach the park's separate picnicking and camping areas from Route 302 in Casco. Take State Park Road to the fork, where you go left to the picnic area or right to Songo Lock and the camping area. Both sections have sandy beaches. Or, from downtown Naples, take Route 11/114 to Thompson Point Road and follow the signs.

Walks and Hikes

The **Lakes Environmental Association** (207/647-8580, www.mainelakes.org) hosts guided hikes, birding programs, talks, and other events throughout the year; check the website for current listings.

DOUGLAS MOUNTAIN PRESERVE

Douglas Mountain (also called Douglas Hill) is one of southern Maine's most popular hikes, so you probably won't be alone. Take a brochure from the registration box, and follow the moderate Woods Trail to the 1,415-foot summit, a

© HILARY NANGLE

Sebago is especially popular with boating enthusiasts.

30-minute walk at most. At the top is a 0.75-mile nature-trail loop, plus a 16-foot stone tower with a head-spinning view. In the fall, the vistas are incomparable. Be eco-sensitive and stick to the trails in this 169-acre preserve. Pets are not allowed. The trails are accessible dawn-dusk. The trailhead is off Route 107 in Sebago: Take Dyke Mountain Road 0.8 mile to Douglas Mountain Road, then follow signs to the parking area ($3).

HOLT POND AND BALD PATE MOUNTAIN

The Holt Pond Preserve comprises 450 mostly wetland acres in Naples and is owned by the **Lakes Environmental Association** (207/647-8580, www.mainelakes.org). A trail with boardwalks makes it easy to spot the flora and fauna in the wetlands and bogs. You can download an interpretive guide from the website. The Town Farm Brook Trail connects to twin-peaked Bald Pate Mountain, part of a 486-acre preserve in South Bridgton maintained by the **Loon Echo Land Trust** (207/647-4352, www.loonecholandtrust.org). Bald Pate's

trail network is open year-round, and there's a kiosk with trail maps at the parking lot (signposted off Rte. 107). The first peak has views to Pleasant Mountain, and the summit peak is bald, with panoramic views. Pack a lunch and plan for a full day if you decide to connect the two preserves. If you come in winter, some of Bald Pate's trails are groomed for cross-country skiing.

PLEASANT MOUNTAIN

Loon Echo Land Trust (207/647-4352, www.loonecholandtrust.org) also manages this nearly 2,000-acre preserve on the eastern sides of the Shawnee Peak alpine resort on Pleasant Mountain in Bridgton. Six interconnecting trails provide access to the main summit—at 2,000 feet it's the highest mountain in southern Maine and a landmark for pilots. The most popular—and relatively easiest for kids—is the Ledges (or Moose) Trail. In late July, allow four hours for the 3.5-mile round-trip so you can pick blueberries on the open ledges midway up. At the top is a disused fire tower and plenty of space for spreading out a picnic overlooking panoramic vistas of woods, lakes, and mountains. The mountain straddles the Denmark-Bridgton town line as well as the Cumberland-Oxford County line. From Bridgton, drive 5.75 miles west on Route 302 to Mountain Road (just after the causeway over Moose Pond). Turn left (south) at signs for Shawnee Peak ski area and go 3.3 miles to the trailhead for the Ledges (or Moose) Trail; parking is limited.

PONDICHERRY PRESERVE

Smack in downtown Bridgton is this 66-acre preserve, with 2 miles of trails, many with boardwalks, lacing woodlands, fields, and wetlands, including a mile of stream frontage. Easiest access is from the public parking lot behind the Magic Lantern Theater. Pick up a trail map at the trailhead kiosk. Leashed dogs are allowed on one designated trail.

Swimming

Besides two sandy beaches at Sebago Lake State Park, you can also take a dip while picnicking at an unmarked picnic area on the island midway across Bridgton's Route 302 Moose Pond causeway. Look for a gated dirt road into the woods on the north side. There are lakeside picnic tables, a small playground, and a portable toilet.

Golf

The 18-hole **Bridgton Highlands Country Club** (Highland Ridge Rd., Bridgton, 207/647-3491, www.bridgtonhighlands.com) course is outstandingly scenic and very popular, especially at the height of summer. Starting times are required. Also here are a handsome clubhouse, tennis courts, a pro shop, and a snack bar.

Less expensive but also scenic is the **Naples Golf and Country Club** (Rte. 114, Naples, 207/693-6424, www.naplesgolfcourse.com), established in 1922. Light meals are available at the clubhouse, and there's a pro shop. On midsummer weekends, call for a starting time.

The championship-level **Point Sebago Golf Club** (Rte. 302, Casco, 207/655-2747, www. pointsebago.com, May-mid-Oct.) is part of a onetime low-key campground transformed into the 800-acre family-oriented Club Med-style Point Sebago Resort. Call for starting times at the 18-hole course, which is open to the public. Golf-and-lodging packages are available.

Water Sports

You can rent a pontoon boat, a powerboat, or if you must, a personal watercraft or PWC, often referred to by the trademark name Jet Ski. The latter have become a major itch on huge Sebago Lake as well as many other Maine lakes, and there's no gray area in the opinion department. The biggest objections are noise pollution and excessive speed. The state requires PWCs to be licensed as powerboats, but regulations are weak, and the state legislature has taken little action, and inadequate funding has led to inadequate enforcement. Each year fatalities occur, spurring towns to try, usually unsuccessfully, to ban or limit PWCs. If you do rent one, play by the rules, exercise caution, and operate at sensible speeds.

Both **Naples Marina** (Rte. 302 and Rte. 114, Naples, 207/693-6254, www.naplesmarina-maine.com) and **Causeway Marina** (Rte. 302, Naples, 207/693-6832, www.causewayma-rina.com) rent powerboats, including pontoon boats, runabouts, and fishing boats.

The **Sports Haus** (103 Main St., Bridgton, 207/647-5100) rents canoes ($30/day, $150/week), kayaks ($25-35/day, $125-180/week), sunfish sailboats (from $125 for three days), paddleboards (from $40/day), and other water toys.

If you've brought a **canoe or kayak,** don't launch it into Sebago Lake; save it for the smaller lakes and ponds, where the winds are more predictable and the boat traffic is less congested. Long Lake is also a possibility if you put in at Harrison on the east side.

ACCOMMODATIONS
Bed-and-Breakfasts

Just around the corner from the Bridgton House and off the main road, ◖ **The Noble**

House (81 Highland Rd., Bridgton, 207/647-3733, www.noblehousebb.com, year-round, $165-275) is a grand turn-of-the-20th-century Victorian with nine warmly decorated guest rooms, all with air-conditioning and Wi-Fi, some with screened porches or jetted tubs. Guests have use of a comfortable sitting room with a TV and a video player, a living room with a grand piano and an organ, and a great veranda. A short walk brings you to Bridgton's Highland Park on the lake, with swimming, picnicking, and boating access. Rates include a full breakfast and access to a guest pantry with a bottomless cookie jar.

Front and center on the action, yet set off the highway just enough to provide privacy, the three-story, brick **Augustus Bove House** (Corner Rtes. 302 and 114, 207/693-6365, www.naplesmaine.com, $145-250) has been welcoming guests since 1851. Innkeepers Arlene and David Stetson have been here for about three decades. The eight rooms, two suites, and two cottages in the main house have a/c, Wi-Fi, TV, and Arlene's handmade quilts. Rooms in the front have lake views; those in the back are quieter. Everyone can enjoy the views from the porch and gardens. A full breakfast is served.

Innkeeper and talented chef Keith Neubert makes his guests feel as important as the Hollywood stars whose names grace the 16 meticulously decorated guest rooms at **The Inn at Long Lake** (15 Lake House Rd., Naples, 207/693-6226 or 800/437-0328, www.innatlonglake.com, year-round, $130-200 d). Built in the early 1900s, the inn is decorated with Victorian Revival flair. All rooms have Wi-Fi; some have lake views. The lovely grounds include a veranda, a gazebo, and a garden. Rates include a multicourse breakfast and afternoon refreshments. Packages with dinner may be available.

Wake up with a morning swim at the lakefront **Pleasant Lake House Bed and Breakfast** (1024 Meadow Rd., Casco, 207/627-6975, www.pleasantlakehouse.com, year-round, $155-250), an especially family-friendly spot. Choose from four guest rooms and a suite in the main house, built in 1836, or a cottage with a full kitchen. Guests have use of the private beach and dock.

Motel

Alyssa's Motel on Thomas Pond (1 Roosevelt Trail, Casco, 207/655-2223, www.alyssasmotel.com, $145-270) has seven rooms and two suites decorated with a light country touch. All face the pond and have TVs, air-conditioning, and Wi-Fi; some have microwaves and fridges. Guests have use of a canoe, a paddleboat, and the dock; there's a public boat launch across the street.

Cottage Colonies and Resorts

Welcome to heaven: At ◖ **Migis Lodge** (Migis Lodge Rd., South Casco, 207/655-4524, www.migis.com, no credit cards), on the east side of Sebago Lake, guests often confirm their next year's July or August booking before they depart for home. Don't let that dissuade you; there often are openings. The rustic elegance of 100-acre Migis, along with attentive service and a fabulous lakeside setting, have drawn big-name guests through the years—ever since the resort was established in the early 20th century as lodging for the parents of summer campers. Guests stay in spacious cabins within steps of the lake; each has a wood-burning fieldstone fireplace and is decorated in inviting Polo Ralph Lauren-meets-L. L. Bean style. Men wear jackets for dinner, and there is a supervised meal and playtime for children during dinner hours. All this comes at a price, which includes almost everything, from sailboats, canoes, and kayaks to island cookouts, waterskiing, tennis courts, and even a weekly lobster bake; exclusions include boats with motors and alcohol. Maine sales tax plus a 15 percent service charge is added on to lodging, food, and beverages. Rates for the 35 lake-view 1-6-bedroom cottages and six lodge rooms begin around $280 pp, varying with the season and the accommodation. This is a fabulous place for an autumn foliage retreat. Pets are not allowed.

Sebago Lake Lodge and Cottages (White's

Bridge Rd., Windham, 207/892-2698, www. sebagolakelodge.com) sit on a point of land with 700 feet of frontage on Sebago Basin adjacent to White's Bridge. Picnic and cookout facilities, free use of canoes and kayaks, boat slips and moorings, and an adults-only fitness room are just a few of the amenities that make this spot special. Accommodations are rustic, dated, and in need of TLC. Guest rooms in the main lodge, with its wonderful wraparound porch, have kitchenettes or kitchen privileges and nice screened porches. A continental breakfast is served in the gathering room, which also has a fireplace and a TV. The lake-view cottages have one or two bedrooms (guests provide their own linen and paper products); most have screened porches. Pets are allowed in the cottages by arrangement for $15/day, but not in the lodge. Lodge rooms ($165-225) rent by the night; cottages are available Saturday-Saturday ($1,050-1,795/week). Discounts apply early and late in the season.

Camping

Camping is especially popular in this part of Maine, and many campgrounds have long-term RV or "immobile" home rentals (also known as "seasonal sites"), so you'll need to plan ahead and reserve sites well in advance. Be forewarned, though, that if you're looking for a wilderness camping experience, especially in midsummer, you probably ought to head for the hills. Many of the campgrounds in this area feature nonstop organized fun, which is fine for enthusiastic families, but the intense activity can be overwhelming for those seeking a quiet respite.

It's crucial to book well ahead to land one of the 250 sites at **Sebago Lake State Park** (11 Park Access Rd., Naples, 207/693-6613 late June-Labor Day, www.parksandlands.com, reservations in Maine 800/332-1501, out of state 207/624-9950 or www.campwithme.com). Despite its popularity, well-spaced sites provide some privacy. Rates are $26 nonresidents, $15 Maine residents with a $2/night reservation fee. Some sites have water and electric hookups ($37.45 nonresidents, $26.75 Maine residents).

Seasonal Rentals

Krainin Real Estate (800/639-2321, www. krainin.com) handles weekly and monthly rentals for cottages on Sebago and Long Lakes as well as many of the surrounding smaller lakes and ponds. Krainin also arranges rentals on **Frye Island,** a 1,000-acre summer community in the middle of Sebago Lake that's accessible only by car ferry.

FOOD

Restaurant hours noted are for peak season but are subject to change. It's always wise to call ahead. Restaurants in this region tend to get swamped in summer, especially when camper parents are dropping off, picking up, or visiting their kids. Reservations are wise, and don't be surprised if the restaurant seems short staffed or slow.

Local Flavors

The **Naples Farmers Market** sets up on the Naples village green, off Route 302, 10am-2pm Thursday early May-mid-September. The **Bridgton Farmers Market** is held 8am-1pm Saturday mid-May-early October on Depot Street, behind Renys.

Conveniently situated across from a lakeside picnic area at the intersection of Routes 302 and 85, **The Good Life Market** (1297 Roosevelt Trail, Raymond, 207/655-1196, www.thegoodlifemarket.com, 7am-7pm daily) is a great place to pick up sandwiches, salads, fresh-baked treats, wine, and specialty foods. There's even a very inexpensive kids' menu.

Just south of downtown Bridgton at the Route 117 intersection is a terrific natural-foods store and café, **Morning Dew** (19 Sandy Creek Rd., Bridgton, 207/647-4003, www. morningdewnatural.com, 9am-6pm Mon.-Fri., 9am-5:30pm Sat., 10am-5pm Sun.). The menu goes far beyond usual natural-foods fare, with sandwiches, grilled items, burritos, salads, soups, and bagels.

Breakfast is an all-day affair at **Chute's Cafe and Bakery** (Rte. 302, South Casco, 207/655-7111, 6am-2pm Mon.-Sat., 6am-1pm Sun.), an always-popular local choice for good home cooking. Prices are low and portions ample. Lunch is served beginning at 11am.

Beth's Kitchen Cafe (108 Main St., Bridgton, 207/647-5211, 7am-3pm daily) is a pleasant spot for breakfast, create-your-own sandwiches, soups, pizzas, and baked goods.

Don't be fooled by the convenience store appearance and the gas pumps. **Standard Gastropub** (233 Main St., Bridgton, 207/647-4100, www.standardgastropub.com, 6am-midnight Mon.-Sat., from 8am Sun., $6-18) is a destination for fans of barbecued and smoked foods. Sure, there are breakfast, lunch, and dinner menus, but don't miss the chalkboard specials. The space is small, the flavors big. Tuck into a picnic table or take it to go, and fill up the gas tank before hitting the road.

Casual Dining

For more than 25 years, the **Black Horse Tavern** (26 Rte. 302, Bridgton, 207/647-5300, www.theblackhorsetavern.com, 11am-9pm Mon.-Sat., 10am-9pm Sun., $9-25) has been a reliable choice for good food in a pleasant, tavern-style atmosphere. A kids' menu is available.

Café by day, bistro by night is the slogan at the **Black Bear Café** (215 Roosevelt Trail, Naples, 207/693-4770, www.theblackbearcafe.com, from 4pm daily $11-23). The pleasant dining area is accented with a tin ceiling and local artwork. Dinner choices—burgers, salads, pizzas, and entrées such as lasagna and chicken saltimbocca—as well as a kids' menu make it easy to please everyone. An early-bird menu served 4pm-5:30pm Monday-Friday is $13 for salad, beverage, entrée, and dessert. On Sunday evenings there's a traditional Irish music session with local musicians.

For brews, burgers, and bands, head to **Bray's Brewpub and Eatery** (Rte. 302 and Rte. 35, Naples, 207/693-6806, www.braysbrewpub.com, from 11:30am daily, $9-20). Bray's, located in a Victorian farmhouse, is the pioneer brewpub in this part of Maine. A pub menu with lighter fare is served all day; heftier entrées are available in the evening. Stick with the simpler fare. Live bands play on weekends.

Merced's on Brandy Pond (770 Roosevelt Trail, Naples, 207/693-5332, www.mercedsonbrandypond.com, 4pm-9pm Mon.-Wed., noon-9pm Thurs.-Sat., 10am-9pm Sun., $10-25), sandwiched between Brandy Pond and Route 302, near the causeway, draws an older clientele. The food's decent, although it tends to be on the heavy side.

Nonguests can dine at **Migis Lodge** (Migis Lodge Rd., South Casco, 207/655-4524, www.migis.com) on Sebago Lake by advance reservation. A five-course dinner is served in the dining room Monday-Thursday, there's a waterside lobster bake on Friday nights, and a buffet dinner is available in the dining room on Saturday nights. Each is $50-55; dining room meals require a jacket.

Built on the site of an old mill, the **Old Mill Tavern** (56 Main St., Harrison, 207/583-9077, www.oldmilltavern.com, 11:30am-9pm daily, $9-36) serves everything from classic club sandwiches to Delmonico steak. The vibe is local, with live entertainment Thursday-Saturday nights and an open mic on Sunday evenings.

Locals recommend **Ruby Slippers Café and Bakery** (103 Norway Rd., Harrison, 207/583-4400, www.rubyslipperscafeandbakery.com, 8am-2pm Tues.-Thurs., 8am-8pm Fri.-Sat., 7am-noon Sun.), for its house-baked breads and hand-dipped chocolates and hearty breakfasts and lunches, but dinner ($7-16) is served on weekends.

INFORMATION AND SERVICES

The **Greater Bridgton Lakes Region Chamber of Commerce** (207/647-3472, www.mainelakeschamber.com) has an attractive information center (with public restrooms) 0.5 mile south of downtown Bridgton on Route 302.

The **Sebago Lakes Region Chamber of Commerce** (Windham 207/892-8265, Naples 207/693-3285, www.sebagolakeschamber.com) operates two information centers, one on Route 302 in Windham, and a seasonal one on the Naples village green.

GETTING THERE AND AROUND

Bridgton is roughly 23 miles or 35 minutes from Cornish via Routes 5 and 117. It's about 23 miles to Poland via Routes 302 and 11. It's 15 miles or 20 minutes to Fryeburg via Route 302 and 40 miles or one hour to Portland via Route 302.

Poland Spring

The section of Route 26 between the Maine Turnpike (I-95) exit in Gray and **Poland** (pop. 1,795) is rich in historical sites and worthwhile attractions, including a wildlife park, the last inhabited Shaker village, the remains of the Poland Spring House, and the source of famed Poland Spring water.

It was the water's fame that helped the Ricker family grow a small hotel into the Poland Spring House, a 300-room hotel that was an architectural and technological marvel. Also on their 5,000-acre property was the world's first resort golf course and one of the first courses designed by Donald Ross. During the resort's heyday in the early 20th century, the richest and most powerful people in the country gathered in Poland Spring to play golf and discuss world policy. Almost every U.S. president from Ulysses S. Grant to Theodore Roosevelt stayed here. Other guests and visitors of note include Babe Ruth, Alexander Graham Bell, Mae West, Betty Grable, and Judy Garland; Charles Lindberg flew over the hotel on July 25, 1927, but was unable to land because of the crowds.

The Poland Spring House was destroyed by fire in 1975, but the Maine State Building and the All Souls Chapel remain open to visitors, and the original spring that started it all can be viewed.

SIGHTS
◖ Poland Spring

Take a tour through the history of one of the world's most famous waters. It was Poland Spring Water that built Hiram Ricker's family empire, and a visit to Poland Spring should include **Poland Spring Preservation Park** (207/998-7143), home to the Poland Spring Museum and Spring House (both free), to learn about the legendary healing power of the water. The Maine State Building and All Souls Chapel are also both maintained by the **Poland Spring Preservation Society** (207/998-4142, www.polandspringps.org, 9am-4pm Thurs.-Sat. late May-early Sept., Fri.-Sat., to mid-Oct., $3 donation requested).

Begin at the **Poland Spring Museum,** where exhibits detail the history of the famed water and explain its origins. The water won the Medal of Excellence at the 1893 Chicago World's Fair, and the Grand Prize at the 1904 St. Louis World's Fair. Also displayed here is the Maine Golf Hall of Fame collection. After touring the exhibits, visit the Spring House. Nature trails lace the grounds and connect to the other sites.

The three-story octagonal **Maine State Building** was built as the state pavilion for the 1893 Chicago World's Fair. Afterward, Ricker bought it for $30,000 and moved it to Maine aboard a special freight train and then via horse-drawn wagon to Ricker Hill, where it was reassembled piece by piece. One year later, it reopened as a library and art museum as part of the Ricker family's centennial celebration of their settlement at Poland Spring. Although it suffered years of neglect in the mid-20th century, it has been restored and is now operated by the Poland Spring Preservation Society as a museum and art gallery.

The Ricker Family built the adjacent **All Souls Chapel** in 1912 with donations from guests and staff of the Poland Spring House. The 1926 Skinner pipe organ and a set of Westminster chimes are still in working order. The chapel is home to a summer concert series (7pm Mon., $7.50).

WESTERN LAKES

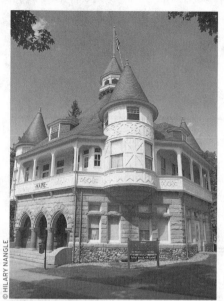

The Maine State Building at Poland Spring was originally built as a pavilion for the 1893 Chicago World's Fair.

© HILARY NANGLE

◖ Shaker Museum

Only a handful of Shakers remain in the world's last inhabited Shaker community, located three miles south of Poland Spring Resort. Nonetheless, the members of the United Society of Shakers, an 18th-century religious sect, keep a relatively high profile with a living-history museum, craft workshops, a store, publications, a mail-order herb and gift business, and even a music CD. (See their website for the wonderful herb and herbal tea catalog.) Each year more than 8,000 visitors arrive at the 1,800-acre **Sabbathday Lake Shaker Community** (707 Shaker Rd., New Gloucester, 207/926-4597, 10am-4:30pm, Mon.-Sat. www. shaker.lib.me.us) to catch a glimpse of an endangered lifestyle, and the Shakers welcome the public to their 10am Sunday religious service, where men and women enter through separate doors and sit separately. The 75-minute basic guided tour ($10 adults, $2 ages 2-12, $30 family) begin at 10:30 and are given every hour on the half hour, with the exception of the last tour of the day, given at 3:15pm. Check the special events calendar for workshops, demonstrations, herb garden tours, and the annual **Maine Festival of American Music: Its Roots and Traditions** concert weekend. No pets permitted on the grounds.

Twice each year on Saturdays in late May and mid-October, the Friends of the Shakers at Sabbathday Lake (www.friendsoftheshakers. org), a nonprofit group (annual membership $30 individual, $40 family), organizes **Friends' Work Day,** when 3-4 dozen volunteers show up at 10am to do spring and fall cleanup chores. The all-day work party includes a communal dinner.

Maine Wildlife Park

If you want to see where Maine's wild things are, visit the **Maine Wildlife Park** (56 Game Farm Rd., Gray, 207/657-4977, www. mainewildlifepark.com, 9:30am-6pm daily mid-Apr.-early Nov., gate closes 4:30pm, $7 ages 13-60, $5 ages 4-12 and over age 60), located four miles south of the Shaker Village. Approximately 30 native species of wildlife can be seen at this state-operated wildlife refuge, including such ever-popular species as moose, black bears, white-tailed deer, and bald eagles. The park began in 1931 as a state-run game farm. For more than 50 years, the Department of Inland Fish and Game reared pheasants here for release during bird-hunting season. At the same time, wildlife biologists and game wardens needed a place to care for orphaned or injured animals.

In 1982 the farm's mission was changed to that of a wildlife and conservation education facility. Today the park is a temporary haven for wildlife, although those who cannot survive in the wild live here permanently.

Among the wildlife that have been in residence at the park are lynx, deer, opossums, black bears, bobcats, porcupines, raccoon, red-tailed hawks, barred and great horned owls, mountain lions, bald eagles, ravens, skunks, woodchucks, and coyotes. Other frequent guests include wild turkeys, fishers, gray foxes, kestrels, turkey vultures, wood turtles, and box turtles. Most are here for protection and healing, and visitors are able to view them at close range.

In addition to the wildlife, there are numerous interactive exhibits and displays to view, nature trails to explore, the Warden Museum, a fish hatchery, a nature store, a snack shack, and even picnic facilities. Special programs and exhibits are often offered on weekends mid-May-mid-September. The park offers a Photographer's Pass, which provides special access to wildlife enclosures, for $50/hour by advance reservation only. Bring quarters to purchase food to feed the critters.

The park is 3.5 miles north of Maine Turnpike (I-95) Exit 63. From the coast, take Route 115 from Main Street in downtown Yarmouth to Gray, and then head north on Route 26 for 3.5 miles.

ENTERTAINMENT

Each summer, **Poland Spring Preservation Society** hosts a series of weekly concerts in the All Souls Chapel. The music varies from acoustic guitar to jazz.

RECREATION
Range Ponds State Park

Brimming with swimmers when the temperature skyrockets, 777-acre **Range Ponds State Park** (Empire Rd., Poland, 207/998-4104) has facilities for swimming, including a lifeguard and a bathhouse, and picnicking as well as a playground and two miles of nature trails. (Part of the trail verges on a marsh; be prepared with bug repellent.) The beach, parking, restrooms, and picnic tables are wheelchair-accessible. Most of the park's acreage was once the estate of Hiram Ricker, owner of Poland Spring Water (it's now owned by Perrier/Nestle). Bring a canoe or kayak and launch it into Lower Range Pond. Admission is $6.50 nonresident adults, $4.50 Maine resident adults, $1.50 nonresident seniors, $1 ages 5-11; the park is open mid-May-mid-October. From Lewiston-Auburn, take Route 202/11/100 South to Route 122. Turn right (east) and continue to

Empire Road in Poland Spring; the turnoff to the park is well signposted.

Pineland Farms

Once a home for Maine's mentally disabled citizens, the 5,000-acre **Pineland** (15 Farm View Dr., New Gloucester, 207/688-4539, www.pinelandfarms.org, $5) campus was closed in 1996. Now the foundation-owned property comprises 19 buildings and 5,000 acres of working farmland, and much of it is open for recreation. Walk or ski the trails, sight birds in the fields and woods, watch cheese being made, stroll through the garden, fish the pond or skate on it in winter, play tennis, go mountain biking or orienteering, or even take a horseback-riding lesson. It's a vast outdoor playground, but your first stop should be the market and visitors center (8am-7pm daily) to see a list of any events (frequent ones include guided farm tours and family experiences), pick up maps, pay any necessary fees, shop for farm-fresh products, or even grab lunch or snacks. From late June into October, four-course farm-fresh, family-style dinners are offered on various dates, with the ticket price ($95) also including live entertainment, drinks, tax, and gratuity; reservations are required ($95). Dogs are not allowed on the grounds.

Golf

The 18-hole **Poland Spring Country Club** (41 Ricker Rd., off Rte. 26, Poland Spring, 207/998-6002) was first laid out in 1896 on the grounds of the long-gone Poland Spring House, a health spa. In 1915, Donald Ross added the second nine. Call for tee times.

Rockhounding

Serious pegmatite collectors should consider **Poland Spring Mining Camps** (207/998-2350), which offers a variety of packages with access to private quarries.

ACCOMMODATIONS

On the shores of Tripp Lake, the **Wolf Cove Inn Bed and Breakfast** (5 Jordan Shore Dr., Poland, 207/998-4976, www.wolfcoveinn.

com, $139-279) is a delightful spot to recoup. Ten guest rooms and suites (eight with private baths, three with fireplaces, all with air-conditioning and Wi-Fi) are named after flowers. Paddle around in one of the inn's canoes, go for a swim in the lake, or hang out in the gazebo. Sunsets are magnificent here. New owners plan upgrades, including private baths.

For dirt-cheap digs with few services, check out the **Poland Spring Resort** (Rte. 26, Poland Spring, 207/998-4351, www.polandspringresort.com). The 500-acre resort comprises three inns, 10 cottages, three restaurants, an 18-hole golf course, and three grass tennis courts; nightly entertainment is offered. Accommodations are Spartan and dated but clean, and all are air-conditioned. The responsive staff aims to please. A five-night, midweek package including buffet-style, all-you-can-eat breakfast and dinner, lodging, and other activities goes for about $200-480 pp for the whole shebang, but be sure to read the details on what's *not* included; nightly rates begin at $99/room. It's not for everyone, but it's a reliable cheap sleep if you're not fussy, and the meals are hearty comfort food.

The handsome **Chandler House Bed & Breakfast** (337 Intervale Rd./Rte. 231, New Gloucester, 207/926-5502, www.chandlerhousebandb.com, $105-175), built in 1903 by Charlie P. Chandler as a wedding gift for his bride, is a serene retreat on 15 country acres in a postcard-perfect village. Four guest rooms and a suite in the main house are furnished with antiques and country pieces; some share bathrooms. Two additional accommodations, one with full kitchen, are located in a separate guesthouse. Massage services, a hot tub, and a sauna are available. The location is convenient both to Route 26 sights and coastal Freeport. Rates include a full breakfast and afternoon sweets.

On the shore of Lower Range Pond, 40-acre **Poland Spring Campground** (Rte. 26, Poland Spring, 207/998-2151, www.polandspringcamp.com) has 130 wooded sites ($30-41 for two adults, two children, and one dog).

Facilities include an outdoor pool, coin-operated showers, a general store, laundry, play areas, and rental canoes, kayaks, and rowboats. There's plenty of organized fun; be prepared for campfires, ice cream parties, hay rides, barbecues, and other activities, although noise rules are monitored. The campground is about 10 miles west of Auburn.

FOOD

You can't go wrong at the **New Gloucester Village Store** (405 Intervale Rd., New Gloucester, 207/926-4224, www.ngvillagestore.com, 6am-9pm Mon.-Sat., 7:30am-8pm Sun.), a bakery/deli with a wood-fired oven. Pizzas, sandwiches on house-made bread, salads, and breakfast fare are available, and there are also prepared foods to go and an extensive selection of wines and beers.

Just a few miles from the Shaker Village is **Bresca and the Honey Bee** (106 Outlet Rd., New Gloucester, 207/926-3388, www.brescaandthehoneybee.com, 11am-4pm Wed.-Sun., daily if the sun is out, late May-early Sept., 9am-sunset Sat.-Sun. fall, winter, spring, but call first), a take-out snack shack with a small café on Outlet Beach. What makes this place special is that it's operated by Krista Kearns Desjarlais, a respected chef who earned national kudos for a restaurant she owned in Portland. Salads, pizzettas, burgers, hot dogs, house-made ice cream, and other specials are served during summer. During the rest of the year, she sells pastries, ployes, savory hand pies, and other goodies. Cash only. If you want access to the beach and lake, admission is $4.50 adults, $3 ages 13-16.

Farm, farm market, bakery, ice cream stand, and pizza and sandwich shop: **Harvest Hill Farms** (Rte. 26, Mechanic Falls, 207/998-3467, www.harvesthillfarms.com, 6am-9pm Mon.-Thurs., 6am-10pm Fri., 7am-10pm Sat., 7am-9pm Sun.) is all that plus there's a slew of kid-friendly fun, including a petting barn, Field of Dreams fun park, and in autumn, a pumpkin park and corn maze. With the exception of 14-inch pizzas, food is under $10, often far less.

Pair a paddle with a meal at **Cyndi's Dockside** (Rte. 26 causeway, Poland Spring, 207/998-5008, www.dockside.me, 11:30am-8pm Sun.-Thurs., 11:30am-10pm Fri., 11:30am-9pm Sat.), a lakeside restaurant with a boat-rental facility on Middle Range Pond. Burgers, sandwiches, fried seafood, and lobster ($6-20) provide something for everyone, and there's a kids' menu too. Kayak, canoe, and paddleboat rentals are $8 for one hour, $25 for four hours.

INFORMATION AND SERVICES

Pick up a copy of the brochure or visit online for more information about the **Gems of Route 26** (www.gemsof26.com).

GETTING THERE AND AROUND

Poland is roughly 23 miles from Bridgton via Routes 302 and 11. It's about 14 miles or 25 minutes to South Paris via Route 26. It's 11 miles or 30 minutes to Lewiston via Route 11.

Oxford Hills

Sandwiched between the Lewiston-Auburn area and the Bethel area, with Sebago and Long Lakes off to the south, the Oxford Hills region centers on **Norway** (pop. 5,014) and **South Paris** (pop. 2,267). The town of Norway shares the banks of the Little Androscoggin River with the community of South Paris, the major commercial center for the town of Paris.

From here it gets really complicated, although it's unlikely to affect a visitor. Oxford County's official seat is Paris, with all the relevant county offices located in South Paris. Next, throw into the mix the town of **West Paris** (pop. 1,812), which is in fact mostly *north* of Paris and South Paris. Within the boundaries of West Paris is the hamlet of North Paris. Fortunately, there's no East Paris, but there is the tiny enclave of **Paris Hill,** a pocket paradise many people never discover.

West Paris gained its own identity when it separated from Paris in 1957, but its traditions go way back. The Pequawket Indian princess Mollyockett, celebrated hereabouts as a healer, supposedly buried a golden treasure under a suspended animal trap, hence the name of Trap Corner for the junction of Routes 26 and 219 in West Paris. No such cache has been uncovered. More recent traditions in West Paris come from Finland, home of many 19th- and early-20th-century immigrants who gravitated to a new life in this area.

Norway, fortunately, is far less complicated. The name, incidentally, comes not from Europe or Norwegian settlers but rather from a variation on a Native American word for waterfalls—cascades on the town's Pennesseewassee (PEN-a-see-WAH-see) Lake (called Norway Lake locally), which powered 19th-century mills. European settlement began in 1786. Norway's downtown National Historic District is slowly being revitalized.

Norway was the birthplace of C. A. Stephens (1844-1931), who wrote weekly stories for a 19th-century boys' magazine, *Youth's Companion,* for 55 years. Colorfully reflective of rural Maine life, the entertaining tales were collected in *Stories from the Old Squire's Farm,* published in 1995. Norway was known as the "Snowshoe Capital of the World" during the early 20th century, when snowshoes made locally by Mellie Dunham were used on the 1909 Peary expedition to the North Pole. The multitalented Dunham also earned fame as one of the nation's top fiddlers.

Waterford (pop. 1,553), is a must-see, especially the National Historic District known as Waterford Flat or Flats, with classic homes and tree-lined streets alongside Keoka Lake in the shadow of Mount Tire'm. It's a 19th-century village frozen in time. Visit during foliage season, and you may never leave.

SIGHTS
【 Paris Hill

On Route 26, just beyond the northern edge of South Paris, a sign on the right marks one end of Paris Hill Road, a four-mile loop that reconnects farther along with Route 26. As you head uphill, past an old cemetery, you'll arrive at a Brigadoon-like enclave of elegant 18th- and 19th-century homes—a National Historic District with dramatic views off to the White Mountains and the lakes below. The centerpiece of the road is Paris Hill Common, a pristine park in front of the birthplace of former Vice President Hannibal Hamlin (1809-1891), which is not open to the public. South of the green stands the **Hamlin Memorial Library & Museum** (16 Hannibal Hamlin Dr., 207/743-2980, www.hamlin.lib.me.us, 11am-5pm Tues., 10am-3pm Sat., also noon-6pm Sunday in summer), the only Paris Hill building open to the public, where you can bone up on the history of this pocket paradise. Visit the library's website to download a copy of the Paris Hill walking tour.

Most children (and adults) get a kick out of entering a public library that was once a town jail. This one, built in 1822, held as many as 30 prisoners until 1896. Three prisoners somehow escaped in the 1830s, abandoning one of their pals stuck in the wall opening they had created. In 1902, the jail became the library, retaining the telltale signs of jail-bar hinges in the granite walls. Admission is free to the library's upper-level museum section, but donations are welcome. The library has no heat, so dress warmly. Hours vary with the seasons.

A great time to visit is on the third Saturday in July, for the annual **Founder's Day Classic Car Exhibit,** when Robert and Sandra Bahre open the garage on the Hamlin estate to share their world-renowned collection. Among the prizes are Packards, Duesenbergs, Stutz Bearcats, a Tucker, Thomas Flyer, vintage race cars, and other models. If you're in the area on the first December weekend in an even-numbered year, inquire about the **Biennial Holiday House Tour,** when a dozen of these elegant homes, decorated exquisitely for Christmas,

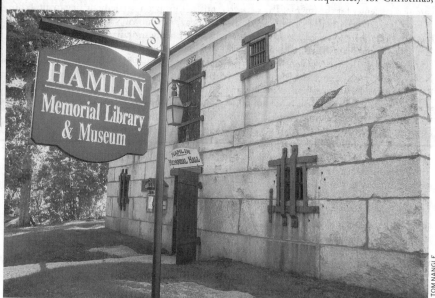

The former jail is now the town library in Paris Hill.

© TOM NANGLE

are open to the public, all to benefit the Paris Hill Community Club.

Finnish-American Heritage Center

In the early 20th century, hundreds of Finnish immigrants moved to Maine's Oxford Hills. The **Finnish-American Heritage Center** (8 Maple St., West Paris, www.mainefinns.org) relates their story. The building, which began life as a hotel before being converted to a boarding house for immigrant Finnish men, then later an American Legion Post, is open to visitors 2pm-4pm Sunday in July-August. Inside are displays, a library, and a gift shop. The center also presents occasional cultural events and meals, which are promoted in local papers.

McLaughlin Garden

In 1997, a little miracle happened in South Paris. For more than 60 years, Bernard McLaughlin had lovingly tended his two-acre perennial garden alongside Route 26, eventually surrounded by commercial development, and he'd always welcomed the public into his floral oasis. In 1995, at the age of 98, McLaughlin died, stipulating in his will that the property be sold. Eager developers eyed it, but loyal flower fans dug in their heels, captured media attention, created a nonprofit foundation, and managed to buy the property—the beginning of the little miracle. The **McLaughlin Garden** (97 Main St., South Paris, 207/743-8820, www.mclaughlingarden. org, 8am-7pm daily May-late Oct., free) lives on, with its 98 varieties of lilacs along with lilies and irises and so much more. The garden's main paths are wheelchair-accessible. Check the website for special events and programs. A gift shop in the house carries gardening items and high-end crafts and gifts, mostly Mainemade. A café may be operating on the premises.

Downtown Norway

After most of **downtown Norway** (www. norwaydowntown.org) burned during the Great Fire of 1894, it was rebuilt in brick and wood, reflecting the Victorian era's considerable embellishments. The Maine Historic Preservation Commission considers the downtown, now a National Historic District, one of the state's best examples of period architecture. It's currently undergoing a two-steps-forward, one-step-back Renaissance, with artists and entrepreneurs breathing new life into vacant storefronts and empty buildings. A historical walking tour, detailing the history of many buildings, is available online.

In 2013, 10 years after the 1894 **Norway Opera House,** with its distinctive clock tower, was designated one Maine's most endangered historical properties, phase one of a massive grassroots preservation effort was completed, and this National Historic Register property is again the town's pride. The first phase addressed structural concerns and reopened the street-level shops. The second phase will rehab and reopen the second-floor opera hall.

RECREATION
Parks and Preserves

A 300-foot gorge on the Little Androscoggin River is the eye-catching centerpiece of **Snow Falls** rest area, an easy-off, easy-on roadside park where you can commandeer a table alongside the waterfall. What better place for a relaxing picnic? There are no grills but some sheltered tables. Trucks whiz by on the highway, but the noise of the water usually drowns them out. The rest area is on Route 26, about six miles north of the center of South Paris.

Western Foothills Land Trust (207/739-2124, www.wfltmaine.org) owns **Roberts Farm Preserve** (64 Roberts Rd.). The 165-acre preserve is webbed with over 7 miles of trails for hiking, Nordic skiing, snowshoeing, and mountain biking and also has a trail for the physically challenged that meets ADA standards. It's a short and easy walk to a lovely vista with views over Lake Pennesseewassee. The preserve is located just off Routes 1887/117, 0.2 mile south of the lake.

Hiking

The most popular Oxford Hills hikes are particularly family-friendly—no killer climbs or even major ascents, no bushwhacking, just darned good exercise and some worthwhile views. July-mid-August, don't be surprised to encounter clusters of summer campers, since camp counselors all over this region regularly gather up their kids and take them out on the trail or paddling the ponds. If you're spending more than a day hiking in this area, pick up a copy at bookstores and gift shops of *Hikes in and around Maine's Lake Region* by Marita Wiser; it's the best available advice on this area.

It's hard to resist a hike up **Mount Tire'm** (1,089 feet)—if only to disprove its name. Actually, it's supposedly a convolution of a Native American name. The only steep section is at the beginning, after the memorial marker dedicated to 19th-century Waterfordite Daniel Brown, for whom the unblazed trail is named. Allow an hour or so for the 1.4-mile round-trip, especially if you're carrying a picnic. Allow time on the summit ledges to take in the views—all the way to Sebago on a clear day. From downtown Waterford (Rte. 35), take Plummer Hill Road about 300 feet beyond the community center. The unmarked trailhead is on the west side of the road where it branches.

Straddling the Paris-Buckfield-Hebron town boundaries, the half-mile **Streaked Mountain** (pronounced STREAK-ed) trail climbs 800 feet, often steeply, to an expansive 1,770-foot summit with communications towers and vistas as far as Mount Washington. Pack a picnic. If you're here in early August, take along a small pail to collect wild blueberries. Late September-early October, it's indescribable, but remember to wear a hunterorange hat or vest once hunting season has started—or tackle the trail on a Sunday, when there's no hunting. Allow about 1.5 hours for the one-mile round-trip, especially if you're picnicking and blueberry-picking. To reach the trailhead from South Paris, take Route 117 west to Streaked Mountain Road, on the right (south); turn and go about 0.5 mile. Park well off the road. (You can also climb Streaked from the east, but it's a much longer hike that requires waterproof footwear.)

Golf

At nine-hole **Paris Hill Country Club** (355 Paris Hill Rd., Paris, 207/743-2371), founded in 1899, you'll find a low-key atmosphere, reasonable greens fees, cart rentals, and a snack bar. No tee times are needed. The rectangular course has all straight shots; the challenges come from slopes and unexpected traps.

It's not just golfers who patronize the nine-hole **Norway Country Club** (Lake Rd./Rte. 118, Norway, 207/743-9840); this is a popular spot to have lunch or kick back on the club porch. The mountain-lake scenery, especially in the fall, is awesome. Starting times are not required; it's first-come, first-served. Established in 1929, the club is a mile west of Route 117.

Spectator Sports

If you're partial to guerrilla warfare on wheels, the place to be is **Oxford Plains Speedway** (Rte. 26, Oxford, 207/539-8865, www.oxfordplains.com), Maine's center for stock-car racing. Late April-mid-September, souped-up high-performance vehicles careen around the track in pursuit of substantial monetary prizes. Almost all races begin at 6:30pm.

Sleigh Rides

Put on your winter warmies, then snuggle under a lap blanket on a 40-minute sleigh ride with **High View Farm** (4 Leander Harmon Rd., Harrison, 207/596-1601, www.high-view-farm.com, $50/sleigh plus $5 pp, $70 minimum). Add a stop in the woods for a bonfire with roasted marshmallows and hot chocolate for $35. Rides are offered 11am-7pm, are private, and are by reservation only.

ENTERTAINMENT

Marcel Marceau wannabes come to study at the nationally famed **Celebration Barn Theater** (190 Stock Farm Rd., South Paris, 207/743-8452, www.celebrationbarn.com), established in 1972 by the late mime master Tony Montanaro. Mime, juggling, dance, clowning, storytelling, and improv comedy performances are open to the public in the 125-seat barn at 8pm most Saturdays June-August. Reservations are required; tickets are $14. Pack a picnic supper and arrive early. The theater also offers residential workshops for aspiring mimes, storytellers, comedians, and the like. Check the website for details. The theater (signposted) is just off Route 117.

The **Oxford Casino** (Rte. 26, Oxford, 207/539-6700, www.oxfordcasino.com) has slot machines and table games.

FESTIVALS AND EVENTS

Wall-to-wall paintings are for sale along Main Street in downtown Norway for the **Norway Arts Festival** (www.norwayartsfestival.org), the second Saturday in July, in which more than 100 artists participate. There's also street entertainment and other events.

Founders' Day (www.hamlin.lib.me.us) brings craft and antiques exhibits, music, and an antique-car open house on Paris Hill Common in Paris Hill the third Saturday in July. A special highlight is a one-day showing of Robert and Sandra Bahre's collection of more than 60 vehicles, including Packards, Duesenbergs, Stutz Bearcats, and more.

The name of North Waterford's **World's Fair** (www.waterfordworldsfair.org) seems sort of cheeky for this three-day country medley of agricultural events, egg-throwing contests, talent show, live music, dancing, and more in mid-July.

The family-oriented four-day agricultural **Oxford County Fair,** "The Horse-Powered Fair," held in mid-September, features 4-H exhibits, a beauty pageant, a pig scramble, live entertainment, an apple-pie contest, and plenty of crafts and food booths at the Oxford County Fairgrounds (www.oxfordcountyfair.com).

SHOPPING

Norway's Main Street has the best selection of independent shops in the area, with many offering works by local artists.

Books

Books-N-Things (430 Main St., Norway, 207/743-7197, www.bntnorway.com) is one of those full-service bookstores that inspire you to buy more than you ever planned. There's an excellent children's section, plentiful toys, and even some specialty foods.

Peruse through more than 13,000 new, used, and out-of-print books as well as artwork at **The Maine Bookhouse** (1545 Main St./Rte. 26, Oxford, 207/743-9300, www.themainebookhouse.com).

Galleries and Gifts

A number of area galleries participate in a First Friday art tour. A gallery guide can be downloaded from www.frostfarmgallery.com/localgalleryguide.html.

The Western Maine Art Group facilitates exhibits for members at the seasonal **Lajos Matolcsy Arts Center** (480 Main St., Norway, 207/739-6161, www.westernmaineartgroup. org), as well as other sites. Check the group's website for info on classes and other events.

Frost Farm Gallery (27 Pikes Hill, Norway, 207/743-8041, www.frostfarmgallery.com) hosts rotating exhibits.

It's hard to resist inhaling deeply upon entering **Maine Balsam Fir Products** (16 Morse Hill Rd., West Paris, 800/522-5726, www. mainebalsam.com), filled with balsam pillows, neck rolls, draft stoppers, trivets, and sachets along with oil, soap, clothing, quilts, and more, all jammed in a one-room shop adjacent to where the balsam products are made. Tours are offered when the schedule permits; just ask.

ACCOMMODATIONS
Sumner

For a complete change of pace, back in time and back of beyond **Morrill Farm Bed and Breakfast** (85 Morrill Farm Rd., Sumner, 207/388-2059, www.morrillfarmbnb.com, $75) is a late-18th-century farm with three unfussy second-floor guest rooms sharing one bath. On the 217-acre working farm are nature and cross-country skiing trails, river fishing, and a menagerie of domestic farm animals. Pets are kenneled on-site for $15/day. The farm is north and east of Norway-South Paris, a mile from Route 219 (West Sumner Rd.). French is spoken.

South Paris

The 200-year-old expanded Cape that now houses the **King's Hill Inn** (56 King Hill Rd., South Paris, 207/744-0204, www.kingshillinn. com, $115-165) was the birthplace of Horatio King, who served as postmaster general under President Buchanan. Inside are three guest rooms and three suites, all with comfortable touches, some with a gas stove, a microwave, and a dining area, a deck entrance, a whirlpool tub, or antiques. The quiet, rural location is convenient to hiking trails and the Celebration Barn Theatre. Rates include an especially bountiful breakfast.

Waterford

Waterford—that lovely little enclave flanked by Norway-South Paris, Bridgton-Naples, and the Lovells—has a couple of fine places to put your head.

Barbara Vanderzanden's traditionally elegant **Waterford Inne** (258 Chadbourne Rd., Waterford, 207/583-4037, www.waterfordinne. com, $125-200), an antiques-filled 19th-century farmhouse on 25 open and wooded acres, is a real treasure. Rooms are bright and airy; some have woodstoves and porches. A delicious breakfast is included; a four-course dinner is available for $40. Children are welcome, and pets are allowed for $15 extra. The inn is close to East Waterford, 0.5 mile west of Route 37. It's open year-round.

The **Bear Mountain Inn** (Rte. 35, South Waterford, 207/583-4404, www.bearmtninn. com), a beautifully updated 1820s B&B overlooking Bear Pond (it's really a lake), is one of those places that's hard to leave, especially after you settle in on the pond-view terrace or the beach. On the premises are boats, docks, hammocks, a lake-view hot tub, picnic tables and a barbecue, even trails up Bear and Hawk Mountains. Five bear-themed guest rooms, with private and shared baths as well as Wi-Fi, go for $120-195; luxury and family suites are $220-325, including breakfast. The self-contained Sugar Bear cottage, with fireplace and kitchenette, is pet-friendly ($20). A rental house that sleeps eight is $600. Also included

are a stocked guest fridge, a TV with a video player and a video library, and, well, just about anything you might desire, within reason.

FOOD
Local Flavors

Many people flock to **The Lake Store** (14 Waterford Rd./Rte. 118 at Rte. 117, Norway Lake, Norway, 207/743-6562) just to check out the crazy collection of Coca-Cola memorabilia, but you can also load up with picnic fixings, pizza, liquor, groceries, and videos.

Homemade soups, salads, and daily specials, occasional concerts and wine tastings, free Wi-Fi, and the area's best coffee make **Café Nomad** (450 Main St., Norway, 207/739-2249, www. cafenomad.com, 7am-4pm Mon.-Fri., 8am-3pm Sat.) an especially popular local spot.

Pop into **Taste of Eden Vegan Café** (238 Main St., Norway, 207/739-6090, www.tasteofedencafe.com, 11am-5:30pm Mon.-Thurs., 11am-2pm Sun.) for inexpensive vegan fare, including soups and sandwiches and daily specials.

A bright spot in the lackluster hubbub on the fast-food strip is **Rising Sun Cafe and Bakery** (130 Main St./Rte. 26, South Paris, 207/743-7046, 6am-4pm Tues.-Fri., 7am-2pm Sat.), a local fave for baked goods, soups, salads, and sandwiches.

"Everything Shirley makes is good," a regular told me as I debated between the scones, cookies, muffins, soups, pies, beans, and other homemade treats at **Hungry Hollow Country Store** (28 Bethel Rd./Rte. 26, West Paris, 207/674-3012, 7am-5pm Mon.-Sat., 10am-5:30pm Sun.). Everything is made from scratch using unbleached flour, natural sea salt and without trans fats.

Local produce, honey, organic meat, perennials, preserves, syrup, cheese, and baked goods are all part of the stock at **Norway Farmers Market**, which sets up downtown at 15 Whiteman St. in the Fare Share parking lot, 2pm-6pm Thursday late May-October.

In addition to fresh produce, **Smedburg's Crystal Spring Farm** (1413 Main St., Oxford, 207/743-6723, 7am-7pm daily) sells fresh bread, pies, prepared foods, condiments, cheeses, and farm-made ice cream. Another farm stand worth a look-see is **Crestholm Farm** (167 Main St., Oxford, 207/539-8832, 9am-9pm daily), which also sells farm-made ice cream and has a free petting zoo.

For exquisite pastries, cakes, tarts, and pies, slip into **Marta's Bakery** (684 Vallen Rd./Rte. 35, North Waterford, 207/583-2250, www.martasbakery.com), where Prague-born Marta Cistecky opened her bakery-café after a career as a baker in Boston. Call for hours as they change frequently.

Casual Dining

Bret and Amy Baker have meticulously renovated an 1896 former judge's mansion into the region's best restaurants at **76 Pleasant St.** (76 Pleasant St., Norway, 207/744-9040, www.76pleasantstreet.com, from 5pm Tues.-Sat., $17-28). The two dining rooms and lounge balance comfortable, contemporary furnishings with former home's architectural elegance. Dining is a treat, with seasonal choices that may include charcoal duck breast, confit of rabbit, or braised lamb shank. Make reservations, as the restaurant only has 24 seats.

Open since 1976, **Maurice Restaurant** (109 Main St./Rte. 26, South Paris, 207/743-2532, www.mauricerestaurant.com, 11am-1:30pm Tues.-Fri., 11am-2pm Sun., and from 4pm Tues.-Sun., $15-24) has stood the test of time and the decor reflects its age. Renowned for French cuisine when it opened, it's had its ups and downs over the decades, but it remains one of the region's more reliable choices.

By reservation, Barbara Vanderzanden will prepare a four-course dinner for guests and nonguests at the peaceful **((Waterford Inne** (258 Chadbourne Rd., Waterford, 207/583-4037, www.waterfordinne.com, no credit cards). The leisurely meal is $40 pp; spring for it, as she does a wonderful job. BYOB.

INFORMATION AND SERVICES

The **Oxford Hills Chamber of Commerce** (4 Western Ave., South Paris, 207/743-2281, www.oxfordhillsmaine.com) produces an annual magazine that's actually an interesting read and far less promotional than the usual CC material.

Downtown Norway Maine (www.norway-downtown.org) covers Norway.

Check out **Norway Memorial Library** (258 Main St., Norway, 207/743-5309, www.norway.lib.me.us).

GETTING THERE AND AROUND

South Paris is roughly 14 miles or 22 minutes from Poland. It's about 24 miles or 45 minutes to Lewiston via Routes 26 and 11. It's 24 miles or 30 minutes to Bethel via Route 26 and 45 miles or 65 minutes to Portland via Route 26 and I-95.

WESTERN LAKES

Lewiston and Auburn

A river runs through the heart of **Lewiston** (pop. 1,795) and **Auburn** (pop. 1,842)—the Androscoggin River, whose headwaters are in the Rangeley Lakes, courses southeastward until it joins the Kennebec River in Merrymeeting Bay near Brunswick. Surging over Great Falls, the mighty Androscoggin spurred 19th-century industrial development of the twin cities, where giant textile mills drew their power from the river and their hardworking employees from the local community of Yankees, then Irish, French Canadian, and other immigrants. The Québécois and Acadian French, who flocked to mills in Lewiston, Biddeford, Sanford, Augusta, and Brunswick, today constitute Maine's largest ethnic minority. In Lewiston and Auburn, the French-accented voting registers reveal long lists of Plourdes and Pomerleaus, Carons and Cloutiers, and the spires of Catholic churches still dominate the skyline.

Long before the falls of the Androscoggin were harnessed, Native Americans recognized the area for its prime salmon fishing and set up seasonal campsites and year-round settlements. Nowadays, their artifacts occasionally turn up along the riverbanks.

European settlers began putting down roots around 1770, earning their keep from small water-powered mills. Quakers established a community as early as 1773. By 1852 the giant Bates Mill (of bedspread fame) began manufacturing cotton, expanding to an annual output of more than 10 million yards by 1900. During the Civil War, Bates was a prime supplier of fabric for soldiers' tents. In 1861, Lewiston was incorporated as a city; Auburn was incorporated in 1869.

By the early 20th century, with a dozen more mills online, taking advantage of the convenient hydropower, the lower reaches of the Androscoggin became polluted, a stinky eyesore until the 1980s when environmental activists took up the cause. Now you can stroll the banks, fish the waters, paddle a canoe, and get up close on the walkways, bridges, and plazas linking the two cities.

Lewiston and Auburn also have quite a sporting heritage in boxing and, believe it or not, skiing. World-class boxer Joey Gamache emerged from the local clubs, and the controversial world title fight between Sonny Liston and Muhammad Ali took place here. Olympic skiers Karl Anderson and Julie Parisien (and her Olympian siblings Anna and Rob) are also local products.

Natural gems are found in the region. Auburn's Mount Apatite has produced record-setting tourmalines, Maine's state gemstone, as well as quartz and feldspar. Now owned by the city, the mountain is open to the prospecting public.

Lewiston and Auburn, known locally as "the other LA," are still not typical vacation destinations, but they deserve more than a drive-through glance. Lewiston is the state's second-largest city and home to Bates College, a highly selective private liberal arts school and a magnet for visiting performers, artists, and lecturers.

Auburn, the Androscoggin County seat, began its industrial career with a single shoe factory in 1836, expanding swiftly in those heady days. By the turn of the 20th century, Auburn's shoe factories were turning out six million pairs a year.

Lewiston and Auburn occupy a pivotal location in southern Maine, with easy access to Portland (35 miles away) and Freeport (28 miles), the western mountains, and the state capital at Augusta (30 miles).

SIGHTS
Bates College
Founded in 1855 on foresighted egalitarian principles, **Bates College** (2 Andrews Rd., Lewiston, 207/786-6255, www.bates.edu) received its current name after major financial

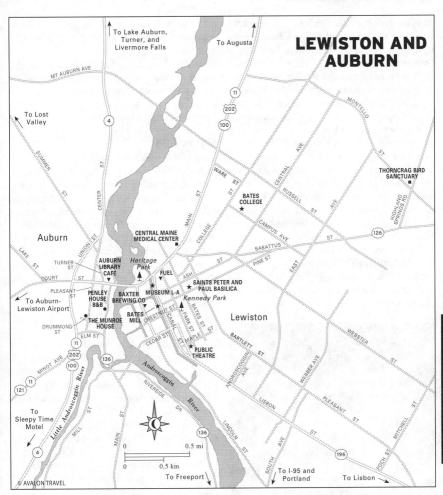

input from Benjamin Bates of the Bates Mill. On a lovely wooded 109-acre campus in the heart of Lewiston, the college earns high marks for small class sizes, a stellar faculty, a rigorous academic program, and a low student-to-faculty ratio. The student body of 1,700 comes from almost every state and about four dozen foreign countries; diversity has always been evident and a point of honor. The oldest campus building is redbrick **Hathorn Hall,** built in 1856 and listed on the National Register of Historic Places; one of the newest buildings, the Olin Arts Center, built in 1986, is an award-winning complex overlooking artificial Lake Andrews.

Within the **Olin Arts Center** (Russell St. and Bardwell St., 207/786-6135) are the **Bates College Museum of Art** (75 Russell St., 207/786-6259) and the 300-seat **Olin Concert Hall.** Most college-sponsored exhibits, lectures, and concerts at the Arts Center are free and open to the public (other organizations also use the concert hall). At 6pm each Thursday mid-July–mid-August, free **lakeside concerts** are presented outside the Arts Center; bring a picnic and a blanket or chair. The **Bates College Museum of Art** (10am–5pm Tues.–Sat., free), with rotating exhibits, is open all year. A significant stop on the Maine Art Museum Trail, it emphasizes works on paper, especially by Maine artists including Lewiston-born modernist Marsden Hartley.

The college has won national and international acclaim for the summertime (mid-July–mid-Aug.) **Bates Dance Festival** (207/786-6161, www.batesdancefestival.org), featuring modern-dance workshops, lectures, and performances. Sellout student and faculty programs, most presented in 300-seat Schaeffer Theater, are open to the public.

Bates is the repository of the **Edmund S. Muskie Archives** (70 Campus Ave., 207/786-6354, 8:30am–noon and 1pm–5pm Mon.–Fri.), containing the papers of the 1936 Bates graduate and former Maine governor, U.S. senator, and U.S. secretary of state who died in 1996.

At the western edge of the campus, at the corner of Mountain Avenue and College Street, walk up **Mount David,** actually a grandly named hill, for a surprisingly good view of the Lewiston-Auburn skyline.

Bates Mill

Thanks to a progressive public-private partnership, the 19th-century Bates Mill complex, on Canal Street in downtown Lewiston, is being revitalized for a variety of new uses. Occupying 1.2 million square feet in 12 buildings spread over six acres, the mill once produced nearly a third of the nation's textiles. Since 1992, much of the hulking brick complex has been undergoing a long-term makeover—offices, studios, shops, restaurants, and even a museum have moved in, ever so slowly, helping the mill to reinvent itself.

MUSEUM L-A

If you want to understand Lewiston and Auburn, visit the fledgling **Museum L-A** (35 Canal St., Lewiston, 207/333-3881, www.museumla.org, 10am–4pm Mon.–Sat., $5 adults, $4 seniors and students). Appropriately situated inside the Bates Mill Complex, a visit immerses you into the region's industrial heyday; it's almost as if you can hear the machines and chatter as you tour the mill space. Exhibits tell the stories of LA's immigrant communities and document the region's textile-, brick-, and shoe-manufacturing industries.

Saints Peter and Paul Basilica

Most distinctive of Lewiston-Auburn's churches is the Gothic Revival Roman Catholic **Saints Peter and Paul Basilica** (27 Bartlett St. at Ash St., Lewiston, 207/777-1200, www.saintspeterandpaul.us), listed on the National Register of Historic Places. Noteworthy is a rose window replica of one in the Chartres Cathedral. It's the second-largest church in New England and capable of seating more than 2,000 for its separate services in English and

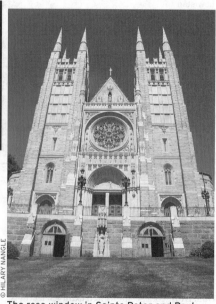

© HILARY NANGLE

The rose window in Saints Peter and Paul Basilica is a replica of the one in Chartres Cathedral.

French. Dedicated in 1938, the recently designated basilica is the only one in New England. Noonday and evening concerts, many featuring the Casavant organ, are scheduled during the summer.

ENTERTAINMENT

Throughout the year, **Bates College** (207/786-6255 weekdays, www.bates.edu) presents a full schedule of concerts, lectures, exhibits, sporting events, and other activities.

The former St. Mary's Church, considered one of the finest examples of Renaissance architecture in the country, has found new life as the **Franco-American Heritage Center** (46 Cedar St., Lewiston, 207/783-1585, box office 207/689-2000, www.francoamericanheritage.org), a performing arts center that presents symphonic, chamber, and choral music concerts as well as other events.

Since 1973, **L/A Arts** (221 Lisbon St., Lewiston, 207/782-7228, www.laarts.org), a respected nonprofit arts-sponsorship organization, has been bringing a whole range of cultural events to the area, including films, concerts, family events, and more. The group sponsors **Sounds of Summer,** with free noontime concerts in Lewiston's Fountain Park and Auburn's Festival Plaza. Check out the "Arts Calendar" link on its website.

Lewiston-Auburn's professional theater company, **The Public Theatre** (31 Maple St., Lewiston, box office 207/782-3200, www.thepublictheatre.org) has been presenting musicals and dramas for more than a decade, leading the way in the twin cities' cultural scene and receiving recognition for the quality of its performances. Ticket prices are about $18 adults, less for students and seniors.

The Maine Music Society (207/782-1403, 207/782-7228 box office, www.mainemusicsociety.org) is the overseer of the 40-voice Androscoggin Chorale and the Maine Music Society Orchestra. Concerts are held in various locations September-May.

Auburn's Festival Plaza is the venue for the extremely popular **Auburn Community Band Concerts** at 7pm Wednesday July-August.

FESTIVALS AND EVENTS

Festival Franco Fun takes place in June at the Franco-American Heritage Center.

The second weekend in July brings the **Moxie Festival** (www.moxiefestival.com), a certifiably eccentric annual celebration of the obscure soft drink Moxie, invented in 1884 and still not consigned to the dustbin of history. Among the activities: a huge offbeat parade, food booths, a Moxie recipe contest, a foot race, and collectibles exhibits and sales. The biggest day is Saturday; it all happens in downtown Lisbon.

The acclaimed annual **Bates Dance Festival** at Bates College in Lewiston mid-July-mid-August features behind-the-scenes classes and workshops as well as performances, which are open to the public.

August brings the **Great Falls Balloon Festival,** with food, entertainment, a carnival, fireworks, and, of course, balloon launches.

The **Dempsey Challenge** run, walk, and cycle fundraiser in October provides an opportunity to see Dr. McDreamy (actor Patrick Dempsey, who grew up in these parts).

RECREATION
Parks and Preserves

The **Androscoggin Land Trust** (www.androscogginlandtrust.org) protects natural area resources. Check the website for places to hike, bike, paddle, and fish; maps; and opportunities such as guided walks or paddles.

Thorncrag Bird Sanctuary

Imagine being able to bird-watch, hike, cross-country ski, and snowshoe on 357 acres within the city limits of Lewiston in one of New England's largest bird sanctuaries. At the **Thorncrag Bird Sanctuary** (Montello St., Lewiston, 207/782-5238, www.stantonbirdclub.org/thorncrg.htm, dawn-dusk daily year-round, free), pick up a trail map at the gate and head out on the three miles of well-maintained, color-coded, easy-to-moderate trails—past ponds, an old cellar hole, stone memorials, and benches and through stands of beeches, hemlocks, white pines, and mixed hardwoods; bring a picnic. Bicycles are banned in the preserve. Throughout the year the **Stanton Bird Club** sponsors close to three dozen lectures and free, open-to-the-public field trips; call or see its website for the schedule. The club also sponsors an excellent junior naturalist program. From downtown Lewiston, take Sabattus Street (Rte. 126) east about three miles to Highland Springs Road. Turn left (north) and continue to the end at Montello Street. You'll be facing the entrance to the sanctuary.

Rockhounding

For sheer fun, spend a few hours searching for apatite, tourmaline, and quartz at **Mount Apatite Park** (Hatch Rd., off Rte. 11/121, Auburn, dawn-dusk), a 325-acre park that's been popular with rock hounds for more than 150 years. For a detailed map, contact the Auburn Parks and Recreation Department (48 Pettingill Park, Auburn, 207/333-6601).

Androscoggin Riverlands

Twelve miles of multiuse trails, and 10 miles of hiking and mountain-biking trails stretching along six river miles lace the 2,345-acre Turner Lands section of **Androscoggin Riverlands State Park** (Center Bridge Rd., Turner, www.parksandlands.com, free). Opt for the Homestead Trail, a 4.5-mile loop with a shorter 2.6-mile option, which follows the river's shoreline.

ACCOMMODATIONS

◖ **The Munroe House** (123 Pleasant St., Auburn, 207/376-3266, www.themunroeinn. com, $120-165), an elegant National Historic Register-listed manse, with exquisite woodwork and stained glass, had stood empty for five years until David and Melanie Davis discovered it on the Internet. They fell in love with the Queen Anne beauty, moved to Maine, and restored and refurnished it. Four spacious, antiques-furnished air-conditioned rooms have Wi-Fi, flat-screen DirecTV, iPod docks, and other niceties. The first-floor rooms, all furnished with period antiques, are equally expansive and lovely, as

is the wraparound porch. Laundry service is available.

The Queen Anne-style **Penley House Bed & Breakfast** (233 Main St., Auburn, 207/786-4800, www.penleyhouse.com, $100-125) is located in Auburn's Historic District, an easy walk from downtown attractions. Each of the four guest rooms has a private bath, but three are detached.

Charmingly retro and immaculately clean, the six-room **Sleepy Time Motel** (46 Danville Corner Rd., Auburn, 207/783-1435, www. sleepytimemotel.com, $79-99) offers a lot of bang for the buck. Perks in the pine-paneled guest rooms include air-conditioning, microwaves, refrigerators, recliners, Wi-Fi, and dining areas. The five-acre property abuts 100 woodsy acres that are laced with three miles of trails for hiking and snowshoeing. Owners Lynn and Mark Klinger are hands-on and helpful. Pets are welcome for $10/night.

FOOD
Local Flavors

Tour and taste at **Baxter Brewing Co.** (130 Mill St., Lewiston, 207/333-6769, www.baxterbrewing.com). Guided tours include at least one free four-ounce sampling. Call for times.

Look for the **Lewiston Farmers Market** at Bates Mill No. 5, 10am-1pm late May-mid-October.

Auburn Library Cafe (49 Spring St., Auburn, 207/784-2300, 7am-4pm Mon.-Fri., 8am-3pm Sat., $4-9) serves all-day breakfast and lunch fare, with menu items named for New England authors.

Maurice Bonneau's Sausage Kitchen (36 Main St., Lisbon Falls, 207/353-5503, www. sausagekitchen.com, 9am-5pm Tues.-Sat.) produces all-natural meat products, including a mind-boggling array of sausages and meat pies.

Named for the river running through town, ◖**Nezinscot Farm Store** (284 Turner Center Rd./Rte. 117, Turner, 207/225-3231, www.nezinscotfarm.com, 6am-6pm Thurs.-Fri., 8am-5pm Sat.-Sun.) is worth the detour. Besides organically grown produce, the farm makes its own organic baked goods, cheeses, charcuterie, cream products, and herbal products and sells plenty of other local goods. There's a café that makes meals to order ($6-10). The shop sells all-natural wool yarns from the farm's sheep, llamas, alpacas, and goats. Pizza and music jams are held the first and third Saturday of the month at 6pm (bring a dish to share or make a donation). The farm is five miles east and north of the junction of Routes 4 and 117 (about 16 miles north of downtown Auburn). Call ahead to confirm hours if you're making a special trip.

The **Italian Bakery Products Co.** (225 Bartlett St., Lewiston, 207/782-8312, 6am-5:30pm Tues.-Fri., 6am-3pm Sat., 6am-noon Sun.) is always bustling. It's a great little place to pick up baked goods such as cannoli or bismark doughnuts, sandwiches, soups, and pizzas for lunch, and daily specials such as Saturday beans. There is no seating.

Hipsters take note: **She Doesn't Like Guthries** (115 Middle St., Lewiston, 207/376-3344, www.guthriesplace.com, 10am-8pm Mon.-Thurs., 10am-10pm Fri., $8-10), a Maine-certified Green Restaurant, has you dialed. Begin with eclectic music, then add local art, live entertainment on Friday nights, and an ecofriendly mission; top it off with inexpensive, well-prepared healthful fare that includes veggie, vegan, and wheat-free choices and even a kids' menu. Expect burritos, quesadillas, soups made from scratch, salads, and similar fare. And don't worry, even if you're not hip, you'll like this place.

Forage Market (180 Lisbon St., Lewiston, 207/333-6840, 7am-7pm Mon.-Fri., 8am-4pm Sat.) is a grab-and-go market selling soups, sandwiches, wood-fired Montreal-style bagels, and daily specials. There's inside seating, and you can go downstairs and see the bakers at work.

Order soups, sandwiches, and specials at the counter at **Marche** (40 Lisbon St., Lewiston, 207/333-3856, www.marchemaine.com, 11am-2pm Mon.-Fri.).

For artisanal breads and excellent sandwiches, salads, and soups, duck into **The Bread Shack** (1056 Center St., Auburn, 207/376-3090, www.thebreadshack.com, 7am-6pm Mon.-Fri., 8am-4pm Sat., 8am-2pm Sun., and 97 Lisbon St., Lewiston, 9am-6pm Mon.-Sat.).

For breakfast, pop into **Rolly's Diner** (87 Mill St., Auburn, 207/753-0171, 7am-6pm Mon.-Fri., 7am-noon Sun., $3-8), where the crepes earn raves.

Family Favorites

In the retrofitted Bates Mill, **DaVinci's Eatery** (150 Mill St., Lewiston, 207/782-2088, www. davinciseatery.com, 11am-9pm Sun.-Thurs., 11am-10pm Fri.-Sat.) specializes in pasta and brick-oven pizza but has a variety of other regional American and Italian entrées in the $11-20 range. Weekdays and Tuesday evenings it features a pizza buffet with a soup and salad bar for about $10.

The area's favorite steakhouse is **Mac's Grill** (1052 Minot Ave., Auburn, 207/783-6885, www.macsgrill.com, from 11:30am daily, $10-21), an often loud and crowded log cabin with a kids' menu.

Casual Dining

Fish Bones American Grill (70 Lincoln St., Lewiston, 207/333-3663, www.fishbonesag. com, 11:30am-9pm Mon.-Sat., $16-28), in a renovated mill with handsome brick-accented decor, serves both light and regular menus with an emphasis on seafood. It also offers a three-course theater menu ($25) and occasional wine dinners.

Warm up on a cool evening at jazzy **◖ Fuel** (49 Lisbon St., Lewiston, 207/333-3835, www. fuelmaine.com, from 5pm Tues.-Sat., $10-30), a country French-inspired bistro and wine bar that opened in 2007 in historic Lyceum Hall. Owner Eric Agren calls the decor "urban cozy," and that seems about right. Expect dead-on service, well-prepared creative fare, an excellent wine list, and chic yet casual surroundings. You might begin with roasted oysters and then move on to cassoulet, coq au vin, or perhaps opt for the four-course chef's tasting menu ($40, add $18 for wine pairings). Lighter fare ($10-12) is served in the bar. Feeling adventuresome, inquire about the Chef's Table in the kitchen.

And then there's a country inn standby:

WESTERN LAKES

Dining is by reservation only at **The Sedgley Place** (54 Sedgley Rd., Greene, 207/946-5990 or 800/924-7778, www.sedgleyplace.com, seatings on the hour from 5pm Tues.-Sun.), in a lovely Federal-style homestead a mile southwest of Route 202 (six miles north of Lewiston). The five-course menu ($32) changes weekly but always includes prime rib, fresh fish, and poultry; request vegetarian and children's portions ahead of time. All of the produce served is certified organic and most of it is grown on the owners' nearby organic farm.

INFORMATION AND SERVICES

The **Androscoggin County Chamber of Commerce** (207/783-2249, www.androscoggincounty.com, www.laitshappeninghere.com) serves as the tourism information center for the entire county.

Housed in a handsome granite 1903 Romanesque Revival building, the **Lewiston Public Library** (105 Park St., Lewiston, 207/784-0135, www.lplonline.org) is one of the sponsors of the Great Falls Forum, presenting monthly lunches with expert speakers on various thought-provoking topics. It's also home to the Marsden Hartley Cultural Center, a meeting and performance venue.

Equally worth a visit is the **Auburn Library** (49 Spring St., Auburn, 207/784-2300), which also has an excellent café serving breakfast and lunch, including specials such as lobster bisque or white bean and chicken chili, Monday-Saturday.

GETTING THERE AND AROUND

Lewiston is roughly 11 miles or 30 minutes from Poland via Route 11. It's 20 miles or 40 minutes to Brunswick via Route 196 and 38 miles or 45 minutes to Portland via I-95.

BACKGROUND

The Land

Maine is an outdoor classroom for Geology 101, a living lesson in what the glaciers did and how they did it. Geologically, Maine is something of a youngster; the oldest rocks, found in the Chain of Ponds area in the western part of the state, are only 1.6 billion years old—more than two billion years younger than the world's oldest rocks.

But most significant is the great ice sheet that began to spread over Maine about 25,000 years ago, during the late Wisconsin Ice Age. As it moved southward from Canada, this continental glacier scraped, gouged, pulverized, and depressed the bedrock in its path. On it continued, charging up the north faces of mountains, clipping off their tops and moving southward, leaving behind jagged cliffs on the mountains' southern faces and odd deposits of stone and clay. By about 21,000 years ago, glacial ice extended well over the Gulf of Maine, perhaps as far as the Georges Bank fishing grounds.

But all that began to change with meltdown, beginning about 18,000 years ago. As the glacier melted and receded, ocean water moved in, covering much of the coastal plain and working its way inland up the rivers. By 11,000 years ago, glaciation had pulled back from all but a

© HILARY NANGLE

few minor corners at the top of Maine, revealing the south coast's beaches and the unusual geologic traits—eskers and erratics, kettleholes and moraines, even a fjord—that make the rest of the state such a fascinating natural laboratory.

TODAY'S LANDSCAPE

Three distinct looks make up the contemporary Maine coastal landscape. (Inland are even more distinct biomes: serious woodlands and mountains as well as lakes and ponds and rolling fields.)

Along the **Southern Coast,** from Kittery to Portland, are fine-sand beaches, marshlands, and only the occasional rocky headland. The **Mid-Coast** and **Penobscot Bay,** from Portland to the Penobscot River, feature one finger of rocky land after another, all jutting into the Gulf of Maine and all incredibly scenic. **Acadia** and the **Down East Coast,** from the Penobscot River to Eastport and including fantastic Acadia National Park, have many similarities to the Mid-Coast (gorgeous rocky peninsulas, offshore islands, granite everywhere), but, except on Mount Desert Island, takes on a different look and feel by virtue of its slower pace, higher tides, and quieter villages.

Turn inland toward the **Maine Highlands**, and the landscape changes again. The Down East mountains, roughly straddling "the Airline" (Route 9 from Bangor to Calais), are marked by open blueberry fields, serious woodlands, and mountains that seem to appear out of nowhere. The central upland—essentially a huge S-shape extending from the Portland area up to the **Kennebec River Valley**, through Augusta, Waterville, and Skowhegan, then on up into **Aroostook County** at the top of the state—is characterized by lakes, ponds, rolling fields, and occasional woodlands interspersed with river valleys. Aroostook County is the state's agricultural jackpot. The northern region—essentially the valleys of the north-flowing St. John and Allagash Rivers—was the last part of Maine to lose the glacier and is today dense forest crisscrossed with logging roads (you can count the settlements on two hands).

The mountain upland, taking in all the state's major elevations and extending from inland York County to Baxter State Park and west through the **Western Lakes and Mountains** is rugged, beautiful, and the premier region for skiing, hiking, camping, and white-water rafting. Here, too, are seemingly endless lakes for swimming, boating, and birding.

GEOGRAPHY

Bounded by the Gulf of Maine (Atlantic Ocean), the St. Croix River, New Brunswick Province, the St. John River, Québec Province, and the state of New Hampshire (and the only state in the Union bordered by only one other state), Maine is the largest of the six New England states, roughly equivalent in size to the five others combined—offering plenty of space to hike, bike, camp, sail, swim, or just hang out. The state—and the coastline—extends from 43° 05' to 47° 28' north latitude, and 66° 56' to 80° 50' west longitude. (Technically, Maine dips even farther southeast to take in five islands in the offshore Isles of Shoals archipelago.) It's all stitched together by 22,574 miles of highways and 3,561 bridges.

Maine's more than 5,000 rivers and streams provide nearly half of the watershed for the Gulf of Maine. The major rivers are the Penobscot (350 miles), the St. John (211 miles), the Androscoggin (175 miles), the Kennebec (150 miles), the Saco (104 miles), and the St. Croix (75 miles). The St. John and its tributaries flow northeast; all the others flow more or less south or southeast.

The Pine Tree State has more than 17 million acres of forest covering 89 percent of the state, 5,900 lakes and ponds, 4,617 saltwater islands, 10 mountains over 4,000 feet, and nearly 100 mountains higher than 3,000 feet. The highest peak in the state is Katahdin, at 5,267 feet. (Katahdin is a Penobscot Indian word meaning "greatest mountain," making "Mount Katahdin" redundant.)

Maine's largest lake is Moosehead, in Greenville, 32 miles long and 20 miles across at its widest point, with a maximum depth of 246 feet.

CLIMATE

Whoever invented the state's oldest cliché—"If you don't like the weather, wait a minute"—must have spent at least several minutes in Maine. The good news, though, is that if the weather is lousy, it's bound to change before too long. And when it does, it's intoxicating. Brilliant, cloud-free Maine weather has lured many a visitor to put down roots, buy a retirement home, or at least invest in a summer retreat.

The serendipity of it all necessitates two caveats: Always pack warmer clothing than you think you'll need. And never arrive without a sweater or jacket—even at the height of summer.

The National Weather Service assigns Maine's coastline a climatological category distinct from climatic types found in the interior. The **coastal category,** which includes Portland, runs from Kittery northeast to Eastport and about 20 miles inland. Here, the ocean moderates the climate, making coastal winters warmer and summers cooler than in the interior (relatively speaking, of course). From early June through August, the Portland area—fairly typical of coastal weather—may have three to eight days of temperatures over 90°F, 25-40 days over 80°F, 14-24 days of fog, and 5-10 inches of rain. Normal annual precipitation for the Portland area is 44 inches of rain and 71 inches of snow (the snow total is misleading, though, since intermittent thaws clear away much of the base).

The **southern interior** division, covering the bottom third of the state, sees the warmest weather in summer, the most clear days each year, and an average snowfall of 60-90 inches. The **northern interior** part of the state, with the highest mountains, covers the upper two-thirds of Maine and boasts a mixed bag of snowy winters, warm summers, and the state's lowest rainfall.

© HILARY NANGLE

a foggy day on the Maine coast

The Seasons

Maine has four distinct seasons: summer, fall, winter, and mud. Lovers of spring need to look elsewhere in March, the lowest month on the popularity scale with its mud-caked vehicles, soggy everything, irritable temperaments, tank-trap roads, and often the worst snowstorm of the year.

Summer can be idyllic—with moderate temperatures, clear air, and wispy breezes—but it can also close in with fog, rain, and chills. Prevailing winds are from the southwest. Officially, summer runs June 20 or 21-September 20 or 21, but June, July, and August is more like it, with temperatures in the Portland area averaging 70°F during the day and in the 50s at night. The normal growing season is 148 days.

A poll of Mainers might well show **autumn** as the favorite season—days are still warmish, nights are cool, winds are optimum for sailors, and the foliage is brilliant. Fall colors usually begin appearing far to the north about mid-September, reaching their peak in that region by the end of the month. The last of the color begins in late September in the southernmost part of the state and fades by mid-October. Early autumn, however, is also the height of hurricane season, the only potential flaw this time of year.

Winter, officially December 20 or 21-March 20 or 21, means deep snow and cold inland and an unpredictable potpourri along the coastline. When the cold and snow hit the coast, it's time for cross-country skiing, ice fishing, snowshoeing, ice skating, ice climbing, and winter trekking and camping.

Spring, officially March 20 or 21-June 20 or 21, is the frequent butt of jokes. It's an ill-defined season that arrives much too late and departs all too quickly. Ice floes dot inland lakes and ponds until "ice-out" in early-mid-May; spring planting can't occur until well into May; lilacs explode in late May and disappear by mid-June. And just when you finally can enjoy being outside, blackflies stretch their wings and satisfy their hunger pangs. Along the coast, onshore breezes often keep the pesky creatures to a minimum.

Northeasters and Hurricanes

A northeaster is a counterclockwise, swirling storm that brings wild winds out of—you guessed it—the northeast. These storms can occur any time of year, whenever the conditions brew them up. Depending on the season, the winds are accompanied by rain, sleet, snow, or all of them together.

Hurricane season officially runs June-November but is most prevalent late August-September. Some years, the Maine coast remains out of harm's way; other years, head-on hurricanes and even glancing blows have eroded beaches, flooded roads, splintered boats, downed trees, knocked out power, and inflicted major residential and commercial damage.

Sea Smoke and Fog

Sea smoke and fog, two atmospheric phenomena resulting from opposing conditions, are only distantly related, but both can radically affect visibility and therefore be hazardous. In winter, when the ocean is at least 40°F warmer than the air, billowy sea smoke rises from the water, creating great photo ops for camera buffs but especially dangerous conditions for mariners.

In any season, when the ocean (or lake or land) is colder than the air, fog sets in, creating perilous conditions for drivers, mariners, and pilots. Romantics, however, see it otherwise, reveling in the womblike ambience and the muffled moans of foghorns. April-October, Portland averages about 31 days with heavy fog, when visibility may be a quarter mile or less.

Storm Warnings

The National Weather Service's official daytime signal system for wind velocity consists of a series of flags representing specific wind speeds and sea conditions. Beachgoers and anyone planning to venture out in a kayak, canoe, sailboat, or powerboat should heed these signals. The flags are posted on all public beaches, and warnings are announced on TV and radio weather broadcasts, as well as on cable TV's Weather Channel and the NOAA broadcast network.

Flora and Fauna

There it was, the State of Maine, which we had seen on the map, but not much like that. Immeasurable forest for the sun to shine on.... No clearing, no house.... The forest looked like a firm grass sward, and the effect of these lakes in its midst has been well compared.... to that of a mirror broken into a thousand fragments, and widely scattered over the grass, reflecting the full blaze of the sun.

Henry David Thoreau, *The Maine Woods*

Looking out over Maine from Katahdin today, as Thoreau did in 1857, you get a view that is still a mass of green stretching to the sea, broken by blue lakes and rivers. Although the forest has been cut several times since Thoreau saw it, Maine is proportionately still the most forested state in the nation.

It also is clearly one of the best watered. Receiving an average of more than 40 inches of precipitation a year, Maine is abundantly endowed with swamps, bogs, ponds, lakes, streams, and rivers. These in turn drain from a coast deeply indented by coves, estuaries, and bays.

In this state of trees and water, nature dominates more than most—Maine is the least densely populated state east of the Mississippi River. Here, where boreal and temperate ecosystems meet and mix, lives a rich diversity of plants and animals.

THE ALPINE TUNDRA

Three continental storm tracks converge on Maine, and the state's western mountains bear the brunt of the weather they bring. Stretching from Katahdin in the north along most of Maine's border with Québec and New Hampshire, these mountains have a far colder climate than their temperate latitude might suggest.

Timberline here occurs at only about 4,000 feet, and where the mountaintops reach above that, the environment is truly arctic—an alpine-tundra habitat where only the hardiest species can live. Beautiful pale-green "map" lichens cover many of the exposed rocks like shapes cut from an atlas, and sedges and rushes take root in the patches of thin topsoil. As many as 30 alpine plant species, typically found hundreds of miles to the north, grow in crevices or hollows in the lee of the blasting winds. Small and low-growing to conserve energy in this harsh climate, such plants as **bearberry willow, Lapland rosebay, alpine azalea, *Diapensia*, mountain cranberry,** and **black crowberry** reward the observant hiker with white, yellow, pink, and magenta flowers in late June-July.

Areas above the tree line are generally inhospitable to most animals other than secretive **voles, mice,** and **lemmings.** Even so, summer or winter, a hiker is likely to be aware of at least one other species: the **northern raven.** More than any of the 300 or so other bird species that regularly occur in Maine, the raven is the bird of the state's wild places, its mountain ridges, rocky coasts, and remote forests. Solid black like a crow but larger and stockier and with a wedge-shaped tail and broad wings, the northern raven is a magnificent flyer—soaring, hovering, diving, and often turning loops and rolls as though playing in the wind. Known to be among the most intelligent of all animals, ravens are quite social, actively communicating with one another in throaty croaks as they range over the landscape in search of carrion and other available plant and animal foods.

At the tree line and below, where conditions are moderate enough to allow black spruce and balsam fir to take hold, fauna becomes far more diverse. Among the wind- and ice-stunted trees, called *krummholz* (crooked wood), **northern juncos** and **white-throated sparrows** forage. The latter's plaintive whistle (often mnemonically rendered as "Old Sam Peabody, Peabody,

Peabody") is one of the most evocative sounds of the Maine woods.

THE BOREAL OR NORTHERN FOREST

Mention the Maine woods and the image that is likely to come to mind is the boreal forests of spruce and fir. In 1857, Thoreau captured the character of these woods when he wrote,

> It is all mossy and moosey. In some of those dense fir and spruce woods there is hardly room for the smoke to go up. The trees are a standing night, and every fir and spruce which you fell is a plume plucked from night's raven wing. Then at night the general stillness is more impressive than any sound, but occasionally you hear the note of an owl farther or nearer in the woods, and if near a lake, the semi-human cry of the loons at their unearthly revels.

Well adapted to a short growing season, low temperatures, and rocky, nutrient-poor soils, spruce and fir do dominate the woods on mountainsides, in low-lying areas beside watercourses, and along the coast. By not having to produce new foliage every year, these evergreens conserve scarce nutrients and also retain their needles, which capture sunlight for photosynthesis during all but the coldest months. The needles also wick moisture from the low clouds and fog that frequently bathe their preferred habitat, bringing annual precipitation to more than 80 inches a year in some areas.

In the lush boreal forest environment grows a diverse ground cover of herbaceous plants, including **bearberry, bunchberry, clintonia, starflower,** and **wood sorrel.** In older spruce-fir stands, mosses and lichens often carpet much of the forest floor in a soft tapestry of greens and gray-blues. Maine is extraordinarily rich in **lichens,** with more than 700 species identified so far—20 percent of the total found in all of North America. **Usnea** is a familiar one; its common name, old man's beard, comes from its wispy strands that drip from the branches of spruce trees. The **northern parula,** a small blue, green, and yellow bird of the wood warbler family, weaves its ball-shaped pendulum nest from usnea.

The spruce-fir forest is prime habitat for many other species that are among the most sought-after by birders: **black-backed** and **three-toed woodpeckers,** the audaciously bold **gray jay** (or camp robber), **boreal chickadees, yellow-throated flycatchers, white-winged crossbills, Swainson's thrushes,** and a half dozen other gem-like wood warblers.

Among the more unusual birds of this forest type is the spruce grouse. Sometimes hard to spot because it does not flush, a **spruce grouse** is so tame that a careful person can actually touch one. Not surprisingly, the spruce grouse earned the nickname "fool hen" early in the 19th century, and no doubt it would have become extinct long ago but for its menu preference of spruce and fir needles, which render its meat bitter and inedible (you can get an idea by tasting a few needles yourself).

Few of Maine's 56 mammal species are restricted to the boreal forest, but several are very characteristic of it. Most obvious from its trilling, far-carrying chatter is the **red squirrel.** Piles of cone remnants on the forest floor mark a red squirrel's recent banquet. The red squirrel itself is the favored prey of another coniferous forest inhabitant, the **pine marten.** An arboreal member of the mustelid family—which in Maine also includes **skunks, weasels, fishers,** and **otters**—the pine marten is a sleek, low-slung predator with blond to brown fur, an orange throat patch, and a long bushy tail. Its beautiful pelt nearly led to the animal's obliteration from Maine through overtrapping, but with protection, the marten population has rebounded.

Nearly half a century of protection also allowed the population recovery of Maine's most prominent mammal, the **moose.** Standing 6-7 feet tall at the shoulder and weighing as much as 1,200 pounds, the moose is the largest member of the Cervidae or deer family. A bull's massive antlers, which it sheds and regrows each year, may span five or more feet and weigh 75 pounds. The animal's long legs and bulbous nose give it an ungainly appearance, but the moose is ideally adapted to a life spent wading through deep snow, dense thickets, and swamps.

Usually the best place to observe a moose is at the edge of a body of water on a summer afternoon or evening. Wading out into the water, the animal may submerge its entire head to browse on the succulent aquatic plants below the surface. The water also offers a respite from the swarms of biting insects that plague moose (and people who venture into these woods without bug repellent). Except for a limited hunting season, moose have little to fear from humans and often will allow close approach. Be careful, however, and give them the respect their imposing size suggests; cows can be very protective of their calves, and bulls can be unpredictable, particularly during the fall rutting (mating) season.

Another word of caution about moose: When driving, especially in spring and early summer, be alert for moose wandering out of the woods and onto roadways to escape the flies. Moose are dark brown, their eyes do not reflect headlights in the way that most other animals' eyes do, and they do not get out of the way of cars or anything else. Colliding with a half-ton animal can be a tragedy for all involved. Pay particular attention while driving in Oxford, Franklin, Somerset (especially Rte. 201), Piscataquis, and Aroostook Counties, but with an estimated 76,000 moose statewide, they can and do turn up anywhere and everywhere—even in downtown Portland and on offshore islands.

Protection from unlimited hunting was not the only reason for the dramatic increase in Maine's moose population; the invention of the chain saw and the skidder have played parts too. In a few days, one or two workers can now cut and yard a tract of forest that a whole crew with saws and horses formerly took weeks to harvest. With the increase in logging, particularly the clear-cutting of spruce and fir, whose long fibers are favored for papermaking, vast areas have been opened up for regeneration by fast-growing, sun-loving hardwoods. The leaves of these young **white birch, poplar, pin cherry,** and **striped maple** are a veritable moose salad bar.

THE TRANSITION ZONE: NORTHERN HARDWOOD FOREST

Although hardwoods have replaced spruce and fir in many areas, mixed woods of sugar maple, American beech, yellow birch, red oak, red spruce, eastern hemlock, and white pine have always been a major part of Maine's natural and social histories. This northern hardwood forest, as it is termed by ecologists, is a transitional zone between northern and southern ecosystems and is rich in species diversity.

Dominated by deciduous trees, this forest community is highly seasonal. Spring snowmelt brings a pulse of life to the newly exposed forest floor as herbaceous plants race to develop and flower before the trees overhead leaf out and limit the available sunlight. (Blink and you can practically miss a Maine spring.) **Trout lily, goldthread, trillium, violets, gaywing,** and **pink lady's slipper** are among the many woodland wildflowers whose blooms make a walk in the forest so rewarding at this time of year. Deciduous trees, shrubs, and a dozen species of ferns also must make the most of their short four-month growing season. In the Maine woods, the buds of mid-May unfurl into a full canopy of leaves by the first week of June.

Late spring and early summer in the northern hardwood forest is also a time of intense animal activity. Runoff from the melting snowpack has filled countless low-lying depressions throughout the woods. These ephemeral swamps and vernal pools are a haven for an enormous variety of aquatic invertebrates, insects, amphibians, and reptiles. Choruses of **spring peepers,** Maine's smallest but seemingly loudest frog, alert everyone with their high-pitched calls that the ice is going out and breeding season is at hand. Measuring only about an inch in length, these tiny frogs with X-shaped patterns on their backs can be surprisingly difficult to see without some determined effort. Look on

FALLING FOR FOLIAGE

The timing of Maine's fall foliage owes much to the summer weather that precedes it, and so does the quality (although the annual spectacle never disappoints). In early September, as deciduous trees ready themselves for winter, they stop producing chlorophyll, and the green begins to disappear from their leaves. Taking its place are the spectacular pigments—brilliant reds, yellows, oranges, and purples—that paint the leaves and warm the hearts of every "leaf-peeper," shopkeeper, innkeeper, and restaurateur in the region.

The colorful display begins slowly, reaches a peak, and then fades—starting in the north in early-mid-September and working down to the southwest corner by mid-October. Peak foliage in far-north Aroostook County usually occurs in late September, about three weeks after the colors have begun to appear. Along the South Coast and Mid-Coast, the peak can occur as late as the middle of October, with the last bits of color hanging on even beyond that.

Trees put on their most magnificent show after a summer of moderate heat and rainfall; a summer of excessive heat and scant rainfall means colors will be less brilliant and disappear more quickly. Throw a September or October northeaster or hurricane into the mix, and estimates are up for grabs.

So predictions are imprecise, and you'll need to allow some schedule flexibility to take advantage of the changes in different parts of the state. Mid-September-mid-October, check the state's **Department of Conservation website** (www.mainefoliage.com) for frequently updated maps, panoramic photographs, and reports on the foliage status (this is gauged by the percentage of dropped leaf in every region of the state). Or call the **Foliage Hotline** (888/624-6345). Another resource for info on driving tours during foliage season is the website of the **Maine Office of Tourism** (www.visitmaine.com).

Fall-foliage trips are extremely popular and have become more so in recent years, so lodging can be scarce in some areas (although you'll often find beds in adjacent towns). Plan well ahead and make reservations, especially if you're headed for the Kennebunks, Boothbay Harbor, Camden, Bar Harbor, Greenville, Rangeley, and Bethel.

the branches of shrubs overhanging the water; males often use them as perches from which to call prospective mates. But then why stop with peepers? There are eight other frog and toad species in Maine to search for too.

Spring is also the best time to look for **salamanders.** Driving a country road on a rainy night in mid-April provides an opportunity to witness one of nature's great mass migrations as salamanders and frogs of several species emerge from their wintering sites and make their way across roads to breeding pools and streams. Once breeding is completed, most salamanders return to the terrestrial environment, where they burrow into crevices or the moist litter of the forest floor. The movement of amphibians from wetlands to uplands has an important ecological function, providing a mechanism for the return of nutrients that runoff washes into low-lying areas. This may seem hard to believe until one considers the numbers of individuals involved in this movement. To illustrate, the total biomass of Maine's **redback salamander** population—just one of the eight salamander species found here—is heavier than the combined weight of all the state's moose.

The many bird species characteristic of the northern hardwood forest are also most in evidence during the late spring and early summer, when the males are engaged in holding breeding territory and attracting mates. For most passerines—perching birds—this means singing. Especially during the early-morning and evening hours, the woods are alive with choruses of song from such birds as the **purple finch, white-throated sparrow, solitary vireo, black-throated blue warbler, Canada warbler, mourning warbler, northern waterthrush,** and the most beautiful singer of them all, the **hermit thrush.**

Providing abundant browse as well as tubers, berries, and nuts, the northern hardwood forest supports many of Maine's mammal species. The **red-backed vole, snowshoe hare, porcupine,** and **white-tailed deer** are relatively abundant and in turn are prey for **foxes, bobcats, fishers,** and **eastern coyotes.** Now well established since its expansion into Maine in the 1950s and 1960s, the eastern coyote has filled the niche at the top of the food chain once held by wolves and mountain lions before their extermination in the state in the late 19th century. **Black bears,** of which Maine has an estimated 25,000, are technically classified as carnivores and will take a moose calf or deer on occasion, but most of their diet consists of vegetation, insects, and fish. In the fall, bears feast on beechnuts and acorns, putting on extra fat for the coming winter, which they spend sleeping (not hibernating, as is often presumed) in a sheltered spot dug out beneath a rock or log.

Autumn is a time of spectacular beauty in Maine's northern hardwood forest. With the shortening days and cooler temperatures of September, the dominant green chlorophyll molecules in deciduous leaves start breaking down. As they do, the yellow, orange, and red pigments (which are always present in the leaves and serve to capture light in parts of the spectrum not captured by the chlorophyll) are revealed. Sugar maples put on the most dazzling display, but beeches, birches, red maples, and poplars add their colors to make up an autumn landscape famous the world over.

Ecologically, one of the most significant mammals in the Maine woods is the **beaver.** After being trapped almost to extinction in the 1800s, this large swimming rodent has recolonized streams, rivers, and ponds throughout the state. Well known for its ability as a dam builder, the beaver can change low-lying woodland into a complex aquatic ecosystem. The impounded water behind the dam often kills the trees it inundates, but these provide ideal nest cavities for **mergansers, wood ducks, owls, woodpeckers,** and **swallows.** The still water is also a nursery for a rich diversity of invertebrates, fish, amphibians, and Maine's seven aquatic turtle species, most common of which is the beautiful but very shy **eastern painted turtle.**

THE AQUATIC ENVIRONMENT

Small woodland pools and streams are, of course, only a part of Maine's aquatic environment. The state's nearly 6,000 lakes and ponds provide open-water and deep-water habitats for many additional species. A favorite among them is the **common loon,** symbol of north country lakes across the continent. Loons impart a sense of wildness and mystery with their haunting calls and yodels resonating off the surrounding pines on still summer nights. Adding to their popular appeal are their striking black-and-white plumage, accented with red eyes, and their ability to vanish below the surface and then reappear in another part of the lake moments later. The annual census of Maine's common loons since the 1970s indicates a relatively stable population of about 4,000 adults and 250 new chicks each summer.

Below the surface of Maine's lakes, ponds, rivers, and streams, 69 freshwater fish species live in the state, of which 17 were introduced. Among these exotic transplants are some of the most sought-after game fish, including **smallmouth and largemouth bass, rainbow trout,** and **northern pike.** These introductions may have benefited anglers, but they have displaced native species in many watersheds.

Several of Maine's native fish have interesting histories in that they became landlocked during the retreat of the glacier. At that time, Maine was climatically much like northern Canada is today, and **arctic char** ran up its rivers to spawn at the edges of the ice. As the ice continued to recede, some of these fish became trapped but nevertheless managed to survive and establish themselves in their new landlocked environments. Two remnant subspecies now exist: the **blue-back char,** which lives in the cold, deep water of 10 northern Maine lakes, and the **Sunapee char,** now found only in three lakes in Maine and two in Idaho.

A similar history belongs to the **landlocked salmon,** a form of Atlantic salmon that many regard as the state's premier game fish and now widely stocked throughout the state and around the country.

Atlantic salmon still run up some Maine rivers every year to spawn, but dams and heavy commercial fishing at sea have depleted their numbers and distribution to a fraction of what they once were. Unlike salmon species on the Pacific coast, adult Atlantic salmon survive the fall spawning period and make their way back out to sea again. The young, or parr, hatch the following spring and live in streams and rivers for the next 2-3 years before migrating to the waters off Greenland. Active efforts are now under way to restore this species, including capturing and trucking the fish around dams. Salmon is just one of the species whose life cycle starts in freshwater and requires migrations to and from the sea. Called anadromous fish, others include **striped bass, sturgeon, shad, alewives, smelt,** and **eels.** All were once far more numerous in Maine, but fortunately pollution control and management efforts in the past three decades have helped their populations rebound slightly from their historic low numbers.

ESTUARIES AND MUDFLATS

Maine's estuaries, where freshwater and saltwater meet, are ecosystems of outstanding biological importance. South of Cape Elizabeth, where the Maine coast is low and sandy, estuaries harbor large salt marshes of **spartina** grasses that can tolerate the frequent variations in salinity as runoff and tides fluctuate. Producing an estimated four times more plant material than an equivalent area of wheat, these spartina marshes provide abundant nutrients and shelter for a host of marine organisms that ultimately account for as much as 60 percent of the value of the state's commercial fisheries.

The tidal range along the Maine coast varies 9-26 vertical feet, southwest to northeast.

Where the tide inundates sheltered estuaries for more than a few hours at a time, spartina grasses cannot take hold, and mudflats dominate. Although it may look like a barren wasteland at low tide, a mudflat is also a highly productive environment and home to abundant marine life. Several species of tiny primitive worms called **nematodes** can inhabit the mud in densities of 2,000 or more per square inch. Larger worm species are also very common. One, the **bloodworm**, grows up to a foot in length and is harvested in quantity for use as sportfishing bait.

More highly savored among the mudflat residents is the **soft-shelled clam,** famous for its outstanding flavor and an essential ingredient of an authentic Maine lobster bake. But because clams are suspension feeders, filtering phytoplankton through their long siphon, or "neck," they can accumulate pollutants that cause illness, including hepatitis. Many Maine mudflats are closed to clam harvesting because of leaking septic systems, so it's best to check with the state's Department of Marine Resources or the local municipal office before digging a mess of clams yourself.

For birds and birders, salt marshes and mudflats are an unparalleled attraction. Long-legged wading birds such as the **glossy ibis, snowy egret, little blue heron, great blue heron, tricolored heron, green heron,** and **black-crowned night heron** frequent the marshes in great numbers throughout the summer months, hunting the shallow waters for mummichogs and other small salt-marsh fish, crustaceans, and invertebrates. Mid-May-early June and then again mid-July-mid-September, migrating shorebirds pass through Maine to and from their subarctic breeding grounds. On a good day, a discerning birder can find 17 or more species of shorebirds probing the mudflats and marshes with pointed bills in search of their preferred foods. In turn, the large flocks of shorebirds don't escape the notice of their own predators: **merlins** and **peregrine falcons** dash in to catch a meal.

THE ROCKY SHORELINE AND THE MARINE ENVIRONMENT

On the more exposed rocky shores—the dominant shoreline from Cape Elizabeth all the way Down East to Lubec—where currents and waves keep mud and sand from accumulating, the plant and animal communities are entirely different from those in the inland aquatic areas. The most important requirement for life in this impenetrable rockbound environment is probably the ability to hang on tight. **Barnacles,** the calcium-armored crustaceans that attach themselves to the rocks immediately below the high-tide line, have developed a fascinating battery of adaptations to survive not only pounding waves but also prolonged exposure to air, solar heat, and extreme winter cold. Glued in place, however, they cannot escape being eaten by **dog whelks,** the predatory snails that also inhabit this intertidal zone. Whelks are larger and more elongate than the more numerous and ubiquitous **periwinkle,** accidentally transplanted from Europe in the mid-19th century.

Also hanging onto these rocks but at a lower level are the brown algae seaweeds. Like a marine forest, the four species of **rockweed** provide shelter for a wide variety of life beneath their fronds. A world of discovery awaits those who make the effort to go out onto the rocks at low tide and look under the clumps of seaweed and into the tidal pools they shelter. Venture into these chilly waters with a mask, fins, and a wetsuit and still another world opens for natural-history exploration. Beds of **blue mussels, sea urchins, sea stars,** and **sea cucumbers** dot the bottom close to shore. In crevices between and beneath the rocks lurk **rock crabs** and **lobsters.** Now a symbol of the Maine coast and the delicious seafood it provides, the lobster was once considered "poor man's food"—so plentiful that it was spread on fields as fertilizer. Although lobsters are far less common than they once were, they are one of Maine's most closely monitored species, and their population continues to support a large and thriving commercial fishing industry.

Sadly, the same cannot be said for most of Maine's other commercially harvested marine fish. When Europeans first came to these shores four centuries ago, **cod, haddock, halibut, hake, flounder, herring,** and **tuna** were abundant, but no longer: Overharvested, their seabed habitat torn up by relentless dragging, these groundfish have all but disappeared. It will be decades before these species can recover, and then only if effective regulations can be put in place soon.

The familiar doglike face of the **harbor seal,** often seen peering alertly from the surface just offshore, provides a reminder that wildlife populations are resilient if given a chance. A century ago, there was a bounty on harbor seals because it was thought they ate too many lobsters and fish. Needless to say, neither fish nor lobsters increased when the seals all but disappeared. With the bounty's repeal and the advent of legal protection, Maine's harbor seal population has bounced back. Scores of them can regularly be seen basking on offshore ledges, drying their tan, brown, black, silver, or reddish coats in the sun. Though it's tempting to approach for a closer look, avoid bringing a boat too near these haul-out ledges, as it causes the seals to flush into the water and imposes an unnecessary stress on the pups, which already face a first-year mortality rate of 30 percent.

Positive changes in our relationships with wildlife are even more apparent with the return of birds to the Maine coast. Watching the numerous **herring gulls** and **great black-backed gulls** soaring on a fresh ocean breeze today, it's hard to imagine that a century ago, egg collecting had so reduced their numbers that they were a rare sight. In 1903, there were just three pairs of **common eiders** left in Maine; today, 25,000 pairs nest along the coast. With creative help from dedicated researchers using sound recordings, decoys, and prepared burrows, **Atlantic puffins** are recolonizing historic offshore nesting islands. **Ospreys** and **bald eagles,** almost free of the lingering vestiges of damage from DDT and other pesticides, now range the length of the coast and up Maine's major rivers.

THE FUTURE

Many Maine plants and animals remain subjects of concern. Too little is known about most of the lesser plants and animals to determine what their status is, but as natural habitats continue to decline in size or become degraded, it is likely that many of these species will disappear from the state. It is impossible to say exactly what will be lost when any of these species cease to exist here, but to quote conservationist Aldo Leopold, "To keep every cog and wheel is the first precaution of intelligent tinkering."

It is clear, however, that life in Maine has been enriched by the recovery of populations of pine marten, moose, harbor seals, eiders, and others. The natural persistence and tenacity of wildlife suggests that such species as the Atlantic salmon, wolf, and mountain lion will someday return to Maine—provided we give them the chance and the space to survive.

This *Flora and Fauna* section was written by William P. Hancock, former director of the Environmental Centers Department at the Maine Audubon Society and former editor of *Habitat Magazine*.

History

PREHISTORIC MAINERS: THE PALEOINDIANS

As the great continental glacier receded northwestward out of Maine about 11,000 years ago, some prehistoric grapevine must have alerted small bands of hunter-gatherers—fur-clad Paleoindians—to the scrub sprouting in the tundra, burgeoning mammal populations, and the ocean's bountiful food supply. Because come they did—at first seasonally and then year-round. Anyone who thinks tourism is a recent Maine phenomenon needs only to explore the shoreline in Damariscotta, Boothbay Harbor, and Bar Harbor, where heaps of cast-off oyster shells and clamshells document the migration of early Native Americans from woodlands to waterfront. "The shore" has been a summertime magnet for millennia.

Archaeological evidence from the Archaic period in Maine—roughly 8000-1000 BC—is fairly scant, but paleontologists have unearthed stone tools and weapons and small campsites attesting to a nomadic lifestyle supported by fishing and hunting (with fishing becoming more extensive as time went on). Toward the end of the tradition, during the late Archaic period, emerged a rather anomalous Indian culture known officially as the Moorehead phase but informally called the Red Paint People; the name is because of their curious trait of using a distinctive red ocher (pulverized hematite) in burials. Dark red puddles and stone artifacts have led excavators to burial pits as far north as the St. John River. Just as mysteriously as they had arrived, the Red Paint People disappeared abruptly and inexplicably around 1800 BC.

Following them almost immediately—and almost as suddenly—hunter-gatherers of the Susquehanna Tradition arrived from well to the south, moved across Maine's interior as far as the St. John River, and remained until about 1600 BC when they, too, enigmatically vanished. Excavations have turned up relatively sophisticated stone tools and evidence that they cremated their dead. It was nearly 1,000 years before a major new cultural phase appeared.

The next great leap forward was marked by the advent of pottery making, introduced about 700 BC. The Ceramic period stretched to the 16th century, and cone-shaped pots (initially stamped, later incised with coiled-rope motifs) survived until the introduction of metals from Europe. Houses of sorts—seasonal wigwam-style dwellings for fishermen and their families—appeared along the coast and on offshore islands.

THE EUROPEANS ARRIVE

The identity of the first Europeans to set foot in Maine is a matter of debate. Historians dispute the romantically popular notion that Norse explorers checked out this part of the New World as early as AD 1000. Even an 11th-century Norse coin found in 1961 in Brooklin (on the Blue Hill Peninsula) probably was carried there from farther north.

Not until the late 15th century, the onset of the great Age of Discovery, did credible reports of the New World (including what's now Maine) filter back to Europe's courts and universities. Thanks to innovations in naval architecture, shipbuilding, and navigation, astonishingly courageous fellows crossed the Atlantic in search of rumored treasure and new routes for reaching it.

John Cabot, sailing from England aboard the ship *Mathew,* may have been the first European to reach Maine, in 1498, but historians have never confirmed a landing site. No question remains, however, about the account of Giovanni da Verrazzano, an Italian explorer commanding *La Dauphine* under the French flag, who reached the Maine coast in May 1524, probably at the tip of the Phippsburg Peninsula. Encountering less-than-friendly Indians, Verrazzano did a minimum of business and sailed onward. His brother's map of the site labels it "The Land of Bad People." Esteban Gomez and John Rut followed in Verrazzano's wake, but nothing came of their exploits.

Nearly half a century passed before the Maine coast turned up again on European explorers' itineraries. This time, interest was fueled by reports of a Brigadoon-like area called Norumbega (or Oranbega, as one map had it), a myth that arose, gathered steam, and took on a life of its own in the decades after Verrazzano's voyage.

By the early 17th century, when Europeans began arriving in more than twos and threes and getting serious about colonization, Native American agriculture was already under way at the mouths of the Saco and Kennebec Rivers, the cod fishery was thriving on offshore islands, Indians far to the north were hot to trade furs for European goodies, and the birch-bark canoe was the transport of choice on inland waterways.

In mid-May 1602, Bartholomew Gosnold, en route to a settlement off Cape Cod aboard the *Concord,* landed along Maine's southern coast. The following year, merchant trader Martin Pring and his boats *Speedwell* and *Discoverer* explored farther Down East, backtracked to Cape Cod, and returned to England with tales that inflamed curiosity and enough sassafras to satisfy royal appetites. Pring produced a detailed survey of the Maine coast from Kittery to Bucksport, including offshore islands.

On May 18, 1605, George Waymouth, skippering the *Archangel,* reached Monhegan Island, 11 miles off the Maine coast, and moored for the night in Monhegan Harbor (still treacherous even today, exposed to the weather from the southwest and northeast and subject to meteorological beatings and heaving swells; yachting guides urge sailors not to expect to anchor, moor, or tie up there). The next day, Waymouth crossed the bay and scouted the mainland. He took five Indians hostage and sailed up the St. George River, near present-day Thomaston. Maritime historian Roger Duncan put it this way:

> The Plimoth Pilgrims were little boys in short pants when George Waymouth was exploring this coastline.

Waymouth returned to England and awarded his hostages to officials Sir John Popham and Sir Ferdinando Gorges, who, their curiosity piqued, quickly agreed to subsidize the colonization effort. In 1607, the *Gift of God* and the *Mary and John* sailed for the New World carrying two of Waymouth's captives. After returning them to their native Pemaquid area, Captains George Popham and Raleigh Gilbert continued westward, establishing a colony (St. George or Fort George) at the tip of the Phippsburg Peninsula in mid-August 1607 and exploring the shoreline between Portland and Pemaquid. Frigid weather, untimely deaths (including Popham's), and a storehouse fire doomed what's called the Popham Colony, but not before the 100 or so settlers built the 30-ton pinnace *Virginia,* the New World's first such vessel. When Gilbert received word of an inheritance waiting in England, he and the remaining colonists returned to the Old World.

In 1614, swashbuckling Captain John Smith, exploring from the Penobscot River westward to Cape Cod, reached Monhegan Island nine years after Waymouth's visit. Smith's meticulous map of the region was the first to use the "New England" appellation, and the 1616 publication of his *Description of New-England* became the catalyst for permanent settlements.

THE FRENCH AND THE ENGLISH SQUARE OFF

English dominance of exploration west of the Penobscot River in the early 17th century coincided roughly with French activity east of the river.

In 1604, French nobleman Pierre du Gua, Sieur de Monts, set out with cartographer Samuel de Champlain to map the coastline, first reaching Nova Scotia's Bay of Fundy and then sailing up the St. Croix River. In midriver, just west of present-day Calais, a crew planted gardens and erected buildings on today's St. Croix Island while de Monts and Champlain went off exploring. The two men reached the island Champlain named l'Isle des Monts Deserts (Mount Desert Island) and present-day Bangor before returning to face the winter with their ill-fated compatriots. Scurvy, lack of fuel and water, and a ferocious winter wiped out nearly half of the 79 men. In spring 1605, de Monts, Champlain, and other survivors headed southwest, exploring the coastline all the way to Cape Cod before heading northeast again and settling permanently at Nova Scotia's Port Royal (now Annapolis Royal).

Eight years later, French Jesuit missionaries en route to the Kennebec River ended up on Mount Desert Island and, with a band of French laymen, set about establishing the St. Sauveur settlement. But leadership squabbles led to building delays, and English marauder Samuel Argall—assigned to reclaim English territory—arrived to find them easy prey. The colony was leveled, the settlers were set adrift

in small boats, the priests were carted off to Virginia, and Argall moved on to destroy Port Royal.

By the 1620s, more than four dozen English fishing vessels were combing New England waters in search of cod, and year-round fishing depots had sprung up along the coast between Pemaquid and Portland. At the same time, English trappers and dealers began usurping the Indians' fur trade—a valuable income source.

The Massachusetts Bay Colony was established in 1630 and England's Council of New England, headed by Sir Ferdinando Gorges, began making vast land grants throughout Maine, giving rise to permanent coastal settlements, many dependent on agriculture. Among the earliest communities were Kittery, York, Wells, Saco, Scarborough, Falmouth, and Pemaquid—places where they tilled the acidic soil, fished the waters, eked out a barely-above-subsistence living, coped with predators and endless winters, bartered goods and services, and set up local governments and courts.

By the late 17th century, as these communities expanded, so did their requirements and responsibilities. Roads and bridges were built, preachers and teachers were hired, and militias were organized to deal with internecine and Indian skirmishes.

Even though England yearned to control the entire Maine coastline, her turf, realistically, was primarily south and west of the Penobscot River. The French had expanded from their Canadian colony of Acadia, for the most part north and east of the Penobscot. Unlike the absentee bosses who controlled the English territory, French merchants actually showed up, forming good relationships with the Indians and cornering the market in fishing, lumbering, and fur trading. And French Jesuit priests converted many a Native American to Catholicism. Intermittently, overlapping Anglo-French land claims sparked locally messy conflicts.

In the mid-17th century, the strategic heart of French administration and activity in Maine was Fort Pentagöet, a sturdy stone outpost built in 1635 in what is now Castine. From here, the French controlled coastal trade between the St. George River and Mount Desert Island and well up the Penobscot River. In 1654, England captured and occupied the fort and much of French Acadia, but, thanks to the 1667 Treaty of Breda, title returned to the French in 1670, and Pentagöet briefly became Acadia's capital.

A short but nasty Dutch foray against Acadia in 1674 resulted in Pentagöet's destruction ("levell'd with ye ground," by one account) and the raising of a third national flag over Castine.

THE INDIAN WARS (1675-1760)

Caught in the middle of 17th- and 18th-century Anglo-French disputes throughout Maine were the Wabanaki (People of the Dawn), the collective name for the state's major Native American tribal groups, all of whom spoke Algonquian languages. Modern ethnographers label these groups the Micmacs, Maliseets, Passamaquoddies, and Penobscots.

In the early 17th century, exposure to European diseases took its toll, wiping out three-quarters of the Wabanaki in the years 1616-1619. Opportunistic English and French traders quickly moved into the breach, and the Indians struggled to survive and regroup.

But regroup they did. Less than three generations later, a series of six Indian wars began, lasting nearly a century and pitting the Wabanaki most often against the English but occasionally against other Wabanaki. The conflicts, largely provoked by Anglo-French tensions in Europe, were King Philip's War (1675-1678), King William's War (1688-1699), Queen Anne's War (1703-1713), Dummer's War (1721-1726), King George's War (1744-1748), and the French and Indian War (1754-1760). Not until a get-together in 1762 at Fort Pownall (now Stockton Springs) did peace effectively return to the region—just in time for the heating up of the revolutionary movement.

COMES THE REVOLUTION

Near the end of the last Indian War, just beyond Maine's eastern border, a watershed event led to more than a century of cultural and political fallout. During the so-called Acadian Dispersal, in 1755, the English expelled from Nova Scotia 10,000 French-speaking Acadians who refused to pledge allegiance to the British Crown. Scattered as far south as Louisiana and west toward New Brunswick and Québec, the Acadians lost farms, homes, and possessions in this *grand dérangement*. Not until 1785 was land allocated for resettlement of Acadians along both sides of the Upper St. John River, where thousands of their descendants remain today. Henry Wadsworth Longfellow's epic poem *Evangeline* dramatically relates the sorry Acadian saga.

In the District of Maine, on the other hand, with relative peace following a century of intermittent warfare, settlement again exploded, particularly in the southernmost counties. The 1764 census tallied Maine's population at just under 25,000; a decade later, the number had doubled. New towns emerged almost overnight, often heavily subsidized by wealthy investors from the parent Massachusetts Bay Colony. With almost 4,000 residents, the largest town in the district was Falmouth (later renamed Portland).

In 1770, 27 Maine towns became eligible, based on population, to send representatives to the Massachusetts General Court, the colony's legislative body. But only six coastal towns could actually afford to send anyone, sowing seeds of resentment among settlers who were thus saddled with taxes without representation. Sporadic mob action accompanied unrest in southern Maine, but the flashpoint occurred in the Boston area.

On April 18, 1775, Paul Revere set out on America's most famous horseback ride—from Lexington to Concord, Massachusetts—to announce the onset of what became the American Revolution. Most of the Revolution's action occurred south of Maine, but not all of it.

In June, the Down East outpost of Machias was the site of the war's first naval engagement. The well-armed but unsuspecting British vessel HMS *Margaretta* sailed into the bay and was besieged by local residents angry about a Machias merchant's sweetheart deal with the British. Before celebrating their David-and-Goliath victory, the rebels captured the *Margaretta,* killed her captain, and then captured two more British ships sent to the rescue.

In the fall of 1775, Col. Benedict Arnold—better known to history as a notorious turncoat—assembled 1,100 sturdy men for a flawed and futile march to Québec" to dislodge the English. From Newburyport, Massachusetts, they sailed to the mouth of the Kennebec River, near Bath, and then headed inland with the tide. In Pittston, six miles south of Augusta and close to the head of navigation, they transferred to a fleet of 220 locally made bateaux and laid over three nights at Fort Western in Augusta. Then they set off, poling, paddling, and portaging their way upriver. Skowhegan, Norridgewock, and Chain of Ponds were among the landmarks along the grueling route. The men endured cold, hunger, swamps, disease, dense underbrush, and the loss of nearly 600 of their comrades before reaching Québec in late 1775. In the Kennebec River Valley, Arnold Trail historical signposts today mark highlights (or, more aptly, lowlights) of the expedition.

Four years later, another futile attempt to dislodge the British, this time in the District of Maine, resulted in America's worst naval defeat until World War II—a little-publicized debacle called the Penobscot Expedition. On August 14, 1779, as more than 40 American warships and transports carrying more than 2,000 Massachusetts men blockaded Castine to flush out a relatively small enclave of left-over Brits, a seven-vessel Royal Navy fleet appeared. Despite their own greater numbers, about 30 of the American ships turned tail up the Penobscot River. The captains torched their vessels, exploding the ammunition and leaving the survivors to walk in disgrace to Augusta or even Boston. Each side took close to 100 casualties, three commanders—including Paul Revere—were court-martialed, and Massachusetts was about $7 million poorer.

The American Revolution officially came to a close on September 3, 1783, with the signing of the Treaty of Paris between the United States and Great Britain. The U.S.-Canada border was set at the St. Croix River, but, in a massive oversight, boundary lines were left unresolved for thousands of square miles in the northern District of Maine.

TRADE TROUBLES AND THE WAR OF 1812

In 1807, President Thomas Jefferson imposed the Embargo Act, banning trade with foreign entities—specifically, France and Britain. With thousands of miles of coastline and harbor villages dependent on trade for revenue and basic necessities, Maine reeled. By the time the act was repealed, under president James Madison in 1809, France and Britain were almost unscathed, but the bottom had dropped out of New England's economy.

An active smuggling operation based in Eastport kept Mainers from utter despair, but the economy still had continued its downslide. In 1812, the fledgling United States declared war on Great Britain, again disrupting coastal trade. In the fall of 1814, the situation reached its nadir when the British invaded the Maine coast and occupied all the shoreline between the St. Croix and Penobscot Rivers. Later that same year, the Treaty of Ghent finally halted the squabble, forced the British to withdraw from Maine, and allowed the locals to get on with economic recovery.

STATEHOOD

In October 1819, Mainers held a constitutional convention at the First Parish Church on Congress Street in Portland. (Known affectionately as "Old Jerusalem," the church was later replaced by the present-day structure.) The convention crafted a constitution modeled on that of Massachusetts, with two notable differences: Maine would have no official church (Massachusetts had the Puritans' Congregational Church), and Maine would place no religious requirements or restrictions on its gubernatorial candidates. When votes came in from 241 Maine towns, only nine voted against ratification.

For Maine, March 15, 1820, was one of those good news/bad news days: After 35 years of separatist agitation, the District of Maine broke from Massachusetts (signing the separation allegedly, and disputedly, at the Jameson Tavern in Freeport) and became the 23rd state in the Union. However, the Missouri Compromise, enacted by Congress only 12 days earlier to balance admission of slave and free states, mandated that the slave state of Missouri be admitted on the same day. Maine had abolished slavery in 1788, and there was deep resentment over the linkage.

Portland became the new state's capital (albeit only briefly; it switched to Augusta in 1832), and William King, one of statehood's most outspoken advocates, became the first governor.

TROUBLE IN THE NORTH COUNTRY

Without an official boundary established on Maine's far northern frontier, turf battles were always simmering just under the surface. Timber was the sticking point—everyone wanted the vast wooded acreage. Finally, in early 1839, militia reinforcements descended on the disputed area, heating up what has come to be known as the Aroostook War, a border confrontation with no battles and no casualties (except a farmer who was shot by friendly militia). It's a blip in the historical time line, but remnants of fortifications in Houlton, Fort Fairfield, and Fort Kent keep the story alive today. By March 1839, a truce was negotiated, and the 1842 Webster-Ashburton Treaty established the border once and for all.

MAINE IN THE CIVIL WAR

In the 1860s, with the state's population slightly more than 600,000, more than 70,000 Mainers suited up and went off to fight in the Civil War—the greatest per-capita show of force of any northern state. About 18,000 of them died in the conflict. Thirty-one Mainers were Union Army generals, the best known being Joshua L. Chamberlain, a Bowdoin College professor, who commanded the Twentieth Maine

regiment and later became president of the college and governor of Maine.

During the war, young battlefield artist Winslow Homer, who later settled in Prouts Neck, south of Portland, created wartime sketches regularly for such publications as *Harper's Weekly*. In Washington, Maine senator Hannibal Hamlin was elected vice president under Abraham Lincoln in 1860 (he was removed from the ticket in favor of Andrew Johnson when Lincoln came up for reelection in 1864).

MAINE COMES INTO ITS OWN

After the Civil War, Maine's influence in Republican-dominated Washington far outweighed the size of its population. In the late 1880s, Mainers held the federal offices of acting vice president, Speaker of the House, secretary of state, Senate majority leader, Supreme Court justice, and several important committee chairmanships. Best known of the notables were James G. Blaine (journalist, presidential aspirant, and secretary of state) and Portland native Thomas Brackett Reed, presidential aspirant and Speaker of the House.

In Maine itself, traditional industries fell into decline after the Civil War, dealing the economy a body blow. Steel ships began replacing Maine's wooden clippers, refrigeration techniques made the block-ice industry obsolete, concrete threatened the granite-quarrying trade, and the output from Southern textile mills began to supplant that from Maine's mills.

Despite Maine's economic difficulties, however, wealthy urbanites began turning their sights toward the state, accumulating land (including islands) and building enormous summer "cottages" for their families, servants, and hangers-on. Bar Harbor was a prime example of the elegant summer colonies that sprang up, but others include Grindstone Neck (Winter Harbor), Prouts Neck (Scarborough), and Dark Harbor (on Islesboro in Penobscot Bay). Vacationers who preferred fancy hotel-type digs reserved rooms for the summer at such sprawling complexes as Kineo House (on Moosehead

Lake), Poland Spring House (west of Portland), or the Samoset Hotel (in Rockland). Built of wood and catering to long-term visitors, these and many others all eventually succumbed to altered vacation patterns and the ravages of fire.

As the 19th century spilled into the 20th, the state broadened its appeal beyond the well-to-do who had snared prime turf in the Victorian era. It launched an active promotion of Maine as "The Nation's Playground," successfully spurring an influx of visitors from all economic levels. By steamboat, train, and soon by car, people came to enjoy the ocean beaches, the woods, the mountains, the lakes, and the quaintness of it all. (Not that these features didn't really exist, but the state's aggressive public relations campaign at the turn of the 20th century stacks up against anything Madison Avenue puts out today.) The only major hiatus in the tourism explosion in the century's first two decades was 1914-1918, when 35,062 Mainers joined many thousands of other Americans in going off to the European front to fight in World War I. Two years after the war ended, in 1920 (the centennial of its statehood), Maine women were the first in the nation to troop to the polls after ratification of the 19th Amendment granted universal suffrage.

Maine was slow to feel the repercussions of the Great Depression, but eventually they came, with bank failures all over the state. Federally subsidized programs, such as the Civilian Conservation Corps (CCC) and the Works Progress Administration (WPA), left lasting legacies in Maine.

Politically, the state has contributed notables on both sides of the aisle. In 1954, Maine elected as its governor Edmund S. Muskie, only the fifth Democrat in the job since 1854. In 1958, Muskie ran for and won a seat in the Senate, and in 1980 he became secretary of state under president Jimmy Carter. Muskie died in 1996.

Elected in 1980, Waterville's George J. Mitchell made a respected name for himself as a Democratic senator and Senate majority leader before retiring in 1996, when Maine became only the second state in the union to have two women senators (Olympia Snowe and Susan Collins, both Republicans). After his 1996 reelection, president Bill Clinton appointed Mitchell's distinguished congressional colleague and three-term senator, Republican William Cohen of Bangor, as secretary of defense, a position he held through the rest of the Clinton administration. Mitchell spent considerable time during the Clinton years as the U.S. mediator for Northern Ireland's "troubles" and subsequently headed an international fact-finding team in the Middle East.

Government and Economy

Politics in Maine isn't quite as variable and unpredictable as the weather, but pundits are almost as wary as weather forecasters about making predictions. Despite a long tradition of Republicanism dating from the late 19th century, Maine's voters and politicians have a national reputation for being independent-minded—electing Democrats, Republicans, or independents more for their character than their political persuasions.

Four of the most notable recent examples are Margaret Chase Smith, Edmund S. Muskie, George J. Mitchell, and William Cohen—two Republicans and two Democrats, all Maine natives. Republican senator Margaret Chase Smith proved her flintiness when she spoke out against McCarthyism in the 1950s. Ed Muskie, the first prominent Democrat to come out of Maine, won every race he entered except an aborted bid for the presidency in 1972. George Mitchell and William Cohen went on to win stellar international reputations. In a manifestation of Maine's strong tradition of bipartisanship, Mitchell and Cohen worked together closely on many issues to benefit the state and the nation (they even wrote a book together).

In the 1970s, Maine elected an independent governor, James Longley, whose memory is still respected (Longley's son was later elected to Congress as a Republican, and his daughter to the state senate as a Democrat). In 1994, Maine voted in another independent, Angus King (now a senator), a relatively young veteran of careers in business, broadcasting, and law. The governor serves a term of four years, limited to two terms.

The state's Supreme Judicial Court has a chief justice and six associate justices.

Maine is ruled by a bicameral, biennial citizen legislature comprising 151 members in the House of Representatives and 35 members in the state senate, including a relatively high percentage of women and a fairly high proportion of retirees. Members of both houses serve two-year terms. In 1993, voters passed a statewide term-limits referendum restricting legislators to four terms.

Whereas nearly two dozen Maine cities are ruled by city councils, about 450 smaller towns and plantations retain the traditional form of rule: annual town meetings. Town meetings generally are held in March, when newspaper pages bulge with reports containing classic quotes from citizens exercising their rights to vote and vent. A few examples: "I believe in the pursuit of happiness until that pursuit infringes on the happiness of others"; "I don't know of anyone's dog running loose except my own, and

I've arrested her several times"; and "Don't listen to him; he's from New Jersey."

When the subject of the economy comes up, you'll often hear reference to the "two Maines," as if an east-west line bisected the state in half. There's much truth to that image. Southern Maine is prosperous, with good jobs (although never enough), lots of small businesses, and a highly competitive real-estate market. Northern Maine struggles along, suffering as much from its immensity and lack of infrastructure as its low population density. The central region lies between the two in every respect; there are a few more population centers and a little more industry. Efforts to stimulate economic development in the less developed areas have experienced fluctuating degrees of success that largely mirror the state of the U.S. economy.

According to state economists, Maine currently faces three challenges. First, slow job growth: Over the past two decades, Maine's has been about half of the national average. Second, changing employment patterns: Once famed for producing textiles and shoes and for its woods-based industries, now health care and tourism provide the most jobs. Third, an aging population: Economic forecasters predict that more than one in five residents will be older than 65 by 2020, which poses a challenge for finding workers in the future.

People and Culture

THE PEOPLE

Maine's population didn't top the one-million mark until 1970. Forty years later, according to the 2010 census, the state had 1,318,301 residents. Along the coast, Cumberland County, comprising the Greater Portland area, has the highest head count.

Despite the longstanding presence of several substantial ethnic groups, plus four Native American tribes (about 1 percent of the population), diversity is a relatively recent

phenomenon in Maine, and the population is about 95 percent Caucasian. A steady influx of refugees, beginning after the Vietnam War, forced the state to address diversity issues, and it continues to do so today.

Natives and "People from Away"

People who weren't born in Maine aren't natives. Even people who *were* born here may experience close scrutiny of their credentials. In Maine, there are natives and *natives*. Every

© HILARY NANGLE

Lobster is Maine's most valuable seafood product.

day, the obituary pages describe Mainers who have barely left the houses in which they were born—even in which their grandparents were born. We're talking roots!

Along with this kind of heritage comes a whole vocabulary all its own—lingo distinctive to Maine, or at least New England.

Part of the "native" picture is the matter of "native" produce. Hand-lettered signs sprout everywhere during the summer advertising native corn, native peas, even—believe it or not—native ice. In Maine, homegrown is well grown.

"People from away," on the other hand, are those whose families haven't lived here year-round for a generation or more. But people from away (also called flatlanders) exist all over Maine, and they have come to stay, putting down roots of their own and altering the way the state is run, looks, and *will* look. Senator Collins is native, but Senator King came from away. You'll find other flatlanders as teachers, corporate executives, artists, retirees, writers, town selectmen, and even lobstermen.

In the 19th century, arriving flatlanders were mostly "rusticators" or "summer complaints"—summer residents who lived well, often in enclaves, and never set foot in the state off-season. They did, however, pay property taxes, contribute to causes, and provide employment for local residents. Another 19th-century wave of people from away came from the bottom of the economic ladder: Irish escaping the potato famine and French Canadians fleeing poverty in Québec. Both groups experienced subtle and overt anti-Catholicism but rather quickly assimilated into the mainstream, taking jobs in mills and factories and becoming staunch American patriots.

The late 1960s and early 1970s brought bunches of "back-to-the-landers," who scorned plumbing and electricity and adopted retro ways of life. Although a few pockets of die-hards still exist, most have changed with the times and adopted contemporary mores (and conveniences).

Today, technocrats arrive from away with computers, faxes, cell phones, and other high-tech gear and "commute" via the Internet and modern electronics.

Native Americans

In Maine, the *real* natives are the Wabanaki (People of the Dawn)—the Micmac, Maliseet, Penobscot, and Passamaquoddy tribes of the eastern woodlands. Many live in or near three reservations, near the headquarters for their tribal governors. The Passamaquoddies are at Pleasant Point, in Perry, near Eastport, and at Indian Township, in Princeton, near Calais. The Penobscots are based on Indian Island, in Old Town, near Bangor. Other Native American population clusters—known as "off-reservation Indians"—are the Aroostook Band of Micmacs, based in Presque Isle, and the Houlton Band of Maliseets, in Littleton, near Houlton.

In 1965, Maine became the first state to establish a Department of Indian Affairs, but just five years later the Passamaquoddy and Penobscot tribes initiated a 10-year-long land-claims case involving 12.5 million Maine acres (about two-thirds of the state) weaseled from the Indians by Massachusetts in 1794. In late 1980, a landmark agreement, signed by President Jimmy Carter, awarded the tribes $80.6 million in reparations. Despite this, the tribes still struggle to provide jobs on the reservations and to increase the overall standard of living. A 2003 and 2011 referenda to allow the tribes to build a casino were defeated.

One of the true success stories of the tribes is the revival of traditional arts as businesses. The Maine Indian Basketmakers Association has an active apprenticeship program, and two renowned basket makers—Mary Gabriel and Clara Keezer—have achieved National Heritage Fellowships. Several well-attended annual summer festivals—in Bar Harbor, Grand Lake Stream, and Perry—highlight Indian traditions and heighten awareness of Native American culture. Basket making, canoe building, and traditional dancing are all parts of the scene. The splendid Abbe Museum in Bar Harbor features Indian artifacts, interactive displays, historic photographs,

and special programs. Gift shops have begun adding Native American jewelry and baskets to their inventories.

Acadians and Franco-Americans

Within about three decades of their 1755 expulsion from Nova Scotia in *le grand dérangement,* Acadians had established new communities and new lives in northern Maine's St. John Valley. Gradually, they explored farther into central and southern coastal Maine and west into New Hampshire. The Acadian diaspora has profoundly influenced Maine and its culture, and it continues to do so today. Along the coast, French is spoken on the streets of Biddeford, where there's an annual Franco-American festival and an extensive Franco-American research collection. The St. John Valley at the tip of Maine is a host for the 2014 Acadian Congress.

African Americans

Although Maine's African American population is small, the state has had an African American community since the 17th century; by the 1764 census, there were 322 slaves and free blacks in the District of Maine. Segregation remained the rule, however, so in the 19th century, blacks established their own parish, the Abyssinian Church, in Portland. Efforts are under way to restore the long-closed church as an African American cultural center and gathering place for Greater Portland's black community. Maine's African Americans have earned places in history books that far exceed their small population. In 1826, Bowdoin's John Brown Russworm became America's first black college graduate; in 1844, Macon B. Allen became the first African American to gain admission to a state bar; and in 1875, James A. Heay became America's first African American Roman Catholic Bishop, when he was ordained for the Diocese of Portland. For researchers delving into "Maine's black experience," the University of Southern Maine, in Portland, houses the African-American Archive of Maine, a significant collection of historic books, letters, and artifacts donated by Gerald

Talbot, the first African American to serve in the Maine legislature.

Finns, Swedes, Lebanese, and Amish

Finns came to Maine in several 19th-century waves, primarily to work the granite quarries on the coast and on offshore islands, the slate quarries in Monson, near Greenville, and to farm in Oxford County.

In 1870, an idealistic American diplomat named William Widgery Thomas established a model agricultural community with 50 brave Swedes in the heart of Aroostook County. Their enclave, New Sweden, remains today, as does the town of Stockholm, and descendants of the pioneers have spread throughout Maine.

At the turn of the 20th century, Lebanese (and some Syrians) began descending on Waterville, where they found work in the textile mills and eventually established St. Joseph's Maronite Church in 1927. One of these immigrants was the mother of former senator George Mitchell.

Amish families are increasingly taking refuge in Maine. What began with one colony in Aroostook County has grown to four, including one in Unity.

Russians, Ukrainians, and Byelorussians

Arriving after World War II, Slavic immigrants established a unique community in Richmond, just inland from Bath. In the 1950s, the town was home to the largest rural Russian-speaking population in the country. Only a tiny nucleus remains today, along with an onion-domed church, but a stroll through the local cemetery hints at the extent of the original colony.

The Newest Arrivals: Refugees from War

War has been the impetus for the more recent arrival of Asians, Africans, Central Americans, and Eastern Europeans. Most have settled in the Portland area, making that city the state's center of diversity. Vietnamese and Cambodians began settling in Maine in the mid-1970s. A handful of Afghanis who fled the Soviet-Afghan conflict also ended up in Portland. Somalis, Ethiopians, and Sudanese fled their war-torn countries in the early to mid-1990s, and Bosnians and Kosovars arrived in the last half of the 1990s. With every new conflict comes a new stream of immigrants—world citizens are becoming Mainers, and Mainers are becoming world citizens.

CULTURE

Mainers are an independent lot, many exhibiting the classic Yankee characteristics of dry humor, thrift, and ingenuity. Those who can trace their roots back at least a generation or two in the state and have lived here through the duration can call themselves natives; everyone else, no matter how long they've lived here, is "from away."

Mainers react to outsiders depending upon how those outsiders treat them. Treat a Mainer with a condescending attitude, and you'll receive a cold shoulder at best. Treat a Mainer with respect, and you'll be welcome, perhaps even invited in to share a mug of coffee. Mainers are wary of outsiders and often with good reason. Many outsiders move to Maine because they fall in love with its independence and rural simplicity, and then they demand that the farmer stop spreading that stinky manure on his farmlands, or they insist that the town initiate garbage pickup, or they build a glass-and-timber McMansion in the midst of white clapboard historical homes.

In most of Maine, money doesn't impress folks. The truth is, that lobsterman in the old truck and the well-worn work clothes might be sitting on a small fortune. Or living on it. Perhaps nothing has caused more troubles between natives and newcomers than the rapidly increasing value of land and the taxes that go with that. For many visitors, Maine real estate is a bargain they can't resist.

If you want real insight into Maine character, listen to a CD or watch a video by one Maine master humorist, Tim Sample. As he often says, "Wait a minute; it'll sneak up on you."

THE ARTS
Fine Art

In 1850, in a watershed moment for Maine landscape painting, Frederic Edwin Church (1826-1900), Hudson River School artist par excellence, vacationed on Mount Desert Island. Influenced by the luminist tradition of such contemporaries as Fitz Hugh Lane (1804-1865), who summered in nearby Castine, Church accurately but romantically depicted the dramatic tableaux of Maine's coast and woodlands that even today attract slews of admirers.

By the 1880s, however, impressionism had become the style du jour and was being practiced by a coterie of artists who collected around Charles Herbert Woodbury (1864-1940) in Ogunquit. His program made Ogunquit the best-known summer art school in New England. After Hamilton Easter Field established another art school in town, modernism soon asserted itself. Among the artists who took up summertime Ogunquit residence was Walt Kuhn (1877-1949), a key organizer of New York's 1913 landmark Armory Show of modern art.

Meanwhile, a bit farther south, impressionist Childe Hassam (1859-1935), part of writer Celia Thaxter's circle, produced several hundred works on Maine's remote Appledore Island, in the Isles of Shoals off Kittery, and illustrated Thaxter's *An Island Garden.*

Another artistic summer colony found its niche in 1903, when Robert Henri (born Robert Henry Cozad, 1865-1929), charismatic leader of the Ashcan School of realist/modernists, visited Monhegan Island, about 11 miles offshore. Artists who followed him there included Rockwell Kent (1882-1971), Edward Hopper (1882-1967), George Bellows (1882-1925), and Randall Davey (1887-1964). Among the many other artists associated with Monhegan images are William Kienbusch (1914-1980), Reuben Tam (1916-1991), and printmakers Leo Meissner (1895-1977) and Stow Wengenroth (1906-1978).

But colonies were of scant interest to other notables, who chose to derive their inspiration from Maine's stark natural beauty and work mostly in their own orbits. Among these are genre painter Eastman Johnson (1824-1906); romantic realist Winslow Homer (1836-1910), who lived in Maine for 27 years and whose studio in Prouts Neck (Scarborough) still overlooks the surf-tossed scenery he so often depicted; pointillist watercolorist Maurice Prendergast (1858-1924); John Marin (1870-1953), a cubist who painted Down East subjects, mostly around Deer Isle and Addison (Cape Split); Lewiston native Marsden Hartley (1877-1943), who first showed his abstractionist work in New York in 1909 and later worked in Berlin; Fairfield Porter (1907-1975), whose family summered on Great Spruce Head Island, in East Penobscot Bay; and Andrew Wyeth (1917-2009), whose reputation as a romantic realist in the late 20th century surpassed that of his illustrator father, N. C. Wyeth (1882-1945).

On a parallel track was sculptor Louise Nevelson (1899-1988), raised in a poor Russian-immigrant family in Rockland and far better known outside her home state for her monumental wood sculptures slathered in black or gold. Two other noted sculptors with Maine connections were William Zorach (1887-1966) and Gaston Lachaise (1882-1935), both of whom lived in Georgetown, near Bath.

Contemporary year-round or seasonal Maine residents with national (and international) reputations include Vinalhaven's Robert Indiana, Lincolnville's Alex Katz, North Haven's Eric Hopkins, Deer Isle's Karl Schrag, Tenants Harbor's Jamie Wyeth (third generation of the famous family), Kennebunk's Edward Betts, and Cushing's Lois Dodd and Alan Magee.

The two best collections of Maine art are at the **Portland Museum of Art** (7 Congress Sq., Portland, 207/775-6148) and the **Farnsworth Art Museum** (16 Museum St., Rockland, 207/596-6457). The Farnsworth, in fact, focuses only on Maine art, primarily from the 20th century. The Farnsworth is the home of the Wyeth Center, featuring the works of three generations of Wyeths.

The **Ogunquit Museum of American Art,** appropriately, also has a very respectable Maine collection (in a spectacular setting), as does the

Monhegan Museum. Other Maine paintings, not always on exhibit, are at the **Colby College Museum of Art** in Waterville and the **Bowdoin College Museum of Art** in Brunswick.

Crafts

Any survey of Maine art, however brief, must include the significant role of crafts in the state's artistic tradition. As with painters, sculptors, and writers, craftspeople have gravitated to Maine—most notably since the establishment in 1950 of the Haystack Mountain School of Crafts. Started in the Belfast area, the school put down roots on Deer Isle in 1960. Craft studios are abundant in Maine, and many festivals include craft displays.

Down East Literature

Maine's first big-name writer was probably the early 17th-century French explorer Samuel de Champlain (1570-1635), who scouted the Maine coast, established a colony in 1604 near present-day Calais, and lived to describe in detail his experiences. Several decades after Champlain's forays, English naturalist John Josselyn visited Scarborough and in the 1670s published the first two books accurately describing Maine's flora and fauna (aptly describing, for example, blackflies as "not only a pesterment but a plague to the country").

Today, Maine's best-known author lives not on the coast but just inland in Bangor—Stephen King (born 1947), wizard of the weird. Many of his dozens of horror novels and stories are set in Maine, and several have been filmed for the big screen here. King and his author wife, Tabitha, are avid fans of both education and team sports and have generously distributed their largesse among schools, libraries, and teams in their hometown as well as other parts of the state.

Other best-selling contemporary authors writing in or about Maine include Carolyn Chute (born 1948), resident of Parsonsfield and author of the raw novels *The Beans of Egypt, Maine* and *Letourneau's Used Auto Parts*; Cathie Pelletier (born 1953), raised in tiny Allagash and author of such humor-filled novels as *The*

Funeral Makers and *The Bubble Reputation*; and coastal-Maine resident Richard Russo (born 1949), author of *Empire Falls*, winner of the 2002 Pulitzer Prize in Fiction and named the year's best novel by *Time* magazine.

CHRONICLERS OF THE GREAT OUTDOORS

John Josselyn was perhaps the first practitioner of Maine's strong naturalist tradition in American letters, but the Pine Tree State's rugged scenic beauty and largely unspoiled environment have given rise to many ecologically and environmentally concerned writers.

The 20th century saw the arrival in Maine of crusader Rachel Carson (1907-1964), whose 1962 wake-up call, *Silent Spring,* was based partly on Maine observations and research. The Rachel Carson National Wildlife Refuge, headquartered in Wells and comprising 10 chunks of environmentally sensitive coastal real estate, covers nearly 3,500 acres between Kittery Point and the Mid-Coast region.

The tiny town of Nobleboro, near Damariscotta, drew nature writer Henry Beston (1888-1968); his *Northern Farm* lyrically chronicles a year in Maine. Beston's wife, Elizabeth Coatsworth (1893-1986), wrote more than 90 books—including *Chimney Farm,* about their life in Nobleboro.

Fannie Hardy Eckstorm (1865-1946), born in Brewer to Maine's most prosperous fur trader, graduated from Smith College and became a noted expert on Maine (and specifically Native American) folklore. Among her extensive writings, *Indian Place-Names of the Penobscot Valley and the Maine Coast,* published in 1941, remains a sine qua non for researchers.

The out-of-doors and inner spirits shaped Cape Rosier adoptees Helen and Scott Nearing, whose 1954 *Living the Good Life* became the bible of Maine's back-to-the-landers.

CLASSIC WRITINGS ON THE STATE

Historical novels, such as *Arundel,* were the specialty of Kennebunk native Kenneth Roberts (1885-1957), but Roberts also wrote *Trending into Maine,* a potpourri of Maine observations

MAINE FOOD SPECIALTIES

Everyone knows Maine is *the* place for lobster, but there are quite a few other foods that you should sample before you leave.

For a few weeks in May, right around Mother's Day (the second Sunday in May), a wonderful delicacy starts sprouting along Maine woodland streams: **fiddleheads,** the still-furled tops of the ostrich fern *(Matteuccia struthiopteris)*. Tasting vaguely like asparagus, fiddleheads have been on May menus ever since Native Americans taught the colonists to forage for the tasty vegetable. Don't go fiddleheading unless you're with a pro, though; the lookalikes are best left to the woods critters. If you find them on a restaurant menu, indulge.

As with fiddleheads, we owe thanks to Native Americans for introducing us to **maple syrup,** one of Maine's major agricultural exports. The annual crop averages 110,000 gallons. The syrup comes in four different colors/flavors (from light amber to extra dark amber), and inspectors strictly monitor syrup quality. The best syrup comes from the sugar or rock maple, *Acer saccharum*. On Maine Maple Sunday (usually the fourth Sunday in March), several dozen syrup producers open their rustic sugarhouses to the public for "sugaring-off" parties—to celebrate the sap harvest and share the final phase in the production process. Wood smoke billows from the sugarhouse chimney while everyone inside gathers around huge kettles used to boil down the watery sap. (A single gallon of syrup starts with 30-40 gallons of sap.) Finally, it's time to sample the syrup every which way—on pancakes and waffles, in tea, on ice cream, in puddings, in muffins, even just drizzled over snow. Most producers also have containers of syrup for sale.

The best place for Maine maple syrup is atop pancakes made with Maine **wild blueberries.** Packed with antioxidants and all kinds of good-for-you stuff, these flavorful berries are prized by bakers because they retain their form and flavor when cooked. Much smaller than the cultivated versions, wild blueberries are also raked, not picked. Although most of the Down East barren barons harvest their crops for the lucrative wholesale market, a few growers let you pick your own blueberries in mid-August. Contact the **Wild Blueberry Commission** (207/581-1475, www.wildblueberries.maine.edu) or the state **Department of Agriculture** (207/287-3491, www.getrealmaine.com) for locations, recipes, and other wild-blueberry information, or log on to the website of the **Wild Blueberry Association of North America** (207/570-3535, www.wildblueberries.com).

The best place to simply *appreciate* blueberries is Machias, site of the renowned annual Machias Wild Blueberry Festival, held the third weekend in August. While harvesting is under way in the surrounding fields, you can stuff your face with blueberry everything—muffins, jam, pancakes, ice cream, pies. Plus you can collect blueberry-logo napkins, T-shirts, fridge magnets, pottery, and jewelry.

Another don't-miss while in Maine is Maine-made **ice cream.** Skip the overpriced Ben and Jerry's outlets. Locally made ice cream and gelato are fresher and better and often come in an astounding range of flavors. The big name in the state is Gifford's, with regional companies being Shain's, Round Top, and Houlton Dairy. All beat the out-of-state competition by a long shot. Even better are some of the one-of-a-kind dairy bars and farm stands.

Finally, whenever you get a chance, shop at a **farmers market.** Their biggest asset is serendipity—you never know what you'll find. Everything is locally grown and often organic. Herbs, unusual vegetables, seedlings, baked goods, meat, free-range chicken, goat cheese, herb vinegars, berries, exotic condiments, smoked salmon, maple syrup, honey, and jams are just a few of the possibilities. The Maine **Department of Agriculture** (207/287-3491, www.getrealmaine.com) provides info on markets.

and experiences (the original edition was illustrated by N. C. Wyeth). Kennebunkport's Booth Tarkington (1869-1946), author of the *Penrod* novels and *The Magnificent Ambersons,* described 1920s Kennebunkport in *Mary's Neck,* published in 1932.

A little subgenre of sociological literary classics comprises astute observations (mostly by women) of daily life in various parts of the state. Some are fiction, some nonfiction, some barely disguised romans à clef. Probably the best-known chronicler of such observations is Sarah Orne Jewett (1849-1909), author of *The Country of the Pointed Firs,* a fictional 1896 account of "Dunnet's Landing" (actually Tenants Harbor); her ties, however, were in the South Berwick area, where she spent most of her life. Also in South Berwick, Gladys Hasty Carroll (1904-1999) scrutinized everyday life in her hamlet, Dunnybrook, in *As the Earth Turns* (a title later "borrowed" and tweaked by a soap-opera producer). Lura Beam (1887-1978) focused on her childhood in the Washington County village of Marshfield in *A Maine Hamlet,* published in 1957, and Louise Dickinson Rich (1903-1972) entertainingly described her coastal Corea experiences in *The Peninsula,* after first having chronicled her rugged wilderness existence in *We Took to the Woods.* Ruth Moore (1903-1989), born on Gott's Island, near Acadia National Park, published her first book at the age of 40. Her tales, recently brought back into print, have earned her a whole new appreciative audience. Elisabeth Ogilvie (1917-2006) came to Maine in 1944 and lived for many years on remote Ragged Island, transformed into "Bennett's Island" in her fascinating "tide trilogy": *High Tide at Noon, Storm Tide,* and *The Ebbing Tide.* Ben Ames Williams (1887-1953), the token male in this roundup of perceptive observers, in 1940 produced *Come Spring,* an epic tale of hardy pioneers founding the town of Union, just inland from Rockland.

In the mid-19th century antislavery crusader Harriet Beecher Stowe (1811-1896), seldom recognized for her Maine connection, lived in Brunswick, where she wrote *The Pearl of Orr's Island,* a folkloric novel about a tiny nearby fishing community.

Mary Ellen Chase was a Maine native, born in Blue Hill in 1887. She became an English professor at Smith College in 1926 and wrote about 30 books, including some about the Bible as literature. She died in 1973.

Two books do a creditable job of excerpting literature from throughout Maine—something of a daunting task. The most comprehensive is *Maine Speaks: An Anthology of Maine Literature,* published in 1989 by the Maine Writers and Publishers Alliance. *The Quotable Moose: A Contemporary Maine Reader,* edited by Wesley McNair and published in 1994 by the University Press of New England, focuses on 20th-century authors.

A WORLD OF HER OWN

For Marguerite Yourcenar (1903-1987), Maine provided solitude and inspiration for subjects ranging far beyond the state's borders. Yourcenar was a longtime Northeast Harbor resident and the first woman elected to the prestigious Académie Française. Her house, now a shrine to her work, is open to the public by appointment in summer.

ESSAYISTS, CRITICS, AND HUMORISTS NATIVE AND TRANSPLANTED

Maine's best-known essayist is and was E. B. White (1899-1985), who bought a farm in tiny Brooklin in 1933 and continued writing for *The New Yorker. One Man's Meat,* published in 1944, is one of the best collections of his wry, perceptive writings. His legions of admirers also include two generations raised on his classic children's stories *Stuart Little, Charlotte's Web,* and *The Trumpet of the Swan.*

Writer and critic Doris Grumbach (born 1918), who settled in Sargentville, not far from Brooklin but far from her New York ties, wrote two particularly wise works from the perspective of a Maine transplant: *Fifty Days of Solitude* and *Coming into the End Zone.*

Maine's best contemporary exemplar of humorous writing is the late John Gould (1908-2003), whose life in rural Friendship has provided grist for many a tale. Gould's hilarious columns in the *Christian Science Monitor* and his steady book output made him an icon of Maine humor.

PINE TREE POETS

Born in Portland, Henry Wadsworth Longfellow (1807-1882) is Maine's most famous poet; his marine themes clearly stem from his seashore childhood (in "My Lost Youth," he wistfully rhapsodized, "Often I think of the beautiful town/That is seated by the sea...").

Widely recognized in her own era, poet Celia Thaxter (1835-1894) held court on Appledore Island in the Isles of Shoals, welcoming artists, authors, and musicians to her summer salon. Today, she's best known for *An Island Garden,* published in 1894 and detailing her attempts at horticultural TLC in a hostile environment.

Edna St. Vincent Millay (1892-1950) had connections to Camden, Rockland, and Union and described a stunning Camden panorama in "Renascence."

Whitehead Island, near Rockland, was the birthplace of Wilbert Snow (1883-1977), who went on to become president of Connecticut's Wesleyan University. His 1968 memoir, *Codline's Child,* makes fascinating reading.

A longtime resident of York, May Sarton (1912-1995) approached cult status as a guru of feminist poetry and prose—and as an articulate analyst of death and dying during her terminal illness.

Among respected Maine poets today are William Carpenter (born 1940); Kate Barnes (1932-2013), Maine's first Poet Laureeate, 1996 to 1999; and her successors to the post: Baron Wormser, 2000-2005; Betsy Scholl, 2006-2010; and Wesley McNair, named in 2011.

CHILDREN'S LITERATURE

Besides E. B. White's children's classics, *Stuart Little, Charlotte's Web,* and *The Trumpet of the Swan,* America's kids were also weaned on books written and illustrated by Maine island summer resident Robert McCloskey (1914-2003)—notably *Time of Wonder, One Morning in Maine,* and *Blueberries for Sal.* Neck-and-neck in popularity is prolific Walpole illustrator-writer Barbara Cooney (1917-1999), whose award-winning titles included *Miss Rumphius, Island Boy,* and *Hattie and the Wild Waves.* Cooney produced more than 100 books, and it seems as if everyone has a different favorite.

C. A. (Charles Asbury) Stephens (1844-1931) for 60 years wrote for the magazine *Youth's Companion.* In 1995, a collection of his vivid children's stories was reissued as *Stories from the Old Squire's Farm.*

Maine can also lay partial claim to Kate Douglas Wiggin (1856-1923), author of the eternally popular *Rebecca of Sunnybrook Farm;* she spent summers at Quillcote in Hollis, west of Portland.

ESSENTIALS

Getting There

Maine has two major airports, two major bus networks, a toll highway, limited Amtrak service, and some ad hoc local transportation systems that fill in the gaps.

AIR

Maine's primary airline gateway is **Portland International Jetport** (PWM, 207/774-7301, www.portlandjetport.org), although visitors headed farther north sometimes prefer **Bangor International Airport** (BGR, 207/947-0384, www.flybangor.com). The "international" in their names is a bit misleading. Military and charter flights from Europe often stop at Bangor for refueling and customs clearance, and Portland has a few flights connecting to Canada, but Boston's Logan Airport is the nearest airport with direct flights from worldwide destinations.

Portland Jetport

Portland's airport is small and easy to navigate. Food options are few, but you won't starve. Visitor information is dispensed from a desk (not always staffed, unfortunately) between the gates and the baggage-claim area. Note: Since Portland is the terminus of most flights, baggage service isn't a priority; expect to hang

© HILARY NANGLE

around for a while. If you have an emergency, contact the airport manager (207/773-8462).

Ground Transportation: The Greater Portland Transportation District's **Metro** (207/774-0351, www.gpmetrobus.com) bus route 5 connects the airport with downtown Portland Monday through Saturday. **Taxis** are available outside baggage claim.

Mid-Coast Limo (207/236-2424 or 800/937-2424) provides car service, by reservation, between Portland and the Mid-Coast and Penobscot Bay regions. **Mermaid Transportation Co.** (800/696-2463, www.go-mermaid.com) services Greater Portland and the Kennebunks.

Car rentals at the airport include **Alamo** (207/775-0855 or 877/222-9075, www.alamo.com), **Avis** (207/874-7500 or 800/230-4898, www.avis.com), **Budget** (207/874-7500 or 800/527-0700, www.drivebudget.com), **Hertz** (207/774-4544 or 800/654-3131, www.hertz.com), and **National** (207/773-0036 or 877/222-9058, www.nationalcar.com).

Bangor Airport

Bangor's airport has scaled-down versions of Portland's facilities but all the necessary amenities. If you need help, contact the airport manager (207/947-0384).

Ground Transportation: Bangor Area Transportation (BAT, 207/992-4670, www.bgrme.org) buses connect the airport to downtown Bangor. Buses run Monday-Saturday. **West's Coastal Connection** (207/546-2823 or 800/596-2823, www.westbusservice.com) has scheduled service along Route 1 to Calais, with stops en route. **Taxis** are available outside baggage claim.

Bar Harbor-Bangor Shuttle (207/479-5911, www.barharborbangorshuttle.com) operates between the airport, Greyhound and Concord Coachlines bus terminals, the Bangor Mall, Hollywood Slots, and Bar Harbor.

Car rentals at the airport include **Alamo** (207/947-0158 or 800/462-5266, www.alamo.com), **Avis** (207/947-8383 or 800/831-2847, www.avis.com), **Budget** (207/945-9429 or 800/527-0700, www.drivebudget.com), **Hertz** (207/942-5519 or 800/654-3131, www.hertz.com), and **National** (207/947-0158 or 800/227-7368, www.nationalcar.com).

Regional Airports

JetBlue partner **Cape Air** (866/227-3247, www.flycapeair.com) flies from Boston to **Hancock County Airport** (BHB, 207/667-7329, www.bhbairport.com) near Bar Harbor, **Knox County Regional Airport** (RKD, 207/594-4131, www.knoxcountymaine.gov) at Owls Head, near Rockland and Camden, and **Augusta State Airport** (AUG, 207/626-2306, www.augustaairport.org). Alaska Air partner **PenAir** (800/448-4226, www.pe-nair.com) provides summer service to Bar Harbor from Boston and year-round service to and from **Northern Maine Regional Airport** (PQI, 207/764-2550, www.flypresqueisle.com), in Presque Isle. Hancock County Airport has rental-car offices for Hertz and Enterprise and is also serviced by the Island Explorer bus late June-Columbus Day. Knox County has car rentals from Budget and Enterprise. Augusta has Hertz rentals. Northern Maine has Avis and Budget.

Boston Logan Airport

If you fly into Boston (BOS), you easily can get to Maine via rental car (all major rental companies at the airport, but it's not pleasant to navigate Logan in a rental car) and Concord Coachlines bus (easiest and least-expensive option). You'll need to connect to North Station to take Amtrak's Downeaster train.

CAR

The major highway access to Maine from the south is **I-95,** which roughly parallels the coast until Bangor, before shooting up to Houlton. Other busy access points are **Route 1,** also from New Hampshire, departing the coast in Calais at the New Brunswick province border; **Route 302,** from North Conway, New Hampshire, entering Maine at Fryeburg; **Route 2,** from Gorham, New Hampshire, to Bethel; **Route 201,** entering from Québec province, just north of Jackman, and a couple of crossing points from New Brunswick into Aroostook and Washington Counties in northeastern Maine.

BUS

Concord Coachlines (800/639-3317, www.concordcoachlines.com) departs downtown Boston (South Station Transportation Center) and Logan Airport for Portland almost hourly from the wee hours of the morning until late at night, making pickups at all Logan airline terminals (lower level). Most of the buses continue directly to Bangor; three daily nonexpress buses continue along the coast, stopping in Brunswick, Bath, Wiscasset, Damariscotta, Waldoboro, Rockland, Camden, Belfast, and Searsport, before turning inland to Bangor. The Portland bus terminal is the Portland Transportation Center, Thompson Point Road, just west of I-295. Buses are clean, movies are shown, and there's free Wi-Fi on most.

Also servicing Coastal Maine but with far less frequent service is **Greyhound** (800/231-2222, www.greyhound.com).

Once-a-day buses to and from Calais coordinate with the Bangor bus schedules. The Calais line, stopping in Ellsworth, Gouldsboro, Machias, and Perry (near Eastport), is operated by **West's Coastal Connection** (207/546-2823 or 800/596-2823, www.westbusservice.com). Flag stops along the route are permitted.

Portland and South Portland have **city bus service,** with some wheelchair-accessible vehicles. A number of smaller communities have established **local shuttle vans** or **trolley-buses,** but most of the latter are seasonal. Trolley-buses operate (for a fee) in Ogunquit, Wells, the Kennebunks, Portland, Bath, and Boothbay. Mount Desert Island and the Schoodic Peninsula have the **Island Explorer,** an excellent free bus service operating late June-early October.

RAIL

It's now possible to travel by train from Boston to Rockland. **Amtrak's Downeaster** (800/872-7245, www.amtrakdowneaster.com) makes daily round-trip runs between Boston's North Station and Brunswick, with stops in Wells, Saco, seasonally in Old Orchard Beach (May 1 to October 31), and the Portland Transportation Center. From Brunswick, take the **Maine Eastern Railway** (866/637-2457, www.maineeasternrailroad.com), a seasonal excursion train between Brunswick and Rockland with stops in Bath and Wiscasset. From the Portland station, Portland's Metro municipal bus service will take you gratis to downtown Portland; just show your Amtrak ticket stub.

FERRY

In 2014, **Nova Star Cruises** (888/216-9018 U.S., 888/762-4058 Canada, www.novastarcruises.com) launched a new international cruise-car-ferry service between Ocean Gateway Terminal, in Portland, Maine, and Yarmouth International Ferry Terminal, in Yarmouth, Nova Scotia. The 528-foot Nova Star provides daily round-trip ferry service from early May through early November. The nine-hour overnight crossing departs Portland at 8pm EST and arrives in Yarmouth 7am AST. The day cruise departs Yarmouth at 9am AST and arrives in Portland at 5pm EST. Ferry amenities include restaurants, casino, live entertainment, theater, art gallery, fitness center, spa, children's area, and duty-free shopping. One-way fares range $79-129 adults and $39-64 kids ages 5-12. Add $19-39 for an assigned recliner chair, $49-89 for a cabin, $129-179 for cars; $49-89 for motorcycles, and $16 -22 for bicycles.

PRONUNCIATION 101: SAY IT LIKE A NATIVE

Countless names for Maine cities, towns, villages, rivers, lakes, and streams have Native American origins; some are variations on French; and a few have German derivations. Below are some pronunciations to give you a leg up when requesting directions along the Maine coast.

- **Arundel**–Uh-RUN-d'l
- **Bangor**–BANG-gore
- **Bremen**–BREE-m'n
- **Calais**–CAL-us
- **Castine**–Kass-TEEN
- **Damariscotta**–Dam-uh-riss-COTT-uh
- **Harraseeket**–Hare-uh-SEEK-it
- **Isle au Haut**–I'll-a-HO, I'LL-a-ho (subject to plenty of dispute, depending on whether or not you live in the vicinity)
- **Katahdin**–Kuh-TA-din
- **Lubec**–Loo-BECK
- **Machias**–Muh-CHIGH-us
- **Matinicus**–Muh-TIN-i-cuss
- **Medomak**–Muh-DOM-ick
- **Megunticook**–Muh-GUN-tuh-cook
- **Monhegan**–Mun-HE-gun
- **Mount Desert**–Mount Duh-ZERT
- **Narraguagus**–Nare-uh-GWAY-gus
- **Naskeag**–NASS-keg
- **Passagassawakeag**–Puh-sag-gus-uh-WAH-keg
- **Passamaquoddy**–Pass-uh-muh-QUAD-dee
- **Pemaquid**–PEM-a-kwid
- **Saco**–SOCK-oh
- **Schoodic**–SKOO-dick
- **Steuben**–Stew-BEN
- **Topsham**–TOPS-'m
- **Wiscasset**–Wiss-CASS-it
- **Woolwich**–WOOL-itch

Getting Around

The Maine Department of Transportation (800/877-9171) operates the Explore Maine site (www.exploremaine.org), which has information on all forms of transportation in Maine.

CAR

No matter how much time and resourcefulness you summon, you'll never really be able to appreciate Maine without a car. Down every little peninsula jutting into the Atlantic lies a picturesque village or park or ocean view.

Two lanes wide from Kittery in the south to Fort Kent at the top, U.S. Route 1 is the state's most congested road, particularly July-August. Mileage distances can be extremely deceptive, since it will take you much longer than anticipated to get from point A to point B. If you ask anyone about distances, chances are good that

you'll receive an answer in hours rather than miles. If you're trying to make time, it's best to take the Maine Turnpike or I-95; if you want to see Maine, take U.S. 1 and lots of little offshoots. That said, bear in mind that even I-95 becomes megacongested on summer weekends, and especially summer *holiday* weekends.

Note that the interstate can be a bit confusing to motorists. Between York and Augusta, I-95 is the same as the Maine Turnpike, a toll highway regulated by the **Maine Turnpike Authority** (877/682-9433 or 800/675-7453 travel conditions, www.maineturnpike.com). All exit numbers along I-95 reflect distance in miles from the New Hampshire border. I-295 splits from I-95 in Portland and follows the coast to Brunswick before veering inland and rejoining I-95 in Gardiner. Exits on I-295 reflect distance from where it splits from I-95 just south of Portland at Exit 44.

Road Conditions

For real-time information on road conditions, weather, construction, and major delays, dial 511 in Maine, 866/282-7578 from out of state, or visit www.511maine.gov. Information is available in both English and French.

Driving Regulations

Seat belts are mandatory in Maine. Unless posted otherwise, Maine allows right turns at red lights after you stop and check for oncoming traffic. *Never* pass a stopped school bus in either direction. Maine law also requires drivers to turn on their car's headlights any time the windshield wipers are operating.

Roadside Assistance

Since Maine is enslaved to the automobile, it's not a bad idea for vacationers to carry membership in AAA in case of breakdowns, flat tires, and other car crises. Contact your nearest AAA office or **AAA Northern New England** (425 Marginal Way, Portland 04101, 207/780-6800 or 800/482-7497, www.northernnewengland. aaa.com). The emergency road service number is 800/222-4357.

Tips for Travelers

WHAT TO TAKE

Weather can be unpredictable in Maine, with fog, rain, and temperatures ranging from the low 30s on a cold spring day to the 90s on a hot summer one. But even summer sees days when a **fleece pullover** or jacket and a **lightweight, weatherproof jacket** are quite welcome. A hat and mittens are a plus when venturing far off shore on a windjammer or whale-watching boat or climbing inland peaks in spring or fall. Other handy items are **binoculars**; a small **backpack** for day trips or light hiking; and a small or collapsible **cooler** for picnics or storing food.

Unless you're dining at the White Barn Inn or Arrows, you won't need fancy clothing. Resort casual is the dress code in most good restaurants and in downtown Portland, with nice T-shirts and shorts being acceptable almost everywhere in beach communities.

In winter and spring, add warm waterproof boots, gloves, hat, and winter-weight clothing to your list.

VISAS AND OFFICIALDOM

Since 9/11, security has been excruciatingly tight for foreign visitors, with customs procedures in flux. For current rules, visit www.usa. gov/visitors/arriving.shtml. It's wise to make two sets of copies of all paperwork, one to carry separately on your trip and another left with a trusted friend or relative at home.

SMOKING

Maine now has laws banning smoking in restaurants, bars, and lounges as well as enclosed areas of public places, such as shopping malls. Few accommodations permit smoking, and if they do, it's only in limited areas or rooms. Many have instituted high fines for smoking in a nonsmoking room. If you're a smoker, motels with direct outdoor access make it easiest to satisfy a craving.

ACCOMMODATIONS

For all accommodation listings, rates are quoted for peak season, which is usually July-August but may extend through foliage (mid-October). Rates drop, often dramatically, in the shoulder and off-season at accommodations that remain open. Especially during peak season, many accommodations require a two- or three-night minimum.

For the best rates, check Internet specials and ask about packages. Many accommodations also provide discounts for members of travel

TIPS FOR THE BUDGET-CONSCIOUS

At first glance, Maine might seem pricey, but take another look. It is possible to keep a vacation within a reasonable budget; here are a few tips for doing so.

For starters, avoid the big-name towns and seek out accommodations in smaller, nearby ones instead. For example, instead of Damariscotta, consider Waldoboro; instead of Camden, try Belfast or Searsport; in place of Bar Harbor, check Trenton or Southwest Harbor. Or simply explore the Down East Coast or inland Maine, where rates are generally far lower than in other regions.

Small, family-owned motels tend to have the lowest rates. Better yet, book a cabin or cottage for a week, rather than a room by the night. Not only can you find reasonable weekly rentals—especially if you plan well in advance—but you'll also have cooking facilities, allowing you to avoid eating all meals out.

Speaking of food, buy or bring a small cooler so you can stock up at supermarkets, farm stands, and farmers markets for picnic meals. Most Hannaford and Shaw's supermarkets have large selections of prepared foods and big salad bars and bakeries, and many local groceries have pizza and sandwich counters.

Do check local papers and bulletin boards for public supper notices. Most are very inexpensive, raise money for a good cause, and provide an opportunity not only for a good meal, but also to meet locals and glean a few insider tips.

Of course, sometimes you want to have a nice meal in a nice place. Consider going out for lunch, which is usually far less expensive than dinner, or take advantage of early-bird specials or of the Friday-night all-you-can-eat fish fries offered at quite a few home-cooking restaurants.

Take advantage of Maine's vast outdoor-recreation opportunities; many are free. Even Acadia, with its miles and miles of trails and carriage roads, and its Island Explorer bus service, is a bargain; buy a park pass and it's all yours to use and explore.

Take advantage of free events: concerts, lectures, farmers markets, art shows and openings, and family events. Most are usually listed in local papers.

Avoid parking hassles and fees and save gas by using local transportation services when available, such as the trolley network on the Southern Coast and the Island Explorer bus system on Mount Desert Island.

Finally, before making reservations for anything, check to see if there's a special Internet rate or ask about any discounts that might apply to you: AAA, senior, military, government, family rate, and so forth. If you don't ask, you won't get.

---

clubs such as AAA, for seniors and for members of the military, and other such groups.

Unless otherwise noted, accommodations listed have private baths.

FOOD

Days and hours of operation listed for places serving food are for peak season. These do change often, sometimes even within a season, and it's not uncommon for a restaurant to close early on a quiet night. To avoid disappointment, call before making a special trip.

ALCOHOL

As in the rest of the country, Maine's minimum drinking age is 21 years—and bar owners, bartenders, and serving staff can be held legally accountable for serving underage imbibers. If your blood alcohol level is 0.08 percent or higher, you are legally considered to be operating under the influence.

TIME ZONE

All of Maine is in the eastern time zone—the same as New York, Washington DC, Philadelphia, and Orlando. Eastern standard time (EST) runs from the last Sunday in October to the first Sunday in April; eastern daylight time (EDT), one hour later, prevails otherwise. Surprising to many first-time visitors is how early the sun rises in the morning and how early it sets at night.

If your itinerary also includes Canada, remember that the provinces of New Brunswick and Nova Scotia are on Atlantic time—one hour later than eastern—so if it's noon in Maine, it's 1pm in these provinces.

Health and Safety

There's too much to do in Maine, and too much to see, to spend even a few hours laid low by illness or mishap. Be sensible—be sure to get enough sleep, wear sunscreen and appropriate clothing, know your limits and don't take foolhardy risks, heed weather and warning signs, carry water and snacks while hiking, don't overindulge in food or alcohol, always tell someone where you're going, and watch your step. If you're traveling with children, you should quadruple your caution.

MEDICAL CARE
In an emergency, dial **911**.

Southern Coast
York Hospital (15 Hospital Dr., York, emergency 207/351-2157); **York Hospital in Wells** (112/114 Sanford Rd., Wells, 207/646-5211, 8am-7pm daily); **Southern Maine Medical Center** (Rte. 111, Biddeford, 207/283-7000, emergency 207/294-5000).

Greater Portland
Maine Medical Center (22 Bramhall St., Portland, 207/662-0111, emergency 207/662-2381); **Mercy Hospital** (144 State St., Portland, 207/879-3000, emergency 207/879-3265).

Mid-Coast
Mid Coast Hospital (Bath Rd., Cooks Corner, Brunswick, 207/729-0181); **Parkview Hospital** (329 Main St., a mile south of Bowdoin College, Brunswick, 207/373-2000); **St. Andrews Hospital and Healthcare Center** (3 St. Andrews Ln., Boothbay Harbor, 207/633-2121); **Miles Memorial Hospital** (Bristol Rd., Rte. 130, Damariscotta, 207/563-1234).

Penobscot Bay
Penobscot Bay Medical Center (Rte. 1, Rockport, 207/596-8000, emergency 207/596-8315); **Waldo County General Hospital** (118 Northport Ave., Belfast, 207/338-2500 or 800/649-2536).

Blue Hill and Deer Isle
The hospital in this region is **Blue Hill Memorial Hospital** (57 Water St., Blue Hill, 207/374-3400, emergency 207/374-2836).

Acadia
Hospitals are **Maine Coast Memorial Hospital** (50 Union St., Ellsworth, 207/664-5311 or 888/645-8829, emergency 207/664-5340) and **Mount Desert Island Hospital** (10 Wayman Ln., Bar Harbor, 207/288-5081).

Down East
Down East Community Hospital (Upper Court St., Rte. 1A, Machias, 207/255-3356); **Regional Medical Center at Lubec** (43 S. Lubec Rd., Lubec, 207/733-5541); **Eastport Health Care** (Boynton St., Eastport, 207/853-6001); **Calais Regional Hospital** (50 Franklin St., Calais, 207/454-7521).

Aroostook
Houlton Regional Hospital (20 Hartford St., Houlton, 207/532-2900); **Aroostook Medical Center** (140 Academy St./Rte. 10, Presque Isle, 207/768-4100); **Cary Medical Center** (163 Van Buren Rd., Caribou, 207/498-3111); **Northern Maine Medical Center** (194 E. Main St./Rte. 1, Fort Kent, 207/834-3155).

Maine Highlands

Millinocket Regional Hospital (200 Somerset St., Millinocket, 207/723-5161); **Charles A. Dean Memorial Hospital** (364 Pritham Ave., Greenville, 207/695-5200); **Mayo Regional Hospital** (43 Dwelley St., Dover-Foxcroft, 207/564-8401); **Eastern Maine Medical Center** (489 State St., Bangor, 207/973-7000); **St. Joseph Hospital** (360 Broadway, Bangor, 207/907-1000).

Kennebec River Valley

Maine General Alfond Center for Health Care (Olde Belgrade Rd. at I-95 Exit 113, Augusta, 207/626-1000); **Redington-Fairview General Hospital** (Fairview Ave./Rte. 104, Skowhegan, 207/474-5121); **Jackman Region Health Center** (376 Main St./Rte. 201, Jackman, 207/668-4300).

Western Lakes and Mountains

Franklin Memorial Hospital (111 Franklin Health Commons, Farmington, 207/778-6031); **Rangeley Region Health Center** (25 Dallas Hill Rd., Rangeley, 207/864-3303); **The Bethel Family Health Center** (32 Railroad St., Bethel, 207/824-2193); **Rumford Hospital** (420 Franklin St., Rumford, 207/369-1000); **Stephens Memorial Hospital** (181 Main St., Norway, 207/743-5933); **Bridgton Hospital** (S. High St., Bridgton, 207/647-6000); **Central Maine Medical Center** (300 Main St., Lewiston, 207/795-0111); **St. Mary's Regional Medical Center** (93 Campus Ave., Lewiston, 207/777-8100).

AFFLICTIONS
Insect Bites and Tick-Borne Diseases

If you plan to spend any time outdoors in Maine April-November, take precautions, especially when hiking, to avoid annoying insect bites and especially the diseases carried by tiny deer ticks (not the larger dog ticks; they don't carry it): **Lyme disease, anaplasmosis,** and **babesiosis.** Mosquito-borne **Eastern Equine Encephalitis** has been found in mosquitoes in Southern Maine, but as of 2013 had not yet been diagnosed in humans.

Wear a long-sleeved shirt and long pants, and tuck pant legs into your socks. Light-colored clothing makes ticks easier to spot. Buy insect repellent with DEET at a supermarket or convenience store and use it liberally; apply permethrin to clothing. Not much daunts the blackflies of spring and early summer, but you can lower your appeal by not using perfume, aftershave lotion, or scented shampoo and by wearing light-colored clothing.

After any hike or prolonged time outdoors in the woods, thick grass, overgrown bushes, or piles of brush or leaves, check for ticks—especially behind the knees and in the armpits, navel, and groin. If you find one, there's a good chance the tick was infected with Lyme disease, a bacterial infection that causes fever, head and body aches, and fatigue and can lead to joint pain and neurological and heart problems. It usually takes 24-48 hours before an attached tick begins to transmit the disease. About 80 percent of Lyme patients get a bull's-eye rash that appears within a month of being bit. Anaplasmosis and babesiosis also exhibit flu-like symptoms. Anaplasmosis can, in rare circumstances, lead to enecephalitis/meningitis; babesiosis can cause anemia and dark urine and is especially problematic for those with weakened immune systems or who have had their spleen removed.

If bitten by a tick, wash the area thoroughly with soap and water and apply an antiseptic, mark the date on a calendar, then monitor your health. If you suspect any of these diseases, see a doctor to be diagnosed and treated immediately; don't put it off. For more information, contact the **Maine Center for Disease Control** (800/821-5821, www.mainepublichealth.gov).

Rabies

If you're bitten by any animal, especially one acting suspiciously, head for the nearest hospital emergency room. For statewide information about rabies, contact the **Maine Center for Disease Control** (800/821-5821, www.mainepublichealth.gov).

Allergies

If your medical history includes extreme allergies to shellfish or bee stings, you know the risks of eating a lobster or wandering around a wildflower meadow. However, if you come from a landlocked area and are new to crustaceans, you might not be aware of the potential hazard. Statistics indicate that less than 2 percent of adults have a severe shellfish allergy, but for those victims, the reaction can set in quickly. Immediate treatment is needed to keep the airways open. If you have a history of severe allergic reactions to *anything*, be prepared when you come to the Maine coast dreaming of lobster feasts. Ask your doctor for a prescription for EpiPen (epinephrine), a preloaded, single-use syringe containing 0.3 mg of the drug—enough to tide you over until you can get to a hospital.

Seasickness

If you're planning to do any boating in Maine—particularly sailing—you'll want to be prepared. (Being prepared may in fact keep you from succumbing, since fear of seasickness just about guarantees you'll get it.) Talk to a pharmacist or doctor about your options.

Hypothermia and Frostbite

Wind and weather can shift dramatically in Maine, especially at higher elevations, creating prime conditions for contracting hypothermia and frostbite. At risk are hikers, swimmers, canoeists, kayakers, sailors, skiers, even cyclists.

To prevent hypothermia and frostbite, dress in layers and remove or add them as needed. Wool, waterproof fabrics (such as Gore-Tex), and synthetic fleece (such as Polartec) are the best fabrics for repelling dampness. Polyester fleece lining wicks excess moisture away from your body. Especially in winter, always cover your head, since body heat escapes quickly through the head; a ski mask will protect ears and nose. Wear wool- or fleece-lined gloves and wool socks.

Special Considerations During Hunting Season

During Maine's fall hunting season (October-Thanksgiving weekend)—and especially during the November deer season—walk or hike only in wooded areas marked No Hunting, No Trespassing, or Posted. And even if an area *is* closed to hunters, don't decide to explore the woods during deer or moose season without wearing a "hunter orange" (read: eye-poppingly fluorescent) jacket or vest. If you take your dog along, be sure it, too, wears an orange vest. Hunting is illegal on Sunday.

Information and Services

MONEY

If you need to exchange foreign currency—other than Canadian dollars—do it at or near border crossings or in Portland. In small communities, such transactions are more complicated; you may end up spending more time and money than necessary.

Typical banking hours are 9am-3pm weekdays, occasionally with later hours on Friday. Drive-up windows at many banks tend to open as much as an hour earlier and stay open an hour or so after lobbies close. Some banks also maintain Saturday morning hours. Automated teller machines (ATMs) are abundant along coastal Maine.

Credit Cards and Travelers Checks

Bank credit cards have become so preferred and so prevalent that it's nearly impossible to rent a car or check into a hotel without one. MasterCard and Visa are most widely accepted in Maine, and Discover and American Express are next most popular; Carte Blanche, Diners Club, and EnRoute (Canadian) lag far behind. Be aware, however, that small restaurants (including lobster pounds), shops, and bed-and-breakfasts off the beaten track might not accept credit cards or nonlocal personal checks; you may need to settle your account with cash or travelers check.

Taxes

Maine charges a 5.5 percent sales tax on general purchases and services; 8 percent on prepared foods, candy, and lodging/camping; and 10 percent on auto rentals.

Tipping

Tip 15-20 percent of the pretax bill in restaurants.

Taxi drivers expect a 15 percent tip; airport porters expect at least $1 per bag, depending on the difficulty of the job.

The usual tip for housekeeping services in accommodations is $1-4 per person, per night, depending upon the level of service.

Some accommodations add a 10-15 percent service fee to rates.

TOURIST INFORMATION AND MAPS

The Maine Office of Tourism has established an excellent website: www.visitmaine.com. You'll find chamber of commerce addresses, articles, photos, information on lodgings, and access to a variety of Maine tourism businesses. The state's toll-free information hotline is 888/MAINE-45 (888/624-6345). The state also operates **Information Centers** in Calais, Fryeburg (May-October), Hampden, Houlton, Kittery, and Yarmouth. These are excellent places to visit to stock up on brochures, pick up a map, ask for advice, and use restrooms. All, except Hamden, offer free Wi-Fi.

The **Maine Tourism Association** (207/623-0363, www.mainetourism.com) also has information and publishes *Maine Invites You* and a free state map.

Peek in any Mainer's car, and you're likely to see a copy of *The Maine Atlas and Gazetteer*, published by DeLorme Mapping Company in Yarmouth. Despite an oversize format inconvenient for hiking and kayaking, this 96-page paperbound book just about guarantees that you won't get lost (and if you're good at map reading, it can get you out of a lot of traffic jams). Scaled at one-half inch to the mile, it's meticulously compiled from aerial photographs, satellite images, U.S. Geological Survey maps, GPS readings, and timber-company maps, and it is revised annually. It details back roads and dirt roads and shows elevation, boat ramps, public lands, campgrounds and picnic areas, and trailheads. DeLorme products are available nationwide in book and map stores, but you can also order direct (800/452-5931, www.delorme.com). The atlas is $19.95 and shipping is $4 (Maine residents need to add 5 percent sales tax).

PHONE AND INTERNET

Maine still has only one telephone area code, 207. For directory assistance, dial 411.

Cell phone towers are now sprinkled pretty much throughout Maine; only a few pockets—mostly down peninsulas and in remote valleys and hollows—are out of cell-phone range. Of course, reception also varies by carrier and getting reception often requires doing the cell-phone hokey pokey—putting your left arm out, your right leg in, and so on to find the strongest signal.

Internet access is widely available at libraries and coffeehouses. Most hotels and many inns and bed-and-breakfasts also offer Internet access.

RESOURCES

Glossary

To help you translate some of the lingo used off the beaten track at places like country stores and county fairs, farm stands and flea markets, here's a sampling of local terms and expressions:

alewives: herring

ayuh: yes

barrens: as in "blueberry barrens"; fields where wild blueberries grow

beamy: wide (as in a boat or a person)

beans: shorthand for the traditional Saturday-night meal, which always includes baked beans

blowdown: a forest area leveled by wind

blowing a gale: very windy

camp: a vacation house (small or large), usually on freshwater and in the woods

chance: serendipity or luck, as in "open by appointment or by chance"

chicken dressing: chicken manure

chowder (pronounced "chowdah"): soup made with lobster, clams, or fish, or a combination thereof; lobster version sometimes called lobster stew

chowderhead: mischief or troublemakers, usually interchangeable with idiot

coneheads: tourists (because of their presumed penchant for ice cream)

cottage: a vacation house (anything from a bungalow to a mansion), usually on saltwater

culch (also cultch): stuff; the contents of attics, basements, and some flea markets

cull: a discount lobster, usually minus a claw

cunnin': cute, usually describing a baby or small child

dinner (pronounced "dinnah"): the noon meal

dinner pail: lunch box

dite: a very small amount

dooryard: the yard near a house's main entrance

downcellar: in the basement

Down East: with the prevailing wind; the old coastal sailing route from Boston to Nova Scotia

dry-ki: driftwood, usually remnants from the logging industry

ell: a residential structural section that links a house and a barn; formerly a popular location for the "summer kitchen," to spare the house from woodstove heat

exercised: upset; angry

fiddleheads: unopened ostrich-fern fronds, a spring delicacy

finest kind: top quality; good news; an expression of general approval; also a term of appreciation

flatlander: a person not from Maine, often but not exclusively someone from the Midwest

floatplane: a small plane equipped with pontoons for landing on water; the same aircraft often becomes a ski-plane in winter

flowage: a body of water created by damming, usually beaver handiwork (also called "beaver flowage")

FR: Fire Road, used in mailing addresses

frappé: a thick drink containing milk, ice cream, and flavored syrup, as opposed to a milk shake, which does not include ice cream (but beware: a frappé offered in other parts of the United States is an ice cream sundae topped with whipped cream)

from away: not native to Maine

galamander: a wheeled contraption formerly used to transport quarry granite to building sites or to boats for onward shipment

gore: a sliver of land left over from inaccurate boundary surveys. Maine has several gores; Hibberts Gore, for instance, has a population of one.

got done: quit a job; was let go

harbormaster: local official who monitors water traffic and assigns moorings; often a very political job

hardshell: lobster that hasn't molted yet (scarcer, thus more pricey in summer)

HC: Home Carrier, used in mailing addresses

hod: wooden "basket" used for carrying clams

ice-out: the departure of winter ice from ponds, lakes, rivers, and streams; many communities have ice-out contests, awarding prizes for guessing the exact time of ice-out, in April or May

Italian: long soft bread roll sliced on top and filled with peppers, onions, tomatoes, sliced meat, black olives, and sprinkled with olive oil, salt, and pepper; veggie versions available

jimmies: chocolate sprinkles, like those on an ice cream cone

lobster car: a large floating crate for storing lobsters

Maine Guide: a member of the Maine Professional Guides Association, trained and tested for outdoor and survival skills; also called Registered Maine Guide

market price: restaurant menu term for "the going rate," usually referring to the price of lobster or clams

molt: what a lobster does when it sheds its shell for a larger one; the act of molting is called ecdysis (as a stripper is an ecdysiast)

money tree: a collection device for a monetary gift

mud season: mid-March–mid-April, when back roads and unpaved driveways become virtual tank traps

nasty neat: extremely meticulous

near: stingy

notional: stubborn, determined

off island: the mainland, to an islander

place: another word for a house (as in "Herb Pendleton's place")

ployes: Acadian buckwheat pancakes

pot: trap, as in "lobster pot"

public landing: see "town landing"

rake: hand tool used for harvesting blueberries

RFD: Rural Free Delivery, used in mailing addresses

roller-skiing: cross-country skiing on wheels; popular among cross-country skiers, triathletes, and others as a training technique

rusticator: a summer visitor, particularly in bygone days

scooch (or scootch): to squat; to move sideways

sea smoke: heavy mist rising off the water when the air temperature suddenly becomes much colder than the ocean temperature

select: a lobster with claws intact

Selectmen: the elected men and women who handle local affairs in small communities; the First Selectman chairs meetings. In some towns, "people from away" have tried to propose substituting a gender-neutral term, but in most cases the effort has failed.

shedder: a lobster with a new (soft) shell; generally occurs in July-August (more common then, thus less expensive than hardshells)

shire town: county seat

shore dinner: the works: chowder, clams, lobster, and sometimes corn on the cob too; usually the most expensive item on a menu

short: a small, illegal-size lobster

slumgullion: tasteless food; a mess

slut: a poor housekeeper

slut's wool: dust balls found under beds, couches, and so on

snapper: an undersize, illegal lobster

soda: cola, root beer, and so on (referred to as "pop" in some other parts of the country)

softshell: see "shedder"

some: very (as in "some hot")

spleeny: overly sensitive

steamers: clams, before or after they are steamed

sternman: a lobsterman's helper (male or female)

summer complaint: a tourist

supper (pronounced "suppah"): evening meal,

eaten by Mainers around 5pm or 6pm (as opposed to flatlanders and summer people, who eat dinner 7pm-9pm)

tad: slightly; a little bit

thick-o'-fog: zero-visibility fog

to home: at home

tomalley: a lobster's green insides; considered a delicacy by some

town landing: shore access; often a park or a parking lot, next to a wharf or boat-launch ramp

upattic: in the attic

Whoopie! Pie: the trademarked name for a high-fat, calorie-laden, cakelike snack that only kids and dentists could love

wicked cold: frigid

wicked good: excellent

williwaws: uncomfortable feeling

Suggested Reading

MAPS

The Maine Atlas and Gazetteer. Yarmouth, ME: DeLorme, updated annually. You'll be hard put to get lost if you're carrying this essential volume; 70 full-page, oversize-format topographical maps with GPS grids.

LITERATURE, ART, AND PHOTOGRAPHY

Curtis, J., W. Curtis, and F. Lieberman. *Monhegan: The Artists' Island.* Camden, ME: Down East Books, 1995. Fascinating island history interspersed with landscape and seascape paintings and drawings by more than 150 artists, including Bellows, Henri, Hopper, Kent, Porter, Tam, and Wyeth.

Maine Speaks: An Anthology of Maine Literature. Brunswick, ME: Maine Writers and Publishers Alliance, 1989.

McNair, W., ed. *The Maine Poets: An Anthology of Verse.* Camden, ME: Down East Books, 2003. McNair's selection of best works by Maine's finest poets.

Spectre, P. H. *Passage in Time.* New York: W. W. Norton, 1991. A noted marine writer cruises the coast aboard traditional windjammers; gorgeous photos complement the colorful text.

Van Riper, F. *Down East Maine: A World Apart.* Camden, ME: Down East Books, 1998. Maine's Washington County, captured with incredible insight and compassion by a master photographer and insightful wordsmith.

HISTORY

Acadian Culture in Maine. Washington, DC: National Park Service, North Atlantic Region, 1994. A project report on Acadians and their traditions in the Upper St. John Valley.

Clark, Stephen. *Following Their Footsteps: A Travel Guide and History of the 1775 Secret Expedition to Capture Quebec.* Shapleigh, ME: Clark Books, 2003.

Duncan, R. F., E. G. Barlow, K. Bray, and C. Hanks. *Coastal Maine: A Maritime History.* Woodstock, VT: Countrymen Press, 2002. Updated version of the classic work.

Isaacson, D., ed. *Maine: A Guide "Down East,"* 2nd ed. Maine League of Historical Societies and Museums, 1970. Revised version of the Depression-era Works Progress Administration guidebook, still interesting for background reading.

Jaster, R. S. *Russian Voices on the Kennebec: The Story of Maine's Unlikely Colony.* Orono, ME: University of Maine Press, 1999. A riveting account of the founding of a Russian-speaking colony in Richmond, Maine, in the 1950s. Superb historical photographs.

Judd, R. W., E. A. Churchill, and J. W. Eastman, eds. *Maine: The Pine Tree State from Prehistory to the Present.* Orono, ME: University of Maine Press, 1995. The best available Maine history, with excellent historical maps.

Paine, L. P. *Down East: A Maritime History of Maine.* Gardiner, ME: Tilbury House, 2000. A noted maritime historian provides an enlightening introduction to the state's seafaring tradition.

LOBSTERS AND LIGHTHOUSES

Bachelder, Peter Dow, and P. M. Mason. *Maine Lighthouse Map and Guide.* Glendale, CO: Bella Terra Publishing, 2009. An illustrated map and guide providing directions on how to find all Maine beacons as well as brief histories.

Caldwell, W. *Lighthouses of Maine.* Camden, ME: Down East Books, 2002 (reprint of 1986 book). A historical tour of Maine's lighthouses, with an emphasis on history, legends, and lore.

Corson, T. *The Secret Life of Lobsters.* New York: HarperCollins, 2004. Everything you wanted—or perhaps didn't want—to know about lobster.

Woodward, C. *The Lobster Coast: Rebels, Rusticators, and the Struggle for a Forgotten Frontier.* New York: Viking, 2004. A veteran journalist's take on the history of the Maine coast.

MEMOIRS

Dawson, L. B. *Saltwater Farm.* Westford, ME: Impatiens Press, 1993. Witty, charming stories of growing up on the Cushing peninsula.

Greenlaw, L. *The Lobster Chronicles: Life on a Very Small Island.* New York: Hyperion, 2002. Swordfishing boat captain Linda Greenlaw's account of returning to life on Isle au Haut after weathering *The Perfect Storm.*

Hamlin, H. *Nine Mile Bridge: Three Years in the Maine Woods.* Yarmouth and Frenchboro, ME: Islandport Press, 2006 [orig. pub. 1945]. Hamlin's experiences as a teacher at a remote lumber camp near the headwaters of the Allagash River, where her husband was a game warden.

Lunt, D. L. *Hauling by Hand: The Life and Times of a Maine Island,* 2nd ed. Frenchboro, ME: Islandport Press, 2007. A sensitive history of Frenchboro (a.k.a. Long Island), eight miles offshore, written by an eighth-generation islander and journalist.

Szelog, T. M. *Our Point of View: Fourteen Years at a Maine Lighthouse.* Camden, ME: Down East Books, 2007. A professional photographer documents in words and photos 14 years at Marsha Point Lighthouse.

NATURAL HISTORY

Bennett, D. *Maine's Natural Heritage: Rare Species and Unique Natural Features.* Camden, ME: Down East Books, 1988. A dated book that examines both the special ecology of the state and how it's threatened.

Conkling, P. W. *Islands in Time: A Natural and Cultural History of the Islands of the Gulf of Maine,* 2nd ed. Camden, ME: Down East Books, and Rockland, ME: Island Institute, 1999. A thoughtful overview by the president of Maine's Island Institute.

Dwelley, M. J. *Spring Wildflowers of New England,* 2nd ed. Camden, ME: Down East Books, 2000. Back in print after several years, this beautifully illustrated gem is an essential guide for exploring spring woodlands.

Dwelley, M. J. *Summer and Fall Wildflowers of New England,* 2nd ed. Camden, ME: Down East Books, 2004. Flowers are grouped by color; more than 700 lovely colored-pencil drawings simplify identification.

Kendall, D. L. *Glaciers and Granite: A Guide to Maine's Landscape and Geology.* Unity, ME: North Country Press, 1993. Explains why Maine looks the way it does.

Maine's Ice Age Trail Down East Map and Guide. Orono, ME: University of Maine Press, 2007. Information on 46 glacial sites, also available online (www.iceagetrail. umaine.edu).

RECREATION
Acadia National Park and Mount Desert Island

Monkman, J., and M. Monkman. *Discover Acadia National Park: A Guide to the Best Hiking, Biking, and Paddling,* 2nd ed. Boston: Appalachian Mountain Club Books, 2005. A comprehensive guide to well-chosen hikes, bike trips, and paddling routes, accompanied by an excellent pullout map.

Nangle, H. *Moon Acadia National Park,* 4th ed. Berkeley, CA: Avalon Travel, 2009. A Mainer since childhood and veteran travel writer is the ideal escort for exploring this region in depth.

Roberts, A. R. *Mr. Rockefeller's Roads,* 2nd ed. Camden, ME: Down East Books, 2012. The story behind Acadia's scenic carriage roads, written by the granddaughter of John D. Rockefeller, who created them.

St. Germain Jr., T. A. *A Walk in the Park: Acadia's Hiking Guide,* 3rd ed. Bar Harbor, ME: Parkman Publications, 2010. The book includes plenty of historical tidbits about the trails, the park, and the island. Part of the proceeds go to the Acadia Trails Forever campaign to maintain and rehabilitate the park's trails. The book is updated regularly; ask for the most recent edition.

Bicycling

Stone, H. *25 Bicycle Tours in Maine: Coastal and Inland Rides from Kittery to Caribou,* 3rd ed. Woodstock, VT: Countryman Press/ Backcountry Guides, 1998.

Birding

Duchesne, B. *Maine Birding Trail: The Official Guide to More than 260 Accessible Sites.* Camden, ME: Down East Books, 2009. Authorized guide to the Maine Birding Trail.

Pierson, E. C., J. E. Pierson, and P. D. Vickery. *A Birder's Guide to Maine.* Camden, ME: Down East Books, 1996. An expanded version of *A Birder's Guide to the Coast of Maine.* No ornithologist, novice or expert, should explore Maine without this valuable guide.

Boating

AMC River Guide: Maine, 4th ed. Boston: Appalachian Mountain Club Books, 2008. Detailed guide to canoeing or kayaking Maine's large and small rivers.

The Maine Island Trail: Stewardship Handbook and Guidebook. Rockland, ME: Maine Island Trail Association, updated annually. Available only with MITA membership (annual dues $45), providing access to dozens of islands along the watery trail.

Miller, D. S. *Kayaking the Maine Coast,* 2nd ed. Woodstock, VT: Countryman Press/ Backcountry Guides, 2006. Thoroughly researched guide by a veteran kayaker; good maps and particularly helpful information. With this book and a copy of *Hot Showers!* you're all set.

The Northern Forest Canoe Trail: Enjoy 740 Miles of Canoe and Kayak Destinations in New York, Vermont, Quebec, New Hampshire, and Maine. Seattle, WA: Mountaineers Books, 2010. Details and maps the waterway, including highlights en route.

Taft, H., J. Taft, and C. Rindlaub. *A Cruising Guide to the Maine Coast,* 5th ed. Peaks

Island, ME: Diamond Pass Publishing, 2008. Don't even consider cruising the coast without this volume.

Wilson, A., and J. Hayes. *Quiet Water Canoe Guide, Maine: Best Paddling Lakes and Ponds for All Ages,* 2nd ed. Boston: Appalachian Mountain Club Books, 2005. Comprehensive handbook, with helpful maps, for inland paddling.

Hiking and Walking

AMC Maine Mountain Guide, 10th ed. Boston: Appalachian Mountain Club Books, 2012. The definitive statewide resource for going vertical, in a handy format.

Clark, Stephen. *Katahdin: A Guide to Baxter State Park and Katahdin,* 6th ed. Shapleigh, ME: Clark Books, 2009. The most comprehensive guide to Katahdin and Baxter State Park.

Collins, J., and J. E. McCarthy. *Cobscook Trails: A Guide to Walking Opportunities around Cobscook Bay and the Bold Coast,* 2nd ed. Whiting, ME: Quoddy Regional Land Trust, 2000. Essential handbook for exploring this part of the Down East Coast, with excellent maps.

Gibson, J. *50 Hikes in Coastal and Southern Maine,* 4th ed. Woodstock, VT: Countryman Press/Backcountry Guides, 2008. Well-researched, detailed resource by a veteran hiker.

Roberts, P. *On the Trail in Lincoln County.* Newcastle and Damariscotta, ME: Lincoln County Publishing, 2003. A great guide to more than 60 walks in preserves from Wiscasset through Waldoboro, with detailed directions to trailheads.

Internet Resources

GENERAL INFORMATION
State of Maine
www.maine.gov
Everything you wanted to know about Maine and then some, with links to all government departments and Maine-related sites. Buy a fishing license online, reserve a state park campsite, or check the fall foliage conditions via the site's Leaf Cam. (You can also access foliage info at www.mainefoliage.com, where you can sign up for weekly email foliage reports in September and early October.) Also listed is information on accessible arts and recreation.

Maine Office of Tourism
www.visitmaine.com
The biggest and most useful of all Maine-related tourism sites, with sections for where to visit, where to stay, things to do, trip planning, packages, and search capabilities as well as lodging specials and a comprehensive calendar of events.

Maine Tourism Association
www.mainetourism.com
Find lodging, camping, restaurants, attractions, services, and more as well as links for weather, foliage, transportation planning, and chambers of commerce.

Maine Emergency Management Association
www.state.me.us/mema/weather/weather. htm
Five-day weather forecasts broken down by 32 zones.

Maine Campground Owners Association
www.campmaine.com
Find private campgrounds statewide.

Portland Papers
www.pressherald.com
Home site for Maine's largest newspaper has current news as well as extensive information on travel, outdoor activities, entertainment, and sports.

Maine Travel Maven
www.mainetravelmaven.com
Moon Maine author Hilary Nangle's site for keeping readers updated on what's happening throughout the state.

TRANSPORTATION

Explore Maine
www.exploremaine.org
An invaluable site for trip planning, with information on and links to airports, rail service, bus service, automobile travel, and ferries as well as links to other key travel-planning sites.

Maine Department of Transportation
www.511maine.gov
Provides real-time information about major delays, accidents, road construction, and weather conditions. You can get the same info and more by dialing 511 in-state.

PARKS AND RECREATION

Department of Conservation, Maine Bureau of Parks and Lands
www.parksandlands.com
Information on state parks, public reserved lands, and state historic sites as well as details on facilities such as campsites, picnic areas, and boat launches. Make state campground reservations online.

Acadia National Park
www.nps.gov/acad
Information on all sections of Acadia National Park. Make ANP campground reservations online.

Baxter State Park
www.baxterstateparkauthority.com
Everything you need for planning a trip to Baxter.

Maine Audubon
www.maineaudubon.org
Information about Maine Audubon's eco-sensitive headquarters in Falmouth and all of the organization's environmental centers statewide. Activity and program schedules are included.

North Maine Woods
www.northmainewoods.org
Essential information for venturing into the privately owned North Woods.

The Nature Conservancy
www.nature.org/wherewework/north
america/states/maine
Information about Maine preserves, field trips, and events.

Maine Land Trust Network
www.mltn.org
Maine has dozens of land trusts statewide, managing lands that provide opportunities for hiking, walking, canoeing, kayaking, and other such activities.

Maine Department of Inland Fisheries and Wildlife
www.state.me.us/ifw
Info on wildlife, hunting, fishing, snowmobiling, and boating.

Healthy Maine Walks
www.healthymainewalks.com
Lists places for walking statewide.

Maine Trail Finder
www.mainetrailfinder.com
Find trails to walk, hike, ski, snowshoe, or mountain bike statewide.

Maine Huts & Trails
www.mainehuts.org
A nonprofit, managed trail system comprising four full-service backcountry lodges on more than 50 miles of wilderness trails.

Bicycle Coalition of Maine
www.bikemaine.org
Tons of information for bicyclists, including routes, shops, events, organized rides, and much more.

Maine Birding Trail
www.mainebirdingtrail.com
A must-visit site for anyone interested in learning more about bird-watching in Maine, including news, checklists, events, forums, trips, and more.

Northern Forest Canoe Trail
www.northernforestcanoetrail.org
Info on more than 350 miles of connected waterways in Maine.

Maine Association of Sea Kayaking Guides & Instructors
www.maskgi.org
Information and links to outfitters and individual guides who meet state requirements to lead commercial trips.

Maine Island Trail Association
www.mita.org
Information about the association and its activities along with membership details.

Maine Windjammer Association
www.sailmainecoast.com
Windjammer schooners homeported in Rockland, Camden, and Rockport belong to this umbrella organization; there are links to the websites of member vessels for online and phone information and reservations.

Ski Maine
www.skimaine.com
The go-to source for information on alpine skiing in Maine.

ARTS, ANTIQUES, AND MUSEUMS

Maine Archives and Museums
www.mainemuseums.org
Information on and links to museums, archives, historical societies, and historic sites in Maine.

Maine Antiques Dealers Association
www.maineantiques.org
Statewide dealers are listed by location and specialty, along with information on upcoming antiques events.

Maine Art Museum Trail
www.maineartmuseums.org
Information on art museums with significant collections statewide, including the Ogunquit Museum of Art in Ogunquit, the Portland Museum of Art in Portland, Bowdoin College Museum of Art in Brunswick, and Farnsworth Art Museum in Rockland.

Maine Antiques Dealers Association
www.maineantiques.org
Lists member dealers statewide by location and specialty and provides information on upcoming antiques events.

FOOD AND DRINK

Maine Department of Agriculture
www.getrealmaine.com
Information on all things agricultural, including fairs, farmers markets, farm vacations, places to buy Maine foods, berry- and apple-picking sites, and more.

Portland Food Map
www.portlandfoodmap.com
A must for culinary travel in Maine's largest city. Information on anything and everything food- and drink-related, including openings and closings and links to reviews.

Index

List of Maps

www.moon.com

DESTINATIONS | ACTIVITIES | BLOGS | MAPS | BOOKS

MOON.COM is ready to help plan your next trip! Filled with fresh trip ideas and strategies, author interviews, informative travel blogs, a detailed map library, and descriptions of all the Moon guidebooks, Moon.com is all you need to get out and explore the world—or even places in your own backyard. While at Moon.com, sign up for our monthly e-newsletter for updates on new releases, travel tips, and expert advice from our on-the-go Moon authors. As always, when you travel with Moon, expect an experience that is uncommon and truly unique.

KEEP UP WITH MOON ON FACEBOOK AND TWITTER
JOIN THE MOON PHOTO GROUP ON FLICKR

MAP SYMBOLS

▨▨▨	Expressway	◖	Highlight	✗	Airfield	⚲	Golf Course
▨▨▨	Primary Road	○	City/Town	✈	Airport	P	Parking Area
▨▨▨	Secondary Road	◉	State Capital	▲	Mountain	⛩	Archaeological Site
‒ ‒ ‒ ‒	Unpaved Road	⊛	National Capital	✦	Unique Natural Feature	⬥	Church
‒ ‒ ‒	Trail	★	Point of Interest			⛽	Gas Station
··········	Ferry	•	Accommodation	⟋	Waterfall		Glacier
⤙⤙⤙	Railroad	▾	Restaurant/Bar	▲	Park		Mangrove
▨▨▨	Pedestrian Walkway	▪	Other Location	▣	Trailhead		Reef
▥▥▥	Stairs	Λ	Campground	✗	Skiing Area		Swamp

CONVERSION TABLES

$°C = (°F - 32) / 1.8$
$°F = (°C \times 1.8) + 32$
1 inch = 2.54 centimeters (cm)
1 foot = 0.304 meters (m)
1 yard = 0.914 meters
1 mile = 1.6093 kilometers (km)
1 km = 0.6214 miles
1 fathom = 1.8288 m
1 chain = 20.1168 m
1 furlong = 201.168 m
1 acre = 0.4047 hectares
1 sq km = 100 hectares
1 sq mile = 2.59 square km
1 ounce = 28.35 grams
1 pound = 0.4536 kilograms
1 short ton = 0.90718 metric ton
1 short ton = 2,000 pounds
1 long ton = 1.016 metric tons
1 long ton = 2,240 pounds
1 metric ton = 1,000 kilograms
1 quart = 0.94635 liters
1 US gallon = 3.7854 liters
1 Imperial gallon = 4.5459 liters
1 nautical mile = 1.852 km

MOON MAINE

Avalon Travel
a member of the Perseus Books Group
1700 Fourth Street
Berkeley, CA 94710, USA
www.moon.com

Editor: Kevin McLain
Series Manager: Kathryn Ettinger
Copy Editor: Alissa Cypher
Graphics and Production Coordinator: Darren Alessi
Cover design: Faceout Studios, Charles Brock
Moon logo: Tim McGrath
Map Editor: Kat Bennett
Cartographer: Stephanie Poulain
Indexer: Rachel Kuhn

430 5W7

ISBN: 978-1-61238-752-9
ISSN: 1531-5606

Printing History
1st Edition – 1998
6th Edition – May 2014
5 4 3 2 1

Front cover photo: © Michele Stapleton
Back cover photo: © Keith Webber Jr. / 123rf.com
Title page photo: © Adam Osgood

Interior color photos: page 6, 7 © Hilary Nangle; page 8 (top) © Hilary Nangle, (bottom) © Adam Osgood; page 9 (all) © Hilary Nangle; page 10 © Ken Lamb, courtesy of the Maine Office of Tourism; page 11 (all) © Hilary Nangle; page 12 © Hilary Nangle; page 14 © Hilary Nangle; page 15 © Hilary Nangle; page 17 © Hilary Nangle; page 18 © Gary Pearl, courtesy of the Maine Office of Tourism; page 19 © Hilary Nangle; page 20 © Hilary Nangle; page 22 © Phil Savignano; page 23 © Hilary Nangle; page 24 (all) © Hilary Nangle

Printed in Canada by Friesens.

KEEPING CURRENT

If you have a favorite gem you'd like to see included in the next edition, or see anything that needs updating, clarification, or correction, please drop us a line. Send your comments via email to feedback@moon.com, or use the address above.